HANDBOOK ON THE HISTORY OF ECONOMIC ANALYSIS VOLUME I

Handbook on the History of Economic Analysis
Volume I

Great Economists since Petty and Boisguilbert

Edited by

Gilbert Faccarello

Professor of Economics, Panthéon-Assas University, Paris, France

Heinz D. Kurz

Emeritus Professor of Economics, University of Graz and Graz Schumpeter Centre, Austria

Edward Elgar
PUBLISHING

Cheltenham, UK • Northampton, MA, USA

Published by
Edward Elgar Publishing Limited
The Lypiatts
15 Lansdown Road
Cheltenham
Glos GL50 2JA
UK

Edward Elgar Publishing, Inc.
William Pratt House
9 Dewey Court
Northampton
Massachusetts 01060
USA

Paperback edition 2018

A catalogue record for this book
is available from the British Library

Library of Congress Control Number: 2015954312

This book is available electronically in the **Elgar**online
Economics subject collection
DOI 10.4337/9781785366642

ISBN 978 1 84980 110 2 (cased)
ISBN 978 1 78536 131 9 (cased 3-volume set)
ISBN 978 1 78536 664 2 (eBook)
ISBN 978 1 78897 237 6 (paperback)
ISBN 978 1 78897 240 6 (paperback 3-volume set)

Typeset by Servis Filmsetting Ltd, Stockport, Cheshire
Printed on FSC approved paper
Printed and bound in Great Britain by Marston Book Services Ltd, Oxfordshire

Contents

Contents (alphabetical)   xiii
List of figures and tables   xxi
List of contributors   xxiii

General introduction   1
Gilbert Faccarello and Heinz D. Kurz

William Petty (1623–1687)   5
Tony Aspromourgos

Pierre Le Pesant de Boisguilbert (1646–1714)   9
Gilbert Faccarello

John Law (1671–1729)   16
Antoin E. Murphy

Richard Cantillon (*c.* 1680/90–1734)   19
Antoin E. Murphy

Charles-Louis de Secondat de Montesquieu (1689–1755)   24
Arnaud Orain

François Quesnay (1694–1774) and Physiocracy   28
Arnaud Orain and Philippe Steiner

Daniel Bernoulli (1700–1782)   40
Gilbert Faccarello

David Hume (1711–1776)   48
Daniel Diatkine

James Steuart [James Denham-Steuart] (1712–1780)   54
Anthony Brewer

Adam Smith (1723–1790)   57
Tony Aspromourgos

Anne-Robert-Jacques Turgot (1727–1781)   73
Gilbert Faccarello

Marie-Jean-Antoine-Nicolas Caritat de Condorcet (1743–1794)   83
Gilbert Faccarello

Jeremy Bentham (1748–1832)   95
Marco E.L. Guidi

Achilles-Nicolas Isnard (1748–1803)   101
Richard van den Berg

Henry Thornton (1760–1815)   104
Jérôme de Boyer des Roches

Thomas Robert Malthus (1766–1834)   107
Catherine Martin

Jean-Baptiste Say (1767–1832)   114
Alain Béraud

David Ricardo (1772–1823)   120
Heinz D. Kurz

Jean-Charles Léonard Simonde de Sismondi (1773–1842)   144
Francesca Dal Degan and Nicolas Eyguesier

Thomas Tooke (1774–1858)   148
Neil T. Skaggs

Robert Torrens (c. 1780–1864)   150
Christian Gehrke

Johann Heinrich von Thünen (1783–1850)   157
Ludwig Nellinger

Barthélemy-Charles Dunoyer de Segonzac (1786–1862)   164
Alain Béraud

Friedrich List (1789–1846)   167
Stefan Kolev and Joachim Zweynert

Frédéric Bastiat (1801–1850)   171
Alain Béraud

Antoine-Augustin Cournot (1801–1877)   174
Alain Béraud

Jules Dupuit (1804–1866)   181
Alain Béraud

John Stuart Mill (1806–1873)   185
Arrigo Opocher

Pierre-Joseph Proudhon (1809–1865)   192
Alain Béraud

Hermann Heinrich Gossen (1810–1858)   196
Heinz D. Kurz

Bruno Hildebrand (1812–1878)   203
Bertram Schefold

Wilhelm Georg Friedrich Roscher (1817–1894)   206
Heinz D. Kurz

Karl Heinrich Marx (1818–1883)   211
Gilbert Faccarello, Christian Gehrke and Heinz D. Kurz

Clément Juglar (1819–1905)   234
Muriel Dal Pont Legrand

Gustave de Molinari (1819–1912)   237
Alain Béraud

Walter Bagehot (1826–1877)   242
Jérôme de Boyer des Roches

Marie-Esprit-Léon Walras (1834–1910)   245
Roberto Baranzini

William Stanley Jevons (1835–1882)   262
John Creedy

Adolph Heinrich Gotthilf Wagner (1835–1917)   268
Rudolf Dujmovits and Richard Sturn

Gustav Friedrich von Schmoller (1838–1917)   272
Johannes Glaeser

Henry Sidgwick (1838–1900)   280
Keith Tribe

Carl Menger (1840–1921)   283
Gilles Campagnolo

Alfred Marshall (1842–1924)   295
Tiziano Raffaelli

Philip Henry Wicksteed (1844–1927)   311
John Creedy

Francis Ysidro Edgeworth (1845–1926)   315
John Creedy

John Bates Clark (1847–1938)   320
Marlies Schütz

Vilfredo Pareto (1848–1923)   323
Michael McLure

Eugen von Böhm-Bawerk (1851–1914)   341
Carl Christian von Weizsäcker

Knut Wicksell (1851–1926)   347
Hans-Michael Trautwein

Friedrich von Wieser (1851–1926)   363
Richard Sturn

Maffeo Pantaleoni (1857–1924)   367
Marco Dardi

Thorstein Bunde Veblen (1857–1929)   374
Alfonso Giuliani

Antonio De Viti de Marco (1858–1943)   379
Amedeo Fossati

John Atkinson Hobson (1858–1940)   382
Michael Schneider

Georg Simmel (1858–1918)   385
Dieter Bögenhold

Enrico Barone (1859–1924)   388
Marco Dardi

Max Weber (1864–1920)   391
Keith Tribe

Mikhail Ivanovich Tugan-Baranovsky (1865–1919)   399
Vladimir Avtonomov and Natalia Makasheva

Gustav Cassel (1866–1945)   404
Hans-Michael Trautwein

Irving Fisher (1867–1947)   410
Harald Hagemann

Ladislaus von Bortkiewicz (1868–1931)   419
Christian Gehrke and Heinz D. Kurz

Vladimir Karpovich Dmitriev (1868–1913)   431
Christian Gehrke

Louis Bachelier (1870–1946)   436
Alain Béraud

Arthur Spiethoff (1873–1957)   440
David Haas

Albert Aftalion (1874–1956)   443
Muriel Dal Pont Legrand

Wesley Clair Mitchell (1874–1948)   446
Malcolm Rutherford

Edwin Walter Kemmerer (1875–1945)   449
Rebeca Gómez Betancourt

Arthur Cecil Pigou (1877–1959)   452
Hansjörg Klausinger

Ralph George Hawtrey (1879–1975)   458
Jérôme de Boyer des Roches

Evgeny Evgenievich Slutsky (1880–1948)   461
Irina Eliseeva

Ludwig Heinrich von Mises (1881–1973)   464
Richard Sturn

John Maynard Keynes (1883–1946)   468
Victoria Chick and Jesper Jespersen

Joseph Alois Schumpeter (1883–1950)   484
Richard Sturn

Frank H. Knight (1885–1972)   498
Ross B. Emmett

Karl Polanyi (1886–1964)   503
Peter Kalmbach

Walter Eucken (1891–1950)   506
Hauke Janssen

Erik Lindahl (1891–1960)   509
Christian Gehrke

Adolph Lowe (1893–1995)   514
Harald Hagemann

Ragnar Anton Kittil Frisch (1895–1973)   518
Olav Bjerkholt

Jacob Marschak (1898–1977)   523
Harald Hagemann

Gunnar Myrdal (1898–1987)   527
Hans-Michael Trautwein

Lionel Charles Robbins (1898–1984)   530
Andreas Rainer

Piero Sraffa (1898–1983)   534
Heinz D. Kurz and Neri Salvadori

Edward Hastings Chamberlin (1899–1967)   552
Rodolfo Signorino

Friedrich August von Hayek (1899–1992)   557
Peter Boettke

Michał Kalecki (1899–1970)   568
Michaël Assous

Roy Forbes Harrod (1900–1978)   575
Michaël Assous

Abba Ptachya Lerner (1903–1982)   578
Volker Caspari

John von Neumann (1903–1957)   581
Manfred J. Holler

Frank Plumpton Ramsey (1903–1930)   587
K. Vela Velupillai and Ragupathy Venkatachalam

Joan Violet Robinson (1903–1983)   592
Harvey Gram

George Lennox Sharman Shackle (1903–1992)   596
Brian J. Loasby

Jan Tinbergen (1903–1994)   599
Mark Knell

John Richard Hicks (1904–1989)   602
Harald Hagemann

Oskar Ryszard Lange (1904–1965)   610
Michaël Assous

Richard Ferdinand Kahn (1905–1989)   613
G.C. Harcourt

Wassily W. Leontief (1905–1999)   616
Olav Bjerkholt

Heinrich von Stackelberg (1905–1946)   621
Ulrich Schwalbe

James Edward Meade (1907–1995)   625
Volker Caspari

Nicholas Kaldor (1908–1986)   628
John E. King

Ronald Harry Coase (1910–2013)   631
Élodie Bertrand

Richard Abel Musgrave (1910–2007)   634
Richard Sturn

Tibor Scitovsky (1910–2002)   638
Viviana Di Giovinazzo

Maurice Allais (1911–2010)   642
Alain Béraud

Milton Friedman (1912–2006)   648
Christian Philipp Schröder and Peter Spahn

Abram Bergson [Abram Burk] (1914–2003)   655
Antoinette Baujard

Paul Anthony Samuelson (1915–2009)   658
Carl Christian von Weizsäcker

Herbert Alexander Simon (1916–2001)   669
K. Vela Velupillai and Ying-Fang Kao

James Tobin (1918–2002)   675
Robert W. Dimand

James M. Buchanan (1919–2013)   682
Viktor J. Vanberg

Hyman Philip Minsky (1919–1996)   685
L. Randall Wray

Kenneth Joseph Arrow (b. 1921)   690
Maurice Salles

Gérard Debreu (1921–2004)   698
Alan Kirman

Don Patinkin (1922–1995)   706
Goulven Rubin

Michio Morishima (1923–2004)   712
Toichiro Asada

Robert Merton Solow (b. 1924)   714
Peter Kalmbach

John Forbes Nash Jr (1928–2015)   718
Robert W. Dimand and Khalid Yahia

Robert Alexander Mundell (b. 1932)   721
Oliver Sauter and Peter Spahn

Takashi Negishi (b. 1933)   725
Toichiro Asada

Amartya Kumar Sen (b. 1933)   728
Wulf Gaertner

Robert E. Lucas (b. 1937)   734
Arash Molavi Vasséi and Peter Spahn

George Akerlof (b. 1940)   737
Olivier Favereau

Joseph Eugene Stiglitz (b. 1943)   741
Max Gödl

Paul Robin Krugman (b. 1953)   748
Max Gödl

Index   755

Contents (alphabetical)

List of figures and tables   xxi
List of contributors   xxiii

General introduction   1
Gilbert Faccarello and Heinz D. Kurz

Aftalion, Albert (1874–1956)   443
Muriel Dal Pont Legrand

Akerlof, George (b. 1940)   737
Olivier Favereau

Allais, Maurice (1911–2010)   642
Alain Béraud

Arrow, Kenneth Joseph (b. 1921)   690
Maurice Salles

Bachelier, Louis (1870–1946)   436
Alain Béraud

Bagehot, Walter (1826–1877)   242
Jérôme de Boyer des Roches

Barone, Enrico (1859–1924)   388
Marco Dardi

Bastiat, Frédéric (1801–1850)   171
Alain Béraud

Bentham, Jeremy (1748–1832)   95
Marco E.L. Guidi

Bergson, Abram [Abram Burk] (1914–2003)   655
Antoinette Baujard

Bernoulli, Daniel (1700–1782)   40
Gilbert Faccarello

Böhm-Bawerk, Eugen von (1851–1914)   341
Carl Christian von Weizsäcker

Boisguilbert, Pierre Le Pesant de (1646–1714)   9
Gilbert Faccarello

Bortkiewicz, Ladislaus von (1868–1931)   419
Christian Gehrke and Heinz D. Kurz

Buchanan, James M. (1919–2013)   682
Viktor J. Vanberg

Cantillon, Richard (*c.* 1680/90–1734)   19
Antoin E. Murphy

Cassel, Gustav (1866–1945)   404
Hans-Michael Trautwein

Chamberlin, Edward Hastings (1899–1967)   552
Rodolfo Signorino

Clark, John Bates (1847–1938)   320
Marlies Schütz

Coase, Ronald Harry (1910–2013)   631
Élodie Bertrand

Condorcet, Marie-Jean-Antoine-Nicolas Caritat de (1743–1794)   83
Gilbert Faccarello

Cournot, Antoine-Augustin (1801–1877)   174
Alain Béraud

Debreu, Gérard (1921–2004)   698
Alan Kirman

De Viti de Marco, Antonio (1858–1943)   379
Amedeo Fossati

Dmitriev, Vladimir Karpovich (1868–1913)   431
Christian Gehrke

Dunoyer de Segonzac, Barthélemy-Charles (1786–1862)   164
Alain Béraud

Dupuit, Jules (1804–1866)   181
Alain Béraud

Edgeworth, Francis Ysidro (1845–1926)   315
John Creedy

Eucken, Walter (1891–1950)   506
Hauke Janssen

Fisher, Irving (1867–1947)   410
Harald Hagemann

Friedman, Milton (1912–2006)   648
Christian Philipp Schröder and Peter Spahn

Frisch, Ragnar Anton Kittil (1895–1973)   518
Olav Bjerkholt

Gossen, Hermann Heinrich (1810–1858)   196
Heinz D. Kurz

Harrod, Roy Forbes (1900–1978)   575
Michaël Assous

Hawtrey, Ralph George (1879–1975)   458
Jérôme de Boyer des Roches

Hayek, Friedrich August von (1899–1992)   557
Peter Boettke

Hicks, John Richard (1904–1989)   602
Harald Hagemann

Hildebrand, Bruno (1812–1878)   203
Bertram Schefold

Hobson, John Atkinson (1858–1940)   382
Michael Schneider

Hume, David (1711–1776)   48
Daniel Diatkine

Isnard, Achilles-Nicolas (1748–1803)   101
Richard van den Berg

Jevons, William Stanley (1835–1882)   262
John Creedy

Juglar, Clément (1819–1905)   234
Muriel Dal Pont Legrand

Kahn, Richard Ferdinand (1905–1989)   613
G.C. Harcourt

Kaldor, Nicholas (1908–1986)   628
John E. King

Kalecki, Michał (1899–1970)   568
Michaël Assous

Kemmerer, Edwin Walter (1875–1945)   449
Rebeca Gómez Betancourt

Keynes, John Maynard (1883–1946)   468
Victoria Chick and Jesper Jespersen

Knight, Frank H. (1885–1972)   498
Ross B. Emmett

Krugman, Paul Robin (b. 1953)   748
Max Gödl

Lange, Oskar Ryszard (1904–1965)   610
Michaël Assous

Law, John (1671–1729)   16
Antoin E. Murphy

Leontief, Wassily W. (1905–1999)   616
Olav Bjerkholt

Lerner, Abba Ptachya (1903–1982)   578
Volker Caspari

Lindahl, Erik (1891–1960)   509
Christian Gehrke

List, Friedrich (1789–1846)   167
Stefan Kolev and Joachim Zweynert

Lowe, Adolph (1893–1995)   514
Harald Hagemann

Lucas, Robert E. (b. 1937)   734
Arash Molavi Vasséi and Peter Spahn

Malthus, Thomas Robert (1766–1834)   107
Catherine Martin

Marschak, Jacob (1898–1977)   523
Harald Hagemann

Marshall, Alfred (1842–1924)   295
Tiziano Raffaelli

Marx, Karl Heinrich (1818–1883)   211
Gilbert Faccarello, Christian Gehrke and Heinz D. Kurz

Meade, James Edward (1907–1995)   625
Volker Caspari

Menger, Carl (1840–1921)   283
Gilles Campagnolo

Mill, John Stuart (1806–1873)   185
Arrigo Opocher

Minsky, Hyman Philip (1919–1996)   685
L. Randall Wray

Mises, Ludwig Heinrich von (1881–1973)   464
Richard Sturn

Mitchell, Wesley Clair (1874–1948)   446
Malcolm Rutherford

Molinari, Gustave de (1819–1912) 237
Alain Béraud

Montesquieu, Charles-Louis de Secondat de (1689–1755) 24
Arnaud Orain

Morishima, Michio (1923–2004) 712
Toichiro Asada

Mundell, Robert Alexander (b. 1932) 721
Oliver Sauter and Peter Spahn

Musgrave, Richard Abel (1910–2007) 634
Richard Sturn

Myrdal, Gunnar (1898–1987) 527
Hans-Michael Trautwein

Nash Jr, John Forbes (1928–2015) 718
Robert W. Dimand and Khalid Yahia

Negishi, Takashi (b. 1933) 725
Toichiro Asada

Neumann, John von (1903–1957) 581
Manfred J. Holler

Pantaleoni, Maffeo (1857–1924) 367
Marco Dardi

Pareto, Vilfredo (1848–1923) 323
Michael McLure

Patinkin, Don (1922–1995) 706
Goulven Rubin

Petty, William (1623–1687) 5
Tony Aspromourgos

Pigou, Arthur Cecil (1877–1959) 452
Hansjörg Klausinger

Polanyi, Karl (1886–1964) 503
Peter Kalmbach

Proudhon, Pierre-Joseph (1809–1865) 192
Alain Béraud

Quesnay, François (1694–1774) and Physiocracy 28
Arnaud Orain and Philippe Steiner

Ramsey, Frank Plumpton (1903–1930) 587
K. Vela Velupillai and Ragupathy Venkatachalam

Ricardo, David (1772–1823)   120
Heinz D. Kurz

Robbins, Lionel Charles (1898–1984)   530
Andreas Rainer

Robinson, Joan Violet (1903–1983)   592
Harvey Gram

Roscher, Wilhelm Georg Friedrich (1817–1894)   206
Heinz D. Kurz

Samuelson, Paul Anthony (1915–2009)   658
Carl Christian von Weizsäcker

Say, Jean-Baptiste (1767–1832)   114
Alain Béraud

Schmoller, Gustav Friedrich von (1838–1917)   272
Johannes Glaeser

Schumpeter, Joseph Alois (1883–1950)   484
Richard Sturn

Scitovsky, Tibor (1910–2002)   638
Viviana Di Giovinazzo

Sen, Amartya Kumar (b. 1933)   728
Wulf Gaertner

Shackle, George Lennox Sharman (1903–1992)   596
Brian J. Loasby

Sidgwick, Henry (1838–1900)   280
Keith Tribe

Simmel, Georg (1858–1918)   385
Dieter Bögenhold

Simon, Herbert Alexander (1916–2001)   669
K. Vela Velupillai and Ying-Fang Kao

Sismondi, Jean-Charles Léonard Simonde de (1773–1842)   144
Francesca Dal Degan and Nicolas Eyguesier

Slutsky, Evgeny Evgenievich (1880–1948)   461
Irina Eliseeva

Smith, Adam (1723–1790)   57
Tony Aspromourgos

Solow, Robert Merton (b. 1924)   714
Peter Kalmbach

Spiethoff, Arthur (1873–1957)   440
David Haas

Sraffa, Piero (1898–1983)   534
Heinz D. Kurz and Neri Salvadori

Stackelberg, Heinrich von (1905–1946)   621
Ulrich Schwalbe

Steuart, James [James Denham-Steuart] (1712–1780)   54
Anthony Brewer

Stiglitz, Joseph Eugene (b. 1943)   741
Max Gödl

Thornton, Henry (1760–1815)   104
Jérôme de Boyer des Roches

Thünen, Johann Heinrich von (1783–1850)   157
Ludwig Nellinger

Tinbergen, Jan (1903–1994)   599
Mark Knell

Tobin, James (1918–2002)   675
Robert W. Dimand

Tooke, Thomas (1774–1858)   148
Neil T. Skaggs

Torrens, Robert (*c*. 1780–1864)   150
Christian Gehrke

Tugan-Baranovsky, Mikhail Ivanovich (1865–1919)   399
Vladimir Avtonomov and Natalia Makasheva

Turgot, Anne-Robert-Jacques (1727–1781)   73
Gilbert Faccarello

Veblen, Thorstein Bunde (1857–1929)   374
Alfonso Giuliani

Wagner, Adolph Heinrich Gotthilf (1835–1917)   268
Rudolf Dujmovits and Richard Sturn

Walras, Marie-Esprit-Léon (1834–1910)   245
Roberto Baranzini

Weber, Max (1864–1920)   391
Keith Tribe

Wicksell, Knut (1851–1926)   347
Hans-Michael Trautwein

Wicksteed, Philip Henry (1844–1927)   311
John Creedy

Wieser, Friedrich von (1851–1926)   363
Richard Sturn

Index   755

Figures and tables

Figures

1	The "Zig-Zag"	32
2	The arithmetic formula	32
3	The main members of the Bernoulli family	40
4	Daniel Bernoulli's representation of the utility of wealth	44
5	Cournot's duopoly	178
6	Short- and long-run equilibriums of a firm in Chamberlin's large-group case	555
7	Kalecki's 1936 diagram	571

Tables

1	Number of men whose labour is required for one year in order to produce a given quantity of cloth and wine	136
2	Triangular-shaped table illustrating the Mengerian exposition of marginal value	286

Contributors

Toichiro Asada, Chuo University, Tokyo, Japan

Tony Aspromourgos, University of Sydney, Australia

Michaël Assous, University of Paris I Panthéon-Sorbonne, France

Vladimir Avtonomov, National Research University Higher School of Economics, Moscow, Russia

Roberto Baranzini, University of Lausanne, Switzerland

Antoinette Baujard, University of Saint-Étienne, France

Alain Béraud, University of Cergy-Pontoise, France

Élodie Bertrand, National Centre for Scientific Research, France

Olav Bjerkholt, University of Oslo, Norway

Peter Boettke, George Mason University, USA

Dieter Bögenhold, Alpen-Adria University Klagenfurt, Austria

Jérôme de Boyer des Roches, University of Paris Dauphine, France

Anthony Brewer, University of Bristol, Great Britain

Gilles Campagnolo, National Centre for Scientific Research, Aix-Marseille School of Economics, France

Volker Caspari, University of Darmstadt, Germany

Victoria Chick, University College London, Great Britain

John Creedy, Victoria University of Wellington, New Zealand

Francesca Dal Degan, University of Lausanne, Switzerland

Muriel Dal Pont Legrand, University of Nice Sophia Antipolis, France

Marco Dardi, University of Florence, Italy

Daniel Diatkine, University of Évry-Val d'Essonne, France

Viviana Di Giovinazzo, University of Milano Bicocca, Italy

Robert W. Dimand, Brock University, Canada

Rudolf Dujmovits, University of Graz, Austria

Irina Eliseeva, Saint Petersburg State University of Economics, Russia

Ross B. Emmett, Michigan State University, USA

Nicolas Eyguesier, University of Lausanne, Switzerland

Gilbert Faccarello, Panthéon-Assas University, Paris, France

Olivier Favereau, University of Paris-Ouest, France

Amedeo Fossati, University of Genoa, Italy

Wulf Gaertner, University of Osnabrück, Germany and London School of Economics, Great Britain

Christian Gehrke, University of Graz, Austria

Alfonso Giuliani, National Centre for Scientific Research, France

Johannes Glaeser, Springer Verlag, Heidelberg, Germany

Max Gödl, University of Graz, Austria

Rebeca Gómez Betancourt, University Lumière, Lyon, France

Harvey Gram, Queens College, City University of New York, USA

Marco E.L. Guidi, University of Pisa, Italy

David Haas, University of Graz, Austria

Harald Hagemann, University of Hohenheim, Germany

G.C. Harcourt, University of Cambridge, Great Britain and University of New South Wales, Australia

Manfred J. Holler, University of Hamburg, Germany

Hauke Janssen, *Der Spiegel*, Germany

Jesper Jespersen, Department of Society and Globalization, Roskilde University, Denmark

Peter Kalmbach, University of Bremen, Germany

Ying-Fang Kao, AI-ECON Research Center, National Chengchi University, Taiwan

John E. King, La Trobe University, Australia and Federation University Australia

Alan Kirman, University of Aix-Marseille, France

Hansjörg Klausinger, WU Vienna University of Economics and Business, Austria

Mark Knell, Nordic Institute for Studies in Innovation, Research and Education, Oslo, Norway

Stefan Kolev, West Saxon University of Applied Sciences Zwickau, Germany

Heinz D. Kurz, University of Graz, Austria

Brian J. Loasby, University of Stirling, Great Britain

Natalia Makasheva, Institute of Scientific Information for Social Sciences, Russian Academy of Sciences, Moscow, Russia

Catherine Martin, University of Paris I Panthéon-Sorbonne, France

Michael McLure, University of Western Australia, Australia

Arash Molavi Vasséi, University of Hohenheim, Germany

Antoin E. Murphy, Trinity College, Dublin, Ireland

Ludwig Nellinger, Federal Ministry of Food and Agriculture, Germany

Arrigo Opocher, University of Padova, Italy

Arnaud Orain, University of Paris-Saint Denis, France

Tiziano Raffaelli, University of Pisa, Italy

Andreas Rainer, University of Graz, Austria

Goulven Rubin, University of Lille, France

Malcolm Rutherford, University of Victoria, Canada

Maurice Salles, University of Caen, France

Neri Salvadori, University of Pisa, Italy

Oliver Sauter, University of Hohenheim, Germany

Bertram Schefold, Johann Wolfgang Goethe-University, Frankfurt am Main, Germany

Michael Schneider, Federation University, Australia

Christian Philipp Schröder, University of Hohenheim, Germany

Marlies Schütz, University of Graz, Austria

Ulrich Schwalbe, University of Hohenheim, Germany

Rodolfo Signorino, University of Palermo, Italy

Neil T. Skaggs, Illinois State University, USA

Peter Spahn, University of Hohenheim, Germany

Philippe Steiner, University of Paris-Sorbonne and Institut Universitaire de France, France

Richard Sturn, University of Graz, Austria

Hans-Michael Trautwein, University of Oldenburg, Germany

Keith Tribe, Independent scholar, Great Britain

Viktor J. Vanberg, Albert-Ludwigs University, Freiburg, Germany

Richard van den Berg, Kingston University, Great Britain

K. Vela Velupillai, Solna, Sweden

Ragupathy Venkatachalam, Goldsmiths, University of London, Great Britain

Carl Christian von Weizsäcker, University of Köln, Germany

L. Randall Wray, Levy Economics Institute of Bard College, New York, USA

Khalid Yahia, McMaster University, Canada

Joachim Zweynert, Witten/Herdecke University, Germany

General introduction

The past is never dead. It's not even past. (William Faulkner)

The aim of this *Handbook on the History of Economic Analysis* is to provide a succinct overview of the development of economics since its systematic inception up until today. The *Handbook* has three volumes. Volume I deals with *Great Economists since Petty and Boisguilbert*. It provides short essays in biography of some of the most important economists in what is known as the "Western World". Volume II deals with *Schools of Thought in Economics*. A school is defined in terms of the analytical method(s) used, the approach chosen in tackling the problem(s) at hand, the results derived and the policy conclusions inferred. Volume III contains summary accounts of *Developments in Major Fields of Economics* reflecting the division of labour within the discipline.

There are different ways of approaching the history of economic thought. The focus of these volumes is on economic theories: their formation, including their philosophical and historical underpinnings, their conclusiveness and place within the field, and their possible use in formulating economic policies. We draw attention to those economists and their doctrines that we regard as especially significant. It hardly needs to be said that our choice unavoidably reflects a subjective element. We would have liked to include the portraits of several more important thinkers, but space constraints prevented us from doing so. The same applies *cum grano salis* to the schools of thought and developments in major fields covered.

Let us however acknowledge, at the outset, some of the important gaps in coverage. The focus is on European intellectual traditions and their continuation in the so-called Western World, but of course it is a fact that all advanced civilizations can point to notable achievements in the exploration of economic life – think of countries such as China or Japan, for example, or civilizations following philosophical or religious traditions such as Buddhism or Islam. In addition to geographic gaps, there are also some gaps in subjects covered, such as the omission of business administration and management theories.

Arthur Cecil Pigou once remarked that the history of economic thought is a history of the "wrong ideas of dead men". Certainly, it is partly also that, but not only, and moreover there is always much to learn from the alleged "errors". While there is progress in economics, there is also occasional regress. This should not come as a surprise: in a discipline dealing with as complex a subject matter as economics, it would be naive not to expect some intellectual "bubbles" that sooner or later burst, necessitating a fundamental re-orientation in the area of investigation under consideration. In the parlance of economists: the market for economic ideas is not a perfectly functioning selection mechanism that preserves all that is correct and valuable and discards whatever is wrong and useless.

This may also contribute to explaining the remarkable fact that certain ideas and concepts in economics, cherished at one time, get submerged and are forgotten afterwards, only to re-emerge in a new garb and liberated of their teething troubles at a later time. As Dennis Robertson once remarked with regard to the history of economics: "If you stand in the same place long enough, the hunted hare comes round again." Or, as Alfred Marshall put it: "We continually meet with old friends in new dresses." One of the most knowledgeable historians of economic thought ever, Joseph Alois Schumpeter, expressed the same view as follows: "Old friends come disguised to the party."

Modern economists frequently seem to believe that it not only suffices to know just the most recent economic doctrines and theories; they even seem to think, echoing Pigou's statement above, that it is detrimental to their intellectual development to expose themselves to the ideas and thoughts of earlier generations of economists. Since by assumption these must be partly or wholly wrong, or at least imperfect, it is not only a waste of time to study the "old masters", it may even be harmful to do so, because it may confuse readers and prompt them to deviate from the correct path to truth and wisdom. This position is a version of what the literary critic Norman Foerster called "provincialism of time", that is, "the measure of past literature by the ideas and moods of a narrow present". It is, among other things, based on the false presumption that it is the privilege of living economists to articulate only correct views.

Even a casual look at the history of economics, its various schools of thought and doctrines, shows that economics always lacked and still lacks a *unité de doctrine*, and that there is no reason to presume that this state of affairs will end any time soon. If economics were characterized by a relentless march towards ever-higher levels of knowledge and truthfulness, this fact would be difficult to explain.

There can be little doubt that the ideas of economists are important. John Maynard Keynes even insisted: "The ideas of economists and political philosophers, both when they are right and when they are wrong, are more powerful than is commonly understood. Indeed the world is ruled by little else." If this happens to be so, it is important to know the ideas of economists, especially when they are wrong. The history of economic analysis is not only a treasure trove of such ideas, it also informs about when and why certain ideas were challenged and some of them eventually rejected, at least in the form in which they were available at the time. Knowing the history of the discipline should help you to resist superstition, hysteria and exuberance in economic and social questions. And it should immunize you against falling victim to the ideas of some "defunct economist" (Keynes) all too easily.

The gestation period of the *Handbook on the History of Economic Analysis* was long – a great deal longer than originally planned. There are many factors that contribute to explaining the delays to the project. With some 140 authors, the probability was high that some of them could not deliver, for various respectable reasons, and had to be replaced. In some cases we had to act as writers of last resort. We also insisted that the three volumes should come out together, which necessitated the completion of them at roughly the same time. Bad health at different periods of time for each of the editors did not exactly help in propelling the project forward. Confronted with these and other difficulties, we are all the more pleased to be able to present the *Handbook on the History of Economic Analysis* to the scientific community. We take this opportunity to thank all of the contributors for their fine work. We are particularly grateful to those who delivered their entries in good time and for their patience thereafter. We also thank the referees we involved in assessing the different versions of the entries and for their useful comments, which helped to improve them.

May this *Handbook on the History of Economic Analysis* contribute to a better under-standing of the path economics took over time up until today and substantiate William Faulkner's claim that "History is not was, it is".

GILBERT FACCARELLO AND HEINZ D. KURZ

A note on the cross-references sections: the volume in which the cross-references appear is listed as follows:

(I)   *Handbook on the History of Economic Analysis Volume I: Great Economists since Petty and Boisguilbert;*

(II)   *Handbook on the History of Economic Analysis Volume II: Schools of Thought in Economics;*

(III) *Handbook on the History of Economic Analysis Volume III: Developments in Major Fields of Economics.*

William Petty (1623–1687)

William Petty was born 26 May 1623 into modest family circumstances in Romsey, Hampshire. A precocious child, with a colourful personality which remained firmly with him in adulthood, Petty made his way in the world with both great ambition and great success. As a result of various happy accidents, he gained a progressive education in France and the Netherlands between 1638 and 1645, and acquired influential patrons, including Thomas Hobbes. After returning to England he studied medicine at Oxford University, acquiring the degree of Doctor of Physic in 1650. Benefiting from the Cromwellian purge of loyalist dons from the university, he was appointed Professor of Anatomy there in 1651.

Petty's ambitions led him to accept the position of physician-general to the English army in Ireland from 1652. More than two decades of his remaining 35 years were spent in that country. He went on to undertake the massive "Down" survey of Ireland which formed the basis for the transfer of Irish lands to the English "adventurers" who had undertaken the military subjugation of Ireland in the 1640s (Larcom 1851; Petty's own long account of the survey). Putting aside any moral judgements about this episode or Petty's involvement in it, the survey provided him with the opportunity to examine in great empirical detail the social and economic condition of an entire people – important material for his later "political arithmetic". His Irish involvements also made Petty a very rich landowner in Ireland.

Petty was an enthusiastic and committed devotee of the English scientific revolution of the seventeenth century, which took much of its inspiration from the reform programme of Francis Bacon. Related to these scientific involvements, he was a founding member of the Royal Society (and its Council) in 1662 and a friend or acquaintance of many leading intellectual figures of the era. Hence as a seminal figure in the formation of a scientific economics in the generic sense, and of classical economics in terms of substantive ideas, Petty comes to economic analysis from a deep and rich philosophical and scientific intellectual background. (This is to be contrasted with the mercantile or commercial background of most of those who contributed to the English economic literature of the seventeenth century.) Marx (1967: 272–3) regards him as the founder of political economy. In significant part following the lead of his early mentor, Hobbes, Petty took mathematics as the model of rational inquiry, at least so long as the mathematical method was combined with well-defined objective, empirical concepts upon which the mathematics could operate (Aspromourgos 1996: 54–72).

Petty was an original and creative thinker who pursued innovation across a range of activities, though not always successfully. The Irish survey itself was a highly innovative exercise. He also tried his hand at various inventions. He had strong ambitions for the advancement of science, technology and policy, *and* his own material interests. This aspect of Petty's temper is captured, albeit in a rather negative way, in a comment of Charles II: "the man will not be contented to be excellent, but is still Ayming at Impossible Things" (Lansdowne 1928: 281).

The intellectual innovation for which Petty is most remembered is the invention of "political arithmetic", first explicitly formulated by him in the early 1670s (Aspromourgos 1996: 41–9, 2001: 79–83; the term originates with him also). It has been retrospectively characterized as the beginnings of "econometrics" (Schumpeter 1954: 209–10); but

Hicks (1983: 17) is closer to the truth in perceiving it as "social accounting". More recently, it has been argued that economists, in claiming Petty as a founding figure in their latter-day discipline, have distorted the character of his political arithmetic project, dislocating it from its context (especially its Irish colonization context) and appropriating it to a Whig history of political economy (McCormick 2009). There is no doubt some truth in this; but while political arithmetic is not political economy, they are not incommensurable projects. As much as Petty's political arithmetic, Adam Smith's political economy is a science designed for State policy.

While Petty's pioneering efforts at the application of quantification to human phenomena has naturally been a source of considerable retrospective interest, not to say fascination, it is important also to recognize that his political arithmetic programme was not merely a large-scale, grand exercise in accumulating quantitative data or "facts" concerning economy, society and polity (as well as other phenomena). In contemplating this question, interpretive debate has often been taken up with rather sterile arguments in terms of inductivism versus deductivism. Putting aside that dichotomy – Petty was, in any case, emphatically an empiricist – it is clear that the quantitative empirical political arithmetic projects from the early 1670s forward, were informed by conceptual and theoretical ideas developed earlier. In particular, latter-day fascination with the essays in political arithmetic (and one large essay in "political anatomy") has drawn attention away from his earlier, and by the standards of the time, large essay, *A Treatise of Taxes & Contributions* (1662, in Hull 1899: 1–97), which contains most of his important conceptual and theoretical ideas, and prefigures the project of a quantitative and objectively grounded form of "social science" (our term), which Petty sought to advance.

The striking feature of the *Treatise* is that it grounds consideration of taxation, tax policy and tax reform in an analysis of production and distribution. The real source of tax revenues (which are partly to fund one of Petty's key reform objectives, the full utilization of the nation's available labour) is society's economic surplus: the gross outputs net of the necessary inputs used up in their production (Hull 1899: 30–31, 42–5, 89–90). In the first instance, Petty is able to conceptualize this idea with clarity by making the simplifying assumption that in agriculture, the output and necessary input are one and the same commodity, so that the surplus may be defined independently of intersectoral relations. But elsewhere he gives expression to the same kind of social surplus concept in more sophisticated forms (Aspromourgos 2005). This conceptualization becomes in the *Treatise* the kernel of a theory of distribution in which the surplus is realized primarily as land-rents and tax revenues – symptomatic of the fact that Petty is theorizing a pre-capitalist economy (Aspromourgos 1996: 22–30). He also outlines a location theory of differential rent (Hull 1899: 48–52).

The surplus analysis is articulated primarily in terms of a division between a society's necessary and total available labour. This framework, in both the *Treatise* and later writings, then informs descriptive and normative analyses of the level and composition of employment in England and Ireland. Petty consistently and persistently argued for grand schemes of socio-economic reform, with a view to maximizing surplus labour and allocating it towards more useful activities. The pursuit of material progress is an underlying motif of his writings, a theme which can also be seen as derivative from Bacon. Petty enunciates as well a kind of labour theory of relative prices, though it might be better interpreted as a cost-of-production theory. This is combined with a market/natural price distinction of similar character to that in later classical writers, and typically of Petty, expressed by way of a preference for objective explanation. Having explained the causes of natural price in terms of labour-time or cost, he adds that as well as these "permanent Causes", there are "contingent Causes", due to commodities having "Substitutes", and the fact that "novelty, surprize . . . and opinion of unexaminable effects do adde or take away from the price of things" (Hull 1899: 90). With regard to monetary analysis, he was also the originator of the concept of the velocity of circulation of money. Although in favour of accumulation of a kind of national precautionary reserve of money, Petty does not fit comfortably into the "mercantilist" mould. A fuller account of all these matters is provided in Aspromourgos (1996: 30–51).

The objectivist temper of Petty's approach to social theory is expressed in many places and in many ways in his corpus of writings (Aspromourgos 1996: 57–64). It is also engagingly captured in a contemporaneous anecdote concerning Petty, recounted by John Aubrey:

> I remember one St Andrewe's day (which is the day of the Generall Meeting of the Royall Society for Annuall Elections) I sayd, Methought 'twas not so well that we should pitch upon the Patron of Scotland's day, we should rather have taken St George or St Isadore (a Philosopher canonized). No, said Sir William, I would rather have had it on St Thomas day, for he would not beleeve till he had seen and putt his fingers into the Holes, according to the Motto *Nullius in verba* [not bound to swear obedience to any man's dogma]. (Dick 1972: 402)

Petty is here referring to the New Testament story of the disciple of Jesus, Thomas – "doubting Thomas" as he has been subsequently known – who, when told that Jesus had risen from the dead, is supposed to have said: "Unless I see in his hands the mark of the nails, and place my finger into the mark . . . I will never believe" (Gospel of St John, 20:25). Evidently, Thomas was the empiricist disciple! This anecdote also incidentally captures something of Petty's personality and sense of humour, which sometimes got him into trouble (see, for example, Bray 1907: 100–101).

Most of Petty's published "economic" works, from the *Treatise* of 1662 forward, including all his published essays in political arithmetic, are in Hull (1899). The most notable published work omitted is Petty (1647), partly inspired by his observations of Holland, a short essay which captures the element of Baconian inspiration for Petty's mature economic thought, prefiguring many of the concerns of his later writings, notably, division of labour, technical progress and labour productivity. Petty (1674), also omitted from Hull (1899) apart from two slight extracts (at pp. 622–4), is significant as well, for its reflections on quantification. Petty left a large archive of manuscripts, which remained in the possession of his descendants for three centuries, but is now in the British Library. Lansdowne (1927) is a collection of selections from this material (also Lansdowne 1928). Matsukawa (1977) is a further and important document from the archive. Interestingly, in another unpublished manuscript from the archive Petty provides a thoughtful argument concerning the *limits* of rational quantification, confounding the image of him in some secondary literature as rather excessive in his pursuit of quantification (Aspromourgos 2000: 66–7). The very large archive of Samuel Hartlib at Sheffield University contains considerable material by and concerning the young Petty, which is also revealing of his formative intellectual development (HROnline 2002). There are two biographies of Petty (Fitzmaurice 1895; Strauss 1954), though McCormick

(2009) is itself primarily an intellectual biography. The latter work is the first comprehensive study more or less singularly devoted to Petty since Roncaglia (1985). The historian of Ireland, T.C. Barnard, has written extensively about Petty's Irish involvements in particular. Aspromourgos (2001) provides a quite comprehensive bibliography of secondary literature on Petty, to the end of the twentieth century.

TONY ASPROMOURGOS

See also:
Mercantilism and the science of trade (II).

References and further reading
Aspromourgos, T. (1996), *On the Origins of Classical Economics: Distribution and Value from William Petty to Adam Smith*, London: Routledge.
Aspromourgos, T. (2000), 'New light on the economics of William Petty (1623–1687): some findings from previously undisclosed manuscripts', *Contributions to Political Economy*, **19**, 53–70.
Aspromourgos, T. (2001), 'The mind of the oeconomist: an overview of the "Petty Papers" archive', *History of Economic Ideas*, **9** (1), 39–101.
Aspromourgos, T. (2005), 'The invention of the concept of social surplus: Petty in the Hartlib circle', *European Journal of the History of Economic Thought*, **12** (1), 1–24.
Bray, W. (ed.) (1907), *Diary of John Evelyn*, vol. 2, London: J.M. Dent & Sons.
Dick, O.L. (ed.) (1972), *Aubrey's Brief Lives*, Harmondsworth: Penguin.
Fitzmaurice, E. (1895), *The Life of Sir William Petty, 1623–1687*, London: John Murray.
Hicks, J. (1983), 'The social accounting of classical models', in J. Hicks, *Classics and Moderns* (*Collected Essays on Economic Theory*, vol. 3), Oxford: Blackwell, pp. 17–31.
HROnline (2002), *The Hartlib Papers: a Complete Text and Image Database of the Papers of Samuel Hartlib (c. 1600–1662) Held in Sheffield University Library*, Sheffield, UK: Humanities Research Institute, University of Sheffield.
Hull, C.H. (ed.) (1899), *The Economic Writings of Sir William Petty together with the* Observations Upon the Bills of Mortality *More Probably by Captain John Graunt*, 2 vols, Cambridge: Cambridge University Press.
Lansdowne, Marquis of [H.W.E. Petty Fitzmaurice] (ed.) (1927), *The Petty Papers*, 2 vols, London: Constable.
Lansdowne, Marquis of [H.W.E. Petty Fitzmaurice] (ed.) (1928), *The Petty–Southwell Correspondence, 1676–1687*, London: Constable.
Larcom, T.A. (ed.) (1851), *The History of the Survey of Ireland, Commonly Called the Down Survey, by Doctor William Petty, A.D. 1655–6*, Dublin: Irish Archaeological Society.
Marx, K. (1967), *Capital: A Critique of Political Economy*, vol. 1, New York: International Publishers (first German edn, 1867).
Matsukawa, S. (1977), 'Sir William Petty: an unpublished manuscript', *Hitotsubashi Journal of Economics*, **17** (February), pp. 33–50.
McCormick, T. (2009), *William Petty and the Ambitions of Political Arithmetic*, Oxford: Oxford University Press.
[Petty, W.] (1647), *The Advice of W.P. to Mr. Samuel Hartlib. For the Advancement of Some Particular Parts of Learning*, London.
Petty, W. (1674), *The Discourse Made Before the Royal Society the 26 of November 1674. Concerning the Use of Duplicate Proportion in Sundry Important Particulars: Together with a New Hypothesis of Springing or Elastique Motions*, London: John Martyn.
Roncaglia, A. (1985), *Petty: the Origins of Political Economy*, New York: Sharpe (Italian edn, 1977).
Schumpeter, J.A. (1954), *History of Economic Analysis*, ed. E.B. Schumpeter, New York: Oxford University Press.
Strauss, E. (1954), *Sir William Petty: Portrait of a Genius*, London: Bodley Head.

Pierre Le Pesant de Boisguilbert (1646–1714)

Pierre Le Pesant de Boisguilbert was born in Rouen (Normandy) on 17 February 1646, in a family of "noblesse de robe" – that is, an aristocratic family which got its rank from holding certain judicial or administrative positions – and died there on 10 October 1714. A distant relative of the playwright Pierre Corneille (1606–1684) and of the *homme de lettres* Bernard Le Bovier de Fontenelle (1657–1757), he was first educated by the Jesuits in Rouen and then in the Jansenist Petites Écoles de Port-Royal near Paris. After studying law in Paris, he held various "charges" or "offices" in Normandy in the Ancien Régime administration of justice and police where he acquired the deserved reputation of being a passionate and bad-tempered person. Like many contemporaries he was struck by the deep and lasting economic and social distress which prevailed in France during the second half of the reign of Louis XIV (1638–1715). Also like many other "men of system" and pamphleteers of the age, he tried to remedy the situation and he proposed, with a remarkable insistence, his solution to the various Contrôleurs généraux des finances (Ministers of the economy and finance), L. Phélypeaux de Pontchartrain (from 1689 to 1699), M. Chamillart (from 1699 to 1708) and N. Desmarets (from 1708 onwards). He remained however unsuccessful in spite of the support of some influential persons like J.-B. Desmarets de Vaubourg – a nephew of Colbert – and the Duke of Saint-Simon (see Hecht 1966b).

The precise dating of most of Boisguilbert's writings is uncertain. While his *Le Détail de la France* was published anonymously in 1695, probably some years after its composition, the greatest part of his works – for example, the *Dissertation de la nature des richesses, de l'argent et des tributs*, the *Traité de la nature, culture, commerce et intérêt des grains*, the first and the second *Factum de la France* – were published all together, with a reprint of the *Détail*, in 1707, in two volumes, under various titles, one of which being particularly misleading: *Testament politique de Monsieur de Vauban* – this generated a lasting confusion between his ideas and those that Marshall Sébastien Le Prestre de Vauban (1633–1707) published the same year in his *Dixme Royale*. Some works were republished in 1843 in the "Collection des principaux économistes", with Guillaumin, in a volume dedicated to the *Économistes financiers du XVIIIe siècle*, but this is a faulty edition because Boisguilbert's vocabulary was sometimes changed by the editor, Eugène Daire, in order to "update" it. Some important unpublished manuscripts and correspondence were discovered later and published in the only complete and reliable collection of Boisguilbert's works: the 1966 INED edition by Jacqueline Hecht (Hecht 1966a).

The interpretation of Boisguilbert's writings is an intricate undertaking. While his works have never ceased to attract attention, the various interpretations offered are conflicting. Boisguilbert was alternatively depicted as a liberal and as a protectionist; as a supporter of capitalism or of socialism; or, to put it briefly, as a "forerunner" of nearly every important economist who wrote after him (see, for example, Horn 1867; Van Dyke Roberts 1935; the studies included in Hecht 1966a, 1989; Faccarello 1986 [1999]). It is true that his style and language do not facilitate the reader's task. Recent research, however, eventually produced a picture of Boisguilbert as a powerful thinker, who, out of a threefold tradition of Bodinian political thought, Cartesian physics and above all Jansenist moral philosophy, founded what is called today the free-trade approach to political economy. Directly or indirectly, his thought influenced the main political economists of the French Enlightenment – Quesnay and Turgot in particular.

Boiguilbert's Approach and the Role of Jansenism

As a Jansenist, Boisguilbert's approach is typically embedded in a dark theological vision based on the fundamental "fact" of the Original Sin – Jansenism being a very pessimistic version of Augustinian thought. After "Adam's sin", man saw his nature totally corrupted and replaced in his heart the love of God with an exclusive love for himself – "amour-propre" or selfishness. Because he is not self-sufficient, he is obliged to work in a hostile environment and to cope with other men's self-loves in an everlasting fight.

Jansenist authors raised in this context three fundamental questions: theological, moral and political. In the first place, if men substituted in their heart their own self-love for the love of God, how could they be saved? – this is the problem of the grace. In the second place, if men act selfishly in all circumstances, no morality can ever exist and any action or thought which looks charitable, altruistic or benevolent from the outside, in reality only conceals strict egoistic motivations. In the third place, and this is the most important point here, the problem of social cohesion is posed: how could a society be maintained in this context of a war of all against all, when "all men are at battle with one another" (Nicole 1671–75 [1700], 3: 116)?

In the Jansenist French tradition, the theologian Pierre Nicole (1625–1695) – and after him the lawyer Jean Domat (1625–1696), both friends of Blaise Pascal – had already given part of the answer: while it is true that man's reason is very weak and his depravity too potent to allow anything other than passions to direct his behaviour, man nevertheless realizes that he cannot achieve his aims if he attempts to use coercion. Unable to "domesticate" his passions through reason, he uses instead his reason to follow his passions: he is thus willing to submit to other men's wishes and self-interest but only in order to fulfil his own desires. Nicole terms this type of conduct "enlightened self-love" ("amour-propre éclairé") and the best example he proposes are market activities.

> For example, when travelling in the country, we find men ready to serve those who pass by and who have lodgings ready to receive them almost everywhere. We dispose of their services as we wish. We command them; they obey . . . They never excuse themselves from rendering us the assistance we ask from them. What could be more admirable than these people if they were acting from charity? It is cupidity which induces them to act. (Nicole 1670 [1677]: 204)

Thanks to this intelligent self-love, a society can endure and develop. This society, which is absolutely deprived of love, actually looks full of charity: moreover passions generate strong positive social results and, as regards the production of material wealth, are incomparably more efficient than charity – all themes picked up later and developed by Boisguilbert, the Protestant theologian Pierre Bayle, Bernard de Mandeville and Adam Smith.

> Would you like that a nation be strong enough to resist her neighbours? Leave the maxims of Christianity to the preachers: keep all this for the theory, and bring back the practice to the laws of Nature . . . which incite us . . . to become richer and of a better condition than our fathers. Preserve the vivacity of greediness and ambition, and just forbid them robbery

and fraud . . . Neither the cold nor the heat, nothing should stop the passion of growing rich. (Bayle 1704 [1705]: 600).

While necessary, this enlightened behaviour is not in fact a sufficient condition for a peaceful social life. Nicole and Domat stress that this attitude and an enduring social order cannot be achieved without the help of bonds of a different kind, the most important of which being the rules of propriety and honour, religion and, above all, the political order ("ordre politique"), that is, a very strong political organization of society implying highly differentiated and stratified estates of the realm and inequality between men (on all these points see, for example, Taveneaux 1965; Viner 1978; Faccarello [1986] 1999; 2006). Nicole's and Domat's conception of society is not market-based and the basic social link is still political and moral. Boisguilbert in contrast obliterates the moral and political order and brings market relationships to the fore.

Economic Equilibrium and "Laissez-Faire"

If we consider the activities of the productive class, we are faced with an intricate network of purchases and sales. Yet, it is possible to discover an order by concentrating on the motivations of the agents, which are the same everywhere and the systematic application of men's self-love to transactions, generating a maximizing economic behaviour: "each man thinks of achieving the greatest degree of individual interest with the greatest ease possible" (Boisguilbert 1691–1714: 749).

What is the main characteristic of a state of wealth or plenty ("équilibre" or "état d'opulence")? Applying here some notions derived from Cartesian physics, Boisguilbert defines this equilibrium as a situation in which economic agents are allowed to realize freely their natural inclinations, that is, to buy and sell, trying to get the most they can out of the various situations they encounter. As each agent is only connected with the other agents by means of markets and of prices, it is not surprising to see Boisguilbert defining a state of equilibrium or plenty as a situation in which a specific price system occurs: the "proportion prices" ("prix de proportion") defined as those prices that generate a "reciprocal utility" or a "shared profit" – in seventeenth-century French language "utility" and "profit" are quite synonymous and are understood in a general way – and make each producer "off loss". This implies that, in each market, demand must equal supply. This condition can be deduced, in particular, from the recurrent passages in which the "tacit condition of exchanges" ("condition tacite des échanges") is referred to. To keep the economy in equilibrium, Boisguilbert insists, each member of the productive class only buys someone else's commodity under the implicit assumption that someone else, directly or indirectly, buys the commodity he sells.

The question, however, lies in the very possibility of the realization of such a structure of relative prices. What about the destabilizing action of self-love? In some striking passages, Boisguilbert seems to admit the necessity for each agent to be aware of the flimsiness of the state of equilibrium. Each man, he writes, cannot obtain his own wealth but from the implementation of the "état d'opulence"; he ought not to forget the necessity of fairness and justice in trade, he has to think of the common good; but, under the pressure of self-love, he acts every day in precisely the opposite way. Nevertheless, Boisguilbert stresses in a rather awkward way, an equilibrium can be reached in such a context: "Providence", he notes, is keeping a watchful eye on the working of markets; a "superior and general authority", a "powerful authority" is seeing to it that the economy is working properly; and he mentions "the harmony of the Republic, that a superior power governs invisibly" (1691–1714: 621).

All this may sound strange today, but the reader should not be misled by this kind of vocabulary. Evoking a "superior and general authority" does not mean a regulatory intervention of the State: Boisguilbert was explicitly against this kind of policy. Nor does the word "Providence" mean "miracle" or represent a rationally unexplainable state of affairs: in seventeenth-century French language, "Providence" refers in the first place to "secondary causes", that is, to the objective laws God installed when creating the world, and which can be discovered through scientific investigation. In Boisguilbert's writings, "Providence" simply refers to the rules of free competition. Competition *is* the "coercive power" – as K. Marx was to put it later – the "general authority" which governs markets. Each seller, Boisguilbert stresses, wants to be free to sell everywhere to anybody he or she wishes and to face the greatest possible number of buyers. As for the buyer, it is in his or her interest to be able to buy from everyone, in any place, and to face a great number of sellers. As maximizing agents wish to sell a commodity at the highest price, or to have it "for nothing", Boisguilbert asserts, then free competition must prevail throughout the economy in order to balance the opposite forces and to oblige people to be reasonable. The conclusion is then straightforward: laissez faire! To illustrate his conviction, Boisguilbert reported the answer a merchant gave to a minister who had asked him how to "re-establish trade":

> [T]he merchant said that there was a very certain and easy method to put into practice, which was that if he and his ilk stop interfering in it [in trade] then everything would go perfectly well because the desire to earn is so natural that no motive other than personal interest is needed to induce action. (Boisguilbert 1691–1714: 795)

Also, restating Nicole's example of the innkeeper, Boisguilbert noted:

> All the commerce of the land, both wholesale and retail . . . [is] governed by nothing other than the self-interest of the entrepreneurs, who have never considered rendering service . . . ; and any innkeeper who sells wine to passers-by never intended to be useful to them, nor did the passers-by who stop with him ever travel for fear that his provisions would be wasted. (Boisguilbert 1691–1714: 748–9)

This is the greatest innovative feature: the basic proposition of liberal political economy unambiguously and powerfully emerges from it. Most of the Jansenist social theory of Nicole and Domat is now obsolete. Man – at least if he is a member of the productive class – has not even to be enlightened; self-love is not destabilizing if embedded in an economic environment of free competition. Society is conceived as market based, and economic transactions form the basic social indirect link between otherwise independent economic agents. In Boisguilbert's words, the realm is just a "general market of all sorts of commodities" (1691–1714: 683). But if Nicole's and Domat's political order disappears, this is not to say that the State has no part to play: its role is to make sure that the rules of free competition actually prevail and, in that respect, it has to "ensure protection and prevent violence" (Boisguilbert 1691–1714: 892).

Destabilizing Shocks and Crises

After having stated the conditions for economic equilibrium Boisguilbert had to deal with the destabilizing shocks on the economy: this also constitutes an *a contrario* proof of the necessity of free trade. Destabilizing shocks originate in the class structure of society.

In Boisguilbert's scheme, a very simple type of society – the "état d'innocence" – existed for some time after the Fall, in which men, though corrupted, cooperated with each other: the number of needs was limited, the division of labour simple and barter was possible. All this came to an end when violence emerged: some men became lords (the rentiers) and the rest, that is, all those who produce goods and services, were subjected to them. This society is called a "state of civilization and magnificence" ("état poli et magnifique").

This transition induced major consequences: (1) with the existence of the rentiers, the number of needs increased and with it professions multiplied; (2) barter was no longer possible and money was introduced in order to facilitate exchanges; (3) the progressive multiplication of the professions, from the most necessary to the most superfluous – the comedian – generates also a kind of ratchet effect, that is, once a profession appears, and even if it is the least necessary, it had to be maintained because any attack on any trade inevitably induces, through the diminution of incomes and expenses, a depressing effect on all the other trades; (4) a one-way flow emerged in the distribution of income, reflecting the class structure of society and the fact that rentiers receive an income from the productive class without giving anything in exchange; and (5) the rentiers are not involved in trade, their behaviour is not checked by competition but by some other rules dictated by the "société de cour" – they know nothing about trade and its necessities and their action has thus to be enlightened. The very existence of a leisure class potentially transforms the economic structure from a stable to an unstable one: Boisguilbert's aim is to show how all destabilizing shocks are caused by the behaviour of those who "only receive" – and particularly the government through the institution of bad forms of taxation and the regulation of economic activities.

For Boisguilbert and in general for most authors during the *Ancien Régime*, the market for agricultural products is basic for two reasons: to satisfy the important needs and consumption habits of the population and because agriculture is the source of income of the leisure class. This is why agricultural crises lead directly to general depressions through significant spillover effects in different markets. But it is Boisguilbert's opinion that agricultural crises are due neither to climatic conditions nor to the mere behaviour of the members of the productive class. Prosperity as well as depression depends on the environment of activities. The role of expectations is crucial here: the same climatic conditions and the same basic behaviour in markets can generate either stabilizing or destabilizing consequences, depending on whether trade is free or regulated.

Let us suppose a strong corn trade regulation such as that which prevailed during the *Ancien Régime*. What happens in times of bad harvest or even when future crops are simply supposed not to be abundant? On the one hand, buyers expect rising prices and demand larger amounts of corn; a supposed crop failure is sufficient to induce strong precautionary behaviour – the formation of precautionary stocks. On the other hand, the sellers amplify the movement. They stress that crops are going to be very bad ones, even if it is not true; they expect a rising corn price, and, therefore, do not bring the usual quantities of corn to the market: they keep back speculative stocks in order to amplify the price movement. Thus, with a higher demand and a reduced supply, the price of corn increases to seven or even ten times its previous value and consumers are greatly impoverished in real terms. The point to note is the stock/flow mechanism on both sides of the market, which is in direct relationship with the expectations of the agents. Of course, the reverse occurs in case of a good harvest. Buyers expect a lower price and demand smaller quantities of corn than they usually do while the sellers, who cannot keep the corn in stock and also anticipate lower prices, increase their supply. The price falls and farmers are led into ruin.

Why do crises occur so regularly in such a context? In a regulated context there is a direct relationship between plenty and shortage of corn, between periods of very low and very high prices. Plenty generates shortage; when prices are low, farmers no longer cultivate poor quality land thus causing a decrease in agricultural production, which produces a shortage at the slightest climatic variation. On the other hand, shortage generates plenty because, owing to the high price of corn, more land is cultivated. Agricultural crises are thus inevitably cyclical and violent, causing in turn ruin on both sides of the market.

However, whenever free trade prevails, Boisguilbert stresses, the price of corn never fluctuates greatly and there are no crises. The proof is always based upon the information available to agents. When bad crops occur, for example, the mere possibility of buying from other places restrains the purchasers from increasing their demand for corn and building up precautionary stocks; the same possibility also restrains the sellers from speculating. As a result, the price does not fluctuate so much and proportion prices are roughly maintained. In this case also Boisguilbert emphasizes the role of expectations; prices are stabilized, he says, even if no corn, or only a small quantity of it, is imported from "foreign" provinces or foreign countries.

Finally, how do agricultural crises turn into general depressions? In the context of a regulated trade, the stock/flow mechanism linked to expectations in agricultural markets amplifies price and quantity movements considerably. A similar stock/flow mechanism, now linked to financial expectations, causes the propagation of the crisis from agriculture to other markets. The agricultural crisis directly affects the income of the leisure class. The rentier is faced with a diminished income flow. His reaction is twofold: because of his lower income, he actually spends smaller amounts of money; but he also spends less because, due to the depressed state of affairs, he is expecting a lower income in the future and he accordingly adopts a precautionary attitude – hoarding. As a result, the crisis is propagated more rapidly and economic movements are amplified.

However, the propagation and deepening of the crisis also takes place in a different way: through price rigidities, for example, in the market for non-agricultural products where downward rigid prices prevail; or in the labour market where a particular emphasis is put on the role of worker coalitions and of downward rigid money wages (on all these points see Faccarello 1986 [1999]).

Two last points must be stressed. First, the essential role played by foreign trade in Boisguilbert's approach is peculiar and still at the root of the free-trade attitude of Quesnay and Turgot during the following century – a kind of specificity of the French followers of the "liberté du commerce". The importance of free foreign trade is, first, qualitative. It is this freedom which acts on the expectations of agents in the grain trade and allows prices to stabilize and avoid crises; the size of the flows of imports or exports are of almost no significance in this context. Secondly, the question of foreign trade is disconnected from that of money. The quantity of circulating medium is of no importance: only the system of relative prices matters. Criticizing the many and persistent complaints about a "lack of money" as the origin of the economic difficulties of the realm, Boisguilbert insisted that this alleged want of circulating medium is only the consequence of the crisis – constitution of precautionary stocks of money, destruction of a great part of the commercial paper which acted as a medium of exchange – and by no means the cause.

GILBERT FACCARELLO

See also:

Marie-Jean-Antoine-Nicolas Caritat de Condorcet (I); French Enlightenment (II); François Quesnay and Physiocracy (I); Adam Smith (I); Anne-Robert-Jacques Turgot (I).

References and further reading

Bayle, P. (1704), reprinted (1705), *Continuation des pensées diverses, écrites à un Docteur de Sorbonne, à l'occasion de la Comète qui parut au mois de décembre 1680, ou Réponse à plusieurs difficultés que Monsieur*** a proposées à l'Auteur*, Rotterdam: Reinier Leers.
Boisguilbert, P. Le Pesant de (1691–1714), 'Correspondance' and 'Œuvres', in J. Hecht (ed.) (1966), *Pierre de Boisguilbert ou la naissance de l'économie politique*, 2 vols, Paris: INED, vol. 1, pp. 245–478, vol. 2, pp. 581–1031.
Domat, J. (1689), *Traité des lois*, in J. Domat (1828–29), *Œuvres complètes*, vol. 1, Paris: Firmin Didot, pp. 1–75.
Faccarello, G. (1986), *Aux origines de l'économie politique libérale: Pierre de Boisguilbert*, Paris: Anthropos, revised edn (1999), *The Foundations of Laissez-faire. The Economics of Pierre de Boisguilbert*, London: Routledge.
Faccarello, G. (2006), 'La *liberté du commerce* et la naissance de l'idée de marché comme lien social', in P. Nemo and J. Petitot (eds), *Histoire du libéralisme en Europe*, Paris: Presses Universitaires de France, pp. 205–53.
Hecht, J. (ed.) (1966a), *Pierre de Boisguilbert ou la naissance de l'économie politique*, 2 vols, Paris: INED.
Hecht, J. (1966b), 'La vie de Pierre Le Pesant, seigneur de Boisguilbert', in J. Hecht (ed.) (1966), *Pierre de Boisguilbert ou la naissance de l'économie politique*, vol. 1, Paris: INED pp. 121–244.
Hecht, J. (ed.) (1989), *Boisguilbert parmi nous*, Paris: INED.
Horn, I.E. (1867), *L'économie politique avant les physiocrates*, Paris: Guillaumin.
Nicole, P. (1670), *De l'éducation d'un Prince*, vol. 2 of *Essais de morale* from 1671 onwards, Paris, revised edn, 1677.
Nicole, P. (1671–75), *Essais de morale*, vols 1 and 3, La Haye: Adrian Moetjens, revised edition, 1700.
Taveneaux, R. (1965), *Jansénisme et politique*, Paris: Armand Colin.
Van Dyke Roberts, H. (1935), *Boisguilbert, Economist of the Reign of Louis XIV*, New York: Columbia University Press.
Viner, J. (1978), 'Religious thought and economic society: four chapters of an unfinished work', J. Melitz and D. Winch (eds), *History of Political Economy*, **10** (1), special issue.

John Law (1671–1729)

John Law (1671–1729) is rare among economists in that he not only attempted to produce a template for addressing monetary and financial crises, but actually implemented this template for a brief time between 1716 and 1720 in France, during a period known as the Mississippi System. The Mississippi System produced the world's first financial bubble which in turn served as a model for the British South Sea Bubble of 1720. By the end of 1720 both bubbles had collapsed and John Law, who had been appointed the equivalent of Prime Minister of France in January 1720, was hastily forced to flee to Brussels and later to Venice where he died in 1729. As such there are two main perspectives against which to examine Law, namely, (1) his role as a macroeconomic/monetary theorist and (2) his activities as a macroeconomic policy-maker. From the first perspective many economists, including Cantillon, Hume, Smith, Marx and Marshall severely criticized Law for his unrealistic and "visionary" theories. Contrastingly, however, Joseph Schumpeter rated Law as "one of the outstanding monetary theorists of all time". From the second perspective it is germane to note that Nicolas Du Tot, a significant contemporary analyst of the Mississippi System, remarked that posterity would not believe that Law had managed to create a specie-less system in France for a short period. It would take another couple of centuries for the global economy to move off the gold standard, an environment that Law had attempted to remove in France between 1716 and 1720.

Law's Background

John Law was born in Edinburgh in 1671. His father was a goldsmith at a time when the Scottish goldsmiths were becoming embryonic bankers by lending money against the deposits that they obtained for safekeeping. Noted for his agile mind and mathematical abilities at school, Law travelled to London in the 1690s acquiring the reputation of a dandy, philanderer and rake. Known as "Beau" Law he killed another "Beau", Edward Wilson in a duel in Bloomsbury Square in 1694. The cause of this duel has been disputed. Law was sentenced to death for Wilson's murder but escaped from prison through the connivance of leading British politicians of the day. He travelled to the Continent where he changed from his hitherto dilettante gambler role to that of the equivalent of an eighteenth-century bookmaker using his mathematical skills to make a fortune at the gambling tables in France and Italy. More importantly Law turned his intellect to money and banking, writing a paper "Essay on a land bank" (now published as *John Law's Essay on a Land Bank* – Law 1994) which he sent to Lord Godolphin in the hope that the English authorities would be interested in his proposal. Rejected by the English, he returned from the Continent to Edinburgh where he wrote *Money and Trade Consider'd with a Proposal for Suppllying the Nation with Money* (1705). This book contained his recommendations to the Scottish Parliament for the establishment of a paper money in Scotland. However, he was turned down by the Scottish Parliament and forced to leave Scotland because of the signing of the Act of Union in 1707. Law, still a convicted murder on the run from British justice, travelled back to the Continent where he attempted over the next nine years to encourage various European monarchs and states to implement his monetary proposals.

Law's Macroeconomics and Monetary Economics

John Law brought remarkable modernity to his economic theorizing. In his first work, "Essay on a land bank", he was the first writer to introduce supply and demand analysis to his theorizing, using it to solve the water/diamonds paradox of value. He then progressed this analysis into monetary economics establishing the concept of the demand for money and arguing that prices would rise when the quantity of money expanded out of line with the demand for money. In explaining inflation in a demand for money/supply of money framework, Law may be regarded as the first monetarist, long before Milton Friedman attempted to analyse the quantity theory of money in this format in 1956. Law's vision, however, extended far beyond monetarism. By one deft change in a preposition he transformed the conceptualization of money from an intrinsically valuable medium of exchange "the value *for* which money is exchanged" to one that held that money did not need to be intrinsically valuable "the value *by* which goods are exchanged" (my italics) (Law, 1994: 55). In this way Law produced a new vista for the monetary economy, one that was not reliant on an intrinsically valuable commodity money. Law's new conceptualization of money permitted the growth not only of paper money but also bank credit and a wide range of near money substitutes. His detractors from Cantillon to Marshall, all metallists at heart, did not grasp the extent to which Law had revolutionized his conceptualization of the monetary system to that which is used in the modern world.

In *Money and Trade* Law continued to advance many of the arguments of the "Essay on a land bank" but the emphasis of his approach changed because he was addressing the problems of a stagnant Scottish economy facing considerable unemployment and underemployment. Law, building on the work of Sir William Petty, developed a circular flow of income analysis and then showed the importance that money had in transforming an economy from a primitive agricultural state to that of a broader economy, embracing manufacturing and other sectors. The title of his book said it all, *Money and Trade*. He saw money as driving trade, a synonym for economic activity. Unemployment and underemployment were signs that there was an insufficient amount of money in the economy. In a strong pre-Keynesian approach Law urged the authorities to expand the money supply and to reduce the rate of interest. For him the way to increase the money supply was to replace the gold and silver metallic system with a new paper credit system. Unlike most monetary theorists Law's recommendations were soon to be implemented as monetary policy.

Law's Mississippi System

It was not till the death of Louis XIV and the arrival of Philippe, duc d'Orléans, as regent of France during the minority of the future Louis XV, that Law's money and banking proposals were accepted. France faced two crises, a monetary crisis, caused by a shortage of money, and a financial crisis, in the form of a high level of state indebtedness due to the late king's over-spending and over-borrowing. Law suggested to the regent that the first crisis could be addressed by the substitution of paper money for gold and silver coins. To achieve this he set up the General Bank in 1716 which was later converted into the Royal Bank. As a quasi-state institution the Royal Bank's paper was made legal tender for the payment and receipt of taxes and its paper banknotes soon became the dominant means of payment. Law addressed the financial crisis by taking over the Company of the West, a company controlling the trading concessions of French Louisiana – a vast area embracing all the land from the Gulf of Mexico to Canada, bordered by the British Carolinas in the east and the Spanish-held Texas in the west. The Company's shares were initially acquired with short-term French government debt (billets d'état) thereby helping to alleviate some of the French national debt problem. As this French debt stood at a hefty discount, the shares could be initially purchased for around 170 French livres. Law then used the Company of the West, which would become known as the Mississippi Company, to take over the other French trading companies, the tobacco monopoly, the mint, the tax farms, and so on, turning it into a giant conglomerate. Further issues of shares were made at 550 livres, 1000 livres and 5000 livres. The main objective of the 5000 livres share issue was to take over the totality of the French national debt.

Through the expansion of the paper note issue and the creation of the Mississippi Company – which issued 624 000 shares – Law appeared to have transformed the French economy. The share price peaked in January 1720 at over 10 000 livres and to honour his achievements John Law was made Contrôlleur Général des Finances, a position equivalent to that of Prime Minister. Unfortunately for Law, he had pushed the System too far and was using the banknote issue of the Royal Bank to support the Mississippi Company's share price. In February 1720 he guaranteed the share price at 9000 livres but this monetization of the shares caused the System to start cracking. In May 1720 he attempted to bring some balance to the financial position by implementing an edict to have staggered monthly reductions in the value of banknotes and shares. The public reacted strongly against this edict. Law was demoted and though he carried out a rearguard action trying to re-structure the System, his efforts failed and he was forced to leave France at the end of 1720.

ANTOIN E. MURPHY

See also:

Richard Cantillon (I); French Enlightenment (II); David Hume (I); Mercantilism and the science of trade (II); Money and banking (III).

References and further reading

Du Tot, N. (1738), *Réflexions politiques sur les finances et le commerce*, The Hague: Les Freres Vaillant et Nicolas Prevost.
Du Tot, N. (1738), *Réflexions politiques sur les finances et le commerce*, ed. P. Harsin, 1935, Paris: E. Droz.
Du Tot, N. (2000), *Histoire du Systême de John Law*, ed. A.E. Murphy, Paris: INED.
Faure, E. (1977), *La Banqueroute de Law*, Paris: Gallimard.
[Law, J.] (1705), *Money and Trade Consider'd with a Proposal for Suppllying the Nation with Money*, Edinburgh: The Heirs and Successors of Andrew Anderson.
Law, J. (1934), *John Law: Oeuvres Complètes*, ed. P. Harsin, Paris; reprint Vaduz, 1980.
Law, J. (1994), *John Law's Essay on a Land Bank*, ed. A. Murphy, Dublin: Aeon.
Murphy, A. (2009), *The Genesis of Macroeconomics*, Oxford: Oxford University Press.
Murphy, A.E. (1997), *John Law Economic Theorist and Policy-Maker*, Oxford: Oxford University Press.

Richard Cantillon (*c.* 1680/90–1734)

Richard Cantillon was born in Ballyheigue, County Kerry in the south west of Ireland probably between 1680 and 1690. Cantillon formed part of a large-scale emigration of Irish Catholics to France after the signing of the Treaty of Limerick, an event that concluded the Jacobite/Williamite war in Ireland. Cantillon's uncle was the Jacobite banker, Daniel Arthur, a man who had been largely instrumental in transferring the financial capital of the Irish Jacobites out of Ireland. This connection probably enabled him to be introduced into the world of bankers and financiers.

Cantillon's Career

Cantillon worked as a deputy to Anthony Hammond, the representative in Spain of the British Paymaster General to the Forces Abroad, James Brydges. Brydges, who later became Lord Carnarvon and still later the Duke of Chandos (henceforth Chandos), was the biggest war profiteer of the age. He amassed a fortune through foreign exchange transactions on money that was converted from sterling into foreign currencies to pay for the armies overseas. Chandos took his percentage on all provisioning contracts ranging from food to horses, to uniforms, to gunpowder, and so on.

By 1717 Cantillon had met up with a far more important personality who was to have a profound effect on the rest of his career. This was the Scotsman, John Law (1671–1729) who had started to put in place his grand design aimed at transforming the French monetary and financial systems – see entry on John Law.

Cantillon's relationship with Law blew hot and cold during the Mississippi System. Initially they were on sufficiently good terms to establish, along with one of the biggest Mississippian speculators, Joseph Gage, a colonizing group to develop a settlement in Louisiana. Cantillon's brother, Bernard, led this group from La Rochelle to New Orleans in 1719. However, as shares in the Mississippi Company rose from 170 to over 2000 in the early summer of 1719 Cantillon believed that there was a definite asset market bubble emerging. He sold his shares and retired to Italy. Cantillon's timing was wrong as the Mississippi shares moved to over 10000 in early January 1720. Cantillon returned to France in the spring of 1720. Then, convinced more than ever that the Mississippi System would explode, he shorted the shares of the Mississippi Company and the French currency. Believing that a similar bubble, emanating from the speculation in the South Sea Company shares, had emerged in Britain, Cantillon took out sizeable put option contracts with Dutch bankers on British shares. Meanwhile in France when the Mississippi Company faced increasing difficulties in the early summer of 1720, John Law invited Cantillon to return to France to assist him in re-structuring the System. Cantillon turned down the offer fearing that his profits, made through shorting the Company's shares and the French currency, would be confiscated when the System eventually collapsed. By the end of 1720 Law was forced to flee from France as his System fell apart. Cantillon, on the other hand, had made sizeable fortunes by shorting Mississippi shares and the French currency along with the put contracts that he had arranged on British shares. He would become known as one of the Mississippian millionaires, classified in the French Visa of 1721 as having made 20 million livres on his French transactions. Cantillon was to find that there were costs associated with making his fortune. Some of his clients, led by Lady

Mary Herbert and Joseph Gage, were responsible for criminal and civil suits against him alleging that he shorted the Mississippi with shares that they had given him as collateral for loans. These charges were never proven but they did mean that Cantillon faced continuous litigation in both Britain and France for the rest of his life. Cantillon was apparently murdered in his bed by a member of his household in 1734 in Albemarle Street, London.

The *Essai*

The *Essai sur la nature du commerce en général*, probably written sometime between 1728 and 1730 was published in Paris in 1755 bearing the fictitious imprint of Fletcher Gyles of London.

Cantillon had an ambitious objective as the title of his work show. He wanted to write an essay on the nature of trade in general. Trade ("le commerce") was a synonym for economic activity at the time. So Cantillon's objective was to produce an essay on the nature of economic activity in general.

To do this Cantillon needed to produce an economic model. This required abstraction which Cantillon produced by assuming initially that the economy consisted of just one single landed estate "which I wish to consider here as if it was unique in the world" (Cantillon 1755: 76).

Building on the abstraction of the single landed estate, with three principal actors (the landlord, supervisors and workers) Cantillon progressively transformed this primitive structure from a command economy to a market economy, from a barter system to a monetary system, and from a closed to an open economy. This transformation involved the introduction of a new series of principal actors, the entrepreneurs, who replaced the supervisors. Despite the continuing power of the proprietor of the landed estate to influence economic activity through his expenditure decisions, he became essentially a mute actor expressing his views through the prices that he was prepared to pay for commodities on the market. He could no longer verbally dictate his commands to the supervisors. The entrepreneurs – there are many of them ranging from entrepreneur producers to entrepreneur wholesalers, to entrepreneur retailers and even entrepreneur beggars – have a key role to play in the price-making process.

Cantillon summarized the role of the entrepreneur in a short sentence. The entrepreneur buys at a known price ("un prix certain") to sell at an unknown price ("un prix incertain"). In other words the entrepreneur knows the price of factors of production that he uses in the form of wages for labour, rent for land and profits for capital. Combining these inputs he produces output at a known price. However, he cannot guarantee that his selling price will cover his costs of production. The entrepreneur faces uncertainty. If he assesses the purchasing decisions of buyers correctly, and prices his commodities appropriately, he will make a profit. If he prices his commodities at excessively high prices and is unable to sell them, then he will be forced off-stage and out of business. Bringing in the distinction between market price and intrinsic value (costs of production plus normal profits), Cantillon showed how resources could be allocated through the market as entrepreneurs moved into sectors where the market price was above the intrinsic value of a commodity and moved out of areas where intrinsic value was above the market price. Smith relied heavily on Cantillon's model in chapter 7, book 1 of the *Wealth of Nations* (Smith 1776 [1976]) when he distinguished between market price and natural price to show the allocation of commodities.

Cantillon was not only interested in the way entrepreneurs ensured the flow of goods and services between markets, he was also concerned with analysing the aggregated flow of goods and services in the economy. Building on the earlier work of Petty and Law, Cantillon traced out in detail the circular flow of income model.

Cantillon's analysis inspired François Quesnay to encapsulate the circular flow process in the *tableau économique*. Cantillon and Quesnay differed in terms of their view on the consequences arising from the *produit net* in agriculture. Quesnay was able to envisage the agricultural surplus producing economic growth. Cantillon believed that any growth in agricultural production would just increase population. Quesnay was more interested in the dynamic income-generating process and the implications that it had for fiscal policy, that is, the possibility of the *produit net* in agriculture supporting the full weight of taxation through the imposition of a single tax – the *impôt unique*. Cantillon had a different objective in mind when analysing the circular flow, for he believed that it would enable him to determine the amount of money required in the economy. He needed to compile an estimate of the output of the economy and then, making allowances for the velocity of circulation of money, derive an estimate of the amount of money required to drive this level of output. He estimated the amount of money required in a state, duly modified by his analysis of the velocity of circulation of money, was one-third of the landlord's rent. As the landlord's rent was one-third of overall output this meant that he estimated the demand for money at one-ninth of output. This, he calculated, was near enough to Petty's estimate that the money in circulation was equal to one-tenth of the produce of the soil.

Cantillon's Analysis of the Monetary Economy

Following his estimation of the demand for money, Cantillon proceeded to demonstrate the different ways in which the money supply could be expanded and to outline the changes that would happen when the money supply moved out of line with the demand for money. This led to his conceptualization of what is now referred to as the "black box transmission mechanism". The black box is meant to describe the different ways in which increases in the money supply permeate through the economy influencing prices, output and the balance of payments. Cantillon's concern was (1) to show the way in which the monetary economy could be meshed in with the real economy to produce an overall equilibrium and then (2) to outline the consequences of an over-expansion of the money supply out of line with the needs of the real economy in terms of inflation, output and the balance of payments. He was not prepared to accept a crude monetarist type that suggested a proportionate relationship between increases in the money supply and an increase in prices. For him there was a need to examine the channels through which monetary expansion could influence expenditure and he was critical of John Locke for not detailing the monetary transmission mechanisms.

Cantillon took up this challenge and provided a detailed taxonomy of these mechanisms outlining four potential sources of monetary expansion: (1) the mining of gold and silver; (2) a balance of trade surplus; (3) capital inflows; (4) invisible earnings.

He then proceeded to show that, depending on the sources of the monetary expansion, the money might be spent, saved or hoarded.

Arising from these decisions, the money could flow either into the commodity market or the financial market. There were two further elements in the chain linking changes in the money supply to changes in expenditure. First it was necessary to consider the openness of the economy and, secondly, the degree of spare capacity in it. Depending on these factors the increased money supply might affect employment and output, or inflation or the balance of payments. Blaug termed the differential effect on prices of an increase in the money supply, arising from different monetary injections, as the "Cantillon Effect" (1962: 21).

Cantillon had witnessed the volatility of financial capital flows across Europe in 1720 and understood how this superstructure of finance could very quickly collapse as investors lost confidence in a particular country.

Cantillon's overall analysis showed the way the real and monetary economies can be meshed together. Consistent with this he recognized the need to keep the rate of monetary expansion, emanating from the financial sector, in line with the size and growth of the real economy. In the case of an over-expansion of the money supply, his analysis of the black box provided a variety of transmission mechanisms so as to identify the pressures that the excessive money supply would generate for output, prices, employment and the balance of payments.

Cantillon realized that this meshing together of the real and monetary economies was a difficult exercise. This arose because there was a further element that needed to be incorporated into the analysis, namely, financial innovation. So far Cantillon had confined his analysis to a specie-based economy. He was a metallist at heart and believed that silver represented the "true sinew of circulation" (Cantillon 1755: 423). He was also a banker and he realized that there were other substitutes for silver money, namely, paper banknotes and bank credit. In his monetary taxonomy Cantillon did not wish to include such types of money in his definition of the money supply. For him they were financial instruments – he referred to them as "fictive money" – that influenced the velocity of circulation of money but not the stock of money. However, in influencing V rather than M he still understood that these financial instruments could have a considerable impact on the economy. As a practising banker Cantillon had witnessed the enormous benefits that the incipient financial revolution had created in Great Britain. Paper money and bank credit had come to Exchange Alley in London, and the Bank of England, which had just managed to escape from the trauma of the South Sea Bubble, was becoming an anchor institution in what would later be called the City. While reluctant to classify paper money and partially backed bank deposits as money, he was prepared to accept the benefits of these new banking innovations in facilitating an increase in the velocity of circulation of money. He was sufficient of a realist to accept a certain amount of financial innovation. In normal times banknotes and bank accounts facilitated the purchase and sale of government stocks and shares. At the same time he fully understood the tension that existed between financial innovation and financial prudence. The scales could tip to the former causing financial prudence to be neglected.

Cantillon fully understood that the financial innovation that had created banknotes and bank credit had greatly increased the potential of financial leverage. It resulted in an environment in which monetary policy was too loose. An excessive amount of money creation, in Cantillon's opinion, pushed equity and property prices too high and generated a bubble. The bubble in turn impacted on the real economy when asset holders attempted to use some of their gains, made in the financial economy, to increase expenditure in the real economy leading inevitably to the destruction of the bubble or "system".

Cantillon identified the dangers created by a financial system, excessively leveraged through financial innovation, for the real economy of "ordinary expenditure": "This example clearly shows that the paper and credit of public and private banks may produce surprising results in everything unconnected with the ordinary expenditure involved in drinking, eating, clothing and other family necessities" (Cantillon 1755: 423).

ANTOIN E. MURPHY

See also:

Balance of payments and exchange rates (III); British classical political economy (II); French Enlightenment (II); David Hume (I); John Law (I); Mercantilism and the science of trade (II); Money and banking (III); Adam Smith (I).

References and further reading

Berg, R. van den (2012), 'Something wonderful and incomprehensible in their economy: the English versions of Richard Cantillon's *Essay on the Nature of Trade in General*', *European Journal of the History of Economic Thought*, **19** (6), 868–907.

Blaug, M. (1962), *Economic Theory in Retrospect*, Homewood, IL: Richard D. Irwin.

Brewer, A. (1992), *Richard Cantillon: Pioneer of Economic Theory*, London: Routledge.

Bordo, M. (1983), 'Some aspects of the monetary economics of Richard Cantillon', *Journal of Monetary Economics*, **12** (2), 235–58.

Cantillon, R. (1755), *Essai sur la nature du commerce en general*, Paris: Guillyn; the publication location bears the fictitious imprint of 'Fletcher Gyles A Londres'.

Cantillon, R. (1931), *Essai sur la nature du commerce en général*, ed. H. Higgs, London: Macmillan.

Cantillon, R. (2015), *Essay on the Nature of Trade in General*, ed. A.E. Murphy, Indianapolis: Liberty Fund.

Hume, D. (1752), *Political Discourses*, Edinburgh: printed by R. Fleming for A. Kincaid and A. Donaldson.

Murphy, A.E. (1986), *Richard Cantillon Entrepreneur and Economist*, Oxford: Oxford University Press.

Murphy, A.E. (1997), *John Law Economic Theorist and Policy Maker*, Oxford: Oxford University Press.

Murphy, A.E. (2009), *The Genesis of Macroeconomics*, Oxford: Oxford University Press.

Smith, A. (1776), *An Inquiry into the Nature and Causes of the Wealth of Nations*, London: W. Strahan & T. Cadell, reprinted 1976, Oxford: Oxford University Press.

Charles-Louis de Secondat de Montesquieu (1689–1755)

Charles-Louis de Secondat, baron de la Brède et de Montesquieu (1689–1755) was born into an aristocratic family at La Brède near Bordeaux. He was educated by the Oratorians at the famous College of Juilly and later at Bordeaux Faculty of Law. He became a lawyer in 1708 and, in 1716, inherited from his uncle the prominent position of *président à mortier* in the Bordeaux *parlement* – at that time a court of justice. Apart from holding this venal office (which he sold in 1726), Montesquieu was also a landowner and a wine merchant. His fame in the Republic of Letters began in 1721 with the publication of the *Lettres persanes* (*Persian Letters*), a critique of absolutism and religion in the form of an epistolary novel. He followed it in 1734 with *Considérations sur les causes de la grandeur des Romains et de leur décadence* (*Considerations on the Causes of the Greatness of the Romans and of their Decline*). Elected to the Académie de Bordeaux in 1716 and to the Académie française in 1728, he travelled throughout Europe, and especially in England, between 1728 and 1731. It was, however, with the publication of *De l'esprit des lois* (*The Spirit of the Laws*) in 1748 that he achieved universal acclaim in the world of political science.

Montesquieu's economic thinking is concentrated in this work (especially in books VII, XIII, XX–XXIII) even if the *Lettres persanes* and the *Considérations* contain reflections on John Law's financial experiment in France (1717–20), considerations on population, trade and luxury goods, and a "history of commerce". Montesquieu does not develop a full-fledged system of economic ideas simply because it is not his intention to do so. His ideas on "commerce" belong to a broader reflection upon the "constitutions" of states and the "general spirit" of nations. In this respect, he reaches a relativistic view of economics embedded in politics and the social process generally. While he clearly supports the idea that individuals, in pursuing their own self-interest, produce goods and services, fulfil their needs, and ultimately increase the wealth of the nation (1748, in Montesquieu 1949–51, bk XX, chs 9–10), he looks to discuss this process within the different political regimes.

His method is well known. He considers a spectrum of causes that create a "spirit" in the nation and the laws, which are adapted (or not) to it. The first cause is "physical" (geography, climates), and the others are religious and related to the manners (*les moeurs*) of the peoples. He then analyses these causes in relation to ideal-types of government: republican, monarchic and despotic. But Montesquieu hones this rather classical three-way division into a contrast between "moderate" and "non-moderate" governments. Monarchies and aristocratic republics are moderate governments; despotic regimes and democratic republics non-moderate. England embodies moderate government. Thanks to its constitution which balances the two great forces (the executive and the legislative powers) and the passions reigning in these opposing camps, political freedom emerges (Montesquieu 1949–51, bk XX, ch. XIX). Not only does it ensure property rights – the citizen does not fear the state or other citizens – but this constitution also means that taxation is more readily accepted than under less moderate or non-moderate governments and that foreign trade flourishes. Indeed, taxes are mainly directed at financing England's maritime superiority. In the "jalousy of trade" (Hume 1987, pt II, essay VI) between European nations, the fiscal-military state of England has a decisive advantage (see Larrère 2001). In contradistinction to the "colonies for conquest" model characterized by wars and the destruction and predation of precious metals (Ancient Rome, the Spaniards in modern times), England promotes "colonies for trade" (this does not preclude aggressive operations to invade warehouses or trading posts). Montesquieu views British foreign commerce as a peaceful relationship between peoples, with the transporting of goods and ideas having civilizing effects. This is the famous *doux commerce* thesis (1748, in Montesquieu 1949–51, bk XX, chs 1–2). Some might concur with Albert O. Hirschman (1977) that Montesquieu theorizes the shift from "passions" to "interests", that is, from an outburst of destructive and bloody territorial conquests to a mutual sharing of the benefits of self-interest between nations. But this way of conceptualizing international trade has been described as a "mantra of modernity" (Reinert 2011: 7), with the "jalousy of trade" leading eighteenth-century European powers to combine war, empires and commerce in a new way that was probably no less destructive than earlier conquests.

However, it would be wrong to imagine Montesquieu as an enthralled worshipper of England and its constitution. He is no great admirer of English culture (especially the place assigned to women) and he judges that its political system is fragile. The liberty of Englishmen is not based on virtue, as in the Ancient Republic, but on self-interest and trade. It is both a strength and a weakness. The passion for money leads to corruption, to a decline of manners and virtues and finally to a possible subversion of the political system. So there should be no question of France adopting the English constitution. The French nation possesses its own "spirit" and its laws, institutions and trade obey their own logic (Cheney 2010: 73).

Montesquieu distinguishes between two kinds of trade. The "carrying trade" ("*commerce d'économie*") is suited particularly to "republics" (that is, republican governments and moderate monarchies) where thrift, a bourgeois spirit of acquisition and a certain equality among citizens prevail. It consists of high volumes of relatively common commodities sold at low prices. By contrast, the "luxury trade" ("*commerce de luxe*") is better suited to monarchic and despotic governments where vanity and pride are the dominant passions of the rich. Such a trade entails higher profits but fewer transactions. Montesquieu clearly states that the two are not exclusive in any nation, but that one or other of these trades dominates in each nation. As far as France is concerned, Montesquieu follows Bernard de Mandeville's *Fable of the Bees* by explaining that monarchies have an absolute requirement for luxury because it is spending by the rich that provides work and income for the poor. Fashions and taste create demand for luxury goods, engendering a luxury industry and trade (1748, in Montesquieu 1949–51, bk XIX, ch. 8–9; bk XXI, ch. 6). In this respect, monarchies such as France (the case of Spain is entirely different), with their hierarchical organization and the vanity and honour of the nobles, could also benefit from the rise of commerce, but in a different way from "republics" such as England or Holland. The path to wealth and the stability of the French "constitution" both depend on maintaining a balance among the constituent parts of the social hierarchy. Nobles should not be traders, but consumers. However, this elite must be open to the merchants (by the acquisition of *offices*) in order to stimulate trade and industry (ibid., bk XX, ch. 21–2) (see also Cheney 2010: 67–71).

Having set out this framework, Montesquieu covers a few points about the role of the state in the economy. He is generally in favour of economic freedom and opposed to monopolies and *compagnies exclusives* (1748, in Montesquieu 1949–51, bk XX, ch. 10).

Montesquieu explains that "monarchies" should not impede trade. Not only do they need the commodities of the carrying trade at low prices, but the enactment of sumptuary laws would tend to diminish spending on the luxury items they require (ibid., bk XX, ch. 4–8). However, he acknowledges that "republics" are entitled to impose restrictions on free trade (navigation acts, customs) in order to protect their carrying trade. As argued in his friend Jean-François Melon's *Essai politique sur le commerce* (1734), "liberty" should not be "licence": trade falls under the sway of the law, and the latter might have to restrict certain lines of trade or trading practices (such as the agreements among traders) in order to protect the general interest of the nation (and its commerce) (1748, in Montesquieu 1949–51, bk XX, chs 7–12). On the question of finance and money, Montesquieu opposes the establishment of banks in "monarchies". One cannot have power on one side and money on the other (ibid., bk XX, ch. 10), simply put, when the power is concentrated in the hands of a prince, he must possess all the money in the state (the "royal treasure"). According to the philosopher, he would be without means otherwise. Montesquieu criticizes public debts in "republics" as well as in "monarchies" on several grounds. If foreigners hold annuity notes, they remove a substantial amount of money from the nation, the burden of taxation to pay the interest on the debt hurts the manufactures and, ultimately, it takes the true revenues from the industrious and transfers them to idle men (ibid., bk XXII, ch. 17). On the question of taxation Montesquieu is against the General-Farm system and for a state *régie*, which should bear mainly upon commodities. He praises the painless character of the English excise duty system. He also holds that any land or personal taxes should be progressive and not proportional (ibid., bk XIII).

Montesquieu subscribes to a quantitative theory of money and remarks on the inflation caused by devaluations (due to the debasement of the coinage or, the most common in the eighteenth-century, the increasing of the value of the coinage in currency of account or numeraire currency, the *livre tournois*). In discussing these matters, he also explains how the rate of interest fell after the discovery of mines in the Americas, which he considered an excellent thing (Keynes was to praise Montesquieu on this), but equally he describes the terrible inflation engendered and finally the loss of gold from Spain to more industrious countries. To his mind, gold and silver are not real wealth, and money should be considered a mere "sign". If the state is driven to manipulate money, it is due to its growing expenses arising from its appetite for war and expansion (ibid., bk XXII, chs 7–14) (see Larrère 2001). Lastly, for Montesquieu, agriculture is clearly a respectable and useful activity, but is not to be placed at the centre of commerce. However, when he comes to discuss the necessity of laws favourable to population growth in Modern Europe, Montesquieu puts forward a few ideas on farming. He is clearly concerned by demography – like many of his contemporaries, and in the absence of statistics, he thinks that population was strongly declining for centuries – and discusses how to increase the number of men and women. Apart from the fact that a despotic government is unfavourable to population growth (1721, in Montesquieu 1949–51, let. CXX–CXXII), Montesquieu sees at least two ways: the state should distribute land to those who have none and facilitate the clearing of land (for example, by cutting taxes) (1748, in Montesquieu 1949–51, bk XXIII, chs 16–18).

De l'esprit des lois made a considerable impact on France. Read by several generations, the work was to promote an interest in economic issues while also spreading a defence of moderate government. Friedrich Melchior Grimm went so far as to say the book caused a "revolution" in the national mind (Grimm 1756 [2007]: 187) and Pierre-Samuel Dupont judged that it was thanks to Montesquieu that France's "finest minds" began to study political economy (Dupont 1769: xii). For the members of the Gournay circle in the 1750s, it became one of the main points of reference for discussion and further elaboration. But beyond their criticism – as in Forbonnais' *Observations sur l'esprit des loix* (1753) and a number of issues (for example, the *noblesse commerçante*) on which the circle opposes the ideas of *De l'esprit des lois* – or their praise of Montesquieu's ideas on the role of self-interest, the effect of trade on the balance of power, taxation, and so on, they made use of the book as a blueprint for developing new methods and a "political" understanding of commerce.

ARNAUD ORAIN

See also:

Pierre Le Pesant de Boisguilbert (I); French Enlightenment (II); François Quesnay and Physiocracy (I); Anne-Robert-Jacques Turgot (I).

References and further reading

Charles, L. (2006), 'L'économie politique française et le politique dans la seconde moitié du XVIIIᵉ siècle', in P. Nemo and J. Petitot (eds), *Histoire du liberalism en Europe*, Paris: Presses Universitaires de France, pp. 279–312.
Cheney, P. (2010), *Revolutionary Commerce. Globalization and the French Monarchy*, Cambridge, MA and London: Harvard University Press.
Dupont, P.-S. (1769), 'Notice abrégée des différens Ecrits modernes qui ont concouru en France à former la Science de l'économie politique', *Éphémérides du Citoyen*, **1**, xi–lii.
Forbonnais, F.V. de (1753), *Observations sur l'esprit des loix*, in *Opuscules de M. F****, ed. É.-C. Fréron, Amsterdam: Arkstée and Merkus.
Grimm, F.M. (2007), *Correspondance littéraire*, vol. 3, Ferney-Voltaire: Centre international d'étude du XVIIIᵉ siècle, first published 1756.
Hirschman, A.O. (1977), *The Passions and the Interest: Political Arguments for Capitalism Before Its Triumph*, Princeton, NJ: Princeton University Press.
Hume, D. (1987), *Essays, Moral, Political, and Literary*, Indianapolis, IN: Liberty Fund, first published 1742–52.
Larrère, C. (2001), 'Montesquieu on economics and commerce', in D.D. Carrithers, M.A. Mosher and P.A. Rahe (eds), *Montesquieu's Science of Politics. Essays on the* Spirit of Laws, Lanham, MD, Boulder, CO, New York and Oxford: Rowman & Littlefield, pp. 335–73.
Larrère, C. (2011), 'Système de l'intérêt et science du commerce: François Véron de Forbonnais, lecteur de Montesquieu', in L. Charles, F. Lebebvre and C. Théré (eds), *Le cercle de Vincent de Gournay. Savoirs économiques et pratiques administratives en France au milieu du XVIIIᵉ siècle*, Paris: Insitut National d'Études Démographiques, pp. 259–80.
Melon, J.-F. (1734), *Essai politique sur le commerce*, Amsterdam: François Changuion.
Montesquieu, C.L. de Secondat de (1949–51), *Œuvres complètes*, ed. R. Caillois, 2 vols, Paris: Gallimard.
Reinert, S. (2011), *Translating Empire. Emulation and the Origins of Political Economy*, Cambridge, MA and London: Harvard University Press.
Sonenscher, M. (2007), *Before the Deluge. Public Debt, Inequality, and the Intellectual Origins of the French Revolution*, Princeton, NJ and Oxford: Princeton University Press.
Spector, C. (2006), *Montesquieu et l'émergence de l'économie politique*, Paris: Honoré Champion.
Steiner, P. (1998), *Sociologie de la connaissance économique. Essai sur les rationalisations de la connaissance économique (1750–1850)*, Paris: Presses Universitaires de France.
Volpihac-Auger, C. (ed.) (2012), 'Débats et polémiques autour de *L'Esprit des lois*', *Revue française d'histoire des idées politiques*, **35** (1), special issue.

François Quesnay (1694–1774) and Physiocracy

Education, Surgery and Medicine

François Quesnay was born into a family of well-to-do ploughmen in the little parish of Méré (near Versailles) on 4 June 1694. The story goes that he only began reading and writing at the age of 11 but that he then went on to study Latin and Greek by himself. What is sure is that after his father's death in 1707 he became the pupil of a surgeon named Jean de la Vigne. With a view to finding a more lucrative profession, Quesnay started an apprenticeship (1711–16) with the engraver Pierre de Rochefort in Paris. He also registered for courses at the Faculty of Medicine and the famous College of Surgery of Saint-Côme. He abandoned engraving and received his letters as a Master in Surgery on 9 August 1718. He had married Jeanne-Catherine Dauphin, the daughter of a minor craftsman from Paris, on 30 January 1717 and they settled down in the city of Mantes to the west of Paris where Quesnay set up as a surgeon. His skill enabled him to become a respected practitioner and he was involved in the controversy on blood-letting with the physician Jean-Baptiste Silva. In 1734 Quesnay became personal surgeon to the Duke of Villeroy and left Mantes for Paris. While under the patronage of Villeroy, Quesnay was also being looked after by François Gigot de La Peyronie, first surgeon to the King, who introduced Quesnay into the Surgeon's College and established him as the secretary of the new Académie de Chirurgie in 1740. During this period, Quesnay concentrated his efforts on the profession of surgeon producing notably the *Essai physique sur l'œconomie animale* and the *Art de guérir par la saignée*, both in 1736, and the *Mémoires de l'Académie de chirurgie* (1743) which he not only edited but drafted almost single-handedly. During the War of Austrian Succession he accompanied the duke of Villeroy to Metz where he had the opportunity to be awarded the title of physician in the Faculty of Pont-à-Mousson (1744). Recommended to the Marquise of Pompadour, mistress of Louis XV, Quesnay became her personal doctor in 1749. Alone – his wife having died in 1728 – he settled in Versailles in his famous small entresol. Having treated the Dauphin for smallpox in 1752 he was rewarded with *lettres de noblesse* and thus able to buy the domain of Beauvoir for his son Blaise-Guillaume. He published his last works on surgery and medicine – *Traité de la suppuration* and *Traité de la gangrene* – in 1749, *Traité des effets et usages de la saignée* in 1750 and, finally, in 1751 the *Traité des fièvres continues*. D'Alembert secured his election to the Académie des sciences in 1751 and he was elected to the Royal Society the year after.

The Beginnings in Political Economy

At the court of Versailles, with access to the king, Quesnay's social network thrived and he was often in contact with some of the leading *philosophes* of the age such as Denis Diderot, Jean Le Rond D'Alembert, Charles Pinot Duclos, Claude-Adrien Helvétius and Étienne Bonnot de Condillac. It seems, however, that it was through the intervention of a close friend, Charles-Georges Leroy, Lieutenant of Hunting in Versailles, that Quesnay was requested to contribute to Diderot and D'Alembert's *Encyclopédie* (Charles and Théré 2008). Quesnay provided several articles but finally only allowed the publication of three of them – "Évidence", "Fermiers" and "Grains" –

in two fields, that is, metaphysics and political economy, but nothing on surgery or medicine. This suggests that it was well known by the mid-1750s that the doctor had turned his attention to these subjects. Everything leads us to believe that he began with philosophy. The second edition of the *Essai sur l'oeconomie animale* (1747) contains major developments on the theory of knowledge, the operation of the understanding and natural law. On these subjects Quesnay was mainly inspired by Locke and the continental empiricist tradition championed by Condillac. The entry "Évidence" published in 1756 in volume 6 of the *Encyclopédie* confirms this: Quesnay argues that our knowledge comes from sensations and that while we are looking for pleasant sensations we try to avoid painful ones. But the end of the article opens the door to another way of thinking. Quesnay denies that morality is based upon perceptions and language, as in Condillac's approach, but links instead his sensationism with the Cartesian tradition. The moral behaviour of man has to comply with a natural order willed by the Creator. To summarize, sensations of pleasure and pain determine our (interested) behaviour, by a sort of calculus, but these pieces of information (sensations) have to be guided by the natural laws, which the theoretician (Quesnay) is able to reveal from faith (Steiner 1998: 43–8, Orain 2006). This outlook finds a natural playground in political economy.

From the study of his library (Cartelier and Longhitano 2012: 193–240), we know that Quesnay did not own any books on economics – in a broad sense – published before 1750. Those published after 1753 are more numerous, but they deal largely with *économie rustique* or agronomy. Now the interest in the cultivation of land was increasing and Quesnay followed the general movement by learning about the economy with the whole generation, which began, by 1750, according to the famous formula of Voltaire, "to argue about grain". It is clear that the entries "Fermiers" (1756) and "Grains" (1757) and also the unpublished "Impôts" and "Hommes" are at the confluence of agronomy and the debate about the freedom of the grain trade (Charles 1999, pt 3, ch. 1). In these texts where Quesnay puts forward the core of his theory which places agriculture at the centre of his thinking, agronomical arguments – the preference for the horse to the ox, the necessity of a three-year crop rotation system – are mixed with economic arguments: the *grande culture*, that of farmers who are real entrepreneurs of agriculture, is praised and contrasted with the *petite culture* of the sharecroppers.

It is in these articles that the important concept of *produit net* appears. By producing an analogy with agricultural accounting where the farmer deducts his costs from the harvest sold, Quesnay defines the "net product" first by the surplus beyond the cost of production – the *prix fondamental*: wages, raw materials and taxes. Here the farmer's profit belongs to the "net product" (Charles 1999, pt 3, ch. 1). Then, in his writings subsequent to the entry "Impôts", the definitive definition of the concept is proposed: the "net product" – called the *revenu* (income) – is a *surplus disponible* (disposable surplus), that is, the rent of the landlords on which to levy taxes for the king and the church. The *avances annuelles* and the *intérêt des avances*, a percentage of the *avances primitives*, the fixed capital of tools and equipment and of the *avances annuelles*, the circulating capital or "the labour costs spent on performing the annual work of one plough" (wages, raw materials, farmer's gain) (Mirabeau and Quesnay 1763: 30), are deducted from the total output. In this definition, more specifically presented in *Philosophie rurale* (Mirabeau and Quesnay 1763), the *fermier* receives two kinds of remuneration that are separated from the landlord's net product (see Charles 1999, pt 3, ch. 1). The first one, "grouped in the expenditures of his annual advances" (Mirabeau and

Quesnay 1763: 131) corresponds to the activity of the agricultural entrepreneur, "the care, the works and the risks of his enterprise". The second, the interest of the advances (*annuelles* and *primitives*), is the return on capital, what the advances "must yield to each one, as in any commerce that entails risks and in which the return of the money advanced requires at least one year, must yield, say I, an interest of 10 per cent" (ibid.: 134). But these incomes of the agricultural entrepreneur are not "available" in Quesnay's vocabulary because, if they decrease, the total output of agriculture is also going to decrease, which is of course undesirable. More precisely, if the gain of the *fermier*, included in the advances, and the interest on the same advances are too low, the entrepreneur could be tempted either to reduce his future advances in order to maintain his remuneration or to abandon his activity. Even if he decides to maintain the level of the future advances, a low remuneration will not enable the agricultural entrepreneur to expand his farming business, the actual aim of all the physiocratic "net product" doctrine. This is why the gain and the profit of the advances must never bear taxes, of any kind, contrary to the landlord's "net product".

In these early texts, Quesnay also puts forward the famous doctrine of the exclusive productivity of agriculture, in other words the idea that there is no "net product" in trade and industry. This idea, which was to take on ever more importance in his thinking, mixes a physical and a value approach: industry does not create new wealth; it gathers pre-existent wealth. In agriculture the value of output exceeds the costs, while in manufacturing the two coincide. The profit and the interest on the advances in trade and industry are, as in agriculture, included in the costs of production. At the end of the process there is no available income, the "gift of nature" which only appears in agriculture. Now, it is the amount of the capital invested in this last sector that determines the amount of the nation's "net product". To increase the national wealth, a large investment in agriculture has to be made and the farmers' profits have to be increased. Only the freedom of the grain trade could produce this movement to Quesnay's mind. However, Quesnay was not entirely consistent on this issue since he acknowledged the existence of what he called "the small net product of commerce" that is the revenue accruing to the countries which had set up an export-led economy (Steiner 1997: 705–6). These countries (or commercial republics) have sacrificed their agricultural sector in keeping the price of food low so that they can offer maritime transport services at a low cost to other countries (agricultural kingdoms). Their service being less costly, commercial republics can spare a part of the money received from the agricultural kingdom as their "small net product". Nevertheless, it would be a complete mistake to follow such a policy in an agricultural kingdom, which must stick to the large net product from the agricultural sector.

The article "Hommes" proposes a five-year framework in two tables (see Steiner 1994, 1998): a stable cost (the *prix fondamental*) but different incomes due to the quantity and prices depending on the harvests each year (from "plentiful" to "bad" year/harvest). The first table presents a country (in reality, France) where the internal traffic of grain within the country is difficult and exports are forbidden. Here grain prices are subjected to a King-Davenant effect: the rises in prices are more than proportional to the deficits of the harvest. The difference between the highest price and the lowest is 20 *livres* (from a range of 10 to 30) but it is only in the "bad" years, when the harvest is poor and the price very high, that the farmer makes (a little) money. In the second table (in reality, England), the freedom of the grain trade causes the effect to vanish despite the same climate changes and the range of prices is considerably narrowed: 4 *livres* (from 16 to 20). By the principle of arbitration, which channels the grain to where people lack it, the country participates in the international market with a stabilized price. Quesnay calls it the *bon prix* (good price). Here the advantages for the kingdom are many. For consumers, the *prix commun de l'acheteur* – that is, the average price paid by the consumer – is almost stable (18 *livres* with freedom versus 17.5 in the prohibitionist state), but for farmers the profits are (substantially) increased and, moreover, they grow richer in four out of every five years and especially so during the "good" harvests. The freedom of the grain trade eliminates the conflict of interests between consumers and producers: everyone has an interest in plentiful harvests. With powerful agriculture, the French kingdom, concluded Quesnay, would be able to maintain a large population and a strong navy so as to sustain the rivalry with England. This theoretical result explains why Quesnay was to try to convince the royal powers, public opinion and the high administration of the benefits of free competition. Before doing so, in the social setting of the court of Versailles, Quesnay had recruited collaborators for their skills in agronomy and arithmetic (Charles-Richard de Butré, Georges Le Roy, Etienne-Claude de Marivetz and Henry Pattulo), who helped him in his works, but who were not his disciples (see Charles and Théré 2008). When he switched from practical economy to the creation of a new science, the doctor needed to create new means and a real school through which to spread his ideas.

The Physiocratic School and the *Tableau économique*

In July 1757 Quesnay met Victor Riqueti, Marquis of Mirabeau, in his entresol. Mirabeau had become famous with the publication, a few months earlier, of *L'ami des hommes*, an agrarian and populationist book. In his own words, Mirabeau was going to bring about his "conversion" and the collaboration between the two men would last up to end of the 1760s. They first worked on a political treatise, the unpublished (before 1999) *Traité de la monarchie*, but the greatest work of Quesnay and Mirabeau at that time was undoubtedly the *Tableau économique*. There exist three early versions of the tableau: one from November/December 1758 and two from 1759. All of them contain the diagram itself (a visual representation of the flow of wealth between three classes in a nation) and a few explanations at the sides or after the figure. This is the "Zig-Zag" which is the fruit of Quesnay's hand (with the help of Charles de Butré for the calculations) and which the doctor tried to explain to Mirabeau. Then, the *Tableau oeconomique avec ses explications* (1760) saw the first collaboration with Mirabeau, who wrote some of the "explanations" but at these dates he and Quesnay, with the help of arithmeticians were working on the *Théorie de l'impôt* (1760) and the *Philosophie rurale* (1763). Finally, the latter book contains a few tables, three "Zig-Zags" and another version without intermediate calculus, the "Précis du Tableau économique". In 1766 this abbreviated formula, transformed once again, became the famous "Formule arithmétique du Tableau économique", that we find with other figures in the *Problème économique* (1766) and *Second problème économique* (1767).

As in Ricardian "Strong cases", the economic table was built in order to explain the functioning of basic principles. Which ones? Two kinds of economic table can be distinguished, even if, as indicated above, one can make room for a third kind with the disequilibrium approach in *Philosophie rurale* (1763), "Premier problème économique" (1766) and "Second problème économique" (1767) (Eltis 1996). The first kind appears in the three successive editions of the "Zig-Zag" set in the years 1758–9 (see Figure 1); the

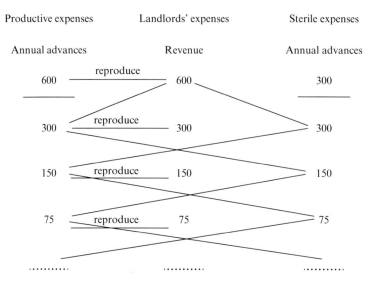

Figure 1   The "Zig-Zag"

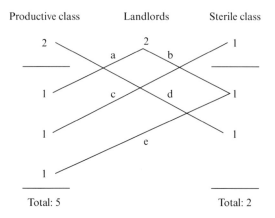

Figure 2   The arithmetic formula

second is limited to the "Analyse de la formule arithmétique du tableau économique" (see Figure 2).

In the "Zig-Zag", the major concern was spending. The formalization showed how the rent paid by the farmers to the landlords (600 *livres*) was successively received and spent by the other two classes (the agricultural or productive class and the artisan or sterile class), giving rise to the same amount of net product (600 *livres*). The initial expenditure of the landlords is divided into two equal sums (300 *livres*), one for the luxury consumption of food and the other for the luxury consumption of furniture, clothes and the like. Then, the sterile class spends half of the money received (150 *livres*) in order to buy food and raw materials from the productive class, the other 150 *livres* are used to reconstitute the capital of the sterile class, possibly with some goods bought abroad. The productive class spends 150 *livres* in order to get manufactured goods from the sterile class, while the 150 left are spent within the sector. The two classes go on spending half the money received until all the money is finally spent. When this spending process is completed the gross total revenue received by the productive class (300 *livres* from the landlords and 300 *livres* from the sterile class) is equal to the circulating capital (or annual advances in Quesnay's language) of this class; consequently, the reproduction of the capital generates a net product of an equal amount, as shown in the central column of the table. In line with Keynesian insights (there is a multiplier equal to two), Quesnay has shown that the sums spent by the landlords are crucial: the various classes are related by flows of money and, to use Michael Kalecki's idea, those in possession of money (landlords) earn what they spend whereas the others spend what they earn. Nevertheless, as mentioned by François Véron de Forbonnais (1767), who carefully studied this version of the economic table, the table is not correct as far as the reproduction of capital is at stake. In the table, the gross revenue (600 *livres*) and the net revenue (300 *livres*) of both the sterile and the productive classes are equal, a result which is clearly at variance with the principle of the exclusive productivity of the productive class (see also Charles and Orain 2016). Aware of this fact, Quesnay, in his commentary on the table, introduced an extra flow (300 *livres*) from the sterile class to the productive class in such a way that the latter obtains a net revenue equal to the initial amount of the net product (600 *livres*). This is a clear sign that the economic table cannot prove the exclusive productivity of one sector alone, and that this exclusive productivity was a hypothesis, and a weak one according to many contemporaries (Graslin 1767; Galiani 1770).

Hence, the formula can be considered as an attempt to overcome the difficulties remaining in the "Zig-Zag" model, that is, to say how the reproduction of the capital (circulating and fixed capital, money capital) results from the monetary flows among the three classes. At the outset, the productive class has 2 units of money, and has invested 10 units of fixed capital and 2 units of circulating capital; the sterile class has only 1 unit of circulating capital; this capital generates a gross production of 5 units of agricultural goods and 2 units of manufactured goods. Then the productive class pays the rent or net product to the landlords, with the 2 units of money. The circulation process begins with (a) landlords spending half of their rent to get luxury food from farmers (1 unit) and (b) luxury goods from artisans (1 unit); thereafter, artisans buy 1 unit of agricultural produce for their food (c) while farmers reconstitute their fixed capital with 1 unit of manufactured goods (d), since this capital suffers from an annual depreciation of one-tenth of its value. Finally, (e) artisans spend this unit of money buying 1 unit of agricultural produce in order to reconstitute their circulating capital.

To sum up, the landlords have spent all the money received as rent in order to consume; the artisans have sold 2 units of manufactured goods, and have spent the corresponding amount of money in order to buy food and to reconstitute their capital; the circulation process has thus allowed these two classes to get in the end what they had in the beginning. What about the productive class? They have sold 3 of the 5 units of agricultural goods produced, they have bought the necessary manufactured goods in order to reconstitute their fixed capital, while the 2 remaining units of agricultural goods reconstitute their circulating capital; finally, the money capital is reconstituted as well, since they have 2 units of money equal to their gross revenue (3 units) minus their expenses (1 unit). Every form of capital is thus reproduced, in value and in use value, by the class, which possessed it formerly: the process of circulation has reproduced the initial conditions of production.

The actual spending of *all* the money received by the various classes is a crucial hypothesis; however, Quesnay adds a further hypothesis since landlords have to spend half of their rent in each sector. If they do not, if they spend more on manufactured goods than on food, then, according to Quesnay, the reproduction of agricultural advances could not be achieved and a process of decline would necessarily ensue. Modern analysis does not corroborate this point, since if artisans go on spending all their money buying agricultural output, agricultural revenue would be left unchanged and the only effect would be a change in the proportion of both sectors in the economy (Cartelier 1991).

At the end of the 1750s, by way of Mirabeau's brother, Quesnay had recruited another disciple in the person of Pierre-Paul Lemercier de la Rivière (1719–1801), who was to be the Intendant of the French West Indies in the early 1760s and the author of *L'ordre naturel et essentiel des sociétés politiques* (1767). But it was also in the former Gournay Circle (Gournay had died in 1759) that Quesnay found new members: Turgot of course, who would rapidly grow apart from the doctor, but also Louis-Paul Abeille (1719–1807), a lawyer and former secretary of the Royal Agricultural Society of Brittany. In 1763, the best recruit was found in Pierre-Samuel Dupont (1739–1817), the future Dupont de Nemours, who would become the great proselyte of Quesnay's ideas and someone who the master really "educated" as a son in economics. In 1764 Quesnay's school, which would become known in history as the Physiocrats, was formed. Two great works were published under the name of Mirabeau: the *Théorie de l'impôt* in 1760, in reality composed by Quesnay, Mirabeau, Butré and two others arithmeticians (Le Grand and Morin) and the *Philosophie rurale* in 1763 by Quesnay (especially chapter 7), Mirabeau and Butré. These books could be seen as the most theoretically accomplished works by these men and the first to present the fiscal theory of the Physiocrats, that of the *impôt unique*. The authors wanted to abolish all the exemptions of the gentleman and all the complexity of the French taxation system so as to propose a single tax upon the "net product" of landlords. In Quesnay's thinking, taxes upon consumption goods or wages increased the cost of production and the prices of agricultural and industrial products. On one hand, the profit and interest of the farmers were diminished and on the other hand the consumers, and especially the landlords, paid more for the goods. The argument was that the last group had already paid – directly or indirectly – the totality of taxes. With a single tax upon the "net product" (the rent) the cost of the levy would be considerably diminished, to the benefit of the landlords. Of course this result appeared quite paradoxical and not readily acceptable to the dominant classes and the semi-private company which collected indirect taxes, the General Farm. After the publication of the *Théorie de l'impôt*, Mirabeau was to be imprisoned and exiled for a few weeks. Quesnay, however, was never troubled.

The Controversies of the 1760s

The Marquise of Pompadour died on 15 April 1764 and Quesnay's influence at court ceased. However, Quesnay's school reached its zenith in the following few years. New members, Guillaume-François Le Trosne (1728–1780), Jean-Nicolas Guérineau de Saint-Péravy (1732–1789) and Nicolas Baudeau (1730–1792) added their force to the

Physiocrat project. Two newspapers: the *Journal d'agriculture, du commerce et des finances* (1765–66) and then the *Éphémérides du citoyen* that the abbé Baudeau put at service of the school from 1767 enabled the Physiocrats' ideas to reach a wider audience. It was in the former that Quesnay started the debate about the sterility of industry and trade in 1766. In the famous dialogues between Mr H and Mr N (the orthodox Physiocrat), Quesnay wanted to prove that industry creates only an "addition" not a "generation" of wealth, in other words that it could not be declared "productive". François Véron de Forbonnais (1722–1800) and Jean-Joseph-Louis Graslin (1727–1790) were unquestionably the authors who most opposed such a doctrine. In their works, they attempted to prove that all the sectors are productive and that the *Tableau* offered a biased vision of the object it was supposed to represent. For Graslin, the very logic of a representation of the circulation of wealth in society by "classes" and by "expenditures" was a nonsense since there were only consumers and producers who exchanged "assets" and "goods" in markets (see Orain 2012). Forbonnais was less categorical, but he criticized the incredible figures, the exaggerations, the errors of calculations, along with the problems of space and time in the circulation of money of the *Tableau* (Charles and Orain 2016). He concluded with a lapidary formula on the uselessness of this whole intellectual enterprise: "The metaphysical obscurity of the Tableau and the whole doctrine that surrounds it proves nothing more than the simple statement of its propositions" (Forbonnais 1767: 284–5). These attacks did not go unanswered. The Physiocrats defend the *Tableau* and the exclusive productivity of agriculture, in particular in the book review of d'Auxiron's *Principes de tout gouvernement* by Baudeau in the *Ephémérides* (1767), where the Physiocrat criticized Forbonnais' ideas at length (see also Baudeau and Graslin 1777). The debate was to continue and to expand upon the question of language in the *Éphémérides* (in October 1767) where Quesnay wrote the "Lettre de M. Alpha sur le langage de la science économique". This was a letter especially opposed to Forbonnais who had signed articles under the penname of Mr A.B.C.D in the *Journal de l'agriculture* mocking the truisms developed by the sect behind their obscure language (Charles and Orain 2016).

At that time, what should be noticed is that Quesnay was looking for a way to complete his system. With the "Observations sur le droit naturel des hommes réunis en société" published in September 1767 in the *Journal de l'agriculture* and then with the title "Le droit naturel" in Dupont's collection *Physiocratie, ou constitution naturelle du gouvernement le plus avantageux au genre humain* in 1767, Quesnay rejected the question of the form of government (monarchy, aristocracy and democracy) in order to insist upon the natural laws that should be discovered and transposed into positive rights by the sovereign: an absolute respect for property and the natural character of inequalities. In the "Maximes générales du gouvernement économique d'un royaume agricole" published also in *Physiocratie*, Quesnay put forward the concept of an "Agricultural government" which had to deploy these natural laws by fighting against mercantilism (the *système des commerçants*), imposing free competition and restoring agriculture. Finally, the "Despotisme de la Chine", serialized in the *Éphémérides* in 1767 proposed a government of a monarch, subject to the laws of natural order (the "legal despotism"), with magistrates who popularized these laws among the population and a society organized around landlords and agricultural entrepreneurs. These views were then developed together with an extensive presentation of the political economy of the physiocratic school by Lemercier de la Rivière in *L'ordre naturel et essentiel des sociétés politiques* (1767). The crucial points were the systematic presentation of a political view by which the politics of the agricultural kingdom were grounded on the hypothesis that there existed a common interest in the growth of the net product for all classes of society; accordingly, politics was no longer an issue of virtue or honour, but of (material) interest. Expertise in political economy became of prime importance since it was, on the one hand, necessary to have a deep knowledge of that science in order to enact laws relevant to the common interest – a task to be performed by the magistrates serving the monarch – and, on the other, the diffusion of the science in public opinion through education was central in their views (Faccarello and Steiner 2008). These political considerations would become the subject of major controversies as well. The abbé de Mably, in particular, in his *Doutes sur l'ordre naturel et essentiel des sociétés politiques* (1768), attacks "legal despotism" and defends the need for counter-forces in every political system. Mocking the notion of *évidence*, Mably does not believe in a natural order: in politics, passions and public opinion are other mistresses much more capricious and powerful than all the so-called "mathematical truths" of the Physiocrats (Ferrand and Orain 2016).

However, at the very end of the 1760s and the beginning of the 1770s, the Physiocrats had to face a greater problem and fierce adversaries. Having promoted and contributed to the first liberalization of the grain trade since 1763–64, Quesnay, Mirabeau and their disciples came under attack during the terrible events that followed this new policy (shortage, riots and punishment). Tension was at its height with the publication of the *Dialogues sur le commerce des blés* of Galiani in the first days of 1770 and, then, Linguet's *Réponse aux docteurs modernes* (1771). Galiani produced a devastating criticism of a policy based on abstract reasoning: having neglected time, geography, opinions, merchants, and so on, the Physiocrats had not understood that grain was not a commodity like others. The subsistence of peoples should be controlled by the authorities (especially in regard to exports), who had to resort exceptionally to the *raison d'état* (see Faccarello 1998; Kaplan 2016a, 2016b). Linguet made the same kinds of claims as Galiani, but insisted also on the consideration of the living body of the people, their pain and suffering, in every matter dealing with policy (Magnot 2015; Orain 2016). These attacks on physiocratic theories were accompanied by an intense campaign of mockery against the "sect". Forbonnais, Galiani and Linguet were again active and joined by Frederic-Melchior Grimm (1723–1807), Louis-Sébastien Mercier (1740–1814), Voltaire and a wide range of anonymous authors of pamphlets, poems and songs. On the one side, the encyclopaedists tried to exclude the Physiocrats from the Enlightenment as a result of their devotion to a master, their jargon of Ancient priests, their trust in eternal truths; on the other side, the high aristocracy, the *parlements* or the craft guilds saw the *philosophes* and Physiocrats alike as dangerous revolutionaries, whose ideas and actions were at the root of a chaos, an inversion of values and a destruction of the social taxonomy (Orain 2015).

The End of the School

At the end of his life, Quesnay turned away from political economy and became interested in geometry (he was almost ignorant of algebra). He prepared two works on trisection of angles and squaring the circle in 1770 and 1771 and remodelled them in the *Recherches philosophiques sur l'évidence des vérités géométriques* published in 1773. The book was clearly insufficient and regarded by scientists as the ravings of an old man. "This is the sun that has become encrusted," said Turgot. Dismissed from favour upon the accession of Louis XVI to the throne, Quesnay left the palace in the summer of 1774 and lived in the Grand-Commun, the building of housekeeping services of the Royal family, in Versailles. It is there that he learned of Turgot's appointment to the General-Control of finances on 25 August, but suffering with gout, he became unable to do anything and finally died on 16 December. He was buried the next day in the church of Saint-Julien in the parish of Notre-Dame in Versailles. His inventory after death by the notary Thibaut, which contains the record of his library, is now conserved in the Archives départementales des Yvelines (see Cartelier and Longhitano 2012). A ceremony was organized in Quesnay's honour in Mirabeau's mansion on 20 December, where the Marquis delivered a glowing eulogy. In the first month of 1775 came a succession of academic tributes. It was to be the beginning of the legend surrounding this sage, credited with beginning a new science among the tumult of Versailles (see Charles and Théré 2007).

As for physiocracy as a movement, Turgot's ministry could be considered a brief period of renewal. Dupont and Condorcet were the principal advisers to the General-Controller, Baudeau revived the movement's periodical under the name of *Nouvelles éphémérides économiques* (December 1774–June 1776 and a single issue in 1788), while Mirabeau multiplied attempts to diffuse the physiocratic doctrines (in the form of catechisms). As the same causes led to the same effects, however, Turgot's liberalization policy raised a wide challenge to the ideas of the Physiocrats and a new campaign against them (see Necker 1775). The resignation of the General-Controller in the spring of 1776 marked the onset of decline of physiocracy as an organized group of scholars. The movement did not die immediately, however, and the works of Dupont, Mirabeau, Baudeau, Saint-Péravy and Lemercier de la Rivière in the 1770s–1780s contributed to the debates preceding and during the Revolution (see Weulersse 1950, 1985; Faccarello and Steiner 1990; Charles and Steiner 1999; Mergey 2010). Beyond the French monarchy, the physiocratic doctrine spread in many European countries, such as the German states, Poland, Sweden and Switzerland (Delmas et al. 1995).

Quesnay's analytical approach to the functioning of the economy had a different and long lasting influence since it was a real *tour de force* to set out the circulation process of a whole nation with three poles and fives arrows. Accordingly, Quesnay's *formule arithmétique* attracted the attention of some major theorists during the following centuries. Karl Marx explicitly referred to Quesnay's "Tableau" and "Formule" when he was studying the circulation process and devising his schemes of reproduction of social capital (see Gehrke and Kurz 1995). Joseph Schumpeter praised Quesnay for having made the first attempt to set forth a general equilibrium approach – an approach he considered as the economists' *Magna Carta*. Finally Wassily Leontief explained that he had Quesnay's scheme in mind when he was modelling the American economy and elaborated his input–output table.

ARNAUD ORAIN AND PHILIPPE STEINER

See also:

Pierre Le Pesant de Boisguilbert (I); Richard Cantillon (I); French Enlightenment (II); Input–output analysis (III); Adam Smith (I); Anne-Robert-Jacques Turgot (I).

References and further reading

Baudeau, N. and J.-J.-L. Graslin (1777), *Correspondance entre M. Graslin, de l'Académie économique de S. Pétersbourg, Auteur de l'*Essai analytique sur la Richesse & sur l'Impôt *et M. l'abbé Baudeau, Auteur des* Éphémérides du citoyen *sur un des Principes fondamentaux de la Doctrine des soi-disants Philosophes Économistes*, London and Paris: Onfroy.

Cartelier, J. (1991), 'L'économie politique de François Quesnay ou l'Utopie du Royaume agricole', in J. Cartelier (ed.), *Physiocratie, Droit Naturel, Tableau économique et autres textes*, Paris: GF-Flammarion, pp. 9–64.

Cartelier, J. and G. Longhitano (eds) (2012), *Quesnay and Physiocracy: Studies and Materials*, Paris: L'Harmattan.

Charles, L. (1999), 'La liberté du commerce des grains et l'économie politique française', PhD dissertation, University Paris 1 Panthéon-Sorbonne.

Charles, L. (2000), 'From the Encyclopédie to the Tableau économique: Quesnay on freedom of grain trade and economic growth', *European Journal of the History of Economic Thought*, **7** (1), 1–21.

Charles, L. (2003), 'The visual history of the Tableau Économique', *European Journal of the History of Economic Thought*, **10** (4), 527–50.

Charles, L. and P. Steiner (1999), 'Entre Montesquieu et Rousseau. La physiocratie parmi les origines intellectuelles de la Révolution', *Études Jean-Jacques Rousseau*, **11**, 83–160.

Charles, L. and C. Théré (2007), 'François Quesnay: a "rural Socrates" in Versailles?', *History of Political Economy*, **39** (1), annual supplement, 195–214.

Charles, L. and C. Théré (2008), 'The writing workshop of François Quesnay and the making of physiocracy (1757–1764)', *History of Political Economy*, **40** (1), 1–42.

Charles, L. and A. Orain (2016), 'François Véron de Forbonnais and the invention of antiphysiocracy', in S.L. Kaplan and S. Reinert (eds), *The Economic Turn: Recasting Political Economy in Eighteenth-Century Europe*, London, New York and Delhi: Anthem Press, forthcoming.

Delmas, B., T. Demals and P. Steiner (eds) (1995), *La diffusion international de la Physiocratie: 18e–19e siècle*, Grenoble: Presses universitaires de Grenoble.

Eltis, W. (1975a), 'François Quesnay: a reinterpretation. 1. The Tableau économique', *Oxford Economic Papers*, **27** (2), 167–200.

Eltis, W. (1975b), 'François Quesnay: a reinterpretation. 2. The theory of economic growth', *Oxford Economic Papers*, **27** (3), 327–51.

Eltis, W. (1996), 'The Grand Tableau of François Quesnay's economics', *European Journal of the History of Economic Thought*, **3** (1), 21–43.

Faccarello, G. (1998), 'Galiani, Necker and Turgot. A debate on economic reform and policy in 18th century France', in G. Faccarello (ed.), *Studies in the History of French Political Economy, From Bodin to Walras*, London: Routledge, pp. 120–85.

Faccarello, G. and P. Steiner (eds) (1990), *La pensée économique pendant la Révolution française*, Grenoble: Presses Universitaires de Grenoble.

Faccarello, G. and P. Steiner (2008), 'Interest, sensationism and the science of the legislator: French "philosophie économique"', *European Journal of the History of Economic Thought*, **15** (1), 1–23.

Graslin, J.-J.-L. (1767), *Essai analytique sur la richesse et sur l'impôt*, London.

Ferrand, J. and A. Orain (2016), 'Sensualism, modern natural law and "science of commerce" at the heart of the controversy between Mably and the physiocrats', in S.L. Kaplan and S. Reinert (eds), *The Economic Turn: Recasting Political Economy in Eighteenth-Century Europe*, London, New York and Delhi: Anthem Press, forthcoming.

Forbonnais, F.V. de (1767), *Principes et observations économiques*, Amsterdam: Marc Michel Rey.

Galiani, F. (1770), *Dialogues sur le commerce des blés*, London.

Gehrke, C. and H.D. Kurz (1995), 'Marx on physiocracy', *European Journal of the History of Economic Thought*, **2** (1), 53–90.

Gilibert, G. (1977), *La costruzione della "macchina della prosperità"*, Milan: Etas Libri.

Herlitz, L. (1996), 'From spending and reproduction to circuit flow and equilibrium: the two conceptions of Tableau économique', *European Journal of the History of Economic Thought*, **3** (1), 1–20.

Kaplan, S.L. (2016a), *Bread, Politics and Political Economy in the Reign of Louis XV*, 2nd edn, London, New York and Delhi: Anthem Press; first published 1976.

Kaplan, S.L. (2016b), 'Galiani: grain and governance', in S.L. Kaplan and S. Reinert (eds), *The Economic Turn: Recasting Political Economy in Eighteenth-Century Europe*, London, New York and Delhi: Anthem Press.

Lemercier de la Rivière, P.-P. (1767), *L'ordre naturel et essentiel des sociétés politiques*, London: Nourse, and Paris: Desaint.

Linguet, S.-N.-H. (1771), *Réponse aux docteurs modernes, ou apologie pour l'auteur de "La Théorie des loix" et des Lettres sur cette théorie. Avec la réfutation du systèmes des philosophes économistes*, n.p.

Mably, G.B. de (1768), *Doutes proposés aux philosophes économistes sur l'ordre naturel et essentiel des sociétés politiques*, in G.B. de Mably (1794–95), *Collection complète des œuvres de l'abbé de Mably*, vol. 11, Paris: Desbrière, pp. 1–256.

Magnot, F. (2015), 'A body without a voice: a literary approach to Linguet's opposition to the physiocrats over the free trade in grain', *European Journal of the History of Economic Thought*, **22** (3), 420–44.

Meek, R.L. (1962), *The Economics of Physiocracy*, London: George Allen and Unwin.

Mergey, A. (2010), *L'État des Physiocrates: autorité et decentralisation*, Aix-en-Provence: Presses Universitaires d'Aix-Marseille.

Mirabeau, V.R. de and F. Quesnay (1763), *Philosophie rurale ou Économie générale et politique de l'Agriculture*, Amsterdam: Les libraires associés.

Mirabeau, V.R. de and F. Quesnay (1999), *Traité de la monarchie*, Paris: L'Harmattan, written in 1757–60.

Necker, J. (1775), *Sur la législation et le commerce des grains*, Paris: Pissot.

Orain, A. (2006), 'Directing or reforming behaviours? A discussion of Condillac's theory of *vrai prix*', *History of Political Economy*, **38** (3), 497–530.

Orain, A. (2012), 'Graslin and Forbonnais against the *Tableau économique*', in J. Cartelier and G. Longhitano (eds), *Quesnay and Physiocracy: Studies and Materials*, Paris: L'Harmattan, pp. 87–111.

Orain, A. (2015), 'Figures of mockery. A cultural disqualification of Physiocracy (1760–1790)', *European Journal of the History of Economic Thought*, **22** (3), 383–419.

Orain, A. (2016), '"One must make war on the lunatics". The physiocrats' attacks on Linguet, the iconoclast (1767–1775)', in S.L. Kaplan and S. Reinert (eds), *The Economic Turn: Recasting Political Economy in Eighteenth-Century Europe*, London, New York and Delhi: Anthem Press, forthcoming.

Quesnay, F. (2005), *Œuvres économiques complètes et autres textes*, ed. C. Théré, L. Charles and J.-C. Perrot, 2 vols, Paris: INED.

Steiner, P. (1994), 'Demand, price and net product in Quesnay's early writings', *European Journal of the History of Economic Thought*, **1** (2), 231–51.

Steiner, P. (1997), 'Quesnay et le commerce', *Revue d'économie politique*, **107** (5), 695–713.

Steiner, P. (1998), *La "science nouvelle" de l'économie politique*, Paris: Presses universitaires de France.

Vaggi, G. (1987), *The Economics of François Quesnay*, London: Macmillan.

Weulersse, G. (1910), *Le mouvement physiocratique en France (de 1756 à 1770)*, Paris: Alcan.

Weulersse, G. (1950), *La Physiocratie sous les ministères de Turgot et de Necker, 1774–1781*, Paris: Presses Universitaires de France.

Weulersse, G. (1985), *La Physiocratie à l'aube de la Révolution, 1781–1792*, Paris: École des Hautes Études en Sciences Sociales.

Daniel Bernoulli (1700–1782)

A Unique Dynasty of Scientists

Daniel Bernoulli is one of the prominent members of the Bernoulli family from Basel, Switzerland, whose members excelled in various theoretical and applied scientific fields – especially in mathematics, probability theory, physics and medicine – in the second half of the seventeenth and in the eighteenth centuries. The family originated from Antwerp, once under the domination of Catholic Spain. It emigrated in 1567 to Frankfurt, Germany, because of its Calvinist faith, and in the end settled in Basel in 1620. Until Niklaus Bernoulli (1623–1708), the important wealth of the family came from the spice trade: Niklaus was himself a merchant and an officer of the city of Basel. But three of his sons, Jakob (1654–1705), Nikolaus (1662–1716) and Johann (1667–1748), took another route. Nikolaus was a painter and a member of the Municipality of Basel. Jakob studied philosophy and theology, and Johann medicine, but they both became renowned mathematicians, developing in particular differential and integral calculus and siding with Gottfried Wilhelm Leibniz in his quarrel with Isaac Newton – the phrase "integral calculus" is due to Jakob.

Daniel Bernoulli, was born in Groningen on 8 February 1700, where his father had taught at the university since 1695, and died in Basel on 17 March 1782. He was Johann's son and the cousin of Nikolaus (1687–1759) – alias Nikolaus I, just as his uncles were named Jakob I and Johann I by historians to distinguish them from the younger members of this dynasty, who had the same Christian names (see Figure 3) – a son of Nikolaus the painter. Daniel was a doctor in medicine and his cousin in jurisprudence but, like their predecessors, their main achievements were in mathematics and the sciences. Also like their predecessors, they travelled in Europe and were part of a network of the most eminent scientists of the time, and members of many scientific academies. (On the main members of the Bernoulli family, see O'Connor and Robertson 1997–98).

As regards the "moral sciences", the works of Jakob, Nikolaus and Daniel are of outstanding interest thanks to their ground-breaking contributions to probability theory (Hacking 1975; Daston 1988; Hald 1990). Jakob is the author of the celebrated *Ars Conjectandi*, mainly written between 1684 and 1689 but posthumously published in 1713. It was the first book written on the theory of probability, this "art of conjecturing"

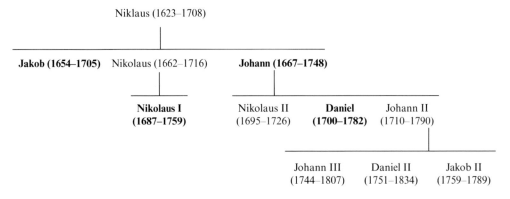

Figure 3   The main members of the Bernoulli family

that he also proposed to call "stochastics". (Pierre Rémond de Montmort's 1708 *Essay d'analyse des jeux de hasard*, the second edition of which was also published in 1713, was in fact written a long time after Jakob Bernoulli drafted his manuscript.) Jakob's book elaborated considerably on Christiaan Huygens's "De ratiociniis in ludo aleæ", a paper included as an appendix in Frans van Schooten's 1657 book, *Exercitationum mathematicarum*. It deals, *inter alia*, with the specification of the concept of (mathematical) expectation proposed by Blaise Pascal and Huygens, the statement and proof of the binomial distribution and the (weak) "law of large numbers" (as Siméon-Denis Poisson called it later). Moreover, it introduced a first clear distinction between objective (frequentist or statistical) probabilities, where the frequencies of events are calculated from experiments or observations, and subjective (or epistemic) probabilities due to our imperfect knowledge and measuring the degree of our belief, or our "reason to believe" (Condorcet), in a statement or a proposition about things or events (see Hald 1990: 28–9, 245–7; and Daston 1988: ch. 4, 1994, for the evolution of these concepts in the eighteenth and nineteenth centuries). In addition, we owe Jakob Bernoulli also "the important distinction between probabilities which can be calculated a priori (deductively, from considerations of symmetry) and those which can be calculated only a posteriori (inductively, from relative frequencies)" (Hald 1990: 247). Finally, the fourth and unfinished part of *Ars Conjectandi*, which contains the statement and proof of the law of large numbers, is entitled "Usum & applicationem præcedentis doctrinæ in civilibus, moralibus & œconomicis" ("The use and application of the previous doctrine to civil, moral and economic affairs"). It posed the fundamental question of the use of the mathematical developments of "expectatio", made for the games of chance, to the more traditional field of the "probability" of judgements developed, for example, in jurisprudence – that is, in modern parlance, the application of probability theory to social and economic matters. Jakob could not bring his project to an end but considered it as "the main part" of his work (to Leibniz, 3 October 1703, in JEHPS 2006: 5). This part was to inspire Nikolaus's approach and, some decades later, Condorcet's research programme.

   Nikolaus who, contrary to the legend, was not the editor of Jakob's book (Kohli 1975; Yushkevich 1987), continued the work of his uncle. In his 1709 thesis, *Dissertatio inauguralis mathematico-juridica de usu artis conjectandi in jure*, and in "Specimina artis conjectandis, ad quaestiones juris applicatae" – an abridged version of his thesis, published in 1711 in a supplement of the Leibnizian *Acta Eruditorum* – he used probability theory to deal with juridical and economic questions such as the reliability of witnesses and of suspicions, marine insurance, the probability of human life, life annuities, or the problem of the "absent" (after how many years can an absent person be considered as dead?) (see, for example, Hald 1990: ch. 21).

Daniel Bernoulli and Moral Sciences

From Basel to Saint Petersburg to Basel

Daniel Bernoulli's father, Johann, wanted his son to become a merchant, but Daniel was more attracted by mathematics. As a compromise he studied medicine but, like his uncle Jakob and his father Johann, wanted to embark on an academic career. He could not immediately obtain a position in Basel. He travelled in Italy and published his first book in 1724, *Exercitationes Quaedam Mathematicae* (*Mathematical Exercises*), a collection of his essays edited with the help of his friend Christian Goldbach, which contains some developments in applied mathematics and physics. It is in this field that he was remarkably inventive, and his fundamental book on hydrodynamics, *Hydrodynamica*, written as early as 1733 but only published in 1738, is still remembered as a milestone in the discipline. From 1725 onwards, Daniel won a number of scientific prizes, ten of them awarded by the Paris Académie des Sciences. In 1725 he reluctantly accepted a position in the Saint Petersburg Imperial Academy of Sciences, newly established at the instigation of Leibniz. While happy to work there with Leonhard Euler (a fellow countryman from Basel) who arrived in 1727, he was nevertheless relieved to leave in 1733 and, in 1734, started botany lectures in Basel, then switched to physiology in 1743 and finally to physics, and held this latter chair from 1750 to 1776.

As regards the moral sciences, Daniel's best known achievements concern the possible applications of probability theory to individual and collective decision-making: first with his celebrated essay, "Specimen Theoriae Novae de Mensura Sortis" ("Proposal of a new theory of the measure of chance") – presented in 1731 in Saint Petersburg and published there in 1738 in the *Annals* of the academy – and, second, with his intervention in the controversy over the desirability or not for the public authority to recommend the inoculation of smallpox to fight against this malady (Bernoulli 1760 [1766]). The theoretical context was a long-standing discussion over the nature and applicability of the calculus of probability, and especially of a central concept: (mathematical) expectation. Many detailed objections were levelled against this calculus, in particular by one of the most celebrated mathematicians and philosophers of the age, Jean Le Rond d'Alembert (Daston 1979; Paty 1988), who also intervened in the controversy over inoculation and reacted to Bernoulli's memoir (Daston 1988: 82–9; Paty 1988: 220–25). The Saint Petersburg paper, which will be dealt with here, belongs to an early stage of this controversy. It forms a milestone in utility theory, the apprehension of risk and the formalisation of economic theory. It is also the symbol of a transformation in the notion of rationality and the definition of the conduct of the "reasonable" man: from a question of justice and equity in jurisprudence and games of chance (with, in particular, aleatory contracts and fair stakes) symbolized by the figure of the disinterested judge abstracting from personal and subjective situations, this conduct changed into that of the prudent man, the model of whom is the merchant in a risky environment (Daston 1980, 1989). Daniel Bernoulli stressed this shift of points of view when, in his essay, he referred to a letter Nikolaus sent him in 1732:

> [H]e [Nikolaus] declared that he was in no way dissatisfied with my proposition on the evaluation of risky propositions when applied to the case of a man who is to evaluate his own prospects. However, he thinks that the case is different if a third person, somewhat in the position of a judge, is to evaluate the prospects of any participant in a game in accord with equity and justice. (Bernoulli 1738 [1954]: 33)

How it all started: Nikolaus's challenge and the first discussions

The long-standing debate on what was called later the "Saint Petersburg paradox" (see, for example, Samuelson 1977; Jorland 1987; Daston 1988: ch. 2; Dutka 1988; Martin 2014) started with a letter of Nikolaus to Montmort, dated 9 September 1713 and immediately published by Montmort, with some other correspondence with Johann and Nikolaus, in the fifth part of the second edition of his *Essay* (Rémond de Montmort

1713: 401–2). Nikolaus proposed five problems for Montmort to solve, the last two being the following:

> *Fourth problem. A* promises *B* to give him one *écu* if, with a normal dice, he obtains six points at the first roll, two *écus* if he succeeds at the second roll, three *écus* if he succeeds at the third roll, four *écus* at the fourth roll, and so on; one asks, what is B's expectation. *Fifth problem*. The same thing is asked if *A* promises *B* to give him *écus* in this progression: 1, 2, 4, 8, 16, etc. or 1, 3, 9, 27, etc. . . . instead of 1, 2, 3, 4, 5, etc. like before. (Ibid.: 402)

Montmort answered (ibid.: 407) that the solution, based on the calculus of the limit of infinite series developed by Nikolaus's uncle Jakob, was easy to find. In a subsequent correspondence however (Dutka 1988: 19; Meusnier 2006: 9–11), Nikolaus pointed out to Montmort two difficulties that the latter had disregarded. Two methods could be used to solve the problem: *B*'s expected gain could be found either as the sum of the terms of an infinite series, as stressed by his correspondent, or using mathematical induction. But while the solution to the fourth problem poses no problem (*B*'s expectation is 6) whatever the method employed, two important discrepancies arise instead in the case of the fifth problem – discrepancies which shake the belief in the meaning and relevance of (mathematical) expectation. In the first place, in the case of the first progression for example – 1, 2, 2^2, 2^3, . . . 2^n . . . – and because the probability to obtain a "six" at every roll is one-sixth, the first method gives a solution:

$$\frac{1}{6}.1 + \frac{1}{6}.\frac{5}{6}.2 + \frac{1}{6}.\left(\frac{5}{6}\right)^2.2^2 + \ldots + \frac{1}{6}.\left(\frac{5}{6}\right)^n.2^n + \ldots = \frac{1}{6}\sum_{n=0}^{\infty}\left(\frac{5}{6}\right)^n.2^n \qquad (1)$$

which is infinite, while, with the second method, the result is different: it is finite and moreover negative: −1/4 (Dutka 1988: 19; Meusnier 2006: 10–11). In the second place, since in games of chance the fair stake was defined as the player's expected gain, another discrepancy arises with what "good sense" would advise: no reasonable player is supposed to pay an infinitely large sum of money – or even only an important sum, compared to his wealth – to play this game.

The first difficulty was very embarrassing and forms the real paradox in this story. After Gabriel Cramer rekindled the debate in 1728 (Montmort had died in 1719), the discussion concentrated on the second difficulty – which was not really a paradox, in spite of the name given to it, but a discrepancy between theory and reality. It involved Cramer, in correspondence with Nikolaus and Georges-Louis Leclerc de Buffon, and Nikolaus with Daniel. An excerpt of this correspondence between Nikolaus and Cramer is quoted at the end of Daniel's essay (Bernoulli 1738 [1954]: 33–5), and the exchange of letters between Buffon and Cramer is recalled in Buffon's "Essai d'arithmétique morale" (Leclerc de Buffon 1777: 75–7). The game considered is now the toss of a coin, with the same progression of possible gains (1, 2, 2^2, 2^3, . . . 2^n . . .). The game goes on if *B* obtains "tails" and stops with "heads". With the first method – the probability to obtain "heads" at every toss being one-half – *B*'s expectation of gain is again infinite:

$$\frac{1}{2}.1 + \frac{1}{2^2}.2 + \frac{1}{2^3}.2^2 + \ldots + \frac{1}{2^{n+1}}.2^n + \ldots = \sum_{n=0}^{\infty}\left(\frac{1}{2}\right)^{n+1}.2^n \qquad (2)$$

The debate thus turned around the possibility to change the definition of expectation because the usual one gave results at odds with "good sense": this was possible by
changing the apprehension of the possible gains. As Cramer put it in 1728 – an approach
which turned out to be the same as Buffon's and Daniel's solutions – the reason for the
discrepancy between the mathematical calculation and common sense "results from the
fact that, *in theory*, mathematicians evaluate money in proportion to its quantity while,
in practice, people with common sense evaluate money in proportion to the use they can
make of it" (Cramer, in Bernoulli 1738 [1954]: 33, translation modified). For the player,
what matters is not the sum of money, but, in Daniel's words, the "emolumentum" – the
benefit, the advantage, usually translated as "utility" – an individual gains from it, which
depends on the wealth already possessed. Daniel formalized and developed this idea in
an outstanding way.

The Book of Daniel
A given sum of money does not have the same importance or utility to different persons
with different wealth. The greater is an individual's wealth ("summa bonorum"), the
less a given increment of it will be of importance to its owner. If, with Daniel Bernoulli,
infinitesimal increments of wealth are considered, this means that what is called today
the marginal utility of wealth is decreasing. This is what had become to be known as
"Bernoulli's hypothesis". It is moreover to be noted that Bernoulli's concept of wealth
is defined in a broad and modern way: it does not only consist in the material wealth
already possessed, but it also takes into account the future incomes that a given human
capital is susceptible to yield (Bernoulli 1738 [1954]: 25). Daniel illustrated his approach
with Figure 4 – which in modern parlance represents the utility of wealth – where the
horizontal axis denotes wealth and its possible increments (not infinitesimal here for
the sake of clarity) and the vertical axis the benefit or utility obtained from them. The
function is concave because of the positive but decreasing marginal utility. *AB* denotes
the initial wealth before the game starts. By convention, the utility of *AB* is nil, so that

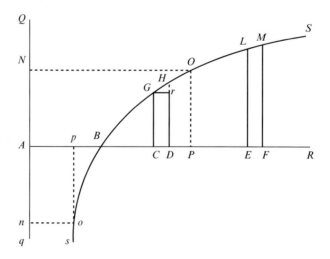

Figure 4   Daniel Bernoulli's representation of the utility of wealth

the utilities *CG, DH, EL* and *FM* of the possible increments of wealth *BC, BD, BE, BF*, can be read easily on the figure.

In order to be more precise and to apply his approach to concrete cases (marine insurance, for example), Daniel advanced a second hypothesis: the increment of utility generated by an infinitesimal increase of wealth is inversely proportional to this wealth (Bernoulli 1738 [1954]: 25). In modern parlance, this is to suppose that the utility function is iso-elastic, the algebraic value of the elasticity of the marginal utility of wealth with respect to wealth being moreover equal to −1.

The (utility) function, Bernoulli writes, can thus be specified. Let α denote the initial wealth *AB*. At any point of the curve (for example, *C*), if *x* denotes the wealth, *dx* its increment, *y* the utility of *x*, and *dy* its increment (the segment *rH* in the graph), then, *b* being a positive constant:

$$dy = b\left(\frac{1}{x}\right)dx \Rightarrow y = b \log x + k \tag{3}$$

where *k* is a constant of integration. Since, by convention, as stated above, *y* = 0 for *x* = α,

$$k = -b \log \alpha \Rightarrow y = b \log \frac{x}{\alpha} \tag{4}$$

Since in a game of chance the mathematical expectation of the monetary gains can no longer be considered as the fair stake a player has to pay, what has to be calculated is instead the "emolumentum medium", that is the "mean utility" or, as Cramer put it in 1728, the "espérance morale" (moral expectation) of the player – Condorcet later spoke of "espérance relative" (relative expectation). The formula of the moral expectation is simply that of the mathematical expectation, the possible gains *BC, BD, BE, BF*, etc. having simply to be replaced with their respective utility *CG, DH, EL* and *FM*, and so on. Suppose that there are *m* independent ways of obtaining *BC, n* of obtaining *BD, p* for *BE, q* for *BF*, and so on. Then, for the player, the "moral expectation" of the gains – *PO* in Figure 4 – is given by:

$$PO = \frac{m.CG + n.DH + p.EL + q.FM + \dots}{m + n + p + q + \dots} \tag{5}$$

with the segment *BP* on the horizontal axis denoting the corresponding (and finite) expected gain.

Now, to get into the game, a player will never pay a sum, the disutility of which is greater than the moral expectation of the gain. As Cramer himself put it in 1728, the stake should be "of such a magnitude that the pain caused by its loss is equal to the moral expectation of the pleasure I hope to derive from my gain" (in Bernoulli 1738 [1954]: 34). How much, then, will a player be ready to pay? Let *po* = *PO* be the disutility of the maximum stake. It is easy to see in Figure 4 that this maximum stake is *Bp* – that is, the diminution of the initial wealth of the player, the disutility of which is precisely equal to *po*. Owing to the concavity of the curve, *Bp* < *BP*, that is, the greatest stake that the player should be prepared to pay is inferior to the expected gain. The values of all the variables can be calculated. In the case of the game of heads or tails mentioned above, the stake would be of a few *écus* only.

This also shows that, whenever the stake is determined on the basis of the usual rule based on the expected gain, the player will always be a loser because the disutility of the stake would always be greater than the utility of the expected gain. However, the two rules of the mathematical and moral expectations are (1) equivalent if utility is directly proportional to the gain, in which case the function becomes a straight line, or (2) nearly equivalent in case the initial wealth is "infinitely great" compared to the greatest possible gain, in which case the graph of the function is approximately a straight line (Corollaries I and II, in Bernoulli 1738 [1954]: 27).

Daniel applied his new method of evaluating risk to questions of trade and insurance (Bernoulli 1738 [1954]: 29–30), for example, to state the conditions of profitable insurance, both for the merchant who thinks about insuring his trade and the insurer who insures the merchant. He showed also that the merchant can reduce his risk in dividing his merchandise and sending it on several boats instead of one single ship (ibid.: 30–31) – "it is advisable to divide goods which are exposed to some danger into several portions rather than to risk them all together" (ibid.: 30). The analysis of a better risk spread can also be extended to other questions. "This counsel will be equally serviceable for those who invest their fortunes in foreign bills of exchange and other hazardous enterprises" (ibid.: 31).

Another important theme can also be found in Daniel's 1738 paper: the definition of risk aversion as a situation in which a player prefers a gain which is certain to a greater but uncertain (expected) gain – a case illustrated nowadays with a concave utility function. As he wrote at the beginning of his text, still referring to the criterion of mathematical expectation:

> Somehow a very poor fellow obtains a lottery ticket that will yield with equal probability either nothing or twenty thousand ducats. Will this man evaluate his chance of winning at ten thousand ducats? Would he not be ill-advised to sell this lottery ticket for nine thousand ducats? To me it seems that the answer is in the negative. (Bernoulli [1738] 1954: 24, s. 3)

Bernoulli's presentation of moral expectation was later taken up and developed in the expected utility theory, and his iso-elastic utility function is still widely used in problems of applied microeconomics. To conclude, two remarks are in order as regards the shape of the utility function. On the one hand, even when Bernoulli's contemporaries accepted his first hypothesis (the decreasing marginal utility of wealth), the second, concerning the value of the elasticity of the marginal utility of wealth with respect to wealth, was contested. Condorcet, in particular, supposed that the absolute value of the elasticity was greater than one – with important consequences in favour of progressive taxation (Faccarello 2006: 26–30). On the other hand, the logarithmic form of the utility function is not the only one contemplated by Daniel Bernoulli. Cramer, in the 1728 letter to Nikolaus, extensively quoted by Daniel at the end of his essay, proposed $y = \sqrt{x}$. It is worth noting that Daniel accepted this specification as a possible solution. The manner in which Cramer expressed "the basic principle . . . that reasonable men should evaluate money in proportion to the use they can make thereof", he wrote, is "in perfect agreement with our view" (in Bernoulli 1738 [1954]: 34, translation modified).

GILBERT FACCARELLO

See also:

Marie-Jean-Antoine-Nicolas Caritat de Condorcet (I); Formalization and mathematical modelling (III); French Enlightenment (II); Uncertainty and information (III).

References and further reading

Bernoulli, D. (1738), 'Specimen Theoriae Novae de Mensura Sortis', *Commentarii Academiae Scientiarum Imperialis Petropolitanae*, **V** (for the years 1730 and 1731): 175–92 (the celebrated figure is to be found as 'fig. 5' of 'Tab. VII', among all the figures of the different papers, at the end of the volume); English trans., D. Bernoulli (1954), 'Exposition of a new theory on the measurement of risk', *Econometrica*, **22** (1), 23–36.

Bernoulli, D. (1760), 'Essai d'une nouvelle analyse de la mortalité causée par la petite vérole, et des avantages de l'inoculation pour la prévenir', in 'Mémoires de Mathématiques et de Physique tirés des registres de l'Académie Royale des Sciences de l'année 1760', *Histoire et Mémoires de l'Académie Royale des Sciences de Paris*, Paris: Imprimerie Royale, 1766, pp. 1–45.

Daston, L. (1979), 'D'Alembert's critique of probability theory', *Historia Mathematica*, **6** (3), 259–79.

Daston, L. (1980), 'Probabilistic expectation and rationality in classical probability theory', *Historia Mathematica*, **7** (3), 234–60.

Daston, L. (1988), *Classical Probability in the Enlightenment*, Princeton, NJ: Princeton University Press.

Daston, L. (1989), 'L'interprétation classique du calcul des probabilités', *Annales. Économies, Sociétés, Civilisations*, **44** (3), 715–31.

Daston, L. (1994), 'How probabilities came to be objective and subjective', *Historia Mathematica*, **21** (3), 330–44.

Dutka, J. (1988), 'On the St. Petersburg paradox', *Archive for History of Exact Sciences*, **39** (1), 13–39.

Faccarello, G. (2006), 'An "exception culturelle"? French Sensationist political economy and the shaping of public economics', *European Journal of the History of Economic Thought*, **13** (1), 1–38.

Hacking, I. (1975), *The Emergence of Probability. A Philosophical Study of Early Ideas about Probability, Induction and Statistical Inference*, Cambridge: Cambridge University Press.

Hald, A. (1990), *History of Probability and Statistics and their Applications before 1750*, Hoboken: Wiley.

JEHPS (2006), 'Quels échanges? Jacob Bernoulli, Gottfried Leibniz', *Journ@l électronique d'histoire des probabilités et de la statistique*, **2** (1), 1–15, accessed May 2015 at http://www.jehps.net/.

Jorland, G. (1987), 'The Saint Petersburg paradox 1713–1937', in L. Krüger, L. Daston and M. Heidelberger (eds), *The Probabilistic Revolution*, vol. I: *Ideas in History*, Cambridge, MA: MIT Press, pp. 157–90.

Kohli, K. (1975), 'Zur Publikationsgeschichte der Ars Conjectandi', in B.L. van der Waerden (ed.), *Die Werke von Jakob Bernoulli*, vol. 3, Basel: Bikhäuser, pp. 391–401.

Leclerc de Buffon, G.-L. (1777), 'Essai d'arithmétique morale', in G.L. Leclerc de Buffon, *Histoire naturelle, générale et particulière. Servant de suite à l'Histoire naturelle de l'homme. Supplément*, vol. IV, Paris: Imprimerie Royale, pp. 46–148.

Martin, R. (2014), 'The St. Petersburg paradox', in E.N. Zalta (ed.), *The Stanford Encyclopedia of Philosophy*, Summer edn, available at http://plato.stanford.edu/archives/sum2014/entries/paradox-stpetersburg/.

Meusnier, N. (2006), 'Nicolas, neveu exemplaire', *Journ@l électronique d'histoire des probabilités et de la statistique*, **2** (1), 1–14, accessed May 2015 at http://www.jehps.net/.

O'Connor, J.J. and E.F. Robertson (1997–98), 'Daniel Bernoulli', 'Jacob Bernoulli', 'Johann Bernoulli', 'Nicolaus Bernoulli', MacTutor History of Mathematics Archive, accessed May 2015 at http://www-history. mcs.st-andrews.ac.uk/.

Paty, M. (1988), 'D'Alembert et les probabilités', in R. Rashed (ed.), *Sciences à l'époque de la Révolution française: études historiques*, Paris: Blanchard, pp. 203–65.

Rémond de Montmort, P. (1713), *Essay d'analyse sur les jeux de hazard. Seconde édition revue et augmentée de plusieurs lettres*, Paris: Jacque Quillau.

Samuelson, P.A. (1977), 'St. Petersburg paradoxes: defanged, dissected, and historically described', *Journal of Economic Literature*, **15** (1), 24–55.

Yushkevich, A.P. (1987), 'Nicholas Bernoulli and the publication of James Bernoulli's *Ars Conjectandi*', *Theory of Probability and its Applications*, **31** (2), 286–303.

David Hume (1711–1776)

Life

Hume was born on 26 April 1711 in Edinburgh. At the age of 12, he entered the University of Edinburgh, where his family encouraged him to pursue legal studies. However, he was only interested in philosophy (including scientific studies). He later stayed in Bristol for several months as a merchant, and then left for France for three years. It was during his stay at La Flèche, in Anjou, between 1733 and 1735 that he wrote his major work, *A Treatise of Human Nature*. Published in 1739 and 1740, this book was given a very disappointing reception. That is why he later decided to publish two versions, deemed more accessible: *An Enquiry Concerning Human Understanding* (1748) and *An Enquiry Concerning the Principles of Morals* (1751).

Upon his return to Scotland in 1740 – where he met Adam Smith, to whom he remained very close throughout his life – he published his first *Essays* in Edinburgh in 1741, spanning a very broad field, ranging from "Of the Delicacy of Taste and Passion" to "Of Civil Liberty". Other essays on widely diverse subjects were to be added over the years. These essays were very successful. However, accused of atheism, Hume failed to obtain a chair at the University of Edinburgh (in 1745) or Glasgow (in 1751). The position of librarian to the Edinburgh Faculty of Advocates enabled him to write *The History of England*, published between 1754 and 1762. After the end of the Seven Years' War, Hume became the personal secretary to the Ambassador of Great Britain in Paris, where he spent three years, frequenting encyclopaedists and philosophers. He returned to Great Britain in 1767, as a member of the government (Under-Secretary of State for the Northern Department). In 1769 he returned to Scotland, working on new editions of his books. He died on 25 August 1776, shortly after the publication of *The Wealth of Nations* by his friend Smith. (On Hume's life, see also Mossner 1954; Ross 2008).

David Hume is unanimously considered as the most important British philosopher of the eighteenth century. His precocity is surprising, since he finished his *Treatise of Human Nature* at the age of 26 (he published the *Abstract of a Treatise of Human Nature* anonymously, which was identified and republished by Keynes and Sraffa in 1938) and its depth is so great that the questions he posed at that time not only awakened Kant from his "dogmatic slumber", but still concern us today.

The *Essays*: Is Money "Oil" or "Blood"?

While nobody questions the place of David Hume in the history of philosophy, opinions about David Hume as an economist are far more divided. Hume's economic writings occupy a minor place in his œuvre. They are mainly to be found in the essays initially published, along with other political essays, under the title of *Political Discourses* in 1752. One final essay in this field, "Of the Jealousy of Trade", was published in 1760.

R. Lucas Jr (Lucas 1996) praised him in his Nobel Lecture "David Hume's marvellous essays of 1752, Of Money and Of Interest", but others, including J.A. Schumpeter, were more reluctant to appreciate his thesis on the neutrality of money. In the *History of Economic Analysis*, for example, Schumpeter wrote: "the genuine quantity theorem that, sometimes in the crudest possible form, became a commonplace for many of the leaders.

It is taken for granted by Genovesi, Galiani, Beccaria and Justi, and Hume reasserted it with an emphasis that was hardly necessary" (Schumpeter 1954: 314–15).

This ambivalent judgement underlines a standard difficulty in Hume's text. On the one hand, Hume shares with Montesquieu and many others the idea of the existence of historical progress. Now this progress is a consequence of the development of commerce. For example, in one of the *Essays Moral, Political and Literary*, "Of the Rise and Progress of the Arts and Sciences", Hume explains "that it is impossible for the arts and sciences to arise, at first, among any people unless that people enjoy the blessing of a free government" (Hume 1742 [1987] I, xiv: 14). He adds: "that nothing is more favourable to the rise of politeness and learning, than a number of neighbouring and independent states, connected together by commerce and policy" (Hume 1742 [1987] I, xiv: 16). It is evident for Hume that international trade implies monetary exchange and is somehow associated with money. In other words, an economy in which the circulation of money is scarce is necessarily a poor economy. In that sense, money seems to be the blood of the social *organism*. On the other hand, Hume seeks to affirm the neutrality of money, which is only the "oil in the wheels" of the economic *mechanism*. How to explain this contradiction between the two propositions?

From the corruption of morals to the danger of imperial expansion
In the first two essays, "Of Commerce" and "Of Refinement in the Arts", Hume takes a stand in the debate concerning the relationship between increasing wealth and virtue. He opposes the classical tradition that associates wealth with political decadence and which interprets the history of Rome as the story of an interminable abandonment of the virtues – especially martial virtues – of the earlier Romans, following the rise in luxury consumption. Hume's thesis is moderate: of course "excessive" luxury may corrupt morals, but under reasonable conditions, commerce promotes both civilization and "the martial spirit" (Hume 1742 [1987], II, ii: 11). Moreover, speaking of Sparta, he writes:

> But though the want of trade and manufactures, among a free and very martial people, may *sometimes* have no other effect than to render the public more powerful it is certain, that, in the common course of human affairs, it will have a quite contrary tendency. . . . Now, according to the most natural course of things, industry and arts and trade increase the power of the sovereign as well as the happiness of the subjects. (Ibid.: II, i, 9)

Then Hume seems to change subjects and the following three essays – "Of Money", "Of Interest" and "Of the Balance of Trade" – express the core of his economic analysis.

All these texts were published in 1752. The final edition of the *Essays* added "Of the Jealousy of Trade". This text, which denounces the use of trade policy as a weapon of war, is inserted prior to the essay "Of the Balance of Power", which has no obvious economic content, and "Of Taxes" and "Of Public Credit", which concern the financing of public expenditure. These are Hume's economic publications in the strictest sense of the term (they were completed with the essays "Of some Remarkable Customs", "Of the Populousness of Ancient Nations" and "Idea of a Perfect Commonwealth"). As the reader can see, the essays are disparate in their themes and subjects. Also, in the economic essays, the questions addressed appear to be very heterogeneous. It is nonetheless easy to find some coherence in the essays published in 1752.

The essay "Of Money" opens with the famous proposition:

> Money is . . . none of the wheels of trade: It is the oil which renders the motion of the wheels more smooth and easy. If we consider any one kingdom by itself, it is evident, that the greater or less plenty of money is of no consequence; since the prices of commodities are always proportioned to the plenty of money. (Hume 1742 [1987], II, iii: 1)

An increase in the quantity of money within an isolated economy has no effect on wealth. That is why money is neutral. Evidently, money is not part of the wealth of either an individual or an economy.

The essay "Of Interest" extends this analysis by seeking to show that a variation in the quantity of money can only have a *transitory* effect on the interest rate, a transition due to the length of time necessary to modify the value of money, caused by the variation in its quantity. The final analysis shows that the effects on money prices concern both the numerator and the denominator of the interest rate, which ultimately remains unchanged following the variation in the quantity of money. It is therefore "real causes" that must explain variations in long-term interest rates.

Finally, the next and most famous essay, "Of the Balance of Trade", is often credited with anticipating the monetary approach to the balance of payments: the argument supposes that any international commercial advantage (disadvantage) can be explained by lower (higher) domestic prices than international prices. This implies an inflow (outflow) of money causing a movement in prices that eliminates the initial advantage (disadvantage) without affecting international prices. Hence, the quantity of money cannot endlessly accumulate within (leave) the economy in question. There is an automatic mechanism which, when international prices are unchanged, determines the equilibrium in the quantity of money. The real effects of a variation in the quantity of money are thus transitory.

Up until this point, Hume had dealt with three seemingly very different themes: the effects of commerce and wealth on martial virtues, the neutrality of money, and the automatic equilibrium of external trade. However, his economic discourse has a coherence that clearly emerges if we read the essay "Of the Balance of Power", omitted from the *Economic Writings* published in 1955 by Rotwein and no longer present in the book *David Hume's Political Economy* edited by Schabas and Wennerlind (2008). Reading this essay, as Hume had intended, after "Of the Balance of Commerce", we move from the balance of foreign trade to the balance of power in Europe, and this is no coincidence.

After arguing that the politics of the balance of power between cities was practised in ancient Greece, Hume expresses surprise at the fact that this maxim had been discarded both by Rome (thus enabling it to build its empire) and by its adversaries (thus allowing the construction of the Roman Empire that caused their downfall). Yet the situation of Great Britain is comparable to that of Rome. The "excess" committed by Great Britain in its struggle against France (initiated in the days following the 1688 Revolution) led to an imminent catastrophe. Under the pretext of implementing the maxim of the balance of power in Europe, the British, animated by "jealous emulation" (Hume [1742] 1987, II, vii: 15), undertook an entirely different policy, characterized by "our own imprudent vehemence" (ibid.) that aimed not to preserve the balance of power in Europe, but to establish British domination on the continent. From then on, the maxim of the balance of power was modified and became a maxim of imperial expansion: "Enormous monarchies are, probably, destructive to human nature; in their progress, in their continuance,

and even in their downfall, which never can be very distant from their establishment"
(Hume [1742] 1987, II, vii, 19). This essay echoes the proposition in "Of Refinement on
Arts" that imputes the decadence of Rome not to an increase in wealth but to the exten-
sion of their empire (Hume [1742] 1987, II, ii: 13).

The role of public credit
These considerations regarding British foreign policy give meaning to the other economic essays. This imperial policy cannot be financed by taxes, and Hume showed that it
cannot be financed by the external trade surplus either, since this is inevitably ephemeral.
The external trade surplus cannot therefore constitute the "English Treasure" evoked by
the mercantilists (Thomas Mun, for instance). The wars can therefore only be financed
by public credit, Hume tells us in "Of Public Credit", the essay that concludes the series
of Political Discourses, the content of which is essentially economic: "It must, indeed, be
one of these two events; either the nation must destroy public credit, or public credit will
destroy the nation" (Hume 1742 [1987], II, ix: 28).

According to Hume, the growth of the public debt threatened Great Britain's constitutional order in three ways. First, in order to reimburse its debt, the government had
to exact a toll to replace the tax that the taxpayers' representatives would not or could
not vote. Consequently, the government had to collect a tribute from the citizens. This
measure brought Great Britain's situation back to one of "Oriental despotism". This
issue signified the *violent* death of public credit and of the Constitution. A second issue
is public bankruptcy, a measure used by continental absolute monarchies that signified
the *natural* death of public credit and, once again, of the Constitution (the "lesser evil"
solution that Hume therefore favoured). Third, otherwise, it seems probable that Great
Britain, no longer able to pursue this policy of the balance of power in Europe due to
lack of resources, would become the victim of invasion by a dominant continental power.
The latter outcome would signify the end of the nation, destroyed by public credit.

The monetary discourse in the *Essays* thus falls within the framework of a coherent
position. Not only does the increase in the wealth of nations not corrupt their military
virtues, but it may also, through public credit, stimulate their nationalism and give rise
to the constitution of new empires financed by the growth of public debt. The real danger
of an increase in wealth therefore does not reside in an excess of moral refinement, but in
the exacerbation of national passions financed by public credit.

The affirmation of the neutrality of money thus serves above all to criticize the mercantilist theories according to which a trade surplus allows the constitution of a war
chest. We must not, therefore, misjudge the essentially political dimension of the *Essays*.
Yet, naturally, the neutrality of money affirmed in the Political Discourses series had to
be argued on economic grounds, as called for by Tucker and Oswald soon after publication of the book (see Rotwein 1955: 190, 197, 202). For instance, they raised the question
of the process through which an increase in the quantity of money would leave real economic variables unchanged. This argument is strong, as Hume himself used the fact that
an economy without money remains backward and poor. Here, we find an expression
of the central tension mentioned above: how can we accept the idea of the neutrality of
money if we accept that a non-monetary economy is necessarily poorer than a monetary
economy? This difficulty gave rise to an abundant literature that is well described in
Wennerlind (2008). It was generally admitted (Rotwein 1955; Schabas 1994; Schabas and

Wennerlind 2008; Wennerlind 2001, 2005) that Hume, along with most of the supporters of the quantity theory of money, accepted the non-neutrality of money in the short term and its neutrality over the long term. Wennerlind (2005) proposes a slightly different interpretation. According to him, Hume contrasted an increase in "endogenous" money, the effects of which would be positive on growth and employment, with an increase in "exogenous" money (imported money) that would be neutral. This interpretation under-lines the importance of the anti-mercantilist dimension of Hume's argument.

Beyond these debates, we find here one of the major difficulties encountered by the quantity theory of money, and this is perhaps why most economists concur (Clower 1969; Lucas Jr 1996) in attributing the paternity of this theory to Hume.

The *Treatise*: A Brief Outline of a Theory of Money?

However, *A Treatise of Human Nature* (Hume 1739–40 [1983]: 520) contains an approach that seems to fundamentally deny the thesis of neutrality (see Diatkine 1992, 2012; Wennerlind 2001). In fact, barter is not only *costly*, it is quite simply *unthink-able*. As Hume writes (1739–40 [1983]: 520): "The transference of property, which is the proper remedy for this inconvenience [the fixity of property], cannot remedy it entirely; because it can only take place with regard to such objects as are present and individual, but not to such as are absent or general."

First, barter (the "transference of property") is costly because it must be immedi-ate; as the exchanged objects must be present. This simultaneity of the transfers is costly, says Hume, because it prohibits inter-temporal trade (1739–40 [1983]: 520). This requires the institution "of the obligation of promises" which is crucial for any theory of justice.

Secondly, because it only concerns individual objects (that is, objects that are identifi-able by means of their owners' identity), barter prohibits the anonymity that is necessary for the generality of trade. The prices of commodities must not depend on the identity of buyers or sellers. Evidently, this is not the case for promises. It is possible to conclude that for Hume, the substitution of a general promise (money) for individual promises is logically necessary for trade. Unfortunately, Hume does not go any further, for his purpose here is to understand the origin of the sentiment of (political) obligation at the heart of his theory of justice, and not to elaborate a theory of money.

Nevertheless, money is therefore an essential element of the economic structure. It is neither the "oil of the wheels of trade" nor the blood of the social body; it is an essential ingredient for social links, and society is neither a mechanism nor an organism.

DANIEL DIATKINE

See also:
Balance of payment and exchange rates (III); Scottish Enlightenment (II).

References and further reading
Blaug, M. (ed.) (1991), *David Hume (1711–1776) and James Steuart (1712–1780)*, Aldershot, UK and Brookfield, VT, USA: Edward Elgar.
Clower, R.W. (1969), 'Introduction', in R.W. Clower (dir), *Monetary Theory*, Harmondsworth: Penguin Books, pp. 17–18.
Deleule, D. (1979), *Hume et la naissance du libéralisme économique*, Paris: Aubier.

Deleuze, G. (1991), *Empiricism and Subjectivity: An Essay on Hume's theory of Human Nature*, New York: Columbia University Press; first published 1953.

Diatkine, D. (1992), 'Hume et Steuart', in G. Faccarello and A. Béraud (eds), *Nouvelle histoire de la pensée économique*, vol. 1: *Des scolastiques aux classiques*, Paris: La Découverte, pp. 204–24.

Diatkine D. (2012), "Promesse et monnaie chez Hume", *Economie et Société* (Série PE), **46**, 122–44.

Forbes, D. (1975), *Hume's Philosophical Politics*, Cambridge: Cambridge University Press.

Haakonssen, K. (1981), *The Science of a Legislator: The Natural Jurisprudence of David Hume and Adam Smith*, Cambridge: Cambridge University Press.

Haakonssen, K. (1994), 'Introduction', in K. Haakonssen (ed.), *Hume, Political Essays*, Cambridge: Cambridge University Press, pp. ix–xxx.

Hont, I. (1993), 'The rhapsody of public debt: David Hume and voluntary state bankruptcy', reprinted in I. Hont (2005), *Jealousy of Trade*, Cambridge, MA: Belknap Press of Harvard University Press, pp. 325–53.

Hume, D. (1739–40), *A Treatise of Human Nature*, reprinted 1983, L.A. Selby-Bigge (ed.), Oxford: Oxford University Press.

Hume, D. (1742), *Essays Moral, Political and Literary*, reprinted 1987, E. Miller (ed.), Indianapolis, IN: Liberty Fund.

Lucas, Jr, R.E. (1996), 'Nobel lecture: monetary neutrality', *Journal of Political Economy*, **104** (4), 661–82.

Mossner, E.C. (1954), *The Life of David Hume*, Austin, TX: University of Texas Press.

Norton, D.F. (1993), *The Cambridge Companion to Hume*, Cambridge: Cambridge University Press.

Pocock, J.G.A. (1985), 'Hume and the American Revolution: the dying thoughts of a North Briton', in J.G.A. Pocock, *Virtue, Commerce, and History: Essays on Political Thought and History, Chiefly in the Eighteenth Century*, Cambridge: Cambridge University Press, pp. 125–41.

Ross, I.S. (2008), 'The emergence of David Hume as a political economist: a biographical sketch', in C. Wennerlind and M. Schabas (eds), *David Hume's Political Economy*, Abingdon: Routledge, pp. 31–48.

Rotwein, E. (1955), *David Hume: Writings on Economics*, Madison, WI: University of Wisconsin Press.

Schabas, M. (1994), 'Market contract in the age of Hume', *History of Political Economy*, **26** (supplement), 117–34.

Schabas, M. and C. Wennerlind (eds) (2008), *David Hume's Political Economy*, Abingdon: Routledge.

Schumpeter, J.A. (1954), *History of Economic Analysis*, London: George Allen and Unwin.

Wennerlind, C. (2001), 'The link between David Hume's *Treatise of Human Nature* and his fiduciary theory of money', *History of Political Economy*, **33** (1), 139–60.

Wennerlind, C. (2005), 'David Hume's monetary theory revisited: was he really a quantity theorist and an inflationist?', *Journal of Political Economy*, **113** (1), 223–37.

Wennerlind, C. (2008), 'An artificial virtue and the oil of commerce: a synthetic view of Hume's theory of money', in C. Wennerlind and M. Schabas (eds), *David Hume's Political Economy*, Abingdon: Routledge, pp. 105–26.

James Steuart [James Denham-Steuart] (1712–1780)

James Steuart's main work, *An Inquiry into the Principles of Political Oeconomy* of 1767, was the first full-length treatise on political economy in Britain. It attracted a fair amount of attention when it was first published but was overshadowed by Adam Smith's *Wealth of Nations* which came out less than a decade later.

Steuart was the son of a successful Edinburgh lawyer. After graduating from Edinburgh University he was called to the bar, but spent five years on a grand tour of the Continent before starting his legal career. While in Rome in 1739, however, he met the Stuart claimant to the British (that is, Scottish and English) throne, starting an entanglement which was to affect the rest of his life. He was openly involved with the Jacobite (Stuart) rising of 1745 and had to go into exile when the rising collapsed, living variously in France, Germany and the Low Countries. Back in Scotland from 1763, he still had to be very careful until 1771 when he was formally pardoned. His *Principles* was published in 1767 but had been mostly constructed in exile. This unusual background meant that he had little experience of conditions in England, the most successful economy of the day.

Political economy, in Steuart's view, exists to provide guidance to the "statesman", his name for an idealized head of government. The aim of the statesman, and hence the aim of political economy, is "to provide food, other necessaries, and employment to every one of society" (Steuart 1767: 28). Since unregulated markets are not to be trusted, the statesman must constantly be ready to intervene in one way or another.

The book starts with population, which depends on "generation" (births) and on food supplies: "generation gives existence, food preserves it". If food supply increases, people multiply, and food becomes scarce again (Steuart 1767: 31, 32). This is essentially the argument later popularized by Malthus – Marx famously accused Malthus of having plagiarized Steuart – but in its essentials it goes back much further. Steuart, like Malthus after him, was expounding his own version of a well-known line of argument.

The main theme of the first two "books" (of five which make up the work) is an account of economic development or, in Steuart's own words, of "the regular progress of mankind, from great simplicity to complicated refinement" (Steuart 1767: 28). Steuart's analysis of development was largely based on arguments which David Hume had published a few years before (Brewer 1997) though Steuart filled in the details more fully and gave it all a rather more pessimistic slant. He divided the population into two classes: "The first is that of the farmers who produce the subsistence; . . . the other I shall call the *free hands*" (Steuart 1767: 43). Non-agricultural activities depend on a supply of food from the agricultural sector, since the "free hands" have to eat. Fortunately, agriculture can (at least potentially) produce a surplus of food over what is needed to support the farmers themselves: "One consequence of a fruitful soil, possessed by a free people, given to agriculture and inclined to industry, will be the production of a superfluous quantity of food, over and above what is necessary to feed the farmers" (Steuart 1767: 42).

This notion of a surplus should be treated with some care. It is a surplus of food potentially available to support the "free hands". It is not the same as the physiocratic "net product" in agriculture, which is a surplus over all costs in value terms. It is not necessarily available to landlords or as tax revenue (as the physiocratic net product is) because the Hume/Steuart marketable surplus of food is normally transferred by exchange.

The key question is, why would farmers want to produce more than they can eat? Without some motive, the surplus will not be produced and population and incomes will be low. To support free hands, an increase in agricultural productivity is needed. But suppose that the agricultural producers are "lazy", that is, that they prefer (at the margin) to work less rather than consume more, or that they live in "such simplicity of manners, as to have few wants". In this case they will find an increased output superfluous to their needs and will, in Steuart's words, "return to their ancient simplicity" (1767: 41) so population could not grow, or (in more moderate cases) population growth would be limited. This was not an abstract hypothesis. Steuart considered that "no country in Europe is cultivated to the utmost" but many were not (he thought) growing. This he called a "moral incapacity" of multiplying (1767: 42).

That said, he recognized that "The great alteration in the affairs of Europe within these three centuries, by the discovery of America and the Indies, the springing up of industry and learning, the introduction of trade and the luxurious arts, . . . have entirely altered the plan of government every where" (Steuart 1767: 24).

A change in tastes leading to a desire for manufactured and exotic goods of all kinds gives farmers the motive to produce food to sell, starting a process of growth characterized by a growing variety of goods and a growing non-agricultural population: "[T]he human species will multiply pretty much in proportion to their industry; their industry will increase according to their wants, and these again will be diversified according to the spirit of the times. . . . Trade, industry, and manufactures, tend only to multiply the numbers of men by encouraging agriculture" (Steuart 1767: 48, 50).

Steuart admitted that foreign trade could have a positive effect as a stimulus to industry but saw many opportunities for it to go wrong, especially since he did not accept Hume's analysis of the self-correcting effects of trade deficits or surpluses through the specie-flow mechanism and the quantity theory of money, arguing that prices depend on supply and demand for individual commodities, which depend in turn on various non-monetary factors. Rich people, for example, may hoard their wealth, reducing demand. The quantity of money could multiply ten-fold without having any necessary effect on prices (Steuart 1767: 345). Overall demand and supply matter, because a deficiency of demand (caused by any of the varied factors which he thought relevant) could lead to unemployment. It was the duty of the statesman to ensure that the people are employed.

According to Steuart, a successful country gains advantages from learning by doing – "every circumstance, in short, becomes more favourable" (1767: 202), but an adept statesman is needed to keep the balance "in vibration as long as possible" (ibid.: 203). When a nation begins to lose ground, when "luxury and extravagance" take hold, "trade will decay where it flourished most" (ibid.: 205). "When a nation . . . finds the balance of trade against her, it is her interest to put a stop to it altogether" (ibid.: 284).

Steuart's economics is often described as mercantilist, but it might be better to think of it as influenced by German cameralism – the state is seen as a business which needs active management by the statesman. He had no confidence in markets, which could produce varied outcomes depending on circumstances, and he emphasized the difference between different countries in the "spirit of the people", in habits and institutions. Each case must be examined in detail in its own terms. The result, if interesting and stimulating, was often inconclusive and difficult to follow. Steuart himself viewed his own work as no more than a first approximation. It is perhaps not surprising that Smith's confidence and optimism carried the day.

Recent years have seen a renewed scholarly interest in Steuart's work and a growing secondary literature (see, for example, Skinner 1966; Tortajada 1999).

ANTHONY BREWER

See also:

Cameralism (II); French Enlightenment (II); David Hume (I); Mercantilism and the science of trade (II); Scottish Enlightenment (II).

References and further reading

Brewer, A. (1997), 'An eighteenth century view of economic development: Hume and Steuart', *European Journal of the History of Economic Thought*, **4** (1), 1–22.
Skinner, A. (1966), 'Introduction', in J. Steuart, *An Inquiry into the Principles of Political Oeconomy*, first printed 1767, ed. A. Skinner, Edinburgh: Oliver and Boyd.
Steuart, J. (1767), *An Inquiry into the Principles of Political Oeconomy*, reprinted in 1966, A. Skinner (ed.), Edinburgh: Oliver and Boyd.
Tortajada, R. (ed.) (1999), *The Economics of James Steuart*, London: Routledge.

Adam Smith (1723–1790)

Adam Smith is one of the great founding figures of the modern social sciences; indeed, he is commonly regarded as *the* seminal figure in the creation of one particular social science, economics or political economy. Smith also stands high in the pantheon of economic and political liberalism. The intertwining of these two dimensions of the retrospective image of Smith is itself symptomatic of the particular proneness of social science to ideological influence. Two roughly coinciding events of the 1970s reflect this characteristic of Smith's standing as a social theorist. From the bicentenary year of his most famous work, *An Inquiry into the Nature and Causes of the Wealth of Nations* (Smith 1776 [1976]; hereafter *WN*), the publication of the "Glasgow Edition of the Works and Correspondence of Adam Smith" (6 vols, 1976–83) provided a comprehensive scholarly edition of all his extant writings. At about the same time, in the anglophone world in particular, there occurs the rise of "neo-conservatism" or "neo-liberalism", with these resurgent conservative or liberal political currents claiming to be in the intellectual tradition of Adam Smith, and aligning themselves with the 1976 celebrations of his book. This intertwining of social science and politics invites some scepticism concerning the contemporary image of Smith and a quest for the historical Adam Smith.

Life

Adam Smith was born in Kirkcaldy, Scotland (baptized 5 June), into a moderately well off family, though his father died five months before Smith was born. From the age of 14 he attended the University of Glasgow, and then from 1740, by way of a scholarship, Balliol College, Oxford, for six years. There Smith studied philosophy and European literature. He was later strongly critical of the quality of education at Oxford. Following some years freelance lecturing in Edinburgh, primarily on rhetoric and "belles-lettres" (essentially, literary criticism), but also the history of philosophy and jurisprudence, in 1751 Smith was appointed Professor of Logic at Glasgow. He shifted to the Chair of Moral Philosophy at Glasgow the following year. In 1764, aged 40, he resigned his professorship to take up the position of travelling tutor to the young Duke of Buccleuch. As a consequence, as well as gaining a life pension of £300 per annum, Smith then spent nearly three years in France. There, partly via the assistance of David Hume, he met a wide range of intellectuals, including François Marie Arouet de Voltaire (in Geneva) and, importantly for Smith's economic thought, François Quesnay and many of the physiocratic school, as well as Anne-Robert-Jacques Turgot.

After returning from France in late 1766, Smith exploited the financial independence provided by his pension to spend six years in Kirkcaldy, drafting and redrafting *WN*. Skinner (1987: 359) notes that the strain of this intellectual work is revealed in Smith's correspondence (Mossner and Ross 1977; hereafter *Corr*). The last three years prior to its publication were spent in London, partly to facilitate completion of empirical aspects of the book. During this period, in May 1767, he was also made a Fellow of the Royal Society, though not admitted until May 1773 (Ross 1995: 225). *An Inquiry into the Nature and Causes of the Wealth of Nations* was published on 9 March 1776, the same year as the death of his closest intellectual friend, David Hume, and the year of the American Declaration of Independence. The latter political conflict figures a little in the book. In 1778, Smith also wrote a memorandum on the Anglo-American conflict for Alexander Wedderburn, British Prime Minister Lord North's Solicitor-General (*Corr*: 377–85). The nation which was subsequently to emerge from that declaration would appear to many to become the clearest embodiment of Smith's political and economic principles.

In February 1778 Smith was appointed a Commissioner of Customs in Edinburgh, a post he held until 1790, adding a salary of £600 per annum to his private pension of £300 per annum. The apparent irony of the political economist who railed against European policies of trade restriction entering into the governance of part of that system has been noticed by many commentators, though a clearer understanding of Smith's policy views much diminishes the paradox (see the section on "Policy" below). He also in these latter years provided advice to British policy-makers on removal of restrictions on Anglo-Irish trade and on the consequences of the loss of the North American colonies. In the last decade of his life he undertook as well significant revisions of *WN*, and even more so of his first book, *The Theory of Moral Sentiments* (Smith 1759 [1976]; hereafter *TMS*). Smith died from a chronic bowel obstruction, in Edinburgh on 17 July 1790. According to one account, his last words to his friends were: "I believe we must adjourn this meeting to some other place" (Ross 1995: 406).

In seeking to sum up the man, Winch (2004: 25–6) notes the elusiveness of his character, partly due to the slight extant correspondence and an absence of autobiographical reflections. This confirms a somewhat reclusive personality though he was not an unsociable man. There are also many anecdotes concerning Smith which indicate a measure of absent-mindedness. There is evidence for a high sense of personal probity as well. He never married. (Further to Smith's biography, see Winch 2004, Ross 1995 and Skinner 1987 upon which the account in this section is based.)

Writings

The corpus of extant Smith writings is quite modest, certainly relative to the published works and manuscripts of many other prominent figures in the history of economics. In part this may be explained by the fact that he wrote slowly and (self-consciously) with difficulty. Smith was also not a prolific correspondent. More interestingly, it is also partly explained by his making a considered decision to have most of his unpublished manuscripts destroyed upon his death. Smith had already expressed a desire for this to be done as early as 1773, in a letter to Hume; and it was, 16 volumes of manuscripts being consigned to the flames in the last days before Smith's death (*Corr*: 168; Stewart 1811 [1980]: 327–8).

The first of his two books, *TMS*, was published in 1759, while he was still Professor at Glasgow, and was well received. There were five further revised editions during Smith's lifetime (1761, 1767, 1774, 1781 and 1790), with the sixth edition in particular involving substantial additions. It was also translated into French in 1764 and German in 1770. Skinner (1996: 3) elegantly sums up its central purpose with regard to descriptive theory (it includes normative theory as well):

> The *TMS* . . . may be regarded as an exercise in social philosophy, which was designed in part to show the way in which so self-regarding a creature as man erects (by natural as distinct from artificial means) barriers against his own passions, thus explaining the observed fact that he is always found in "troops and companies". The argument places a good deal of emphasis on the

importance of general rules of behaviour which are related to experience and which may thus vary in respect of content.

Prior to *TMS* Smith had published just two pieces of work, both anonymously and both in the short-lived *Edinburgh Review*: a review of Samuel Johnson's 1755 *Dictionary* and a long "Letter to . . . the *Edinburgh Review*" (1755 and 1756 respectively) – though he had also written the (unsigned) preface to a 1748 book of poems by William Hamilton, and probably the dedication to the 1758 second edition (for all these, see Wightman et al. 1980: 227–62; hereafter *EPS*). The review of Johnson reflects Smith's early and continuing interest in language. The "Letter" is concerned with the comparative character of learning and intellectual temper in Britain and France, including discussion of the *Encyclopédie* (1751 forward, five volumes having appeared by 1755) and particularly, Jean-Jacques Rousseau's *Discours* on the origin and foundations of human inequality (1755; commonly called the "Second Discourse"). Nothing else was published by Smith before *TMS*, nor between *TMS* and *WN* (with the exception of one essay noted below), nor between *WN* and Smith's death, apart from the revised editions of the two books themselves. But this publication history says more about the difference between intellectual culture in eighteenth-century Europe and academic culture in the contemporary world, than it does about Smith particularly.

Hence, as a result of *TMS*, when *WN* appeared in 1776 it was the work of a person with an already high intellectual reputation in Europe. The book gained good sales, with four further revised editions during Smith's lifetime (1778, 1784, 1786 and 1789). The 1784 third edition in particular involved significant changes. It was also quickly translated into German and French during 1776–78 and 1781. (For studies of the reception and diffusion of *WN*, see Lai 2000; Carpenter 2002; Tribe 2002.) The character and contents of Smith's more famous book on political economy are examined in detail below. But it may be mentioned here (and also taken up further below) that the question of the relationship between the doctrines enunciated in Smith's two books has been an ongoing source of controversy, at least since the latter half of the nineteenth century.

Smith had most of his manuscript writings destroyed at the time of his death but not all of them. The exceptions consist of six essays which were subsequently published together in 1795 as *Essays on Philosophical Subjects* (re-edited and published in *EPS*: 1–225). The first three of the essays concern the history of science – astronomy, ancient physics, and "ancient logics and metaphysics", respectively – with the first of these much the largest. The dates of their writing are uncertain but the astronomy essay appears to be largely an early composition, and almost certainly completed prior to 1758. It has figured prominently in interpretations of Smith's thought as a whole, his conception of the character and progress of astronomy being understood as implying his view of the nature of science in general. The remaining three essays primarily concern aesthetics: sense perception, the fine or "imitative" arts (together with an appendix on "the Affinity between Music, Dancing, and Poetry"), and a comparative analysis of English and Italian verse. Only the last of these three can be dated with any precision, at about 1782.

Since the end of the eighteenth century the corpus of Smith's known extant writings has been importantly augmented, most particularly, by the discovery of three sets of student lecture notes, all large documents. In 1958 J.M. Lothian discovered a set of student notes from Smith's 1762–63 "Lectures on Rhetoric and Belles Lettres", publishing an edition of them in 1963 (re-edited and published in Bryce 1983a: 1–200; hereafter *LRB*). This is a highly detailed transcription of 30 lectures, averaging almost seven pages in modern print per lecture. The character and significance of language is a central motif of these lectures, as it is also in the latter essays in *EPS*. Smith's no longer extant 1751 dissertation for his appointment as Professor of Logic, entitled "De origine idearum", appears also to have been concerned with language, depending on the sense of "idea" there. Recall also that his first publication, the review of Johnson's *Dictionary*, concerns language as well. In 1761 he published an essay on "Considerations concerning the first formation of languages, and the different genius of original and compounded languages", subsequently republishing it in the third to sixth editions of *TMS*.

In relation to Smith's economic thought, it is the further two sets of subsequently discovered lecture notes which are of particular interest. They are fairly parallel texts on "jurisprudence", together amounting to over 550 pages in modern print (though the earlier of the two is much the larger), resulting from two equivalent courses of lectures given in 1762–63 and 1763–64. The latter set of notes, which happens to coincide with Smith's last teaching session at Glasgow, was discovered by Edwin Cannan and published by him in 1896 (re-edited and published in Meek et al. 1978: 395–558; hereafter *LJB*). The former set was discovered also by Lothian in 1958, in the same private library where he found the 1762–63 lecture notes on rhetoric and belles lettres (re-edited and published in Meek et al. 1978: 1–394; hereafter *LJA*). These documents contain a quite substantial quantity of economic analysis, enabling some comparison between the state of Smith's economic thinking at this time and in 1776 (see further to this, the section on "Controversies" below). The only further Smith manuscripts are an early draft of a small part of *WN* (hereafter *edWN*), and two slight fragments on division of labour, all three dating from the 1760s, discovered by W.R. Scott and published by him in 1937 (re-edited and published in Meek et al. 1978: 562–86). Strictly speaking, all three sets of lecture notes are not Smith "writings"; but there are considerable grounds for supposing their veracity.

The *Wealth of Nations*

The *Wealth of Nations* confirms the old adage, that a "classic" is a book that every-body's heard of and nobody's read. In the case of this classic, that fate has undoubtedly been assisted by its being, at 950 pages in modern print (in the Glasgow edition), a very large work. The book is itself divided into five books. The first is concerned with the pricing of commodities and the functional distribution of income (most particularly, wages, profits and rents); though importantly, it opens with three chapters on technical change and labour productivity growth ("division of labour"). Book II examines capital accumulation and economic growth. Roughly speaking, these first two books together, amounting to a little under two-fifths of the text as a whole, constitute Smith's core economic theory. Books III to V then consider successively: the actual historical course of economic development in Europe, contrasted with the "natural" course of development; the actual policy regimes in place in Europe ("the mercantile system" or mercantilism), with a final chapter here also evaluating Physiocracy; and, finally, public finance at great length (259 pages in the Glasgow edition).

While Smith is capable of a fine prose style, *WN* is not an elegant work in its overall construction and character. Nevertheless, there is a clear unity of purpose. The central theoretical theme is the causes of economic development (economic growth involving qualitative change), including in this, rising living standards extending down to the mass of society. The "wealth" referred to in the title of the book is the flow of annual national product. It is the causes of the dynamics of this, and its distribution and allocation, which Smith explores. The primary policy theme is a critique of government policies that are restrictive of economic freedom or discriminatory, contrasted with Smith's preferred "system of natural liberty". The highlighting in the title of the book of "the nature" as well as the "causes" of wealth points to this: critique of mercantilism and its alleged mis-conception of the nation's wealth as its stock of precious metals.

Political Economy: Theory

Putting aside the analysis of *WN's* first three chapters for the moment, the theory of prices is built around the distinction between "natural price" and market prices, where the former refers to what may be called, in latter-day language, the equilibrium competitive supply-price of a commodity, and the latter refer to actual particular prices at which market transactions occur. For each commodity, the unique natural price is determined by the production method in use (tacitly, the dominant method in use) and natural rates of remuneration for the collaborating inputs of labour, capital and land required for its production. (Hence Smith appears to make land-rent price-determining, a doctrine which would be overturned in the subsequent forty years.) Market prices result from the interaction of supplies and demands, with imbalances between aggregate supply of a commodity and "effectual demand" causing deviations between market prices and the natural commodity price. When supply is fully adapted to effectual demand – the aggregate demand for a commodity, forthcoming when the natural price has to be paid – market prices align with natural price. Competition, understood especially as the free mobility of capital, is the dynamic which brings about this adaptation, in response to the abnormal profitability which results from deviations between natural and market prices.

What then determines the natural rates of remuneration of labour, capital and land? The theory of wages is partitioned into an account of the general level of wages, or the wages of "common" labour (or the lowest-skill form of labour), and an account of wage differentials for heterogeneous labour. The determination of the general level of wages is conceived of in terms of the balance of bargaining power around the labour contract, with that balance in general favouring the employers. In the limit, wages will be pushed to a subsistence level, where that subsistence consumption is understood as a customary, historically determined minimum. (In extreme circumstances, the consumption of at least the unemployed can fall below subsistence: *WN*: I.viii.26.) The balance between the growth of labour demand (driven by the rate of capital accumulation) and population and workforce growth serves as a proxy for the balance of power, so that high real wages can result from a liberal, competitive economic society which has high rates of capital accumulation and growth. Wage differentials (putting aside the influence of policy) are due to the relative "disagreeableness" of occupations, the costs of acquiring skills or human capital, the irregularity or otherwise of employments, "the small or great trust" involved in employments, and differential risk (*WN*: I.x.a–b).

On profits, Smith offers only a vague and indeterminate notion of competition between capitals tending to reduce profit rates in general, though maximum and minimum normal ("ordinary") profit rates are defined (*WN*: I.ix.18–21). (In any case, this attempt at a theory of profit rates separate from the theory of real wage rates was later rendered redundant by the determinate inverse functional relation between real wages and rates of profit, for given production methods, first enunciated by David Ricardo.) Competitive profit differentials are explained by differential risks and "the agreeableness or disa-greeableness" of alternative employments of capital, with the former the more important factor (*WN*: I.x.b.33–4). The highly unsatisfactory attempt at a theory of rents, notably, in the final chapter of book I of *WN* (the longest chapter of *WN*, near one-eighth of the entire text), is even more problematic than the theory of profit rates, seeming to make land-rent, at one and the same time, price-determined as well as price-determining. (For an attempt at a more positive and charitable interpretation, see Brewer 1995.)

Economic growth is understood by Smith to have two proximate causes: division of labour and capital accumulation, with human capital explicitly included (but not the term). These two factors in turn are seen as derivative from underlying propensi-ties of human nature, which are treated as parameters for the purposes of the political economy: "the propensity to truck, barter, and exchange" is the source of division of labour; "the desire of bettering our condition", the driving force of saving and accu-mulation (*WN*: I.ii.1, II.iii.28). In the opening three chapters of *WN* he enunciates the doctrine that labour specialization, the source of labour productivity growth, is limited or enabled by the size of the market. This is perhaps second only to the "invisible hand" as the doctrine for which Smith is most well known, though it is not original to him. The division of labour doctrine is a doctrine of *ongoing* technical change, expressing Smith's basic technological optimism, though he is careful to allow also, that at least some natural scarcities will likely become more binding as commercial societies grow, so that real wages measured in such commodities might fall (*WN*: I.xi). Smith has been criticized for over-emphasizing the importance of labour specialization at the expense of the role of mechanization in economic development, but introduction of new machinery is a very common accompaniment in his commentaries on division of labour.

In any case, since in the social economy Smith theorizes, wages are part of the capital advanced by employers, capital accumulation is the necessary prerequisite to division of labour and the realization of technical progress. The role of capital accumulation is also articulated in terms of the distinction between "productive" and "unproductive" labour, inherited, somewhat transformed, from the Physiocrats. (He also takes over from them a distinction between circulating and fixed capital.) There are inconsistencies in the manner in which Smith draws the productive/unproductive distinction; but his primary intention is to distinguish between labour devoted to capital accumulation and growth, versus labour devoted to the production of luxury consumption. In short, the coherent and important conception of productive labour in Smith's text is labour devoted to the production of capital goods, keeping in mind that capital for Smith includes the wages or consumption of the productive workers themselves. The rate of capital accumulation appears as driving the growth process, Smith being able to avoid the issue of any possible aggregate demand constraints upon the growth of the capital stock, and hence of output capacity, by recourse to a saving-is-spending doctrine (*WN*: II.iii.18). In effect, this doc-trine facilitates an avoidance of the question of the coordination of saving and invest-ment (in general undertaken by different classes of economic agents, even in 1776), by treating saving and investment as one and the same thing (Aspromourgos 2009: 164–78, 192–6; also Eltis 1984: 68–105). To that extent, Smith's theory is really a theory of how production capacity can grow, or one may say, a theory of *potential* growth.

With regard to monetary theory, Smith firmly endorses a commodity-standard for currency (*WN*: I.v.41–2, I.xi.g.5, I.xi.m.20). The conventional unit of account should be fixed in terms of a quantity of a precious metal. He is well aware of the history of actual currency debasements. Smith believes also that, as a matter of fact, it is the quantity of the commodity currency (not quantity in terms of the conventional unit of account) which agents have regard to in monetary exchange. Under these conditions, equilibrium money prices are just a particular case of equilibrium relative prices, or of the theory of natural prices: those money prices will be determined by the relative natural costs of production (including natural profits and rents) of the money commodity versus other commodities, and with the quantity of commodity money in circulation demand-determined. Interest rates are understood to be regulated by the profitability of capital in production, the differences between the two sets of rates of return being primarily determined by the distribution of risk-bearing between lenders and borrowers (*WN*: I.ix.16–22). Smith also has much to say about banking, the most notable theoretical element of which is his "real bills" doctrine, that secure and adequate collateralization of at least short-term loans with real assets ensures no excess issue of paper currency or credit, a doctrine further developed by the Banking School in the nineteenth century (*WN*: II.ii.26–106; Green 1992: 114–27; and further to Smith's monetary thought in general, Rockoff 2013).

Political Economy: Policy

Smith is famous for at least supposedly being a thoroughgoing advocate of an economic-liberal policy regime, aimed at minimizing the role of the state and its involvements or interventions in economic life and activity. Indeed, that liberal temper is nicely captured in his prescriptive definition of political economy:

> POLITICAL œconomy, considered as a branch of the science of a statesman or legislator, proposes two distinct objects; first, to provide a plentiful revenue or subsistence for the people, or more properly to enable them to provide such a revenue or subsistence for themselves; and secondly, to supply the state or commonwealth with a revenue sufficient for the publick services. It proposes to enrich both the people and the sovereign. (*WN*: IV.1)

Notice the two asymmetries here, in relation to the people versus the state: plenty for the former but just sufficiency for the latter; and rather than providing for the people, enabling them "to provide . . . for themselves", whereas the state is implicitly treated as unable to so self-provide. Smith's notion of the "unproductive" character of government activity and labour ultimately rests upon a conception of the public sector as, largely, if not quite entirely, not producing capital in Smith's sense but merely using up as inputs commodities produced by the private sector (Aspromourgos 2009: 166–9). At another level, at least some part of the infrastructure of government, notably, that required for ensuring property rights, is essential to the very existence of liberal capitalism (not his term) or "commercial society", and orderly private economic activity. Smith, the historian and theorist of property rights in the lectures on jurisprudence was by no means oblivious to that fact.

Hence *WN* is not merely a work of economic theory in the contemporary sense, though

Smith certainly is self-consciously utilizing political economy understood as a system of "theory" in the book (Aspromourgos 2009: 10–17, 238–40). *WN* is also a vigorous, sustained and polemical critique of "the policy of Europe" or "the mercantile system" (*WN*: I.x.b.8, II.v.37, IV.viii.46–IV.ix.3) understood as systems of government regulation which constrain the liberty of the owners of labour, produced means of production and land, and hence, obstruct the free mobility between alternative uses of these potentially productive inputs, or which discriminate in their treatment of different economic activities. "Mercantilism" is the shorthand which has come down to us to characterize the object of Smith's attack, and it is an expression of his success that this term remains in common use. However, it may be emphasized that restrictive or discriminatory policy with respect to imports, exports and international financial flows (the usual latter-day sense of mercantilism) is by no means the whole target. For example, legal restrictions on entry to professions and trades, and other restrictions on the liberty of workers to choose both location and occupation of work, are important considerations in Smith's critique.

The underlying theoretical position supporting this general policy stance is that economic activity levels and growth depend upon the overall quantity of capital advanced in production and the rate of overall capital accumulation over time; and that restrictive and discriminatory policies cannot favourably influence these, but rather, will serve only to reduce overall value added or output growth. However, as mentioned above in the context of Smith's theory of growth, there is nothing in that theory to ensure that capital utilization and capital accumulation are not constrained by the level of the demand for the outputs of the capital stock (for a fuller account of this issue, see Aspromourgos 2009: 205–9, 214–18, 223–5). The later divide between marginalist orthodoxy and Keynes, as to whether economic activity levels and growth are supply-determined or demand-determined, is relevant here. These later contending theoretical approaches both have something Smith lacks: a theory of the coordination of saving and investment at the system level, in a decentralized economy.

In any case, while Smith certainly has a general presumption in favour of economic liberalism, in *WN* he in fact allows what add up to a very considerable number of exceptions to that general rule. These are comprehensively detailed in Aspromourgos (2009: 225–8), following the lead given by Viner (1927) and Skinner (1996: 183–208), and include, for example: sumptuary laws; restriction of paper money and credit; product quality validation; legal prohibition of wage payments in kind rather than money; laws obliging private owners to cultivate their land, at pain of forfeiture; preventative public health policies; and allowance that government can successfully run commercial enterprises (postal services being the best example). Smith even makes some mild recommendations in favour of progressive taxation (*WN*: V.i.d.5; V.ii.b.6n; V.ii.e.6). More generally and more fundamentally, in book V, chapter i of *WN* he examines the three legitimate roles ("duties") of government, in enforcement of justice, external defence and public works (*WN*: IV.ix.51–2), the latter in particular involving transport infrastructure and education.

In relation to the second of these, there also arises a further notable exception to thoroughgoing economic liberalism: the requirements for external defence must prevail over economic freedom if the two come into conflict; hence Smith's support for navigation acts that protect the nation's naval capacity (*WN*: IV.ii.30). But the first two duties do not, in and of themselves, constitute government "intervention" in the conventional sense. In truth, they amount to something more fundamental: the provision of the legal and enforcement infrastructure to enable the very existence of "private" economic activity via individual liberty and secure property rights, pointing to the fact that the "system of liberty", however "natural" (*WN*: IV.vii.c.44, IV.ix.51), is not a spontaneously self-creating order. (That which is "private" – beyond the intrusion of the state – is defined by the state or by law.) Provision of this infrastructure also requires taxation, which is effectively a form of restriction upon private property rights.

In relation to the third duty, Smith also endorses compulsory education (*WN*: V.i.f.57). There is one particular aspect of the role of education which is further revealing of the rather nuanced character of his stance towards liberal capitalism or "commercial society", as against mere unqualified endorsement of the system. In the opening chapters of *WN*, division of labour appears as the vehicle for ongoing technical progress and rising labour productivity. Together with free competition and the high capital accumulation that Smith expects to occur in competitive commercial society, these dynamics are predicted to generate high, rising and widely distributed consumption per capita, an outcome he strongly favours (Aspromourgos 2009: 205–14) – though this is consistent with real wages growing less rapidly than labour productivity and so, rising inequality (*edWN*: 567). But in book V of *WN* (V.i.f.50–61) it is argued that this labour specialization, in rendering labourers machine-like, greatly degrades their minds and their sensibilities. Education is Smith's suggested solution for this problem. Whether or not that response may be regarded as adequate, by so fully acknowledging this negative consequence of a central dynamic in his conception of liberal capitalism, Smith strikingly evidences that he is not an ideologue. An ideologue or mere apologist for liberal capitalism would suppress or downplay such uncomfortable consequences.

However extensive in Smith's political economy the roles of government and the exceptions to strict non-interventionism may be, he *is* an economic liberal. That is his general policy presumption. But at a deeper level, concerning the relation between theory and practice, Smith is very self-consciously a moderate in his view of how theory should inform policy. He does not embrace the conclusion that policy should be a mere straightforward application of right theory; correct policy is not necessarily a simple embodiment of the ideal. He pursues this line of thought consciously, and at many points in his writings; so much so, that one may say Smith has the rudiments of a kind of meta-theory of the relation between theory and practice. The moderateness, the aversion to intellectual and political zealotry, is not merely an instinct of temperament on Smith's part; it is a thought out, reasoned conclusion. His science of political economy is certainly for the service of legislation or policy. But Smith takes the view that the authentic legislator will exercise prudence, particularly by way of taking into account the history and situation of the particular nation under policy consideration. He firmly repudiates engineering society on the mere basis of theoretical reasoning or principles, even sound theory, without attention to the concrete situation and the history from which that situation has arisen (for detailed textual exegesis, see Aspromourgos 2009: 241–7). This temper is bolstered by a certain confidence in human nature, even under imperfect policy regimes:

> in the political body, the natural effort which every man is continually making to better his own condition, is a principle of preservation capable of preventing and correcting, in many respects, the bad effects of a political œconomy, in some degree, both partial and oppressive.

Such a political œconomy, though it no doubt retards more or less, is not always capable of stopping altogether the natural progress of a nation towards wealth and prosperity, and still less of making it go backwards. If a nation could not prosper without the enjoyment of perfect liberty and perfect justice, there is not in the world a nation which could ever have prospered. (*WN*: IV.ix.28)

Political Economy and Smith's Wider Thought

At first glance, Smith's political economy project, aimed at understanding production, distribution and growth, with a view to generalized high and rising consumption, might appear narrow, but ultimately, the factors relevant to that purpose embrace everything which shapes the two narrowly "economic" factors that are the proximate causes, labour productivity growth and capital accumulation. This includes, for example, political governance and the forms of legal regulation (especially property rights); the particular histories of nations for which policy is being formulated; and the "moral sentiments" which form the social framework of norms and conventions within which production and exchange take place. The moral sensibilities of peoples have a history too (*TMS*: V, VII. iv.36–7). There is a legitimate and fruitful intellectual division of labour which enables a "narrow" political economy to proceed in *WN*, by taking various factors as given; but there is also a larger frame of reference pointing to the possibility of a unified science of society. (Further to Smith and political economy as a distinct science, see Winch 1978: 6, 184–7; 1996.)

That larger frame of reference for the political economy is evident in other of Smith's writings. The lectures on jurisprudence are in large measure devoted to the history and theory of property rights. The theory of justice to be found there, and in *TMS*, underpins the economic liberalism of *WN* by defending private wealth and incomes against any possible justifications for redistribution by policy. In a very real sense, for Smith, justice is laissez-faire: people are literally to leave each other alone (*TMS*: II.ii.1.9, II.ii.3.3, III.6.10–11). The lectures also provide substantial illustrations of the strong historical sensibility Smith brings to bear in all his intellectual endeavours, with respect to all variety of human phenomena. Most notable in relation to economics is his recourse to a four-stages theory of the history of human economic and wider development, an approach to history with a strongly "materialist" character, though not mechanically deterministic (*WN*: V.i.a.1–10, V.i.b; *LJA*: 14–16, 200–244; *LJB*: 404–17, 459–60).

Much more could be said (and has been) about the relation between Smith's two books, an issue taken up also, a little further, in the next section. Suffice it to add one key point here. It would be a misleading presumption to suppose that Smith's conception of self-interested behaviour versus moral behaviour can be understood in terms of a dualism or dichotomy in which the former as egoism (or vice) and the latter as altruism (or virtue) are mutually exclusive phenomena. There is conflict between self-interest and virtue, with Smith supposing principles intrinsic to human nature (notably, 'sympathy', though understood in a particular, technical sense) which incline human beings to act sociably. Hence the very first sentence of *TMS* (I.i.1.1): "How selfish soever man may be supposed, there are evidently some principles in his nature, which interest him in the fortune of others, and render their happiness necessary to him".

Sociable or moral behaviour is not merely an artificial imposition on natural self-interestedness. It is this which inclines humans to a natural self-restraint of their pursuit of their own interests. Indeed, Smith, much influenced by Stoicism, comes to regard self-command as *the* primary human virtue (Raphael and Macfie 1976: 6). However, a certain self-regard is an element of virtue for Smith too, an expression of a sensibility more humanist than Christian. He speaks at one point of our negative moral judgements upon those who neglect their own well-being. This is not a grave moral defect, but it is nevertheless a *moral* defect (*TMS*: VI.i.14, VII.ii.3.16, VII.ii.4.8). More generally and more importantly, the "virtue" of "prudence" is precisely the characteristic which epitomizes the savers who drive capital accumulation in *WN* (*TMS*: VI.i, VII.ii.3.16–17; Raphael and Macfie 1976: 8–9).

Smith's famous (or infamous) "invisible hand" metaphor also is best understood in the context of his disposition in favour of historical analysis. The term appears only three times in his writings (*EPS*: 49; *TMS*: IV.1.10; *WN*: IV.ii.9). While three references are not suggestive of an important role for the notion, at core, the invisible-hand metaphor expresses a concept of unintended system-consequences of individuals' behaviours, where those system-effects are usually socially beneficial, though they need not be so in all cases. This generic idea finds much more frequent application in his writings. See, for example, the historical argument concerning political power ceded away as a result of economic forces (*WN*: III.iv.9–17); the discussion concerning the profound consequences for history and civilization of "a mere accident", the invention of gunpowder (*WN*: V.i.a.43); and the analysis of the decline in the temporal power of the clergy, due to economic development (*WN*: V.i.g.21–30).

Perhaps the most important narrowly economic instances of such unintended consequences are the tendency for profit maximization under free competition to eliminate above- and below-normal profits; and for high rates of accumulation and growth, together with technical change, to lead to high and rising real wages. Smith also more than once appeals to "invisible chains" of causal explanation in the "History of Astronomy" (esp. *EPS*: 45–6, 48; the *EPS*: 49 invisible-hand instance is really a case of this, albeit involving spurious explanation). Smith's political economy, similarly, is intended to grasp and reveal that which is invisible to the individual participants in society, as individual participants: the system-consequences of individual behaviour, including the feedbacks of such systematic forces upon individual behaviours. Notably, with regard to feedbacks, individuals' pursuit of material self-betterment generates competition as a system-consequence, and also technical innovation to improve productivity; but competition in turn drives innovation (e.g., *WN*: V.i.e.26).

Smith's wider set of writings beyond *WN* can serve to enhance our understanding of his political economy project, and how it was conceived of by him as part of an even more ambitious, larger species of social science (not Smith's term). Skinner (1987: 358) and Winch (2004: 16–17, 19), drawing on the contemporaneous account of John Millar (reported in Stewart 1811 [1980]: 273–6) have both drawn attention to how three of the four parts of Smith's early lectures are reflected in elements of the corpus of Smith writings and lecture notes: the lectures dealt successively with natural theology, ethics, jurisprudence and political economy; and subsequently, we have *TMS*, *LJA/LJB* and *WN*. (No written Smith texts survive that particularly concern the first part, natural theology.)

However, these do not constitute the limits of his intellectual ambition. In a prefatory note to the 1790 sixth edition of *TMS* (p. 3 of the Glasgow edition), which appeared shortly before his death, Smith draws attention to a promise he had made in the last paragraph of the book, in all five previous editions, to publish "an account of the general principles of law and government, and of the different revolutions which they had undergone in the different ages and periods of society", covering both "justice" (or "jurisprudence") and political economy. *WN* had fulfilled the latter part of that promise but Smith admits to little hope of completing the former. The lecture notes on jurisprudence give us some idea of what such a work might have looked like. Smith writes also in 1785: "I have . . . two other great works upon the anvil: the one is a sort of Philosophical History of all the different branches of Literature, of Philosophy, Poetry and Eloquence; the other is a sort of theory and History of Law and Government' (*Corr*: 286–7). As the editors of the correspondence point out (*Corr*: 287n), elements of all this are preserved in *EPS*, *LRB* and *LJA/LJB*. In the same letter Smith admits the unlikelihood of his plans being brought to completion.

In this wide-ranging, even comprehensive, ambition one sees Smith's vision for achieving that unified social science to which the eighteenth century aspired, a "science of man". Indeed, a good part of the fascination in recent decades with the whole corpus of Smith's writings, and their interrelations, is perhaps due to our seeing in the comprehensiveness of Smith's treatment of the human condition something latter-day social science has lost as a result of disciplinary and sub-disciplinary specialization. There is an irony here, since Smith is famous for his division of labour doctrine, and himself explicitly applies this principle for labour productivity growth to science (for example, *WN*: I.i.9). The irony is compounded by the fact that his own intellectual labours did not prove productive enough to succeed in achieving a projected outcome, the pursuit of which amounted to a refusal to acquiesce in intellectual specialization. (For a wide-ranging collection of essays covering all aspects of Smith's thought see Berry et al. 2013.)

Controversies

It should not be surprising that a very large and wide-ranging work like *WN* should be the source of considerable interpretive controversy. The scope for differences of opinion are only compounded when such a large book is in turn but one element of a much larger body of writings, covering a very wide range of human phenomena, writings which have many possible real or imagined interrelations. Here we draw attention to just three key issues in interpretation.

With respect to Smith's economic theory, one may ask how it contrasts with marginalist or so-called "neo-classical" economics, built around supply and demand functions for commodities and factors of production, in turn supposedly derived from constrained individual optimization with autonomous individual preferences and substitution possibilities in production and consumption. This theoretical approach arose in the late nineteenth century and became dominant in academic economics during the first half of the twentieth century. Of all the founders of marginalism, Alfred Marshall in particular sought to portray a theoretical continuity between classical and marginalist theory (for a valuable commentary, see Groenewegen 1993 [2003]). So the interpretive controversy here has turned upon whether the economics of Smith, and indeed the classical economists more generally, can properly be understood as belonging to the same theoretical framework as marginalism; or whether his economics is to be understood as in a classical tradition running from William Petty to Ricardo and Karl Marx, which has a distinctly different theoretical structure to the later marginalist theory. The latter view derives in particular from the work of Piero Sraffa. Hollander (1973) is perhaps the best example of the former view of Smith.

I am firmly of the view that Smith's political economy does not share a fundamental theoretical continuity with marginalism. Whatever may be said of the veracity of the twentieth-century perceptions of Smith in relation to liberal politics and economic policy, the image of Smith as economic theorist is distorted by assimilating him to the marginalist tradition. Much could be said about this matter but suffice it to here make these key points. Two distinctive and related features of the marginalist theory, essential to its characteristic results under competitive conditions, are the marginal productivity theory of functional income distribution, and the adaptation of labour demand to labour supply, with equilibrium entailing full utilization of resources (Garegnani 1983, 1984, 1987; Kurz and Salvadori 1995: 379–467). Nothing resembling either mechanism is to be found in Smith's theory.

On the contrary, if there is any adjustment between labour demand and supply the causation runs from the former to the latter (for example, *WN*: I.viii.40). With regard to functional distribution, Smith theorizes it in terms of distribution of a social surplus, with the outcome decisively dependent upon the balance of bargaining power. The classical concept of "surplus" refers to that part of the gross product of the economic system which is available for free disposal, after replacement of the inputs used up in the production of that gross output, including among those inputs the necessary or subsistence consumption of the labour employed – or more particularly, in Smith's case, the *productive* labour employed. For Smith, the surplus is realized in the income forms of land-rents, pure profits (that is, profits net of risk premia) and a part of wages, depending on that balance of bargaining power, behind which lies a complex of economic and social factors (Aspromourgos 2009: 97–101, 196–202).

The second issue concerns, in particular, how indebted Smith's political economy is to Physiocracy and Turgot; but this may also be treated as part of a larger question, as to how original Smith's economics is more generally. (Smith's contact in the mid-1760s with Quesnay, the Physiocrats and Turgot was noted above.) The upshot on the narrower issue is that it seems inescapable that Smith was decisively indebted to Quesnay and Turgot on the subject of capital theory, the role of capital in growth, and the competitive tendency towards equalization of net profit rates on capital. None of this capital-related theory, which is clear and evident in Quesnay or Turgot or both, and is also in *WN*, is to be found in the economic parts of *LJA* and *LJB*, both sets of lectures having been given before Smith's French travels, though "stock" plays some role in the lectures (Aspromourgos 2009: 164). The significance of this evident debt cannot be overstated. Capital is absolutely fundamental to the theory of *WN*, books I and II, both the treatment of functional income distribution and commodity prices, and of output and productivity growth. In both dimensions, the allocation and accumulation of capital are central to the dynamics of competition. At one point, Smith was intending to dedicate *WN* to Quesnay (Stewart 1811 [1980]: 304).

On the wider question of the originality of Smith's economics more generally, it is possible to find antecedents for many if not most of the particular propositions and doctrines of his political economy. One could treat this lack of originality on particulars as an indictment, throwing into question the legitimacy of Smith's canonical status in the history of economics. Rashid (1998) is a recent example of this stance. In fact, Smith's friend, Dugald Stewart (1811 [1980]: 322–3), certainly not of an anti-Smith disposition, tends also toward the view that Smith's contribution was more as systematizer of extant economic ideas, than as an original genius; but this is not thereby regarded as a slight achievement:

> [P]erhaps the merit of such a work as Mr Smith's is to be estimated less from the novelty of the principles it contains, than from the reasonings employed to support these principles, and from the scientific manner in which they are unfolded in their proper order and connection. . . . [I]n questions of so complicated a nature as occur in political economy, the credit . . . belongs . . . to the author who first established their solidity, and followed them out to their remote consequences; not to him who, by a fortunate accident, first stumbled on the truth.
>   . . . The skill and the comprehensiveness of mind displayed in his arrangement, can be judged of by those alone who have compared it with that adopted by his immediate predecessors. And perhaps, in point of utility, the labour he has employed in connecting and methodizing their scattered ideas, is not less valuable than the results of his own original speculations . . .

Smith's achievement in this regard is to have successfully fashioned a system for a new science. If there is any genuine sense in which he is the "founder" of economics, this is it. Interestingly, while in *WN* Smith barely acknowledges intellectual debts, he was not slow to take offence when he thought his own ideas were being borrowed without attribution (Bryce 1983b: 3; Ross 1995: 105–7, 191, 230, 404; Winch 2004: 26).

Finally, there has been long-running controversy concerning the relationship between *TMS* and *WN*. The question here, put bluntly, is whether there is consistency between the moral philosophy in *TMS* and the supposed philosophy of selfishness in *WN* (Raphael and Macfie 1976: 20–25; Montes 2003). Some interrelations between the accounts of human behaviour in the two books were noted in the previous section. Suffice it merely to add here that there is currently a substantial consensus that no significant contradictions exist between the doctrines of the two books.

However, it is one thing to argue that there are no fundamental contradictions; it is another to suppose that the two books together provide a completely unified and consistent conception of human nature, behaviour and society, without any tensions between the two. Here, a somewhat cheeky comment by Jacob Viner (1927: 201) remains pertinent:

> It is a commonplace among the authorities on Adam Smith that it is impossible fully to understand the *Wealth of Nations* without recourse to the *Theory of Moral Sentiments*. The vast bulk of economists, however, who have read the *Wealth of Nations* without reading the *Theory of Moral Sentiments*, have not regarded Smith's masterpiece as an obscure book, as one especially hard to understand. On the other hand, the very authorities who are most emphatic in asserting the need of reference to the *Theory of Moral Sentiments* to understand the *Wealth of Nations*, once they embark upon their self-imposed task of interpreting the latter in the light of the former, become immersed in difficult problems of interpretation for which scarcely any two writers offer the same solution.

There is still truth in these comments on the interpretation of *TMS*, more than 80 years after Viner wrote them, though whether *WN*, by contrast, is so easy to understand is another matter!

TONY ASPROMOURGOS

See also:
British classical political economy (II); Scottish Enlightenment (II).

References and further reading

Aspromourgos, T. (2009), *The Science of Wealth: Adam Smith and the Framing of Political Economy*, London: Routledge.

Berry, C.J., M.P. Paganelli and C. Smith (eds) (2013), *The Oxford Handbook of Adam Smith*, Oxford: Oxford University Press.

Brewer, A. (1995), 'Rent and profit in the *Wealth of Nations*', *Scottish Journal of Political Economy*, **42** (2), 183–200.

Bryce, J.C. (ed.) (1983a), *Adam Smith. Lectures on Rhetoric and Belles Lettres* (Glasgow Edition of the Works and Correspondence of Adam Smith, vol. 4), Oxford: Clarendon.

Bryce, J.C. (1983b), 'Introduction', in J.C. Bryce (ed.) *Adam Smith. Lectures on Rhetoric and Belles Lettres*, Oxford: Clarendon.

Carpenter, K.E. (2002), *The Dissemination of the* Wealth of Nations *in French and in France, 1776–1843*, New York: Bibliographical Society of America.

Eltis, W.A. (1984), *The Classical Theory of Economic Growth*, London: Macmillan.

Garegnani, P. (1983), 'The classical theory of wages and the role of demand schedules in the determination of relative prices', *American Economic Review*, **73** (Papers and Proceedings), 309–13.

Garegnani, P. (1984), 'Value and distribution in the classical economists and Marx', *Oxford Economic Papers*, **36** (2), 291–325.

Garegnani, P. (1987), 'Surplus approach to value and distribution', in J. Eatwell, M. Milgate and P. Newman (eds), *The New Palgrave: a Dictionary of Economics*, vol. 4, London: Macmillan, pp. 560–74.

Green, R. (1992), *Classical Theories of Money, Output and Inflation: A Study in Historical Economics*, London: Macmillan.

Groenewegen, P.D. (1993), 'Marshall on Ricardo', in M. Baranzini and G.C. Harcourt (eds), *The Dynamics of the Wealth of Nations: Growth, Distribution and Structural Change. Essays in Honour of Luigi Pasinetti*, London: Macmillan, pp. 45–70; reprinted in P.D. Groenewegen (2003), *Classics and Moderns in Economics: Essays on Nineteenth- and Twentieth-Century Economic Thought*, vol. 2, London: Routledge, pp. 29–49.

Hollander, S. (1973), *The Economics of Adam Smith*, Toronto: University of Toronto Press.

Kurz, H.D. and N. Salvadori (1995), *Theory of Production: a Long-Period Analysis*, Cambridge: Cambridge University Press.

Lai, C.-C. (ed.) (2000), *Adam Smith Across Nations: Translations and Receptions of* The Wealth of Nations, Oxford: Oxford University Press.

Meek, R.L., D.D. Raphael and P.G. Stein (eds) (1978), *Adam Smith. Lectures on Jurisprudence* (Glasgow Edition of the Works and Correspondence of Adam Smith, vol. 5), Oxford: Clarendon.

Montes, L. (2003), 'Das Adam Smith problem: its origins, the stages of the current debate, and one implication for our understanding of sympathy', *Journal of the History of Economic Thought*, **25** (1), 63–90.

Mossner, E.C. and I.S. Ross (eds) (1977), *The Correspondence of Adam Smith* (Glasgow Edition of the Works and Correspondence of Adam Smith, vol. 6), Oxford: Clarendon.

Raphael, D.D. and A.L. Macfie (1976), 'Introduction', in D.D. Raphael and A.L. Macfie (eds), *Adam Smith. The Theory of Moral Sentiments*, Oxford: Clarendon.

Rashid, S. (1998), *The Myth of Adam Smith*, Cheltenham, UK and Northampton, MA, USA: Edward Elgar.

Rockoff, H. (2013), 'Adam Smith on money, banking and the price level', in C.J. Berry, M.P. Paganelli and C. Smith (eds), *The Oxford Handbook of Adam Smith*, Oxford: Oxford University Press, pp. 307–32.

Ross, I.S. (1995), *The Life of Adam Smith*, Oxford: Clarendon.

Skinner, A.S. (1987), 'Smith Adam (1723–1790)', in J. Eatwell, M. Milgate and P. Newman (eds), *The New Palgrave: a Dictionary of Economics*, vol. 4, London: Macmillan, pp. 357–75.

Skinner, A.S. (1996), *A System of Social Science: Papers Relating to Adam Smith*, 2nd edn, Oxford: Clarendon.

Smith, A. (1759), *The Theory of Moral Sentiments*, London: Millar and Edinburgh: Kincaid and Bell; reprinted in DD. Raphael and A.L. Macfie (eds) (1976), *Adam Smith. The Theory of Moral Sentiments* (Glasgow Edition of the Works and Correspondence of Adam Smith, vol. 1), Oxford: Clarendon.

Smith, A. (1776), *An Inquiry into the Nature and Causes of the Wealth of Nations*, 2 vols, London: Strahan and Cadell; reprinted in R.H. Campbell, A.S. Skinner and W.B. Todd (eds) (1976), *Adam Smith. An Inquiry into the Nature and Causes of the Wealth of Nations* (Glasgow Edition of the Works and Correspondence of Adam Smith, vol. 2), 2 vols, Oxford: Clarendon.

Stewart, D. (1811), 'Account of the life and writings of Adam Smith, LL.D.', in D. Stewart, *Biographical Memoirs of Adam Smith, LL.D. of William Robertson, D.D. and of Thomas Reid, D.D*, Edinburgh: Creech, Bell and Bradfute et al. (1st edn, 1794); reprinted in W.P.D. Wightman, J.C. Bryce and I.S. Ross (eds) (1980), *Adam Smith. Essays on Philosophical Subjects*, Oxford: Clarendon, pp. 263–351.

Tribe, K. (ed.) (2002), *A Critical Bibliography of Adam Smith*, London: Pickering & Chatto.

Viner, J. (1927), 'Adam Smith and laissez faire', *Journal of Political Economy*, **35** (2), 198–232; reprinted in J.M. Clark et al. (1928), *Adam Smith, 1776–1926: Lectures to Commemorate the Sesquicentennial of the Publication of 'The Wealth of Nations'*, Chicago, IL: University of Chicago Press, pp. 116–55.

Wightman, W.P.D., J.C. Bryce and I.S. Ross (eds) (1980), *Adam Smith. Essays on Philosophical Subjects* (Glasgow Edition of the Works and Correspondence of Adam Smith, vol. 3), Oxford: Clarendon.

Winch, D. (1978), *Adam Smith's Politics: an Essay in Historiographic Revision*, Cambridge: Cambridge University Press.

Winch, D. (1996), *Riches and Poverty: an Intellectual History of Political Economy in Britain, 1750–1834*, Cambridge: Cambridge University Press.

Winch, D. (2004), 'Smith, Adam (bap. 1723, d. 1790)', in H.C.G. Matthew and B. Harrison (eds), *Oxford Dictionary of National Biography*, vol. 51, Oxford: Oxford University Press, pp. 15–28.

Anne-Robert-Jacques Turgot (1727–1781)

Anne-Robert-Jacques Turgot was born on 10 May 1727 in Paris, where he died on 18 March 1781. He was the youngest son of Michel-Étienne Turgot, Marquis of Sousmont, a magistrate and "Prévost des marchands" (Lord Mayor) of Paris. While first destined by his family to an ecclesiastical estate – he studied theology and was admitted to the Maison de Sorbonne – Turgot devoted his career to serving the State. Already during his lifetime he acquired the status of an emblematic figure as the grand reforming civil servant of the Ancien Régime, particularly through two important positions: first as Intendant of the Généralité of Limoges (1761–74), that is, representative of the King in some of the poorest provinces in France (Limousin, Marche and Angoumois); and then as Contrôleur général des Finances (minister of the economy and finance, August 1774–May 1776). In this last position, during less than two years, he tried to progressively implement free trade; to put an end to traditional structures limiting the establishment in trades – such as "jurandes" (craft-guilds) – or regulating the labour force; and to abolish hurtful and inefficient obligations like the "corvée royale" (royal chore). He was also aiming at reforming the political regime of France and had a project of transferring some powers held by the King into the hands of a pyramid of elected assemblies – municipal, provincial and national. (On all these points, see the many developments by Gustave Schelle in Turgot 1913–23.)

Turgot had a serious philosophical training. He was a follower of the sensationist approach proposed by John Locke and developed in France by Étienne Bonnot de Condillac (1714–1780) and he approved of Rousseau's *Contrat social*. He also had an encyclopedic mind like many French *philosophes* of the time. While he published relatively little during his lifetime – some of his writings circulated and were known from various sources – his influence proved to be huge and lasting.

Texts and Themes

Among his youthful works, his two 1750 discourses in Sorbonne – "Les avantages que la religion chrétienne a procurés au genre humain", and "Tableau philosophique des progrès successifs de l'esprit humain" – are well known. They introduced important themes like a philosophy of history based on a development of societies in three stages, the unbounded perfectibility of the human mind and the notion of progress. A 1749 letter to the abbé de Cicé on paper-money and his "Plan d'un ouvrage sur le commerce, la circulation et l'intérêt de l'argent, la richesse des États" (*c.* 1753–54) are also indicative of his early interest in money and trade. During this period he also contributed to volumes 6 (1756) and 7 (1757) of Diderot and D'Alembert's *Encyclopédie, ou Dictionnaire raisonné des sciences, des arts et des métiers* with the entries "Étymologie", "Existence", "Expansibilité", "Foire" and "Fondation". He was a member of the group of young intellectuals gathered around Jacques-Claude-Marie Vincent, Marquis of Gournay (1712–1759), Intendant du commerce, who played an important role in the translation and/or circulation in France of some significant writings by Richard Cantillon, David Hume, Josiah Child, and so on, and in the "acclimatization" of the British "science of trade". Turgot himself translated two writings by Josiah Tucker, one of which – the 1751 *Reflections on the Expediency* . . . – was published under the title *Questions importantes sur le commerce* . . .

(1755). Some developments in this literature – for example, on the importance of the level of the interest rate, or on money – are to be found later in Turgot's thought. He wrote his celebrated "Éloge de Vincent de Gournay" (1759) after the death of the Intendant du commerce: he attributed to him however some of his own ideas on free trade, thus distorting the perception that posterity had of Gournay (Tsuda 1983).

Having made the acquaintance of Quesnay, Turgot adopted some of his views. This is probably the reason why his approach was for a long time either confused with Physiocracy or seen as a "dissenting" view of it. He developed in fact a powerful approach of his own which can be termed "sensationist political economy" (Faccarello 1992, 2006). His theoretical principles are presented in five fundamental texts: (1) a short treatise, *Réflexions sur la formation et la distribution des richesses*, written *c.* 1766 and published by instalments in 1769–70 by Pierre Samuel Dupont (1739–1817) in *Éphémérides du citoyen*; (2) his 1767 comments on two memoirs on indirect taxation respectively written by Jean-Joseph-Louis Graslin and Guérineau de Saint-Péravy; (3) the uncompleted entry "Valeurs et monnaies" (*c.* 1769) intended for André Morellet's *Dictionnaire du commerce*; (4) *Mémoire sur les prêts d'argent* (*c.* 1770) against the Scholastic doctrine of usury; and (5) "Lettres au Contrôleur général sur le commerce des grains" (1770) reassessing the necessity of a free grain trade – which forms also an implicit critique of Ferdinando Galiani's 1770 *Dialogues sur le commerce des blés* (Faccarello 1998). Important aspects of his theories are also to be found in his correspondence and in other writings.

Shortly after Turgot's death, both Dupont and M.-J.-A.-N. Caritat de Condorcet (1743–1794) – his most outstanding disciple – published a life of Turgot (Dupont 1782; Condorcet 1786). Condorcet's *Vie de M. Turgot* greatly contributed to maintain and develop Turgot's legend in France and abroad. It was translated into English as early as 1787 and appreciated by British reformers. In his *Autobiography* John Stuart Mill noted how Condorcet's book – which he compared to Plutarch's *Lives* – deeply impressed him and induced him to abandon all sectarian attitude and spirit (Mill 1873: 115–17).

It is important to keep in mind the peculiar status of Turgot's texts. First, the greatest part of his writings are just first – and sometimes incomplete – drafts. This is even the case for the 1766 *Réflexions*. This treatise was published in the *Éphémérides* on the insistence of Dupont, but Turgot had the intention to use a special offprint to thoroughly revise and expand the piece – yet he did not find the time for this revision. This probably explains some fluctuations in the vocabulary and in the presentation of some themes, for example, the rate of return on capital. Secondly, Dupont modified some texts to make them match better with the Physiocratic doctrine. This is the case for the *Réflexions*: Turgot had to demand that he print a separate edition of the original manuscript. Thirdly, a great number of Turgot's writings were published after his death, from sometimes undated manuscripts – their dating is thus occasionally uncertain.

A first edition of Turgot's work, by Dupont, was published in 1808–10 but this edition is unfaithful because of the changes made by the editor – in particular he reprinted his faulty version of the *Réflexions*. Three decades later two volumes of the "Collection des principaux économistes", published in 1844 with Guillaumin and edited by Eugène Daire and Hippolyte Dussard, are also devoted to Turgot's writings and correspondence, but they mainly reproduce Dupont's versions (Schelle, in Turgot 1913–23, I: 3–4). The most comprehensive edition is, to date, the one prepared by Gustave Schelle (Turgot 1913–23)

– all the references hereafter refer to this edition. Whenever it was possible, the texts were based on the manuscripts or some reliable documents – but some manuscripts having disappeared, Dupont's version remained occasionally the only source. Yet even Schelle's edition is not totally reliable (see, for example, Meek 1973: 3–4; van den Berg 2014). A new edition of Turgot's works and correspondence is certainly needed, which at long last is possible since the French Ministry of Culture bought Turgot's manuscripts in February 2015 (the previous owners had denied access to them).

Turgot's contribution to political economy is decisive. He powerfully developed Boisguilbert's free-trade approach, reinforcing at the same time its foundations. Elaborating upon the hitherto common – but rather vague – supply and demand framework, he developed, on the supply side, a systematic approach in terms of capital competition and, on the demand side, a subjective theory of value and prices – what allowed him also to reconsider the doctrine of usury and propose the first economic theory of the rate of interest. He also proposed some views on the successive stages of development of societies and on the origin and effect of the division of labour (Meek 1971, 1973); he put forward the main themes of what was to be called public economics, based on market failures and on the *quid pro quo* approach (Faccarello 2006); and he engaged in a polemic with Galiani on how to efficiently reform a society and implement a transition from a regulated to a free-trade economy (Faccarello 1998). The secondary literature is abundant. For the above-quoted and other aspects of his work and some divergent interpretations, see, for example, Groenewegen (1970, 1971, 1983), Brewer (1987), Faccarello (1991, 1992), Ravix and Romani (1997). In this entry, the focus will be on competition, value and the rate of interest.

Competition, Capital and Profit

Turgot shared many views with Quesnay, notably the belief in the efficiency of free trade, the hypothesis of the exclusive productivity of agriculture and the fundamental importance of the "avances" (capital) in production and trade. However by systematically referring to the concepts of competition, he distanced himself from the "sect". As he wrote to Dupont, criticizing the Physiocrats: "I find that . . . you do not make sufficient use of this less abstract principle, but . . . more enlightening, more fruitful or at least forceful for its simplicity and without exception because of its generality: the principle of competition and of free trade" (Turgot 1913–23, II: 507). In this respect the 1766 *Réflexions* marked a watershed. The most important paragraphs are those concerned with capital, its definition, forms, origin and logic.

While insisting there, like Quesnay, on the need to invest large sums of capital in agriculture, Turgot generalizes this idea and applies it to all kinds of activities. He focuses on the word "capital" – defined as a quantity of value which can be embodied in all sorts of objects and adopt any form. This is a first polemical position against the Physiocrats since it establishes an equivalence between all sorts of "accumulated value": land ownership is only one of many forms of capital, and the landowner a capitalist.

Quesnay and his disciples struggled with the question of the origin of capital. While restating the usual Physiocratic arguments – savings by the landowners, lack of competition which allows entrepreneurs to appropriate part of the "produit net" – Turgot, more importantly, emphasizes an alternative explanation. Breaking with the prevailing approach which, from Boisguilbert to Quesnay, put a stress on the necessity of "expense" to maintain prosperity, he develops a vibrant apology of savings and the "esprit d'économie" as the main source of the accumulation of capital and wealth (see also his comments on Saint-Péravy, Turgot 1913–23, II: 649 ff.). He insists on the fact that savings in no way cause a decrease in global demand: while they are not a simple "expense" – that is, a purchase of final goods for consumption – they are no hoarding either but a formation of capital. Whether they are spent directly or indirectly on the means of production, this produces beneficial effects for growth, productivity and employment. Furthermore, Turgot claims, savings are made by entrepreneurs themselves, out of their profits, and profits are earned in all activities.

The motive for investment and capital accumulation is "income or annual profit". Why would an individual invest in agricultural, industrial or commercial enterprises if he did not in return receive his expenses and the amortization of fixed capital, a compensation for his effort and the risks incurred, and – Turgot insists – a surplus equivalent to that which he would have received, without work and risk, had his capital been used to buy land? The logic of the argument is clear. The particular branch of production is of little importance: individuals invest in it if the return is not less than the minimal expected remuneration. If this return is higher elsewhere, movements of capital take place: capital leaves trades in which the rate of return is relatively low towards those activities where it is more attractive. The mobility of capital, through its action on relative supplies and demands, modifies relative prices and the rates of return tend to be equalized throughout the economy, all things being equal: "the products of the different employments limit themselves each other, and are maintained . . . in a kind of equilibrium" (Turgot 1913–23, II: 591).

> [A]s soon as profits which result from any employment of money, increase or decrease, capitals are withdrawn from other employments and directed to it – or withdrawn from it and directed to the other employments – what necessarily changes, in each employment, the ratio between the capital and the annual product . . . [B]ut regardless of how money is employed, its return cannot increase or decrease without all the other employments experiencing a proportionate increase or decrease. (Ibid.: 592)

A situation of equilibrium is thus defined by this equalization of the rates of return, or, more precisely, by a stable hierarchy of global rates of return, if we take into account the elements of risk proper of each activity, and the contribution of the entrepreneur. The lowest rate is the rate on land, that is, the rent rate calculated on the value of the land – Turgot evidently thought that he could thereby eliminate differences in land quality because the best pieces of land are more expensive. The highest rates are the profit rates for agricultural, industrial and commercial enterprises. The rate of interest lies in between: as a result of the risk incurred by the lender, it is higher than the rent rate; but it is lower than the rates related to employments which, apart from risk, also include work. It is important to note here that the hierarchy and levels of the rates of return are established at equilibrium – contrary to what Eugen von Böhm-Bawerk asserts (1884: ch. 3), this is not an explanation of the rent and profit rates through the interest rate and Turgot's explanation is not "an explanation in a circle" (ibid.: 65).

This approach will later form the core of classical political economy. But it also seemingly undermines Physiocratic theory: the emphasis on the existence of profits in all activities poses the problem of the compatibility of this perspective with the dogma of the exclusive productivity of agriculture and the assertion that all the "produit net" is appropriated by the landowners. Turgot seems to be aware of the problem but his texts do not present a clear solution. The answer to this question however appears clearly in the work of one of his followers, Pierre-Louis Rœderer (1754–1835), in 1787, and is developed in Rœderer's subsequent writings (Faccarello 1991). Rœderer (1787: 14–26) explains that the net product of the economy, while generated in agriculture, has to be distributed equitably among all the amounts of capital in the economy, whatever form they take and in proportion to the amounts invested. This is what he calls "le droit des capitaux" or "la loi du niveau" – "the rights of capitals" and "the law of the level". The general profit rate is thus given at the aggregate level by the value of the "produit net" divided by the total value of the capital invested in all activities, including land. It is striking that Marx later adopted a similar approach in Book III of *Capital* for resolving the problem of the transformation of values into production prices.

Some significant consequences are to be drawn from this analysis. A first consequence is the modification of the class structure of the economy. While Turgot first started from the Physiocratic triad of a land-owning class, a productive class and a sterile class, he ended with another threefold division based on the ownership of land, capital and labour – because, while the land-owning class is homogeneous, the productive and sterile classes are not: each of them is divided "in two categories of men, that of the entrepreneurs or capitalists who make all the advances, and that of the simple wage-earning workers" (Turgot 1913–23, II: 572). As Turgot insists in his comments on Graslin: "These are . . . two very different categories of men who contribute in a very different way to the grand work of the annual reproduction of wealth" (ibid.: 633). It could be asserted, however, that Turgot could also have ended with only two classes, the landowners being only, in his view, a sub-group among the owners of capital. J.C.L. Simonde de Sismondi was later to draw this consequence.

A second consequence is the determination of a sort of minimal price for each commodity – a cost of production *lato sensu* – beneath which the agents decrease their production or stop producing altogether. In his comments on Saint-Péravy (Turgot 1913–23, II: 655–6) and in a letter to David Hume (25 March 1767; ibid.: 663) Turgot calls it "prix fondamental" (fundamental price). Under the effect of the action of competition and the migrations of capital, the "prix courant" or market price, directly determined by supply and demand, tends towards this fundamental price – in the above-mentioned letter to Hume, Turgot extends this analysis to the labour market (Turgot 1913–23, II: 663–4). This theme was to be developed later in classical economics as the gravitation of market prices around natural prices (for an interpretation of Turgot as a classical economist, see Brewer 1987; Ravix and Romani 1997). However, Turgot's interest is almost exclusively directed to the determination of "prix courant" which only exist in trade (Turgot 1913–23, III: 176). Moreover, the elements of the "prix fondamental" are themselves determined by supply and demand.

Another consequence was to be clearly stated by Condorcet and Rœderer: the theory of capital helps in explaining the hierarchy of wages. The minimum wage is what is necessary to sustain the worker and his family. Any additional amount is just the remuneration of the capital invested in the person, through education, training, and so on.

Note finally that, in addition to this path-breaking approach, Turgot's texts include other innovative aspects. For example, in his 1767 comments on a memoir by Saint-Péravy, and in searching for the optimal quantity of "avances" – the number of units of labour – to be employed with a given quantity of a fixed factor in agriculture – a certain quantity of seed employed on a given piece of land – Turgot clearly states the law of non-proportional returns: the physical marginal product of the variable factor is first increasing and then diminishing. He clearly distinguishes between intensive and extensive diminishing returns and also points out the fact that it is always advantageous, in physical terms, to go beyond the point of maximal average product till the marginal product becomes nil (Turgot 1913–23, II: 643–5).

Utility, Value and Prices

A person is "merely a bundle of needs", Turgot states in "Plan d'un mémoire sur les impositions" (Turgot 1913–23, II: 293). Satisfying these needs brings about utility; the effort spent on this goal involves a pain (disutility). On the basis of this sensationist approach, Turgot developed a theory of subjective value, which allows him to determine equilibrium prices, which, in the short period, equilibrate supply and demand. This is a remarkable step, which also makes him embark on two genuine tours de force. (1) In the first place, while retaining the whole edifice of the free trade approach developed by Boisguilbert, he gave it a different foundation. Sensationist philosophy now explains the selfish and maximizing behaviour of agents in markets, in place of the theological dogma of the Original Sin and the Fall of Man. (2) In the second place, he showed that the traditional debates about usury were misconceived and that the problem of the nature and the determination of the rate of interest can easily be solved on the basis of his theory of value and price.

The question of value is investigated at some length in the 1766 *Reflections* but a more extensive analysis is formulated in the *c.* 1769 uncompleted text "Valeurs et monnaies". What is value? To answer this question, Turgot, probably on the celebrated model of the statue Condillac developed in his 1754 *Traité des sensations*, first imagines a man alone facing nature. This "savage" has to produce the goods he requires to satisfy his needs, but he must first determine the value each of these goods has for him. This "valeur estimative" or "esteem value" is the subjective "degree of esteem which he attaches to the different objects of his desires" (Turgot 1913–23, II: 87) – the "degree of utility" as Turgot puts it in the 1770 *Mémoire sur les prêts d'argent* (Turgot 1913–23, III: 175). The isolated individual thus establishes a preference-ordering – "order of utility" (ibid.: 86, 97) – on all of the goods, taking into account (1) the ability of each object to satisfy a kind of need, (2) the temporal element generated by foresight, and (3) the scarcity of the desired object. As a result of this calculation, he attributes a certain "esteem value" to each quantity of each object: this reflects the proportion of his "faculties" which he is prepared to devote to obtaining it, all other things being the same. He also distributes all of his faculties in such a way as to procure the different goods "according to their *importance* for . . . his well-being" (1913–23, III: 87), that is, by searching for the greatest possible well-being. It should be noted that Turgot poses the question of the measuring of values, and opts for a purely relative understanding of these. The reason for this is that the unity – the "faculties" – to which the values refer cannot be evaluated. However, the text sometimes presupposes this measurement, that is, cardinality, as it is the case in the determination of the equilibrium price.

Turgot then supposes that there are two agents and two goods, in absence of production. Each agent has an initial endowment of a good and needs part of the quantity of the good owned by the other agent; the situation is thus of a bilateral monopoly in a pure exchange economy. The two agents engage in a bargain under the following assumptions: (1) each agent determines for himself the "esteem values" he attributes to the different parts of the endowment he wishes to exchange, as well as to the parts of the other agent's endowment which he could receive in exchange; (2) the agents do not reveal their preferences: these values are kept a secret by each individual; (3) on this basis, each agent determines the states of indifference, in other words, the reservation price from which the exchange is possible; (4) each of them follows a maximizing behaviour, that is, is animated by "the interest to keep the largest quantity possible of his own good and to acquire in exchange the largest quantity of the other's good" (Turgot 1913–23, II: 90) – a typical eighteenth-century formulation of the mathematical problem of "maximis et minimis".

In order for a transaction to take place, it is necessary for each agent to attribute to the quantity of the object received a higher "esteem value" (say λ) than that which he assigns to the quantity of the good given in exchange (λ^*): $\lambda > \lambda^*$. As Turgot states: "each would stay as he is unless he finds an interest, a personal profit, to exchange; unless he estimates more what he receives than what he gives" (Turgot 1913–23, II: 91). The gains from exchange are clear: (1) free exchange implies an increase in total utility for both parties; (2) moreover, whenever production is possible, exchanges also allow a division of labour and result in an increase of the quantities of goods available to the agents (ibid.: 93).

Turgot assumes that the bargaining process converges towards a price on which both agents agree, in between the reservation prices of the two agents. This equilibrium price – called by Turgot "valeur appréciative" – is unique and is determined simultaneously with the quantities exchanged. The final agreement is defined as a situation in which the difference of the "esteem values" of the quantity of the received good over that of the quantity of the good given in exchange is equal for both parties – which could be symbolized, for two agents i and j: $\lambda_i - \lambda_i^* = \lambda_j - \lambda_j^*$. This is the reason why this equilibrium price is termed "average esteem value".

This solution, however, could not be satisfactory for those who note that there is a priori no unique solution in the case of a bilateral monopoly. But this approach is nevertheless remarkable for its originality and rigour: it was probably inspired by the celebrated pages on justice and exchange in Aristotle's *Nicomachean Ethics* and finds an interpretation in terms of cooperative games (Dos Santos Ferreira 2002). The explanation given by Turgot remains however questionable: this "valeur appréciative" is necessarily attained because, he notes, should the differences between the "esteem values" of the goods be different between agents, it would be in the interest of one of the two agents to continue the bargaining process. But how could the agents know each other's differences when preferences are not revealed – and moreover utilities are not comparable?

Having established his argument for two contracting parties, Turgot intended to generalize it to a large number of agents and goods. The article "Valeurs et monnaies" unfortunately concludes after taking into consideration a larger number of agents in a two goods context; Turgot assumes that as a result of competitive arbitrages a single price would be established. The general situation (many agents and goods) is only dealt with incidentally in *Mémoire sur les prêts d'argent* and the 1770 "Lettres" to Terray. Turgot simply reaffirms his conviction in the realization of a general equilibrium. Nevertheless, two remarks formulated on these occasions are of interest. First, the process by which equilibrium is achieved is explicitly described in the "Lettres" as a process of "tâtonnement" (Turgot 1913–23, III: 326). It is however a real "tâtonnement" since exchanges are made outside equilibrium: but according to Turgot, no one's interest would really be damaged – at least statistically – since, given that the variations are made by "imperceptible degrees", the "losses" and "gains" would compensate for each other in the end. Secondly, Turgot stresses in the *Mémoire*, while prices are actually determined from a subjective basis, they acquire in the end a misleading "objective" appearance in markets. It is this illusion which has given rise to a belief in the existence of an "intrinsic value", "real value" or "natural price": but nothing of the like exists in reality (ibid.: 175–6).

The Rate of Interest and the Problem of Usury

One important aspect of Turgot's work relates to the rate of interest. In some sections of the *Réflexions* (Turgot 1913–23, II: 577–86) and particularly in the 1770 *Mémoire sur les prêts d'argent* (Turgot 1913–23, III: 154–202) his line of thought is double. On the one hand, taking up traditional arguments for and against usury, he shows the "frivolity" of the latter and the possibly correct, but not truly decisive, aspect of the former. On the other hand, he supplies his own reasons, the most important of which displaces the controversy. The question of usury, he stresses, is traditionally badly posed. Once the terms are correctly defined, it becomes a simple problem of economic theory and more specifically an application of the theory of value (ibid.: 174–80).

One of the traditional arguments in favour of the prohibition of usury was that – founded in Roman law – of the fungible and consumable character of some objects, money included: destroyed by the use which is made of them, they cannot be lent at interest because their transfer to the borrower necessarily involves a transfer of property. This argument, Turgot stresses, supposes that the transaction is about the physical object – for example, a quantity of coins, or a given weight of a precious metal – and it cannot but lead to the above-mentioned conclusion. However, the transaction relates instead to a quantity of value and implies the utilities of the contracting parties: "where have our quibblers seen that the only thing to be considered in the loan is the weight of the metal borrowed and returned, and not its value and its utility for the lender and the borrower?" (Turgot 1913–23, III: 177). The interest rate is just a price like any other and its determination falls in the field of the theory of value. Two principles are essential here: (1) an exchange can only be implemented if the utility of the quantity of the commodity received is higher, for each agent, than the utility of the quantity of the commodity given up in exchange; (2) time preference: the depreciation, in terms of "esteem value", of a good available in the future compared to the same good available now (ibid.).

At the time of the transaction the lender compares the utility of the sum of money he owns with a promise of reimbursement in the future. If no interest is stipulated, and as the lender estimates the promise to reimburse tomorrow to be worth less than the identical sum today, an agreement in these conditions is impossible because it would involve a loss of utility for the lender. In order that the transaction takes place, it is therefore necessary that the promise of reimbursement in the future be for a higher amount than the sum which is lent, so that the "esteem value" the lender attributes to it be higher than the value he attributes to the sum in question. If the elements of risk and disutility are reintroduced, then this difference – the interest – measures (1) time preference, (2) the risks incurred and (3) the disutility experienced because of the momentary unavailability of the amount of money. This analysis is obviously novel and path-breaking: the link with the theory of value, in particular, is fundamental.

Turgot's studies at the Sorbonne could have been of some help here, because a similar development had been made, more than a century and a half before, by the Flemish Jesuit Leonard de Leys (Lessius): his "carentia pecuniae" already referred to a kind of time preference. However in Lessius' writings this element was just an empirical fact observed in the market (van Houdt 1998). Turgot instead linked it to his subjective theory of value. It is also to be noted that the reasoning in terms of time preference seems to have been widespread among confessors and casuists during the seventeenth century because Pope Innocent XI, in 1679, had to condemn the proposition that a present sum of money being "more precious" than the same sum available in the future, "the lender may demand from the debtor something more in addition to the loan, and on that title can be excused from usury" (quoted in Delumeau 1990: 118).

Two last points must be mentioned to conclude. The first regards the interest rate; it is definitely not a monetary variable. While a type of monetary quantitativism prevails – probably a legacy of Cantillon and Hume – the interest rate is subject to the logic of the loanable funds market and, being a price like any other, must be determined freely between agents. The second point concerns money as a measure of value and a medium of exchange. As noted above, values cannot be expressed as such. In particular the "valeur appreciative" of a commodity is essentially relative. It is thus expressed, in an isolated transaction, by the quantity of the good against which it is exchanged; or in general by each of the quantities of every other commodity against which it can be exchanged. Turgot deduces from this the money form properly speaking: thanks to its intrinsic qualities, related to the requirements of the functions of measure of values and medium of exchange, one commodity detaches itself from the rest, and all the other commodities, by convention, express their value in terms of this good, which therefore becomes the unique form of expression of value, "gage universel" (Turgot 1913–23, II: 554). This analysis is to a great extent taken up and developed by Morellet in his "Digression" on money which he included in his 1769 *Prospectus d'un nouveau diction-naire de commerce*, and from there probably handed over to Condillac in his 1776 *Le commerce et le gouvernement considérés relativement l'un à l'autre*. Above all, Karl Marx later adopted and developed it in his analysis of the "forms of value" in book I of *Capital*.

GILBERT FACCARELLO

See also:

Daniel Bernoulli (I); Pierre Le Pesant de Boisguilbert (I); British classical political economy (II); Marie-Jean-Antoine-Nicolas Caritat de Condorcet (I); French Enlightenment (II); François Quesnay and Physiocracy (I).

References and further reading

Translating Turgot is not an easy task. Modern English translations of some of Turgot's writings are by Ronald L. Meek (*Precursors of Adam Smith*, London: Dent, 1973, and *Turgot on Progress, Sociology and Economics*, Cambridge: Cambridge University Press, 1973) and Peter Groenewegen (*The Economics of A.R.J. Turgot*, The Hague: Martinus Nijhoff, 1977). Some of them, completed with older translations of other texts, are republished in *The Turgot Collection* (David Gordon, ed., 2011, Auburn: Ludwig von Mises Institute). In this entry, however, we use our own translations. The references are to the Schelle edition (Turgot 1913–23).

Böhm-Bawerk, E. von (1884), *Kapital und Kapitalzins: I. Geschichte und Kritik der Kapitalzinstheorien*; English trans. (1890), *Capital and Interest. A Critical History of Economical Theory*, London: Macmillan.
Bordes, C. and J. Morange (eds) (1981), *Turgot, économiste et administrateur*, Paris: Presses Universitaires de France.
Brewer, A. (1987), 'Turgot: founder of classical economics', *Economica*, **54** (November), 417–28.
Condorcet, M.-J.-A.-N. Caritat de (1786), *Vie de M. Turgot*, [London].
Delumeau, J. (1990), *L'aveu et le pardon. Les difficultés de la confession, XIIIᵉ–XVIIIᵉ siècle*, Paris: Fayard.
Dos Santos Ferreira, R. (2002), 'Aristotle's analysis of bilateral exchange: an early formal approach to the bargaining problem', *European Journal of the History of Economic Thought*, **9** (4), 568–90.
Dupont [de Nemours], P.-S. (1782), *Mémoires sur la vie et les ouvrages de M. Turgot, ministre d'Etat*, [Philadelphia].
Faccarello, G. (1989), 'L'évolution de la pensée économique pendant la Révolution: Alexandre Vandermonde ou la croisée des chemins' in *Französische Revolution und Politische Ökonomie*, Trier: Schriften aus dem Karl-Marx-Haus, pp. 75–121.
Faccarello, G. (1991), 'Le legs de Turgot: aspects de l'économie politique sensualiste de Condorcet à Roederer', in G. Faccarello and P. Steiner (eds), *La pensée économique pendant la Révolution française*, Grenoble: Presses Universitaires de Grenoble, pp. 67–107.
Faccarello, G. (1992), 'Turgot et l'économie politique sensualiste', in A. Béraud and G. Faccarello (eds), *Nouvelle histoire de la pensée économique*, vol. 1, *Des scolastiques aux classiques*, Paris: La Découverte, pp. 254–88.
Faccarello, G. (1998), 'Galiani, Necker and Turgot: a debate on economic reform and policy in 18th century France', in G. Faccarello (ed), *Studies in the History of French Political Economy*, London: Routledge, pp. 120–95.
Faccarello, G. (2006), 'An "exception culturelle"? French Sensationist political economy and the shaping of public economics', *European Journal of the History of Economic Thought*, **13** (1), 1–38.
Grœnewegen, P. (1970), 'A reappraisal of Turgot's theory of value, exchange and price determination', *History of Political Economy*, **2** (1), 177–96.
Grœnewegen, P. (1971), 'A reinterpretation of Turgot's theory of capital and interest', *The Economic Journal*, **81** (2), 327–40.
Grœnewegen, P. (1983), 'Turgot's place in the history of economic thought: a bicentenary estimate'. *History of Political Economy*, **15** (4), 585–616.
Meek, R.L. (1971), 'Smith, Turgot and the "four stages" theory', *History of Political Economy*, **3** (1), 9–27. Also in R.L. Meek (1977), *Smith, Marx and After*, London: Chapman and Hall, pp. 18–32.
Meek, R.L. (1973). 'Introduction', in R.L. Meek (ed.), *Turgot on Progress, Sociology and Economics*, Cambridge: Cambridge University Press, pp. 1–40.
Mill, J.S. (1873). *Autobiography*, in *Collected Works of John Stuart Mill*, in J.M. Robson and J. Stillinger (eds), vol. 1, Toronto: University of Toronto Press, pp. 1–290.
Ravix, J.-T. and P.-M. Romani (1997), 'Le système économique de Turgot', in A.-R.-J. Turgot, *Formation et distribution des richesses*, Paris: GF/Flammarion, pp. 1–63.
Rœderer, P.-L. (1787), *Questions proposées par la commission intermédiaire de l'Assemblée provinciale de Lorraine, concernant le reculement des barrières, et observations pour servir de réponse à ces questions*, n.p.
Tsuda, T. (1983), 'Un économiste trahi: Vincent de Gournay (1712–1759)', in T. Tsuda (ed), *Traités sur le commerce de Josiah Child et remarques inédites de Vincent de Gournay*, Tokyo: Kinokuniya, pp. 445–85.
Turgot, A.-R.-J. (1913–23). *Œuvres de Turgot et documents le concernant, avec biographie et notes par Gustave Schelle*, 5 vols, Paris: Félix Alcan.
Van den Berg, R. (2014), 'Turgot's Valeurs et monnaies: our incomplete knowledge of an incomplete manuscript', *European Journal of the History of Economic Thought*, **21** (4), 549–82.
Van Houdt, T. (1998), '"Lack of money": a reappraisal of Lessius' contribution to the scholastic analysis of money-lending and interest-taking', *European Journal of the History of Economic Thought*, **5** (1), 1–35.

Marie-Jean-Antoine-Nicolas Caritat de Condorcet (1743–1794)

Mathematics and Philosophy

Condorcet is considered as the last of the eighteenth-century French *philosophes* who powerfully shaped the intellectual landscape in France and Europe. Born on 17 September 1743 in Ribemont, in the province of Picardie, he was first educated at the Jesuit school in Reims and the celebrated Collège de Navarre in Paris. Possessed of a talent for mathematics, he studied with the mathematician and *philosophe* Jean Le Rond d'Alembert (1717–1783) – the co-editor, with Denis Diderot (1713–1784), of the flagship of the French Enlightenment, the *Encyclopédie, ou Dictionnaire raisonné des sciences, des arts et des métiers* (1751–72). He quickly gained the reputation of a prominent *géomètre*, his domains of predilection being integral calculus and probability theory. But as many scientists and *philosophes* of the time he had an encyclopaedic mind, and he showed a great interest in the "sciences morales et politiques" or "sciences sociales" (see, for example, Granger 1956; Baker 1975; Kintzler 1984; Crépel and Gilain 1989; McLean and Hewitt 1994).

During the 1760s and early 1770s, he became a disciple and friend of Voltaire (1694–1778) and Turgot (1727–1781). He later published a celebrated *Vie de M. Turgot* (1786) – immediately translated into English (1787) and much appreciated by the British reformers – and a *Vie de Voltaire* (1789). A promising member of the clan of the Encyclopaedists, he was quickly elected at the Académie des Sciences (1769) – of which he became the *secrétaire perpétuel* in 1776 – and the Académie Française (1782). Thanks to Turgot, he also held the official position of Inspecteur des Monnaies from 1775 to 1791. His first publications in economics, such as "Monopole et monopoleur" (1775) and *Réflexions sur le commerce des blés* (1776), were made to support Turgot's free trade program of reforms during his ministry (August 1774–May 1776). After the fall of Turgot, he turned back to mathematics and sciences but never abandoned his political and philosophical concerns. This can be seen in particular in *Vie de M. Turgot*, or in his attempts to apply mathematics and probability either to the traditional problems of insurance – for example, in some 1784 texts for C.-J. Panckoucke's *Encyclopédie Méthodique*: "Absent", "Arithmétique politique (supplément)" or "Assurances maritimes" – or to the fields of law (decisions to be taken by a panel of judges) and elections. He shared Turgot's project to transform the French political system with a series of elected assemblies: he wished not only to define their tasks but also sought the best way to organize ballots and decisions. These last points were mainly developed in the voluminous and complex *Essai sur l'application de l'analyse à la probabilité des décisions rendues à la pluralité des voix* (1785), in *Essai sur la constitution et les fonctions des assemblées provinciales* (1788), *Lettres d'un bourgeois de New Haven à un citoyen de Virginie, sur l'utilité de partager le pouvoir législatif entre plusieurs corps* (1788) or *Sur la forme des élections* (1789).

While not elected to the 1789 États Généraux du Royaume – the convening of which is the emblematic starting point of the French Revolution – he was an enthusiast supporter of the revolutionary process, either as a member of the Commune de Paris or as a careful observer and journalist in various newspapers. He was also the co-founder of a political club, the Société de 1789, and two periodicals, *Bibliothèque de l'homme public* in 1790 and *Journal d'instruction sociale* in 1793. Finally elected to the Assemblée Législative in 1791 and to the Convention Nationale in 1792, he demanded the deposition of the

King and the proclamation of the Republic after a failed attempt by the Royal family to leave the country. His activities encompassed a wide range of subjects: money, finance, taxes, public debt, public instruction and the new constitution – continuing also his former fights in favour of the equality of men and women and the abolition of slavery. As regards political economy proper, the most significant texts from this period are "Sur l'impôt progressif" and "Tableau général de la science, qui a pour objet l'application du calcul aux sciences politiques et morales", both published in 1793 in *Journal d'instruction sociale*. After he refused to vote for the death sentence for the King – he was against capital punishment – and criticized the Jacobins in power, the Convention decreed his arrest. While hiding, he wrote his philosophical testament, *Esquisse d'un tableau historique des progrès de l'esprit humain*, posthumously published in 1795, which provoked T.R. Malthus's *Essay on the Principle of Population* (1798) and formed the starting point of some nineteenth-century developments in political philosophy. After having been arrested, Condorcet died in jail, probably on 30 March 1794.

The large number of Condorcet's writings on mathematics, philosophy, politics and economics present a problem of interpretation (for a brief history of some reactions, see Faccarello 1989). Commentaries generally referred to a vague theory of evolution and progress associated with the 1795 *Esquisse*, and, after the Second World War, to his ideas on elections to which Georges-Théodule Guilbaud (1952), Gilles-Gaston Granger (1956), Duncan Black (1958) and Kenneth Arrow (1963) drew attention – they had been almost forgotten for some 150 years, with the exceptions of Edward John Nanson (1882 [1907]) and Charles Lutwidge Dodgson (alias Lewis Carroll 1876 [1958]). While much is still to be done, recent research has made it possible to identify a quite different intellectual stature of Condorcet. Leaving aside the widely commented *Esquisse* – which is a small part of a wider project, the *Tableau historique des progrès de l'esprit humain* proper (Condorcet 2004), of which it was supposed to be the *Prospectus* – it is first necessary to understand the main characteristics of his approach.

Sensationism, Knowledge and Probability

Probability and the nature of knowledge
Unlike many of his contemporaries, including d'Alembert, but like Turgot, Condorcet thought that progress was possible in the new moral and political sciences and that it was also possible to reach there the same degree of "certainty" than in the more traditional fields of, for example, physics, chemistry or astronomy (see, for example, the first pages of the 1785 *Essai*). This conviction, however, ought to be understood properly. While it implies that the nature of knowledge is basically the same in all fields of inquiry, this nature is such that nowhere is it possible to find propositions that are absolutely certain. This is not only because no science has achieved, or could ever reach, its highest degree of perfection. The reason lies with the nature of knowledge itself. Following Locke and Turgot's sensationist philosophy, and insisting on the importance of Turgot's entry "Existence" in the *Encyclopédie*, Condorcet stressed that any knowledge of the existence and properties of objects comes from our senses and our ability to think about our sensations and combine them. While it is also based on the idea that there exist constant laws for the various observable phenomena, this constancy is only an hypothesis and, by nature, this knowledge can never produce any absolute certainty, whatever the field of

inquiry – mathematics included because this hypothesis also concerns the human under-standing, and not only external phenomena. It only leads to a more or less strong confi-dence that these phenomena, in the same circumstances, will happen again in the future.

This is the reason why, when Condorcet speaks of "certainty", he does so only metaphorically to express a great degree of assurance – the word "assurance" is, in his view, more adapted in this context (Condorcet 1785: xvi, 1994a: 523), and a better choice than the ambiguous phrase "certitude morale" (moral certainty). It is also why, in sciences and in everyday life, this assurance is called by Condorcet a probability – founded on past experience and measuring a "motif de croire" (reason to believe). "The knowledge that we call certain is . . . nothing else than a knowledge based on a very high probability" (1994a: 602) that in most cases it is meaningless to calculate (Condorcet 1785: xiv). Hence his statement that all propositions "belong to this part of the calculus of probability where one judges the future order of unknown events on the basis of the order of known events" (Condorcet 1994a: 291) and the parallel explicitly made with a classical example in probability theory:

> The reason to believe that, from ten million white balls and one black, it is not the black one that I will pick up at the first go, is of the same nature as the reason to believe that the sun will not fail rising tomorrow, and these two opinions only differ as to their lower or higher prob-ability. (Condorcet 1785: xi)

However, Condorcet did not follow the sceptical tradition (for further developments, see Rieucau 2003). He believed in the progress and usefulness of knowledge, and he often denounced "the absurdity of absolute scepticism" (Condorcet 1994a: 602). The systematic collectioning of data and the organization of accurate experiences permit an undisputable progress in sciences, and what happened in physics or astronomy will also happen in the new fields concerning society. Politics or political economy, with time, and with the knowledge of human nature based on sensationist philosophy, are liable to approach the same degree of assurance in the truths they establish.

Probability and the conduct of life

Condorcet's probabilistic approach has also important consequences on a more practi-cal level. In all fields of life where decisions are to be taken, Condorcet stresses, people almost always have to face uncertainty. D'Alembert did not see that

> in the sciences the aim of which is to teach how to act, as in the conduct of life, man can content himself with higher or lower probabilities, and that . . . the right method consists less in search-ing rigorously proven truths than in choosing among probable propositions, and above all in knowing how to estimate their degree of probability. (Condorcet 1994a: 544)

In this perspective probability theory is an indispensable tool for estimating in an accu-rate way the data of the problems and the outcomes of alternative choices, and this theory had been developing since the seventeenth century (see Hacking 1975; Daston 1988; Hald 1990). Lively controversies never ceased about the meaning of the main con-cepts of the theory (about mathematical expectation, for example) and their use or abuse in various applied fields, and one prominent critic was d'Alembert himself. In defence of probability theory – and of the use of mathematical expectation – Condorcet developed an important reflection on the nature and significance of its concepts, especially in his 1784–87 "Mémoire", his 1785 *Essai* and in various other texts and manuscripts, such as *Éléments du calcul des probabilités*. In his view, while the probability of an event is a "purely intellectual consideration" (Condorcet 1994a: 289) that "does not pertain to the real order of things" (ibid.: 291) and does not predict its occurrence – the contrary event can happen – nevertheless "we judge of all the things of life from this probability and it rules our conduct" (ibid.). This probability is the measure of our reason to believe in the occurrence of this event.

It is finally to be noted that Condorcet also calls "probability" the number of votes in favour or against a candidate or a proposal in an election or decision-making process, particularly in his 1785 *Essai*. While this could seem confusing, it is not in the perspective of voting as judgement aggregation: in absence of any other usable evidence regarding the relevant qualities of two candidates, the number of votes may be taken as the best probabilistic indicator of those qualities.

From Political Arithmetic to "Social Mathematic"

The main question is how to use the calculus of probability in a legitimate way. Calculation should be handled cautiously because it can be dangerous in the hands of "charlatans" (Condorcet 1994a: 337): in politics, it is so easy to impress people with the use of some numbers in order to influence their opinions and choices. Some "ridiculous" applications of calculus to political questions have also been made, but "how many applications, just as ridiculous, have not been made in each part of physics?" (Condorcet 1785: clxxxix). In his 1771–72 correspondence with Piero Verri (Condorcet 1994a: 68–74), Condorcet had also criticized Verri's attempt, with the aid of the mathematician Paolo Frisi, to formalize economic theory in the sixth edition of his *Meditazioni sulla Economia Politica*. He considered that this was a complex undertaking which could not be achieved with simple and careless solutions – the same erroneous method was still to be applied less than three decades later by two *géomètres*, Nicolas-François Canard in his *Principes d'économie politique* and above all Charles-François de Bicquilley in his *Théorie élémentaire du commerce*, both works presented at the Institut in 1799 and respectively published in 1801 and 1804 (Crépel 1998).

All these critiques notwithstanding, the use of calculus could no longer be dispensed with. Condorcet stressed that with its help it is possible to reason in a more precise way, to go further than "what reason alone can do", and avoid the negative influence of vague impressions due to imperfect knowledge, prejudices, interests or passions. In this perspective, he had the ambitious project to develop "political arithmetic" into a systematic science – this field being defined as "the application of calculus to political sciences" in his 1784 eponymous entry for the *Encyclopédie méthodique*. In his eyes, the first attempts by William Petty or John Graunt were almost insignificant. Serious things only started with the works of Jan De Witt and, above all, Jakob Bernoulli (1654–1705) (*Ars Conjectandi*, posthumously published in 1714) and his nephew Nicolas I Bernoulli (1687–1759) (*Dissertatio Inauguralis Mathematico-juridica, de Usu Artis Conjectandi in Jure*, 1709). Probability theory was used there to solve economic and juridical questions of marine insurance, life annuities, calculation of interest or the problem of the "absent" (after how many years can an absent person be considered as dead with a sufficient probability?). However, the science was new, and all remained to be done. It is this same science that Condorcet, in an even more ambitious way than before, called "social mathematic" in his 1793 "Tableau général" (on the different editions of this important text and their shortcomings, see Crépel and Rieucau 2005):

> I prefer the word *mathematic*, although now no longer used in the singular, to arithmetic, geometry or analysis because these terms refer to particular areas of mathematics . . . whereas we are concerned . . . with the applications in which all these methods can be used. . . . I prefer the term *social* to *moral* or *political* because the sense of these words is less broad and less precise. (Condorcet 1994b: 93–4, original emphasis)

Condorcet died the following year and could not accomplish his programme. However, he had already some outstanding achievements to his credit.

Economic Behaviour in the Face of Uncertainty and Risk

In the first field of "social mathematic", that is, at the individual level, Condorcet's developments were mainly in line with those of the Bernoullis. But he went further, especially in the questions related to the problem of the absent or marine insurance (Crépel 1988, 1989). In particular, generalizing his analysis of the behaviour of both a merchant and his insurer facing uncertainty and risk in maritime trade, he conceived of any economic activity as an uncertain and risky undertaking – "undertakings in which men expose themselves to losses in view of a profit" (Condorcet 1994a: 396) – and used probability theory to describe the entrepreneurs' decisions to invest (Rieucau 1998). A parallel is made with the traditional analysis of "fair" games of chance, in which a fair stake is equal to the mathematical expectation of gain: but Condorcet explains that, in economic activity, additional constraints and calculations arise because the analogy between a gambler and an entrepreneur is somewhat misleading.

> When a merchant makes a conjecture [fait une spéculation] implying a significant risk, it is not enough that his profit be such that the mean value of his expectations be equal to his stake [sa mise] plus the interest that a riskless trade would have brought him. In addition he must have . . . a very high probability that he would not suffer a loss in the long run. To submit this kind of project to calculus, one should thus determine, for the funds that each trader could successively employ in such a risky trade, what is the excess of profit that he must obtain in order either to have a sufficient probability not to lose his entire funds, or to lose only part of them, or to just get them back, or to get them back with a profit. (Condorcet 1986: 561–2)

However, a second field for "social mathematic" is related to the collective level (public economics, social choice). Here Condorcet is clearly continuing Turgot's analysis of public economics, who had already made some definite advances concerning the political organization of a modern state in a free society based on the respect of human rights, and the nature of public interventions in markets – for example, the definition and classification of public goods, a reflection on the nature of taxation from a *quid pro quo* perspective, the taking into account of externalities and the free rider problem (Faccarello 2006). Of particular interest are Condorcet's ideas on taxation and decision-making processes.

Rules for a Just and Optimal Taxation

Two significant developments on taxation are to be found in the 1793 paper "Sur l'impôt progressif" – they do not explicitly use mathematics but they entail an implicit formalization. The first consists in providing a theoretical proof of the fact that a progressive income tax complies with justice: this is done in the "equal absolute sacrifice" perspective, assuming a decreasing marginal utility of wealth (one of Daniel Bernoulli's hypotheses) and an elasticity of the utility of marginal income with respect to income greater than unity (Faccarello 2006: 26–30).

The second 1793 development on taxation consists in the determination of what is called today the optimal volume of public expenses and taxation, with a reasoning that is probably the first to refer to an equilibrium at the margin. A question debated at that time was that a theory of public finance cannot be limited to the affirmation that the state should not spend too much and that the normal financing of its expenditure should be made through taxation in a *quid pro quo* perspective. It is also important to determine what public goods and services should be produced, and in which quantities. The list of the goods and services useful to society could be long and it is generally impossible to provide them at once. Choices must be made, and, in a given period, a criterion to determine the optimal volume of public spending is needed. The essence of Condorcet's answer is the following (Faccarello 2006: 19–21). Amounts of public expenses may be classified according to the decreasing order of utility they produce. One might then imagine (although Condorcet does not do so explicitly) a plan in which one would have, as abscissa, the successive volumes of public spending, and as ordinate, the levels of utility engendered by each supplementary volume of expense (the curve of decreasing "marginal" utility of public spending). But public spending must be financed by taxes, taxation meaning a diminution of the disposable income. As Condorcet accepted Bernoulli's hypothesis of a diminishing marginal utility of wealth, successive increases in public spending necessarily entail an increasing marginal disutility of taxation. As a consequence, it is also possible to imagine an increasing "marginal" disutility curve for public expenditure; in the same schema as before, this disutility is shown along the ordinate while the successive volumes of taxation (equal to those of public spending) is represented along the abscissa. The two curves cross. Public expenses "have a limit: the point where the utility of the expense becomes equal to the evil generated by the tax" (Condorcet 1793, in 1847–49, XII: 629). In other words, their volume is determined by the point at which their marginal utility is equal to the marginal disutility they entail, the "margins" being here broadly defined.

But in a modern state, all these decisions about public expenses and taxation are taken by an elected assembly. How to choose its members and which decision-making process should they follow in order to take just and true decisions?

"Social Mathematic" and Social Choices

The most spectacular example of "mathématique sociale" concerns elections or, more generally, social choices: it deals with the way in which to take decisions in any kind of assembly, be it a political assembly or a tribunal. The subject was of foremost importance because Condorcet shared Turgot's ideas of political reforms and because of the discussions Condorcet had with Turgot and Voltaire about the problem of the decisions of justice. But the subject was also important because Condorcet's aim was to develop some ideas presented by Jean-Jacques Rousseau in *Du contrat social* (1762), a treatise Turgot himself had praised, and in particular to clarify Rousseau's concept of "general will" (see, for example, Barry 1964, 1965: 292–3; Baker 1975: 229–31; Grofman and Feld 1988; Estlund et al. 1989). It was not clear how this "general will" could be known, especially when voters could not abstract from their own interests and passions, from factions or lobbies. The "general will", Rousseau stressed, was to be distinguished from the "will of all":

> [T]he general will is always right [droite] and always tends toward the public utility. But it does not follow that the people's deliberations always have the same rectitude. . . . There is often a considerable difference between the will of all and the general will. The latter considers only the common interest, while the former considers private interest and is merely a sum of particular wills. (Rousseau 1762 [2012], II, iii: 182)

Moreover Rousseau's statement that if we remove "from these same wills the pluses and minuses, which mutually cancel each other out, . . . the remaining sum of the differences is the general will" (ibid.) – probably alluding to differential and integral calculus (Philonenko 1986) – was puzzling.

Condorcet's 1785 *Essai* deals with the various ways to organize a vote, to fix the majority needed for the decision, and to estimate their relative advantages – building, as G.-G. Granger (1956: ch. 3) called it, a model of "homo suffragans". The cases studied are numerous, and in this also Condorcet's project was realized only in part: starting with a set of strong simplifying hypotheses, the analysis becomes only programmatic when some of these hypotheses are relaxed. In the first part of the book (Condorcet 1785: xxi–xxii, 3), it is supposed that voters (1) are equally enlightened, (2) try honestly to answer the question asked (nobody tries deliberately to influence others, there are no lobbies, no parties), (3) have only the public good in mind and abstract from their own interests.

All these hypotheses Rousseau had already invoked in *Contrat Social*. Condorcet's approach is however more detailed and systematic, with some significant differences: (1) the object of the vote must not necessarily be a "general object", that is, a law, but also any decision which needs to be taken in the public or private sphere; (2) the outcome of the voting process must comply with "truth" (the voting process is a collective quest for "truth") and not only be "right" and honest because emanating from the assembly of virtuous citizens; (3) in the political sphere, Condorcet is in favour of a representative assembly: the most important thing is the truth of the decision, and the size of the assembly should be adapted according to the degree of enlightenment of its members (below); (4) in this perspective, Condorcet introduces an additional and central variable, the probability for each voter to make the "true" choice, and an additional simplifying assumption: this probability is the same for all.

Note that Condorcet also formulated the condition of independence of irrelevant alternatives (Young 1988; McLean 1995). It is in this context that the attention focused on two main points, stated for the most simple case in the first pages of the *Essai* (1785: 3–11).

The Jury Theorem

The first point concerns what has been called Condorcet's "jury problem" (Black 1958) or "jury theorem". Let v (v for "vérité", that is, truth) be the probability for each voter to make the right choice, and e (e for error) the probability of being mistaken: $e = (1 - v)$. Suppose a dichotomous choice situation (for example, is a person guilty or not guilty of a crime?) in which the number of voters is n and q is the required majority expressed in terms of a number of votes. For Condorcet, two questions are of particular importance: (1) before the vote, what is the probability p to obtain a decision complying with truth? (2) Once the decision is taken, what is, for an external observer, the probability $p*$ that this decision complies with the truth? In modern parlance (see, for example, Granger 1956: 105–6), probability p is found using Bernoulli's binomial distribution. It is the sum, for all x, $q \leq x \leq n$, of the probability $v^x(1 - v)^{n-x}$ that a decision is true when it obtains x votes, multiplied by the possible number of occurrences $\binom{n}{x} = \frac{n!}{x!(n-x)!}$ of this event:

$$p = \sum_{x=q}^{n} \binom{n}{x} v^x (1 - v)^{n-x} \tag{1}$$

Probability $p*$ is found using the Bayes–Laplace theorem and is given by:

$$p* = \frac{v^q}{v^q + (1 - v)^q} \tag{2}$$

From the first equation, $p \to 1$ when $n \to \infty$ if $v > 0.5$, but $p \to 0$ in the opposite case. (Note that in case $v = 0.5$, $p = 0.5$ for all n.) This is the "jury theorem": in an assembly in which the probability for each voter to make the right choice is greater than 0.5, the probability for the outcome to be true increases with the number of voters – and conversely, when $v < 0.5$, the probability of the outcome to be true is a decreasing function of this number (Condorcet 1785: xxiii–xxiv, 6–9). From the second equation – in which the number of voters plays no role – it is possible to conclude that, all other things being equal, $p*$ is an increasing function of v and q.

These are both positive and negative results. The positive side of the story is the proposition that – under the very restrictive conditions noted above – an assembly could collectively have a degree of wisdom superior to its individual members, and that, if $v > 0.5$, this degree increases with the number of voters. This is the kind of statement already made by Aristotle when, examining the different possible political regimes, he declared that it is possible that many individuals, of whom no one is "virtuous", are collectively better when they are assembled than the best ones among them (*Politics*, III, 11, 1281-a). Condorcet's theorem could thus be taken as a powerful argument in favour of democracy.

The negative aspect arises if $v < 0.5$. Then the opposite conclusion applies: "it could be dangerous to give a democratic constitution to an unenlightened people: a pure democracy could even only suit a people much more enlightened, much more freed of prejudices than is any of those we know in history" (Condorcet 1785: xxiv). In these circumstances, nevertheless, a pure democracy would be acceptable if decisions are "limited to what regards the maintaining of safety, liberty and property, all objects on

which a direct personal interest can enlighten everybody" (ibid.; see also ibid.: 135) –
these being precisely among the "general" or "universal" objects in Rousseau's
approach. Otherwise the assembly, to decide on an issue, could designate a committee
composed of its most enlightened members and then judge, not the decision itself, but
whether the decision does not hurt justice or some of the fundamental human rights
(ibid.: 7).

However, while aware of the novelty and complexity of his developments on the forms
of elections or choices made in the various parts of the book, Condorcet in the end rela-
tivized the importance of the choice to be made between the different possible devices.
For him, the key variable remains the probability for each voter to be right or wrong;
hence his tireless action in favour of public instruction.

> [T]he happiness of men depends less on the form of assemblies that decide their fate than on
> the enlightenment of those who compose them, or, in other words, . . . the progress of reason
> affects more their happiness than the form of political constitutions. (1785: 136; see also
> ibid.: lxx)

The Condorcet Effect

What happens when there is more than one alternative? Voters, Condorcet states,
must rank them following a procedure of pairwise comparisons. What has been
called the "Condorcet winner" is the proposal or candidate who would win a two-
candidate election against each of the other proposals or candidates (for a possible
tension between Condorcet's probabilistic and social choice approach, see Black
1958: ch 18; Young 1988). In this context, the second main point which attracted the
attention in the 1785 *Essai* is what G.-T. Guilbaud called "the Condorcet effect" and
K. Arrow called the "paradox of voting", which expresses the possible intransitivity
of social choices resulting from the aggregation of individual choices made by rational
voters.

Suppose that voters have to express their preferences among three candidates or proposals A, B and C, through pairwise comparisons (Condorcet 1785: 120–21). For each
voter, there are a priori eight possibilities ("XY" meaning "X is preferred to Y"): (1) AB,
AC, BC; (2) AB, AC, CB; (3) AB, CA, BC; (4) AB, CA, CB; (5) BA, AC, BC; (6) BA,
AC, CB; (7) BA, CA, BC; and (8) BA, CA, CB. A rational voter will never choose choices
(3) and (6) which are not transitive. But, at the social level, outcomes (3) and (6) are possible. Among 31 voters, imagine that nine vote for (1), two for (2), seven for (4), four for
(5), six for (7) and three for (8). Eighteen voters prefer AB against 13, 19 BC against 12,
and 16 CA against 15, with the "cycling" result ABCA.

This outcome has significant consequences for any social choice theory based on an
aggregation of individual choices. The logic of the problem has been made explicit in the
general framework of Arrovian social choice theory: Arrows's so-called impossibility
theorem shows that there is no procedure for the aggregation of individual choices guar-
anteeing a transitive social ranking, while at the same time respecting some seemingly
mild axioms expressing "individualistic concerns" (that is, that the social choice should
reflect individual choices at least in some minimal way).

Condorcet, however, did not think that the paradox of voting was such an important
problem, even when the numbers of alternatives and voters grow – and it has been shown

that the probability to have a Condorcet effect quickly increases with them. He did not get locked in a logical dilemma, but proposed solutions out of the impasse (Black 1958: ch. 18; Young 1988, 1995; Monjardet 2008), which, in modern terms, are the maximum likelihood estimation, Kemeny's rule or the search for a median in a metric space. In particular, in the three-alternative cases dealt with above, one simple solution (Condorcet 1785: 122) consists in respecting the total number of votes that each candidate or proposal obtains against the two others. In the above example, AB and AC obtain together 18 + 15 = 33 votes, BA and BC 13 + 19 = 32 votes and CA and CB 16 + 12 = 28 votes. The winner is A.

To conclude, an essential aspect of Condorcet's thought must again be emphasized. All his developments are aimed at discovering "the truth", even in decisions that do not deal with justice but with choosing the right proposal or candidate in an assembly. He was convinced that on all these occasions, thanks to reason and science, there exists a truth, never imposed from above but which could be known provided those who decide are enlightened enough and follow the right procedure. As Rousseau had already insisted, a member of an assembly, when voting, must not express his own preferences but decide whether the proposal under examination does or does not comply with the common good. The "will of all" can differ from the "general will" whenever individuals are unable to abstract from their particular or partisan interests. The same is true with Condorcet. Hence, while Arrow's impossibility theorem can take as a starting point the Condorcet cycle, there is a fundamental difference between the problems Condorcet and Arrow are concerned with. The distinction between preference and judgement is concerned – and the recent developments of the theory of judgement aggregation, in a way initiated by Guilbaud (Mongin and Dietrich 2010, Mongin 2012), while more faithful to Condorcet, do not cancel the difference. For Condorcet, the problem does not consist in aggregating individual preferences and obtaining social choices respecting the "particular wills" or "private interests": the result would be the "will of all", not the "general will". Two different conceptions of democracy and the role of the State are at stake here.

> When he [a man] submits himself to a law which is contrary to his opinion, he must say to himself: *It is not here a question of myself alone, but of all; I thus must not behave according to what I believe to be reasonable, but according to what all, abstracting, like me, from their opinion, must consider as complying with reason and truth.* (Condorcet 1785: cvii, emphasis in the original)

GILBERT FACCARELLO

See also:

Daniel Bernoulli (I); Formalization and mathematical modelling (III); French Enlightenment (II); Social choice (III); Anne-Robert-Jacques Turgot (I); Uncertainty and information (III).

References and further reading

After the death of Condorcet, his widow Marie-Louise Sophie de Grouchy edited the *Œuvres complètes de Condorcet* with the collaboration of A.-A. Barbier and the *idéologues* P.J.G. Cabanis and D.J. Garat (Condorcet 1804). This edition, by no means complete, was followed four decades later by another edition, the *Œuvres de Condorcet*, by his daughter Elisa, his son-in-law, Arthur O'Connor, and the scientist and republican François Arago (Condorcet 1847–49). Nor is this edition complete: many important texts, like the 1785 *Essai*, are missing, as well as his entries for *Encyclopédie méthodique* or his writings on mathematics and probability – for example, "Mémoire sur le calcul des probabilités" (published by instalments, 1784–87) or *Éléments du calcul des probabilités et son application aux jeux de hasard, à la loterie et aux jugemens des hommes* (1789–90, posthumously published in 1805). Moreover, in both editions, a huge amount of manuscripts were disregarded: it was only recently that they started to be explored systematically (see, for example, Condorcet 1994a, 2004, two models of edition). His correspondence is now also re-examined (Rieucau 2014).

Arrow, K.J. (1963), *Social Choice and Individual Values*, 2nd edn, New York: John Wiley & Sons.
Badinter, E. and R. Badinter (1988), *Condorcet. Un intellectuel en politique*, revised edn 1990, Paris: Fayard.
Baker, K.M. (1975), *Condorcet. From Natural Philosophy to Social Mathematics*, Chicago, IL: University of Chicago Press.
Barry, B. (1964), 'The public interest', *Proceedings of the Aristotelian Society*, Suppl. vol. 38, 1–18, as in A. Quinton (ed.) (1977), *Political Philosophy*, Oxford: Oxford University Press, pp. 112–26.
Barry, B. (1965), *Political Argument*, London: Routledge and Kegan Paul, New York: Humanities Press.
Black, D. (1958), *The Theory of Committees and Elections*, Cambridge: Cambridge University Press.
Condorcet, M.-J.-A.-N. Caritat de (1785), *Essai sur l'application de l'analyse à la probabilité des décisions rendues à la pluralité des voix*, Paris: Imprimerie Royale. (The important 'Discours préliminaire' is reproduced in M.-J.-A.-N. Caritat de Condorcet (1986), *Sur les élections et autres textes*, Paris: Fayard, pp. 9–177.)
Condorcet, M.-J.-A.-N. Caritat de (1804), *Œuvres complètes de Condorcet*, 21 vols, Brunswick and Paris: Vieweg and Heinrichs.
Condorcet, M.-J.-A.-N. Caritat de (1847–49), *Œuvres*, eds A. Condorcet-O'Connor and F. Arago, 12 vols, Paris: Firmin Didot.
Condorcet, M.-J.-A.-N. Caritat de (1883), *Correspondance inédite de Condorcet et de Turgot, 1770–1779*, ed. C. Henry, Paris: Charavay.
Condorcet, M.-J.-A.-N. Caritat de (1986), *Sur les élections et autres textes*, Paris: Fayard. (Note that the important table on pp. 606–7 is erroneously reproduced.)
Condorcet, M.-J.-A.-N. Caritat de (1994a), *Condorcet. Arithmétique politique: textes rares ou inédits (1767–1789)*, ed. with comments B. Bru and P. Crépel, Paris: INED.
Condorcet, M.-J.-A.-N. Caritat de (1994b), *Condorcet. Foundations of Social Choice and Political Theory*, trans. and eds I. McLean and F. Hewitt, Aldershot, UK and Brookfield, VT, USA: Edward Elgar.
Condorcet, M.-J.-A.-N. Caritat de (2004), *Tableau historique des progrès de l'esprit humain. Projets, esquisse, fragments et notes (1772–1794)*, ed. with comments J.-P. Schandeler, P. Crépel and the Groupe Condorcet, Paris: INED.
Crépel, P. (1988), 'Condorcet, la théorie des probabilités et les calculs financiers', in R. Rashed (ed.), *Sciences à l'époque de la Révolution française: études historiques*, Paris: Blanchard, pp. 267–325.
Crépel, P. (1989), 'A quoi Condorcet a-t-il appliqué le calcul des probabilités?', in P. Crépel and C. Gilain (eds), *Condorcet: mathématicien, économiste, philosophe, homme politique*, Paris: Minerve, pp. 76–86.
Crépel, P. (1998), 'Mathematical economics and probability theory: Charles-François Bicquilley's daring contribution', in G. Faccarello (ed.), *Studies in the History of French Political Economy. From Bodin to Walras*, London: Routledge, pp. 120–85.
Crépel, P. and C. Gilain (eds) (1989), *Condorcet: mathématicien, économiste, philosophe, homme politique*, Paris: Minerve.
Crépel, P. and N. Rieucau (2005), 'Condorcet's social mathematics, a few tables', *Social Choice and Welfare*, **25** (2–3), 243–85.
Daston, L. (1988), *Classical Probability in the Enlightenment*, Princeton, NJ: Princeton University Press.
Dodgson, C.L. (1876), *Suggestions as to the best method of taking votes, where more than two issues are to be voted on*, in D. Black (1958), *The Theory of Committees and Elections*, Cambridge: Cambridge University Press, pp. 222–34.
Estlund, D.M., J. Waldron, B. Grofman and S.L. Feld (discussion between) (1989), 'Democratic theory and the public interest: Condorcet and Rousseau revisited', *American Political Science Review*, **83** (4), 1317–40.
Faccarello, G. (1989), 'Introduction' ('Condorcet: au gré des jugements') to Part III (Economics), in P. Crépel and C. Gilain (eds), *Condorcet: mathématicien, économiste, philosophe, homme politique*, Paris: Minerve, pp. 121–49.
Faccarello, G. (2006), 'An "exception culturelle"? French Sensationist political economy and the shaping of public economics', *European Journal of the History of Economic Thought*, **13** (1), 1–38.
Granger, G.-G. (1956), *La mathématique sociale du marquis de Condorcet*, Paris: Presses Universitaires de France.
Grofman, B. and S.L. Feld (1988), 'Rousseau's general will: a Condorcetian perspective', *American Political Science Review*, **82** (2), 567–76.
Guilbaud, G.-T. (1952), 'Les théories de l'intérêt général et le problème logique de l'agrégation', *Economie Appliquée*, **5**, 501–51; reprinted 2012 in *Revue Économique*, **63** (4), 659–720; English trans. 2008, *Journ@l*

électronique d'histoire des probabilités et de la statistique, **4** (1), accessed May 2015 at http://www.jehps. net/.

Hacking, I. (1975), *The Emergence of Probability. A Philosophical Study of Early Ideas about Probability, Induction and Statistical Inference*, Cambridge: Cambridge University Press.

Hald, A. (1990), *History of Probability and Statistics and their Applications before 1750*, Hoboken, NJ: Wiley.

Kintzler, C. (1984), *Condorcet, l'instruction publique et la naissance du citoyen*, Paris: Minerve; reprinted 1987, Paris: Gallimard.

McLean, I. (1995), 'Independence of irrelevant alternatives before Arrow', *Mathematical Social Sciences*, **30** (2), 107–26.

McLean, I. and F. Hewitt (1994), 'Introduction', in M.-J.-A.-N. Caritat de Condorcet, *Condorcet. Foundations of Social Choice and Political Theory*, trans and eds I. McLean and F. Hewitt, Aldershot, UK and Brookfield, VT, USA: Edward Elgar, pp. 1–90.

McLean, I. and A.B. Urken (1997), 'La réception des œuvres de Condorcet sur le choix social (1794–1803): Lhuilier, Morales et Daunou', in A.-M. Chouillet and P. Crépel (eds), *Condorcet. Homme des Lumières et de la Révolution*, Fontenay-aux-Roses: ENS Éditions, pp. 147–60.

Mongin, P. (2012), 'Une source méconnue de la théorie de l'agrégation des jugements', *Revue économique*, **63** (4), 645–57.

Mongin, P. and F. Dietrich (2010), 'Un bilan interprétatif de la théorie de l'agrégation logique', *Revue d'économie politique*, **120** (6), 929–72.

Monjardet, B. (2008), 'Mathématique sociale and mathematics. A case study: Condorcet's effect and medians', *Journ@l électronique d'histoire des probabilités et de la statistique*, **4** (1), accessed May 2015 at http://www. jehps.net/.

Nanson, E.J. (1882), 'Methods of election', *Transactions and Proceedings of the Royal Society of Victoria*, 1883, **19**, 197–240, accessed 15 December 2015 at http://www.biodiversitylibrary.org/bibliography/50009#/ summary; reprinted 1907 in *Parliamentary Papers, Reports from HM Representatives in Foreign Countries and in British Colonies Respecting the Application of the Principle of the Proportional Representation to Public Elections*, London: HMSO, pp. 123–41.

Philonenko, A. (1986), 'Jean-Jacques Rousseau 1712–1778. Contrat social, 1762', in F. Châtelet, O. Duhamel and É. Pisier (eds), *Dictionnaire des œuvres politiques*, Paris: Presses Universitaires de France, pp. 983–99.

Rieucau, N. (1998), '"Les entreprises où les hommes s'exposent à une perte dans la vue d'un profit": Condorcet et l'héritage de d'Alembert', *Revue économique*, **49** (5), 1365–405.

Rieucau, N. (2003), 'Les origines de la philosophie probabiliste de Condorcet. Une tentative d'interprétation', *Studies on Voltaire and the Eighteenth Century*, **12**, 245–82.

Rieucau, N. (ed.) (2014), *La correspondance de Condorcet. Documents inédits, nouveaux éclairages, 1775–1792*, Ferney-Voltaire: Centre international d'étude du XVIIIe siècle.

Rousseau, J.-J. (1762), *Du contract social, ou principes du droit politique*, Amsterdam: Marc Michel Rey. English trans., *On the Social Contract*, in J.T. Scott (ed.) (2012), *The Major Political Writings of Jean-Jacques Rousseau*, Chicago and London: Chicago University Press, pp. 153–272.

Young, H.P. (1988), 'Condorcet's theory of voting', *American Political Science Review*, **82** (4), 1231–44.

Young, H.P. (1995), 'Optimal voting rules', *Journal of Economic Perspectives*, **9** (1), 51–64.

Jeremy Bentham (1748–1832)

Jeremy Bentham is universally reputed to be the founder of modern utilitarianism, although various aspects of this philosophy were developed before him (Rosen 2003). He was born in Houndsditch, London, into a wealthy family, on 15 February 1749. He graduated at Queen's College, Oxford, in 1764, and subsequently studied law at Lincoln's Inn, London. Though called to the bar in 1769, he never practised. Instead, he decided to devote his life to writing on matters of law and institutional reform. In a work entitled *An Introduction to the Principles of Morals and Legislation* (hereinafter *IPML*), printed in 1780 although published only in 1789, he laid down the groundwork of utilitarian philosophy. The latter is based on the "greatest happiness principle" (GHP), according to which both individuals in their private sphere and governments in the public sphere ought to promote "the greatest happiness of the greatest number" (Bentham 1983: 309–10). This ethical doctrine is based on the assumption that individuals seek pleasure and avoid pain. Therefore, an action is morally right and morally obligatory if and only if it promotes the greatest amount of pleasure and minimizes the pain of those who are affected by it, independently of any other quality they may have (principle of impartiality). This implies that individuals must be able to calculate the "value" of pleasures and pains. In chapter 4 of *IPML* Bentham argued that such a value depends on various "circumstances", including intensity, duration, probability, propinquity, number of persons affected, and the secondary dimensions of "fecundity" and "purity" (meaning, respectively, the amount of either pleasure or pain that follows an initial pleasure, or vice versa the amount of either pain or pleasure that follows an initial pain) (see Schofield 2009).

After visiting his brother Samuel in White Russia between 1785 and 1788, Bentham devoted most of his energies to promoting the "Panopticon", a circular model prison based on the "inspection principle", according to which convicts were constantly under the eye of a gaoler who could watch them without being seen. This "simple architectural idea" would ensure, according to him, the "moral reform" of prisoners. The project was initially supported by William Pitt's government, but Bentham was left alone in battling for it until, in 1803, the new Addington administration decided to drop the plan. Interpreters indicate in the bitter disappointment Bentham experienced at that time one of the main causes of his political evolution towards radicalism (see Semple 1993). In the last 30 years of his long life (Bentham died on 6 June 1832), the "recluse" of Queen's Square Place denounced the corruption and waste of the British government and became an active supporter of parliamentary democracy based on universal suffrage and annual elections (see Schofield 2006).

Since the beginning, Bentham's "genius" for the science of legislation included an interest in political economy. Unfortunately, pending the announced new critical edition of Bentham's (1748–1832) *Writings on Political Economy* as part of *The Collected Works of Jeremy Bentham* (Bentham, forthcoming), and in the light of the critiques addressed by various scholars to Werner Stark's edition of *Jeremy Bentham's Economic Writings* (1952–54), any interpretation of Bentham's economic thought at the time of writing may be subject to rapid obsolescence.

Beyond this problem, Bentham's place in the development of classical political economy has always been a puzzle. Since Schumpeter (1954: 408–9), the prevailing opinion has been that his influence was limited to the supposed utilitarian credo of classical economists. However, if the Mills, father and son, and Jean-Baptiste Say became in their own way partisans of utilitarianism, the same cannot be said of David Ricardo and Thomas Robert Malthus. On the other hand, Bentham wrote his first published essay on political economy, *Defence of Usury* (1787, hereafter *DU*), partially as a response to Smith's views on the legal limit to the rate of interest. Also, he was a personal acquaintance of Ricardo, Nassau Senior, Say, Charles Dunoyer, Charles Comte, Pellegrino Rossi, and Gaspar Melchor de Jovellanos.

Bentham's contributions to political economy were partially published during his life, and to a larger extent remained unpublished until recently. To the set of published works, aside from *DU*, belong a series of texts composed by the philosopher in his youth, and published in 1811 by his editor, Étienne Dumont, as Book 4 of *Théorie des peines et des récompenses*, under the title of *Manuel d'économie politique* (hereafter *Manuel*). At the outbreak of the French Revolution, Bentham wrote a series of works he addressed to the French National Assembly and Convention. Among them there was a pamphlet entitled *Emancipate your Colonies!*, privately printed in 1793 and published only in 1830. Another draft written for the French was reformulated and published in 1795 under the title *Supply without Burthen; or Escheat vice Taxation: being a proposal for saving in taxes by an extension of the law of escheat; including strictures on the taxes on collateral succession*. Another tract, *A Protest against Law Taxes* was printed in 1793 and published in 1795 together with *Supply without Burthen*. The only other published essays on an economic subject are the twin essays respectively entitled *Defence of Economy against the Right Honourable Edmund Burke*, and *Defence of Economy against the Right Honourable George Rose*, both written in 1810 although published only in 1817. All these publications went through various editions along Bentham's life, and he attached a great importance to them in his correspondence with various economists. *Defence of Usury* and *Manuel* were translated in various languages and contributed to Bentham's reputation as a partisan of laissez-faire. However, many other papers remained in manuscript, as is the case of a series of practical proposals on monetary and banking issues composed between 1799 and 1801, and of some tracts on colony emancipation and free trade addressed to the Spanish *Cortes* in the early 1820s.

The difficulty of identifying Bentham's place in the history of economic thought mainly derives from the nature of one of his main "theoretical" works, the *Manuel*. The subjects examined in this text are not those on which classical economics was based, that is, the distinction between market and natural prices, that between "use" and "exchange value", the analysis of the respective role of cost of production and utility in the determination of value, the relationship between value, distribution and growth, the quantitative theory of money, and so on. The theoretical assumptions on which Bentham's analysis is based are quite simple: (1) the law of demand and supply; (2) a primitive version of the law of markets based on a sort of aggregate production function whose elements are the number of labourers, the amount of capital, the allocation of capital, the productivity of labour, and the "avantage du commerce", that is, (absolute) advantage in international trade; and (3) the assumption that individuals are both the best judges of their own interests and the best placed to obtain the relevant information for their choices. These assumptions led Bentham to the conclusion that the amount of aggregate income can be increased only by variations of any of the above mentioned factors, and the market spontaneously maximizes this output – a conclusion summarized by the argument that "trade is limited by capital". On this ground Bentham examined the most widespread policy measures for the encouragement of industry and trade: capital loans, capital transfers, bounties on production, drawbacks on production, bounties on exportation, prohibition of rival manufactures, maximums, and selective taxation. The only other subjects analysed in the *Manuel* were population, colonies, and usury laws. The general conclusion was typically laissez-faire: "Political economy is a science rather than an art. There is a lot to learn and little to do" (Bentham 1829–30, II: 201).

As to *DU*, the text contains no analysis of the determination of the interest rate. The main argument is that usury laws – setting a cap on the maximum interest rate that can be levied – do not contribute to lower it, as they encourage either risky illegal loans or other practices of evasion. Furthermore, they have adverse selection effects on borrowers, by excluding innovators (projectors), who could obtain loans only at rates beyond the legal maximum. This was an explicit critique of Adam Smith, who in book II, chapter 4 of *Wealth of Nations* had argued in favour of usury laws (Hollander 1999).

Among Bentham's unpublished projects, the most interesting is a bulky manuscript translated by Dumont as *Sur les prix*, whose publication was discouraged by Ricardo. This text contains an analysis of the British credit system and of the phenomena of inflation, forced saving and the instability of credit markets. Bentham argues in favour of a flexible role of central banks as gatekeepers against these risks, and at the same time as stimuli to production via credit creation, an unorthodox approach that cost Bentham the disapproval of his friend.

Another focus of Bentham's economic analysis is represented by public finance or, as he called it, "financial economy", or "economy as applied to office". The pamphlets he published on this subject dealt with taxation and its effects on individual choice on the one hand, and on the ways of making public expenditure more efficient on the other hand. In *A Protest against Law Taxes*, Bentham argued that taxes on legal proceedings are the worst possible type of tax, because they cannot be foreseen, apportioned or insured, and because failure to pay them in full operates as a complete exclusion from justice. The consequences are that lawsuits become inaccessible to poor plaintiffs, and justice is not encouraged. Finally, in *Supply without Burthen* he suggested that taxing collateral inheritance could be the best way to redistribute wealth and finance government expenditure, as this measure did not disappoint legitimate expectations.

Bentham's pamphlets on public economics belong to the period 1808–32, when he became a radical campaigner for representative democracy based on universal suffrage. Aside from the two *Defences of Economy*, most of the legal and political works of this period contain an interesting analysis of the means to minimize public expenditure and maximize its efficacy (a collection of articles published in 1830, entitled *Official Aptitude Maximized, Expense Minimized*, testifies to Bentham's attitude towards innovation in the language of social sciences; Bentham 1830 [1993]). Reducing public expenditure implies minimizing salaries, abolishing civil and religious sinecures and useless offices, optimizing the number of employees for every office, and avoiding every opportunity for corruption. Bentham's proposals range from rules of transparency (including transparency of public buildings according to panoptic principles) (Blamires 2008), contract management, an idiosyncratic revival of the sale of offices, and an interesting mechanism combining public examinations for verifying moral and intellectual "aptitude", with a "patriotic auction" for minimizing salaries. Utopian as they may appear, these proposals aimed at selecting a class of political representatives and public officers who, without being altruists, are more interested in reputation and self-fulfilment than in pecuniary motives.

So, what makes Bentham's approach to political economy so peculiar and apparently so distant from the typical concerns of classical economists, except for the laissez-faire conclusions?

An eye at chronology may offer a first answer to this question. In the timeline going from Smith's *Wealth of Nations* (1776) to Malthus's *Principles* (1820), the earliest significant "neo-Smithian" contributions are Say's *Traité d'économie politique* (1803), Sismondi's *De la Richesse commerciale* (1803) and James Mill's *Essay on the Impolicy of a Bounty on the Exportation of Grain* (1804). Burke's *Thoughts and Details on Scarcity* date from 1795 and Malthus's *Essay on Population* was published in 1798. Bentham's interest in political economy originated in his early years. In a letter to James Anderson, dated 28 March 1783, he defines himself "a mere novice in political economy", while already showing awareness of the principles later illustrated in the *Manuel*. He wrote most of the materials employed by Dumont between 1785 and 1795, and he published *DU* in between. There was no classical canon at that time, and the reinterpretation and exploitation of Smith's contribution was still potentially open to different alternatives. The shelves of Bentham's mental library were peopled by Smith's *Wealth of Nations*, as well as by James Steuart's *Inquiry* (1767), Montesquieu's *Esprit des lois* (1748), Josiah Tucker's *Elements of Commerce* (1755), Condillac's *Le Commerce et le Gouvernement* (1776), Anderson's *Observations on the Means of Exciting a Spirit of National Industry* (1777), John Howlett's *Examination of Dr. Price's Essay on Population* (1781), Arthur Young's *Annals of Agriculture* (1784–1815), and Hume's *Political Essays* (1751).

However, most importantly, the connection Bentham established between political economy and the science of legislation is the reason that explains the conceptual structure of his economic reasoning. Very early, and certainly by the mid-1770s at least, Bentham conceived an ambitious plan to compose a complete body of law. In opposition to Blackstone, whose *Commentaries on the Laws of England* (1765–69) he critically examined in the *Fragment on Government* (1776), and in opposition also to Smith, parts of whose analysis of British law he could find in *Wealth of Nations*, Bentham was interested in the principles of law-making, rather than in the study of "law as it is". Many of the materials employed by Dumont for the *Traités de législation civile et pénale* (1802) and the *Théorie* (1811) derive from the manuscripts of the *Projet d'un corps de loix complet à l'usage d'un pays quelconque*, a text on which Bentham worked in the 1780s possibly in response to a competition announced by the Société économique de Berne. The basic ingredients of Bentham's approach to the science of legislation comprise two: on the one hand, every branch of legislation must be based on some specific "ends" which the law must promote to make a nation happy. These ends are, for Bentham, essentially four, although particular branches of legislation may have additional ones: security, subsistence, abundance, and equality; on the other hand, the law must create a set of appropriate incentives and penalties that influence individual decisions, and, as Élie Halévy (1901–04 [1905]) wrote, "artificially harmonise" and direct them towards those ends. Bentham wrote *IPML* to give an exact foundation to this logical structure. In the light of the utilitarian doctrine exposed in that work, the ends of legislation are interpreted as so many specifications of the GHP – they are in fact "subordinate ends" – while the exact measure of reward and punishment is based on the "felicific calculus". The subordinate ends are the necessary guidelines to translate the GHP into a body of laws aiming at regulating social interactions. The arithmetic of pleasures and pains, combined with Bentham's admonition that "[m]en calculate, some with less exactness, indeed, some with more: but all men calculate" (Bentham 1789 [1996]: 173–4), grounds the mechanics of laws on the "economic" assumption that individuals react to incentives.

Bentham considered political economy as a branch of the "art-and-science" of legislation. In a text probably dating from 1814, he describes the connection with other branches of law as follows:

> Ends of Political Economy:
> These are the same as the distributive branch of law. Wherein, then, lies the difference? Answer: In so far as political economy is the object, so it is, that to two of those objects, viz. subsistence and abundance, a more particular and direct attention is paid, than either to security or to equality.
> By distributive law, is declared what on as many occasions as shall happen to have been taken into view, shall be each man's own. By political economy, is endeavoured to be ascertained how far, and for what particular purposes, chiefly for the general purposes of abundance and subsistence (i.e. security for subsistence), the use which otherwise under distributive law each man might make of his own, shall, for the more effectual fulfilment of these several ends, be directed and restricted. (Bentham 1838–43: III, 295)

The doctrine of political economy as "a branch of the science of a statesman or legislator" (Smith 1776, IV: I.1), although variously interpreted, was commonplace in Bentham's times. However, whereas writers such as Steuart and Anderson employed it to prescribe how to "direct" and "restrict" private initiative, the "capital limits trade" principle drove Bentham to the conclusion that governments had very little to do in this field, and that the "natural rewards" awarded by market laws were the best incentives to promote the ends of subsistence and abundance (Sigot 2001). On this point he agreed with Smith, who had famously argued that the main aim of political economy was "to provide a plentiful revenue or subsistence for the people, *or more properly to enable them to provide such a revenue of subsistence for themselves*" (Smith 1776, IV: I.1, emphasis added). Conversely, Bentham showed how the measures recommended by other writers offered adverse incentives to individuals, reducing, instead of increasing, the "matter of wealth" and therefore the stock of subsistence and opulence. The demonstration of the errors made by governments in manipulating incentives is the main focus of the *Manuel*, as well as of *DU* and of all other economic works written or published by Bentham, including those on "financial economy".

Far from believing he was interested only in some aspects of the Smithian economic discourse, Bentham was convinced that he had translated the core of Smith's political economy into a more coherent set of principles, avoiding useless digressions and a certain disorganization in the order of arguments, not because he had amended the flaws of Smith's theory of value or distribution, but because he had scrutinized the relationship between market laws and the ends of government in the mirror of an utilitarian science of legislation.

MARCO E.L. GUIDI

See also:

British classical political economy (II); French classical political economy (II); John Stuart Mill (I); Jean-Baptiste Say (I); Utilitarianism and anti-utilitarianism (III).

References and further readings
Bentham, J. (1789), *An Introduction to the Principles of Morals and Legislation*, reprinted 1996, J.H. Burns and H.L.A. Hart (eds), with new introduction by F. Rosen, Oxford: Clarendon Press.
Bentham, J. (1829–30), *Œuvres de Jérémie Bentham*, 3 vols, Brussels: Hauman.
Bentham, J. (1830), *Official Aptitude Maximized; Expense Minimized*, reprinted 1993, P. Schofield (ed.), Oxford: Clarendon Press.
Bentham, J. (1838–43), *The Works of Jeremy Bentham*, 11 vols, Edinburgh: Tait.
Bentham, J. (1952–54), *Jeremy Bentham's Economic Writings*, ed. W. Stark, 3 vols, London: Allen & Unwin.
Bentham, J. (1977), *A Comment on the Commentaries and A Fragment on Government*, eds J.H. Burns and H.L.A. Hart, London: Athlone Press.
Bentham, J. (1983), *Deontology together with A Table of the Springs of Action and the Article on Utilitarianism*, ed. A. Goldworth, Oxford: Clarendon Press.
Bentham, J. (forthcoming), *Writings on Political Economy*, ed. M. Quinn, 5 vols, Oxford: Clarendon Press.
Blamires, C. (2008), *The French Revolution and the Creation of Benthamism*, Basingstoke: Palgrave Macmillan.
Halévy, É. (1901–04), *La Formation du radicalisme philosophique*, 3 vols, reprinted 1995, Paris: Presses Universitaires de France.
Hollander, S. (1999), 'Jeremy Bentham and Adam Smith on the usury laws: a "Smithian" reply to Bentham and a new problem', *European Journal of the History of Economic Thought*, **6** (4), 523–51.
Rosen, F. (2003), *Classical Utilitarianism from Hume to Mill*, London and New York: Routledge.
Schofield, P. (2006), *Utility and Democracy. The Political Thought of Jeremy Bentham*, Oxford: Oxford University Press.
Schofield, P. (2009), *Bentham. A Guide for the Perplexed*, London and New York: Continuum.
Schumpeter, J.A. (1954), *History of Economic Analysis*, London: Allen & Unwin.
Semple, J. (1993), *Bentham's Prison. A Study of the Panopticon Penitentiary*, Oxford: Clarendon Press.
Sigot, N. (2001), *Bentham et l'économie: Une histoire d'utilité*, Paris: Economica.
Smith, A. (1776), *An Inquiry Into the Nature and Causes of the Wealth of Nations*, Glasgow edition, reprinted 1976, Oxford: Oxford University Press.

Achilles-Nicolas Isnard (1748–1803)

During the 1780s and 1790s, after the decline of the physiocratic school and before the publication of J.B. Say's *Traité d'économie politique*, few French authors made lasting contributions to economic theory. A clear exception is Achilles-Nicolas Isnard, even though recognition of his work had to wait until the late nineteenth century. Even in 1954 Schumpeter observed that Isnard had "as yet to conquer the position in the history of economic theory that is due to him as a precursor of Léon Walras" (1954 [1994]: 217). Since then the engineer's early contributions to value theory have been recognized more widely as well as the relevance of his conceptions for input–output theory. Still, Isnard's contributions to mathematical economics have often been appraised in isolation and their relation to his wider social and economic thinking has rarely been studied.

Achilles-Nicolas Isnard was born in Paris, most probably in 1748. Though the names of his parents are unknown, it appears that the Isnards were a relatively well-to-do bourgeois family. At the age of 19 Isnard entered the *École royale des Ponts et Chaussées*, at that time the foremost institution of technical education in France. In his seven years at the school he received a solid training in subjects such as map design and architecture, and various branches of mathematics in which he obtained such proficiency that for a time he ended up teaching the classes in algebra and calculus. In the same period he also established friendly contacts with at least one prominent physiocrat, P.S. du Pont, and studied their works.

In early 1775 he was given his first posting as assistant engineer at Arbois. From the beginning Isnard's career progression was hampered by a perceived lack of deference to his superiors and for two decades he did not gain any promotion. In 1781, for example, he was not only reported for not dealing firmly with farmers who refused the *corvée*, which he considered an oppressive institution, but he was also reprimanded for having his *Traité des richesses* published in Lausanne, across the Swiss border, without the required permission of his superiors. From 1785 Isnard was stationed at Evreux where he busied himself with writing on engineering subjects and experiments with electricity. During the early years of the Revolution he became a prolific, though unsuccessful, pamphletist. His initial enthusiasm for the Revolution cooled fast when it became clear that it would not deliver his ideal of a reformist and liberal monarchy guided by natural laws. In 1795, after the death of his wife Catherine, Isnard resigned from the engineering corps and for some years lived in straitened circumstances with his three surviving children in Paris. However, at the beginning of 1800 he was elected to the Tribunat, where he spoke frequently on fiscal matters and public works. He knew his fellow *tribun*, J.-B. Say, and soon became part of the "liberal opposition" against Bonaparte. Dismissed as a result, he took up the post of engineer, this time at Lyon. There he died of tuberculosis on 25 February 1803.

Isnard published 12 works over a tumultuous 20-year period, a body of work that adds up to over 3000 (octavo) pages, but his modern reputation is based solely on a few mathematical passages in his first book the *Traité des richesses* of 1781. Although those passages have often been read in isolation, they are in fact elements of a more or less coherent formal analysis of value, reproduction and distribution that forms the central part of a more comprehensive economic theory. This economic theory is in turn part of a much wider social science to which Isnard aspired and which he referred to as the "science of man".

As in Quesnay's work, the notion of reproduction is fundamental in Isnard's economic theory. Indeed, the engineer develops his conception as part of a critique of Quesnay's depiction of circular flow and reproduction in the *Tableaux économiques* (van den Berg 2002). Isnard's alternative construction is remarkable for its abstraction and clarity. The simplest of these *systèmes de richesses*, which is the earliest two-sector model, reads:

$$10 \text{ M} + 10 \text{ M}' \text{ produce } 40 \text{ M}$$
$$5 \text{M} + 10 \text{ M}' \text{ produce } 60 \text{ M}'$$

where M and M' are physical units of different commodities. The device illustrates at least three distinctive ideas. In the first place, it expresses the engineer's view that any process of production is formally the same in the sense that "[i]t produces through the aggregation and separation of forms [that is, inputs], qualities, capacities and properties that are useful to men [that is, outputs]" (Isnard 1789: 22). Second, "productivity", in the sense of production in excess of strict reproductive requirements, is recognized as a property of the economic system as a whole. Isnard (1781, I: 36) comments on the above example: "Thus to produce the total of the two products a consumption of 15M + 20M' is required, and the value of the disposable wealth [*richesses disponibles*] is 25M + 40M'". Third, like Quesnay, Isnard conceives reproduction-with-a-surplus as a process that is irreducibly circular (outputs are used as inputs) and as irreducibly social (some of the outputs are produced in other "sectors"). Unlike Quesnay however, he realizes that this necessitates an explicit theory of value and exchange.

This Isnard provides at the very beginning of his *Traité* by deriving relative values using simultaneous algebraic equations. Starting with the case of the exchange of given quantities of two commodities, he observes that "the value of each unit will . . . be in inverse ratio to the number of units that is offered for exchange" (Isnard 1781, I: 18). Extending his analysis to the many-commodity case he observes that in order to find relative values between units of all commodities "one would have to formulate as many equations as there are commodities" (ibid.: 19). While noting that "[s]uch calculations would be very complicated in a system with a great number of commodities" (ibid.: 26–7), the engineer provides an illustration (or proof) of his seminal idea by calculating the relative values for the case of given quantities of three types of commodities (ibid.: 20). The historical importance of this piece of analysis is highlighted by Ingrao and Israel (1990: 64) who note that "Isnard was . . . the first to suggest the condition of equality between the number of equations and the number of unknowns that, until the early twentieth century, was to remain the theory's only answer to the problems of the existence and uniqueness of the vector of equilibrium prices".

Isnard sees the valuation of products in exchange and their reproduction as two distinct moments in an ongoing economic process. Equilibrium values obtained in the market decide the distribution of the system's disposable wealth and inform the subsequent decisions of producers about what and how much to produce. But Isnard does not offer views about the "normal" distribution of the surplus. Despite very clear statements of the tendency towards a uniform rate of profit in different applications of capital, there is no attempt in the *Traité* to determine prices and the rate of profit simultaneously.

Besides the fundamental issues of value, reproduction and distribution, the work contains interesting discussions of consumption, the theory of money, the valuation of capital goods, foreign trade and taxation. Isnard's *Cathéchisme social* (1784) supplements his economics with a theory of human action and society. It is based on an original combination of sensationist psychology and natural law sociability, which underpins the radical liberal economic notions of the *Traité*.

Until the 1870s the influence of Isnard's ideas was negligible, even within the so called French "econo-engineering tradition" (Ekelund and Hébert 1999). The classical political economists do not seem to have known the *Traité des richesses*, with the notable exception of J.R. McCulloch (1845), who called it a "learned and valuable work". In 1878 Léon Walras was the first to recognize Isnard's contributions to mathematical economics. Jaffé (1969) presents detailed evidence to argue that Walras did in fact borrow, without explicit acknowledgment, a significant number of ideas from the engineer in the construction of his theory of general equilibrium. More recently, similarities of Isnard's reproductive schemes to those of Leontieff have been discussed (Steenge and van den Berg 2001). Kurz and Salvadori (2000) have noted especially the "striking similarity" of the two sector model of the *Traité* with the one Leontieff discusses in his early article "Die Wirtschaft als Kreislauf" (1928). Isnard's work is a principal example of how in economics fundamental ideas can be overlooked for a long time.

RICHARD VAN DEN BERG

See also:

Formalization and mathematical modelling (III); French Enlightenment (II); General equilibrium theory (III); Input–output analysis (III); Wassily W. Leontief (I); François Quesnay and Physiocracy (I); Marie-Esprit-Léon Walras (I).

References and further reading

Ingrao, B. and G. Israel (1990), *The Invisible Hand. Economic Equilibrium in the History of Science*, Cambridge, MA: MIT Press.

Isnard, A.-N. (1781), *Traité des richesses contenant l'analyse de l'usage des richesses en general et de leurs valeurs*, 'Londres' [Lausanne]: Grasset.

Isnard, A.-N. (1784), *Cathéchisme social ou Instructions élémentaires sur la morale sociale, à l'usage de la jeunesse*, Paris: Guillot.

Isnard, A.-N. (1789), *Réponses aux principales objections à faire contre l'impôt unique*, [n.p.].

Isnard, A.-N. (1791), *Les devoirs de la seconde legislature ou des législateurs de France*, Paris: Mecquignon.

Isnard, A.-N. (1801), *Considerations théoriques sur les caisses d'amortissement de la dette publique*, Paris: Duprat.

Jaffé, W. (1969), 'A.N. Isnard, progenitor of the Walrasian general equilibrium model', *History of Political Economy*, **1** (Spring), 19–43.

Kurz, H. and N. Salvadori (2000), 'Classical roots of input–output analysis: a short account of its long prehistory', *Economic Systems Research*, **12** (2), 153–79.

McCulloch, J.R. (1845), *The Literature of Political Economy*, London: Longman, Brown, Green and Longmans.

Schumpeter, J.A. (1954), *History of Economic Analysis*, reprinted 1994, London: Routledge.

Steenge, A.E. and R. van den Berg (2001), 'Generalising the Tableau économique: Isnard's Système des richesses', *International Journal of Applied Economics and Econometrics*, **9** (2) 121–46.

Van den Berg, R. (2002), 'Contemporary responses to the Tableau économique', in S. Boehm, C. Gehrke, H.D. Kurz and R. Sturn (eds), *Is There Progress in Economics? Knowledge, Truth and the History of Economic Thought*, Cheltenham, UK and Northampton, MA, USA: Edward Elgar, pp. 295–316.

Van den Berg, R. (2006), *At the Origins of Mathematical Economics. The Economics of A.N. Isnard (1748–1803)*, London and New York: Routledge.

Henry Thornton (1760–1815)

Henry Thornton (1760–1815) was a banker, philanthropist, Evangelical, one of the founders of the Clapham Sect and the treasurer of several evangelist societies, a politician and an economist. From a rich merchant family, he left his studies and began his career as a banker at the age of 18, in 1778. In 1784, he joined a private bank whose name became *Down, Thornton and Free*. This bank experienced difficulties from 1810 on and was close to bankruptcy in 1815, the year of Thornton's death. Henry should not be confused with his brothers: Robert, Governor of the East India Company, and Samuel, Governor of the Bank of England from 1799 to 1801. From 1782 until 1815, Henry sat in Parliament as an independent MP. He argued for progressive income tax and the abolition of the slave trade. He supported the younger William Pitt (1783–1806) and distinguished himself in banking and monetary debates. In 1797 and 1802, he argued in favour of the suspension of gold payments on Bank of England notes. In 1803 and 1804 he played a leading role in the debate on the Irish currency question. In 1810 he was appointed chairman of the Bullion Committee, together with Francis Horner, a Whig, and William Huskisson, a Tory.

In 1802, Thornton published *An Enquiry into the Nature and Effects of the Paper Credit of Great Britain* (Thornton 1802 [1939]). Translations in French and German were published the following year. An American edition came out in Philadelphia in 1807. Except for a private reproduction by J.R. McCulloch in 1857, *Paper Credit* was not republished in Great Britain during the nineteenth century. However, Thornton's influence on the Banking School in England and the Credit School in the United States is obvious. Hayek's edition (1939) of *Paper Credit* contains Thornton's evidence to the Parliament's Committees of Secrecy on the Bank of England in March and April 1797, and the two speeches he made in May 1811 when the bullion report went into debate. His book and speeches reveal Thornton as a major economist. He made three main contributions to monetary and banking economics: (1) he stated the first theory of the central bank as lender of last resort; (2) he was the first to describe the gold points mechanism, which explains how a low exchange rate causes a rise in the market price of gold in a country where the gold standard is suspended; (3) he was the first to describe the interest rate mechanism by which new issues of money may entail a rise in monetary prices. He saw his analysis as a challenge to that of Smith.

Smith's *Wealth of Nations* (1776 [1976]) does not deal with central banking, but with competitive banking. The prevailing idea at the end of the eighteenth century was that, although it was bigger and more solvent, the Bank of England was similar to other banks and provided liquidity according to the same rules: it granted credit by issuing bank notes, thus taking both credit and liquidity risks, and had to diminish its issues when its cash reserve fell. Thornton challenged this view by taking into account the velocity of circulation of bank notes. He explained that bank notes belong to a wide range of paper credit – which he refers to as a "circulating medium" – and that the velocity of the different kinds of credit varies with the interest rate and confidence. When confidence is high, traders prefer to hold commercial paper, which yields interest, and accept country bank notes in payment so that the demand for Bank of England notes and specie is low. On the contrary, when distrust reigns, traders prefer to hold specie and Bank of England notes, rejecting both commercial bills and country bank notes, so that banks face liquidity difficulties and call for the rediscounting of bills by the Bank of England. When the velocity of circulation of country bank notes increases, while the velocity of the Bank of England notes decreases, the banking system becomes illiquid, even though it is solvent. All banks, including the Bank of England, have a low cash reserve. Now, in this case, if the Bank of England, following the Smithian rule, refuses to grant new loans to country banks and traders in order to issue the notes required, it will fuel this distrust, thus aggravating the liquidity crisis. By lending in last resort, on the contrary, the Bank restores confidence and reverses the crisis process. This monetary policy rule was to be harshly criticized by Ricardo's followers.

Thornton also understood the bank liquidity risk caused by the operation of the currency market. Unlike David Hume, he introduced capital transfers into the analysis of international gold flows. For that purpose, he formulated the gold points mechanism, whereby a transfer of capital from England to the Continent can give rise to an outflow of gold even if there is no excess in the quantity of money circulating in England. Thus a subsidy sent by the English government to its continental allies may lead to a supply of sterling in the currency markets strong enough to diminish the exchange rate so that it reaches the gold export point, that is, the point at which it is profitable to sell foreign currency and buy sterling with a view to buying gold and silver in England and exporting it. If bank notes are convertible into gold and silver, precious metals are sold at fixed prices by the Bank of England, causing its cash reserves to shrink. In the context of inconvertibility, on the contrary, the Bank no longer sells gold and silver at fixed prices, and hence the market prices of gold and silver rise. Ricardo was to harshly reject this explanation of the high price of bullion during the Napoleonic wars.

Thornton's political view was that the war was responsible both for the panic that led to the suspension of convertibility in February 1797 and for the necessity to maintain the suspension as long as the hostilities lasted. In addition, the war necessitated the payment of subsidies to foreign allies, which in turn caused a high market price of gold and silver. However, Thornton did not rule out the idea that an excess issue of bank notes may cause a deficit in the balance of payments. On the contrary, he explained that a gap between the rate of profit and the usury interest rate may induce an excess issue of Bank of England notes, therefore an increase in prices, followed by a balance of trade deficit. He added that price inflation reduces the real value of the interest rate, thereby strengthening the inflationary process. Credit rationing may be implemented to remove this cumulative process which leads to outflows of gold, bringing about either bank illiquidity or a high price of bullion, depending on whether there is convertibility or not. These developments regarding the interest rate and price levels foreshadow Alfred Marshall's and Knut Wicksell's analyses, and can be considered fundamental contributions to quantity theory.

JÉRÔME DE BOYER DES ROCHES

See also:

Walter Bagehot (I); Balance of payments and exchange rates (III); Banking and currency schools (II); British classical political economy (II); Bullionist and anti-bullionist schools (II); Ralph George Hawtrey (I); David Hume (I); Alfred Marshall (I); Money and banking (III); David Ricardo (I); Adam Smith (I); Thomas Tooke (I); Knut Wicksell (I).

References and further reading

Arnon, A. (2011), *Monetary Theory and Policy from Hume and Smith to Wicksell: Money, Credit, and the Economy*, Cambridge: Cambridge University Press.

de Boyer des Roches, J. (2003), *La pensée monétaire, histoire et analyse*, Paris: Les Solos.

de Boyer des Roches, J. (2013), 'Bank liquidity risk: from John Law (1705) to Walter Bagehot (1873)', *European Journal of the History of Economic Thought*, **20** (4), 547–71.

de Boyer des Roches, J. and R. Solis Rosales (2003), 'Les approches classiques du prêteur en dernier ressort: de Baring à Hawtrey', *Cahiers d'Économie Politique*, **2003/2** (45), 79–100.

Hayek, F.A. von (1939), 'Introduction', in H. Thornton, *An Enquiry into the Nature and Effects of the Paper Credit of Great Britain (1802): together with his evidence given before the Committees of Secretary of the two Houses of Parliament in the Bank of England, March and April, 1797, some manuscript notes, and his speeches on the bullion report, May 1811*, F.A. von Hayek (ed.), London: Allen & Unwin.

Hicks, J. (1967), *Critical Essays in Monetary Theory*, Oxford: Clarendon Press.

Laidler, D. (2003), 'Two views of the lender of last resort, Thornton and Bagehot', *Cahiers d'Économie Politique*, **2003/2** (45), 61–78.

Murphy, A. (2003), 'Paper credit and the multi-personae Mr. Henry Thornton', *European Journal of the History of Economic Thought*, **10** (3), 429–53.

Rist, C. (1938), *Histoire des doctrines relatives au crédit et à la monnaie depuis John Law jusqu'à nos jours*, Paris: Sirey; English edition 1940, *History of Monetary and Credit Theory, from John Law to the Present Day*, London: Thoemmes Press.

Smith, A. (1776), *An Inquiry into the Nature and Causes of the Wealth of Nations*, reprinted 1976, R.H. Campbell and A.S. Skinner (eds), Oxford: Oxford University Press.

Thornton, H. (1802), *An Enquiry into the Nature and Effects of the Paper Credit of Great Britain (1802): together with his evidence given before the Committees of Secretary of the two Houses of Parliament in the Bank of England, March and April, 1797, some manuscript notes, and his speeches on the bullion report, May 1811*, reprinted 1939, with an introduction by F.A. von Hayek (ed.), London: Allen & Unwin.

Thomas Robert Malthus (1766–1834)

As Schumpeter noted, since the publication of the *Essay on Population*, Malthus has been "the subject of equally unreasonable, contradictory appraisals. He was a benefactor of humanity. He was a fiend. He was a profound thinker. He was a dunce. . . . Marx poured on him his vitriolic wrath. Keynes glorified him" (1954: 480–81).

Setting the Stage

Thomas Robert Malthus was born on 13 February 1766 at The Rookery, near Dorking in Surrey and died in Bath on 29 December 1834. His father, Daniel Malthus, was a friend of David Hume and a great admirer of Jean-Jacques Rousseau and his philosophical novel *Émile*. Three weeks after Robert's birth these two philosophers came to visit him. Robert was educated first by his father and then, until he was 16, by Richard Graves, a clergyman friend of his father. In 1782, he went to the famous Dissenting Academy at Warrington, Lancashire, to be taught by a "heretical" clergyman, Gilbert Wakefield, a disciple of Rousseau. Malthus went to Jesus College, Cambridge, in 1784, where he studied mathematics, science and classics. In 1788, he graduated as Ninth Wrangler, and took orders. After he had left Cambridge, one of his tutors, William Frend, was removed from his fellowship because of his advocacy of Unitarianism and his opposition to the war with the French Republic.

In 1793, Malthus was elected to a fellowship by his college, and took a curacy at Okewood, near his family's home. In 1803, he was instituted rector of Walesby, Lincolnshire, and held the living for the rest of his life without having resided there. The following year, he married Harriet Eckersall. In 1805, he was appointed Professor of Political Economy at the East India College, situated from 1809 at Haileybury, where he lived until his death, thus becoming the first Professor of Political Economy in England. Most of Malthus's contemporaries, even those who disagreed with his opinions, described him as a lovable man of considerable humour and underlined his affectionate and loyal nature and his intellectual honesty.

In 1796, Malthus wrote his first pamphlet, *The Crisis, a View of the Present Interesting State of Great Britain, by a Friend to the Constitution*, in order to criticize Pitt's administration. He failed to find a publisher, and the manuscript has unfortunately been lost. Nevertheless, some passages quoted by his two friends and biographers, William Empson and Bishop William Otter, indicate that he was already prompted by the desire to reduce the hardship of the poor and, more widely, interested in social problems of political economy. A close reading of his work cannot but convince the reader that his desire to improve the condition of the labouring classes would remain all his life; and that he intended to understand the true causes of their conditions, whether by poverty or by unemployment, in order to find appropriate remedies. In the introduction of the first edition of his *Principles of Political Economy* published in 1820, Malthus emphasizes the main difficulties inherent in such a task, particularly by stressing the principal cause of error in political economy: "a precipitate attempt to simplify and generalize" (1820b: 5). Simplifying by not acknowledging "the operation of more causes than one in the production of particular effects" (1820b: 6) and generalizing by not taking into account "the necessity of limitations and exceptions in a considerable number of important propositions" (1820b: 7) led to "crude and premature theories" (1820b: 6). Furthermore, on 26 January 1817, in a letter to Ricardo, Malthus writes: "A writer may, to be sure, make any hypothesis he pleases; but if he supposes what is not at all true practically, he precludes himself from drawing any practical inferences from his hypotheses" (Malthus in Ricardo 1951–73, VII: 122). Malthus's willingness to account for complexity, limitations and exceptions in political economy could explain most of his disagreements with Ricardo and that the hope the latter expressed on 20 August 1818 in a letter to his friend: "I wish to have an opportunity of judging of your system as a whole" (Ricardo 1951–73, VII: 284) could not be realized.

The *Essay on the Principle of Population* and the Poor Laws

The six successive editions of the *Essay on the Principle of Population*, from 1798 to 1826, illustrate Malthus's willingness to acknowledge when he was wrong. Malthus wrote the first edition of the *Essay*, which was published anonymously, mainly in order to attack the utopian ideas of Godwin and Condorcet. Population, when unchecked, has a tendency to increase at a higher rate than subsistence to support it: "Population, when unchecked, increases in a geometrical ratio. Subsistence increases only in an arithmetical ratio" (Malthus 1798 [1970]: 71). This implies the operating of checks, either preventive, reducing the birth rate, or positive – increasing the death rate (because of diseases, plague, famine and war) and entailing "misery and vice". Accordingly, the poor laws may be said "in some measure to create the poor which they maintain" (1798: 97): by contributing to increase the price of subsistence – an increased demand facing a constant supply – they "impoverish that class of population whose only possession is labour" (1798: 98); and "though they may have alleviated a little the intensity of individual misfortune . . . have spread the evil over a larger surface" (1798: 94). A chapter is also devoted to set out the "probable error of Dr Adam Smith in representing every increase of the revenue or stock of a society as an increase in the funds for the maintenance of labour" and to stress that "an increase of wealth can have no tendency to better the condition of the labouring poor" (1798: 183). According to Keynes, Malthus's first *Essay* is "a work of youthful genius. . . . He believed that he had found the clue to human misery" (1933 [1972]: 86).

Partly in order to collect further information concerning the principle of population, Malthus undertook two study tours: one of Norway, Sweden and Finland in 1799, and one of France and Switzerland in 1802. In August 1800, he published, again anonymously, a pamphlet, *An Investigation of the Cause of the Present High Price of Provisions*, in order to explain why the price of provisions had risen much more than could be explained by the actual deficiency in the harvest. He relates this fact to the poor laws and not to the increased quantity of money: "I should be inclined to consider it rather as the effect than the cause of the high price of provisions. This fullness of circulating medium, however, will be one of the obstacles in the way to returning cheapness" (Malthus 1800 [1970]: 25). According to Keynes "in this Pamphlet, Malthus's conception of 'effective demand' is brilliantly illustrated" (1933 [1972]: 88). It is known that Malthus was so struck by this idea while riding from Hastings to London that he worked solidly "sitting up till two o'clock to finish [this pamphlet] that it might come out before the meeting of parliament" (ibid.).

In the Preface to the second edition of the *Essay on Population* published in 1803, Malthus writes that "it may be considered as a new book" (Malthus 1803 [1989]: I,

2). The introduction of the "moral restraint", consisting of postponing marriage until people could support a family, is presented as an important change since it consists of a check to population "which does not come under the head of either vice or misery" (1803 [1989]: I, 3). Malthus emphasizes also his endeavour "to soften some of the harshest conclusions of the first *Essay*" (1803 [1989]: I, 3): particularly, he proposes a plan for a "gradual" abolition of the poor laws, underlining in a letter to Whitbread published in 1807 that this abolition should not be undertaken carelessly "till the poor themselves could be made to understand that they had purchased their right to a provision by law, by too great and extensive a sacrifice of their liberty and happiness" (1807b [1970]: 34); hence the necessity of education.

In the third edition published in 1806, he emphasizes that "both humanity and true policy imperiously require that we should give every assistance to the poor" (1806 [1989]: I, 357) in case of bad harvest. In the fourth edition published in 1807, Malthus admits that, under the present circumstances, the poor laws should not be said to encourage early marriages and population and adds in a note: "should this be true, many of the objections which have been urged in the *Essay* against the poor laws will of course be removed" (1807a [1989]: II, 226). Malthus was not reluctant to admit his errors: Donald Winch deplores that this acknowledgment has not been regarded as "an example of honesty in the face of the facts that ran contrary to one of his predictions" (1987: 97). In his *Principles*, Ricardo wrote: "Of Mr. Malthus's *Essay on Population*, I am happy in the opportunity here afforded me of expressing my admiration. The assaults of the opponents of this great work have only served to prove its strength" (Ricardo 1951–73, I: 398).

From the Bullion Controversy . . .

Malthus intervened in the Bullion Controversy with articles in the *Edinburgh Review*. In "Depreciation of paper currency", which appeared anonymously in February 1811, he reviewed pamphlets on bullion, among them Ricardo's *High Price of Bullion* and his *Reply to Bosanquet*. Although praising Ricardo for his analysis of the depreciation of bank notes, he considers that "the great fault of Mr. Ricardo's performance is the partial view which he takes of the causes which operate upon the course of Exchange" (Malthus 1811a [1963]: 74). He reproaches Ricardo for "considering redundancy and deficiency of currency as the mainspring of all commercial movements" (ibid.: 91), for attributing "a favourable or unfavourable exchange *exclusively* to a redundant or deficient currency" and for overlooking "the varying desires and wants of different societies, as an original cause of a temporary excess of imports above exports, or exports above imports" (ibid.: 75, author's emphasis). This represents for Malthus a signal instance of one of the principal causes of error in political economy. In the fourth edition of the *High Price of Bullion* published in April 1811, Ricardo added an important appendix, mainly to answer the Edinburgh reviewers – he did not know yet that Malthus was the author. On 22 June 1811, Ricardo and Malthus met on the latter's initiative having written a letter to Ricardo six days before: "As we are *mainly* on the same side of the question, we might supersede the necessity of a long controversy in print respecting the points in which we differ, by an amicable discussion in private" (Malthus in Ricardo 1951–73, VI: 21, author's emphasis). The discussion must have been amicable indeed: from this meeting began a fascinating correspondence and a friendship, which lasted until Ricardo's death in 1823. Malthus's "Pamphlets on the bullion question" appeared in August 1811. A few days before finishing it, Malthus wrote to Ricardo: "It will have nothing to do with our controversy which appears to me to be too nice a question for the generality of readers to be interested about" (Malthus in Ricardo 1951–73, VI: 48). However, at the end of the article, Malthus, dealing with the problem concerning the return to cash payments, alludes to "the valuable suggestion of Mr. Ricardo" in his plan for bullion payments, outlined in his appendix to the fourth edition to the *High Price of Bullion*. He supported Ricardo's view that the government should indulge the Bank of England's directors and "merely compel them, at the expiration of two years, to pay their notes above £20, and no other, in guineas, standard bar gold, or foreign gold of the same value" (Malthus 1811b [1963]: 127).

. . . to the Corn Laws Debate

Malthus contributed to the public debate about the Corn Laws with three pamphlets. After publishing in 1814 *Observations on the Effects of the Corn Laws, and of a Rise or Fall in the Price of Corn on the Agriculture and General Wealth of the Country* in which he sets out the arguments for and against the Corn Laws, he released *An Inquiry into the Nature and Progress of Rent* on 3 February 1815 and *The Grounds of an Opinion on the Policy of Restricting the Importation of Foreign Corn* a week later. In his *Essay on Profits* which appeared exactly two weeks later, Ricardo writes that he is indebted to Malthus for developing so ably the principles which regulate rent, and, in a letter of 13 February: "You have yourself said, and I very much admire that passage, that the last portion of capital employed on the land yields only the common profits of stock, and does not afford any rent" (Ricardo 1951–73, VI: 177). Nevertheless, Ricardo disagrees with his friend's support of the existing Corn Laws. The difference between them rests on two sets of arguments. The first set refers to the principles of political economy. Particularly, Malthus claims that the price of corn does not depend only on the difficulty of its production and that demand has to be taken into account; that restrictions, by increasing the price of corn, can increase the profits and improve the conditions of the labourers. This was because of such a rise of money wages, which enabled them to purchase more of other commodities. In short, Malthus did not think that a low price of corn was always an advantage. The second set of arguments consists of the political dangers of being dependent for any considerable quantity of food on foreign supply (in case of war or of bad harvest occurring abroad). Concerning the latter set of arguments, Ricardo, although not sharing Malthus's fears, considers that the political dangers are not easy to estimate and writes to him that "those who are for an open trade in corn may underrate them, and it is possible that you may overrate them" (Ricardo 1951–73, VI: 177). Malthus's Whig friends felt dismayed by his support to the Corn Laws, and in spite of his claiming in the *Grounds*: "If I were convinced that to open our ports would be permanently to improve the conditions of the labouring classes of society, I should consider the question as at once determined in favour of such a measure" (Malthus 1815b [1970]: 154), he was accused of defending the interest of landlords to the detriment of others. Later on, after Ricardo's death, Malthus's position on the Corn Laws will change, calling into question the necessity of agricultural protection, "of any forced encouragement given to agriculture, which would probably defeat the very end in view" (1823a [1963]: 180–81).

The Possibility of a General Glut

Another major subject of disagreement with Ricardo concerns Malthus's assertion of the possibility for the progress of wealth to be checked while the powers of production remain undiminished or, even, are increased, throwing labourers out of employment. This possibility rests on the lack of willingness among capitalists to consume unproductively, to spend their revenue either on luxuries or on employing unproductive labourers. In his *Principles of Political Economy*, published in 1820, Malthus considers that, after a great and sudden increase in agricultural and manufacturing productivity, farmers and manufacturers might choose not to convert their new increased revenue into capital and, given that the taste for luxuries is "a plant of slow growth" (Malthus 1820b: 314), might prefer indolence, that is to say "the luxury of doing little or nothing to the luxury of possessing conveniences and luxuries" (ibid.: 337). This would "occasion a want of demand for the returns of the increased powers of production supposed and throw labourers out of employment" (ibid.: 313). However, in Malthus's eyes, two points are much more important and preoccupying than indolence. On the one hand there is the possibility that capitalists, after such a great increase in the powers of production, choose neither indolence nor unproductive consumption, but to convert their new increased revenue into productive consumption, into capital. On the other hand the possibility exists that capitalists decide to deprive themselves of their usual conveniences and luxuries and to convert unproductive labourers into productive labourers, saving from their revenue to add to their capital. In these two cases, the lack of willingness amongst capitalists to consume unproductively results in an increase in production and supply of commodities destined for the maintenance of labour.

For Malthus, commodities are produced by numerous capitalists. When the increase in production is excessive, each capitalist becomes afraid of not being able to sell all his commodities. The competition between capitalists leads them to lower the money prices of commodities "in a much greater degree than in proportion to the increase" in production (Malthus 1823a [1963]: 200), which sinks "their value below the costs of production" (1820b: 374). Considering that "for many years together the money-price for labour remains the same" (1827: 55), Malthus concludes that "the same produce, though it might have *cost* the same quantity of labour as before, would no longer *command* the same quantity" (1820b: 309, author's emphasis). Since Malthus considers that "we must at last resort to labour as the only standard of the real value of everything, and of the effectual demand for it" (1836: 319) – that is, the quantity of labour which commodities command – the situation described above means for him that sometimes "an increase of supply is so far from increasing demand that it diminishes it" (1827: 45). When this happens for all commodities, there is a glut which is "evidently general not partial" (1820b: 308). Thus:

> If the conversion of revenue into capital pushed beyond a certain point must, by diminishing the effectual demand for produce, throw the labouring classes out of employment, it is obvious that the adoption of parsimonious habits in too great a degree may be accompanied by the most distressing effects at first, and by a marked depression of wealth and population permanently. (1820b: 325)

In his *Notes on Malthus*, Ricardo comments on this passage: "Here the difference between Mr. Malthus and me is fairly stated. The reader must judge on which side truth lies" (Ricardo in Malthus 1820b: 325). The difference is clear and consists in the fact that Ricardo does not agree with his friend on the very *possibility* for what Malthus calls a general glut: a deficiency in effectual demand for all commodities, which throws labourers out of employment. Obviously, this difference is not of the same nature as that which Ricardo stated a few years previously in a letter to his friend, on 24 January 1817, according to which Malthus is more interested in "the immediate and temporary effects of particular changes", whereas Ricardo put these effects aside, fixing his attention "on the permanent state of things which will result from them" (Ricardo 1951–73, VII: 120). Malthus answered two days later: "I agree with you that one cause of our difference in opinion is that which you mention" (in Ricardo 1951–73, VII: 121–2).

Of course, the "certain point" beyond which the conversion of revenue into capital is pushed too far, "the resources of political economy are unequal to determine. It must depend upon a great variety of circumstances, particularly upon fertility of soil and the progress of invention in machinery" (Malthus 1820b: 422). Nevertheless, what is sure is that one cannot rely on capitalists to realize the adequate proportion between productive and unproductive consumption: the latter one "is not consistent with the actual habits of the generality of capitalists. The great object of their lives is to save a fortune" (ibid.: 423). The passion for accumulation is inherent in the nature of capitalists, and constitutes a threat to society, to labourers and to capitalists themselves. On the basis of this analysis, Malthus advises not only that: "a knowledge of the effects of unproductive consumers on national wealth will make us proceed with more caution in our efforts to diminish them" (ibid.: 446), but also that "public works, the making and repairing the roads, and a tendency among persons of fortune to improve their grounds, and keep more servants, are the most direct means within our power of restoring the demand for labour" (ibid.: 446).

Even if Marx disagreed with Malthus's analysis, should not he have praised him for highlighting the dangers of the passion for the accumulation of capital, as he did himself? As for Keynes, even if he agreed with Malthus with regard to the possibility for effectual demand to be deficient, and its consequence concerning employment, should not he have underlined the differences between their analyses? In particular, this possible deficiency is caused for Malthus by the desire to accumulate too much, for Keynes by a lack of incentive to invest.

CATHERINE MARTIN

See also:

British classical political economy (II); Bullionist and anti-bullionist schools (II); Population (III); David Ricardo (I).

References and further reading

Cremashi, S. (2014), *Utilitarianism and Malthus's Virtue Ethics. Respectable, Virtuous and Happy*, Abingdon and New York: Routledge.
Hollander, S. (1997), *The Economics of Thomas Robert Malthus*, Toronto: University of Toronto Press.
James, P. (1979), *Population Malthus. His Life and Times*, London: Routledge and Kegan Paul.
Keynes, J.M. (1933), *Essays in Biography*, London: Macmillan, new edn in E. Johnson and D. Moggridge (eds), *The Collected Writings of John Maynard Keynes*, vol. 10, 1972, London: Macmillan for the Royal Economic Society.
Malthus, T.R. (1798), *An Essay on the Principle of Population, as it affects the future Improvement of Society,*

with Remarks on the Speculation of Mr. Godwin, M. Condorcet, and other Writers, London: J. Johnson, reprinted 1970, A. Flew (ed.), London: Pelican.

Malthus, T.R. (1800), *An Investigation of the Cause of the Present High Price of Provisions*, by the Author of the Essay on the Principle of Population, London: J. Johnson, reprinted 1970 in *The Pamphlets of Thomas Robert Malthus*, New York: A.M. Kelley.

Malthus, T.R. (1803), *An Essay on the Principle of Population*, 2nd edn, in P. James (ed.), *An Essay on the Principle of Population*, variorum edition, 1989, 2 vols, Cambridge: Cambridge University Press.

Malthus, T.R. (1806), *An Essay on the Principle of Population*, 3rd edn, in P. James (ed.), *An Essay on the Principle of Population*, variorum edition, 1989, 2 vols, Cambridge: Cambridge University Press.

Malthus, T.R. (1807a), *An Essay on the Principle of Population*, 4th edn, in P. James (ed.), *An Essay on the Principle of Population*, variorum edition, 1989, 2 vols, Cambridge: Cambridge University Press.

Malthus, T.R. (1807b), *A Letter to Samuel Whitbread on his Proposed Bill, for the Amendment of the Poor Laws*, London: J. Johnson and J. Hartchard, reprinted 1970 in *The Pamphlets of Thomas Robert Malthus*, New York: A.M. Kelley.

Malthus, T.R. (1811a), 'Depreciation of paper currency', *Edinburgh Review*, February, **17** (34), 339–72, reprinted 1963 in B. Semmel (ed.), *Occasional Papers of T.R. Malthus*, New York: Burt Franklin.

Malthus, T.R. (1811b), 'Pamphlets on the bullion question', *Edinburgh Review*, August, **18** (36), 448–70, reprinted 1963 in B. Semmel (ed.), *Occasional Papers of T.R. Malthus*, New York: Burt Franklin.

Malthus, T.R. (1814), *Observations on the Effects of the Corn Laws, and of a Rise or Fall in the Price of Corn on the Agriculture and General Wealth of the Country*, London: J. Johnson, reprinted 1970 in *The Pamphlets of Thomas Robert Malthus*, New York: A.M. Kelley.

Malthus, T.R. (1815a), *An Inquiry into the Nature and Progress of Rent, and the Principles by which it is Regulated*, London: J. Murray, reprinted 1970 in *The Pamphlets of Thomas Robert Malthus*, New York: A.M. Kelley.

Malthus, T.R. (1815b), *The Grounds of an Opinion on the Policy of Restricting the Importation of Foreign Corn, intended as an Appendix to 'Observations on the Corn Laws'*, London: J. Murray and J. Johnson, reprinted 1970 in *The Pamphlets of Thomas Robert Malthus*, New York: A.M. Kelley.

Malthus, T.R. (1817), *An Essay on the Principle of Population*, 5th edn, in P. James (ed.), *An Essay on the Principle of Population*, variorum edition, 1989, 2 vols, Cambridge: Cambridge University Press.

Malthus, T.R. (1820a), *Principles of Political Economy: Considered with a View to their Practical Application*, London: J. Murray.

Malthus, T.R. (1820b), *Principles of Political Economy*, excerpts of the 1st edn in *The Works and Correspondence of David Ricardo, 1951–73*, vol. II, Cambridge: Cambridge University Press.

Malthus, T.R. (1820c), *Principles of Political Economy: Considered with a View to their Practical Application*, variorum edition, 2008, J. Pullen (ed.), 2 vols, Cambridge: Cambridge University Press.

Malthus, T.R. (1823a), 'Political economy', *Quarterly Review*, January 1824, **60**, 297–334, reprinted 1963 in B. Semmel (ed.), *Occasional Papers of T.R. Malthus*, New York: Burt Franklin.

Malthus, T.R. (1823b), *The Measure of Value Stated and Illustrated, with an application of it to the altercations in the value of the British currency since 1790*, London: John Murray.

Malthus, T.R. (1826), *An Essay on the Principle of Population*, 6th edn, in P. James (ed.), *An Essay on the Principle of Population*, variorum edition, 1989, 2 vols, Cambridge: Cambridge University Press.

Malthus, T.R. (1827), *Definitions in Political Economy*, London: John Murray.

Malthus, T.R. (1836), *Principles of Political Economy*, 2nd edn, London: W. Pickering.

Ricardo, D. (1951–73), *The Works and Correspondence of David Ricardo*, P. Sraffa (ed.), with the collaboration of M.H. Dobb, 11 vols, Cambridge: Cambridge University Press.

Schumpeter, J.A (1954), *History of Economic Analysis*, London: Oxford University Press.

Waterman, A. (1998), 'Reappraisal of "Malthus the Economist", 1933–97', *History of Political Economy*, **30** (2), 293–334.

Winch, D. (1987), *Malthus*, Oxford: Oxford University Press.

Winch, D. (1996), *Riches and Poverty, an Intellectual History of Political Economy in Britain, 1750–1834*, Cambridge: Cambridge University Press.

Jean-Baptiste Say (1767–1832)

Jean-Baptiste Say was born in Lyon, on 5 January 1767, in a Protestant family. At the age of 15, he started an apprenticeship in a trading house in Paris, then went to England and, in 1787, Étienne Clavière, a Swiss businessman, took him on in the insurance company he was managing. Say took an active part in the Revolution. He worked at a newspaper, the *Courrier de Provence*, published by Gabriel-Honoré de Mirabeau, and was close to the Girondins, to whom Clavière, who was for a time Minister of Finance in 1792, had introduced him. In 1794, Sébastien-Roch de Chamfort involved him in the foundation of the periodical *La Décade philosophique, littéraire et politique, par une société de républicains* and as its managing editor. The incapacity of the Directoire to stabilize the Revolution led Say and his friends, the "Idéologues", to support Napoleon Bonaparte's *coup d'état* on 18 Brumaire of Year VIII (9 November 1799). He became secretary of the Legislative Committee of the Conseil des Cinq-Cents and then, after the new Constitution of Year VIII, a member of the Tribunat. The first edition of his *Traité d'économie politique* was published in 1803. In March 1804, with some other members of this assembly, he was eliminated from the Tribunat because of his opposition to Bonaparte. "From the texts written during this period, Say appears . . . as an committed intellectual . . . who never betrayed his republicanism" (Steiner 1990: 176). He was and remained a Republican (Whatmore 2000: 12). In his *Cours complet d'économie politique pratique* (Say 1828–29 [2010], II: 954), he stated again the idea that "the representative government . . . is the necessary outcome of the economic progress of societies", but was in the end disappointed by his experience and was led to reject the idea that political freedom is the condition of economic progress. "Wealth is independent of the nature of government, a State can thrive if it is well administrated . . . The forms of public administration have only an indirect and accidental influence on the formation of wealth, which is almost entirely the work of individuals" (Say 1803 [2006]: 2).

The first edition of his *Traité d'économie politique* opens with this statement. A second, heavily revised edition was prepared quickly but, for political reasons, the publication had to wait until the fall of Napoleon in 1814. After the fall of the Empire, Say went again to England, where he met James Mill, David Ricardo and Jeremy Bentham. When back in Paris, he lectured at the *Athénée*, a private institution, which was a kind of political club for the liberal opposition to the policy of the Restoration. In 1819 a chair at the Conservatoire des Arts et Métiers was installed on his behalf: his lectures were published as the *Cours complet* in 1828–29. It is only after the 1830 Revolution that the government considered political economy as a field of science. A chair of political economy was created at the Collège de France; Say was the first to hold this chair until his death in Paris on 14 November 1832.

The Legacy of Smith and Bentham

Very critical of the Physiocrats, Say affirms that political economy did not exist before Adam Smith. It is true that predecessors advanced true propositions, but Smith was the first to show why they were true. Smith's merit is to have applied the scientific method to political economy, "starting from observed facts and deducing the general laws, of which they are the consequences" (Say 1814 [2006]: 34). French liberals – particularly

Germaine de Staël and Benjamin Constant – had a critical attitude towards utilitarianism (Faccarello and Steiner 2008: 34–46). Say (1833 [2003]: 133), instead, praises Bentham. He interprets him stating that the best way for an individual to look after his or her "interest well understood" is to adhere to the principle of utility, to evaluate his or her interests for such things with the utility they have for human beings, that is, for the greatest good for the greatest number. He relies on this principle when he states that public utility – and not the consent of the majority – is the rational foundation of the activity of the state.

Production

Say proposes a new definition of production: it is not a creation of matter, but of utility. It is not measured in physical units, but in utility degrees (Say 1803 [2006]: 78). The Physiocrats maintained that craftsmen were unproductive because they did not produce any surplus, the value of their products being equal to that of their consumption. Say disagrees: craftsmen produce at least the interest of the capital used. For Smith (1776 [1976]: 330) the labour not embodied in some material object does not produce any value and is unproductive. For Say, instead, this labour renders useful services and produces an "immaterial product". He admits however that this labour cannot be accumulated and cannot increase the national capital. Charles Dunoyer (1827: 68) accused him of being inconsequent: the fact that a product is immaterial does not imply that it cannot be accumulated, as the example of knowledge clearly shows.

Say, moreover, does not think that the division of labour can alone explain the progress of wealth – well-being augmented because men learned how to better exploit natural resources. Sciences are the basis of industry and wealth, but this is not enough: it is necessary to know how to exploit its discoveries in order to satisfy the human needs. This task is performed by industry. Invention and innovation lie at the heart of the development process, of which scientists and entrepreneurs are the deciding agents.

Value

In the first edition of the *Traité*, Say developed his view of value from the *Wealth of Nations*. There were of course some nuances: the word "value" disappeared, but the main development relied on the gravitation of the market price around the natural price. In the second edition (1814), the analysis is modified. Utility is now "the first base of the value of things" (1803 [2006]: 592), and the cost of production the second. The link between the two is supply and demand. Say first studies the role of the individuals' choices and the distribution of income in the relation between the price of a good and the demand for it. Individuals have different needs they rank according to their degree of importance for them, they satisfy first the most urgent ones, then those that are less so, and so on. However, to derive the total demand from individuals, the distribution of income must be taken into account. Say describes it as a pyramid: only a few consumers are rich, many are poor. When the price is high, only a few persons can afford the good; when it is low, almost all can. On the other hand, Say (1826a [2006]: 619) stresses that, when the demand for a good increases, the demand for the productive services that are necessary to produce it and their prices increase too. He concludes that, while some economists like Ricardo wrote that the cost of production regulate the price of products, they were right in this sense that products are never sold for a long time at a price lower than their cost of production; but when they said that demand does not influence their value, they were wrong . . .: demand influences the value of the productive services, increases the cost of production and rises the value of products while not exceeding the cost. (Ibid.).

Income Distribution

For Say, there are three kinds of income: the remuneration of labour, interest and rent. No category is homogeneous: for example, there is no reason that the earnings of a scientist are the same as that of a worker. This classification is partly due to Say's analysis of the role of the entrepreneur. For Smith, in the typical situation the entrepreneur is the capitalist, who invested the capital. He deals with profits as a whole and stresses that they are not the remuneration of a labour of inspection and direction – such tasks can be performed "by some principal clerk" (Smith 1776 [1976]: 66). For Say, it is of no importance whether or not the entrepreneur owns a fraction of the capital of the firm: what is important is that he manages it. In his income, the remuneration of his work and the interest of his capital must be distinguished. Smith disregarded this and "ran into difficulties" (Say 1803 [2006]: 730n).

The prices of the productive services are, like those of the products, determined by supply and demand. The demand for services is indirect: "when a product is in demand, all the services, which concur to its production, are also in demand" (Say 1828–29 [2010], II: 705) and their demand rises with that of the goods. Thus, when wealth increases, the amount of capital increases, interest declines and wages rise.

The rent of land is determined in the same way as wages and profits. Land differs in location and fertility: each kind of land is the object of a specific demand, which determines its remuneration. Say consequently criticizes the Ricardian theory of rent and particularly the principle that rent is not a constituent part of the price of commodities. Increasing human needs certainly lead to high prices, which induce the cultivation of land of poorer quality and allow the payment of a rent on more fertile land. However, this proposition applies to all productive services. It does not permit either to exclude rent from costs, or to state that the existence of poorer land is the cause of the rents made on the more fertile land.

One difficulty remains however. Land is not the only natural agent that is productive; why is it the only one that generates an income? This is because it is the soil, which can be appropriated by men. This ownership must thus be justified. Say (1819 [2006]: 793) advances an utilitarian argument: "Land is cultivated, and we obtain its products in some abundance, thanks to its appropriation."

Money and Crises

Say defines money as a means of payment. Its value is determined by supply and demand. Its value is thus not inversely proportional to its quantity in circulation: it also depends on the quantity demanded. Say had lived through the period of the "assignats". He was thus led to investigate the causes of the value of an inconvertible paper money. He had first thought that "money is accepted in exchanges . . . because it is a commodity, which has a value" (Say 1803 [2006]: 456). In this perspective a paper money could not have circulated. That the assignats experiment could go on was thanks to the measures taken by the government: not only were the assignats fiat money but producers were obliged to accept it against the commodities, the price of which was fixed by the State. In 1814 however, Say, in England, read Ricardo's analysis of the 1797 Bank Restriction Act. He then came to think that the value of paper money is not due to a possible reimbursement in specie, but is a consequence of the need of a medium of exchanges. "It is the proportion of notes, and not discredit, which influence their value" (Say 1815 [1996]: 75).

With money as a means of payment, it could be thought that products do not sell because the quantity of money is too small. Say discards this idea in the celebrated chapter "Des débouchés" of *Traité* – the source of the so-called Say's law. However, in the different editions, the arguments change. In 1803, he maintained that any agent, even if he deals with important sums during a period, has at the end of it approximately the same cash balance than at the beginning. He thus justified what was called later Say's identity: the sum of the excess demands, money excluded, is identically nil. However he abandoned this idea in 1814 and stated that "when money falls short of the needs of commerce, it is easily replaced" (Say 1814 [2006]: 248). For want of money, one pays with notes, cheques and bills of exchange. An excess demand for money can possibly correspond to an excess supply of goods, but it will soon disappear because other means of payment replace money proper (Baumol 1977: 159). The idea of an equality replaces that of an identity: in equilibrium, demand for and supply of money are equal, and the sum of the excess demands for goods is nil.

However, when Say examined the 1825 British crisis, he put the blame on banks: "the spirit of speculation was excessively excited by the banks, which in England all have the power of issuing notes payable to the bearer" (Say 1826b: 43). The abundance of the circulation provoked a fall of the value of specie relative to bullion, and there was a run at the banks to convert notes into specie in order to melt it into bullion. The reserves were depleted, banks were unable to discount bills of exchange and entrepreneurs, unable to face their commitments, went bankrupt. Say does not deny the possibility of crises, but he rejects the idea that they are due to an excessive production or a too rapid accumulation of capital.

"Il mondo va da se"

Say liked to repeat the motto attributed to Vittorio Fossembroni: "Il mondo va da se" ("The world turns by itself"; see Faccarello 2010: 734). People "need not been governed ... The State exists without receiving an impulse, without the need of a *system of administration*, a *thought of government*" (Say 2003: 324, original emphases). Several times, during the Revolution, "all the springs of authority were broken ... there was no government ... All was functioning as usual" (Say 1819 [2003]: 101). When a public institution fails, people know how to replace it for the best. Governments wrongly try to influence production, to stimulate the production of goods, the consumption of which they judge preferable, or to dictate the way in which they have to be produced. Worse, they sometimes want to create manufactures. Far from being an alleged source of wealth, these establishments were instead a cause of loss. The state is a bad producer because "it only acts through ... the intermediary of persons, who have a particular interest different from its own – a particular interest which they prefer" (Say 1803 [2006]: 382).

While a government is not an essential part of social organization, this does not mean that it is useless, but that the principle of utility alone can justify its intervention. Some consumptions "can only be made in common, with persons to which one is tied by the political organization" (Say 1803 [2006]: 920). They are characterized by two elements: (1) they concern needs that an individual can only satisfy in society, and they require the intervention of an institution with a coercive power; and (2) they also deal with the production and diffusion of knowledge, because scientists obtain from their works a smaller benefit than that enjoyed by society. It is thus necessary, for example, to support "a small number of outstanding schools, where the stock of knowledge is not only preserved . . . but the field of science always extended" (ibid.: 955). It is also necessary to give all the citizens the knowledge they need to know where their enlightened interest lies and where that of society is. "A nation is not civilized . . . when some do not know how to read, write and count" (ibid.: 957).

Say maintains that the government must erect and maintain works like the means of communication, which, while being in the public interest, cannot be the outcome of private interest. He rejects the idea that they must be wholly financed by those who use them. Tolls ration the use of utilities by many persons, who cannot afford them. They deprive society from a part of the potential benefits these works could bring. The principle that a means of communication should not be made if its exploitation does not cover its costs is also ill-founded because it neglects the fact that such a means would stimulate production in the provinces it serves.

Say, like Ricardo, Mill and Malthus, developed his analyses from his reading of the *Wealth of Nations*. They all are Smith's heirs, and they could, for this reason, be described as classical. However, the idea of a school – of the existence, as Hollander wrote (2005), of a "Classical canon in economics" – can be a source of mistakes if it leads to the neglect of the divergences that, despite long and friendly discussions, divide these authors. On some central questions – the theory of prices and of distribution in particular – Say developed his own views, different from Ricardo's, because he did not conceive in the same way the role of demand in the determination of the prices of goods and productive services.

ALAIN BÉRAUD

See also:

Jeremy Bentham (I); French classical political economy (II); Thomas Robert Malthus (I); John Stuart Mill (I); David Ricardo (I); Barthélemy-Charles Dunoyer de Segonzac (I); Jean-Charles Léonard Simonde de Sismondi (I); Adam Smith (I).

References and further reading

Baumol, W. (1977), 'Say's (at least) eight laws, or what Say and James Mill may really have meant', *Economica*, New Series, **44** (174), 145–61.
Béraud, A. (2003), 'Jean-Baptiste Say et la théorie quantitative de la monnaie', in J.-P. Potier and A. Tiran (eds), *Jean-Baptiste Say, nouveaux regards sur son œuvre*, Paris: Economica, pp. 447–70.
Blanc, E. and A. Tiran (2003), 'Introduction générale', in E. Blanc and A. Tiran (eds), *Jean-Baptiste Say, Œuvres complètes*, vol. V, *Œuvres morales et politiques*, Paris: Economica, pp.
Dunoyer, C. (1827), 'Traité d'économie politique par Jean-Baptiste Say', *Revue Encyclopédique*, **34**, 63–90.
Hollander, S. (2005), *Jean-Baptiste Say and the classical canon in economics, the British connection in French classicism*, London: Routledge.
Faccarello, G. (2010), 'Bold ideas. French liberal economists and the state: Say to Leroy-Beaulieu', *European Journal of the History of Political Economy*, **17** (4), 719–58.

Faccarello, G. and P. Steiner (2008), 'Political economy and religion in early 19th century France', in B.W. Bateman and H.S. Banzhaf, *Keeping Faith, Losing Faith: Religious Belief and Political Economy*, *History of Political Economy*, **40**, annual supplement, 26–61.

Gehrke, C. and H.D. Kurz (2001), 'Say and Ricardo on value and distribution', *European Journal of Economic Thought*, **8** (4), 449–86.

Ricardo, D. (1817), *On the principles of political economy and taxation*, London: John Murray, reprinted in P. Sraffa and M. Dobb (eds) (1951), *The Works and Correspondence of David Ricardo*, vol. I, Cambridge: Cambridge University Press.

Say, J.-B. (1803), *Traité d'économie politique*, Paris: Deterville, reprinted in J.-B. Say (2006), *Œuvres complètes*, vol. 1, Paris: Economica.

Say, J.-B. (1814), *Traité d'économie politique*, 2nd edn, Paris: Renouard, reprinted in J.-B. Say (2006), *Œuvres complètes*, vol. 1, Paris: Economica.

Say, J.-B. (1815), *De l'Angleterre et des anglais*, Paris, Bertrand, reprinted in C. Mouchot (ed.) (1996), *Jean-Baptiste Say, Cours d'économie politique et autres essais*, Paris: GF-Flammarion.

Say, J.-B. (1817), *Traité d'économie politique*, 3rd edn, Paris: Deterville, reprinted in J.-B. Say (2006), *Œuvres complètes*, vol. 1, Paris: Economica.

Say, J.-B. (1819), *Traité d'économie politique*, 4th edn, Paris: Deterville, reprinted in J.-B. Say (2006), *Œuvres complètes*, vol. 1, Paris: Economica.

Say, J.-B. (1819), *Cours à l'Athénée*, reprinted 2003 in J.-B. Say, *Œuvres complètes*, vol. IV, Paris: Economica.

Say, J.-B. (1826a), *Traité d'économie politique*, 5th edn, Paris: Rapilly, reprinted in J.-B. Say (2006), *Œuvres complètes*, vol. 1, Paris: Economica.

Say, J.-B. (1826b), 'De la crise commerciale en Angleterre', *Revue Encyclopédique*, **32** (October), 40–45.

Say, J.-B. (1828–29), *Cours complet d'économie politique pratique*, Paris: Rappily, reprinted in J.-B. Say (2010), *Œuvres complètes*, vol. 2, Paris: Economica.

Say, J.-B. (1833), 'Essai sur le principe d'utilité', in C. Comte (ed.), *Mélanges et correspondance d'économie politique*, Paris, Chamerot, reprinted 2003 in *Œuvres Complètes de J.B. Say*, vol. 4, *Leçons d'économie politique*, Paris, Economica.

Say, J.-B. (2003), *Politique pratique*, in *Jean-Baptiste Say, Œuvres complètes*, vol. 5, *Œuvres morales et politiques*, Paris, Economica.

Smith, A. (1776), *An inquiry into the nature and causes of the wealth of nations*, London: Strahan and Cadell, reprinted in R.H. Campbell and A.S. Skinner (eds) (1976), *The Glasgow Edition of the Works and Correspondence of Adam Smith*, vol. 1, Oxford: Oxford University Press.

Steiner, P. (1990), 'Comment stabiliser l'ordre social moderne? J.-B. Say, l'économie politique et la révolution', *Œconomia*, Cahiers de l'ISMEA (13), 173–93.

Steiner, P. (2006), 'Les *Traités d'économie politique*, 1803, 1814, 1817, 1819, 1826, 1841', in J.-B. Say (2006), *Œuvres complètes*, vol. 1, *Traité d'économie politique*, Paris: Economica, pp. ix–lii.

Whatmore, R. (2000), *Republicanism and the French Revolution*, Oxford: Oxford University Press.

David Ricardo (1772–1823)

Life and Work

Ricardo was born into a prolific Sephardic Jewish family in London on 18 April 1772. His father, a well-to-do stockbroker, had moved his business from Amsterdam to London shortly before David's birth. Ricardo was for the most part privately instructed. According to a memoir written by his brother Moses, David already at a young age "showed a taste for abstract and general reasoning" (Ricardo 1951–73, X: 4; hereafter *Works*). This taste he refined over time. As one commentator was to remark in 1820, Ricardo "meets you upon every subject that he has studied with . . . opinions in the nature of mathematical truths" (*Works* VIII: 152, n. 2).

At the age of 14, David joined his father's business and assumed a profound knowledge of the financial trade and the London Exchange. On 20 December 1793, at the age of 21, he married Priscilla Ann Wilkinson, an English Quaker. His mother especially, adamantly opposed this marriage and his parents fell out with him. Ricardo, depending on himself, started a career at the Stock Exchange on his own. He benefited from the support of important members of the London Exchange and soon became more successful than his father. He acquired great recognition in the profession and was widely considered with admiration not only because of his skills and knowledge, but also because of his personal integrity and reliability. From a financial point of view, his best year was 1815. Four days before the battle of Waterloo on 18 June, the British government had raised the largest loan during the entire war with Napoleon Bonaparte and his allies. The size of the loan and the uncertainty about the outcome of the battle depressed the stock exchange quotation of the state obligation. Ricardo bet on the victory over the Napoleonic troops and was proved right.

His "most favourite subject"

Ricardo's interest in political economy was ignited during a stay in Bath towards the end of 1799, where he had brought his wife for a cure vacation after she had fallen ill when their third daughter and fourth child had been stillborn. As a pastime Ricardo began to read Adam Smith's *Wealth of Nations* (1776 [1976]), which he had discovered in a circulating library. He was deeply impressed and fascinated by the book and ordered a copy to be sent to his home. Political economy advanced to his "most favourite subject" (*Works* VI: 263). Economic and political events amplified his interest in it. In February 1797 the Bank of England had suspended the convertibility of its bank notes into gold, and inflationary tendencies arose in Great Britain. These events triggered the so-called "Bullion Controversy" in which Ricardo was a major participant. He published his first article anonymously in 1809 on "The Price of Gold" in *The Morning Chronicle*. A year later followed his pamphlet *The High Price of Bullion, a Proof of the Depreciation of Banknotes*. These made him quickly known in learned and political circles. The Bullionists and Ricardo argued that the Bank of England's increase of the circulation of money was responsible for rising prices, whereas the anti-Bullionists maintained that the money supply was driven by the "needs of trade" reflected by the real bills presented to the Bank for discount. The "Bullion Report" to the House of Commons was strongly influenced by Henry Thornton, a Bullionist, but reflected also ideas of Ricardo. In several letters to the *Morning Chronicle* and in a pamphlet titled *Reply to*

Mr. Bosanquet's 'Practical Observations on the Report of the Bullion Committee' (1811), Ricardo defended the Bullion Report and attacked the Bank of England, whose policy, while benefiting a few, harmed the interests of the nation at large.

Elaborating "a very consistent theory"
Ricardo got to know James Mill and Thomas Robert Malthus. Mill, impressed by Ricardo's sharpness and talent, incessantly urged him to write down his ideas and publish them. With Malthus, Ricardo engaged in numerous controversial discussions until the end of his life especially on the theory of value and distribution, the problem of what would be a good measure of value and the problem whether a general "glut" of commodities, that is, a lack of aggregate effectual demand, was possible. It was Malthus's relentless criticism that prompted Ricardo to rethink his positions and develop what he eventually considered "a very consistent theory" (*Works* VII: 246).

Prompted by a move before Parliament to restrict the corn trade in early 1813, Ricardo started to investigate the impact of such a restriction on the accumulation of capital and on income distribution — the rents of land, the rate of profits and wages. He scrutinized critically Adam Smith's doctrine and found it wanting. His efforts resulted in March 1814 in some "papers on the profits of Capital", which unfortunately have never been found, and in February 1815 in the publication of his *Essay on the Influence of a Low Price of Corn on the Profits of Stock; Shewing the Inexpediency of Restrictions on Importation*. Thereafter the problem of income distribution in a developing economy was at the centre of Ricardo's research agenda. The *Essay* laid the ground for Ricardo's magnum opus, *On the Principles of Political Economy, and Taxation*, published in April 1817. The book sold out in a few months. A second, substantially revised edition came out in 1819, and a third, containing the new chapter "On Machinery," in which Ricardo responded inter alia to the movement of the Luddites, in 1821. Ricardo identified the "principal problem in Political Economy" to consist in unravelling the "laws" that regulate the distribution of the product between landowners, capitalists, and workers in conditions of changing relative scarcities of natural resources and changing technical conditions of production due to "improvements" (*Works* I: 5).

Napoleon's fall, Ricardo's rise
Consequent upon the enormous fortune he had made on the occasion of Napoleon's defeat, Ricardo by late 1815 decided to withdraw from the Stock Exchange and turn his time and energy to political economy. He invested a great part of his money in landed estates. According to his theory of income distribution as expounded in the *Essay*, with a growing population corn production must be increased, which requires extending the cultivation of land to ever less fertile plots of land or intensifying the cultivation of given plots. The scarcity of land(s) increases and yields its proprietors rising rents per acre. In parallel the general rate of profits and, in its wake, the rate of interest tend to fall. Since the price of an acre of a particular plot of land is a perpetuity that is equal to the ratio of the rent per year and the rate of interest, with the numerator rising and the denominator falling, the price of land will rise. According to Immanuel Kant, there is nothing more practical than a good theory, a wisdom Ricardo expressed repeatedly and followed in practical life: he bought large plots of land. He retired from his activities at the Stock

Exchange to his country house Gatcombe Park near Minchinhampton, Gloucestershire, which he had acquired in 1814.

In February 1816 Ricardo published some *Proposals for an Economical and Secure Currency* (see *Works* IV: 43–141), in which he put forward anew his "Ingot Plan". The plan suggested a return to the Gold Standard by making bank notes convertible not into specie (coins), but into bullion (gold ingots), which implied the demonetization of gold in domestic circulation. This would have several desirable effects: it would allow Britain to continue to use paper money as the actual means of payment, which Ricardo endorsed; it would reduce the need for gold reserves held by the Bank of England and thus mitigate the upward pressure on the value of gold; and, last but not least, it would curb the huge profits pocketed by the governors and directors of the Bank (which remained a private institution until 1946), who benefited from the appreciation of gold. These profits, Ricardo insisted, belonged to the public. The House of Commons decided on a plan for the gradual return to note convertibility in bullion, starting in early 1820 and ending in May 1821 at the pre-1797 parity. During this period Ricardo's Ingot Plan was implemented. However, immediately after the old parity had been restored, the Bank of England decided to return to note convertibility in coin. This led to huge profits reaped by its directors, who in anticipation of the move had accumulated large amounts of gold, which they now sold to their bank at very favourable terms – precisely the kind of self-enrichment Ricardo chastised.

In 1823 Ricardo composed a *Plan for the Establishment of a National Bank*, which was published posthumously in February 1824 (see *Works* IV: 271–300). His plan had first taken shape in 1815 while he was composing the pamphlet *Economical and Secure Currency* and was then put forward in the first edition of the *Principles* (*Works* I: 361–3). Of the two operations that the Bank of England performed – issuing paper currency and advancing loans to merchants and so on – the former should be taken away from it and given to independent commissioners, who act as bankers to the government, but are "totally independent of the control of ministers". This would not thwart the provision of the economy with money, but "in a free country, with an enlightened legislature" (*Works* I: 362) transfer a part of the profits of the Bank to the national Treasury and thus to the public.

In Parliament
On 30 September 1814 James Mill in a letter flattered Ricardo that he "might be of great use to a favourite science, and to a most important department of practical politics, which altogether depend upon such a science". This, Mill added, "ought to be sufficient motive with him, to improve every hour and every moment, nay to place himself in that situation in which his tongue, as well as his pen might be of use" (*Works* VI: 138). With the *Principles* Ricardo had attended to his duty with his "pen". When in 1819 he became a Member of Parliament by buying the seat of Portarlington, Ireland, the time had come for his "tongue" to follow suit. Ricardo participated in several debates, mostly on monetary, financial and currency matters, but also, in 1821–22, in committees dealing with agricultural distress. He spoke up on behalf of civic rights, secret ballots, the equal treatment of religions, penal reform and the abolition of the haggling over seats in the House of Commons (see Milgate and Stimson 1991; King 2013: ch. 6). His suggestion in 1819 to repay the whole of the national debt that had accumulated during the Napoleonic wars

in a few years by means of a lump-sum tax on property became famous. He argued that such a tax would not diminish total wealth and would also not unduly hurt the propertied classes because the capital value of the current taxes levied on them to cover interest and amortization of the national debt was probably in the range of the property tax suggested. It was not implemented. In 1821 Ricardo became a member of the influential "Political Economy Club" in London and participated in several of its meetings.

After the publication of the first edition of the *Principles*, Ricardo was predominantly concerned with the problems of value and distribution, the measure of value, and the machinery question. The second edition, published in 1819, brought substantial changes in the chapter "On Value". For a detailed account of these changes as well as the changes from the second to the third edition, published in 1821, see Sraffa's "Introduction" in *Works* (Sraffa 1951: xiii–lxii). In the third edition, the most important change concerned the question of whether technical change was always a universal blessing or whether there were types of it that were harmful especially to the labouring class. Ricardo now recanted his earlier optimistic view as to the swift compensation of labour displacement due to the introduction of improved machinery: in the case of technical progress that reduced the gross produce, the resulting unemployment may persist and exert a lasting downward pressure on wages.

Controversy with Malthus

In 1820 Thomas Robert Malthus published his *Principles of Political Economy*, which were designed as a response to Ricardo's *Principles*. Ricardo replied with his *Notes on Malthus*, which he circulated privately; they were published only posthumously (see *Works* II). Ricardo disagreed with Malthus essentially in the following regards. First, Malthus had argued that both "market" and "natural" prices are regulated by supply and demand. To this Ricardo objected that while market prices may deviate from natural prices, "this does not overturn the doctrine that the great regulator of price is cost of production" (*Works* II: 39). Also, in a letter to Malthus dated 9 October 1820, he wrote: "You say demand and supply regulates value – this, I think, is saying nothing" (*Works* VIII: 279). On 24 November he explained:

> I do not dispute either the influence of demand on the price of corn and on the price of all other things, but supply follows close at its heels, and soon takes the power of regulating price in its own hands, and in regulating it he is determined by cost of production. I acknowledge the intervals on which you so exclusively dwell, but still they are only intervals. (*Works* VIII: 302)

Without the elaboration of a *theory* of demand and supply, invoking the two terms does not explain anything.

Secondly, Malthus had questioned Ricardo's view of the connection between capital accumulation and the rate of profits, but Ricardo found Malthus's argument not convincing (see below). Third, Malthus had argued that too much saving will entail a "general glut" of commodities. However, since he had endorsed the view that every act of saving will be accompanied by an act of investment of equal size, Ricardo was at a loss to understand how Malthus could then contend that there might be a lack of aggregate effectual demand. Also, when Malthus suggested that the interests of the landlord and of the state coincide and that a class of spendthrifts or "unproductive consumers" – the landlords – was needed in order to stabilize demand, Ricardo commented drily: "A body of unproductive labourers are just as necessary and as useful with a view to future production, as a fire, which should consume in the manufacturers warehouse the goods which those unproductive labourers would otherwise consume" (*Works* II: 421).

In 1822 Ricardo, his wife and his two youngest daughters embarked on a tour to several countries on the Continent that lasted for a couple of months during which Ricardo met a handful of economists, including the Swiss Jean-Charles Léonard Simonde de Sismondi and the Frenchman Jean-Baptiste Say. His opinion on the two economists' views did not improve upon their encounter.

When back in England, Ricardo continued his discussions and correspondence with Malthus, Mill, McCulloch, Robert Torrens and others. He made a further attempt to solve the still unsettled problem of value and distribution during the last few weeks of his life and composed a complete rough draft and an unfinished later version entitled "Absolute Value and Exchangeable Value" (see *Works* IV: 357–411). In them he elaborated on his own view of what would be an ideal measure of value and criticized the views entertained by other authors. However, it is clear that the search for such a measure was essentially a search for a coherent theory of value and distribution, as Sraffa remarked perceptively.

Ricardo died unexpectedly at his country seat on 11 September 1823 at the age of 51 from an "infection of the ear, which ultimately extended itself to the internal part of the head" (*Works* X: 12).

On the life, times and works of Ricardo, see also Weatherall (1976), De Vivo (1987), Henderson and Davis (1997), King (2013) and Heertje in Kurz and Salvadori (2015).

Debunking Some Myths

Before we enter into a discussion of Ricardo's contributions to economic theory, a few myths about his doctrine ought to be debunked, followed by a specification of Ricardo's particular method of analysis.

Myths about Ricardo
According to John Maynard Keynes (1972: 95, 98; hereafter *CW* X), "Ricardo was the abstract and *a priori* theorist" – a man "with his head in the clouds". Ricardo did indeed defend economic theory against the "vulgar charge" of those who are "all for fact and nothing for theory. Such men can hardly ever sift their facts. They are credulous, and necessarily so, because they have no standard of reference" (*Works* III: 160, 181). However, this does not mean that he did not care for facts. Ricardo was a man with a considerable practical sense, experience and financial success. A stockjobber, his knowledge about money, finance and banking came second to none in his time, and there is compelling evidence that he kept abreast with the latest technical and organizational improvements in agriculture, manufacturing, commerce and trade (see Davis 2005; Morgan 2012).

Another myth says that Ricardo's doctrine of value and distribution "is radically fallacious" since it involves more unknowns than equations (Jevons 1871 [1965]: 258–9; see also Walras 1874 [1954]: s. 368; Schumpeter 1954: 569). Yet as Knut Wicksell ([1893] 1954: 34–40) already argued, this criticism cannot be sustained. It resulted from looking at Ricardo's surplus approach as if it was an early marginalist or demand-and-supply explanation of income distribution. Yet, Ricardo explained the real wage rate and the rate of profits asymmetrically, taking the former as given and ascertaining the latter residually, and not symmetrically, as the marginalists, in terms of the demand and supply of labour and capital.

A further myth is that Ricardo was "piling a heavy load of practical conclusions upon a tenuous groundwork" – the so-called "Ricardian vice" (Schumpeter 1954: 1171). While Ricardo frequently employed bold cases to "elucidate" the principle at hand and to draw attention to what in his view were the most important aspects of the problem under consideration, he did not seek to prevent his readers from trying out less restrictive assumptions, nor did he himself abstain from doing so. Ricardo heralded an approach in economics that requires a clear statement of the premises from which policy recommendations are derived. What Schumpeter chastised as a vice is nowadays considered a virtue (see Kurz 2008).

It is frequently contended that Ricardo was a staunch advocate of Malthus's "law of population". While Ricardo invoked the "law" in his discussions with Malthus about value and distribution, he did so because then the real wage rate could be taken as a given magnitude, which rendered the explanation of profits in terms of the surplus product a great deal easier. This does not mean that Ricardo endorsed the law. He rather stressed the historical and social dimensions of the natural wage (*Works* I: 96–7) and insisted that "population may be so little stimulated by ample wages as to increase at the slowest rate – or it may even go in a retrograde direction" (*Works* I: 169). "Better education and improved habits" may break the connection between population and necessaries (*Works* II: 115). Workers may get "more liberally rewarded" and thus participate in the sharing out of the surplus product (*Works* I: 48). If this happens to be the case for a longer period of time, a sort of ratchet effect may be observed: the higher real wages become customary and define a new level of "natural" wages. As early as in the *Essay on Profits*, Ricardo stressed that "it is no longer questioned" that improved machinery "has a decided tendency to raise the real wage of labour" (*Works* IV: 35; see also VIII: 171; Jeck and Kurz 1983). More generally, the concept of "natural wages" in Ricardo is defined with reference to the wealth of a society and the growth regime experienced. Ricardo thus felt the need to replace the concept of a given real (that is, commodity) wage rate by a share concept, or "proportional wages" (Sraffa 1951: lii), that is, "the proportion of the annual labour of the country . . . devoted to the support of the labourers" (*Works* I: 49). It was on the basis of this wage concept that he asserted his fundamental proposition on distribution: the rate of profits depends inversely on proportional wages (see Gehrke 2011).

Ricardo's method of analysis
The theory Ricardo sought to elaborate shared with Adam Smith's important features. First, the theory had to be general in the sense that it had to deal with the economic system as a whole and the interlocking of its various parts. Second, it had to come to grips with the capitalist economy's inherent dynamism, a system that is continually changing from within because of capital accumulation, population growth, the scarcity of renewable (land) and exhaustible (mines) resources, and technological change. What are the laws governing the system and, especially, what are the laws governing the distribution of a growing social product among the different strata of society – workers, capitalists and landlords? Third, Smith and Ricardo studied the system in terms of what

is known as the long-period method. It focuses attention on a comparison of situations in which, in the ideal case of free competition, a uniform rate of profits and uniform rates of wages and of rents for each particular quality of labour or of land are obtained. Competitive forces are taken to let "market prices" and the distributive variables gravitate towards (or oscillate around) their "natural" levels. The latter were seen to reflect the persistent and systematic forces at work in the economic system, whereas the former also reflect the impact of temporary and accidental forces. Natural prices, wages and so on are the theoretical magnitudes on whose explanation the classical authors focused attention on the grounds that market prices would commonly not deviate by too much and for too long from their "centres of gravitation", that is, their natural levels (see *Works* I: 92).

In a first step of the analysis Ricardo typically studied the situation of an economy in a given place and time. In a second step he then investigated the path the economy would take according to the "natural course of things". By this he meant the path the system would hypothetically follow, if there were no further technological progress or "improvements". The order according to which lands of different "fertility" will be cultivated upon the first settling of a country, as discussed in his chapter II, "On Rent", reflects well Ricardo's method of counterfactual reasoning: the system expands, but technical knowledge is taken to be frozen. In a third step he then expounded the effects of different types of technical progress on income distribution and economic growth.

The focus of much of Ricardo's analysis is on steps one and two. Setting aside technical progress was motivated by the fact that little can be known today about future technical breakthroughs. What could at most be done was to assess the impact of different well-specified forms of improvements on the economic system. This procedure appears to have misled some commentators to see in Ricardo a technical pessimist, who expected the stationary state to lurk around the corner – which is another myth (see Kurz 2010: 1184, 1195).

Main Themes

These fields will be dealt with in this section: money and currency; value and distribution; capital accumulation, technical progress and economic growth; foreign trade and comparative advantage; and taxation.

Money and currency
Ricardo is typically portrayed as a representative of orthodox monetary views and a strict advocate of a narrow quantity theory of money (see Blaug 1995: 31, who echoes Schumpeter 1954: 703). However, this view does not do justice to Ricardo and ignores the fact that his monetary theory, while characterized by a remarkable continuity, was not something that stood on its own feet. It rather developed in close correspondence with the elaboration of his theory of value. Here we focus on the most advanced views Ricardo put forward on money and currency, that is, those we encounter in the *Principles*.

In his book Ricardo had pointed out the important role of a standard of value, which was to provide a solid basis upon which to assess the causes of changes in the prices of commodities; see his chapter I, "On Value". After some deliberation he decided to take gold to be a standard that performed reasonably well vis-à-vis the requirement of being an "invariable standard of value" in the sense that it was produced across time with roughly always the same amount of labour needed directly and indirectly per ounce. On the one hand, gold was a commodity like any other commodity, and its value was regulated as that of other commodities by the amount of labour expended in its production. On the other hand, gold served as money under the gold standard and as such was not a commodity; see his chapter XXVII, "On Currency and Banks". The "*only use*" of the standard, Ricardo insisted, "is to regulate the quantity, and by the quantity the value of a currency" (*Works* IV: 59; emphasis added). If the state coins money and charges a seignorage for coinage, "the coined piece of money will generally exceed the value of the uncoined piece of metal by the whole seignorage charged" (*Works* I: 353). Hence the value of gold (of a given weight and fineness) and the value of money will differ and the difference will depend on the quantity of money provided. Ricardo was concerned with proposing an ideal monetary system, which he defined in the following way: "A currency is in its most perfect state when it consists wholly of paper money, but of paper money of an equal value with the gold which it professes to represent." (*Works* I: 361). Hence the quantity of paper money in circulation "should be regulated according to the value of the metal which is declared to be the standard" (*Works* I: 354). This does not require that paper money should be payable in specie to secure its value. It suffices that "paper might be increased with every fall in the value of gold, or, which is the same thing in its effects, with every rise in the price of goods" (*Works* I: 354). According to Ricardo the increase in the price level during the suspension of the convertibility of bank notes between 1797 and 1821 was the result of printing too much money and of disregarding the role of the monetary standard.

In Ricardo we encounter the purchasing power theory of exchange rates and the theory of a gold currency including the mechanism that is seen to bring about an equalization of the balance of payments. In the Bullion Controversy, which generated important insights into the functioning of a monetary system without convertibility, Ricardo fought on the side of the "bullionists" who argued in favour of a swift return to the Gold Standard. An increase of the domestic relative to the foreign price level leads via the flow of commodities and capital to a falling external value of the domestic currency and thus prompts a tendency towards the parity of its purchasing power at home and abroad.

For a through treatment of Ricardo's monetary theory, see also Laidler (1975), Marcuzzo and Rosselli (1991), Arnon (2011) and Deleplace in Kurz and Salvadori (2015).

Value and distribution
The theory of value and distribution forms the backbone of all other economic theory in Ricardo. This explains why it was at the centre of debates ever since its inception. Our understanding of Ricardo, and the classical authors more generally, has dramatically improved thanks to the publication of the Royal Economic Society (RES) edition of *The Works and Correspondence of David Ricardo* (Ricardo 1951–73), Piero Sraffa's introductions, especially to volume I of the edition, and the latter's 1960 resumption of and elaboration on the "standpoint of the old classical economists from Adam Smith to Ricardo" (Sraffa 1960: v). (For an account of the difficulties Sraffa met when editing Ricardo's works, see Gehrke and Kurz (2002). On Sraffa's elaboration of his interpretation of the classical theory of value and distribution, see Garegnani (1987), Gehrke and Kurz (2006) and Kurz (2011).)

Market prices and "natural" prices   As regards the assumed gravitation of the market levels of prices and the distributive variables to their "natural" levels, Ricardo closely followed Smith with perhaps a single, but important difference. This concerns the greater emphasis given to the decisions of profit-seeking capitalists and the role of the "moneyed class", that is, financial capitalists, in particular. He stressed that the "restless desire on the part of all the employers of stock, to quit a less profitable for a more advantageous business, has a strong tendency to equalize the rate of profits of all" (*Works* I: 88). He then drew the attention to moneyed men and bankers. These are possessed of "a circulating capital [liquid funds] of a large amount", and since "There is perhaps no manufacturer, however rich, who limits his business to the extent that his own funds alone will allow: he has always some portion of this floating capital, increasing or diminishing according to the activity of the demand for his commodities" (ibid.). This floating capital is said to speed up the process of gravitation and the formation of a uniform rate of profits in competitive conditions (or a given structure of profit rates reflecting different risks and so on).

   The natural price of a commodity covers all necessary costs of production (wages, raw materials, and the wear and tear of fixed capital) plus the normal rate of return on the capital advanced. Costs reflect the "difficulty of production" of the commodity in given circumstances in terms of the inputs (means of subsistence and of production) that of necessity have to be used up in order to obtain the commodity. If the market price exceeds the natural price, typically above-normal profits will be obtained in the industry. Self-seeking behaviour will tend to eliminate the deviation: attracted by the above-normal profitability, capital (and labour) will move into the industry, increase productive capacity and output relative to effectual demand and thus lead to a falling market price, which eliminates above-normal profits; conversely in an industry that initially exhibits below-normal profits.

   In the simple case of single-product industries and thus circulating capital only, and normalizing gross output levels of the different industries as unity, the price equations Ricardo can be said to have aimed at can be written as

$$\mathbf{p} = (1 + r)(\mathbf{M} + \mathbf{S})\mathbf{p} \text{ or } \mathbf{p} = (1 + r)\mathbf{A}\mathbf{p}, \tag{1a}$$

where $\mathbf{p}$ is the n-dimensional price vector $(p_1, p_2, \ldots, p_n)^T$, r is the general rate of profits, $\mathbf{M}$ is the $n \times n$ matrix of material means of production, $\mathbf{S}$ is the matrix of the necessary subsistence of workers and $\mathbf{A} = \mathbf{M} + \mathbf{S}$. On the simplifying assumption of a given and uniform real wage per unit of labour employed in production, defined in terms of the number of units w of an elementary consumption bundle given by vector $\mathbf{c} = (c_1, c_2, \ldots, c_n)$, and denoting the quantities of (direct) labour needed per unit of output in the different industries by $\mathbf{l} = (l_1, l_2, \ldots, l_n)^T$, $\mathbf{S} = w\mathbf{l}\mathbf{c}^T$, we can replace equation (1a) by

$$\mathbf{p} = (1 + r)(\mathbf{M} + w\mathbf{l}\mathbf{c}^T)\mathbf{p} \tag{1b}$$

With $\mathbf{M}$, $\mathbf{l}$ and $\mathbf{c}$ given, and taking a bundle of non-negative quantities of the different commodities $\mathbf{d} = (d_1, d_2, \ldots, d_n)^T$ as the standard of value, that is,

$$\mathbf{d}^T\mathbf{p} = 1, \tag{2}$$

the general rate of profits r and the prices in terms of the standard $\mathbf{d}$ can be ascertained, as Ricardo had maintained (see Sraffa 1960: ch. II, Garegnani 1984; Kurz and Salvadori 1995: ch. 4). No other data or known variables (and especially no demand and supply functions) are needed to determine the unknowns. Hence the contention put forward by Jevons et al. that Ricardo tried to determine two (or several) unknowns from a single equation is false.

The fundamental law of distribution "Profits come out of the surplus produce" (*Works* II: 128). What applies to a particular level of the real wage rate applies to all levels compatible with a non-negative rate of profits. This led Ricardo to his fundamental law of distribution – the inverse relationship between the rate of profits (r) and wages (w), which was arguably one of his most important analytical discoveries. As he put it in a letter to McCulloch of 13 June 1820: "The greater the portion of the result of labour that is given to the labourer, the smaller must be the rate of profits, and vice versa" (*Works* VIII: 194). While the formalization above revolves around the real wage rate and implies $\partial r/\partial w < 0$, the argument applies also to the case with proportional wages.

A quick look at the path along which Ricardo gradually elaborated his remarkable propositions is in order. In his Introduction to the *Principles* in *Works* I, Sraffa interpreted Ricardo's 1815 *Essay on Profits* as being based on the idea that there was a trade or sector in the economy that was "in the special condition of not employing the products of other trades while all the others must employ *its* product as capital" (*Works* I: xxxi; emphasis in the original). The sector under consideration is the growing of corn (wheat), a fact that led Sraffa to speak of the "corn-ratio theory". It allows one to determine the rate of profit in the sector under consideration in purely material terms as the surplus (exclusive of rent) obtained in the sector, a quantity of corn, divided by the capital advanced in the sector, another quantity of corn – without any reference to values. However, the rate of profit so determined is also the general rate of profits since in the case of free competition all other trades or sectors which are supposed to need corn as an input yield the proprietors of capital the *same* rate of profits by an adjustment of the prices of their product relative to that of corn (see also Sraffa 1960: 93). Corn in this interpretation is a "basic" commodity (and actually the only basic in the system), since it is needed directly or indirectly in the production of all commodities (Sraffa 1960: 7), whereas all the other commodities are non-basics. In his Introduction to volume I of the *Works* Sraffa stressed: "The numerical examples in the *Essay* reflect this approach; and particularly in the well-known table which shows the effects of an increase of capital, both capital and the "neat produce" are expressed in corn, and thus the profit per cent is calculated without need to mention price" (*Works* I: xxxii).

Sraffa draws the attention to Malthus's criticism of "the fault of Mr. Ricardo's table", since circulating capital (which includes real wages) typically does not only consist of corn, but includes "tea sugar cloaths &c for the labourers" (ibid.: xxxii, n. 4). Ricardo stuck to his basic vision that the rate of profits could be conceived of in purely physical terms. A deeper analysis was needed than Malthus's shallow proposition that "the profits of the farmer no more regulate the profits of other trades, than the profits of other trades regulate the profits of the farmer" (*Works* VI: 104). This proposition was of no use at all in understanding *how* that regulation was actually meant to work.

In the *Principles* Ricardo suggested rendering heterogeneous commodities commensurate in terms of the amounts of labour bestowed upon them in their production. The labour theory of value was the device by means of which he intended to overcome as best as he could the impasse in which he found himself, lacking a fully consistent and general theory of value. This was clearly seen by him as a makeshift solution, which, he opined, came close to the correct one he was unable to establish. Interestingly, the labour theory of value did not make him entirely abandon his conviction that the question of income distribution could be discussed independently of the theory of value: in all three editions of the *Principles* we encounter a numerical example that satisfies the homogeneity condition of output and capital, but now no longer with regard to a single industry (corn production) only, but with regard to the aggregate of several industries (corn, hats and coats) taken together (see *Works* I: 50, 64–6). Taking into account a multiplicity of wage goods therefore does not spell trouble for the latter's grand vision of the factors affecting the general rate of profits and the possibility of conceiving of it in physical terms. The rate, Ricardo insisted, depends on the conditions of production in all industries that directly or indirectly contribute to the production of wage goods, while it does not depend on the conditions of production of "luxuries". Ricardo's numerical example thus could be said to elevate the corn-ratio theory from its previous single (or compound composite) commodity conceptualization to an explicitly multicommodity conceptualization.

Ricardo was keen to avoid getting entangled in a myriad of complex relationships, whose precise form neither he nor anyone else knew at the time. In a letter to Malthus of 17 April 1815 he spoke of his "simple doctrine", designed to "account for all the phenomena in an easy, natural manner" and thus stay away from "a labyrinth of difficulties" (*Works* VI: 214). Yet Ricardo obstinately insisted, as he wrote in a letter to McCulloch on 13 June 1820, that "After all[,] the great questions of Rent, Wages, and Profits must be explained by the proportions in which the whole produce is divided between landlords, capitalists, and labourers, *and which are not essentially connected with the doctrine of value*" (*Works* VIII: 194; emphasis added). Ricardo was not able to prove the fruitfulness of his remarkable intuition; a proof had to wait until Sraffa (1960: ch. IV).

The measure of value   Intimately related to what has just been said, there is the remarkable fact that much of Ricardo's thoughts and debates with friends, especially Malthus, revolved around the problem of an ideal or "invariable" measure of value. Originally the concept was designed to allow comparisons between one and the same economy at different times and between different economies at the same time, that is, intertemporal and interspatial comparisons. An ideal measure of value, Ricardo stressed, would be a commodity that at all times is produced by the same quantity of labour. If some other commodity rose or fell in value relative to the invariable standard, the cause of this must be found in the changing conditions of production of the former.

After Ricardo had discovered that relative prices do not only depend on relative quantities of labour embodied in the different commodities, but also on income distribution, he had to adapt his concept of invariability. He struggled with the issue until the end of his life; see the draft and manuscript fragment on "Absolute Value and Exchangeable

Value" written in 1823 (*Works* IV) shortly before he passed away. Since the time profiles of the quantities of labour bestowed on the various commodities typically differ from one another and since wage payments are to be discounted forward at the general rate of profits, a change in that rate (and a corresponding contrary change in wages) is bound to affect relative prices. Ricardo's attention therefore focused on the "different circumstances" under which commodities are produced (*Works* IV: 368). The extreme cases would be a commodity produced by direct labour alone, on the one hand, and a commodity produced by means of a large amount of durable capital goods and hardly any direct labour at all, on the other. With a rise in the rate of profits and a corresponding fall in the real wage rate, the latter commodity would become more expensive compared with the former due to compound interest. A commodity, however, which exhibited the "medium between the extremes" (*Works* IV: 373), that is, the medium proportion of direct labour to means of production, would be a measure that is invariant with respect to changes in income distribution, because its profit component would rise by as much as its wage component would fall.

Ricardo's arguments serve the purpose of elaborating a coherent theory of value and distribution. While Ricardo at first thought that he might be able to solve the two requirements of invariance of the measure of value – one concerning production, the other one distribution – in terms of a single commodity, he eventually understood that he was chasing a will-o'-the wisp, because the former referred to an environment with a changing and the latter with a given technology; see on this Kurz and Salvadori (1993). Only the latter problem of invariance can be solved analytically in a cogent way (provided a solution exists), as Sraffa (1960) showed with his construction of the "Standard commodity". The former problem requires the construction of index numbers.

Choice of technique   In agreement with Adam Smith, Ricardo insisted that competitive conditions enforce cost-minimizing behaviour of producers. This means that a method of production will be chosen if it minimizes unit costs, that is, the amount of labour needed directly and indirectly in the production of one unit of the commodity. If new methods of production lead to "improvements" in the different sectors of the economy (agriculture, manufacturing, commerce, and trade) the following effects will result on the assumption that the real wage rate is given and constant. If the improvement concerns an industry that produces wage goods, that is, "necessaries", or industries that directly or indirectly provide inputs for the production of wage goods, the price of the commodity will fall relative to the other commodities and the general rate of profits will rise. In the case of "luxuries" the improvement will lead only to a reduction in price, but leave the general rate of profits unaffected. If, Ricardo stressed,

> by the extension of foreign trade, or by improvements in machinery, the food and necessaries of the labourer can be brought to market at a reduced price, profits will rise [,] . . . but if the commodities obtained at a cheaper rate . . . be exclusively the commodities consumed by the rich, no alteration will take place in the rate of profits. (*Works* I: 132; see also 143)

The role of consumed commodities in Ricardo has been studied by D'Alessandro and Salvadori (2008) and Salvadori and Signorino (forthcoming). As Ricardo stressed: "the labouring class have no small interest in the manner in which the net income of the country is expended" (*Works* I: 392).

The analogy Ricardo drew between improvements and foreign trade explains why he advocated free trade: it will cheapen many commodities, which benefits consumers, and it will frequently imply a rise in the rate of profits, given the real wage rate, which can be expected to speed up capital accumulation and economic growth and, as a consequence, increase wages.

Ricardo insisted that technical progress, by itself, never decreases the rate of profits. Marx tried to disprove him in this regard, but failed (see Kurz 2010). Ricardo may be said to have anticipated what became known as the "Okishio theorem": for a given real wage rate cost-minimizing behaviour implies that new methods of production will be adopted if and only if they raise the general rate of profits or leave it constant (in the case of non-basics) (see also Bortkiewicz 1906–07; Samuelson 1959; Sraffa 1960).

Rent theory   Up until now we have put on one side scarce natural resources such as land, which Ricardo assumed to be possessed of "original and indestructible powers" (*Works* I: 69). In chapter I of the *Principles* he abstracted from them on the ground that his argument applied to no-rent (later called: "marginal") land, on which the level of the rate of profits was decided for any given level of (real or proportional) wages. In chapter II, "On Rent", he then elaborated the principles of extensive and intensive diminishing returns in agriculture, reflecting a growing scarcity of land. While Ricardo was not the first to discover these principles, he deserves credit for having incorporated them into a fairly coherent system of political economy whose main aim was the determination of the general rate of profits.

With extensive diminishing returns, lands of different quality (or location) can be brought into a ranking of natural "fertility" that corresponds to the order according to which the different qualities of land will be cultivated. With low levels of production of corn, only land of the highest fertility (that is, lowest unit cost) will be cultivated and there will be no rent, for essentially the same reason "why nothing is given for the use of air and water, or for any other of the gifts of nature which exist in boundless quantity" (*Works* I: 69). It is only as capital accumulates and population grows that land of second, third and so on quality will have to be cultivated in order to satisfy a growing social demand. As a consequence, the price of corn will rise relative to that of other commodities. The price being determined by costs of production (including profits at the normal rate) on no-rent-bearing land, the owners of intra-marginal lands obtain differential rents reflecting lower unit costs. From this Ricardo concluded against Smith that rent "cannot enter in the least degree as a component part of its price" (*Works* I: 77). Rent was not an expression of the generosity of nature, as Smith had argued echoing the Physiocratic doctrine, but of its "niggardliness": it was not the cause, but the effect of a high price of corn.

With intensive diminishing returns, the amount of labour and other inputs will be increased per acre of a given quality of land; it will result in an increase in output per acre, though at a diminishing rate. (The case of intensive diminishing returns was later generalized by marginalist authors indiscriminately to all factors of production and all industries alike. In this way all prices and distributive variables were taken to be subject to a single principle only: that of universal scarcity or marginal productivity. However, as Knut Wicksell already understood, this generalization meets with considerable difficulties; see Kurz and Salvadori 1995: ch. 14; Kurz 2000).

Ricardo dealt also with exhaustible natural resources, such as coal or metals, especially in chapter XXIV of the *Principles*, "Doctrine of Adam Smith Concerning the Rent of Land". He criticized Smith for confounding profits and rents, which ought to be carefully distinguished, because in the course of the development of a country, and setting aside technical progress, they typically move in opposite directions. Ricardo was, of course, aware of the principal exhaustibility of certain resources, but did not think that the problem was imminent: first, because "new and more productive mines may be discovered"; second, because "Improvements may be made in the implements and machinery used in mining, which may considerably abridge labour"; and third, because "the facilities of bringing [the resource] to the market may be increased" (*Works* I: 86). While these factors tend to reduce the value of the metal, "the increasing difficulty of obtaining [it], occasioned by the greater depth at which the mine must be worked [and so on]" (ibid.), tend to increase it.

All things considered, Ricardo felt entitled to approach the problem of exhaustible resources in terms of his theory of differential rent. Since there will generally be deposits of different fertility, the working of each of which is subject to a capacity constraint that limits the amount of the resource that can be extracted per unit of time, effectual demand will typically be met by working several deposits simultaneously. As in the theory of the rent of land, there will be a marginal, no-rent, deposit worked together with several intra-marginal deposits that will yield their proprietors differential rents, which are higher the lower the costs of extraction are of one unit of the resource. (For a comparison of Ricardo's approach with the Hotelling model, see Kurz and Salvadori (2009, 2011). The Hotelling rule maintains that in competitive conditions the preservation of a resource must yield its proprietor the same general rate of profits as is obtained in production and trade, which implies that the price of the resource *in situ*, which is capital to the proprie-tor, will have to rise with that rate. Empirically, the Hotelling rule does not perform well and precisely for the reasons given by Ricardo.)

Capital accumulation, technical progress and economic growth

Say's law   Ricardo advocated what is known as Say's law, but it is important to see precisely what he meant by it. He stated that there cannot "be accumulated in a country any amount of capital which cannot be employed productively, until wages rise so high in consequence of the rise [of the prices] of necessaries, and so little consequently remains for the profits of stock, that the motive for accumulation ceases" (*Works* I: 290; see also Gehrke and Kurz 2001). In this regard Ricardo followed Adam Smith who had insisted that any act of savings will swiftly lead to an act of investment of the same magnitude, so that there cannot be a lack of aggregate effective demand and a corresponding "general glut" of commodities that would depress profits, as Malthus had contended. There may be disequilibria in single markets, "but this cannot be the case with respect to all com-modities" (*Works* I: 291).

Say's law in this conceptualization applies only to commodities whose production is motivated by the aim of making profits, but does not apply to labour as in later theory, beginning with the wage fund doctrine and leading up to the marginalist concept of the labour market. It thus does not imply any tendency towards the full employment of labour. This becomes very clear in the famous chapter "On Machinery", added to the third edition of the *Principles* (1821), in which Ricardo discussed a form of technical progress that is detrimental to the labouring class, because it is accompanied by lasting unemployment. The latter can only be removed, if due to an increase in profitability capital accumulation accelerates and increases the "demand for hands".

A falling tendency of the rate of profits　Setting aside improvements in agriculture and elsewhere in the system and assuming a given and constant real wage rate, an extension of the cultivation of land, while increasing the surplus product, involves an ever larger part of it being appropriated as differential rent and an ever smaller one as profits. The landed gentry benefits from economic growth to the detriment of the capitalist class. Ricardo emphasized that the "natural tendency" of the rate of profits therefore is to fall (*Works* I: 120). This fall is neither due to an intensified "competition of capitals", as Smith had contended, nor to an increase in the real wage rate. It is rather due to diminishing returns in agriculture (and mining). This does not mean that Ricardo was a technological pessimist; he in fact saw improvements in all sectors of the economy as thwarting time and again this "natural tendency". This brings us to Ricardo's view of the technological dynamism of modern society.

Different types of technical progress　Ricardo was clear that technical change was an essential part of the development of modern society and that different types of it have to be distinguished because they typically have different effects (see also Schefold 1976). He saw the historical course of an economy as largely shaped by two opposing forces: the "niggardliness of nature", on the one hand, and man's ingenuity and creativity reflected in new methods of production and new commodities, on the other. Ricardo also saw clearly that new technical knowledge may at first not be adopted, because it would not be profitable to do so, but may be adopted at a later time as a consequence of the economic environment having changed from within: this is the case of what later was called "induced technical change".

　Already in *The Essay on Profits* of 1815 Ricardo wrote: "we are yet at a great distance from the end of our resources, and . . . we may contemplate an increase of prosperity and wealth, far exceeding that of any country which has preceded us" (*Works* IV: 34). In a letter to Hutches Trower on 5 February 1816 he concluded from a fall in grain prices since 1812 that "we are happily yet in the progressive state, and may look forward with confidence to a long course of prosperity" (*Works* VII: 17). Also, in his entry on the "Funding System", published in September 1820, he stressed with regard to England that "it is difficult to say where the limit is at which you would cease to accumulate wealth and to derive profit from its employment" (*Works* IV: 179). The widespread view (see, for example, Rostow 1990: 34, 87; and more recently Blaug 2009; Solow 2010) that Ricardo saw the stationary state lurking around the corner cannot be sustained. It seems to mistake Ricardo's method of counterfactual reasoning for factual statements about economic development.

　Ricardo studied various types of technical progress and their effects. In chapter II of the *Principles* the focus is on land and capital alias labour-saving forms of improvements in agriculture (see Gehrke et al. 2003). In the machinery chapter the emphasis is on improvements in the production of necessaries (see Eltis 1984; Kurz 2010). While Smith had seen the manufacturing sector as essentially producing only luxuries, Ricardo can be said to have glimpsed its key role in economic development. He even contemplated the limiting case of a fully automated system of production and observed: "If machinery could do all the work that labour now does, there would be no demand for labour. Nobody would be entitled to consume any thing who was not a capitalist, and who could not buy or hire a machine" (*Works* VIII: 399–400).

Technical progress, Ricardo was clear, was not an unambiguous blessing for all members of society. The system, he now maintained, may experience prolonged periods of what later was called "technological unemployment". In short, maximizing profits and maximizing employment levels are different things, contrary to what Ricardo had thought before the third edition of his magnum opus. He explained:

> My mistake arose from the supposition, that whenever the net income [profits] of a society increases, its gross income [net income plus wages, which equal a year's labour] would also increase; I now, however, see reason to be satisfied that the one fund, from which . . . capitalists derive their revenue, may increase, while the other, that upon which the labouring class mainly depend, may diminish, and therefore it follows . . . that the same cause which may increase the net revenue of the country, may at the same time render the population redundant, and deteriorate the condition of the labourer. (*Works* I: 388)

In the chapter "On Machinery" Ricardo constructed an example that was designed to illustrate precisely this possibility. Since the progressive replacement of labour by fixed capital is a characteristic feature of modern economic development, the case under consideration is of great relevance. Marx translated Ricardo's particular case into a rising "organic composition" of capital – the ratio between dead labour incorporated in capital goods and living labour actually performed – and interpreted it as *the* form of technical progress induced by the capitalist mode of production (see Kurz 1998: 119). The labour displacing effect is taken to give rise to an "industrial reserve army of the unemployed". Marx contended that this particular form of technical progress is also responsible for a falling tendency of the general rate of profits, because by increasing the organic composition it decreases the maximum rate of profits. However, Marx's reasoning cannot be sustained.

As regards induced innovations, Ricardo pointed out that "Machinery and labour are in constant competition and the former can frequently not be employed until labour rises" (*Works* I: 395). According to the natural course of things, necessaries (in particular corn) tend to become more expensive and, for a given real wage rate, money wages tend to rise. However, "The same cause that raises labour [money wages], does not raise the value of machines [which are produced under constant or even increasing returns], and, therefore with every augmentation of capital, a greater portion of it is employed in machinery" (*Works* I: 395). An endogenous change in relative prices and the money wage rate may eventually induce the adoption of an invention, which at first had fallen flat to the ground.

Foreign trade and comparative advantage

Like Adam Smith before him, Ricardo advocated free trade (setting aside a number of exceptions), but found the Scotsman's advocacy of it wanting. In the tensely written chapter VII, "On Foreign Trade", all major threads of which the fabric of Ricardo's theory is made meet and are being discussed in a quick succession on just a few pages.

Table 1   Number of men whose labour is required for one year in order to produce a given quantity of cloth and wine

	Cloth	Wine
In Portugal	90	80
In England	100	120

This fact is partly responsible for the frequent misapprehension of Ricardo's argument and its distortion beyond recognition in textbook presentations. (The misapprehension started with James and John Stuart Mill; see Sraffa, 1930, who corrected their error.) It was only recently that new attempts were made to come to grips with Ricardo's argument; see the entries by Faccarello, Maneschi and Parrinello in Kurz and Salvadori (2015); see also Faccarello (2015), Gehrke (2015) and Kurz (2015: s. 8). Here only the gist of Ricardo's argument can be given.

Assume with Ricardo in terms of his famous numerical example here reproduced in Table 1 – his "four magic numbers" (Samuelson 1969) – that all commodities can be produced at lower labour costs abroad, in Portugal, than at home, in England. Does this mean that there are no opportunities for mutually beneficial trade? Ricardo's answer is a resounding no: it would be advantageous for England to export cloth in exchange for wine imported from Portugal, and for Portugal to export wine in exchange for cloth from England. Under these circumstances "England would give the produce of the labour of 100 men, for the produce of the labour of 80" (*Works* I: 135).

A stockjobber, versed in seeking out arbitrage opportunities, Ricardo could easily see the profitable business to merchants in view of the fact that the price of cloth relative to wine differs in the two countries. Assume now that the numbers represent domestic currencies, Real (R) in Portugal and Pounds (£) in England, that are non-convertible. Take the case of an English merchant. He may buy for £100 a given quantity of cloth at home, ship it to Portugal and sell it there for 90 R. With this sum of money he may then buy wine from a Portuguese wine grower and get altogether $90/80 = 9/8$ units of wine, where one unit costs 80 R. This quantity of wine he then ships to England and sells it for $9/8 \cdot £120 = £135$. He thus obtains a profit of £135 − £100 = £35 or a rate of profit of 35 per cent on an investment of £100 over the time it took to export cloth and import wine. An analogous consideration applies to a Portuguese merchant. Both the English and the Portuguese merchant can use one and the same ship to export and to import goods. The remarkable fact here is that while goods are exported and imported, the currencies of the two countries do not cross borders. As Ricardo stressed with regard to a different case: "without the necessity of money passing from either country, the exporters in each country will be paid for their goods" (*Works* I: 138).

We may now look at the problem also from the perspective of another monetary regime. Assume specie (gold coins) to be the universal means of exchange and unit of account. The total amount of gold (a producible commodity) in the system (comprising the two countries) is given and fixed. The four numbers now refer to the gold prices of given quantities of cloth and wine in autarky in Portugal and England. Both commodities are more expensive in England, which again implies profitable business for merchants: goods will be shipped from the country in which they are cheaper (Portugal) to the country in which they are dearer (England). Ships would leave Portugal fully laden, but return to her empty. English producers are bound to stop producing both commodities and Portuguese producers would like to expand production and meet effectual demands in both countries.

Portugal would experience a trade surplus and England a trade deficit. This would imply a flow of specie from England to Portugal. The quantity of money in Portugal (England) would increase (decrease) and money prices rise (fall). Foreign trade would thus affect prices and the value of money in the two countries.

This, however, brings about "such a state of prices as would make it no longer profitable to continue these transactions" (*Works* I: 139). This is indeed the case, as the following consideration shows. Assume for simplicity that prices in each country increase or decrease proportionately, leaving relative (domestic) prices unaffected. Then it is clear that a point will come when English cloth will become less expensive than Portuguese cloth, while English wine will still be substantially more expensive than Portuguese wine. At that point the direction of the cloth trade would be redirected from England to Portugal. A new distribution of the precious metals, Ricardo emphasized, "would in some degree have changed [the value of money] in the two countries, it would be lowered in [Portugal] and raised in [England]. Estimated in money, the whole revenue of [England] would be diminished; estimated in the same medium, the whole revenue of [Portugal] would be increased." (*Works* I: 141)

These considerations show that Portugal's (England's) original absolute advantages (disadvantages) in the production of both commodities will not prevail: the specie-flow mechanism will undermine the initial situation and lead to a new pattern of specialization. The important point to note is this. *The direction of change in absolute cost advantages will bring to the fore the principle of comparative advantage*: as prices rise in Portugal and fall in England, the point will come where English cloth becomes less expensive than Portuguese cloth, while English wine is still more expensive than Portuguese wine. Portugal will thus end up having both a comparative and absolute advantage in the production of wine and England a comparative advantage in the production of cloth, which is reflected in an absolute one in price terms.

What applies to the specialization among countries (or regions within countries) applies also to that among people. The glad tidings of joy of Ricardo's theorem of comparative advantage read: if a person happens to be inferior to some other person in each and every respect, he or she may nevertheless enter a mutually advantageous division of labour with his or her counterpart. Ricardo thus adds an important verse to Adam Smith's hymn on the beneficial effects of the division of labour.

Malthus challenged Ricardo's stance in favour of free trade by emphasizing a conflict with national security. Against this Ricardo insisted that restrictions on corn export are not sustainable, especially if trade expectations have induced large investments in agriculture; see Salvadori and Signorino (2015).

Taxation

In the *Principles* a substantial space, organized in ten chapters, and a great deal of attention is devoted to taxation and especially the problem of tax incidence and the impact of taxes on the pace of capital accumulation and economic growth. Ricardo insisted that "There are no taxes which have not a tendency to lessen the power to accumulate.

All taxes must either fall on capital or revenue" (*Works* I: 152). However, he added, the burden of a tax is not necessarily borne by whoever pays it (*Works* I: 152). This insight is then illustrated in a number of cases involving both direct and indirect taxes. For example, on the premise that workers are paid a subsistence wage a tax on wages could not be borne by workers: nominal wages would rise leaving real wages constant and the tax would accordingly be shifted to capitalists. A similar reasoning applies to the case in which a tax is laid on wage goods or "necessaries". The price of the wage goods and as a consequence the nominal wage would increase. Taxes on "luxuries" on the contrary "fall on those only who make use of them" (*Works* I: 205).

In full accordance with his doctrine that rent does not enter the price of commodities Ricardo insisted that "A tax on rent would affect rent only; it would fall wholly on landlords, and could not be shifted to any class of consumers" (*Works* I: 173). A tax on profits would increase the prices of the products: "if a tax in proportion to profits were laid on all trades, every commodity would be raised in price" (*Works* I: 205). Depending on the consumption patterns of the different classes of society this would affect their respective members differently. A rise in the price of wage goods would again entail a corresponding adjustment of nominal wages: "Whatever raises the wages of labour, lowers the profits of stock; therefore every tax on any commodity consumed by the labourer, has a tendency to lower the rate of profits" (*Works* I: 205), and, as a consequence, the rate of capital accumulation.

Ricardo's treatment of taxes, while containing numerous interesting ideas and suggestions, is generally not considered the strongest part of his book and is said to suffer from a bad arrangement of the material and an argument that is frequently tied to excessively restrictive assumptions. For more complete treatments of the subject, see Shoup (1960), O'Brien (2004) and Dome (2004).

Reception and Impact

According to Keynes (*CW* VII: 32), "Ricardo conquered England as completely as the Holy Inquisition conquered Spain. Not only was his theory accepted by the city, by statesmen and by the academic world. But controversy ceased" – meaning that Malthus' alternative theory of effective demand ceased to be discussed. This contention cannot be sustained. Soon after Ricardo's death his influence in England began to dwindle (Blaug 1958). With the advent of the "marginal" method, Ricardo's different surplus-based approach to the problem of value and distribution actually began to meet with serious problems of understanding as can be seen by the misapprehension of his theory by major marginalist economists. What can be said, however, is that there are few economists who had a comparable impact on the development of political economy. For a study of the reception of Ricardo's doctrine in continental Europe and Japan, see Faccarello and Izumo (2014).

About Ricardo opinions differed sharply across time and space. Besides glowing admirers we encounter ardent critics. To Karl Marx (1968: 166) Ricardo was the last great representative of classical political economy, who is to be credited with having laid the "basis, the starting-point for the physiology of the bourgeois system – for the understanding of its internal organic coherence and life process". William Stanley Jevons (1871 [1965]: xlvi and li) called Ricardo an "able but wrongheaded man [who] shunted the car of economic science on to a wrong line" and based his analysis on "mazy and preposterous assumptions". Léon Walras ([1874] 1954) praised Ricardo's theory of rent, but criticized the fact that the underlying principle of scarcity had not been generalized from land to all factors of production, including labour and capital. He also completely failed to grasp the different analytical structure of Ricardo's theory (see Kurz and Salvadori 2002). Alfred Marshall (1890 [1977]: 629, 416–17) praised Ricardo's "strong constructive originality [which] is the mark of the highest genius in all nations" and insisted "that the foundations of the theory [of value] as they were left by Ricardo remain intact", boldly re-interpreting Ricardo in terms of his own demand and supply approach. Among the marginalist writers Knut Wicksell was perhaps the one who understood best Ricardo's surplus approach to an explanation of profits and observed: "Since, according to Ricardo, wages represent a magnitude fixed from the beginning, . . . [i]t is neither possible nor necessary to explain capital profit in other ways" (Wicksell 1893 [1954]: 36–7). He added that "Ricardo's theory of value is . . . developed with a high degree of consistency and strictness" (ibid.: 40). The Austrian economists, especially Eugen von Böhm-Bawerk, objected that not cost of production but utility – more precisely: marginal utility – is the principle that regulates value. In equilibrium, however, Böhm-Bawerk insisted, relative prices are strictly proportional to relative labour costs – a result he could only reach by reckoning with simple interest, when, as Ricardo was clear, compound interest was strictly necessary.

Ricardo is considered a founder of a rigorous analytics in economics. Shortly after Ricardo's death we see attempts to formalize his theory. The first authors in this regard were William Whewell and John Edward Tozer, later followed Vladimir K. Dmitriev (1904 [1974]) and Ladislaus von Bortkiewicz (1906–07) and in more recent times Paul Samuelson (1959), Luigi Pasinetti (1960) and Michio Morishima (1989; see also Kurz and Salvadori 1992). See also Kaldor (1956.)

The most important reconsideration, reformulation and revival of the classical and especially Ricardian intellectual heritage we owe to Piero Sraffa. His edition (with the collaboration of Maurice H. Dobb) of *The Works and Correspondence of David Ricardo* (1951–73) triggered a thorough re-engagement with the doctrines of Ricardo and the classical economists. Sraffa's introduction to volume I and his 1960 book clarified the specific logical structure of the classical theory of value and distribution and demonstrated that it was fundamentally different from the later marginalist (or "neoclassical") theory. He also showed that the theory can be formulated in a consistent way and does not stand or fall with the labour theory of value. Starting from his new interpretation and formalization of the classical theory of value and distribution, several authors have developed it in various directions; for an overview, see, for example, Kurz and Salvadori (1995).

Sraffa's Ricardo edition was widely considered an editorial masterpiece and earned him in 1961 the golden Söderström medal of the Royal Swedish Academy of Sciences. Sraffa's surplus-based interpretation of the classical theory of value and distribution at first met with almost unanimous approval. Only when it gradually transpired, especially after the publication of his 1960 book, that it implied a radical break with the Whig history of economics according to which there was continuous progress of the subject from its early beginnings to its modern pronouncements, that opposition arose. John Hicks, Paul Samuelson (1978) and particularly Samuel Hollander (1979) tried to counter Sraffa's new view and interpreted Ricardo again essentially in the received Marshallian mould as an advocate of demand and supply theory with the demand side still in its infancy. The revisionist point of view was criticized, among others, by Krishna Bharadwaj, John Eatwell, Alessandro Roncaglia, Giancarlo de Vivo and particularly Pierangelo Garegnani (2007). Mark Blaug variously attacked what he called the "Sraffians", but in a controversy with Garegnani, Kurz and Salvadori eventually opined that the difference between his interpretation and theirs was only "a question of emphasis" (Blaug 2009: 232). Terry Peach (1993) attacked Hollander's view from a non-Sraffian angle, but was also critical of certain elements of Sraffa's interpretation. For a critical account of the debates, see King (2013: chs 7, 8) and Mongiovi in Kurz and Salvadori (2015).

Remarkably, even nowadays Ricardo's work is still capable of stirring debates about the foundations of economics to which leading representatives of the subject contribute. Could there be some better evidence on behalf of the lasting importance of his contribution? Maria Edgeworth, a writer and friend of the Ricardos, deserves the final word about the most classical of all classical authors:

> I never argued or discussed a question with any person who argues more fairly or less for victory and more for truth. He gives full weight to every argument brought against him, and seems not to be on any side of the question for one instant longer than the conviction of his mind on that side. It seems quite indifferent to him whether you find the truth, or whether he finds it, provided it be found (*Works* X: 168–9).

Heinz D. Kurz

See also:

British classical political economy (II); Bullionist and anti-bullionist schools (II); Growth (III); International trade (III; Thomas Robert Malthus (I); Karl Heinrich Marx (I); Money and banking (III); Paul Anthony Samuelson (I); Adam Smith (I); Piero Sraffa (I).

References and further reading

On each and every theme dealt with in this entry, see also the corresponding entries in *The Elgar Companion to David Ricardo* (Kurz and Salvadori 2015), in *The Elgar Companion to Classical Economics* (Kurz and Salvadori 1998) and in King (2013). A detailed bibliography of contributions on Ricardo can also be found in King (2013).

Arnon, A. (2011), *Monetary Theory and Policy from Hume and Smith to Wicksell: Money, Credit, and the Economy*. Cambridge: Cambridge University Press.
Blaug, M. (1958), *Ricardian Economics. A Historical Study*, New Haven, CT: Yale University Press.
Blaug, M. (1995), 'Why is the quantity theory of money the oldest surviving theory of economics?', in M. Blaug, W. Eltis, D. O'Brien, R. Skidelsky and D. Patinkin (eds), *The Quantity Theory of Money. From Locke to Keynes and Friedman*, Aldershot, UK and Brookfield, VT, USA: Edward Elgar, pp. 27–49.
Blaug, M. (1997), *Economic Theory in Retrospect*, 5th edn, Cambridge: Cambridge University Press.
Blaug, M. (2009), 'The trade-off between rigor and relevance: Sraffian economics as a case in point', *History of Political Economy*, **41** (2), 219–47.
Bonar, J. (1923), 'Ricardo's ingot plan: a centenary tribute'. *Economic Journal*, **33** (131), 281–304.
Bortkiewicz, L. von (1906–07), 'Wertrechnung und Preisrechnung im Marxschen System', three parts, *Archiv für Sozialwissenschaft und Sozialpolitik*, **23**, 1–50; **25**, 10–51, 445–88; English trans. of parts 2 and 3 in 1952, 'Value and price in the Marxian system', *International Economic Papers*, **2**, 5–60.
D'Alessandro, S. and N. Salvadori (2008), 'Pasinetti *versus* Rebelo: two different models or just one?', *Journal of Economic Behavior & Organization*, **65** (3–4), 547–54.
Davis, T. (2005), *Ricardo's Macroeconomics: Money, Trade Cycles and Growth*, Cambridge: Cambridge University Press.
De Vivo, G. (1987), 'Ricardo, David, 1772–1823', in J. Eatwell, M. Milgate and P. Newman (eds), *The New Palgrave: A Dictionary of Economics*, vol. 4, London: Macmillan, pp. 183–98.

Dmitriev, V.K. (1904), *Economic Essays on Value, Competition and Utility*, originally published in Russian, English trans. M.D. Nuti (ed.) (1974), Cambridge: Cambridge University Press.

Dome, T. (2004), *The Political Economy of Public Finance in Britain 1767–1873*, London and New York: Routledge.

Eltis, W. (1984), *The Classical Theory of Economic Growth*. London: Macmillan.

Faccarello, G. (2015), 'A calm investigation into Mr Ricardo's principles of international trade', *European Journal of the History of Economic Thought*, **22** (5), 754–90.

Faccarello, G. and M. Izumo (eds) (2014), *The Reception of David Ricardo in Continental Europe and Japan*, London and New York: Routledge.

Findlay, R. (1987), 'Comparative advantage', in J. Eatwell, M. Milgate and P. Newman (eds), *The New Palgrave: A Dictionary of Economics*, vol. 1, London: Macmillan, pp. 514–17.

Garegnani, P. (1984), 'Value and distribution in the classical economists and Marx', *Oxford Economic Papers*, **36** (2), 291–325.

Garegnani, P. (1987), 'Surplus approach to value and distribution', in J. Eatwell, M. Milgate and P. Newman (eds), *The New Palgrave: A Dictionary of Economics*, vol. 4, London: Macmillan, pp. 560–74.

Garegnani, P. (2007), 'Professor Samuelson on Sraffa and the classical economists', *European Journal of the History of Economic Thought*, **14** (2), 181–242.

Gehrke, C. (2011), 'Price of wages: a curious phrase', in R. Ciccone, C. Gehrke and G. Mongiovi (eds), *Sraffa and Modern Economics*, vol. 1, London: Routledge, pp. 405–22.

Gehrke, C. (2015), 'Ricardo's discovery of comparative advantage revisited: a critique of Ruffin's account'. *European Journal of the History of Economic Thought*, **22** (5), 791–817.

Gehrke, C. and H.D. Kurz (2001), 'Say and Ricardo on value and distribution', *European Journal of the History of Economic Thought*, **8** (4), 449–86.

Gehrke, C. and H.D. Kurz (2002), 'Keynes's and Sraffa's "difficulties with J.H. Hollander": a note on the history of the RES edition of the works and correspondence of David Ricardo', *European Journal of the History of Economic Thought*, **9** (4), 449–86.

Gehrke, C. and H.D. Kurz (2006), 'Sraffa on von Bortkiewicz: reconstructing the classical theory of value and distribution', *History of Political Economy*, **38** (1), 91–149.

Gehrke, C., H.D. Kurz and N. Salvadori (2003), 'Ricardo on agricultural improvements: a note', *Scottish Journal of Political Economy*, **50** (3), 291–6.

Henderson, J.P. and J.B. Davis (1997), *The Life and Economics of David Ricardo*, Boston, MA: Kluwer.

Hollander, S. (1979), *The Economics of David Ricardo*. Toronto: University of Toronto Press.

Jeck, A. and H.D. Kurz (1983), 'David Ricardo: Ansichten zur Maschinerie', in H. Hagemann and P. Kalmbach (eds), *Technischer Fortschritt und Arbeitslosigkeit*, Frankfurt am Main: Campus, pp. 38–166.

Jevons, W.S. (1871), *The Theory of Political Economy*, London: Macmillan, reprinted in 1965, New York: Kelley.

Kaldor, N. (1956), 'Alternative theories of distribution', *Review of Economic Studies*, **23** (2), 83–100.

Keynes, J.M. (1972), *Essays in Biography*, in A. Robinson and D. Moggridge (eds), *The Collected Writings of John Maynard Keynes*, vol. X, London: Macmillan, pp. 71–103.

Keynes, J.M. (1973), *The General Theory of Employment, Interest and Money*, in A. Robinson and D. Moggridge (eds), *The Collected Writings of John Maynard Keynes*, vol. VII, London: Macmillan.

King, J.E. (2013), *David Ricardo*, Basingstoke: Palgrave Macmillan.

Kurz, H.D. (1998), 'Marx on technological change: the Ricardian heritage', in R. Bellofiore (ed.), *Marxian Economics. A Reappraisal*, vol. 2, Basingstoke: Macmillan, pp. 119–38.

Kurz, H.D. (2000), 'Wicksell and the problem of the "missing" equation', *History of Political Economy*, **32** (4), 765–88.

Kurz, H.D. (2008), 'Ricardian vice', in W.A. Darity (ed.), *International Encyclopedia of the Social Sciences*, vol. 7, 2nd edn, Detroit, MI: Macmillan Reference, pp. 243–7.

Kurz, H.D. (2010), 'Technical progress, capital accumulation and income distribution in classical economics: Adam Smith, David Ricardo and Karl Marx', *European Journal of the History of Economic Thought*, **17** (5), 1183–222.

Kurz, H.D. (2011), 'On David Ricardo's theory of profits. The laws of distribution are "not essentially connected with the doctrine of value"', *The History of Economic Thought*, **53** (1), 1–20.

Kurz, H.D. (2015), 'David Ricardo: on the art of "elucidating economic principles" in the face of a "labyrinth of difficulties"', *European Journal of the History of Economic Thought*, **22** (5), 818–51.

Kurz, H.D. and N. Salvadori (1992), 'Morishima on Ricardo', *Cambridge Journal of Economics*, **16** (2), 227–47.

Kurz, H.D. and N. Salvadori (1993), 'The "Standard commodity" and Ricardo's search for an "invariable measure of value"', in M. Baranzini and G.C. Harcourt (eds), *The Dynamics of the Wealth of Nations:*

Growth, Distribution, and Structural Change: Essays in Honour of Luigi Pasinetti, New York: St. Martin's Press, pp. 95–123.

Kurz, H.D. and N. Salvadori (1995), *Theory of Production: A Long-Period Analysis*, Cambridge: Cambridge University Press.

Kurz, H.D. and N. Salvadori (eds) (1998), *The Elgar Companion to Classical Economics*, 2 vols, Cheltenham, UK and Northampton, MA, USA: Edward Elgar.

Kurz, H.D. and N. Salvadori (2002), 'One theory or two? Walras's critique of Ricardo', *History of Political Economy*, **34** (2), 365–98.

Kurz, H.D. and N. Salvadori (2009), 'Ricardo on exhaustible resources and the Hotelling rule', in A. Ikeo and H.D. Kurz (eds), *The History of Economic Theory. Festschrift in Honour of Takashi Negishi*, London: Routledge, pp. 68–79.

Kurz, H.D. and N. Salvadori (2011), 'Exhaustible resources: rents, profits, royalties and prices', in V. Caspari (ed.), *The Evolution of Economic Theory. Essays in Honour of Bertram Schefold*, London: Routledge, pp. 39–52.

Kurz, H.D. and N. Salvadori (eds) (2015), *The Elgar Companion to David Ricardo*, Cheltenham, UK and Northampton, MA, USA: Edward Elgar.

Laidler, D. (1975), *Essays on Money and Inflation*. Manchester: Manchester University Press.

Malthus, T.R. (1820), *Principles of Political Economy Considered with a View to Their Practical Application*, London: John Murray, reprinted in D. Ricardo (1951–73), *The Works and Correspondence of David Ricardo*, ed. P. Sraffa with M.H. Dobb, vol. 2, Cambridge: Cambridge University Press.

Marcuzzo, M.C. and A. Rosselli (1991), *Ricardo and the Gold Standard. The Foundations of the International Monetary Order*, London: Macmillan.

Marshall, A. (1890), *Principles of Economics*, reprinted 1977, London: Macmillan.

Marx, K. (1968), *Theories of Surplus Value*, pt II, Moscow: Progress.

Milgate, M. and S. Stimson (1991), *Ricardian Politics*, Princeton, NJ: Princeton University Press.

Morgan, M. (2012), *The World in the Model. How Economists Work and Think*, Cambridge: Cambridge University Press.

Morishima, M. (1989), *Ricardo's Economics: A General Equilibrium Theory of Distribution and Growth*, Cambridge: Cambridge University Press.

O'Brien, D. (1975), *The Classical Economists*, Oxford: Oxford University Press.

Pasinetti, L.L. (1960), 'A mathematical formulation of the Ricardian system', *Review of Economic Studies*, **27** (2), 78–98.

Peach, T. (1993), *Interpreting Ricardo*, Cambridge: Cambridge University Press.

Ricardo, D. (1951–73), *The Works and Correspondence of David Ricardo*, ed. P. Sraffa with the collaboration of M.H. Dobb, 11 vols, Cambridge: Cambridge University Press.

Rostow, W.W. (1990), *Theories of Economic Growth from David Hume to the Present*, New York: Oxford University Press.

Salvadori, N. and R. Signorino (2015), 'Defense versus opulence? An appraisal of the Malthus–Ricardo 1815 controversy on the corn laws', *History of Political Economy*, **47** (1), 151–84.

Salvadori, N. and R. Signorino (forthcoming), 'From stationary state to endogenous growth: international trade in the mathematical formulation of the Ricardian system', *Cambridge Journal of Economics*, **73** (1 and 2), first published online 1 April 2015, doi: 10.1093/cje/bev018.

Samuelson, P.A. (1959), 'A modern treatment of the Ricardian economy: I. The pricing of goods and of labor and land services; II. Capital and interest aspects of the pricing process', *Quarterly Journal of Economics*, **73**, 1–35, 217–31.

Samuelson, P.A. (1969), 'The way of an economist', in P. Samuelson (ed.), *International Economic Relations. Proceedings of the Third Congress of the International Economic Association*, London: Macmillan, pp. 1–11.

Samuelson, P.A. (1978), 'The canonical model of classical political economy', *Journal of Economic Literature*, **16** (4), 1415–34.

Schefold, B. (1976), 'Different forms of technical progress', *Economic Journal*, **86**, 806–19.

Schumpeter, J.A. (1954), *History of Economic Analysis*, New York: Oxford University Press.

Shoup, C.S. (1960), *Ricardo on Taxation*, New York: Columbia University Press.

Smith, A. (1776), *An Inquiry into the Nature and Causes of the Wealth of Nations*, 2 vols, reprinted in R.H. Campbell and A.S. Skinner (eds) (1996), *The Glasgow Edition of the Works and Correspondence of Adam Smith*, Oxford: Oxford University Press.

Solow, R.M. (2010), 'Stories about economics and technology', *European Journal of the History of Economic Thought*, **17** (5), 1113–26.

Sraffa, P. (1930), 'An alleged correction of Ricardo', *Quarterly Journal of Economics*, **44** (3), 539–44.

Sraffa, P. (1951), 'Introduction', in D. Ricardo, *The Works and Correspondence of David Ricardo*, ed. P. Sraffa with M.H. Dobb, vol. 1, Cambridge: Cambridge University Press, pp. xiii–lxii.

Sraffa, P. (1960), *Production of Commodities by Means of Commodities: Prelude to a Critique of Economic Theory*, Cambridge: Cambridge University Press.

Walras, L. (1874), *Elements of Pure Economics*, English trans. by W. Jaffé (1954), London: Allen & Unwin.

Weatherall, D. (1976), *David Ricardo: A Biography*, The Hague: Martinus Nijhoff.

Wicksell, K. (1893), *Über Wert, Kapital und Rente nach den neueren nationalökonomischen Theorien*, Jena: G. Fischer, original in German, English trans. 1954, *Value, Capital, and Rent*, London: George Allen & Unwin.

Jean-Charles Léonard Simonde de Sismondi (1773–1842)

Jean-Charles Léonard Sismondi was born in Geneva (1773) into an upper-class Calvinist family. Like many Swiss intellectuals, Sismondi was forced to emigrate, first to England during the Swiss revolutionary episode (1792–94), and then to Italy (Tuscany) in the last years of the eighteenth century, before eventually returning to his native Geneva in 1800. He continued to visit Italy regularly where he collected material relevant for the composition of his *History of Italian Republics* (1808–17). He also claimed to find in Italy the so-called origin of his family, the Sismondi of Pisa, and, subsequent to this discovery, changed his name from "Simonde" to "Simonde de Sismondi". His own personal experience of an era saddled between revolution and reaction and his familiarity with different political traditions (both republican and liberal) encouraged him to elaborate an idiosyncratic interpretation of the economic and social context in which he lived. His different positions on various issues were shaped by his lifelong preoccupation with finding the moral and cultural means necessary to ensure political liberty and economic development while qualitatively improving social well-being (measured not as an abstraction but concretely in terms of the genuine *bonheur* of all members of society). Within the much larger framework of his collected works, Sismondi's economic writings represent quantitatively only a minor share (albeit one which is undeniably central) of a much larger intellectual project. Actually, Sismondi's contemporaries were more familiar with his work as an historian than as an economist. For example, the *Edinburgh Review* called him the 'first living historian' (*Edinburgh Review*, 1815, vol. XXV: 437).

Sismondi actively participated in the Coppet circle with Benjamin Constant and Germaine de Staël. These intellectual associations influenced his attempts to reconceptualize at once the relationship between the individual and society and ways of creating shared values grouped around the idea of the public good. The English tradition of historical and constitutional thought as propagated by jurists such as Jean-Louis Delolme, William Blackstone and Richard Wooddeson had an important formative influence on Sismondi's conviction that it was necessary to establish institutional guarantees ensuring political and civil liberty within the framework of a well-functioning economic system. In Italy he discovered the tradition of civic humanism, which, with its central focus on the importance of civic virtues, became a pivotal reference for him.

Sismondi also kept in touch with the anglophone world through friends and family. Sismondi's familiarity with British concerns had a great impact on his understanding of the precise working conditions of the then most advanced capitalist economy, and his writings were read and discussed in Britain as well – for example, Thomas Carlyle translated his 'Political Economy' for the *Edinburgh Encyclopedia*.

Sismondi's economic writings can be characterized by their distinctly historical approach, which led him to analyse political and economic phenomena in their respective contexts and eclectically to enlarge his research interests to various fields of knowledge and experience. In contrast with "pure political economists" such as Ricardo and his followers who, in Sismondi's eyes, were guilty of abstracting economic laws from their social and historical context, Sismondi tried to establish links between economics and other disciplines, first politics, in order to give a more subtle account of economic causality. In this regard, he always claimed to be faithful to the prior approach of Adam Smith.

In Tuscany, Sismondi led the life of a gentleman farmer, taking part in various agrarian activities and regularly examining and experimenting with new technological instruments and processes for improving agricultural production. The outcome of Sismondi's time in Tuscany was his *Tableau de l'agriculture toscane* (1801), which constitutes the first sketch of an institutional analysis that would become the distinguishing feature of his economic writings. This study would be followed by a two-volume work designed to clarify how wealth was created and distributed: *De la richesse commerciale* (1803). In this work, Sismondi criticized the centralizing, monopolistic and protectionist economic policies of Bonaparte and their effects on his native Geneva, which was a small, open market economy based on free trade and a highly decentralized network of producers of high quality goods.

In 1819, after the post-Napoleonic war depression, Sismondi published his magnum opus, the *Nouveaux principes d'économie politique* (second edition, 1827), essentially a development of his earlier article 'Political Economy' (written in 1817, translated by Carlyle and published in 1825 in Brewster's *Edinburgh Encyclopedia*). Underscoring the importance of historical time and transition phases, Sismondi notably defended the idea that overproduction is not fortuitous, but inherent to an economy based on wage labour. The advent of modern capitalist economies represented in his eyes the emergence of 'an entirely new state of society, [a] universal competition which degenerates into hostility between the wealthy class and the working class' (Sismondi 1827, 2: 434): thus, modern capitalist economies, endemically generate pauperism and unemployment, and, as a consequence, are at their root politically unstable.

Sismondi's most striking thesis (famously expressed in the *Nouveaux principes* among other places) is about the balance between consumption and production. In modern capitalist economies in which property is concentrated in a few hands, workers have no choice but to accept the lowest possible wages. This downward pressure on wages leads necessarily to under-consumption. On the other hand, capitalists produce for an invisible, potentially boundless market, and are forced, by competition, to produce the most possible goods at the lowest possible price, leading necessarily to overproduction. This mechanism constitutes a vicious circle, in so far as mass-production and machinery further exacerbate inequalities and market instability and certainly do nothing to attenuate poverty.

Criticisms of this argument – as made by R. Torrens, J.R. McCulloch, T.R. Malthus, J.-B. Say, D. Ricardo – as well as Sismondi's diverse responses to them, constitute an important chapter in the controversy over Say's law of supply and demand and, therefore, are an integral part of the history of economic thought. Sismondi's approach to political economy has also been recognized as the first attempt to articulate a genuine dynamic analysis of economic processes as well as one of the most adequate contemporary accounts of transitional phenomena. As Schumpeter put it: 'his great merit is that he used, systematically and explicitly, a schema of periods, . . . that he was the first to practice the particular method of dynamics that is called period analysis' (Schumpeter 1954: 496).

Sismondi's last economic work, *Études sur l'économie politique* (1837), itself part of a much larger work – *Études sur les sciences sociales* – contains no major theoretical novelty, but summarizes all of Sismondi's main concerns (regarding slavery, the machinery question, landed property, and so on) and constitutes a strong plea against industrialism and the concomitant glorification of production, a matter which at the time was widely debated among advocates of economic liberalism.

Sismondi's plea in favour of erecting a 'social power' to moderate the 'wealth power', and Marx's influential characterization of Sismondi in the *Communist Manifesto* (the 'head of the school of petty-bourgeois socialism') have led him to be criticized by both liberals and socialists alike and have contributed to his unwarranted reputation for having been an indecisive, middle-of-the-road economist. Nevertheless, Sismondi had a crucial critical influence on economists concerned with the question of industrialization, running from French liberals such as J.A. Blanqui to the Russian Populists; and Sismondi is regularly 'rediscovered' on the occasion of each new economic crisis.

FRANCESCA DAL DEGAN AND NICOLAS EYGUESIER

See also:

French classical political economy (II); French Enlightenment (II); Institutional economics (III); Thomas Robert Malthus (I); Non-Marxian socialist ideas in France (II); Political philosophy and economics: freedom and labour (III); Population (III); Poverty (III); David Ricardo (I); Jean-Baptiste Say (I); Technical change and innovation (III).

References and further reading

The best biography of Sismondi remains Jean-René De Salis (1932). For a survey of Sismondi's intellectual education, see Francesca Sofia (1983) and Helmutt Otto Pappe (1963). Pappe also wrote a concise introduction to Sismondi's political thought in English (Pappe 1979). On this theme, see also Francesca Sofia (1983). On Sismondi's economic analysis, see Richard Arena (1981, 1982). Thomas Sowell (1972) contains a chapter about Sismondi. For a Marxist perspective, see Henry Grossmann (1924) and, on Sismondi's methodology, Jean-Jacques Gislain (1998, 2002). A "humanistic" interpretation of Sismondi is presented by Mark A. Lutz (1999). Note that several Sismondi-related conference proceedings have been published: notably *Atti del colloquio internazionale su Sismondi* (Rome: Accademia Nazionale di lincei, 1973); *Sismondi Européen* (Geneva: Slatkine and Paris: Honoré Champion, 1976); *Histoire, socialisme et critique de l'économie politique* (Paris: ISMEA, 1976); and *Sismondi e la civiltà toscana* (Florence: Leo S. Olschki, 2001).

Arena, R. (1981), 'Note sur les apports de Sismondi à la théorie classique', *L'Actualité économique*, **58** (4), 565–88.
Arena, R. (1982), 'Réflexion sur l'analyse sismondienne de la formation des prix', *Revue économique*, **33** (1), 132–49.
De Salis, J.-R. (1932), *Sismondi, 1773–1842. La Vie et l'Œuvre d'un cosmopolite philosophe*, Paris: Champion.
Gislain, J.-J. (1998), 'Sismondi and the evolution of economic institutions', in G. Faccarello (ed.), *Studies in the History of French Political Economy. From Bodin to Walras*, London and New York: Routledge, pp. 229–53.
Gislain, J.-J. (2002), 'Entre marché et circuit: la relation salariale selon Sismondi', *Storia del pensiero economico* (43–4), 79–112.
Grossmann, H. (1924), *Simonde de Sismondi et ses théories économiques. Une nouvelle interprétation de sa pensée*, Warsaw: Sumptibus Universitatis Liberae Poloniae.
Lutz, M.A. (1999), *Economics for the Common Good. Two Centuries of Social Economic Thought in the Economic Tradition*, London: Routledge.
Pappe, H.O. (1963), *Sismondis Weggenossen*, Geneva: Droz.
Pappe, H.O. (1979), 'Sismondi's system of liberty', *Journal of the History of Ideas*, **40** (2), 251–66.
Schumpeter, J.A. (1954), *History of Economic Analysis*, New York: Oxford University Press.
Sismondi, J.C.L. Simonde de (1801), *Tableau de l'agriculture toscane*, Geneva: Paschoud.
Sismondi, J.C.L. Simonde de (1802), *Statistique du département de Léman*, reprinted 1971 Geneva: A. Jullien.
Sismondi, J.C.L. Simonde de (1803), *De la Richesse commerciale*, 2 vols, Geneva, Paschoud.
Sismondi, J.C.L. Simonde de (1808–17), *Italian Republics; or the Origin, Progress, and Fall of Italian Freedom*, reprinted 1832, London, Longman.
Sismondi, J.C.L. Simonde de (1819), *Nouveaux principes d'économie politique ou De la richesse dans ses rapports avec la population*, 2 vols, Paris: Delaunay.
Sismondi, J.C.L. Simonde de (1825), *Political economy*, reprinted 1966, New York: August M. Kelley.

Sismondi, J.C.L. Simonde de (1827), *Nouveaux principes d'économie politique ou De la richesse dans ses rapports avec la population*, 2nd edn, Paris: Delaunay (this volume contains his famous articles against the Ricardian school, 'Examen de cette question: le pouvoir de consommer s'accroît-il toujours dans la société avec le pouvoir de produire?' and 'Sur la balance des consommation avec les productions').

Sismondi, J.C.L. Simonde de (1827a), *New Principles of Political Economy. Of Wealth in Its Relation to Population*, reprinted 1997, trans. R. Hyse, foreword by R. Heilbrorner, New Brunswick, NJ: Transaction.

Sismondi, J.C.L. Simonde de (1837), *Études sur l'économie politique*, 2 vols, Paris: Treuttel et Wurtz.

Sismondi, J.C.L. Simonde de (2012–17), *Œuvres économiques complètes*, 6 vols: vol. I *Tableau de l'agriculture toscane et Statistique du département de Léman*; vol. II *De la richesse commerciale*; vol. III *Écrits d'économie politique 1799–1815*; vol. IV *Écrits d'économie politique 1816–1842*; vol. V *Nouveaux principes d'économie politiques*; vol. VI *Études sur les sciences sociales*, Paris: Economica.

Sofia, F. (1981), 'Sul pensiero politico-istituzionale del giovane Sismondi', *Rassegna storica del risorgimento*, **68** (2), 131–48.

Sofia, F. (1983), *Una biblioteca ginevrina del Settecento: i libri del giovane Sismondi*, Rome: Edizioni dell'Ateneo & Bizzari.

Sowell, T. (1972), *Say's Law, an Historical Analysis*, Princeton, NJ: Princeton University Press.

Thomas Tooke (1774–1858)

Thomas Tooke (29 February 1774–26 February 1858) was one of the most influential political economists in Great Britain over the course of five decades. Tooke was born in a village near St Petersburg, Russia, the eldest son of the Reverend William Tooke, the chaplain of the "English Factory" at St Petersburg. He received a general education and entered into mercantile endeavours at an early age, soon becoming a partner in one of the largest of London's "Russian houses" engaged in the trade between Russia and Great Britain. Early in his commercial career Tooke began gathering and evaluating price data on various commodities, an activity that led to the publication of seven books focusing on price data and four more publications focusing on the currency and on monetary policy.

Over the course of his long life Tooke became a well-known figure in the world of political economy as a collector and publisher of price data, as a monetary theorist and as a social reformer.

Tooke developed a reputation as an expert on economic issues long before he began writing on the subject. In 1810 he was called to give evidence before the Select Committee on the High Price of Gold Bullion. In 1819 Tooke testified before the parliamentary committee considering the return to convertibility of the pound sterling. Later that same year he was also called to state his opinions before the Lords' Committee investigating the state of the Bank of England as the return to convertibility neared. Over the next 13 years Tooke was involved with five other parliamentary committees. In 1833 Tooke was chosen as one of the 15 commissioners who were appointed to oversee the implementation of the Factory Act. He also served as one of three commissioners on the Central Board. Besides these duties, Tooke was one of the founders of the Political Economy Club in 1821, presided over the St Katherine's Dock Company, was one of the founders of the Statistical Society, was one of the promoters of the Birmingham Railway and wrote the Merchants Petition in favour of free trade. But Tooke's greatest achievements as a political economist were in the area of monetary theory and policy.

Tooke's first book focusing primarily on monetary issues was *Considerations on the State of the Currency* (1826). At this point in his career, Tooke could be characterized as a moderate bullionist. While Tooke was a political ally of David Ricardo, he objected to Ricardo's bullion plan, in which all gold coins would be withdrawn from circulation, while all international payments would be made in gold bars. Ricardo believed that the quantity of gold needed to accommodate the British economy could thereby be sharply reduced. Tooke disagreed with Ricardo on the grounds that David Hume's price-specie-flow theory, upon which Ricardo based his bullion plan, depended upon "tight linkages," while in the world of commerce actual linkages were "loose". Tooke maintained that the price-specie flow mechanism did not, in the real world, work automatically and with the speed required to enable a great trading nation to make its payments without holding a large gold reserve with which to pay its international debts, as they often came due before the payment inflows from British exports were received. In many ways Tooke's "early stage" monetary theory resembled Henry Thornton's theory of money. However, over the course of the 1830s and early1840s Tooke radically revised his view of how the British monetary system actually worked, a shift that led him to rethink his approach to monetary theory.

Great Britain's monetary system experienced significant problems in the 1820s, 1830s, and into the 1840s. During this period, the English banking system expanded greatly, to a large extent through the creation of joint-stock banks. In 1844 the British government took advantage of the legal opportunity to revise the Bank of England's charter. The government followed the Currency School's quantity theoretic approach in reshaping the Bank, following the theories of J. Horsley Palmer, Samuel Jones-Loyd (Lord Overstone), Robert Torrens and other monetary thinkers who subscribed to a quantity-theoretic approach to monetary policy. The Bank was divided into two departments, the Issue Department, which issued more notes only as it acquired more gold to back those notes, and a Banking Department that operated as a commercial bank, free of obligations to the Issue Department.

Tooke opposed the Bank Act primarily because he rejected the currency principle, which maintained, in his words, that "bank notes in circulation should be made to conform to the gold into which they are convertible not only in value but in amount" (1844: 2). The note issue should vary just as a fully metallic currency would. Tooke rejected this theory, arguing that the Bank lacked the ability to control the quantity of its own notes. Taking a Banking School approach, Tooke argued that credit conditions determined the quantity of notes in circulation, rather than the other way around. Tooke predicted that, if the currency principle were ensconced in law, financial crises would ensue. His prediction proved correct. While the convertibility of the pound sterling was maintained, the Bank Act, that is, the rule of issuing notes, was temporarily suspended three times within two decades, in 1847, 1857 and 1866.

NEIL T. SKAGGS

See also:

Banking and currency schools (II); Bullionist and anti-bullionist schools (II); Money and banking (III); David Ricardo (I); Henry Thornton (I).

References and further reading

Arnon, A. (1991), *Thomas Tooke: Pioneer of Monetary Theory*, Ann Arbour, MI: University of Michigan Press.

Skaggs, N.T. (2003), 'Thomas Tooke, Henry Thornton, and the development of British monetary orthodoxy', *Journal of the History of Economic Thought*, **25** (2), 177–96.

Smith, M. (2003), 'On central banking rules: the Bank Charter Act of 1844', *Journal of the History of Economic Thought*, **25** (1), 39–61.

Smith, M. (2009), 'Thomas Tooke on the Corn Laws', *History of Political Economy*, **41** (2), 343–82.

Smith, M. (2011), *Thomas Tooke and the Monetary Thought of Classical Economics*, London: Routledge.

Tooke, T. (1823), *Thoughts and Details of High and Low Prices of the Last Thirty Years, in Four Parts*, London: John Murray.

Tooke, T. (1826), *Considerations on the State of the Currency*, London: John Murray.

Tooke, T. (1838–57), *History of Prices and of the State of the Circulation during the Years 1703–1856*, 6 vols, vols 1–3, London: Longman, Orme, Brown, Green and Longmans, vol. 4, London: Longman, Brown, Green and Longmans, vols 5–6, with W. Newmarch, London: Longman, Brown, Green, Longmans and Roberts.

Tooke, T. (1844), *An Inquiry into the Currency Principle: the Connexion of the Currency with Prices and the Expediency of a Separation of Issue from Banking*, London: Longman, Brown, Green, and Longmans.

Robert Torrens (*c.* 1780–1864)

Robert Torrens was born in Ireland around 1780 (the exact date of birth is not known) into a family with clergymen ancestry, received a classical education at Derry Diocesan School in his home parish of Tamlaght O'Crilly, and joined the Marines as an ensign at age 16. He married in 1801 and fathered five children, but later "divorced" his Irish wife in order to marry a minor English heiress. He died in London on 27 May 1864.

Torrens led a long and busy life with several distinguished careers. He was a professional soldier – a Lieutenant-Colonel and later Major in the Marines, who was decorated for gallantry at the battle of Anholt – from 1796 to 1834 (though only on half pay after 1823). In 1821 he became the editor and principal proprietor of *The Traveller*, which he merged with *The Globe* a year later, making it England's second-largest daily and dominant evening paper. He retired as managing editor in 1826, but continued to influence the paper's policy and management until at least 1858. Torrens briefly entered Parliament for the Borough of Ipswich in 1826–27, and then again in 1831 as Member for Ashburton. After the Reform Bill of 1832 he was re-elected as Member for Bolton. Shortly after he had lost the next election in 1835 he became Chairman of the Board of Commissioners for the Colonialization of South Australia, a post he held until 1841, when after South Australia's bankruptcy he was forced to resign. Torrens was a Fellow of the Royal Society and a founding member of the Political Economy Club, of which he remained an active member until 1851. Apart from his contributions to economics, Torrens also published two novels, *Coelibia choosing a Husband* (1809), and *The Victim of Intolerance: or, the Hermit of Killarney* (1814); the latter contained an interesting dialogue on physiocracy, probably deriving from his readings for his first work in economics, *The Economists Refuted* (Torrens 1808 [2000]). (For further biographical details see Moore 2016.)

Torrens was a prolific writer and managed to publish some 90 books and pamphlets. However, there is a fair amount of repetition in his work, since he was not diffident about recycling previously used material several times over. He was also a gifted controversialist, who did not shy away from vigorously attacking arguments and theoretical positions that he himself had held before (often without informing his readers about this). Since it would be quite impossible to go through all his books and pamphlets and their various editions, the following discussion of his contributions will be arranged thematically.

Theory of Value and Distribution

Torrens's thinking on the theory of value and distribution developed in close relation to that of Ricardo, and comprised phases and elements of acknowledging, adopting, opposing, and rejecting Ricardo's ideas. Characteristically, Torrens's anti-Ricardian stance became markedly more pronounced after the latter's death in 1823, and it was Torrens who, in 1831, declared in the Political Economy Club that "all the great principles of Ricardo's work had been successively abandoned", and that "his theories of value, Rent and Profits were now generally acknowledged to have been erroneous" (Political Economy Club of London 1921: 225).

In his *Essay on the External Corn Trade* (Torrens 1815 [2000]), which was published on the same day as Ricardo's *Essay on Profits* (1815 [1951–73], IV), Torrens still adhered to Smith's "adding-up of components" theory of value and accordingly maintained that an increase in wages must raise all prices. He also had not yet absorbed the theory of differential rent (which he could have picked up from Malthus's *Inquiry*), and his entire treatment of distribution suffered from a lack of systematic order and coordination. But soon after he had read Ricardo's pamphlet, Torrens became "quite a convert" to Ricardo's ideas on the theory of distribution. In particular, he picked up from Ricardo's *Essay on Profits* (1815 [1951–73], IV) the idea of determining the rate of profits by assuming homogeneity between product and capital and also adopted Ricardo's proposition regarding the inverse wage–profit relationship. The only part of the theory of distribution to which Torrens contributed something substantial in the first edition of his *External Corn Trade* is the theory of wages. Its novelty was not so much his definition of natural wages as equal to the level of the subsistence require-ments of the worker and his family, but rather his stress on the importance of customs and habits in determining this level. Moreover, Torrens also emphasized that "the natural price of labour, . . . though it varies under different climates, and with the dif-ferent stages of natural improvement, may, in any given time and place, be regarded as very nearly stationary" (1815 [2000]: 64–5). This idea of treating the normal wage as given was not a novelty, of course, but Torrens spelt it out more clearly than any of his predecessors.

In his review of Ricardo's *Principles*, entitled "Strictures on Mr Ricardo's Doctrine respecting Exchangeable Value" (1818 [2000]), Torrens then put forward a scathing criti-cism of the labour theory of value, which Ricardo had found it necessary to adopt in the first edition of his *Principles* in order to generalize his propositions on the inverse wage–profit relationship beyond the "corn-ratio" reasoning of the *Essay*. Torrens pointed out that:

> the results obtained by the employment of equal capitals will be of equal worth in the market; and therefore, as equal capitals generally put unequal quantities of labour in motion, or, what comes to the same thing, as equal quantities of labour are put in motion by unequal capitals, the products of equal quantities of labour will be of unequal value. (1818 [2000]: 336)

His (valid) objections to Ricardo's "embodied labour" based reasoning led him to advocate (what has later been called) a "capital theory of value": That "it is always the amount of capital, and never the quantity of labour, expended on production, which determines the exchangeable value of commodities" (Torrens 1818 [2000]: 337). But Torrens soon had to admit that this "theory" had serious weaknesses, which eventually forced him to abandon it – and to have recourse to labour value reasoning again. First, there was the problem of defining "equal amounts of capital", as Ricardo (1951–73, IX: 359–60) was quick to point out. When Torrens tried to solve this problem by specifying "equal amounts of capital" to mean "equal amounts of accumulated labour" in his *Essay on the Production of Wealth* (1821), the whole conception turned out to involve him in circular reasoning: "To disproof that commodities exchange according to labour embod-ied, Torrens starts from assuming that the commodities which constitute their capitals do so exchange" (De Vivo 2000, III: x–xi). Secondly, Torrens's theory, as opposed to Ricardo's labour-value based reasoning, does not allow the determination of the rate of profits, except by assuming the particular conditions of production for which homo-geneity between product and capital obtains (that is, except when no theory of value is necessary to determine the rate of profits). Nonetheless, Torrens's numerical examples were sufficient to demonstrate the incompatibility between exchange in proportion to labour embodied and a uniform rate of profits, and the way in which Torrens posed the problem had some affinities with Marx's formulation of the transformation problem. In his "Strictures" (1818 [2000]: 337; see also 1821 [2000]: 28), Torrens also introduced the idea of treating fixed capital as a joint-product, which subsequently was adopted also by Ricardo, Malthus and Marx, but then fell into oblivion until it was revived by Sraffa (1960).

The main interest of Torrens's subsequent contributions to the theory of distribution derives from his attempts to determine the general rate of profits without making use of the labour theory of value. In the second edition (1820) of the *Essay on the External Corn Trade* he formulated the "corn-ratio" theory of profits, that is, a determination of the rate of profits as a ratio between two physical amounts of corn (see De Vivo 1985, 2000, II: xxii). He also stated explicitly that given the agricultural rate of profits the prices of other commodities relative to corn are determined:

> It may be laid down as a general principle, that in whatever proportion the *quantity* of produce obtained from the soil exceeds the *quantity* employed in raising it, in that proportion the *value* of manufactured goods will exceed the *values* of the food and material expended in producing them. (Torrens 1820 [2000]: 362; emphasis added)

However, Torrens did not content himself with "corn-ratio" reasoning, but also generalized the idea of a physically determined profit rate based on homogeneity between product and capital. He did so by formulating numerical examples in which the commodities enter into the net social product in the same composition in which they enter into the aggregate social capital, so that the general rate of profits can be determined as a physical ratio between two different quantities of a "composite commodity", with no need to determine prices (1820 [2000]: 354). In the Preface to the third edition (1826) of the *Essay on the External Corn Trade* Torrens then constructed numerical examples which showed that Ricardo's inverse wage–profit relationship need not necessarily hold true if non-wage capital was properly taken into account: productivity-enhancing technical change could raise the general rate of profits without a fall of proportional wages (see Torrens 1826 [2000]: xv–xvi; see also De Vivo 2000, II: xxviii–xxix). Torrens's demonstration anticipated Marx's later criticism of Ricardo for his neglect of non-wage capital in his observations on profits and wages, which, according to Marx, had precluded him from recognizing the true cause of the tendency towards a falling rate of profit, that is, the rising organic composition of capital and the associated fall in the maximum rate of profits. (However, it must be mentioned that in *The Budget* (1844 [2000]: xxviii) Torrens later recanted this valid criticism, and claimed that Ricardo's argument could be extended also to cases in which non-wage capital is taken into account.)

International Trade Theory and Trade Policy

In his first publication, *The Economists Refuted* (1808 [2000], Torrens made a plea for free trade along Smithian lines, and argued that gains from trade can be reaped from exploiting productivity gains which emanate from the "territorial division of labour" (a phrase coined by Torrens). But Torrens's use of this phrase is certainly insufficient to justify his later claim to priority with regard to the formulation of the theory of comparative advantage, which gave rise to a famous debate between Edwin R. Seligman and Jacob H. Hollander (for a review, see Viner 1937: 441–4), and which has continued to attract the attention of historians of economic thought (see, for instance, Aldrich 2004). There is more substance to it with regard to his *Essay on the External Corn Trade* (1815), where Torrens had stated that if the costs of producing cloth relative to corn were lower in England than in Poland it would be advantageous for her "to neglect tracts of her territory . . . *even though they should be superior to the lands in Poland*, . . . and [to import] a part of her supply of corn . . . from that country" (1815 [2000]: 264; emphasis added). However, this statement is still somewhat vague and ambiguous, as compared to Ricardo's lucid exposition in chapter 7 of the *Principles*. The comparative costs principle was clearly stated by Torrens, and neatly illustrated in terms of a comparison of cost ratios, only in the fourth edition of the *Essay on the External Corn Trade* (1827). However, in his one general work on political economy, the *Essay on the Production of Wealth* of 1821, Torrens did make the unusual and interesting point that international trade could be harmful for a country that specializes in necessaries rather than luxuries (1821 [2000]: 272–80).

The *Letters on Commercial Policy* (1833 [2000]) mark the beginning of a partial volteface with regard to Torrens's stance on trade policy. He was among the first to make clear that a tariff might turn the terms of trade in favour of the country imposing it, and to base thereon a theory of reciprocity in commercial policy. However, it must be stressed that Torrens was not against free trade in general, and did not advocate a policy of import tariffs in order to turn the terms of trade in favour of his own country. He rather argued that unilateral tariff reduction would be disadvantageous for England, and therefore supported a policy of reciprocity and a colonial *Zollverein*. Finally, in his *Letters on Commercial Policy* (1833) and in *The Budget* (1844, but partly published in instalments previously in 1841–43) Torrens began to elaborate, but did not quite arrive at, the theory of "reciprocal demands" (a term first used by Torrens) for determining the terms of trade. While Torrens can perhaps be credited with independent discovery in this regard, it must be admitted that John Stuart Mill's constructions, in his famous essay "Of the Laws of Interchange between Nations", were clearly superior to Torrens's rather vague formulations. At any rate, Torrens's statements in the *Budget* induced Mill to publish his essay, which he had written already in 1829–30, in his *Essays on some Unsettled Questions of Political Economy* of 1844.

Colonization Policy

Torrens contributed rather more to colonization policy, and in particular to the colonization of South Australia, than to colonization theory, where he was chiefly an ardent expounder of Edward Gibbon Wakefield's ideas. In *Colonization of South Australia* (1835) he expounded Wakefield's principles of "systematic colonization", based on "self-supporting emigration", "a hired labour price for land", and "self-supporting colonization". Following Wakefield, he argued that colonial immigrants should not be supplied with free land because this would lead to too much dispersion of population, landholdings of sub-optimal size, and low agricultural productivity. Instead, the price of land should be set sufficiently high to prevent emigrant workers from becoming independent farmers until after they had worked for some years as labourers for hire. Moreover, the proceeds from the land sales could be used as a means of financing the expenses for sending out emigrants. Torrens's fervent support of colonization was primarily based on his view that it could counteract the falling rate of profit from decreasing returns in agriculture. Colonization was seen as a remedy for improving the living conditions of the Irish peasants and of preventing them from moving to England, and thereby causing a fall in the standard of living of the English working class.

Monetary Theory and Policy

Torrens is probably best known for his contributions to money and banking, and in particular as a major representative of the Currency School in the controversies of the 1830s and 1840s. However, in the monetary debates of the Restriction period Torrens was essentially an anti-Bullionist. In his *Essay on Money and Paper Currency* (1812 [2000]) he started out as a staunch advocate of the banking principle, taking an extreme position by defending the system of inconvertible paper on the basis of the real bills doctrine. Torrens continued to argue along those lines in his *Letters to Lauderdale* (1816 [2000]) and *A Comparative Estimate* (1819 [2000]), but in the late 1820s or early 1830s he changed sides and became a Ricardian in respect of monetary theory and policy. This almost inexplicable U-turn has long puzzled students of Torrens. The most plausible explanation was provided by O'Brien (1965), based on a (previously unpublished) memorandum titled "On the means of establishing a cheap, secure, and uniform Currency", which Torrens had drafted in 1826 and which contains a sort of "half-way house" between his early and his later views on monetary theory. Apart from political opportunism Torrens was apparently driven into the Bullionist camp by a fear of over-issue. Torrens's new position is already visible in parliamentary speeches of 1833, and in the following years he became a leading proponent of the currency principle, together with Norman and Overstone. In his *Letter to Lord Melbourne* (1837 [2000]) he advocated the separation of the two departments of the Bank of England and their adherence to strict rules in order to avoid over-issue. Torrens's recommendations of 1837 and his proposals in the ensuing controversies with Thomas Tooke in the early 1840s were largely responsible for the legislation that was adopted in Peel's Bank of England Charter Act 1844. After the monetary crises of 1847 Torrens vigorously defended this legislation, first in *On the Operation of the Bank Charter Act of 1844, as it Affects Commercial Credit* (1847 [2000]), and then in *The Principles and Practical Operation of Sir Robert Peel's Bill of 1844* (1848 [2000]), in which he also provided a critical analysis of his opponents' views, especially Tooke and Fullarton.

Conclusion

Torrens was one of the leading political economists in Britain in the post-Ricardian era, but after 1850 his books and pamphlets ceased to attract much attention. This only began to change when Seligman (1903) included him among the "neglected British economists" whom he sought to rescue from oblivion. Viner (1937) and Robbins (1958) then did much to give Torrens his due for his contributions to the theory of international trade and to monetary theory and policy. However, Torrens's contributions to the theory of value and distribution were not adequately appreciated by Robbins, who described him as "the most eminent of the minor English Classical Economists"

(Robbins 1958: v). It was only with Sraffa's reconstruction of Ricardo's theory of value in his "Introduction" to Ricardo's *Works* (Sraffa 1951) that Torrens's role in the development of the classical approach to the theory of value and distribution came to be better understood.

CHRISTIAN GEHRKE

See also:

British classical political economy (II); Karl Heinrich Marx (I); Money and banking (III); David Ricardo (I); Adam Smith (I).

References and further reading

Aldrich, J. (2004), 'The discovery of comparative advantage', *Journal of the History of Economic Thought*, **26** (3), 379–99.

De Vivo, G. (1985), 'Robert Torrens and Ricardo's "corn-ratio" theory of profits', *Cambridge Journal of Economics*, **9** (1), 89–92.

De Vivo, G. (2000), 'Introduction', in G. de Vivo (ed.), *Collected Works of Robert Torrens*, 8 vols, London: Thoemmes Press.

Mill, J.S. (1844), *Essays on Some Unsettled Questions of Political Economy*, in J.M. Robson (ed.) (1967), *Collected Works of John Stuart Mill*, vol. 4: *Essays on Economics and Society 1824–1845*, Toronto: University of Toronto Press, pp. 229–339.

Moore, P.L. (2016), *Biography of Robert Torrens*, forthcoming (parts of the unfinished manuscript were kindly made available by the author).

O'Brien, D.P. (1965), 'The transition in Torrens's monetary thought', *Economica*, New Series, **32** (127), 269–86.

Political Economy Club of London (1921), *Minutes of Proceedings, 1899–1920, Roll of Members, and Questions Discussed, 1821–1920*, vol. VI, London: Macmillan.

Ricardo, D. (1951–73), *The Works and Correspondence of David Ricardo*, ed. by P. Sraffa with the collaboration of M.H. Dobb, 11 vols, Cambridge: Cambridge University Press.

Robbins, L. (1958), *Robert Torrens and the Evolution of Classical Economics*, London: Macmillan.

Seligman, E.R.A. (1903), 'On some neglected British economists', *Economic Journal*, **13** (51), 335–63.

Sraffa, P. (1951), 'Introduction', in *The Works and Correspondence of David Ricardo*, vol. I, pp. xiii–lxii.

Sraffa, P. (1960), *Production of Commodities by Means of Commodities*, Cambridge: Cambridge University Press.

Torrens, R. (1808), *The Economists Refuted*, in G. de Vivo (ed.) (2000), *Collected Works of Robert Torrens*, vol. VI, London: Thoemmes Press.

Torrens, R. (1812), *Essay on Money and Paper Currency*, in G. de Vivo (ed.) (2000), *Collected Works of Robert Torrens*, vol. VII, London: Thoemmes Press.

Torrens, R. (1815), *Essay on the External Corn Trade*, in G. de Vivo (ed.) (2000), *Collected Works of Robert Torrens*, vol. II, London: Thoemmes Press.

Torrens, R. (1816), *Letters to Lauderdale*, in G. de Vivo (ed.) (2000), *Collected Works of Robert Torrens*, vol. VII, London: Thoemmes Press.

Torrens, R. (1818), 'Strictures on Mr Ricardo's Doctrine respecting Exchangeable Value', in G. de Vivo (ed.) (2000), *Collected Works of Robert Torrens*, vol. VIII, London: Thoemmes Press.

Torrens, R. (1819), *A Comparative Estimate*, in G. de Vivo (ed.) (2000), *Collected Works of Robert Torrens*, vol. VII, London: Thoemmes Press.

Torrens, R. (1820), *Essay on the External Corn Trade*, 2nd edn, in G. de Vivo (ed.) (2000), *Collected Works of Robert Torrens*, vol. II, London: Thoemmes Press.

Torrens, R. (1821), *Essay on the Production of Wealth*, in G. de Vivo (ed.) (2000), *Collected Works of Robert Torrens*, vol. III, London: Thoemmes Press.

Torrens, R. (1826), *Essay on the External Corn Trade*, 3rd edn, in G. de Vivo (ed.) (2000), *Collected Works of Robert Torrens*, vol. II, London: Thoemmes Press.

Torrens, R. (1827), *Essay on the External Corn Trade*, 4th edn, in G. de Vivo (ed.) (2000), *Collected Works of Robert Torrens*, vol. II, London: Thoemmes Press.

Torrens, R. (1833), *Letters on Commercial Policy*, in G. de Vivo (ed.) (2000), *Collected Works of Robert Torrens*, vol. VIII, London: Thoemmes Press.

Torrens, R. (1835), *Colonization of South Australia*, in G. de Vivo (ed.) (2000), *Collected Works of Robert Torrens*, vol. IV, London: Thoemmes Press.

Torrens, R. (1837), *Letter to Lord Melbourne*, in G. de Vivo (ed.) (2000), *Collected Works of Robert Torrens*, vol. VII, London: Thoemmes Press.

Torrens, R. (1844), *The Budget*, in G. de Vivo (ed.) (2000), *Collected Works of Robert Torrens*, vol. V, London: Thoemmes Press.

Torrens, R. (1847), *On the Operation of the Bank Charter Act of 1844, as it Affects Commercial Credit*, in G. de Vivo (ed.) (2000), *Collected Works of Robert Torrens*, vol. VII, London: Thoemmes Press.

Torrens, R. (1848), *The Principles and Practical Operation of Sir Robert Peel's Bill of 1844*, in G. de Vivo (ed.) (2000), *Collected Works of Robert Torrens*, vol. VI, London: Thoemmes Press.

Torrens, R. (2000), *Collected Works of Robert Torrens*, 8 vols, ed. and introduction by G. de Vivo, London: Thoemmes Press.

Viner, J. (1937), *Studies in the Theory of International Trade*, New York: Harper & Brothers.

Johann Heinrich von Thünen (1783–1850)

The works of several great economists had at first a relatively small impact on the development of economics because they were born into an environment that was not ready for them. Johann Heinrich von Thünen's work is a particularly glaring case in point. The first edition of Part I of his magnum opus *Der Isolierte Staat* was published in 1826 and a second edition in 1842, while the first section of Part II, containing marginal productivity theory, was published in 1850. Translations in French, Russian and Italian followed soon, whereas English editions had to wait until 1960, 1966 and 2009. However, despite the path-breaking achievements contained in Thünen's works, up until now their full content has not yet been secured, as Samuelson (1983) emphasized.

Life and Works

Thünen was born in Canarienhausen in Northern Germany in 1783. He inherited a strong interest in, and talent for, mathematics and at an early age received private lessons in calculus. An agricultural professional training followed from 1799 to 1802 before Thünen went to the Agricultural Academy of Lucas Staudinger near Hamburg for one year. Noting the different farming systems in the area, he got an idea of the structure of agriculture around a central market and, at the age of 19, put forward his first primitive Isolated State Model in the short treatise *Description of the Agriculture in the Village of Gross-Flottbeck*. He then spent a year in Albrecht Thaer's famous Agricultural Institute in Celle. Both institutes propagated the modern English crop rotation system applied by progressive farmers. Thünen completed his theoretical education at the University of Göttingen in 1803–04, where he also attended lectures in economics.

In 1806 he married and in 1810 he bought the estate of Tellow, which he developed into a profitable agricultural model farm, which soon attracted visitors from far and wide. There he elaborated the first model of a closed economy, which combined a realistic account of the production technology used at his time with an analysis of rational decision-making in competitive markets.

He put much energy into the estate's bookkeeping to obtain records of labour, capital and other inputs and outputs of agricultural production processes between 1810 and 1819. His main economic ideas were developed between 1815 und 1830 (Thünen 1817, 1823–50). He published numerous papers on a large number of issues, including the "Social Question", in local periodicals. In 1818/19 he wrote the first draft of Part I of *The Isolated State*, which was published only in 1826.

In the early 1820s, Thünen in all probability studied intensively the works of major economists, including David Ricardo, Jean-Baptiste Say and Thomas Robert Malthus. He then worked out the main propositions of his theory of distribution, centred around the concept of marginal productivity and on the capital formation model dealing with the "natural wage" (*naturgemäßer Lohn*), which was published in Part II of *The Isolated State* only in 1850. He derived a wage rate that is higher than the subsistence wage. His manuscripts of these years, comprising some 250 pages, contain *inter alia* the concept of optimization of individual objective functions, the solution of systems of equations and the formulation of a two-factor Cobb–Douglas production function (capital and labour). While Thünen was mainly interested in income distribution, he also contributed to monetary, trade and resource economics.

Between 1830 and 1850 Thünen refined his economic system. He contrasted his "natural wage" model with the prevailing subsistence wage theory and was particularly keen to find a "law" in production, relating inputs, outputs and the return on capital. He also applied his findings to real-world problems, for example, taxation, trade, agricultural education, improvements of infrastructure and technical progress.

In 1842 he drafted a complete outline for an extended Isolated State opus, which he was not able to realize. In the posthumous Schumacher edition (1863) we find only fragments of his manuscripts and an incomplete manuscript on forestry economics.

With the advent of democratization and unification of the German regional kingdoms and dominions and in fear of a social revolution, political questions got the upper hand between 1840 and 1850. Thünen was elected to the National Assembly in Frankfurt, but due to bad health he never attended any meeting.

Besides his research and farm management Thünen was an adviser to his farmer colleagues, the regional government and foreign visitors. His main economic contributions with respect to these activities were published in the agricultural journal *Neue Annalen der Mecklenburgischen Landwirtschaftsgesellschaft*, and include essays on the improvement of urban farming (Thünen 1831b), taxation, the introduction of a credit system (Thünen 1817) and a deposit bank (Thünen 1831a), and on improved agricultural technology. Thünen's social commitment, his political conviction and his philosophical outlook are well documented in his published letters (Rieter 2011).

Owing to his scientific achievements and his activities on behalf of common welfare he was awarded a PhD *honoris causa* by the University of Rostock in 1830 and was made an honorary citizen of the town of Teterow in 1848.

Thünen died in September 1850, half a year after the first section of Part II of *The Isolated State* was published. According to his instructions his natural wage formula was engraved on his tombstone: $A = \sqrt{ap}$ (A = wage; a = subsistence wage; p = average product of labour).

Thünen's Achievements

In the introduction to the second edition in 1842 of *The Isolated State* (Part I) Thünen states that his theoretical-cum-empirical "method of analysis has illuminated – and solved – so many problems in my life, and appears to me to be capable of such widespread application, that I regard it as the most important matter contained in all my work". Thünen's ingenious models are based on abstract, but never arbitrary assumptions; he makes judicious use of mathematics, particularly calculus, and comparative statics; and he verifies his theorems in terms of empirical data, primarily from his own estate's accountancy.

Thünen's basic analytical workhorse is the model of a closed economy on a flat plane with homogenous soil and a city in the centre as an idealized economic space, and a long-term steady state as an idealized situation with respect to time. Production techniques in agriculture, the price of grain in the city, the real wage and the interest rate are constants in Part I of *The Isolated State*. The model determines the prices of agricultural products, the location of their production, production intensities and the land rent. The model in

Part II comprises his theory of marginal productivity and of capital formation, enabling the calculation of steady state wages and interest rates. In his posthumously published works and his unpublished manuscripts he discusses different scenarios with respect to the extension and structure of the Isolated State and the resulting functional income distribution (different populations, replacement of the monocentric by a polycentric model, formation of capital by workers and capitalists).

Thünen defines self-interest in terms of objective functions, that is, the maximization of rents by the proprietors of land and renewable resources, of capitalists' pure profits and of a "surplus wage rent" of the capital accumulating workers (as "marginal" producers of capital).

Thünen's spatial models of agricultural production and prices as well as his marginal productivity theory are the first static equilibrium models. The core elements of his models are the following:

1. Diminishing returns to factor inputs, including capital: "*Every additional capital, additionally invested in an enterprise or trade, brings less return than capital previously invested*" (Thünen 1850: 98, original emphasis).
2. Marginal products equal factor prices: "*The return which capital as a whole gives when lent out is determined by the return of the last unit of the capital*" (ibid.: 100). "*The value of the labour of the last worker employed is also his wage*" (ibid.: 182, original emphases).
3. Factor prices and factor substitution:

    By producing one and the same product, *p*, a part of the capital can be substituted by increased labour; and again, a part of labour can be substituted by increased capital; in this way capital is like a coworker that competes with the wage earner . . . The entrepreneur who knows and follows his own interest will increase his relative capital, *q*, until the cost of the work of the capital and the cost of the work of a human being are in the same proportion as their efficiency in production. (Ibid.: 123)

4. Income distribution:

    The significance of capital we have measured by the increase in the product of labour of a man which results from an increase in the capital with which he works. Here labour is a constant, capital a varying magnitude. When on the other hand we consider capital as remaining constant and the number of workers as varying, we realize in a large business, that the significance of labour and the share of labour in the product is determined by the increase in the product which results from another labourer. (Ibid.: 190)

5. Dynamic equilibrium condition. With respect to the relation between the value of stocks and the flows resulting from these stocks he states: "*As wages of labour are related to the amount of revenue which the same amount of labour produces if that labour is used for the production of capital, so are capital and interest related*" (ibid.: 92).

As these conditions are taken to hold with regard to every good, and as market forces equalize interest rates and wages as well as the prices of each good (in the same location), Thünen develops equations that are reminiscent of the production equations of Sraffa

(1960) in order to calculate the relative prices of produce in circumstances in which there are no rents of land, using labour as the numeraire (see Nellinger 2014c). These equations are also used in passages on trade theory in his unpublished manuscripts, the stock-flow problem in the economy of natural resources (Böventer, 1984: 142) and in his monetary theory. To simplify matters, Thünen variously used simple interest, although compound interest would have been appropriate. As Kurz (1995) observed, Thünen wrongly thought that his findings in a model with a single capital good produced by unassisted labour carry over to a system in which heterogeneous capital goods are produced by means of themselves.

Thünen did not demonstrate that the dynamic process converges to a steady state, he simply assumed that the system was stable. He expected, but did not prove, that deviations from the long-term steady state path would be corrected smoothly.

While the demand side in Thünen's analysis is rather primitive, he may be said to have adopted ideas of the German "Gebrauchswertschule" (useful value school). However, a paternalistic proprietor of an estate and a member of the educated classes ("Bildungsbürger"), he could not fully endorse utilitarian ideas.

For a long time, economists saw a contradiction between Thünen's marginal productivity concept of the wage rate and his tombstone formula wage. According to Thünen this wage should obtain if land is freely available (for example, in North America at his times) and population is constant. Yet Dorfman (1986), Samuelson (1986) and van Suntum (1988) have clarified that Thünen's correctly derived natural wage equals the marginal productivity of labour at an optimal capital–labour ratio. Hence there is no contradiction; what remains obscure, however, is the objective function Thünen postulates with regard to the workers.

In his unpublished manuscripts Thünen also investigates the actual wage in central Europe, which according to his empirical analysis was somewhat higher than the subsistence wage. Thünen deplored the fact that workers typically spent the difference to raise more children rather than investing it in a better education for their children or on capital goods.

Thünen then introduced human capital in the production function to theoretically explain the low wages of workers in Europe and to demonstrate how to improve them (see Nellinger 2014c). Real capital formation, whether physical or human, has to yield a uniform interest rate, considering that the upbringing and education of children is an investment as any other investment. The investment in workers' human capital – by own savings or public schooling and apprenticeship – will increase the product of their labour and, *a fortiori*, their wages. The resulting $\sqrt{ap}$-wage will always be higher than the subsistence wage, unless the population relative to the available natural resources increases greatly – which Thünen believes depends on the labourers' reproduction behaviour. Capital formation by capitalists and workers or technical progress may defer the limitations of individual well-being. At this point Thünen merges the contemporary ideal of a well-educated citizen, perfecting his mind and controlling his sexual drives, with his pure economic analysis based on rational behaviour.

Part III of *The Isolated State* is titled "Principles for the Determination of Rent, the Most Advantageous Rotation Period and the Value of Stands of Varying Age in Pinewoods" and contains Thünen's work on forestry optimization under different technical conditions and factor scarcities. It is superior to, and far more detailed than, many subsequently published works, but inferior to the so-called Faustmann approach (see Faustmann 1849).

Johann Heinrich von Thünen's contributions to the problem of the commons – hidden in an 1831 article about urban agriculture (Thünen 1831b) and in an unpublished manuscript (see Nellinger 2014b) – have been totally neglected until now. It deserves to be mentioned that he published his ideas about the core problem of the commons two years earlier than William Forster Lloyd. He not only presented the correct allocation criteria for the open access and the regulated scenario but additionally developed a framework on (1) how to obtain the maximal resource rent through an auction system – drafting the first demand table; (2) how to redistribute the gains to the communal property owners – developing an adequate compensation mechanism; and (3) how to establish this institutional innovation democratically – thereby anticipating important elements of Elinor Ostrom's common property rights framework (1990: 182).

A 60-page manuscript on monetary questions written by Thünen (1823–50: 35–95) has been discovered recently (see Nellinger 2014a). It contains an algebraic equation of exchange, analyses the interaction between the monetary interest rate and the rate of return on real capital and provides a synthesis of an extended quantity theory and the production cost theory of money. Thünen's monetary theory includes important elements foreshadowing the development in monetary economics in the late nineteenth and the early twentieth century mainly influenced by contributions of Irving Fisher, Knut Wicksell and John Maynard Keynes.

Thünen's Legacy in Economics

According to Blaug (1968: 321), Thünen was "the first truly modern economist" and, as another commentator emphasized:

The depth and the real significance of his theoretical developments – in particular the unity of his thinking, the interrelationships between the various parts of his analyses, the greatness of the basic structure of the whole opus – have yet to be given the full credit they deserve in the history of scientific ideas. (Böventer 1984: 138)

One reason for the unsatisfactory reception was that Thünen's successors did not fully understand the treasures hidden in his works – which can be inferred from the disappointing posthumous edition of the second section of Part II in 1863 and 1875 by his student Hermann Schumacher and by many superficial comments of his contemporaries. According to Blaug this may partially be the responsibility of the author himself as *The Isolated State* stands out as "a collection of notes, comments, arithmetical examples and mathematical formula in which the main lines of argument can frequently only be discerned with the benefit of hindsight" (Blaug 1992: xi). Another main reason was that only a few scholars were aware of the huge amount of unpublished manuscripts and the important contributions published in the *Neue Annalen*.

However, among Thünen's admirers were major economists such as Alfred Marshall, Joseph Schumpeter and Paul A. Samuelson. They credited him with path-breaking achievements in economic analysis, mathematical economics and econometrics and ranked his work even above the work of his famous contemporary David Ricardo. Karl Marx regarded Thünen as far superior to the German economists of his time, and not belonging to the "vulgar" brand.

Alfred Marshall read *The Isolated State* around 1869 and, according to Peter Hall (1966: xi), central issues of his work derive from Thünen. They have become part of the toolbox of English economic thought: the treatment of marginal productivity, the analysis of rent, the careful distinction between partial and general equilibrium, the separation of the short and the long term. Through Marshall, Thünen's *Isolated State* became a precursor of neoclassical theory.

Thünen's monocentric space model provided the basis from which the German dominated location theory was erected, mainly by Alfred Weber, Oskar Engländer, Andreas Predöhl, Walter Christaller and August Lösch. In his posthumously published papers, Thünen provided a systematic account of factors explaining economic agglomeration, which, according to Fujita (2012), made him a precursor of the New Economic Geography.

Thünen's achievements in human and in real capital theory, in resource economics and in monetary theory could not exert any influence up until now as they have been unknown until a short while ago. They add to the impressive performance of this genius economist.

LUDWIG NELLINGER

See also:

Economic geography (III); German and Austrian schools (II); Paul Robin Krugman (I); Formalization and mathematical modelling (III); David Ricardo (I); Adam Smith (I).

References and further reading

Blaug, M. (1968), *Economic Theory in Retrospect*, Homewood, IL: Richard D. Irwin.
Blaug, M. (1992), *Johann von Thünen (1783–1850), Augustin Cournot (1801–1877), Jules Dupuit (1804–1866)*, Cambridge: Cambridge University Press.
Böventer, E. von (1984), 'The von Thünen–Hotelling Rule', in H. Hauptmann, W. Krelle and K.C. Mosler (eds), *Operations Research and Economic Theory. Essays in Honor of Martin J. Beckmann*, Berlin and Heidelberg: Springer, pp. 137–50.
Dorfman, R. (1986), 'Comment: P.A. Samuelson, Thünen at Two Hundred', *Journal of Economic Literature*, **24** (4), 1773–76.
Faustmann, M. (1849), 'Berechnung des Werthes, welchen Waldboden, sowie noch nicht haubare Holzbestände für die Waldwirthschaft besitzen', *Allgemeine Forst- und Jagd-Zeitung*, December, 441–55.
Fujita, M. (2012), 'Thünen and the New Economic Geography', *Regional Science and Urban Economics*, **42** (6), 907–12.
Hall, P. (1966), *Von Thünens Isolated State*, Oxford: Pergamon Press.
Kurz, H.D. (1995), 'Thünen und die allmähliche Herausbildung der marginalistischen Theorie. Eine Antwort auf Ernst Helmstädter', in H. Rieter (ed.), *Studien zur Entwicklung der ökonomischen Theorie* XIV: *Johann Heinrich von Thünen als Wirtschaftstheoretiker*, Berlin: Duncker & Humblot, pp. 165–180.
Nellinger, L. (2014a), 'Über die Natur und das Wesen des Geldes. J.H. von Thünens unveröffentlichtes Manuskript zur Geldtheorie', *Jahrbücher für Nationalökonomie und Statistik*, 234/1, 85–110.
Nellinger, L. (2014b), *An Unexpected Discovery: Johann Heinrich von Thünen and the Tragedy of the Commons*, Rostock: Thünen-Series of Applied Economy 135.
Nellinger, L. (2014c), 'Thünens umfassendes Raumwirtschaftsmodell, Studien zur Entwicklung der ökonomischen Theorie', in H.-M. Trautwein (ed.), *Studien zur Entwicklung der ökonomischen Theorie XXIX*, Berlin: Duncker & Humblot, pp. 57–126.
Ostrom, E. (1990), *Governing the Commons. The Evolution of Institutions for Collective Action*, Cambridge: Cambridge University Press.

Rieter, H. (2011), 'Johann Heinrich von Thünen in seinen Briefen', in J.H. von Thünen, *Briefe*, ed. G. Viereck, Marburg: Metropolis, pp. 31–86.

Samuelson, P.A. (1983), 'Thünen at two hundred', *Journal of Economic Literature*, **21**, 1468–88.

Samuelson, P.A. (1986), 'Yes to Robert Dorfman's vindication of Thünen's natural-wage derivation', *Journal of Economic Literature*, **24** (4), 1777–85.

Sraffa, P. (1960), *Production of Commodities by Means of Commodities*, Cambridge: Cambridge University Press.

Suntum, U. van (1988), 'Vindicating Thünen's tombstone formula', *Jahrbücher für Nationalökonomie und Statistik*, 204/5, 393–405.

Thünen, J.H. von (1817), 'Ueber die Einführung eines Kreditsystems in Mecklenburg und über die Bestimmung des Pfandwerths der Mecklenburgischen Landgüter', *Neue Annalen der Mecklenburgischen Landwirtschaftsgesellschaft*, 2/4, 401–544.

Thünen, J.H. von (1823–50), manuscripts (partially published and transcribed), accessed 15 January 2014 at http://www.thuenen.info ('Digitales Archiv') and https://www.uni-hohenheim.de/uniarch/FTA%20E%20 XVII/index.html.

Thünen, J.H. von (1826), *Der Isolirte Staat in Beziehung auf Landwirthschaft und Nationalökonomie, erster Teil: Untersuchung über den Einfluß, den die Getreidepreise, der Reichthum des Bodens und die Abgaben auf den Ackerbau ausüben*, Hamburg: Perthes; 2nd (extended) edn (1842) Rostock: Leopold.

Thünen, J.H. von (1831a), 'Vorschlag zur Errichtung einer Deposital-Zettelbank in Mecklenburg', *Neue Annalen der Mecklenburgischen Landwirtschaftsgesellschaft*, 1/17, 2–10.

Thünen, J.H. von (1831b), 'Erachten über die Verbesserung des Ackerbaus der Städte', *Neue Annalen der Mecklenburgischen Landwirtschaftsgesellschaft*, 1/17, 337–99.

Thünen, J.H. von (1842), *Der isolirte Staat in Beziehung auf Landwirthschaft und Nationalökonomie. I. Theil. Untersuchungen über den Einfluss, den die Getreidepreise, der Reichthum des Bodens und die Abgaben auf den Ackerbau ausüben*, 2nd edn, Rostock: Leopold.

Thünen, J.H. von (1863), *Der naturgemäße Arbeitslohn und dessen Verhältniß zum Zinsfuß und zur Landrente. Zweite Abtheilung*, ed. H. Schumacher, Rostock: Leopold.

Thünen, J.H. von (1850), *Der Isolirte Staat in Beziehung auf Landwirthschaft und Nationalökonomie, zweiter Teil, erste Abtheilung: Der naturgemäße Arbeitslohn und dessen Verhältnis zum Zinsfuß und zur Landrente*, Rostock: Hinsdorff.

Thünen, J.H. von (2009), *The Isolated State in Relation to Agriculture and Political Economy. Part III: Principles for the Determination of Rent, the Most Advantageous Rotation Period and the Value of Stands of Varying Age in Pinewoods*, trans. K. Tribe from the posthumous German edn (1863), ed. U. van Suntum, Chippenham and Eastbourne, UK: Palgrave Macmillan.

Barthélemy-Charles Dunoyer de Segonzac (1786–1862)

Charles Dunoyer was born on 20 May 1786 in the department of Lot. He studied in Paris, first at the Académie de Jurisprudence and then at the École de Droit. Hostile to Napoleon, he supported the Provisional Government in 1814 after the first fall of the imperial regime. He was however dissatisfied with Louis XVIII's "Charte octroyée" and, with Charles Comte – J.-B. Say's son-in-law – he founded a periodical, *Le Censeur*, to defend liberal ideas. The publication, first made on a weekly basis and then in thick volumes in order to avoid a censorship, which was limited to publications of less than 320 pages, came to an end for a while. It resumed under the name of *Censeur européen*, but, in June 1817, Comte and Dunoyer were prosecuted. Comte left the country but Dunoyer was arrested and sentenced to one year of imprisonment. After the Revolution of July 1830, he returned to politics, supported the new regime of Louis-Philippe and was appointed as a Préfet and became a member of the Conseil d'État. Elected to the Académie des sciences morales et politiques, he was a co-founder of the Société d'économie politique, of which he became the president. He opposed Louis-Napoléon Bonaparte's putsch of 2 December 1851 and resigned from all official positions. He died in Paris on 4 July 1862.

For Dunoyer (1827a: 368), the eighteenth-century *philosophes*, and especially Montesquieu and Rousseau, analysed the organization of society abstracting from the laws of its progress and without inquiring into the proper aim of social activity. Politics only consisted in a discussion of the nature and forms of governments. The economists, on the other hand, thought that politics had no influence on wealth and prosperity and that "wealth was basically independent of public organization" (Say [1803] 2006: 3). Dunoyer instead wanted to understand the links between politics and the economy, starting from the idea Benjamin Constant (1814: 8) had put forward that "today the unique aim of human nations is quietness, and wealth with quietness, with industry as the source of wealth". When in 1815 the editors of *Le Censeur* were obliged to suspend its publication, they were wondering whether the liberal opposition had a proper object: and they admitted that "in general one did not know, and did not even ask, where society had to go, and in view of what general object it had to be established" (Dunoyer 1827a: 374). Dunoyer tried to give an answer.

It is first necessary to know what liberty is. Dunoyer discards the traditional definition that it is the possibility to do what one wants to do. He also rejects the idea of liberty as a natural right as stated in the Declaration of Human Rights. For him, liberty is a situation in which a person can use his or her faculties without any impediment (1825: 29; 1845, I: 24). Liberty is not a right. It is a power that can be obtained.

What organization in political power does comply with a market economy? Do men therein live in harmony or conflict? Montesquieu (1748, II: 2) wrote that "the natural effect of commerce is to bring peace. Two nations that trade together render themselves mutually dependent if one has an interest in buying and the other in selling". Louis de Bonald (1796, II: 449) stated instead that "even the most honest trade necessarily puts men in a constant state of war" and, as a consequence, he proposed a specific organization of the political system:

> Civilized countries ... could not have existed ... without the formation, from the very nature of man and society, of a barrier ... which placed in the lower part of the society the wish

and the duty to get rich through work and industry, and in the upper part, where fortune has already been made, the duty and even the ambition of public careers. (Bonald 1822: 32)

One must be wealthy in order to be allowed to participate in political power.

Dunoyer rejects this view. Industry alone, defined as all the useful activities, is capable of giving society prosperity, morality and peace. Political and social organization must favour this development. What must be removed is the opposition between a dominated class, doomed to work, and a politically ruling and leisure class. What must and will be instituted is a society in which "the working classes have taken precedence . . . , in which the passion for work prevails instead over the passion for power . . . and labour is the sole avowed means to get rich" (Dunoyer 1825: 323).

Like Dunoyer, Claude-Henri de Saint-Simon (1823) defended "industrialisme", but he disagreed with him on the role of the government. Dunoyer (1827a: 381) criticized him for considering political power as the authority in charge of "directing all the industrial activities towards a common aim", and put forth instead the idea that the government's activity is an industry like any other, as it can be seen from the nature of public expenses. Say had rejected Adam Smith's opposition between productive and unproductive labour, but nevertheless had maintained a distinction between unproductive consumption, which meets the immediate satisfaction of a need, and reproductive consumption, which produces a deferred satisfaction (Say 1803 [2006]: 863). Public expenses mainly concern "immaterial products" and are thus unproductive (ibid.: 937), a destruction of values, a diminution of wealth. Against Say, Dunoyer (1827b) maintains that, if they are suitably done, public expenses are productive even if they take the form of services. With an industrious people:

> government itself has the character of an industrial undertaking, with the sole difference that, instead of being done for particular persons or associations, . . . it acts on behalf of the general society, which entrusts it to people of its choice, at a price and conditions it judges to be the most advantageous. (Dunoyer 1825: 323–4)

In an industrial society, the government plays the part that society assigns to it and by which it is not ruled.

ALAIN BÉRAUD

See also:

French classical political economy (II); Gustave de Molinari (I); Jean-Baptiste Say (I); Adam Smith (I).

References and further reading

Benkemoune, R. (2009), 'Charles Dunoyer and the emergence of the idea of an economic cycle', *History of Political Economy*, **41** (2), 271–95.
Bonald, L. de (1796), *Théorie du pouvoir politique et religieux dans une société civile démontrée par le raisonnement et par l'histoire*, Constance: n.p.
Bonald, L. de (1815), *Réflexions sur l'intérêt général de l'Europe, suivi de quelques considérations sur la noblesse*, Paris: Le Normant.
Bonald, L. de (1822), *Discours dans la discussion du projet de loi relatif aux feuilles périodiques*, Paris: Hacquart.
Comte, C. (1815), Review of Louis de Bonald's *Réflexions sur l'intérêt général de l'Europe*, Le Censeur, **4**, 133–210.
Constant, B. (1814), *De l'esprit de conquête et de l'usurpation dans leurs rapports avec la civilisation européenne*, London: J. Murray.

Dunoyer, B.-C. (1825), *L'industrie et la morale considérées dans leur rapport avec la liberté*, Paris: Sautelet.

Dunoyer, B.-C. (1827a), 'Esquisse historique des doctrines auxquelles on a donné le nom d'*Industrialisme*, c'est-à-dire, des doctrines qui fondent la société sur l'*Industrie*', *Revue encyclopédique*, **33** (2), 368–93.

Dunoyer, B.-C. (1827b), 'Compte-rendu de la 5ème édition du *Traité d'économie politique* par J.-B. Say', *Revue encyclopédique*, **34** (1), 63–90.

Dunoyer, B.-C. (1830), *Nouveau traité d'économie sociale, ou simple exposition des causes sous l'influence desquelles les hommes parviennent à user de leurs forces avec le plus de liberté, c'est-à-dire avec le plus facilité et de puissance*, Paris: Sautelet et Mesnier.

Dunoyer, B.-C. (1845), *De la liberté du travail, ou simple exposé des conditions dans lesquelles les force humaines s'exercent avec le plus de puissance*, Paris: Guillaumin.

Faccarello, G. (2010), 'Bold ideas. French liberal economists and the state: Say to Leroy-Beaulieu', *European Journal of the History of Political Economy*, **17** (4), 719–58.

Hart, D.M. (1994), 'Class analysis, slavery and the industrialist theory of history in French liberal thought, 1814–1830: the radical liberalism of Charles Comte and Charles Dunoyer', unpublished doctoral dissertation, King's College, Cambridge.

Leroux, R. (2015), *Au fondement de l'industrialisme, Comte, Dunoyer et la pensée libérale en France*, Paris: Hermann.

Liggio, L.P. (1977), 'Charles Dunoyer and French Classical Liberalism', *Journal of Libertarian Studies*, **1** (3), 153–78.

Montesquieu, C.L. de Secondat de (1748), *De l'esprit des lois*, Geneva: Barillot, reprinted 1772, Paris: Nourse.

Penin, M. (1991), 'Charles Dunoyer, 1786–1862, l'échec d'un libéralisme', in Y. Breton and M. Lutfalla (eds), *L'économie politique en France au XIXᵉ siècle*, Paris: Economica, pp. 33–81.

Saint-Simon, C.-H. de (1823), *Le catéchisme industriel*, Paris: Imprimerie du Setier.

Say, J.-B. (1803), *Traité d'économique politique*, Paris: Deterville, variorum edn in J.-B. Say (2006), *Œuvres complètes*, vol. 1, Paris: Economica.

Say, J.-B. (1814), *Traité d'économique politique*, 2nd edn, Paris: Renouard, variorum edn in J.-B. Say (2006), *Œuvres complètes*, vol. 1, Paris: Economica.

Say, J.-B. (1826), *Traité d'économique politique*, 5th edn, Paris: Rapilly, variorum edn in J.-B. Say, *Œuvres complètes*, vol. 1, Paris: Economica.

Villey, E. (1899), *L'œuvre économique de Charles Dunoyer*, Paris: Librairie de la société du recueil général des lois et arrêts.

Weinburg, M. (1978), 'The social analysis of three early 19th century French liberals: Say, Comte, and Dunoyer', *Journal of Libertarian Studies*, **2** (1), 45–63.

Friedrich List (1789–1846)

Friedrich List has been characterized as one of the most renowned German economists, along with Karl Marx (Häuser 1989: 30). Like Marx, he was not a person involved only in academia, and thus his economic œuvre cannot be understood without knowledge of his political vision of a free and united Germany. In this respect List was a typical nationalist of his age, attempting to merge nationalism and liberalism into an inseparable whole.

Biographical Notes

List was born in 1789 in Reutlingen in south-west Germany (for biographical details, see Henderson 1983; Wendler 2013). In the course of the territorial re-organizations of the Napoleonic era he aimed for a career in the public administration. During his early reform attempts within the bureaucratic apparatus of the Kingdom of Württemberg, the Faculty of State Sciences (Staatswissenschaftliche Fakultät) was founded at the University of Tübingen, and List, possessing neither a high school diploma nor a university degree, was appointed Professor of Administration Practice. After the Restoration, he had to leave the university owing to his liberal convictions. In the following years he was entirely committed to the introduction of a German customs union (Zollunion), which was eventually realized in 1834, partly based on his efforts.

After authoring a petition against the illiberal practices of the Kingdom of Württemberg he was forced into exile, eventually settling in the United States, where he spent the years 1825–30 as a highly successful entrepreneur in the emerging railroad industry. It was during this period that he first developed the idea of a protective duty. With this idea he joined the presidential campaign of the Democratic candidate Andrew Jackson and, after the latter's victory, used his political connections to get back to Germany, eventually returning as an American envoy to the Kingdom of Saxony. Here he acted as a major figure in the development of the German railroad system, in his view a key factor (along with the customs union) for the industrialization of the country. After some disappointments in this field, he left Germany for Paris, and between 1839 and 1840 wrote his major work, *Das nationale System der politischen Ökonomie* (*The National System of Political Economy*), published in 1841. Following further serious setbacks in his last years in Germany, he committed suicide in 1846 at the age of 57.

Works

The principal goal of *Das nationale System der politischen Ökonomie* is to integrate the idea of the nation into political economy. The nation has to be considered an important intermediate layer between the individual and the rest of mankind, especially owing to the role of power in nation-state politics (List 1841 [1928]: 141–56). List's sharp critique of Smith and Say for having omitted this intermediate layer of the nation is already contained in his *Outlines of American Political Economy*, published in 1827 amid his participation in the economic policy debates in the United States (List 1827 [1996]).

The *National System* can be seen as an important precursor to the German Historical Schools (Rieter 2002: 140–41) owing to List's conviction that the economic policy strategy for a specific country can only be chosen adequately when bearing in mind the development stage of that country. In the German debate he thus introduces the notion of the temporal and spatial relativity of economic policy recommendations, a concept which would become crucial for the German approach of "Nationalökonomie" (incidentally a name substantially inspired by the title of List's book) in the second half of the nineteenth century.

According to List, the level of a nation's economic development is characterized not only by its varying wealth but also by different stages of development or civilization, beginning with "original barbarism" and culminating, after several intermediate steps, in an interconnected "agricultural-manufacturing-commercial condition" – concepts already contained in his earlier work *The Natural System of Political Economy* (List 1837 [1983]). Opposed to the policy recommendation of Ricardo's famous wine-and-cloth example, List underscores that if the wine-producing nation indeed happens to specialize in agriculture, its stage of development and particularly its power will remain low, resulting in a dependency (especially in military terms) on the industrialized nations. The essential issue in List's view is that the catch-up of the agricultural nation will not take place automatically, but will need temporary protection: only after it has reached a comparable stage of civilization vis-à-vis the non-agricultural country can it be opened to free trade for the mutual benefit of all. He is in favor of industrialization and technical progress, but considers them not as an aim in themselves but rather as a means of supporting the process of civilization.

The stark contrast in the way he sees and interprets the classical economists stems from List's notion that it is not only material wealth which drives development but the interplay of material and immaterial (mental) factors. This idea is at the basis of his "theory of the powers of production" and constitutes his most significant theoretical contribution. The original idea of "inner goods" and the links to material and "moral" determinants of economic development, however, had already been developed by the German-Russian classic Heinrich von Storch in his 1815 *Cours d'économie politique* whose ideas influenced many French classical economists, above all Charles Dunoyer. It is, however, surprising that despite the importance of the theory in List's thinking, the concept is not precisely defined anywhere. The often quoted sentence that "the power of producing wealth is . . . infinitely more important than wealth itself" (List 1841 [1928]: 108) only implicitly circumscribes the concept of the productive powers. What can be inferred from List's usage of the term is that it is the "mental capital" ("geistiges Kapital") of mankind or of a specific nation which is at the center of the concept of productive powers.

Thus List can be seen as a precursor to the twentieth-century theory of human capital. With this stress on the macroeconomic aspects of human capital – as opposed to the microeconomic focus of classical economists, such as Smith and Say, as well as of modern conceptualizations – he can be seen as advocating a view similar to the later representatives of the "old" or "original institutionalism" of Thorstein Bunde Veblen and John Roger Commons. Both List and the institutionalists are convinced that not only quantifiable factors should be analyzed by economists, but rather the economic process in its interplay with the societal whole: a stance which can justly be interpreted as a plea for integrated social sciences as opposed to isolated economics. This can be seen when the "proto-institutionalist" List is the first to point to an issue which has been highly relevant for economics ever since, and plays a prominent role in the famous "Methodenstreit" of Gustav Schmoller and Carl Menger: should the science of economics engage only in economic issues in the strict sense, or should it also incorporate the societal context in which human thought and action are embedded, and if so, to what extent?

Regarding List's macroeconomic development perspective, secondary literature often refers to the nexus with Adam Müller. Müller formulates very similar positions in his *Elemente der Staatskunst* of 1809/10, in which he attributes British prosperity to the combination of human (mental) and physical capital. As already mentioned, however, Heinrich von Storch, who is referred to in the *National System*, certainly is the more important influence here.

In conclusion, neither the stage theory of economic development (already present in Smith) nor the protective duty argument are in a strict sense List's inventions; the ideas of "mental capital" or "productive powers" also already existed in the earlier literature. However, to paraphrase Schumpeter, if an innovation consists of combining already known elements into a new entity, then List is an innovator *par excellence*. The reason for such a classification is his masterly linking of the theory of economic development with the theory of the powers of production, thus transforming the protective duty ("Schutzzoll") argument into an argument for a development or educational duty ("Erziehungszoll"). This is more than a rhetorical achievement: while the protective duty is aimed at conserving existing structures, the development duty is targeted at enabling progress and catch-up that would otherwise not materialize.

List's heritage is ambiguous. Even though his idea of the special role of the nation aims at a world that should become a "universal union" once – with the help of his duty system – nations have reached comparable stages of development, his work can be seen as the beginning of the German "Sonderweg" in nineteenth-century economics. His opposition to the individualism of classical economics, the endorsement of holistic notions of economy and society, and the emphasis on relativism in political economy of different nations have made him an attractive figure not just in the eyes of the Historical Schools, but also – in complete disregard of his deeply rooted democratic convictions which entailed existential difficulties during his entire lifetime – of National Socialism. This twentieth-century reception of his work lets List appear once more as a truly tragic figure.

STEFAN KOLEV AND JOACHIM ZWEYNERT

See also:

British classical political economy (II); Development economics (III); French classical political economy (II); Historical economics (II); Institutionalism (II); International trade (III); Carl Menger (I); David Ricardo (I); Jean-Baptiste Say (I); Gustav Friedrich von Schmoller (I); Barthélemy-Charles Dunoyer de Segonzac (I); Adam Smith (I); Thorstein Bunde Veblen (I).

References and further reading

Häuser, K. (1989), 'Friedrich List: Sein Leben und Wirken', in K. Häuser, W. Lachmann and H. Scherf (eds), *Vademecum zu einem schöpferischen Klassiker mit tragischem Schicksal*, Düsseldorf: Verlag Wirtschaft und Finanzen, pp. 29–47.
Henderson, W.O. (1983), *Friedrich List. Economist and Visionary, 1789–1846*, London: Frank Cass.
List, F. (1827), *Grundriß der amerikanischen politischen Ökonomie* (*Outlines of American Political Economy*), reprinted 1996, ed. M. Liebig, Wiesbaden: Dr. Böttiger.
List, F. (1837), *The Natural System of Political Economy*, reprinted 1983, trans. and ed. W.O. Henderson, London: Frank Cass.
List, F. (1841), *The National System of Political Economy*, reprinted 1928, trans. S.S. Lloyd, London: Longmans, Green & Co.

List, F. (1841), *Das nationale System der politischen Ökonomie*, in E. von Beckerath (ed.), *The Collected Works*, vol. 6, reprinted 1930, Berlin: Reimar Hobbing.

Müller, A. (1809/10), *Die Elemente der Staatskunst*, 1922 reprint of the original Berlin edn, Jena: Gustav Fischer.

Rieter, H. (2002), 'Historische Schulen', in O. Issing (ed.), *Geschichte der Nationalökonomie*, 4th edn, Munich: Franz Vahlen, pp. 131–68.

Storch, H. von (1815), *Cours d'économie politique: ou exposition des principes qui déterminent la prospérité des nations*, 1997 reprint of the original St Petersburg edn, Hildesheim: Olms-Weidmann.

Wendler, E. (2013), *Friedrich List (1789–1846). Ein Ökonom mit Weitblick und sozialer Verantwortung*, Wiesbaden: Springer Gabler.

Frédéric Bastiat (1801–1850)

Born in Bayonne on 30 June 1801, Frédéric Bastiat became an orphan at an early age and had to leave the religious school he attended before obtaining his Baccalauréat diploma. In 1818, he started to work in the trade company of his uncle but soon got bored. He left and lived in a landed property that his family possessed in Mugron, in the Landes, but, rather than managing the estate, he preferred to study philosophy, history and political economy – in particular the works of the French classics: Jean-Baptiste Say, Charles Comte and Charles Dunoyer.

Bastiat's first writings date from 1830 and support a liberal candidate to the Parliament, François Faurie. He was himself an unsuccessful candidate during the 1831 elections, but was elected in 1833 to a local position, as Conseiller général of the Canton of Mugron. In 1844, in England, he attended some meetings of the Anti-Corn Laws League and met its leaders. He kept in touch with Richard Cobden and translated into French, in 1845, the main speeches of the League leaders. Bastiat also published his first article in *Journal des économistes* – "De l'influence des tarifs français et anglais sur l'avenir des deux peuples" – which was successfully received. Following the English model, he tried to organize a Free Trade movement: in 1846 he created the Association bordelaise pour la liberté des échanges, and then a similar association in Paris. The 1848 Revolution opened new perspectives. Bastiat realized that he had not only to fight against protectionism but also socialism – first that of Louis Blanc, and then of Pierre-Joseph Proudhon. Elected to the Assemblée Constituante, he voted sometimes with the Right, sometimes with the Left. In particular, he declared himself against the prosecution of Louis Blanc, and against the death penalty. Re-elected to the Assemblée Législative in 1849, he was in favour of the right of coalition for the workers. He died in Rome on 24 December 1850 where he had decided to go with the hope that the climate would dampen his sufferings due to a larynx disease. It is during the last year of his life that he published his most well-known book, *Les harmonies économiques*.

Bastiat's short career can be divided into two periods. It started with the defence of free trade. French protectionists maintained that tariffs should be sufficiently high to cover the difference between the price of domestic and foreign commodities: competition can be free only if costs are equal. In order to discard this argument, Bastiat made use of two classical ideas. He stressed first that such a measure was an attack against the very principle of exchange, which was based on the diversity of the conditions of production. He explained that employment in France could not suffer from the competition of countries which enjoyed more favourable conditions. If, initially, foreign prices were lower, if free trade would lead to a deficit of the balance of trade, the increase of the demand for foreign products and the monetary transfers would generate a rise in prices abroad and domestic prices would again become competitive. However, he wanted to go further and show that those which benefit most from free trade are the less favoured countries. In each product, he explained, "nature collaborates with labour. But the contribution of nature is always free. Only that part which is due to human labour is the object of exchange and consequently of a remuneration" (Bastiat 1845: 353). If prices depend only on the labour of the producers, a country will gain more from exchange than its partners that are possessed of natural resources which it does not have, because it will benefit freely from these resources. However,

Bastiat's main argument is moral. Exchange is a natural right: anyone who produces or acquires a product should be able to give it to anyone on earth against the objects that he desires.

The 1848 Revolution radically modified the context. The enemy changed and Bastiat started to fight the socialists. He maintained that, while the economists rightly defended liberty, they did not know how to solidly establish their starting point, that is, the idea that "interests, left to themselves, tend to the preponderance of the general interest" (Bastiat 1850 [1982]: 5). Still worse, they advanced statements, which socialists used in order to maintain that private interests are in conflict with one another: they stated that the natural agents of production – land in particular – have a value. Landowners sell the power of production of land (the gifts of God) to the farmers. Socialists concluded that this was an injustice. Ricardo explained that the price of the means of subsistence was determined on the land of the poorest quality among all lands cultivated. With the increase in population, men must give for their subsistence a growing quantity of labour, and rent must increase. The inequality is fatal. Malthus, on the other hand, explained that population grows faster than subsistence. Only two remedies are thus possible: a diminution of the number of births or an increase of mortality. Malthus was in favour of the moral constraint, but this remedy, to be efficient, must be universal: it is thus impossible to count on it. Pauperism is unavoidable.

To fight against socialism, it is necessary to discard these classical propositions and reconstruct the theory of value, that is, discard at the same time Say's thesis that utility is the foundation of value, and Ricardo's that the expense of labour determines the price of goods. Their price, Bastiat maintains, is not determined by the labour of the producer, but by the labour saved to the buyer. The natural agents do not create any value: what land is worth is "the human labour which improved it, the capital sunk in it" (Bastiat 1850 [1982]: 279). The landowner is the owner of a value that he himself has created; his rent remunerates the services he provides. The ownership of land is legitimate because its origin is labour.

When more intensive techniques of production are introduced, Ricardo said, costs of production must increase. Bastiat (1850 [1982]: 280) maintains that they decrease instead. Of course, when the quality of land is improved, the successive crops are charged with the interest of the capital invested, but the quantity of labour necessary to cultivate land diminishes and every crop is thus obtained in less expensive conditions. Against the Ricardian approach Bastiat proposed a vision of an economy where, as capital accumulates, the sum total of wages increases both absolutely and relatively, while the sum total of profits increases in absolute but diminishes in relative terms.

The human society is harmonious: "all the interests tend towards a great outcome . . . : the convergence of all the social classes towards an always growing level; in other terms: the *equalisation* of individuals with a general *improvement*" (Bastiat 1850 [1982]: 115).

ALAIN BÉRAUD

See also:

Jean-Baptiste Say (I); Pierre-Joseph Proudhon (I); French classical political economy (II); David Ricardo (I); Adam Smith (I); Thomas Robert Malthus (I); Gustave de Molinari (I).

References and further reading

Baslé, M. and A. Gélédan (1991), 'Frédéric Bastiat, 1801–1850, Théoricien et militant du libre échange', in Y. Breton and M. Lutfalla (eds), *L'économie politique en France au XIXème siècle*, Paris: Economica.

Bastiat, F. (1844), 'De l'influence des tarifs français et anglais sur l'avenir des deux peuples', *Journal des économistes*, **9**, 244–71.

Bastiat, F. (1845), 'Sophismes économiques', *Journal des économistes*, **11** (41), 1–16, **11** (44), 345–60, **12** (47), 201–15.

Bastiat, F. (1850), *Harmonies économiques*, Paris: Guillaumin, 2nd edn, 1851, Paris: Guillaumin, reprinted 1982, Geneva and Paris: Slatkine.

Bastiat, F. (1854–55), *Œuvres complètes*, P. Paillottet and R. de Fontenay (eds), Paris: Guillaumin, reprinted 1862–64, Paris: Guillaumin.

Bastiat, F. (2011), *The Collected Works of Frédéric Bastiat*, Jacques de Guenin (ed.), Indianapolis, IN: Liberty Fund.

Leroux, R. (2008), *Lire Bastiat, Science sociale et libéralisme*, Paris: Hermann.

Leroux, R. (ed.) (2011), *Political Economy and Liberalism, the Contribution of Frédéric Bastiat*, Abingdon: Routledge.

Antoine-Augustin Cournot (1801–1877)

Antoine-Augustin Cournot was born on 28 August 1801 in Gray, in the province of Franche-Comté, and died in Paris on 31 March 1877. He was admitted to the École Normale at the age of 20, but the school was closed in 1822 for political reasons. He then studied at the Faculty of Sciences and defended in 1829 his main thesis in mechanics and a secondary thesis in astronomy.

The mathematical papers he published attracted the attention of Siméon-Denis Poisson and, thanks to him, in 1834 he became professor of mechanics and analysis at the Faculty of Sciences in Lyon. In October 1835, he became "Recteur" of the Académie de Grenoble and taught mathematics at the Faculty. In 1836 he replaced André-Marie Ampère as general inspector of education. While working for these three positions, he wrote his *Recherches sur les principes mathématiques de la théorie des richesses*, published in 1838. He came back to mathematics and published, in 1841, the *Traité élémentaire de la théorie des fonctions et du calcul infinitésimal* and, in 1843, his book on probability theory, *Exposition de la théorie des chances et des probabilités*. He then directed his attention to the philosophy of sciences with his *Essai sur les fondements de nos connaissances* (1851) and *Traité de l'enchaînement des idées fondamentales dans les sciences et dans l'histoire* (1861). From 1854 to 1862, he was "Recteur" of the Académie de Dijon but, in 1862, because of his blindness, he left this position. He continued to do research until his death. He returned to economics in *Principes de la théorie des richesses* (1863) which put in literary form the ideas he advanced in 1838. This book, however, shows a change in his views and the influence of John Stuart Mill and Friedrich List: Cournot's dissatisfaction with liberalism became more evident. The idea that "the greatest good for society must necessarily be the resultant of the forces generated by private interests" (Cournot 1863 [1981]: 275) seems ill founded; on the one hand, the notion of an optimum is not clearly defined and, on the other hand, it is impossible to prove that particular interests necessarily lead to a collective well-being.

Mathematics, Economics and Philosophy

Cournot was a mathematician, an economist and a philosopher. In the preface to his 1838 *Recherches* he writes that he intends to apply "the forms and symbols of mathematical analysis" to the theory of wealth (1838 [1980]: 3). He is led to use the theory of continuous functions and of infinitesimal calculus, of which he gave an elementary exposition three years later (1841). It is, however, less easy to understand whether his economic analyses benefited from his reflection on probabilities, history and philosophy of science.

In *Théorie des chances et des probabilités* (1843) Cournot stresses that the word probability has two meanings, being either the measure of our ignorance or the measure of the possibility of things. However, when he applies his theory to aleatory markets and insurance, this point is not stressed. What characterizes his approach is his rejection of Bernoulli's solution of the Saint Petersburg paradox. While admitting that, for an individual, the importance of a sum of money depends on his wealth, he does not think that it is possible to measure utility and to establish a functional relationship between the utility of a sum of money and this wealth. He analyses a random market without referring to the notion of moral expectation.

In *L'enchainement des idées fondamentales dans les sciences et dans l'histoire* (1861), he deals with economic optimism and maintains that the idea that the greatest general good necessarily results from conflicting private interests is not susceptible of a logical proof. If the motto *Laissez faire, Laissez passer* must triumph in the end, it is not because of a theoretical proof in its favour, but because only artificial and arbitrary rules are proposed against it.

The 1838 *Recherches* are devoted to the mathematical principles of the theory of wealth. In the 1863 *Principes* Cournot came back to his former approach but referred also to his *Esssai sur le fondement des connaissances* (1851) and to the analysis he made there of the Platonic opposition between science and opinion. From this point of view, political economy is in an ambiguous position. Cournot (1863 [1981]: 326) states "that it does not admit and will never completely admit the regular, systematic and always progressive construction, which belong to the sciences ... and never completely rely on unshakable and universally accepted bases". First, while some propositions of the theory of wealth could be rigorously proved, their meanings depend on considerations drawn from "social economics" and this last field is not based on science but on opinion. As an example, he contrasts the scientific definition of wealth as the sum of the values of the goods, to the meaning the word well-being has in social economics. The value of income does not measure men's well-being.

Secondly, the abstractions to which economists must resort to simplify questions are not shared by all economists and could sometimes appear artificial and arbitrary. Depending on the facts they judge essential or of secondary importance, economists formulate hypotheses and reach different conclusions even if they all reason correctly. Cournot does not abandon his 1838 ambition, but he feels it necessary to stress its dangers: "The mathematical apparatus ... leads us unfortunately to think that one confers to these hypotheses a value that they effectively have in the interpretation of natural phenomena, but that they cannot have to the same degree in the interpretation of social phenomena" (1863 [1981]: 329–30).

The Axioms of the Theory of Prices

Cournot (1877 [1982]: 91) considers his theory of prices as his main contribution to economic theory. He breaks with his predecessors not only because he uses mathematics and proposes new tools, but also because his approach is different. The classics viewed monopoly as an exceptional case. For Cournot, instead, it is a point of departure to study duopoly and "infinite" competition.

For what concerns the theory of value, Cournot refers to "only one axiom ... that everybody tries to get the greatest possible value from his thing or labour" (1838 [1980]: 35). He applies this axiom to explain the behaviour of producers who want to maximize their profits, but he refuses to use it as regards the demand for commodities or to estimate the benefit an individual gets from exchange: "there is nothing in common between the feeling of pleasure or pain and the mathematical notion of quantity in mathematics" (1851 [1975]: 233).

However, the axiom that anybody tries to get the maximum income from his or her resources is not Cournot's sole hypothesis. He affirms many times the principle of the uniformity of a price, which originates in the very notion of market understood as "the whole territory, the parts of which are united through free trade, so that prices are easily and quickly levelled" (Cournot 1838 [1980]: 40).

Cournot's framework is partial equilibrium, justified by the "principle of compensation". While it is true that "the economic system is an entity, the parts of which are linked together and act on each other" Cournot 1838 [1980]: 99), yet it is possible, as a first approximation, to abstract from such effects. Suppose that the production of a good diminishes from D_0 to D_1, and that its price increases from p_0 to p_1. The revenue of its producers changes from $p_0 D_0$ to $p_1 D_1$. Despite the rise in price, some consumers maintain their demand, but the new price reduces their income, available to buy the other goods, of an amount equal to $(p_1 - p_0)D_1$. Some other consumers instead stop buying the good and spend the sum saved $p_0(D_0 - D_1)$ to buy other commodities. Globally, Cournot writes, the income effect is nil. "Thus, when we consider the totalities of the producers and the consumers of the good in question, one finds that the same annual sum is available for the demand for all the other goods" (ibid.: 101). It is thus possible that this sum will be spent as before, among the other commodities, and that their prices will not change. Such a possibility is however exceptional and Cournot recognizes that the prices of the other commodities will change, but the consequence on the good, which initially was subject to the first change, will only be of a second order and can be ignored in a first approximation.

To analyse the formation of prices, Cournot's approach is the same for monopoly, duopoly or "infinite" competition: the seller(s) fix(es) the price. This point has been long discussed (Magnan de Bornier 1992, 2000, 2001; Morrison 2001). It is effectively possible to think that, after having supposed that a monopolist firm fixes the price of the good it produces, Cournot also supposes that, for other forms of markets, the quantity produced is the strategic variable while the price is determined by supply and demand. In fact, when he deals with duopoly, he does not reason on the demand function but on the reciprocal function. However, Cournot (1838 [1980]: 60; 1863 [1981]: 73) explicitly states that each entrepreneur fixes the volume of his sales "in changing adequately the price". The entrepreneur supposes the production of his competitor as given and reasons like a monopolist; at the same time he sees him facing the residual – and not the total – demand. When we read that "firms form conjectures *à la* Cournot", it is not pretended that firms take the quantities, and not prices, as the decision variable. To make a conjecture *à la* Cournot means that the entrepreneur supposes that his competitors will not change the quantities of the goods they sell if he changes the price.

The "Loi du débit"

Cournot thinks that the relationship between the price and the quantity produced – the "débit" – cannot be established theoretically. The law of demand is empirical and must be based on observations. He just supposes demand to be a generally decreasing function, $f(p)$, of price. The demand of a small number of agents is a discontinuous function, but, when dealing with a great number of agents, it is possible to consider it as continuous and that its variations are proportional to those in prices when they are small compared to their initial level.

Monopoly

When the cost of production is nil or when it only consists in overhead costs, the profit is maximal when the final revenue $pf(p)$ is at a maximum. As f is a continuous function, the total revenue is a continuous function of price. It is increasing or decreasing as the elasticity of demand – Cournot introduces the notion, if not the phrase – is smaller or greater than 1. When it is a maximum, the marginal revenue $f(p) + pf'(p)$ is nil. Cournot shows that there exists at least one maximum but that it is mathematically possible to have more than one solution – he discards however this possibility because he is convinced that "in real facts, and taking into account all the conditions of an economic system, there is no good, the price of which is not fully determined" ([1838] 1980: 82). A good model must only entail one solution.

If the total cost is a function $\phi(p)$ of the quantity produced, the profit $pf(p) - \phi[f(p)]$ is a maximum when $f(p) + pf'(p) - \phi'f'(p) = 0$, that is, when marginal revenue equals marginal cost. Cournot contrasts manufactures on the one hand and agriculture and mining on the other, and many followed him in this. While in the former, marginal costs are taken to be decreasing – at least as long as the increase in production does not increase the prices of raw materials and wages – in agriculture and mining where marginal costs are taken to be increasing. The logical conclusion is that "powerful capitalists or great companies can . . . artificially constitute monopolies, with profits superior to the usual rate of profits" (Cournot, 1863 [1981]: 79). However, Cournot does not judge this evolution negatively. To be sure, the monopoly price is higher than the competitive price, but the consumer benefits from lower prices due to a decrease in costs.

Cournot then studies the effects of the introduction of a tax. If the tax is based on the net revenue of the monopoly, it affects neither the price of the good nor the quantity produced. Its only consequence is to lower the rent of the monopolist. If the tax is based on each unit produced, it increases the price and diminishes production. The producer's loss is the reduction of his or her net income and is greater than the product of the tax. An idea advanced by Quesnay is thus met again: it is better to tax the net revenue than the products. However, what is the consumers' loss? Cournot calculates the additional expense that the consumers, who still buy the good in spite of its higher price, have to meet. He abstracts from the loss experienced by the consumers who stop buying the good: "this kind of damage cannot be evaluated" (1838 [1980]: 103). Cournot deliberately closes a door that Dupuit was to open later to measure the consumer's surplus.

Duopoly

Two firms, which produce the same good, have an interest in agreeing with each other to fix a monopoly price, but each of them can increase its profit through an increase in its production. The cooperative equilibrium, Cournot stresses, is unstable: "it could not persist unless a formal link is established; because one cannot . . . suppose . . . men making no errors or not being careless" (1838 [1980]: 62). Each producer tries to increase his revenue and must take into account the reaction of his competitor. He supposes that his competitor's output is given: this is what is called Cournot's conjecture. Taking an example in which each firm could alone meet demand at no cost, Cournot supposes that each firm fixes its production in order to maximize its revenue, given the output of

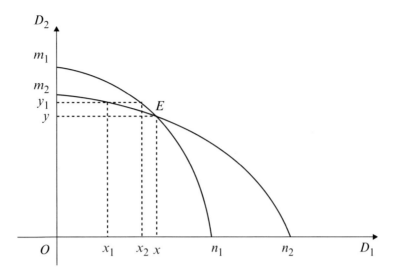

Source: Cournot (1838 [1980]: 60).

Figure 5   Cournot's duopoly

its competitor. He thus expresses reaction functions using the inverse demand function $p = f^{-1}(D_1 + D_2)$:

$$f^{-1}(D_1 + D_2) + D_1 f'^{-1}(D_1 + D_2) \tag{1}$$

$$f^{-1}(D_1 + D_2) + D_2 f'^{-1}(D_1 + D_2) \tag{2}$$

In Figure 5, the $m_i n_i$ curve represents the reaction function of firm i, $i = 1, 2$. An equilibrium is reached at point E where each firm fixes its production at the level anticipated by its competitor.

Cournot could have supposed that the decision variable is the price instead of the quantity. Each firm would thus have fixed its price in such a way that $p = [f(p) - D_j]$ is a maximum, D_j being the production level of its competitor. The result would have been the same. Each firm behaves as a monopolist, the demand for its product being the residual demand.

To study stability, Cournot describes a dynamical process where each firm fixes its production in turn, supposing that its rival will maintain its output at the level of the previous period. If the output of firm 1 is Ox_1, firm 2 will produce Oy_1, that is, a quantity such as to maximize its profits for a given Ox_1. However, for the same reason firm 1 will produce Ox_2. Cournot maintains that this process leads firms 1 and 2 to produce in the end respectively Ox and Oy. The equilibrium is stable. "If either of the two producers . . . momentarily departs [from equilibrium], he will be brought back to it by a series of reactions, the magnitude of which will be constantly diminishing" (Cournot 1838 [1980]: 61).

Cournot's duopoly theory and stability analysis were criticized almost 50 years after the publication of *Recherches.* Joseph Bertrand (1883: 503) maintained that the situation described by Cournot was not an equilibrium: "Whatever could be the common price adopted, if one competitor diminishes its price, he would attract . . . the whole sales and double his revenues if his competitor does not react." He discards the hypothesis of a uniform price and replaces the Cournot conjecture with the supposition that each firm takes the price of its rival as given. Edgeworth (1897: 117–18) picked up the idea and introduced a simple form of decreasing returns in the model: the production capacity of each firm is limited. He concluded that the outcome is indeterminate: the price will continuously fluctuate between a minimum required by the firm's capacity, and a maximum, that is, the monopoly price. Irving Fisher (1898: 126) criticized all his predecessors and maintained that no firm supposes that its competitors will not react when it changes the level of production or the price. It is in the situation of a chess player: its problem is to know how its rivals will react to its decisions. Later, the work of John Nash led to an understanding of Cournot, which discards dynamics: Cournot's solution is interpreted as an application of the theory of non-cooperative equilibria to duopoly analysis.

From Duopoly to "Infinite" Competition

The analysis of duopoly is generalized: the number of firms in a market is increased and costs of production are introduced. Supposing n firms, let $\phi_i(D_i)$ be the cost of production of firm i. Its profit $pD_i - \phi_i(D_i)$ is at a maximum when $D_i + pf'(p) - \phi_i'(D_i)f'(p) = 0$. Cournot shows that, in these circumstances, the price is lower than in monopoly conditions, in spite of a greater marginal cost.

The "infinite" competition is a limit, when D_i is negligible for all i, with respect to the total production $f(p)$ and to its derivative $f'(p)$ "so that the partial production D_i could be deleted [from the total production] without any appreciable change in the price of the good" (Cournot 1838 [1980]: 69). In such a case the price equals the marginal cost. It is thus possible to consider the supply of each firm as a function of the price and, in addition, obtain a total supply which is necessarily an increasing function of price. The equilibrium price is determined by supply and demand.

Cournot's Achievement

Using the theory of arbitrary functions, Cournot provided a new answer to the question of the determination of the prices of commodities. His point of departure is monopoly: it is the simplest problem to solve because the entrepreneur must not deal with the reactions of competitors. He then extends his model to the case of a competition between several firms. "Infinite" competition thus appears as a limit, where the decisions of no firm can affect prices. He thus introduced all the notions still in use in microeconomics today.

ALAIN BÉRAUD

See also:

Daniel Bernoulli (I); Jules Dupuit (I); Competition (III); Industrial organization (III); John Forbes Nash Jr (I); Uncertainty and information (III); Marie-Esprit-Léon Walras (I).

References and further reading

Bertrand, J. (1883), 'Compte-rendu de Théorie de la richesse sociale par Léon Walras et de Recherches sur les principes mathématiques de la théorie des richesses par Augustin Cournot', *Journal des Savants*, September, 499–508.
Cournot, A.-A. (1838), *Recherches sur les principes mathématiques de la théorie des richesses*, Paris: Hachette, reprinted 1980 in *Œuvres Complètes de A.A. Cournot*, vol. 8, Paris: J. Vrin.
Cournot, A.-A. (1841), *Traité élémentaire de la théorie des fonctions et du calcul infinitésimal*, Paris: Hachette, reprinted 1984 in *Œuvres Complètes de A.A. Cournot*, vol. 6, Paris: J. Vrin.
Cournot, A.-A. (1843), *Exposition de la théorie des chances et des probabilités*, Paris: Hachette, reprinted 1984 in *Œuvres Complètes de A.A. Cournot*, vol. 1, Paris: J. Vrin.
Cournot, A.-A. (1851), *Essai sur les fondements de nos connaissances et sur les caractères de la critique philosophique*, reprinted 1975 in *Œuvres Complètes de A.A. Cournot*, vol. 2, Paris: J. Vrin.
Cournot, A.-A. (1861), *Traité des idées fondamentales dans les sciences et dans l'histoire*, Paris: Hachette, reprinted 1982 in *Œuvres Complètes de A.A. Cournot*, vol. 3, Paris: J. Vrin.
Cournot, A.-A. (1863), *Principes de la théorie des richesses*, Paris: Hachette, reprinted 1981 in *Œuvres Complètes de A.A. Cournot*, vol. 9, Paris: J. Vrin.
Cournot, A.-A. (1877), *Revue Sommaire des Doctrines Économiques*, Paris: Hachette, reprinted 1982 in *Œuvres Complètes de A.A. Cournot*, vol. 10, Paris: J. Vrin.
Dos Santos Ferreira, R. and R. Ege (2013), 'General equilibrium as competitive equilibrium: the significance of Walras' achievement from a Cournotian viewpoint', *European Journal of the History of Economic Thought*, **20** (4), 625–45.
Edgeworth, F.Y. (1897), 'Teoria pura del monopolio', *Giornale degli Economisti*, **15**, 13–21, 307–20, 405–14, English trans. in F.Y. Edgeworth (1925), *Papers Relating to Political Economy*, London: Macmillan, vol. 1, pp. 111–42.
Fisher, I. (1898), 'Cournot and mathematical economics', *Quarterly Journal of Economics*, **12** (1), 119–38.
Magnan de Bornier, J. (1992), 'The "Cournot–Bertrand Debate": a historical perspective', *History of Political Economy*, **24** (3), 623–56.
Magnan de Bornier, J. (2000), 'Cournot avant Nash: grandeur et limites d'un modèle unitaire de concurrence', *Cahiers d'économie politique*, **37**, 101–25.
Magnan de Bornier, J. (2001), 'Magnan de Bornier on Cournot–Bertrand: a rejoinder to Clarence Morrison', *History of Political Economy*, **33** (1), 167–74.
Magnan de Bornier, J. (2007), 'Cournot et l'économie: quelques repères', in J.-P. Touffut (ed.), *La société du probable: les mathématiques sociales après Cournot*, Paris: Albin Michel, pp. 21–36.
Martin, T. (1996), *Probabilités et critique philosophique selon Cournot*, Paris: Vrin.
Morrison, C. (2001), 'Magnan de Bornier on Cournot–Bertrand', *History of Political Economy*, **33** (1), 161–5.

Jules Dupuit (1804–1866)

Jules Dupuit was born on 18 May 1804 in Fossano, in Piedmont, where his father was Inspecteur des finances. At the age of 18, he was admitted to the École Polytechnique in Paris. He then studied also in École des Ponts et Chaussées. From 1827 onwards, as engineer of the Ponts et Chaussées administration, he worked in the Département of Sarthe, and, from 1844, in Angers, where he had to deal with the floods of the River Loire. He started to collaborate with the *Journal des économistes* in 1849. In 1850 he became chief engineer in Paris, director of the municipal administration, and general inspector of the civil engineers in 1855. He died in Paris on 5 September 1866.

Engineer and Economist

The phrase "French ingénieurs économistes" usually designates mathematicians such as Antoine-Augustin Cournot as well as engineers like Dupuit, but their approaches are often different. The approach of the mathematicians is most of the time abstract: Cournot's ambition was to develop a mathematical theory of wealth. Dupuit instead, like most engineers, started from concrete problems, for example, how to know whether a public investment – a bridge, a road – would be useful enough to justify its construction? Must it be financed by a toll and, if so, at which level should it be fixed?

In order to find a solution to these problems, Dupuit used economic theory. He reasons in exactly the same way when dealing with the determining tolls or the distribution of water (Chatzis 2009: 668). He thought that theory alone can explain natural phenomena and the engineer or the economist must rely on it, and not only on experience, when trying to solve concrete problems.

French liberals discussed for a long time the nature and object of political economy. Henri Baudrillart (1863: 250) maintained that political economy is a moral science and differed from physics or mathematics because a role has to be given to opinions. Dupuit disagreed. Political economy, being the science of society, is not dependent as regards its principles on opinions. One of its most outstanding features "is that it presents a set of principles that can be demonstrated rigorously and form a dense doctrine, on which every intelligent man is not susceptible to have an opinion" (Dupuit 1863 [2009]: 153).

Dupuit did not explicitly use mathematics in his economic articles, but he always stated that political economy would benefit from such a use. He compared the role of mathematics with that of machines: they allow a smaller amount of expenses, time and labour. They favour the exactness of the result while our mind always runs the risk of being lost in a complex chain of arguments. He takes Jean-Baptiste Say (1803 [2006]: 519) as an example, who was mistaken when he advanced that doubling the quantity of wine produced would half its price. Mathematics would have allowed him to state rigorously the relationship between the abundance of production and the price, and would have avoided his error and, still better, would have shown that, while the price is a decreasing function of the quantity produced, it also depends on many other data.

Utility is a Measurable Quantity

Dupuit's contemporaries ignored his analyses. It was Jevons who, in 1879, drew attention to him. The problem was that he stated that Dupuit's analysis of utility was basically the same as the analysis he himself developed in his *Theory of Political Economy*. However, this assertion is misleading. For Jevons (1871 [1879]: 49) the utility of a good is the satisfaction obtained by the consumer. Dupuit instead considers that it is impossible to measure rigorously the faculty of things to satisfy human needs and that "political economy must take, for the measure of the utility of an object, the greatest sacrifice that a man would be ready to make in order to obtain it" (Dupuit 1844 [2009]: 214). This conception is coherent with his object. In order to estimate the utility of a public investment, it is not necessary to know the satisfaction of its users: what matters is the price these are ready to pay for the use of it.

To illustrate his statement, Dupuit (1849 [2009]: 276) often gave the example of a bridge for pedestrians, the user cost of which is nil. Suppose that an agent $h = 1, \ldots, k$ considers as equivalent the initial situation in which he or she does not cross the bridge and keep an amount of money x_m^h, and a situation in which the bridge is crossed and a diminished amount $(x_m^h - \Delta x_m^h)$ of money is left. The absolute utility of the bridge for agent h is Δx_m^h. For all the agents, it is $\sum_{h=1}^{k} \Delta x_m^h$. This presentation does not entail any interpersonal comparison of utility, nor any hypothesis about the marginal utility of money. Dupuit simply adds up the amounts of money that the agents are ready to pay to cross the bridge (Allais 1981 [1989]: 165).

The relative utility – the benefit that consumer h draws from buying the good – is the difference between the absolute utility of the good and the price p_1 he or she must pay to obtain it – a price for the time being supposed to be uniform: $\Delta x_m^h - p_1$. If the relative utility is positive for the first j agents and negative for the others, the total relative utility – the consumer's surplus in modern parlance – is $\sum_{h=1}^{j} (\Delta x_m^h - p_1)$.

Dupuit generalizes the result to the case where each agent can consume several units of the good. "Each consumer attaches a different utility to the same object, according to the quantity he can consume. So, a consumer who bought 100 bottles at 10 cents would only buy 50 at 15 cents, and only 30 at 20 cents" (Dupuit 1844 [2009]: 209). He introduces the cost of production (ibid.: 215) and analyses the effects of a technical progress that diminishes the cost: it increases utility because it allows new consumers to buy the good and the former consumers to buy more of the good. He studies the effects of an indirect tax and shows that the measure of the loss incurred is not the sum of the tax collected. What constitutes a loss is the fact that some agents stop consuming the good, which is now too expensive for them.

In the case of a bridge, for example, the problem of the determination of the level of the toll is of the utmost importance to Dupuit. If it is too high, a considerable part of the utility the public investment could have would be lost, and if it is too low it would be impossible to get back the sums invested. To fix it properly, it is necessary to know what it is aimed at. A private company would try to maximize its profit. The state would fix the level of the toll to get back a sum equal to the interest of the investment, the maintenance and the depreciation. The amount fixed by the private company would be larger than that requested by the state. However, for Dupuit, this is not important. The sum that "the company gets in excess over that obtained by the State form a profit for the shareholders who gain exactly what the users lose. Had the tariff no other result, one could say that it has no influence on the public wealth, it just modifies its distribution" (Dupuit 1849 [2009]: 280). The public investment is nevertheless preferable because the higher private tariff would entail a loss for all: those who would stop using the service would be deprived of something, which would have cost nothing, in Dupuit's example, to the company.

However, if the uniform public toll is preferable, it is not the best one. What would be a rational toll? If it were nil, relative and absolute utilities would be equal, but the financing of the investment should be made through taxes; and if the investment is of no utility to those who pay taxes, this would be unjust. One must in consequence establish a toll and fix it at such a level that those who use it pay a sum proportional to the utility they get (Dupuit 1844 [2009]: 286). It is thus necessary to abandon the idea of a uniform price, and differentiate the toll in order not to prevent its use by anyone who is ready to pay a duty, which exceeds the cost of the service.

Utility, Natural Right and Liberalism

Public utility is at the origin of the laws and determines the interventions of the state. Dupuit refers to this principle on a great number of occasions, for example, to justify his position on patents, on free external trade or on the management of the means of communication.

Many liberals referred to natural rights to justify private property. "Property exists before the law; the law is in charge to have property respected everywhere it is formed" (Bastiat 1848: 186). Dupuit disagrees: "all the economists who tried to justify economic phenomena referring to equity and justice have been mistaken . . . Justice is not the principle of society . . . It is public utility, the public good, because it is for this purpose . . . that society is established" (Dupuit 1862 [2009]: 643).

A firm producing a means of communication between two cities must not be afraid of competitors because it enjoys "a *de facto* monopoly" (Dupuit, SEP 1853 [Dupuit 2009], I: 574). A newcomer would have to face many geographical, economic and financial obstacles. The first firm had chosen the most convenient route, and its possible competitor must content itself with a second best. The sums to be invested are considerable and, for this investment to be profitable, the newcomer must be able to attract an important part of the customers. But, owing to habits, this is unlikely. This is why, Dupuit concludes (1852–53 [2009], I: 520), "the new firm would have harmed the first one, and ruined its own shareholders . . . The means of communication, the construction and exploitation of which require considerable expenses, are necessarily monopolies".

If the management is left to a private company, prices will be fixed so as to maximize its profits while the state can content itself with a lower fare, which will be enough to cover its costs. The high price demanded by a private firm would discourage a fraction of the potential customers and a great part of the utility they could have obtained from the means of communication would be lost. Which solution should be chosen? The answer, Dupuit states, lies in the principle of utility (1852–53 [2009], I: 452): "Any means of communication, which is a monopoly, must be exploited by the State; any means of communication open to competition must be exploited by privately owned firms".

Dupuit brought solutions to a series of practical and theoretical questions raised either by the administration or the economists. He can be seen as one of the founders of modern microeconomics (Ekelund and Hebert 1999).

ALAIN BÉRAUD

See also:
Maurice Allais (I); French classical political economy (II); Jean-Baptiste Say (I); Antoine-Augustin Cournot (I).

References and further reading
Allais, M. (1981), 'La théorie générale des surplus', *Économies et Sociétés*, série Économie Mathématique et Économétrie, 8 and 9, new edn 1989, Grenoble: Presses Universitaires de Grenoble.
Bastiat, F. (1848), 'Propriété et loi', *Journal des économistes*, **20** (80), 171–91.
Baudrillart, H. (1863), 'Observations du rédacteur en chef', *Journal des économistes*, **37** (36), 249–53.
Chatzis, K. (2009), 'Jules Dupuit, Ingénieur des ponts et chaussées', in J. Dupuit, *Œuvres économiques complètes*, Y. Breton and G. Klotz (eds), vol. 1, Paris: Economica, pp. 675–92.
Dupuit, J. (1844), 'De la mesure de l'utilité des travaux publics', *Annales des Ponts et Chaussées*, **116**, 332–75, in J. Dupuit (2009), *Œuvres économiques complètes*, Y. Breton and G. Klotz (eds), vol. 1, Paris: Economica, pp. 203–41.
Dupuit, Jules (1849), 'De l'influence des péages sur l'utilité des voies de communication', *Annales des Ponts et Chaussées*, **207**, 170–248, in J. Dupuit (2009), *Œuvres économiques complètes*, Y. Breton and G. Klotz (eds), vol. 1, Paris: Economica, pp. 243–307.
Dupuit, Jules (1852–53), 'Eau, Péage, Ponts et Chaussées (Corps de), Routes et chemins, Voies de communication', in C. Coquelin and C. Guillaumin (eds), *Dictionnaire de l'économie politique*, Paris: Guillaumin, in J. Dupuit (2009), *Œuvres économiques complètes*, Y. Breton and G. Klotz (eds), vol. 2, Paris: Economica, 'Eau', vol. 1, pp. 535–59, 'Péage', vol. 1, pp. 517–29, 'Pont et Chaussées (Corps)', vol. 2, pp. 227–35, 'Routes et chemins', vol. 1, pp. 453–66, 'Voies de communication', vol. 1, pp. 431–52.
Dupuit, J. (1862), 'De la justice au point de vue économique et relativement à la propriété', note manuscrite pour la réunion de la Société d'Economie Politique du 6 octobre 1862, in J. Dupuit (2009), *Œuvres économiques complètes*, Y. Breton and G. Klotz (eds), vol. 2, Paris: Economica, pp. 641–5.
Dupuit, Jules (1863), 'Réponse de M. Dupuit à M. Baudrillart au sujet de l'article "L'économie politique est-elle une science ou une étude"', *Journal des économistes*, **37** (37), 474–82, in J. Dupuit (2009), *Œuvres économiques complètes*, Y. Breton and G. Klotz (eds), vol. 2, Paris: Economica, pp. 151–61.
Dupuit, Jules (2009), *Œuvres économiques complètes*, Y. Breton and G. Klotz (eds), 2 vols, Paris: Economica.
Ekelund, R.J. and R.F. Hebert (1999), *Secret Origins of Modern Microeconomics*, Chicago, IL: University of Chicago Press.
Ekelund, R.J. and R.F. Hebert (2012), 'Dupuit and the railroads', *History of Political Economy*, **44** (1), 97–111.
Etner, F. (1983), 'Note sur Dupuit', *Revue Économique*, **34** (5), 1021–35.
Jevons, W.S. (1871), *The Theory of Political Economy*, 2nd edn 1879, London: Macmillan.
Numa, G. (2012), 'Dupuit and Walras on the natural monopoly in transport industries: what they really wrote and meant', *History of Political Economy*, **44** (1), 69–95.
Poinsot, P. (2011), *La relecture de l'œuvre de Jules Dupuit à l'aune de la notion de bien-être: intérêt général, bien-être et utilité publique*, thesis, University of Paris I.
Say, J.-B. (1803), *Traité d'économie politique*, Paris: Deterville, 2006 édition variorum des six éditions établie par Claude Mouchot, in *Œuvres complètes*, vol. 1, Paris: Economica.
Simonin, J.-P. and F. Vatin (eds) (2002), *L'œuvre multiple de Jules Dupuit (1804–1866). Calcul d'ingénieur, analyse économique et pensée sociale*, Angers: Presses Universitaires d'Angers.
Société d'économie politique (SEP) (1853), 'Séance du 10 mars 1853', *Journal des économistes*, 1st series, **35** (144), 148–51.

John Stuart Mill (1806–1873)

The Fortunes of Mill

John Stuart Mill's fortunes as an economist varied substantially though time, and the assessment of his lasting contributions to economics is to some extent controversial.

From the publication of his *Principles* (Mill 1848 [1965]) to about the end of his life in 1873, Mill was the unrivalled authority of economic theory both for the general public and the scientific community, similar to what Adam Smith had been until the advent of Malthus and Ricardo. During his lifetime, his treatise was published in seven "library editions" (and one successful "People's edition"), promptly translated into the main European languages, and printed for the US public. Worldwide, "it rapidly eclipsed in popular favor the preceding treatises" (Mitchell 1967: 573), becoming "the most successful treatise of the period [between 1790 and 1870]" (Schumpeter, 1954: 527) and "probably the longest-lived textbook our discipline has ever had or ever will have" (Viner 1949: 380). It also marked an epoch for the scientific community: for a quarter of a century it was the basis of the apprenticeship of "most . . . English economists" (Marshall 1876 [1925]: 119) and was responsible for "the greatest triumphs of the classical political economy in the applied fields" (Hayek, 1934: vi).

The "marginal revolution" challenged and eventually overcame Mill's intellectual domain. Jevons (1871: vi) openly claimed that "authority was on the wrong side" and, in 1875–76, he warned his students at Owens College, Manchester, that "Mill's Political Economy is disfigured by a series of fallacies" (Jevons, 1977: 3). Jevons, Menger, and Walras abandoned the traditional theory of value and offered an alternative which was more sophisticated from a mathematical point of view and occupied the centre of a more integrated and abstract theoretical system. A new mainstream was being established. Mill's fortunes were decidedly on the decline, and afterwards, according to Stigler (1982: 160), they "reached a nadir in the generation between the two world wars".

Since the second half of the twentieth century there has been a Mill revival. Doubtless this has been made possible by the enduring reputation of Mill the philosopher, social reformer and theorist of liberalism, but also some peculiar features of his economics, such as the important economic role of changing human institutions, have reawakened an interest in Mill's achievements. In particular, Robbins, Hayek, Schumpeter, and Stigler contributed to this "resurrection" in the 1950s. The publication during 1963–91 of Mill's collected works and the "centenary conference" held at the University of Toronto precisely one century after Mill's death were but two of the many circumstances which facilitated the reappraisal of Mill as an economist.

Mill's Exposition of the Ricardian Theories

During a century and a half of alternating fortunes, reputable commentators agreed on just one point: Mill's *Principles* contained (but by no means consisted of) a large, systematic, and effective exposition of what he considered the most accomplished achievements of Smith, Malthus, and mostly Ricardo. In a letter to John Austin written when he was completing the *Principles* for print, Mill wrote: "I doubt if there will be a single opinion (on pure political economy) in the book, which may not be exhibited as a corollary from his [Ricardo's] doctrines." (Mill to John Austin, 22 February 1848, in Mill 1963, XIII: 731). A non-controversial aspect of Mill's contribution consists therefore in the exceptional literary and logical power of his exposition. He established a standard for economic theory by passing the existing theories through the scrutiny of his logic, his taste for proportion, order, and detail, and his sense of intellectual duty. He borrowed the core of the Ricardian doctrines, incorporating the best of the Malthusian theory of population and the Smithian large view of the division of labour. It is widely agreed that this was Mill's modest original intention. According to his leading biographer, M.St.J. Packe, "he did not aspire to anything more than a blending and a thorough exposition of already existing treatises" (Packe 1954: 295). In the words of Mitchell, "it was a matter of arranging an ordered exposition of principles which had been formulated by his predecessors" (Mitchell 1967: 559).

The precise reasons why Mill set out in fall 1845 to write a treatise of political economy after the great success of his *Logic* (Mill 1843 [1973]) is partially a matter of speculation. In 1844 he had published a book containing some old essays on political economy (Mill 1844 [1967]) which had remained unpublished for some fourteen years, but at that time he had won his outstanding reputation not as an economist but as a philosopher. Presumably, the *Principles* were intended to be a continuation of the *Logic* (not of the *Essays*). As Schumpeter (1954: 530) remarked, "The original preface [of the *Principles*] is worth reading. He might with little change have reprinted the preface to the *Logic*". The *Principles* were then "a natural descent from the theory of knowledge as a whole to a detailed enquiry into the field of human activity" (Packe 1954: 296). This descent took for granted what he already knew – the works of his predecessors. He strongly believed during all his lifetime in a "religion of humanity" in which the ultimate goal of science was to help mankind better its lot, and political economy was central in this effort. The subtitle of the *Principles*, "with some of their applications to social philosophy", reflects the fact that he was interested not so much in establishing new principles as in shaping the existing principles to make them consistent with his system of logic and amenable to his social philosophy. There was a "double message" (Mitchell 1967: 560): one concerned pure economic theory, and the other concerned its application to social philosophy, where "social philosophy is the larger, the controlling element in Mill's mind" (Mitchell 1967: 562).

Some Biographical Notes

A biographical digression is proper here. James Mill, who was a close friend of David Ricardo and an economist himself, started to instruct his son John Stuart (born in London, 20 May 1806) in political economy when he was only about 13 years of age. J.S. Mill's *Autobiography* (Mill 1873 [1981]) is a legendary testimony of the extraordinary education he received under the spell of his father. We are told that he learned Greek and Latin from him in his childhood and read the main classical historians by the age of 8. Then he studied mathematics, philosophy, social science, and eventually political economy. His father (who attended the University of Edinburgh at the expense of Sir John Stuart – after whom the first son was to be named – in exchange for James's teaching of Stuart's daughter) wanted to methodically build a pure "thinking machine" out of him, making a *tabula rasa* of any preconceptions, unreasoned thinking, and even personal feelings, with the exception of love for knowledge; to this end, the young Mill was educated entirely at home, in the absence of boy companions. During their daily walks, James delivered to his son a complete course of political economy based on Ricardo's recently published "great work" and asked him to write an account of each lecture the next day. Afterwards Mill read Ricardo's and Smith's treatises, sharing with his father the opinion that the latter was "more superficial" and the former had "superior lights" (Mill 1873 [1981]: 31). In May 1820 he went to Paris, with a letter of presentation from his father to J.-B. Say with whose family he spent nine days, before moving to the south, guest for over one year of Sir Samuel Bentham, the younger brother of Jeremy Bentham, the great master of James Mill. On returning to England, he worked on the manuscript of his father's *Elements of political economy* (Mill 1821), writing short abstracts of every paragraph. Mill did not attend a university, even though Sir John Stuart bequeathed to him a sum of money for the express purpose of sending him to Cambridge: he "already knew more than he could learn" (Packe 1954: 49). A third phase of his economic apprenticeship began in 1825 with his participation in debating societies with economic interests (after his participation in the Benthamite "Utilitarian society"), in the spare time left by his clerkship at the East India Company (where he made an outstanding carrier until his retirement in 1858). The meetings of the "Grote group" were organized on the basis of reading systematic treatises, and the first choice was James Mill's *Elements*.

After a period he called a "mental crisis", he returned to economic theory, writing the *Essays*. Afterwards his efforts were gradually absorbed by study of the philosophical problems of knowledge, which eventually led to the publication of the *Logic*. At the time of his "mental crisis", the poetry of Wordsworth led him to appreciate the importance of feeling and sympathy in social relations, and the Benthamite attitude against sentimentality became intolerable to him. He cultivated new intellectual contacts and gradually became critical of the Philosophic radicals to whom he had been introduced by his father. The younger disciples of Coleridge aroused in him an interest in German romanticism. Thomas Carlyle, with whom Mill had a long, affectionate friendship, helped him to understand and appreciate the reasons of mysticism. In a letter of 1834 to Carlyle, Mill wrote: "if I have any *vocation*, I think it is exactly this, to translate the mysticism of others into the language of Argument" (Mill to Carlyle, 2 March 1834, in Mill 1963, XII: 219, original emphasis). The French Saint-Simonians, whom he met at the London Debating Society at the end of the 1820s, also influenced him significantly: "I read nearly everything they wrote. Their criticism on the common doctrines of Liberalism seemed to me full of important truth; and it was partly by their writings that my eyes were opened to the very limited and temporary value of the old political economy" (Mill 1873 [1981]: 173–5). The death of James Mill in 1836 made his dissent from the strict Benthamite doctrine more explicit. However, the most important biographical source in the development of Mill's social philosophy was his relationship from the early 1830s with Harriet Taylor, who became Mrs Mill in 1851. Mill took advantage of any occasion, and of his *Autobiography* in particular, to passionately acknowledge the influence of Harriet on his views of human progress. She strongly reinforced Mill's favourable attitude toward the ethical aims of utopian socialism and encouraged him to give those aims a firmer logical ground. Hayek (1951) has provided a masterly reconstruction of the documental evidence of their intellectual and personal relationship, which ended with Harriet's premature death in 1858 in Avignon; Mill died in the same town, on 8 May 1973.

Mill's Original Contributions

The exposition of previous economic theories in J.S. Mill's *Principles* must, of course, have included some original elements. A new tone and fresh perspectives were intertwined with new knowledge and insights, which, however, were far from self-evident. Mill's style, which did not call attention to his original achievements (see Stigler 1982: 160) and had no regard to parentage (see Stigler 1955: 296), set an obstacle to the assessment of his originality. Nor did the structure of Mill's treatise, so different from both that of Ricardo and that of Smith, reflect Mill's originality: the organizing principle was in the main borrowed from the structure of the treatises of Say and James Mill. "Production", "Distribution", and "Consumption of wealth" were the subjects of the three books of Say's treatise; "Production", "Distribution", "Interchange", and "Consumption" were those of James Mill. The first three books of J.S. Mill's treatise addressed "Production", "Distribution", and "Interchange"; the fifth (and last) book basically addressed taxation, like Say's and J. Mill's books on "Consumption". The subject matter of the fourth book, "Influence of the progress of society on production and distribution", was of course an innovation.

In order to assess Mill's contribution to economics we need to distinguish between progress depending on his social philosophy, on the one hand, and "technical" achievements in pure economic theory, on the other.

Some authors tended to downplay the degree of Mill's cross-fertilization between economics and social philosophy. Samuelson (1978), for example, plainly placed Mill's theory in the "canonical model" of Smith, Malthus, and Ricardo, as if Mill's insistence on the possibility of social progress, conditioned by his sympathy for utopian socialism, was an aside which left his economic theory virtually untouched. Viner argued that Mill failed in the integration of competition-based economic principles with other social principles based on customs, laws, and other social institutions (see Viner 1949: 380). Similarly, Stigler characterized Mill's insistence on "the immutability of the laws of production vs. the social plasticity of the laws of distribution" as "at least unhappy" (Stigler 1955: 296).

Other commentators, to the contrary, insisted that Mill succeeded in his intent to "humanize" (to use Mitchell's phrase) economic theory and that his claim that the "Distribution of wealth . . . is a matter of human institution only" (Mill 1848 [1954]: 199) was quite well reasoned and far reaching. Ashley (1909: xxii) strongly supported the "validity of the distinction between the laws of Production and the modes of Distribution"; Edgeworth (1926: 759) recognized that "there is surely a very intelligible difference, in degree at least, between the two classes of 'laws'"; Schumpeter (1955: 531) stressed that Mill's claim was at the basis of the "warm-hearted humanitarianism" which pervaded his book; the excellent exposition of Schwartz (1972) also supports this view.

The principle of competition, so central in any theory of distribution, is explicitly put by Mill into the context of changing habits, laws, and institutions. There was nothing "natural", in his eyes, in the fact that real wages remained at a subsistence level while rents increased with economic progress. Much depended on the comparative habits of the workers' families in respect of comfort and in respect of population (see Mill 1848 [1965], II: 341–3). In his essay on *The claims of labour* (Mill 1967 [1845]), Mill distinguished quite explicitly between two different inferences from Malthus's population principle: an early, mistaken inference "was at first announced as an inexorable law, which, by perpetuating the poverty and degradation of the mass of mankind, gave a *quietus* to the visions of indefinite social improvement" (Mill 1848 [1967]: 366); and a later, correct inference "afforded a sure hope, that whatever accelerates [human] progress would tell with full effect upon the physical condition of the labouring classes" (ibid.: 368). According to Mill, an increase in real wages, however occasioned, could modify workers' habits in favour of comfort and against fertility (see ibid.: 379). A series of other customs and institutions contributed to this end. School education was fundamental, like the "spontaneous education" brought about by the diffusion of newspapers, lectures, and discussions, as well as by collective deliberations on questions of common interest (Mill 1848 [1965], III: 763–6). Peasant proprietorship was another means by which the general progress of society could be turned permanently in favour of workers, because it led to higher productivity and promoted a sense of independence and self-respect (see Mill 1848 [1965], II: 252–77). A similar effect was produced in trade and industry by the diffusion of co-operatives and profit sharing (see ibid.: 769–98).

Mill had a clear vision of the main issues concerning the progress of the working classes which became central in the decades to come (as in Ludlow and Jones 1867 [1973]) and reshaped the problem of the improvability of their living conditions. He recognized that the real wages can be permanently increased by legislation or combination, thus departing from the wage fund doctrine, which he explicitly recanted in 1869 (Mill 1869 [1967]). To say the least, this inspired further theorizing. Marshall borrowed directly from Mill the fundamental aim of economic theory, which he passed on to later generations. Evidence of the Millian origin of Marshall's keen interest in the living condition of the working classes is his 1873 conference on "The future of the working classes" (Marshall 1876 [1925]). According to Groenewegen, "the problem which guided Marshall's work throughout the whole of his life [was that of] raising the standards of life of the working class until they had reached those of 'gentlemen'" (Groenewegen 1994: 278). In his biography of Keynes, Harrod insists that "that vision of the good life . . . animated his endeavours, of which his readers catch glimpses all through his works" (Harrod 1951: 186). However, Mill's application of the theory of distribution bore some theoretical fruits as well. According to him, the possibility of increasing wages depended on how extra wages (and more leisure) were to be used. Marshall applied the same potential self-reinforcing mechanism and asked, "what is the connection between changes in the manner of living and the rate of earnings; how far is either to be regarded as the cause of the other, and how far as the effect?" (Marshall 1920: 689; see Opocher 2010). It would not be too far off the mark even to suggest that modern theories of endogenous growth and evolutionary approaches to growth were anticipated by Mill's (and Marshall's) insights into the creation of habits and institutions.

In a variety of fields, Mill has also been credited with progress in pure economic theory. According to Marshall, hidden in Mill's theory of value was a general law of supply and demand of which his "law of cost of production" was a corollary: "he explains this briefly, perhaps too briefly, at the beginning of the third book" (Marshall 1876 [1925]: 127–8). More recently, after a long period of eclipse, some modern authors have re-evaluated Mill as a forerunner of supply and demand theory. Schumpeter (1954: 603) claims that "Mill's own main contribution was to develop the supply-and-demand analysis so fully that . . . there remained not so very much to do beyond removing loose ends and adding rigour in order to arrive at something not far distant from Marshallian analysis"; and that in this effort he was second only to Cournot. Stigler (1955: 298) and Samuelson (1962: 10–12) proposed a similar interpretation. A by-product of Mill's sketch of analysis of demand schedules was his solution to the problem of competitive pricing in the case of commodities produced jointly in fixed proportions (Stigler 1955: 297; also Kurz 1986: 23–5). In this view, Mill is seen as "a figure of transition and, implicitly, as the starting point for the first generation of the 'moderns'" (Groenewegen 2005: 27). It should not be forgotten, however, that for Mill the law of supply and demand was relevant only "with respect to all commodities not susceptible of being multiplied at pleasure" and that such commodities were "exceptions", even though "the principle of the exception stretches wider, and embraces more cases, than at first supposed" (Mill 1848 [1965]: 468). For the generality of commodities, "this point of exact equilibrium may be as momentary, but is nevertheless, as real, as the level of the sea" (Mill 1869 [1967]: 636).

Other distinct hints at future developments in economic theory have been stressed, mainly by Stigler (1955). One is Mill's "recognition of the barriers to mobility erected by the costs of education" (Stigler 1955: 297). The presence of non-competing groups in labour has been considered also by Mitchell as a "characteristic modification of Ricardo's theory of wages" (Mitchell 1967: 563) and is at the basis of modern theoretical explanations of differential wages. Finally, Mill's argument that, theoretically, a system of protection under "Corn laws" was inferior to a system of free trade accompanied by a tax indemnifying the landlords has been rightly considered an anticipation of the "compensation principle" of welfare economics (Stigler 1982: 161).

The Saint of Rationalism

The intellectual stature of John Stuart Mill cannot be adequately measured only by the depth and persistence of his scientific achievements; nor can it be identified with one major discovery. Rather, it should be measured mainly by the exceptional extension and open-mindedness with which the various questions were elaborated by his mind. In no field was he an apologist. It is characteristic of him that seemingly opposite doctrines stand together in harmony, not merely by virtue of a verbal artifice inspired by eclecticism, but because he discovered points of view which were better than the conventional ones. He was the champion of both liberalism and evolutionary socialism; he was consistently a theorist and a social reformer, an economist and a philosopher; as an economist, he presented at the same time a synthesis of old theories, their application to the main issues of his time, and a sketch of the logical kernel of theories to come. This all-embracing variety is mirrored by his personal life: outwardly it was singularly uneventful, but in respect of his inner experience it was of the most exceptional kind. He was at the same time a "thinking machine" and a candid man; he professed no religious beliefs, but set no limits to the dignity of human life and its improvability. In the words of Hayek, he was

> a great moral figure . . . in whom even his purely intellectual achievements are mainly due to his profound conviction of the supreme moral value of unrelenting intellectual effort. Not by temperament but out of a deeply ingrained sense that this was his duty did Mill grow to be the "Saint of rationalism", as Gladstone once so justly described him. (Hayek 1951: 16)

ARRIGO OPOCHER

See also:

British classical political economy (II); Income distribution (III); Thomas Robert Malthus (I); Alfred Marshall (I); Non-Marxian socialist ideas in Britain and the United States (II); David Ricardo (I); Henry Thornton (I).

References and further reading

Ashley, W.J. (1909), 'Introduction', in J.S. Mill, *Principles of Political Economy, with Some of Their Applications to Social Philosophy*, London: Longmans, pp. v–xxvi.
Edgeworth, F.Y. (1926), 'John Stuart Mill', in H. Higgs (ed.), *Palgrave's Dictionary of Political Economy*, London: Macmillan, pp. 756–63.
Groenewegen, P. (1994), 'Alfred Marshall and the Labour Commission 1891–1894', *European Journal for the History of Economic Thought*, **1** (2), 273–95.
Groenewegen, P. (2005), 'Was John Stuart Mill a classical economist?' *History of Economic Ideas*, **13** (3), 9–31.
Harrod, R.F. (1951), *The Life of John Maynard Keynes*, London: Macmillan.
Hayek, F.A. (1934), 'Introduction', in F.A. Hayek (ed.), *The Collected Works of Carl Menger*, vol. 1, London: London School of Economics, pp. v–xxxviii.
Hayek, F.A. (1951), *John Stuart Mill and Harriet Taylor. Their Friendship and Subsequent Marriage*, New York: A.M. Kelly.
Jevons, W.S. (1871), *The Theory of Political Economy*, London: Macmillan.
Jevons, W.S. (1977), *Lectures on Political Economy 1875–1876*, in R.D. Collison Black (ed.), *Papers and Correspondence of William Stanley Jevons*, vol. 6, London: Macmillan.
Kurz, H.D. (1986), 'Classical and early neoclassical economists on joint production', *Metroeconomica*, **38** (1), 1–37.
Ludlow, J.M. and L. Jones (1867), *Progress of the Working Class 1832–1867*, London, Alexander Strahan, reprinted 1973, New York: A.M. Kelley.
Marshall, A. (1873), 'The future of the working classes', in A.C. Pigou (ed.), *Memorials of Alfred Marshall*, reprinted 1925, New York, A.M. Kelley, pp. 101–18.
Marshall, A. (1876), 'Mr Mill's theory of value', in A.C. Pigou (ed.), *Memorials of Alfred Marshall*, reprinted 1925, London: Macmillan, pp. 119–33.
Marshall, A. (1920), *Principles of Economics*, 8th edn, London: Macmillan.
Mill, J. (1821), *Elements of Political Economy*, London: Baldwin, Cradock, and Joy.
Mill, J.S. (1843), *A System of Logic Ratiocinative and Inductive*, in J.M. Robson (ed.) (1973), *Collected Works of John Stuart Mill*, vols VII and VIII, Toronto: University of Toronto Press.
Mill, J.S. (1844), *Essays on Some Unsettled Questions of Political Economy*, in J.M. Robson (ed.) (1967), *Collected Works of John Stuart Mill*, vol. IV, Toronto: University of Toronto Press, pp. 229–339.
Mill, J.S. (1845), 'The Claims of Labour', in J.M. Robson (ed.) (1967), *Collected Works of John Stuart Mill*, vol. IV, Toronto: University of Toronto Press, pp. 363–89.
Mill, J.S. (1848), *Principles of Political Economy, with Some of Their Applications to Social Philosophy*, in J.M. Robson (ed.) (1965), *Collected Works of John Stuart Mill*, vols II and III, Toronto: University of Toronto Press.
Mill, J.S. (1869), 'Thornton on Labour and Its Claims', in J.M. Robson (ed.) (1967), *Collected Works of John Stuart Mill*, vol. V, Toronto: University of Toronto Press, pp. 631–68.
Mill, J.S. (1873), *Autobiography*, in J.M. Robson (ed.) (1981), *Collected Works of John Stuart Mill*, vol. I, Toronto: University of Toronto Press.
Mill, J.S. (1963), 'Earlier letters, 1812–1848', in J.M. Robson (ed.), *Collected Works of John Stuart Mill*, vols XII and XIII, Toronto: University of Toronto Press.
Mitchell, W.C. (1967), *Types of Economic Theory*, vol. 1, New York: A.M. Kelley.
Opocher, A. (2010), 'The future of the working classes: a comparison between J.S. Mill and A. Marshall', *European Journal of the History of Economic Thought*, **17** (2), 229–53.
Packe, M.St.J. (1954), *The Life of John Stuart Mill*, London: Secker and Warburg.
Samuelson, P.A. (1962), 'Economists and the history of ideas', *American Economic Review*, **52** (1), 1–18.
Samuelson, P.A. (1978), 'The canonical classical model of political economy', *Journal of Economic Literature*, 16 (4), 1415–34.
Schumpeter, J.A. (1954), *History of Economic Analysis*, New York: Oxford University Press.
Schwartz, P. (1972), *The New Political Economy of J.S. Mill*, London: Weidenfeld and Nicolson.
Stigler, G.J. (1955), 'The nature and role of originality in scientific progress', *Economica*, **22** (88), 293–302.
Stigler, G.L. (1982), *The Economist as Preacher*, Oxford: Basil Blackwell.
Viner, J. (1949), 'Bentham and J.S. Mill: the utilitarian background', *American Economic Review*, **39** (2), 360–82.

Pierre-Joseph Proudhon (1809–1865)

Born in Besançon on 15 January 1809 into a humble family, Pierre-Joseph Proudhon worked in a printing workshop from 1827 onwards. Together with three friends he bought himself such a workshop in 1836 but without commercial success. He obtained the Baccalauréat diploma and, in 1838, a grant which allowed him to resume his studies. Elected to the Parliament in 1848, he was condemned on 28 March 1849 to three years' imprisonment for having insulted the president of the Republic, Louis-Napoléon Bonaparte. He published in 1858 *De la justice dans la révolution et dans l'Église* but the book was seized and Proudhon condemned, on 2 June 1858, to three years' imprisonment for "outrage on the public and religious morals" and having "turned into derision a cult legally recognised by the State". He had to flee to Belgium but was pardoned in December 1860. He returned to Paris in 1862 where he died on 19 January 1865.

Proudhon published many works, and his complete writings number 26 volumes. As an economist, his main works are his three pamphlets on property (1840, 1841a, 1841b), *Système des contradictions économiques* (1846) and the part of *De la création de l'ordre dans l'humanité* (1843) dedicated to political economy. The content of *Théorie de la propriété* (1866) shows an evolution in his thought at the end of his life.

Proudhon has a peculiar place among the 1848 revolutionaries. He reproached the socialists, the communists and the Saint-Simonians for having considered the political revolution as a means and the social revolution as an end. They wanted to conquer the power to transform the society. For Proudhon, the social revolution is the means, and the political revolution – liberty – the end. He proclaimed himself an anarchist (Proudhon 1840: 229). The social structure must be organized on the basis of contracts because free associations are the only form of a just society. He was in favour of federalism and the systematic abolition of any governmental function, the regalian ones included (1851: 286).

In 1839, taking part in a competition organized by the Académie of Besançon, he wrote *De l'utilité de la célébration du Dimanche, considérée sous les rapports de l'hygiène publique, de la morale, des relations de famille et de cité*. He not only defended the Sunday rest against "those philanthropists . . . who suffer . . . from the fact that the poor only work six days for an insufficient wage and invariably conclude that they must work one day more" (1839: 41), but proclaimed that "the equality of conditions . . . is the aim of society" (ibid.: 44). He used some ideas he found in the French and English classical economists. He was convinced that, once the errors that vitiated its teaching are removed, economics could provide the positive conception of the new order of things. From the incoherent disorder in which, in his opinion, economic doctrines were at that time, he pretended to create a science, which would have formed "the head of the human encyclopaedia".

Property is Theft

According to Proudhon, the aim of economics is justice (1846, II: 510). The first question is that of property. To justify its existence, liberals maintained that the basis of property is labour. Charles Comte (1834, I: 61) justified this statement, writing that labour was a pain to which people voluntarily submit themselves only in order to obtain its fruits. Proudhon objected, one cannot justify in this way the appropriation of natural resources. People who cleared land, improved and cultivated it, have the property of the products of their labour, but not of land itself. "To whom belongs the rent of land? To be sure, to the producer of land. Who made the land? God. In this case, landowner, go away" (Proudhon 1839: 70).

However, if one admits, with Comte (1834, I: 60), that the values a man created can only belong to him, how is it possible to maintain that the value of the products made by the workers do not belong entirely to them? How can Comte affirm that, if the workers increase the value of a piece of land by clearing it, "it is paid to them with the food they get and the price of their working days: land becomes the property of the capitalist"? (ibid.: 155–6) It is true that the capitalist who advanced the raw products and the subsistence of the workers should have a part of the product. However, this right does not suppress that of the workers: "the worker keeps a natural right on the property of the product he made, even after the payment of his wage" (Proudhon 1839: 90).

For Proudhon, "property is theft", but it has a function: if men had benefited from the progress of their productivity, they had soon ceased to work. "*Man must work*! It is for this purpose that theft . . . was instituted, organized, sanctified! If the owner had become tired to take, the proletarian had soon become tired to produce" (Proudhon 1846, II: 517).

The Collective Working Force

Adam Smith had explained how the division of labour increases productivity. Proudhon (1843: 357) stresses the importance of this analysis, but thought that Smith did not understand the fecundity of this principle: he did not state "the law of the collective working force". When a clock is made by 50 workers rather than by one alone, this is as if it had been produced by one worker with 50 heads and 100 arms. The workers do not act independently of each other: they are associated and, in this way, co-responsible; they are not competing with each other, but solidary. This means that it is impossible to evaluate the contribution of each worker to the product. The division of labour and the collective labour force are two sides of the same law.

Proudhon then uses the concept of a collective force to analyse the distribution of income. As the force of 100 workers is incomparably greater than 100 times the force of one worker, this force is not paid with the wages of 100 workers. The difference between the value of the product and the amount of the wages does not legitimately belong to the capitalist. It is between the workers and the capitalist that the product must be shared, and the law forbidding the coalitions of workers must be repealed.

How to divide the product between workers? According to the Saint-Simonian motto: to each depending on his capability, to each capability depending on its works; or according to Fourier's statement: to each depending on his work and capability? Proudhon discards these view. He does not deny the diversity of tasks and talents but, as associates, men are equal and one of them must not be paid more than another.

Value as an Expression of Justice

For Proudhon, the value of things is measurable because they are all the produce of the collective working force. "Any product is a representative sign of labour and can consequently be exchanged against another product . . . Delete labour: only some more or less great utilities remain, which, possessing no human character, are incommensurable" (1846, I: 68). A product has an absolute value, namely, what it costs in labour and expenses.

When Proudhon states that the labour time determines value, his aim is to define the conditions for an equitable exchange between free men who voluntarily agree. Exchange must be deprived of any inequality: there is "a moral obligation that no contractor gains at the expense of the other" (1840: 107). *A contrario* "the worker who gives the labour of his arms for a piece of bread . . . is not free. The master for whom he is working does not become his associate through their exchange of a wage for a service, he is his enemy" (ibid.: 108). When exchange takes place between free and equal men, it must be done for equal values. The exchange between the worker and the entrepreneur is not fair.

The Organization of Credit and the Solution to the Social Question

When in April 1848 the Revolution seemed to take a wrong path, Proudhon restated his fundamental thesis on the occasion of presenting his project of a Bank of the People: the solution to the social question is to be sought in a radical transformation of the economic organization, not in a political reform (Haubtmann 1982: 843). He proposed to abandon any reference to a gold or silver standard: the notes issued by the Bank must be based on products, not on metallic reserves or on properties. The bank must issue its notes by discounting bills presented by its clients. Such notes would be perfectly safe because they would have as collaterals the effective values of a service done, of a commodity the delivery of which is either already made or warranted and certain (Proudhon 1848: 28). The issuing of such notes could not be excessive because it would only be made against real bills and follow the demands for discount. Granting credit would be easier as the lending activity of the bank would no more be limited by its metallic reserve. Moreover – and this is the main aspect of the project – the bank would be able to charge a very low interest rate, just to cover its costs. In such conditions, the interest rate would be nil or almost nil, and credit would be free. The reorganization of credit is the solution to the social question.

Proudhon had an important influence on the labour movement through anarcho-syndicalism and revolutionary unionism. His followers opposed those of Marx in the International Workingmen's Association. Proudhon's work is heterodox: it was defended by Georges Sorel (1892) and criticized by authors as different as Marx (1847), Bastiat (Bastiat and Proudhon 1849–50) and Walras (1860): but the works they devoted to him shows its importance in their eyes.

ALAIN BÉRAUD

See also:

Frédéric Bastiat (I); Karl Heinrich Marx (I); Non-Marxian socialist ideas in France (II); Adam Smith (I).

References and further reading

Bastiat, F. and P.-J. Proudhon (1849–50), 'Gratuité du crédit', *La voix du Peuple*, Paris: Guillaumin.

Comte, C. (1834), *Traité de la propriété*, Paris: Chamerot, Ducollet.

Gaillard, C. and G. Navet (eds) (2011), *Dictionnaire Proudhon*, Brussels: Éditions Aden.

Gioia, V., S. Noto and A. Sánchez Hormigo (eds) (2015), *Pensiero critico ed economia politica nel XIX secolo: da Saint-Simon a Proudhon*, Bologna: il Mulino.

Haubtmann, P. (1982), *Pierre-Joseph Proudhon, sa vie et sa pensée, 1809–1849*, Paris: Beauchesne.

Haubtmann, P. (1988), *Pierre Joseph Proudhon, sa vie et sa pensée 1849–1865*, vol. 1: 1849–1855, vol. 2: 1855–1865, Paris: Desclée de Brouwer.

Marx, K. (1847), *Misère de la philosophie. Réponse à la philosophie de la misère de M. Proudhon*, Paris: A. Franck.

Proudhon, P.-J. (1839), *De l'utilité de la célébration du dimanche considérée sous les rapports de l'hygiène publique, de la morale, des relations de famille et de cité*, Besançon: Bintot, Tubergue and Jacquot.

Proudhon, P.-J. (1840), *Qu'est-ce-que la propriété? Ou recherche sur le principe du droit et du gouvernement. Premier mémoire*, Paris: J.-F. Brocard.

Proudhon, P.-J. (1841a), *Lettre à M. Blanqui, Professeur d'économie politique au conservatoire des arts et métiers, sur la propriété*, deuxième mémoire, Paris: Librairie de Prévot.

Proudhon, P.-J. (1841b), *Avertissement aux propriétaires ou lettre à M. Considérant, rédacteur de la Phalange, sur la défense de la propriété*, Paris: Librairie de Prévot and Besançon: Chez l'Auteur.

Proudhon, P.-J. (1843), *De la création de l'ordre dans l'humanité ou principes d'organisation politique*, Paris: Librairie de Prévot, Besançon: Bintot.

Proudhon, P.-J. (1846), *Système des contradictions économiques ou philosophie de la misère*, Paris: Guillaumin.

Proudhon, P.-J. (1848), *Organisation du crédit et de la circulation et solution du problème social*, 2nd edn, Paris: Garnier.

Proudhon, P.-J. (1849), *Les confessions d'un révolutionnaire pour servir à l'histoire de la révolution de février*, Paris: Au bureau du journal *La Voix du Peuple*.

Proudhon, P.-J. (1851), *Idée générale de la révolution au XIXème siècle*, Paris: Garnier.

Proudhon, P.-J. (1866), *Théorie de la propriété*, 2nd edn, Paris: A. Lacroix, Verboeckhoven and Cie.

Sorel, G. (1892), 'Essai sur la philosophie de Proudhon', *Revue philosophique de la France et de l'étranger*, **33**, 622–38 and **34**, 41–68.

Walras, L. (1860), *L'économie politique et la justice, examen critique et réfutation des doctrines économiques de M. P.-J. Proudhon*, Paris: Guillaumin.

Hermann Heinrich Gossen (1810–1858)

Little has come down to us about the bachelor who spent a life in obscurity. We do not even know what he looked like. Most of what we know about him we owe to Léon Walras (1885 [1952]). William Stanley Jevons draws Walras's attention to Gossen in a letter and in the second edition of *The Theory of Political Economy* (1879) he mentions several precursors of his own ideas and of the use of mathematics in economics, including Gossen's *Entwickelung der Gesetze des menschlichen Verkehrs, und der daraus fließenden Regeln für menschliches Handeln* (1854). He rightly calls Gossen's "fundamental theory even more general and thorough" than his own (Jevons 1879: xxxviii). Walras gets hold of Gossen's book, is deeply impressed by it and seeks to learn more about the "économiste inconnu". He contacts Gossen's nephew, Hermann Kortum, a professor of mathematics, who provides him with information about his uncle, on the basis of which Walras publishes a paper in the *Journal des économistes*, in which he calls Gossen "one of the most remarkable economists that has ever lived" (Walras 1885 [1952]: 71). For details of Gossen's life, see Blum (n.d.) and Georgescu-Roegen (1983).

Heinrich Wilhelm Joseph Hermann Gossen was born on 7 September 1810 into a family of civil servants in Düren near Cologne, at the time a part of the Napoleonic Imperium. His father worked as a tax collector for the French administration and later leased and managed a manor estate, which yielded the family a decent income and wealth. His mother was a devout Catholic who educated her children strictly according to her religious faith. Gossen's reaction was to become a life-propagating hedonist with a distinctive anticlerical inclination.

His father pushed his son to embark on a career in the civil service. Gossen studied law, without much enthusiasm, in Bonn and Berlin, and is reported to have read writings by Jeremy Bentham and a widely used economics textbook by Karl Heinrich Rau. In late 1834 he became a law clerk in Cologne. For years he fails to get promoted and was removed to other posts, because he did not take his profession seriously and spent more time in pubs than in his office. Apparently he followed the maxim he was to formulate in his book: "*Man should organize his life so that his total life pleasure becomes a maximum*" (Gossen 1983: 5, original emphasis). In 1847 he resigned from office thus pre-empting being given a dishonourable discharge. This happened shortly after his father had passed away and spared the son embarrassing explanations for his failure. Gossen inherited a substantial fortune, which allowed him to live on a private income together with his two sisters, who looked after him. He founded an insurance company with a Belgian, but soon withdrew his capital from it. He had by then firmly decided to write down ideas he had developed over the years and which he considered to be epochal. He was convinced that their publication would make him famous and gain him an academic career. In January 1853 he finished his work, but was unable to find a publisher. He finally self-published the manuscript at his own expense. *Entwickelung der Gesetze* appeared in summer 1854; it was the only work Gossen would ever publish. In the same year he fell ill with jail-fever, which permanently damaged his health.

The fate of his book did not cheer him up. Only ten copies were sold and for about two decades the scientific community took no notice of it. It was as if the book had never been written. Shortly before his death he withdrew the unsold copies from the publisher. On 13 February 1858 a pulmonary tuberculosis carried off the enfeebled Gossen at the age of 47 in Cologne. The harbinger of the principle of pleasure maximization died disappointed and bitter. All his insights into the "true nature of man" were of little help to him. If only he had anticipated the fame that would be bestowed on his book long after his death!

The Book

Gossen's book contains a theodicy: it attempts to establish the fact that "this is the best of all possible worlds", to use the famous phrase of the German philosopher Gottfried Wilhelm Leibniz (1646–1716) (see Kurz 2009; Steiner 2011). In the conflict between the (Catholic) church and the natural sciences Gossen sides firmly with the latter. He prides himself on having shown for the first time in history beyond any doubt the "real purpose of man's life, willed by his Creator" (Gossen 1983: 4). This, he is convinced, justifies a comparison with Copernicus: "I believe I have accomplished for the explanation of the relations among humans what a Copernicus was able to accomplish for the explanation of the relations of heavenly bodies" (ibid.: cxlvii). In fact, the sciences and his *Entwickelung*, he surmises, form the "true religion", with him as one of its "priests" (ibid.: 208–9). Moral commandments enunciated by men frequently contradict the will of the Creator and thwart his intentions, engraved in "the laws of pleasure" or "laws of enjoyment". The "denunciation" of pleasure and "egoism" by the Christian churches is based on an egregious misunderstanding of the Plan of Creation. God is accused of being "a dilettante by the standards of our intelligence and, hence, we have to hurry to correct His mistake . . . That is why the Creator was provided with Heaven, Purgatory, and Hell – so that he may keep order among the wayward human creatures!" (ibid.: 207–8) Yet Gossen insists: "*The Creation is perfect.*" (ibid.: 207, original emphasis) In order to see this, one simply has to follow the gospel of "true [that is, Gossen's] economics".

True economics must use mathematics, because when creating the world, God is said to have made detailed calculations. More precisely, in economics the problems to be solved are typically problems of determining a minimum or a maximum: the *condition humaine* amounts to solving an optimization problem. "*Man! Investigate the laws of my creation and act according to these laws*" (Gossen 1983: 4, original emphasis), he hears the Creator speak at the beginning of his book. If man obeys the command, he concludes at its end in bold letters, "Then there is nothing further wanting in the world to make it a perfect paradise" (ibid.: 298). Gossen is convinced that the self-seeking behaviour of man does not get him into conflict with his neighbours, because when maximizing utility he who respects the laws of pleasure will at the same time contribute to the well-being of all humans.

Gossen's construction is based on two axioms: (1) the law of the falling marginal utility until there is satiety together with the time constraint man faces to keep his egoism and passions in rein, and (2) because of the benefits accompanying the division of labour, exchange and trade, men enter into forms of mutually favourable cooperation and thus become dependent upon each other. The social good is not to be sought in socialism or communism, Gossen concludes, but in acting out one's self-seeking traits. In the sequel Gossen is concerned with re-interpreting all behaviour that at first sight looks socially harmful as actually being socially beneficial. In fact, Gossen wishes to establish that a society that is exclusively based on the self-interest of people is (in modern parlance) statically and dynamically efficient. Gossen, Bernard de Mandeville and Voltaire's Dr Pangloss may be said to be brothers in spirit. We now understand perhaps why Gossen (1983: v) prepends his book with parts of Friedrich Schiller's poem 'An die Freude'. It suffices to cite the text of the chorus:

> O ye millions, now embrace ye
> Boundless love for all his world.
> Brothers, somehow there in Heaven
> Must live a sweet Father.

(German original: "*Seid umschlungen, Millionen! Diesen Kuß der ganzen Welt! Brüder, überm Sternenzelt – Muß ein lieber Vater wohnen!*"/The sweet father above the sky, other than Gossen's own father, does not force anyone to do things they dislike and punish them for things they like, following their own nature).

Gossen intends to elaborate a general analysis of the economy and society, based on a few elementary premises. He begins with a discussion of the isolated individual, then turns to the problem of pure exchange between two and then several individuals, followed by a discussion of the division of labour, trade and the emergence of money, culminating in an analysis of the pattern of specialization across the entire globe. Productivity gains are said to result from specialization, a reallocation of resources and the worldwide diffusion of technical knowledge. Without too great a stretch of the imagination we may say that what Gossen had in mind was an optimal dynamical economic development emerging from the self-seeking behaviour of agents in competitive conditions.

The isolated individual Gossen discusses in terms of a Robinsonade (Gossen 1983: 54–5). This is based on two axioms, the first part of the first of which is well known in microeconomics as "Gossen's First Law": "*The magnitude [intensity] of pleasure decreases continuously if we continue to satisfy one and the same enjoyment without interruption until satiety is ultimately reached*" (ibid.: 6, original emphasis). The second part is less well known and draws attention even more explicitly to an aspect of Gossen's argument that has been largely ignored in the history of the reception of his contribution: consumption occurs in time, it is a time-consuming process. He maintains:

> *A similar decrease of the magnitude* [intensity] *takes place if we repeat a previously experienced pleasure. Not only does the initial magnitude* [intensity] *of the pleasure become smaller, but also the duration of the pleasure shortens, so that satiety is reached sooner. Moreover, the sooner the repetition, the smaller the initial magnitude* [intensity] *and the shorter the duration of pleasure.* (Gossen 1983: 6, original emphasis)

Hence, Gossen is first and foremost concerned with analysing a possibly complex time profile of enjoyment and thus with the dynamic properties of optimal consumption. It is truly remarkable that even Jevons and Walras missed the time dimension of Gossen's argument. All people indiscriminately face a time constraint, Gossen insists, and many of them in addition an income constraint. Even man in the land of plenty — the land of Cockaigne — would have to solve an economic problem, because consumption takes time, and time is limited. This is the reason why Gossen focuses attention essentially on the problem of utility maximization subject to a time constraint. He assumes an additive-separable utility function (that is, the different needs are independent of one another and the utilities can be aggregated):

$$U = U_1(t_1) + U_2(t_2) + \ldots + U_n(t_n), \tag{1}$$

where U is total utility and U_i and t_i ($i = 1, 2, \ldots, n$) designate the partial utility derived from and the time devoted to the enjoyment of good i; it is assumed that "the quantity consumed is proportional to time" (Gossen 1983: 33), that is, $t_i = \tau_i c_i$, where τ_i is the amount of time needed to consume one unit of good i and c_i is the total amount consumed. This utility function is to be maximized subject to:

$$T = t_1 + t_2 + \ldots + t_n = \tau_1 c_1 + \tau_2 c_2 + \ldots + \tau_n c_n, \tag{2}$$

with T as the total amount of time available to spend consuming goods. Notice that the time budget constraint is an equation and not a weak inequality. This expresses the fact that the time at one's disposal one has to spend – it can neither be saved nor "killed".

Gossen does not know yet the term "marginal utility" or *Grenznutzen* (a word invented by Friedrich von Wieser), but he knows the concept: he speaks of the last "atom" of enjoyment (Gossen 1983: 33–4). He assumes a linear marginal utility curve whose intersection with the abscissa gives the satiety level. He is optimistic that one day it will be possible to measure the level of enjoyment at each moment of time. Utility is assumed to be cardinally measurable and interpersonally comparable. Interestingly he sees man's needs and wants as hierarchically or lexicographically ordered (which precludes the existence of a utility function). His analysis foreshadows Carl Menger's division of goods in goods of various orders.

However, how should the optimizing agent proceed? First, he has to respect his satiety levels. Disregarding them makes man miserable (Gossen 1983: 14). Secondly:

> *In order to maximize his total pleasure, an individual free to choose between several pleasures but whose time* [!] *is not sufficient to enjoy all to satiety must proceed as follows: However different the absolute magnitudes of the various pleasures might be, before enjoying the greatest pleasure to satiety he must satisfy first all pleasures in part in such a manner that the magnitude* [intensity] *of each single pleasure at the moment when its enjoyment is broken off shall be the same for all pleasures.* (Gossen 1983: 14, original emphasis)

This amounts to the maxim:

$$(\partial U_1/\partial c_1)/\tau_1 = (\partial U_2/\partial c_2)/\tau_2 = \ldots = (\partial U_n/\partial c_n)/\tau_n \tag{3}$$

Here the consumption time "cost" per unit of good i, τ_i, is found in place of the price of the good in conventional representations of "Gossen's Second Law". Gossen is very clear that this is not a description of how people actually consume, but how they ought to consume.

In case a person is constrained by both time and income, the argument has to be modified. Gossen discusses in some detail the case in which man makes a living by working. He introduces the concept of disutility or "discomfort" of labour and states that maximizing life pleasure now amounts to equalizing the marginal disutility of labour and the marginal utility of the pleasure obtained by the product of labour: "*the intensity of pleasure of the last atom produced shall be equal to the magnitude [intensity] of the discomfort experienced by him at the very moment of his expenditure of effort*" (Gossen 1983: 53; original emphasis).

Gossen then shows that pure exchange may increase the pleasure of all agents. He thus anticipates the discussion in Jevons and Walras. As regards production, Gossen points out labour-saving effects of the division of labour. He expresses the opinion that in competitive conditions each agent gets what he deserves, that is, the system is not only efficient, it is also just. He rejects the view that man, in order to maximize his life time pleasure, must not only be possessed of a full knowledge of all alternatives he faces over time and the effects associated with them, but must also be possessed of an infinite capacity to calculate pleasures and discomforts and weigh them against each other. Gossen speculates that the emergence of money as a means of exchange and market prices will solve this problem – after all, the Creation is perfect, as we have already heard. He contends that while single individuals may err, the market will not. Self-seeking is all that is needed to bring about a social optimum. If sentiments of compassion happened to interfere with the distribution of the product, they would hamper efficiency. Wherever Gossen looks, he sees the beneficent effects of an "overabundant horn of plenty" poured out over men.

In the rest of his book Gossen criticizes received views and applies his theory to problems of economic and social policy. Interestingly, he sees cases of market failure, for example, with regard to credit markets and child labour. There is especially one obstacle in the way of a paradise on earth: private ownership of land and its uneven distribution. This is said to prevent an efficient allocation of people across the globe. Gossen therefore elaborates a Plan for the Nationalization of Land, which is very similar to what Léon Walras was to propose (and before them, in the 1820s and 1830s, Auguste Walras and Antoine-Elisée Cherbuliez).

Impact

Why does nobody during two decades after its publication take notice of Gossen's book? The publisher has little incentive to promote it, the book's title is not very attractive, the author's preface, bristling with self-praise, is off-putting, the text lacks any subdivision, the reader is swiftly immersed in tedious mathematical formulas and numerical examples – not an easy fare, especially for Germans brought up with the Historical School. Spiegel (1968: 210) calls the *Entwickelung* "fundamentally un-German", Schumpeter (1954: 463) opines that the book was far ahead of its time and therefore bound to founder, Georgescu-Roegen (1983: lviii) maintains that Gossen "only happened to write in the wrong country". (Gossen's *Entwickelung*, published in 1927, may thus be compared to Antoine Augustin Cournot's *Recherches* of 1838.) All of these reasons certainly contribute to explaining the book's lack of early success, but they do not get us very far. First, at the time when Gossen wrote, German was still a widely spoken language in the economics profession. Secondly, some of the ideas Gossen advocated were not new, but had been put forward by representatives of the German so-called "use value school" with Karl Heinrich Rau as one of its leading protagonists (Chipman 2005: 159). Also, mathematics had been introduced in the profession by authors such as Johann Heinrich von Thünen and Friedrich Benedict Wilhelm Hermann in the first half of the nineteenth century.

Thirty years after Gossen's death, in 1889 his nephew brought out the unsold copies of the book with a new front page and preface as a "new edition". Apart from Jevons and Walras, Maffeo Pantaleoni (1889 [1898]) was particularly effective in propagating the book. By the turn of the twentieth century Gossen's contribution was well known to, and highly regarded by, the majority of economists. "Gossen's Laws" found their way into microeconomic textbooks and several essays were devoted to the man and his work; see, for example, Kraus (1910), Liefmann (1910, 1927) and Beyerhaus (1926). In 1927 a "third edition" of his book was published; however, it was nothing but a reprint of the 1889 edition, enriched by an introduction written by Friedrich August von Hayek. Yet only a small number of Gossen's propositions are picked up and then frequently reproduced in a distorted way. Its religious exaltations are set aside. Gossen's concern with consumption as a process that takes time and the optimal allocation of scarce time to alternative activities is almost entirely ignored and never makes it into microeconomics. Authors that took seriously the time aspect of consumption did so without any reference to Gossen; see, for example, Linder (1970) and Winston (1982). Only in more recent times have we seen attempts to make good the lacuna. Georgescu-Roegen (1983, 1985) was the first, followed by Steedman (2001), who, starting from Gossen, investigated in detail how the presence of two constraints rather than one – time and income – affects the agent's behaviour not just quantitatively, but also qualitatively, compared with the behaviour typically assumed in microeconomic textbooks. This is shown to have important implications for the theory of consumption and welfare economics.

It is a remarkable fact that while, on the one hand, the many insights contained in Gossen's important contribution have been only gradually rediscovered and developed further, on the other hand, the man and his message seem to fall into oblivion. Gossen is no longer even mentioned in some of the most widely used contemporary microeconomics textbooks; see, for example, Varian (1978) and Mas-Colell et al. (1995). A subject that forgets its history runs the danger of forgetting some of its major findings and is bound to reinvent the proverbial wheel. Economics without its history is not a very efficient undertaking.

HEINZ D. KURZ

See also:

German and Austrian schools (II); William Stanley Jevons (I); Karl Heinrich Marx (I); Adam Smith (I); Johann Heinrich von Thünen (I); Marie-Esprit-Léon Walras (I).

References and further reading

Beyerhaus, G. (1926), 'Hermann Heinrich Gossen und seine Zeit', *Zeitschrift für Volkswirtschaft und Sozialpolitik*, new series, **5**: 522–39.
Blum, K.R. (n.d.), 'Hermann Heinrich Gossen: Eine Untersuchung über die Entstehung seiner Lehre', unpublished manuscript. (This is a PhD thesis submitted to the University of Gießen, Germany, in 1933, which was not accepted. The author of the thesis was a Jew.)
Bousquet, G.H. (1958), 'Un centenaire: L'oeuvre de H.H. Gossen (1810–1858) et sa véritable structure', *Revue d'économie politique*, **68**: 499–523.
Chipman, J.S. (2005), 'Contributions of the older German schools to the development of utility theory', in C. Scheer (ed.), *Die Ältere Historische Schule: Wirtschaftstheoretische Beiträge und wirtschaftspolitische*

Vorstellungen. Studien zur Entwicklung der ökonomischen Theorie XX, Berlin: Duncker and Humblot, pp. 157–259.

Cournot, A. (1838), *Recherches sur les principes mathématiques de la théorie de la richesse*, Paris: L. Hachette.

Georgescu-Roegen, N. (1983), 'Hermann Heinrich Gossen: his life and work in historical perspective', in H.H. Gossen (1983), *The Laws of Human Relations and the Rules of Human Action Derived Therefrom*, trans. R.C. Blitz, introduced by N. Georgescu-Roegen, Cambridge, MA, and London: MIT Press, pp. xi–cxlv.

Georgescu-Roegen, N. (1985), 'Time and value in economics and in Gossen's system', *Rivista internazionale di scienze economiche e commerciali*, 32: 1120–40.

Gossen, H.H. (1854), *Entwickelung der Gesetze des menschlichen Verkehrs, und der daraus fließenden Regeln für menschliches Handeln*, Braunschweig: Friedrich Vieweg and Sohn.

Gossen, H.H. (1927), *Entwickelung der Gesetze des menschlichen Verkehrs, und der daraus fließenden Regeln für menschliches Handeln*, with an introduction by F.A. von Hayek, Berlin: R.L. Prager.

Gossen, H.H. (1983), *The Laws of Human Relations and the Rules of Human Action Derived Therefrom*, trans. R.C. Blitz, introduced by N. Georgescu-Roegen, Cambridge, MA, and London: MIT Press.

Jevons, W.S. (1879), *Theory of Political Economy*, 2nd edn, London: Macmillan.

Kraus, O. (1910), 'Gossen', *Allgemeine Deutsche Biographie*, vol. 55, Leipzig: Duncker and Humblot, pp. 483–8.

Krelle, W. (1987), 'Über Gossens "Gesetze des menschlichen Verkehrs"', in W. Krelle and H.C. Recktenwald (eds), *Gossen und seine "Gesetze" in unserer Zeit. Vademecum zu einem frühen Klassiker*, Düsseldorf: Verlag Wirtschaft und Finanzen GmbH, pp. 13–42.

Kurz, H.D. (2008), 'Hermann Heinrich Gossen (1810–1858)', in H.D. Kurz (ed.), *Klassiker des ökonomischen Denkens*, vol. 1, Munich: C.H. Beck, pp. 196–215.

Kurz, H.D. (2009), 'Wer war Hermann Heinrich Gossen (1810–1858), Namensgeber eines der Preise des Vereins für Socialpolitik?', *Schmollers Jahrbuch*, **129** (3), 473–500.

Liefmann, R. (1910), 'Hermann Heinrich Gossen und seine Lehre', *Jahrbücher für Nationalökonomie und Statistik*, **40**: 483–98.

Liefmann, R. (1927), 'Neuere Literatur über H.H. Gossen', *Zeitschrift für die gesamte Staatswissenschaft*, **83**, 500–517.

Linder, S.B. (1970), *The Harried Leisure Class*, New York and London: Columbia University Press.

Mas-Colell, A., M.D. Whinston and J.R. Green (1995), *Microeconomic Theory*, New York and Oxford: Oxford University Press.

Pantaleoni, M. (1889), *Principii di economia pura* (*Pure Economics*), English trans. 1898, London: Macmillan.

Riedle, H. (1953), *Hermann Heinrich Gossen, 1810–1858*, Winterthur: Keller.

Schumpeter, J.A. (1954), *History of Economic Analysis*, New York: Oxford University Press.

Spiegel, H.W. (1952), *The Development of Economic Thought*, New York: Wiley.

Steedman, I. (2001), *Consumption Takes Time. Implications for Economic Theory*, in *The Graz Schumpeter Lectures*, London: Routledge.

Steiner, P. (2011), 'The creator, human conduct and the maximisation of utility in Gossen's economic theory', *European Journal of the History of Economic Thought*, **18** (3), 353–79.

Stigler, G.J. (1959), 'The development of utility theory', in two parts, *Journal of Political Economy*, **58**, 307–327, 373–96, reprinted in G.J. Stigler (1965), *Essays in the History of Economics*, Chicago, IL: Chicago University Press.

Varian, H.R. (1978), *Microeconomic Analysis*, New York and London: W.W. Norton.

Walras, L. (1885), 'Un économiste inconnu: Hermann-Henri Gossen', *Journal des économistes*, 4th series, **30**, 60–90; a shortened English version is contained in H.W. Spiegel (1952), *The Development of Economic Thought*, New York: Wiley.

Winston, G.C. (1982), *The Timing of Economic Activities*, Cambridge: Cambridge University Press.

Bruno Hildebrand (1812–1878)

Bruno Hildebrand is known as one of the three founders of the German Historical School. His book *Die Nationalökonomie der Gegenwart und Zukunft* (*The Economics of the Present and the Future*) became a classic in the history of economic thought (Hildebrand 1844). He was born on 6 March 1812 in Naumburg (Saale, Thüringen), of modest origins. He participated at the age of 14, without the knowledge of his parents, in a competition for admission to the famous elite school Schulpforta and succeeded, being accepted with a grant. The thorough knowledge of the ancient languages and of history obtained there remained important in his later life as a basis for his studies of the economic history of the ancient world and for his understanding of history. His liberalism was inspired by classical ideals of humanity and citizenship, but also by the intellectual currents of his time; it was less based on individualism and the desire to minimize state action than the liberalism of the classical English economists. He participated in the student movements, which fought for constitutional government. He studied theology only briefly at Leipzig, then philosophy, languages and history, obtained his doctorate in 1836 and, having taught at a gymnasium, became Extraordinary Professor in 1839 and was called to Marburg as Full Professor of Staatswissenschaften (Economics) in 1841. The range of his lectures was characteristically much wider than that of his publications.

Hildebrand served as Vice Rector of the University of Marburg in 1845, parliamentarian in the National Assembly in 1848 and in the Parliament of Kurhessen, representing Bockenheim 1845 and 1850. He was persecuted for his political activities and went into exile in Switzerland, the only country in Europe where the revolution of 1848 really had succeeded. He was made Professor of the University of Zurich (and honorary citizen of the city) and later moved to the University of Berne where he founded the Swiss Statistical Office. He returned to Germany with his family in 1861 and became Professor at Jena. He founded the *Jahrbücher für Nationalökonomie und Statistik* in 1863 and the Statistical Office of Thüringen. He died in Jena on 29 January 1878. His oldest son Richard Hildebrand became a respected economist in turn; another son a famous sculptor, who was ennobled (Adolf von Hildebrand). Hildebrand's practical work was connected with his economic convictions. His work for the railways combined entrepreneurship and the creation of infrastructure; thanks to him, Jena, as the last university town in Germany, was linked with the railway network. His belief in the importance of the institutions of credit for economic development led him to help founding country banks, to support credit cooperatives and pension funds for widows. A quite different background to his writings is his acquaintance with the nascent communist movement. Hildebrand visited the Club of German Communists in London in 1846. They hotly disputed whether the state or private initiative should build up the mechanized industries, which, as both sides hoped, would eventually free the workers from drudgery.

Some minor writings by Hildebrand deserve attention. His inaugural speech as Vice Rector of the University of Marburg in 1845, in Latin, focuses on Xenophon and tries to reconstruct a Socratic theory of economics. It stands in contrast to more recent interpretations, which deny the idea that the Greeks and Romans saw the economy as a special subsystem of society. The point is that Hildebrand, in this speech, already adopts the point of view of the Historical School and interprets the economy in relation to ethics, like the philosophers of antiquity. Hildebrand here also touches on the problem of credit and quotes Ciceronian passages to show that credit cannot exist without mutual trust, which must be restored after crises of confidence.

Hildebrand is remembered for his theory of stages, which he maintained up to the end of his life, asserting that economic development leads to higher levels of culture. His theory of stages distinguished a natural economy, a money economy and, ultimately, a credit economy. The first stage could be identified with the economy of the Middle Ages, when there was little trade and much of that was based on barter and when the surplus was produced by the labour of the serfs or delivered in kind. The money economy emerges in the early modern period, and Hildebrand believed that the credit economy would dominate the future.

The stage theory, which at first looks like a sequence of different states of the economy, characterized only by their instruments of circulation, was proposed to demonstrate the link between economics and ethics and culture. The natural economy of the medieval period was based on direct personal relationships of authority and loyalty. Money made the individuals independent and gave them freedom to pursue their own interests, but it led to large discrepancies in the distribution of income, and the poor were left to their own devices. The credit economy gave the hope of uniting the solidarity of the earliest period with the possibilities of independent action of the second, in that credit would be given, not only for deferred payment as in earlier times, but, more fundamentally, as a means to undertake. Hence, credit could be given, within a limit, without securities other than the good character of the borrower, whom the lender judged to be an able entrepreneur. Thus even the poor could become masters of their own destiny. This was Hildebrand's answer to the challenge of communism.

The core idea was developed in later publications (Hildebrand 1864), but it was first formulated in his book of 1848, which was published in the same year as the Communist Manifesto; surprisingly, passages of the book are similar in expression to the flowery sentences by Marx and Engels.

Various criticisms of this theory of stages have been advanced. Hildebrand himself tried to overcome the contrast between what he knew about credit in ancient Rome and his thesis that the credit economy was primarily a matter of the future. He formulated the hypothesis, in a paper in 1869, that the primary assets, which the rich could buy in antiquity, were slaves and land, so landlords were the main capitalists (Hildebrand 1869).

His 1848 book shows that Hildebrand shared a certain predilection for the social cohesion of the Middle Ages with romantic authors such as Adam Müller or Sismondi, but Müller suffers, in Hildebrand's eyes, from the illusion of being able to restore feudalism. A critical assessment of the achievements of Adam Smith follows. His system is regarded as ingenious but historically specific. Friedrich List has the merit of having understood Smith, but also of having shown that the Smithian doctrine needed to be modified for backward countries like Germany. Much of the remainder of the book is a critique of Engels's *Die Lage der arbeitenden Klasse in England*, which had been published in Leipzig in 1845. Hildebrand is first concerned with Engels's theory in his paper "Umrisse zu einer Kritik der Nationalökonomie"; the so-called "contradictions" could not be solved by eliminating private property, since even a socialist society would require rules for distribution in accordance with the social need to organize production. Hildebrand proposes instead that bonds, which had existed in the natural economy and had been dissolved by the money economy, could be restored in a credit economy by a reaffirmation of ethical principles. Some modern interpreters praise this vision as prophetic, others regard it as naive. Hildebrand here affirmed the belief, so typical of the later Historical School, that the growth of technology, economic progress, ethical improvement and cultural refinement belonged together and all had to be objects of policy.

Hildebrand never published the second volume in which he would have had to describe his political strategy, but it is clear that he was an uncompromising advocate of economic freedom, coupled with state action to raise the productive forces and improve education. His 1848 book is indispensable for understanding the common concerns felt and the divergent solutions proposed at the time when the heritage of cameralism and liberalism bifurcated and the Historical School and Marxism originated.

BERTRAM SCHEFOLD

See also:

Historical economics (II); Friedrich List (I); Marxism(s) (II); Adam Smith (I).

References and further reading

Conrad, J. (1878), 'Bruno Hildebrand', *Jahrbücher für Nationalökonomie und Statistik*, **30**, 1–16.
Eisermann, G. (1956), *Die Grundlagen des Historismus in der deutschen Nationalökonomie*, Stuttgart: Enke.
Hildebrand, B. (1844), 'Friedrich Engels: Umrisse zu einer Kritik der Nationalökonomie', *Deutsch-Französische Jahrbücher*, Paris, reprinted in K. Marx, *Friedrich Engels: Werke*, vol. 1, Berlin: Dietz Verlag, reprinted 1976, pp. 499–524.
Hildebrand, B. (1845), *Xenophontis et Aristotelis de oeconomia publica doctrinae illustratae*, Marburg: Typis Bayrhofferi Academicis.
Hildebrand, B. (1848), *Die Nationalökonomie der Gegenwart und Zukunft*, Frankfurt am Main: J. Rütten, reprinted 1998 with commentary, in B. Schefold (ed.), *Vademecum zu einem Klassiker der Stufenlehren*, Düsseldorf: Verlag Wirtschaft und Finanzen.
Hildebrand, B. (1864), 'Natural-, Geld- und Credit-Wirtschaft', *Jahrbücher für Nationalökonomie und Statistik*, **2**, 1–24.
Hildebrand, B. (1869), 'Die soziale Frage der Verteilung des Grundeigentums im klassischen Altertum', *Jahrbücher für Nationalökonomie und Statistik*, **12**, 1–25, 139–55.
Pierenkemper, T. (2005), 'Bruno Hildebrand – ein deutscher Liberaler in Vormärz, Revolution und liberaler Ära', in C. Scheer (ed.), *Studien zur Entwicklung der ökonomischen Theorie*, vol. 20, Berlin: Duncker and Humblot, pp. 107–23.
Rothschild, E. (1998), 'Bruno Hildebrands Kritik an Adam Smith', in B. Schefold (ed.), *Vademecum zu einem Klassiker der Stufenlehren*, Düsseldorf: Verlag Wirtschaft und Finanzen, pp. 133–72.
Schefold, B. (2005), 'Bruno Hildebrand: Die historische Perspektive eines liberalen Ökonomen', in C. Scheer (ed.), *Studien zur Entwicklung der ökonomischen Theorie*, vol. 20, Berlin: Duncker and Humblot, pp. 125–56.

Wilhelm Georg Friedrich Roscher (1817–1894)

Roscher was born on 21 October 1817, in Hanover into a family of civil servants. From 1835 he studied history, philosophy and linguistics in Göttingen and then classical philology and history in Berlin. He obtained his doctorate in Göttingen in 1838, his habilitation in 1840 and then became a lecturer there in history and economics and public finance (*Staatswissenschaften*). In 1842 he published his historical study about Thucydides and only one year later his *Grundriß zu Vorlesungen über die Staatswirthschaft, nach geschichtlicher Methode* (*Outline of Lectures on the Public Economy, Using the Historical Method*). This work made him, together with Bruno Hildebrand (1812–1878) and Karl Knies (1821–1898), one of the founders of the so-called "Older Historical School of Economics" in Germany. In 1848 he was appointed to a chair at the University of Leipzig, where he worked on his monumental magnum opus *System der Volkswirthschaft. Hand- und Lesebuch für Geschäftsmänner und Studierende* (*System of Economics. Hand- and Reading Book for Businessmen and Students*), which comprises altogether five volumes and whose first volume saw numerous editions. For the history of the sciences in Germany, a project launched by the historical commission of the Bavarian Academy of Sciences, Roscher contributed his *Geschichte der National-Oekonomik in Deutschland* (*History of Political Economy in Germany*) in 1874, a work of more than 1000 pages. In 1892 he published *Politik: Geschichtliche Naturlehre der Monarchie, Aristokratie und Demokratie* (*Politics: Historical Natural Doctrine of Monarchy, Aristocracy and Democracy*), which contains an encyclopaedia of the history of political constitutions in Europe and is a most important early German contribution to what became political science.

Roscher lived in seclusion. His deep rootedness in the Protestant faith is reflected in his long-term activity in the Leipzig Protestant mission society and in poor relief. See in this context also Roscher (1896). Politically he was conservative and supported German colonialism and imperialism on the grounds that Germany needed a secure supply of raw materials and an outlet for its products (see Roscher 1885). Roscher died on 4 June 1894 in Leipzig.

Roscher advocated what he called the "historico-physiological method", which he contrasted with the "idealistic method" (see Weber 1922; Priddat 1995). While the former tried to take due account of the historical specificities in the economic, social, cultural and political development of different nations, the latter abstracted from them and focused attention on ideal or optimal states. While the former was positive economics, the latter was essentially normative. The former saw "organic unities", where the latter saw only abstract principles at work. As a studied historian Roscher endorsed the historical-inductive method, which was designed to provide a realistic picture of the economy, capturing its essential institutional and cultural features. His focus was on socio-economic development, which he saw unfold in a succession of stages characterized by differences in terms of political constitution and social institutions, property rights, the labour process up to the aspirations and mind-sets of people. In an analogy to the life of humans, Roscher distinguished between four stages of development: childhood, youth, manhood and old age. While Friedrich List had advocated the view that development is only ascending, Roscher saw both ascending and descending phases. He carried out comparative studies of different economies and people, and saw them belonging to different phases in the process of development, which, while not linear and uniform,

exhibited certain common patterns and similarities. The emphasis was on comparative dynamics and historical relativism. An important message was that people behave
differently in different socio-economic regimes, and it was important to understand
how historical conditions shaped the behaviour. It was clear that from such a holistic
perspective the idea of "methodological individualism", that is, of reconstructing the
economy and society by starting from autonomous individuals and their economically
driven interaction, was unacceptable. Roscher's historicism did not, however, prompt
him, as it did members of the younger Historical School, to downplay or even deny the
importance of economic theory. In fact, Roscher elaborated several theoretical economic
concepts and relationships between magnitudes (variables) himself, typically seeking to
find empirical support for them. His historical-inductive approach therefore did not
imply an uncompromising opposition to the idealistic-deductive method. Roscher was,
rather, concerned with identifying the precise role of each and the best way of combining
the two. He stressed that, to him, politics was the doctrine of the laws of development
of the state, with political economy and statistics being facets of politics. He claimed to
have reflected upon each and every law of development through comparing the epochs
of the life of the various nations and peoples he knew of. In short, he saw economics as a
part and parcel of "universal history".

In Roscher's view, major representatives of the idealistic method were the classical
economists, who in one part of their analyses derived economic laws from hypotheses
about people's behaviour and the economic problems they faced. He felt that some of
the classical economists had gone too far by claiming that there existed definite causal
relationships that are valid at all times and in all circumstances, whereas he was convinced there existed only historically contingent patterns of behaviour. This criticism
would have applied more to marginal theory, which was on the rise in the last quarter
of the nineteenth century. In fact, there are close similarities between Roscher and
Adam Smith, who also judiciously combined theoretical and historical analyses and
whom Roscher esteemed highly. Both were of the opinion that historical analysis was
indispensable because it informed about the subject matter of economics. They were
convinced that while the historical material illustrates economic theory and defines the
confines within which the latter is applicable, economic theory makes the material speak
to us. From this point of view economic development is both the expression of abstract
economic laws or regularities and of the specific cultural and institutional particularities
of a nation, of its "character" and "mentality" (*Sinnesart*); see also Salin (1968).

In his *Ansichten der Volkswirtschaft aus dem geschichtlichen Standpunkte* (*Views of
Economics from the Historical Point of View*), first published in 1861, Roscher develops
a three-stages theory of socio-economic development, which revolves around changes in
the relative importance of the three "factors" of production – nature (land), labour and
capital – in various epochs in history (1861: ch. 1). In it Roscher applies the concept of
factor substitution, which he discusses in great detail, in a historico-philosophical way.
He comes back to his concept of history as unfolding in stages in *Politik* (1892), but
now uses a different classification according to different types of government – from
patriarchal kingdom via the aristocracy of knights and priests to absolute monarchy and
then democracy. Degenerate forms are plutocracy and "Caesarism", which amounts to
military dictatorship. As Schefold (1987: 221) remarked: "Roscher did not systematically
attempt an integration of his theory of political development and the stages of economic

evolution." There is not, at any rate, the idea that certain economic stages imply certain types of government; while there are some correspondences, there is no one-to-one fit.

In his treatise "Zur Lehre von den Absatzkrisen" ("On the doctrine of sales crises"), first published in 1849, and in several other essays, Roscher traces slumps back to a deficiency of aggregate effective demand and develops views that may perhaps be said to foreshadow elements of Keynes's. In particular, he rejects Say's law (that is, he sees in it only an identity) with reference to the fact, already noted by John Stuart Mill, that in a monetary economy, in which money is also used as a store of value, acts of sales and acts of purchases may be separated from another. Sales crises, Roscher insisted, are triggered by commercial excess speculation (see Hagemann 1995, 2011). Schumpeter (1954: 740), however, plays down the achievements of Roscher's respective analysis, whose content he circumscribes in the following terms: "crises will occur if anything of sufficient importance will go wrong". He adds that Roscher's theory "can only be described as a fricassee of most of the ideas that were current at the time he wrote" (ibid.). While this judgement is not entirely false, it is also not entirely fair.

Die Grundlagen der Nationalökonomie (*The Foundations of Economics*), volume 1 of his magnum opus, *System der Volkswirthschaft*, which was first published in 1854, saw its twenty-sixth edition in 1922 and came out in an English translation in 1878. Roscher, on the one hand, develops the argument along seemingly classical lines of thought. He deals with production (and credit), circulation, distribution, consumption and population. He adopts essentially a cost of production explanation of relative prices; in determining rent he has recourse to Ricardo's principle of extensive diminishing returns, but confounds it with earlier physiocratic conceptions; and as regards wages and population he moves in the footsteps of Malthus's theory of population. His theory of profits reflects various influences, especially the idea of profits as some sort of wage (an idea Smith had vigorously rejected) and as a compensation for "abstinence". He accepts Smith's premise that individuals are self-interested, but he sees this principle complemented with, and corrected by, another principle, namely, human conscience and empathy, which expresses Roscher's piety. However, there are also elements in his analysis that clearly foreshadow marginalist ideas. The reference to demand and supply is, of course, not new and does not mean much unless it is supplemented with an analysis of how demand and supply are determined. In this regard Roscher emphasizes some ideas that became prominent with marginalism, especially the marginal productivity principle. Johann Heinrich von Thünen had stated this principle, with whose *Isolated State* Roscher was familiar. Roscher was no historicist in the strict sense of the word. Whether he was "a very meritorious follower of the English 'classics'", as Schumpeter (1954: 508) opined, is however dubious. More to the point is Streissler (1994), who saw in Roscher's work the culmination of the "German proto-neoclassical theory".

There is an empirical-cum-historical part of the *Grundlagen* in which Roscher provides accounts of the history of the main types of income, wages, profits, interest and rent, of the development of population and of the prices of major "necessary goods" and also of some "luxuries". The other four volumes of *System* deal with the economics of land cultivation and of the related primary production (vol. 2, 1859); the economics of trade and industry (vol. 3, 1881); the system of public finance (vol. 4, 1886); and the system of poor relief and the poor laws (vol. 5, 1894).

Roscher also contributed some new ideas and insights in other fields of economic inquiry. These include the theory of property rights and of incentives and its effects. In a talk on *Betrachtungen über die geographische Lage der großen Städte* (*Considerations on the Geographical Location of Large Cities*) he gave in 1871 in Leipzig, he stresses that decisions about settlements and the building of towns and cities was hardly ever based on purely economic considerations, but involved numerous other aspects.

Basically all of Roscher's contributions contain a fair share of observations on important precursors of ideas and doctrines. His magnum opus in this regard is his *Geschichte*. According to Edgar Salin (1968) it is Roscher's "only work of lasting significance". The book reflects well his erudition and comprehensive knowledge of the history of economic thought in Germany, focusing attention on cameralism and the German Use Value School (*Nutzwertschule*), but assessing also early contributions to mathematical economics, such as those of von Thünen and Friedrich Benedikt Wilhelm Hermann. Roscher holds Thünen especially in high esteem. While Roscher was keen to take account of anything that happened in the German economics profession since its beginnings, he missed out some important works, including Hermann Heinrich Gossen's conceptualization of economic activities as time-constrained processes and his formalization of marginal utility theory (Gossen 1854). Schumpeter (1954) benefited from Roscher's work, but felt that Roscher's judgements were not always reliable.

Roscher was one of the most important and influential economists of Germany in the nineteenth century, which can already be inferred from the success of his textbook, the *Grundlagen*. However, soon after his death his work fell into almost complete oblivion. A reason for this may be that he was more learned than original and that his huge tomes were considered rather forbidding. Another reason could be that he frequently only sketched his ideas, but did not fully develop them. Hence it remains somewhat unclear how deep his understanding was.

During his life, however, he was a towering figure of German economics. Carl Menger dedicated his *Grundsätze der Volkswirthschaftslehre* (1871) to him and Alfred Marshall expressed his indebtedness especially to Thünen, from whom he had taken the marginal productivity principle, but also to Roscher. Marx who repeatedly referred to the *Grundlagen* accused its author, whom he dubbed "Wilhelm Thukydides Roscher", of syncretism, "eclectic professorial twaddle" and "ingenious apologetic fancies" (Marx 1954: 209, 95n., 199n.). Schumpeter called Roscher "the incarnation of professorial learning" (1954: 809). While he bowed to Roscher's erudition, he criticized him for "his almost Keynesian dislike of laissez faire" (1954: 284n.); his entire failure to grasp the "true meaning" of Thünen's theory (1954: 465); and his inclination "to extoll [the] merits [of some authors – here the reference is to Oresme], particularly its originality, beyond all reason" (1954: 95). (This inclination is quite frequent among historians of economic thought.) More recently there has been a resurgence of interest in Roscher and more generally in the German Historical School. Erich Streissler revisited Roscher's works and, interestingly, called him "an economic theorist of world-class and of lasting world-class" (1994: 37).

HEINZ D. KURZ

See also:

German and Austrian schools (II); Bruno Hildebrand (I); Historical economics (II); Karl Heinrich Marx (I); Carl Menger (I); Joseph Alois Schumpeter (I); Johann Heinrich von Thünen (I).

References and further reading

Gossen, H.H. (1854), *Entwickelung der Gesetze des menschlichen Verkehrs, und der daraus fließenden Regeln für menschliches Handeln*, Braunschweig: Friedrich Vieweg und Sohn.
Hagemann, H. (1995), 'Roscher and the theory of crisis', in J. Backhaus (ed.), 'Wilhelm Roscher and the "Historical Method"', *Journal of Economic Studies*, **22** (3–5), 171–86.
Hagemann, H. (2011), 'Wilhelm Roscher's crises theory: from production crises to sales crises', in D. Besomi (ed.), *Crises and Cycles in Economic Dictionaries and Encyclopaedias*, Abingdon: Routledge, pp. 197–208.
Kurz, H.D. (2005), 'Roscher, Wilhelm Georg Friedrich', in *Neue Deutsche Biographie* (*NDB*), vol. 22, Berlin: Duncker & Humblot, pp. 39–41.
Marx, K. (1954), *Capital*, vol. I, trans. from the 3rd German edn by S. Moore and E. Aveling, ed. F. Engles, London: Lawrence and Wishart.
Priddat, B.P. (1995), 'Intention and failure of W. Roscher's historical method of national economics', in P. Koslowski (ed.), *The Theory of Ethical Economy in the Historical School*, Berlin and Heidelberg: Springer, pp. 15–34.
Roscher, W. (1842), *Leben, Werk und Zeitalter des Thukydides*, Göttingen: Vandenhoeck & Ruprecht.
Roscher, W. (1843), *Grundriß zu Vorlesungen über die Staatswirthschaft, nach geschichtlicher Methode*, Göttingen: Dieterich.
Roscher, W. (1849), 'Zur Lehre von den Absatzkrisen', reprinted in W. Roscher (1878 [1861]), pp. 279–398.
Roscher, W. (1854–1894), *System der Volkswirthschaft*, 5 vols, Stuttgart: Cotta.
Roscher, W. (1859), *Nationalökonomie des Ackerbaus und der verwandten Urproduktionen*, vol. 2 of *System der Volkswirthschaft*, Stuttgart: Cotta.
Roscher, W. (1861), *Ansichten der Volkswirthschaft aus dem geschichtlichen Standpunkte*, Leipzig and Heidelberg: Winter, reprinted 1878 with some additional material, in W. Roscher, *Grundlagen der Nationalökonomie*, vol. 1 of *System der Volkswirthschaft*, Stuttgart: Cotta.
Roscher, W. (1870), *Zur Gründungsgeschichte des deutschen Zollvereins*, Berlin: Carl Habel.
Roscher, W. (1871), *Betrachtungen über die geographische Lage der grossen Städte*, Leipzig: Hinrichs.
Roscher, W. (1874), *Geschichte der National-Oekonomik in Deutschland*, Munich: Oldenbourg.
Roscher, W. (1878), *Grundlagen der Nationalökonomie*, vol. 1 of *System der Volkswirthschaft*, trans. from 13th edn by J.J. Lalor in 1954, *Principles of Political Economy*, 2 vols, New York: Henry Holt & Co.
Roscher, W. (1881), *Nationalökonomie des Handels und Gewerbefleißes*, vol. 3 of *System der Volkswirthschaft*, Stuttgart: Cotta.
Roscher, W. (1885), *Kolonien, Kolonialpolitik und Auswanderung*, Leipzig: Winter.
Roscher, W. (1886), *System der Finanzwissenschaft*, vol. 4 of *System der Volkswirthschaft*, Stuttgart: Cotta.
Roscher, W. (1892), *Politik: Geschichtliche Naturlehre der Monarchie, Aristokratie und Demokratie*, Stuttgart: Cotta.
Roscher, W. (1894), *System der Armenpflege und der Armenpolitik*, vol. 5 of *System der Volkswirthschaft*, Stuttgart: Cotta.
Roscher, W. (1896), *Geistliche Gedanken eines National-Oekonomen*, Leipzig: Weimann.
Salin, E. (1968), 'Roscher, Wilhelm', in *International Encyclopedia of the Social Sciences*, New York: Columbia University Press.
Schefold, B. (1987), 'Roscher, Wilhelm Georg Friedrich', in J. Eatwell, M. Milgate and P. Newman (eds), *The New Palgrave. A Dictionary of Economics*, vol. 4, London: Macmillan, pp. 221–2.
Schefold, B. (ed.) (1994), *Vademecum zu einem Klassiker der Historischen Schule: Wilhelm Roscher und seine 'Ansichten der Volkswirtschaft aus dem geschichtlichen Standpunkte'*, Düsseldorf: Handelsblatt-Verlag.
Schumpeter, J.A. (1954), *History of Economic Analysis*, New York: Oxford University Press.
Streissler, E. (1994), 'Wilhelm Roscher als führender Wirtschaftstheoretiker', in B. Schefold (ed.), *Vademecum zu einem Klassiker der Historischen Schule: Wilhelm Roscher und seine 'Ansichten der Volkswirtschaft aus dem geschichtlichen Standpunkte'*, Düsseldorf: Handelsblatt-Verlag, pp. 37–121.
Weber, M. (1922), 'Roschers historische Methode', in M. Weber, *Gesammelte Aufsätze zur Wissenschaftslehre*, 2nd edn, Tübingen: Mohr, pp. 3–42.

Karl Heinrich Marx (1818–1883)

Life and Writings

The formative years

Karl Marx was born on 5 May 1818 the eldest son of Heinrich and Henriette Marx in the provincial town of Trier in the Rhineland, where his father practised as a lawyer. On his father's side Karl was descended from a Jewish family with a long-standing tradition of rabbis. But his father Herschel (or, since 1814, Heinrich) Mordechai had converted to Protestantism in 1816 in order to escape the Prussian restrictions against the Jews, and he also had Karl and his six brothers and sisters baptized as Protestants. Heinrich Marx was a cultured man, who had great admiration for Leibniz, Lessing, and Kant, and raised his children as liberal and law-abiding Protestants. His wife Henriette, née Pressburg, was the daughter of a Jewish merchant from Nijmegen in the Netherlands.

The person who exerted the most important intellectual influence on the young Karl, apart from his father, was Johann Ludwig von Westphalen, a high-ranking civil servant, who treated the talented young neighbour's boy and schoolmate of his son Edgar as an equal partner in discussions on literary and philosophical themes. While his father acquainted him with the German and French enlightenment philosophers, Karl would learn about Homer, Shakespeare and the Romantics from his future father-in-law. Presumably, it was also Baron von Westphalen who introduced him to the ideas of Henri de Saint-Simon, in which he took a keen interest himself. Until his twelfth year, Karl was educated privately by his father and the local bookseller. In the gymnasium, which he attended from 1830 to 1835, he was conspicuous mainly for his diligence and for his strong interest in literature and fine arts.

From 1835 to 1841 Marx studied at the universities of Bonn and Berlin. Following his father's advice, he enrolled at Bonn University as a student of law, but attended courses also in history, medicine, and theology. In 1836 he changed over to the University of Berlin, where at first he continued his studies in law, but then devoted his time and energy mainly to philosophy, after he had come into contact with some of the so-called Young Hegelians, who gathered around the radical theologian and religious critic Bruno Bauer (1809–1882). In 1841 he earned a doctorate with a philosophical dissertation on "The difference between the Democritean and the Epicurean philosophy of nature" at the University of Jena. However, he quickly realized that there was little chance of success for an academic career, in view of the strict actions of the Prussian authorities against radical left-wing Hegelians: his mentor Bruno Bauer, whom he had intended to follow to the University of Bonn, was deprived of his lecture rights. Being thrown back on his own financially by the unexpected death of his father, Marx turned to journalism and began to write articles for the *Rheinische Zeitung* in Cologne, which had been founded by enlightened citizens and industrialists in early 1842. In October, Marx took over the editorship of the liberal and anti-clerical, and under Marx's influence increasingly more radical, newspaper. Being watched with mounting suspicion by the censorship authorities, the *Rheinische Zeitung* was banned in March 1843.

Revolutionary turmoil in Europe

In June 1843 Karl Marx and Jenny von Westphalen, the daughter of J.L. von Westphalen, got married. In October the young couple moved to Paris, then the centre of radical thinking and political activism in Europe, where Marx came in contact with men such as Heinrich Heine (1797–1856), Georg Herwegh (1817–1875), Pierre-Joseph Proudhon (1809–1865), and Michail Bakunin (1814–1876), and where he planned to edit, together with Arnold Ruge (1802–1880), a literary-political magazine called the *Deutsch-Französische Jahrbücher*. The first (and only) issue of these "yearbooks" was published in 1844. It contained *inter alia* Friedrich Engels's contribution "Umrisse zu einer Kritik der Nationalökonomie" ("Outlines of a critique of political economy") and two articles by Marx, "Zur Judenfrage" ("On the Jewish question") and "Zur Kritik der Hegelschen Rechtsphilosophie" ("A contribution to the critique of Hegel's philosophy of right"). Marx was very impressed by Engels's contribution and the first meeting of the two men marked the beginning of a lifelong friendship. In Engels (1820–1895), the son of an industrialist from Barmen, Marx found a most congenial intellectual ally, who would subsequently stand by him in his scientific and political activities as a critical commentator, occasional co-author, generous financial helper, and editor of his unfinished works.

Shortly after his meeting with Engels, in autumn 1844, Marx began to study seriously political economy. He filled several notebooks with excerpts and commentaries on the economic writings of Boisguilbert and the French physiocrats, and of Smith, Malthus, and Ricardo (which he first read in French). He then used his "Paris notebooks" for drafting out a long text that he himself had not considered for publication, but which was published posthumously in 1932 as the so-called *Ökonomisch-philosophische Manuskripte von 1844* (*Economic and Philosophic Manuscripts of 1844*). In these manuscripts Marx formulated a critique of Hegel's philosophy and also discussed the specific forms that "alienation" assumes under capitalistic production relations. (On Marx's early writings, see Colletti 1975.)

In early 1845 Marx was expelled from France at the instigation of the Prussian embassy in Paris. With his wife and his newly born daughter "Jennychen" he flew to Brussels, where he continued to pursue his studies in political economy. In *Die deutsche Ideologie* (*The German Ideology*), written jointly with Engels in 1845–46, he again discussed critically Hegel's philosophy and developed the main ideas of what was to be called the materialist conception of history (on the so-called "dialectical materialism", see Colletti 1969 [1973]), which he later summarized as follows in his celebrated "Introduction" to the critique of political economy:

> In the social production of their existence, men inevitably enter into definite relations, which are independent of their will, namely relations of production appropriate to a given stage in the development of their material forces of production. The totality of these relations of production constitutes the economic structure of society, the real foundation, on which arises a legal and political superstructure and to which correspond definite forms of social consciousness. The mode of production of material life conditions the general process of social, political and intellectual life. It is not the consciousness of men that determines their existence, but their social existence that determines their consciousness. At a certain stage of development, the material productive forces of society come into conflict with the existing relations of production or — this merely expresses the same thing in legal terms — with the property relations within the framework of which they have operated hitherto. From forms of development of the productive forces these relations turn into their fetters. . . . In broad outline, the Asiatic, ancient, feudal

and modern bourgeois modes of production may be designated as epochs marking progress in the economic development of society. The bourgeois relations of production are the last antagonistic form of the social process of production . . . but the productive forces developing within bourgeois society create also the material conditions for a solution of this antagonism. The prehistory of human society accordingly closes with this social formation. (Marx 1859 [1987]: 263–4)

In 1846 Marx also published a scathing polemic against Proudhon, entitled *Misère de la Philosophie* (*The Poverty of Philosophy*) (1847) – thus ridiculing the title of Proudhon's book *Philosophie de la misère* (*Philosophy of Poverty*) (1846). In this text as well as in a short tract on "Wage labour and capital", which emanated from a set of lectures that he had delivered in 1847 at the German Workers' Association in Brussels, Marx first set out his theory of value and surplus value. In Brussels, Marx and Engels also founded the "Communistisches Korrespondenz-Kommittee" (Communist Correspondence Committee) in early 1846, which aimed at the unification of the revolutionary German and international workers. They established an international Communist party by merging with Wilhelm Weitling's "Bund der Gerechten" (League of the Just). At the first joint congress in London in November 1847 Marx and Engels succeeded in establishing the "Bund der Kommunisten" (the Communist League). From the mandate given to Marx and Engels at the second congress in 1848 to write a declaration of principle emanated the famous *Manifesto of the Communist Party* – which in fact was written by Marx alone after both had agreed that Engels's preliminary drafts were unsuitable.

In spring 1848, when the revolutionary movements began to spread throughout Europe after the February revolution in Paris, Marx was briefly imprisoned and then expelled from Belgium. Upon an invitation from the newly installed French government he first returned to Paris, but after the March revolution in Germany he and Engels moved to Cologne in order to lead the revolutionary movement in the Rhine provinces and edit the re-established *Neue Rheinische Zeitung*. After the failure of the revolution, the popular daily paper was increasingly subjected to censorship and finally banned in May 1849. Marx was expelled from Prussia and deprived of his citizenship. After a brief interval in Paris he moved into exile with his family to England and settled down in London, where he was to stay until the end of his life.

Exile in London

Over the next 30 years Marx devoted much of his time and energy to political economy. He used to work in the reading room of the British Museum, studying the available literature on political economy as well as the so-called Government Blue Books, the economic and financial sections of newspapers and magazines, and various other sources that provided information on the economic and social conditions in Britain and in the rest of the world, filling several hundred notebooks and thousands of pages with excerpts, commentaries, and bibliographic references. In the evenings and at night he then used his extensive notes in producing first drafts of sections and chapters of his planned books.

The economic crisis of 1857 induced him to summarize the results of his economic studies in a first manuscript on political economy of some 800 pages. In the "Introduction" he grouped the topics to be dealt with into six "books": "(1) Of Capital (with some pre-chapters). (2) Of landed property. (3) Of Wage-labour. (4) Of the State.

(5) Foreign Trade. (6) World Market." This manuscript, which Marx composed from August 1857 to March 1858, was first published in 1939–41 under the title *Grundrisse der Kritik der Politischen Ökonomie (Rohentwurf) 1857–1858*. It is often referred to as a "rough draft" of *Das Kapital (Capital)*, but Marx's original plan was in fact much wider in scope. The three volumes of his later main work, *Das Kapital*, in fact cover only the contents of the first "book" of the originally planned six "books". In the course of working out this part, Marx realized the impossibility of finishing the huge task he had set himself and was forced to postpone work on "books" 4, 5 and 6, while those on "landed property" and on "wage-labour" were partly integrated into his main work (in volumes I and III of *Capital* and in the *Theories of Surplus Value*).

In 1859 Marx managed to prepare a revised version of the first part of the 1857–58 "Rough draft" for publication: *Zur Kritik der Politischen Ökonomie (Erstes Heft) (A Contribution to the Critique of Political Economy)*. However, this book, in which Marx first presented his value theory in full, did not have the desired impact, which prompted him to revise his publication plans again. As preliminary drafts for his major work, which was now meant to consist of four "books" (in three volumes), he wrote two extensive sets of manuscripts, which have been published as *Ökonomische Manuskripte von 1861–63* and *Ökonomische Manuskripte von 1863–67* in the new MEGA edition. On the basis of these manuscripts he then managed to complete and prepare for publication, in 1867, only the first volume of *Capital*, entitled *Das Kapital. Kritik der Politischen Ökonomie. Erster Band. Buch I: Der Produktionsprozeß des Kapitals*. He did not succeed in bringing the remaining volumes to completion. These were published only posthumously by Friedrich Engels from the extant sets of manuscripts, with many changes and additions, in 1885 and 1894, and by Karl Kautsky, in 1905–10. During the 1870s Marx repeatedly interrupted his work on the planned volumes II and III of *Capital* and devoted his attention to various other research fields (such as Russian society, the Asiatic mode of production, linguistics, mathematics, and the latest developments in the natural sciences, in particular chemistry); in the early 1880s he ceased to work on them altogether.

Engels's edition of volumes II and III of *Capital* does not meet today's editorial standards. As the basis of the text Engels used the manuscripts written by Marx between 1863 and 1867, which he merged with manuscript fragments from later working periods and "supplemented" by insertions, changes, and additions of his own, without properly indicating the latter. The full extent of Engels's editorial intrusions can be assessed only since the original manuscripts have been published in the new MEGA edition.

According to Marx's plan, the second volume was meant to comprise the "Circulation process of Capital (Book II) and the Process as a whole (Book III)", but in Engels's edition book II became volume II and book III became volume III of *Capital*. According to Marx's plan, the final and third volume was to be the "History of the Theory" ("Book IV" in Marx's outline); this was published in three volumes from 1905–10 under the editorship of Karl Kautsky as *Theorien über den Mehrwert (Theories of Surplus Value)* from a set of manuscripts that Marx had written during 1861–63. (For a detailed account of the gestation of Marx's economic writings, culminating in the three volumes of *Capital* and the *Theories of Surplus Value*, see Rosdolsky 1968 [1977]; Oakley 1983; and the volumes published in the new MEGA edition as "Abteilung II. Vorarbeiten zum Kapital".)

During the years in London, Marx and his family suffered from material deprivation, in spite of continuous financial support from Engels. Bad housing conditions, malnutrition, and lack of medical care led to the worsening of Marx's health and that of his wife, as well as to the early death of four of his seven children. He took on various journalistic jobs, but these did not earn him a regular income. His work as European correspondent of the *New York Daily Tribune*, for which he wrote hundreds of articles (see Ledbetter 2007), forced him to keep himself well informed about British and European politics. From 1864 to 1872 Marx also often had to interrupt his scientific work because of his multifarious commitments in the International Workingmen's Association, the so-called "First International", in whose foundation he was actively involved in 1864. From London he also tried to foster the foundation of a revolutionary socialist party in the German states. At first he distanced himself from Ferdinand Lassalle's reform-oriented "Allgemeiner Deutscher Arbeiterverein", which then however was merged with the "Sozialdemokratische Arbeiterpartei" in 1875, which Wilhelm Liebknecht had founded six years earlier in close collaboration with Marx, to form the "Sozialistische Arbeiterpartei Deutschlands", from which the German "Social Democratic Party", the SPD, was later to emerge.

In his last years Marx was plagued by serious health problems. He suffered from chronic liver and lung problems, and also from carbuncles, which are diagnosed today as psychologically caused. In spite of several cure treatments at the English seaside, in Karlsbad and in Algiers, his health further deteriorated. His wife Jenny, who fell fatally ill in 1880, died the following year. Marx only survived her by a little more than two years. He died, presumably from the after-effects of lung tuberculosis that had never been properly treated, on 14 March 1883 in London.

Marx's Approaches to Value – Socio-Historical, Dialectical, Classical

The theory of labour value: basic concepts

Marx begins his study of capitalistic production with an analysis of commodities, because, "for bourgeois society, the commodity-form of the product of labour, or the value-form of the commodity, is the economic cell-form" (1867 [1976]: 90). Commodities have a use-value and an exchange-value. According to Marx, this "double character" of the products of labour is a source of "contradictions". While from a societal point of view economic activities aim at the production of use-values to satisfy the needs and wants of the members of society, the interest of the individual capitalist is directed at the production of exchange-values and profit – he "wants to produce a commodity greater in value than the sum of the values of the commodities used to produce it, namely the means of production and the labour-power" (1867 [1976]: 293). What, then, determines the exchange values of commodities? Since every commodity can be exchanged against any other, the exchange relations between commodities, Marx insists, must be based on a common "something": "The exchange values of commodities must be reduced to a common element, of which they represent a greater or lesser quantity" (1867 [1976]: 127). He adds:

> This common element cannot be a geometrical, physical, chemical or other natural property of commodities. Such properties come into consideration only to the extent that they make the commodity useful, i.e. turn them into use-values. . . . As use-values, commodities differ above

all in quality, while as exchange-values they can only differ in quantity, and therefore do not contain an atom of use-value. If then we disregard the use-value of commodities, only one property remains, that of being products of labour. (Marx 1867 [1976]: 127–8)

The relative values of commodities are thus taken to be governed by the relative amounts of embodied labour. Labour itself, however, also has a double character. In the production process, with all its technical and intellectual specificities due to education and formation, it is heterogeneous, "concrete labour", qualitatively different according to productive necessities. However, as the "substance" and "magnitude" of value, Marx stresses, it is "abstract labour", "labour in general", and as such directly comparable to any other quantity of abstract labour embodied in some other commodity. For some given prevailing technical conditions of production, the amount of abstract labour spent in the production of a commodity is called "socially necessary labour" (1867 [1976]: 129).

These are the first basic concepts on which Marx's reasoning is built. Their understanding, however, is not self-evident, and Marx himself published several versions of his presentation of his theory of value, for example, first in the 1859 *Contribution to the Critique of Political Economy*, then in 1867 in the first section of the first edition of *Capital* – to which he added an appendix, "Die Werthform" (the value-form), placed as an afterthought at the end of the book – a section modified for the 1872–75 French edition and again in the fourth German edition (posthumously published in 1890). Marx was not only facing misunderstandings from his readers, as he wrote, he was also struggling with important analytical difficulties. One problem is the way in which he "derived" the statement that the only thing that commodities have in common is labour, leaving "out of consideration the use-value of commodities". Eugen von Böhm-Bawerk (1884 [1890]), Philip Henry Wicksteed (1884) and Vilfredo Pareto (1902), for example, pointed out that this mode of reasoning is not conclusive: eliminating some items in a list of qualities to retain the remaining one cannot be a proof because the substance of value could well originate in an item omitted from the list; moreover, Marx's approach could also be turned in favour of utility because, just as "abstract labour", as distinct from "concrete labour", is alleged to be the substance of value, "abstract utility", as distinct from "concrete utility", could well form the substance of value.

This aspect is only a symptom of deeper difficulties in Marx's approach. In particular, the meaning of the central concept of "abstract labour", "labour in general", is not clear. Several definitions can be found, which are not compatible with one another. These definitions express different strands of Marx's thought concerning value, money and capital – socio-historical, dialectical and classical (see Faccarello 1983a, 1997, 2000a).

The socio-historical approach to value
A first definition of "abstract labour" is purely socio-historical – or "sociological" – and is tightly connected to the phenomenon of fetishism (see, for example, "The fetishism of the commodity and its secret", Marx 1867 [1976]: 163–77). We encounter it in passages in which Marx stresses the "phantom-like objectivity" (ibid.: 128) and the "mystical character" (ibid.: 164) of the products of labour in a market society and speaks of "labour in general" as the "common social substance" of these products, and of the commodity as a "social hieroglyph". "Not an atom of matter enters into the objectivity of commodities as values", Marx stresses, and adds:

Commodities possess an objective character as values only in so far as they are expressions of an identical social substance, human labour, . . . their objective character as values is therefore purely social. From this it follows self-evidently that it can only appear in the social relation between commodity and commodity. (1867 [1976]: 138–9)

Marx's purpose here is to define the "specific difference" presented by the capitalist mode of production as compared with other forms of society. This is an important task, which he deduced from his youthful criticism of Hegel's philosophy along Feuerbachian lines. In this perspective, "value" is supposed to express this *differentia specifica*. What matters is the qualitative side of the analysis. However, the sociological or qualitative characterization of value inevitably involves a quantitative determination, which proves to be at variance with the traditional "labour incorporated" analysis (below).

To single out the specificity of a market-based economy, Marx refers, in *Contribution* and *Capital*, to four other forms of society: "Robinson on his island", the "dark European Middle-Ages", the rural and patriarchal family, and a "society of free and equal men". In these non-capitalist societies, Marx writes, (1) only "concrete labour" matters, (2) the products of labour are not commodities and (3) social relations of production are transparent. In a market society, on the contrary, (1) concrete labour does not matter as such, (2) products are commodities and (3) the social relations of production are hidden behind the apparent equality in exchange relations. Why do such differences arise?

First, Marx argues, in a non-capitalist society there is an immediate correspondence between (1) the different kinds of concrete labour, (2) the produced use values and (3) the needs of the members of society. There is no place for a break between a "private" and a "social" side of activities: it is "the distinct labour of the individual in its original form, the particular features of his labour and not its universal aspect that formed the social tie" (Marx 1859 [1987]: 275). Second, the cause of this state of things lies in the existence of a community that acts prior to production and coordinates it. All the societies he mentions are, in some way, planned: "the individual labour powers, by their very nature, act only as instruments of the joint labour-power" (Marx 1867 [1976]: 171).

The "specific difference" presented by the capitalist mode of production is thus defined as the lack of any community prior to production. Producers are independent and isolated; they work privately and their activities are not coordinated *ex ante*. This is why the "natural" forms of labour are not immediately social. The social link forces itself upon the system *ex post* through the market. It is by transforming their products into commodities that independent producers constitute a coherent set of relationships, that is, a society, and that their private labour is – or is not – validated as a social commodity. The market is the locus of social integration. In this socio-historical line of argument, Marx called "abstract" or "general" labour the concrete labour that is socially validated through the exchange of its products in the market, a "concrete labour" that proves itself part of the "social division of labour". It is a result of exchange, defined simultaneously with the exchange rate. "Abstract labour" is not a "substance" prior to exchange nor does it determine it. "Universal social labour is consequently not a ready-made prerequisite but an emerging result" (Marx 1859 [1987]: 286; translation modified).

If abstract or general labour is not a substance which exists prior to exchange, value cannot be defined other than as the quantity of money for which a commodity is exchanged: this quantity acts both as the determining factor and the measure of value.

We can now understand the meaning of such sentences as "universal labour time itself is an abstraction, which, as such, does not exist for commodities" (Marx 1859 [1987]: 286). Money acts as the social link for labours expended independently of each other, without social coordination. It regulates production. It is, in Marx's own words, the community (an indirect, abstract community) that seems to be lacking in a society based on market exchange and the private ownership of means of production. Producers meet as owners and

> exist for each other only as things, something that is merely further developed in the money relation, in which their community itself appears as an external and hence a casual thing with respect to all. . . . Since . . . they are not subsumed under any naturally evolved community . . . this community must . . . exist as an independent, external, casual thing . . . with respect to them as independent subjects. That is precisely the condition for their simultaneously being in some social connection as independent private persons. (Marx 1858 [1987]: 468)

This "sociological" approach is thus at variance with the traditional, or classical, interpretation of *Capital* (below). Its most striking feature is the inversion of the deduction of value and money. If, in the classical approach, money is deduced from the concepts of abstract labour and value – it is a commodity which itself has a value and can consequently act as a measure of value, a medium of exchange and a store of value – in the socio-historical approach abstract labour and value are deduced from the concept of money.

The dialectical approach
The second definition of "abstract", "general" labour is purely conceptual. Abstract labour can be seen as an "indeterminate abstraction", as the category that, in thought, embraces all imaginable kinds of concrete labour: "the mental product of a concrete totality of labours" (Marx 1857–58 [1973]: 104) – just as the concept of "fruit" denotes concrete fruits like apples, pears, mangos, and so on. The concept is here hypostatized, in an idealist way that it is a priori surprising to find in Marx. However, it is in fact in line with Marx's second line of argument, which can be called the "dialectical approach" and which stems from Marx's plan to build his theoretical construction on a rigorous chain of deductions of concepts, from the commodity concept to that of money, from money to capital and then to wage-labour and the different kinds of capital – a plan which is visible in *Grundrisse*, in *Contribution* and the manuscript of it, and of course in *Capital*.

In Marx's eyes the theoretical introduction of money from the sociological approach is no doubt insufficient because all the concepts are given simultaneously and are not deduced from one another. This creates a break in his chain of reasoning: once money and value are given, there seems to be no place left for a rigorous deduction of the concepts of capital and wage labour, and a picture emerges eventually of a rather harmonious society of independent producers, whereas in Marx's opinion a monetary economy is necessarily a capitalist one. This is why, of the preceding considerations, Marx retains only the necessary transformation of products into commodities. He then stresses that a commodity has a twofold character (exchangeable value and use value) and that these two are "contradictory". Then, from this basic "opposition", he dialectically deduces money, capital, wage labour and the different kinds of capital.

To use Marx's Hegelian language, what is this "opposition" stemming from the analysis of the two sides of a commodity and why is there a "contradiction" between them? How and with the help of which logical tools is the concept of money generated as a result of the development of this alleged basic "contradiction"? Marx asserts that, on the one hand, a commodity is not immediately a value, but "has to become so". On the other hand, it is not immediately a use value, but it has also to become so. Of course the exchange process realizes a commodity as a value (for the seller), just as it simultaneously realizes it as a use value (for the buyer). In Marx's opinion, this means a "contradiction": the "realization" of use value presupposes in his eyes the realization of the commodity as value, and conversely the "realization" of value presupposes that of use value. As the solution of each problem implies that of the other, we therefore face an endless theoretical regression from one determination of the concept of commodity to the other. In order to generate this opposition and the endless regression, the classical meanings of value and use value have been modified. Use value is now defined as a direct utility relationship between a thing and its owner, and value is defined as the quantity of such and such commodities for which it can be exchanged.

The "inner" contradiction of the commodity, Marx continues, brings about the "equivalent form", in which a given commodity assumes the "relative" value form, and the received commodity acts as a "particular" equivalent. The commodity is then equated with different quantities of all other commodities, which act as many particular equivalents: it is the "developed" equivalent form. Marx stresses, however, that every attempt to transcend a particular equivalent in order to give value its "general form" is bound to fail: a commodity can be successively equated with every other commodity, but each of them nevertheless remains a particular equivalent. Here we encounter once again a theoretically endless regression from one determination to another. To obtain the "general equivalent", the "money form", Marx simply reverses the sequence of the particular equivalents, which, by means of this operation, express their value in a determined amount of one and the same commodity.

The meaning of this analysis of the "value forms", that is, the development of the original "contradiction" of the two aspects of commodity – stated at the beginning of *Contribution* and *Capital* – and the final reversal which generates the concept of money, is problematic. (1) The reversal can be interpreted as a mere subjective reasoning on the part of the dealer who considers his or her commodity as a general equivalent for all other commodities. However, in this case no theoretical derivation of money is accomplished: if each dealer wants his commodity to be accepted by the other dealers as the general equivalent, no commodity can assume this role (Marx 1867 [1976]: 180). (2) The development of the "value forms" could also be interpreted in an idealist way, implying the progressive realization of a universal element (value) that aims at a manifestation appropriate to its concept (money), as Hegel would have put it. In both cases the dialectical deduction of the concept of money is questionable, and the concept of "abstract" labour, "substance" of value, either vanishes, or is at best to be understood as an "indeterminate abstraction" (the definition noted above).

Marx's classical approach to value

Two further definitions of "abstract labour" can be found in Marx's texts, referring to the usual classical understanding of Marx's economics. The first conveys a "physiological" conception, which, as for Ricardo at the end of his life, puts stress on the expense of energy that all labour always involves. "Tailoring and weaving, although they are qualitatively different productive activities, are both a productive expenditure of human brains, muscles, nerves, hands etc., and in this sense both human labour" (Marx 1867 [1976]: 134). This is why Marx states that "all labour is an expenditure of human labour-power, in the physiological sense, and it is in this quality of being equal, or abstract, human labour that it forms the value of commodities" (1867 [1976]: 137).

The second definition of "abstract" or "general" labour stresses the growing indifference of labourers vis-à-vis their tasks and kinds of labour, an indifference that results from the development of the labour market and from a process of deskilling imposed by technological progress (Marx 1863–66 [1976]). "Indifference towards specific labours corresponds to a form of society in which individuals can with ease transfer from one labour to another, and where the specific kind is a matter of chance for them, hence of indifference" (Marx 1857–58 [1973]: 104). This is evident in the United States: "Here, then, for the first time, the point of departure of modern economics, namely the abstraction of the category 'labour', 'labour as such', labour pure and simple, becomes true in practice" (ibid.: 104–5).

In Marx's texts, the line of argument expressed by these definitions is closely connected to the traditional analysis of *Capital* and to its stress on the determination of values in terms of incorporated quantities of labour. This approach links the analyses of *Capital* directly to those of classical political economy and, in systematically developing a quantitative and positive economic analysis, confers a "naturalistic" flavour on the theory of value. From this point of view the so-called "socially necessary labour" that must be spent directly and indirectly to produce a commodity, and which forms its value, is defined with respect to technical factors, that is, to what can be considered as the "normal" or "average" technical conditions in each industry at a given place and time. The "substance" of value, "abstract labour", is also to be understood in the same perspective. This is why, among the different definitions that can be found in Marx, only the "physical" ones can be coherently accepted: that is, either the one that stresses the "energetical" nature of abstract labour, or the one that, in pointing out the process of development in the labour market, in the end simply identifies "concrete" and "abstract" labour. This kind of "technological" or "naturalistic" approach, of course, does away with a socio-historical specification of value. It is also at odds with the dialectical deduction of concepts: it is impossible to see to what extent its concepts of value and use value (value is supposed to be a quantity of labour, and use value expresses the physical and concrete aspects of the product of labour) are "opposed" to each other.

Finally, it is important to note that the ideas expressed by Marx in his different approaches to value – including the classical approach with the attempt to "prove" that the only thing that commodities have in common is labour – owe a great deal to Hegel's philosophy: not only to Hegel's *Science of Logic* but also, and perhaps to a greater extent, to his *Philosophy of Right*, and that this source of inspiration is also important for the deductions of the concept of "capital in general", wage labour and the different forms of capital (see Reichelt 1970; Faccarello 1983a: chs 14–16, 1997, 2000a).

Note that the three conflicting approaches coexist in Marx's texts in different proportions, with the classical definition being dominant in *Capital*. This coexistence of conflicting conceptualizations is a source of dire controversies and confusions. In the following we focus on the classical concept of value in Marx.

Main Themes in Marx's Classical Approach

From value to surplus value
According to Marx, it is a specific characteristic of the capitalist mode of production that human labour-power also assumes commodity-form. Its value is determined, just like that of any other commodity, by the amount of socially necessary labour required in its (re)production. In order to (re)produce his labour-power the labourer needs certain amounts of means of subsistence (for himself and his family), that is, a certain consumption basket, the size and composition of which is determined, at any given time and place, by physiological, historical, and cultural circumstances: "Therefore the labour-time necessary for the production of labour-power is the same as that necessary for the production of those means of subsistence; in other words, the value of labour-power is the value of the means of subsistence necessary for the maintenance of its owner" (Marx [1867] 1976: 274). That the workers' remuneration cannot systematically exceed the subsistence level Marx explains with reference to competitive pressures on the labour market that result from the existence of an "industrial reserve army", that is, especially from the existence of a pool of unemployed workers, which is continuously replenished by the displacement of workers consequent upon the introduction of labour-saving technical progress.

The use-value of the commodity labour-power consists in its "productive consumption" in the production process: the capitalist "consumes" the commodity labour-power he has purchased at its labour-value v by employing it, together with various means of production whose aggregate labour value is given by c, in the production of a certain commodity. Marx called the raw materials, intermediate products, and the means of production purchased by the capitalist "constant" capital, because their value is merely transferred onto the product without any change, either in a single production cycle (raw materials and intermediate products) or else over a number of production cycles (tools and machines). With the "variable" part of the capital advances labour-power is purchased, which reproduces not only its own value but generates an additional value conferred to the product. The value of the product, λ, is given by the amount of (socially necessary) labour which has been used up in its production in the form of "direct" or "living" labour, l, and in the form of "indirect" or "previously expended" labour, which is "congealed" in the means of production, c, that is:

$$\lambda = c + l = c + v + s \qquad (1)$$

The term s denotes what Marx calls "surplus value". Its existence obviously derives from the fact that a part of the "living" labour performed by the worker consists of "unpaid" or "surplus labour", because the labourer has to work longer than is necessary for reproducing his means of subsistence ($l > v$). In volumes I and II of *Capital*, Marx supposed all commodities, including the commodity labour power, to exchange at their (labour-) values. Accordingly, "exploitation" is not "explained" by him from wages being "too low," that is, from assuming that workers have to sell their commodity – their labour power – below its value. Exploitation, Marx insisted, is a phenomenon that is not generated in the sphere of circulation, but in that of production.

The "transformation problem"

In volume I of *Capital* Marx maintained that the value of a commodity is given by the quantity of socially necessary abstract labour required in its production. The exchange ratios between any two commodities are then given, by definition, by the ratio of their labour values. However Marx, who had carefully studied the contributions of Smith and Ricardo, was of course aware of the fact that the "prices of production" (or "natural prices", as his precursors called them) must generally deviate from labour values. He was convinced, however, that he understood much better than his predecessors why these deviations occur and how their magnitudes can be ascertained. What had prevented his precursors from developing a correct solution to the problem? According to Marx, the reason for their failure is to be found in Adam Smith's erroneous idea that the annual social product (exclusive of rent) can be entirely reduced to wages and profits; an idea which had also been implicitly adopted by Ricardo when he supposed in his determination of the general rate of profits that all capital can be reduced to advanced wage capital in a finite number of steps. Both had overlooked that a part of the annual product, which Marx called "constant capital", must be used in order to replace the used-up means of production. If this is taken into account, it becomes immediately obvious that the deviations of production prices from labour values are caused by the differences in the proportions of the two capital components in the production of the various commodities, that is, by differences in the proportions between "living labour" and "dead labour" (*vorgetane Arbeit*). If the constant capital is again assumed for simplicity to consist only of circulating capital, the value of an industry's annual product is equal to $c + l$, where c is the value of the constant capital (the quantity of "indirect" labour) and l is the quantity of "living" (or "direct") labour. Denoting by v the value of the wages advanced in this industry – Marx's "variable capital" – the industry's costs of production in value terms amount to $c + v$, and the surplus value generated in this industry is given by $s = (c + l) - (c + v) = l - v$. The rate of profit in value terms of this industry is then given by:

$$r = \frac{s}{c + v} = \frac{s/v}{(c/v) + 1} \tag{2}$$

It is thus seen to depend on two magnitudes: on s/v, a ratio that Marx calls "rate of surplus value" or "rate of exploitation", and on c/v, which expresses the so-called "organic composition of capital". Under competitive conditions (and on the assumption of the mentioned deskilling of labour and the emergence of a uniform length of the working day) the rate of surplus value must be the same in all industries. The organic composition of capital, however, is determined by technology and will in general differ across industries. An exchange of commodities at their labour values would therefore be associated with different profit rates across industries. The tendency towards uniform rates of profit in competitive conditions therefore leads to systematic deviations of relative prices from labour values. These deviations are necessary in order to relate the surplus value of the economic system as a whole, S, which was generated in the individual industries in proportion to the industries' variable capitals, to the capital of the economic system as a whole, $C + V$.

Marx believed that for the system as a whole these deviations of production prices from labour values must exactly compensate each other, so that the general rate of profits is the same as the one which emerges if the economy as a whole is considered as a single industry, that is, the same as:

$$r = \frac{S}{C + V} \tag{3}$$

where S, C, and V denote total surplus value, total constant capital, and total variable capital, respectively. In Marx's view, the labour theory of value, although it does not directly give a correct theory of relative prices, nevertheless provides the basis of such a theory. That Marx felt justified to make use of the labour theory of value in volumes I and II of *Capital* was therefore due to his conclusion, at which he had already previously arrived (but from which we now know that it is untenable) that the general rate of profits calculated at production prices is the same as the value rate of profits. However, if this mode of exposition may have seemed justified to Marx as being easily comprehensible for his readers, with the benefit of hindsight it was a mistake, which has seriously impeded the understanding of his work. The fact that volumes II and III of *Capital* became available only much later has contributed to the solidification of the misconception that Marx had meant to determine relative prices *directly* by means of the labour theory of value.

When Marx, in section 2 of volume III of *Capital*, explicated his idea of the redistribution of surplus value in the course of the transformation of labour values in prices of production, he noted explicitly that his transformation procedure was not fully accurate, because the means of production have to be evaluated at production prices rather than at labour values (1894 [1981]: 259–60, 264–5). He overlooked, however, the important implication that he then also had no justification for supposing that the ratio of total profits to total capital is the same as if commodities were exchanged at labour values, that is, he overlooked that his "successivist", two-step procedure for the determination of the general rate of profits and relative prices, as Ladislaus von Bortkiewicz (1906–07 [1952]: 38) called it, was thereby undermined.

Reproduction, accumulation, and crises

As Marx explained in his Foreword to *Capital*, "it is the ultimate aim of this work to reveal the economic law of motion of modern society" (1867 [1976]: 92). Accordingly, the analysis of the dynamism of the capitalist development process formed a central element in Marx's work. In this analysis, as in Marx's thinking generally, the concept of "reproduction" occupied a prominent place. Social relations and social formations exist, Marx argued, because the prevailing mode of production systematically reproduces them. In capitalist societies the reproduction of capital is associated with the reproduction of the class relations: at the end of the production and circulation process the capitalist has reproduced his advanced capital, together with surplus value, whereas the labourer has reproduced only his labour power. If social production is organized capitalistically, the production process itself thus reproduces capitalists and labourers as social classes.

Accumulation of capital requires that part of the previously generated surplus value is used in the production process again. If the reinvested surplus were used only for increasing the activity levels of the existing production processes, the constant capital and the variable capital would be increased proportionately, and there is "reproduction on an extended scale". However, this need not be the case. In general, the accumulation process is bound up with changes in the structure and organization of capital and in production relations; new machinery and new methods of production, of transportation, or of organization are introduced, and new products and new markets are developed. The competitive process forces each individual capitalist to search constantly for less costly methods of production, better product quality, new markets, and so on. In addition, Marx argued that the accumulation process is also bound up with an increasing concentration and centralization of capital: larger capitals displace smaller capitals owing to the exploitation of increasing returns to scale and scope, and capital becomes ever more centralized by means of take-overs of competitors.

The schemes of "simple" and "extended reproduction" in chapters 20 and 21 of volume II of *Capital*, which Marx developed on the basis of François Quesnay's *Tableau économique*, are widely regarded as one his finest analytical achievements (see Gehrke and Kurz 1995). The model of simple reproduction depicts the commodity circulation between two sectors. The first sector produces capital goods for itself and for the second sector producing consumption goods, and receives in return the consumption goods required for the alimentation of the workers and the capitalists' consumptions. For this simple two-sectoral model with circular production relations Marx showed the conditions for a stationary reproduction equilibrium. In the next step, he then turned to the analysis of extended reproduction and showed by means of simple numerical examples that balanced capital accumulation must be associated with an expansion of the two sectors in lock-step, that is, with steady-state growth. The original manuscripts published in the MEGA edition show that Marx had also worked out more elaborate versions of the reproduction schemes with six sectors, which in terms of their analytical structure are similar to the three-sector models of Feldman (1928 [1964]), Mahalanobis (1953), and Lowe (1976); see Mori (2007).

In Marx's writings there is no consistently elaborated cycle theory, but there are several approaches to the explanation of crises. One of these relates to the reproduction schemes and locates the source of crisis-ridden developments in disproportions that occur in the accumulation process and that tend to reinforce themselves. In addition, Marx also put forward theoretical explanations based on under-consumption arguments, which refer to insufficient purchasing power of the working class as triggering an insufficient overall effective demand. However, Marx's most elaborate explanation for crises and economic stagnation derives from his "law of the tendency of the rate of profits to fall", which he set out in volume III of *Capital*.

The law of the tendency of the rate of profits to fall

Like his predecessors, Marx tried to provide an explanation for the supposed empirical phenomenon of the tendency of a falling rate of profits. His approach must be seen in connection with the alternative one suggested by David Ricardo, who had argued that in the course of the accumulation process the wage share must rise, because the production of foodstuff is subject to increasing costs as a consequence of the need to have recourse to less and less productive soils or methods of land cultivation. Accordingly, nominal wages must rise to keep real wages constant and the rate of profit and the profit share are bound to fall. Ricardo had also suggested that the rise in money wages could lead to the substitution of machinery for labour, that is, to the introduction of machines which have been available already before, but which could not be profitably introduced at the lower money wages. This can temporarily retard the fall of the rate of profits, but not ultimately prevent it. In his argument Ricardo explicitly set aside technical progress proper.

Marx had detected an important error in Ricardo's reasoning. Ricardo had maintained that the rate of profits depends only on "proportional wages", that is, the share of wages in the total product measured in labour terms. With a rise in the latter the former is bound to fall. In his argument, Ricardo had assumed for simplicity that the advanced capital consists only of wages, or could be reduced to direct and indirect wages in a finite number of steps; but such a reduction is possible only with "unidirectional" production processes, that is, when the reduction series comprises a production stage at which only "original" factors of production like labour and land are needed in the production of the means of production. If Ricardo's error is corrected and the existence of circular production relations is taken into account, Marx insisted, the true cause of the falling rate of profits is revealed.

If we designate the rate of profits with r, the value of the social product with Y, wages with W, profits with Π, and the wage share with ω, then Ricardo determined the rate of profits as:

$$r = \frac{\Pi}{W} = \frac{Y - W}{W} = \frac{1 - \omega}{\omega} \tag{4}$$

In the special case contemplated by Ricardo, the rate of profits corresponds to the rate of surplus value: Ricardo thus derived the falling rate of profits from a falling rate of surplus value (see Marx 1861–63c [1989b]: 73).

Denoting the total quantity of living labour by L, and the maximum rate of profits by R, the following relationship can be derived (reckoning in terms of labour values, where $Y = L$, $W = V$ and $\Pi = S$):

$$r = \frac{S}{C + V} = \frac{S/L}{C/L + V/L} = \frac{1 - \omega}{1/R + \omega} = \frac{R(1 - \omega)}{1 + R\omega} \tag{5}$$

This shows that the rate of profits depends on *two* magnitudes, not one (as Ricardo thought): on the wage share ω – or the rate of surplus value, $(1 - \omega)/\omega$ – and on the maximum rate of profits, R. If the latter falls, the rate of profits must also fall, given the rate of surplus value. Even a moderately rising rate of surplus value cannot prevent this tendency of a fall in the general rate of profits.

For Marx the law of the tendency of the rate of profits to fall had two fascinating aspects. First, he regarded it as a striking refutation of Ricardo's view, according to which the falling rate of profits is caused by the "niggardliness of nature", which gives rise to increasing production costs of subsistence goods. For Ricardo, the introduction of agricultural improvements or new machinery in manufacturing was a counteracting factor, which could temporarily retard, but not ultimately prevent, the fall in the rate of profits. Marx believed he could demonstrate that the rate of profits falls not in spite of, but precisely *because of* technical progress, since the latter is bound up with a rising organic composition. Secondly, the law also revealed, in Marx's view, one of the major contradictions inherent in the capitalistic mode of production: the progressive element in this mode of production is its capacity to develop the social forces of production and to raise labour productivity. However, since technical progress under capitalistic production must inevitably take the form of replacing living labour by machinery – or, in Marx's terminology, of a rising organic composition of capital – it paradoxically deprives the capitalistic system also of one of its constituting elements, since surplus value cannot be generated by "dead", but only by living, labour.

However, as the original manuscripts published in the new MEGA edition show, Marx entertained doubts about the general validity of the "law" (see, in particular, Marx 1863–67 [2012]). On the one hand, he was clear about the fact that not all forms of technical progress are necessarily associated with a rising organic composition of capital. Moreover, even if the organic composition were rising and the maximum rate of profits were exhibiting a tendency to fall, this need not necessarily imply a fall in the actual rate of profit, since the former could be accompanied by a rise in the rate of surplus value. (For a more detailed account, see Kurz 2010, 2012–13.)

From the point of view of the development of the surplus approach to value and distribution it was perhaps one of Marx's most important analytical achievements to have carried the analysis of prices and income distribution which he had inherited from his precursors a step forward: by resurrecting the aspect of circular production relations he could demonstrate the existence of a maximum rate of profits and show its importance for the analysis of distribution, accumulation, and technical change.

Reception and Influence

It is not possible to summarize the reception and influence of Marx's economic work, which has spanned more than 150 years, in its entirety within the confines of this entry. In order to show some of the main lines of development, it will be convenient to make use again of the thematic division introduced above. It is, however, worth noting that Marx's work, although he was widely considered as the scientific head of the international socialist movement after the publication of volume I of *Capital*, was at first largely ignored by the so-called "bourgeois economists". This was not owing to ideological reasons alone, but also had to do with the fact that at first only volume I of *Capital* was available, and this only in German (a French and a Russian edition were published from 1872 onwards – the French translation having been published by instalments until 1875). Until the turn of the century, the scientific discussion of Marx's work was therefore mainly confined to Germany and Russia, and to some extent also to France and Italy. In England, where Marx had been living since 1849, he remained largely unknown during his lifetime. (For more detailed assessments of the reception of Marx's economics, see Howard and King 1989, 1992 and Steedman 1995.)

The theory of value and prices
From the beginning the discussion of Marx's work centred on the theory of value and prices. When Friedrich Engels, in his Foreword to the second volume of *Capital*, rejected the idea that Marx had plagiarized the theory of value and surplus value from Johann Karl Rodbertus, he invited the economists to show "how an average rate of profit can and must come about, not only without violating the law of value, but precisely on the basis of this law" (Engels 1885 [1978]: 102), and announced that the third volume would contain Marx's definitive solution of the problem. Of the contribu-

tions to Engels's "prize essay competition", which came *inter alia* from Wilhelm Lexis, Julius Wolff, Achille Loria, Conrad Schmidt and P. Fireman, none was convincing. When the third volume of *Capital* was published in 1894, the interest centred mainly on Marx's solution to the so-called "transformation problem". (For a detailed history of the controversies, see Dostaler 1978 and Faccarello 1983a, 2000b.)

From the standpoint of the neoclassical theory Marx's theory of value and prices was criticized by, among others, Philip H. Wicksteed (1884, 1885) and Vilfredo Pareto (1902). One of the most influential critiques of Marx's procedure for the transformation of values to prices (and of the rate of surplus value to the rate of profits) was Eugen von Böhm-Bawerk's "Zum Abschluß des Marxschen Systems" ("Karl Marx and the close of his system") (1896 [1949]). Böhm-Bawerk accused Marx of having given up the value theory expounded in vol. I of *Capital* with his theory of prices of production expounded in vol. III. Between the first and the third volume of *Capital*, he contended, there is "an irreconcilable contradiction". He declared that a determination of the general rate of profits and of relative prices in the way Marx intended was impossible and that Marx's theoretical work has "a past and a present, but no permanent future". But although Böhm-Bawerk failed to notice the real shortcomings of Marx's theoretical construction, Rudolf Hilferding ([1904] 1949), who was to play the leading role in defending Marx in the ensuing debates, could not counter Böhm-Bawerk's attack convincingly. Note however that, in his 1904 answer to Böhm-Bawerk and in his book *Das Finanzkapital* (1910 [1981]), Hilferding started a sociological interpretation (see above) of Marx's theory of value, which was to be taken up later by a few authors such as Nikolaï Boukharin in *Economic Theory of the Leisure Class* (written in 1914, published in 1927) and Rosa Luxemburg in her posthumously published *Einführung in die Nationalökonomie* (1925) – a line of thought above all developed in Isaak Illich Rubin's writings in the 1920s (Rubin 1927 [1978], 1928 [1972]), especially his 1928 *Essays on Marx's Theory of Value* (Faccarello 1983b, 2000b; for a historical setting of Rubin, see Boldyrev and Kragh 2015).

Ladislaus von Bortkiewicz (1906–07 [1952], 1907) deserves the credit for having first demonstrated the errors of Marx's transformation algorithm, and for presenting a correct solution procedure. Bortkiewicz demonstrated, first for the case of unidirectional production processes (where he harked back to a contribution by Vladimir K. Dmitriev (1898 [1974]) and then also for a circular, three-sectoral production system, that the rate of profits and relative prices can be determined on the basis of Marx's set of data by solving a system of simultaneous equations. Similar findings were presented in two neglected contributions by Georg von Charasoff (1909, 1910), who not only anticipated some of the arguments that were proposed later in the discussion of Marx's "transformation problem", but also noted the duality properties of the price and quantity system. Moreover, in the course of his investigation he defined and made use of the concepts of a "production series" (*Produktionsreihe*), of "original capital" (*Urkapital*), and of "basic products" (*Grundprodukte*), thus anticipating Piero Sraffa (1960) with regard to the related concepts of a reduction series to dated quantities of labour, the Standard commodity, and the basics/non-basics distinction. Bortkiewicz's approach to a solution of the transformation problem, which was first made available in an English translation by Paul M. Sweezy in 1942, was subsequently generalized by Josef Winternitz (1948), Francis Seton (1957), and Paul A. Samuelson (1957).

A milestone in the understanding and further development of the surplus approach of the classical economists and Marx was Piero Sraffa's *Production of Commodities by Means of Commodities* (1960). Without entering into an explicit critique of Marx's economic theory, Sraffa demonstrated that the general rate of profits can be ascertained on the basis of the classical set of data (given quantities, given real wage rate, and given methods of production) only simultaneously with the prices. The implications of Sraffa's modern reformulation of the surplus approach to the theory of value and distribution for Marx's theoretical construction were concisely stated by Ian Steedman (1977): on the basis of the classical set of data a consistent determination of the general rate of profits and of relative prices is possible; the recourse to labour values is dispensable. Moreover, Steedman also stressed that labour values and prices more generally depend on income distribution if there is a choice of technique and that Michio Morishima's "Fundamental Marxian theorem", according to which "the equilibrium rate of profit is positive if and only if the rate of exploitation is positive" (1973: 6) need not hold in systems with (pure) joint production.

While Sraffa (1960) and Steedman (1977) have implicitly or explicitly shown that Marx's (labour) value-based reasoning is difficult to sustain, there have been various attempts to defend or reinterpret it. Here it suffices to mention only the reconstruction of Marx's labour theory of value suggested independently from each other by Duncan Foley (1982) and Gérard Duménil (1983). The reconstruction emphasizes the relation between money and labour time that preserves the rigorous quantitative relation between paid and unpaid labour, on the one hand, and the aggregate wages bill and aggregate gross profits, on the other. It became known as "the new solution" to the transformation problem, which is a misnomer, because the punchline of the argument is that there is no transformation problem. The "new view" has been criticized for, among other things, not being a faithful interpretation of Marx and that it wrongly conveys the impression that the classical surplus-based approach to the theory of value and distribution stands or falls with the labour theory of value.

Theory of capitalist development
At centre stage in discussions about Marx's theory of capitalist development has been the validity of the law of the tendency of the rate of profits to fall, on which a large amount of literature exists. An important contribution was made by Nobuo Okishio (1961, 1963), who proved that for a constant real wage rate the rate of profits cannot fall with technical progress (now known as the "Okishio theorem"). It ought to be mentioned, however, that Okishio's results are clearly foreshadowed in Ricardo's analysis and have been anticipated by Samuelson (1959) and Sraffa (1960). For many economists this demonstrates the invalidity of Marx's entire theoretical construction, because a central element of his accumulation theory and his crises theory has been shown to be false. However, as was argued above, Marx seems to have had doubts about the correctness of his "law" himself, and it is unclear whether he meant to suppose a constant wage share (or given rate of surplus value) or a constant real wage rate. Moreover, his argument seems to have been meant to refer, following Ricardo, to technical changes induced by changes in income distribution, that is, to "induced innovations", rather than to technical progress proper.

Marx's schemes of simple and extended reproduction inspired the development of multi-sectoral models of growth and cycles. Michail Tugan-Baranovsky (1905) and

Henrik Grossmann (1929) developed cycle and crises theories from those schemes; Rosa Luxemburg (1913 [1951]) used the reproduction schemes for the development of a theory of imperialism; and Russian economists like G.A. Feldman (1928 [1964]) developed multi-sectoral planning models from them (for a comprehensive survey, see Turban 1980). Marx's schemes also influenced Wassily Leontief's input–output analysis and the associated literature. (Piero Sraffa's "first equations", which he elaborated in 1927–28, however, were developed independently of Marx's reproduction schemes; see Kurz and Salvadori (2015).)

Marx's analysis of the interrelationship between capital accumulation and income distribution in an evolving economic system has led to the development of a still growing class of non-linear cyclical growth models, which generate endogenous cycles around a growth path on the basis of the "predator–prey" model developed by Richard M. Goodwin (1967). Strongly influenced by Marxian ideas about the introduction and diffusion of technical progress and the dynamics of capitalist development is also a branch of the evolutionary economics literature inspired by Joseph A. Schumpeter's *Theorie der wirtschaftlichen Entwicklung* (*Theory of Economic Development*) (1912). The macroeconomic effects of the tendency towards monopolization and capital concentration, emphasized by Marx, have been investigated by Rudolf Hilferding (1910 [1981]), Josef Steindl (1952), and Paul A. Baran and Paul M. Sweezy (1966).

GILBERT FACCARELLO, CHRISTIAN GEHRKE AND HEINZ D. KURZ

See also:

Ladislaus von Bortkiewicz (I); British classical political economy (II); Vladimir Karpovich Dmitriev (I); Marxism(s) (II); Non-Marxian socialist ideas in France (II); Non-Marxist socialist ideas in Germany and Austria (II); Non-Marxian socialist ideas in Britain and the United States (II); Pierre-Joseph Proudhon (I); David Ricardo (I); Value and price (III); Piero Sraffa (I).

References and further reading

There still is no complete edition of Marx and Engels's writings. The *Karl Marx. Friedrich Engels. Historisch-kritische Gesamtausgabe. Werke. Schriften. Briefe* – called MEGA for *Marx-Engels Gesamtausgabe* – started to be published in 1927 at the Marx-Engels Institute in Moscow, under the direction of David Riazanov until 1931, and then of V.V. Adoratski, after Riazanov had been eliminated at the request of Stalin. This programme was stopped in 1935 after 13 volumes had been published.

After World War II a new publication was started. The 39 volumes (plus four supplementary volumes) of the *Marx-Engels Werke* (MEW) series, which were published jointly by the Institutes for Marxism-Leninism in Moscow and in East Berlin (in Russian and in German), contain the most important writings and correspondence.

An attempt to bring out a complete critical edition called the *Marx-Engels Gesamtausgabe* – thus the second MEGA – was started by the same institutes in 1970, but interrupted by the breakdown of the German Democratic Republic and the Soviet Union. In 1990 the Internationale Marx Engels Stiftung (IMES) assumed the scientific responsibility for the continuation of the project. The editorial plans were revised and the originally envisaged 164 volumes were cut down to 114 volumes, of which 62 have been published by 2015. The manuscripts published in the (second) MEGA edition, in particular those relating to Marx's preliminary work on volumes II and III of *Capital*, necessitate revising the assessment of parts of Marx's work.

Baran, P.A. and P.M. Sweezy (1966), *Monopoly Capitalism*, New York and London: Monthly Review Press.
Berlin, I. (1939), *Karl Marx. His Life and Environment*, London: Thornton Butterworth.
Böhm-Bawerk, E. von (1884), *Kapital und Kapitalzins*, vol. I: *Geschichte und Kritik der Kapitalzinstheorien*, Innsbruck: Verlag der Wagner'schen Universitäts-Buchhandlung, English trans. 1890, *Capital and Interest. A Critical History of Economic Theory*, London: Macmillan.
Böhm-Bawerk, E. von (1896), 'Zum Abschluß des Marxschen Systems', in O. von Boenigk (ed.), *Staatswirtschaftliche Arbeiten. Festgaben für Karl Knies*, Berlin: Haering, English trans. 1949, 'Karl Marx

and the close of his system', in P.M. Sweezy (ed.), *Karl Marx and the Close of his System by Eugen von Böhm-Bawerk, and Böhm-Bawerk's Criticism of Marx by Rudolf Hilferding*, New York: A.M. Kelley, pp. 3–118.

Boldyrev, I. and M. Kragh (2015), 'Isaak Rubin: historian of economic thought during the Stalinization of social sciences in soviet Russia', *Journal of the History of Economic Thought*, **37** (3), 363–86.

Bortkiewicz, L. von (1906–07), 'Wertrechnung und Preisrechnung im Marxschen System', *Archiv für Sozialwissenschaft und Sozialpolitik*, in three instalments, **23**, 1–50, **25**, 10–51, 445–88, English trans. of Parts 2 and 3 in 1952, 'Value and price in the Marxian system', *International Economic Papers*, **2**, 5–60.

Bortkiewicz, L. von (1907), 'Zur Berichtigung der grundlegenden theoretischen Konstruktion von Marx im 3. Band des 'Kapital', *Jahrbücher für Nationalökonomie und Statistik*, **34**, 319–35.

Bukharin, N. (1927), *The Economic Theory of the Leisure Class*, New York: International Publishers.

Charasoff, G. von (1909), *Karl Marx über menschliche und kapitalistische Wirtschaft*, Berlin: Bondy.

Charasoff, G. von (1910), *Das System des Marxismus. Darstellung und Kritik*, Berlin: Bondy.

Colletti, L. (1969), *Il marxismo e Hegel*, Bari: Laterza, English trans. of Part II by L. Garner (1973), *Marxism and Hegel*, London: New Left Books.

Colletti, L. (1975), 'Introduction' to K. Marx, *Early Writings*, London: Penguin Books and New Left Review, pp. 7–56.

Dmitriev, V.K. (1898), 'David Ricardo's theory of value. An attempt at a rigorous analysis', in V.K. Dmitriev (1974), *Economic Essays on Value, Competition and Utility*, English trans. of a collection of Dmitriev's essays published in 1904 in Russian, ed. with an introduction by D.M. Nuti, Cambridge: Cambridge University Press.

Dostaler, G. (1978), *Valeur et prix: histoire d'un débat*, Grenoble: Presses Universitaires de Grenoble et François Maspéro.

Duménil, G. (1983), 'Beyond the transformation riddle: a labor theory of value', *Science and Society*, **47** (4), 427–50.

Engels, F. (1885), 'Preface', in K. Marx, *Das Kapital. Kritik der politischen Ökonomie. Zweiter Band. Der Zirkulationsprozess des Kapitals*, ed. by F. Engels, Hamburg, Meissner, as in MEW, vol. 24, Berlin: Dietz, 1963, English trans. 1978 by D. Fernbach, *Capital*, vol. II, London: Penguin Books and New Left Review pp. 83–102.

Faccarello, G. (1983a), *Travail, valeur et prix. Une critique de la théorie de la valeur*, Paris: Anthropos.

Faccarello, G. (1983b), 'La loi de la valeur et le problème de la coordination des activités économiques', *L'Homme et la Société*, **67–8**, 153–77.

Faccarello, G. (1997), 'Some reflections on Marx's theory of value', in R. Bellofiore (ed.), *Marxian Economics Revisited*, vol. 1, London: Macmillan, pp. 29–47.

Faccarello, G. (2000a), 'Karl Marx et la critique de l'économie politique: 'Le purgatoire du temps présent'', in A. Béraud and G. Faccarello (eds), *Nouvelle histoire de la pensée économique*, vol. 2: *Des premiers mouvements socialistes aux néoclassiques*, Paris: La Découverte, pp. 62–170.

Faccarello, G. (2000b), 'Les controverses autour du *Capital*: les débats autour de la loi de la valeur', in A. Béraud and G. Faccarello (eds), *Nouvelle histoire de la pensée économique*, vol. 2: *Des premiers mouvements socialistes aux néoclassiques*, Paris: La Découverte, pp. 171–201.

Feldman, G.A. (1928), 'On the theory of growth rates of national income', in N. Spulber (ed.) (1964), *Foundations of Soviet Strategy for Economic Growth*, Bloomington, IN: Indiana University Press.

Foley, D.K. (1982), 'The value of money, the value of labor power, and the Marxian transformation problem', *Review of Radical Political Economics*, **14** (2), 37–47.

Foley, D.K. (1986), *Understanding Capital. Marx's Economic Theory*, Cambridge, MA: Harvard University Press.

Gehrke, C. (2012), 'Marx's critique of Ricardo's theory of rent: a re-assessment', in C. Gehrke, N. Salvadori, I. Steedman and R. Sturn (eds), *Classical Political Economy and Modern Theory. Essays in Honour of Heinz D. Kurz*, London and New York: Routledge, pp. 51–84.

Gehrke, C. and H.D. Kurz (1995), 'Karl Marx on physiocracy', *European Journal of the History of Economic Thought*, **2** (1), 54–92.

Gehrke, C. and H.D. Kurz (2006), 'Sraffa on von Bortkiewicz: reconstructing the classical theory of value and distribution', *History of Political Economy*, **38** (1), 91–149.

Goodwin, R.M. (1967), 'A growth cycle', in C.H. Feinstein (ed.), *Socialism, Capitalism, and Economic Growth*, Cambridge: Cambridge University Press, pp. 54–8.

Grossmann, H. (1929), *Das Akkumulations- und Zusammenbruchsgesetz des kapitalistischen Systems (Zugleich eine Krisentheorie)*, Leipzig: Hirschfeld.

Hilferding, R. (1904), 'Böhm-Bawerks Marx-Kritik', *Marx-Studien*, vol. 1, Vienna, pp. 1–61, English trans., 'Böhm-Bawerk's criticism of Marx' in P.M. Sweezy (ed.) (1949), *Karl Marx and the Close of his System by Eugen von Böhm-Bawerk, and Böhm-Bawerk's Criticism of Marx by Rudolf Hilferding*, New York: A.M. Kelley, pp. 119–96.

Hilferding, R. (1910), *Das Finanzkapital*, Vienna: Wiener Volksbuchhandlung, English trans. 1981 by M. Watnick and S. Gordon, ed. T. Bottomore, *Finance Capital*, London: Routledge and Kegan Paul.

Howard, M.C. and J.E. King (1989), *A History of Marxian Economics. Vol. I: 1883–1929*, Princeton, NJ: Princeton University Press.

Howard, M.C. and J.E. King (1992), *A History of Marxian Economics. Vol. II: 1929–1990*, Princeton, NJ: Princeton University Press.

Kurz, H.D. (1995), 'Marginalism, classicism and socialism in the German-speaking countries, 1871–1932', in I. Steedman (ed.), *Socialism and Marginalism in Economics 1870–1930*, London and New York: Routledge, pp. 7–86.

Kurz, H.D. (2010), 'Technical change, capital accumulation and income distribution in classical economics: Adam Smith, David Ricardo and Karl Marx', *European Journal of the History of Economic Thought*, **11** (5), 1183–222.

Kurz, H.D. (2012–13), 'Das Problem der nichtintendierten Konsequenzen: Zur Politischen Ökonomie von Karl Marx', *Marx-Engels-Jahrbuch*, 75–112.

Kurz, H.D. and N. Salvadori (1995), *Theory of Production. A Long-Period Analysis*, Cambridge: Cambridge University Press.

Kurz, H.D. and N. Salvadori (2015), *Revisiting Classical Economics. Studies in Long-Period Analysis*, London: Routledge.

Ledbetter, J. (2007), *Dispatches for the New York Tribune: Selected Journalism of Karl Marx*, London and New York: Penguin Books.

Lowe, A. (1976), *The Path of Economic Growth*, Cambridge: Cambridge University Press.

Luxemburg, R. (1913), *Die Akkumulation des Kapitals*, Berlin: Buchhandlung Vorwärts Paul Singer, English trans., A. Schwarzschild (1951), *Accumulation of Capital*, London: Routledge and Kegan Paul.

Luxemburg, R. (1925), *Einführung in die Nationalökonomie*, Berlin: E. Laub'sche Verlagsbuchhandlung, English trans. 2014, *Introduction to Political Economy*, in *The Complete Works of Rosa Luxemburg*, vol. I, New York: Verso.

Mahalanobis, P. (1953), 'Some observations on the process of growth of national income', *Sankhya*, **12** (4), 307–12.

Marx, K. (1844), *Ökonomisch-philosophische Manuskripte von 1844*, MEW (1973), vol. 40, Berlin: Dietz.

Marx, K. (1847), *Misère de la Philosophie. Réponse à la philosophie de la misère de M. Proudhon*, Brussels: C.G. Vogler, Paris: A. Frank.

Marx, K. (1857–58), *Grundrisse der Kritik der Politischen Ökonomie (Rohentwurf)*, Berlin: Dietz, 1953, 1st edn Moscow, 1939–41, English trans. 1973 by M. Nicolaus, New York: Vintage Books.

Marx, K. (1858), 'Fragment des Urtextes von "Zur Kritik der politischen Ökonomie"', in K. Marx (1953), *Grundrisse der Kritik der Politischen Ökonomie (Rohentwurf)*, Berlin: Dietz, pp. 871–947, English trans. 1987 in *Karl Marx, Frederick Engels: Collected Works*, London: Lawrence & Wishart, vol. 29: *Economic Works 1857–61*, pp. 430–507.

Marx, K. (1859), *Zur Kritik der Politischen Ökonomie*, MEW, vol. 13, Berlin: Dietz. English trans. 1987, *A Contribution to the Critique of Political Economy*, in *Karl Marx, Frederick Engels: Collected Works*, London: Lawrence & Wishart, vol. 29: *Economic Works 1857–61*, pp. 257–417.

Marx, K. ([1861–63a] 1988), *Economic Works 1861–1863. Economic Manuscript of 1861–63. A Contribution to the Critique of Political Economy ['Theories of Surplus Value']*, in *Karl Marx, Frederick Engels: Collected Works*, vol. 30, London: Lawrence & Wishart.

Marx, K. ([1861–63b] 1989a), *Economic Manuscript of 1861–63. A Contribution to the Critique of Political Economy ['Theories of Surplus Value']*, in *Karl Marx, Frederick Engels: Collected Works*, vol. 31, London: Lawrence & Wishart.

Marx, K. ([1861–63c] 1989b), *Economic Manuscript of 1861–63. A Contribution to the Critique of Political Economy ['Theories of Surplus Value']*, in *Karl Marx, Frederick Engels: Collected Works*, vol. 32, London: Lawrence & Wishart.

Marx, K. ([1861–63d] 1991), *Economic Manuscript of 1861–63. A Contribution to the Critique of Political Economy ['Theories of Surplus Value']*, in *Karl Marx, Frederick Engels: Collected Works*, vol. 33, London: Lawrence & Wishart.

Marx, K. (1863–66), 'Das Kapital. Erstes Buch, Der Produktionsprozeß des Kapitals. Sechstes Kapitel. Resultate des unmittelbaren Produktionsprozesses', in *Arkhiv Marksa i Engelsa*, vol. II (VII) (Moscow, 1933), pp. 4–266, English trans. 1976 by B. Fowkes in *Capital*, vol. 1, London: Penguin Books and New Left Review, pp. 948–1084.

Marx, K. (1863–67), *Ökonomische Manuskripte 1863–1867. Teil 2. (Manuskript 1863/65 zum 3. Buch des Kapital)*, MEGA II 4/2, 2012, 2nd edn (1st edn 1993), Berlin: Akademie Verlag.

Marx, K. (1867), *Das Kapital. Kritik der politischen Ökonomie. Erster Band. Der Produktionsprozeß des Kapitals*, Hamburg: Meissner, 4th edn, 1890, in MEW, 1962, vol. 23, Berlin: Dietz, English trans. of the 4th edn 1976 by B. Fowkes, *Capital*, vol. 1, London: Penguin Books and New Left Review.

Marx, K. (1885), *Das Kapital. Kritik der politischen Ökonomie. Zweiter Band. Der Zirkulationsprozeß des Kapitals*, ed. by F. Engels, Hamburg: Meissner, as in MEW, 1963, vol. 24, Berlin: Dietz, English trans. 1978 by D. Fernbach, *Capital*, vol. II, London: Penguin Books and New Left Review.
Marx, K. (1894), *Das Kapital. Kritik der politischen Ökonomie. Dritter Band. Der Gesamtprozeß der kapitalistischen Produktion*, ed. F. Engels, Hamburg: Meissner, as in MEW, 1964, vol. 25, Berlin: Dietz, English trans. 1959 by D. Fernbach, *Capital*, vol. 3, London: Penguin Books and New Left Review.
Marx, K. (1905–10), *Theorien über den Mehrwert*, 3 vols, ed. K. Kautsky, MEW 1968, 26 (1–3), Berlin: Dietz.
Marx, K. (1975), *Early Writings*, trans R. Livingstone and G. Benton, London: Penguin Books and New Left Review.
Marx, K. and Engels, F. (1846), *Die deutsche Ideologie*, MEW 1969, vol. 3, Berlin: Dietz.
Marx, K. and Engels, F. (1848), *Manifest der Kommunistischen Partei*, MEW 1959, vol. 4, Berlin: Dietz.
McLellan, D. (1973), *Karl Marx. His Life and Thought*, London: Macmillan.
Mehring, F. (1918), *Karl Marx. Geschichte seines Lebens*, Berlin: Leipziger Buchdruckerei.
Mori, K. (2007), 'Eine dogmenhistorische Dualität in der Reproduktions- und Preistheorie: Georg von Charasoff und Kei Shibata', *Marx-Engels Jahrbuch 2006*, 118–41.
Morishima, M. (1973), *Marx's Economics. A Dual Theory of Value and Growth*, Cambridge: Cambridge University Press.
Nikolaevskij, B. and O. Mänchen-Helfen (1963), *Karl Marx. Eine Biographie*, Hanover: J.H.W. Dietz.
Oakley, A. (1983), *The Making of Marx's Critical Theory: A Bibliographical Analysis*, London: Routledge and Kegan Paul.
Okishio, N. (1961), 'Technical changes and the rate of profit', *Kobe University Economic Review*, 7 (1), 85–99.
Okishio, N. (1963), 'A mathematical note on Marxian theorems', *Weltwirtschaftliches Archiv*, 91 (2), 287–99.
Pareto, V. (1902), *Les systèmes socialistes*, Paris: V. Giard & R. Brière.
Petri, F. (1998), 'Labour theory of value', in H.D. Kurz and N. Salvadori (eds), *The Elgar Companion to Classical Economics*, vol. 2, Cheltenham, UK and Northampton, MA, USA: Edward Elgar, pp. 12–22.
Proudhon, P.-J. (1846), *Système des contradictions économiques ou Philosophie de la misère*, 2 vols, Paris: Guillaumin.
Quesnay, F. (1972), *Quesnay's Tableau Economique [1759]*, eds M. Kuczynski and R.L. Meek, London: Macmillan.
Reichelt, H. (1970), *Zur logischen Struktur des Kapitalsbegriffs bei Karl Marx*, Frankfurt am Main: Europäische Verlagsanstalt.
Ricardo, D. (1951), *On the Principles of Political Economy and Taxation*, vol. 1 of *The Works and Correspondence of David Ricardo*, ed. P. Sraffa with the collaboration of M.H. Dobb, Cambridge: Cambridge University Press.
Rosdolsky, R. (1968), *Zur Entstehungsgeschichte des Marxschen 'Kapital'*, Frankfurt: Europäische Verlagsanstalt, English trans. 1977, *The Making of Marx's 'Capital'*, 2 vols, London: Pluto Press.
Rubin, I.I. (1927), 'Abstrakte Arbeit und Wert im Marxschen System', German trans. in I.I. Rubin, S.A. Bessonov et al., *Dialektik der Kategorien*, Berlin: Verlag für das Studium der Arbeiterbewegung, 1975, pp. 7–53, English trans. from German 1978, 'Abstract labour and value in Marx's system', *Capital and Class*, 2 (2), 109–39.
Rubin, I.I. (1928), *Essays on Marx's Theory of Value*, 3rd edn, Moscow: Gosudasrstvennoe Izdatel'stvo, English trans. 1972, by M. Samardžija and F. Perlman, Detroit, MI: Black and Red.
Samuelson, P.A. (1957), 'Wages and interest: a modern dissection of Marxist economic models', *American Economic Review*, 47 (6), 884–912.
Samuelson, P.A. (1959), 'A modern treatment of the Ricardian economy: I. The pricing of goods and of labor and land services; II. Capital and interest aspects of the pricing process', *Quarterly Journal of Economics*, 73 (1), 1–35, 217–31.
Schumpeter, J.A. (1912), *Theorie der wirtschaftlichen Entwicklung*, Leipzig: Duncker & Humblot.
Seton, F. (1957), 'The transformation problem', *Review of Economic Studies*, 24 (3), 149–60.
Sraffa, P. (1960), *Production of Commodities by Means of Commodities*, Cambridge: Cambridge University Press.
Steedman, I. (1977), *Marx after Sraffa*, London: Verso.
Steedman, I., P. Sweezy, E.O. Wright, G. Hodgson, P. Bandyopadhyay, M. Itoh et al. (1981), *The Value Controversy*, London: Verso.
Steedman, I. (ed.) (1995), *Socialism and Marginalism in Economics 1870–1930*, London and New York: Routledge.
Steindl, J. (1952), *Maturity and Stagnation in American Capitalism*, Oxford: Blackwell.
Sweezy, P.M. (1942), *The Theory of Capitalist Development*, New York: Oxford University Press.
Tugan-Baranowsky, M. (1905), *Theoretische Grundlagen des Marxismus*, Leipzig: Duncker & Humblot.

Turban, M. (1980), *Marxsche Reproduktionsschemata und Wirtschaftstheorie*, Berlin: Duncker & Humblot.
Wheen, F. (1999), *Karl Marx. A Life*, London: Fourth Estate.
Wicksteed, P.H. (1884), 'Das Kapital. A criticism', *Today*, **2** (October), 388–409.
Wicksteed, P.H. (1885), 'The Jevonian criticism of Marx: a rejoinder', *Today*, **3** (April), 177–9.
Winternitz, J. (1948), 'Values and prices: a solution of the so-called transformation problem', *Economic Journal*, **58** (June), 276–80.

Clément Juglar (1819–1905)

Joseph Schumpeter (1954: 1123) described Clément Juglar as being "among the greatest economists of all times" and proposed the so-called Juglar-cycle, which lasts between eight and ten years. However, Juglar's contribution was not confined to the analysis of business cycles: he wrote papers on demography and on monetary and credit theories (see Allisson et al. 2009). These works are of interest not only because they are original and reflect the debates of the nineteenth century, but also because they provide a more comprehensive view of Juglar's vision.

Juglar was born in Paris in 1819 and initially trained as a physician (see Frobert and Hamouda 2008). He defended his thesis in medicine, 'De l'influence des maladies du coeur sur les poumons', in 1846, but in 1848, shocked by the revolution, and the three years of the Republican regime and the 1847 recession, he decided to become an economist. There was a transition period (1851–52) when, after travelling to Algeria, Juglar published several papers on the French colonies (Frobert 2009) before turning his attention to the French population movements. His statistical investigations led him to identify a regular cycle of weddings, births, and so on, a *retour périodique*, which he progressively linked to the economic context. Then began his focus on economics: in 1856 he was introduced to the Société d'économie politique by Louis Wolowski, and in 1860 he became one of the founding members of the Société de statistique de Paris.

His first paper on the commercial crises was published in 1856 in the *Annuaire de l'économie politique et de la statistique*. However, his most famous piece was published in 1863 and was a reduced version of the 1862 essay for which he was awarded the prize of the Académie des Sciences Morales et Politiques. At that time, Juglar was not yet a member of this Académie: after several attempts to become a member, in 1892 he was successfully nominated to Jean-Gustave Courcelle-Seneuil's seat (Longchamp 2009).

Juglar's business cycle approach was explicit: there are external causes that can be considered impulses for cycles, but economists need to propose a general theory that explains the recurrence (with a periodicity of seven to ten years) of this phenomenon and also its international synchronization. What Juglar proposes in the main is a business cycle analysis which considers cycles as natural and unavoidable movements, due essentially to the predispositions of modern economies, that is, the development of credit. In considering such crises as general and partly endogenous, he contradicts a strict interpretation of Say's law, an element which contributed to his isolation among contemporary French liberal economists (see Courcelle-Seneuil 1889 for an example of a 'sceptical' reception of Juglar's business cycle theory).

Although Juglar is unequivocal that in the absence of credit there will only be monetary crises, provoked by decreasing metal reserves, he nevertheless considers the development of credit as a necessary element for industry's activities. Commercial crises, defined as brutal disturbances of commercial activities characterized by bankruptcies, are the most fundamental types. But Juglar never directly blames the banks (although he sometimes regrets their lack of prudence); he considers their data – especially evolution of the discount rate – as adequate barometers of the cycle. Juglar blames speculative behaviour and all kinds of excesses generated during periods of prosperity. The crises, and more specifically the liquidation phases, are seen as corrections of those excesses.

A second edition of his 1862 book was published in 1889, augmented by new data but also revealing a (slight) theoretical evolution. Juglar strengthens his explanation of the three business cycle phases, namely, prosperity, crisis, and liquidation, and better explains why they are so strongly intertwined. In the interval between the two editions, Juglar had concentrated much of his attention on monetary economics: in 1865, he edited eight volumes analysing the English banking system, and monetary and credit circulation, and in 1868 he published a collection of his articles on these topics. These investigations of monetary economics contributed to clarifying price dynamics (which initially relied mainly on speculative behaviour) as well as the role of credit in his business cycle theory.

Juglar published many papers that provide accurate and detailed historical data, and interpretations of various crises, and identify ten or so that occurred in France between 1802 and 1882. The (unavoidably) repetitive character of his work, as well as his strong desire to forecast the course of a cycle, and perhaps also his deep religious commitment – his contribution was heavily influenced by his Jansenist beliefs (Dal Pont Legrand and Frobert 2010) – led some French economists to describe him, not without some degree of irony, as 'le prophète des crises' (see, for example, Beauregard 1908). It should be noted also that the unexpectedly long stagnation (1873–97) did not provide a favourable context for Juglar's predictions.

It is true that Schumpeter (1954) admired Juglar's approach to political economy which was characterized by a systematic use of theory, history, and statistics. Schumpeter identified two fundamental points of business cycle analysis specifically highlighted by Juglar. First, a crisis is not a purely monetary phenomenon although monetary data are excellent barometers of the course of a cycle; second, the only cause of recession is prosperity, so crises are interpreted as the turning point between phases of prosperity and liquidation. Schumpeter also identified theoretical limits of Juglar's business cycle theory, such as the absence of an analysis of prosperity factors, an element which according to Schumpeter prevented Juglar from proposing a complete business cycle theory (Dal Pont Legrand and Hagemann 2007).

It was not only Schumpeter who referred to Juglar as a pioneer of modern business cycle theory; economists such as Wesley Clair Mitchell and Alvin Hansen also considered his work to be ground-breaking. However, it is less obvious that these latter had read Juglar carefully, and the translation of the second edition of his book into English in 1893 may have been the main source of his fame and reputation at the international level (Besomi 2011). Schumpeter (1954: 1124) concludes his assessment of Juglar's contribution as follows:

> [T]oday Juglar's work reads like an old story very primitively told. And at the end of the period stands a work that, on the one hand, was entirely conceived in his spirit, and on the other hand, ushered in a most important part of the cycle analysis of our own time: Wesley C. Mitchell's *Business Cycles*.

MURIEL DAL PONT LEGRAND

See also:
Banking and currency schools (II); Wesley Clair Mitchell (I); Money and banking (III); Jean-Baptiste Say (I); Joseph Alois Schumpeter (I); Arthur Spiethoff (I).

References and further reading

Allisson, F., L. Bréban and P. Bridel (2009), 'Bibliographie des écrits de Clément Juglar (1846–1904)', in P. Bridel and M. Dal Pont Legrand, *Clément Juglar (1819–1905). Les origines de la théorie des cycles, Revue Européenne des Sciences Sociales*, **47** (143), 107–24.

Beauregard, P. (1908), 'Notice sur la vie et les travaux de Clément Juglar', *Académie des Sciences Morales et Politiques*, Comptes Rendus 71, 153–79.

Besomi, D. (2011), 'The fabrication of a myth: Clément Juglar's commercial crises in the secondary literature', *History of Economic Ideas*, **19** (3), 69–111.

Courcelle-Seneuil, J.C. (1889), 'Compte rendu de Cl. Juglar, Des crises commerciales et de leur retour en France, en Angleterre et aux Etats-Unis', *Journal des économistes*, October–December, 446451.

Dal Pont Legrand, M. and H. Hagemann (2007), 'Business cycles in Juglar and Schumpeter', *The History of Economic Thought*, **49** (1), 1–18.

Dal Pont Legrand, M. and L. Frobert (2010), 'Le "prophète des crises". Economie politique et religion chez Clément Juglar', *Astérion* (7), accessed 17 December 2015 at http://asterion.revues.org/document1642.html.

Frobert, L. (2009), 'Clément Juglar, l'Algérie et les Colonnies', in P. Bridel and M. Dal Pont Legrand, *Clément Juglar (1819–1905). Les origines de la théorie des cycles, Revue Européenne des Sciences Sociales*, **47** (143), 95–105.

Frobert, L. and O. Hamouda (2008), 'The influence of the study of Medecine on Clément Juglar's first take on the economic cycle, 1846–1862', *Journal of the History of Economic Thought*, **30** (2), 173–98.

Juglar, C. (1856), 'Des crises commerciales en France de l'an VIII à 1855', *Annuaire de l'économie politique et de la statistique*, **13**, 555–81.

Juglar, C. (1862), *Des Crises Commerciales et de leur retour périodique en France, en Angleterre et aux Etats-Unis*, Paris: Guillaumin.

Juglar, C. (1863), 'Crises commerciales', in M. Block, *Dictionnaire général de la politique* Paris: O. Lorentz, vol. 1, pp.615–27 (offprint: 13p. Strasbourg, Berger – Levrault).

Juglar, C. (1865), *Extraits des enquêtes parlementaires anglaises sur les questions de banque, de circulation monétaire et de crédit, traduits et publiés par la Banque de France sous la direction de Coullet et Juglar*, 8 vols, Paris: Furne: 1. *Enquête de 1810, 1818, 1819, 1841. Bullion Report. – Intérêt de l'argent. – Paiements en espèces*; 2. *Enquête de 1832 sur le renouvellement de la charte de la Banque d'Angleterre*; 3. *Enquête de 1840 sur les banques d'émission*; 4. *Enquête de 1848 sur la crise commerciale de 1847 (Chambre des Communes*; 5. *Enquête de 1848 de 1848 sur la crise commerciale de 1847 (Chambre des Lords)*; 6 and 7. *Enquête de 1857 sur la législation des banques*; 8. *Enquête de 1858 sur la législation des banques*.

Juglar, C. (1868), *Du change et de la liberté d'émission*, Paris: Guillaumin.

Juglar, C. (1889), *Des Crises Commerciales et de leur retour périodique en France, en Angleterre et aux Etats-Unis*, 2nd edn, Paris: Alcan.

Juglar, C. (1893), *A Brief History of Panics and their Periodical Occurrence in the United States*, English trans. and ed. with an introductory essay setting out the indications of approaching panic by D.W. Thom, New York: G.P. Putnam's Sons.

Longchamp, O. (2009), 'Clément Juglar et l'Académie des Sciences Morales et Politiques', in P. Bridel and M. Dal Pont Legrand, *Clément Juglar (1819 – 1905). Les origines de la théorie des cycles, Revue Européenne des Sciences Sociales*, **47** (143), 13–15.

Schumpeter, J.A. (1954), *History of Economic Analysis*, London: Allen & Unwin.

Gustave de Molinari (1819–1912)

Gustave de Molinari was born in Liège, at that time a part of the Low Countries, on 3 March 1819. He went to Paris at the beginning of the 1840s where he became a journalist specializing in economic matters. He wrote especially in *La Nation*, *Le Courrier français* and *La Réforme*. In 1846 he was the co-founder of the Association pour la liberté des échanges, of which Frédéric Bastiat was the general secretary. During the 1848 Revolution he was a republican and opposed both monarchists and socialists. His first book, *Les soirées de la rue Saint-Lazare* was published in 1849. An opponent to Louis-Napoléon Bonaparte, he returned to Belgium after the 2 December 1851 *coup d'état*. He acted as a professor of political economy at the Musée royal de l'industrie belge and at the Institut de commerce in Antwerp. He came back to France in 1867 and in 1871 became the chief editor of the *Journal des débats*. He remained in Paris during the siege of Paris and the Paris Commune, analysing the question of subsistence and the relevance of the rationing measures. From 1881, after the death of Joseph Garnier, until 1909 he served as the chief editor of the *Journal des économistes*. He died in Adinkerque, in Belgium, on 28 January 1912.

Molinari thought that "human societies organize themselves, develop and progress by themselves, in accordance with laws inherent in their nature" (1861, I: v) and that "it is sufficient . . . to ensure each member of the society the free usage of his activity and the ownership of the fruits of this free activity, to reach the *maximum* possible wealth and justice" (ibid.: xxx, original emphasis). He does not limit himself to stating that competition is efficient in economic matters, but he maintains that this is also true in politics and that "no government should have the right to prevent another government to establish itself and compete with it" (1849b: 279). He thus appears as the founder of a liberal and anti-statist tradition (Hart 1979, 1981–82).

Competition and Just Price

Molinari (1851: 127) maintains that competitive market prices are just: they remunerate everybody in proportion to his or her effort. However, labour markets are local markets in which employers can exploit the workers. The spontaneous evolution of these markets will change their functioning and allow the workers to sell their services at their just prices when the market becomes general.

Natural and market price

Molinari accepts Smith's distinction between the natural and market price for the products as well as for the productive services. The market price is determined by supply and demand. While the quantity supplied is a datum inherited from the past, demand is a decreasing function of the price: (1) fewer agents demand a good when its price rises and (2) the utility of a good and the price an individual is prepared to pay for it diminish as the consumed quantity rises (Molinari 1855a, I: 103). Molinari insists that a change in the supply entails a proportionally greater change in price: if supply rises, proceeds diminish. He justifies his view with empirical and theoretical arguments. When the quantity of a thing increases, it becomes both less rare and less useful.

The natural price of a good is equal to the cost of production – the remuneration of capital and labour directly or indirectly necessary to production, rent being excluded from costs – plus a proportional part of the net product. The same applies for the productive services. "Workers must be seen as machines . . . which require . . . expenses for their maintenance and renewal, in order to work in a regular and continuous way. These expenses . . . form the *minimum of subsistence* of the worker" (Molinari 1855a, I: 194, original emphasis). The minimum price of the productive service of capital entails three elements: its depreciation, a risk premium and a remuneration for the immobilization of capital, that is, the interest on the invested capital. Changes in the quantity of the factors of production depend on their remunerations. In equilibrium each of them must receive a proportional fraction of the net product. Adding it to the cost of production gives their natural price.

Gravitation always brings back the market price to the level of the natural price (Molinari 1851: 117, 1891: 313–15), with a general and permanent tendency towards an equilibrium between production and demand at the necessary price, that is, the price which allows the producer to continuously supply the market.

Market imperfections
The above-described mechanism only works if the produced commodities and services are available at the time and place, where they generate the greatest profit. Over long periods of time, this condition was not fulfilled because markets were small and insulated. This condition is, however, fulfilled now for the commodity markets and the services of capital. Labour markets are still local. Workers, obliged to sell their labour, face few or even only a single employer and do not have the possibility of selling their services elsewhere. They do not take into account whether, far away from their home, they could find a job and what wages they could obtain. In Belgium, for example (Molinari 1855b: 1), the development of wealth only benefited the upper classes, and real wage decreased. The solution lies, Molinari states (1891: 338), in the transformation of the labour market in line with what happened to the products and capital markets:

> In the present state of things the free worker is still generally obliged to act both . . . as a producer and a merchant of labour. While he has the full capacity to be a producer, he has neither time, nor resources, nor the necessary information to be a successful merchant. Like all the producers . . . he needs some intermediary to sell his commodity.

Some entrepreneurs, in order to reduce the costs of hiring and managing their personnel, use the services of "marchandeurs" who recruit workers and re-sell their labour. The intervention of such intermediaries was seen to involve the exploitation of workers, and was forbidden by law on 2 March 1848. However, if these intermediaries did not fulfil their task well, it is because they acted on too small a scale. Molinari proposes the formation of powerful societies of bargaining, which would buy and pay for the services of the workers and supervise their labour. He maintained that they could reduce costs because, having to recruit and supervise workers for specific functions, they would be more competent in choosing personnel and would recruit them from the best and cheapest places.

The extension of the markets for products and capital generated the creation of commodity and stock exchanges, which circulated the information needed by merchants and bankers. The extension of the labour market would have had the same effect. The intermediaries – the job placement offices and the emigration corporations – would wish to know on a daily basis the situation prevailing on local markets. Labour exchanges would provide this information. Molinari (1893: 162) stresses that this kind of institution aimed at mobilizing labour "would be spontaneously created and would develop by itself as soon as the spirit of enterprise and capitals would find an interest in its creation, that is, as soon as it will bring them a profit. It would be enough to *laissez-faire*". As Benkemoune (2008: 258) stresses, Molinari's aim is to show that civil society, left to its own devices, can solve the problem of the deficiency of information and that the extended market would appear spontaneously without any necessity of a state intervention.

The Social Organization of Competition

Government, Dunoyer (1825: 323–4) wrote, "has the character of an industrial undertaking with the sole difference that, instead of performing for particular persons or associations only, . . . it acts on behalf of the society at large, which entrusts it to people of its choice, at a price and conditions it judges the most advantageous", but its functions, Dunoyer specified, are so specific that "they cannot be assumed by private activity" (1845, III: 353). This thesis Molinari rejected in 1849: he defended the idea that it is in the interest of the consumers that the production of security be supplied in competitive conditions. Later, he abandoned this position and adopted the right to secession.

The production of security must be submitted to competition
In 1849, when Molinari published *Les soirées de la rue Saint-Lazare*, the sovereignty of the people was constantly invoked – in particular, the new Constitution, adopted on 4 November 1848, stated that "sovereignty lies in the universality of the French citizens". Governments based on such a principle, he thought, were to be preferred to monarchies of divine right, but the alleged democratic republics are not the expression of the sovereignty of the people. In a representative democracy, the right of the minority can be neglected.

> There is no durable security in this system . . . because the persons and the properties of all are at the mercy of a majority, be it blind or enlightened, moral or immoral. The right of the greatest number to tyrannize the will of the fewer could also . . . generate a civil war. (Molinari 1849a: 326–7)

This is the reason why the idea that competition satisfies the needs of the consumer at the lowest cost should be applied to the production of security.

Molinari's position perplexed his friends (Coqulin 1849; Société d'économie politique (SEP) 1849 [1889]). In order for the exchanges in markets to be fair, fraud and violence should be excluded. A superior authority should regulate markets and, if necessary, intervene in conflicts between participants and condemn them. Competitive conditions cannot exist without a state that has the monopoly on legitimate use of force – a natural, unavoidable monopoly. What puts a limit on the power of the government are the constitutional guarantees and the regular intervention of the citizens in public affairs. Competition is within the representative institutions of the state: political parties compete with each other and offer their services to the public, which chooses the one it prefers any time it votes (Dunoyer, in SEP 1849 [1889]: 83). While Molinari did not trust representative democracy, most of the French liberals saw it as the only principle allowing the citizens to control those who govern.

The right to secession

Molinari was probably shaken by these critiques and implicitly gave up the idea of competitive firms supplying services of security. He admitted the specificity of public services: "they benefit, by nature, the totality of inhabitants . . . [H]ence the obligation, for the individual, either to leave the territory or to contribute proportionally to the costs of these services. It is a natural servitude" (1887: 262). However, in the present system an individual is obliged to pay for all the services supplied by the public authority. It is an abuse because this individual, while not being able to refuse collective services – security, public lighting, sewage system – is susceptible not to want to use individual services – schools, churches, theatres – financed by the authority. Those who do not use them do not have to pay for them. How to put an end to this "political servitude"? By means of the right to secession, Molinari maintains.

In between the consumer and the government, there are at least two intermediaries: the province and the municipality. If citizens in a municipality find that they are obliged to pay for services they do not want, they should be allowed to use their right to secession in two ways. If the municipality is extended, those who live in a rich area could secede and form a new municipality or merge with another one. If it is small, the only possibility for them is to leave for another place. The municipality itself receives form the province, and the province from the state, services of domestic or external security, and of means of communication. In the present organization, municipalities are helpless in case the province asks a high price for its services or if these services are of poor quality. In Molinari's scheme, it will be possible for it to secede and ask its inclusion in another province. In the same way, a province could leave a state to become independent or join another state. Molinari maintains that the right to secession creates competition between provinces and states and an incentive to provide better services at a lower price. Individual services and taxes would disappear. Collective services themselves would not be produced by local authorities: it would be less expensive to buy them from private competitive firms. Finally, because any province could secede, the wars of conquest would be purposeless and would disappear

For Molinari, it is possible to go further. Citizens accept the financing of military expenses to protect themselves from the risk of foreign aggression.

> Suppose that, for nations, a collective assurance replaces an isolated assurance, as it happened for individuals. The situation immediately changes and the unlimited risk of wars disappears. With it also disappears the necessity to give the government in charge of the security of the nation the unlimited right to requisition the life, the property and the liberty of individuals. (Molinari 1899: 70–71)

It would then be enough to maintain a military force sufficient to enforce the decisions of the international justice. Molinari opined optimistically that the use of force could soon stop being applied.

As Hart states (Hart 1981, II: 426) the origin of the evolution of Molinari's thought is the distinction he makes between individual and collective services. It is true that, in

1849, he admitted the existence of collective services but he maintained that they should be submitted to the law of competition – a point of view that he abandoned subsequently, accepting Charles Coquelin's objection that these services are natural monopolies. Some industries are not open to competition and, consequently, must be managed by the state or some territorial authority.

ALAIN BÉRAUD

See also:

Frédéric Bastiat (I); Barthélemy-Charles Dunoyer de Segonzac (I); French classical political economy (II); Jean-Baptiste Say (I).

References and further reading

Benkemoune, R. (2008), 'Gustave de Molinari's bourse network theory: a liberal response to Sismondi's informational problem', *History of Political Economy*, **40** (2), 243–63.

Coquelin, C. (1849), 'Compte-rendu des Soirées de la rue Saint-Lazare', *Journal des économistes*, **24** (104), 364–72.

Dunoyer, B.-C. (1825), *L'industrie et la morale considérées dans leur rapport avec la liberté*, Paris: Sautelet.

Dunoyer, B.-C. (1845), *De la liberté du travail*, Paris: Guillaumin.

Faccarello, G. (2010), 'Bold ideas. French liberal economists and the state: Say to Leroy-Beaulieu', *European Journal of the History of Political Economy*, **17**(4), 719–58.

Hart, D.M. (1979), 'Gustave de Molinari and the anti-statist liberal tradition', thesis, Macquarie University, Sydney.

Hart, D.M. (1981–82), 'Gustave de Molinari and the anti-state liberal tradition', *Journal of Libertarian Studies*, **5** (3), 263–90, **5** (4), 399–434, **6** (1), 83–104.

Minard, G. (1912), *Gustave de Molinari, pour un gouvernement bon marché dans un milieu libre*, Paris: Institut Charles Coquelin.

Molinari, G. de (1849a), *Les soirées de la rue Saint-Lazare*, Paris: Guillaumin.

Molinari, G. de (1849b), 'De la production de sécurité', *Journal des économistes*, **22** (95), 277–90.

Molinari, G. de (1851), 'Observations sur la formation des prix', *Journal des économistes*, **29** (122), 111–28.

Molinari, G. de (1855a), *Cours d'économie politique professé au musée royal de l'industrie belge*, Brussels: Librairie Polytechnique d'A. Decq.

Molinari, G. de (1855b), 'Un moyen d'améliorer le sort des classes ouvrières', *L'économiste belge*, **1** (18), 1–3.

Molinari, G. de (1861), *Questions d'économie politique et de droit public*, Paris: Guillaumin.

Molinari, G. de (1863), *Cours d'économie politique*, 2nd edn, Brussels and Leipzig: Lacroix & Verboeckhoven, Paris: Guillaumin.

Molinari, G. de (1887), *Les lois naturelles de l'économie politique*, Paris: Guillaumin.

Molinari, G. de (1891), *Notions fondamentales d'économie politique et programme économique*, Paris: Guillaumin.

Molinari, G. de (1893), *Les bourses du travail*, Paris: Guillaumin.

Molinari, G. de (1899), *Esquisse de l'organisation politique et économique de la société future*, Paris: Guillaumin.

Société d'économie politique (SEP) (1849), 'Séance du 10 octobre 1849', in A. Courtois (ed.) (1889), *Annales de la Société d'économie politique*, Paris: Guillaumin, pp. 81–6.

Walter Bagehot (1826–1877)

Walter Bagehot (1826–1877) was an English banker, journalist and essayist. He was 18 years old when Parliament passed the 1844 Bank Charter Act. He studied mathematics in London, obtained a master's degree in 1848 and joined his father's bank in 1852. In 1857 he published his first article in the influential newspaper, *The Economist*, which was founded by James Wilson, his father-in-law and a supporter of the Banking School. In 1861, Bagehot became editor of *The Economist*. Bagehot is famous for his book on law and politics, *The English Constitution*, published in 1867. The second and revised edition (1872) became a classic. In 1873 he published a second book that would also become a classic, but in the field of economics: *Lombard Street: A Description of the Money Market*. In 1876–77, Bagehot proposed the creation of the "Treasury Bill": a new kind of public debt that would be more liquid and consequently less expensive. Bagehot died in March 1877. He was in the process of writing a book on British political economy. The unfinished manuscript was published in 1880 as *Economic Studies*.

As an economist, Bagehot's formative years were characterised by the controversy between the Banking and the Currency Schools. When he was 22 years old, in 1848, he published two articles in the *Prospective Review*. One concerned the rules governing the issue of banknotes enacted by the 1844 banking reform; Bagehot argued in favour of the currency principle, but approved the 1847 suspension of the rules. The second paper was a laudatory review of John Stuart Mill's *Principles of Political Economy*. From 1857, he published articles on several contemporary economic topics: international bimetallism, finance in France, India and the United States, and the British banking crises of 1857 and 1866. *Lombard Street* was published seven years after the 1866 crisis. This book was inspired by the financial consequences of the Franco-Prussian War (1870–71), which, according to Bagehot, could have undermined the functioning of the British banking system. The book contains recommendations for strengthening the Bank of England. Fourteen editions of *Lombard Street* were published between 1873 and 1915. Along with Hume's price-specie flow mechanism, Bagehot's banking and monetary thought constitutes one of the two pillars of the British monetary orthodoxy that prevailed from the 1870s through to Word War I.

Bagehot provided Ricardian monetary doctrine with a theory of the lender of last resort. The challenge was a difficult one. Ricardo's "Plan for a National Bank" and the currency principle introduced a separation between credit and currency, between the granting of credit and the issue of banknotes. This led to the division of the Bank of England into two departments in 1844: the Banking Department that granted credit but could not issue banknotes, and the Issue Department that could not grant credit but did issue banknotes. Banknotes could be issued or withdrawn only in exchange for gold; and the gold reserve of the Issue Department was not available to the Banking Department for lending. This had been established in accordance with Hume's price-specie flow mechanism, whereby every inflow of gold into the country indicates that additional currency is needed, and symmetrically, that every outflow of gold indicates that there is an excess of currency. Bagehot agreed with this.

However, for Bagehot, while the banking reform made sense with respect to the rules governing the issue of banknotes by the Issue Department, it misinterpreted the activity of the Banking Department. Contrary to the understanding of the governors of the Bank of England, the Banking Department was not a bank like any other. Historically, the Banking Department had acquired the function of sustaining the British credit system. British banks were accustomed to working with low levels of shareholder funds and a low cash reserve, and having access to loans from the Bank of England in the event of a credit crisis on the money market. As a constitutional theorist, it was Bagehot's opinion that a republican system would be preferable, but he believed that history had confirmed the monarchy in England and that his questioning would have a destabilizing effect. Similarly, influenced by the Free Banking School, he thought that a competitive system comprising several large banks would be preferable, but that calling the dominant position of the Bank of England into question had become impossible. In exchange, the Banking Department had to recognize and assume its responsibility to the general interest, and not aim for the payment of a maximum dividend per share.

For Bagehot, a credit crisis was a situation where traders and banks are reluctant to lend because they fear that they will not be able to borrow. If the Banking Department was to act like an ordinary bank and refuse to increase its loans when this occurs, it would feed the credit crisis. According to him, the Banking Department has to act as the lender of last resort, following three rules: first, to lend freely in order to re-establish confidence in the availability of loans on the money market; second, to lend only against bona fide collateral, to ensure that it only lent to solvent banks; and third, to lend at a high rate to deter banks from unnecessary borrowing. However, in order to achieve these goals, Bagehot did not suggest that the Banking Department should issue banknotes or borrow banknotes from the Issuing Department, or that the Issuing Department should grant credit on the money market. These are Banking School ideas. Bagehot's proposal was that the Banking Department should increase its shareholders' funds, in order to increase the reserve of legal tender that it could loan to the banks.

Bagehot's main contribution was not stating the three rules for acting as a lender of last resort: lending freely, to solvent banks, at a high rate. The first rule was already present in Henry Thornton (1802) and Thomas Tooke (1844, 1848); the second in Thornton, Tooke and the 1873 Coe Report of the New York Clearing House (in Sprague 1910: 91–103); and the third in Tooke (1844, 1848), but with a balance of payments argument. Bagehot's main contribution was that he made the lender of last resort theory compatible with Ricardian monetary theory. He did so by developing an original approach to lender-of-last-resort theory. Contrary to Thornton's approach, the lender of last resort does not respond to a demand for money, but to a demand for credit. The money that is loaned is not going to be held, but used as a means of payment. Therefore, there is not one classical theory of the lender of last resort, but two.

It is worth noting that Bagehot did not use the phrase "lender of last resort". Nor did Thornton. Francis Baring (1797 [1968]) qualified the Bank of England on two occasions as the "*dernier ressort*" (last resort). The expression is absent from Ricardo's writings and from those of the Banking School. However, the expression "the bank of last resort in panic" can be found in a Parliamentary report of 1858. The first explicit and significant use of the phrase "lender of last resort" appeared in Hawtrey's book, *The Art of Central Banking*, in 1932.

JÉRÔME DE BOYER DES ROCHES

See also:

Balance of payments and exchange rates (III); Banking and currency schools (II); Bullionist and anti-bullionist schools (II); Ralph George Hawtrey (I); Money and banking (III); Henry Thornton (I); Thomas Tooke (I).

References and further reading

Bagehot, W. (1867), *The English Constitution*, reprinted from the *Fortnightly Review*, London: Chapman and Hall.

Bagehot, W. (1873), *Lombard Street: A Description of the Money Market*, London: Kegan Paul & Co.

Bagehot, W. (1880), *Economic Studies*, ed. R.H. Hutton, London: Longmans, Green, & Co.

Bagehot, W. (1986), *The Collected Works of Walter Bagehot: Volumes 1–15*, ed. N.S. John-Stevas, New York: Oxford University Press.

Baring, Sir F. (1797), 'Observations on the establishment of the Bank of England and on the paper circulation of the country', reprinted in Bank of England (1968), *Selected Tracts 1694–1804*, London: Gregg International.

Coe Report (1873), Report of the Committee appointed by the New York Clearing-House Association, 11 November, reprinted in O.M.W. Sprague (1910), *History of Crises under the National Banking System*, National Monetary Commission, Washington, DC: Government Printing Office, pp. 91–103.

de Boyer des Roches, J. (2003), *La pensée monétaire, histoire et analyse*, Paris: Les Solos.

de Boyer des Roches, J. (2013), 'Bank liquidity risk: from John Law (1705) to Walter Bagehot (1873)', *European Journal of the History of Economic Thought*, **20** (4), 547–71.

de Boyer des Roches, J. and S.R. Ricardo (2003), 'Les approches classiques du prêteur en dernier ressort: de Baring à Hawtrey', *Cahiers d'Économie Politique*, **2003/2** (45), 79–100.

Fetter, F.W. (1965), *The Development of British Monetary Orthodoxy, 1797–1875*, Cambridge, MA: Harvard University Press.

Forrest, H.C., H. Forest and G. Wood (2006), *The Lender of Last Resort*, London: Routledge.

Hawtrey, R.G. (1932), *The Art of Central Banking*, London: Longmans, Green, & Co.

Humphrey, T.M. (1992), 'Lender of last resort', in P. Newman, M. Milgate and J. Eatwell (eds), *The New Palgrave Dictionary of Money and Finance*, vol. 2, London: Macmillan; pp. 571–3.

Laidler, D. (2003), 'Two views of the lender of last resort, Thornton and Bagehot', *Cahiers d'Économie Politique*, **2003/2** (45), 61–78.

Sprague, O.M.W. (1910), *History of Crises under the National Banking System*, National Monetary Commission, Washington, DC: Government Printing Office.

Thornton, H. (1802), *An Enquiry into the Nature and Effects of the Paper Credit of Great Britain (1802): together with his evidence given before the Committees of Secretary of the two Houses of Parliament in the Bank of England, March and April, 1797, some manuscript notes, and his speeches on the bullion report, May 1811*; reprinted 1939, ed. and introduction by F.A. von Hayek, London: Allen & Unwin.

Tooke, T. (1838–56), *A History of Prices and of the State of the Circulation from 1792 to 1856*, 5 vols, London: Longman, Brown, Green, and Longmans, reprinted 1972, New York: Johnson.

Tooke, T. (1844), *An Inquiry into the Currency Principle, the Connection of Currency with Prices and the Expediency of a Separation of Issue from Banking*, 2nd edn, London: Longman, Brown, Green, and Longmans, reprinted 1996, London: Routledge/Thoemmes Press.

Tooke, T. (1848), A History of Prices and of the State of the *Circulation from 1839 to 1847* Inclusive, London: Longman, Brown, Green, and Longmans.

Marie-Esprit-Léon Walras (1834–1910)

The presentation of Walras's work is problematic because it is both central to economic theory and highly controversial. The general economic equilibrium theory occupies a privileged place in post-war theoretical developments; a boldly stripped-down version of the general economic equilibrium model forms the basis even of macroeconomic approaches such as the real business cycles and dynamic stochastic general equilibrium theories. At the same time, the reconstruction of Walras's contribution made considerable progress beyond what it was in the 1980s, thanks to the publication of Auguste and Léon Walras's *Œuvres économiques complètes* (hereafter OEC followed by the volume, page if appropriate and page of English translation if available and adequate). New interpretations have thus appeared, sometimes conflicting with each other.

The purpose of this entry is to give a summary account of Léon Walras's political and social economy in his work as a whole. A particular attention is paid to the three main volumes – the famous "triptych": *Éléments d'économie politique pure*, *Études d'économie sociale* and *Études d'économie appliquée*. This corpus is presented following the way the Walrasian historiography has evolved over the past 50 years, and the themes reflect the purpose Walras gave to his work: the scientific solution to the *question sociale*, or rather "to two social questions plus one": the traditional social question, the problem of monopolies, and that of money.

An Unlikely Path

In April 1905, the Nobel Peace Prize award committee received an application from Léon Walras, then a retired professor from the University of Lausanne. As in 1905 he had submitted it after the deadline, he applied again, unsuccessfully, in 1906. A persevering man, he tried again in 1907, but his "La paix par la justice sociale et le libre échange" ("Peace by means of social justice and free trade") failed to convince the committee. Neither dementia nor foolish ambition led Walras to this, but rather his belief in a consistent, fundamental scientific project. Walras was convinced that he had supplied the necessary tools to rid the world of poverty, and of the clash between social classes, he had provided, or so he thought, a scientific answer to the social question.

Walras's youth and the first draft of the Walrasian system

Marie-Esprit-Léon Walras was born on 16 December 1834, at Evreux, in Normandy. He was the second of four children. His parents, Louise Aline Sainte-Beuve (1811–1893) and Antoine-Auguste Walras (1801–1866) belonged to the provincial bourgeoisie. Walras is one of the great names in economics (like, for example, John Stuart Mill and John Maynard Keynes) that are marked by the influence of towering father figures. A radical anticlerical intellectual, Antoine-Auguste was not a very successful economist. A former graduate from the French École Normale, he never managed to achieve a real academic career, mainly for political reasons. Nevertheless, he lavished his attention on his son, and had a decisive influence on Léon's choices.

After studying literature in Caen and Douai, Léon Walras obtained his Bachelor's Degree in literature in 1851. He then specialized in mathematics, an inevitable path for those who intended to graduate from French elite schools. Despite his Bachelor of

Science degree, he failed the École polytechnique entrance examination twice: however, in 1854 he was accepted as an external student at the École impériale des Mines. He stayed there only for a short time: his marks were too low in the technical and practical tests, and he was excluded from the prestigious school in summer 1856. Walras was more interested in a literary career. He published, at his own expense, his first and only novel, *Francis Sauveur* (1858). However, a tragic event – the death of his younger brother Louis – convinced him to dedicate himself to continuing his father's work. This was called the "oath of the Reeds", the name of the villa in front of which Léon made the solemn promise to his father to walk in his steps.

The publicist period: researching the Social Ideal
It was at this point that Léon Walras's career as an economist and publicist properly began. He benefited from a rich philosophical heritage: a French heritage, based on Victor Cousin and Théodore Jouffroy, but also on the doctrine of natural law; and a political economic heritage, based on physiocracy, Condorcet, Turgot, Destutt de Tracy and Saint-Simonism. Antoine-Auguste was also a true mentor and sought to help his son in his efforts to gain acceptance in the world of economists. He prompted Léon to participate in the Congrès international de l'impôt (International Congress on Taxes), held in Lausanne in 1860, and organized at the initiative of the Vaud Radical Party. Unconvincing in the eyes of Joseph Garnier, who strongly disliked Walras's support to the collective property of land, Walras impressed the Vaud authorities, who therefore invited him to teach a course in political economy. Unfortunately Walras took only fourth place in the contest following the Congrès, but this episode remained a decisive factor in his future academic career.

Auguste's contribution was not confined to giving good advice. He helped his son to write "Théorie critique de l'impôt". He was also very helpful in the drafting of his son's *Concours* (competitive exam) paper. More importantly, he made available to his son the notes he wrote on Proudhon in 1859, which Léon used extensively in his *L'économie politique et la justice* (OEC V). The Walrases were opposed to Proudhon's doctrine, and were keen to demonstrate that getting maximum utility can be achieved only under a regime of absolutely free competition.

At that time, Léon tried to collaborate with influential journals such as the *Journal des Économistes* and *La Presse*, which he joined almost simultaneously in 1860. His contribution to both journals lasted less than two years, as he then tried to launch his own newspaper, *L'Économiste* – but failed to get authorization for publication.

In 1862, Walras's co-operativist years began, during which he turned to practical work. His co-operativism is of a peculiar kind, far from the socialist tradition, supported by business circles, rather than emanating from workers. In 1863, while occuping the position of Director of railways for the Rothschilds, he developed an advance bank to facilitate pooling modest savings so as to enable the working class to access ownership of their homes. While working in 1864 for the *Caisse d'escompte des associations populaires* chaired by Léon Say, Walras managed to direct his own newspaper. In 1866, he published *Le Travail, organe international des intérêts économiques de la classe laborieuse, revue du mouvement coopératif*. He was careful not to advocate the co-operative form as the only desirable form of organization. Disagreements emerged with the Belgian owner of the newspaper, Constant Leirens; Léon Say for a while supported the publication in France, until it was finally discontinued in 1868, for lack of subscribers and in conjunction with the decline in popularity of co-operative ideas. That same year, the *Caisse d'escompte* was liquidated.

Léon Walras's early years in France (1853–1870) were plagued with failure and he confessed himself that his career "was the career of a man living in the wrong homeland" (OEC V 19). He had failed both his literary career and his cooperatives projects and activities; he was an unsuccessful economist and publicist, too; in 1870, he had a job as a junior clerk at Hollander Bank. Salvation came from another country and from a city he already knew: Switzerland and Lausanne.

The Vaud authorities' bet on the Walrasian project
In the Canton de Vaud, the new 1869 law on the *Académie de Lausanne* provided the opening of the first chair in political economy. Jules Ferry suggested Walras's name to Louis Ruchonnet, a young lawyer that Walras had met in 1860. Ruchonnet had become an influential politician, and was in charge of Waldensian Public Education. On September 6, 1870, Léon Walras sent his official application. He was appointed as Adjunct Professor on 12 November 1870 and Full Professor on 24 July 1871. His appointment to the first chair of political economy at the University of Lausanne owes much to his ideological proximity with Vaud radicalism (Dumez 1985). His pure economics, almost non-existent at the time, cannot be said to have resulted in getting "that French man with no university degree" appointed; actually, he owed his professorship far more to his "Republican political economy", as this matched perfectly this "reformist nebula" (Bourdeau 2005). In the early 1860s, Walras deployed a real research program directed towards the scientific resolution of the *question sociale*, and it was this program that was his key asset.

In the early years in Lausanne, his pure economics courses did not incorporate the fundamentals of marginalism or of general equilibrium. His mathematical economics was not yet formally developed. In 1873, during a lecture at the Académie des sciences morales et politiques in Paris on the "Principle of a mathematical theory of exchange", Walras publicly presented the concept of *rareté* that he had inherited from his father, but the mathematics in it proved problematic, particularly to Louis Wolowski and Emile Levasseur, who is credited with the famous phrase "Freedom cannot be put into equations". As he could not find publishers in Paris, it was thanks to the support of Louis Corbaz in Lausanne that he managed to publish the first instalment of the first edition of *Éléments d'économie politique pure ou théorie de la richesse sociale* in the summer of 1874. Part I, "Object and divisions of political and social economy", presented the Walrasian research programme and enshrined its pure economics within his political and social economy. In the second part, "Theory of exchange", he presented the formulation of trade between several commodities and the relationship between demand and utility. The third part, "Of *Numéraire* and Money", deals with the issue of a medium of exchange. The second instalment of this first edition of *Éléments* did not come out until 1877. It contained a fourth part on pricing in a production economy, a fifth part including capital commodities, and it ended with considerations on the impact of monopolies and taxes on various incomes and products.

Continuing his work in this direction, he published, in 1877 in France, his *Théorie mathématique de la richesse sociale*, a collection of papers written in 1875–76 for the *Société vaudoise des sciences naturelles* and integrated later into the *Éléments*. Gerolamo Boccardo – who translated and published the text entitled "Une branche nouvelle de la mathématique" in the *Giornale degli Economisti*, that Walras completed in 1876, but failed to publish in France – undertook to publish the *Théorie mathématique* in Italian (1878) as well. The German edition was not published until 1881. Walras added four extra papers and, in 1883, completed a more comprehensive book with the same title. In that same year, two more episodes were added to the already endless controversy regarding the mathematization of political economy. In a joint review of Cournot's *Recherches* and of Walras's *Théorie mathématique*, Joseph Bertrand (1883) pointed out, among other things, the impact on endowments of trade out of equilibrium, as well as their consequences for the determination of equilibrium. Walras explicitly replied in 1885 in a note, fully assuming the no-trade-out-of-equilibrium hypothesis. As for mathematics as a method, Walras advocated, in his private correspondence with Carl Menger, the idea that mathematics is altogether a method of research, demonstration and presentation, whereas Menger claimed that mathematics cannot be a research method but is, at best, only an auxiliary tool (Jaffé 1965).

However, it is the monetary issue that attracted most of his attention. To the lessons on credit and on the stock market that he was preparing for his *Cours d'économie politique appliquée*, three more texts must be added: the "Théorie mathématique du billet de banque" (1881), "Monnaie d'or avec billon d'argent régulateur" (1884) and *Théorie de la monnaie* (1886). In July 1889, delayed only by the studies on the issue of money, the second edition of the *Éléments* was eventually published, with major changes. Walras added an introduction to the mathematics used in his book (OEC VII: 236–60) and he changed the order in which chapters were organized. While the actual definition of social wealth still implies three general facts (property, value in exchange and industry), in the second edition, a fourth science was added: pure moral science, which was seen as affecting the relationships among sciences (see below). The theory of capitalization was fully developed and, above all, he drastically altered his monetary theory. Financial and monetary issues had always preoccupied him, owing to their potentially destabilizing nature, and the causes of the crisis were gradually "endogenized" into a very sophisticated monetary theory. The publication of the second edition revived the controversy over pricing and another controversy was raised, this time with Francis Ysidro Edgeworth (1889) who criticized Walras's *tâtonnement* (trial and error). The exchange of letters between the two men only demonstrates they utterly misunderstood each other, and Walras asked Ladislaus von Bortkiewicz to respond to Edgeworth's criticism. Which he did, in his review of the *Éléments* (1890).

Retirement, relinquishing the triptych and the completion of pure economics

Walras's health had not been good for some time, but it began to deteriorate and caused him to retire in 1892. This raised the matter of his succession to the chair of political economy. When Bortkiewicz turned it down, Walras – following Maffeo Pantaleoni's advice – supported the appointment of Vilfredo Pareto.

Freed from the burden of teaching, Walras believed at first he would be able to complete his research programme by finalizing the triptych, but he had to give up. From the beginning of his lectures in Lausanne, Walras directed his teaching not only towards pure economics, but also to applied and social economics. As in the case of his pure economics lectures, these were to contribute to his fundamental works. He intended to complete his *Éléments d'économie politique pure* with *Éléments d'économie politique appliquée* and *Éléments d'économie sociale*, but these were eventually published in the form of incomplete *Études*. The publications in 1896 of *Études d'économie sociale (Théorie de la répartition de la richesse sociale)* and, two years later, of *Études d'économie politique appliquée (Théorie de la production de la richesse sociale)* included mostly previously published works.

At the time of the publication of the two *Études*, Walras developed his *Éléments*; in the third edition, he added three appendices and moved four lessons, focusing on the theory of money, to the *Études d'économie politique appliquée*. His way of dealing with money in the *Éléments* was increasingly akin to the classical dichotomy and, in parallel, the disturbing aspects (dynamic) were moved to applied political economics.

In the fourth edition, Walras introduced the *tâtonnement* on bonds, and turned back to fixed production coefficients. It finally enabled him to confer its timeless character to his general economic equilibrium, and provided the ultimate response to Bertrand's criticism. At the same time, it probably contributed to his intuition of the difficulty inherent to the heterogeneity of capital.

An "intestinal thrombophlebitis" got the better of him, while he lived in Tavel-sur-Clarens, on 5 January 1910, a few months after the *Jubilée* – a ceremony organized by the State Council of the Canton of Vaud for his fiftieth birthday as an economist. On this occasion, Walras had delivered a speech that was a tribute to the person who had made it possible for him to join the University of Lausanne, but, in many respects, it may be described as his scientific testament: "Ruchonnet et le socialisme scientifique".

The *Éléments d'économie politique pure*

With four editions during his lifetime (1874–77, 1889, 1896, 1900) and a posthumous fifth (1926), the *Éléments d'économie politique pure* are probably the most accomplished and important part of Walras's work. In it Walras provides a formulation of the general economic equilibrium with which he wishes to analyse the interdependencies of markets. He assumes as given (1) initial resources, (2) production technology, (3) economic agents' preferences and (4) their initial endowments. He then shows that, on the assumption of absolutely free competition, it is possible to determine the quantity and price of any traded commodity and any input in production in such a way that the maximum utility position reached by each economic agent is compatible with those of all other agents. This state of general economic equilibrium is the maximum production of social wealth.

The first part of *Éléments d'économie politique pure* is dedicated to the definition of the subject, and to the divisions of its political and social economy arising from Walras's research programme directed towards the scientific resolution of the social question.

The object of study is social wealth, which Walras defines as "all things, material or immaterial . . . that are *scarce*, that is to say, on the one hand *useful* to us, and on the other hand, only available to us *in limited quantity*" (OEC VIII: 45 [65], original emphases). From this definition, Walras draws a triple consequence: (1) useful things limited in quantity are appropriable, (2) they are valuable and exchangeable, and (3) they are industrially producible or reproducible (OEC VIII: 49 [66]). This triple consequence of scarcity defines three distinct groups of facts, therefore three sciences: (1)

social economics (or the theory of the distribution of social wealth), (2) pure economics (or the theory of the value of social wealth) and (3) applied economics (or the theory of the production of social wealth) – each with a specific validation criterion.

The general economic equilibrium deals with value in exchange: "*pure economics* is, in essence, the theory of the determination of prices under a hypothetical regime of [absolutely] free competition" (OEC VIII: 11 [40], original emphasis). This is a hypothetical scheme, in that Walras supposes "that the market is perfectly competitive, just as in pure mechanics we suppose, to start with, that machines are perfectly frictionless" (OEC VIII: 71 [84]).

Absolute free competition is said to prevail when economic agents cannot influence prices by their own personal supplies or demands. Thus, since the value of social wealth "does not result either from the will of the buyer or from the will of the seller or from any agreement between the two" (OEC VIII: 50 [69]), its determination under an absolutely free competition regime is a natural fact; therefore, the science that deals with it meets the criterion of truth. Then, since producing social wealth results from exercising man's will over things, applied economics meets the criterion of usefulness. Finally, social economy "is guided by considerations of justice" (OEC VIII: 61 [75]), because the distribution of social wealth consist of a "relationship between persons and persons designed for the mutual co-ordination of the destinies of the persons concerned" (OEC VIII: 42 [63]).

After this introductory and methodological part, Walras presents the core of the general equilibrium approach, moving from simple to more complex phenomena.

> [I]t becomes possible to arrive successively at: (1) a determination of the prices of consumer's goods and services by means of *the theory of exchange*; (2) a determination of the prices of raw materials and productive services by means of the *theory of production*; (3) a determination of the prices of fixed capital goods by means of *the theory of capitalization*; and (4) a determination of the prices of circulating capital goods by means of *the theory of circulation*. (OEC VIII: 12 [40], original emphases)

In the Walrasian terminology, economic agents are distinguished depending on the nature of the factors of production they possess, that is, what Walras calls (fixed) capitals. These can be natural, such as land; personal, such as the ability to work; or capitals proper, such as plant and equipment; they are distinguished from incomes (or circulating capitals) because they are not exhausted after having been used once. Thus, landowners own the land, workers own personal capacities and capitalists own plant and equipment.

There are also the entrepreneurs who, through access to credit, have the opportunity to acquire inputs and assemble them, so as to minimize production costs of commodities, with given technology as known to them. These commodities are sold as consumer, intermediate or capital goods, in such quantities that maximize entrepreneurs' profits. However, in a state of equilibrium, neither excess-profits (*bénéfices*) nor losses (*pertes*) can exist since the absolutely free competition mechanism is such that one "bought his services and sold his products by auction, and . . . decreased his output in case of loss and always increased it in case of a profit" (OEC VIII: 284 [225]). The mechanism of absolutely free competition implies that buyers at the auction bid higher and sellers offer tenders at a discount; this is assumed to cause the price of a commodity to fall when supply exceeds demand, and rise when demand exceeds supply.

Exchange of two commodities and several commodities for one another
Walras first tries to show that it is possible to solve the problem of exchange between two persons of two commodities, and find the equilibrium prices and quantities. Walras "proves" the existence of the equilibrium by counting the (equal) number of equations and of unknowns. At that time this equality was considered to be sufficient as a proof: Irving Fisher (1892), for example, whose mathematical skills were much superior to Walras's very limited ones, proceeded in the same way, despite this being neither a necessary nor a sufficient condition. In the discussion of demand curves, Walras also addresses the issue of the uniqueness of equilibrium, and identifies the decreasing excess demand as a stability criterion. Thus, in his conceptualization the questions of the existence, uniqueness and stability of equilibrium were clearly separated.

The generalization of this reasoning to many commodities raises difficulties: in particular a generalized direct or indirect barter could no longer lead to a solution. Walras solved the problem by adopting at the same time a concept of equilibrium which rules out arbitrage (OEC VIII: 161–2), and a *numéraire*. The introduction of the *numéraire*, that is, "the commodity in terms of which the prices of all the others are expressed" (OEC VIII: 171 [161]), reduces the number of markets and prices and de facto forces all exchanges to be made against or through the *numéraire*.

Walras also generalizes the budget constraint of each agent in the two-commodity model, where obtaining a commodity required the sale of the other one, with a simultaneous equilibrium in both markets. In the case of many commodities, if all markets except one are in equilibrium, then the latter is necessarily in equilibrium, to the extent that consumers have met their budget constraints. This is what Oskar Lange called "Walras's Law" (1942: 51, n. 2).

What Walras secondly tries to show is "that this selfsame problem of exchange of which we just have furnished the theoretical solution is also the problem that is solved [practically] on the market by the mechanism of free competition" (OEC VIII: 173 [163]). Imagine a market in which all commodities and all economic agents are present and where prices are set at random. If by sheer chance every demand and supply are in equilibrium, the problem is solved. Otherwise, other prices should be set so that, through trial and error, by *tâtonnement*, supplies and demands in each market end up coinciding. If, among the newly set prices, at least one assures the equilibrium for a commodity, only the others unbalancing prices are set again. And so on for all markets. However, by balancing markets one after the other, the previously balanced markets end up unbalanced. Walras then distinguishes between the direct effects and indirect effects and assumes that the former are larger than the latter (OEC VIII: s. 130). This makes him think that he obtains convergence towards equilibrium prices and is thus able to formulate the law of price determination in the case of trading several commodities one for the other. It should be noted that exchange is assumed not to take place until after the equilibrium prices have been found for all commodities (OEC IX: 312 [251]).

Production, capitalization and money
As early as the second edition, Walras deals with the exchange values of the factors of production (Part IV) after having dealt with that of commodities, and before the part (VI) on money. With the introduction of the "equations of production", the *tâtonnement* is complicated by the fact that quantities of commodities are not given, but depend on

production. So, if the set prices are not such that in each market demand equals supply, new prices are set, but it is also necessary to manufacture other amounts of products. Only with the fourth edition of *Éléments* does Walras believe he has found a convincing solution: "In the theory of production, I no longer represented the preliminary *tâton-nements* towards equilibrium as it takes place effectively, but I assumed, instead, that it was done by *means of tickets* [*sur bons*]" (OEC VIII: 5–7, original emphases). However, integrating production in general equilibrium remains problematic, especially in Part V, when Walras takes into account heterogeneous capital goods, as he had done for the other productive services, labour and land services. Already, when solving the produc-tion equations, the issue of the initial conditions matters and Walras, in the first edition of the *Éléments* resorts to the expedient of a foreign market where entrepreneurs find services in indefinite quantities. In the theory of capitalization, to determine the quanti-ties and prices of new capital goods, the available physical quantities of produced means of production are given data and hence include those of capital goods per se. However, "we cannot expect that configuration of capital stocks to be the most "appropriate" to the production of the outputs required by the preferences of the consumers" (Garegnani 1990: 16) and to obtain a uniform rate of net income (or profits) to obtain. With the fourth edition, Walras seems to realize the problem when he says that:

> It is not at all certain that the amount of savings . . . will be adequate for the manufacture of new fixed capital goods proper in just such quantities as will satisfy the last *l* equations [which determine the quantities of new fixed capital goods proper to produce] of the above system. (OEC VIII: 431 [308])

Thus, in the static context of general equilibrium, Walras admits that net income rates differ from one another, and that in a progressive society he could only postulate that they are uniform.

The construction of the general economic equilibrium is supplemented by taking money into account, in its payment function, because the unit of account function has already been introduced with the *numéraire* on the occasion of trading several commodi-ties for each other. As noted earlier, monetary theory is the subject that underwent the most extensive changes throughout the four editions of the *Éléments*.

In the first edition, the part on money concludes the first instalment, after studying the exchange of several commodities. Money is the necessary intermediary of exchange because "we cannot directly exchange commodities against commodities" (OEC VIII: 541). So, from the very beginning, Walras does not think in terms of a generalized barter system, but a Clower-like monetary economy and "there is a perfect analogy between the intervention of money and the intervention of *numéraire*" (OEC VIII: 228). Walras addresses the issue of determining the value of money from the fact that "the [total] value of the money that has bought the commodities is equal to the value of commodities that were sold against money" (OEC VIII: 468), which he formalizes in a "veritable exchange equation" that anticipates Fisher's equation.

The publication of the second edition of the *Éléments* "was delayed only by the studies that I had undertaken on the question of money" (OEC VIII: 4). His results, including those stated in *Théorie de la monnaie* (1886), lead Walras to change the order of chapters by shifting the part on money after that of capitalization and credit. Thus, money is now considered as a circulating capital, in the dual form of circulating money and savings money (for the purchase of new capital), and the determination of its value is not only made in aggregate terms of the needs of the circulation, but in an individual perspective of desired cash balance to finance daily transactions. However, the most important change consists in the separation between pure and applied monetary theory that refers to a distinction between the steady-state equilibrium of pure economics and the dynamic, unbalancing aspects of applied economics. Following this logic, four lessons in the third edition (lessons 37–40) were removed and returned to the *Études d'économie appliquée*. The fourth edition continues along these lines, on the one hand, with the timeless general economic equilibrium, and, on the other hand, with the introduction of the demand for money in individual utility functions. Money is used to purchase capital and other commodities, thus it provides a service that Walras called *d'approvisionnement* (service of availability). So, he can finally put the equation of the equality of the supply and demand for money no longer "apart from the other equations and as empirically given . . . [but] deduced rationally" (OEC VIII: 9 [38]).

Finally, four subjects, organized in two parts, conclude the *Éléments*. In Part VII, outside his atemporal general equilibrium, Walras moves his thoughts on economic progress – including the theorem of marginal productivities – together with a critique of pure systems of political economy, that is, the Physiocrats and the English classical economists'. The last part deals with tariffs, monopolies and taxes.

The Triptych and Pure Moral Science

The literature on Walras, since his death and up to the 1970s, focused on *Éléments d'économie politique pure*, and, with a few exceptions, set aside applied and social economics. It was not until William Jaffé's latest contributions that Walras's social economics began to be examined, at least by historians of economic thought. Applied economics hardly fared better. With the publication of the *Œuvres économiques complètes*, most historians of economic thought extended the corpus to the triptych and beyond. It is not uncommon now to encounter references to *Mélanges d'économie politique et sociale* – an interesting volume, planned to be published in 1892, though it did not come off the press except as part of the *Œuvres* (OEC VII) in 1987 – *Cours d'économie sociale* and *Cours d'économie politique appliquée* (OEC XII), and *Notes d'humeur* (OEC XIII). The problem of the relationships between the various components of Walras's political and social economics is thus raised. We have seen that a triple consequence was drawn from the definition of social wealth, and from it three general facts, which give rise to three sciences: pure economics dealing with exchange value; applied economics dealing with industry; and social economics dealing with property. To study social wealth comprehensively, exchange value had to be dealt with (the theory of general economic equilibrium), but also the conditions under which social wealth is produced (applied economics) and, of course, how it is distributed (applied social economics).

However, to solve the social question, Walras introduced a fourth science in 1879: pure moral science, or history, understood as the path towards the realization of human destiny, which eludes, Walras believes, man's will, and is therefore natural, hence inevitable. Pure moral science is also the science of justice, as Walras introduced it in his essay on "Théorie de la propriété" ("Theory of property"). Therefore, the triptych actually covers four sciences, because the *Études d'économie sociales* contains pure (Parts I and II) and applied (Parts III and IV) moral science. This results in a general architecture of political and social economics that relies on explicit ontological considerations, through two natural theories (in Walras's sense of the term) – of property and of the determination of the exchange value – to develop the reforms necessary to achieve the inevitable economic and social ideal. As Walras sees it, it is precisely failing to deal with one or more of these aspects that caused those who, before him, tackled the social question to fail. Ignoring the exchange value, giving precedence to morality or utility perspectives, and a general lack of command of good scientific methods, these are some of his predecessors' mistakes.

Social Economics and the Distribution of Social Wealth

In 1896, Walras published the *Études d'économie sociale*, a collection of a dozen articles on the theory of the distribution of social wealth. Although this volume did not have the systematic nature of *Éléments*, its structure is clear, and it speaks for itself: "I. Seeking the social ideal", "II. Property", "III. Realization of the social ideal" and "IV. Taxes". Based on considerations sometimes ontological (I), Walras lays the foundation for a pure theory of property (II) and develops the necessary measures for the implementation of the theory (III): the abolition of income tax and the repurchase of land by the state.

Following a well-established tradition that came down to him through his father, Léon Walras takes up again, already in his early writings, an opinion he himself calls "neo-physiocratic", consisting of a tax system reduced to "a single tax on rents" (OEC IX: 348). In the general considerations on taxes with which Walras opened his contribution to the 1860 Congrès international de l'impôt, he expresses a clear position based on the principle of "the identity of the two problems of ownership and taxes". Starting from the idea that the fruits of labour and savings belong to the natural domain of private property, and that the land belongs to the natural domain of collective property – thus solving the problem of property – Walras intended to solve also the tax issue, "because, since the State would own the land capital, it would levy the land-income; thereby, the amount of rent would become the natural tax" (OEC V: 440). Thus, "conceding the land to the State solves the problem of taxation by abolishing it" (OEC IX: 192 [146]). In fact, the rent would be the only (legitimate) state revenue. The writings in the last part (IV) of *Études* document Walras's reflections on the transitional phase, when the revenue from land rent accruing to the State is insufficient to finance its operations.

The solution of the social question: collective land ownership and abolition of income taxes
In 1896, Walras published in the *Revue socialiste* the "Théorie de la propriété", which, he believed, was to fill a gap between his ontological and his (applied) social economics considerations. Written "in geometrical form [which] is the true form of the science of justice if this science, like that of space, consists of analytical deduction of relationships and laws concerning ideal types abstracted from reality [by] definition" (OEC IX: 177 [135]), it is, together with pure economics, the reference to the theories on reforming distribution and organizing production.

Although ownership applies to all social wealth, Walras clarified beforehand that it is sufficient to develop a theory of the ownership of personal abilities, and a theory of land ownership, as those of other components (other assets, services and so on) derive from them. Regarding personal faculties, they "are, by natural law, owned by the *individual*"

(OEC IX: 185 [142]). What he calls "Theorem I" of the "Théorie de la propriété" follows directly from the definition of the human being as such, that is, "fulfilling a farsighted and free destiny" (OEC IX: 102). In other words, for Walras, a human being "feels, knows and possesses himself. He has a destination and he pursues it, and he does so while knowing that he has a destination, and that it is he himself who has to pursue it." (OEC IX: 102 [77]). This implies that his personal faculties belong to him, so that he might enjoy them based on their efforts, according "to the principle of inequality of positions" (OEC IX: 186 [142]).

Conversely, land ownership is based on "the principle of equality of conditions" because all human beings "must be able to benefit equally from the natural resources available" (OEC IX: 189 [144]) to pursue their purpose and fulfil their destinations. "Theorem II" states that "*land* is, by natural law, the property of the *State*", and Walras thus asserts that "any alienation of land is against natural law, because it wrongs future generations. In legal terms, humanity is the owner and the present generation is the usufructuary of the land" (OEC IX: 189 [145]).

Walras had already advocated the ethical need for the state to redeem all of the land, but it is only in "Théorie de la propriété" that he is able to fully justify his opinions. Walras considers land as a factor of production. Moreover, he notes that "for all, the land owner is a man who sells, at the price of rent, the natural fertility of land" (OEC XII: 236). If the land has intrinsic value, rent is natural and therefore cannot accrue to individuals, but must return to the community, that is, the state that represents its present and future interests. Rent collected by individuals is therefore contrary to distributive justice, since the only legitimate income for individuals is the one provided by their own labour and savings. Taxing rents is justified. If, according to justice, rent accrues to the state, it means it must be the owner of the land that generates it; otherwise we would face a contradiction with Lemma I of the "Théorie de la propriété", according to which "*the owner of a thing is the owner of its service.*" (OEC IX: 178 [136], original emphasis). Therefore, land is, on account of natural law, the property of the State.

However, while it is fair that the State should become the owner of all the land, it is still necessary that this ownership should be legitimate. On this point Walras's position is clear: The State has no right to expropriate property owners, but must respect Lemma II, "*the owner of a thing is the owner of its price*" (OEC IX: 178 [136], original emphasis). The State must therefore redeem the land. "Théorie mathématique du prix des terres et de leur rachat par l'État" (1880) is devoted to the cost and financing of this acquisition: Walras takes up again H.-H. Gossen's theory, and thereby considers he had demonstrated that "the State could therefore redeem all the land by amortizing the purchase price by means of rents" (OEC XII: 360). However, the equilibrium price of an asset in an efficient market is equal to the sum of discounted expected earnings (the rents in this case) and, therefore, the internal rate of return of the asset coincides with the discount rate. Nevertheless, since the net income rate corresponds to the interest rate paid on the debt that the state has incurred to buy the land, it is impossible for future rents to write off the debt. Walras considers that individuals underestimate the upward trend of rent in a progressive economy, which only the state can anticipate properly, ultimately as the increase in land rent is largely due to improvements in infrastructure, decided by the State.

Applied Economics and the Political Organization of the Market

To solve the social question, the fair distribution of social wealth is not enough; it is also necessary that its production should be "as plentiful as possible" (OEC IX: 56 [39]). Applied economics is the theory of how to organize production, according to the criterion of usefulness.

The book *Études d'économie politique appliquée* was published in 1898, and the table of contents tells us more about the subjects that preoccupied Walras, than about the true content of separating political from social economics. Three-quarters of the volume are devoted to money and finance; the rest is divided into three roughly equal parts – between the study of monopolies, of agricultural studies, of industry and commerce and the "Esquisse d'une doctrine économique et sociale". In Part I, "Money" – more than a third of the book – Walras presents again the chapters that had been expurgated from the third edition of *Éléments*, the *Theory of money* and half a dozen articles published in scientific journals and newspapers. The part entitled "II. Monopolies" consists of only one substantial study dating back to 1875, "L'État et les chemins de fer", that had been turned down by the *Journal des économistes*. Part III contains three articles whose titles speak for themselves: "The influence of communication between markets on the situation of rural communities", "Applied economics and the protection of wages" and "Theory of free trade". Three parts follow, on credit, banking (with a text that is crucial to understand Walras's monetary theory, "Mathematical theory of banknotes") and stock markets. The book concludes with "Outline of an economic and social doctrine".

Organization of production and the second social question

Organizing production for it to be *"convenable"* ("suitable") means primarily finding a solution to monopolies, something that increasingly preoccupies Walras probably since the revision of Lesson 29 in the 1887 edition of *Cours d'économie politique appliquée* (Potier 1998). Ultimately, he claims that "a second social question would remain to be solved: The production of wealth by people in society, while preventing certain entrepreneurs from making greater profits than under the normal condition of free competition" (OEC X: 425 [372]).

Walras distinguishes three types of monopolies: economic, moral and artificial. Economic monopolies are "natural and necessary" (OEC X: 427 [373]). He quotes extractive industries, but also postal mail: crucial economic activities with high fixed costs are a barrier for potential competitors. As a price maker, the monopolistic contractor imposes an exchange procedure that does not respect man's freedom and farsighted nature; he obviously violates the neutrality of the exchange, to the extent that the price he sets allows him to profit illegitimately. He can also establish a discrimination that violates price uniqueness. In short, the monopolist deprives price of its natural character. To avoid "an onerous levy, *laisser faire* should no longer be allowed in certain cases, on the contrary the State, should intervene to exercise the monopoly itself, or to organize it so that it is exercised without profit or loss. In this way, economic monopolies, based on social interest, will arise" (OEC X: 189) – private monopolies transformed into state monopolies or into monopolies granted by the state.

These economic monopolies must be distinguished from the moral monopolies – also managed by the state, but whose nature is different. Indeed, this second type of monopoly is related to commodities and services – Walras describes them as "the public interest" – that the production would not be right without state intervention, as these are commodities that include externalities or that, from the natural law perspective, are merit goods. Moreover, the products of moral monopolies are usually free commodities.

In fact from a theoretical perspective, Walras was especially concerned with a third sort of monopoly: artificial monopolies, resulting from competition among enterprises.

> I am mainly working on pure political economics, that is, the analysis of the free competition mechanism considered in itself. But . . . this study . . . convinced me that this mechanism is far from being always absolutely self-driven and self-regulating, as argued by official and orthodox school economists. I find it rather conclusively demonstrated that free competition, in many cases, has a natural tendency to lead to monopolies. (Jaffé 1965, letter to H. Blabed, dated 7 February 1892)

The development of this third type of monopoly places state intervention outside the ordinary context and, in the same period, the early 1870s, Walras started his thoughts on the "collectivism of production". Ultimately, the issue is about the extent of state intervention, as an entrepreneur or as a supervisor of production under concessions.

Thus, the "entrepreneur unique" who, in 1875, simply meant the monopolistic contractor (OEC X: 191), becomes the conjecture of collective production of the social wealth in the text "L'économie appliquée et la défense des salaires" (1897): "All enterprises could possibly be supposed collective, but they cannot all be supposed private. Collective production is materially possible and would not, in itself, be contradictory to liberty, equality, order or justice. It is a simple matter of social utility" (OEC X: 251 [221]). Such collectivism – "where the State would be the entrepreneur unique", and which, in the first manuscript version, is "perhaps the formula for the future" (OEC X: 481, n. 18) – differs from Marxian communism, which Walras had studied, in that all capitals except land are still private. Moreover, the matter of the entrepreneur unique is not confined to applied economics: in his fourth edition of the *Éléments*, Walras introduced it and, in the *Préface*, he indicates the addition: "Free competition among entrepreneurs is, as I explain in §188, not the only means of bringing selling price into equality with cost of production. It is the role of applied economics to inquire whether free competition is always the best means" (OEC VIII: 11 [40]). At the end of the day, Walras does not decide on the matter, but suggests to "establish, under conditions as serious as possible, a great experience." (OEC X: 251).

Money, credit and crises: a third question sociale?

Because of its redistributive implications, the problem of the value of money may constitute the third social question: the fixity of the value of money is "indispensable for the exercise of the right of property" (OEC IX: 184 [141]). The solution that Walras reaches in 1900 is a perfectly exogenous money managed by the state (Baranzini 2005).

The young Walras began his career as a follower of the Banking School and supporter of gold-monometallism. But for the rest of his life he advocated a "Gold money with regulating silver token" together with the abolition of the net issue of bank notes. In 1884, at the International Monetary Conference for the Prolongation of the Latin Union, he presented a scheme the benefits of which would be "the reform of our monetary system by means of regulating the variation in the value of money, the reform of our credit system by getting rid of fictitious drawing credit, the redemption of part of the public debt" (OEC X: 43 [37]). This was supposed to stabilize the value of money and reduce the magnitude of crises.

As early as the first edition of the *Éléments* (s. 195), Walras refers to transactions made without the medium of precious metals; but he is aware of the difficulties inherent to the matter, and postpones any conclusion to a later specific study. In 1880, he publishes the "Théorie mathématique du billet de banque", which contains "singular and interesting results, which I for one had not expected," (Jaffé 1965) as he writes to Jevons in March that same year. Banknotes are not a substitute for other means of payment: they are added to them and cause crises because their issue occurs through credit operations. Issuing banknotes expands credit beyond savings as well as distorting the respective maturities of deposits and loans. Walras had anticipated both the forced savings theory and the cumulative processes theory, and this enabled him to find an explanation to crises, as triggered by the complexities of reabsorbing banknotes. "I am increasingly convinced that in fact the issue of banknotes could not be reimbursed at a moment's notice without social upheaval, nor be reduced without considerable economic difficulty" (OEC X: 16 [12]).

In the 1882 text, "De la fixité de la valeur de l'étalon monétaire" (OEC XI), Walras showed that the gold-money system with a silver token regulator (separate from money in coins and notes) provides greater stability than a bimetallic system, let alone a monometallic one. However, that kind of stability is relative and it is still necessary that the state should add or subtract an appropriate amount of the regulating token, and be the only one to influence the amount of money in circulation. From this point of view, "the general equilibrium ... is based not on the theoretical neutrality of money assertion, but on its political neutralization" (De Caro 1988: 111). Thus, the money circulation problem would be completely solved, by correcting "the slow, persistent variation in the value of money, which affect ownership and disturb general economic equilibrium" (OEC X: 359 [312]).

Concluding Remarks

Since the early 1990s, most monographs about Léon Walras contain a section on his philosophy, and several articles have been published on this topic. More recently, alongside epistemological issues, Walrasian ontology has also been investigated and these aspects have been used to interpret his work, making it possible to elucidate two fundamental points.

The first point is the question of the *referent* of pure economics, that is, of the entity that general equilibrium refers to. Walras was greatly influenced by Étienne Vacherot, whose *La métaphysique et la science ou principes de métaphysique positive* (1858) used to be his "favorite bedside book". Walras considers pure economics as a rational science, not an experimental science. From economic facts, the subject gets immediate perceptions organized in real types. Freed by the abstraction process from their contingencies, real types become ideal types. Pure economics is the set of mathematical propositions obtained by deduction from ideal types (exchange value, for example) that determine the equilibrium price vector, under a hypothetical system of absolute free competition. The only "empiricist" aspect of his method is that it is grounded in facts, but the construction of ideal types is not achieved through an inductive process. "Collecting facts has nothing to do with a scientist's work . . . it is a ragman's job" (OEC XIII: 552).

Empirical analysis is also *a posteriori* dismissed, since a theory does not need verification (OEC VIII: s. 30). Moreover, regardless of the method used to confront theory with reality, the former cannot possibly be validated, because the "perfection, or the absolute, is the principal constituent of theory and science [but] imperfection, or that which is relative, is the principal constituent of practice and art" (Walras, OEX IX: 15 [8]). In other words, reality is necessarily inadequate compared to science. "Mr. P[areto] believes the goal of science is to approach reality increasingly closely, by means of successive approximations. For my part, I think the ultimate goal of science is to bring reality closer to a particular ideal; that's why I formulate this ideal" (OEC XIII: 567).

Ideal types are perfect, and capture the essence of things, or things per se. The resulting theory has strong foundations and can claim to stand as the true nature of the objects of knowledge. Walras asserts that essences exist, as do ideal types, and their knowledge is possible. He is a realist – in the philosophical sense of the word – both ontologically and epistemologically. However, the conceptual existence of ideal types precedes that of singular things, as essences are not yet completed in historical time, "the world is a reality that starts empirically and that afterwards returns and acts upon itself to organize itself according to a rationally generated ideal" (OEC XIII: 552). Thus, the referent of pure economics, of Walras's general economic equilibrium, is an ideal cognitive product that has not yet achieved full correspondence in reality, but that will gradually materialize. This is Walras's teleological realism, a realism that does not involve *realisticness* (Mäki 1998).

The second point, which has to do with the relations between pure and applied economics, is closely linked to the first, because it is precisely through the materialization of the ideal that applied sciences play a crucial role. Applied economics points out provident reforms to implement sound practices, which are essential to the realization of the ideal economy, and to the materialization of essences. Applied economics provides the – institutional, not formal – conditions for the existence of the ideal as grasped by pure economics. Implicitly, applied sciences account for the gap between the historical appearance of phenomena and their essence. From this perspective, pure economics and applied economics are consubstantial in knowledge and Walras dodges the idealistic bias.

Finally, if, as suggested by Jaffé, we take into account the final purpose of Walras's political and social economy – that is, the solution of the social question in its three facets – as well as the underlying ontology and epistemology, as called for by De Caro and Dockès, some controversial features in his thought can be explained. The (a)temporal structure of *Éléments* and the expulsion of disturbing (dynamic) factors from the general economic equilibrium are no longer understood as related to an inconsistency owing to Walras's (declining) intellectual health, and some key concepts such as *tâtonnement* become more intelligible. This approach makes it possible to remove a number of contradictions, such as that between neutral money as found in *Éléments* and the money responsible for crises in applied economics, or between absolutely free competition and the unique entrepreneur. More generally, this interpretative line explains why Walras suggests reforms that seemed useless if the theory was accurate. In fact, these reforms are necessary for the pure theory to be true and so the state intervention is not conceived by Walras as limited to correct market failures.

Léon Walras's political and social economy, as it emerges from recent studies, is rather distant from the École de Lausanne general economic equilibrium, and this distance can help us to understand the evolution of economic theory during the following 150 years.

ROBERTO BARANZINI

See also:

Ladislaus von Bortkiewicz (I); Capital theory (III); Antoine-Augustin Cournot (I); Francis Ysidro Edgeworth (I); Formalization and mathematical modelling (III); Hermann Heinrich Gossen (I); General equilibrium theory (III); William Stanley Jevons (I); Carl Menger (I); Non-Marxian socialist ideas in France (II); Vilfredo Pareto (I).

References and further reading

Baranzini, R. (2005), *Léon Walras e la moneta senza velo*, Torino: UTET Libreria.
Baranzini, R. (2014), 'Pour une histoire de la théorie économique de Léon Walras', in J.-P. Potier (ed.), *Les marmites de l'histoire. Mélanges en l'honneur de Pierre Dockès*, Paris: Classiques Garnier, pp. 285–98.
Bertrand, J. (1883), 'Théorie des richesses: Théorie mathématique de la richesse sociale, par Léon Walras – Recherches sur les principes mathématiques de la théorie des richesses, par Augustin Cournot', *Journal des savants*, September, 499–508.
Bortkiewicz, L. von (1890), 'Léon Walras, *Éléments d'économie politique pure, ou Théorie de la richesse sociale. 2e édition*', *Revue d'économie politique*, **4** (1), 80–96.
Bourdeau, V. (2005), 'L'économie politique républicaine de Léon Walras. Philosophie républicaine et économie politique en France au XIXe siècle', doctoral thesis, UFR de Philosophie, Université de Franche-Comté.
Bridel, P. (1996), *Le chêne et l'architecte: un siècle de comptes rendus bibliographiques des 'Éléments d'économie politique pure' de Léon Walras*, with R. Baranzini, Geneva: Droz.
Bridel, P. (1997), *Money and General Equilibrium Theory. From Walras to Pareto (1870–1923)*, Cheltenham, UK and Northampton, MA, USA: Edward Elgar.
De Caro, G. (1985), *Léon Walras dalla teoria monetaria alla teoria generale della produzione di merci*, in L. Walras, *L'economia monetaria*, vol. 1, Rome: Istituto della Enciclopedia Italiana Treccani, pp. 5–200.
De Caro, G. (1988), 'Le monde atemporel de Léon Walras', *Économies et Sociétés*, **22** (10), 105–32.
Dockès, P. (1996), *La société n'est pas un pique-nique: Léon Walras et l'économie sociale*, Paris: Economica.
Dockès, P. (2011), 'Lire Walras et les autres: une "note d'humeur"', in R. Baranzini, A. Legris and L. Ragni (eds), *Léon Walras et l'équilibre économique général. Recherches récentes*, Paris: Economica, pp. 1–17.
Dockès, P. and J.-P. Potier (2001), *La vie et l'œuvre économique de Léon Walras*, Paris: Economica.
Dumez, H. (1985), *L'économiste, la science et le pouvoir: le cas de Walras*, Paris: Presses Universitaires de France.
Edgeworth, F.Y (1889), 'The mathematical theory of political economy', *Nature*, **40**, 434–6.
Fisher, I. (1892), 'Mathematical investigations in the theory of value and prices', *Transactions of the Connecticut Academy*, **8**, 1–124.
Garegnani, P. (1990), 'Quantity of capital', in J. Eatwell, M. Milgate and P. Newman (eds), *The New Palgrave: Capital Theory*, London: Macmillan, pp. 1–78.
Jaffé, W. (ed.) (1965), *Correspondence of Léon Walras and Related Papers*, Amsterdam: North Holland.
Jaffé, W. (1983), *William Jaffé's Essays on Walras*, D.A. Walker (ed.), Cambridge: Cambridge University Press.
Jolink, A. (1996), *The Evolutionist Economics of Léon Walras*, London: Routledge.
Lallement, J. (2014), 'Walras between holism and individualism', in R. Baranzini and F. Allisson (eds), *Economics and Other Branches. In the Shade of the Oak Tree: Essays in Honour of Pascal Bridel*, London: Pickering & Chatto, pp. 15–30.
Lange, O. (1942), 'Say's Law: a restatement and criticism', in O. Lange et al. (eds), *Studies in Mathematical Economics and Econometrics*, Chicago, IL: Chicago University Press, pp. 49–68.
Mäki, U. (1998), 'Realisticness', in J.B. Davis, D. Wade Hands and U. Mäki (eds), *The Handbook of Economic Methodology*, Cheltenham, UK and Northampton, MA, USA: Edward Elgar, pp. 409–13.
Potier, J.-P. (1994), 'Classification des sciences et divisions de l'"économie politique et sociale" dans l'œuvre de Léon Walras: une tentative de reconstruction', *Économies et Sociétés*, **28** (10–11), 223–77.

Rebeyrol, A. (1999), *La pensée économique de Walras*, Paris: Dunod.
Van Daal, J. and A. Jolink (1993), *The Equilibrium Economics of Léon Walras*, London and New York: Routledge.
Walker, D.A. (1996), *Walras's Market Model*, Cambridge: Cambridge University Press.
Walker, D.A. (2006), *Walrasian Economics*, Cambridge: Cambridge University Press.
Walras, A. and L. Walras (1987–2005), *Œuvres économiques complètes*, 14 vols, P. Dockès, et al. (eds), Paris: Economica.
Walras, L. (1858), *Francis Sauveur*, Paris: E. Dentu.
Walras, L. (1954), *Elements of Pure Economics*, London: George Allen & Unwin.
Walras, L. (2005), *Studies in Applied Economics*, Abingdon: Routledge.
Walras, L. (2010), *Studies in Social Economics*, Abingdon: Routledge.

William Stanley Jevons (1835–1882)

William Stanley Jevons (1835–1882) was in every sense a pioneer of neoclassical economics. He is perhaps best known as an enthusiastic proponent of the use of mathematics in economics and for his successful introduction of a marginal utility analysis of exchange, being closely followed by Menger and Walras. Yet over his short life he made many original contributions to other areas of economics as well as a wide range of other disciplines. After spending two years at University College London, where he largely concentrated on chemistry and botany, he was offered the position of assayer to the new mint in Sydney, Australia. In view of the failure of his father's firm in 1847, this offer was financially attractive and Jevons arrived in Sydney in 1854, where he remained for five years. He returned to England and University College London in 1859, this time concentrating on logic, mathematics and political economy. Following a period as tutor at Owens College, Manchester, in 1866 Jevons became Professor of Logic and Mental and Moral Philosophy and Cobden Professor of Political Economy at Owens College. Ten years later he became Professor of Political Economy at University College London, resigning this post in 1880. He drowned while swimming near Hastings, on the south coast of England.

Jevons displayed a restless curiosity and astonishing capacity for original thought. During his time in Sydney, Jevons became a pioneer social statistician, meteorologist (building an experimental machine to produce different types of cloud and writing on the climate of Australia), and photographer. In attempting to produce cirrus clouds in 1857, Jevons discovered what, 100 years later, became known as "salt fingers". Heat diffuses much more rapidly than salt, causing rising and sinking tendrils of water to develop where warm salty water lies on top of cooler fresher water. This process is thus associated with vertical mixing in oceans. As a skilled pianist he invented his own music notation system. His work on logic developed alongside his economics, producing in 1869 a machine, the "logic piano", a pioneer mechanical computer capable of deriving conclusions from a set of premises. His *Elementary Lessons in Logic*, published in 1870, was widely read, and in 1874 he published his massive *The Principles of Science*. This impressive volume contained, in a short section, his discussion of factorization, leading to what is now known as "Jevons's number" and later important developments in cryptography. He asked, "Can the reader say what two numbers multiplied together will produce the number 8,616,460,799? I think it unlikely that anyone but myself will ever know" (1874: 123). In 1903, D.N. Lehmer showed that 89 681 times 96 079 gives Jevons's number.

Jevons's early work in economics was applied and policy-related. His pioneering work on index numbers included his *A Serious Fall in the Value of Gold* (1863). His book on *The Coal Question* (1865) was on resource depletion that attracted much attention, including the interest of Gladstone. This book includes his conjecture, now referred to as "Jevons's paradox", that technological change which improves efficiency in the use of a resource, by lowering its relative cost, causes the use of that resource to increase. His later works included *Money and the Mechanism of Exchange* (1875), *A Primer on Political Economy* (1878), and *The State in Relation to Labour* (1882). After his death *Methods of Social Reform* was published and, after a further interval, *Investigations in Currency and Finance* (1884) was edited by his friend Foxwell. Among other things, this book contains Jevons's analyses of a possible link between sunspots and commercial crises, via the effect of sunspots on the weather and hence agricultural production. In particular, he stressed the link between high prices in India and the UK balance of payments.

However, there is no doubt that Jevons is best remembered for his *Theory of Political Economy*, published in 1871. Some of the central ideas had been contained in his short "Notice of a general mathematical theory of political economy", which was presented to the Cambridge meeting of Section F of the British Association in 1862. Jevons's confidence about the value of this work and his concern that it may be neglected are both reflected in his letter to his brother, which stated:

> Although I know pretty well the paper is perhaps worth all the others that will be read there put together, I cannot pretend to say how it will be received . . . I shall watch it like an artilleryman watches the flight of a shell or shot, to see whether its effects equal his intentions. (Quoted by Keynes 1936: 532)

Jevons's article appeared in print four years later in the *Statistical Journal*, and is most easily found in later editions of his *Theory of Political Economy*.

Having failed to hit his mark, Jevons delayed producing his full-scale treatment until Fleeming Jenkin's important paper on "The graphic representation of the laws of supply and demand" in 1870 stimulated him to publish his own work more quickly in book form, in order to establish priority. This book was not an immediate success, meeting with a negative review by Cairns and a grudging and anonymous review by Marshall. It is not clear if Jevons ever knew the identity of the author. Marshalls' complex attitude to Jevons is discussed by Keynes (1936: 534–6). However, Jevons received support from the mathematician George Darwin, son of Charles Darwin. An anonymous piece in the *Saturday Review* attacked Jevons's use of mathematics, which was said to, "wrap up a plain statement in a mysterious collection of letters" (see Black 1981: 157).

However, Jevons's *Theory of Political Economy* has long been regarded as a major foundation stone of neoclassical economics. Nevertheless it is sometimes unfairly caricatured as being merely an early application of mathematics and the marginal utility analysis of demand to economics, while at the same time criticisms are directed at Jevons for not explicitly deriving demand curves from utility functions, and also illegitimately applying the theory to aggregates of a number of traders rather than single individuals.

It is therefore important to stress that Jevons's primary emphasis was on exchange as the "central" problem in economics. Indeed, Hicks (1984) referred to the early neoclassical economists as "catallactists", in order to emphasize their exchange focus. This neologism (of Whately, used also by Edgeworth) was extensively used by Hearn (1864) in his *Plutology*, which appears to have had some influence on Jevons, who attended a lecture by Hearn while in Australia. In the introduction to his *Theory of Political Economy* Jevons also praised Hearn. Hicks stressed that:

> while the classics looked at the economic system primarily from the production angle, the catallactists looked at it primarily from the side of exchange. It was possible, they found, to construct a 'vision' of economic life out of the theory of exchange, as the classics had done out of the social product. It was quite a different vision. (1984: 250)

Jevons and the other neoclassical writers provided a foundation for their exchange model in the form of a utility analysis and this (the ability to talk about individuals being "better off" in a particular sense) provided the basis of what came to be called welfare economics. Hicks stated that "welfare economics was captured by the catallactists and it has never got quite free" (1984: 253).

Only when the perceived central position of exchange analysis is recognized, with utility maximization as the foundation, is it possible to appreciate the enthusiasm of Jevons for his pioneering approach, nicely reflected in Edgeworth's later remark that:

> "Mécanique sociale" may one day take her place along with "Mécanique céleste", throned each upon the double-sided height of one maximum principle, the supreme pinnacle of moral as of physical science ... the movements of each soul, whether selfishly isolated or linked sympa-thetically, may continually be realising the maximum energy of pleasure, the Divine love of the universe. (1881: 12)

Of course, Jevons was more prosaic than Edgeworth, but Jevons's excitement is clear in letters to his sister and brother. Writing to his sister, he suggested that, "in treating of Man or Society there must also be general principles and laws which underlie all the present discussions & partial arguments . . . each individual must be a creature of cause and effect": see Black (1977: 361). His letter to his brother stated that he had, "fortu-nately struck out what I have no doubt is the true theory of economy, so thorough-going and consistent, that I cannot now read other books on the subject without indignation": see Black (1977: 410). There had, of course, been earlier attempts to introduce a utility analysis into economics: Jevons was not only successful where others had failed, but he saw clearly its far-reaching implications. He later took great pains to unearth earlier pre-cursors, particularly of the use of mathematics in economics. His interest in the history of the subject led to his rediscovery of the work of Cantillon.

Jevons's exchange model can be described briefly as follows, using a mixture of his own and modern notation. Persons A and B hold endowments, a and b respectively, of goods X and Y. Where x and y are the amounts exchanged, utility after trade takes place can therefore be written as $U_A = U_A(a - x, y)$ for trader A, while for B it is $U_B = U_B(x, b - y)$. Jevons actually used additive utility functions. The "keystone" of the theory is the result that for utility maximization, "*the ratio of exchange of any two commodities will be the reciprocal of the ratio of the final degrees of utility of the quantities of commodity avail-able for consumption after the exchange is complete*" (Jevons 1871, in 1957: 95, original emphasis). This gives rise to his famous "equations of exchange", which can be expressed as:

$$-\frac{\partial U_A/\partial x}{\partial U_A/\partial y} = \frac{dy}{dx} = -\frac{\partial U_B/\partial x}{\partial U_B/\partial y} \qquad (1)$$

The term $\frac{dy}{dx}$ is the ratio of exchange of the two commodities at the margin. Jevons recog-nized that the integration of these differential equations presents formidable difficulties, and for this reason he restricted his attention to price-taking equilibria, using his "law of indifference" whereby there are no trades at disequilibrium ratios of exchange and "the last increments in an act of exchange must be exchanged in the same ratio as the whole quantities exchanged" (1957: 94). This means that $\frac{y}{x}$ can be substituted for $\frac{dy}{dx}$ in (1), giving two simultaneous equations in x and y. The price-taking equilibrium amounts traded are given by the solution to these two equations. With prices introduced, the equation for each person is easily arranged into the familiar "equi-marginal principle" (marginal utility per unit of money is the same for both goods), and of course (following Edgeworth) the tangency solution regarding indifference curves and the budget constraint. But Jevons was more interested in exchange rather than individual optimization.

Jevons recognized that $\frac{y}{x}$ is equivalent to the ratio of prices of the two goods, $p = \frac{p_x}{p_y} = \frac{y}{x}$, but he preferred to leave p out of the equations until the equilibrium values of x and y are obtained. Recognizing that in general the equations in (1) would be nonlinear, he did not take their formal analysis further, although he added the important but rather cryptic comment that the theory is "perfectly consistent with the laws of supply and demand; and if we had the functions of utility determined, it would be possible throw them into a form clearly expressing the equivalence of supply and demand" (1957: 101).

Jevons was subsequently criticized for describing his parties to the exchange as "trading bodies", which appeared to consist of more than one trader on each side of the market. This seems to have been Jevons's rather clumsy solution to a problem raised in correspondence with Fleeming Jenkin, who raised the question of indeterminacy with just two traders who were not price takers. This was before completion of the *Theory of Political Economy* and arose from the publication of the Jenkin's paper on trade unions in 1868. Jenkin sent the paper to Jevons, who in reply sent a copy of his own paper which he read to the British Association in 1862. The highly revealing letters from Jenkin (in Black 1977: 166–78) devote a great deal of attention to the case of exchange between two persons. The basic difference between them was that Jevons, as explained above, explicitly assumed price-taking behaviour, whereas Jenkin examined barter. He could not see why two isolated individuals should accept the price-taking equilibrium, writing:

> There is no motive operating on their minds to induce them to agree on this rate [of exchange]. Jones would like more cotton for his silk, Brown would like more silk for his cotton and I do not see how any considerations as to the rate at which their desires fluctuate with the quantity can determine their desire for any one quantity. This must it seems to me be determined by wholly different considerations. You appear to me to assume that the ratio of exchange would be that fixed by the intersection of the curves . . . but in order that this should be true it would be necessary that the aggregate utilities to each party should increase up to that point which is not true. (Black 1977: 177)

As Edgeworth later made clear, in the desire to focus on price-taking behaviour for which there is a determinate solution (or solutions) to his equations of exchange, Jevons was really considering the behaviour of two typical individuals in a large market: see Edgeworth (1881: 109) who also referred to individuals "clothed with the properties of a market". The tension arising from his model of two traders and this need for price-taking clearly led Jevons to his unfortunate term "trading body". Around 1879 Edgeworth came into contact with Jevons, a near neighbour in Hampstead, through a mutual friend, James Sully, and their membership of the Savile Club. This led to Edgeworth's rapid shift of attention from moral philosophy towards economics, marked by his *Mathematical Psychics* published in 1881. Edgeworth's concern was precisely the role of the number of traders, and he showed that with a sufficient number of competitors the range of indeterminacy in exchange, in a barter context, shrinks to the price-taking equilibria.

Jevons clearly realized that in his model, partial equilibrium demand and supply curves are not appropriate: the diagrammatic treatment had to wait for Edgeworth's eponymous box diagram. Nevertheless Jevons discussed the precise form of the famous King–Davenant law of demand, suggesting a functional form whose parameters he "estimated", comparing his "fitted" values with the original "data". Jevons did not realize that the "law" followed a cubic equation. See Creedy (1986) for details.

However, his further discussion of complex cases showed his confident handling of a range of subtleties. He examined situations where one dealer has very large initial stocks compared with the other trader, the extension to three traders dealing in three goods, and the case of two individuals holding stocks of one good while a third person holds stocks of the second good: these cases are examined in detail in Creedy (1992). In a section on "Failure of the Laws of Exchange", Jevons discussed cases in which some indeterminacy would result. His most notable example was of house sales, where it was suggested that indeterminacy would result from the discrete nature of the good being exchanged. Jevons then proceeded to apply his utility analysis to other contexts. In particular he provided a treatment of labour supply, producing an elegant diagram. By extending his analysis to capital, and emphasizing the two dimensions of quantity and the time period of production, Jevons was adopted by the later "Austrian School" of economists.

These "equations of exchange" illustrate both a point of similarity and difference between Jevons and Walras (1874 [1954]), who later (with help from Paul Piccard) produced the same two simultaneous equations and, importantly, also concentrated on price-taking solutions. Despite Walras's famous *tâtonnement* process, in the formal models it is hard to escape the fact that, just as in Jevons's approach, individuals are price takers and, in the equilibria considered, all exchange takes place at the corresponding prices. As explained above, Jevons left the equations expressed in terms of quantities exchanged, leaving the equilibrium price ratio to be determined by the resulting ratio of quantities. Recognizing their non-linear nature, Jevons knew that explicit solutions could not generally be obtained. Before adding a utility analysis, Walras had extended Cournot's model of trade between two regions to produce a non-utility analysis of the exchange of two goods between two traders. He produced his general equilibrium curves in which the quantity demanded or supplied is expressed as a function of the relative price, and he had explored the form these curves might take. Hence, when faced with the equations of exchange, he realized that instead of trying to solve them in terms of quantities of the two goods, the concept of reciprocal supply and demand allowed him to replace one of the quantities with the product of a relative price and the other quantity, since $\frac{y}{x} = \frac{p_x}{p_y}$. Walras therefore showed how general equilibrium demand and supply functions can be derived from utility functions (though he gave no explicit examples, Laundhart being the first). However, these are not partial equilibrium demand functions: for further details see Creedy (1999).

The journals and correspondence of Jevons, collected in the multi-volume edition by R.D.C. Black, clearly reveal his personal characteristics and particularly his introspective nature. His own summary, made at the young age of 22 while he was in Australia and embarking on an astonishingly fertile period of self-education and discovery, provides a fitting description of the man, and is worth quoting in full:

I am not so much a storehouse of goods as I am a machine for making those goods. Give me a few facts or materials, and I can work them up into a smoothly arranged and finished fabric of theory, or can turn them out in a shape which is something new. My mind is of the most regular structure, and I have such a strong disposition to classify things as is sometimes almost painful. I also think that if in anything I have a chance of acquiring the power, it is that I have some originality, and can strike out new things. This consists not so much in quickness of forming new thoughts or opinions, but in seizing upon one or two of them and developing them into something symmetrical. It is like a kaleidoscope; just put a bent pin in, or any little bit of rubbish, and a perfectly new and symmetrical pattern will be produced. (Quoted by Keynes 1936, p. 546)

JOHN CREEDY

See also:

British marginalism (II); Capital theory (III); Competition (III); Formalization and mathematical modelling (III); German and Austrian schools (II); Hermann Heinrich Gossen (I); Income distribution (III); Alfred Marshall (I); Carl Menger (I); Marie-Esprit-Léon Walras (I).

References and further reading

Black, R.D.C. (1977), *Papers and Correspondence of William Stanley Jevons*, vol. 2. London: Macmillan.
Black, R.D.C. (1981), *Papers and Correspondence of William Stanley Jevons*, vol. 7. London: Macmillan.
Creedy, J. (1986), 'On the King–Davenant law of demand'. *Scottish Journal of Political Economy*, **33** (3), 193–212.
Creedy, J. (1992), 'Jevons's complex cases in the theory of exchange', *Journal of the History of Economic Thought*, **14** (Spring), 55–69.
Creedy, J. (1999), 'The rise and fall of Walras's demand and supply curves'. *Manchester School*, **67** (2), 192–202.
Edgeworth, F.Y. (1881), *Mathematical Psychics*. London: Kegan Paul.
Hearn, W.E. (1864), *Plutology: Or the Theory of Efforts to Satisfy Human Wants*. London: Macmillan.
Hicks, J.R. (1984), *The Economics of John Hicks*, D. Helm (ed.), Oxford: Basil Blackwell.
Jevons, W.S. (1863), *A Serious Fall in the Value of Gold*, London: Edward Stanford.
Jevons, W.S. (1865), *The Coal Question*, London: Macmillan.
Jevons, W.S. (1870), *Elementary Lessons in Logic*, London: Macmillan.
Jevons, W.S. (1874), *Principles of Science*, London: Macmillan.
Jevons, W.S. (1875), *Money and the Mechanism of Exchange*, London: D. Appleton and Co.
Jevons, W.S. (1878), *A Primer on Political Economy*, London: Macmillan.
Jevons, W.S. (1882), *The State in Relation to Labour*, London: Macmillan.
Jevons, W.S. (1883), *Methods of Social Reform and Other Papers*, London: Macmillan.
Jevons, W.S. (1884), *Investigations in Currency and Finance*, ed. H.S. Foxwell, London: Macmillan.
Jevons, W.S. (1957), *The Theory of Political Economy*, 5th edn, ed. H.S. Jevons, New York: Augustus Kelly.
Keynes, J.M. (1936), 'William Stanley Jevons (1835–1882): a centenary allocation on his life and work as economist and statistician', *Journal of the Royal Statistical Society*, **99**, pt III, 516–55.
Schumpeter, J.A. (1954), *History of Economic Analysis*, London: Allen and Unwin.
Walras, L. (1874), *Elements of Pure Economics*, trans. 1954 W. Jaffé, London: Allen and Unwin.

Adolph Heinrich Gotthilf Wagner (1835–1917)

Adolph Heinrich Gotthilf Wagner was born on 25 March 1835 in Erlangen (near Nuremberg) and died on 8 November 1917 in Berlin. Rudolf Wagner, his father, was a physiologist and university professor. Adolph Wagner finished his study of economics at the University of Heidelberg in 1857. His academic career included positions at the Handelshochschulen (Merchants Superior Schools) in Vienna and Hamburg, chairs at the universities of Dorpat (Livonia), Freiburg in Breisgau and, finally, the prestigious Humboldt University in Berlin, where he held the chair of *Staatswissenschaften* (sciences of the state) from 1870 until 1916; he was succeeded by Werner Sombart.

In terms of directly traceable influence on subsequent developments in public economics, Adolph Wagner is probably the most influential member of the triad of German *Finanzwissenschaft* (public finance) in its Golden Age (a phrase coined by Richard Musgrave), comprising also Lorenz von Stein and Albert Schäffle. Even today, he is fairly well known to students of public economics as the author of Wagner's Law, referring to the tendency of an increasing relative size and functional importance of the public sector in the development process of market societies, characterized by the secular trends that became clearly visible in the nineteenth century: industrialization, urbanization, and unprecedented economic growth. His successful academic career made him a figure with some influence not only in academia, but also in German tax and social policy. Nor was his reputation confined to the German-speaking academic world: apart from countries such as Italy, he had some influence in the US (see Wagner 1886, 1891; Senn 1997).

Wagner is in at least two respects the protagonist of a third way: he holds an "intermediate" position in the *Methodenstreit* (battle of methods) between theory-oriented and historical economists and in the confrontation of liberal individualism and collectivistic socialism. His so-called "state socialism" is basically an attempt to give individualist, socialist, and conservative principles their due, with the market and the state as functionally complementary institutions.

Wagner is a foremost protagonist of the "socialists of the chair", a group of conservative academics influential in social policy issues in Bismarck's Germany. Bismarck (whom Wagner regarded as a state socialist) implemented social insurance systems much along the lines advocated by that group. Wagner is also an early member of the Christian-Social Party founded in 1878, whose social policy orientation was combined with the kind of anti-Semitism characteristic of many Christian-social-conservative movements in continental Europe of that time. Wagner seems to have endorsed some kind of pseudo-scientific anti-Semitism, speculating about an eventual correlation of the aptness of Jews for capitalist business and their alleged lack of concern for the public interest (Wagner 1893: 818). Even though such leanings attenuated during the second half of his life, he was praised by Wilhelm Vleugels (1935) for having anticipated some of the socio-economic tenets popular among the Nazi intellectual milieus, while E.A. Clark (1940) discussed those links in a denunciatory tone.

Wagner's personal temper seems to have been somewhat belligerent, once earning him a challenge to a duel. He stressed disagreements even with scholars endorsing a by-and-large similar vision of socio-economic affairs in theory and policy. Conflicts are reported in cases where no major theoretical antagonism seems to have been at stake (for example, with von Stein in his Vienna years). Notwithstanding this, some differences with the contemporary currents were indeed substantial, notably with respect to the Historical School. He considered its weakness as it regards economic theory a real problem, not least because he felt that the Marxian current of socialism was clearly superior in that respect. Wagner (1891: 320) stressed that German writers "would wish not to be judged abroad by the narrow opinions of the younger historical school, more particularly . . . Professor Schmoller".

The following characteristic features of Wagner's approach to economics indicate his position among different currents.

Methodological stance

Wagner stresses that the methods must be adapted to the problems at hand and the different levels of scientific investigation. The different levels of study include: (1) the development of adequate concepts capturing the essential properties of economic phenomena; (2) explaining the present state and the development of those phenomena in terms of a combination of psychological motifs and structural conditions; (3) normative economic reasoning determining socially desirable developments; and (4) implementation problems regarding those desirable changes (see, for example, Wagner 1886: 124–8). Notice that the distinction of positive and normative economics is generally deemed useful for public economics, as is the recognition of the specificities of implementation. Conceptual analysis nowadays does not command as much respect, yet Wagner employs it effectively, for example, regarding collective wants/goods. Levels (1) to (4) prepare the stage for a research architecture in which economic theory, political philosophy, empirical study, and institutional details play specific roles.

Background and strategic perspectives of his thought

Wagner is influenced by a specific mix of philosophic currents in nineteenth-century Germany, including Krause, von Gierke, Ahrens, Roeder, and Ihering (see Corado and Solari 2010). Those influences led to a particular kind of natural rights perspective, which is clearly at odds with the individualist perspective of the Lockean tradition regarding private property rights. Instead, there is a foundational interdependence of private property (including the market) and the state, implying a critical stance regarding traditions in which the state is a necessary evil, justified solely as an enforcement agency for pre-political property rights. In short, there is no such thing as (modern) property rights without a state. The ideal type of the bourgeois property-owning agent with its historical and theoretical contingencies must not be mistaken for the human condition in general. Compared to a Locke-inspired framework, modern taxation thus can much more easily be reconstructed as a legitimate mechanism of distribution adequate for a modern society; socialization of natural monopolies and social insurance can be justified, even if seemingly violating principles of private property and contract freedom. More generally, the idea of a quantitative expansion of the public sector going along with a qualitative transformation is close at hand. Within modern economic development, the "prevention principle" becomes more important as a guiding principle of public agency, complementing the traditional principle of repression.

Other influences include Malthus (whose population theory he endorsed) and the classical economists. He emphasized that achievements such as Ricardo's rent theory are of lasting importance for the study of economics. His respect for more theory-oriented

German economists is obvious, notably for Karl-Heinrich Rau, whose public finance textbook was re-edited by Wagner several times, with an ever increasing amount of additional material (see Wagner 1876).

The style of his scholarly work

It can be summarized as comprehensive and synthetic, including an emphasis on the methodological and the conceptual level along with economic theorizing, a great quantity of institutional details, and a historical-empirical perspective. Not surprisingly, this kind of style led to volumes of enormous size. His specific version of the more common German critique of one-sided individualism in "British economics" deserves to be emphasized. It played a constructive role regarding choice-based approaches to the public sector. More specifically, a pluralist horizon regarding psychological motives with respect to choices within the public sector is stressed, including what in modern behavioural economics is called "social preferences".

Wagner's normative stance reflects his conservative leanings. His critique of Marxian socialism is informed by some ontology of the good life supporting the non-malleability of human nature. Informed by his Malthusian perspectives, he rejects any optimism regarding the development of the forces of production overcoming the constraints imposed by a limited generosity of nature.

Wagner's influence in public economics

His most lasting influence is his reasoning on the functions of the state including Wagner's law. His conceptualizations of collective needs and collective goods must not only be seen as a conclusive summary of pertinent German reasoning since Hermann, but also as a starting point of the development of modern public goods theory and merit wants: considering writings by Sax, Wicksell (1896), Lindahl and Cassel, Adolph Wagner is the point of reference. Moreover, he foreshadowed Musgrave's tripartite division of the subject, stressing allocation and distribution as separate branches of public sector economy: Wagner distinguished between "social-welfare" purposes of taxation and its functional role as revenue for financing government expenditures.

RUDOLF DUJMOVITS AND RICHARD STURN

See also:

German and Austrian schools (II); Public economics (III).

References and further reading

Clark, E.A. (1940), 'Adolf Wagner: from national economist to National Socialist', *Political Science Quarterly*, **55** (3), 378–411.
Corado, D. and S. Solari (2010), 'Natural law as inspiration to Adolph Wagner's theory of public intervention', *European Journal of the History of Economic Thought*, **17** (4), 865–79.
Senn, P.R. (1997), 'Problems of determining the influence of Gustav Schmoller and Adolph Wagner on American fiscal policy and taxation systems', in J.G. Backhaus (ed.), *Essays on Social Security and Taxation: Gustav von Schmoller and Adolph Wagner reconsidered*, Marburg: Metropolis-Verlag, pp. 35–141.
Vleugels, W. (1935), 'Adolph Wagner, Gedenkworte zur 100ten Wiederkehr seines Geburtstages', *Schmollers Jahrbuch für Gesetzgebung, Verwaltung und Volkswirtschaft*, new series, **59** (2), 1–13.
Wagner, A. (1876), *Allgemeine oder theoretische Volkswirthschaftslehre. Erster Theil. Grundlegung*, Mit Benutzung von Rau's Grundsätzen der Volkswirtschaftslehre, K.H. Rau (ed.), completely reworked by A. Wagner and E. Nasse, *Lehrbuch der politischen Oekonomie*, 1. Band, Leipzig and Heidelberg: C.F. Winter'sche Verlagshandlung.

Wagner, A. (1886), 'Wagner on the present state of political economy', *Quarterly Journal of Economics*, **1** (1), 113–33.

Wagner, A. (1891), 'Marshall's principles of economics', *Quarterly Journal of Economics*, 5 (3), 319–38.

Wagner, A. (1893), *Grundlegung der politischen Oekonomie. Erster Theil. Grundlagen der Volkswirthschaft. 2. Halbband. Buch 4 – 6*, substantially reworked and enlarged 3rd edn, A. Wagner et al. (eds), *Lehr- und Handbuch der politischen Oekonomie*, 1. Hauptabtheilung, Leipzig and Heidelberg: C.F. Winter'sche Verlagshandlung.

Wicksell, K. (1896), *Finanztheoretische Untersuchungen*, Jena: G. Fischer.

Gustav Friedrich von Schmoller (1838–1917)

Gustav Friedrich von Schmoller was the leading economist of Imperial Germany at the turn of the twentieth century. He was the most important representative of the Younger Historical School, also called the "historical-ethical school", which dominated German economics until the outbreak of World War I. As one of the founders and long-time chairman of the Verein für Socialpolitik, the most important association of economists in Germany until today, he had a strong influence on social and economic politics in Imperial Germany. Because of his aim to improve the situation of the working class by means of moderate social reforms and education, he and other members of the Verein, such as Lujo Brentano and Adolph Wagner, were often ridiculed as "socialists of the chair" (Oppenheim 1872). His political ideas even influenced Bismarck's social legislation, and today he is considered as one of the pioneers of the German welfare state. Schmoller also had a strong influence on the Prussian education politics and used his relations to Friedrich Althoff (1839–1908), who was in charge of the Prussian university system at the Ministry of Education in Berlin, to control the appointment of important academic positions in Prussia.

Many German economists after World War I, who tried to catch up with the international theoretical development in economics and favoured an economic science free of value-judgments, considered the Younger Historical School an aberration, which cut the ties to classical economics and delayed progress in German economics for half a century. Historicism was considered as "anti-theoretical", Schmoller as a "dead dog" (Kempski 1964: 200), and his major work, the *Grundriß der allgemeinen Volkswirtschaftslehre*, as an "unassailable mountain" (Salin 1967: 140). In his article in *Schmollers Jahrbuch*, Joseph Schumpeter was giving a more differentiated recognition of Schmoller's merits compared with most of his contemporaries (Schumpeter 1926). However, Schumpeter later complained in the *History of Economic Analysis* that in Germany "economic theory as understood in England was in many places almost completely in abeyance for several decades" (Schumpeter 1954: 804). In the past two decades, the general dissatisfaction with mainstream formal theorizing and neoliberal economic policy has led to a growing interest in Schmoller's historical, institutional, interdisciplinary, and ethical approach, and to a less prejudiced reception of his writings (Peukert 2001).

Biography

Schmoller was born in 1838 in Heilbronn as the son of a Württemberg civil servant. His father, Ludwig Friedrich David Schmoller, was an administrator of the district treasury. In the business office of his father, the young Schmoller learned about the financial and administrative practices of the small kingdom and was exposed to the business world. The economic flourishing of his hometown, Heilbronn, served Schmoller as a lively illustration for his future economic studies. After his mother's passing in 1846, the young Schmoller spent his summer vacations in Calw, an industrial town close to Heilbronn, in the household of his grandfather and his great-grandfather, Carl Friedrich Gärtner and Joseph Gärtner. Both were famous natural scientists and biologists and belonged to a rich and well-known trading family. Their household was an intellectual centre of the city. His grandfather studied the reproduction of plants, had correspondence with

Charles Darwin, and was honoured by the Dutch Academy of Science (Hansen 2012: 396–7). He set an example for Schmoller in conducting sound scientific research, not driven by personal gain or position (Schmoller 1918).

After Schmoller finished his school, he worked for a short time in the office of his father before enrolling at the University of Tübingen in 1857. He studied *Staatswissenschaften*, a discipline derived from cameral science combining economics, administrative science, history, statistics, and public finance in order to train future civil servants how to administrate the state. In order to gain a broader perspective, Schmoller also attended classes in natural science and philosophy. The economists of the university, Carl von Schütz and J.A.R. Helferich, did not leave a lasting impression on Schmoller. The practical and empirical knowledge Schmoller had accumulated in his father's office allowed him to skip many classes (Schmoller 1918). After he finished his dissertation on the economic opinions prevailing during the reformation period, for which he was also awarded a prize, Schmoller worked for a short period as a civil servant in the statistical department of the Württemberg civil service. His brother-in-law, Gustav Rümelin, with whom he shared the admiration of the Prussian state, directed the department. Here, Schmoller was assigned the task of evaluating the Württemberg state's industrial craft census of 1861, published in 1862 in the *Württembergische Jahrbücher*. In 1862, Schmoller also anonymously published a work about the Prussian–French trade treaty of 1861. The treaty of 1861 had prevented the inclusion of Austria into the German tariff union; and Württemberg as one of the states in the south of Germany had been on the side of Austria. Because of his pro-Prussian views in the article, Schmoller had to quit his career as a civil servant in Württemberg.

Schmoller's analysis and evaluation of the Württemberg state's industrial craft census and the support of the Prussian trade minister Rudolf Delbrück gave Schmoller the opportunity to become a Professor of Economics in Halle. During his time in Halle, he wrote his famous article entitled "Die Arbeiterfrage" ("Problems of the labour force") published in the *Preußische Jahrbücher* in 1864 and 1865. In this article, he outlined the social problems caused by technical progress and the transition to an industrial society, which included the replacement of handicraft by machines and factories, the flight of the population from the rural regions to the cities, high unemployment, and missing accommodations for workers. In Halle, he married Lucie Rathgen, the daughter of a government official from Weimar, and became a city counsellor in 1864. In this position, he gained more practical experience in the administrative routines and economic policies of the city.

Schmoller was very critical towards the doctrine of laissez-faire. He conceded that Adam Smith and the classical economists had identified the positive effects of free markets on economic development. However, in his monograph about the evolution of the German small-scale industry and crafts in the nineteenth century (1870), he critically reassessed the hopes in the effects of liberal trade reforms in Prussia. The empirical material, including field inquiries and statistical data, highlights the downside of the economic transformation processes: increasing inequality in the distribution of wealth and displacement of small crafts by the factory system. Like other members of the Historical School, such as Lujo Brentano, Schmoller did not consider the laissez-faire capitalism of the Manchester liberals as an adequate cure for the pressing social problems. He was sceptical whether social harmony was the outcome of unrestrained self-interest and warned that without legal restrictions and moral norms, the economic freedoms could change into pure egoism, fraud, and gambling. In a public lecture in 1874 in Berlin with Kaiser Wilhelm, the German emperor, in the audience, Schmoller went so far as to contend that one cannot make millions in contemporary Germany without one's sleeves touching the walls of a jail (Stieda 1921: 223). At the same time, Schmoller feared the growing Marxist threat and a socialist revolution. He shared with other like-minded academics the conviction that the so-called "social question" could neither be solved by the "natural laws" of the economy alone nor by the abolishment of private ownership of the means of production. Instead, he was advocating moderate social reforms by the state and a humanistic education policy to improve the well-being of the working classes, and to prevent a revolution.

Schmoller wanted to preserve the prevailing social order in Germany, with private ownership of capital, with parliamentary democracy, and with the emperor as the head of the German nation. He felt that the Prussian state had the obligation to mediate between the working class and the other classes, and to integrate the working class into the institutions of the monarchy. The enlightened and socially conscious sovereign (*soziales Königtum*) was assigned the role to ensure the establishment of a unified economic territory and to improve the living standards of the working class by social legislation (1874). Schmoller expected scholars and civil servants to take a neutral position between the conflicting classes and egoistic interests and to serve the common good. He also wanted to complement economic and social policy with the idea of justice, which is based on conventional norms and values (see Schmoller 1893–94). In Schmoller's view, income distribution was not only the outcome of market laws, but also a result of legal norms such as property rights, inheritance, and contract law.

Together with other German economists such as Adolph Wagner, Lujo Brentano, Wilhelm Roscher, Johannes Conrad, Ernst Engel, Georg Friedrich Knapp and Julius Eckhardt, Schmoller founded the Verein für Socialpolitik in 1872 in order to discuss the pressing social and economic problems and to propose legislative measures within the institutions of the constitutional monarchy. The preliminary talks were held in his house in Halle. This new association was intended to pursue two goals: to allow academic debates on socio-economic issues and to find political agreement. It was open to academics, businessmen, journalists and politicians. In the opening speech at the inauguration of the first meeting of the Verein, Schmoller emphasized its practical orientation and the aim to influence public opinion. During the first meeting of the new association in Eisenach in 1872, the members prepared resolutions demanding factory legislation, a reform of stock corporations, and restrictions of working hours for women and children.

In 1872, shortly after the foundation of the Verein, Schmoller joined to the University of Strasbourg. After the Franco-Prussian war of 1870–71 and the foundation of the German nation, large parts of the provinces Alsace und Lorraine were re-annexed to Germany, and the University of Strasbourg became a German university. During his time in Strasbourg, he wrote his work about the clothing and weaver guilds of Strasbourg (1879), in which he discussed the modernization and liberalization of crafts and industry. In 1874–75 he had a bitter controversy on the notion of social reform with the historian Heinrich von Treitschke, who considered him a "Gönner des Sozialismus" ("patron of socialism"). In 1881, Schmoller became the editor-in-chief of the *Jahrbuch für Gesetzgebung, Verwaltung und Volkswirtschaft im Deutschen Reich*, which later came to be known as *Schmollers Jahrbuch*.

In 1882, Schmoller was appointed to a chair at the University of Berlin where he stayed until 1913. In his major work, the *Grundriß der allgemeinen Volkswirtschaftslehre*, published in two volumes in 1900 and 1904 (Schmoller [1978]), he described technical and economic development in conjunction with other social, cultural and moral factors. Like the members of the older Historical School, such as Hildebrand and Bücher, he developed a theory of the stages of economic development; he distinguished them in terms of economic constitution and various other economic and cultural features.

In Berlin, Schmoller was granted many positions and honours: he had a seat in the Prussian state council (1884), became a member of the Prussian Academy of Sciences (1887), and represented the Berlin University in the Prussian Upper House (1899). He also became editor of the *Acta Borussica*, a large-scale collection of sources and reports on the history of Prussia. Finally, he was ennobled in 1908. Schmoller died in 1917 at the age of 79 while on vacation in Bad Harzburg, Germany.

Schmoller and the Methodological Debates of His Time

In the second half of the nineteenth century, economics was not yet established as a discipline in Germany and was only gradually gaining an independent profile alongside other already well-established disciplines such as philosophy, jurisprudence and history. The suitable methods and topics of economics still had to be identified and assigned in the course of the differentiation and specialization of the various academic disciplines. In the philosophy of science, Wilhelm Dilthey (1833–1911) and the New Kantians, Wilhelm Windelband (1848–1915) and Heinrich Rickert (1863–1936), were searching for an appropriate method for the humanities and distinguished between nomothetic and ideographic approaches.

Against this background, the question arose whether economics should be considered as part of the arts and humanities or as part of the natural sciences. The Historical School was influenced by the concept of historicism, which interpreted all human institutions, activities and events in a relativist manner as the result of unique historic constellations and not as fixed unchanging laws. Methodologically, historicism demanded a primarily hermeneutic and descriptive method, which aims at a better comprehension of the individual characteristics of human phenomena. As a consequence, Schmoller and the Historical School understood their approach as a part of the humanities (Schmoller 1887: 593; see also Häuser 1988). However, in the 1870s, the "marginal revolution" took place, which aimed to have general economic laws based on assumptions about the economic behaviour of individuals.

Immediately after Schmoller had joined the University in Berlin, he got involved in a methodological controversy with the Viennese economist Carl Menger (1840–1921), the Austrian marginal theory theorist and founder of the Austrian School of Economics. The so-called *Methodenstreit* (battle of methods) of the 1880s was essentially a dispute over an appropriate methodology for the understanding of economic phenomena, a dispute between advocates of the inductive and deductive method. The *Methodenstreit* started in 1883 with a review article by Schmoller of a methodological work written by Menger in the same year. In this work, Menger asserted the necessity of applying abstract logical reasoning to political economy and emphasized that empirical observations already require theories and concepts. In his review article, Schmoller defended the historical method and stressed the importance of collecting historical and empirical knowledge. He was sceptical whether abstract economic laws were applicable to all periods and circumstances. He criticized Menger and the Austrian marginal utility school for premature generalization and for reducing human economic motives to individual utility maximization. Menger reacted in 1884 with his polemical pamphlet *Die Irrthümer des Historismus* (*The Errors of Historicism*). Schmoller refrained from answering this second attack and left the task to some of his younger followers. Schumpeter perceived the two decades of quarrel about methodology essentially as a "history of wasted energies" (1954: 782).

The views of Schmoller and Menger were actually not as far apart as was generally assumed. The old verdict that Schmoller was completely hostile to theory is certainly not true. Schmoller did not consider himself purely as a historian. He also wanted to make general statements about reality and to discover economic laws. The dispute between Menger and Schmoller was not about whether economics should be theoretical, but about the proper methodology to arrive at theoretical statements. Schmoller put more emphasis on the inductive method and aimed to be in a position to make general statements by means of wide-reaching empirical-historic studies. He always insisted that economic theories should rest on an empirical base, and he criticized the method of abstract modelling for relying on empirically questionable axioms. However, he was not totally opposed to abstract modelling and theoretical deduction. Schmoller was searching for reconciliation between deduction and induction. Although he put more emphasis on induction, he considered both approaches as necessary and complementary to each other "as the left and the right foot are both necessary for walking" (Schmoller 1893 [1949]: 61).

Schmoller did not manage to build an economic theory upon his empirical-historical analysis. However, his conception of economics differs from neoclassical economics in that he tried to reconcile economic theory with the vast empirical and historical material (Schefold 1989). He aimed for a more interdisciplinary approach that also takes into account psychological, sociological and philosophical aspects. His account of historical development analyses the interplay between the technical-economical and the cultural-moral factors. In the *Grundriß der allgemeinen Volkswirtschaftslehre*, he discusses, for example, different economic virtues and shows that economic behaviours, such as profit and money making, only stimulate economic development if they are embedded in legal and moral norms.

The second major dispute Schmoller was involved in was the *Werturteilsstreit* (value judgment dispute), which was a dispute within the Historical School – between Schmoller and his successors Max Weber (1864–1920) and Werner Sombart (1863–1941). It was largely a controversy on whether political economy should be understood as an ethical discipline, entitled to hold normative views in research as well as in economic policy. In line with economic thinkers in ancient philosophy and medieval scholasticism, Schmoller and the other members of the historical-ethical school were aiming for a holistic economic thinking that does not only describe economic phenomena but also delivers value judgements about the desirability of economic circumstances and actions in order to give meaningful and concrete policy recommendations. As described by their contemporaries, Schmoller, as well as Lujo Brentano and Adolph Wagner, fulfilled the "ideal of the professor who preaches reform and denounces obstructing interests" (Schumpeter 1954: 770). Robert Wilbrandt portrays Schmoller, his former PhD adviser, as a statesman, who not only tried to demonstrate empirically his practical statements, but also knew how to appeal and personally convince others (Wilbrandt 1926: 87).

The *Werturteilsstreit* began at the Vienna conference of the Verein für Socialpolitik in 1909. In Vienna, Schmoller and his followers strove to define a measure of economic productivity and welfare, which was supposed to describe not only material well-being but also social and cultural progress, such as better life quality for the working classes. This debate on a normatively better justified measure of economic welfare gave Max Weber (1864–1920) and Werner Sombart (1863–1941) the opportunity to criticize the mixture of descriptive and normative semantics (Glaeser 2014). Weber and Sombart insisted that the normative validity of value judgements cannot logically be derived from descriptive statements about reality. In consequence, economists should restrict themselves to an economic science free of value judgements. Weber and Sombart's critique questioned the two-fold character of the Verein as a scientific and at the same time politically oriented organization. After the Vienna conference, many other economists, such as Heinrich Herkner, Gustav Cohn, Lujo Brentano, Julius Wolf, Ludwig Pohle, and others, published statements on the question of value neutrality and the debate finally culminated in a non-public session in the committee of the Verein in Berlin.

In this dispute, Schmoller was not as one-sided as he is usually described in the history of economic thought. Schmoller defended the two-fold character of the Verein and considered moral and legal questions as an integral part of political economy. However, Schmoller always emphasized that there are competing value judgements, which vary with regional origin and class. He warned students not to frivolously take sides in a particular interest. Furthermore, he recommended Prussian civil servants and scholars should keep the necessary distance from the politics of the day and carefully balance between the different standpoints to find positions acceptable for all parties. In his article "Die Volkswirtschaft, die Volkswirtschaftslehre und ihre Methode", published in 1893 long before the actual outbreak of the value judgement dispute, Schmoller was already looking for a methodological foundation for the political and ethical orientation of the Historical School. In it he pointed to the ethical systems since ancient times, which combined empiricism with teleology to understand the meaning and direction of human development (Schmoller 1893 [1949]: 22–6). Schmoller believed in ethical progress, and in the last chapters of the *Grundriß* he gives an illustrative account of the historical refinement of norms and values. However, Schmoller remained sceptical. He did not claim that his "evolutionary ethics" could be deducted logically from history. As a consequence, Schmoller recommended economists should – for the time being – abstain from personal value judgments (ibid.: 29). It is surprising that despite this moderate stand, Schmoller was the main target of Weber's and Sombart's attacks in the value judgement dispute.

Schmoller did not achieve his goal to combine the extensive empirical, historical and statistical material consistently and to build a general economic theory. After the war and the death of Schmoller in 1917, a deep-set cultural crisis emerged (see Häuser 1994; Janssen 2012). With the end of the German monarchy new social problems arose, and the political institutions as well as the norms and values of the Wilhelminian time lost their relevance and legitimacy. The experience of World War I and the abasement of

Germany in the Treaty of Versailles dispelled the belief in ethical progress in Germany. Schmoller's major work, the *Grundriß*, was not reprinted after 1923, but the heritage of the Historical School lived on in the works of some younger German economists, such as Max Weber, Werner Sombart, Heinrich Herkner, Edgar Salin, and Arthur Spiethoff (Hennis 1987; Häuser 1994; Schefold 1994). Even though Weber and Sombart, whom Schumpeter called the "youngest historical school", rejected the belief in historical progress, they did not abandon the task to analyse the transformation of economic forms and understand the logic of economic development in relation to cultural factors.

JOHANNES GLAESER

See also:

German and Austrian schools (II); Economics and philosophy (III); Bruno Hildebrand (I); Historical economics (II); Institutional economics (III); Institutionalism (II); Carl Menger (I); Wilhelm Georg Friedrich Roscher (I); Joseph Alois Schumpeter (I); Adolph Heinrich Gotthilf Wagner (I); Max Weber (I).

References and further reading

Glaeser, J. (2014), *Der Werturteilsstreit in der deutschen Nationalökonomie. Max Weber, Werner Sombart und die Ideale der Sozialpolitik*, Marburg: Metropolis.
Hansen, R. (2012), 'Gustav Schmoller as a scientist of political economy', in J.G. Backhaus (ed.), *Handbook of the History of Economic Thought*, Heidelberg: Springer, pp. 389–413.
Häuser, K. (1988), 'Historical School and "Methodenstreit"', *Journal of Institutional and Theoretical Economics*, **144** (3), 532–42.
Häuser, K. (1994), 'Das Ende der historischen Schule und die Ambiguität der deutschen Nationalökonomie in den Zwanziger Jahren', in K.W. Nörr, B. Schefold, and F. Tenbruck (eds), *Geisteswissenschaften zwischen Kaiserreich und Republik*, Stuttgart: Franz Steiner, pp. 47–74.
Hennis, W. (1987), *Max Webers Fragestellung*, Tübingen: Mohr Siebeck.
Janssen, H. (2012), *Nationalökonomie und Nationalsozialismus. Die deutsche Volkswirtschaftslehre in den dreißiger Jahren des 20. Jahrhunderts*, 4th edn, Marburg: Metropolis.
Kempski, J. (1964), 'Stein, Schmoller, Weber und die Einheit der Sozialwissenschaften', in N. Kloten, W. Krelle, H. Müller and F. Neumark (eds), *Systeme und Methoden in den Wirtschafts- und Sozialwissenschaften*, Tübingen: J.C.B. Mohr, pp. 191–206.
Oppenheim, H.B. (1872), *Der Katheder-Sozialismus*, Berlin: Oppenheim.
Peukert, H. (2001), 'The Schmoller renaissance', *History of Political Economy*, **33** (1), 71–116.
Salin, E. (1967), *Politische Ökonomie. Geschichte der wirtschaftspolitischen Ideen von Platon bis zur Gegenwart*, Tübingen: J.C.B. Mohr.
Schefold, B. (1989), 'Schmoller als Theoretiker', in H.C. Reckenwald (ed.), *Gustav von Schmoller (Vademecum)*, Düsseldorf: Verlag Wirtschaft und Finanzen, pp. 77–103.
Schefold, B. (1994), 'Nationalökonomie und Kulturwissenschaften: Das Konzept des Wirtschaftsstils', in K.W. Nörr, B. Schefold, and F. Tenbruck (eds), *Geisteswissenschaften zwischen Kaiserreich und Republik*, Stuttgart: Franz Steiner, pp. 215–42.
Schmoller, G. (1862), *Der französische Handelsvertrag und seine Gegner. Ein Wort der Verständigung von einem Süddeutschen*, Frankfurt am Main: J.D. Sauerländer's Verlag.
Schmoller, G. (1864–65), 'Die Arbeiterfrage', *Preußische Jahrbücher*, **14**, 393–424, 523–47, and **15**, 32–63.
Schmoller, G. (1870), *Zur Geschichte der deutschen Kleingewerbe im 19. Jahrhundert*, Halle: Verlag der Buchhandlung des Waisenhauses.
Schmoller, G. (1874), 'Die soziale Frage und der preußische Staat", *Preußische Jahrbücher*, **33**, 323–42.
Schmoller, G. (1879), *Die Strassburger Tucher- und Weberzunft. Urkunden und Darstellung*, Strasbourg: Verlag von Karl J. Trüber.
Schmoller, G. (1887), 'Nachschrift zu Wilhelm Hasbach, Ueber eine andere Gestaltung des Studiums der Wirthschaftswissenschaften', *Jahrbuch für Gesetzgebung, Verwaltung und Volkswirtschaft im Deutschen Reich*, **11**, 587–94.
Schmoller, G. (1893), 'Volkswirtschaft, Volkswirtschaftslehre und –methode', in *Handwörterbuch der Staatswissenschaften*, vol. 6, pp. 527–63, reprinted in A. Skalweit (ed.) (1949), *Die Volkswirtschaft, die Volkswirtschaftslehre und ihre Methode*, Frankfurt am Main: Klostermann.
Schmoller, G. (1893–94), 'The idea of justice in political economy', *Annals of the American Academy of Political and Social Science*, **4**, 697–737.

Schmoller, G. (1900–1904), *Grundriß der allgemeinen Volkswirtschaftslehre*, 2 vols, Berlin: Duncker and Humblot, reprinted 1978.

Schmoller, G. (1911), 'Volkswirtschaft, Volkswirtschaftslehre und -methode', in *Handwörterbuch der Staatswissenschaften*, vol. 8, 3rd edn, Jena: Fischer, pp. 426–501.

Schmoller, G. (1918), 'Meine Heilbronner Jugendjahre', in *Von schwäbischer Scholle. Kalender für schwäbische Literatur und Kunst*, Heilbronn: Eugen Salzer, pp. 53–61.

Schumpeter, J.A. (1926), 'Gustav Schmoller und die Probleme von heute', *Schmollers Jahrbuch*, **50**, 337–88.

Schumpeter, J.A. (1954), *History of Economic Analysis*, New York: Oxford University Press.

Stieda, W. (1921), 'Zur Erinnerung an Gustav Schmoller und seine Strassburger Zeit', *Schmollers Jahrbuch*, **45**, 219–57.

Wilbrandt, R. (1926), 'Das Ende der historisch-ethischen Schule', *Weltwirtschaftliches Archiv*, **24**, 73–108, 228–74.

Henry Sidgwick (1838–1900)

The modern reputation of Henry Sidgwick is that of a later nineteenth-century Cambridge moral philosopher, whose 1874 *Methods of Ethics* is a landmark text in the consideration of the moral foundations of human action: whether there were any general principles governing how one should act. This is the view of modern philosophers, among whom Sidgwick's stock has been rising in recent years; but the scope of Sidgwick's work and influence is greater than this reputation might suggest. As Knightbridge Professor of Moral Philosophy at Cambridge from 1883 until his death in 1900, Sidgwick was chiefly responsible for the Moral Sciences Tripos, the tripos on which Alfred Marshall taught from 1885 until the establishment of his own, Independent Economics Tripos in 1902. Most of the young men that Marshall regarded as his brightest students – Sydney Chapman (1898), Alfred Flux (1889), Joseph Shield Nicholson (1876), D.H. Macgregor (1901) and of course A.C. Pigou (1900) – were products of the Moral Sciences Tripos, which was the means through which Marshall created the first generation of Cambridge economists. Sidgwick also wrote a substantial treatise on political economy, *Principles of Political Economy* (1883), which *inter alia* laid the foundations for Pigou's welfare economics and introduced the conception of externalities. Further, in 1891 he published *The Elements of Politics*, building upon Bentham and Mill. And so, in later nineteenth-century Cambridge, Sidgwick represented philosophy, politics and economics, all rolled into one.

Henry Sidgwick was born in Skipton, West Riding, on 31 May 1838, the fourth of six children of the Reverend William Sidgwick, headmaster of Skipton Grammar School. William Sidgwick, a graduate of Trinity College, Cambridge, died in 1841, after which the family moved away from Skipton, Henry being schooled privately. In 1852 Henry entered Rugby School, his mother also settling nearby in 1853, so that Henry lived at home with his family until he entered Trinity College in October 1855. Also living with them at Rugby was Edward White Benson, a cousin of William Sidgwick, a young master at Rugby, a future Archbishop of Canterbury and also, after marrying Henry's younger sister Mary in 1859, his brother-in-law. In 1876 Henry himself married Eleanor Balfour, sister of Arthur Balfour, a former pupil of Henry and one of the first students to be examined in the reformed Moral Sciences Tripos of 1876, a Conservative Member of Parliament from 1875, and Prime Minister from 1902 to 1905 of the Conservative government that broke on the issue of tariff reform. Henry Sidgwick died on 28 August 1900 of cancer, his death giving rise to numerous tributes testifying to the widespread respect he commanded.

He had entered Trinity College in 1855, graduating in 1859 with firsts in both Classics and Mathematics. In the same year he had been appointed to a college lectureship in Classics at Trinity College, but during the early 1860s he read widely in philosophy, theology and languages, entertaining the possibility of making himself eligible for one of the two chairs in Arabic at Cambridge. By the mid-1860s this strategy was abandoned and he focused his attention on the one chair for moral philosophy, the Knightbridge chair. In 1869 he exchanged his Assistant Tutorship in classics for a College Lectureship in moral philosophy, orienting himself to the Moral Sciences Tripos as reformed by John Grote. Also, since John Grote had died in 1866, Sidgwick came to represent the tripos in Cambridge, especially following his appointment to the Knightbridge Chair in 1883.

The shift from classics to moral philosophy in 1869 was associated with Sidgwick's growing doubt in the status of the truths enshrined in the 39 Articles, embodying the principles of Anglican faith which all college fellows had to profess. Maynard Keynes notoriously remarked in a letter of March 1906, after reading the memorial volume to Sidgwick prepared by his wife and sister, that "He [Sidgwick] never did anything but wonder whether Christianity was true and prove that it wasn't and hope that it was" (Harrod 1951: 116). Later, in writing his biographical memoir on Alfred Marshall, Keynes elaborated on this offhand judgement, sketching a later nineteenth-century Cambridge riven by scepticism and rationalism. However, we should also note the relationship between faith and rationalism which Sidgwick represented. In the earlier part of the century scepticism about Anglican theology and religious practice was more likely to result in the embrace of Dissent: David Ricardo married a Quaker, and converted from Judaism to Unitarianism. The Anglicanism of Robert Malthus was the exception among progressive thinkers, bankers and merchants in early nineteenth-century England, and of course Scotland had long been Presbyterian. We too easily assume today that scepticism and religious doubt must end in lack of any faith.

Sidgwick's insistence on submitting the tenets of faith to rational examination also prompted his interest in psychical research, leading to a keen interest in verifying the claims by various mediums that they could communicate with the dead. A founding member of the Society for Psychical Research in 1882, this was an interest he shared with his wife. Another common interest was university education for women, and the Sidgwicks were closely involved in the foundation of Newnham College in 1880. One outcome of this was the naming of Sidgwick Avenue in Cambridge in his honour; and it is on the post-war Sidgwick Site that Cambridge's Faculty of Economics and Politics can be found.

In 1869 Sidgwick had joined with others to establish unofficial lectures for women students, an initiative that led in 1871 to the purchase of a house for these students. It was in this context that Alfred Marshall first lectured on political economy, also meeting his future wife, Mary Paley, and jointly authoring with her his first book, *The Economics of Industry* (1879). College fellows had to surrender their appointment on marriage, and so Marshall's marriage in 1877 took him first to University College, Bristol, then briefly to Oxford, before his return to the Cambridge chair in 1885. By this time Marshall was well advanced in the composition of *Principles*. Sidgwick's election to the Knightbridge chair ensured that his subsequent interest in political economy would be confined to occasional lectures and involvement with Royal Commissions on university and secondary education, and taxation.

Nonetheless, Sidgwick's *Principles of Political Economy* went into a second edition in 1887, and a third in 1901. The first two of its three books dealt with the "Science of Political Economy", a broadly Millian account of production, distribution and exchange. Even in the early pages the influence of Jevons can be seen at work, in the idea that the relative market values of goods corresponds to "variations in the comparative estimates formed by people in general, not of the *total* utilities of the amounts purchased of such articles, but of their *final* utilities" (1883: 74–5, original emphases), this being complemented with the observation that a given commodity is "more useful when bought by the poor, because the poor have fewer luxuries and therefore get more enjoyment out of what they have" (1883: 76). In Book Three, on the art of political economy,

Sidgwick returns to examine the problem raised by his treatment of wealth and utility: if the wealth of a country depends on its distribution among its inhabitants, then government policy with respect to taxation and tariffs can increase or diminish the wealth of a country. Here he also puts forward the idea that public goods exist, that for example "it may easily happen that the benefits of a well-placed lighthouse must be largely enjoyed by ships on which no toll could be conveniently imposed" (1883: 412–13).

KEITH TRIBE

See also:

Cambridge School of economics (II).

References and further reading

Since Sidgwick is today read as a moral philosopher, no reliable evaluation exists of his political and economic arguments. However, his significance for Cambridge economics is outlined in Backhouse (2006). The best treatment of Sidgwick's thought remains Schneewind (1977); Schultz's intellectual biography (2004) is very long, but far from comprehensive. Stefan Collini has written on Sidgwick in various places, summarized in his *Oxford Dictionary of National Biography* entry.

Backhouse, R. (2006), 'Sidgwick, Marshall, and the Cambridge School of Economics', *History of Political Economy*, **38** (1), 15–44.
Collini, S. (2004), 'Sidgwick, Henry (1838–1900)', in *Oxford Dictionary of National Biography*, Oxford: Oxford University Press.
Harrod, R. (1951), *The Life of John Maynard Keynes*, London: Macmillan.
Schneewind, J.B. (1977), *Sidgwick's Ethics and Victorian Moral Philosophy*, Oxford: Oxford University Press.
Schultz, B. (2004), *Henry Sidgwick: Eye of the Universe. An Intellectual Biography*, Cambridge: Cambridge University Press.
Sidgwick, Henry (1874), *The Methods of Ethics*, 7th edn 1907, London: Macmillan.
Sidgwick, Henry (1883), *The Principles of Political Economy*, London: Macmillan.
Sidgwick, Henry (1891), *The Elements of Politics*, London: Macmillan.

Carl Menger (1840–1921)

Vienna, the capital city of Mitteleuropa, was at the turn of the nineteenth to twentieth century the place where modernity broke away from received ways of thinking in the fields of philosophy (Wittgenstein), psychology (Freud), architecture (Loos), painting (Klimt), literature (Musil), music (Schönberg) – and many more. Vienna also hosted the founder of the school later known as the "Austrian school of economic thought", Carl Menger. At the same time as Léon Walras and William Stanley Jevons, Menger developed the marginalist method in economics and especially marginal-utility reasoning, and paved the way to the so-called "neo-classical" economics and provided a basis for a renewal of economic liberalism.

Johann Heinrich von Thünen and Hermann Heinrich Gossen anticipated part of what the three authors were credited with, but Menger's views on economic utility set him apart from these lesser-known predecessors as well as from his contemporaries; indeed, his stress on subjectivity and dynamics differentiates him from the other two founding fathers of marginalism. The way Menger incorporated the subjectivity of economic agents into a rigorous methodological individualism – a phrase coined by his disciple Friedrich von Wieser and popularized by Josef Schumpeter – made Menger stand against the German Historical School in the so-called "Methodenstreit" ("dispute over the methods"). The role Menger attributed to ignorance, time, human cognition and the environment set the Austrian mode of reasoning apart from the other strands of marginalism, a fact that has been overlooked for a long time, until "de-homogenization" of these views was undertaken (see Jaffé, 1976; Campagnolo, 2010).

Life

Carl Menger was born on 28 February 1840, second of three brothers, in Neu-Sandesz, Western Galicia – then Austro-Hungarian, now partly Polish and partly Ukrainian – the offspring of a family of imperial civil servants and army officers. The Mengers can be traced back to the early seventeenth century in Bohemia. Carl's grandfather bought land in Galicia during the Napoleonic wars. Menger's father died in 1848, when Carl was 8 years old. The three brothers were raised by their mother. All three continued the family tradition by serving the Emperor – Carl would be a tutor to Crown Prince Rudolf – while attempting to contribute to the modernization of the outdated imperial structures they had experienced particularly strongly in the Eastern provinces. Max, the elder, became a successful entrepreneur and a representative at the Imperial Parliament for the national-liberal party. Anton Menger, the younger brother, would become a famous Law Professor at Vienna University. He tended towards socialism, contributed the first Austrian codex of consumer laws and, though opposing Karl Marx and Johann Karl Rodbertus, authored a treatise on the claim by workers to the full produce of their labour (Menger 1886 [1962]). Anton's approach was close to that of the Historicists as well. As to Carl, he was to take a completely opposite direction resulting in major changes in the whole field of what was then called political economy ("Volkswirtschaftslehre").

Carl started studying law in Prague (1859–63), became a Doctor in Law at Krakow University and began his career as a journalist in Lemberg (today Lviv, Ukraine). Menger's formative years (Yagi 1993) were in the city gazette, but he quickly quit to enter the Civil Service. In 1873 he became *Extraordinarius* (professor without a tenure) at Vienna University and was made *Ordinarius* (full professor) in 1879. He worked there until he retired in 1903; his notebooks show he was active until 1911.

Carl Menger also acted as a columnist and a high civil servant, closely related to the media world (Menger at times had a column in the *Neue Freie Presse*, whose founder and director was his friend Moritz Szeps), and in touch with ministerial offices: he was a major adviser in the monetary "Valutareform" of the early 1890s. From 1876 to 1878, he had tutored Crown Prince Rudolf in a trip over Western Europe giving him temporary relief from the Court world and, at the age of 62, he himself had a son, Karl, who became a famous mathematician.

Menger died in 1921. He had worked half a century on a revised edition of his 1871 *Grundsätze der Volkswirthschaftslehre* (*Principles of Political Economy*). In 1923 his son re-edited the masterwork, whose first version had never been republished by his father. As the 1923 modified version bears witness to a different epoch and to the son's philosophical background, the 1871 version remained the founding stone of Austrian economics. The 1923 edition could have brought some confusion, despite the dearest faithfulness claimed by the son, but the 1871 version remained the most widespread. One reason is that, in the 1930s, Friedrich von Hayek re-edited the 1871 version. Now, the changes that Menger wanted can be precisely described by exploring his archives. So, while his son did not publish exactly what his father wished, Hayek, since conversely he did not use the archives at all, may also be said to have "ignored" partly what Menger had to say.

In order to know Menger's own final wording, it is necessary to consult the archives at Hitotsubashi University, Tokyo, to which Menger's widow sold her late husband's private collection (Campagnolo 2012), and at Duke University (North Carolina, USA), where the Perkins Library hosts mostly notebooks brought to the USA by his son as he fled the Anschluss in 1938, together with von Neumann, Morgenstern and many German and Austrian scholars.

Carl Menger was also a bibliophile. He had collected more than 20 000 volumes, many of which contain annotations that bear witness to Menger's deep knowledge in all fields of the social sciences and the history of political economy. The collection in Japan was mainly studied by Kauder, Yagi and Campagnolo, while the archives at Duke University were studied by Caldwell, Yagi and Campagnolo.

Archives are particularly helpful in retracing Menger's sources: the Ancients, especially Aristotle, British seventeenth-century political philosophers, French writers of the Enlightenment and French Liberals of the nineteenth century, such as Jean-Baptiste Say and Pellegrino Rossi. Menger fought against Classical economists and their historicist opponents, the German Historical School, alike. Menger also stands apart from German authors sometimes labeled "proto-neoclassical" (Streissler 1990), like Karl Heinrich Rau, whose textbook Menger annotated heavily, almost using it as a draft for his own ideas. Today Menger's archives can no longer be ignored: although still partly unpublished, they are indispensable to supplement published texts gathered by Hayek in *Carl Menger Gesammelte Werke*.

A New Path for Economics: Menger's *Principles of Economics*

According to his son's introduction to the 1923 edition of the *Grundsätze*, Carl Menger started the deeper study of economics in the fall of 1867. A renewal in science was long overdue, especially because, as was later reported by Wieser and Hayek, Menger did find a deeply unsatisfactory and blatant discrepancy between theories taught at academic level and economics practically used in ministerial offices and in the business world, especially at the stock exchange, which Menger had analysed as a journalist.

When Menger entered the field, the Classical School (Adam Smith, David Ricardo and John Stuart Mill) was under heavy criticism by the so-called "Historicists", who based their attack on the works of Wilhelm Roscher in the 1840s and his method of drawing historical parallels based upon factual investigation. They tended to combine a variety of elements into a somewhat arbitrary perspective since the criteria for selecting facts were not all clear and depended much on the creativity of the historian. Philosophers also built various theories of knowledge upon which Menger would draw in his private notes, albeit showing signs of doubt as to their validity. Yet, Menger dedicated his 1871 *Principles* to Roscher and also wrote an obituary of him in 1894.

While Menger kept Roscher in high esteem, he fiercely opposed Roscher's successors. The historical method displayed too many flaws, widespread in journals and edited series (see Grimmer-Solem 2003). After Roscher, Karl Knies and Bruno Hildebrand had indeed raised the issue and tried to mend the method. The form later given to it by Gustav von Schmoller, the leader of the so-called "Younger historical school", Menger met with hostility. Conversely, Schmoller discarded Menger's innovative work. In fighting Schmoller, Menger displayed talents in polemics because of which he was labelled "anti-historical". The fact however is that Menger rebuked the claim that history – or any other inductive methodology for that matter – might ever provide a theory for economics. Rather, a reform was needed in political economy to put research therein at par with the causality method operated in sciences regarded as truly scientific, first of all in the natural sciences, and then in economics. Against (historical) relativism and without confusion between sciences, Menger offered a new methodology that brought to the fore a theoretical science of economics.

Menger's own *Grundsätze* were indeed meant to provide such grounds. He states the point in the first opening sentences of the *Grundsätze*. Menger wishes to bring *rigorous* causal analysis to socio-economic phenomena. Menger thus ranks in the history of economics with innovators such as François Quesnay or Adam Smith, and his own contemporaries Walras and Jevons. Menger's theory revolves around three concepts: human satisfaction of needs, availability of resources and saleability (or marketability). The exchange of goods between human beings depends on the relationship between the agent's economic self and the quantities of things found to be both satisfying his/her needs and available and marketable in the environment at the moment the need is felt. Menger does not make any difference between the need for goods or for services. It is granted that all agents are set in a certain environment due to history and geography, local customs and climate, as the Historicists stressed. Yet, agents nevertheless all have basic needs, like hunger, thirst, accommodation and so on which need analysis at theoretical level. And only these objects that are satisfying/available/marketable become goods, and can be properly called economic goods.

Menger then ranks those goods, from first order (meaning "direct consumption") up to higher orders: second order goods are used to produce first order ones, third order goods to make second order ones, and so on. No limits exist in the number of orders, and new productive methods may always introduce new stages of production between the most basic raw materials and the finished products. This hierarchy of needs and wants thus fits the time structure of production, yet they are different approaches. Such a scale adequately meets the "natural" worries and needs of human beings: at first survival, then a "normal life" (given the existing living standards in a society) and eventually a "good life", contemplating the idea of the good and the ultimate goals of mankind. Menger followed the Aristotelian philosophy of a life aiming at the good in itself.

The ranking of one good that is considered in a given "line" of production does not depend upon the nature of this good, but upon the position it takes in both production and consumption. Its rank is not determined by any given quantity of labour used in it, nor by any intrinsic feature else than its natural power to satisfy a need under given (subjectively known) cognitive circumstances: indeed, in any two different processes where it enters, the same good may perfectly be ranked differently – wheat used as a seed and wheat to make bread are differently ranked.

Moreover, Menger's basic principles leave plenty of room to express the subjectivity of the agent – and that was a revolution against the objectivist views borne by both the Classics and the Historicists. Whether Menger fully completed this revolution, that is in itself a controversial issue (for a negative view, see Lachmann 1978). Anyhow, Menger formulates a new law of value, from reasoning on "marginal value", the last unit used by the consumer. This is the core of his *Grundsätze*, Chapter 3 entitled "Die Lehre vom Werthe". Menger provided his new economic thinking within his version of marginalist reasoning. A subsection bears the title "subjective factor" and aims at measuring the *original* value of goods along such new principles illustrated in a triangular-shaped table (Table 2).

In this famous table, magnitudes of value (Arabic numerals) are the weight that the agent attributes to "units" of goods, whose classes (in Roman numerals) are ranked, top line, by order of the "importance" they have for the agent who wishes to satisfy needs

Table 2   Triangular-shaped table illustrating the Mengerian exposition of marginal value

I	II	III	IV	V	VI	VII	VIII	IX	X
10	9	8	7	6	5	4	3	2	1
9	8	7	6	5	4	3	2	1	0
8	7	6	5	4	3	2	1	0	
7	6	5	4	3	2	1	0		
6	5	4	3	2	1	0			
5	4	3	2	1	0				
4	3	2	1	0					
3	2	1	0						
2	1	0							
1	0								
0									

Source: Menger (1871 [1968–70], I: 93).

he or she subjectively feels. The table reads in columns, along successive units of goods: the agent attaches an intensity of 10 to the first unit of good I, of 9 to a second unit of the same, and so on by decreasing intensity. So as to obtain maximum satisfaction, the agent would do all he could to get the first unit (as "10" only occurs once in the table): say, a glass of water, were he dying of thirst in a desert. A second unit of the same would already bring less enjoyment ("9") and could be traded for a first unit of good II, and so on. Despite cardinality being used with numerals, only ranking is important and this scheme is ordinal, a point later much debated, when comparing the Austrian notion of marginal utility with "utility functions". Value that lies at the "margin" of an agent's needs displays the value of the good. The last unit thereof the agent wants is what determines what the agent is ready to trade for it. This "marginal" position in the triangle thus indicates the measure of substitutes the agent would be ready to give away to be satisfied. The intensity of needs is ranked and value derives only from such a subjective individual valuation.

Choice widens as needs become less urgent. Once water is provided in the desert, one may choose between dates or a cereal grown in some oasis nearby: Menger himself draws on such examples. Unit after unit of good, by recurrence, his reasoning operates until all needs get satisfied. For instance, as thirst gets finally quenched, one more glass of water bears no more "value", hence "zero" value lies at the end. Differences of magnitude in the *significance* that goods bear *subjectively* explain the ranking of units enjoyed. At the individual level, the "diamonds versus water" story of classical economics seems to fade away, as Menger offers no wholly sociological analysis of diamonds as instruments to signal riches and power but purely subjective terms.

Menger then begins Chapter 4 of the *Grundsätze*, entitled "Die Lehre vom Tausche", quoting Smith only to rebuke Smith's supposed human "inner tendency to exchange", then rejecting in turn labour-commanded theory and labour-value alike. Only the notions of need, availability and marginal utility are needed by Menger in his new principles to ground economics.

Like Menger, Walras and Jevons were concerned with properly understanding value. In discovering the reasoning "at the margin" and in explaining the process of utility-maximizing that combines a subjective valuation of needs with the scarcity of available resources, Menger, Walras and Jevons brought about a "revolution". They were somehow anticipated by Gossen (and Thünen as regards marginal productivity theory). Some other German thinkers such as Karl Heinrich Rau or Karl-Hans von Mangoldt ought to be mentioned as well. Menger indeed read part of their works (as reported by Kauder 1957), but mainly opposed them; see his manuscript *marginalia* and his notebooks and drafts. Maffeo Pantaleoni later accused Menger of having plagiarized Gossen. The archives however show that this accusation cannot be sustained, since Menger (who noted down the date of acquisition of his books) got hold of, and read Gossen's volume (published in 1854) only after 1880, therefore after he had published his own *Grundsätze*.

To be fair, Menger acknowledged the laws Gossen had elaborated. Yet, Gossen focused on the fact that consumption takes time, whereas Menger changed the insight that the intensity of pleasure decreases with time into the idea that the degree of value that an individual subjectively attributes to goods decreases with "more units of goods" and determines pricing, which is the goal that Menger pursues in assessing marginal value. Besides the two fundamental "laws" which Gossen rightly drew through complex geometrical construction and analysis, especially the law of maximization (Gossen's so-called "second law"), Menger judges all the rest in Gossen as being erroneous and condemns him together with Bastiat. He writes:

> Gossen fails: to his mind, (technical) labour occupies a place indeed absolutely exceptional . . . [Also] all defects coming from the mathematical methods in the field of psychological investigations may be found there. Only enjoyment [*Genießen*] and enjoyment only – and not what is effective for life and for human welfare (the utmost enjoyment of one's whole life). Only labour and enjoyment, just like in Bastiat.

Whether Menger is right or wrong, this note (our translation) that appears at the back of the first flyleaf of his own copy of Gossen's 1854 exposition shows that Menger reproaches Gossen with a lack of adequate concepts that the (then incipient) mathematical method cannot mend in his eyes, and the use of deficient labour-value while Menger would insist on *differentiating* hedonistic pleasure and subjective satisfaction of needs to determine value based upon "self-felt" utility.

Menger parted company also with the other two "fathers of marginalism", Walras and Jevons. He reasoned in terms of process and the dynamics by which individuals act: while seeking satisfaction, they discover how beneficial exchange is for that purpose. The science of exchange (or "catallactics", a term later coined by Hayek) and Menger's attention to praxis ("praxeology", a term later coined by Ludwig von Mises) find their origins in Chapter 4 of the *Grundsätze*, describing why and how agents trade. As the quantities of goods they need may be more or less available and saleable, trade between agents prevails. Jevons also stressed that point as early as 1871. Menger firmly rejected the notion that labour-value may ever be a determining factor for pricing goods on markets in real life: it is never the case that what it costs to produce (to the seller) is what determines the final selling price, but only what it means to the buyer to acquire and what the seller is ready to trade for. Discussing the limits within which buyer and seller agree to trade (horses against cows, and then cereals for horses in examples developed in Chapters 4 and 5), Menger does not seek equilibrium but a range of relative prices emerges, between whose limits exchange will actually happen.

From the following quote that Menger takes from Rossi, it may be inferred that it was precisely this process the Viennese was looking for: "if you could follow the thousands vicissitudes of the market, the contracting partners, and analyse rigorously the positions they take, *and weigh, so to speak, the needs that explain them, then you would truly have solved the whole issue*" (handwritten in the copy owned by Menger of the original French edition; Menger 1871 [1968–70], I: 108, Menger's emphasis).

In his *Grundsätze*, as in later methodological writings, Menger speaks of "Atomismus" (atomism). Just as reasoning upon "units" of good and ranking orders set conditions for the satisfaction of needs to be a decreasing function of units being further enjoyed, Menger also treats agents as discrete, thus referring to "atoms". The economist can observe such agents and see they are akin to individuals endowed with subjectivity. Their needs are understandable, and ultimately preferences can be assigned to agents who are not mere "material" atoms but express feelings, emotions, are more or less rational, more or less ignorant. Menger did not speak of "revealed preferences". He better defined a strictly individual basis for economic analysis, later to be called "methodological individualism". Max Weber later admitted adopting this view.

A parallel existed between marginal reasoning and a then very well-known experimental law, the so-called "fundamental Law of Psychophysics" (or Weber–Fechner Law, from Ernst Weber and Gustav Fechner) stating that sensation increases with stimulus after an initial threshold is overcome and before satiety sets in. Whether pleasant (a soft touch, the satisfaction of some need, like quenching thirst) or painful (fatigue from labour, for instance), would this process take in the description of individual satisfaction of economic needs reckoned by Menger? The economist acknowledged an analogy but he rejected the view that this "law" could be a basis for economic theory. The result of experiments could always be debased by new experiments, while other psychological researches are surely to happen regarding the nature of the mind, and that was not Menger's object. Menger argued in favour of pure theory, based on the logic of individual decision.

It is not coincidental that archives show that Menger wanted to change the title of his 1871 *Grundsätze* to *Reine theoretische Wirtschaftslehre* (*Pure Theoretical Economics*). The contents of the volume indeed make Menger's intentions clear: Chapters 5 to 7 display the necessary elements to build a pure theory of how prices emerge (Chapter 5), how to distinguish "value-in-use and value-in-exchange" (Chapter 6) and how to gradually extend the analysis to all kinds of commodities and market (dual trade, monopoly, general competition: Chapter 7). Menger retains that trade gets done within price ranges, which themselves derive from negotiations on available quantities wished for and effectively take into consideration all sorts of conditions that he lists.

In the last chapter (Chapter 8) of his *Grundsätze*, Menger seemed to insert a historical analysis of money, a fact which has sometimes puzzled commentators, as if there appeared some inconsistency. Quite the contrary: Menger echoes therein Karl Knies's *Das Geld* (1885), the book that was then the reference on historicist monetary theory, yet only to overturn the latter's method. Menger rejects inductive inquiry and conceives of the emergence of money as illustrating his concept of increasing "Absatzfähigkeit" ("saleability") in payment systems. Menger reiterated his views in his 1892 essays on "*Geld*" (money), a series of different, yet matching texts in German, French and English (Latzer and Schmitz 2002; Campagnolo 2005).

Menger's *Investigations into the Method*

Following the publication of his theory, many methodological issues became bones of contention, as Menger had to convince fellow German economists that his new theoretical principles were well grounded. In the *Grundsätze*, he displayed circumstances in which subjective action occurs and looked at things in a way exactly opposite to that of the German Historicists. While the latter sought to gather facts so as to induce at best regularities, Menger provided deductive schemes starting from basic concepts, only then illustrating his framework by using facts when needed to show better what the reasoning (and not factual inquiry) must have already made clear. That divergence was the focus of the famous "Methodenstreit" in the 1880s.

Much later Schumpeter would see that dispute as a substantial waste of energy (Schumpeter 1954). It can be argued otherwise. Menger and Schmoller fought a battle that resulted in re-orienting economic research. There was the time of the "Great Crossroads" at the end of the nineteenth century, after which German Historicism declined, while marginalism rose and, thanks to Menger's methodology, the role of a pure and exact theory was regained upon an individualistic basis.

It must be noted that Menger and Schmoller were opponents less with respect to their common rejection of the sole use of mathematics as proof of science (a claim which they both opposed, albeit for different reasons), than regarding the role of other sciences that aimed at dominating the field of the *Geisteswissenchaften*, namely history and psychology. As regards mathematical economics, which had been developed by Thünen, Cournot, Gossen, Auspitz and Lieben and, of course, by Walras and Jevons, the archives show that Menger annotated critically some works, like Auspitz and Lieben's *Zur Theorie des Preises* (1887). However, while Schmoller regarded mathematization as pointless (except for the benefit of shorthand writing) given the historical "nature" of human beings and economic phenomena, Menger thought that mathematics suffered from the limits of a tool imported from a different field, whose use would only support views favourable to static analysis instead of a much needed theory in terms of pure dynamics. The inner logic thereof brought him not to not seek equilibrium, unlike Walras, but the conditions and the limits within which trade would occur. While Walras's *tâtonnement* (trial and error gradual process) is set to ultimately reach a given set of price-quantities at general equilibrium, Menger stresses how exchange brings in all kinds of uncertainty. Instability is inherent to market relationships. Even though the role of a strict causality and accuracy in methodological and theoretical foundations gave "resemblances" to their theories, these were reflected differently (Menger to Walras, 27 January 1887, in Jaffé 1965).

Menger saw mathematics as a method for illustration and representation, for exposition and demonstration at best, not as a heuristic or research tool. Therefore, if any economic law could be "clothed" in formulas and expressed through graphics, its usefulness still stopped short of affecting the essence of conceptual research (literally in Jaffé 1965: 768). Menger rejected equilibrium-oriented marginalism, be it Jevons's partial equilibrium or Walras's general equilibrium. Nowadays, such a gap still exists between Austrians and the so-called "mainstream", despite the widespread use of differentials to mimic dynamics in equations.

In his times and for his purpose of raising economics to a science, Menger feared less the threat of invasive mathematics than that of history and psychology in German-speaking academia. Ambitious designs of unilateral supremacy over all social sciences were carried by schools of historicism and (experimental) psychology under the guidance of Schmoller and Wilhelm Wundt respectively. Menger opposed both. A file, by the title "*Gegen* [against] *Wundt*", is kept in the archives at Duke University. On the other side Menger openly challenged Schmoller in his "open letters", *Die Irrthümer des deutschen Historismus* (*The Errors of German Historicism*, 1884), to this day a piece of masterly academic polemics.

In 1883 Menger published his methodological masterwork *Untersuchungen über die Methode der Socialwissenschaften und der Politischen Oekonomie insbesondere*, fighting the cold reception of his *Grundsätze* by Schmoller and providing his own philosophy of the social sciences. A reception even more bitter by the same followed (Schmoller 1883 [1888]). Against Schmoller, Menger supported the combination of marginalist reasoning with subjective individualism and the notion of value-neutrality ("Wertfreiheit"), a theme later endorsed by Weber. While Menger was critical of historicism, he did not deny history a role, as an illustrative inquiry. This can be seen in his treatment of institutions.

As he had done in Chapter 8 of his *Grundsätze* on monetary evolution, Menger paid much attention to institutions and showed, in Part III of his *Untersuchungen* (Menger 1968–70, vol. II), that they may arise from either "pragmatic" self-conscious planning or through "organic" spontaneous development. While Historicists tended to stress exclusively the former, the latter appears to Menger to be more often the case; see, for example, money, the state and so on. In that perspective, Menger rejected Schmoller's method of pointing to convergences and divergences between epochs and places within German history as being an endless inquiry, moreover pointless inasmuch as it remained strictly irrelevant to draw a theory as such. The "Methodenstreit" was useful in reorienting endeavours misdirected in the Historical School – so much so that even Schmoller felt compelled to qualify his statements against theory and argued famously (yet also wrongly in Menger's view) that induction and deduction were "like the two legs of a walking man" (Schmoller 1874–97 [1898]: 222).

Menger had not only to face historicism, but also overbearing "psychology". For Menger, economists should strongly separate economics from psychology: he reckoned the heuristic value of psychology (as in the aforementioned Weber–Fechner Law), but rejected any interference with economics. Menger denied that, despite analogies, psychology could serve as a ground for economics, since confusion between academic fields only caused havoc. Weber would later call for the same strict divide. Hayek and Mises would later make Menger's warning their own as well. Scientific economics bears realistic implications but it is solely anchored in a theoretical understanding of human economic behaviour. Menger rejected the denomination "Psychologenschule" sometimes used for his movement (Kraus 1905; Campagnolo 2008). Menger never denied the major roles of history or psychology, even in political economy, but staunchly rejected the dominating role they both claimed in his times.

Menger's warnings resulted in his new classification of economic sciences:

1. *Theory*. Theory deals with what is general (like in Aristotle). It is divided into an exact orientation of pure concepts (what, in essence, a "good" is, what makes it "economic", what "prices" consist in, for example) and a realistic-empirical orientation where types of economic behaviour are studied as *"Realtypen"* ("real types" compare for the closeness of their resemblance with Weber's later "ideal types", *Idealtypen*).
2. *History of economic facts and ideas*. It is the knowledge of facts according to time and place, where inductive method and inquiry are in order. Menger calls it "individual" as it deals with what happens only once. One mistake made by the Historicists was to multiply concepts of "collective entities" and "spirit" (like the *Volksgeist* or "spirit of the people"). Weber also opposed such collective notions (*Kollektivbegriffe*).
3. *Practical sciences*. These "applied" parts of economics include finance, policy-making, what consultants advise the Prince to do, firm management, household economics, and so on. Again, the Historicists, seeing themselves as heirs to the German Cameralists, had presumptuously turned into modern experts while experience cannot do what theoretical knowledge must do.

This tripartite classification of economics is put to use as early as the first chapter of the *Untersuchungen* and onwards. Furthermore, it is detailed in the Appendices in contrast to classical and historical views. This tripartite divide also supported Menger's fundamental realism, causal analysis and deductive method, while keeping strictly apart the various *Geisteswissenschaften* (the classical German academic name for what we today call both the 'sciences of the mind' and most of the humane and social sciences). Menger provided this new terminology and methodology to clearly divide subfields, lines and schemes in economic research. Using deduction apart from induction also leads to an abductive method (Milford 1990). Grounding his views both on realism and causality theory, Menger remained consistent throughout with the claim made in the opening of his 1871 *Grundsätze* in favour of a strict use of causality in economics.

The Founder of the Austrian School of Economics

Through his two masterworks of 1871 and 1883, Menger heralded a new era in economics. Commentators are strongly disputing whether he conscientiously founded a school to spread the word. In any case, Menger's economics became known as "Austrian" because of their Viennese originator. Even if Menger may have somehow caricatured historicism – as some historicists such as Emil Sax, Gustav Schönberg or Hans von Scheel had themselves criticized "ultra-historical" views – Menger had been cautious to refrain from entering debates on ontological issues. Also, because he provided economic research with the lineaments of a nascent epistemology based on a fully individualistic approach, he is rightfully said to have originated this school of thought.

There is evidence from letters to the Austrian ministry that Menger was indeed at least conscious that initiating a new school against the dominating German Historical School made sense in his fight. He spent much energy in it. His followers would develop some of his themes and the Austrian school would become famous for paying attention to socio-economic phenomena taken in a multifaceted perspective: the economics of "time and ignorance", the idea of the "*roundaboutness*" of production, imputation theory. Neither Menger nor his disciples managed to solve all the queries that had been raised. Yet, from Eugen von Böhm-Bawerk and Wieser to more recent followers, Austrian disciples would deal with themes that Menger originated: information (Hayek), uncertainty (Frank Knight), entrepreneurship (Israel Kirzner), and so on. Thus, the work of Menger still remains to this day seminal in debates about all sorts of conditions in trade, on the role of time, information, location and allocation of resources, legal conditions, the birth and growth of institutions.

While so-called Austrians picked on the mainstream, some of their arguments also slowly made their way into it, like information into agency cost theory. Some Austrian traits remain specific, such as a rigorous methodological individualism and their interest in subjectivity, which sometimes pervades neighbouring sciences, like sociology. The views of Menger and his followers also diverged at times: for example, his understanding of empirical studies contrasts with the "extreme a-priorism" defended in *Human Action* (1949) by Mises and, later on, Murray Rothbard. More divergences can be spotted with recent Austrians: "free-banking" is widely upheld among them, while it is a far cry from Menger's say, notably that "states, or groups of states may decree the quantity of money they emit" in order to provide a stable measure for the varying prices of commodities (Menger 1892 Campagnolo [2005]: 259). However, Menger's views on the evolution of payment systems remain topical (Latzer and Schmitz 2002).

A seminal thinker, Menger, whose legacy is still an object for inquiry, initiated a major current of thought. Many economic policies would be advocated in his name (free-trade policies and radical economic liberalism), although he may not have upheld all of these as the inspiring founder of the school. In this regard and through the new sense he gave to what doing research means in economics, Menger stands in historical significance on a par with Quesnay, Smith, Marx or Keynes.

GILLES CAMPAGNOLO

See also:

Eugen von Böhm-Bawerk (I); German and Austrian schools (II); Hermann Heinrich Gossen (I); Friedrich August von Hayek (I); William Stanley Jevons (I); Ludwig Heinrich von Mises (I); Wilhelm Georg Friedrich Roscher (I); Gustav Friedrich von Schmoller (I); Marie-Esprit-Léon Walras (I); Friedrich von Wieser (I).

References and further reading

Archives of Carl Menger: (1) Allgemeines Verwaltungsarchiv, Staatsarchiv, Vienna: Mengers Personalakten; (2) Menger's collection of books and pamphlets (approx. 20000 volumes), Centre for the Literature of Western social sciences, Hitotsubashi University (Japan); (3) Notebooks at Perkins Library, Duke University (North Carolina) – both (2) and (3) are catalogued.
Auspitz, Rudolf and Richard Lieben (1887), *Zur Theorie des Preises*, Leipzig: Duncker und Humblot.
Caldwell, B. (ed.) (1990), *Carl Menger and His Legacy in Economics* (*History of Political Economy*, **22**, supplement), Durham, NC: Duke University Press.
Campagnolo, G. (2005), 'Money as measure of value. A presentation of Menger's essay in monetary thought' (followed by the translation thereof by the same: 'La monnaie, mesure de valeur', *Revue d'économie politique*, **6**, 159–75), *History of Political Economy*, **37** (2), 233–61.
Campagnolo, G. (2008), 'Was the Austrian School a "Psychologenschule" in the realm of economics in Carl Menger's view?', in G. Campagnolo (ed.), *Carl Menger. Discussed on the Basis of New Findings*, Frankfurt am Main and Vienna: Peter Lang Verlag, pp. 165–86.
Campagnolo, G. (2009), 'Origins of Menger's thought in French liberal economists', *Review of Austrian Economics*, **22** (1), 53–79.
Campagnolo, G. (2010), *Criticisms of Classical Political Economy. Menger, Austrian Economics and the German Historical School*, Abingdon and New York: Routledge.
Campagnolo, G. (2012), 'Deutsche Archive in Japan und das Beispiel: Carl Menger und sein Verständnis der Nikomachischen Ethik des Aristoteles', in H. Kurz (ed.), *Der Einfluss deutschsprachigen Wirtschaftswissenschaftlichen Denkens in Japan*, Schriften des Vereins für Socialpolitik Gesellschaft für Wirtschafts- und Sozialwissenschaften, **115** (XXVII) new series, Berlin and Vienna: Duncker and Humblot, pp. 131–77.
Gossen, H.H. (1854), *Entwickelung der Gesetze des menschlichen Verkehrs, und der daraus fliessenden Regeln für menschliches Handeln*, Braunschweig: F. Vieweg und Sohn.
Gossen, H.H. (1854), *Laws of Human Relations and the Rules of Human Action Derived Therefrom*, trans. 1983 by R.C. Blitz (with an introductory essay by N. Georgescu-Roegen), Cambridge, MA: MIT Press.
Grimmer-Solem, E. (2003), *The Rise of Historical Economics and Social Reform in Germany 1864–1894*, Oxford: Oxford University Press.
Hayek, F. von (1934), 'Einleitung', Introduction to *Carl Menger Gesammelte Werke*, reprinted 1968–70, Tübingen: J.C.B.Mohr, pp. vii–xxxvi.
Jaffé, W. (1965), *Correspondence of Léon Walras and Related Papers, vol. I: 1857–1883*, Amsterdam: North Holland.
Jaffé, W. (1976), 'Menger, Walras and Jevons De-Homogeneized', *Economic Inquiry*, **14** (4), 511–24.
Kauder, E. (1957), 'Intellectual and political roots of the older Austrian School', *Zeitschrift für Nationalökonomie*, **17**, 411–25.
Kirzner, I. (1978), 'The entrepreneurial role in Menger's system', in R. Wagner (ed.), *Carl Menger and Austrian Economics*, special issue of the *Atlantic Economic Journal*, **6** (3), 31–45.
Knies, K. (1885), *Das Geld. Darlegung der Grundlehre von dem Gelde*, 2nd edn, Berlin: Weidmannsche Buchhandlung.

Kraus, O. (1905), 'Die aristotelische Werttheorie in ihren Beziehungen zu den Lehren der moderner Psychologenschule', *Zeitschrift für die gesamte Staatswissenschaft*, **61** (4), 573–92.

Lachmann, L. (1978), 'Carl Menger and the incomplete revolution of subjectivism', in R. Wagner (ed.), *Carl Menger and Austrian Economics*, special issue of the *Atlantic Economic Journal*, **6** (3), 57–9.

Latzer, M. and S. Schmitz (eds) (2002), *Carl Menger and the Evolution of Payment Systems*, Cheltenham, UK and Northampton, MA, USA: Edward Elgar.

Menger, A. (1886), *Der Recht auf den vollen Arbeitsertrag in geschichtlicher Darstellung*, Stuttgart: Cotta.

Menger, A. (1886), *The Right to the Whole Produce of Labour*, trans. 1900 by J. Foxwell (ed.), London, reprinted 1962, New York: Kelley.

Menger, C. (1871), *Principles of Economics*, trans. in 1950 by J. Dingwall and B. Hoselitz (eds), Glencoe, IL: Free Press, reprinted 1981, New York: New York University Press.

Menger, C. (1883), 'Problems of economics and sociology', partly trans. in 1963 by F. Nock, Urbana, IL: University of Illinois, revised, completed by L. White (1985), *Investigations into the Method of the Social Sciences with Special Reference to Economics*, New York: New York University Press.

Menger, C. (1884), *Die Irrthümer des deutschen Historismus*, Vienna: A. Hölder.

Menger, C. (1892), 'Money', trans. M. Streissler, in L.M. and S. Schmitz (eds) (2002), *Carl Menger and the Evolution of Payment Systems*, Cheltenham, UK and Northampton, MA, US: Edward Elgar, pp. 7–125.

Menger, C. (1892), 'La monnaie mesure de valeur', *Revue d'économie politique*, **6**, 159–75, English trans. G. Campagnolo (2005), 'Money as measure of value. A presentation of Menger's essay in monetary thought' (followed by the translation thereof by the same: 'La monnaie, mesure de valeur', *Revue d'économie politique*, **6**, 159–75), *History of Political Economy*, **37** (2), 233–61.

Menger, C. (1968–70), *Carl Menger Gesammelte Werke*, ed. F. Hayek, 4 vols, 1934–36, 2nd edn, Tübingen: Mohr; vol. I: (first published 1871) *Grundsätze der Volkswirthschaftslehre*, Wien: Braumüller; vol. II: (first published 1883) *Untersuchungen über die Methode der Socialwissenschaften und der Politischen Oekonomie insbesondere*, Leipzig: Duncker und Humblot; vol. III: (first published 1880–1910) *Kleinere Schriften zur Methode und Geschichte der Volkswirthschaftslehre*; vol. IV: (first published 1880–1910) *Schriften über Geldtheorie und Währungspolitik* includes *Geld* pp. 1–116 (originally in J. Conrad et al. (eds), *Handwörterbuch der Staatswissenschaften*, vol. 4, Jena: Fischer, pp. 555–610).

Menger, K. (ed.) (1923), *Carl Menger's Grundsätze der Volkswirtschaftslehre*, revised edn, Wien: Hölder-Pichler-Tempsky, as in R. Schüller (ed.) (1994), *Carl Menger's Grundsätze der Volkswirtschaftslehre*, Leipzig: G. Freytag.

Milford, K. (1989), *Zu den Lösungsversuchen des Induktionsproblems und des Abgrenzungsproblems bei Carl Menger*, Wien: Verlag der österreichischen Akademie der Wissenschaften.

Milford, K. (1990), 'Menger's methodology', in B. Caldwell (ed.), *Carl Menger and His Legacy in Economics* (ann. suppl. to vol. 22, *History of Political Economy*), Durham, NC and London: Duke University Press.

Mises, L. von (1949), *Human Action*, New Haven, CT: Yale University Press.

Schmoller, G. von (1874–97), *Über einige Grundfragen der Socialpolitik und der Volkswirtschaftslehre*, reprinted 1898, Leipzig: Duncker und Humblot.

Schmoller, G. von (1883), 'Die Schriften von C. Menger und W. Dilthey zur Methodologie der Staats- und Sozialwissenschaften', *Jahrbuch für Gesetzgebung, Verwaltung und Volkswirthschaft im deutschen Reiche*, **7** (3), 239–60, revised edn (1888), *Zur Litteratur-geschichte der Staats- und Sozialwissenschaften*, Leipzig: Duncker und Humblot, pp. 275–304.

Schumpeter, J.A. (1954), *History of Economic Analysis*, London: Allen and Unwin.

Streissler, E. (1990), 'The influence of German economics on the works of Menger and Marshall', in B. Caldwell (ed.), *Carl Menger and His Legacy in Economics*, Durham, NC: Duke University Press, pp. 31–68.

Yagi, K. (1993), 'Carl Menger's Grundsätze in the making', *History of Political Economy*, **25** (4), 697–724.

Alfred Marshall (1842–1924)

Alfred Marshall was born on 26 July 1842 in the London suburb of Bermondsey into a lower middle-class family, which subsequently moved to the suburb of Clapham. After attending the Merchant Taylors' School, thanks to a loan from an Australian uncle and an open exhibition to St John's College he entered Cambridge University and in 1865 completed the Mathematical Tripos. A Fellow of St John's, in 1868 he was appointed Lecturer in Moral Science and lectured on political economy. In 1875 he visited the United States to study at first hand the costs and benefits of protectionism. The manuscripts he was working on, collected in Whitaker (1975), were partly printed by Henry Sidgwick in 1879 under the titles *The Pure Theory of Foreign Trade* and *The Pure Theory of Domestic Values*. After his marriage to Mary Paley, one of his women students of the foundation that was to become Newnham College, in 1877, he had to resign his Fellowship, as celibacy requirements at Cambridge University were not removed until 1882. The young couple moved to Bristol, where Alfred became Principal of University College and later Professor of Political Economy. In 1879 Alfred and Mary published *The Economics of Industry*, a primer of political economy. In 1881 he resigned his posts and spent a year in Palermo, where he started to compose *Principles of Economics*. After another year spent in Bristol, and one in Oxford as lecturer to candidates for the Indian Civil Service, in January 1885 he returned to Cambridge as Professor of Political Economy, a chair he held until 1908, when he resigned. In 1903 he achieved the goal of establishing an independent Tripos in Economics and Politics. In 1890 he published *Principles of Economics. Vol. I*, which from the sixth edition, in 1910, became *Principles of Economics. An Introductory Volume*. A condensation of this book, *Elements of the Economics of Industry*, meant to replace the early *Economics of Industry*, which he had come to dislike, was published in 1892. In 1891–94 he was engaged as a member of the Royal Commission on Labour. Part of the material that should have been printed in volumes II and III of *Principles* was printed separately as *Industry and Trade* (1919) and *Money, Credit and Commerce* (1923). Marshall died on 13 July 1924. After his death, two of his pupils collected his occasional writings and his contributions to government inquiries, respectively in *Memorials of Alfred Marshall*, edited by Arthur Cecil Pigou in 1925, and *Official Papers of Alfred Marshall*, edited by John Maynard Keynes in 1926 (a supplement to the latter has been edited by Groenewegen in 1996).

The language of modern and contemporary economic analysis is greatly indebted to Marshall. Thanks to his work, "'marginal productivity,' 'elasticity,' 'substitution,' the distinction between long and short periods, 'quasi-rent,' 'prime' and 'supplementary' cost, the elegant and serviceable expository device of plane-curves, became the stock-in-trade of the professional economist" (Shove 1942: 313).

Second wrangler in 1865, Marshall put his mathematics to task "to disentangle the interwoven effects of complex causes" (Guillebaud 1961, II: 173). His self-taught training in economics consisted in translating "Ricardo's reasonings into mathematics", in the endeavour "to make them more general" (Keynes 1924: 328), and "[Mill's] doctrines into differential equations as far they would go; and as a rule, rejecting those which would not go" (Pigou 1925: 412).

Meanwhile, before engaging in the study of economics, as a young philosopher and aspiring psychologist Marshall was fascinated by the "inquiries into the possibilities of the higher and more rapid development of human faculties" (Keynes 1924: 320). As he later recollected, around 1871–72 he was uncertain whether to devote his life to psychology or economics and spent a year in doubt (Whitaker, 1966, II: 285). In an early manuscript he contrived a model of the functioning of the human mind that would later act as the frame of reference for economic analysis (Raffaelli 1994: 116–32). The model conveys the idea of a decomposable, cumulative set of mental devices in continuous evolution. It displays not only the source of Marshall's lifelong interrogation on the shortcomings of the mathematics of the physical sciences when applied to economics, but also the origin of his firm conviction that biology is the economist's Mecca (Marshall 1898: 43, 1920: xiv).

If one adds the young Marshall's keen interest in theories of human progress (Cook 2009), his two-faced attitude towards economic analysis becomes almost obvious. On the one hand, he argued that analytical "machinery" is essential, and its growth coincides with scientific progress:

> When the same operation has to be performed over and over again in the same way, it generally pays to make a machine to do the work. . . . Similarly in knowledge, when there are processes of investigation or reasoning in which the same kind of work has to be done over and over again in the same kind of way; then it is worth while to reduce the processes to system, to organize methods of reasoning and to formulate general propositions to be used as machinery for working on the facts and as vices for holding them firmly in position for the work. (Marshall 1920, app. C: 779)

On the other hand, this analytical machinery is but an "organon", "an engine for the discovery of concrete truth, similar to, say, the theory of mechanics" (Pigou 1925: 159). Its main weakness consists in the intrinsic inability to deal with the evolutionary character of economics, as of any other human science: "every movement that takes place in the moral world alters the magnitude *if not* the character of the forces that govern succeeding movements" (Whitaker 1975, II: 163; emphasis added, see below). Though Marshall tried to circumscribe the problem, in order to extend the applicability of his analytical tools, he could not avoid it when dealing with increasing returns and distribution, where irreversibility is prominent and demand–supply equilibrium analysis fails. Far from being exceptions, these two cases reveal the inner structure of Marshall's analysis and the difficulties and ambiguities it met with.

After Marshall's death, his concepts were recast into the mainstream of economic theory, represented by general equilibrium theory. Economics took from Marshall what suited the new paradigm, relegating the rest to the old curiosity shop. This gave rise to the paradox of a science that bought up Marshall's analytical tools, relocating them in an allogeneous setting. Recent developments in industrial and evolutionary economics have triggered a revival of interest in Marshall's original programme.

These are the main coordinates of the puzzle that was Marshall: the theoretician who greatly contributed to modern economic analysis; the almost disparaging critic of the growing tendency to freely explore the potentialities of abstract, mathematical theory; the pioneer of evolutionary economics, whose intuitions were lost along the main road taken by twentieth-century economics. What follows aims to put Marshall's quandaries into their historical and cultural context, avoiding the temptation to break them apart as if there were two Marshalls, irreconcilable with each other.

The Role of Mathematical Reasoning in Economics

Entering the study of economics, Marshall set himself the task of enhancing its scientific status to the standard of the natural sciences. Economics, as he found it in the late 1860s, was in a mess. Marshall held a high opinion of the classics, Ricardo in particular, who "never went wrong" (Whitaker 1996, III: 270), as his "genius" enabled him "to tread his way safely through the most slippery paths of mathematical reasoning, though he had no aid from mathematical training" (Pigou 1925: 99). However, post-Ricardian economics had become akin to a book of recipes, "confidently proclaiming the solution of the most intricate problems by a few cut-and-dried formulae" (ibid.: 166). Notwithstanding his high moral and intellectual status, Mill could not go very far in his attempt to restore reputation to the discipline, as his style was "literary: & therefore full of error" (Whitaker 1996, I: 168). Lacking Ricardo's mathematical "instincts", Mill could but be "unequal to the task" (Marshall 1920: 836). Marshall's aim was to write "a general treatise of a similar scope to Mill's" (Keynes 1924: 329), succeeding where Mill had failed.

Mathematics helped Marshall to build up the analytical machinery of book V of *Principles*, often considered to be the only part of his system that survived the test of time. To better understand Marshall's views on the use of mathematics in economics, we need to look at his mathematical training. In his time, Cambridge mathematics was outdated when compared with France, where Lagrange and Laplace had established "the supremacy of analytic over synthetic-geometric mathematics" (Becher 1980: 1). The "impure" character of Cambridge nineteenth-century mathematics laid stress on the calculations needed for mathematical physics to the detriment of pure mathematics. In 1848, the reform of the tripos restrained the diffusion of analysis, "undermining the analysts' emphasis on pure mathematics" and "preserving the tradition conducive to the development of physics" (ibid.: 46). Whewell, who fathered this counter-revolution, thought of mathematics as strictly connected to the natural, inductive sciences and of its basic concepts as founded on intuitions of space and time relationships. In his view, "mathematics and physics were one" (ibid.: 17). Excessive dependence on the mathematical machinery was seen as an encumbrance to the intuitive power of the mind to grasp the fundamental ideas of the science to which that machinery was applied. By contrast, Whewell favoured the "method of curves", as "order and regularity are more readily and clearly recognised, when thus exhibited to the eye in a picture, than they are when presented to the mind in any other manner" (quoted in Maas and Morgan 2002: 110; see also Dardi 2016).

Given this background, Marshall almost naturally came to think that the fundamental ideas of classical economics could be clarified by the use of functions that correlated variable quantities:

> The most powerful engines for such a purpose are supplied by the various branches of the mathematical calculus. But diagrams are of great service, wherever they are applicable, in interpreting to the eye the processes by which the methods of mathematical analysis obtain their results. . . . Diagrams present simultaneously to the eye the chief forces which are at work, laid out, as it were, in a map. (Whitaker 1975, II: 133)

The mechanical model of the balance of forces, that originally belonged "to the older science, physics" (Marshall 1898: 43), was transferred, by analogy, to the "balance between efforts and the satisfactions resulting from them" (Marshall 1920: 353).

The theories of value and distribution of the early manuscripts bear witness to Marshall's excitement at the discovery of how far mathematics could go to improve the consistency and perspicuity of economic doctrines. "On value" presents a whole set of equilibrium models, "depending mainly on the length of the period of time to which the investigation applies" (Whitaker 1975, I: 134). Similar models are applied to earnings, money, taxation and other economic issues. Stable and unstable equilibria are clearly defined, and the main potentialities of these analytical tools are explored.

At first sight, Marshall's initial enthusiasm for the applications of mathematics to economics looks to be in sharp contrast with his later critical remarks on the "mathematical toys", which make Arthur Bowley lose touch with the real world (Whitaker 1996, II: 301). Similar charges are levelled against Edgeworth, who "has crushed his instincts between the cog wheels of his mathematical machinery" (Whitaker 1996, II: 307; see also III: 130). This leads to thinking of a life parabola, owing to the progressive loss of mathematical competencies that Marshall himself avows (Whitaker 1996, III: 91). Harshness aside, however, there is nothing new in these criticisms. The same concern about excessive trust in mathematical analysis permeates the early review of Edgeworth's *Mathematical Psychics* (Whitaker 1975, II: 267), and the late warnings against pure mathematical exercises remind us of the "mist of symbols" that worried Whewell (Becher 1980: 17), and was censured in the student's guide to the tripos.

When Marshall thought of mathematical training as a privileged way of accessing the study of economics, and successfully strove to attract students from the Mathematical Tripos, he looked for students who were trained in applied rather than pure mathematics, and had "mastered some branch of the physical sciences" (Guillebaud 1961, II: 173).

Evolution in Human and Social Affairs

Soon after graduating, Marshall plunged into the philosophical controversies of the time (Raffaelli 1994), sharing the "wave of Darwinian enthusiasm" that was pervading Cambridge (Clifford 1886: 24–25). Though the spur came from many a source, and Marshall later indistinctly referred to Spencer, Hegel, and others, Darwin's theory best highlights the basic elements of the evolutionary process Marshall had in mind: variation, selection and heredity. In Darwin, selection between individual carriers of casual variation is worked out by survival probability, while genetic heredity preserves those variations that make individuals survive. Similar three-dimensional views of evolution were already applied within and outside of the biological sciences, with different characterization of one or more of the three elements. In Spencer's *Psychology*, pleasure–pain selection discriminates between actions that are experienced by the individual, giving rise to a process of learning by doing. The role of heredity is here played by habit and instinct at the individual level and by custom at the social level. With regard to variation, the human world presents an additional causal factor: power to at least partially foresee the consequences of any new action and to plan its execution accordingly. This opens the door to Spencer's non-casual view of evolution, in which variation is performed purposefully. Directionality is reinforced by the cultural transmission of acquired habits. What further distinguishes Spencer's from Darwin's theory, and lays it open to criticism and ridicule, is the possibility that acquired habits are genetically transmitted.

In "Ye machine", a paper delivered in the late 1860s, Marshall drew a sophisticated model of how a mechanical mind evolves over time. In its routine activity the machine relies on automatic actions stored in previously acquired instincts. When a novel situation occurs that defies existing automatisms, the machine tries accidental variations until it hits one that succeeds, directly or in a roundabout way. If all these "contrivances" fail, and the stimulus persists, the machine resorts to a higher mental circuit capable of foreseeing the consequences of each action before choosing which one to perform. Successful "contrivances", wherever they have been first performed, either at the lower or the higher level, not only restore equilibrium, but tend to become part of the machine's normal behaviour, changing the way it will act in future circumstances. Repetition makes the performance of any new action easier, so that in the end it is stored as a new instinct. Each machine's "character" consists in its peculiar set of accumulated automatisms, and varies over time. Character introduces a new level of causality, which partakes of biological systems: each action is directed by the machine's character, which itself is slowly changed by the actions that are performed. If we consider the machine's ability to foresee and plan the variations, causation is not merely biological. However, selection is always worked out by "purely mechanical agencies" (Raffaelli 1994: 119). The model is not Spencerian in its denigratory meaning. Though it does not rule out genetic transmission of acquired habits, the issue is set aside as not of primary concern, as it will also be in the major works (ibid.; Marshall 1919: 163–4 n, 1920: 248 n). Marshall's failure to reach the economist's Mecca is often attributed to his Lamarckian–Spencerian leanings (Hodgson 1993; Moss 1982), but the conclusion is unwarranted. Marshall's model is made up of the three basic evolutionary elements that consist in innovation, selection and routine. The fact that variation in human affairs can be consciously planned, and is not due to pure chance, does not contradict the neo-Darwinian theory of genetic variation, which is said to have played havoc with Marshall's forays into economic biology. Intentional directionality instead of pure chance in the emergence of variations, and cultural instead of genetic transmission, characterize the evolution of human ideas and artefacts differently from biological evolution.

The model performs two functions in Marshall's economic analysis. On the one hand, it explains how the mind works, thanks to its specific mechanisms: variation can be either casual or designed, pleasure and pain provide the selective test, and instinct is where successful variations are preserved. On the other hand, with different specifications of the three components, the model reproduces the steps through which any system evolves, be it a firm, an institution, a society. This detailed model of the cumulative growth of human knowledge is applied to economics from the very beginning: "when a man works he produces two effects, one on his work, and another on himself" (Whitaker 1975, II: 55). Variation and innovation are of primary concern in any field, from industrial economics to education: "the tendency to variation is a chief cause of progress" (Marshall 1920: 355). Competition fosters innovation and is the most powerful selective mechanism in the economy. At different levels, habit, custom, and standardization offer a corpus where variations can be preserved and stored: "Custom standardizes unconsciously and crudely processes and products alike. The modern science of industrial technique deliberately standardizes some products and many processes" (Marshall: 1919: 201).

Both functions of the model help understand Marshall's insistence on the limits of the mathematics he knew when applied to economics. Restoration of the equilibrium, which is exhaustively represented by the mechanical analogy, does not bring an end to the story. It neglects the change that takes place in the mechanism itself and affects the way it will work in the future.

Partial Equilibrium Analysis versus General Equilibrium Analysis

The analytical apparatus of book V of the *Principles* is firmly rooted in Marshall's mathematical training, though here, unlike in the early manuscripts, the mathematics occupies a less prominent position, being confined to footnotes and appendices. Marshall's ambition to be read by lay people is usually blamed for this rearguard practice, in open contrast with what was happening in modern economics. According to this interpretation, an excessive pretension to be "realistic" prevented Marshall from ascending to the level of abstraction required for the full development of equilibrium analysis. A hierarchy is thus established with Walras's "general" equilibrium on top and Marshall's "partial" equilibrium lower down. The words themselves tell the difference, causing the latter to be thought of as an approximation to the former, more useful for practical applications, but less satisfying from a theoretical point of view. This simple and attractive assessment of the relative standing of these two paradigms of economic analysis overlooks their radical difference, which the early model of the mind illuminates. Marshall's reluctance to sever the links between analysis and history and his midway position in the *Methodenstreit* (Pigou 1925: 437; Whitaker 1996, II: 179) depend on his research programme, not on any attempt "to compromise" (Whitaker 1996, III: 184). History matters because the action of economic laws changes over time, and the analytical apparatus must be continuously revised: "if the subject-matter of a science passes through different phases of development . . . the laws of the science must have a development corresponding to that of the things of which they treat" (Marshall 1920: 764). Analysis, on the other hand, is essential – "facts by themselves are silent" (Pigou 1925: 166) – but Marshall's analysis is not made up of the same ingredients as Walras's. As Dardi (2006: 215) convincingly argues: "Marshall's and Walras's theories of equilibrium are irreconcilable because of the different motivations from which they originated. Marshall used equilibrium as an analogy intended to transfer a mental framework devised in classical mechanics to phenomena of a completely different nature, such as those studied in economics".

Whereas Walras identified economics with mechanics, Marshall pointed out the limits of the mechanical analogy (Marshall 1898: 39), however valuable it is to grasp the instantaneous action of economic forces. In economics, alterations concern "the character *as well as* the magnitude of economical and social forces . . . the catastrophes of mechanics are caused by changes in the quantity and not in the character of the forces at work; whereas in life their character changes also" (Marshall 1898: 42, emphasis added). In the former case, the mechanical law of the composition of forces can work; in the latter, the mechanical analogy proves defective. Nevertheless, the latter must not be abandoned too "hastily", as it helps cope with situations in which change takes place at different levels, mastering them one by one. By way of example, Marshall selects mechanical systems whose movement can be broken up into separate components, each with its own laws of motion, if any. They go from packing the parcels on the rack of a moving train (Marshall 1898: 38) to studying the movement of a pendulum "standing on an inclined ledge" (ibid.: 42), hanging in the troubled water of a mill-race, or held by a hand whose movements are "partly rhythmical and partly arbitrary" (Marshall 1920: 346). Economics has much to learn from such mechanical systems as "the economic pendulum does not swing back along the course by which it came" (Guillebaud 1961, II: 71). Unsurprisingly, to illustrate Marshall's way of reasoning, Frisch (1950) invites the reader to look at the economy in terms of a succession of equilibria nested into one another, like a system composed of three pendula, one suspended from the other, with the heaviest, which stands for long period equilibrium, on top, and the lightest, representing temporary equilibrium, at the bottom (the middle pendulum stands for short-term equilibrium). Under some assumptions, the oscillation of each of the three pendula can be studied on its own, "splitting the problem into separate movements". Frisch's discussion of the relationships between Marshall's analytical tools – marginal and average, variable and total, prime and supplementary cost – provides a clear account of normal equilibrium period analysis.

Partial equilibrium is the only way of dealing with economic change. Any disequilibrium is characterized by the subset of variables it affects. The standard example is the fishing industry (Marshall 1920: 369–71). Day-to-day oscillations of the fish price, owing to the weather, do not call for any change on the supply side, and equilibrium is restored by variations in demand. A cattle plague, which raises the demand for fish for a couple of years, causes variations at a deeper level, inducing fishermen to set afloat boats not especially fit for fishing. If "the disuse of meat causes a permanent distaste for it", disequilibrium will affect the shipbuilding industry. Each case has to be studied on its own, impounding the movements that still take place at the other levels in the *ceteris paribus* clause. Day-to-day oscillations still happen when we consider the effects of the cattle plague, or the dietary change, but have no influence on the equilibrium we are looking for. Similarly, long period movements happen while we look for the temporary or short period equilibrium price, but their influence is negligible.

The fishing industry shows that complex problems must be broken up to be subjected to scientific machinery: "the human mind has no other method than this; that a complex problem is broken up into its component parts" (Pigou 1925: 164). To treat variables as constants "is the only method by which science has ever made any great progress in dealing with complex and changeful matter, whether in the physical or moral world" (Marshall 1920: 380 n). Marshall's *ceteris paribus* clause attempts to do this. It refers to the time period under consideration, without necessarily implying that the rest of the system is in equilibrium as it should (and could not) be if the clause were applied from a general equilibrium perspective. It only assumes that the adjustments that take place in other parts of the system are either too quick or too slow to affect the equilibrium of the period in question. Time is a key component of the clause, and this introduces a difference from applications of the clause that are common to "almost every scientific discipline", mechanics included: "the condition that time must be allowed for causes to produce their effects is a source of great difficulty in economics. For meanwhile the material on which they work, and perhaps even the causes themselves, may have changed". (Marshall 1920: 36)

The clause is rather hazardous in the long period, when slow movements that do not directly affect the market under consideration "may produce great effects ... if they happen to act cumulatively". Therefore "violence is required for keeping broad forces in the pound of *Cæteris Paribus* during, say, a whole generation, on the ground that they have only an indirect bearing on the question in hand" (Marshall 1920: 379 n). Time period analysis is how partial equilibrium works. The latter is not a sub-system which, if the *ceteris paribus* clause were removed, would end up in static general equilibrium. The stationary state is a fiction, a device useful "only to illustrate particular steps in the argument, and to be thrown aside when that is done" (ibid.: 366 n).

Marshall's economic analysis cannot be cut off from this conceptual framework, which makes sense of it. Though expressed in the language of marginal analysis that marked the new paradigm of economic science, his analytical tools perform different functions, as emerges almost at every step. Marshall's concept of margin itself is instrumental and far from univocal, as it should be if it were taken for the cause of value. The margin "does not govern price, but . . . focuses the causes which do govern price" (Marshall, 1920: 428; see also ibid.: 411). Like a valve, it is the locus where the opposing forces can be measured, but these forces alone can be said to govern price. On the demand side, consumers, who have to decide whether or not to buy an additional quantity of a commodity, compare its marginal utility with its price. Marshall's assumption of constant marginal utility of money, vindicated by Georgescu-Roegen (1968), allows consumers to take their decision without the need to inspect the whole range of potential consumption (Leijonhufvud 2006: 327). On the supply side, when price falls below average fixed cost, the marginal cost curve does not coincide with the individual producer's supply curve: "fear of spoiling the market" acts to restrain production below the level of the marginal cost curve (Marshall 1920: 374–5, 458–9, 498). In general, even when working "at the margin", productive units face different sets of problems and their margins are dispersed through a multidimensional space. Some firms, at the beginning of their activity, strive to strengthen their position, others are decaying or switching to different products. Looking for the equilibrium of the industry, the representative firm "comes to our aid" (Marshall 1920: 459), establishing a link between equilibrium analysis and the study of the growth of the industry. To distinguish the representative firm from the tools of pure equilibrium analysis, Marshall emphasizes that "the concept is biological rather than mechanical" (Marshall 1898: 50). What marginal analysis does, in Marshall's system, is to show how equilibrium is worked out in a given set of circumstances. Demand and supply curves can be relied upon only in the neighbourhood of the equilibrium point (Whitaker 1975, I: 137; Marshall 1920: 133, 384 n); any larger movement irreversibly destabilizes the connection between prices and quantities which the curves represent.

The driving force that guides human action to equalize marginal uses is the "principle of substitution". This too cannot be identified with the maximizing tool of the marginalist school, as it performs a supplementary function, dynamic or rather biological, mixing up "optimization within a given technology with a change of technology" (Loasby 1990: 121–2). The principle is "a special and limited application of the law of survival of the fittest" (Marshall 1920: 597), "one form of competition" (ibid.: 540), which is itself "one of the many agencies through which natural selection works" (Guillebaud 1961, II: 75). It applies to "almost every field of economic inquiry" (Marshall 1920: 341), consumer's theory included. Its more relevant applications, however, are those of "the alert business man", who "strives so to modify his arrangements as to obtain better results with a given expenditure, or equal results with a less expenditure" (ibid.: 355), and "is ever seeking for the most profitable application of his resources" (ibid.: 514).

Marshall's use of the concept of normal provides further proof of the incompatibility between his analysis and general equilibrium theory. Supply and demand curves reflect a "normal" way of working of the economic system: "every use of the term normal implies the predominance of certain tendencies which appear likely to be more or less steadfast and persistent in their action over those which are relatively exceptional and intermittent" (Marshall 1920: 34). This sets the reference point which, when brought into disequilibrium, will tend to re-establish itself. Perfect competition is ruled out as "the term [normal] has often to be applied to conditions in which perfectly free competition does not exist" (ibid.: 35) and "Normal does not mean Competitive" (ibid.: 347). This relativistic attitude is not due to any inconsistency, or unwillingness to follow the requirements of rigorous analysis. It is an ingrained habit, following from Marshall's evolutionary approach. Any change that takes place is not from scratch. It happens in a given setting and ends up in a slightly different one, according to the principle of continuity – *natura non facit saltum* – that well describes how evolution was conceived to work, both in the natural and the human world, at least before the theory of punctuated equilibria. Single changes are slight, it is their cumulative effects that revolutionize the system. This is how Marshallian competition works. It does not immediately subvert every behavioural rule, habit, or custom it finds on its way. It does so slowly, until in the end the passive resistance of custom is overcome by the active force of competition (Marshall and Marshall 1881: vi–vii; see Schlicht, 2006: 302–3). In the meantime however, other rigidities, due to newly established routines, will have replaced the old ones, and the system is never perfectly competitive. Imperfections are essential to evolution: no imperfection, no evolution could be Marshall's motto. Once "perfect adaptation" sets in, the system stops evolving and this is undesirable "for perfectly stable businesses would be likely to produce men who were little better than machines" (Marshall 1919: 195).

Marshall was at pains to insist that competitive markets are far from perfect, first because perfect competition "requires a perfect knowledge of the state of the market" and this is "an altogether unreasonable assumption" (Marshall 1920: 540). Marshallian competition is a lively force, based on guesses and expectations, far from its mechanical neighbour of general equilibrium theory. If productive routines make firms different from each other, consumers too have their own idiosyncratic preferences. Therefore, individual firms in a competitive market do not face the perfectly elastic demand curve of perfect competition theory. They compete starting from varying degrees of consumers' fidelity and their market is made up of separate groups of buyers, which Marshall classifies under two headings, the particular and the general market (Marshall 1919: 182; 1920: 458–9). In the 1930s, market imperfections were considered a major innovation only because they had been removed from the standard version of Marshall's theory.

Another anomaly of Marshall's analysis is that he drew his diagrams with prices as functions of quantities. These diagrams do not indicate the optimal quantities that are demanded or supplied at a given price, but the maximum or minimum prices at which they can be sold or supplied. The Marshallian cross is drawn from the point of view of the producer, who tries to determine the price at which different quantities can be supplied and sold: "the cost of production per unit is deduced from the amount expected to be produced, and not *vice versa*" (Marshall 1920: 457 n). The same view was already stated in *The Economics of Industry*: "Every producer of a commodity calculates the price at which he will be able to sell it, and the Expenses of producing it. He thus determines whether to increase or diminish his production" (Marshall and Marshall 1879

[1994]: 76). According to the advocates of the "marginalist revolution", the classics had failed to see how demand governs value. In appendix I of *The Principles* Marshall openly criticizes Jevons's opinion that "value depends on utility", and sympathizes with the classical doctrine that in the long run cost of production governs value.

To close this section, it may be appropriate to quote Leijonhufvud's (2006: 226–7) remark that "nothing better illustrates our confusion than the universal habit of drawing Walrasian schedules in Marshallian space".

Its Unfitness to Deal with Increasing Returns . . .

The confusion lamented by Leijonhufvud derives from the habit of isolating Marshall's analysis from its aim and context. Marshall bears some responsibility for this, because he stretched the mechanical analogy beyond the limits he had set and tried to shield it from its deficiencies, reserving their treatment to a further stage that he never achieved. However, the unfitness of ordinary curves to represent the evolution of the economic system becomes insurmountable in the theories of increasing returns and distribution. They are dealt with respectively in this and the following section.

Increasing returns follow, among others, the pattern of the growth of knowledge as conceived in "Ye machine": variations produce innovations that in the long run irreversibly change the operating system. Book IV of the *Principles* and *Industry and Trade* show the model at work in shaping the organization of the industry, in a relentless succession of innovation and standardization. This evolutionary model cannot be envisaged through the lens of static equilibrium analysis.

The issue of increasing returns troubled Marshall from the beginning. They were first introduced as part of the analytical machinery in curve D of the early essay "On value", meant to explain long-term equilibrium. A letter to Neville Keynes shows that, when writing the *Principles*, Marshall was in doubt as to whether to resurrect the analysis of the early essay, initially set aside because of fear of "over-complexity" (Whitaker 1996, I: 278). In the first edition, increasing returns found their proper place in chapter V of book V, the core of value theory. Marshall's fear of over-complexity must soon have had a comeback, as he felt unhappy with this collocation, and changed it in subsequent editions. Ultimately, in edition V, increasing returns were relegated to appendix H. The irreversibility problem was shut up in a sort of "Pandora's box" (Bharadwaj 1972: 46), together with the limitations of the statical method that could have undermined the fundamentals of equilibrium analysis. The final location is emblematic of Marshall's worries on how to match the biological foundations of economics with static equilibrium analysis. While emphasizing the biological character of key concepts of equilibrium analysis, such as the principle of substitution and the representative firm, he strove to preserve his tools from getting lost in the *mare magnum* of economic biology.

Given the fact that irreversibility is an essential feature of increasing returns, they were a source of trouble, which, though it could not be ignored, was to be segregated, "softening the impact of the remark of the non-rigidity of the curves with the claim that its relevance was limited to the case of increasing returns only, with no substantial consequences for the other cases" (Dardi 2006: 224). Hence the decision to treat them in the appendix almost as if they were an anomaly. As Dardi observes, this decision leads readers astray, as it makes them believe that increasing returns are an exception to the rule that supply curves unproblematically provide a perfect representation of the economic forces at work. When Marshall faces the "exception", in appendix H, the supply curves become two. The "true" supply curve plots the prices at which any quantity can be produced, assuming that quantity be the overall level of production. This curve adequately represents the case of increasing returns, with its intrinsic irreversibility. Beside it, Marshall drew the "particular expenses curve", always positively inclined, which embodies the conditions under which different quantities of a commodity are produced under the assumption that total supply is fixed. Equilibrium along this curve coincides with the cost of the marginal producer. The "true" supply curve cannot be derived from the particular expenses curve. As Andrews (1951: 148) notes, "the reasoning is of general application", and, here as elsewhere, "the blunt facts of increasing returns saved Marshall from the use of constructions which . . . would have led to misleading conclusions".

Increasing returns deprive the concept of margin itself of meaning:

> [T]he term "margin of production" has no significance for long periods in relation to commodities the cost of production of which diminishes with a gradual increase in the output . . . Therefore, when we are discussing the special conditions of value of those commodities which conform to that tendency, the term "margin" should be avoided (Marshall 1920: app. H).

To prevent the problem from disrupting the theory of the equilibrium of the individual firm, Marshall assumed that "a tendency to increasing returns does not exist generally for short periods" (ibid.). For the long period, the problem was dealt with by resorting to the representative firm, which has access to the internal and external economies dependent on the expansion of production (Marshall 1920: 317). The representative firm is meant to explain why internal economies do not lead to monopoly, as mathematical equilibrium theory inexorably infers from its premises (Whitaker 1996, II: 227).

Though relegated to the appendix, increasing returns are not an oddity, but bring to the forefront the irreversibility problem, which is ubiquitous in Marshall's economics. Hysteresis regards demand curves too, whenever new patterns of consumption, established by price variations, change the consumer's preferences after prices have returned to their former level (Marshall 1920: 808; cf. also Whitaker 1975, II: 163). Such phenomena defy the tools of static equilibrium analysis. Given the mathematics he knew, Marshall could not do much better, but he never accepted the idea that statics has autonomous scientific status: "Statics is but a branch of Dynamics" (Marshall 1920: 366 n). The term dynamics itself, however, is deceptive, as it fails to seize the essential elements of the problem. While the analogy between economic and mechanical statics is fruitful, that between economic and mechanical dynamics is misleading: "the Mecca of the economist is economic biology rather than economic dynamics" (Marshall 1898: 43). Like biology, economics has to do with qualitative change. When human agents are changed by the action of economic forces, they are different in a sense which does not coincide with the way in which physical forces are changed by the action of other forces. The irreversibility of the pendulum is caused by mechanical forces that do not affect its law of swinging; the same does not hold in economics. There is an unbridgeable gap between the tools of economic analysis of book V and the cognitive tasks of advanced economics. A different, rather indeterminate kind of equilibrium analysis is required in biology:

[I]n the earlier stages of economics, we think of demand and supply as crude forces pressing against one another, and tending towards a mechanical equilibrium; but in the later stages, the balance or equilibrium is conceived not as between crude mechanical forces, but as between the organic forces of life and decay. (Marshall 1898: 43)

. . . and with Distribution Theory

Another spectacular failure of static analysis is distribution theory. Marshall is known for his marginal productivity theory. The marginal shepherd of the "Preliminary survey" of book VI of the *Principles* is taken as an epitome (sometimes a caricature) of the unit of a factor of production, which, when added to other factors, causes an increase in net production that determines its remuneration. This is an instance of Marshall's many generalizations of Ricardo's theory; in this case it is brought about by dropping the assumption that the technical coefficients of production are fixed. The theory is a mere consequence of the application of the principle of substitution to the derived demand for agents of production: the "alert business man" employs as many units of each agent as are capable of repaying their cost, so that, "in its marginal application, the cost is proportionate to the additional net product resulting from its use" (Marshall 1920: 515).

However, as Marshall repeatedly emphasizes, the law of substitution and the marginal product do not provide the backbones of a theory of distribution. As usual with Marshall, the determining causes lie on the supply side: "Marshall in true classical vein sees factor supply conditions as having the dominant effect in determining wage and interest rates in the long period" (Whitaker 2006: 322). In the long run, supply conditions regulate the price of labour, like any other price, and "Ricardo and his followers seem to have been rightly guided by their intuitions, when they silently determined that the forces of supply were those, the study of which is the more urgent and involves the greater difficulty" (Marshall 1920: 525).

In the case of labour, Marshall explicitly rejects the idea that marginal productivity determines its remuneration. The true causal link runs the other way around: increase in wages leads to increased productivity. Moreover, the effects are cumulative because of the indirect effects on the rearing of children. The word "cumulative(ly)" is repeated six times in chapter IV of book VI, in connection with the evil effects of low wages.

Likewise, when dealing with capital Marshall rejects Böhm-Bawerk's theory that interest depends on the increased productivity of roundabout methods of production (Marshall 1920: 583 n). Supply conditions determine whether interest has to be paid for the use of capital. In principle, interest can be negative (ibid.: 232, 582 n), and even when it is positive there is no necessary relationship between its rate and the level of saving. It all depends on the motives which lie behind the supply of saving.

With his analytical tools on hand, Marshall outlines a general overview of distribution in book VI of *Principles*. The book is of paramount importance in his system of thought because it verges on the "high theme of economic progress". In particular, the final chapter (final two, from the fifth edition) leads the way to higher level economic and social research, as Marshall states in *Distribution and Exchange*:

In Book V the theory of oscillations about a point of equilibrium is prominent, but not in Book VI. There we have very little to do with oscillations of a mechanical sort about a centre of equilibrium. We discuss demand and supply in their general relations, but ever more and more from a biological point of view. Especially is that the case in the final chapter, which gives a slight partial sketch of the "Influence of Progress on Value." Every page of that chapter is dominated by conceptions of provisional equilibria of opposing forces. An endeavour is made, by their latent aid, to present at once whole chords, instead of single notes. But the equilibria themselves never appear. The chapter aims at being dynamical, if that phrase must be used; but I prefer to regard it as biological. (Marshall 1898: 54)

Distribution is fundamental since in the long run it exercises a decisive influence on the uses of wealth and thereby on social and economic evolution. Increase in the standard of life and incentives to capital accumulation are two leading forces of economic progress, and the distribution of wealth decides whether they become stronger or not. The analytical machinery of equilibrium analysis is almost useless in dealing with the long period perspective, in which irreversible and cumulative processes are pervasive. This is the main reason why, as Shove remarked, Marshall "never actually applied his supply and demand curves to the agents of production". They would be applicable only to a very limited extent, as "the irreversibility of the process to be analysed is even more patent here. The rising long-period supply price of labour definitely depends on the effect of high earnings on habitual standards of life" (Shove, 1942: 324).

Interpreters have often noted a contrast between the evolutionary character of book IV and the static equilibrium analysis of book V. Book VI goes one step further, taking into account the evolution of the economic system, and investigates how the earnings of the agents of production of Book IV, in compliance with the theory of value of book V, react on their future performance and shape the overall functioning of the economic system.

The Abandonment of Marshall's Programme and its Resurrection

After Marshall's death, his research programme was abandoned in favour of more exact theorizing (Hart 2013). Pigou, unanimously considered the guardian of the Marshallian tradition, paid little attention to the limits of the "organon". One of the most striking instances of this change of mind is Pigou's welfare economics that ignores irreversibility problems. Bharadwaj (1972) reconstructs Marshall's annoyance at Pigou's handling of the subject, as is revealed by Marshall's comments on his personal copy of *Wealth and Welfare*:

> His [Marshall's] criticism of Pigou is directed against Pigou's application of the statical method to the case of increasing returns without the qualifications that he himself had laid down. . . . His criticism raises questions which are not confined to Pigou's application of the statical method to the problem of welfare, but relate more generally to the validity of the statical approach to the theory of equilibrium itself. (Bharadwaj 1972: 44, 46)

Another episode, which shows Pigou's disposition, is the substitution of the representative firm with the equilibrium firm, defined in such a way that its marginal cost is equal to the supply price of the industry. This makes it easy to think of as if "all the firms contained in it [the industry] were individually in equilibrium" (Pigou 1928: 239). In a perfectly competitive market, the equilibrium firm has no internal economies and increasing returns are only due to the economies originating from the expansion of the output of the whole industry. When Robbins (1928) attacked the representative firm, it had already disappeared from view. Loasby's summary of the episode is worth quoting at length:

> the representative firm is the device by which Marshall seeks to preserve the continuity between a process theory of the firm and an equilibrium analysis of price. Pigou's decision to replace it by an equilibrium firm . . . destroyed the link. Marshall's achievement in having Pigou elected as his successor had consequences which he neither intended nor desired. . . . the form of Marshall's ideas triumphed over their substance. (Loasby 1990: 124; see also Hart 2003; O'Brien 2006)

The substitution of the equilibrium firm for the representative firm can be seen as a typological fallacy. The two concepts answer different theoretical problems: whereas the former aims to explain how equilibrium holds notwithstanding the evolution of the industry, the latter focuses on the evolution of the industry, in which equilibrium constitutes but a provisional step.

Soon afterwards, the 1930 *Economic Journal* Symposium led the way to the replacement of Marshall's equilibrium of the industry with the equilibrium of the firm which characterized the theories of imperfect and monopolistic competition. Sraffa (1926) had shown that Marshall's partial equilibrium analysis was incompatible with static general equilibrium and increasing returns "incompatible with competitive conditions". Robertson tried to rescue both internal economies and the representative firm from Robbins's and Sraffa's devastating critiques, as well as from Pigou's concessions, but, without directly challenging the theory of the market for the competitive manufacturing business, he was "downed" by Sraffa (Andrews 1951: 157). As a result, "a whole department of economic analysis has disappeared into the gulf that he [Sraffa] opened up" (ibid.: 139).

Sraffa's "destructive criticism" was followed by Shove's "constructive suggestions", which, though at the time quite uninfluential, set the pace for later attempts to rescue Marshall's theory from oblivion. Market imperfections and time constraints take centre stage in Shove's subdivision of internal economies into economies of individual expansion and concentration, with the former alone compatible with competitive equilibrium, as well as in his substitution of the representative firm with a stochastic theory of the distribution of firms, later revived by Newman and Wolfe (1961).

The resurrection of Marshall's research programme came from two breakthroughs in industrial and economic analysis: the competence theory of the firm and the advent of evolutionary economics. As for the former, after Andrews (1951) had revived Marshall's industrial analysis, dropping the assumptions for the individual firm of short-term decreasing returns and equality between marginal cost and price, Penrose's (1959) theory focused on the inner structure of the firm, conceived as an evolving bundle of resources and competencies. This approach, developed by Richardson, is now a well-established trend of research — rightly labelled post-Marshallian – that complements Coase's transaction costs theory of the firm (Loasby 1999, Langlois 2011). The focus lies on the effort by the firm to build up a growing asset of capabilities, similar to what was achieved by Marshall's ideal machine. This determines the competitive advantage of the firm that often depends on specific, non-transferable forms of cooperation between factors of production. As for evolutionary economics, Nelson and Winter (1982) can be taken as the turning point. Their hero, however, was Schumpeter, with Marshall in a subordinate position, as he had been in the heyday of general equilibrium. Since the evolutionary turn gained momentum, Marshall's role has been reconsidered, and his evolutionary model given more credit as a source of inspiration. The alternation of innovation and routine, order and creativity, variation and standardization is the base element of modern evolutionary theories, as it was of Marshall's. New mathematical tools help tackle some of the problems Marshall left unsolved (Foster 1993; Metcalfe 2007). The road to the Mecca has definitely reopened.

TIZIANO RAFFAELLI

See also:

British marginalism (II); Cambridge School of economics (II); Francis Ysidro Edgeworth (I); Evolutionary economics (III); German and Austrian schools (II); Lausanne School (II); John Stuart Mill (I); Arthur Cecil Pigou (I); Marie-Esprit-Léon Walras (I).

References and further reading

Andrews, P.W.S. (1951), 'Industrial analysis in economics, with special reference to Marshallian doctrine', in T. Wilson and P.W.S. Andrews (eds), *Oxford Studies in the Price Mechanism*, Oxford: Clarendon Press, pp. 139–72.

Becher, H.W. (1980), 'William Whewell and Cambridge mathematics', *Historical Studies in the Physical Sciences*, **11** (1), 1–48.

Bharadwaj, K. (1972), 'Marshall on Pigou's *Wealth and Welfare*', *Economica*, **39** (153), 32–46.

Clifford, W.K. (1886), *Lectures and Essays*, London: Macmillan.

Coase, R.H. (1937), 'The nature of the firm', *Economica*, new series, **4** (16), 386–405.

Cook, S. (2009), *The Intellectual Foundations of Alfred Marshall's Economic Science: A Rounded Globe of Knowledge*, Cambridge: Cambridge University Press.

Dardi, M. (2006), 'Partial equilibrium and period analysis', in T. Raffaelli, G. Becattini and M. Dardi (eds), *The Elgar Companion to Alfred Marshall*, Cheltenham, UK and Northampton, MA, USA: Edward Elgar, pp. 215–25.

Dardi, M. (2016), 'Philosophy and psychology of mathematics according to Alfred Marshall', *Cambridge Journal of Economics*, **40** (1), 283–308.

Foster, J. (1993), 'Economics and the self-organization approach: Alfred Marshall revisited', *Economic Journal*, **103** (419), 975–91.

Frisch, R. (1950), 'Alfred Marshall's theory of value', *Quarterly Journal of Economics*, **64** (4), 495–524.

Georgescu-Roegen, N. (1968), 'Revisiting Marshall's constancy of marginal utility of money', *Southern Economic Journal*, **35** (2), 176–81.

Groenewegen, P. (1995), *A Soaring Eagle: Alfred Marshall 1842–1924*, Cheltenham, UK and Northampton, MA, USA: Edward Elgar.

Groenewegen, P. (ed.) (1996), *Official Papers of Alfred Marshall. A Supplement*, Cambridge: Cambridge University Press.

Guillebaud, C.W. (ed.) (1961), *Alfred Marshall's Principles of Economics*, 2 vols, London: Macmillan.

Hart, N. (2003), 'From the representative to the equilibrium firm: why Marshall was not a Marshallian', in R. Arena and M. Quéré (eds), *The Economics of Alfred Marshall. Revisiting Marshall's Legacy*, London: Macmillan, pp. 158–81.

Hart, N. (2013), *Alfred Marshall and Modern Economics. Equilibrium Theory and Evolutionary Economics*, London: Palgrave Macmillan.

Hodgson, G.M. (1993), 'The Mecca of Alfred Marshall', *Economic Journal*, **103** (417), 406–15.

Keynes, J.M. (1924), 'Alfred Marshall 1842–1924', *Economic Journal*, **34** (135), 311–72.

Langlois, R. (2011), 'Marshall's (real) influence on present-day industrial economics', in T. Raffaelli, T. Nishizawa and S. Cook (eds), *Marshall, Marshallians, and Industrial Economics*, London Routledge, pp. 308–19.

Leijonhufvud, A. (2006), 'Market adjustment processes', in T. Raffaelli, G. Becattini and M. Dardi (eds), *The Elgar Companion to Alfred Marshall*, Cheltenham, UK and Northampton, MA, USA: Edward Elgar, pp. 226–36.

Loasby, J.B. (1990), 'Firms, markets, and the principle of continuity', in J.K. Whitaker (ed.), *Centenary Essays on Alfred Marshall*, Cambridge: Cambridge University Press, pp. 108–26.

Loasby, J.B. (1999), 'Marshall's theory of the firm', in R.E. Backhouse and J. Creedy (eds), *From Classical Economics to the Theory of the Firm*, Cheltenham, UK and Northampton, MA, USA: Edward Elgar, pp. 175–93.

Maas, H. and M. Morgan (2002), 'Timing history: the introduction of graphical analysis in 19th century British economics', *Revue d'histoire des sciences humaines*, no. 7, 97–127.

Marshall, A. (1898), 'Distribution and exchange', *Economic Journal*, **8**, 37–59.

Marshall, A. (1919), *Industry and Trade*, London: Macmillan.

Marshall, A. (1920), *Principles of Economics*, 8th edn, London: Macmillan.

Marshall A. and M.P. Marshall (1879), *The Economics of Industry*, reprinted 1994, Bristol: Thoemmes Press.

Marshall, A. and M.P. Marshall (1881), *The Economics of Industry*, 2nd edn, London: Macmillan.

Metcalfe, S. (2007), 'Alfred Marshall's Mecca: reconciling the theories of value and distribution', *The Economic Record*, **83** (special issue), S1–S22.

Moss, L.S. (1982), 'Biological theory and technological entrepreneurship in Marshall's writings', *Eastern Economic Journal*, **8** (1), 3–13.

Nelson, R.R. and S.G. Winter (1982), *An Evolutionary Theory of Economic Change*, Cambridge, MA: Belknap Press.

Newman, P. and J.N. Wolfe (1961), 'A model for the long-run theory of value', *Review of Economic Studies*, **42** (1), 51–61.

O'Brien, D.P. (2006), 'The theory of the firm after Marshall', in T. Raffaelli, G. Becattini and M. Dardi (eds), *The Elgar Companion to Alfred Marshall*, Cheltenham, UK and Northampton, MA, USA: Edward Elgar, pp. 625–33.

Penrose, E.T. (1959), *The Theory of the Growth of the Firm*, Oxford: Oxford University Press.

Pigou, A.C. (1928), 'An analysis of supply', *Economic Journal*, **38** (150), 238–57.

Pigou, A.C. (ed.) (1925), *Memorials of Alfred Marshall*, London: Macmillan.

Raffaelli, T. (ed.) (1994), 'Alfred Marshall's early philosophical writings', *Research in the History of Economic Thought and Methodology, Archival Supplement*, **4**, 51–159.

Raffaelli, T. (2003), *Marshall's Evolutionary Economics*, London: Routledge.

Robbins, L. (1928), 'The representative firm', *Economic Journal*, **38** (151), 387–404.

Robertson, D.H., P. Sraffa and G.F. Shove (1930), 'Increasing returns and the representative firm. A symposium', *Economic Journal*, **40** (157), 79–116.

Schlicht, E. (2006), 'Custom and competition', in T. Raffaelli, G. Becattini, and M. Dardi (eds), *The Elgar Companion to Alfred Marshall*, Cheltenham, UK and Northampton, MA, USA: Edward Elgar, pp. 304–6.

Shove, G.F. (1942), 'The place of Marshall's *Principles* in the development of economic theory', *Economic Journal*, **52** (208), 294–329.

Sraffa, P. (1926), 'The laws of returns under competitive conditions', *Economic Journal*, **36** (144), 535–50.

Whitaker, J.K. (ed.) (1975), *The Early Economic Writings of Alfred Marshall, 1867–90*, 2 vols, London: Macmillan.

Whitaker, J.K. (ed.) (1996), *The Correspondence of Alfred Marshall Economist*, 3 vols, Cambridge: Cambridge University Press.

Whitaker, J.K. (2006), 'The theory of distribution: an overview', in T. Raffaelli, G. Becattini, and M. Dardi (eds), *The Elgar Companion to Alfred Marshall*, Cheltenham, UK and Northampton, MA, USA: Edward Elgar, pp. 319–27.

Philip Henry Wicksteed (1844–1927)

Philip Henry Wicksteed (1844–1927) was an English economist who was also a Unitarian theologian (succeeding James Martineau at the Little Portland Street Chapel in London in 1874, and resigning in 1897), translator and classicist (with a particular interest in Dante) and literary critic: Wicksteed's life is described by Herford (1931). Turning to economics after reading Henry George's (1879) *Progress and Poverty*, for many years he gave University of London Extension Lectures on economics (as part of an adult education programme). Robbins (1933: v) makes the point that "there can be few men who have so successfully combined such a wide range of intellectual pursuits with such conspicuous excellence in each of them". The greatest influence on his economics was Jevons's *Theory of Political Economy*, and he can be described, with Edgeworth, as a disciple of Jevons and a careful exponent of the subjectivist approach in which cost is interpreted in terms of foregone alternatives rather than as a "real cost". Robbins (1931: 229) describes how Wicksteed's copy of the second edition of Jevons's *Theory*, purchased in 1882, is covered with marginal annotations.

Wicksteed's first publication in economics was his 1884 criticism of Marx, the first along Jevonian lines by a British economist, and which led to a debate with George Bernard Shaw. He published his first economics book, *The Alphabet of Economic Science* in 1888. This is primarily a pedagogic work expounding the utility theory of value, with a long introductory section on basic calculus. In this, he is responsible for introducing the term "marginal utility" as an improvement on Jevons's "final utility". This was followed in 1894 by the celebrated *Essay on the Co-ordination of the Laws of Distribution* in which, in contrast to the earlier work, he states in the preface that, "I address myself only to experts", although at the same time "without any claim to originality" (Wicksteed 1894: 3). Although the main elements of the marginal productivity theory of distribution, according to which factors receive their marginal revenue product (marginal physical product multiplied by marginal revenue, which in a competitive goods market is equal to price or average revenue), had been proposed by a number of authors, Wicksteed is famous for his original argument that the total remuneration of all factors will precisely exhaust total revenue. Hence there is no "residual" available for distribution (in contrast to the classical approach in which rent is regarded as a residual). This led to the famous review by Alfred Flux (a Cambridge Senior Wrangler in mathematics in 1887 who, as a student of St John's College, came into contact with Alfred Marshall). Flux made the important point that Wicksteed had implicitly assumed constant returns to scale, or linear homogeneous, production functions and, in addition, that the result is immediately given by the application of Euler's theorem for homogeneous functions. For $f(x_1, \ldots, x_n)$ homogeneous of degree k, then Euler's theorem states that:

$$\sum_{i=1}^{n} x_i \frac{\partial f(x_1, \ldots, x_n)}{\partial x_i} = kf(x_1, \ldots, x_n) \qquad (1)$$

Hence for $k = 1$ and perfectly competitive markets, the "product exhaustion" result follows. Flux (1894: 310) suggested that, "there seems no need for delaying to prove a relation so well known as this, as Mr. Wicksteed does". It may have been "well known" to mathematicians, but Wicksteed was not a trained mathematician; indeed Herford

(1931: 200) mentions that he had been taking lessons in calculus from John Bridge, a mathematics tutor at University College London.

The assumption of linear homogeneity, along with the continuous substitutability of factors in production, was subsequently strongly criticized by Pareto, Barone and a bad-tempered Walras who unfairly accused Wicksteed of plagiarism. For further discussion of Wicksteed's contribution, see Stigler (1941: 38–60). Furthermore, it elicited the following comment by Edgeworth, made in his unique style: "There is a magnificence in this generalization which recalls the youth of philosophy. Justice is a perfect cube, said the ancient sage; and rational conduct is a homogeneous function, adds the modern savant". Edgeworth's "ancient sage" is Aristotle, who in his *Nicomachean Ethics* argued that justice requires equality in all directions. As a result of these attacks, Wicksteed himself became somewhat dissatisfied with his argument, though not, of course, with the main points of the marginal productivity theory.

In 1910 Wicksteed published his massive *Common Sense of Political Economy*, described by Robbins (1931: 235) as "the most exhaustive non-mathematical exposition of the technical and philosophical complications of the so-called 'marginal' theory of pure economics, which has appeared in any language". Again, Wicksteed makes no claims of originality, but this book does contain a strong criticism of the partial equilibrium analysis of supply and demand, suggesting that it does not pay adequate attention to the role of stocks of goods. He went so far as to describe the standard diagrammatic analysis as "profoundly misleading" (1910, [1933], II: 785) and actually stated that there is "no such thing" as a supply curve. He argued that although it is useful to separate the supply and demand sides of the market in considering the process of adjustment by which an equilibrium may be reached, it was of dubious value in examining the determinants of that price. He suggested that:

> the cross curves of demand and supply, so often employed by economists, are really no more than two sections of the true collective curve of demand, separated out from each other, and read, for convenience, in reverse directions. These cross curves, then, as usually presented, confuse the methods by which the equilibrating price is arrived at with the conditions that determine what it is. (Wicksteed 1910 [1933] II: 797–8)

The situation he had in mind was not of firms producing only for sale but, along with other major neoclassical economists, for exchange. He envisaged the standard exchange situation in which individuals hold stocks of a good which are brought to a market. His examples include the results of a harvest, or the "catch" of a fishing fleet (Wicksteed 1910 [1933], II: 787). Those who hold stocks also consume the good and therefore have a demand for it comparable with that of individuals who do not hold stocks. This context is thus the same as that of Jevons and Walras, Mill and Marshall (when considering international trade) and Edgeworth, yet Wicksteed took a quite independent position: See Wicksteed (1910 [1933], I: 229–34, II: 772–96, II: 797–800, II: 822–6). He referred to the conventional supply curve as a "reverse demand curve" and argued: "I say it boldly and baldly: there is no such thing . . . what is usually called the supply curve is in reality the demand curve of those who possess the commodity" (1910 [1933], II: 785).

Wicksteed's preferred diagram showed a curve relating the price to the total demand of possessor and non-possessors (on the horizontal axis). The equilibrium price is then obtained by the intersection of this total demand curve with a vertical line drawn from the total stock of the good available. He went on to suggest that: "a change in its initial distribution (if the collective curve is unaffected, while the component or intersecting curves change) will have no effect on the market, or equilibrating price itself, which will come out exactly the same". (1910 [1933], II: 785–6).

However, this result was simply assumed by Wicksteed, who failed to recognize that the basic assumption, that a change in the allocation of stocks does not affect the total demand curve, requires very special conditions and generally will not hold; for details see Creedy (1991). In criticizing the partial equilibrium demand and supply analysis, Wicksteed simply replaced it with another partial equilibrium approach, instead of using the exchange context of Jevons, Walras and Edgeworth which in fact made explicit the stocks of goods held by traders in exchange.

Wicksteed's strong rejection of the supply curve is of course associated with his "Austrian" view that all productive resources are ultimately fixed in "supply" and that cost must be seen in terms of opportunity cost; see, for example, Hutchison (1953: 104). Again, this is entirely consistent with an emphasis on exchange. As stressed by Fraser (1937: 104), the view of cost in terms of foregone alternatives is "merely the extension of the exchange relationship to the whole range of economic life", which was of course the agenda set out by Jevons. This makes Wicksteed's approach rather curious.

His interest in Jevons also led Wicksteed to criticize Jevons's discussion of the famous King–Davenant law of demand, where Jevons provided a functional form which he "fitted" to the basic data which were presented by Davenant in tabular form. Wicksteed actually recognized that a third degree polynomial fits the data points exactly, and gave the parameters, adding that it "can hardly fail to stimulate curiosity as to the origin of this most interesting estimate, and the grounds on which it was formed" (1910 [1933], II: 738). He acknowledged the help of Bridge in finding the polynomial, using the "method of differences". Yet it is interesting that neither Wicksteed nor Jevons recognized that Whewell had earlier given the precise form of the polynomial, and yet Jevons explicitly referred to Whewell; for details see Creedy (1986).

Wicksteed's reputation stands because of his serious and extended analyses of fundamental theoretical questions. Although these analyses attracted the attention of only a small number of his contemporaries, they were without question the leaders of the economics profession. At a time when economics was becoming dominated by established academics, this was a remarkable achievement by someone who was clearly an "outsider". More general readers are indeed likely to find his expansive style difficult to penetrate, yet it is likely that those concerned with basic questions will continue to find much interest and food for thought in his works.

JOHN CREEDY

See also:

British marginalism (II); Competition (III); Francis Ysidro Edgeworth (I); General equilibrium theory (III); Hermann Heinrich Gossen (I); William Stanley Jevons (I); Alfred Marshall (I); Vilfredo Pareto (I); Arthur Cecil Pigou (I); Value and price (III); Marie-Esprit-Léon Walras (I); Welfare economics (III).

References and further reading
Creedy, J. (1986), 'On the King–Davenant law of demand'. *Scottish Journal of Political Economy*, **33** (3), 193–212.

Creedy, J. (1991), 'The role of stocks in supply and demand analysis: Wicksteed's problem', *Oxford Economic Papers*, **43** (4), 689–701.
Flux, A.W. (1894), 'Review of an essay on the co-ordination of the laws of production'. *Economic Journal*, **9**, 308–13.
Fraser, L.M. (1937), *Economic Thought and Language*, Edinburgh: A. & C. Black.
Herford, C.H. (1931), *Philip Henry Wicksteed*, London: J.M. Dent and Sons.
Hutchison, T.W. (1953), *A Review of Economic Doctrines 1870–1929*, Oxford: Clarendon Press.
Robbins, L. (1931), 'The economic works', in C.H. Herford, *Philip Henry Wicksteed*, London: J.M. Dent and Sons, pp. 228–47.
Robbins, L. (ed.) (1933), 'Introduction', in P.H. Wicksteed, *The Common Sense of Political Economy*, reprint of 1910 first edn, London: Macmillan.
Stigler, G.J. (1941), *Production and Distribution Theories: The Formative Period*, New York: Macmillan.
Wicksteed, P.H. (1884), 'Das Kapital: a criticism', *To-Day*, **2**, 388–409.
Wicksteed, P.H. (1888), *The Alphabet of Economic Science*, London: Macmillan.
Wicksteed, P.H. (1894), *An Essay on the Co-ordination of the Laws of Production*, London: Macmillan.
Wicksteed, P.H. (1910), *The Common Sense of Political Economy*. London: Macmillan, reprinted in 1933, L. Robbins (ed.), 2 vols, London: Routledge.

Francis Ysidro Edgeworth (1845–1926)

Francis Ysidro Edgeworth (1845–1926) was a leading figure in the rapid development of economics during the last quarter of the nineteenth century and the first quarter of the twentieth century. He held the Drummond Chair at Oxford from 1891 and was regarded as second only to the great Cambridge economist Alfred Marshall. He was a prolific and highly original author who, in a cosmopolitan age, had probably the widest correspondence with economists all over the world. For a full-length treatment of Edgeworth's economics, see Creedy (1986), and for a biography, see Barbé (2010). He was a man of enormously wide reading and considerable linguistic skills. He was the first editor of the *Economic Journal*, published by the newly formed Royal Economic Society. He was President of Section F of the British Association in 1889 and 1922.

He achieved eminence as a statistician as well as an economist, becoming a Guy Medallist (Gold) of the Royal Statistical Society in 1907 and was President of the Society, 1912–14. Indeed, of about 170 papers, roughly three-quarters are concerned with statistical theory. His main contributions to statistics concern work on inference and the "law of error", the correlation coefficient, transformations (what he called "methods of translation"), and the "Edgeworth expansion". The latter, a series expansion which provides an alternative to the Pearson family of distributions, has been widely used (particularly since the work of Sargan 1976) to improve on the central limit theorem in approximating sampling distributions. It has also been used to provide support for the bootstrap in providing an Edgeworth correction. His third and final book was *Metretike: or the Method of Measuring Probability and Utility* (1887). These contributions are not examined here; see Bowley (1928) and Stigler (1978). Edgeworth's work in probability and statistics has been collected by McCann (ed.) (1996).

His name is familiar to all economists, if only because of the "Edgeworth box", one of the most widely used analytical devices in the subject. This diagrammatic tool was introduced by Edgeworth in 1881 in his first publication in economics, *Mathematical Psychics: An Essay on the Application of Mathematics to the Moral Sciences*. This small book is remarkable for its highly original and far-reaching contributions to economics; indeed, Marshall began his review with the statement that, "This book shows clear signs of genius". However, it was written in such a terse and unique style that it took many years before its contributions were fully appreciated, despite the fact that Edgeworth became one of the most prominent economists of his age. The title itself does not clearly signal a book on economics, and his use of sophisticated mathematics put it well beyond the reach of most of the economists of the period. The technical difficulty of much of his published output contributed to its slow assimilation into text books and he continues to remain relatively neglected in texts on the history of economic analysis.

Mathematical Psychics provides the key to all his later work and his lasting importance to economics. He wrote extensively on a wide range of topics, but the central theme of Edgeworth's work is clear in his revealing statement, taken from his Presidential address to Section F of the Royal Society, that "It may be said that in pure economics there is only one fundamental theorem, but that is a very difficult one: the theory of bargain in a wide sense" (1925, II: 288).

Taking as his starting point Jevons's (1871 [1957]) basic analysis of exchange of two goods between two traders, Edgeworth supposed that the objective of each trader is to maximize utility, considered to be a general function of the quantities of the goods held and consumed after trade is concluded. The utility-maximizing approach was immediately congenial to Edgeworth, who was steeped in Utilitarian moral philosophy. He first concentrated on the nature of barter, instead of describing the characteristics of an equilibrium set of prices, that is, one which ensures that the individuals' responses are mutually consistent. If the traders in barter are allowed freely to vary the terms of provisional "contracts", Edgeworth showed that there is a range of "final settlements", from which no further "recontracting" would take place. In a rectangular box where the base and height are determined by the initial stocks of the two goods, these final settlements define what Edgeworth called the "contract curve". These settlements are also efficient trades, in the sense that if a settlement is not on the contract curve, movement to it can make one person better off without the other being worse off: this original idea of efficiency later came to be called Pareto efficiency. Movement along the contract curve involves one trader becoming worse off while the other gains.

Edgeworth then defined indifference curves for a trader as showing combinations of amounts consumed for which utility is constant. Using several approaches, he demonstrated that the contract curve is the locus of points of tangency between traders' indifference curves, between limits given by their pre-trade curves (those going through the initial endowment point in the box). The existence of a range of final settlements has important implications. First, without introducing further structure to the barter framework, it is not possible to say what the implied rate of exchange is, given only information about preferences and endowments of individuals. It results in "indeterminacy" whereby all that can be said is that the actual trade depends on the relative bargaining strength of the traders.

On the argument that such higgling is widespread, Edgeworth stated in his unique style that, "The whole creation groans and yearns, desiderating a principle of arbitration, and end of strifes" (1881: 51). His next argument involved two steps. First, he showed that the Utilitarian principle of maximizing total utility places individuals on the contract curve, because the mathematical conditions are equivalent to the tangency of indifference curves. Indeed, if it is possible to make someone better off without someone being worse off, total utility cannot be a maximum and individuals cannot be on the contract curve. While this may seem a small step, to Edgeworth it was of great significance. He suggested, "It is a circumstance of momentous interest that one of the in general indefinitely numerous settlements between contractors is the utilitarian arrangement . . . the contract tending to the greatest possible total utility of the contractors" (1881: 53).

However, he recognized that this result is not sufficient to justify the use of Utilitarianism as a principle of arbitration; it is only a necessary condition. Edgeworth's justification for Utilitarianism as a principle of justice, comparing points along the contract curve, was as follows:

> Now these positions lie in a reverse order of desirability for each party; and it may seem to each that as he cannot have his own way, in the absence of any definite principle of selection, he has about as good a chance of one of the arrangements as another . . . both parties may agree to commute their chance of any of the arrangements for . . . the utilitarian arrangement. (1881: 55)

The important point to stress about this statement is that Edgeworth clearly considered willingness to accept the Utilitarian arbitration in terms of choice under uncertainty.

His argument is that the contractors, faced with uncertainty about their prospects but viewing alternatives along the contract curve as equally likely, would choose to accept an arrangement along Utilitarian lines. Thus a crucial component of this argument is the use of equal a priori probabilities, something that was later important to Edgeworth in his statistical work. In taking this second step Edgeworth believed that he had provided an answer to an age old question, stating, "by what mechanism the force of self-love can be applied so as to support the structure of utilitarian politics, neither Helvetius, nor Bentham, nor any deductive egoist has made clear" (1881: 128).

The importance to him of this new justification of Utilitarianism cannot be exaggerated. Indeed, the whole of *Mathematical Psychics* seems to be imbued with a feeling of excitement generated by his discovery of this justification based on a "social contract". This provided the crucial link between "impure" and "pure" utilitarianism in a more satisfactory way than his earlier appeal to evolutionary forces, made in his book on *New and Old Methods of Ethics*, written in 1877, before turning to economics.

The nature of price-taking behaviour – involving an equimarginal principle whereby the ratio of prices must be equal, for both traders, to the ratio of their marginal utilities for each of the relevant goods, had been explored with great originality by Jevons with his "equations of exchange". Edgeworth made important extensions to this analysis, as well as providing his succinct diagrammatical synthesis (which included showing, in 1881: 113, how Marshall's "offer curves" can be derived from indifference curves). He showed how his box diagram can be used to illustrate a price-taking equilibrium. This arises where one or more of the mutual tangency positions of indifference curves along the contract curve also corresponds to tangency with a straight line going through the endowment point. This line represents a common budget constraint for the choices of the individuals, whereby the slope represents the exchange ratio and hence the relative price. In equilibrium, individuals acting in isolation and taking prices as given (in contrast to those engaged in barter) have mutually consistent demands and supplies. A price-taking equilibrium, as such a tangency position, must therefore correspond to a point on the contract curve.

Edgeworth was thus able to clarify the sense in which a price-taking (often called competitive) equilibrium is "optimal", fully recognizing that it is just one of many Pareto optimal points. This gives rise to what is now referred to as the "First Fundamental Theorem" of welfare economics – that a price-taking equilibrium is Pareto efficient. The use of price-taking also provides a considerable reduction in the amount of information required by traders compared with barter. Individuals only need to know the equilibrium prices, whereas in barter they have to learn a considerable amount of information about other individuals' preferences and endowments. Of course, this merely describes the properties of an equilibrium and does not, as Edgeworth was fully aware, explain how it may be achieved in practice. However, he later showed that a sequence of price adjustments, where trading – at the minimum of demand and supply – takes place at disequilibrium prices, leads to a point on the contract curve although precisely where is indeterminate.

Edgeworth then returned to the indeterminacy in barter, asking whether this indeterminacy results from the absence of competition in the simple two-person market. Edgeworth quickly moved on to examine the implications of introducing further pairs of traders. The analysis of barter with numerous traders again involves Edgeworth's stylized description of the recontracting process of barter mentioned above. With more traders, the importance of the recontracting process, apart from allowing the dissemination of information, lies in the fact that it makes it possible to analyse the use of collusion among some of the traders. Individuals are allowed to form coalitions in order to improve bargaining strength. Recontracting enables the coalitions to be broken up by outsiders who may attract members of a group away with more favourable terms of exchange.

The analysis of many traders, where coalitions can be temporarily formed and broken up by the offer of improved terms from other traders, would appear to present formidable difficulties. Yet Edgeworth rapidly demonstrated, again using his famous box diagram, that the introduction of further similar pairs of traders gradually reduces the range of indeterminacy; that is, the length of the contract curve shrinks. With a sufficiently large number of traders, the range of indeterminacy shrinks to the finite number of price-taking equilibria. Barter thus replicates price-taking behaviour. Given that coalitions among traders are allowed in the recontracting process, a price-taking equilibrium cannot be "blocked" by a coalition of traders. In this sense the competitive equilibrium is robust.

The argument that a complex process of bargaining among a large number of individuals produces a result which is identical to a price-taking equilibrium is an important result that is far from intuitively obvious. The recontracting process can be said to represent a competitive process, and the contract curve shrinks essentially because of the competition between suppliers of the same good, although it is carried out in a barter framework in which explicit prices are not used. The price-taking equilibrium, in contrast, does not actually involve a competitive process. Individuals simply believe that they must take market prices as given and outside their control. They respond to those prices without any reference to other individuals. But the result is that the price-taking equilibrium looks just like a situation in which all activity is perfectly coordinated.

Great stress was placed by Edgeworth on comparison with Lagrange's "Principle of least action" in examining the overall effects produced by the interactions among many particles. The connection with Edgeworth's analysis of competition, involving interaction among a large number of competitors to produce a determinate rate of exchange, is clear. The fact that in the natural sciences so much could be derived from a single principle was important for both Jevons and Edgeworth. However, Edgeworth took this to its ultimate limit in arguing that the comparable single principle in social sciences, that of maximum utility, would produce results of comparable value. Referring to Laplace's massive work, *Mécanique Céleste*, he suggested that:

> Mécanique Sociale may one day take her place along with Mécanique Céleste, throned each upon the double-sided height of one maximum principle, the supreme pinnacle of moral as of physical science ... the movements of each soul, whether selfishly isolated or linked sympathetically, may continually be realising the maximum energy of pleasure, the Divine love of the universe. (1881: 12)

A strong belief in the value of mathematical analysis in economics, even where the precise numerical form of the relevant relationships cannot be known, imbues all of Edgeworth's work. When this is combined with his strong adherence to Utilitarianism, it is not difficult to see how Edgeworth was excited to be showing not only why this principle may be accepted in the form of a "social contract", but how the actions of many utility maximizing individuals in a market can lead to a determinate solution. Thus, while the comparison with Laplace may seem fanciful to some readers, it was far from fanciful to Edgeworth. These elements provide the "plan" with which virtually all his work in economics could be viewed. It is no wonder that Alexander Pope's statement, in his *Essay on Man*, that it presents "A mighty maze, but not without a plan" was borrowed by Edgeworth to describe the competitive barter process. It also nicely fits Edgeworth's own œuvre. Although he went on to write on a wide range of economic topics, and to make original contributions to mathematical statistics which alone would guarantee a lasting reputation, an appreciation of the preoccupations leading towards, and nature of, this first work is important in placing everything else in perspective: his economic papers are collected in Edgeworth (1925).

It is clear from even a small sample of Edgeworth's work that the writer brings to it not just a deep and fertile originality, but also a vast range of knowledge covering natural sciences and literature. His writing is highly allusive and contains quotations from Greek and Latin classics as well as a range of English poets. It displays a sharp wit of a kind found in no other writing on the subject, and continues to repay repeated reading.

JOHN CREEDY

See also:

British marginalism (II); Competition (III); General equilibrium theory (III); Hermann Heinrich Gossen (I); William Stanley Jevons (I); Alfred Marshall (I); Vilfredo Pareto (I); Arthur Cecil Pigou (I); Value and price (III); Marie-Esprit-Léon Walras (I); Welfare economics (III); Philip Henry Wicksteed (I).

References and further reading

Barbé, L. (2010), *Francis Ysidro Edgeworth: A Portrait with Family and Friends*, Cheltenham, UK and Northampton, MA, USA: Edward Elgar.
Bowley, A.L. (1928), *Edgeworth's Contribution to Mathematical Statistics*, London: Royal Statistical Society.
Creedy, J. (1986), *Edgeworth and the Development of Neoclassical Economics*, Oxford: Basil Blackwell.
Edgeworth, F.Y. (1877), *New and Old Methods of Ethics: or Physical Ethics and Methods of Ethics*, Oxford: Parker.
Edgeworth, F.Y. (1881), *Mathematical Psychics: An Essay on the Application of Mathematics to the Moral Sciences*, London: Kegan Paul.
Edgeworth, F.Y. (1887), *Metretike, or the Method of Measuring Probability and Utility*, London: Temple.
Edgeworth, F.Y. (1925), *Papers Relating to Political Economy*, 3 vols, London: Macmillan, for the Royal Economic Society.
Jevons, W.S. (1871), *The Theory of Political Economy*, 5th edn 1957, ed. H.S. Jevons, New York: Augustus Kelly.
McCann, C.R. (ed.) (1996), *F.Y. Edgeworth: Writings in Probability, Statistics and Economics*, 3 vols, Cheltenham, UK and Northampton, MA, USA: Edward Elgar.
Sargan, J.D. (1976), 'Econometric estimators and the Edgeworth expansion', *Econometrica*, **44** (3), 421–48.
Stigler, S.M. (1978), 'Francis Ysidro Edgeworth, statistician', *Journal of the Royal Statistical Society*, series A, **141** (3), 287–322.

John Bates Clark (1847–1938)

John Bates Clark was born in Providence, Rhode Island on 26 January 1847. His child-hood was characterised by a strict and religious upbringing and his parents set high value on the education of their three children. Clark was educated at Brown University, Rhode Island and Amherst College, Massachusetts and graduated from Amherst in 1872 at the age of 25. During his studies at Amherst College, J. Seelye, president of the College at that time, piqued Clark's interest in political economy when Clark participated in one of his lectures. Clark spent three years of his studies (1872–75) in Heidelberg as well as in Zurich. In Heidelberg he was taught by C. Knies, a representative of the German Historical School. After returning to the United States in 1875, Clark was appointed to his first chair for political economy and history at Carleton College in Minnesota. In the same year he married Myra Smith with whom he had three children.

His time at Carleton College was important for two reasons (Henry 1999): first, he met T.B. Veblen – one of his most famous students – and, second, he published a range of arti-cles (Clark 1879a, 1879b, 1882, and so on) which made him known to the economic com-munity and to the public. In these articles Clark clarified his view on the capitalist order in consideration of the transformation of the US economy at that time from a system of free competition to one with oligopolistic and monopolistic tendencies ('trusts'). He was convinced that these developments resulted in rising inequality of income distribution and an aggravation of living conditions for the working class. He considered it as justi-fied that the working class formed unions to defend their rights, since "[l]abor imparts utilities to matter, and the impulse to it is that these may be enjoyed by the laborer. To be enjoyed they must be owned; the fruits that the laborer raises or the implements that he fashions must belong to him, and to no other" (Clark 1882: 843). Also worthy of note is his moral and spiritual arguing in these early works, which earned him the reputation of a 'Christian socialist' (see Henry 1999). His publishing activities at Carleton culminated in 12 articles and three book reviews mainly printed in *The New Englander*, which later became known as *The Yale Review*. Eight out of these 12 articles later formed the core of his first book *The Philosophy of Wealth* (1886). Clark was influenced in this period by the German Historical School, even if this school of thought never dominated his academic work and thinking.

At the beginning of the 1880s Clark left Carleton College and took a professorship for political science and history at Smith College in Northampton, Massachusetts. His early work at Smith College saw the transformation of Clark from a putative 'Christian socialist' to a neoclassical economist; his last public spiritual argument can be found in *Christianity and Modern Economics* (1887). Further, Clark no longer supported the posi-tion that oligopolistic and monopolistic tendencies are inevitably harmful to society (and in particular to the working class), but instead held the view that a non-competitive order is not condemnable and can be part of a capitalist order. Thereupon, Clark developed his theory of property rights, which was formulated against the works of K. Marx and H. George. In his time at Smith College, a further series of articles emerged (Clark 1888, 1889, 1890, 1891, 1894), where Clark continually developed his general theory of distri-bution, strengthening his neoclassical position. In addition, through these works Clark did the preparatory work for his magnum opus *The Distribution of Wealth. A Theory of Wages, Interest and Profits* (hereafter DoW), which was first published in 1899.

In 1892 Clark returned to Amherst College and held a chair for political economy. At the same time he gave a few lectures at Johns Hopkins University, partly acting in place of R. Ely. Noteworthy during his short stay at Amherst is the debate between Clark and E. von Böhm-Bawerk which lasted from 1893 until 1907. This debate on the theoretical meaning of capital and interest led to a vivid correspondence between the two and was carried out publicly in the *Quarterly Journal of Economics*. In 1894 Clark was elected to the presidency of the third chairman of the American Economic Association (AEA), which reflected his academic reputation.

In 1895 Clark was offered a chair at Columbia University where he remained until his retirement in 1923, except for the period 1898–99 when he replaced I. Fisher at Yale University, who was recovering from severe illness. During his time at Columbia University, Clark mainly researched in the field of industrial organization and published some of his most influential books, among them his magnum opus DoW as well as *The Control of Trusts* (1901) and *The Essentials of Economic Theory* (1907). At the core of his distribution theory developed in DoW lies the idea that in capitalist societies under competitive conditions each factor of production gets its share in the social product according to what it has contributed to the production of the former: "It is the purpose of this work to show that the distribution of the income of society is controlled by a natural law, and that this law, if it worked without friction, would give to every agent of production the amount of wealth which that agent creates" (DoW 1899: preface).

Thus, some natural law for the distribution of the social product exists and Clark considered every intervention in this natural law as harmful to the capitalist order — even if non-competitive tendencies are prevailing. What also today is associated with Clark's main contribution to economic theorizing is the extension of the Classical law of diminishing returns on land for the explanation of the rent to the explanation of all factor incomes:

> Wages then, conform to the product of the final increment of social labor and interest to the product of the final increment of social capital. Both of these incomes may be translated into the form of rents of concrete producers; and these, like all products, are elements of determining values. (Clark 1899: 843)

Yet, how to measure and, above all, in what unit should the share of each factor in the social product be expressed? While a physical measurement of labour did not constitute a severe problem, Clark was aware that a universal measure of capital was lacking. However, he only treated this severe problem in passing (see Kurz 1999). In developing his theory of distribution Clark borrowed heavily from J.H. von Thünen – especially concerning the marginal productivity principle – and from F.B.W. Hermann. However, only few references to them can be found in DoW. As Hagemann (2009) stresses, the distinction and complementarity between statics and dynamics is a crucial element in Clark's theory of distribution since in order to explain the distribution of the social product among the different factors of production an abstraction from dynamic forces is required. Instead concentrating on a static state of a stationary equilibrium is necessary:

> A static state, however, is imaginary. All natural societies are dynamic; and those which we have principally to study are highly so. [. . .] Yet this does not invalidate the conclusions of a static theory; for static laws are nevertheless real laws. [. . .] All the forces that would work in

the unchanging world are not only working in the changeful one, but are even the dominant forces in it. (Clark 1899: 29–30)

Apart from his vivid academic life at Columbia, Clark actively participated in the local political and cultural life and gave several talks and lectures at the Cooper Union Forum and the Lake Mohonk Conferences. As a confident pacifist, Clark was involved in ongoing discussions about the eradication of wars. In 1911 Clark was consigned by the Carnegie Endowment for International Peace with directing the department of economics and history, which he held until his retirement.

Clark died on 21 March 1938. In honour of Clark, since 1947 the AEA awards the prestigious 'John Bates Clark Medal' to young American economists every two years. The first awardee of this medal was P.A. Samuelson, who called John Bates Clark 'America's first great theorist' (Samuelson 1999: 55).

MARLIES SCHÜTZ

See also:

Eugen von Böhm-Bawerk (I); British marginalism (II); Capital theory (III); German and Austrian schools (II); Income distribution (III); William Stanley Jevons (I); Karl Heinrich Marx (I); Marie-Esprit-Léon Walras (I).

References and further reading

Clark, J.B. (1879a), 'Business ethics, past and present', *The New Englander and Yale Review*, **38** (149), 157–69.
Clark, J.B. (1879b), 'The nature and progress of true socialism', *The New Englander and Yale Review*, **38** (151), 565–82.
Clark, J.B. (1882), 'Non-competitive economics', *The New Englander and Yale Review*, **41** (171), 837–47.
Clark, J.B. (1886), *The Philosophy of Wealth: Economic Principles Newly Formulated*, Boston, MA: Ginn & Company, Publishers.
Clark, J.B. (1887), 'Christianity and modern economics', *The New Englander and Yale Review*, **47** (208), 50–60.
Clark, J.B. (1888), *Capital and its Earnings*, American Economic Association Monographs, vol. 3, Baltimore, MD: American Economic Association.
Clark, J.B. (1889), 'The possiblity of a scientific law of wages', *Publications of the American Economic Association*, **4** (1), 39–69.
Clark, J.B. (1890), 'The law of wages and interest', *Annals of the American Academy of Political and Social Science*, **1** (1), 43–65.
Clark, J.B. (1891), 'Distribution as determined by a law of rent', *Quarterly Journal of Economics*, **5** (3), 289–318.
Clark, J.B. (1894), 'A universal law of economic variation', *Quarterly Journal of Economics*, **8** (3), 261–79.
Clark, J.B. (1899), *The Distribution of Wealth. A Theory of Wages, Interest and Profits*, New York and London: Macmillan.
Clark, J.B. (1901), *The Control of Trusts: An Argument in Favor of Curbing the Power of Monopoly by a Natural Method*, New York and London: Macmillan.
Clark, J.B. (1907), *The Essentials of Economic Theory: As Applied to Modern Problems of Industry and Public Policy*, New York and London: Macmillan.
Hagemann, H. (2009), 'John Bates Clark', in H.D. Kurz (ed.), *Klassiker ökonomischen Denkens*, vol. 2, Munich: Verlag C. H. Beck oHG, pp. 9–25.
Henry, J.F. (1999), 'John Bates Clark: Leben und Werk', in K.-D. Grüske (ed.), *John Bates Clarks 'The Distribution of Wealth': Vademecum zu einem amerikanischen Neoklassiker*, Düsseldorf: Verlag Wirtschaft und Finanzen, Verlagsgruppe Handelsblatt GmbH, pp. 33–54.
Kurz, H.D. (1999), 'Das natürliche Gesetz der Einkommensverteilung. John Bates Clark und die Grenzproduktivitätstheorie', in K.-D. Grüske (ed.), *John Bates Clarks 'The Distribution of Wealth': Vademecum zu einem amerikanischen Neoklassiker*, Düsseldorf: Verlag Wirtschaft und Finanzen, Verlagsgruppe Handelsblatt GmbH, pp. 77–103.
Samuelson, P.A. (1999), 'Amerikas erster großer Theoretiker', in K.-D. Grüske (ed.), *John Bates Clarks 'The Distribution of Wealth': Vademecum zu einem amerikanischen Neoklassiker*, Düsseldorf: Verlag Wirtschaft und Finanzen, Verlagsgruppe Handelsblatt GmbH, pp. 55–75.

Vilfredo Pareto (1848–1923)

Fritz Wilfrid Pareto was born in Paris on 15 July 1848. His mother, Marie Méténier, was a French citizen and his father, the Marchese Raffaele Pareto, was an Italian supporter of fellow exile Giuseppe Mazzini, the activist leader of Giovine Italia who advocated the unification of Italy. It would be pure speculation to reflect on why a French woman and Italian man decided to christen their son with German given names, but he continued to use those names during his student life, writing "Fritz Wilfrid" Pareto on formal documents and "Wilfrid" on his letters. But from early adulthood he consistently Italianized his given names in most documents, including his published works, which refer to him as Vilfredo Pareto, although the passport issued to him by the Free State of Fiume is in the name of "Fedrigo Vilfredo Pareto".

The Pareto family moved to Italy in 1854, initially to Genoa (Busino 2002; Mornati 2015: 7). When living in Turin, "Vilfredo" progressively completed: his matriculation ("la licenza di maturità") to qualify for university entry in 1864; the certificate in mathematics and physics at the University of Turin in 1867; and the diploma of "graduate engineer" at the University of Turin's Scuola di Applicazione per Ingegneri in 1870. Between 1870 and 1890 he worked in Italy's emerging ironworks industry, initially as an engineer at the Società Anonima delle Strade Ferrate (Railways Company Limited) in Florence between 1870 and 1873. He then took a senior engineering post with the Società dell'Industria del Ferro (Iron Industry Company) in 1873 and rose to become the Director General of that company in 1880 when it was reorganized and renamed as the Società delle Ferriere Italiane (Italian Ironworks Company). However, he was "retired" from that position in 1890 after he had compromised the firm's financial position through his dealings on the London iron market (Busino 1987: 800), which gave him time to devote his energies to studying and writing on economic issues, which he had taken an interest in as a young man (even becoming a founding member of the Florence-based Adam Smith Society in 1874). Also in 1890, Pareto met Léon Walras, Professor of Political Economy at the University of Lausanne, and Maffeo Pantaleoni, one of the directors and editors of the *Giornale degli Economisti*.

In 1893 Pareto succeeded Walras at the University of Lausanne, from where he continued to make important contributions to the *Giornale degli Economisti*, some of a purely scholarly character while others, such as his *Cronaca* for the journal, were essentially critical and partisan commentaries on the economic, fiscal and military policies of the Italian Government and the state of the Italian economy. He also commenced writing his series of influential scholarly books from Switzerland, most notably the two-volume *Cours d'Économie Politique* (1896–97), the two-volume *Les systèmes socialistes* (1901–02) and the *Manuale di Economia Politica* (1906) and the subsequent French edition the *Manuel d'Économie Politique* (1909). Pareto retired from the University of Lausanne in 1911, which freed him up to work intensively on his *Trattato di Sociologia Generale* (1916). After a long period of illness, Pareto died in Céligny on 21 August 1923.

Like most giants of intellectual history, Pareto's contribution to thought evolved, but the evolution of his ideas is especially important to an understanding of his contribution to intellectual history as he made significant contributions during all phases of his scholarship. Consequently, this entry is structured around three discrete periods in Pareto's scholarly life. First, the initial phase between 1890 and 1899 is considered. During this early stage his contributions were primarily associated with the application of Walras's conception of economic equilibrium to a range of topics – like welfare, trade and rent – although all such applications were undertaken within a different methodological context to that employed by Walras. Second, the intermediate phase between 1900 and 1911 is considered. His greatest single contribution during this period is associated with a shift in focus from "applied" theory to the pure theory of economics via his work on choice theory. Thirdly, the last phase of his scholarly life, which runs from 1912 until his death in 1923, is considered. During this time Pareto developed a sociological theory that is relevant to economists because it considers when sociological investigation of the economic phenomenon is necessary, which extends to issues that would later be considered in a modern context through the "Social Welfare" function. This discussion of Pareto concludes with a brief overview of his legacy and influence on the development of economic ideas.

1890–99: A Positive and Pluralistic Approach to Walras's Theory

At the start of the initial phase of his scholarly life, Pareto was an active contributor to the *Giornale degli Economisti*. His articles published in that journal, plus his preparations for the economics programme taught at the University of Lausanne, provided the platform from which he wrote his two-volume *Cours* late in that initial phase. The discussion that follows on each of the main themes of scholarship that Pareto worked on during the initial phase will generally commence with reference to Pareto's early economic articles, typically published by the *Giornale degli Economisti*, and conclude with reference to his contribution to that theme in the *Cours*. To that end, this section considers the issues of "Walras, general equilibrium and successive approximations", "pure economic theory", the "application of pure theory" to issues like welfare economics, international trade and rent, and the issue of "applied empirical economics", as represented by the Pareto distribution.

Walras, general equilibrium and successive approximations
After initially dismissing the economic theory of Léon Walras as too metaphysical in orientation, Pareto was persuaded by Maffeo Pantaleoni to study Walras's *Éléments d'Économie Politique Pure* more carefully. Having done so, he came to endorse Walras's general equilibrium theories of exchange, production and capital formation, and the associated formal conditions of equilibrium, as the subject of "pure economics" for conditions of free competition. However, Pareto significantly de-emphasized the issue of the equilibration process by not following Walras in giving prominence to *tâtonnement* within pure economics as the mechanism for establishing the path to equilibrium prices. The origin of Pareto's concern with Walras's approach to the equilibration process is implicitly discussed in 1892, in the first part of the five-part article "Considerazioni sui principii fondamentali dell'economia politica pura" (Pareto 1892–93 [2007]), when he drew attention to Walras's paraphrasing of an interlocutor who had questioned the necessity of demonstrating how prices adjust in the face of excess demand and excess supply, and took the side of the interlocutor:

in this case we must confess that it was his [Walras's] interlocutor who was right, only he did not defend himself well. He should have said that it is from direct observation that we deduce the law about prices rising when demand is greater than supply, and vice versa. And he should also add: since these are elementary, simple direct observations, if you no longer wish to take them as the basis of your reasoning, but as its consequences, then you must show that the replacements are more elementary, simpler and more direct. (Pareto 1892 [2007]: 4)

Pareto makes reference to the equilibrating role of the haggling process in the *Cours*, although he used the French word *marchandage* instead of Walras's term *tâtonnement* (Lendjel 1999) and his support for treating this process in pure theory was brief and limited. His almost ambivalent position on the issue was most likely due to his realization that a formal theory on the process of adjustments to equilibrium would require economic equations to be specified on a dynamic basis using functional calculus, but he was unable to develop such a study for economic analysis (Donzelli 2006: 513). As a consequence, he largely settled on a static representation of equilibrium for pure theory, with the haggling process briefly presented as an almost incidental justification for the use of given prices in pure theory under conditions of free competition. His contributions to economic theory in subsequent phases of his scholarship did not even include indirect allusions to *tâtonnement*. As a consequence, the extensive secondary literature on *tâtonnement* within the Walrasian system of equilibrium is not matched by an equivalent literature on *marchandage* in the Paretian economic system.

To accommodate this reduction in emphasis on the equilibration process, with a corresponding increase in emphasis on applied economics, Pareto set general equilibrium within his own distinctly non-Walrasian methodological framework that he referred to as "successive approximations", which he took directly from the physical and natural sciences. When the *Cours* was being published, Pareto wrote a letter to Maffeo Pantaleoni (19 February 1897) saying: "I recognize that I have taken the idea of equilibrium from Walras, to which I have added the idea of successive approximations" (Pareto 1960: 36).

Under the methodological approach outlined in the *Cours*, the concrete economic phenomenon is explained by a synthetic union of the theoretical analysis of the conditions of economic equilibrium (the first approximation) and applied economic studies (the second approximation), be it the application of pure theory to particular problems (for example, the theories of welfare economics, international trade and rent) or laws deduced from empirical uniformities derived from statistical observation (for example, the distribution of income). But Paretian successive approximation also has an explicit pluralistic dimension: it is not limited to a relationship between theoretical and empirical economic analysis, it also extends to a synthesis of theory and applied studies pertinent to the economic phenomenon but which come from the other social sciences. So Pareto attempted to accommodate third, fourth and subsequent approximations, which were considered synthetically when uniting analyses from a range of disciplines when compiling a picture of the general economic phenomenon under particular circumstances.

To accommodate the successive approximations approach, Pareto introduced his neologism, ophelimity, and set about distinguishing it from utility. The abstract quality of acts that lead to physical, intellectual and moral development is termed "utility", which may be considered with respect to the individual, the social aggregate, or the species as a whole. However, Pareto regarded such a notion as having too many dimensions to be clearly defined for use in theoretical analysis, so he introduced the one-dimensional notion of ophelimity, which is a sub-class of utility that is limited to the subjective and abstract quality of acts that satisfy an individual's needs or desires irrespective of their legitimacy or usefulness. This distinction supported the pluralistic approach to social science that Pareto tried to accommodate because utility, and its sub-class ophelimity, are divided into different species: economic utility concerns the development of material well-being and economic ophelimity concerns the satisfaction of material desires irrespective of whether they are useful; moral utility concerns the development of more perfect morals while moral ophelimity concerns the subjective benefit from satisfying moral needs and desires irrespective of whether it is useful; and so on. Within that context, the abstraction *homo œconomicus* – and not a real person – was the subject of Pareto's pure economics, as its actions were undertaken solely in response to the economic forces of "elementary" (marginal) ophelimity.

From this, Pareto also recognized that the approximate relationship between fact and theory is not equally accurate across each of the general equilibrium theories of exchange, production and capital formation, as "disturbances" from errors of judgement are common, most especially in relation to capital formation and the transformation of savings into a diverse range of capital goods. Consequently, the *Cours* concedes that observed equilibrium modifies itself continuously as the technical and economic conditions of production change with the real state being one of continuous oscillations around a central point of equilibrium which also changes (Pareto 1896–97 [1971]: 177). This general conclusion mirrors Walras's view of equilibrium, but, to Pareto, the difference between theory and fact served to reinforce the need for a methodology that is based on successive approximations, a methodology that Walras was reluctant to embrace.

Pure economic theory

Pareto's contributions to pure theory during this initial stage were significant, although modest in comparison to his subsequent achievements, and primarily fell within the areas of consumer theory and the pure theory of distribution. In regard to the former, his contribution was largely positive in the sense that it culminated in an enhancement of demand analysis. In regard to the latter, his contribution was largely negative in the sense that it culminated in a rejection of the strict marginal theory of productivity and distribution. Importantly, he also extended Walras's analysis based on free competition to cover the case of monopoly.

By way of context, it should be noted that at this stage in his academic career, Pareto adopted the then prevailing practice of using cardinal valuations. His introduction of terms like ophelimity and *homo œconomicus* when framing pure theory, as outlined above, was not motivated by a desire to introduce ordinal preference rankings in pure theory and his early contributions to consumer theory, as reflected in his "Considerazioni" (1892–93 [2007]), are best seen in that light. He addressed the issue of demand based on two main assumptions: first, that an individual's final degree of utility (in 1892–93 Pareto used Jevons's phrase) from the acquisition of a good is a function of the quantity of that good only; and second, that Daniel Bernoulli's general theorem, concerning the diminishing final degree of utility, is valid. Pareto was of the view that people only have a clear perception of variations in utility from the prevailing existing social state and he appreciated that total utility may not exist when economic values are path dependent. These assumptions were important to him as they were a deliberate simplification from which he could consider the consequences for the demand relationship when the final degree of utility diminishes in a manner that was independent of the consumption of other goods. He was also motivated to consider this relationship in light of his newly acquired understanding of Walrasian interdependence, as he employed comparative static analysis to derive a downward sloping demand curve without resort to Marshall's practice of keeping marginal utility constant for the economic good that serves the function of money. In the process of this demonstration, Pareto introduced Hessian determinants to economic analysis. This work on consumer theory also has an important legacy, as Pareto's solution to the downward sloping demand curve became the basis from which Slutsky developed his analysis of consumer demand to isolate the income and substitution effects (Chipman 1976; Dooley 1983; Weber 1999).

Pareto also undertook extensive investigations of the potential functional forms that can show variations in the final degree of utility that are consistent with theory and observation, including the specification of a logarithmic utility function with the main characteristics of the Cobb–Douglas utility function (Weber 1998). Pareto subsequently summarized his early contributions to consumer theory in the *Cours*, although in a less extensively developed manner as that book was intended as a textbook for students at the University of Lausanne and he adopted Marshall's practice of limiting mathematical formalization to the footnotes.

Pareto's contribution to the pure theory of production and distribution has its genesis in his landmark paper "Il Massimo di utilità dato della libera concorenza" (Pareto 1894b [2008]), where variable coefficients of production were introduced to the mathematical formalization of Walras's theory for the purposes of applying that theory to an investigation of the welfare consequences of varying the combination of productive services used in the production of consumer goods. Pareto does not explicitly discuss the distributional implications of minimizing his unit cost equations for distribution theory, but marginal properties are implied by the cost minimizing conditions he identified.

In the *Cours*, however, Pareto largely rejects the marginal theory of production and distribution. Henry Schultz (1929, 1932) and John Hicks (1932a, 1932b) subsequently entered into an insightful, albeit heated, debate on the extent to which Pareto abandoned marginal productivity theory. Pareto's stated concern with the marginal theory of distribution was related to the need to account for the use of both fixed and variable coefficients of production, which served to constrain the capacity for substituting productive services. In addition, he recognized that interdependence between coefficients of production can also influence production and distribution. However, he was not motivated by a desire to interrogate the mathematical properties of production equations and functions. Rather, it was a reflection of a more basic view that the general parameters of distribution are largely established by historical conditions, which gives some context to his empirical study of the distribution of income over very long periods of time. Consequently, to the extent that his approach to production accommodates the marginal theory of production, it appears to be regarded by Pareto as limited to the static space around local equilibrium. It should be noted that Pareto's contribution to this issue also persuaded others of the limits of marginal production theory and influenced Enrico Barone and Philip Wicksteed in their decisions to abandon that theory (Schultz 1929; Dorfman 1964).

Finally, the *Cours* is important for recognizing that Walras's general equilibrium system need not be limited to the state of free competition. Pareto formally introduced the theory of monopoly to general equilibrium, in which the equilibrium profit is not zero, as in the case of free competition. This laid a foundation for subsequent discussion in the *Manual* concerning strategic behaviour aimed at altering prices.

Application of pure theory
During this stage of Pareto's career, his main applications of general theory were to the study of "virtual" economic movements, especially in the areas of welfare economics, international trade, and the theory of rent.

Pareto's seminal "Il Massimo di utilità dato dalla libera concorenza" (Pareto 1894b [2008]) is one of his more important economic papers. In addition to introducing variable coefficients of production to economics, it demonstrates that a point of equilibrium under free competition must yield an economic maximum when the cost of productive services is minimized by the competitive process. He does this formally by showing that when society moves from an initial state that is not a point of free equilibrium to a subsequent one that is a cost minimizing state of free equilibrium, an economic residual (surplus measured in terms of the *numéraire* good) is generated from the more efficient use of productive services. Importantly, Pareto introduces the criterion in this article that social welfare is increased when the coefficients of production are altered in a manner that increases the product returned to each individual member of society but harms no one. Consequently, this is the article in which both the Pareto criterion and the first theorem in welfare economics (an economic maximum, in terms of the Pareto criterion, is given by a point of equilibrium under free competition) are outlined. In addition, the "compensation principle" is, as Chipman (1976 [1999]: 178) has reported, introduced in this article when Pareto discusses variation in the coefficients of production in socialist economies, when the second law of welfare economics (any point of economic maximum can be realized under conditions of free exchange) is also broached – but imperfectly. Nevertheless, he did demonstrate that redistributional goals are not achieved efficiently when pursued by altering the coefficients of production (for example, increasing wages paid for labour services).

This analysis of welfare generally, and welfare in socialist countries in particular, is further developed in the *Cours* (1896–97 [1971]: 722–34). However, the weak point of the article is also preserved in the *Cours*, with analysis focusing on production (albeit with variable coefficients of production) while largely setting aside the issue of exchange, which is necessary in a general specification of the fundamental theorems of welfare economics.

The application of general equilibrium theory to the study of international trade was initially undertaken by Pareto in "Teoria matematica dei cambi forestieri" (Pareto 1894a [2008]), which was subsequently extended (Pareto 1895b [2008]). Pareto modified Walras's system to accommodate two markets (countries) for consumer goods, with the quantities of consumer consumption sourced from domestic production and from imports determined in equilibrium from new exogenously given international prices, subject to the constraint that the value of exports equals the value of imports in each market. Analysis in the *Cours* consolidated Pareto's earlier work on this subject by illustrating the equalization of the price of traded goods and the welfare gains from free trade. As Andrea Maneschi (1993) reported, Bertil Ohlin was astonished that the Anglo-Saxon trade literature had totally overlooked Pareto's application of mutual interdependence theory to several markets and not just one.

Pareto's main original contribution to the theory of economic rent is outlined in the *Cours* (Gross and Tarascio 1998). He presented economic rents for produced goods as variations in income that derive from movement from complete free equilibrium to an incomplete state of free equilibrium. The new equilibrium state is incomplete because savings are not uniformly transformed into heterogeneous capital in the proportion required by relative prices under the new equilibrium or because of other obstacles to price adjustment. The acquisition of rent from the ownership of a particular capital good is the difference between the realized return on that particular good and the notional return that would have been earned if the return on particular capital goods was in line with the general rate of return on savings that are transformed into capital. Consequently, the "rent acquired" from the services of a particular capital good is the difference between its rate of return and the general rate of return on savings. Importantly, the rent acquired may be positive or negative, depending on whether the movement to the new equilibrium places upward or downward pressure on the price of particular capital goods. Consequently, this notion of rent depends largely on different time constraints pertaining to the production of heterogeneous capital items. More generally, Pareto saw rents as a consequence of "obstacles to transformation" which, in addition to time, includes the Ricardian scarcity of natural resources as well as other limitations imposed by technology, costs and savings (Bird and Tarascio 1992 [1999]: 483).

Applied empirical economics – Pareto's law
In the area of applied economics, Pareto is most well known for his attempts to establish general empirical uniformities, especially his research on income distribution. In the "La Courbe de la répartition de la richesse" (1896) and the *Cours* Pareto undertook empirical study of income based on taxation records from England, Prussia, Peru and towns in Italy, to consider the form of distribution of income. For the levels of income above some arbitrarily determined minimum cut-off point, he found that the distribution of income in many societies over longer periods of time was largely captured by a general equation, which, in reduced form, is represented by equation 1 below; and by the corresponding double log version of that equation, which is given by equation (1*):

$$N_x = \frac{A}{x^\alpha} \tag{1}$$

$$\log N_x = A - \alpha(\log x) \tag{1*}$$

where
x : a level of income
N_x : number of people with an income of at least x
A, α : parameters.

Three basic scientific uniformities emerged from this research. First, the distribution of income is not given by chance but still follows a general pattern (that is, an income distribution function exists and it is not normally distributed). Second, a characteristic of this general distribution is that income inequality is a uniform social phenomenon across different societies and across different periods of history. Third, empirical investigation of income data using the Pareto distribution shows that the value of α was generally close to 1.5, with empirical estimates ranging from 1.13 to 1.89. Francis Y. Edgeworth (1896, 1897) and Pareto (1897) debated this issue with vigour, focusing mainly on whether the form of the distribution function is best represented by Pareto's equations or other distributions, most notably the Pearson distribution.

But perhaps most controversial was Pareto's examination of the question of income inequality. To that end, he suggested that a suitable index of inequality in income distribution (u_x) is given by the quotient of the number of people accruing some arbitrary level of income, x, or more (N_x), and the number of people accruing a minimum income, h, or more (N_h). Given the form of the Pareto distribution, that index of inequality can be represented by equation (2).

$$u_x = \left(\frac{N_x}{N_h}\right) = \frac{\dfrac{A}{x^\alpha}}{\dfrac{A}{h^\alpha}} = \left(\frac{h}{x}\right)^\alpha \tag{2}$$

According to Pareto, inequality diminishes when the index number given by equation (2) increases. Consequently, inequality falls in the face of a rise in the minimum income h and/or a reduction in the parameter α, which indicates that the slope of the log form of Pareto's income distribution curve becomes less steep and, as a result, increases the number of people with an income of at least x). As these events are also indicative of economic growth, Pareto put forward the proposition, now known as Pareto's law, that real per capita growth is necessary "to increase the level of the minimum income or to reduce the inequality of income" (Pareto 1896–97 [1971]: 1097). Pigou (1912), however, refused to accept this proposition and was vigorous in his rejection of Pareto's law, although his analysis was based on a flawed reading of Pareto's *Cours* (McLure 2013).

1900–1911: A Dualistic Methodology and Choice Theory

By 1900 Pareto's methodology had evolved into an essentially dualistic, but still positive, approach. The genesis of this change in Pareto's methodology was his shift toward a political sociology and the development of the distinction between logical and non-logical action. As a result of this distinction, the Walrasian core of Pareto's theory diminished with the recognition that consistency of choice in unchanged circumstances is an important aspect of logical action, culminating in the emergence of choice theory based on preference ordering. As in the previous section, the discussion of the main themes will generally commence with reference to Pareto's early economic articles and conclude with reference to his contribution to that theme in his books, which during this phase were the Italian and French editions of the *Manual of Political Economy*. The work from this phases was crowned by Pareto's "Économie mathématique" (1911), which was published in *Encyclopédie des Sciences Mathématiques Pures et Appliqués*. The main themes covered over this period concern methodology, pure economic theory, and welfare economics.

Emergence of a dualistic methodology – logical versus non-logical action
Pareto's new dualistic approach was a direct result of the distinction between logical and non-logical action that he set out in "Un'applicazione di teorie sociologiche" (1900a [1980]). The starting point for this study was the proposition that there are three forms of phenomena, each of which need to be investigated: (1) the objective form (the relationship between real objects); (2) the subjective form (the relationship between psychological states); and (3) how "real phenomenon act to alter the subjective phenomenon and vice-versa" (Pareto 1900a [1980]: 181). He attempted to consider the rise and fall of aristocracies in term of these three forms. As societies rose and then fell (the objective) Pareto noted "sentiment", such as feelings of support for, or opposition to, socialism, nationalism, humanism, imperialism, and so on (the subjective), grew more intense in opposition to the prevailing aristocracy and noted that the path of the rise and fall of elites was interdependent with sentiment for or against the government (the subjective acting to alter the objective and the objective acting to alter the subjective). This theme was greatly expanded by Pareto in his *Les systèmes socialistes* (1901–02), which introduced the term "elites" in place of "aristocracies".

At the theoretical level, the fundamental point is that Pareto regarded Sociology as the study of social phenomena where the subjective view is interdependent with objective phenomena; and the associated action was characterized by Pareto as "non-logical", not because it was illogical, but because it could not be analysed on the presumption of a logical nexus between means and ends. The study of logical action, however, is reserved for situations in which there is a stable and unique relationship between the objective (or real) phenomena and subjective intent. This permits "ends" to be taken as given, with the means to ends associated with choices being directly observed. Pure economic theory was, to Pareto, a study of logical action, which he also associated with the observed consistency of repeat choices when circumstances are unchanged.

Pure economic theory – logical action and the "fact of choice"
The theoretical formalization of choice theory was initially developed by Pareto in his two part article, "Sunto di alcuni capitoli di un nuovo trattato di economia pura" (1900b [2008]), which demonstrated that, for a system of indifference curves in which each curve is labelled by an index number, the shape of the indifference curves is unaltered when an arbitrary transformation function is used to change the index numbers. The system of index numbers applied to different consumption bundles could reflect the (cardinal) measure of pleasure as a quantity, but this would be just one of an infinite range of possible index number systems, none of which would alter the shape of indifference curves or the resulting equilibrium outcomes. As a result, ordinal preferences or cardinal utilities may be used to determine the same equilibrium state.

However, the introduction of ordinalist indexes was not "an end" to Pareto; rather, it was a means to the end of making economics a more experimental science by focusing on the "fact of choice" and dispensing with considerations on the motives for choice. The statistical problem presented here depends on data from the observation of choice, which Pareto characterized as "facts" that may be obtained through either binary choice experiments (when investigating potential movement in choice space) or interpolation (to estimate the equation for indifference curves in the area that is close to equilibrium). As noted in the *Manual*:

> The notions of *lines of indifference* and *lines of preference* were introduced into the science by Professor F.Y. Edgeworth. He started out from the concept of *utility* (ophelimity), which he assumed to be a known quantity, and from it deduced the definition of these lines. I have inverted the problem. I have shown that, starting from indifference lines, given directly by experience, we can immediately obtain the determinateness of economic equilibrium and work back to certain functions, including ophelimity if it exists; or at any rate we can deduce the ophelimity indices. (Pareto 1906 [2014]: 273, emphasis added)

Interestingly the early literature on ordinalism by Hicks (1934), Lange (1934), and Hicks (1939) all referred extensively to the French-language *Manuel* (1909) with some noting that systems of ophelimity were sometimes set up ordinally but with cardinal restrictions also imposed – most notably in the extended appendix – which some commentators consider confused. However, in the earlier Italian *Manuale*, Pareto took much greater care to clarify exactly when index numbers (I) are considered: one, as a function (Φ) of consumer goods on the basis that ophelimity is a quantity (cardinal function); or two, as a function (Ψ) of consumer goods when indifference curves are determined from direct observation. This can be seen first-hand in the English language variorum edition of Pareto's *Manual* (1906, 1909 [2014]).

The *Manual* also re-specified economic equilibrium as a general theory of transformations. Specifically, Walras's economic theories of exchange, production and capital formation are absorbed within a more general formulation where equilibrium is considered as the balance between an individual's "tastes", defined by individual's choices, and "obstacles" represented by the costs of transforming goods in response to tastes, either through exchange or the production process.

The equilibrium between tastes and obstacles is then considered for three types of phenomena. Type I phenomena characterizes the case where individuals act economically to realize a direct benefit with market conditions determined by voluntary pursuit of direct tastes without strategic interaction. Type II phenomena characterizes the case where individuals act to increase the indirect benefits from their actions through strategic behaviour that modifies the market price. Kirman (1987: 806) has highlighted the originality of Pareto's analysis of the type II phenomenon because it explicitly recognized actions to influence prices and examined equilibrium in the context of what is now termed monopolistic competition, well before monopolistic competition was integrated within general equilibrium frameworks in the 1960s. Type III phenomena characterizes the case where collectivist action is intended to maximize a given notion of welfare (for example, a socialist state).

Welfare economics

In response to Gaetano Scorza (1902) claiming that Pareto's finding that equilibrium under free competition is an economic maximum (today's first law of welfare economics) is nothing but "gross sophistry", Pareto returned to the mathematical treatment of welfare economics. As his work on welfare economics had, until that time, largely focused on production, there were some grounds for Scorza's critique. Pareto's reaction, while full of sarcasm and scorn, was also substantive as he extended his previous analysis of welfare to include both exchange and production. In the process, he provided economics with its first, analytically sound, first-order demonstration of the first fundamental theorem of welfare economics. Full treatments of the fascinating and lively polemic between Pareto and Scorza can be found in Chipman (1976) and McLure (2000).

After the polemic, Pareto again returned to the issue of economic maximization through his analysis of types I and II phenomena in the *Manual*. The type I phenomenon yields an economic maximum for perfect competition because no movement from that point satisfies the criterion that at least one person gains and no one is harmed:

$$\delta U = 0 = \frac{1}{\varphi_{1a}}\delta\Phi_1 + \frac{1}{\varphi_{2a}}\delta\Phi_2 + \frac{1}{\varphi_{3a}}\delta\Phi_3 + \ldots \tag{3}$$

U = ophelimity
1, 2, 3 =individuals 1, 2, and 3
φ_a = elementary ophelimity (marginal utility) of numeraire good A
Φ_i = total ophelimity for individual i.

In contrast, the type II phenomenon does not yield an economic maximum. The investigation of the type III phenomenon in the *Manual* contains aspects of the second fundamental welfare theorem but the conclusion is largely unchanged from the earlier *Cours*: a socially planned distribution of income can achieve an economic maximum when production is efficiently coordinated by the "ministry of production", but he goes on to stress that pure economics alone does not give us a truly decisive criterion for choosing between an organization of society based on private property and a socialist organization (1906 [2014]: 185).

Finally, the *Manual* is important to the history of diagrams in economics, as the famous Edgeworth, or Edgeworth–Bowley, box was also first introduced to economics in the *Manual* (1906, 1909 [2014]: 95, 180). This box diagram has played an important didactic role in the teaching of welfare analysis over many years.

1912–23: A Sociological Approach to Equilibrium and Welfare

By 1912 Pareto's scientific thought had shifted almost entirely to the non-logical side of his methodological dual and was centred on the development of a sociological approach to equilibrium. His most important article in that regard was "Il Massimo di utilità per una collettività in sociologia" (Pareto 1913 [1999]), which was followed by his grand three-volume *Sociologia* (1916 [1935]). Pareto's last article on economics "Economia sperimentale" (1918 [2008]), which was published when he was 70, was a mature reflection on the relationship between economics and sociology.

From economic welfare to social welfare
In "Il Massimo di utilità per una collettività in sociologia" Pareto extended his economic theory of collective welfare, in which direct interpersonal comparison of each individual's ophelimity is prohibited, to a sociological theory of social welfare, which specifies social utility in homogenous terms based on the interpersonal utility comparisons by individuals and government.

This sociological work on the maximization of utility is based on the proposition that each individual has a view about the relative benefits to society from their own consumption and from the consumption of other members of society. To maximize utility in this social sense, Pareto outlined a two-step process to measure "social utility". In the first step, every individual subjectively weights the welfare of themselves and the welfare of every other individual in the community to establish each individual's social utility function, as shown in equation (4):

$$\left.\begin{array}{l} \text{Person 1's social utility maximum: } 0 = \alpha_1' \delta\Phi_1 + \alpha_2' \delta\Phi_2 + \alpha_3' \delta\Phi_3 \ldots \\ \text{Person 2's social utility maximum: } 0 = \alpha_1'' \delta\Phi_1 + \alpha_2'' \delta\Phi_2 + \alpha_3'' \delta\Phi_3 \ldots \\ \ldots \end{array}\right\} \qquad (4)$$

where:
Φ_1 is person 1's welfare
Φ_2 is person 2's welfare . . .
α_i' is person 1's weightings of each individual i's welfare
α_i'' is person 2's weightings for each individual i's welfare.

In the second step, the government weights each person's assessment of social utility to derive a social welfare function in which utility is a homogeneous quantity with cardinal properties, which can be maximized through government policy in accordance with equation (5):

$$\text{Collective social utility maximum: } \quad 0 = M_1 \delta\Phi_1 + M_2 \delta\Phi_2 + M_3 \delta\Phi_3 + \ldots \qquad (5)$$

where:

$M_1 = \alpha_1' \beta' + \alpha_1'' \beta'' + \alpha_1''' \beta'''$

$M_2 = \alpha_2' \beta' + \alpha_2'' \beta'' + \alpha_2''' \beta''' \ldots$

β' political weighting of person 1's weighting of social utility
β'' political weighting of person 2's weighting of social utility . . .
other symbols, as per equation 4.

Unlike Pareto's economic approach to maximization, his sociological approach is not necessarily constrained by the Pareto criterion (that is, the requirement that no one be harmed and at least one person gain) and there is obviously no prohibition on interpersonal comparisons of utility. Furthermore, there is no suggestion that utility for the purposes of social welfare considerations is an ordinal measure – in this sociological context Pareto treated social utility as a homogeneous quantity (over the period for which the prevailing social equilibrium is stable) for society as a whole. Pareto himself described his work in this area as a first step towards a "theory of social utility".

Social equilibrium and its economic aspects

Pareto's conception of social equilibrium was developed in its most expansive form in the final volume of his *Sociologia*. It considers the social state with respect to: the distribution of conformist and nonconformist behaviour by individual members of a society; the political balance between individualist and collectivist social organization; and the general economic equilibrium between the activities of high-risk-taking speculators and risk-averse rentiers. The key positive issue that Pareto seeks to address is whether the social equilibrium is stable, in which case the prevailing pattern of social, political and economic action continues, or unstable, in which case forces of change are overcoming the forces of conservation with the relative proportions of speculators and rentiers among economic elites starting to change and the political balance influenced by pressures to alter the proportions of individuals among governing elites who are pro-individualist (decentralizing) and pro-collective (centralizing). As such, instability in social equilibrium is associated with elite conflict and changes in patron–client relations among political and economic elites.

After systematic reflection on written texts that outline social and economic doctrines, Pareto concluded that the (quasi)logic used to justify social theories tended to rest on the acceptance of some residual sentiment. He called this observed residual sentiment "residues" and referred to the form of language in which residues are expressed and rationalized as "derivations", because they derive from sentiment and constitute the form in which ideology is rationalized. Pareto briefly considered whether the study of social equilibrium with reference to residues and derivations could be undertaken on the same bases as economics, with residues being akin to subjective "tastes". However, he quickly rejected that approach because derivations are a variable and endogenous influence on non-logical human action:

> [I]n activity based on residues human beings use derivations more frequently than strict logical reasonings . . . Residues are not, like tastes, merely sources of conduct; they function throughout the whole course of the conduct developing from the source, a fact which becomes apparent in the substitution of derivations for logical reasonings. (Pareto 1916 [1935]: 1442–3)

As a first approximation, Pareto considered the theory of social equilibrium with reference to the two main classes of residues: class I, instinct for combinations, and class II, persistence of aggregates. The instinct for combinations is the subjective force for change associated with a faith in the effectiveness of reordering social concepts and social arrangements. Persistence of aggregates is the subjective force for preserving the prevailing social relations, such as relations within the family, and between places and social groups. Derivations linked to class I residues may advocate reformist ideologies (irrespective of the character of change being advocated) while derivations linked to class II residues may advocate conservative ideologies (irrespective of the social arrangement being preserved). He then used those notions to specify his "fundamental sociological theorem", namely, that a general and rough explanation of social change is evident from the relative proportions of class I and class II residues among the ruling class and among the subject classes (Pareto 1916 [1935]: 1921). In relation to economics, the main consequence of non-logical action evident from this fundamental theorem and the economic balance between *speculators* and *rentiers* related to long-run economic growth and development:

> In our day, for instance, the enormous development of economic production, the spread of civilisation to new countries, the remarkable rise in the standard of living among all civilized

peoples, are in large part the work of speculators. But they have been able to do that work because they came from populations in which class II residues were numerous and strong. (Pareto 1916 [1935]: 1578)

Economic phenomena and their economic and sociological parts
Pareto's final contribution to the *Giornale degli Economisti*, "Economia sperimentale" (Pareto 1918 [2008]) attempted to make evident the economic implications of his sociological theory of social equilibrium. He did so by differentiating between the economic part of the economic phenomenon, which is limited to local action when subjective tastes can be given exogenously, and the sociological part of the economic phenomenon, which extends to non-logical action and is influenced by endogenous derivations.

> there is almost no concrete problem that is exclusively economic, and not economic and sociological at the same time. In fact, very often the sociological part prevails over the economic part; examples of this are: the problem of free trade, or tariff protection; many monetary problems; almost all taxation problems; and other similar problems. . . . one does not leave the experimental field if one studies the economic and sociological parts separately. (Pareto 1918 [2008], 558)

When the economic phenomenon is significantly influenced by public policy, the interplay between residues and derivations are an endogenous influence on individuals' views on their behaviour and welfare, then the mature Paretian position was that economic policy should be considered from both the economic and sociological perspectives. Consequently, economic theories of trade, money and public finance need to be complemented by the sociology of trade and protection, the sociology of money and fiscal sociology. This is because they all influence the distribution of economic goods among members of society – sometimes for welfare enhancing policy reasons but, in Pareto's view, more often in response to relations between governing elites and their client economic elites. His concern is fundamentally the same as Adam Smith's fear that legislators had introduced laws that benefited manufacturers and merchants but harmed the other great social orders and society in general. However, to examine such issues, Pareto concluded that sociological theories were more insightful than economic theories. He even asserted that the history of economists' theories and doctrines on the government's role in matters related to trade, monetary and fiscal policy was relevant to developing a sociological understanding of government activities in these areas.

Pareto's Influence on the Development of Economics

Just as the preceding discussion of Pareto's body of work was necessarily limited and selective, so too is the following discussion of his legacy. However, a more extensive treatment of Pareto's influence on the development of economic ideas is available from Roberto Marchionatti (2006).

As Pareto's intellectual debt to Walras was enormous, especially during the initial phase, the first point that must be made in regard to Pareto's legacy is that he played a major role in popularizing and continuing the work of Walras's programme in economic theory. Indeed, the early reaction to Pareto in Europe, most especially Italy, was in the context of the economic approach associated with the University of Lausanne. Notable in that regard is Enrico Barone, who is sometimes grouped with Walras and Pareto as a leading contributor to the Lausanne tradition in economics. However, it must also be added that Pareto's influence on economics and public finance in Italy during the early twentieth century was to become so directly influenced by his works from the intermediate and final phases of his scholarship that it is legitimate to refer to a "Paretian School" within Italy (McLure 2007; Pomini and Tusset 2009; Pomini 2014), which is distinct in many important ways from the tradition that Walras initiated at Lausanne.

In the area of pure equilibrium theory, Pareto's unique international legacy was perhaps most important in the 1930s when ordinal preferences were systematically integrated within utility theory by Hicks (1934, 1939), with the combined effect motivating Paul Samuelson (1938) to initiate the formalization of choice theory based on revealed preference. However, Pareto's influence in pure theory also extends to: consumer theory, through the inspiration that he gave Slutsky (1915); pioneering and fundamental studies of economic dynamics by Luigi Amoroso, Giulio La Volpe, Eraldo Fossati, Guiseppe Palomba and Arrigio Bordin (Pomini and Tusset 2009; Pomini 2014); and investigations into monopoly by Amoroso (Edgeworth 1922). Furthermore, Pareto's treatment of attempts to alter market prices under type-II phenomena in the *Manual* dealt with issues that were being addressed with the emergence of a much later general equilibrium literature on monopolistic competition (Kirman 1987: 806).

Pareto's contribution to welfare studies is the one major issue that he continued to make original, important and enduring contributions across each phase of his scholarship: introducing the Pareto criterion, the compensation criterion and the first law of welfare economics in the first phase, albeit limited to the case of production; extending the analysis of efficiency to include exchange and formalizing the "surplus" approach to quantifying the gains from free competition in the intermediate period; and introducing his sociological approach to issues of social welfare in the final phase. However, the legacy among the economics profession (especially outside Italy) from Pareto's work in this area is mainly related to his contributions in the first two phases. Three examples are worthy of particular note. First, Enrico Barone's classic study "Il Ministro della Produzione nello Stato Collettivista" (1908) was inspired directly from Pareto's work. Second, the new approach to welfare economics associated with J.R. Hicks was directly inspired by Pareto's work on ordinalism. Finally, and perhaps most importantly, a profound and original contribution to welfare economics was made by Maurice Allais (1975), who revised and extended Pareto's surplus approach to the issue of welfare. Outside Italy, Pareto's sociological works of collective welfare were not noticed by economists, which represented something of a lost opportunity as John Chipman (1976) and Vincent Tarascio (1968) suggest that Pareto's sociological work on welfare anticipates the social welfare function. However, in Italy, Pareto's contribution to welfare studies from the final phases of his scholarship was not lost, with Pareto's most direct followers attempting to integrate his economics and sociology through the development of a fiscal sociology.

Finally, in regard to empirical economics, interest in the Pareto distribution and Pareto's law was almost immediate, starting with Rudolfo Benini (1897) in Italy, and Edgeworth (1896, 1897) in the English-speaking world. The interest, debate and controversy associated with the Pareto distribution and its relevance to a range of circumstances and the particular issue of inequality continued for more than half a century (Wood and McLure 1999, 4: 1–299), with the most recent historical review of that issue undertaken by Terenzio Maccabelli (2009). However, it is also relevant that the range of applications for which the Pareto distribution is used has extended beyond the issue of income distribution to include finance (Mandelbrot) and the growth and distribution of firm size (Steindl) – as well as stochastic processes compatible with the generation of a Pareto distribution (Champernowne).

MICHAEL McLURE

See also:

Maurice Allais (I); Enrico Barone (I); John Richard Hicks (I); Lausanne School (II); Maffeo Pantaleoni (I); Evgeni Evgenievich Slutsky (I); Marie-Esprit-Léon Walras (I).

References and further reading

Allais, M. (1975), 'The general theory of surplus and Pareto's fundamental contribution', *Convegno Internazionale Vilfredo Pareto (Roma 25–27 ottobre 1973)*, Atti dei Convegni Lincie 9, Roma: Accademia Nazionale Dei Lincei, pp. 109–63, reprinted in J.C. Wood and M. McLure (eds) (1999), *Vilfredo Pareto: Critical Assessments*, vol. 1, London: Routledge, pp. 428–73.
Barone, E. (1908), 'Il Ministro della produzione nello stato collettivista', *Giornale degli Economisti*, **2** (September/October), 267–93, 392–414, trans. as 'The Ministry of Production in the collectivist state', in F.A. Hayek, ed. (1935), *Collectivist Economic Planning*, London; Routledge, pp. 245–90.
Benini, R. (1897), 'Di Alcune curve descritte da fenomeni economici avanti relazione colla curva del reddito o con quella del patrimonio', *Giornale degli Economisti e Rivista di Statistica*, **7** (14), 177–214.
Bergson, A. (1983), 'Pareto on social welfare', *Journal of Economic Literature*, **21** (1), 40–60.
Bird, R. and V.J. Tarascio (1992), 'Paretian rent theory versus Pareto's rent theory: a clarification and correction', *History of Political Economy*, **24** (4), 909–23, reprinted in J.C. Wood and M. McLure (eds) (1999), *Vilfredo Pareto: Critical Assessments*, vol. 2, London: Routledge, pp. 473–84.
Busino, G. (1987), 'Vilfredo Pareto', in J. Eatwell, M. Milgate and P. Newman (eds), *The New Palgrave: A Dictionary of Economics*, vol. 3, London: Macmillan, pp. 799–804.
Busino, G. (2002), 'Introduzione alla lettura dell'opera di Vilfredo Pareto', G. Manga (ed.), *Vilfredo Pareto (1848–1923): L'Uomo e Lo Scienziato*, Sondrio and Milan: Banca Popolare do Sondrio and Libri Schweiwiller.
Chipman, J.S. (1976), 'The Paretian heritage', *Revue Européene des Sciences Sociales*, no. 37, 65–173, reprinted in J.C. Wood and M. McLure (eds) (1999), *Vilfredo Pareto: Critical Assessments*, vol. 2, London: Routledge, pp. 157–257.
Dardi, M. (2006), 'Choice, preference and rationalizability in Pareto's theory of economic behavior', *International Review of Economics*, **53** (4), 476–90.
Donzelli, F. (2006), 'Walras and Pareto on the meaning of the solution concept in general equilibrium theory', *International Review of Economics*, **53** (4), 491–530.
Dooley, P.C. (1983), 'Slutsky's equation is Pareto's solution', *History of Political Economy*, **15** (4), 513–17.
Dorfman, J. (1964), 'Wicksteed's recantation of the marginal productivity theory', *Economica*, **32** (123), 294–95.
Edgeworth, F.Y. (1896), 'Supplementary notes on statistics'' *Journal of the Royal Statistical Society*, **59** (September), 529–39.
Edgeworth, F.Y. (1897), 'La curva delle entrate e la curva di probabilità', *Giornale degli Economisti*, **7** (14), 215–18.
Edgeworth, F.Y. (1922), 'The mathematical economics of Professor Amoroso', *Economic Journal*, **32** (September), 400–407.
Gross, M. and V.J. Tarascio (1998), 'Pareto's theory of choice', *History of Political Economy*, **30** (2), 171–87.
Hicks, J.R. (1932a), 'Marginal productivity and the principle of variation', *Economica*, **12** (35), 79–88.
Hicks, J.R. (1932b), 'A reply', *Economica*, **12** (37), 297–300.
Hicks, J.R. (1934), 'A reconsideration of the theory of value – part 1', *Economica*, **1** (1), 52–76.
Hicks, J.R. (1939), 'The foundations of welfare economics', *Economic Journal*, **49** (196), 696–712.
Kirman, A.P. (1987), 'Pareto as an economist', in J. Eatwell, M. Milgate and P. Newman (eds), *The New Palgrave: A Dictionary of Economics*, vol. 3, London: Macmillan, pp. 804–9.

Lange, O. (1934), 'The determinateness of the utility function', *Review of Economic Studies*, **1** (3), 218–25.

Lendjel, E. (1999), 'Tâtonnement Walrassien et marchandage Parétien: une approche comparative', *Revue Européenne des Sciences Sociales*, **37** (16), 295–314.

Maccabelli, T. (2009), 'Measuring inequality: Pareto's ambiguous contribution', *History of Political Economy*, **41** (1), 183–208.

Maneschi, A. (1993), 'Pareto on international trade theory and policy', *Journal of the History of Economic Thought*, **15** (Fall), 210–28.

Marchionatti, R. (2006), 'At the origin of post-war mainstream of economics: on Pareto's influence on economic theory', *International Review of Economics*, **53** (4), 538–59.

McLure, M. (2000), 'The Pareto–Scorza polemic on collective economic welfare', *Australian Economic Papers*, **39** (3), 345–69.

McLure, M. (2007), *The Paretian School and Italian Fiscal Sociology*, Basingstoke: Palgrave Macmillan.

McLure, M. (2013), 'A.C. Pigou's assessment of Pareto's law', *Cambridge Journal of Economics*, **37** (4), 775–89.

Mornati, F. (2015), *Una Biografia Intellettuale di Vilfredo Pareto: I, Dalla Scienza alla Libertà (1848–1891)*, Rome: Edizioni di Storia e Letteratura.

Pareto, V. (1892–93), 'Considerazioni sui principii fondamentale dell'economia politica pura', Parts 1 to 5, *Giornale degli Economisti*, **2** (4), 389–420, **2** (5), 119–57, **3** (6), 1–37, **3** (7), 279–321, English trans. V. Savini and J. Kinder, R. Marchionatti and F. Mornati (eds) (2007), *Considerations on the Fundamental Principles of Pure Political Economy*, London: Routledge.

Pareto, V. (1894a), 'Teoria matematica dei cambi forestieri', *Giornale degli Economisti*, **4** (8), 142–73, English trans. J. Cairncross, J. Chipman (ed.) (2008), 'Mathematical theory of foreign exchanges', *Giornali degli Economisti e Annali di Economia*, **67** (3), 361–86.

Pareto, V. (1894b), 'Il Massimo di utilità dato dalla libera concorrenza', *Giornale degli Economisti*, **4** (9), 48–66, English trans. J. Cairncross, J. Chipman (ed.) (2008), 'The maximum of utility given by free competition', *Giornali degli Economisti e Annali di Economia*, **67** (3), 387–403.

Pareto, V. (1895), 'Teoria matematica del commercio internazionale' *Giornale degli Economisti*, **5** (10), 479–98, English trans. J. Cairncross, J. Chipman (ed.) (2008), 'Mathematical theory of international trade', *Giornali degli Economisti e Annali di Economia*, **67** (3), 405–24.

Pareto, V. (1896), 'La Courbe de la répartition de la richesse', Université de Lausanne, Faculté de Droit à l'occasion de l'Exposition nationale Suisse: Lausanne, English trans. J. Cairncross, J. Chipman (ed.) (2008), 'The curve of the distribution of wealth', *History of Economic Ideas*, **17** (1), 132–43.

Pareto, V. (1896–97), *Cours d'Économie Politique*, Lausanne: Rouge, Italian trans. *Corso di Economia Politica*, 1971, Torino: Unione Tipographico-Editrice Torinese.

Pareto, V. (1897), 'Ultima risposta al prof. Edgeworth' *Giornale degli Economisti*, **7** (14), 219–20.

Pareto, V. (1900a), 'Un'applicazione di teoria sociologiche', *Rivista Italiana di Sociologia*, reprinted in G. Busino (ed.) (1980), *Œuvres Complètes 22: Écrits Sociologiques Mineurs*, Geneva: Librairie Droz, pp. 178–238.

Pareto, V. (1900b), 'Sunto di alcuni capitoli di un nuovo trattato di economia pura del Prof. Pareto', *Giornali degli Economisti*, **2** (20), 216–35, 511–49, English trans. J. Cairncross, J. Chipman (ed.) (2008), 'Summary of some chapters of a new treatise on pure economics by Professor Pareto', *Giornali degli Economisti e Annali di Economia*, **67** (3), 453–504.

Pareto, V. (1901–02), *Les Systèmes Socialistes*, Paris: Giard et Briére, Italian trans. (1974), *I Sistemi Socialisti*, Torino: Unione Tipografico-Editrice Torinese.

Pareto, V. (1902), 'Di un nuovo errore nello interpretare le teorie dell'economia matematica', *Giornale degli Economisti*, **12** (15), 401–33; translated into English by J. Cairncross and J. Chipman (ed.) (2008), 'On a new error in the interpretation of the theories of mathematical economics', *Giornali degli Economisti e Annali di Economia*, **67** (3), 515–44.

Pareto, V. (1906), *Manuale di Economia Politica*, Milan: Società Editrice Libraria, revised and translated in French as *Manuel d'Économie Politique* (1909), Paris: Giard et Briére, with the Italian and French edns trans. into English, A. Montesano, A. Zanni, L. Bruni, J.S. Chipman and M. McLure (eds) (2014), *Manual of Political Economy: A Critical and Variorum Edition*, Oxford: Oxford University Press.

Pareto, V. (1911), 'Économie mathématique', in J. Monk (ed.), *Encyclopedie des Sciences Mathématiques Pures et Appliqués*, **4** (1), Paris: Gauthier-Villars, English trans. J.I. Griffin (1955), 'Mathematical economics', *International Economic Papers*, **5**, 58–102.

Pareto, V. (1913), 'Il Massimo di utilità per una collettività in sociologia', *Giornale degli Economisti e Rivista di Statistica*, **23** (46), 337–41, English trans. reprinted in J.C. Wood and M. McLure (eds) (1999), *Vilfredo Pareto: Critical Assessments*, vol. 3, London: Routledge, pp. 307–10.

Pareto, V. (1916), *Trattato di Sociologia Generale*, Florence: Barbara, English translation (1935), *The Mind and Society*, New York: Harcourt, Brace and Company.

Pareto, V. (1918), 'Economia sperimentale', *Giornale degli Economisti e Rivista di Statistica*, **28** (57), 1–18,

English trans. V. Savini, in M. McLure (ed.) (2008), 'Experimental economics', *Giornali degli Economisti e Annali di Economia*, **67** (3), 545–66.

Pareto, V. (1960), *Lettere a Maffeo Pantaleoni*, vol. 2, ed. G. de Rosa, Rome: Banca Nazionale del Lavoro.

Pareto, V. (1965–2005), *Œuvres Complètes, Vols I to 32*, ed. G. Busino, Genevae: Librairie Droz.

Pigou, A.C. (1912), 'Pareto's law', in A.C. Pigou, *Wealth and Welfare*, London: Macmillan, pp. 71–7.

Pomini, M. (2014), *The Paretian Tradition During the Interwar Period: From Dynamics to Growth*, London: Routledge.

Pomini, M. and G. Tusset (2009), 'Habits and expectations: dynamic general equilibrium in the Italian Paretian School', *History of Political Economy*, **41** (2), 311–42.

Samuelson, P.A. (1938), 'A note on the pure theory of consumer behaviour', *Economica*, **5** (17), 61–71.

Schultz, H. (1929), 'Marginal productivity and the general pricing process', *Journal of Political Economy*, **37** (5), 505–51.

Schultz, H. (1932), 'Marginal productivity and the Lausanne School', *Economica*, **12** (37), 285–96.

Scorza, G. (1902), 'Osservazioni su alcuni teorie di economia pura', *Giornale degli Economisti*, **2** (25), 503–16.

Slutsky, E. (1915), 'Sulla teoria del bilancio del consumatore', *Giornale degli Economisti*, **51** (July), 1–26, English trans. O. Ragusa, in G.J. Stigler and K E. Boulding (eds) (1952), 'On the theory of the budget of the consumer', *Readings in Price Theory*, Homewood, IL: Irwin, pp. 27–56.

Tarascio, Vincent J. (1968), *Pareto's Methodological Approach to Economics*, Chapel Hill, NC: University of North Carolina Press.

Volterra, V. (1906), 'L'Economia matematica e il nuovo manuale del Prof. Pareto', *Giornale degli Economisti*, **16** (33), 296–301.

Weber, C.E. (1998), 'Pareto and the Wicksell–Cobb–Douglas functional form', *Journal of the History of Economic Thought*, **20** (2), 203–10.

Weber, C.E. (1999), 'More on Slutsky's equation as Pareto's solution', *History of Political Economy*, **33** (3), 575–85.

Wilson, E.B. (1935), 'Generalisation of Pareto's demand theorem', *Quarterly Journal of Economics*, **49** (4), 715–17.

Wood, J.C. and M. McLure (eds) (1999), *Vilfredo Pareto: Critical Assessments*, London: Routledge.

Eugen von Böhm-Bawerk (1851–1914)

Eugen Ritter von Böhm-Bawerk is best known to us for his theory of capital and interest. It will also be the main topic of this entry. Nevertheless, there are other relevant contributions of Böhm-Bawerk to economic theory and policy.

Life

Böhm-Bawerk was born on 12 February 1851 in Brünn (Brno) in the Czech part of the Austrian-Hungarian Empire. His father was a high civil servant. Böhm-Bawerk studied law in Vienna and then entered the civil service. He soon took leave to become an economist by studying in Heidelberg, Leipzig and Jena. In 1880 he obtained his Habilitation at the Faculty of Law in Vienna as a student of Carl Menger. His Habilitation thesis "Whether legal rights and relationships are economic goods" was published in 1881. In this he deals with the question of whether immaterial property like patent rights or goodwill positions in markets could be seen as part of net national wealth. In opposition to earlier writers such as Albert Schäffle and also to his own mentor Carl Menger, he gave a negative answer by emphasizing the similarity with loans which also could not be seen as part of net national wealth. The private value of such immaterial property rested on the fact that other people in the future will pay more for material goods than their cost of production. If these margins were considered to be paid above cost as a future burden of consumers, their capitalized value just cancels the capital value of the immaterial property.

In 1880 Böhm-Bawerk was appointed professor of economics in Innsbruck. During his Innsbruck years he wrote his most important work on the theory of capital and interest, *Kapital und Kapitalzins*. It was published in two volumes, the first in 1885, the second in 1889. In 1889 he went back to the Imperial Ministry of Finance. His job was first to design a reform of the Austrian income tax and then to head a commission studying the question of whether Austria-Hungary should return to the gold standard. He then was appointed Minister of Finance in a caretaker cabinet; after the resignation of the cabinet he became president of a high court of administrative law. For several years, depending on the actual politics in Vienna, he moved between the two positions. In 1904 he resigned as Minister of Finance in protest against large increases of military expenditure. Having declined the well-paid position of Governor of the Imperial Central Bank, he went back to academic life, this time as a professor at the University of Vienna. He was appointed a member of the Austrian upper house. Böhm-Bawerk died in 1914.

Works

Apart from his great work on capital theory and his Habilitation book mentioned above, Böhm-Bawerk wrote three other important pieces: first and foremost his 1896 evaluation of Karl Marx's *Capital* after the posthumous appearance of volumes II and III of that great work; then, not long before he died, his incisive critique of Schumpeter's "dynamic theory of capital" and, third, a policy-oriented newspaper article on the balance of payments in which, in a very clear manner, he laid down the (full employment) theory of foreign trade: that capital exports and imports drove the balance of trade rather than the other way round (1914).

In the first volume on the theory of interest (1885) Böhm-Bawerk surveys and criticizes the whole history of theories which tries to explain the positive rate of interest. In the second volume (1889), the *Positive Theory*, he gives his own explanation. We best understand his theory as a general equilibrium theory of the stationary state – and it was of course that theory which then in his *Theory of Economic Development* (1912) Schumpeter tried to replace. Böhm-Bawerk writes (1889):

> As a rule goods available now have a higher subjective value than future goods of the same kind and quantity. And, since the result of subjective valuations determines the objective exchange value, present goods, as a rule, have a higher exchange value and price than future goods of the same kind and quantity.

This kind of reasoning was new at the time and was an extension of Carl Menger's subjective value theory to an inter-temporal calculus.

Böhm-Bawerk gives three causes for this lower valuation of future goods. The first is the potential or real discrepancy between the inter-temporal structure of wants to be satisfied by material goods and the inter-temporal structure of the availability of those goods. Thus, there is a desire to shift goods through time. However, future goods cannot physically be shifted backward towards the present, whereas present goods can be shifted forward in time by storing them. This induces superior value of present goods. Bortkiewicz and others have criticized this argument by pointing to the costs of storage. To this Böhm-Bawerk replied that in a market economy operating with money people only need to store money which has a storage cost of zero.

The second cause is impatience of individuals, basically what then later has been termed "time preference" by Irving Fisher.

The third cause is what Böhm-Bawerk called the "incremental productivity of greater roundaboutness of production". This general law implies that earlier availability of inputs allows a greater roundaboutness of production and thus a greater labour productivity in the provision of consumption goods for a given future point in time. As this third cause is expressed in comparative or quantitative terms of "more roundaboutness" Böhm-Bawerk had to offer a measure for the degree of roundaboutness of production. This was what later would be called the average period of production or, for short, the period of production. It can be understood as the average time distance between the labour inputs and the consumption good output produced by these labour inputs. Böhm-Bawerk essentially argues in terms of a vertically fully integrated virtual factory which only buys labour inputs and only sells final consumption goods. All intermediate goods, including machinery, buildings, and so on are made and used internally by the virtual factory itself. Production starts with unassisted labour.

Owing to these three causes, the real rate of interest is positive in a stationary general equilibrium.

Many economists then were impressed by Böhm-Bawerk's achievements, but at the same time were critical of the details. Of the great economists of the time, nobody accepted Böhm-Bawerk's theory fully. Neither Wicksell, nor Irving Fisher, nor John Bates Clark, nor Gustav Cassel, nor even Carl Menger – Böhm-Bawerk's teacher – accepted the concept of the average period of production as a good measure for the roundaboutness of production and the corresponding capital requirements of the economy.

Later, the Austrians, in particular Hayek and Mises, used Böhm-Bawerkian concepts to develop their severe criticism of an easy money policy. According to them, such a policy would first lead to overinvestment and then later on to a slump owing to the excess capacities thereby generated. To show this they built on Böhm-Bawerk's temporal capital theory. Eucken further developed the Böhm-Bawerk theory by generalizing the input flows which were allowed in the model. Throughout the first half of the twentieth century many economists commented on Böhm-Bawerk's theory.

After the introduction of the Solow model, and thus after the beginning of neoclassical growth theory in 1956, Böhm-Bawerk's temporal capital theory basically was discarded. Whereas the idea of the roundaboutness of production continued to be used as a *façon de parler* (manner of speech) the analytical tool of the average period of production was replaced by the Solow macroeconomic production function. The severe criticism of the Solow approach by the Cambridge School (Sraffa, Joan Robinson, Kaldor, Pasinetti, Garegnani, Harcourt, Schefold and others) did not lead them back to Böhm-Bawerk, but rather to David Ricardo and Karl Marx. In his *Capital and Time. A Neo-Austrian Approach* (1973) John Hicks came back to Böhm-Bawerk. He argued that a temporal theory of capital was more suitable for a dynamic analysis than was the Solowian production function approach. Already in his much earlier "classic" *Value and Capital* (1939) he gave reasons why a period of production might better be defined in terms of present values of labour inputs rather than in terms of raw physical quantities, as Böhm-Bawerk had defined it. However, in both books Hicks considered the period of production to be a useless concept for an economy with fixed capital such as buildings or machinery.

What do we make of the three causes for a lower valuation of future goods today? In analysing Böhm-Bawerk's reasoning we can admire his sharp intellect, yet we may feel sorry for him that he did not know the mathematical-axiomatic method which has allowed modern theory substantially greater clarity in the concepts used to do economic theory. Like Ricardo or Marx he worked with numerical examples; and this probably also was a reason that he used simple interest rather than the compound interest calculus.

The first Böhm-Bawerkian cause, the incongruence of the inter-temporal structure of wants with the inter-temporal structure of the availability of goods, is not generally valid. Storage costs are a problem, notwithstanding the availability of money as a store of value. Money as "inside money", for example, in the form of bank deposits for constant purchasing power, presupposes the existence of a sufficient number of borrowers who provide collateral which is real capital like buildings, equipment and inventories. All of these forms of real capital imply storage costs or costs in the form of wear and tear. Outside money, like gold, is not able, without substantial effort involving again inside money, to guarantee constant purchasing power. Moreover, today, with the high life expectancy of people, the desire to hold wealth for consumption purposes in old age may be larger than the availability of real capital even at a real rate of interest of zero.

The second cause, time preference, is valid, but may be quantitatively constrained. No doubt, other things being equal, a greater degree of time preference implies a higher real rate of interest. However, this does not necessarily mean that with the empirically observed time preference the real rate of interest is positive.

The third cause, greater productivity of greater roundaboutness of production, is not valid beyond any limits. This is basically admitted by Böhm-Bawerk in the first part of his "Exkurs I". Exkurs I, as the other "Exkurses", was written in answer to criticisms raised against his theory by several authors including Irving Fisher, Bortkiewicz, Gustav Cassel, Taussig and others. But Böhm-Bawerk maintains that in the real world of his time the potential for exploiting incremental productivity of greater roundaboutness had not yet been fully used. He continues in this "Exkurs I" to give quite a bit of evidence as to why he concludes that this is so. Given the substantial changes in technology and wealth which have occurred in a century after Böhm-Bawerk finished his work, we can no longer be sure whether there are still unexploited opportunities for a higher productivity of greater roundaboutness.

Modernization of Böhm-Bawerkian Concepts

The best way to find out whether today the three causes are sufficient to generate a positive real rate of interest is to use very Böhm-Bawerkian analytical tools: the "modernized" period of production and an analogous "waiting period". Both are defined in terms of present values.

We may look at the price p_i of consumption good i in a competitive economy with a given nominal wage rate w and a given rate of interest r; thus $p_i = f_i(w; r)$. It then can be shown that $\frac{\partial f_i}{\partial r} = T_i f_i(w; r)$ where T_i is the "modernized" Böhm-Bawerkian period or production as applied to consumption good i. Thus the percentage increase of the price of consumption good i, as the rate of interest rises one percentage point, equals the period of production of the labour inputs which directly and indirectly (via intermediate products) enter into the production of that good. This is a quite general result which does include models with fixed and circulating capital and as many capital goods and consumption goods as you like. It has a forerunner in Hicks's *Value and Capital*, chapter XVII.

The result has consequences which very much vindicate Böhm-Bawerk's idea of measuring capital intensity and roundaboutness by means of the average period of production. The first observation is that as the rate of interest rises techniques with a higher period of production induce a faster price rise than techniques with a lower period of production. Thus there is a tendency to switch to techniques with lower periods of production as the rate of interest rises. This can be called the substitution theorem of capital theory. The second observation is marginal productivity. Böhm-Bawerk claimed that at the equilibrium period of production the percentage increment in productivity resulting from a lengthening of the period of production by a (small) time unit will be equal to the equilibrium rate of interest. Indeed, as the period of production rises by one unit the cost of the product directly and indirectly produced by one hour of labour rises by r in percentage terms. But since the period of production at the prevailing interest rate has been selected so as to minimize unit costs this must mean that the labour productivity in the production of good i must have risen by exactly the same percentage, which is r. Hence the private and social marginal productivity of roundaboutness is reflected in the rate of interest, as Böhm-Bawerk said. But we must remember that in comparison to Böhm-Bawerk the period of production is somewhat "modernized".

The third vindication of Böhm-Bawerk is the fact that the aggregate period of production serves as a good aggregate measure of roundaboutness and capital intensity. For this we observe that – beyond Böhm-Bawerk – we can define a parallel concept on the side of private households. It is the waiting period. Any given rate of interest ρ used to compute the present values induces a particular system of weights by which the weighted labour inputs along the time axis and the weighted consumption good outputs are used to find the period of production and the waiting period of consumers/savers. The waiting period is the average time distance between wage income and consumption good expenditures. For a steady-state economy growing at a constant rate of growth g it can then be shown that a general equilibrium of that economy exhibits an endogenously determined equilibrium real rate of interest r with the following property: there exists a notional rate of interest ρ which lies between g and r such that with present value weights induced by ρ the period of production T and the waiting period Z are equal. We may then speak of T as an aggregate measure of the demand for capital and speak of Z as an aggregate measure of the supply of capital. Thus, for a steady-state economy, these modernized Böhm-Bawerkian concepts serve as a useful aggregation device for millions of different capital goods.

On these three results, see von Weizsäcker (1971: pt IV). They are also quite useful for actual policy issues such as, for example, public debt. We should by no means discard Böhm-Bawerk's important contributions to economic theory.

CARL CHRISTIAN VON WEIZSÄCKER

See also:

Capital theory (III); John Bates Clark (I); German and Austrian schools (II); Income distribution (III); Karl Heinrich Marx (I); Carl Menger (I); Joseph Alois Schumpeter (I); Knut Wicksell (I); Friedrich von Wieser (I).

References and further reading

Böhm-Bawerk, E. von (1881), *Rechte und Verhältnisse vom Standpunkte der volkswirtschaftlichen Güterlehre*, Innsbruck: Wagner, trans. 'Whether legal rights and relationships are economic goods', in E. von Böhm-Bawerk (1962), *Shorter Classics*, South Holland, IL: Libertarian Press.

Böhm-Bawerk, E. von (1885), *Kapital und Kapitalzins. Erste Abteilung: Geschichte und Kritik der Kapitalzins-Theorien*, Innsbruck: Wagner, 2nd edn, 1900, 3rd edn, 1914, 4th edn, 1921, Jena: Fischer, trans. 1st edn (1890), *Capital and Interest*, London: Macmillan, trans. 4th edn (1959), *Capital and Interest*, vol. 1. South Holland, IL: Libertarian Press.

Böhm-Bawerk, E. von (1886), 'Grundzüge der Theorie des wirthschaftlichenGüterwerthes'. *Jahrbücher für Nationalökonomie und Statistik*, **13**, 1–82, 477–541, reprinted separately (1932), London: London School of Economics.

Böhm-Bawerk, E. von (1889), *Kapital und Kapitalzins. Zweite Abteilung: Positive Theorie des Kapitales*, Innsbruck: Wagner, 2nd edn, 1902, 3rd edn, 2 vols, 1909 and 1912; 4th edn 2 vols, 1921, Jena: Fischer, trans. 1st edn (1891), *The Positive Theory of Capital*, London: Macmillan, trans. 4th edn (1921), *Capital and Interest*, vols 2 and 3, South Holland, IL: Libertarian Press.

Böhm-Bawerk, E. von (1896), 'Zum Abschluss des Marxschen Systems', in O. von Boenigk (ed.), *Staatswissenschaftliche Arbeiten, Festgaben für Karl Knies*, trans. (1898), *Karl Marx and the Close of his System*, London: Fisher Unwin, reprinted in P.M. Sweezy (ed.) (1949), *Karl Marx and the Close of his System by Eugen von Böhm-Bawerk and Böhm-Bawerk's Criticism of Marx*, New York: Kelley, trans. as 'Unresolved contradictions in the Marxian economic system', in E. von Böhm-Bawerk (1962), *Shorter Classics*, South Holland, IL: Libertarian Press.

Böhm-Bawerk, E. von (1913), 'Eine "dynamische" Theorie des Kapitalzinses', *Zeitschrift für Volkswirtschaft, Sozialpolitik und Verwaltung*, **22**, 520–85, 640–57.

Böhm-Bawerk, E. von (1914), 'Macht oder ökonomisches Gesetz?', *Zeitschrift für Volkswirtschaft, Sozialpolitik und Verwaltung*, **23**, 205–71, reprinted in F.X. Weisz (ed.) (1924), *Gesammelte Schriften*, Vienna and Leipzig: Hölder-Pichler-Tempsky.

Böhm-Bawerk, E. von (1926), *Kleinere Abhandlungen über Kaptial und Zins*, Vienna and Leipzig: Hölder-Pichler-Tempsky.

Böhm-Bawerk, E. von (1962), *Shorter Classics*, South Holland, IL: Libertarian Press.

Cassel, G. (1903), *The Nature and Necessity of Interest*, London: Macmillan.

Clark, J.B. (1899), *The Distribution of Wealth*, New York: Macmillan.
Eucken, W. (1934), *Kapitaltheoretische Untersuchungen*, 2nd edn, Tübingen: Mohr.
Fisher, I. (1907), *The Rate of Interest*, New York: Macmillan.
Hayek, F.A. von (1931), *Preise und Produktion*, Vienna: Springer, trans. (1931), *Prices and Production*, London: Routledge.
Hayek, F.A. von (1941), *The Pure Theory of Capital*, London: Routledge.
Hennings, K. (1997), *The Austrian Theory of Value and Capital: Studies in the Life and Work of Eugen von Böhm-Bawerk*, Cheltenham, UK and Northampton, MA, USA: Edward Elgar.
Hicks, J.R. (1939), *Value and Capital*, Oxford: Clarendon Press.
Hicks, J.R. (1967), 'The Hayek story', in J.R. Hicks, *Critical Essays in Monetary Theory*, Oxford: Clarendon Press.
Hicks, J.R. (1973), *Capital and Time. A Neo-Austrian Approach*, Oxford: Clarendon Press.
Hilferding, R. (1904), 'Böhm-Bawerks Marx-Kritik', in M. Adler and R. Hilferding (eds), *Marx Studien 1*, trans. 'Böhm-Bawerk's criticism of Marx', in P.M. Sweezy (ed.) (1949), *Karl Marx and the Close of his System by Eugen von Böhm-Bawerk and Böhm-Bawerk's Criticism of Marx*, New York: Kelley.
Lutz, F.A. (1956), *Zinstheorie*, Tübingen: Mohr, trans. (1967), *The Theory of Interest*, Dordrecht: Reidel.
Schäffle, A.E.F. (1870), *Kapitalismus und Sozialismus*, Tübingen: Laupp.
Schumpeter, J.A. (1912), *Theorie der wirtschaftlichen Entwicklung*, Leipzig: Duncker & Humblot, trans. (1934), *The Theory of Economic Development*, Cambridge, MA: Harvard University Press.
Schumpeter, J.A. (1914), 'Das wissenschaftliche Lebenswerk Eugen von Böhm-Bawerks', *Zeitschrift für Volkswirtschaft, Socialpolitik und Verwaltung*, **23**, 454–528, trans. J.A. Schumpeter (ed.) (1952), *Ten Great Economists*, London: Allen & Unwin.
Sweezy, P.M. (ed.) (1949), *Karl Marx and the Close of his System by Eugen von Böhm-Bawerk and Böhm-Bawerk's Criticism of Marx*, New York: Kelley.
Weizsäcker, C.C. von (1971), *Steady State Capital Theory*, Berlin: Springer.
Wicksell, K. (1893), *Über Wert Kapital und Rente nach neueren nationalökonomischen Theorien*, Jena: Fischer, trans. (1954), *Value, Capital and Rent*, London: Allen & Unwin.
Wicksell, K. (1911), 'Böhm-Bawerkskapitalteori och kritikendärav', *Ekonomisk Tidskrift*, **13**, 39–49, trans. K. Wicksell (1958), *Selected Papers on Economic Theory*, London: Allen & Unwin.

Knut Wicksell (1851–1926)

The Swedish economist Knut Wicksell is well known for his contributions to the marginal productivity theory of distribution and the theory of capital and interest, where he tried to create a unified framework from a synthesis of ideas of David Ricardo, Léon Walras and Eugen von Böhm-Bawerk. Nowadays he is perhaps even better known for his pioneering works in monetary economics, where his approach paved the way for both Austrian and Keynesian economics. It has recently even seen a renaissance in dynamic stochastic general-equilibrium models. Moreover, Wicksell has made a strong contribution to the theory of public finance, giving impetus to the development of welfare economics and public choice. Both as "a pioneer and a follower-up", Wicksell has thus earned the recognition of an "economist's economist", while he "was not only an ingenious scholar, but also a radical political thinker and untiring social reformer of great caliber" (Lindahl 1958: 9).

Life

Johan Gustav Knut Wicksell was born in Stockholm on 20 December 1851, the youngest of the six children of grocer Johan Wicksell and his wife Catharina. He lost his mother at the age of 6 and his father at 15. Yet family life with his father and sisters, who loved to discuss anything in the spirit of a debating club, made a lasting impression on him. In school, Wicksell was regarded as very talented, but also reprimanded for his "rebellious attitude". During adolescence, he fell under the spell of the Lutheran Awakening movement that was widely popular in the mid-nineteenth century. After seven years of intensive Bible studies, he came across the works of Charles Darwin, David Friedrich Strauß and Henrik Ibsen. They led him into a deep crisis of faith, from which he emerged as an atheist and free thinker. By then, in 1873, Wicksell had already earned his first degrees in philosophy, history, Latin, Nordic languages, astronomy and mathematics at Uppsala University. He aspired to become a professor of mathematics, but his advanced studies took 12 years, partly due to financial problems, but mostly because he intensively engaged in social and political activities. He completed his studies in 1885, at the age of 35, but by that time he had abandoned his ambitions for a chair in mathematics.

Wicksell's life took a new direction in the late 1870s, when he read George Drysdale's *Elements of Social Science* (1878), a book on the 'Three primary social evils: poverty, prostitution, and celibacy'. He began to study Malthusian theories of population and gave a public lecture in 1880, in which he presented overpopulation as the main cause of poverty and alcoholism in Sweden. The lecture was received with admiration and indignation, as Wicksell fervently advocated birth control. It drew such large audiences that it was repeated several times and printed in several thousand copies. It earned Wicksell the reputation of a radical liberal with a social mission, who argued with wit and tact. Within a short time he was able to make a living as a lecturer and writer of articles and pamphlets about poverty, liberty and social reform. Some critics pointed out, however, that he lacked deeper understanding of the economic causes of overpopulation. As it came from highly regarded authorities in public debate, such as the Uppsala professor David Davidson, Wicksell took this criticism very seriously and turned to extensive studies of classical political economy. Between 1885 and 1889, he used a small inheritance and several grants from the Lorén Foundation to travel to London, Paris, Strasbourg, Vienna and Berlin, where he talked to social reformers, such as Drysdale and Annie Besant, and attended lectures of Georg Friedrich Knapp, Carl Menger and Adolph Wagner – without, however, being much impressed. Of more importance was his close reading of the classics, in particular the works of Thomas Malthus, David Ricardo and John Stuart Mill. He also studied the marginalist writings of Stanley Jevons, Menger and Walras that are nowadays regarded as the pioneering works of neoclassical economics.

When Wicksell discovered Böhm-Bawerk's *Positive Theory of Capital* in a Berlin bookshop in 1889, it came as "a revelation" to him. As he remembered in his obituary for Böhm-Bawerk 25 years later, the book had helped him

> to penetrate theoretically the phenomenon of interest and the overall problem of economic distribution when it is complicated by the presence of capital. . . All of a sudden I saw. . . the roof being erected on a scholarly edifice. Ever since the days of Ricardo, economists had only managed to construct its lower floors and otherwise had to be content with collecting more or less useful building materials. (Wicksell 1914: 322)

Böhm-Bawerk's theory inspired Wicksell to draft a series of lectures on the new marginalist theories of value, capital and rent. Since *Stockholms högskola*, the University College of Stockholm (now Stockholm University), refused to let Wicksell give his lectures on its premises, he presented them to Arbetarföreningen, the Workers' Association in Stockholm. The first lecture attracted an audience so large that it had to be moved to a bigger hall. When Wicksell came to the details of value theory, however, that hall quickly became too big (Gårdlund 1956: ch. 6). Their humble origins notwithstanding, the lectures were translated into German and came out in print in 1893, published by Gustav Fischer at Jena. The book carried the title *Über Wert, Kapital und Rente*, and it was Wicksell's first major contribution to economic theory, favourably received by both Böhm-Bawerk and Walras.

It did not take long before further contributions followed, with Wicksell endeavouring to qualify for an academic position at the University College of Stockholm. Apart from his passion for scientific research he had private motives. In summer 1888, during holidays in Copenhagen, he had met Anna Bugge, a teacher from Kristiania (now Oslo). After a few dances in the summer night, they had parted and started a long and intensive correspondence with each other. In summer 1889 Knut had visited Anna at her parents' home and eventually convinced her, to the disapproval of her parents, to take part in a civil marriage contract and to move to Stockholm with him. With the birth of their two sons, Wicksell now had a family to feed. This he could hardly manage as a freelancing lecturer and writer, especially since he never compromised on his radically liberal views. For the same reason, he failed to find employment at the University College, although it was more formally pointed out that he lacked a doctoral degree. His 1893 treatise on value theory was not accepted as a doctoral dissertation, so he began to work on a thesis on tax incidence and justice in taxation. This led eventually to a larger study of public finance which was published under the title *Finanztheoretische Untersuchungen nebst Darstellung und Kritik des Steuerwesens Schwedens* (1896). The first part of the book is largely identical to the thesis for which Wicksell was awarded the doctoral degree by Uppsala University in 1895. It may have been produced as a merely formal requirement, but it came to exert a notable influence on further developments in the fields of public finance and political economy.

Yet there were further obstacles to Wicksell's academic career. At that time, economics in Sweden was taught at the faculties of law. A law degree was a prerequisite to an appointment as lecturer or professor in economics. In his mid-forties and in a precarious financial condition, Wicksell thus had to study legal matters. As he found this extremely boring, he continued to do economic research in his free time, with a little help from his friends and some grants. In 1898 he presented "a study of the causes regulating the value of money". This is the subtitle of the famous treatise on "interest and prices", *Geldzins und Güterpreise*, which contains a theory of inflation based on differences between market rates of interest and the rates of return to real investment – an idea that Wicksell had outlined as early as 1889 (Boianovsky and Trautwein 2001a). As a by-product of boredom with legal matters, this path-breaking idea now saw daylight, but it took a few more decades for it to leave its mark on the evolution of macroeconomic thinking.

In 1899, Lund University created the position of a professor extraordinarius in economics. Wicksell applied, in competition with Gustav Cassel and two others. Despite protracted resistance of the Bishop of Lund, Wicksell was appointed professor in late 1901. Even conservatives argued that Sweden could afford to have at least one radical free thinker. In 1904 Wicksell was promoted to the position of a full professor. Finally, at the age of 52, he had secured his living and could concentrate on academic work.

During his professorship in Lund, Wicksell published many articles and other papers, but no more books. The only exceptions were the two volumes of his *Lectures on Political Economy*, published in Swedish in 1901 and 1906. The *Lectures* essentially combined and refined Wicksell's earlier theories of value, distribution and money. In addition to his academic work, Wicksell continued to propagate social reforms and to give lectures in the service of enlightenment and the freedom of speech. He tested the constitutional right to the latter in 1908, when he opposed the prison sentence that the liberal agitator Ljungdahl had received for blasphemy. Wicksell provoked the authorities, giving a public lecture on "the throne, the altar, the sword, and the money bag". Examining the dogma of Immaculate Conception, which had been attacked by Ljungdahl, he surmised that:

> Joseph, the betrothed of the Virgin Mary . . . must in all piety have grumbled to himself, when nobody else heard it: "Why the hell didn't the Holy Ghost let me father my little Jesus myself?" But then the world could not have been saved. That's it, you see: . . . Private interests must give way to the general interest. (Translated from Gårdlund 1956: 279)

As a consequence, Wicksell himself was tried for blasphemy and sentenced to two months in prison. There he spent his time writing a tract on demography and translating Adam Smith's *Wealth of Nations* into Swedish.

Stubborn as Wicksell was in his conflicts with the temporal and spiritual authorities, he impressed his contemporaries with his unconventional and unassuming behaviour. His biographer Gårdlund (1956: 371) described him as giving

> the impression of a strong inner conflict, almost a split personality in fact. He was a wild agitator and an objective scholar at one and the same time, a hot-headed polemic, but sensitive and considerate of everybody near to him; he attacked and reviled religion, while singing hymns and

revering jubilating deans; he expressed his admiration for the most stubborn rightists, while his place was on the extreme left.

This may appear to stand in contrast with Schumpeter's high praise for Wicksell: "No finer intellect and no higher character have ever graced our field. If the depth and originality of his thought do not stand out more clearly than they do, this is only owning to this lovable modesty" (1893 [1954]: 862). There is, of course, no contradiction between these two descriptions.

After retirement in 1916, Wicksell and his wife Anna moved back to Stockholm, his beloved hometown. Anna Bugge made a political career in the women's suffrage movement and the peace movement. As a Swedish delegate to the League of Nations and member of the Permanent Mandates Commission she travelled much and was away from home for long spells. Wicksell suffered from depression, but remained productive in his research work, setting the focus on capital theory and monetary policy, which had become a first-order social issue after the First World War, when the gold standard was suspended and Sweden suffered from waves of inflation and deflation. A consultant to the governor of Riksbanken, the Swedish central bank, since 1915, Wicksell came to be in high demand as an expert in parliamentary committees on banking, taxation and other matters. At the initiative of David Davidson, Eli Heckscher and other friends, the Political Economy Club (Nationalekonomiska föreningen) was founded in his honour, and Wicksell was made its first chairman. The club became an important debating forum and contributed significantly to the formation of the Stockholm School (or Swedish School), which in the 1930s came to expand Wicksell's monetary theory into a more general mode of thinking about macroeconomic fluctuations. Yet Wicksell did not live to see the renewed interest in his theory of interest-rate gaps. He died on 3 May 1926 in Stockholm, at the age of 74.

Works

Wicksell was a prolific writer on a large variety of political and economic issues. The excellent bibliography by Knudtzon and Hedlund-Nyström (1976) listed more than 800 publications, prompting the rediscovery of much more material, partly unpublished. In the following, the focus is on Wicksell's most eminent contributions to the theories of income distribution, taxation, capital, interest and inflation. Their connection may be seen in Wicksell's untiring endeavours to provide a unified framework for economic analysis on the basis of the marginal principle.

Marginal analysis
In the introduction to his theory of value in the first volume of the *Lectures* (1901 [1934]: 14), Wicksell emphasized that:

> [m]odern investigations in the theory of value have led to the setting up of a principle – or rather to the generalization and establishment of a principle already known and applied – called the *marginal principle*, whose application extends far beyond the actual province of the exchange of goods into the fields of production, distribution, and capital. In other words, it governs every part of political economy. (Original emphasis)

It is a well-known result of neoclassical economics that, in the general equilibrium of a market system with perfect competition, the prices of goods are fully determined by the marginal utility of their consumption and the marginal productivity of the factors used in their fabrication. This is standard fare in modern textbooks. In the 1890s, neoclassical economics was not yet a coherent framework of analysis. Different schools were forming at Lausanne, Vienna, Cambridge and elsewhere, and dividing lines were drawn between their concepts of value, markets, equilibrium and the methods of reasoning in general. Wicksell attempted to transform the diverse constructs of Walras, Böhm-Bawerk, Jevons and Alfred Marshall into a unified body of theory, and to add a few missing parts. He took, moreover, frequent recourse to the classical theories of Ricardo and Johann Heinrich von Thünen, systematically proceeding from the history of economic thought to the logical steps in his own analysis. In marked contrast to his arch-rival Cassel, Wicksell never forgot to acknowledge the contributions of others. He sported an extreme form of Swedish understatement, often hiding his light under a bushel. Conspicuous examples of such modesty can be found in Wicksell's contributions to the neoclassical theory of income distribution.

Distribution

Wicksell's recipe for synthesis has been aptly described by Uhr (1951: 842) as:

> using the marginal-utility-marginal-productivity theories of Jevons and Menger, adding to these the derived Böhm-Bawerkian analysis of capital, and fusing the product within a Walrasian framework of general equilibrium to reveal the multiple causal interrelations of the theoretical edifice. In this process he became the founder of the marginal productivity theory of functional distribution.

That theory has actually many fathers, notably John Bates Clark and Philip Wicksteed. Wicksell has nevertheless helped to make the theory more precise, and he has taken it to its limits.

The core of the theory can be expressed in terms of two propositions. The first is that, in competitive equilibrium, the prices of the factors of production (wage, interest and rent) correspond to the marginal productivity of the factors. In classical political economy, only rent is determined by the scarcity of the corresponding factor of production – "land" or, more generally, "the external natural forces at the service of man" (Wicksell 1901 [1934]: 107). The neoclassical theory of value, on the other hand, is based on scarcity as the general principle of the explanation of the prices of goods and factors of production. This use of the notion of scarcity implies that demand and supply are independently determined by given tastes and technology. It also implies that the prices that match supply and demand in the markets lead to an efficient allocation of resources, so that production cannot systematically exceed or fall short of the demand that follows from the incomes it generates.

The second proposition of the neoclassical theory of distribution is thus the exhaustion theorem: if all factors of production are paid according to their marginal productivity, aggregate output (the "social product") will correspond exactly to aggregate income, and aggregate demand will thus suffice to absorb aggregate supply. While Clark only asserted this in 1889, Wicksell demonstrated it in 1893 (1893: 146–53), even though his proof was less elegant than that accomplished by Wicksteed a year later. When Walras claimed to have been the first to prove the exhaustion theorem, Wicksell (1900, 1902) countered by declaring Wicksteed to be the main pioneer of marginal productivity theory, completely ignoring his own contribution of 1893. He also showed that, contrary to Walras's claims, the exhaustion theorem is valid only in the special case of an aggregate production function that is linear and homogenous of degree one (Wicksell 1900 [1958]: 97–100). Moreover, Wicksell pointed out that Wicksteed's analysis was limited in scope because of the underlying assumption of constant returns to scale. According to Wicksell, this condition was not as innocent and plausible as Wicksteed had claimed. Yet Wicksell also demonstrated that the condition of constant returns holds in perfect competition, as the firms achieve their profit maximum in this setting at the point of minimal average costs, where they pass from increasing to diminishing returns (1902 [1958]: 123–30). In an extended version of this argument Wicksell had proved a year earlier, in his *Lectures* of 1901 ([1934] 125–31), that a remuneration of labour and land according to their marginal productivity would lead to excessive claims on the social product in the case of increasing returns to scale, and to insufficient claims in the case of decreasing returns. For the reference case of exact exhaustion he used a linear and homogenous production function where the scale elasticity is equal to one. This special form was later promoted to the standard formula for the neoclassical theory of production and distribution – by Charles Cobb and Paul Douglas.

In all his enthusiasm for marginal analysis Wicksell did not forget to point out that factor pricing at marginal productivity may lead to suboptimal results at the individual and the social level. Taking issue with Ricardo's analysis of the income effects of labour-saving technical progress, Wicksell (1901 [1934]: 133–44) drew attention to cases in which technical change lowers the marginal productivity of labour even while total output is growing. If free competition prevails in the labour market, this could easily happen, as the displacement of labour will tend to reduce wages. Competing with the firms that have introduced the new labour-saving methods, other firms may find it profitable to re-employ the displaced workers at the lower wage level, in plants that use less productive older methods. Given the pressure on wages, Wicksell concluded that technical progress may result in a decline of both marginal productivity and the wage level.

In view of the miseries of overpopulation, his old nemesis, Wicksell drove the argument further:

> Nor is the result any different if we assume that wages are already at the subsistence level (and cannot, according to the usual view, fall lower). In reality, wages can not only be forced below it for a little, but can remain below it indefinitely, if the labourers and their families can make up the difference by poor relief, as happened in England to a great extent at the end of the eighteenth and the beginning of the nineteenth centuries. (1901 [1934]: 141)

This insight led Wicksell to advocate wage subsidies that preserve full employment. In logical consequence he rejected minimum wages and reductions of working hours, arguing that such measures would lead to persistent unemployment and impoverishment. This view, which he had actually propagated since the early 1890s, cost him a lot of sympathy from his old friends in the workers' association and the trade unions. Yet it provided neoclassical foundations for the theoretical justification of employment policies in welfare states. Wicksell pointed out that wage subsidies could be financed out of the increase in the social product generated by labour-saving technical progress. He thus argued in favour of a redistribution of incomes by way of taxes, suggesting that such corrections of the primary "functional" income distribution support growth by way of reducing the costs of unemployment.

Collective goods and principles of taxation
The scope of Wicksell's contributions to the theory of public finance is not limited to social policies that correct dysfunctional outcomes of the market process. The first part of his "studies in the theory of public finance" (*Finanztheoretische Untersuchungen*, Wicksell 1896: 1–75) sets the focus on tax incidence and compares the distributional effects of direct and indirect taxes. In this context Wicksell demonstrated that a (direct) tax on profit is to be preferred to (indirect) specific taxes and *ad valorem* taxes, since the latter induce welfare-reducing effects on prices and quantities.

The greater innovation is found in the second part of the studies where Wicksell developed "a new principle of just taxation" (1896: 76–164). He criticized the dualist practices and doctrines of his time, which dealt with state revenues and expenditures as if they were completely separate entities, where revenues are tailored to what taxpayers can afford to pay, while expenditures are autonomously governed by the state's interests. Wicksell considered it to be unjust to define the distribution of the tax burdens, and thereby determine the state revenues, independently of the decisions taken about the supply of "collective goods", such as roads, mail services and theatres. The order should be reversed: the benefits to the taxpayers should determine the corresponding distribution of the tax burden. Wicksell argued that the principle of voluntary exchange, or quid pro quo, should apply to the public sector, too, so that the marginal principle could become effective (with some exceptions, duly defined). He deemed it possible to offer enough options for the distribution of the costs of collective goods that general consent on their finance could be reached in each and every case. "[I]f the corresponding expenditure promises any value that exceeds the costs, it will doubtlessly be considered as beneficial and, hence, might even be approved unanimously" (1896: 113, my translation). In principle, Wicksell insisted on unanimous votes, in order to remain close to the rules of voluntary exchange. "For practical reasons", however, Wicksell (1896: 116–17) defined the lower boundaries of "relative unanimity" at the levels of 90 or even 75 per cent. Any failure to achieve these levels should be considered as sufficient proof that the social benefits of the projects in question are smaller than their costs. In this case they should be rejected. Above these levels, however, state expenditures and the supply of collective goods could be expanded up to the point where their marginal benefits equal their marginal costs. Wicksell's application of the marginal principle to the public sector helped to provide another set of neoclassical arguments for welfare-state policies.

For Wicksell (1896: 125) the great advantage of his consensus rule was a higher degree of legitimacy and acceptance. Instead of regarding the taxes they have to pay as an unjust burden, citizens would consider them as the means to provide for their need of collective goods. Wicksell admitted that the consensus could be abused and undermined by way of vetoing holdups and free riding. Yet he believed these risks to be rather small and amenable to regulation. He nevertheless insisted that the consensus rule for taxation would work only if there was a fair distribution of wealth and income right from the start. "Otherwise it is impossible to speak of equal exchange, and of the equality of the sacrifices made; it is no 'service' to the state, nor a 'sacrifice' that could be accepted as such, if a person is made to return to it what he had unjustly possessed" (1896: 143, my translation). From this followed Wicksell's distinction between allocative and redistributive sections of the taxation system. In addition to consensual taxation for the provision of collective goods there ought to be inheritance tax and taxes on accidental gains, based on democratic voting (1896: 142–60). As Samuelson (1988: 30) has pointed out, Wicksell believed that Adam Smith's invisible hand needed the helping hand of redistribution by taxes and transfers in order to make the marginal utilities of different members of society "ethically comparable".

Capital and interest

Wicksell's contributions to the theories of distribution and public finance would have been fully sufficient to secure him a place in the history of economic thought. His pioneering works in the fields of capital theory and monetary theory have made him even more prominent, and they are connected with each other through the phenomenon of interest rates. Böhm-Bawerk's theory of capital may have provided a strong ingredient of Wicksell's synthesis in the neoclassical theory of distribution, and Wicksell never forgot to give strong praise to Böhm. However, his untiring attempts to make Böhm's concepts more precise – from his first treatise (*On Value, Capital and Rent*, 1893) until the very last article (published posthumously in 1928) – led him further and further away from Böhm, into fundamental criticism and modifications of his own analysis (cf. Uhr 1960: chs 4–7; Sandelin 1998; Kurz 2000). Already in his earliest treatise, Wicksell (1893: 87–8) had criticized Böhm and many of his predecessors for not strictly distinguishing between the theory of capital and the theory of interest. Exploring the implications of that distinction made Wicksell increasingly aware of the pitfalls of Austrian capital theory.

Wicksell's admiration for Böhm-Bawerk had its origins in two fundamental conundrums of the neoclassical theory of distribution. The first conundrum is the determination of the size of the capital stock, the second is in the observation that the consumption of capital services, unlike the use of labour, reproduces the capital and generates a permanent income at one and the same time. If factor prices are to be explained by the scarcity of the respective factors, the latter's quantities must be determined independently of factor prices. The originary factors of production, land and labour, may to some extent be quantifiable in physical units of area and time, such as working hours and acres. Hence, Wicksell developed his theory of production and distribution in the *Lectures* (1901 [1934]: 108–44) in a thought experiment of "non-capitalistic production", with land and labour as the only inputs. In this way, he could show that the marginal-productivity approach provides a consistent explanation of income distribution, if the production functions are linear and homogenous, and if competition is perfect. The capital stock of economy, on the other hand, consists of heterogenous capital goods and cannot generally be measured in a unit that is independent of the rate of interest, the actual *explanandum*. A consistent explanation would have to be based on dubiously specific constructs, such as the reduction of the spectrum of products to a single good that is malleable enough to serve for investment and consumption in every relevant respect.

In addition to the difference in measurability, there is a fundamental difference between labour and capital in terms of factor property (stocks) and income (flows). Wicksell (1901 [1934]: 146) pointed out that:

[i]f anybody makes a spade, a plane, or any other capital good, he obtains, by its use, compensation for his work – and he has no obvious claim to anything more. What is enigmatic is that the possession of capital, apparently at least, does procure something more, namely a permanent income in the form of interest, either without sacrifice of capital or while capital is being constantly replaced . . . We must not simply take it for granted that capital can claim the whole of the surplus.

Why did Wicksell refer to Böhm-Bawerk for the solution of these conundrums? The reason is Böhm's emphasis on the importance of time in processes of production and the intertemporal nature of consumption plans. In Wicksell's view (1901 [1934]: 172), "the time element. . . is the real kernel of the capital concept". Different processes of production require different inputs of capital over different numbers of periods, yet they must yield a uniform rate of interest (per period) in competitive equilibrium. Böhm defined the rate of interest as a premium for waiting, a compensation for income foregone and diminished utility of instant consumption. However, Wicksell did not accept Böhm's concept of "time preference for consumption" as a general explanation of the existence and levels of interest rates. He reduced time preference to a determinant of the speed of capital accumulation and, hence, an indirect determinant of the size of the capital stock.

In Wicksell's view, the equilibrium rate of interest is basically determined by Böhm's "Third Ground", the superior productivity of more roundabout (that is, time-consuming) methods of production – in other words, it is determined by the marginal productivity of capital. At first, Wicksell (1893) had praised Böhm for having given the notion of marginal productivity a precise and generally quantifiable meaning by his concept of the "average period of production". In the *Lectures* (1901 [1934]: 184), he still retained Böhm's notion of the "marginal productivity of waiting" as "a concise general principle, reflecting the essence of productive capital". Yet he also pointed out that Böhm's method of determining the rate of interest by way of the average period of production, on the one hand, and time preference, on the other, is applicable only under extremely specific assumptions, if at all. Wicksell argued that the average period of production is not independent of the rate of interest if the more general method of compounding is used to calculate the average time distance between input and output. In a similar vein, Wicksell (1901 [1934]: 149) had criticized the circular reasoning of the "Walrasian School", where the rate of interest is determined by the value of capital, which is deduced from its costs of production, these being determined, in turn, by the size of the capital stock and the rate of interest. In the end (as we shall see below), Wicksell himself escaped from such conundrums and tautologies only by taking the aggregate value of capital as given.

Wicksell's theory of "capitalistic production", as expounded in his *Lectures* (1901 [1934]: 144–206) from the second edition (1911) onwards, amounts to determining the rate of interest by the marginal products of dated services of land and labour. Capital is defined as "saved-up labour and saved-up land" (1901 [1934]: 154), a conglomerate of land and labour services of earlier periods. In general equilibrium, the marginal products of these dated services, valued at their prices in the goods markets, correspond to the rent rate and wage rate, multiplied with compound interest. Accordingly, "[i]nterest is the difference between the marginal productivity of saved-up labour and land and of current labour and land" (ibid.).

Since capital is reckoned "as a sum of exchange value – whether in money or as an average of products, . . . each particular capital-good is measured by a unit extraneous to itself" (1901 [1934]: 149). In Wicksell's view, this "is a theoretical anomaly which disturbs the correspondence which would otherwise exist between all the factors of production" (ibid.). Failing to close his own model in any other admissible way, Wicksell eventually took recourse to the assumption of a given value sum of "social capital" in order to determine the rate of interest – a procedure that he admitted to be valid only under rather restrictive conditions of static analysis (1911 in Wicksell 1958: 183–4, 1928: 208). Moreover, he demonstrated (in terms of comparative static analysis) that, after a rise in the capital stock of an economy, competition for labour and land makes the marginal productivity of social capital fall below the (representative) rate of interest (1901 [1934]: 148–9). This "curious divergence" from the standard result of the marginal-productivity theory of income distribution was later called the "Wicksell effect" (Uhr 1951: 850–52). It came to play an important role in the Cambridge controversies on the neoclassical theory of capital.

Money and credit
Ever since he had begun to work on monetary issues, Wicksell, like Ricardo before him, was searching for an invariable standard for the valuation of goods and capital. The common standard of value is money, but its own exchange value in terms of goods, measured by changes in the general price level or by the rate of inflation, is rather volatile. In his treatise on *Interest and Prices*, Wicksell (1898 [1936]: ch. 1) declared the stability of the value of money to be of highest importance for the preservation of a fair social order. Inflation has adverse effects on those who receive fixed nominal incomes and have no market power. Moreover, it induces "unhealthy speculation. . . and culminates in over-expansion of credit, credit disturbances, and crisis" (1898 [1936]: 2). Deflation is "no less significant an evil" as "[b]usiness is paralysed, and growing unemployment and falling wages result" (ibid.). In order to develop his proposal for making money a "stable and invariable standard of value", Wicksell set off to analyse the causes of inflation and deflation.

Wicksell (1898 [1936]: ch. 5) argued that the venerable quantity theory of money is the only framework capable of explaining the changes in the value of money consistently. Yet he criticized the traditional approach for being far from reality, as it proceeded from exogenous variations in the volume of money and assumed the velocity of its circulation to be invariable in the short run. Writing in the late nineteenth century, Wicksell pointed out, with some foresight, that modern economies are characterized by financial systems in which money proper (in terms of cash) is almost completely substituted by bank deposits. These are endogenously created in the process of bank lending, and payments are effectuated simply by transfers of bank deposits. Wicksell's special trick of adapting the quantity theory to such modernities was to define both the long-term evolution of money and banking and the short-run variations in the volume of "deposit money" as "changes in the virtual velocity" of the circulation of cash, the monetary base (1898 [1936]: ch. 6) The latter is but a liquidity reserve for the banking system as a whole and circulates only in cases of "external drains".

Wicksell accordingly developed his modernized quantity theory under the assumption of a "pure credit economy". In its extreme form, the banks face no reserve constraints at all, as they operate in a worldwide system where no drains can happen. In such a system, the banks make profits on the spreads between the deposit and the loan rates of interest. They can increase the volume of "deposit money" or "credit money" at any rate, as long as they expand their business in step, netting out their claims on each other in the clearing process. Wicksell understood as early as 1898 that global financial markets have a tendency to increase both the credit and the money supply.

Interest and prices

Wicksell's special version of the equation of exchange amounted to treating the monetary base as invariable and the velocity of its circulation in terms of bank deposits as infinitely variable. With this trick and the insight that loans create deposits, he set the focus on the level of loan rates as their main determinant. The decisive factor is not this "market rate of interest" per se, but its changes in proportion to the prospective rate of return on real investment – or rather, its inertia in view of ever-changing yields on real investment. For the latter, Wicksell (1898 [1936]: ch. 8) used a physical concept as a virtual benchmark for monetary equilibrium, even though he was well aware of the problems of measuring the marginal productivity of capital in physical units. Referring to the competitive equilibrium of a (fictitious) barter economy, he defined as "the natural rate of interest" the rate of return that would match aggregate investment and saving if all borrowing and lending were made in kind, that is, in the form of real capital goods. In more general definitions, he used the notions of a "neutral" or "normal rate of interest" with reference to the market rate that leaves the price level unchanged, as the cost of financing investment projects corresponds to the latter's marginal return.

Wicksell argued that the optimizing behaviour of commercial banks tends to make the market rate of interest sticky, whereas the natural rate is highly variable. It depends on the impact of innovations, disasters and other factors that affect supplies and demands – in short, "on all the thousand and one things which determine the current economic position of a community; and with them it constantly fluctuates" (Wicksell 1898 [1936]: 106). Once the natural rate rises above the money rate of interest, it becomes profitable for entrepreneurs to borrow additional funds for new investments. Given the conventionally required collaterals (whose values tend to rise during a credit boom), it will also be profitable for the banks to lend, and thus the supply of deposit money adjusts endogenously to the demand for credit. Under Wicksell's standard assumption of full employment, aggregate demand exceeds aggregate supply and goods prices will start to rise. The upward movement of prices will become self-reinforcing over time. It will "create its own draught" (1898 [1936]: 96), as expectations of further inflation begin to enter the process of price formation.

The cumulative process of changes in the price level will continue as long as there remains a gap between the money rate of interest and the neutral rate. Wicksell (1898 [1936]: 117) asserted that the gap will always be closed by a convergence of the market rate of interest on the natural rate: "[T]he Bank rate, or more generally the money rate of interest, will always coincide eventually with the natural capital rate, or rather that it is always tending to coincide with an ever-changing natural rate." However, as Wicksell's critics Davidson, Cassel and Ludwig von Mises pointed out, he failed to explain why that should happen in a pure credit economy at all, and why it would not lead to the adjustment of the rate of return on real investment to the market rate of interest, rather than vice versa.

Wicksell considered cumulative deflation to be essentially symmetric to inflation. He admitted that a fall of the natural rate of interest below the market rate might not only lower the price level, but output and employment, too. Yet he considered such real effects to be of second-order and non-cumulative.

Apart from what has been pointed out above, Wicksell's theory of cumulative changes in the price level is noteworthy for at least five reasons. The first is that it provided one of the earliest frameworks of macroeconomic analysis, in which the movements of prices and quantities in the markets for goods, finance and labour were systematically connected at the aggregate level. The second reason is its clear conceptualization of inflation and deflation as interacting failures of the inter- and intra-temporal price mechanisms. Every change in the unobservable "natural rate of interest" carries the risk that the observable intertemporal price, embodied in the money rate of interest, fails to coordinate investment with planned saving. As a consequence the intra-temporal price mechanism in the goods markets will translate the excess demands for present goods into a rise in the price level. A "false price" (the money rate of interest) in one market induces adjustments in other markets (for labour and goods) that do not lead to a self-correction of that price (the interest rate). The third reason is Wicksell's fundamental distinction between the stability properties of the price structure and the price level: the system of relative prices is stable. "Every movement away from the position of equilibrium sets forces into operation – on a scale that increases with the extent of the movement – which tend to restore the system to its original position" (Wicksell 1898 [1936]: 101). In the case of the general price level, on the other hand, the final equilibrium position will differ from the original one, as market forces do not automatically correct for past inflation (or deflation). The fourth reason is that Wicksell did not see his monetary theory as an explanation of the business-cycle phenomenon. In his view, which he outlined in few sketches only, the basic cause of cyclical fluctuations is to be found in the asynchronous occurrence of technical progress and changes in aggregate demand (Wicksell 1906 [1935]: 209–14; Boianovsky and Trautwein 2001b). The fifth reason for the prominence of Wicksell's monetary theory is the simple rule for the stabilization of the price level that he deduced from it. The current natural rate of interest is unobservable, but the rate of inflation can be ascertained with only a short lag. If it rises above zero, the central bank ought to increase its lending rates until the inflation stops. In the case of deflation, it should correspondingly lower its lending rates. In this way, monetary policy could produce a stable and relatively invariable standard of value.

Impact

Wicksell published all his major works in German, then a universal language of science. From early on he had letter correspondences and other exchanges with many of the great economists of his time. Yet, outside of Sweden, the world took very little notice of his contributions while he lived. A notable exception was the Austrian von Mises (1912) who discussed Wicksell's theory of the credit economy in some detail and based his business cycle theory on it.

Public finance

Erik Lindahl was the last Swedish economist to write his doctoral dissertation in German. With reference to Wicksell (1896) he proposed in *Die Gerechtigkeit der Besteuerung* (1919), translated as *Just Taxation: A Positive Solution* (1958), that citizens pay for the provision of a public good according to their marginal benefits. Two of the most prominent twentieth-century authors in public finance based their contrary views on Wicksell's and Lindahl's works. Richard Musgrave, who was an émigré from Nazi Germany, used them in his 1937 Harvard PhD thesis, and made them known to the English-speaking world (Musgrave 1939). They were subsequently refined into what Samuelson (1987: 910) has described as the "Wicksell–Lindahl–Musgrave–Samuelson–Vickrey theory of pure public goods". In a nutshell, it leads to the following proposition:

> When private goods consumed by a single person only are supplemented by a public good that is simultaneously enjoyed by many people, Pareto optimality requires that production of the public good be carried to a point where its marginal (opportunity) cost just equals the sum of all citizen's marginal-rates-of substitution between the public good and any private good. (Ibid.)

Yet, Samuelson also added that "[r]elying on a hoped-for Scandinavian consensus or 'unanimity', Wicksell perhaps worried too little about the 'free rider' problem (that results from the fact that every citizen in a Lindahl market is tempted to pretend not to much want the public good)" (ibid.).

At the same time, Wicksell's radical liberalism stimulated the development of public choice theory, as James Buchanan, the latter's founder, has emphasized in his Nobel lecture of 1986 (Buchanan 1987). Buchanan has contributed a translation of Wicksell's "new principle of taxation" to Musgrave's and Peacock's anthology of classics in the theory of public finance (1958). An English version of the "theory of tax incidence" was made available in Wicksell's *Selected Essays in Economics*, edited by Bo Sandelin (Wicksell 1997: 57–115).

Theories of distribution and capital

Between the 1950s and 1970s, Wicksell effects played a central role in the Cambridge debates on the neoclassical theory of capital. The main adversaries in these controversies were Piero Sraffa, Luigi Pasinetti and Joan Robinson in Cambridge (UK) on the one hand, and Paul Samuelson and Robert Solow in Cambridge (Massachusetts) on the other. The central, interrelated questions were (1) whether an economy's capital stock in the aggregate can be determined independently of the rate of interest, and (2) whether the choice of the technique of production is independent of the distribution of income. Cambridge, Massachusetts, affirmed, whereas Cambridge, England, denied categorically. Dissecting the original Wicksell effect into a price effect and a real effect, it was shown that the objections of the English side were essentially correct. The controversies did not, however, end in consensus and progress. Nowadays most economists prefer to remain silent on the birth defects of the neoclassical theory of distribution, if they are aware of them at all. Wicksell, who had openly addressed them and who had untiringly attempted to repair them, would certainly not have approved of such negligence.

Macroeconomics
Wicksell's theory of inflation has inspired the development of modern macroeconomics in many ways. Coordination failures of the interest-rate mechanism were at the centre of macroeconomic thinking in the 1920s and 1930s, and most of the more prominent approaches that discussed intertemporal disequilibrium can be described as having a Wicksell connection (Leijonhufvud 1981). In view of the macroeconomic instabilities of the inter-war period – with its waves of inflation and deflation, and finally the Great Depression – it was quite natural to use Wicksell's theory of cumulative processes for explanations of cycles and crises. The Austrians Ludwig von Mises and Friedrich A. Hayek did it, and so did – with a fundamentally different approach – Erik Lindahl, Gunnar Myrdal, Bertil Ohlin and other members of the Stockholm School. In his *General Theory of Money, Interest and Employment* (1936), John Maynard Keynes chose the opposite version of Wicksell's cumulative process: he emphasized that, even in free competition with flexible prices, changes in quantities may happen before price changes, and that they may even prevent the latter. He considered the price level to remain more or less constant, while reductions of effective demand lead to lower real output and underemployment in multiplier processes. Wicksell had delivered the methodical key for Keynes's proposition that market forces will not always tend to produce full employment.

However, Wicksell's ideas can also be found in monetarist and New Classical macroeconomics that firmly oppose the Keynesian approach. Milton Friedman (1968) coined the term "natural rate of unemployment" with reference to Wicksell's natural rate of interest, in order to postulate the automatic restoration of labour market equilibrium once people learn to adapt to inflation. It is doubtful, though, that Wicksell would have consented to Friedman's transfer of notions, as he had a rather different view of unemployment (Boianovsky and Trautwein 2003).

Modern macroeconomics has in recent years reached a consensus view that is generally described as the "New Neoclassical Synthesis". The core contribution to this view, Michael Woodford's *Interest and Prices* (2003), has the title in common with Wicksell's 1898 treatise. Moreover, its combination of New Classical and New Keynesian elements is described as "the neo-Wicksellian model". It is a framework in which deviations of actual output from potential output are caused by discrepancies between the interest rates that are set by the central bank and the natural rate of interest. The discrepancies can be eliminated by feedback rules (such as a Taylor rule) that bear resemblance to Wicksell's rule for monetary policy. However, the new synthesis proceeds from the basic assumption that the system is continuously in intertemporal equilibrium, essentially determined by the rate of time preference. Wicksell would hardly have approved of this turn away from his focus on imbalances of investment and saving plans. There are good reasons to assume that the creative potential of Wicksell's ideas has not been exhausted yet.

HANS-MICHAEL TRAUTWEIN

See also:

Eugen von Böhm-Bawerk (I); James M. Buchanan (I); Capital theory (III); Income distribution (III); Erik Lindahl (I); Thomas Robert Malthus (I); Ludwig Heinrich von Mises (I); Money and banking (III); Richard Abel Musgrave (I); Public economics (III); David Ricardo (I); Stockholm (Swedish) School (II); Marie-Esprit-Léon Walras (I).

References and further reading

Boianovsky, M. and H.-M. Trautwein (2001a), 'An early manuscript by Knut Wicksell on the bank rate of interest', *History of Political Economy*, **33** (3), 485–516.

Boianovsky, M. and H.-M. Trautwein (2001b), 'Wicksell's lecture notes on economic crises (1902/05)', *Structural Change and Economic Dynamics*, **12** (3), 343–65.

Boianovsky, M. and H.-M. Trautwein (2003), 'Wicksell, Cassel and the idea of involuntary unemployment', *History of Political Economy*, **35** (3), 385–436.

Buchanan, J. (1987), 'The constitution of economic policy', *American Economic Review*, **77** (3), 243–50.

Drysdale, G. (1878), *The elements of social science; or, physical, sexual, and natural religion. An exposition of the true cause and only cure of the three primary social evils: poverty, prostitution, and celibacy*, enlarged 17th edn, London: E. Truelove.

Friedman, M. (1968), 'The role of monetary policy', *American Economic Review*, **54** (1), 1–17.

Gårdlund, T. (1956), *Knut Wicksell. Rebell i det nya riket*, Stockholm: Bonniers, trans. 1958, *The Life of Knut Wicksell*, Stockholm: Almqvist & Wiksell.

Henriksson, R. (1991), 'The Political Economy Club and the Stockholm School, 1917–1951', in L. Jonung (ed.), *The Stockholm School of Economics Revisited*, Cambridge: Cambridge University Press, pp. 41–74.

Keynes, J.M. (1936), *The General Theory of Employment, Interest and Money*, London: Macmillan.

Knudtzon, E. and T. Nyström-Hedlund (eds) (1976), *Knut Wicksells tryckta skrifter 1868–1950*, Lund: CWK Gleerup.

Kurz, H.D. (2000), 'Wicksell and the problem of the "missing" equation', *History of Political Economy*, **32** (4), 765–88.

Leijonhufvud, A. (1981), 'The Wicksell connection: variations on a theme', in *Information and Coordination. Essays in Macroeconomic Theory*, New York: Oxford University Press, pp. 131–202.

Lindahl, E. (1958), 'Introduction: Wicksell's life and work', in K. Wicksell, *Selected Papers on Economic Theory*, ed. E. Lindahl, London: Allen & Unwin, pp. 9–48.

Musgrave, R. (1939), 'The voluntary exchange theory of public economy', *Quarterly Journal of Economics*, **53** (2), 213–37.

Musgrave, R. and A. Peacock (eds) (1958), *Classics in the Theory of Public Finance*, London: Macmillan.

Samuelson, P. (1987), 'Wicksell and neoclassical economics', in J. Eatwell, M. Milgate and P. Newman (eds), *The New Palgrave: A Dictionary of Economics*, vol. 4, London: Macmillan, pp. 908–10.

Samuelson, P. (1988), 'Wicksells Werk und Persönlichkeit', in P. Samuelson, R.A. Musgrave and B. Sandelin, *Knut Wicksells Opus. Eine kritische Würdigung*, Düsseldorf: Handelsblatt Verlag (Klassiker der Nationalökonomie), pp. 25–36.

Sandelin, B. (1998), 'Three features of Wicksell's theory of capital', in E. Streissler (ed.), *Knut Wicksell als Ökonom, Studien zur Entwicklung der Ökonomischen Theorie*, vol. 18, Berlin: Duncker & Humblot, pp. 112–30.

Schumpeter, J.A. (1954), *History of Economic Analysis*, London: Allen & Unwin.

Uhr, C. (1951), 'Knut Wicksell – a centennial evaluation', *American Economic Review*, **41** (5), 829–60.

Uhr, C. (1960), *Economic Doctrines of Knut Wicksell*, Berkeley and Los Angeles, CA: University of California Press.

von Mises, L. (1912), *Theorie des Geldes und der Umlaufsmittel*, Munich and Leipzig: Duncker & Humblot, trans. 1934, *Theory of Money and Credit*, London: Jonathan Cape.

Wicksell, K. (1893), *Über Wert, Kapital und Rente. Nach den neueren nationalökonomischen Theorien*, Jena: Gustav Fischer, trans. 1954, *On Value, Capital and Rent*, London: Allen & Unwin.

Wicksell, K. (1896), *Finanztheoretische Untersuchungen nebst Darstellung und Kritik des Steuerwesens Schwedens*, Jena: Gustav Fischer, trans. Part I: 'On the theory of tax incidence', in K. Wicksell (1997), *Knut Wicksell – Selected Essays in Economics*, vol. 1, ed. by B. Sandelin, London: Routledge, pp. 57–115, Part II: 'A new principle of just taxation', in R. Musgrave and A. Peacock (eds) (1958), *Classics in the Theory of Public Finance*, London: Macmillan, pp. 72–118.

Wicksell, K. (1898), *Geldzins und Güterpreise. Eine Studie über die den Tauschwert des Geldes bestimmenden Ursachen*, Jena: Gustav Fischer, trans. 1936, *Interest and Prices. A Study of the Causes Regulating the Value of Money*, London: Macmillan.

Wicksell, K. (1900), 'Om gränsproduktiviteten såsom grundval för den nationalekonomiska fördelningen', *Ekonomisk Tidskrift*, **3**, 305–37, trans. K. Wicksell (1958), *Selected Papers on Economic Theory*, ed. E. Lindahl, London: Allen & Unwin. pp. 93–120.

Wicksell, K. (1901), *Föreläsningar i nationalekonomi*, I: *Teoretisk nationalekonomi*, Lund: Berlingska Boktryckeriet, trans. 1934, *Lectures on Political Economy*, vol. 1: *General Theory*, London: Routledge, Kegan & Paul.

Wicksell, K. (1902), 'Till fördelningsproblemet', *Ekonomisk Tidskrift*, **5**, 424–33, trans. in K. Wicksell (1958), *Selected Papers on Economic Theory*, ed. E. Lindahl, London: Allen & Unwin, pp. 121–30.

Wicksell, K. (1906), *Föreläsningar i nationalekonomi*, vol. II: *Penningar och kredit*, Lund: Berlingska Boktryckeriet, trans. 1935, *Lectures on Political Economy*, vol. 2: *Money*, London: Routledge, Kegan & Paul.

Wicksell, K. (1914), 'Lexis och Böhm-Bawerk', *Ekonomisk Tidskrift*, **16**, 294–300, 322–34, trans. in K. Wicksell (1997), *Knut Wicksell – Selected Essays in Economics*, vol. 1, ed. B. Sandelin, London: Routledge, pp. 26–40).

Wicksell, K. (1928), 'Zur Zinstheorie (Böhm-Bawerks Dritter Grund)', in H. Mayer, F. Fetter and R. Reisch (eds), *Die Wirtschaftstheorie der Gegenwart*, vol. 3: *Einkommensbildung*, Vienna: Julius Springer, pp. 199–209, trans. in K. Wicksell (1997), *Knut Wicksell – Selected Essays in Economics*, vol. 1, ed. B. Sandelin, London: Routledge, pp. 41–53.

Wicksell, K. (1958), *Selected Papers on Economic Theory*, ed. E. Lindahl, London: Allen & Unwin.

Wicksell, K. (1997), *Knut Wicksell – Selected Essays in Economics*, vol. 1, ed. B. Sandelin, London: Routledge.

Woodford, M. (2003), *Interest and Prices, Foundations of a Theory of Monetary Policy*, Princeton, NJ: Routledge.

Friedrich von Wieser (1851–1926)

Friedrich von Wieser was born 10 July 1851 in Vienna. His father Leopold von Wieser was a high-ranked civil servant in the Ministry of War. Owing to his merits in the war of 1859 against Italy, Leopold von Wieser was ennobled. Later, he became Vice-President of the Court of Audit. His sons Hyacinth and Friedrich inherited Leopold von Wieser's inclinations towards the fine arts. While Hyacinth gained some reputation as a painter, Friedrich is said to have been among the first to recognize the importance of the composer Hugo Wolf.

Friedrich attended the elite Schottengymnasium where Eugen von Böhm-Bawerk (who was to become his friend and brother-in-law) was his classmate. In 1868 Wieser and Böhm enrolled in the Law Faculty of Vienna University. As a part of the curriculum in legal studies, some education in economics was on offer at this academic institution. Both young men entered the civil service and, in 1875, took a two-year leave in order to continue their economic studies with some of the most prominent German professors in the field, Karl Knies, Bruno Hildebrand and Wilhelm Roscher. Wieser passed his habilitation (with Menger) in economics in 1883 and was appointed associate professor at the University of Prague in 1884 (full professor 1889). He succeeded Menger in the chair of economic theory at Vienna University in 1903. Wieser was the most influential teacher among the first generation of the Austrian School: Schumpeter, Mises and Hayek were his students. He became a member of the Austrian Herrenhaus (House of Lords) and served as Minister of Commerce in the last Austrian government under the Habsburg monarchy (1917–18). He died on 23 July 1926 in St Gilgen, a lakeside resort not far from Salzburg.

Wieser is commonly portrayed as an original thinker with occasionally powerful rhetoric and pre-analytical visions of extraordinarily wide scope, whose originality is not matched by analytical clarity. This impression may be related to the fact that his research programme has a multi-disciplinary background: his economics is complemented by a sociological approach to the phenomena of power, elite and mass. He is a multi-disciplinary social theorist in the best sense of the word, and his intellectual background is rich and diverse. Wieser was one of the first to read Menger's *Principles*; he was impressed by Herbert Spencer and influenced by Marx.

Over and above all, in the more specific field of economics his thought is sufficiently multi-faceted to earn him the title of the "odd man out" of the Austrian School. He is sometimes said to have been a follower of Walras rather than of Carl Menger. Indeed, more than the other Austrian economists of the first generation, Wieser was very much interested in general equilibrium interdependences, and in the long-period position (see Kurz and Sturn 1999: 85–7). This implies a certain tension vis-à-vis the causal-genetic approach of the Austrians. Unlike Menger and Mises, Wieser moreover did not categorically reject the use of mathematics in price theory. He was not himself engaging in mathematical modelling and was far from endorsing it as enthusiastically as Schumpeter.

Wieser differs from most other Austrians in one further respect. While all Austrians emphasize the value-neutrality of economic analysis, most of them are staunch defenders of some kind of free market-liberalism. By contrast, Wieser envisaged a mixed economy, eventually including distributive policies.

In an article in the *Economic Journal*, Wieser (1891) emphasizes parallels between the Austrians, Walras and Jevons. By way of introduction, he offers a crisp account of his views on method, defending the use of suitably idealized models by drawing the parallel with a geographical map, which "sharpens our vision in view of the complexities of reality" and is "a means not to deception but to more effective guidance". But the bulk of Wieser (1891) is devoted to explaining his pioneering (though not entirely successful) attempts to solve the imputation problem by the marginal productivity theory of distribution, dealing with the question of whether the marginal product of the contributing factors would exhaust the product. This theme was already pursued in his habilitation thesis '*Über den Ursprung und die Hauptgesetze des wirtschaftlichen Werthes*' ('On the origin and the main laws of economic value') (Wieser 1884: 170–79).

His habilitation thesis furthermore deals with a couple of other foundational concepts. *Inter alia*, he defines the essence of costs as foregone utility. No clearer statement of the opportunity cost-concept can be found in the literature before Wieser's (1884: 101) pertinent passages. Moreover, he coins the term "marginal utility" ("*Grenznutzen*"), while Jevons had used the expression "final degree of utility". After having explained the "law of marginal utility" ("*Gesetz des Grenznutzens*") without production (Wieser 1884: 126–39), he proceeds to the so-called Wieser's Law of Cost: he is credited for having stated for the first time the equimarginal principle with respect to production.

However, Wieser's contributions are not limited to terminological innovations and conceptual clarifications. They include more over-arching issues, which are related to subsequent developments in Austrian economics and beyond, most notably the debates on economic planning (another term promoted by Wieser) and their theoretical underpinning. In the final parts of Wieser (1884) and in Wieser (1889), we find a clear idea of a kind of normative economics conceptualized as an institution-free allocation theory, guided by equimarginal principles of efficient allocation. Wieser emphasizes that those principles hold good for any kind of "economic planning" (capitalist or socialist) and are practically relevant irrespective of the prevailing mode of social and economic organization. Economic planning under socialism (and in the public sector of a capitalist economy) to a certain extent needs to mimic the working of an efficient price system – or it will fail to be rational. In particular, rational socialist planning cannot dispense with (1) marginal valuations, (2) the use of information summarized by prices, and (3) the use of a monetary measuring rod.

However, while Wieser seems to leave open (or even to suggest, see Wieser 1884: 210) the possibility that shadow prices may be used for the purpose of planning, his student Mises twisted the argument, suggesting the impossibility of rational calculation under socialism. In absence of market prices, socialist planners would be "groping in the dark". Hayek (1945), another student, expanded on the informative nature of prices which is already anticipated by Wieser (1884: 166).

Wieser's *Der natürliche Werth* (1889) was edited by William Smart as *Natural Value* (1893). In this book he shows that the principles of efficient allocation can be analytically separated from issues of distribution: natural value reflects the efficiency conditions of a competitive economy framed by utilitarian principles of distribution: "In natural value goods are estimated simply according to their marginal utility; in exchange value, according to a combination of marginal utility and purchasing power" (Wieser 1893, II.vi). Marginal valuations corresponding to this natural value also could be thought of as ethically defensible criteria with respect to issues such as the allocation of public funds.

Further writings deal with themes in monetary theory (for example, Wieser 1910), in which he remains interested throughout his live. Indeed, one of his last publications is the entry on money in the *Handwörterbuch der Staatswissenschaften* (Wieser 1927a).

Wieser's third important book in economics, *Theorie der gesellschaftlichen Wirtschaft*, is a volume commissioned for the monumental collection of contemporary social and economic science *Grundriss der Sozialökonomik*. This was translated as "*Social Economics*" and edited by Wesley Mitchell (Wieser 1927b). It is a textbook-like account of Wieserian economics, which is applied to various topics (part III offers the "theory of the public economy", part IV the "theory of the world economy"). Passages on the different forms of enterprises and entrepreneurs are remarkable for the parallels to Schumpeterian themes and concomitant terminology.

Wieser's last book *Das Gesetz der Macht* (*The Law of Power*, 1926) summarizes his sociological reasoning with specific regard to the role of power in social organizations (see also Wieser 1914, 1927b). Wieser conceptualizes power-driven processes subject to the "law of small numbers" (as opposed to the anonymous forces of the law of large numbers). As the key power he identifies the power over mental models and moods. We find a couple of ideas looming large in contemporary discourses of the first third of the twentieth century, related to mass psychology and leadership. Wieser suggests some power-related "laws", such as the "law of circulation of power" (dealing with the social conditions for the reproduction of malleable power elites) or the "law of decreasing coercion" in the development of civilization.

It is fair to say that Wieser is not an unchanging adherent of what are commonly regarded to be the central tenets of Austrian economics. Nonetheless, many of his ideas have a distinctly Austrian background. Some of those ideas later became relevant in economic theory beyond the Austrian School. Examples are his views related to the informative function of prices and entrepreneurship. Concepts such as opportunity cost, shadow prices, and the general idea of using efficiency conditions in order to derive an institution-free yardstick for economic planning which is relevant irrespective of the institutional framework (be it a perfectly competitive private-ownership economy or some other variety of capitalism, or the public sector of a mixed economy, or socialism, or multi-divisional private firm, or something else) became indispensable ingredients to the welfare-theoretic approach to allocation theory.

RICHARD STURN

See also:

Eugen von Böhm-Bawerk (I); German and Austrian schools (II); Friedrich August von Hayek (I); Carl Menger (I); Ludwig Heinrich von Mises (I); Joseph Alois Schumpeter (I).

References and further reading

Hayek, F.A. (1945), 'The use of knowledge in society', *American Economic Review*, **35** (4), 519–30.
Kurz, H.D. and R. Sturn (1999), 'Wiesers *Ursprung* und die Entwicklung der Mikroökonomik', in H. Hax (ed.), *Vademecum zu einem Klassiker der Österreichischen Schule*, Düsseldorf: Handelsblatt Verlag, pp. 59–103.
Mayer, H., R.A. Fetter and R. Reisch (1927), *Die Wirtschaftstheorie der Gegenwart*, 4 vols, Vienna: Springer.
Schumpeter, J.A. (1952), 'Friedrich Wieser (1851–1926)', in J.A Schumpeter, *Ten Great Economists*, London: George Allen & Unwin, pp. 298–301.
Wieser, F. von (1884), *Über den Ursprung und die Hauptgesetze des Wirtschaftlichen Werthes*, Vienna: Alfred Hölder.
Wieser, F. von (1889), *Der natürliche Werth*, Vienna: Alfred Hölder.

Wieser, F. von (1891), 'The Austrian School and the theory of value'. *Economic Journal*, **1**, 108–21.
Wieser, F. von (1893), *Natural Value*, trans. of *Der natürliche Werth* by C.A. Malloch, ed. and preface by W. Smart, London: Macmillan.
Wieser, F. von (1910), 'Der Geldwert und seine Veränderungen', *Schriften des Vereins für Socialpolitik*, vol. 132, Leipzig: Duncker & Humblot, reprinted in F. von Hayek (ed.) (1929), *Friedrich von Wieser, Gesammelte Abhandlungen*, Tübingen: J.C.B. Mohr.
Wieser, F. von (1914), 'Theorie der gesellschaftlichen Wirtschaft', in *Grundriss der Sozialökonomik*, vol. 1: *Wirtschaft und Wirtschaftswissenschaft*, Tübingen: J.C.B. Mohr, pp. 125–444.
Wieser, F. von (1926), *Das Gesetz der Macht*, Vienna: Julius Springer.
Wieser, F. von (1927a), 'Geld', in L. Elster, A. Weber and F. Wiese (eds), *Handwörterbuch der Staatswissenschaften*, 4th edn, vol. 5, Jena: G. Fischer.
Wieser, F. von (1927b), *Social Economics*, trans. of 'Theorie der gesellschaftlichen Wirtschaft' by A. Ford Hinrichs, introduction by W.C. Mitchell, New York: Adelphi Company.

Maffeo Pantaleoni (1857–1924)

Life and Personality

Pantaleoni was by general consent one of the protagonists, if not *the* protagonist, of the renaissance in Italian economic thought from the "prostration" of the 1870s to the eminent position it came to occupy on the international scene at the turn of the century (Barucci 1972). He masterminded the spread of marginalism in Italy, spotted and encouraged potential talents such as Pareto and Barone, launched a new series of the languishing *Giornale degli economisti*, and pursued a line of research in which marginal analysis was instrumental in supporting his liberal convictions and in outlining a suggestive sketch of a theory of social dynamics. By no means a tranquil academic, his career was interrupted twice for political reasons. The first time was in 1892, when reactions to his attacks on the government's protectionist policies forced him to resign from his post as director of the Scuola Superiore di Commercio of Bari. Reinstated as professor at the University of Naples, he quit again in 1896 after the clamour caused by his denunciation of secret deals concerning the failure of the colonial campaign in Abyssinia. For a while he went into voluntary exile in Switzerland, where he held a chair at the University of Geneva from 1897 to 1900. He also acted as a manager of the Cirio food company, as liquidator and supervisor of bank affairs (this role involved him in particularly bitter disputes), and as a Member of Parliament elected with the votes of the extreme left in 1900 (a temporary alliance that broke down well before his resignation in 1904). He settled definitively as a professor at the University of Rome in 1902, but this did not calm his political activism. From about 1910 on he veered towards extreme right-wing positions, to the point of participating in D'Annunzio's self-proclaimed regency of Fiume in 1920 and acting as economic adviser for the first Mussolini cabinet from 1922. Sudden death in 1924 put an end to a restless political itinerary. Reconstructions of episodes in Pantaleoni's life can be found in Michelini (1998, 2011) and Magnani (2003); a complete bio-bibliographical sketch in Augello and Michelini (1997); in English, see the essays collected in Baldassarri (1997) and Groenewegen (1998).

Some personal features of Pantaleoni can be traced back to his origins and early years. He was the son of an Irish lady of patrician lineage and a liberal Italian patriot, Diomede Pantaleoni, a physician, scholar, and collaborator of Cavour. Half-Irish birth and early education in French and German schools account for his fluency in the main European languages and the international bent of his personality: for example, announced as a guest at a party given by the Marshalls at Balliol Croft, visiting Edgeworth at Nuffield College and endorsing him for election to a professorship, being offered a chair (declined) at the University of Chicago while in difficulty at Naples, addressing the British Economic Association (BEA) annual meeting in 1898, being extended the honour of a session devoted to his ideas on dynamics at the 1909 American Economic Association (AEA) meeting. Devotion to his father's political ideals may account for the reactionary brand of liberalism that he professed all through his life, his blunt opposition to all forms of socialism, and his condemnation of both the corruption of the emerging business class during the Crispi years and Giolitti's tendency to appease social strife by means of concessions to the labour movement. The absence of a party committed to a liberal agenda on the Italian parliamentary scene may have been responsible for Pantaleoni's swinging from one extreme to the other of the political spectrum. The brief idyll with the socialists of the early 1900s gave way to his turning to nationalism during World War I and to fascism later on, finding no stopping-place in the middle. Moreover, in his later years he tended to spice his political tirades with a charge of violent anti-Semitism, which cast a shadow on his international reputation (Dalton 1923). As argued below, Pantaleoni the economist cannot be fully understood without considering the direction and intensity of his political involvement.

Despite the unpleasant drift of his later years, Pantaleoni's personality was attractive to the point of inducing characters as far from his political leanings as his lifelong friend De Viti de Marco (1925) and the young communist Piero Sraffa (1924) to commemorate him in singularly warm terms. Behind the vast public display of energies was a private man of stunning erudition, a sharp reasoner, a brilliant speaker and an even more brilliant teacher. In contrast to his acknowledged role as the herald of pure economics in Italy, he was little equipped with mathematical training and inept at formal analysis, which he could not master beyond elementary geometry and calculus. Correspondence with Pareto (1960) and Barone (Magnani and Bellanca, 1991) shows the two friends patiently tutoring him in the fundamentals of mathematics. However, in economics he seems to have been the master of himself.

Formation and Early Work

Pantaleoni studied law as did most economists in Italy in those days – the "Scuole Superiori di Commercio" were to start later in the century – graduating from the University of Rome with a thesis on the theory of the shifting of taxation that became his first published work (Pantaleoni 1882). "He chose economics by chance", de Viti recollected, "I can't remember how it was that we stumbled upon Stanley Jevons' little book which, unlike the university courses, engrossed us enormously" (De Viti de Marco 1925: 168). For Pantaleoni marginalism meant Jevons's conditions for the optimal allocation of a common resource among different uses, rather than the integration of these into a general equilibrium system as in Walras's theory. Walrasian general equilibrium was hard to understand for the innumerate young Pantaleoni, and remained a secondary interest even later, in spite of his intellectual closeness to Pareto. It is also to be noted that the channel through which he approached marginalism in the course of the 1880s was, as emphasized by Buchanan (1960) and Barucci (1972), the theory of public finance, that is, a special field in which economic analysis is in close contact with political philosophy.

Apart from a few allusions to the final degree of utility, the analysis of tax shifting in Pantaleoni (1882) was entirely based on a conventional, pre-marginalist supply and demand framework. The terms of the political dispute between a free-trade interpretation of the role of the state, prevented from interfering in the distribution of wealth brought about by market competition, and the socialist view, according to which the state should take sides and represent the interests of one class against another, were clearly stated but left undecided. Just one year later, however, in an 1883 essay on the optimal distribution of public expenditure (reprinted in Pantaleoni 1904: 49–110; partially translated in Musgrave and Peacock 1967: 16–27), Pantaleoni availed himself of Jevons's utility maximization conditions in order to arrive at a precise definition of the role of the state. How to characterize an optimal tax-expenditure plan – was the essay's central issue. The answer was in two parts. First, the batch of services provided by the state should be such that, in the given technical conditions, their production cost is lower if they are produced jointly and for citizens all together, rather than separately and for citizens one by one. Secondly, the entire tax revenue should be distributed among types of expenditure so as to equalize their weighted marginal utilities as perceived by the "average intelligence of Parliament". Marginalist foundations for a notion of a minimal state were thus established: this is a state that acts as a *homo oeconomicus* on the basis of the "hedonic principle" in an efficient division of labour scheme.

Further questions naturally followed from such an approach. Alert as he was to the problem of public corruption in *fin de siècle* Italy, Pantaleoni could not be content with the vague formula of the "average intelligence of Parliament". Exactly whose utility does the state maximize? In general, how is the hedonic principle to be applied when the decision-maker is a collective entity? In the *Principii di economia pura* of 1889 Pantaleoni prepared the ground for his subsequent investigation. Slighted as "old truths in fresh associations" by A.W. Flux (1898: 360), the volume in fact contained a number of original hints, two of which provide clues to what was to come. First, Pantaleoni stressed a dual interpretation of the hedonic principle, which he took to mean a search either for maximum individual advantage or for maximum advantage of the group to which the individual belongs, as he or she understands it. He dubbed the two interpretations, respectively, "individual" and "species" ("tribal" in Bruce's English translation of the volume) egoism, a duality that he may have derived from the Italian tradition of eighteenth century utilitarianism as well as from Edgeworth and Sidgwick. Secondly, he began to develop the practice, which would become habitual with him, of identifying common logical patterns behind apparently different social phenomena, so that these could be subjected to analogous analytical treatment. In the *Principii* he followed Ferrara in subsuming exchange and production under a general notion of transformation, arguing that this move would lay bare the continuity between marginalism and the classical theory of value from Ricardo to Cairnes. Later, this practice would lead him to deal with coercion as just another manifestation of the hedonic principle alternative to contract, justifying the extension of marginal analysis from the field of economic to that of political action.

Between Economics and Political Ideology

The casual (as it seems) meeting between Pantaleoni and Pareto in 1890 marked the beginning of a friendship and intellectual exchange that were to deeply affect the development of the ideas of both. A first notable episode occurred in conjunction with Pantaleoni and Bertolini's 1892 essay on individual and collective optima (reprinted in Pantaleoni 1904: 281–340). Here, the above-mentioned duality between individual and species egoism was developed into an inchoate theory of the mechanisms of social choice, classified according to their being based on voluntary individual participation, as in all the cases ruled by the law of contract, or on coercion, as in the case of socialism and all systems in which one social group has the power to impose a particular view of collective interest which other groups would reject if they had the possibility. The essay contained the seeds of all the fundamental problems of the still unborn theory of social choice. Among these, the point to which Pareto responded immediately was the divergence between utility as seen by the individual who experiences it and as seen by an external observer. "Reading your work showed me even more clearly that it is necessary to establish whether the hedonic principle is to be considered only from a *subjective* or also from an *objective* point of view" (Pareto 1960, I: 101–2, original emphasis). This was probably the cue that prompted Pareto to make a distinction between ophelimity and utility in his *Cours* and, after further elaboration, to distinguishing between the *economic* ophelimity frontier of a collectivity – nowadays, the set of Pareto optima – and the sociological problem of choosing a point of the frontier according to a political assessment of what is good for the collectivity (Pareto 1913). Pantaleoni was to adopt Pareto's ophelimity/utility distinction in his successive works but did not adhere to the separation of economics from politics implied by the second distinction. Pareto's and Pantaleoni's ways went in the same direction, but were also distinct from the very beginning.

In the 1892 essay, questions of meaning and implementation of collective optima were intertwined with the question of who has what power in society. Pantaleoni (1898), and the related 1901 essay on "the characters of initial positions" (Pantaleoni 1904: 387–421), contain further enquiries into the matter. When there is a clear imbalance of force between two interacting social parties, the "hedonic calculus of the stronger" will naturally lead the latter to exploit its advantage and to enforce a state of affairs in which the weaker will be subjected to predatory or parasitic spoliation. Only if force is evenly distributed, or if there is no clear understanding of which is the stronger side, will the situation be settled peacefully by means of a contract voluntarily entered into by both sides. Thus, the hedonic principle provides basic fuel to two kinds of social phenomena: those that involve actual or threatened violence and result in power exerted by one group over others, and those that arise out of common interests of independent parties free to arrange agreements of mutual collaboration – respectively, the fields of sociology (as intended in Pantaleoni's times) and of economics. While Pantaleoni insisted on the separation of the two disciplinary fields, that of economics being limited to the action of ophelimity in a free choice context, the point of the whole essay is that, as a matter of fact, the two kinds of phenomena never come about in their pure state and unequal power relations lurk everywhere in economic transactions. "Whilst we are always constructing economics on the basis of ophelimity, we are also continually falling out of our role and introducing other criteria" in order to take the political side of economic phenomena into account (Pantaleoni 1898: 200–201). The conclusion of the essay is that the space of economics is characterized not by freedom from force, but by the latter being distributed in such a complex way as to make it impossible to tell apart power from negotiation.

Indeed, the overlapping of free contract and political force in the making and unmaking of the institutions through which a competitive economy works is the subject of a series of essays on syndicates of firms, trade unions and co-operatives written in the early 1900s and containing some of Pantaleoni's finest pages (most of them collected in Pantaleoni 1924–25 [1963]). What these institutions have in common is the attempt to build up a force differential by means of coalitions based on common egoistic interests (the "species" or "tribal" egoism recalled above), with each coalition trying to realize a surplus the origin of which is either the new wealth created by the superior efficiency of the coalition with respect to the unorganized group of its members, or wealth plundered from the social groups that have become relatively weaker. It might appear that the theoretical background of this analysis should lie in Pareto's and Barone's demonstration that a general competitive equilibrium always belongs to the ophelimity frontier: a coalition is a creator of wealth, or a plunderer, or a wealth destructor, according to whether or not it is able to imitate competition in implementing cost-minimizing productive formulas. In fact, Pantaleoni was rather late in acknowledging the relevance of the notion of Pareto's frontier and continued for a while to think in terms of collective hedonistic maxima. Moreover, the relationship between competitive equilibrium and efficiency could not suit his purposes because Pantaleoni's competitive markets were not the fictional atomistic markets of the welfare theorems. Price-cutting was only the final manifestation of that complex of heterogeneous activities, involving both contract and coercion, in which competition consisted for him. "Competition is invention" (Pantaleoni 1924–25 [1963], II: 204), and the question whether the starting of an innovative line of action, by either an economic or a political body, will move the system towards a collective optimum or away from it, runs into the difficulty that the optimum is an imaginary locus that never coincides with the actual position, and that locating and even conceiving it is shrouded in doubt (ibid.: 206).

The interest that prompted Pantaleoni's theoretical research was not only scientific, but also political. In fact, he aimed to channel the scientific prestige of the new marginalist economics into a support for his main political thesis, according to which all kinds of working-class organizations (co-operatives and trade unions alike) concealed forms of protection backed by political power and therefore acted as parasites of the social system. However, there was the fact (Pantaleoni 1924–25 [1963], II, 277 ff.) that also firm syndicates introduced elements of monopoly and protection into the competitive game, and it was not clear why they should be treated differently from workers' coalitions. In 1911 Pantaleoni believed that he had found a way to separate the two cases. "Every modification in the social régime comes to light in the form of a change in prices" (Pantaleone 1911: 114), he affirmed, and consequently introduced a distinction between what he called "political" and "economic prices": the former were prices that vary depending on who — in the sense of census, class belonging and the like — one of the parties of the underlying transaction is. But he had to recognize that there may also be perfectly economic prices that discriminate between purchasers, although on a non-political basis, and therefore that the distinction had no objective foundation and relied entirely on the intentions – political or otherwise – of the price setter (ibid.: 21–3). The ultimate criterion is perhaps to be found in another principle to which Pantaleoni held consistently all through his life, one which asserts that, while purely economic (that is, contractual) social arrangements are self-supportive, parasitic or predatory arrangements are either self-defeating or are supported by some tributary economic system.

In order to be applicable, Pantaleoni's principle naturally needed a dynamic frame of reference. In essays written from 1901 (Pantaleoni 1904: 387–421, 1924–25 [1963], II: 177–209) to the fundamental Pantaleoni (1909) he elaborated a theory of his own in which dynamics, differently from the moving temporary equilibrium envisaged by Pareto, involved some kind of discontinuity in the premises on which a state of equilibrium is based; psychological and sociological attitudes, technology, political institutions and the like. If such a disturbance happens to displace a system from its equilibrium, it then sets it in motion along a path that will not return to the original position, nor to a new equilibrium, for a stretch of time that is "too long to fall within our purview, or long enough to allow a non-economic system to replace the present economic one" (Pantaleoni 1909: 113). This "type 2" dynamics (as he dubbed it in the Italian version of the 1909 paper, to differentiate it from the equilibrium-related dynamics of "type 1") did away with Pareto's equilibrium-efficiency pair, and focused instead on those processes of redistribution of wealth and privilege that were consequent upon changes in the balance of force between social groups, which was Pantaleoni's main concern. However, he was unable to go beyond a rough sketch of how a dynamic analysis of this kind could be elaborated.

The previous reconstruction makes it clear that disagreements with Pareto on points of theory were inevitable, although these never went beyond their private correspondence. It was only after Pareto's death that Pantaleoni (1923) distanced himself publicly from general equilibrium theory and proclaimed that it had reached a dead end. No prediction has ever been more inaccurate, but Pantaleoni had his reasons for wishing that it be true. Pareto wanted economics to be rigorously separated from sociology so as to avoid the exactness of the "first approximation" being spoilt by the jumble of illogical factors that operate outside it. On the contrary Pantaleoni, never the pure economist, had tried all his life to blur the dividing line in an attempt to bring economics to bear upon what he perceived as the political problem of his age: how to prevent tribal egoism, of which he recognized the positive economic role, from turning into a regressive force by taking hold of the state and using it as an instrument for the protection of particular interests. He had other reasons for disagreeing, such as his penchant for psychological explanations (which Pareto dismissed), and his idea that price adjustments are better studied with reference to groups of "connected commodities" rather than in a general equilibrium perspective (see Pantaleoni 1924–25 [1963], I: 191–4, II: 267 ff.). However, the urgency of his political concerns seems to have been the main motive behind his theoretical choices.

Marco Dardi

See also:

Competition (III); Economic dynamics (III); Vilfredo Pareto (I); Public economics (III); Social choice (III).

References and further reading

Augello, M.M. and L. Michelini (1997), 'Maffeo Pantaleoni (1857–1924). Biografia scientifica, storiografia e bibliografia', *Il pensiero economico italiano*, **5** (1), 119–206.
Baldassarri, M. (ed.) (1997), *Maffeo Pantaleoni: At the origin of the Italian school of economics and finance*, London and New York: Macmillan and St Martin's Press.
Barucci, P. (1972), 'The spread of marginalism in Italy, 1871–1890', *History of Political Economy*, **4** (2), 512–32.
Buchanan, J.M. (1960), '"La scienza delle finanze": the Italian tradition in fiscal theory', in J.M. Buchanan, *Fiscal Theory and Political Economy: Selected Essays*, Chapel Hill, NC: University of North Carolina Press, pp. 24–74.
Dalton, H. (1923), 'Pantaleoni fascist', *Economic Journal*, **33** (129), 66–9.
De Viti de Marco, Antonio (1925), 'Maffeo Pantaleoni', *Giornale degli economisti e rivista di statistica*, 4th series, **65**, 165–77.
Flux, A.W. (1898), '*Pure Economics*. By Professor Maffeo Pantaleoni', *Economic Journal*, **8** (31), 355–60.
Groenewegen, P.D. (1998), 'Maffeo Pantaleoni', in F. Meacci (ed), *Italian Economists of the 20th Century*, Cheltenham, UK and Northampton, MA, USA: Edward Elgar, pp. 44–68.
Magnani, I. (2003), *Dibattito tra economisti italiani di fine ottocento*, Milan: Franco Angeli.
Magnani, I. and N. Bellanca (1991), 'Un carteggio inedito Pantaleoni–Barone', *Rivista di diritto finanziario e scienza delle finanze*, **50** (I), 24–80.
Michelini, L. (1998), *Marginalismo e socialismo: Maffeo Pantaleoni (1882–1904)*, Milan: Franco Angeli.
Michelini, L. (2011), *Alle origini dell'antisemitismo nazional-fascista. Maffeo Pantaleoni e 'La Vita italiana' di Giovanni Preziosi (1915–1924)*, Venice: Marsilio.
Musgrave, R.A. and A.T. Peacock (1967), *Classics in the Theory of Public Finance*, London and New York: Macmillan and St Martin's Press.

Pantaleoni, M. (1882), *Teoria della traslazione dei tributi. Definizione, dinamica e ubiquità della traslazione*, Rome: Tipografia Paolini.

Pantaleoni, M. (1889), *Principii di economia pura*, reprinted 1970, Padua: CEDAM, English trans. T. Boston Bruce (revised by the author) (1898), *Pure Economics*, London: Macmillan.

Pantaleoni, M. (1898), 'An attempt to analyse the concepts of "strong and weak" in their economic connection', *Economic Journal*, **8** (30), 183–205.

Pantaleoni, M. (1904), *Scritti varii di economia*, Milan, Palermo and Naples: Remo Sandron.

Pantaleoni, M. (1909), 'The phenomena of economic dynamics', *American Economic Association Quarterly*, **11** (1), 112–22, this is an abstract of 'Di alcuni fenomeni di dinamica economica', reprinted in M. Pantaleoni (1924–25), *Erotemi di economia*, vol. 2, reprinted 1963, Padua: CEDAM, pp. 75–125.

Pantaleoni, M. (1911), 'Considerazioni sulle proprietà di un sistema di prezzi politici', *Giornale degli economisti e rivista di statistica*, 3rd series, **17**, 9–29, 114–33.

Pantaleoni, M. (1923), 'Obituary. Vilfredo Pareto', *Economic Journal*, **33** (132), 582–90, an extended Italian version appeared in *Giornale degli economisti* in 1924.

Pantaleoni, M. (1924–25), *Erotemi di economia*, 2 vols, reprinted 1963, Padua: CEDAM.

Pareto, V. (1913), 'Il massimo di utilità per una collettività in sociologia', *Giornale degli economisti e rivista di statistica*, 3rd series, **46**, 337–41.

Pareto, V. (1960), *Lettere a Maffeo Pantaleoni*, ed. G. de Rosa, 3 vols, Rome: BNL.

Sraffa, P. (1924), 'Obituary. Maffeo Pantaleoni', *Economic Journal*, **34** (136), 648–53.

Thorstein Bunde Veblen (1857–1929)

Thorstein Bunde Veblen was born in Cato, Wisconsin, 30 July 1857 to Thomas and Kary Veblen, Norwegian immigrants. He grew up in a Lutheran, mainly rural agricultural community, where waste and excess were condemned. Although his mother tongue was Norwegian, he quickly learned English and, later on, five other languages. From these early years, he learned values that would remain crucial for his entire life and work: the family and social solidarity and the devotion to handicraft – both values as sources of growth.

Formative Years

In 1874, together with his brother Andrew, he enrolled in a program at Carleton College Academy of Northfield for careers in Pastoral Ministry. The focus of the college on religious matters provided Thorstein with a narrow and isolated set of studies, which he broadened by reading the works of David Hume, Jean-Jacques Rousseau, Immanuel Kant, John Stuart Mill and Herbert Spencer. However, it was following the courses of John Bates Clark that he developed an interest for economics (see Forges Davanzati 2006). His relationships with the other students and professors were difficult. This was also due, in part, to his complex and difficult personality.

In 1880, one year ahead of time, he successfully graduated with a BA, earning high marks. His dissertation consisted in a critique of Mill in the wake of the philosophical thinking of Hamilton. In 1881, Thorstein enrolled at Johns Hopkins University, along with his brother. Here, he chose philosophy. Among his educators were the historian Henry Brooks Adams, the mathematician and philosopher Charles Sanders Pierce, the philosopher George S. Morris and the economist Richard T. Ely. During this period, Veblen furthered his studies of anthropology, sociology and psychology, which would become fundamental for developing his own research approach. He left Johns Hopkins University in 1882 and transferred to Yale, where he earned a PhD in philosophy in 1884, with a dissertation on "Ethical grounds of a doctrine of retribution". At Yale, Veblen met William Graham Sumner and Noah Porter and importantly he acquired in-depth knowledge of Spencer's theory. All of these elements contributed to the evolution of his thinking (Tilman 2007: 288).

After a long period of inactivity, he enrolled in 1891 in a post-doctoral course in economics at Cornell University. There he met James Laurence Laughlin who, when Veblen transferred to Chicago in 1892, helped him to get a fellowship and placed him on the editorial board of the *Journal of Political Economy*. This is when Veblen published his first article on waste: "The economic theory of woman's dress" (Veblen 1894). In Chicago he also met Jacques Loeb, a famous evolutionary biologist.

In the same period, he wrote book reviews on Karl Marx, Enrico Ferri, Antonio Labriola, Werner Sombart and Gabriel Tarde. He also published some articles that were important to his career, such as "The Beginnings of Ownership" (Veblen 1898). All these articles can be seen, *ex post*, as progressive steps leading him towards his best-known book: *The Theory of Leisure Class* (Veblen 1899). In all these papers he criticized the classical and neoclassical economic theory and its idea of immutable economic laws, based on the laws of nature (the term "neoclassical" was probably coined by him

(Rutherford 2011: 7, fn 4). Instead, he insisted that the new science of economics should focus on the application of the methodology provided by Darwinian Evolutionism, which defined social phenomena as cumulative processes (Veblen 1898).

Three main concepts define the originality of Veblen's social theory: instincts, habits of mind and institutions. Instincts are at the basis of his vision of historical change, that is, a continuous comparison between the old institutions and new thinking brought about by new technological data. According to Veblen, in fact, there are social instincts: the instinct of workmanship, parental bent, idle curiosity, which promotes community and social wealth or welfare. However, there are also antisocial instincts: instincts of self-regarding, predatory impulses that destroy aspects of the cultural fabric and intensify individualism. Nevertheless, these instincts are moderated or re-shaped by rational thought and intelligence (Weed 1981: 72).

These instincts combine to create a technical knowledge, which is an endogenous variable to the system. When instincts and technical knowledge are considered together, they develop institutions. Institutions consist in the habits of mind predominant in a society. In these processes, technological knowledge plays a pre-eminent role as engine for cultural change (Veblen 1898). There is a need to identify the mental attitudes prevalent in a society in order to understand their interactions with the societal environment and relate them back to economic analysis. For instance, it is imperative that modern science studies the mental attitudes of the businessmen (Vianello 1961: 226). For this approach, Veblen is considered a founding father of American institutionalism (see Rutherford 2011).

Maturity

In 1899 Veblen published his main work, entitled *The Theory of Leisure Class: An Economic Study of the Evolution of Institutions* – reprinted in 1912 with the title *The Theory of Leisure Class: An Economic Study of Institutions* (Veblen 1899 [1912]). Starting from the observation of American society, he delves deeply into the concept of conspicuous consumption, going beyond the satisfaction of basic needs to include what he qualified as waste. According to him, the ruling class is driven and propelled by the financial emulation to consume in order to preserve its reputation within the circles to which it relates, while maintaining a social distance from the underclass. This invidious comparison encourages more individuals to consume in order to gain and grow in social status and power. Conspicuous consumption and invidious comparison are also part of the critical argument against neoclassical theory, which implies that the consumer is perfectly rational. Conspicuous consumption and invidious comparison are formidable instruments for safeguarding capitalism. The working class is driven to emulate leisure-class consumption and this behaviour overcomes the social conflict between the parasitic class and the productive class. The purchased social power of the wealthier class also perpetuates control of the institutions, like in the US university system (Veblen 1918). Notwithstanding the negative judgement by the academic world, Veblen's theories became an alternative for socialists in search of a non-Marxist critique of capitalism (see Edgell and Townshend 1993).

Veblen also wrote an article on "Gustav Schmoller's economics" (Veblen 1901). Contrary to other American institutionalists, he criticized the German Historical School but did appreciate Schmoller.

In *The Theory of Business Enterprise* (Veblen 1904) – which can be considered as his main work in economics proper – he proposed a theory of credit. Here, Veblen concentrates on the businessman's habits in order to understand the social mutations and the habits of mind prevalent in society. The mentality of the businessman oriented toward profit making and toward large financial speculation is driven by a predatory instinct, with a total disinterest in the industrial process, which is in the hands of technical professionals. Enterprises and their captains, thanks to a credit system – always endowed with better performance and the issuance of stocks and obligations – overcapitalize their tangible and intangible assets, such as goodwill and brand. Enterprise ownership through shareholding is subsequently defined by Veblen also as absentee ownership (1923). If technicians, who are driven by workmanship, controlled production in the interest of community, thereby increasing output and lowering prices and the financial value of the enterprise, this would cause a loss of power of the financial ownership through a loss in the value of shares. The ownership therefore feels justified in sabotaging the production system by an artificial limitation of production. Therein lies the possibility, for the businessmen, to alter the price system and increase the value of enterprises. One of the main consequences of this arrangement is unemployment. According to Veblen, the means of production (capitalist property), in order to be productive, must be articulated with community's technological knowledge (immaterial equipment). For Veblen, knowledge is produced by the community thanks to experience and experimentation handed down from generation to generation. For this reason, he equated the pecuniary gain of capital goods to rent while criticizing patent systems that draw rent from community knowledge. It follows that to limit production for financial purposes and not on behalf of society is a social waste. This is the Veblenian dichotomy between business and industry.

In his studies of American trusts, Veblen focused on quasi-monopoly and oligopoly price, even in the absence of a formal analysis able to explain the relationship between price and quantity. Veblen attempted to combine microeconomics with macroeconomics, examining different industries and the effect they had on the whole production of goods and services. The author concluded that, from a microeconomic point of view, the politics of prices determined in oligopoly to the advantage of businessmen, created a distortion of the flow of individual revenue, altering general consumption and investments. Therefore, the maximization of profits at the microeconomic level corresponded to a drop in the national production at the macroeconomic level (Vianello 1961: 236–7). Indeed, with the industrial concentration process, the short-term interests of the world of finance overruled the medium- and long-term interests of the production system. This contradiction could lead to a crisis of capitalism.

Veblen's Chicago period was the most prolific in his academic career. It ended in 1906, when he was forced to resign from the university, officially because of marital infidelity but most probably because the university's president learned of his manuscript against the US university system.

Last Years

In 1914 Veblen published *The Instinct of Workmanship and the State of Industrial Arts* (Veblen 1914) – which he declared to be his most important work because it delivered the psychological and anthropological foundations of his approach in the most complete way (see also Hodgson 2004: 143) – and, in the following year, *Imperial Germany and the Industrial Revolution* (Veblen 1915). The capacity of a developing nation (as Germany was at that time) to attain and develop the most advanced technology was presented as a significant advantage. In contrast to England, Germany had imported the most advanced technology, creating conditions whereby its development would not be hampered by old institutions, as is typical of a more mature economy. Veblen's views were considered supportive of German interests. According to US espionage legislation, he was denied the possibility to sell his book by mail order. Moreover, because his political position was considered un-American, he was no longer allowed to teach at Cornell University. In 1917 his new work – *An Inquiry Into the Nature of Peace and the Terms of its Perpetuation* – predicted the birth of a new world order and proposed conditions for a long-lasting peace.

In 1918, he began an editorial collaboration with *The Dial*, a literary and political magazine advocating internationalism and the refoundation of industrial and scholastic systems. His reflections about this period, originally appearing in *The Dial*, were subsequently published as *The Vested Interest and the State of Industrial Arts* (Veblen 1919b). *The Dial* editorial staff debated subjects ranging from the Soviet organization, the Treaty of Versailles and the conditions of war reparations at the end of the First World War. At this time, Veblen dedicated himself to political matters and wrote, for example, "Bolshevism is a menace – to whom?" (Veblen 1919a). In 1919, he ended his partnership with *The Dial*, owing to the review's financial and political problems, and joined the New School for Social Research of New York. Because of cutbacks in research projects, the best among his colleagues, including Wesley Clair Mitchell and Charles Austin Beard, resigned. Veblen had no alternative but to remain. In 1920, the year his wife Anne died, he wrote a review of John Maynard Keynes's *The Economic Consequences of the Peace* (1919), in which he affirmed that the conditions imposed by the hegemonic powers were subtended to the destruction of Soviet Russia.

From that time on, he continued to focus on technocratic systems and published *The Engineers and Price System* (Veblen 1921) – one of his most controversial and quasi-utopian works, which combined two previous articles published in *The Dial*. The book imagined a technocratic system organized by a Soviet of Technicians, who could oversee production processes and eliminate the waste of resources with the aid and efficient expertise of engineers. This was, in his eyes, the opposite of an industrial system based on the interests of absentee ownership.

Veblen left his economic and sociological studies in 1926 and moved to Palo Alto, California, where he died on 3 August 1929 of a heart attack.

ALFONSO GIULIANI

See also:

Institutionalism (II); Non-Marxian socialist ideas in Britain and the United States (II).

References and further reading

Dorfman, J. (1972), *Thorstein Veblen and his America*, 7th edn, New York: A.M. Kelley.
Edgell, S. and J. Townshend (1993), 'Marx and Veblen on human nature, history, and capitalism: Vive la Différence!', *Journal of Economic Issues*, **27** (3),721–39.
Fiorito, L. (1999), 'The present significance of Thorstein Veblen's contribution in the centennial of *The Theory of the Leisure Class*: foreword', *History of Economic Ideas*, **7** (3), 81–3.

Forges Davanzati, G. (2006), *Ethical Codes and Income Distribution: A Study of John Bates Clark and Thorstein Veblen*, London and New York: Routledge.
Hodgson, G.M. (2004), *The Evolution of Institutional Economics. Agency, Structure and Darwinism in American Institutionalism*, London and New York: Routledge.
Keynes, J.M. (1919), *The Economic Consequences of the Peace*, London: Macmillan.
Rutherford, M. (2011), *The Institutionalist Movement in American Economics, 1918–1947*, New York: Cambridge University Press.
Tilman, R. (2007), *Thorstein Veblen and the Enrichment of Evolutionary Naturalism*, Columbia, MO: University of Missouri Press.
Veblen, T. (1894), 'The economic theory of woman's dress', *Popular Science Monthly*, **46**, 198–205.
Veblen, T. (1898), 'Why is economics not an evolutionary science?', *Quarterly Journal of Economics*, **12** (4), 373–97.
Veblen, T. (1899), *The Theory of the Leisure Class: An Economic Study of Institution*, reprinted 1912, New York: The Macmillan Company.
Veblen, T. (1901), 'Gustav Schmoller's economics', *Quarterly Journal of Economics*, **16** (1), 69–93.
Veblen, T. (1904), *The Theory of Business Enterprise*, New York: Charles Scribner's Sons.
Veblen, T. (1914), *The Instinct of Workmanship and the State of the Industrial Arts*, New York: Macmillan.
Veblen, T. (1915), *Imperial Germany and The Industrial Revolution*, New York: Macmillan.
Veblen, T. (1917), *An Inquiry Into the Nature of Peace and the Terms of its Perpetuation*, New York: Macmillan.
Veblen, T. (1918), *The Higher Learning In America: A Memorandum On the Conduct of Universities By Business Men*, New York: B.W. Huebsch.
Veblen, T. (1919a), 'Bolshevism is a menace – to whom?', *The Dial*, **26** (February), 174–9.
Veblen, T. (1919b), *The Vested Interest and The State of Industrial Arts. (The Modern Point of View and the New Order)*, New York: B.W. Huebsch.
Veblen, T. (1921), *The Engineers and Price System*, New York: B.W. Huebsch.
Veblen, T. (1923), *Absentee Ownership and Business Enterprise in Recent Times: The Case of America*, New York: Viking Press.
Vianello, M. (1961), *Thorstein Veblen*, Milan: Edizioni di Comunità.
Weed, F.J. (1981), 'Interpreting "institutions" in Veblen's evolutionary theory', *American Journal of Economics and Sociology*, **40** (1), 67–78.

Antonio De Viti de Marco (1858–1943)

Antonio De Viti de Marco was born in Lecce on 30 September 1858, the son of Raffaele De Viti who, having been adopted by his godmother, the Marquise Costanza De Marco, inherited the title and added de Marco to his family name. He graduated in law at the University of Rome in 1881, and immediately began his academic career. He first lectured at the University of Naples, and then taught Political Economy at the Universities of Camerino and Macerata, and, finally, Public Finance in Pavia. In 1887–88, he obtained a Chair of Public Finance at the University of Rome, which he held until 1931, when he retired at the age of 73, refusing to take the oath of allegiance to the Fascist government. He was responsible for the spread of marginalism in Italy for his role as co-owner and co-director of the *Giornale degli economisti*. From the beginning, he worked as an intense and passionate writer and publisher in order to promote liberalism. In the years 1901–22, as a member of the Italian Parliament, he struggled to achieve his dream of reshaping Italian political institutions towards a liberal democracy. With the advent of the Fascist regime, he retired from politics and returned to his scientific work. He died in Rome on 1 December 1943.

The first scientific interest of De Viti concerned money and banking, and lasted throughout his life. In fact, his first theoretical book on the topic is an essay on money (De Viti 1885), followed by articles on specific topics in the *Giornale degli economisti*, and then by the long article on banking (De Viti 1898), which was expanded and revised later (see De Viti 1934a). De Viti (1885) contains an exposition of the quantity theory of money, based on a definition of money that includes only the metals. The Devitian theory rests on a clear separation between money and credit, based on the distinction between the functions of medium of exchange and unit of account. Therefore, the banking principle adjusts the volume of fiduciary media, while movements in the price-level are determined by changes in the amount of money based on the quantity theory. His analysis covers the open economy and therefore also international adjustments, and the business cycle. In this analysis, however, money and credit are not considered as a major cause of crises, but are only important in the propagation of the business cycle. Since his approach to banking is closely linked to his idea of money, he believes that the payment function is the true function of banks. Bank loans are considered as a means to develop the payment system, and based on the real-bills doctrine, the solvency of banks does not depend on deposits, but on the quality of portfolios. Overall, his contribution to the theory of money and banking exhibits a certain eclecticism because of his extreme version of metallism, but does not display a high amount of originality. However, there are some original ideas, from the role played by the imperfect information in the dynamics of the business cycle to some elements that prefigure the new monetary economics according to which monetary theory depends on the institutional framework.

However, the main interest of De Viti concerned public finance. Actually, he is generally regarded as the most eminent scholar of the early Italian tradition, in which marginalism was used to define the optimum allocation of public expenditures among alternative uses. In *Il carattere teorico dell'economia finanziaria* (De Viti 1888), he proposed a scientific explanation of the activity of the state based on marginal analysis, like the Austrian Emil Sax. In addition, this pioneering study can be interpreted as a reaction to the previous Italian *scienza delle finanze* in order to foster the scientific approach.

De Viti refused the organicist conception of the state, namely, he did not consider the state as a sentient being, and his approach has been explicitly based on the assumption that government intervention has not only economic effects, but is also fundamentally economic in nature. He then proposed the same explanatory principles used in economics, in particular the idea that the economic agents exhibit a maximizing behaviour, even though he was aware that, in public economics, political problems are also involved. For these reasons, De Viti's contribution is conventionally regarded as the origin of the Italian tradition in public finance theory, understood as a coherent and comprehensive structure, based on marginal utility.

He considered polar cases of the state basing on political assumptions regarding the behaviour of the dominant class: (1) monopolistic state, where a social class exerts power in its exclusive interest; and (2) cooperative state, where, as in a cooperative enterprise, everybody participates, directly or through appointed agents, in their collective interests. It was only in the 1888 book that De Viti hinted at a third polar case, where the power, absolute but paternalistic, is managed in order to promote the welfare of all consumers. However, he was interested in the cooperative state only, which he thought to be very similar to modern states, apart from more or less important deviations due to political elements. In fact, he considered that historically the cooperative state represented a point of arrival and political equilibrium. His doctrine is based on the idea of public needs intended as a mere premise of fact: the economic activity of the state provides for the satisfaction of public needs in terms of the production of public services. Thus, his approach is based on the productive aspect of public activity, as far as the state is not anything but the public, organized for the production of certain goods as in a cooperative enterprise.

With time, he softened his position vis-à-vis the opportunity to use marginal analysis in the general theory of public finance. At any rate, since the very beginning, in the cooperative state the crucial principle is the cost pricing. However, in his subsequent work from *I primi principî dell'economia finanziaria* (De Viti 1928) to *Principî di economia finanziaria* (De Viti 1934b), he enlarged the scope and range of the material considered, from the economic and political theory of proportional and progressive taxation to the shifting and incidence of taxation and the theory of public debt; from the double taxation of savings to the theory of tariffs and the fiscal theory of custom duties. For example, as regards De Viti's seminal work on the effects of taxation, its original characters are both the Paretian idea of market interdependence, and the necessity of considering the expenditure of the tax income. As regards the theorem of the double taxation of savings (J.S. Mill, I. Fisher and L. Einaudi), he argued that no double taxation occurs because the new tax is the counterpart of new public services, at least in the limit of the cooperative state, in which public services are true productive factors. As regards the different effects of debt and extraordinary taxation, he has built on the Ricardian model. He specified the assumptions of the model and extended it to agents without capital income (workers and professionals). In contrast to Ricardo, he reached the conclusion that, for the community, public debt is more efficient than an extraordinary tax, but arrived at the Ricardian conclusion that the burden cannot be shifted to future generations. The work on public debt by the Italian scholars in the first half of the twentieth century (including Benvenuto Griziotti's approach) has been largely a development of the De Vitian analysis.

AMEDEO FOSSATI

See also:
Money and banking (III); Public economics (III).

References and further reading
Benham, F.C. (1934), 'Review: [untitled, German edition of the *First Principles*]', *Economica*, New Series, **1** (3), 364–7.
Buchanan, J. (1960), '"La scienza delle finanze": the Italian tradition in fiscal theory', in J. Buchanan, *Fiscal Theory and Political Economy: Selected Essays*, Chapel Hill, NC: University of North Carolina Press, pp. 24–74.
Cardini, A. (1985), *Antonio De Viti de Marco: la democrazia incompiuta*, Bari: Laterza.
Cardini, A. (1995), 'Guida bibliografica agli scritti di Antonio De Viti de Marco', in A. Pedone (ed.), *Antonio De Viti de Marco*, Bari: Laterza, pp. 237–308.
Cesarano, F. (1991), 'De Viti de Marco as monetary economist', *History of Political Economy*, **23** (1), 41–59.
De Viti de Marco, A. (1885), *Moneta e prezzi, ossia il principio quantitativo in rapporto alla questione monetaria*, Città di Castello: Lapi.
De Viti de Marco, A. (1888), *Il carattere teorico dell'economia finanziaria*, Rome: Pasqualucci.
De Viti de Marco, A. (1898), 'La funzione della banca, nota del corrispondente Prof. De Viti de Marco' (seduta del 16 gennaio 1898), *Rendiconti della R. Accademia dei Lincei, classe di scienze morali*, 5th series, **8** (1), 7–38.
De Viti de Marco, A. (1928), *I primi principî dell'economia finanziaria*, Rome: Sampaolesi, German translation, with enlargements, 1932, *Grundlehren der Finanzwirtschaft*, Tübingen: J.C.B. Mohr, Spanish translation from the German, 1934, *Principios fundamentales de economia financiera*, Madrid: Editorial Revista de derecho privado.
De Viti de Marco, A. (1934a), *La funzione della banca. Introduzione allo studio dei problemi monetari e bancari contemporanei*, Torino: Einaudi, German translation, 1935, *Die Funktion der Bank. Einführung in der gegenwärtingen Geld und Bankproblem*, Vienna: J. Springer.
De Viti de Marco, A. (1934b), *Principî di economia finanziaria*, Torino: Einaudi, 2nd edn, 1939, Torino: Einaudi, English translation 1936, *First Principles of Public Finances*, London and New York: Jonathan Cape and Harcourt Brace.
Dehove, G. (1946), 'L'œuvre financière de A. De Viti', *Revue d'Economie publique*, nos 3 and 4, 249–91 and 436–56.
Fossati, A. (2006), 'Needs, the principle of minimum means, and public goods in De Viti de Marco', *Journal of the History of Economics Thought*, **28** (4), 427–43.
Kayaalp, O. (1998), 'Antonio De Viti de Marco', in F. Meacci (ed.), *Italian Economists of the 20th Century*, Cheltenham, UK and Northampton, MA, USA: Edward Elgar, pp. 95–113.
Pedone, A. (ed.) (1995), *Antonio De Viti de Marco*, Bari: Laterza.
Rossi, E. (1926), 'Le prime basi teoriche della finanza dello stato democratico', *La Riforma Sociale*, **37** (1), 140–56.
Simons, H.C. (1937), 'Review of *First Principles of Public Finance* (1936) and *Grundlehren der Finanzwirtschaft* (1932)', *Journal of Political Economy*, **45** (5), 712–17.

John Atkinson Hobson (1858–1940)

Aptly self-described in his later years as an economic heretic, John Atkinson Hobson (1858–1940) made two substantial contributions to economic analysis, one major and one relatively minor. His major contribution was to revive interest in the underconsumption theory. His relatively minor contribution was as a critic of the marginal productivity theory of distribution. These contributions were initially unrelated, though later the distribution of income came to play an important part in Hobson's exposition of the underconsumption theory.

Hobson was "born – on 6 July 1858 – and bred in the middle of the middle class of a middle-sized Midland industrial town" (Hobson 1931: 13), to wit, Derby, where his father was the founder, joint proprietor and editor of *The Derbyshire Advertiser and Journal*. After proceeding to an open scholarship at Lincoln College, Oxford, and graduating in 1880, he was employed by schools in Faversham and Exeter, where he taught classics for seven years; during that time, in 1885, he married Florence Edgar, who hailed from New Jersey. In 1887 he abandoned school teaching in order to take up journalism, moving for that reason to West London. After this move he became a university extension lecturer, offering a course in political economy from 1888, and was thereafter a prolific writer on matters economic and societal. The best account of his life is to be found in Lee (1972).

Hobson's first contribution to economic analysis came with the publication in 1889 of *The Physiology of Industry*, of which the businessman A.F. Mummery (who died while mountaineering in 1895) was co-author (Mummery and Hobson 1889). By Hobson's admission it was Mummery who converted him to the theory of underconsumption, which although it had already been advanced more than 50 years earlier by Malthus among others had since then been rejected by economists on the ground that for an economy as a whole supply can never exceed demand.

In their version of the underconsumption theory Hobson and Mummery assumed not only a given technology at any one time, but also fixed coefficients of production. On this basis, to summarize their theory, they argued that if the output of consumption goods were constant, a given quantity of capital stock would be required to produce it. From this it followed that if the output of consumption goods were growing, the capital stock required to produce it would grow at the same rate. In other words, the required addition to the capital stock, that is to say, the investment required, is determined by the rate of growth of demand for consumption goods. Additions to the capital stock in excess of this amount were referred to by Hobson and Mummery as "over-investment", reflecting "over-saving", alternatively described as "underconsumption". Hobson and Mummery argued that since such excessive capital stock is unprofitable it would be allowed to run down, leading to an economic depression such as that of the mid-1880s, with accompanying unemployment whose ultimate cause is underconsumption. They noted that remedies for this unemployment include war expenditure, luxury consumption and public works.

The only reviews of *The Physiology of Industry*, by Edgeworth (1890) and by W.A.S. Hewins (1891), were both highly critical, and the unorthodox views expressed in the book led to Hobson being refused inclusion on the London Society for the Extension of University Teaching's list of lecturers in the field of economics, because of an adverse reference written by Foxwell (not by Edgeworth, as was once supposed). The reputation of *The Physiology of Industry* was, however, eventually retrieved by Keynes, who devoted six pages of the *General Theory* (Keynes 1936) to praise of its general line of argument. Nonetheless, Keynes rejected the view that unemployment is due to excessive investment, arguing instead that unemployment is due to investment falling short of full employment saving, a more inclusive demand-deficiency explanation.

Subsequently, however, in comparing Hobson with Keynes, Domar (1947: 52) argued that Hobson was dealing with a "different, and possibly also a deeper problem. . . . suppose savings are invested. Will the new plants be able to dispose of all their products?" Hobson thus pointed the way to the Harrod–Domar growth theory, as Joan Robinson (1949: 79) implied when she stated that "Mr. Harrod's analysis provides the missing link between Keynes and Hobson".

Between 1889 and 1938 Hobson continued to be a strenuous advocate of the under-consumption theory, in numerous books and articles, though he expanded his exposition in two ways. First, as argued by Craig Medlen (2012), from *The Evolution of Modern Capitalism* (Hobson 1894) onwards Hobson attached increasing importance to the economic consequences of institutional change from competitive to monopolistic industrial structures, contending in particular that monopolistic firms engage in investment in excess of that needed to produce their output which they restrict in the interests of profit maximization. Second, and more important, *The Problem of the Unemployed* (Hobson 1896) marked the beginning of Hobson's association of underconsumption with the unequal distribution of income, the remedies recommended in that book including taxation of "unearned income" (see below) and a rise in wages through trade union action. Over time Hobson's political views also changed, moving to the left, his resignation from the Liberal Party in 1916 being followed by membership first of the Independent Labour Party and then, in 1924, of the Labour Party.

In an 1898 *Contemporary Review* article entitled "Free trade and foreign policy" Hobson used his underconsumption theory to develop a then innovative theory of imperialism, which he attributed to pressure on governments by capitalists who thereby hoped to relieve the domestic glut of consumption goods by obtaining exclusive access to markets overseas. C.P. Scott, the editor of the *Manchester Guardian*, having had his attention drawn to this article by L.T. Hobhouse, in 1899 sent Hobson as a correspondent to South Africa shortly before the outbreak of the Boer War, an outcome being the expansion of Hobson's theory of imperialism to be found in *Imperialism: A Study* (1902), which in turn was an acknowledged major source of Lenin's Marxist theory of imperialism.

Hobson's other substantial contribution to economics was in the field of income distribution. In "The law of the three rents", published in the *Quarterly Journal of Economics* in 1891, Hobson extended the Ricardian theory of rent so as to make it equally applicable to all three factors of production. He argued that rent is payable not only on intra-marginal land, but also on intra-marginal capital and intra-marginal labour. This provided the basis of a theory of income distribution advanced notably in *The Economics of Distribution* (Hobson 1900). Hobson divided the income received by a factor of production into three parts, namely, reward for effort or sacrifice, and two forms of what Hobson termed "unearned income". One form of unearned income he named monopoly rent (later renaming it marginal rent) received by all owners of a particular "grade" of a factor of production, explained by lack of competition between factor grades. The other he named differential rent, received by those who are more productive than the least productive owners of that factor "grade".

More provocative was the criticism of the marginal productivity theory of distribution to which this theory led. In *The Economics of Distribution* Hobson argued that the withdrawal of a unit of a factor of production reduces the productivity both of the remaining units of that factor of production and of the other factors of production with which it was previously combined, and that the separate contribution of a last unit of a factor therefore cannot be calculated. Unfortunately none of Hobson's attempts to illustrate this criticism by an example was successful; Marshall rightly criticized one such attempt on the ground of inappropriate choice of numbers representing factor units, an assessment with which Joan Robinson, otherwise sympathetic to Hobson, agreed, pointing out that merely allowing for half-units of factors would undermine the criticism. However, Hobson's principal objection to the marginal productivity theory was that in reality very few factors of production conform to its assumption of infinite divisibility; an example dropping this assumption so as to illustrate a Hobsonian scenario is to be found in Schneider (1996: 55–6). Hobson's criticisms notwithstanding, the marginal productivity theory of distribution survived, no doubt due to the absence of a better alternative.

In conclusion, to adapt Keynes, these contributions to economic analysis indicate that while not a general, Hobson was at least a major in the brave army of economic heretics.

MICHAEL SCHNEIDER

See also:

British marginalism (II); Business cycles and growth (III); Francis Ysidro Edgeworth (I); Industrial organization (III); John Maynard Keynes (I); Labour and employment (III); Non-Marxian socialist ideas in Britain and the United States (II).

References and further reading

Domar, E.D. (1947), 'Expansion and employment', *American Economic Review*, **37** (1), 34–55.
Edgeworth, F.Y. (1890), 'Review of *The Physiology of Industry*', *Journal of Education*, new series, **12**, 194.
Hewins, W.A.S. (1891), 'Review of *The Physiology of Industry*', *Economic Review*, **1**, 133–4.
Hobson, J.A. (1891), 'The law of the three rents', *Quarterly Journal of Economics*, **5**, 263–88.
Hobson, J.A. (1894), *The Evolution of Modern Capitalism: A Study of Machine Capitalism*, London: W. Scott.
Hobson, J.A. (1896), *The Problem of the Unemployed*, London: Methuen.
Hobson, J.A. (1898), 'Free trade and foreign policy', *Contemporary Review*, **64**, 167–80.
Hobson, J.A. (1900), *The Economics of Distribution*, New York: Macmillan.
Hobson, J.A. (1902), *Imperialism: A Study*, London: Constable.
Hobson, J.A. (1931), *Towards Social Equality*, London: Oxford University Press.
Hobson, J.A. (1938), *Confessions of an Economic Heretic*, London: Allen & Unwin.
Keynes, J.M. (1936), *The General Theory of Employment Interest and Money*, London: Macmillan.
Lee, A. (1972), 'Hobson, John Atkinson (1858–1940)', in J.M. Bellamy and J. Saville (eds), *Dictionary of Labour Biography*, vol. 1, London: Macmillan, pp.176–81.
Medlen, C. (2012), 'A historiographical exhumation of J.A. Hobson's over-saving thesis: general theory versus historiography', *European Journal of the History of Economic Thought*, **19** (5), 785–95.
Mummery, A.F. and J.A. Hobson (1889), *The Physiology of Industry: Being an Exposure of Certain Fallacies in Existing Theories in Economics*, London: J. Murray.
Robinson, J. (1949), 'Mr. Harrod's dynamics', *Economic Journal*, **59** (233), 68–85.
Schneider, M. (1996), *J.A. Hobson*, London: Macmillan.

Georg Simmel (1858–1918)

Georg Simmel (born in Berlin 1858, died in Strasbourg 1918) counts as a classic in the social sciences. Although his major book was entitled *The Philosophy of Money*, Simmel is regarded as a sociologist. His academic career was not successful, since he repeatedly failed to obtain a chair at a university until, finally, four years before he passed away, he was appointed to a professorship at Strasbourg University. The reasons for his failures are diverse.

Simmel's Jewish background has often been mentioned as one cause for being neglected; another reason was certainly that he was not mainstream. In 1908 he was considered for a chair in philosophy at Heidelberg University, following Max Weber's recommendation. In the end, a majority in the university council decided to withdraw the call for Simmel, since he could not be clearly categorized as a member of one or the other discipline, and many committee members qualified his writing style as insufficiently academic and too essayist-narrative.

Simmel studied history, psychology and philosophy. He submitted a work on music as PhD thesis, which was rejected, and he replaced his submission with a study on Kant, which was finally accepted. Two years later, he encountered similar problems with his "habilitation" thesis: a first submission was accepted only after a long process of confrontational debate, and his first "habilitation" defence lecture was rejected, so that a second lecture became necessary.

Simmel had no real financial problems, since he was able to live on an inheritance left to him by a benefactor. He lectured with the status of a *Privatdozent* and attracted a large number of students, because his lectures always served as a kind of cultural event. In 1911, he received a doctoral degree *honoris causae* in economics at Freiburg University in recognition of his works on defining and initiating sociology.

Simmel published around 30 books and more than 200 articles and papers. His achievements were considered an attempt to consolidate sociology as an independent discipline. Sociology was always thought of as a branch of science with a specific and unique object, which can be distinguished from and defended against other sciences, but sociology was also regarded as a method of historic and social sciences in general, which deals with issues of human action. Sociology works with findings delivered by history or anthropology or other sciences, and tries to form a synthesis of empirical material, perspectives, and interpretation. Much of Simmel's sociological discussion of empirical phenomena is based on his impressions gained in Berlin, where the speed of the modernization process was very rapid and the span of lifestyles and social diversity was very broad (Moebius 2002; Helle 2015).

In its first steps, network research also goes back to Georg Simmel, even if he was not a genuine network researcher by any formal definition. He was, however, a researcher who thought in categories, which are quite similar to network approaches nowadays. He portrayed society in dualistic terms to which, for example, the binary wordings of universality and particularity, continuity and change, or conformism and distinction belonged. Also, human beings are regarded as dualistic. Simmel thinks about dualism as a driving force of development, which causes change. Society is regarded as a place of permanent conflict of different sorts. Individual human agents are part of a uniform collectivism as well as pieces of specific individual accentuation. The very central idea of interdependence ("*Wechselwirkung*") corresponds to the idea of dualism in Simmel's thinking.

In the early days of sociology, society was thought of as a geometry of social relations. In the same sense that geometry deals with forms through which matter becomes a body, the analysis of abstract forms was a major part of Simmel's work. Social formations are characterized and constituted through continuous repetition. Simmel's crossing of social circles looks similar to the modern analysis of cliques, as they are discussed in contemporary network analysis. Different dispositions of individual actors differ according to their positions in a network, and personality in a sense of individuality is a result of the crossing of circles (Simmel 1908). Networks function as a mode of social differentiation *and* societal trends of standardization. Finally, social structures are conceptualized as relational – and principally changing – links between human actors and organizations.

Society is the result of interdependences, in which everything is related to every other thing. Reality is always the outcome of permanent and diverse interplays between different agencies. Even an accidental interaction between different human beings can be portrayed as society. According to Simmel, these are elementary forms of social interdependence. Besides informal or episodic forms of interaction, Simmel has bigger and more stable forms of social organization in mind, namely, classes or families. Again, interdependencies keep society working, and society is a permanent process.

Simmel published many articles, which appeared in collections of essays. He discussed various topics of everyday life and he also addressed topics such as religion, fashion, family, gender or ethnicity. There is hardly a topic on which Simmel did not reflect. Alongside a great number of shorter works, Simmel's most ambitious work was *Die Philosophie des Geldes* (first published in 1900, English translation, *The Philosophy of Money*, Simmel 2011). The title reflects the fact that philosophy at that time promised greater success than "sociology", which did not really exist in Germany at that time. However, Simmel was not greatly concerned about differences between philosophy and sociology, but assumed fluid borders between both areas of discussion and knowledge.

The Philosophy of Money discusses money as a mirror of the process of rationalization in capitalist life (Dietz 1997). Money is like a spider weaving the net of society. It documents the impersonality of society and it is simultaneously its cause. Money fosters neutrality of life in a positive and a negative understanding. Finally, life-styles and social rationalities are discussed intensively against the new historical fact of a money economy. *The Philosophy of Money* gives proof of Simmel's cultural critique. He reflects on ambiguities of progress and freedom to choose, and insists on rising contradictions, needs, and processes of a loss of social coherence (Deflem 2003). *The Philosophy of Money* is a treatise that deals with money from the perspective of a non-economist. While economists deal with money almost in an empirical way, Simmel argues as a socio-economist, underlining the social embeddedness of money, the extra-economic, social basis of modern money (Zelitzer 1989). Human knowledge and cognition in society is highly dependent upon the evolution of the money economy. In this sense, the sphere of finance has generated its own dynamics, which underpin and transport societal and economic development and relations (Poggi 1993).

Simmel was generally interested in the outlines of the modern style of life at a time when society was not only experiencing cultural change, but was also going through turbulent economic changes as well. In *The Philosophy of Money* he examined in detail this modern "style of life", which complicates human relationships. Complications were seen in the ever-increasing detachment in social circles and the replacement of traditional rhythms in social life by more complex forms as well as in an increase in the tempo in which society was changing. These distinctions in everyday culture can be seen as a growing "multiplicity" of cultural styles that are forever changing (Bögenhold 2001).

Today, Simmel serves as a classic and founding father of sociology, especially of the sociology of culture, but he is also well known in the history of economic thought, especially as a figure of heterodoxies throwing light on extra-economic dimensions. He was – compared with other scholars of his time – discovered and discussed quite recently in Anglo-American sociology (Levine 1995), but he also represents a starting-point for many specific discussions. Aesthetics, sociology of design and fashions, or sociology of religion all have Simmel as one of their progenitors.

DIETER BÖGENHOLD

See also:

German and Austrian schools (II); Non-Marxist socialist ideas in Germany and Austria (II).

References and further reading

Bögenhold, D. (2011), 'Social inequality and the sociology of life style material and cultural aspects of social stratification', *American Journal of Economics and Sociology*, **60** (4), 829–47.

Deflem, M. (2003), 'The sociology of the sociology of money: Simmel and the contemporary battle of the classics', *Journal of Classical Sociology*, **3** (1), 67–96.

Dietz, R. (1997), 'Georg Simmel's contribution to a theory of the money economy', in P. Koslowski (ed.), *Methodology of the Social Sciences, Ethics, and Economics in the Newer Historical School Studies in Economic Ethics and Philosophy*, Berlin and New York: Springer, pp. 115–44.

Helle, H.J. (2015), *The Social Thought of Georg Simmel*, Los Angeles, CA: Sage.

Levine, D.N. (1995), *Visions of the Sociological Tradition*, Chicago, IL: University of Chicago Press.

Moebius, S. (2002), *Simmel lesen: Moderne, dekonstruktive und postmoderne Lektüren der Soziologie von Georg Simmel*, Stuttgart: Ibidem-Verlag.

Poggi, G. (1993), *Money and the Modern Mind: Georg Simmel's Philosophy of Money*, Berkeley, CA: University of California Press.

Simmel, G. (1908), 'Die Kreuzung sozialer Kreise', in G. Simmel, *Soziologie. Untersuchungen über die Formen der Vergesellschaftung*, Berlin: Duncker & Humblot, pp. 305–44.

Simmel, G. (1989–2015), *Gesamtausgabe*, ed. O. Rammstedt, 24 vols, Frankfurt am Main: Suhrkamp.

Simmel, G. (2011), *The Philosophy of Money*, London: Routledge.

Zelitzer, V.A. (1989), 'The social meaning of money: "special monies"', *American Journal of Sociology*, **95** (2), 342–77.

Enrico Barone (1859–1924)

Born in Naples, Enrico Barone was educated in military schools in Naples and Turin, receiving the mix of technical and humanist education typical of those institutions. From 1880 on he climbed the ranks of a regular military career in the army up to general staff colonel, but he suddenly resigned in 1906 – apparently after a clash with his superiors on matters of national defence. Economics was only one of the many interests of this renowned teacher and prolific writer in strategic and historical matters. Yet while still in the army, in the early 1890s, he managed to establish himself as one of the leading Italian economists, although not in an academic position until 1910 when he became full Professor of Political Economy at the University of Rome. He contributed to the literature on mathematical marginalism on a par with Walras, Pareto, Wicksell and other eminent economists of the age. As with Pareto, Pantaleoni acted as mentor in directing Barone's considerable talent towards pure theory. The range of his interests was much wider than that, however. His economic writings – most of which are collected in Barone (1894–1924 [1936–37]) – are concentrated in two periods, 1894–96 and 1906–24, and apart from mathematical economics they cover a variety of topics such as public finance, colonial, transport and war economics, industrial syndicates, and tariffs. Many other interests – journalism, politics and public debate, even film making – competed with economics for his attention. Einaudi, a good friend of his, remarked that "had he been less distracted by the most diverse engagements [. . .] and less unwilling to spend time in refining his own works, he would have left a much more remarkable imprint" (in Finoia 1980: 105). Barone died in Rome in 1924. Most of his personal papers were lost in the bombings of World War II. For a detailed biographical study see Gentilucci (2006).

As a pure analyst, Barone worked mainly in the wake of Walras's general equilibrium approach, but his mathematical skill and nonsectarian spirit set him apart in the tangle of misunderstandings, disputes and personal rivalries of the period. In a compact assessment of his contributions, Kuenne (1972) wrote that Barone's mathematical background was superior to that of Walras and Pareto, which is certainly true of the former but very doubtful of the latter. Probably the impression is due to Barone's treasuring concise and crystal-clear expression, while Pareto cared little for form and always wrote as if in a hurry, driven by an urge to cover more and more ground. An interesting linkage concerning the mathematics is provided by the physicist Galileo Ferraris: a fellow student of Pareto's at the University of Turin, where they both attended the lectures of the mathematician Angelo Genocchi, Ferraris taught Barone physics and rational mechanics at the Turin military academy about 20 years later. An acknowledgement of Barone's superior clarity came from Schumpeter, who had Barone's 1908 textbook, *Principles of Political Economy*, translated into German in order to introduce his German-speaking colleagues to general equilibrium theory (Schumpeter 1927).

Personally less touchy than Walras or Pareto, Barone disliked controversies and if necessary would act as a peacemaker. Although he himself had reasons to complain about the British, he was unwilling to comply with the creeping rivalry between continental and British marginalists. Loyal to Walras, he was ready to adopt Marshallian concepts and methods whenever they were handy, as was the case with the hypothesis of constant marginal utility of money and with the measure of net utility gains through producers' and consumers' rents. In papers written for the *Giornale degli Economisti* in

1894 (Barone 1894–1924 [1936–37], I: 57–114), Barone sided with Edgeworth against Nicholson in defending rent, and provided a precise characterization of the different behavioural assumptions underlying Walras's and Marshall's price-quantity functional relations. He also argued that, whereas the former provided exact tools for comparative statics, the latter were more effective for investigating the "approximate equilibrium" dynamics of an economy subject to a continuous flow of small perturbations. Notably, in this pioneering attempt at applying general equilibrium theory to the analysis of dynamical questions Barone never mentioned – and implicitly distanced himself from – Walras's *tâtonnement* procedure. To the best of my knowledge, the only case in which Barone resorted to *tâtonnement* was as a device for computing the accounting prices needed by his "Ministry of production" in the famous 1908 paper "Il Ministro della Produzione nello Stato Collettivista".

Another line of research attesting to Barone's originality is represented by his development of a fully blown theory of equilibrium of the competitive firm, combining Wicksteed's notion of the production function (launched in the latter's 1894 *Essay on the Coordination of the Laws of Distribution*) with the conditions of the entrepreneur's "net product" maximization. Walras, who in the second edition of the *Eléments* had stuck to the hypothesis of constant coefficients of production, was at first puzzled by Barone's formulation, neatly presented for the first time in a letter to him of 20 September 1894 (Jaffé 1965: 619–21). A complicated chain of reactions followed (for the details, see Jaffé 1964; Kuenne 1972). On Walras's part, the resolve to take Barone's perspective into account led to important changes in the treatment of production in the definitive edition of the *Eléments*. Barone formalized his ideas in a long 1896 paper on distribution (Barone (1894–1924 [1936–37], I: 145–228), outlining a theory of equilibrium business profits based on free entry to match Walras's notion of an entrepreneur "making neither profit nor loss". Before this, in reviewing Wicksteed's *Essay* for the *Economic Journal* on Edgeworth's invitation, he had also shown how a marginalist theory of distribution could be derived without needing to assume first-degree homogeneity of the production function. The review, however – a French version of which has survived among Walras's papers (Jaffé 1964: 68–73) – was inexplicably rejected by the journal with what Barone perceived as embarrassment on the part of Edgeworth. Walras and Pareto took it as a sign of Marshall's underhand manoeuvring, a suspicion that has since become history although there is no evidence for it – indeed, why should Marshall have acted so maliciously in a matter in which he had no direct interest? Barone, while at first piqued, ended by assuming a forgiving attitude, but the episode continued to fuel hostility between continental and British economists for a while. Finally, Pareto, who was not keen on considering the firm as the kernel of distribution and disparaged the production function in favour of the greater flexibility of production coefficients, in a letter to Pantaleoni of 1896 boasted of having persuaded Barone of the validity of his own approach. No surprise, then, if in the "Ministry of production" paper Barone, too, used a production coefficients representation of technology.

This 1908 paper doubtless represents Barone's chief claim to international renown. Made available to the English reading public by Hayek in the 1930s (Hayek 1935: 245–90), it has since become a point of reference for two main lines of economic literature of the twentieth century, the theory of socialist planning and the so-called "new welfare economics". On both accounts the primary inputs came from Pareto, but

Barone, once again, managed to rework them with characteristic originality and clarity. Neither the theoretical importance of this contribution (see, for example, Petretto 1982) nor its political and ideological background (Michelini 2005) can be adequately illustrated here. Suffice it to recall that the possibility of using perfectly competitive equilibrium as an algorithm for tracing the efficient states of a generic social system, be it planned or decentralized, was investigated by Barone without any reference to individual utilities, simply by using the net social product evaluated at competitive equilibrium prices as an index the maximization of which guarantees, on the grounds of a revealed preference argument, that no possibility of Pareto improvement remains unexploited. Further, the paper contained the first clear statement of the role of lump-sum transfers of income or of property as a device to select among efficient states according to ethical and social criteria.

MARCO DARDI

See also:

British marginalism (II); Lausanne School (II); Vilfredo Pareto (I); Marie-Esprit-Léon Walras (I); Welfare economics (III).

References and further reading

Barone, E. (1894–1924), *Le opere economiche*, 3 vols, reprinted 1936–37, ed. A. Piperno, Bologna: Zanichelli.
Barone, E. (1908), 'Il Ministro della Produzione nello Stato Collettivista', reprinted in E. Barone (1894–1924), *Le opere economiche*, 3 vols, reprinted 1936–37, ed. A. Piperno, Bologna: Zanichelli, vol. 1, pp. 231–97.
Finoia, M. (ed) (1980), *Il pensiero economico italiano 1850–1950*, Bologna: Cappelli.
Gentilucci, C.E. (2006), *L'agitarsi del mondo in cui viviamo. L'economia politica di Enrico Barone*, Turin: Giappichelli.
Hayek, F.A. von (ed.) (1935), *Collectivist Economic Planning*, London: Routledge.
Jaffé, W. (1964), 'New light on an old quarrel', *Cahiers Vilfredo Pareto* (3), 61–102.
Jaffé, W. (ed.) (1965), *Correspondence of Léon Walras and Related Papers*, vol. 2, Amsterdam: North-Holland.
Kuenne, R.E. (1972), 'Barone, Enrico', in D.L. Sill (ed.), *International Encyclopaedia of the Social Sciences*, New York: Macmillan and The Free Press, pp. 16–19.
Michelini, L. (2005), 'Innovazione e sistemi economici comparati: il contributo di Enrico Barone e il pensiero economico italiano (1894–1924)', *Società e storia*, **28** (110), 741–97.
Petretto, A. (1982), 'Enrico Barone e i fondamenti della moderna teoria dell'allocazione delle risorse', *Rivista internazionale di scienze sociali*, **90** (1–2), 89–118.
Schumpeter, J.A. (1927), 'Introduction' to E. Barone, *Grundzüge der theoretischen Nationalökonomie*, Bonn: Schroeder.

Max Weber (1864–1920)

The scholarly reputation of Max Weber (1864–1920) has undergone extensive revision in recent years. In the mid-twentieth century he became a canonical figure for the development and dissemination of modern sociology and political science. This movement chiefly originated in the United States, and was based on a limited number of translations of his writings, and a particular interpretation of these translations. From the mid-1960s this wave met increasing opposition from a growing interest in the work of Karl Marx as the central theorist of modern capitalism, for whom economic interests and class conflict were the motor of human development. Weber's apparent emphasis upon rationalization as the principal narrative of modernity, together with what seemed an apolitical advocacy of value neutrality for the sciences, was widely considered a deficiency in comparison to Marx. However, during the 1980s interest in Marx's account of capitalism and historical development waned; and scholars began to demonstrate that Weber's contribution to the development of the social sciences, and to our understanding of modernity in general, was far more coherent and wide-ranging than had hitherto been generally realized. In 1984 the first of many volumes in a new *Max Weber Gesamtausgabe* (*MWG*) was published; and although this project was still unfinished 30 years later, the creation of an authoritative complete edition from his extensive and scattered writings, correspondence and lectures has played a significant part in raising the standard of international discussion of the history, present and future of the social sciences. Max Weber is no longer the founding father of "modern sociology"; he is instead now seen more clearly as the critical figure in the transformation of ancient discourses of law, politics and economics into the modern social sciences. To understand what this means we begin with his personal biography, link this to his activities and writings, and conclude by indicating some of his key theoretical innovations.

Family Background

Max Weber was born on 21 April 1864 in Erfurt, the eldest son of Max Weber (1836–1897) and Helene Fallenstein (1844–1919). Alfred Weber (1868–1958), who in 1909 published his important study of industrial location, was a younger brother. Max Weber senior's family had been active in the cloth trade around Bielefeld, but by mid-century their fortunes were declining; when he met Helene in Berlin in 1860 he was working for the Berlin City Council and was already active in politics. The family of Helene Fallenstein (née Souchay) had made its money in the Frankfurt cloth wholesale trade. Although Max Weber senior's career as a National Liberal politician would dominate the household in which Max Weber junior grew up, the family's wealth came through his wife (Roth 2001: 631–42). It would be the same, later, with Max Weber junior. When on 20 September 1893 he married his great-niece Marianne Schnitger (1870–1954) he had no regular source of income; he did in 1894 become Professor of Political Economy and Financial Science at Freiburg, but only nine years later he resigned his Heidelberg chair and in so doing lost his salary. Max and Marianne were for a period substantially dependent on Helene Fallenstein's generosity, until in 1907 Marianne finally came into a significant inheritance. From then on Max was supported financially by his wife (Radkau 2005: 450–52). Max and Marianne had no children.

He died in Munich on 14 June 1920 of pneumonia, following an infection of the lung contracted earlier that month. His posthumous reputation was quickly provided for by his widow, who saw a number of works through the press, collected correspondence, and then in 1926 published a biography that remains a central source for understanding the life and work of Max Weber (Hanke 2009).

In 1869 Max senior moved the family back to Berlin where he became first a city councillor, and then a deputy in the post-Unification Reichstag. Max Weber junior began his career as a law student in the summer semester of 1882 at Heidelberg University. After three semesters he moved to Strasbourg for one year of military service, following which he enrolled in Berlin for two semesters of Roman and German law. For the Winter Semester of 1885–86 he prepared for his state examinations in Göttingen, passing in May 1886; he then moved back into his parent's home in Berlin, where he would live until he moved to Freiburg in 1894.

He became an unpaid court clerk in Berlin and at the same time worked under the supervision of Levin Goldschmidt, Professor of Commercial Law, on a dissertation for which he was awarded a doctorate in August 1889 (Kaelber 2003: 6–9). In October 1890 Weber passed the second state law examination which formally qualified him to practise, but instead of pursuing this he turned to the study of Roman agrarian law. He attended Meitzen's seminar on agrarian history, and in October 1891 published for his Habilitation the *Römische Agrargeschichte*, qualifying on this basis to lecture on 1 February 1892. From the summer semester of 1892 he lectured in the Law Faculty, and when in May 1892 Goldschmidt had a stroke he also took over the lecturing of his former supervisor. He was not however made an "extraordinary" (that is, unpaid adjunct) professor of German and Commercial Law in the University of Berlin until November 1893.

His Early Career

In February 1892, soon after he had gained the right to teach, he agreed to write up a study of East Elbian rural labour relations, part of a national survey of rural labour that had been organized by the Verein für Sozialpolitik. By the end of the year he had worked through the survey questionnaires and written them up into a very substantial volume, on the basis of which he then made a summary presentation at the Verein meeting held in Berlin in March 1893. This presentation stood out clearly from all others both for its analytical clarity and substantive detail. The following month his Freiburg appointment was confirmed. He continued to lecture and write on these and related topics until the end of the decade, weaving his account of the development of agrarian capitalism in Eastern Germany into an analysis of the politics and economics of German social development (Tribe 1983).

The second project with which Weber became involved at about this time related to contemporary debate over the appropriate regulatory regime for German stock and commodity trading. It is not entirely clear when or where this involvement originated; before 1894 he had written nothing on the subject, but by December 1896 he was already recognized as one of Germany's leading financial economists and appointed as a scientific expert to a government committee alongside the elite of the business community and East Elbian landowners. During the summer of 1894 he completed a popular guide to stock and commodity exchanges for Friedrich Naumann's "Workers' Library", and also worked on a longer multipart article commissioned for the *Zeitschrift für das Gesammte Handelsrecht* on financial markets and regulation. During the winter semester of 1895–96 Weber lectured twice a week on "Money, Banking and Exchanges", and with this became the first professor to lecture on stock and commodity exchanges in a German university (Borchardt 1999: 103–4).

Having successfully made his entrance into the domain of contemporary economics in Freiburg, Weber succeeded Carl Knies as Professor of Political Economy in Heidelberg, teaching there from the summer semester of 1897. Knies, the last surviving member of the "Older Historical School" and whose lectures Weber had attended some 15 years before, wished to retire, and Weber was marked out as a promising young successor. For his theory lectures in the summer of 1898 he published an extensive reading list together with a partial outline, suggesting that he had in mind the publication of his own textbook (Tribe 2010). But during the summer semester he suffered some kind of breakdown while delivering his lecture course. Recovering from this, he then prepared a course on applied economics for the following winter semester, but again broke down while presenting it; subsequently he ceased lecturing, and eventually resigned his post.

The hiatus in Weber's life that his breakdown brought about is sometimes used to suggest that when, some five or six years later, Weber once again began to write and publish intensively, this represented a new beginning in which he discovered his true vocation, shifting the focus of his writing and of his thinking, creating in this way the canonical figure with whom we are familiar today. At this *Stunde Null* there can be found the 1903–05 essay on Roscher and Knies together with the 1904 "Objectivity" essay as foundational "methodological" works, and also of course the 1904–05 essays on the *Protestant Ethic* which went on to become his most well-known and accessible text. However, this only appears to be a new beginning for those unfamiliar with what went before. His trip to the USA in 1904 was brought about by an invitation to give a public lecture at the Universal Exposition in St Louis, where he presented a resumé of work he had done ten years previously. Peter Ghosh has pointed out that the conception of *Herrschaft* exposed here in the analysis of German rural relations links forward to formulations in the pre-war manuscripts from 1913–14, as well as to the formulation in 1919–20 of a "typology" of rulership as presented in *Economy and Society*, part I, chapter 3 (Ghosh 2005: 357 n. fe). Likewise, Weber's initial engagement with the German Sociological Society in 1910 was connected with his interest in the organization of a wide-ranging survey of the modern media, for which he drafted a detailed research proposal (Weber 1998), confirming his continuing interest in empirical social research. There are also a number of rhetorical and substantive affinities between his Freiburg inaugural lecture of 1895 and his lecture "Science as a Vocation", given in November 1917. Lack of familiarity with his extensive, and specialized, writings on agrarian social structure, ancient history, finance and law during the 1890s too often becomes a justification for their relegation to a formative "early" phase which can be duly neglected. This is however mistaken; while there is indeed a lull in Weber's activity, 1898–1903 were by no means the "lost years" that Marianne Weber later suggested, and only in 1901 did Weber publish nothing at all. Furthermore, there is a real continuity from his earliest writings on ancient economic history right through to his last lecture course in 1919–20, which presents an account of the development of capitalism in Europe; while much of the material which went into *Economy and Society* originates in this "early" period (Bruhns 2006).

While the period 1903–06 was indeed a highly productive one for Weber, there are other, similar, phases throughout his adult life: in, for example, 1892–95, 1913 and 1919–20.

The *Archiv*, the Protestant Ethic and the *Grundriss der Sozialökonomik*

In July 1903 Edgar Jaffé purchased the academic journal *Archiv für soziale Gesetzgebung und Statistik* from its owner Heinrich Braun largely, it seems, with Max Weber in mind. Werner Sombart had previously been in discussion with Braun concerning the future of the journal, and all three men now became the new editors of the retitled *Archiv für Sozialwissenschaft und Sozialpolitik* (Ghosh 2010). This rapidly established itself as the world's leading social science journal, very much due to the editorial direction which Max Weber gave, and not least to the fact that most of his essays henceforth appeared in its pages. The first issue appeared in April 1904, for which the "Objectivity" essay was composed as a set of guidelines on the management of a journal devoted to a new domain of study – the *Sozialwissenschaften* – as well as to topical problems of the day – *Sozialpolitik*. As an instance of the latter, in August 1906 Weber published in the *Archiv* his 250-page "essay" on the aftermath of the 1905 Russian Revolution, representing the kind of political journalism which the new journal sought to foster. In February the following year the journal carried his critique of Rudolf Stammler, which was to provide a red thread in his thinking through the 1913 essay on sociological categories, to his lecture course in Vienna in 1918, to chapter 1 of *Economy and Society*. The *Protestant Ethic* was also published here as two essays in November 1904 and June 1905, his replies to various critics reaching through to 1910. During these years he also wrote for newspapers about university politics, became involved in the creation of the German Sociological Society, and contributed to discussions at meetings of the *Verein für Sozialpolitik*. However, in terms of his core intellectual interests, the *Archiv* was the key vehicle for scholarly writing, besides providing him with a means of constructing an academic network for the new social sciences.

This would prove crucial for another project; alongside his work on the *Archiv* Weber also became the editor of a major new social science reference work, the *Grundriss der Sozialökonomik*, for which *Economy and Society* was conceived and written. Max Weber's work is today linked firmly to the publishing house of Mohr Siebeck; but this link was first developed through the publication of the *Archiv*. It was from this connection that the *Grundriss* emerged as a major project led by Weber.

In the early 1900s Paul Siebeck was the publisher of a well-known economics reference work, Schönberg's *Handbuch der politischen Ökonomie*. This had first appeared in 1882 as a two-volume work, but by 1896 revisions had expanded it to five volumes. By 1905 the text was seriously in need of updating, but Schönberg was by this time very old and no longer capable of undertaking the kind of revision that Siebeck thought necessary, and so in April he turned for advice to Max Weber. After protracted negotiations and, importantly, the death of Schönberg in January 1908, Max Weber agreed to take on the project of replacing the *Handbuch*, and he at once set to work devising a new structure and finding suitable contributors (Schluchter 2009). This all took up an inordinate amount of time, and eventually the first part was not published until August 1914, scarcely the most propitious time to be launching a comprehensive German account of "modern capitalism". Weber decided that there was no prospect of continuing his own work for the project until the war was concluded, and when he did so in 1919 the world looked very different from the way that it had in 1914. The final volume was not published until well into the 1920s, but the *Grundriss* as a whole remains an important indication of the breadth of Weber's interests and scholarly contacts, as well as suggestive of his very empirical interest in "capitalism", the recurring motif of contributions on trade, transport, credit, economic geography, forestry, agriculture and industrial structure.

Weber's own contribution to the *Grundriss* has come down to us as *Economy and Society*, which was assembled from his papers by Marianne Weber and Melchior Palyi shortly after his death. Only the first three chapters can be said to represent Weber's intentions at the time of his death, the remainder of the text dating from before the war and representing material that he would have extensively reworked. Quite how extensive such reworking would have been can be seen from a comparison of the 1913 essay on "Sociological Categories" with the eventual first chapter, "Basic Sociological Concepts". In fact the first three chapters of *Economy and Society* present a systematic template for the new interpretive social sciences and historical analysis; but these chapters have hardly ever been read in such terms, nor is it now possible to discern precisely what shape *Economy and Society* would have taken had Weber completed the process of revision that was ended so abruptly with his death.

The War: Political Activity and a Return to the University

When the European war broke out in the summer of 1914 Weber was broadly aligned with German national sentiment, although he also hoped that involvement in a European war would lead to major changes in Russian society. Quite how this would turn out is not something he fully anticipated; but the political analysis that he developed in wartime journalism and public speaking provided him with the means for his increasingly vocal critique of the German imperial government's conduct of the war, his parallel criticism of leftists and anarchists in the immediate post-war crisis, and positive arguments for the shaping of a new German democratic republic. His intensive programme of public speaking from 1917 to 1919 and involvement in the foundation of the German Democratic Party in 1918 suggests that a post-war career in liberal politics would have been a possibility; but his decision in 1919 to accept appointment as Lujo Brentano's successor in Munich's Chair of Political Economy is a strong indication that, despite his misgivings following his semester in Vienna the previous year, he now saw his future as an academic, and not as a politician.

It is, however, instructive to consider what he published during wartime. On the one hand, there are his political writings, ranging from journalism opposing unrestricted submarine warfare to his programmatic "Parliament and Government in a Reordered Germany: A Political Critique of Bureaucratic and Party Organization" (May 1918). On the other hand, all of the substantive new essays that went into the three-volume collected writings on the sociology of religion – on Confucianism, Buddhism and Judaism – were published in the *Archiv* between 1915 and 1918, representing almost the entirety of his wartime scholarly publication. As noted above, during this period he simply put to one side work on the *Grundriss*. If this disjuncture is of any significance, then it suggests two things.

First, we could perhaps view this intensive engagement with ancient religious systems as a form of wartime therapy; this work involved no academic controversy, rather it was a personal project whose prosecution required simply that he read, think and write. When he did during wartime present his scholarly credo in the form of the lecture "Science as a Vocation", delivered on 7 November 1917, the very day that the Bolshevik Revolution erupted in Petrograd, the main argumentative components of this are simply boilerplated from work that goes back in places to the 1890s. The lectures he gave in Vienna during the summer semester of 1918 systematized work he had already done in 1913. The essays on the sociology of religion represent by contrast a different level of work.

However, we also know that Weber was not a religious person, that he described himself as "unmusical" in this respect. If he ended up being thought of as a "sociologist of religion" this was certainly not his intention. As Peter Ghosh has observed, throughout the twentieth century Weber's most famous work, *The Protestant Ethic and the Spirit of Capitalism*, was discussed largely as if it were a book mostly "about" religion; whereas for Weber it was primarily "about" capitalism. If we are forced to summarize his work in two sentences, this would run as follows. He was driven by one question, and by the agenda which was its corollary. The question is, why did capitalism take root and flourish in Western Europe, and only in the West? The agenda that follows from this question is, the investigation of the "cultural problems of capitalism" as the prime task of an empirical social science. The latter is forcefully stated in the "Objectivity" essay of 1904, which is first and foremost a rubric for the new journal:

> [W]e characterize the prime work of our journal as the scientific investigation of *the general cultural significance of the social-economic structure of human communal life* and its historical forms of organization. . . . The social science that we wish to pursue is a *science of reality*. Our aim is an understanding of the *uniqueness* of the lived reality within which we are placed. We wish to understand on the one hand the context and cultural *significance* of individual phenomena as presently constituted; and on the other, the reasons for their being historically so and not otherwise. (Weber 2004: 370, 374, original emphases)

We could also reformulate the above question, and consequent agenda, as follows: the answer to the question is to be found in the relationship between acting human beings and the structures within which they find themselves; and so an agenda directed to the elaboration of the social sciences is the means of forming an adequate answer to the question.

Weber had already referred to elements of "agrarian capitalism" in his book on Roman agrarian history as well as in his essays on East Elbian rural structure. However, Werner Sombart's *Der moderne Kapitalismus* of 1902 was the first work to present an account of the formation of modernity in terms of capitalism, moving from the economic foundations to the creation of an urban culture and new forms of consumption. For Sombart the emergence of "capitalism" as a dominant form of European economic organization was chiefly attributable to double-entry book-keeping and the rationalization that it implied. Importantly the book II, part III, of the text was devoted to "The Genesis of the Capitalist Spirit", where he argues that the idea that Protestantism, and Calvinism especially, had played an important role in the development of capitalism, was too well-known to require any further discussion (Sombart 1902, I: 380–81).

So, if there is a "Weber thesis" about the rise of capitalism it cannot be what Sombart here offhandedly dismisses. Weber's leading question is the origin and continuing advance of occidental capitalism, as opposed to all that had once emerged in Rome, Byzantium, India and China but which, at one point or another, had simply been overwhelmed, or become ossified. Instead, Max Weber's two essays of 1904 and 1905 on the Protestant ethic sketch an account of the formation of a way of living life through the influence of religious belief – a social mechanism which first creates the "individual", then sets that individual to work in a rational and calculating manner pursuing not wealth for its own sake, but rather an ascetic, rational way of life pursued for its own sake. As it happens, this way of leading a life is undermined by the very thing that its practice creates: a capitalist order which becomes a "steel housing" displacing the values of ascetic Protestantism. The *Protestant Ethic* is therefore directed to rational "life conduct" (*Lebensführung*), its genesis, practice and consequences, as Wilhelm Hennis forcefully argued in his 1982 essay (Hennis 2000). If there is a "Weber thesis", then this is it.

Once this is clearly established it becomes easier to understand quite where Weber's arguments concerning the role of values in the prosecution of scholarship fit in. He has a question which implies an evaluation; but response to this question requires that values be first acknowledged, then set aside. This argument runs through the "Objectivity" essay, the 1913 memorandum written in response to Verein's discussion of the issue, and finally "Science as a Vocation". There Weber points out that without values there would be no science; for science cannot itself provide a rationale for doing science, that rationale is a product of the values of the human beings who dedicate themselves to the scientific life. In this respect "science" is the new religion of modernity.

KEITH TRIBE

See also:

Eugen von Böhm-Bawerk (I); German and Austrian schools (II); Karl Heinrich Marx (I); Wilhelm Georg Friedrich Roscher (I); Gustav Friedrich von Schmoller (I); Utilitarianism and anti-utilitarianism (III).

References and further reading

The best introduction in English to Max Weber's work remains Albert Salomon's "Max Weber's methodology" (1934). Although Weber himself detested "methodology", Salomon here summarizes skilfully and reliably both the continuity in his interests and the underlying arguments he advanced in the wide variety of his writings. The best single reader remains Gerth and Mills (1948), not least because all subsequent collections are modelled upon it. More specialized collections that can be recommended for the quality of their translations are (Weber 1994) and Dreijmanis (2008). Currently the most reliable edition of the *Protestant Ethic* is the Penguin edition of the 1904–05 essays (Weber 2002). Weber (1975) remains the single most useful biographical source for Weber's life. Recent developments in our understanding of Max Weber's life and work are best exemplified by Scaff (2011).

Borchardt, K. (1999), 'Einleitung', in K. Borchardt and C. Meyer-Stoll (eds), *Börsenwesen. Schriften und Reden 1893–1898, Max Weber Gesamtausgabe*, vol. I/5, Tübingen: Mohr Siebeck, pp. 1–111.
Bruhns, H. (2006), 'Max Weber's basic concepts in the context of his studies in economic history', *Max Weber Studies*, supplement I, 39–66.
Dreijmanis, J. (2008), *Max Weber's Complete Writings on Academic and Political Vocations*, trans. G.C. Wells, New York: Algora.
Gerth, H.H. and C. Wright Mills (1948), *From Max Weber*, London: Routledge.
Ghosh, P. (2005), 'Max Weber on the rural community: a critical edition of the English text', *History of European Ideas*, **31** (3), 327–66.
Ghosh, P. (2010), 'Max Weber, Werner Sombart and the *Archiv für Sozialwissenschaft*: the authorship of the "Geleitwort" (1904)', *History of European Ideas*, **36** (1), 71–100.

Hanke, E. (2009), '"Max Weber's Desk is now my Altar": Marianne Weber and the intellectual heritage of her husband', *History of European Ideas*, **35** (3), 349–59.

Hennis, W. (2000), 'Max Weber's central question', in W. Hennis, *Max Weber's Central Question*, trans. K. Tribe, 2nd edn, Newbury: Threshold Press, pp. 3–51.

Kaelber, L. (2003), 'Max Weber's dissertation in the context of his early career and life', in M. Weber, *The History of Commercial Partnerships in the Middle Ages*, trans. L. Kaelber, Lanham, MD: Rowman and Littlefield, pp. 1–47.

Radkau, J. (2005), *Max Weber. Die Leidenschaft des Denkens*, Munich: Carl Hanser Verlag.

Roth, G. (2001), *Max Webers deutsch-englische Familiengeschichte 1800–1950*, Tübingen: Mohr Siebeck.

Salomon, A. (1934), 'Max Weber's methodology', *Social Research*, **1** (2), 147–68.

Scaff, L. (2011), *Max Weber in America*, Princeton, NJ: Princeton University Press.

Schluchter, W. (2009), 'Entstehungsgeschichte', in *Max Weber Gesamtausgabe*, vol. I/24, Tübingen: J.C.B. Mohr (Paul Siebeck), pp. 1–31.

Sombart, W. (1902), *Der moderne Kapitalismus*, 2 vols, Leipzig: Duncker and Humblot.

Tribe, K. (1983), 'Prussian agriculture – German politics: Max Weber 1892–7', *Economy and Society*, **12**, 181–226, reprinted 1989 in *Reading Weber*, London: Routledge, pp. 85–130.

Tribe, K. (2010), 'Max Weber and the new economics', in H. Hagemann, T. Nishizawa and Y. Ikeda (eds), *Austrian Economics in Transition. From Carl Menger to Friedrich Hayek*, Basingstoke: Palgrave Macmillan, pp. 62–88.

Weber, M. (1975), *Max Weber. A Biography*, trans. H. Liebersohn. New York: John Wiley.

Weber, M. (1984–), *Max Weber Gesamtausgabe*, Tübingen: J.C.B. Mohr (Paul Siebeck).

Weber, M. (1994), *Political Writings*, eds P. Lassman and R. Speirs, Cambridge: Cambridge University Press.

Weber, M. (1998), 'Preliminary report on a proposed survey for a sociology of the press', *History of the Human Sciences*, **11** (2), 111–20.

Weber, M. (2002), *The Protestant Ethic and the 'Spirit' of Capitalism*, ed. and trans. by P. Baehr and G.C. Wells, London: Penguin Books.

Weber, M. (2004), 'The objectivity of knowledge in social science and social policy', trans. K. Tribe, in S. Whimster (ed.), *The Essential Weber*, London: Routledge, pp. 359–404.

Mikhail Ivanovich Tugan-Baranovsky (1865–1919)

Mikhail Ivanovich Tugan-Baranovsky was born on 8 January 1865, in the village of Solenoye near Kharkov (in Ukraine, at that time part of the Russian Empire). He received a classical education in Kiev and Kharkov. In 1883, he enrolled at St Petersburg University (physics and mathematics faculty). In 1886, he was arrested and exiled from St Petersburg to Kharkov for his participation in a student demonstration. He continued his education in Kharkov and in 1888 graduated from the law and science faculties of Kharkov University. In 1894, he received a Master's degree from Moscow University for a dissertation on industrial cycles and crises published in the same year (*Industrial Crises in Contemporary England, Their Causes and Immediate Influence on National Life*). His doctoral dissertation, on economic history, was published in 1898: *Russian Factory in Past and Present. Historical Development of the Russian Factory in the Nineteenth Century*.

His academic career was hampered by his political views and public activity. It was interrupted in 1899 when he was dismissed for 'political unreliability' and had to leave St Petersburg, spending five, albeit very productive, years on his estate in Poltava Province (Ukraine). During these years he was very active as an author, editor and founder (along with P.B. Struve) of two pro-Marxist journals, *Novoe slovo* (*New Word*) and *Nachalo* (*The Beginning*). His articles were published in *Mir Bozhii* (*God's World*), *Nauchnoe obozrenie* (*Scientific Review*), and other journals.

Tugan-Baranovsky returned to St Petersburg University in 1905, but finally moved to St Petersburg only in 1911. He also taught at the Polytechnic Institute (St Petersburg) and the Shanyavsky People's University (Moscow). Shortly after the February Revolution he returned to Ukraine and in August 1917 accepted the post of Minister of Finance in the Ukrainian Central Rada government. After the fall of the Central Rada in January 1918, he spent some months in Moscow before returning to Ukraine to become the dean of the law faculty at Kiev University and a founder of the Ukrainian Academy of Sciences and the Ukrainian cooperative movement. In January 1919, he was appointed head of the Ukrainian financial mission to France. He died of a heart attack on 21 January 1919, on his way from Kiev to Odessa to board a ship for France. He was buried in Odessa.

Tugan-Baranovsky had an extremely wide range of academic, social and spiritual interests. Like many other members of the Russian intelligentsia of his time he was deeply concerned with the political, social and economic prospects of Russian development, including the potential of capitalism and socialism in this country. He was not only involved in academic discussions on these matters, but also took part in the democratic movement and the political struggle. Like many Russian intellectuals he was deeply influenced by Marxism. He was attracted by its social ideal and sided with the Russian Marxists in their disputes with the *narodniki* (populists), arguing in favour of the possibility and reality of capitalist development in Russia. His 1898 historical and economic work – *Russian Factory in Past and Present* – contained a detailed analysis of industrial development in Russia and related socioeconomic trends, including the development of large- and small-scale industry in different historical periods, state policy, changes in legislation, and so on. This book became a weighty argument in support of the thesis that capitalist development in Russia was inevitable and already on the way.

Differences between Tugan-Baranovsky and the Marxists came to light at the very beginning of his research activities. V.I. Lenin called Tugan-Baranovsky, and also N.A. Berdyaev and S.N. Bulgakov, "legal Marxists". This became something of a cliché used in virtually all publications on the history of Russian thought. With this description, Lenin expressed his disapproval of the readiness of these economists to discuss the country's socioeconomic problems and Marxist issues in the legal (according to Lenin, bourgeois) press. But these differences had deeper roots and were connected with the attitude to Marxism in general. In contrast to Lenin, who took a rather dogmatic and radical view of Marxism, Tugan-Baranovsky assessed different aspects of Marx's economic theory differently, criticizing some of its key elements such as the labour theory of value and the theory of surplus value.

Business Cycle Analysis

Though the range of his investigations in economic theory and policy was very broad, Tugan-Baranovsky's place in the history of economics is primarily due to his works on business cycles and crises. The publication of his *Industrial Crises in Contemporary England* (1894) immediately attracted the attention of Russian and foreign economists. A final completely revised edition appeared in 1914 under the title *Periodic Industrial Crises. A History of English Crises. A General Theory of Crises.* In the author's lifetime, the book was published in German (1901) and French (1913); a Japanese translation appeared in 1931. Tugan-Baranovsky located the problem of crises in the context of a more general perspective on business cycles, which he considered inevitable in capitalist economy. He proposed an explanation of the cycle mechanism proper and pointed out the economic, institutional, social and political factors that influenced (in different periods in varying degree) the character of particular cycles and crises. Among these factors he identified long-term trends in capital accumulation, concentration of production, international division of labour and emergence of new markets, trade and monetary regimes, changes in central bank gold reserves, political events, and so on. He assigned an important role to changes in the social structure and income distribution, and to the trade union movement. He also studied the influence of current business conditions on the position of the working class. Thus, an entire section in the third edition of *Industrial Crises* (1914) was devoted to social topics.

An important part of the book was devoted to an empirical study of the history of English business cycles, which is impressive both in scope and depth. One of the most important topics discussed was the periodization of British economic history, specifying different sub-periods with regard to prevalent trade policy and monetary policy regimes, which affected the amplitude of cycles and crises. He also analysed the sequence of events happening during specific crises in the nineteenth century. His analysis provided empirical arguments for a decisive role of investment in capital goods in shaping the cyclical dynamics of production. Tugan-Baranovsky, followed by Arthur Spiethoff in Germany, paid special attention to the dynamics of prices of pig iron, which coincided with phases of business cycles. According to him cyclical fluctuations are transferred from industries producing capital goods to the economy on the whole. In the article "Krizisy, ekonomicheskie" ("Crises, economic") written for *The Brockhaus and Efron Encyclopedic Dictionary* he provided a typology of economic crises, dividing them into monetary, credit, and trade-industrial crises, and emphasized that business cycles do not have any fixed duration.

The second part of the book was devoted to a critical analysis of existing theories of gluts and business cycles and development of the author's own concepts. Tugan-Baranovsky argued both against the position of the classical economists, who claimed that general overproduction was impossible (Say's law), and against the position of their opponents, who pointed to the insolubility of the "realization problem" in the expanding capitalist economy (Malthus, Sismondi).

Like his contemporaries Tugan-Baranovsky did not provide any coherent theoretical model of business cycles, but explored several relevant issues, giving important impetus to subsequent research. One of the issues was the

> antagonistic nature of the capitalist economy, with the workers considered only as a means of production. An inadequate distribution of income did not provide sufficient purchasing power to working classes. The large share of income, which was received by capitalists in the form of profits, had no immediate link to consumption and entailed a possible risk of crises. However, arguing against the theories which base the explanation of business cycles on underconsumption (Sismondi etc.), and using Marxian reproduction schemes, Tugan-Baranovsky showed that consumption does not set a limit on production because the driving force of capitalist production is not consumption but the accumulation of capital. Thus an expanding reproduction could in principle take place (even with a declining consumption) through the increase of produced capital goods. But all the produced goods should be sold, and this requires an allocation of capital and labour between industries in a certain proportion. Otherwise there will be an overproduction of some commodities and, since all industries are interrelated, a state of the market known as a general overproduction of commodities (general glut), characterized by a mass of unsold goods and falling prices. (Tugan-Baranovsky 1894: 434)

Crises are inevitable under capitalism because of the lack of any mechanism for coordinating different industries. This issue the author called "disproportionality".

Another issue investigated by Tugan-Baranovsky in his theory of cycles was the interaction between two processes: the accumulation of real capital, mainly in industry and construction, and the movement of finance capital, primarily of the part he called free money capital or free loanable capital, stored in banks in the form of short-term or demand deposits. The sources of this capital, he believed, were the profits of those entrepreneurs who did not invest their capital in the areas where these profits were generated, but mostly the savings of those whose earnings were not directly associated with the business cycle. This meant that its accumulation was relatively stable. In the expansion phase of the business cycle these accumulated funds were spent for financing industrial projects and became exhausted raising the interest rates. However, during the contraction phase a large amount of liquid assets seeking profitable investment was accumulated. Because of the chaotic nature of the capitalist economy free loanable capital could not initially find profitable use, but when it became abundant enough to "break the resistance of industry" it was invested in industry. This ushered in the upward phase of the cycle.

Economic Theory of Socialism

In the field of the economic theory of socialism, Tugan-Baranovsky addressed two essential problems: the problem of the value of goods under socialism and the problem of achieving a social optimum, that is, of determining how the planning authorities should act in order to guarantee the corresponding allocation of resources that would lead to "the maximum of public benefit". As he saw it, direct accounting in terms of labour inputs not through wages but in working hours – was possible, though not easy, under socialism; it was a way to avoid treating labour as a commodity and so to follow the Kantian ethical principle. In addressing the second task, he referred to his very first published work – the article entitled "A doctrine of marginal utility of economic goods, as a cause of their value" (1890). In this paper, he tried to combine a labour theory of value explaining the objective factor of value and a marginal utility theory dealing with the subjective factor of value. On the basis of his arguments N. Stolyarov formulated in 1902 a "theorem" which purported to prove quantitative correlations of labour inputs and marginal utilities for freely reproducible goods in the case of an optimal allocation of resources: "the relations of marginal utilities of freely reproduced products and their labour costs are equal" (Stolyarov 1902: 4). Tugan-Baranovsky believed that the government could reveal individual preferences by using a price mechanism similar to the Walrasian auctioneer. Characteristically, Walrasian relative prices turn out to be genuine prices of the socialist economy, while the medium of accounting – the Walrasian *numéraire* – reflects the essence of money under socialism: "a mere symbol with no value at all". So, in the economic theory of socialism Tugan-Baranovsky was to a certain extent a predecessor of the theory of market socialism.

The Methodology of Political Economy

Tugan-Baranovsky identified two components of political economy: theoretical (subdivided into abstract and concrete) and practical (or economic policy). The task of abstract theoretical political economy, as he saw it, was to reveal general objective laws and regularities in economic life. This task was to be achieved in two stages: (1) a description leading to the construction of a system of general concepts; (2) an explanation resulting in a set of causal regularities. The main method here is deduction. Induction is used in concrete political economy, which studies historically specific types of economies. For Tugan-Baranovsky there is no impenetrable wall between these two parts: empirical analysis often precedes theoretical analysis and is used to evaluate a theory. Theoretical political economy is contrasted with practical political economy, closely associated with some ethical principles. According to Tugan-Baranovsky, the only ethical principle that could provide an acceptable normative basis for practical political economy was the Kantian principle of the supreme value and equipollence of the human personality. Tugan-Baranovsky advocated a separation of the two parts of political economy, emphasizing that the penetration of ethics into scientific analysis calls into question the objectivity of science. However, he admitted that in view of the specific subject matter of political economy the ethical element is already present at the stage of the description and concept formation. That is why he saw the problem of the objectivity of economic knowledge as a very difficult one. He hoped that a scholar seeking objective knowledge would not mix the normative and positive approaches. His main complaint against Marxism was that Marxists based their theory on the class approach, so casting doubt on its objectivity. He believed that many of the mistakes of Marxism, including the thesis about the tendency of the rate of profit to fall and the resulting inevitable collapse of the capitalist economic system, were ultimately associated with this methodological bias.

VLADIMIR AVTONOMOV AND NATALIA MAKASHEVA

See also:

Albert Aftalion (I); Enrico Barone (I); Business cycles and growth (III); Corporatism (III); Economics and philosophy (III); Clément Juglar (I); Karl Heinrich Marx (I); Marxism(s) (II); Russian School of mathematical economics (II); Arthur Spiethoff (I).

References and further reading

Barnett, V. (2005), *A History of Russian Economic Thought*, New York: Routledge.
Howard, M.C. and J.E. King (1989), *A History of Marxian Economics*, vol. 1. Princeton, NJ: Princeton University Press.
Makasheva, N.A. (2008), 'Searching for an ethical basis of political economy', in V. Barnett, and J. Zweynert (eds), *Economics in Russia*, Aldershot and Burlington, VT: Ashgate, pp. 75–90.
Nove, A. (1998), 'Tugan-Baranovsky, Mikhail Ivanovich', in J. Eatwell, M. Milgate and P. Newman (eds), *The New Palgrave. A Dictionary on Economics*, vol. 4, New York and Basingstoke: Palgrave, pp. 705–6.
Stolyarov, N. (1902), *Analiticheskoe dokazatel'stvo predlozhennoi g. M. Tugan-Baranovskim politiko-ekonomicheskoi formuly: Predel'nye poleznosti svobodno proizvedennykh blag proportzionalny ich trudovym stoimostyam* (*Analitical Proof of the Political-Economic Formula Proposed by Mr. M. Tugan-Baranovsky, According to Which Marginal Utilities of Freely Produced Goods Are Proportional to Their Labour Values*), Kiev: S.V. Kulzhenko.
Tugan-Baranovsky, M.I. (1890), 'Uchenie o predel'noi poleznosti khozyaistvennych blag, kak prichine ich stoimosti' ('A doctrine of marginal utility of economic goods as a cause of their value'), *Yuridicheskii vestnik*, **1**: 192–230.
Tugan-Baranovsky, M.I. (1894), *Promyshlennye krizisy v sovremennoi Anglii, ich prichiny i blizhayshee vliyanie na narodnuyu zhizn'* (*Industrial Crises in Contemporary England, Their Causes and Immediate Influence on National Life*), St Petersburg: I.N. Skorokhodov Printing House.
Tugan-Baranovsky, M.I. (1898), *Russkaya fabrika v proshlom i nastoyashchem: Istoricheskoe razvitie russkoi fabriki v XIX veke* (*Russian Factory in Past and Present. Historical Development of Russian Factory in the Nineteenth Century*), St Petersburg: L.F. Panteleev.
Tugan-Baranovsky, M.I. (1901), *Studien zur Theorie und Geschichte der Handelskrisen in England*, Jena: G. Fischer.
Tugan-Baranovsky, M.I. (1908), 'Metodologiya politicheskoi ekonomii' ('Methodology of political economy'), *Obrazovanie*, **12**, 1–19.
Tugan-Baranovsky, M.I. (1909), *Osnovy politicheskoi ekonomii* (*Foundations of Political Economy*), St Petersburg: Printing House 'Slovo'.
Tugan-Baranovsky, M.I. (1913), *Les crises industrielles en Angleterre*, Paris: M. Giard and É. Brière.
Tugan-Baranovsky, M.I. (1914), *Pereodicheskie promyshlennye krizisy. Istoriya angliyskikh krizisov. Obshchayy teoriya krizisov*, St Petersburg: Tovarishchestvo O.N.Popovoy.
Tugan-Baranovsky, M.I. (1917), *Bumazhnye den'gi i metal* (*Paper Money and Metal*), Petrograd: Book Store 'Law'.
Tugan-Baranovsky, M.I. (1918), *Socializm kak polozhitel'noe uchenie* (*Socialism as a Positive Doctrine*), Petrograd: Kooperaciya.
Tugan-Baranovsky, M.I. (1931), *Eikoku Kyoukou Shiron*, Tokyo: Nihon Hyouron Sya.

Gustav Cassel (1866–1945)

Opinions about the Swedish economist Gustav Cassel (1866–1945) have varied over time. Before the First World War, he made himself known as a progressive liberal who advocated social reform and trade unions as means to increase labour productivity and economic growth. In the 1920s, he was considered to be "the most influential leader of our science" (Schumpeter 1954: 1154). He advised the League of Nations and national governments on monetary policy issues, and attracted worldwide attention as a lecturer and writer of textbooks, pamphlets and articles. In the wake of the Great Depression, Cassel fell out of favour with public opinion, due to his opposition to the "new economics" of the Stockholm School, Keynes and other advocates of fiscal activism. His image shifted from that of a skilful popularizer of complex theory and "pragmatic truths" to that of a conceited vulgarizer, if not plagiarizer of Walras. In the 1980s, Cassel was reappraised as a "pioneer" of growth theory, monetary targeting, the notion of revealed preferences, and other concepts. Since then, many of these claims have been disputed or downsized.

Life

Karl Gustav Cassel was born into a merchant family in Stockholm in 1866. After taking a doctoral degree in mathematics in 1895, Cassel turned to studies in economics. In 1898 and 1899 he went to Germany to attend lectures of Gustav Schmoller, Adolph Wagner and other representatives of the historical school and *Kathedersozialisten* (socialists of the chair). On visits to England in 1901 and 1902 he made the acquaintance of Alfred Marshall and Sidney and Beatrice Webb. The encounter with German *Kathedersozialismus* and British Fabianism left its traces in Cassel's book on social policy (1902), in which he made a case for improvements in the living conditions of the working class, with the aim of increasing the productivity of labour. He argued that general economic progress would be fostered by workers' education, by giving trade unions responsibility for wages and employment, and by using public works to counter unemployment (Boianovsky and Trautwein 2003). With regard to capital, Cassel published a treatise on *The Nature and Necessity of Interest* (1903), in which he rejected Böhm-Bawerk's utility-based theory of interest and defined the rate of interest as the "price for waiting". According to Cassel, this price – just as all other prices of factors and goods, relative and in terms of money – is governed by the "principle of scarcity", which he expounded from his first "outline of an elementary theory of prices" (1899) to his last writings in the 1940s. His magnum opus was the *Theory of Social Economy* (*Theoretische Sozialökonomie*, 1918). This was a textbook originally designed for the German language area and completed by 1914. Owing to the war, the book was not published before 1918. Even though Cassel made few additions and no substantial changes in the many editions and translations to other languages that followed, the book advanced to a leading text in the interwar years (Sandelin and Trautwein 2010). This success is explained by Cassel's clear, didactic writing style, and by his reputation as leading economist that he acquired in Sweden before the First World War, and on the international level shortly after.

In 1901 Cassel had competed unsuccessfully with Knut Wicksell for a professor's position at the University of Lund. From 1904 until retirement in 1933 Cassel was professor of political economy and public finance at the University of Stockholm. Working as adviser to the government, lecturing and writing articles for newspapers (more than 1500 over the years), all on a wide range of political issues, he became a public authority in Sweden (Carlson and Jonung 2006).

After the First World War, Cassel rose to international prominence. On invitation of the League of Nations, he spoke at high-level conferences and wrote two important memoranda on *The World's Monetary Problems* (Cassel 1921). He recommended a return to the gold standard as a means to restore international economic order, but warned against the risks of deflation and depression which would result from returning to pre-war parities. Cassel (1921) proposed to fix exchange rates in terms of purchasing power parities, in line with his quantity-theoretical approach to exchange-rate determination that he had developed in his textbook (1918: ch. 12). Throughout the 1920s and 1930s, Cassel published and lectured intensively about the monetary policy issues of the day. Together with John Maynard Keynes, he criticized the Versailles treaty on German war reparations as a threat to the international economic order. The zenith of his career was reached in 1928, when he was invited to speak to the US House of Representatives, where he was introduced as "the world's foremost economist" (Cassel 1940: 315).

In September 1931 the Great Depression had reached the point at which Britain abandoned the gold standard. Cassel "saw the event as a worldwide economic disaster and stressed that Sweden must mobilize all resources to defend the connection between the krona and gold" (Carlson 2011: 33). A few days later, however, when Sweden was forced to let exchange rates float, it was Cassel who drafted the finance minister's statement that the aim was now "to defend the internal purchasing power of the Swedish krona with all means at hand" (ibid.: 34). Together with Erik Lindahl, Cassel was a driving force behind the experiment of price-level targeting, carried out successfully by the Swedish central bank between 1931 and 1937 – long before this strategy became popular in the 1970s.

In social matters, however, Cassel had turned from a social liberal, who hailed trade unions as promoters of economic progress, to a conservative, who gave them much of the blame for mass unemployment. He argued that the depression could not be cured by public works or other fiscal policies, which would only crowd out private investment. Instead Cassel advocated monetary policies that stop deflation, plus downward adjustments of money wages to lowered price levels – a policy resisted by the unions. Already in 1926, when German unemployment had risen strongly within a short time, Cassel had run a widely debated article campaign in German newspapers and journals, in which he denounced public works and unemployment benefits as measures that distort the price system and increase unemployment (Sandelin and Trautwein 2009: 84). In his critique of Keynes's diagnosis of unemployment as an effective demand failure, Cassel (1937) insisted on the general validity of Say's law. He argued that the Great Depression was caused by flawed monetary policies, state interventionism and irresponsible behaviour of the unions. He found himself increasingly isolated, as the tides of academic views and public opinion had changed in favour of a more active role for the state. Cassel's voluminous memoirs, which carry the self-confident title *In the Service of Reason* (1940: 315, 1941: 195), end with some bitterness and the following words: "It fell to my lot to work in the service of reason . . . He who fights for reason must give himself to the struggle, sticking it out though he finds himself standing alone" (quoted after Carlson and Jonung

2006: 522). Cassel died in January 1945. It is reported that his last words were: "A world currency!" (Gustafsson 1987: 377).

Works

It is no easy task to assess Cassel's contributions to economics. His success as a popularizer of economics was, in his own view, based on his emphasis on simplification of theory to bring out its "essentials", on realism, and on political engagement in the non-partisan "service of reason". Cassel's critics argued, however, that his general equilibrium framework was simplistic and incomplete, that he confused positive and normative thinking, and that, in his conceited manner, he was incapable of contributing to a fruitful discourse. With hindsight it might nevertheless be argued that Cassel managed to set some impulses for the progress of economic thinking.

According to Cassel, it all started in the summer of 1898, in the little university town of Tübingen, a place in Southern Germany that he liked for its mountains and plane tree-lined avenues. "The economic teaching, on the contrary, I found most unsatisfactory and almost ridiculous", he remembered in his memoirs (1940: 15). Rejecting the widely taught, but "worthless" concepts of value, Cassel became fully convinced of his historical mission: "During these weeks, my decision to abolish the whole theory of value and build up an economic theory directly on a study of price formation came to maturity" (ibid.). Soon thereafter Cassel published his outline of an elementary theory of prices, explaining in the introduction: "Of the authors that can . . . be regarded as my predecessors, only Walras be mentioned here. It is deplorable that he deprived himself of a wider readership by using an extraordinarily clumsy mathematical apparatus." (1899: 396, my translation). Cassel simplified Walras's general equilibrium theory to the extent of doing away with "utility metaphysics", and value theory in general, in favour of the "universal principle of scarcity". In his *Sozialökonomie* (1918), he used this principle to integrate the quantity theory of money and business cycle theory with a general equilibrium analysis in which all prices are expressed in terms of money. He no longer referred to Walras: "Since the theory is based on foundations that differ strongly from the conventional, the examination of other opinions would mostly have been rather sterile" (Cassel 1918: v, my translation).

Moreover, Cassel's unifying use of the scarcity principle did not imply that he had overcome the neoclassical dichotomy of the determination of relative prices and money prices – on the contrary:

> In the general economic theory we must reckon all values in a unit of money. The value of this unit itself cannot be determined there. To do this is the separate function of the theory of money. The central point of this theory is that the value of the unit is determined by the scarcity of the means of payment valid in the given monetary system. (Cassel 1918 [1932], vol. 1: v–vi)

Likewise, business cycles were described in terms of the scarcity of savings, where variations in the production of fixed capital result from "an over-estimate of the supply of capital, or of the amount of savings available for taking over the real capital produced" (Cassel 1918 [1932] vol. 2: 649).

Even though Cassel (1918) refused to refer to Walras, he helped to revive interest in Walrasian general equilibrium analysis, which had been largely lost out of sight by the 1890s. Chapter 4 of his *Sozialökonomie* (1918) contains a model of a perfectly competitive, closed and stationary economy, in which goods are produced by making use of factor services, with a technology defined by fixed technical coefficients. The system consists of several sets of equations. The first, in Cassel's order, describes the prices of final goods as equal to their production costs in "free competition". The second set determines the demand for each final good as a function of the prices of all final goods. The third set states the market clearing conditions for all goods: "[T]he fixing of prices in accordance with the principle of scarcity has to restrict the demand until it can be met out of the available supply of commodities" (Cassel 1918 [1932] vol. 1: 137). The fourth set uses technical coefficients of the production functions to state the market clearing conditions for the factors of production. All four sets constitute a system of simultaneous equations by which equilibrium prices, costs and quantities are determined jointly. As the number of unknowns in the system is equal to the number of equations, the system satisfies the criterion of completeness. To Cassel, this was sufficient proof of the existence of a unique general equilibrium solution. He argued, though only verbally, that this proof could also be given for a "uniformly progressing economy", in which factor supplies and demands for goods are increased at a fixed identical rate such that aggregate output grows along a steady-state path.

Ignoring the complexities of value theory, Cassel managed to model the interaction of markets in a price system, where only consumer preferences, technology and factor endowments are exogenous. His analytical framework became thus the "proximate starting point of the development of modern neoclassical general equilibrium theory" (Kurz and Salvadori 1995: 408). Using the logic of this framework, Cassel invoked Say's law to argue, contra Keynes and others, that there is nothing such as involuntary unemployment, as long as factor prices (both wages and interest) are allowed to move freely (Boianovsky and Trautwein 2003).

Impact

The first reactions to Cassel's *Theory of Social Economy* were not all positive. Wicksell (1919) wrote a long and devastating review, in which he drew attention to numerous inconsistencies and shortcomings, starting from the demonstration that Cassel's rejection of value theory is flawed, because "scarcity and marginal utility are fundamentally one and the same thing" (1919 [1934]: 221). Furthermore, Wicksell chided Cassel for not giving due credit to Walras and other old masters for the ideas that he had taken from them. In Swedish academia, Wicksell's review amounted to a severe blow to Cassel's reputation.

Later, the Stockholm School came to work with Wicksell's ideas rather than Cassel's. However, Gunnar Myrdal, Bertil Ohlin, Erik Lundberg and other members of the Stockholm School had been students of Cassel, and some of their main contributions clearly bear traces of Cassel's influence. The origin of Ohlin's (1933) theory of interregional trade, which became the core of neoclassical trade theory, was an attempt to extend Cassel's model of price determination in one economy to a model of exchange between several economies. Cassel's name could easily be added to the "Heckscher–Ohlin" label of that theory, even if Ohlin greatly expanded the scope of Cassel's general equilibrium analysis, not only by extending it to the multi-economy case, but also by endogenizing the technical coefficients as cost-minimizing variables (Samuelson 2002). Myrdal's (1927) dissertation on price formation and change extended Cassel's static system to more dynamic considerations of uncertainty and the formation of expectations. It marked the beginning of the Stockholm School, which developed from central macroeconomic insights of Wicksell, but sided with Cassel in critique of Wicksell's value-theoretical concept of the natural rate of interest. The other impacted dissertation, often taken to mark the end of the Stockholm School, is Lundberg's *Studies in the Theory of Economic Expansion* (1937), which contains a formalization of Cassel's "uniformly progressing economy". In his sequence analysis of unstable growth processes, Lundberg made use of that formalization to work out the Harrod–Domar conditions for steady-state growth – several years before Harrod and Domar did it (Berg 1991). In terms of domestic impact, it should finally be noted that Gösta Rehn, one of the architects of the post-war "Swedish model" of economic policy, was a student of Cassel. Some of the core ideas of this social-democratic strategy of "structural rationalization", such as the combination of solidaristic wage policy ("equal pay for equal work") and mobility-enhancing labour market policy, can be traced back to Cassel (1902).

As the leading textbook in the interwar period, Cassel's *Sozialökonomie* also gave impulses for theoretical advances outside Sweden, especially in the fields of exchange-rate determination, Walrasian general equilibrium theory and business cycle theory. Cassel's concept of purchasing power parity (PPP) as a fundamental explanation of exchange rates among "free and independent currencies" has been generally acknowledged as the base of modern exchange-rate theories. In the field of Walrasian general equilibrium theory, Cassel's contribution to progress was more indirect. Cassel's claim to have proved the existence of a unique general equilibrium by the criterion of completeness was critically examined by Hans Neisser (1932), Frederik Zeuthen (1932), and Heinrich von Stackelberg (1933), who (in this order) showed that completeness is not sufficient to guarantee a solution that makes economic sense (in terms of non-negative prices), that the system ought to be written as inequalities, and that it could be overdetermined. These problems provoked debate in Karl Menger's Mathematical Colloquium at Vienna and led, in 1935–36, to Abraham Wald's proof of the existence of a unique equilibrium in a stationary Walras–Cassel economy, which in turn prepared the ground for the Arrow–Debreu model, nowadays the standard of Walrasian general equilibrium theory.

Another area in which Cassel made an impact is business-cycle theory. In the 1920s and 1930s, the German language arena saw lively debates about the compatibility of general equilibrium analysis with a general explanation of industrial fluctuations. Together with Arthur Spiethoff, Cassel was the most prominent proponent of a non-monetary overinvestment theory of business cycles, while his general equilibrium framework became the representative target of attack from all camps. Friedrich Lutz (1932) criticized Cassel extensively for explaining cyclical fluctuations by populistic mixes of theory and stylized facts, instead of consistently sticking to general equilibrium analysis proper. Lutz argued that cycles could all be explained within the latter's confines, since they either represent exogenous changes in the data or endogenous reactions of the system – a view that resembles the use of Ragnar Frisch's "impulse-propagation" terminology in modern mainstream economics.

Yet it was precisely Cassel's skilful mix of a primitive relativity theory of market interaction with pragmatic shortcuts to the explanation of stylized facts that made both

Cassel and Walrasian-style theory popular in the 1920s. When general-equilibrium approaches to business cycle theory became popular in the 1980s, Cassel was rediscovered as a pioneer of business cycle theory, growth theory, monetary targeting, revealed preferences and other concepts (Brems 1989). Such claims have later been disputed and downsized (Samuelson 1993), but it may still be argued that Cassel's provocative simplifications have had catalytic effects on the development of economic thinking.

HANS-MICHAEL TRAUTWEIN

See also:

Business cycles and growth (III); General equilibrium theory (III); Open economy macroeconomics (III); Stockholm (Swedish) School (II); Marie-Esprit-Léon Walras (I); Knut Wicksell (I).

References and further reading

Berg, C. (1991), 'Lundberg, Keynes, and the riddles of a general theory', in L. Jonung (ed.), *The Stockholm School of Economics Revisited*, Cambridge: Cambridge University Press, pp. 205–28.

Boianovsky, M. and H.-M. Trautwein (2003), 'Wicksell, Cassel and the idea of involuntary unemployment', *History of Political Economy*, **35** (3), 385–436.

Brems, H. (1989), 'Gustav Cassel revisited', *History of Political Economy*, **21** (2), 165–78.

Carlson, B. (2011), 'From the gold standard to price level targeting: Swedish monetary policy in the daily press', *Sveriges Riksbank Economic Review*, **2011** (1), 29–64.

Carlson, B. and L. Jonung (2006), 'Wicksell, Cassel, Heckscher, Ohlin and Myrdal on the role of the economist in public debate', *Econ Journal Watch*, **3** (3), 511–50.

Cassel, G. (1899), 'Grundriss einer elementaren Preislehre', *Zeitschrift für die gesamte Staatswissenschaft*, **55** (4), 395–458.

Cassel, G. (1902), *Socialpolitik*, Stockholm: Gebers.

Cassel, G. (1903), *The Nature and Necessity of Interest*, London: Macmillan.

Cassel, G. (1918), *Theoretische Sozialökonomie*, Leipzig: C.F. Winter, English trans. 1923, 2nd edn 1932, *The Theory of Social Economy*, 2 vols, London: Ernest Benn.

Cassel, G. (1921), *The World's Monetary Problems: Two Memoranda*, London: Constable.

Cassel, G. (1937), 'Keynes' *General Theory*', *International Labour Review*, **36** (4), 437–45.

Cassel, G. (1940), I förnuftets tjänst, vol. 1, Stockholm: Natur och kultur.

Cassel, G. (1941), I förnuftets tjänst, vol. 2, Stockholm: Natur och kultur.

Gustafsson, B. (1987), 'Cassel, Gustav', in *The New Palgrave Dictionary of Economics*, vol. 1, 2nd edn, London: Palgrave Macmillan, pp. 375–77.

Kurz, H.D. and N. Salvadori (1995), *Theory of Production. A Long-Period Analysis*, Cambridge: Cambridge University Press.

Lundberg, E. (1937), *Studies in the Theory of Economic Expansion*, London: P.S. King.

Lutz, F. (1932), *Das Konjunkturproblem in der Nationalökonomie*, Jena: Gustav Fischer.

Myrdal, G. (1927), *Prisbildning och föränderligheten*, Uppsala: Almqvist & Wiksell.

Neisser, H. (1932), 'Lohnhöhe und Beschäftigungsgrad im Marktgleichgewicht', *Weltwirtschaftliches Archiv*, **36** (2), 415–55.

Ohlin, B. (1933), *Interregional and International Trade*, Cambridge, MA: Harvard University Press.

Samuelson, P. (1993), 'Gustav Cassel's scientific innovations: claims and realities', *History of Political Economy*, **25**, 515–27.

Samuelson, P. (2002), 'My Bertil Ohlin', in R. Findlay, L. Jonung and M. Lundahl (eds), *Bertil Ohlin. A Centennial Celebration (1899–1999)*, Cambridge, MA: MIT Press, pp. 51–62.

Sandelin, B. and H.-M. Trautwein (2010), 'The Baltic exchange: mutual influences between economists in the German and Swedish language areas', in H.D. Kurz (ed.), *Studien zur Entwicklung der ökonomischen Theorie XXIV*, Berlin: Duncker & Humblot, pp. 65–96.

Schumpeter, J.A. (1954), *History of Economic Analysis*, London: Allen & Unwin.

Stackelberg, H. von (1933), 'Zwei kritische Bemerkungen zur Preistheorie Gustav Cassels', *Zeitschrift für Nationalökonomie*, **4**, 456–72.

Wicksell, K. (1919), 'Professor Cassels nationalekonomiska system', *Ekonomisk Tidskrift*, **21**, 195–226, English trans. 1934, in *Lectures on Political Economy*, vol. 1, London: Routledge, Kegan & Paul, pp. 219–57.

Zeuthen, F. (1932), 'Das Prinzip der Knappheit, technische Kombination und ökonomische Qualität', *Zeitschrift für Nationalökonomie*, **4** (1), 1–24.

Irving Fisher (1867–1947)

Life

Irving Fisher was praised by Schumpeter in his obituary as America's "greatest scientific economist" (Schumpeter 1948 [1951]: 223). Fisher was born on 27 February 1867 in Saugerties-on-Hudson, New York, as the son of a clergyman. His mother Ella Wescott descended from an old New England family. Thus Fisher grew up in a religious environment which probably contributed to the missionary zeal that characterized his personal life. He graduated from the Smith Academy, St Louis in June 1884. A few weeks later his father died because of tuberculosis, just after Fisher had been admitted to Yale College. Fisher remained closely associated with Yale for the rest of his life. With his remarkable mathematical abilities, he graduated first in his class with a BA degree in 1888. Furthermore, he published poems and political commentaries and was a successful rower.

Fisher remained at Yale for graduate studies mainly in mathematics and economics but also in philosophy and the sciences. His mentor was the physicist and mathematician Josiah Willard Gibbs. In economics he got stimulus from the industrial economist and later president of Yale University, Arthur Twining Hadley, who induced him to read the works of Francis Amasa Walker, the founding president of the American Economic Association. His main influence, however, was William Graham Sumner, with whose free market and Social Darwinist views he did not agree, but who suggested that he engage more in mathematical economics and study the newly published work *Investigations on the Theory of Price* by the two Austrians Auspitz and Lieben (1889). In April 1891 Fisher earned a PhD from Yale as the first doctoral candidate in pure economics with his meanwhile classical *Mathematical Investigations in the Theory of Value and Prices* (1892) which, according to Samuelson (1967: 22), was the "greatest Ph.D. dissertation ever written in economics". Shortly afterwards the mathematical department appointed Fisher as assistant professor.

In June 1893 Fisher married Margaret Hazard (1867–1940) with whom he had two daughters and one son who became his biographer (Fisher 1956). They spent the next 14 months in Europe where Fisher developed closer personal contacts with almost all leading contemporary economists who would play a role in his own work: Francis Y. Edgeworth in Oxford, Alfred Marshall in Cambridge, Léon Walras and Vilfredo Pareto in Lausanne, Maffeo Pantaleoni in Rome, Enrico Barone in Florence and Carl Menger, Eugen von Böhm-Bawerk, Friedrich von Wieser and Richard Lieben in Vienna. During his stay in Berlin, Fisher preferred to study with the mathematician Ferdinand Georg Frobenius and the physicist Hermann von Helmholtz rather than with Gustav Schmoller and Adolph Wagner.

Back in New Haven, Fisher resumed his teaching activity with a course on the theory of numbers in September 1894. In the following year he transferred from the mathematics department to the political economy department where he was appointed full professor in 1898. Shortly afterwards he fell ill with tuberculosis and spent the next three years in a sanitorium. After recovery Fisher, who had already been a vegetarian refusing alcohol and tobacco before his disease, started a lifelong crusade for a healthier nutrition and a more hygienic lifestyle. Thus most American soldiers in World War I had Fisher's pamphlet on "The effect of diet on endurance" (1907b) in their knapsack. Moreover Fisher was an ardent eugenicist who in 1913, together with Harold A. Ley, co-founded the Life Extension Institute. With its acting manager, Eugene Lyman Fisk, he wrote *How to Live. Rules for Healthful Living Based on Modern Science* (1915) which soon became the standard textbook on hygiene for high schools and colleges, and went into 21 editions until 1945 (Allen 1993: 139–40).

After Fisher had resumed teaching at Yale, there followed a period of extremely high scientific productivity. Before his disease, he had already published some articles on capital and the monograph "Appreciation and interest" (1896), in which he aimed at showing that changing interest rates tend to compensate for rising and falling prices. With his important works on *The Nature of Capital and Income* (1906), *The Rate of Interest* (1907a) and *The Purchasing Power of Money* (1911b) Fisher now became America's leading economic theorist.

Furthermore, he wrote a textbook *Introduction to Economic Science* (1910), which in its revised version *Elementary Principles of Economics* (1911b) went into three further editions. "Copious use is made of diagrams, perhaps making it the first Marshallian text in America" (Samuelson 1967: 21). In 1918 he was elected President of the American Economic Association, and later, as a co-founder, he became the first President of the Econometric Society in 1930. He was also President of the American Statistical Association in 1932.

Fisher's lifelong crusade for good causes also included his fight for peace. At the end of World War I he became a strong advocate of American participation in the League of Nations. Fisher was also a restless inventor, best known for his patented visible card index. With his own firm, the Index Visible company, founded in 1913, sold to its greatest competitor Kardex Rand in 1925 and in another merger to Remington Rand in 1927, Fisher became a successful businessman. However, his acquired wealth did not last for long. In the stock market crash of 1929 and the subsequent Great Depression, Fisher not only lost all his private wealth but as an enthusiastic speculator even after the crash became heavily indebted for the rest of his life. Yale University had to buy his house to prevent Fisher and his family from being evicted. What was worse for Fisher was the fact that his optimism that recovery was just around the corner, which he continued for some months even after the crash, impaired his academic reputation. "Until the 1950s the name Irving Fisher was without honour in his own university. Except for economic theorists and econometricians, few members of the community appreciated the genius of a man who lived among them for 63 years" (Tobin 1987: 371).

The economist Irving Fisher, however, reacted to the stock market crash and the subsequent events, analysed *Booms and Depressions* (1932) and developed "The debt-deflation theory of great depressions" (1933) which attributed the deep crisis to over-indebtedness and the bursting of a credit bubble. Over-investment and over-speculation are often essential features of a boom, but if they are conducted mainly with borrowed money, then the consequences of a recession are much more dangerous. The bursting of the credit bubble unleashes a series of negative effects which in an interaction between an excessive real burden of debt and deflation seriously aggravates the crisis which evolves into a depression. According to Fisher, reflation, and not deflation was the remedy. Fisher's remarkable debt-deflation analysis of the depression remained largely unnoticed among contemporary economists due to his loss of reputation at the beginning of the depression. However, it was revitalized by Tobin (1980) against the historical background of the high costs of disinflation, and gained further ground after the world-wide Great Recession burst out in 2008–09. Tobin argued convincingly that this "Fisher effect", triggered by too great a fall in asset prices and business profits, dominates the Pigou or real balance effect which is related to outside money. The increased real burden of debt due to deflation or much higher real rates of interest in a period of unexpected disinflation imposed on firms, farmers or home-owners make the number of bankruptcies and defaults much greater in size. It was the consequential negative downward spiral of the real economy with the collapse of economic activity and mass unemployment which worried Fisher.

Fisher was also an economic policy crusader, as comes out best in his (unsuccessful) proposal to require that banks should keep 100 per cent reserves against checkable deposits instead of lending out these funds (1935). In the same year he retired from Yale. After the death of his wife he continued to stay active as in his last book *Constructive Income Taxation* (1942), jointly written with his brother Herbert, in which Fisher made a strong plea for a radical tax reform advocating an expenditure tax rather than an income tax. Fisher died of cancer in New York City on 29 April 1947.

Work

Fisher's *Mathematical Investigations in the Theory of Value and Prices* (1892) brought general equilibrium analysis to North America. Stimulated by Jevons's *Theory of Political Economy* (1871) and the recent book by Auspitz and Lieben, Fisher had largely invented the masterly exposition of general equilibrium theory for himself. He came to know the works of Walras and Edgeworth only when he had finished his book. In his generalized mathematical formulation of utility functions and their maximization Fisher treats the utility of every commodity as a function of the quantities consumed of all commodities. This differs from the analysis of Walras who made the quantity consumed of every commodity a function of prices. Fisher constructed indifference curves as Edgeworth (1881) had done before him, but in contrast to Edgeworth refused the penetration of psychology into economics as dangerous and inappropriate. In his early renouncing of utility as a psychic entity he "anticipated in substance the line of argument that then runs on from Pareto to Barone, Johnson, Slutsky, Allen and Hicks, Georgescu, and finally to Samuelson" (Schumpeter 1948 [1951]: 225). He points out that for the determination of equilibrium neither an interpersonal comparison of utility nor a cardinal measurement of utility for each individual would be necessary. Although Fisher thus can be considered as having pioneered the idea of ordinal theory of utility, which had been elaborated a decade later by Pareto, unlike Pareto, Fisher did not give up "Measuring marginal utility" (1927) empirically.

In his general equilibrium system Fisher (1892) also drew attention to two types of interdependent goods, in modern utility theory later distinguished as substitutes and complements. However, the supply side, including technology and available factors of production, is not elaborated. Furthermore, Fisher's early model of general equilibrium does not contain capital and interest. This should change with his later works, beginning with *Appreciation and Interest*. In this work, with which he also intervened into the bimetallic controversy, the focus is on the connection between monetary appreciation and the rate of interest. It is here that in the discussion of a redistribution of wealth between creditors and debtors, he makes the important distinction between expected and unexpected changes in the value of money. Expected changes have no real effects because they are neutralized by interest rates adjustments through arbitrage. Fisher (1896 [1961]: ch. II) develops the interest parity formula in which the difference in interest between two commodities is exactly matched by the expected change in their relative price. If i is the interest rate for gold and j is the interest rate for wheat, and a is the rate at which gold appreciates relatively to wheat in one interest interval, then the equilibrium condition is $1 + j = (1 + i)(1 + a)$ or $j = i + a + ia$.

The rate of interest in the (relatively) depreciating standard is equal to the sum of three terms, namely, the rate of interest in the appreciating standard, the rate of appreciation itself, and the product of these two elements (1896: 9) Each commodity has its own rate of interest depending on the expectations of the development of its price in the future. As long as future changes in the purchasing power of money are anticipated, there would be no real effects since they are neutralized by adjustments in interest rates. Contrary to a widespread view, a growing scarcity of gold, resulting in falling wheat prices relative to gold, need not necessarily harm farmers who have taken a credit in gold. "[T]he farmer who contracts a mortgage in gold is, *if the interest is properly adjusted*, no worse and no better off than if his contract were in a 'wheat' standard or a 'multiple' standard" (ibid.: 16, original emphasis).

The problem of non-neutrality, however, arises with unexpected changes in the purchasing power of money. Fisher considered wrong expectations mainly as a short-run phenomenon since people would learn from experience and adjust their expectations, although with a lag. Fisher became a pioneer of the statistical analysis of distributed lags. Fisher (1926) correlates unemployment with a distributed lag of inflation. However, it has to be pointed out that in this article, which had been reprinted in 1973 as "I discovered the Phillips curve" in a leading journal, causality runs from changes in the value of money to unemployment, whereas in the Phillips curve it is the unemployment rate which affects changes in the wage (inflation) rate.

Modern monetary macroeconomics started with Wicksell's *Interest and Prices* (1898 [1936]) and Fisher's *The Purchasing Power of Money*; whereas Humphrey in his thorough comparative analysis of Fisher's and Wicksell's different interpretations of the quantity theory comes to the conclusion "that Wicksell was ... every bit as much a quantity theorist as Fisher. Evidence reveals that he, like Fisher, understood and indeed enriched the theory's postulates" (Humphrey 1999: 73), it must not be overlooked that there is a direct line from Fisher's forceful restatement and statistical verification of the quantity theory of money, to Milton Friedman's modern revival of quantity theory (the "Fisher connection"). Wicksell's critical, although respectful, re-examination of quantity theory, on the other hand, gave much stimulus to various savings-investment business-cycle theories in the interwar debates, as shown in Leijonhufvud's famous diagram of the "Wicksell Connection" (1981: 133).

Schumpeter (1954: 1096) as well as most other contemporary economists considered Fisher's *Purchasing Power of Money* as an "outstanding achievement", as "quantity theory analysis at its highest", that is, as the best and most complete explanation in the entire economic literature before the modern revival by Friedman et al. However, it is interesting to note that Friedman's version is in fact based on the Cambridge approach which Keynes so strongly opposed to Fisher's. Fisher generalized the quantity theory to a long-run or equilibrium theory of price level/inflation determination, taking up the classical propositions of neutrality, equiproportionality, causality running from the quantity of money to prices, and independence of the supply and demand of money. Fisher extended the equation of exchange, as had been formulated by Simon Newcomb to whom he dedicated the book, to, in obvious notation, $MV + M'V' = PT$, which soon became Fisher's equation of exchange or Yale equation, in contrast to the Cambridge version of the quantity equation (based on the demand for money) as formulated by Marshall and Pigou, who wrote the equation in terms of income, whereas Fisher preferred to write it in terms of transactions.

> If the principles here advocated are correct, the purchasing power of money – or its reciprocal, the level of prices – depends exclusively on five definite factors: (1) the volume of money in circulation [M]; (2) its velocity of circulation [V]; (3) the volume of bank deposits subject to check [M']; (4) its velocity [V']; and (5) the volume of trade [T]. (Fisher 1911a: vii)

Fisher extended Newton's equation by taking into account the rising importance of bank deposits. While the equation of exchange in itself is a "truism", asserting no causal relationship between the quantity of money and the price level, nevertheless it holds empirically that after the transition period "a change in M produces a proportional change in M', and no changes in V, V', or the Q's [T], there is no possible escape from the conclusion that a change in the quantity of money (M) must normally cause a proportional change in the price level (the p's)" (ibid.: 157), where the p's and Q's are individual prices and quantities.

After the transition period, that is, in long-run equilibrium the "Fisher equation" holds, according to which the nominal interest rate i fully reflects a change in the inflation rate $\hat{p}$, leaving the real interest rate r unaltered, that is, $i = r + \hat{p}$. Like the equation of exchange the Fisher equation is an identity in the sense that an unobservable real interest rate can be calculated as the difference of the other two variables. More interesting is the application of the equation as an equilibrium condition for financial markets for which the expected rate of inflation $\hat{p}_e$ has to be included. Whereas in long-run equilibrium it holds that $\hat{p} = \hat{p}_e$, it is a characteristic of adjustment processes that changes in the inflation rate are only imperfectly anticipated in the nominal rate of interest. The real rate of interest which matters for investment decisions very often is too low in the upswing and too high in the downswing. This was particularly the case in the Great Depression of the early 1930s with its strong deflation.

These short-run deviations implying a non-neutrality of money were considered by Fisher as the principal causes of booms and depressions. For Schumpeter the most important insights of Fisher's analysis are contained in chapters IV to VI of *The Purchasing Power of Money* where Fisher deals with transition periods, explicitly recognizing changes in the velocity of money – which Wicksell regarded as one of the flimsiest variables in the economy so that an elaborated quantity theory in particular has to analyze the factors which cause changes in the velocity of circulation of money – and the tardiness (lags) of interest adjustment to price movements. While conceding that the quantity theory is not strictly true during transition periods, Fisher (1911a: 159–62), however, is downplaying these temporary disturbances and "bent all his forces to the task of arriving actually at a quantity-theory result . . . I cannot help thinking that the scholar was misled by the crusader" (Schumpeter 1948 [1951]: 234–5). Whereas the equation of exchange first of all is an identity, the causal content is injected by propositions such as making the velocity an institutional constant independent of the quantity of money, assuming that the volume of bank deposits varies proportionally with legal-tender money, and the independence of the volume of trade from the quantity of money. The outcome of the analysis of this "essentially 'mechanistic' mind" (ibid.: 235) is "that *one of the normal effects of an increase in the quantity of money is an exactly proportional increase in the general level of prices*" (Fisher 1911a: 157, original emphasis). Fisher's restatement of the quantity theory of money has survived more than a century of monetary debates without major revisions. This is best indicated by the formula for the reference value for the growth of the monetary aggregate M3 by the European Central Bank.

Fisher was convinced that fluctuations in the purchasing power of money were the main cause of most severe macroeconomic problems. This belief explains his life-long crusade for stable money and a stable managed currency. His various proposals for stabilizing the general price level induced him to engage in a persistent quest of the best index for measuring the value of money. Whereas in 1911 he had opted for the Paasche price index, and also seemed to favour the idea of chain indexes, in his later *The Making of Index Numbers* (1922), he postulated various criteria for a successful price index formula and elaborated a host of formulas of which he favoured the geometric mean of the Laspeyres (base-year weighted) and the Paasche (current-year weighted) formulas as coming closest to an "ideal index". In January 1923 Fisher also founded the Index Number Institute.

Fisher's masterpiece is *The Theory of Interest* (1930), a revised and elaborated version of his earlier *The Rate of Interest* (1907a), which he dedicated to the memory of John Rae and Eugen von Böhm-Bawerk. "[T]he book is a wonderful performance, the peak achievement . . . of the literature of interest" (Schumpeter 1948 [1951]: 230). Owing to its clear exposition "it is hard to imagine a better book to take with you to a desert island than this 1930 classic" (Samuelson 1967: 18). The core of Fishers's theory of interest comes out best in the subtitle "As determined by impatience to spend income and opportunity to invest it". It is central for Fisher's thought that the present value of the capital stock equals the discounted value of the flow of future net incomes derived from an investment project, at the going rate of interest. Fisher held the view that "income is the alpha and omega of economics" (1930: 13) and controversially insisted that income consists solely of consumption (1906, 1930: ch. I). It is a basic idea of his interest theory that a trade-off exists between current and future consumption. In this sense investment is not a part of income but acts only as a means for the distribution of consumption over time, i.e. saving (investment) implies the sacrifice of current for the benefit of future consumption. The dated quantities of consumption goods are the only object of choice.

Thereby a two-stage decision rule applies (Fisher separation theorem). First, on the investment opportunity side the decision-maker chooses that technique of production which maximizes the expected marginal rate of return over cost r_i of all available real investment projects (production optimum). Second, intertemporal consumption is maximized by comparison of the rate of time preference δ and the market rate of interest i which decides whether an individual becomes a borrower or a lender (consumption optimum). Fisher makes a clear distinction between production and exchange opportunities. His graphical illustration of the two sub-decisions which nicely shows the interplay of investment opportunities, time-preference (impatience) and the market rate of interest (which is a given data for the individual) for the simple case of two time periods has entered many textbooks.

In equilibrium the marginal rate of return over cost and the marginal rate of time preference equal the market rate of interest, that is, $r = i = \delta$. Fisher's main aim "is to show how the *rate* of interest is caused or determined" (1930: 13, original emphasis). Here the interplay between the rates of return on investment and rates of time preferences of all individuals is decisive. But most of his considerations are made from the perspective of an individual for whom the rate of interest is given within a partial equilibrium framework. In oscillating from the level of an individual investor (for whom the price system and interest rate are given) to the economy as a whole, a dilemma of Fisher's theory of interest becomes apparent. The connection between the interest rate and the price system, which can only be treated simultaneously, is dissolved into two allegedly isolated subsystems, so that on the one hand in his price theory he assumes a given interest rate whereas in his theory of interest he assumes given prices (1930: 131). Owing to this fixed-price assumption Fisher can express all variables in money terms and operate with the investment of value sums. Alas, this is not possible because commodity prices and the wage rate have to be determined simultaneously with the interest rate. Fisher's partial analysis and the associated fixed-price assumption are inadequate since a theory of interest has to be elaborated within a general equilibrium analysis. In such a framework interest rates affect the flow of net incomes of alternative investment projects via changes in the wage rate and product prices.

Fisher himself recognizes this "complication", that is, the interdependence between the interest rate and prices which is most clearly visible in his discussion of the ranking of alternative investment projects (1930: 170 ff.). There he expresses that not only the choice of the investment project but even the range of choice depends upon the rate of interest, because "[i]f the rate of interest is changed, a change is produced not only in the present values of the income items but in the income items themselves" (ibid.: 171). However, he downplays this complication as "more intricate than important", and therefore refrains from drawing consequences for his theory of capital and interest. Although Fisher, besides Walras, can be regarded as the second ancestor of a modern version of a general equilibrium theory, to which he gave decisive impulses with regard to the temporal disaggregation, he remained engrained in a partial equilibrium framework in his theory of interest.

Legacy

As is well known, Keynes pointed out in his *General Theory* that "Professor Fisher uses his 'rate of return over cost' in the same sense and for precisely the same purpose as I employ 'the marginal efficiency of capital'" (Keynes 1936 [1971]: 141), "nor is there any material difference . . . between my schedule of the marginal efficiency of capital or investment demand-schedule and the demand curve for capital contemplated by some of the classical writers" (ibid.: 178). As has been demonstrated, however, by Alchian (1955) and Garegnani (1978, 1979) from different perspectives, it is impossible to construct an investment demand curve exclusively by varying the rate of interest, holding all other prices constant.

Fisher's theory of investment, interest and capital has been elaborated in modern economic theory by Hirshleifer (1970) who has shown that the two alternative criteria developed by Fisher for an investment decision, the net-present-value rule and the internal-rate-of return rule, only lead to identical results in the two-period case or the perpetuity case. The two criteria may lead to different results in the multiperiod case where the net-present-value should be applied, because of the reinvestment problem and the possibility of multiple internal rates of return (see also Hagemann 1987).

Solow (1963) has taken up Fisher's concept of the rate of return on investment and modified it as the "social rate of return" which is defined solely in terms of changes in consumption streams: the perpetual gain in consumption is compared to the sacrifices in consumption during the transition period. Solow's aim was to formulate "a theory of interest rates, not a theory of capital" and to present the social rate of return as "the central concept in capital theory" (ibid.: 16) which was intended to form a surrogate for the marginal productivity of capital in a world with heterogeneous capital goods. The parallels with Samuelson's attempt to construct a surrogate production function to rescue vital results of the Clark–Ramsey parable in a world of heterogeneous capital goods are close at hand, and caused a major controversy between Pasinetti and Solow within the two Cambridge controversies on the theory of capital. The debate stimulated Dougherty (1980) to come to the defence of Fisher, to elaborate the Fisherian analysis and to provide a comprehensive account of interest and profit in a modern setting, giving credit to Fisher even for phenomena such as capital reversing and reswitching.

The continuous relevance of Fisher's analytical contributions for modern debates in economics is indicated by Tobin (1985), the publication of a 14-volume edition of *The Works of Irving Fisher* (Fisher 1997), edited by William J. Barber on behalf of the American Economic Association, or the more recent collections edited by Loef and Monissen (1999), Dimand and Geanakoplos (2005), Dimand (2007), and the special issue of the *European Journal of the History of Economic Thought* (**20** (2), April 2013) on *The Purchasing Power of Money*.

HARALD HAGEMANN

See also:

Capital theory (III); Macroeconomics (III); Monetarism (II); Money and banking (III); Milton Friedman (I); Knut Wicksell (I).

References and further reading

Alchian, A.A. (1955), 'The rate of interest, Fisher's rate of return over costs and Keynes' internal rate of return', *American Economic Review*, **45** (5), 938–43.
Allais, M. (1968), 'Irving Fisher', in D.L. Sills (ed.), *International Encyclopedia of the Social Sciences*, vol. 5, London and New York: Macmillan, pp. 475–85.
Allen, R.L. (1993), *Irving Fisher. A Biography*, Cambridge, MA and Oxford: Blackwell.
Auspitz, R. and R. Lieben (1889), *Untersuchungen über die Theorie des Preises*, Leipzig: Duncker & Humblot.
Dimand, R.W. (ed.) (2007), *Irving Fisher, Critical Responses*, 3 vols, London and New York: Routledge.
Dimand, R.W. and J. Geanakoplos (eds) (2005), *Celebrating Irving Fisher, the Legacy of a Great Economist*, Oxford: Oxford University Press.
Dougherty, C. (1980), *Interest and Profit*, London: Methuan and Co.
Edgeworth, F.Y. (1881), *Mathematical Physics. An Essay on the Application of Mathematics to the Moral Sciences*, London: C. Kegan Paul & Co.
Fisher, I. (1892), *Mathematical Investigations in the Theory of Value and Prices*, New Haven, CT: Connecticut Academy of Arts and Sciences, Transactions 9, reprinted 1961, New York: Augustus M. Kelley.

Fisher, I. (1896), 'Appreciation and interest', *AEA Publications*, third series, **XI** (4), 331–442, reprinted 1961, New York: Augustus M. Kelley.

Fisher, I. (1906), *The Nature of Capital and Income*, New York: Macmillan.

Fisher, I. (1907a), *The Rate of Interest*, New York: Macmillan.

Fisher, I. (1907b), 'The effect of diet on endurance', *Transactions of the Connecticut Academy of Arts and Sciences*, **13**, 11–46.

Fisher, I. (1910), *Introduction to Economic Science*, New York: Macmillan.

Fisher, I. (1911a), *The Purchasing Power of Money. Its Determination and Relation to Credit, Interest and Crises*, with H.G. Brown, New York: Macmillan.

Fisher, I. (1911b), *Elementary Principles of Economics*, New York: Macmillan.

Fisher, I. (1922), *The Making of Index Numbers*, Boston, MA: Houghton Mifflin.

Fisher, I. (1926), 'A statistical relation between unemployment and price changes', *International Labour Review*, **13** (June), 785–92, reprinted 1973, as 'Lost and Found: I discovered the Phillips curve – Irving Fisher', *Journal of Political Economy*, **81** (March–April), 496–502.

Fisher, I. (1927), 'A statistical method for measuring "marginal utility" and testing the justice of a progressive income tax', in J.H. Hollander (ed.), *Economic Essays Contributed in Honor of John Bates Clark*, New York: Macmillan.

Fisher, I. (1930), *The Theory of Interest*, New York: Macmillan.

Fisher, I. (1932), *Booms and Depressions*, New York: Adelphi.

Fisher, I. (1933), 'The debt-deflation theory of great depressions', *Econometrica*, **1** (4), 337–57.

Fisher, I. (1935), *100% Money*, New York: Adelphi.

Fisher, I. (1997), *The Works of Irving Fisher*, 14 vols, ed. William J. Barber, assisted by R.W. Dimand and K. Foster; cons. ed. J. Tobin, London: Pickering & Chatto.

Fisher, I. and H.W. Fisher (1942), *Constructive Income Taxation. A Proposal for Reform*, New York: Harper & Brothers.

Fisher, I. and E.L. Fisk (1915), *How to Live. Rules for Healthful Living Based on Modern Science*, New York: Funk and Wagnalls.

Fisher, I.N. (1956), *My Father Irving Fisher*, New York: Comet Press.

Fisher, I.N. (1961), *A Bibliography of the Writings of Irving Fisher*, New Haven, CT: Yale University Library.

Garegnani, P. (1978), 'Notes on consumption, investment and effective demand, I and II', *Cambridge Journal of Economics*, **2** (December), 335–53.

Garegnani, P. (1979), 'Notes on consumption, investment and effective demand, I and II', *Cambridge Journal of Economics*, **3** (March), 63–82.

Hagemann, H. (1987), 'Internal rate of return', in J. Eatwell, M. Milgate and P. Newman (eds), *The New Palgrave. A Dictionary of Economics*, vol. 2, London, New York and, Tokyo: Macmillan, pp. 892–94.

Hirshleifer, J. (1970), *Investment, Interest and Capital*, Englewood Cliffs, NJ: Prentice Hall.

Humphrey, T.M. (1999), 'Irving Fisher and Knut Wicksell: different interpretations of the quantity theory?', in H.-E. Loef and H.G. Monissen (eds), *The Economics of Irving Fisher, Reviewing the Scientific Work of a Great Economist*, Cheltenham, UK and Northampton, MA, USA: Edward Elgar pp. 59–78.

Jevons, W.S. (1871), *The Theory of Political Economy*, London: Macmillan.

Keynes, J.M. (1936), *The General Theory of Employment, Interest and Money*, in *The Collected Writings of John Maynard Keynes*, vol. VII, London: Macmillan and Cambridge University Press, reprinted 1971.

Leijonhufvud, A. (1981), 'The Wicksell connection: variations on a theme', in A. Leijonhufvud, *Information and Coordination. Essays in Macroeconomic Theory*, New York and Oxford: Oxford University Press, pp. 131–202.

Loef, H.-E. and H.G. Monissen (eds) (1999), *The Economics of Irving Fisher, Reviewing the Scientific Work of a Great Economist*, Cheltenham, UK and Northampton, MA, USA: Edward Elgar.

Samuelson, P.A. (1967), 'Irving Fisher and the theory of capital', in W. Fellner (ed.), *Ten Economic Studies in the Tradition of Irving Fisher*, New York: Wiley, pp. 17–38.

Schumpeter, J.A. (1948), 'Irving Fisher's econometrics, *Econometrica*, **6**, 219–31, reprinted in J.A. Schumpeter (1951), *Ten Great Economists, From Marx to Keynes*, London, Oxford and New York, pp. 222–38.

Schumpeter, J.A. (1954), *History of Economic Analysis*, New York: Oxford University Press and London: George Allen & Unwin.

Solow, R.M. (1963), *Capital Theory and the Rate of Return*, Amsterdam: North-Holland.

Tobin, J. (1980), *Asset Accumulation and Economic Activity*, Oxford: Basil Blackwell.

Tobin, J. (1985), 'Neoclassical theory in America', *American Economic Review*, **75** (6), 28–38.

Tobin, J. (1987), 'Fisher, Irving (1867–1947)', in J. Eatwell, M. Milgate and P. Newman (eds), *The New Palgrave*, vol. 2, London: Macmillan, pp. 369–76.

Wicksell, K. (1898), *Geldzins und Güterpreise. Eine Studie über die den Tauschwert des Geldes bestimmenden Ursachen*, Jena: Gustav Fischer, English trans. R.F. Kahn (1936), *Interest and Prices. A Study of the Causes Regulating the Value of Money*, London: Macmillan.

Ladislaus von Bortkiewicz (1868–1931)

Life

Ladislaus von Bortkiewicz, of Polish descent, was born in St Petersburg on 7 August 1868. His father was a colonel and military instructor teaching artillery and mathematics. Ladislaus studied several subjects – law at the university of his home town, where he graduated in 1890, political economy and statistics first in Strasbourg from 1891 to 1892, then under the supervision of the eminent German statistician Wilhelm Lexis in Göttingen in 1892, followed by study visits to Vienna and Leipzig. He received his PhD in 1893 from Göttingen University. From 1895 to 1897 he lectured on statistics and actuarial science as a Privatdozent in Strasbourg. He returned to Russia, where he worked as a clerk and then as a teacher until 1901, when he became an extraordinary professor of statistics at the Friedrich-Wilhelms University of Berlin. In 1920 he was appointed to the chair of statistics and political economy. He stayed in Berlin until he passed away on 15 July 1931.

Bortkiewicz received several honours, including membership of the Royal Swedish Academy of Sciences, the Royal Statistical Society, the American Statistical Association and the International Statistical Institute. It is perhaps interesting to note that when Walras's health deteriorated and caused him to retire from his chair in Lausanne in 1892, he asked Bortkiewicz whether he would become his successor, reflecting an enormous esteem for the 24-year-old. It was only after Bortkiewicz had told him that he had turned to statistics and was not interested that Walras, upon Maffeo Pantaleoni's advice, supported the appointment of Vilfredo Pareto.

Bortkiewicz published over 100 articles and a number of books. His work is wide-ranging, covering mathematical statistics, actuarial science, economics, mathematics and physics. He was well read in all major economic theories, including those of David Ricardo, Karl Marx, Léon Walras, Eugen von Böhm-Bawerk and Vilfredo Pareto, and he was keen to identify the differences and similarities between them and whether and when there was progress in the discipline. For example, his observations on major authors, such as Ricardo, Marx, or Böhm-Bawerk, were typically embedded in more general discussions and assessments of the developments in economic analysis. Bortkiewicz's main interest was the theory of value, capital and income distribution. He admired David Ricardo, but also Marx and Walras. His analytic mind was acute and uncompromising. He did not allow sloppy arguments to pass unnoticed and therefore was feared as a "taskmaster" in the profession. Joseph Schumpeter (1954: 851) severely underestimated his achievements by calling him a "comma hunter", who "had no eye for the wider aspects and deeper meanings of a theoretical model". More to the point, he and Bortkiewicz held fundamentally different views about what the latter dubbed the "touchstone" of an explanation of interest (that is, profits) (see below).

In this entry the main focus is on Bortkiewicz's contributions to economics. A brief summary account of his works on statistics is followed by a discussion of his "collaboration" with Léon Walras. Then his comparative assessment of the theories of value and distribution of David Ricardo and Karl Marx are dealt with.

Contributions to Statistics

Bortkiewicz worked on mathematical statistics and its applications especially to actuarial science. There the focus of his work was on mortality tables. Examining life expectancy in a growing population he showed that contrary to received opinion life expectancy was not a function of the observed birth and death rates, but could only be computed from mortality tables. He published several articles on the issue (see Bortkiewicz 1903, 1904, 1911; see also Samuelson 1976). He also applied his statistical methods to such diverse fields as radioactivity, order statistics, and legal studies.

It has been argued that it would be more appropriate to call the Poisson distribution the Bortkiewicz distribution, because it had been established for the first time in a book entitled *Das Gesetz der kleinen Zahlen* (*The Law of Small Numbers*) published in 1898. In it Bortkiewicz studied events with a low frequency in a large population and showed that these followed a Poisson distribution even when the probabilities of the events varied. The case he had investigated was the number of soldiers annually killed by horse kicks per Prussian army corps. The observation period encompassed 20 years and he examined 14 corps. While the risk of lethal horse kicks varied across time and corps, a Poisson distribution fitted the overall distribution surprisingly well (Gumbel 1968).

Bortkiewicz was critical of Karl Pearson's approach to statistics. He claimed that Pearson's formulas designed to match observed results lacked a theoretical underpinning and were thus of no value. John Maynard Keynes in the *Treatise on Probability* (1921), while praising Bortkiewicz's mathematical brilliance, questioned the meaning of his respective argument and maintained that it remained unclear what it really amounted to. Bortkiewicz's approach to mathematical statistics did not gain general acceptance.

Bortkiewicz and Walras

The relationship between Bortkiewicz and Léon Walras was largely unknown until William Jaffé's edition of the correspondence of Walras (1965). It turned out that Bortkiewicz had written to Walras when he was barely 20 years of age and that the latter had found it rewarding to exchange altogether 56 letters with him, 31 of them written by Walras, in the period between 1887 and 1899. As a reflection of their discussions and in an attempt to defend Walras against some criticisms put forward by Francis Y. Edgeworth, Bortkiewicz published a review article of the second edition of the *Éléments* (Bortkiewicz 1890). Later followed a short review of *Etudes d'économie sociale* (Bortkiewicz 1898b). For summary accounts of the debate amongst the three authors, see Marchionatti (2007) and Bridel (2008). The main themes discussed in the "triangular debate" were essentially the following: (1) capital theory and especially the role of production costs in the determination of the prices of new capital goods; (2) the theory of exchange and the concept of competition; and (3) the concept of *tâtonnement*. Walras apparently tried to manipulate the young Russian on his behalf in his controversy with Edgeworth, but Bortkiewicz was far too clever to get tricked by the old man.

Bortkiewicz questioned the validity of Walras's proof of the "theorem of maximum utility of newly produced capital goods proper", with regard to which Walras contended that the costs of production of the goods played no role. As later discussions demonstrated, Bortkiewicz was right in this regard, but he could not convince Walras.

In his review of the second edition of the *Éléments*, Edgeworth (1889: 435) maintained that Walras went "too far in the way of abstraction when he insists that the ideal *entrepreneur* should be regarded as 'making neither gain nor loss'" (original emphasis). This was in fact a criticism of too narrow a concept of competition Walras was said to have entertained. Bortkiewicz rushed to Walras's defence by arguing that only the ideal entrepreneur is compatible with Walras's concept of general equilibrium. Soon afterwards, however, he appears to have got doubts and was willing to admit that there is a difference between competition in industry and in commerce.

Edgeworth had also objected to Walras's construction that "the equations of exchange are of a statical, not a dynamical, character. They define a position of equilibrium, but they afford no information as to the path by which that point is reached" (Edgeworth 1889: 435). Walras, who had prided himself with having elaborated a general analysis of the gravitation to equilibrium, was mistaken. Bortkiewicz in his reply to Edgeworth, which was endorsed by Walras, defended the concept of a "realistic" process of *tâtonnement*, but admitted that there might be several methods of arriving at the equations and that Walras's assumption that there is no trade out of equilibrium might be replaced by one that reflects the actual "practices in markets". The real problem under discussion was, of course, whether the equilibrium, if it existed, was stable or not. This was crucial, because if it happened to be unstable, what was the use of equilibrium theory?

Later in his economic writings, Bortkiewicz variously referred to Walras's general equilibrium theory and in one of his latest papers even suggested to incorporate the classical cost of production equations into a Walrasian system (see Bortkiewicz 1921). In this way he sought to integrate the objectivism of the classical authors and Marx, on the one hand, and the subjectivism of the marginalists, on the other, in a single theory. It can however be shown that Walras, up until the fourth edition of the *Éléments*, was (erroneously) of the opinion that his system reflected a long-period equilibrium, characterized by a uniform rate of net profits, and that the proposed equations satisfied the "law of cost of production" (see Kurz and Salvadori 1995: 24–5, 439–41).

Bortkiewicz on Böhm-Bawerk

In his criticism of "the cardinal error" of Eugen von Böhm-Bawerk's theory of capital and interest (profits), Bortkiewicz criticized the "Three Grounds" put forward by the Austrian in favour of a positive rate: (1) the differences between wants and provision in different periods of time; (2) the systematic underestimation of future wants and the means available to satisfy them; and (3) the technical superiority of present compared with future goods of the same quality and quantity. Bortkiewicz focused attention on the third ground – according to Böhm-Bawerk (1889 [1902]: 286) the "main pillar" of his theory – which referred allegedly to a "purely objective factor" (Bortkiewicz 1906: 945).

Bortkiewicz distinguished between three types of approaches to the theory of interest, only one of which met what he called the "touchstone" of the theory of profits:

> I believe that this can be regarded as *the touchstone of such a theory*: whether it is able to show the *general cause of interest* also for the case in which not only *no technical progress*, of whichever type, takes place, but also *the length of the periods of production appears to be technically predetermined*, so that *no choice* is possible between different methods. (Bortkiewicz 1906: 970–71; emphases added)

In other words, interest ought to be explained in conditions of a given system of production and neither in the context of a choice of technique problem nor as a fruit of technical progress. As Bortkiewicz made clear, two of the most popular theories of profits at the time did not meet these criteria: John Bates Clark's marginal productivity theory of capital and Eugen von Böhm-Bawerk's "Austrian" theory of capital and interest. The former explained profits in terms of the marginal productivity of capital and thus did not start from a given technical system of production, and the latter presupposed a variable length of the average period of production and thus a dynamic element. Elsewhere Bortkiewicz expounded the implications of his postulate with regard to the theory of value:

> Now my opinion is that in general the value of goods can only depend upon such *technical knowledge as is applied in practice*. But the value of goods remains unaffected by *knowledge, which, on whatever grounds, is not utilized*. The result thus obtained can be summed up in the following brief formula: *for [the determination of] the value of goods there come into consideration only actual methods of production, and not merely potential ones.* (Bortkiewicz 1907b: 1299; emphases added)

As regards Böhm-Bawerk's third ground, Bortkiewicz turned to a numerical example in the *Positive Theory of Capital* meant to illustrate the superiority of "more roundabout" processes of production. The example, Bortkiewicz maintained, was misleading because Böhm-Bawerk had given only an incomplete picture of the case under consideration. The example concerns production processes started in consecutive years. Alas, Böhm-Bawerk had assumed without any justification that all processes stop at the end of the process started first. If each process was instead taken to break off after the same number of years as the first one, we arrive at a uniformly staggered system of production. Now the process started first is no longer superior to all other processes with regard to all future time periods, because after its truncation the other processes still generate outputs, whereas the first one no longer does. Bortkiewicz (1906: 958) concluded that, "seen from a purely formal point of view, [Böhm-Bawerk] did not reason correctly. His argumentation, on which he puts the main weight, suffers from an internal mistake."

Bortkiewicz was also critical of the other two grounds and particularly of Böhm-Bawerk's argument in favour of a positive rate of time preference. He insisted that one ought to be "extremely cautious" with any sort of "psychological reasoning" and (as Friedrich von Wieser, Böhm-Bawerk's brother-in-law, had argued before him) that it would have to be shown that a positive time preference exists independently of the phenomenon of interest, because if the latter is positive, the former must necessarily be positive too: a positive time preference would have to be shown to be the "*prius*" relative to the phenomenon of interest (Bortkiewicz 1906: 948). He also attacked the view that a positive time preference follows from the fact that all future possessions are more or less uncertain. Since Böhm-Bawerk was concerned with explaining interest proper, that is, net interest as opposed to gross interest, which includes a risk premium designed to take account of the element of uncertainty just mentioned, myopic behaviour due to uncertainty can play no role in his argument. "Taken all together", Bortkiewicz concluded, "the purely subjective foundation of Böhm-Bawerk's doctrine turns out to be uncertain and precarious" (Bortkiewicz 1906: 950).

Which theory, if any, met the touchstone criteria? According to Bortkiewicz it was the theory of the classical economists in the form David Ricardo gave it. Bortkiewicz drew attention to this fact especially in his essay "Wertrechnung und Preisrechnung im Marxschen System" ("Value and price in the Marxian system"), published in three instalments in 1906–07 (only parts 2 and 3 have been translated into English; see Bortkiewicz 1952).

Bortkiewicz on Ricardo and Marx

The essay is actually as much about Ricardo as it is about Marx. In his essay Bortkiewicz referred to the work of the Russian mathematical economist Vladimir K. Dmitriev, who in a paper published in Russian in 1898 had formalized Ricardo's approach to the theory of value and distribution. Dmitriev had shown that the rate of profits and relative prices can be determined, once "the technical conditions of production of commodities (including the commodity labour-power) are given" (Bortkiewicz 1906–07, pt 2: 39). Besides the system of production and the real wage rate (that is, the remuneration of the "commodity labour power") no other data were needed.

Prices and profits

Bortkiewicz (1906–07) took Dmitriev's formalization as the starting point of his own analysis and assumed unidirectional production processes of finite duration, that is, one-way avenues starting from what Ricardo had called "unassisted labour" via a number of intermediate products or capital goods to final outputs. In such "time-phased" production processes prices of commodities can also be conceived in terms of what Sraffa (1960) called "dated quantities of labour", with the dated wage bills paid at the consecutive stages of production properly discounted forward at the current rate of profits r. Let l_{-1j} be the amount of labour expended during the last year before the completion of one unit of commodity j, l_{-2j} the amount expended two years before, l_{-3j} three years before, and so on. If the process has been started T years ago, and if wages are paid at the beginning of each year (*ante factum*), where w is the real wage rate in terms of some commodity, which also serves as standard of value, then we get the following reduction to dated quantities of labour for commodity j:

$$p_j = (1 + r)wl_{-1j} + (1 + r)^2wl_{-2j} + (1 + r)^3wl_{-3j} + \ldots + (1 + r)^Twl_{-Tj} \qquad (1)$$

$$(j = 1, 2, \ldots, n)$$

With a given w and a standard fixed as indicated, there are n equations to determine r and the remaining $n - 1$ prices. Hence, Ricardo's determination of the rate of profits was perfectly sound and was not marred by an insufficient number of independent equations to ascertain the unknowns, as critics like William Stanley Jevons and Walras had contended. Bortkiewicz agreed with Knut Wicksell who had defended Ricardo against these accusations.

Bortkiewicz then extended the framework to analyse (1) the problem of a choice of technique, (2) fixed capital and (3) scarce natural resources that are non-exhaustible (land).

Choice of technique
As regards the first problem, with several alternative ways to produce a given commodity we get as many reduction equations as there are technical alternatives. Obviously, and flukes apart, different methods of production do not support the same rate of profits r, given the real wage rate. Bortkiewicz corroborated Ricardo's finding that in competitive conditions the method will be chosen that minimizes unit costs. If the method that does so is at the same time a method employed directly or indirectly in the production of wage goods, its adoption will entail an increase in the general rate of profits. Otherwise, in the case of "luxuries", it will only lead to a reduction in the price of the commodity in the production of which the new method is used (and in the prices of commodities in whose production the commodity enters as a means of production).

This argument anticipates already why Bortkiewicz refuted Marx's attempt at explaining a falling tendency of the rate of profits in terms of technical progress. Technical progress implies that new methods of production become available, and for a given real wage rate they will be adopted by cost-minimizing producers if and only if they allow to reduce costs of production, which however means that the general rate of profits will either rise or stay constant. This result became known later as the "Okishio theorem".

Fixed capital
Next Bortkiewicz turned to the case of fixed capital. Ricardo had defined fixed capital in the following way: "According as capital is rapidly perishable, and requires to be frequently reproduced, or is of slow consumption, it is classed under the heads of circulating, or of fixed capital" (Ricardo 1951–73, I: 52). However, he did not deal in detail with the particular difficulties the presence of durable instruments of production involves in the theory of value and distribution. Without much ado the highly successful stockjobber had rather assumed that the problem can be dealt with in terms of annuities.

Bortkiewicz (1906–07, pt 2: 27–32) credited Ricardo with having integrated fixed capital in his theory of value and distribution in a satisfactory way. He then formalized Ricardo's approach, which implicitly dealt with the case of constant efficiency of a machine. Assume that a (new) machine can be used for n years and the price of the brand new item is given by p_{m0}. At the end of the t-th year of its employment its book value is $p_{m,t}$, $t = 1, 2, \ldots, n$, whereas at the end of its life the price is taken to be nil. (This means implicitly that it has neither a scrap value nor incurs disposal costs.) The difference between the prices of the machine in two consecutive years is equal to the machine's depreciation. Since the law of one price for the commodity produced holds, this implies that the yearly charge in terms of profits and depreciation – the annuity – must be constant across the entire life of the machine. Let z be the charge, then the following i equations hold true:

$$z = rp_{m,t} + p_{m,t} - p_{m,t+1} \tag{2}$$

for $t = 0, 1, 2, \ldots, n - 1$. ($p_{m,n} = 0$ by assumption.) Multiplying the i-th equation by $(1 + r)^{-i}$, $i = 1, 2, \ldots, n$, and adding the equations, all terms on the RHS except p_{m0} cancel out and we get:

$$p_{m0} = \frac{z}{1 + r} + \frac{z}{(1 + r)^2} + \ldots + \frac{z}{(1 + r)^n} \tag{3}$$

Solving the sum of this geometric series for the annual charge on the machine z gives:

$$z = p_{m0}\frac{r(1 + r)^n}{(1 + r)^n - 1} \tag{4}$$

The constant annuity represents that component of the price of a commodity that is due to the use of the fixed capital item, as a share of the price of the brand new durable instrument of production employed.

Bortkiewicz observed that compared to Ricardo's treatment of fixed capital, Marx's was inferior and applied strictly only in the special case of $r = 0$. In this case the labour theory of value holds as a theory of relative prices and depreciation is linear, that is, it equals period after period the nth fraction of the value of the brand new instrument until it has been entirely written off.

The so-called "transformation problem"

Probably best known among Bortkiewicz's writings is an essay in which he sought to correct Marx's attempt to "transform" labour values in prices of production in volume III of *Capital*, posthumously edited by Friedrich Engels in 1894 (see Bortkiewicz 1907a, 1949). Marx had approached the problem in the following way. (We assume for simplicity only circulating capital.) He had stipulated that the "law of value" holds in the aggregate and that therefore the ratio of the sum total of surplus values produced in the various sectors of the economy, $S = \Sigma_i s_i$, and the sum total of constant and variable capitals, $K = \Sigma_i(c_i + v_i)$, gives the correct value of the general rate of profits in the system, ρ, that is:

$$\rho = S/K = \Sigma_i s_i/\Sigma_i(c_i + v_i) \ (i = 1, 2, \ldots, n) \tag{5}$$

He then used this rate to discount forward the values of constant and variable capitals in the different sectors in order to arrive at prices of production:

$$p_i = (1 + \rho)(c_i + v_i) \ (i = 1, 2, \ldots, n), \tag{6}$$

where p_i designates the production price of commodity i in whose production the same rate of profits is earned in competitive conditions as in all other sectors of the economy. Marx was aware that this procedure was deficient, because it implied that inputs were sold and bought at labour values, whereas outputs were sold and bought at production prices. However, he appears to have been of the opinion that transforming also the constant and variable capitals in production prices would not undermine the validity of his determination of the general rate of profits in labour value terms.

The fact that in conditions of free competition and the corresponding tendency towards a uniform rate of profits commodities cannot exchange at labour values had been noticed already by readers of volume I of *Capital*. It had prompted Engels when editing volume II in his foreword to defy economists to show "in which way an equal average rate of profit can and must come about, not only without a violation of the law of value, but on the very basis of it." Interestingly, one of the economists who accepted the challenge was Wilhelm Lexis (Bortkiewicz's supervisor in 1892 in Göttingen). According to Engels, none of the people participating in the "prize essay competition", including Lexis, succeeded in solving the riddle and so the publication of volume III of *Capital*, which was announced as containing the solution, was eagerly anticipated. However, the book did not keep its promises. While several people criticized the procedure Marx had suggested, very few were able to grasp its shortcoming, let alone suggest an algorithm that would solve the transformation problem for good, provided a solution existed. Probably the most effective criticism of Marx came from Eugen von Böhm-Bawerk (1896), who, however, failed to see the slip in Marx's argument and contented himself with pointing out a "fundamental contradiction" between values and prices in Marx.

In 1907 Bortkiewiz published a paper in which he achieved two aims at once: he solved the transformation problem, but in doing so he also showed that the magnitudes in the numerator and in the denominator of the expression giving the general rate of profits were generally affected by the transformation and could not be taken to be invariant with regard to it, as Marx had assumed. The implication of this was that the general rate of profits, r, was not equal to the one ascertained in labour value terms, ρ. Bortkiewicz argued that Marx's "successivist" procedure – determining the general rate of profits first and only after this had been accomplished determining prices of production – was inadmissible in general and had to give way to a "simultaneous" determination of both, the rate of profits and prices.

Bortkiewicz established these results within a circular framework of production with three "departments", department 1 producing means of production, department 2 wage goods and department 3 luxury goods consumed by capitalists. He assumed a stationary economy, that is, simple reproduction, which implied that the sum total of wages (or variable capitals) is entirely spent on wage goods and the sum total of profits (surplus value) entirely on luxury goods. He formulated the following system of simultaneous equations:

$$(c_1x + v_1y)(1 + r) = (c_1 + c_2 + c_3)x \tag{7}$$

$$(c_2x + v_2y)(1 + r) = (v_1 + v_2 + v_3)y \tag{8}$$

$$(c_3x + v_3y)(1 + r) = (s_1 + s_2 + s_3)z \tag{9}$$

In it the c_is, v_is and s_is ($i = 1, 2, 3$) are known labour value magnitudes, from which Marx had started his reasoning; x, y and z are price coefficients that may be interpreted as value-price transformation coefficients; and r is the general rate of profits. The system has three equations and four unknowns: x, y, z and r. Fixing a standard of prices by setting x, y or z equal to unity (for example, $z = 1$, as Bortkiewicz did) allows one to determine the remaining unknowns, including the general rate of profits. It turns out that except in very special technological conditions (or with particular normalizations) none of Marx's invariance postulates holds: the sum of values is not equal to the sum of prices, the sum of surplus values is not equal to the sum of profits, and the sum of capital advances in labour value terms is not equal to the sum in price terms, and, most importantly, $r \neq \rho$. The "law of value" turned out not to provide the solid basis upon which the edifice of political economy could safely be erected, as Marx had thought. This does not mean that Bortkiewicz sided with the critics of Marx: these, he maintained, had thrown out the valuable along with the undesirable. Marx's idea of transforming labour values in prices of production did not imply chasing a will-o'-the-wisp. It can be done, but when it was done correctly, it necessitated important revisions of Marx's doctrine. Last but not least, while Marx had assumed that the (labour) values of commodities are known magnitudes, it is clear that in a circular (as opposed to a unidirectional) framework they can only be ascertained by also solving a system of simultaneous equations. This system reflects a very special constellation of the sharing out of the product. To emphasize this fact, Sraffa in the early 1940s coined the term "Value theory of labour" (see Sraffa Papers D3/12/44: 3, D3/12/46: 24): values are proportional to labour quantities if and only if there are no profits (setting aside the exceedingly special case of uniform input proportions across all industries of the economy).

Bortkiewicz (1906–07: 56) traced Marx's ineptitude to provide correct solutions to the problems he raised back to the "meagreness of his mathematical abilities". He praised instead Ricardo for having provided sufficiently correct answers on a number of issues with regard to which Marx failed.

Rent theory

Bortkiewicz published two papers devoted to the treatment of land in the theory of value and distribution. In both papers the attention focuses on the theories of rent of the German economist Karl Rodbertus, on the one hand, and Marx, on the other, and on whether these theories involved any progress with respect to Ricardo's theory (Bortkiewicz 1910–11, 1919). In volume III of *Capital* Marx had criticized Ricardo for having missed the concept of "absolute rent", that is, rent obtained by the proprietor of "marginal" land. Absolute rent emerges, because the competitive process is said to be imperfect and thus fails to channel surplus value produced in agriculture, which is taken to exhibit a lower organic composition of capital than manufacturing, away from it in an amount necessary to bring about a uniform rate of profit. Some of the non-redistributed surplus value is said to allow the proprietors of marginal land to pocket a rent. Marx located the deeper reason for Ricardo's inability to see this in his failure to distinguish between constant and variable capital. Ricardo is therefore also accused of having missed an important element at work in the transformation (or lack thereof) of (labour) values in prices of production.

While there is a correct element in Marx's criticism in so far as Ricardo had indeed tended to neglect the existence of non-wage capital when determining the rates of profit and rent (see Gehrke 2012), two observations are apposite. First, as Bortkiewicz stressed, Ricardo did not advocate a "law of value" in the sense of Marx (see also Kurz and Salvadori 2013). Secondly, without free competition across all sectors of the economy the results would differ from those obtained. There is nothing surprising here, as the classical theory of differential profit and wages rates, originating with Smith and further developed by Ricardo, shows (see 1951–73, I, ch. I, s. II). As Bortkiewicz demonstrated, Ricardo's theory of rent emerges largely unscathed (see also Gehrke 2012). Its substance stands up to criticism, but certain formulations Ricardo used turn out to be misleading or untenable and more general formulations of the theory are possible.

The question was close at hand: did Marx's theory involve only regress compared with Ricardo's? Bortkiewicz was not of this opinion, but credited Marx essentially with a single important achievement only: his explanation of the "source of profits". In the third instalment of his 1906–07 essay, Marx is said to have had the illuminating idea of building a scheme in which, while commodities exchange according to labour values, there is surplus value and thus profits. In this way Marx was able to refute both the vulgar idea that profits are the result of raising prices above their values and the proposition that profits are a payment for the "productive services" of capital. Marx was able to show conclusively that profits reflect "unpaid labour", and thus exploitation, and imply a "deduction" from the produce of labour, as Adam Smith had already argued.

Sraffa on von Bortkiewicz

It is interesting to note that among Piero Sraffa's unpublished papers there is a notebook of 1942–43 with extensive excerpts from, and critical comments on, three contributions of Bortkiewicz: his criticism of Böhm-Bawerk's theory of capital and interest (Bortkiewicz 1906, 1907b) and his essay on "Value and price in the Marxian system" (Bortkiewicz 1906–07). Sraffa in his comments on Bortkiewicz's essay on the "cardinal error" in Böhm-Bawerk's theory of interest approved of Bortkiewicz's specification of the task of interest theory – a task Sraffa had in fact established independently of him and accomplished (with regard to single production) with his "second equations" relating to an economy with a surplus and given real (that is, subsistence) wages elaborated towards the end of 1927. Sraffa held Bortkiewicz in high esteem because of his "dictum" concerning the criteria that the theory of value and distribution ought to satisfy, but he also accused him of having put forward misleading interpretations of Ricardo and Marx and of inconsistencies in the 1906–07 article. Sraffa's main criticism concerned the fact that Bortkiewicz, who had considered Marx's analysis as a "regression" from the state of the classical theory of value and distribution achieved by Ricardo, had not seen that Marx had indeed contributed a major analytical insight. He had shown that with circular production relations, which Ricardo had for simplicity set aside in his analysis of the wage–profit relationship, the rate of profits is always bounded from above (that is, there is a finite maximum rate of profits) – with important implications for the theory of distribution, capital accumulation, and technical change. (For an in-depth discussion of Sraffa's comments on Bortkiewicz, see Gehrke and Kurz 2006.) As regards Bortkiewicz's treatment of the "transformation problem", Sraffa objected that while Bortkiewicz had assumed different organic compositions of capital between the three departments under consideration, he had implicitly assumed the same organic compositions of all industries within each department.

CHRISTIAN GEHRKE AND HEINZ D. KURZ

See also:

Vladimir Karpovich Dmitriev (I); Francis Ysidro Edgeworth (I); General equilibrium theory (III); Karl Heinrich Marx (I); David Ricardo (I); Piero Sraffa (I); Value and price (III); Marie-Esprit-Léon Walras (I).

References and further reading

Böhm-Bawerk, E. von (1889), *Kapital und Kapitalzins*, vol. 2: *Positive Theorie des Kapitales*, 2nd edn 1902, Innsbruck: Wagner'sche Universitätsbuchhandlung.

Böhm-Bawerk, E. von (1896), 'Zum Abschluss des Marxschen Systems', in O. von Boenigk (ed.), *Staatswirtschaftliche Arbeiten. Festgaben für Karl Knies*, Berlin: Haering.

Bortkiewicz, L. von (1890), 'Book review article of Léon Walras, *Eléments d'économie politique pure, ou Théorie de la richesse sociale*, 2nd edn', *Revue d'économie politique*, **4** (1), 80–96.

Bortkiewicz, L. von (1893), *Die mittlere Lebensdauer. Die Methoden ihrer Bestimmung und ihr Verhältnis zur Sterblichkeitsmessung*, Jena: Gustav Fischer.

Bortkiewicz, L. von (1898a), 'Die Grenznutzentheorie als Grundlage einer ultraliberalen Wirtschaftspolitik' [book review of Vilfredo Pareto, *Cours d'économie politique*], *Schmollers Jahrbuch für Gesetzgebung, Verwaltung, und Volkswirtschaft im deutschen Reich*, **22**, 1177–216.

Bortkiewicz, L. von (1898b), 'Book review of Léon Walras, *Etudes d'économie sociale*', *Jahrbuch für Gesetzgebung, Verwaltung, und Volkswirtschaft im deutschen Reich*, **22**, 1075–8 (new series: **22** (3), 369–72).

Bortkiewicz, L. von (1898c), *Das Gesetz der kleinen Zahlen*, Leipzig: B.G. Teubner.

Bortkiewicz, L. von (1903), 'Über die Methode der "Standard Population"', *Bulletin de l'Institut International de Statistique*, **14** (1), 145ff, **14** (2), 418ff.

Bortkiewicz, L. von (1904), 'Die Theorie der Bevölkerungs- und Mortalitätsstatistik nach Lexis', *Jahrbücher für Nationalökonomie und Statistik*, **27**, 230–54.

Bortkiewicz, L. von (1906), 'Der Kardinalfehler der Böhm-Bawerkschen Zinstheorie', *Schmollers Jahrbuch*, **30**, 943–72.

Bortkiewicz, L. von (1906–07), 'Wertrechnung und Preisrechnung im Marxschen System', three parts, *Archiv für Sozialwissenschaft und Sozialpolitik*, **23**, 1–50, **25**, 10–51, 445–88.

Bortkiewicz, L. von (1907a), 'Zur Berichtigung der grundlegenden theoretischen Konstruktion von Marx im 3. Band des *Kapital*', *Jahrbücher für Nationalökonomie und Statistik*, **34**, 319–35.

Bortkiewicz, L. von (1907b), 'Zur Zinstheorie. II. Entgegnung', *Schmollers Jahrbuch*, **31**, 1288–307.

Bortkiewicz, L. von (1910–11), 'Die Rodbertus'sche Grundrententheorie und die Marx'sche Lehre von der absoluten Grundrente', *Archiv für die Geschichte des Sozialismus und der Arbeiterbewegung*, **1**, 1–14, 391–434.

Bortkiewicz, L. von (1911), 'Die Sterbeziffer und der Frauenüberschuss in der stationären und in der progressiven Bevölkerung. Zugleich ein Beitrag zur Frage der Berechnung der verlebten Zeit', *Bulletin de l'Institut International de Statistique*, **19** (1), 63–183.

Bortkiewicz, L. von (1919), 'Zu den Grundrententheorien von Rodbertus und Marx', *Archiv für die Geschichte des Sozialismus und der Arbeiterbewegung*, **8**, 248–57.

Bortkiewicz, L. von (1921), 'Objektivismus und Subjektivismus in der Werttheorie', *Ekonomisk tidskrift*, **21** (1), 1–22.

Bortkiewicz, L. von (1923–24), 'Zweck und Struktur einer Preisindexzahl', pts 1, 2, 3, *Nordisk statistisk tidskrift*, **2**, 369–408, **3**, 208–52, 494–516.

Bortkiewicz, L. von (1925), 'Böhm-Bawerks Hauptwerk in seinem Verhältnis zur sozialistischen Theorie des Kapitalzinses', *Archiv für die Geschichte des Sozialismus und der Arbeiterbewegung*, **11**, 161–72.

Bortkiewicz, L. von (1949), 'On the correction of Marx's fundamental theoretical construction in the "Third Volume of *Capital*"' (English trans. of L. von Bortkiewicz (1907), 'Zur Berichtigung der grundlegenden theoretischen Konstruktion von Marx im 3. Band des *Kapital*'), in P.M. Sweezy (ed.), *Karl Marx and the Close of his System*, New York: Kelley, pp. 199–221.

Bortkiewicz, L. von (1952), 'Value and price in the Marxian system' (English trans. of pts 2 and 3 of L. von Bortkiewicz (1906–07), 'Wertrechnung und Preisrechnung im Marxschen System'), in *International Economic Papers*, **2**, 5–60.

Bortkiewicz, L. von (1971), *La teoria economica di Marx e altri saggi su Böhm-Bawerk, Walras, e Pareto*, ed. L. Meldolesi, Turin: Giulio Einaudi.

Bridel, P. (2008), 'Bortkiewicz et Walras. Notes sur une collaboration intellectuelle avortée', *Revue d'économie politique*, **118** (5), 711–42.

Dmitriev, V.K. (1974), *Economic Essays on Value, Competition and Utility*, Cambridge: Cambridge University Press, English trans. of a collection of Dmitriev's essays published in Russian in 1904, ed. D.M. Nuti, Dmitriev's essay on Ricardo's theory of value originally published in 1898.

Edgeworth, F.Y. (1889), '"The mathematical theory of political economy", review of L. Walras's *Éléments d'économie politique pure*, 2nd edn', *Nature*, **40** (5 September), 434–6.

Gehrke, C. (2012), 'Marx's critique of Ricardo's theory of rent: a re-assessment', in C. Gehrke, N. Salvadori, I. Steedman and R. Sturn (eds), *Classical Political Economy and Modern Theory. Essays in Honour of Heinz Kurz*, London: Routledge, pp. 51–84.

Gehrke, C. and H.D. Kurz (2006), 'Sraffa on von Bortkiewicz: reconstructing the classical theory of value and distribution', *History of Political Economy*, **38** (1), 91–149.

Gumbel, E.J. (1968), 'Ladislaus von Bortkiewicz', in D.L. Sills (ed.), *International Encyclopedia of the Social Sciences*, vol. 2, New York: Macmillan, pp. 128–31.
Keynes, J.M. (1921), *A Treatise on Probability*, London: Macmillan.
Kurz, H.D. and N. Salvadori (1995), *Theory of Production. A Long-Period Analysis*, Cambridge: Cambridge University Press.
Kurz, H.D. and N. Salvadori (2013), 'On the "vexata questio of value": Ricardo, Marx and Sraffa', in L. Taylor, A. Rezai and T. Michl (eds), *Social Fairness and Economics. Economic Essays in the Spirit of Duncan Foley*, London: Routledge, pp. 213–27.
Marchionatti, R. (2007), 'On the application of mathematics to political economy. The Edgeworth–Walras–Bortkiewicz controversy, 1889–1891', *Cambridge Journal of Economics*, **31** (2), 291–307.
Ricardo, D. (1951–73), *The Works and Correspondence of David Ricardo*, 11 vols, ed. P. Sraffa, with the collaboration of M.H. Dobb, Cambridge: Cambridge University Press.
Samuelson, P.A. (1976), 'Resolving a historical confusion in population analysis', *Human Biology*, **48** (3), 559–80.
Schumpeter, J.A. (1954), *History of Economic Analysis*, New York: Oxford University Press.
Sraffa Papers, unpublished papers of Piero Sraffa, Trinity College Library, Cambridge, UK (numbers refer to the catalogue prepared by Jonathan Smith, archivist).
Sraffa, P. (1960), *Production of Commodities by Means of Commodities*, Cambridge: Cambridge University Press.
Walras, L. (1965), *Correspondence of Léon Walras and Related Papers*, ed. W. Jaffé, 3 vols, Amsterdam: North Holland.

Vladimir Karpovich Dmitriev (1868–1913)

Vladimir K. Dmitriev (1868–1913) was a Russian mathematical economist who published three major essays on economic theory. Born near Smolensk, Dmitriev studied medicine and political economy at the University of Moscow before he took up a post as an excise controller in the provincial town of Von'kovitsy in 1896. Three years later he had to give up this post, because he had contracted pulmonary tuberculosis, and chronic illness and notorious financial problems plagued him for the rest of his life. (For further biographical details, see Nuti 1974.)

In 1898 Dmitriev published an essay (in Russian) on Ricardo's theory of value, followed in 1902 by two further articles on Cournot's theory of competition and on the theory of marginal utility. In 1904, the three essays were published together (in Russian) in a book entitled *Economic Essays. First Series: Attempt at an Organic Synthesis of the Labour Theory of Value and the Theory of Marginal Utility*. A French translation of this collection of essays was published in 1968 (Dmitriev 1968) and an English translation in 1974 (Dmitriev 1974); the three essays are also available in Italian, Spanish and German translations (Schütte 2003). Dmitriev's further writings include a survey on statistical theory, a study on the problem of alcoholism, and several survey articles and book reviews on economic theory. (For a bibliography, see Nuti 1974: 30–31.)

Ricardo's Theory of Value

In his first essay of 1898, entitled "The theory of value of David Ricardo. An attempt at a rigorous analysis", Dmitriev made important contributions to classical economics. In particular, he demonstrated that (1) prices can be decomposed into wages and profits via a "reduction to dated quantities of labour"; (2) relative prices are proportional to relative labour values only with zero profits or with "equal organic composition"; (3) Ricardo's concept of the inverse relationship between the general rate of profits and the real wage rate, given the technical conditions of production, that is, the wage–profit relationship, can be given a precise analytical expression; (4) the data of Ricardo's approach (that is, the real wage rate and the technical conditions of production in the wages goods industry) suffice to determine relative prices and the general rate of profits simultaneously.

Reduction to dated quantities of labour
Dmitriev investigated first how the total amount of labour expended in the production of a commodity can be ascertained. He considered a single product system that can be represented, in matrix notation, as:

$$v = l + Av \tag{1}$$

where A is the $n{\times}n$ matrix of commodity inputs, l is the n-vector of direct labour inputs, and v is the n-vector of direct and indirect labour inputs. Then:

$$v = l + Al + A^2l + \ldots + A^tl + \ldots \tag{2}$$

or

$$v = l_0 + l_1 + l_2 \ldots + l_t + \ldots,$$

where $l_t = A^t l$. Dmitriev set out the simultaneous equation system (1) and concluded that since there are as many equations as unknowns v is determined, given A and l. He thus disposed of the common misconception that a "historical digression" would be needed in order to ascertain the total labour contents of commodities:

> [W]e can always find the total sum of the labour directly and indirectly expended on the production of any product *under present-day production conditions*. . . . the fact that all capital under *present-day* conditions is itself produced with the assistance of other capital in no way hinders a precise solution of the problem. (Dmitriev 1974: 44)

However, in the following, Dmitriev then assumed that the series of dated quantities of labour in (2) is finite, and thus implicitly adopted an "Austrian" perspective: Dmitriev's representation of production processes in terms of a finite series of dated quantities of labour corresponds to Austrian processes of the "flow input–point output" type, and presupposes the non-existence of basic commodities (Kurz and Salvadori 1995: 176–8). Within this framework, Dmitriev then confirmed the proposition, originally proposed by Smith and adopted by Ricardo, that the price of every commodity can be entirely resolved into wages and profits. Following the classical authors, wages are supposed to be paid *ante factum* and prices are explained in terms of a reduction to a finite stream of dated quantities of labour, that is:

$$p = (1 + r)w[l + (1 + r)Al + (1 + r)^2 A^2 l + \ldots + (1 + r)^k \, A^k l] \tag{3}$$

or

$$p = (1 + r)w[l_0 + (1 + r)l_1 + (1 + r)^2 l_2 + \ldots + (1 + r)^k l_k]$$

Proportionality of prices and labour values

Dmitriev next turned to the investigation of relative prices, which in his framework are given by:

$$\frac{p_i}{p_j} = \frac{(1 + r)we_i^T[l + (1 + r)Al + (1 + r)^2 A^2 l + \ldots + (1 + r)^k A^k l]}{(1 + r)we_j^T[l + (1 + r)Al + (1 + r)^2 A^2 l + \ldots + (1 + r)^k A^k l]} \tag{4}$$

or

$$\frac{p_i}{p_j} = \frac{l_{i0} + (1 + r)l_{i1} + (1 + r)^2 l_{i2} + \ldots + (1 + r)^k l_{ik}}{l_{j0} + (1 + r)l_{j1} + (1 + r)^2 l_{j2} + \ldots + (1 + r)^k l_{jk}}$$

where $l_{it} = e_i^T l_t$. Dmitriev confirmed Ricardo's finding that relative prices are proportional to relative labour values in two special cases only: the first, when the series of dated quantities of labour are linearly dependent pairwise, that is, when the commodities exhibit "identical organic composition"; and the second when the rate of profits is zero.

Wage–profit relationship

Dmitriev next turned to the analysis of the general rate of profits and of natural prices. He praised Ricardo for having clearly specified the factors which determine the general rate of profits, that is, the real wage rate and the technical conditions of production in the industries producing wage goods or means of production used (directly or indirectly) in the production of wage goods: "Ricardo's immortal contribution was his brilliant solution of this seemingly insoluble problem" (1974: 58, first published in 1898). Dmitriev suggested that Ricardo had accomplished the solution of this problem because he recognized "that there is one production equation by means of which we may determine the magnitude of *r directly* (that is, without having recourse for assistance to the other equations)" (ibid.: 59, original emphasis). In Dmitriev's reading, Ricardo had adopted the simplifying assumption that the real wage basket consists only of corn, that is:

$$w = p_c c, \tag{5}$$

with *c* as the amount and p_c as the price of corn, respectively. In this case the rate of profits is determined from the price equation of the corn industry alone, without recourse to the price system, since:

$$p_c = (1 + r)p_c c e_c^T [\mathbf{l} + (1 + r)A\mathbf{l} + (1 + r)^2 A^2 \mathbf{l} + \ldots + (1 + r)^k A^k \mathbf{l}] \tag{6}$$

or

$$\frac{1}{c} = (1 + r)e_c^T [\mathbf{l}_0 + (1 + r)\mathbf{l}_1 + (1 + r)^2 \mathbf{l}_2 + \ldots + (1 + r)^k \mathbf{l}_k]$$

so that, with $l_{ct} = e_c^T \mathbf{l}_t$, it follows that $r = f(l_{c0}, l_{c1}, l_{c2}, \ldots, l_{ck}; c)$. Dmitriev then generalized this model by considering the case of many wage goods and vindicated Ricardo's proposition – which had been disputed by Marx – that the general rate of profits is not affected by changes in the conditions of production of the "non-basic" industries, that is, industries which produce neither wage goods nor means of production used directly or indirectly in the wage goods industries.

Simultaneous determination of prices and distribution

Next, Dmitriev refuted Léon Walras's contention (1874 [1954], lesson 40, s.368) that Ricardo's "cost of production explanation of prices" involved circular reasoning, because the number of unknowns exceeds the number of equations in the classical approach to value and distribution. Dmitriev deserves the credit for having demonstrated that the data of Ricardo's approach, that is, the real wage rate and the technical conditions of production, suffice to determine relative prices and the general rate of profits simultaneously.

In the remainder of his essay, Dmitriev also discussed the theory of competition, the problem of the choice of technique, the problem of fixed capital, and the theory of rent. In the course of his investigation he also introduced the concept of "total requirements for gross output" and thereby anticipated some elements of the so-called "hypothetical extraction method" of modern input–output analysis (see Mariolis and Rodousaki 2011);

he also provided the first clear statement of the so-called "(dynamic) non-substitution theorem". Although he aimed at "an organic synthesis" of classical and marginal utility theory, Dmitriev nevertheless retained the fundamental asymmetry in the treatment of the distributive variables which characterizes the classical approach to economic analysis, arguing that the investigation of the conditions affecting the level of real wages "falls outside the scope of political economy" (Dmitriev 1974: 74).

Dmitriev's formalization of Ricardo's theory of prices and distribution was a major source of inspiration for Ladislaus von Bortkiewicz, who praised his essay of 1898 as a "remarkable work", which "bears evidence of an exceptional theoretical talent and presents something really new" (Bortkiewicz 1952: 20, n. 31). As von Bortkiewicz pointed out, Vladimir K. Dmitriev introduced the idea of solving systems of simultaneous equations into the classical analysis of prices and distribution and contributed to the clarification of the analytical structure of the classical approach to economic theory.

Cournot's Theory of Competition

In the second essay, Dmitriev critically examined Cournot's theory of competition and made some steps towards the development of a theory of competition with strategic interaction. He anticipated some elements of Chamberlin's approach to imperfect competition theory and showed that a homogeneous oligopoly has a determinate solution which corresponds to an implicit collusion (Schütte 2003: 160–72). The starting point of his argument is the observation that Cournot's analysis, in which each seller is supposed to seek a "temporary profit" (Cournot's "*bénéfice momentané*") from expanding his individual output until in equilibrium price equals marginal costs (or costs of production), is based on the assumption that other sellers cannot react immediately by increasing their market supplies. Rejecting this premise, Dmitriev argued that in competitive conditions producers will hold inventories and/or excess capacity for strategic reasons, that is, as a threat to competitors (1974: 148). Dmitriev indeed provided the same explanation for (implicit) cooperative behaviour as modern game-theoretic approaches to oligopoly theory. In fact, by separating the producers' decisions on production from those on sales (by means of inventories or excess capacities), he introduced sunk costs and a two-step recursive solution procedure, in precisely the same way as in sequential games for oligopolistic markets of the 1970s and 1980s (for example, Spence, Dixit, Rotemberg).

Marginal Utility Theory

In the third essay Dmitriev provided a detailed account of the genesis of marginal utility theory. This essay is mainly of interest from the perspective of the history of economic thought, because Dmitriev disputed the occurrence of a major break in the development of economic theory in terms of a "marginal revolution" in the 1870s by arguing that important contributions to marginal utility theory had been made already much earlier by economists such as Gossen, Senior, Rossi, Dupuit, and Molinari, and that, indeed, "we find *all the information* needed for the construction of a *finished* theory of marginal utility in the work of such an 'old' economist as Galiani" (Dmitriev 1974: 182, original emphases). He also maintained that "*the Austrian School* as such (Menger, Böhm-Bawerk, von Wieser, and others) *added very little* (unless much significance is given to the introduction of new terms) *to what had been done* before them *for the solution of the problem*" (ibid.: 181, original emphases). Important contributions had only been made by economists who used the mathematical method, including "Walras (who may justifiably be regarded as the creator of marginal utility theory), Launhardt, Auspitz and Lieben and Jevons" (ibid.: 182). Dmitriev neatly summarized these contributions, but he showed no awareness that utility need not be cardinally measurable and did not himself contribute to the further development of marginal utility theory.

CHRISTIAN GEHRKE

See also:

Ladislaus von Bortkiewicz (I); British classical political economy (II); Neo-Ricardian economics (II); David Ricardo (I); Russian School of mathematical economics (II); Piero Sraffa (I).

References and further reading

Bortkiewicz, L. von (1906–07), 'Wertrechnung und Preisrechnung im Marxschen System', *Archiv für Sozialwissenschaften und Sozialpolitik*, **23** (1906), 1–50, **25** (1907), 10–51, 445–88.

Bortkiewicz, L. von (1952), 'Value and price in the Marxian system', *International Economic Papers*, **2**, 5–60, English trans. of L. von Bortkiewicz (1907), 'Wertrechnung und Preisrechnung im Marxschen System', *Archiv für Sozialwissenschaften und Sozialpolitik*, **25**, 10–51, 445–88.

Dmitriev, V.K. (1968), *Essais économiques. Esquisse de synthèse organique de la théorie de la valeur-travail et de la théorie de l'utilité marginale*, French trans. of a collection of Dmitriev's essays published in 1904 in Russian, ed. and introduction by A. Zauberman, postface by H. Denis, Paris: Edition du CNRS.

Dmitriev, V.K. (1974), *Economic Essays on Value, Competition and Utility*, English trans. of a collection of Dmitriev's essays published in 1904 in Russian, ed. and introduction by D.M. Nuti, Cambridge: Cambridge University Press.

Kurz, H.D. and N. Salvadori (1995), *Theory of Production. A Long-Period Analysis*, Cambridge: Cambridge University Press.

Mariolis, T. and E. Rodousaki (2011), 'Total requirements for gross output and intersectoral linkages: a note on Dmitriev's contribution to the theory of profits', *Contributions to Political Economy*, **30** (1), 67–75.

Nuti, D.M. (1974), 'V.K. Dmitriev: a biographical note', in V.K. Dmitriev, *Economic Essays on Value, Competition and Utility*, ed. and introduction by D.M. Nuti, Cambridge: Cambridge University Press, pp. 29–32.

Ricardo, D. (1951–73), *The Works and Correspondence of David Ricardo*, ed. P. Sraffa, with M.H. Dobb, 11 vols, Cambridge: Cambridge University Press.

Schütte, F. (2003), *Die ökonomischen Studien V.K. Dmitrievs. Ein Beitrag zur Interpretation und theoriehistorischen Würdigung unter besonderer Berücksichtigung der russischen Volkswirtschaftslehre*, doctoral dissertation submitted to the Faculty of Economic Sciences at the Technical University of Chemnitz, accessed 23 November 2015 at http://www.qucosa.de/fileadmin/data/qucosa/documents/5136/data/start.html.

Walras, L. (1874), *Eléments d'économie politique pure*, Lausanne: Corbaz, English trans. W. Jaffé (ed.) (1954), *Elements of Pure Economics*, London: Allen and Unwin.

Louis Bachelier (1870–1946)

Louis Bachelier was born in Le Havre on 11 March 1870. He stopped his studies in 1889 on the death of his father and managed the family business. He enrolled in 1992 in the Paris Faculty of sciences and, in 1900, defended his thesis on 'Théorie de la speculation'. His supervisor was Henri Poincaré. His academic career was difficult: he only obtained his first position in 1919 as lecturer at the University of Besançon. From there, he lectured in Dijon from 1922 to 1925 and in Rennes from 1925 to 1927. He became a professor in 1927 in Besançon and died on 26 April 1946 in Saint-Servan-sur-Mer.

Bachelier was not aiming at "analysing the causes, which act on the stock prices; this research would be vain and would only lead to errors" (Bachelier 1914 [1993]: 176–7). The evolution of the stock prices cannot be forecast: it is submitted to the law of chance. Bachelier, however, does not discard determinism: the variations of stock prices have causes, but they are unknown and, worse, unknowable. One must thus reason as if chance alone was acting. But while the evolution of prices cannot be determined, it is perhaps possible to find the law of probability, which governs them. "It is precisely because one wants to ignore everything that it is possible to know" (ibid.).

As an illustration of his research, Bachelier examines the 3 per cent rent, which was at that time the object of the greatest number of transactions. As a matured coupon of 0.75 franc was paid monthly, the price of the bond increased every month by 25 cents. It was necessary to eliminate this drift and Bachelier takes into account what he calls the true price, net of the mature coupon. He finds it, moreover, convenient to norm the present market price at zero. When he writes that, at instant t, the price of the bond is x_t this means that x_t is the difference between the true price at t and the actual price of the bond.

Bachelier's developments rely on three principles: the principles of the mathematical expectation, of indifference and of uniformity. Jules Regnault (1863: 34, original emphasis) in his *Calcul des chances*, wrote that at the stock exchange:

> the mechanism of the game boils down to . . . two opposite probabilities: the *increase* or the *decrease* . . . At any moment, the probability of the one is not superior to the probability of the other; as we ignore the future result, it is absolutely indifferent to bet for or against, . . . to buy rather than sell or sell rather than buy.

Bachelier develops this idea. At a given moment, in the market, some speculators expect a rise in price, some others a fall. However, as the equality between supply and demand determines the market price, "it seems that *at a given moment*, all the speculators must neither believe in a rise nor in a fall since, for any quoted price, there are as many sellers and buyers" (Bachelier 1900: 31–2, original emphasis). The mathematical expectation of any operation is nil.

Regnault (1863: 38) maintained that, at the stock exchange:

> the player is always tempted to forecast what should happen on the basis of what happened, so that, after three or four days of falling prices, he tends to believe in a rise the next day, but at some other times he will think that the fall will continue, despite the fact that these various effects are totally independent.

This statement can be seen as the origin of what Bachelier calls the principle of independence: the changes in the market price at a given moment are independent from the past variations and from the price that is quoted at the given instant. Quotations follow a random walk, a random process without any memory, where the future only depends on the past through the present.

The principle of uniformity states that the instability of the market prices does not vary through time. Bachelier (1912: 286) justifies this by maintaining that the market does not have any reason to believe that the probability of the given variation in prices would be different tomorrow from what it is today. But this hypothesis does not have the same importance as the principle of indifference. It is a simplifying device for computations, but most of the results obtained by Bachelier remain valid without it.

On these bases, Bachelier determines the law of probability of the price. Let $p_{z,t}dz$ be the probability that, at instant $t = t_1 + t_2$, the price of the bond is included between z and $z + dz$. We seek the probability that the price z be quoted at epoch $t_1 + t_2$, the price x having been quoted at epoch t_1. It is equal to the probability $p_{x,t_1}dx$ that in t_1 the price will be x, multiplied by the probability $p_{z-x,t_2}dz$ that z will be quoted in $t_1 + t_2$, knowing that x was quoted in t_1. Hence $p_{z,t}dz = p_{x,t_1}p_{z-x,t_2}dxdz$. Through integration, the probability that, at instant t, the price will be z is:

$$p_{z,t}dz = \int_{-\infty}^{+\infty} p_{x,t_1}p_{z-x,t_2}dxdz \tag{1}$$

Bachelier then shows that, if the principle of uniformity is verified and if k is the coefficient of instability, a solution is:

$$p_{x,t} = \frac{e^{-\frac{x^2}{4\pi k^2 t}}}{2\pi k\sqrt{t}} \tag{2}$$

At instant t, the bond price follows a standard normal distribution. The probability is a function of time, increases until a certain time and decreases thereafter. In order to study the law of probability followed by the market prices, and as they are the effects of "unanalysable" factors, Bachelier must face the problem of the sum of small independent hazards. He thought that the shocks, which create price fluctuations, are of the same nature and not too scattered, so that their variance is finite. This restrictive hypothesis was the only one possible at that time: the addition of small random magnitudes can generate other laws than the Gaussian distribution, but it is only in the 1930s that Paul Lévy and Alexandre Khintchine established this point.

Prior to Bachelier, many scientists applied mathematics to economic phenomena, but their tools were well known. Cournot is a typical example. Bachelier instead introduces new mathematical tools to deal with questions, which, admittedly, had been broached upon by some predecessors like Regnault, but were left unanswered. "It is above all from the point of view of pure science", he wrote, "that the theory of speculation was useful . . . It generated the theory of the radiation of probabilities and the theory of continuous probabilities . . . If speculation did not exist, one should imagine it in order to better understand the laws of chance" (Bachelier, 1914 [1993]: 177–8). The number of discoveries he made in economics and mathematics is remarkable. He started the analysis of the Brownian motion and of the Markovian processes, introduced the idea of a random walk and of efficient markets. Not surprisingly, such a novel and path-breaking work was not understood for a long time.

Mathematicians were among the first to recognize Bachelier's contribution to the mathematical theory of the Brownian motion (Kolmogorov 1931: 417). Economists kept silent. The idea was prevailing, in general, that it was impossible to rely on the probability calculus to study moral sciences. "When men are together, they do not decide any more by chance and independently from each other; they interact" (Poincaré 1907: 275). It was this interaction that had to be understood.

It is through two apparently independent ways that Bachelier's work became known to economists. Paul Samuelson (Taqqu 2001: 25) writes that, in the 1950s, Leonard J. Savage drew the attention of his colleagues to the book *Le jeu, la chance et le hasard*, in which Bachelier intended to spread his ideas among a larger public. Samuelson, while looking for this book in the library of the Massachusetts Institute of Technology (MIT) discovered *La théorie de la spéculation*. He advised one of his students, Richard Kruizenga, to read it. The latter used Bachelier's analysis of the value of options in his thesis (Kruizenga 1956).

The idea that the price of financial assets could not be forecast had imposed itself progressively. M.F. Maury Osborne, who wrote in this tradition, showed that the probability distribution of the variations of the logarithms of the prices was precisely that of a particle in a Brownian motion (1959a: 145). When he was writing this paper, Osborne did not know Samuelson or Bachelier, but when he read his predecessors, he acknowledged the importance of *Théorie de la spéculation*:

> I believe the pioneer work on randomness in economic time series, and yet most modern in viewpoint, is that of Bachelier . . . [He] proceeds, by quite elegant mathematical methods, directly from the assumption that the expected gain (in francs) at any instant on the Bourse is zero, to a normal distribution of price changes, with dispersion increasing as the square root of the time, in accordance with the Fourier equation of heat diffusion. . . To him is due credit for major priority on this problem (Osborne 1959b: 808).

As soon as Bachelier's contribution was recognized, a debate arose and the two hypotheses, on which he relied – the variations of prices are independent random variables, and they follow a normal distribution – were scrutinized. The second was discussed first. Benoît Mandelbrot (1963), while studying the evolution of the price of cotton, showed that it exhibited extreme variations, which could not be explained by a Gaussian distribution: "A great number of small variations of prices ran alongside . . . huge ones . . . just as huge legions of poor co-exist with some privileged plutocrats" (Mandelbrot and Hudson 2004 [2005]: 183). To the normal standard distribution, Mandelbrot (1962) and Eugene Fama (1963) proposed to substitute a power law such as the one used by Pareto to express the distribution of income.

Bachelier supposed that the successive variations of prices are independent random variables. Mandelbrot (1963: 418) maintained that this is not so: "large changes tend to be followed by large changes – of either sign – and small changes tend to be followed by small changes". This scheme, which is neither regular nor predictable, shows the existence of a long-term memory through which the past influences the present. The idea that prices follow a random walk, that the probability distribution of the variations of prices at instant *t* neither depends on the level of prices at this instant, nor on its past evolution, was thus rejected.

The current mainstream in modern finance is based on the foundations Bachelier laid in 1900. Its critics often rely on Mandelbrot's propositions. However, while Mandelbrot discards Bachelier's hypotheses, his admiration for the man is real (Mandelbrot and Hudson 2004 [2005]: 65 ff.).

ALAIN BÉRAUD

See also:

Financial economics (III); Paul Anthony Samuelson (I).

References and further reading

Bachelier, L. (1900), 'Théorie de la spéculation', *Annales scientifiques de l'École Normale Supérieure*, 3rd series, **17**, 21–85, reprinted 1995, Sceaux: Jacques Gabay.
Bachelier, L. (1912), *Calcul des probabilités*, Paris: Gauthier-Villars.
Bachelier, L. (1914), *Le jeu, la chance et le hasard*, Paris: Flammarion, reprinted 1993, Sceaux: Jacques Gabay.
Bachelier, L. (2006), *Theory of Speculation*, trans. and commentary by M. Davis and A, Etheridge, Princeton, NJ: Princeton University Press.
Courtault, J.-M. and Y. Kabanov (eds) (2002), *Louis Bachelier. Aux origines de la finance mathématique*, Besançon: Presses Universitaires Franc-Comtoises.
Fama, E.F. (1963), 'Mandelbrot and the stable Paretian hypothesis', *Journal of Business*, **36** (4), 420–29.
Jovanovic, F. and P. Le Gall (2001), 'Does God practice a random walk? The financial physics of a nineteenth-century forerunner, Jules Regnault', *European Journal of the History of Political Economy*, **8** (3), 332–62.
Kolmogorov, A. (1931), 'Uber die analytischen Methoden in der Wahrscheinlichkeitsrechnung', *Mathematische Annalen*, **104**, 415–58.
Kruizenga, R. (1956), 'Put and call options: a theoretical and market analysis', PhD thesis, MIT.
Mandelbrot, B. (1962), 'Sur certains prix spéculatifs: faits empiriques et modèle basé sur les processus stables additifs de Paul Levy', *Comptes rendus hebdomadaires des séances de l'Académie des sciences*, **254** (3), 3968–70.
Mandelbrot, B. (1963), 'The variation of certain speculative prices', *Journal of Business*, **36** (4), 394–419.
Mandelbrot, B. and R.L. Hudson (2004), *The (Mis)Behavior of Markets. A Fractal View of Risk, Ruin and Reward*, New York: Basic Books, French trans. 2005, Paris: Odile Jacob.
Osborne, M.F.M. (1959a), 'Brownian motion in the stock market', *Operations Research*, **7** (2), 145–73.
Osborne, M.F.M. (1959b), 'Reply to "Comment on Brownian Motion in the Stock Market"', *Operations Research*, **7** (6), 807–11.
Poincaré, H. (1907), 'Le hasard', *La revue du mois*, **3** (15), 257–76.
Regnault, J. (1863), *Calcul des chances et philosophie de la bourse*, Paris: Mallet-Bachelier and Castel.
Taqqu, M.S. (2001), 'Bachelier and his time: a conversation with Bernard Bru', *Finance and Stochastics*, **5** (1), 3–32.
Walter, C. (1996), 'Une histoire du concept d'efficience sur les marchés financiers', *Annales. Histoire, Sciences Sociales*, **51** (4), 873–905.

Arthur Spiethoff (1873–1957)

The German economist Arthur Spiethoff was born in Düsseldorf in 1873. He studied economics and politics in Berlin and was an assistant of Gustav Schmoller between 1899 and 1908. In 1905 he received a PhD for his work on economic crises. After finishing his habilitation in 1907 Spiethoff became full professor at the German University of Prague in 1908. From 1918 until his retirement in 1939 he was professor at the University of Bonn. Arthur Spiethoff died in 1957 in Tübingen. On Spiefhoff's life and academic record, see Clausing (1958) and Kamp (1969).

Arthur Spiethoff is known for his work on economic methodology and business cycles. In the *History of Economic Analysis* Joseph A. Schumpeter notes that Spiethoff is one of "most eminent members" of "a 'youngest' historical school" and that "[t]he international reputation of Arthur Spiethoff . . . rests upon his outstanding performance in the field of business cycle research" (Schumpeter 1954: 815–16).

Between Spiethoff and Schumpeter there is both a personal and intellectual connection. As noted by Kurz (2013), they were not only friends but also shared similar methodological positions. Schumpeter was influenced by what Spiethoff termed "historical" or "observational theory". Observational theory building starts with empirical and historical investigations of the phenomenon under consideration in order to identify and isolate its essential regularities. Then it tries to provide a causal explanation of the essential regularities using theoretical concepts and tools (see Spiethoff 2002a: 109–12). In his later methodological work, Spiethoff further aimed at reconciling pure theory and historical studies by developing a theory of "economic styles" (see, for example, Gioia 1997). Two of Spiethoff's methodological publications in English are "The 'historical character' of economic theories" (Spiethoff 1952) and in 1953 "Pure theory and economic Gestalt theory: ideal and real types" (Spiethoff 1953).

Moreover, both Spiethoff and Schumpeter studied business cycles and "were convinced of the *endogenous* nature of the ups and downs of economic activity and sought to understand the 'beat of the heart' of the capitalist economy" (Kurz 2013: 152, original emphasis). Spiethoff's most important work on business cycles is his famous essay "Krisen" ("Business cycles") published in 1925 in German (Spiethoff 1925). The English translation was published as *Business Cycles* in 1953 (see Spiethoff 2002a). The essay builds on his 1902 article "Vorbemerkungen zu einer Theorie der Überproduktion" ("Preliminary remarks to a theory of overproduction") (see Spiethoff 2002b), which marks the beginning of Spiethoff's analysis of crises and cycles. The follow-up book *Die wirtschaftlichen Wechsellagen. Aufschwung, Krise, Stockung* (*Economic Cycles. Upswing, Crisis and Stagnation*) was published in 1955 (Spiethoff 1955). The two volumes include both a reprint of his 1925 essay and the large amount of statistical material on which his theory of the business cycle is based.

For Spiethoff, the endogenous business cycle is a relatively new phenomenon but nonetheless a very significant one: "The 'normal state' is neither the upswing, nor the downswing, nor, least of all, the crisis. What is normal in a free, highly capitalist market system based on money, is the business cycle" (Spiethoff 2002a: 200). This view on economic fluctuations was shared by Schumpeter, who states that "with the possible exception of Marx, Spiethoff was the first to recognize explicitly that cycles are not merely a non-essential concomitant of capitalist evolution but that they are the essential form of capitalist life" (Schumpeter 1954: 1127).

Spiethoff's explanation of endogenous business cycles rests on three elements: (1) the profit motive as the driver of the system, (2) a distinction between the role of investment and consumption goods in explaining business cycles and (3) overproduction as an unavoidable consequence of any upward movement. On some important differences between the theories of Spiethoff and Schumpeter, see Kurz (2013).

The upswing consists of two phases: revival and expansion. The revival is a child of the slump, in which interest rates and wages are low due to capital laying idle and owing to high unemployment. However, these circumstances alone do not suffice to bring about an upswing, but profit expectations must turn positive to induce an expansion of economic activity: "The ultimate cause of the upward movement is of a psychological rather than of an economic nature" (Spiethoff 2002a: 181). The psychological momentum facilitating the upswing is provided by pioneers, who engage in risky investment projects. If they succeed their high profit margins induce others to revise their profit expectations for the better in the light of promising investment opportunities. What is needed are "brave, enterprising men . . . willing to risk a large part of their fortune . . . They can, however, set the pace for investment and for the upswing only to the extent to which they are blessed with a success which will be as visible as a beacon" (Spiethoff 2002a: 182–3).

Spiethoff argues that the success of the pioneers is mostly due to their conquest of "fields of new profits" (2002a: 183) and that rising expected profitability "appears to have originated chiefly in two wide fields: the expansion of world trade, i.e. the opening up of fresh markets, and technical development" (ibid.: 183). A higher expected profitability leads to an increase in real capital formation and therefore an increase in the demand for investment goods.

After a successful take-off, the economy expands and booms. The boom is characterized by a "chain of upswing phenomena". Spiethoff explains: "As with a rolling snowball, each turn expands the sphere: increased investment, increased consumption, rising prices and profits, together with the expansion of production and of capital formation and then again increased investment etc. . . . . The result is a constant spiral-like self-raising movement" (Spiethoff 2002a: 188).

The essential feature of the upswing are rising consumption of certain capital goods and rising prices of those goods. In his empirical studies, Spiethoff singled out iron consumption per capita as a good indicator of economic fluctuations.

The end of every boom is brought about by overproduction of durable capital goods. Spiethoff emphasizes disproportions between different spheres of production owing to uneven expansion of different sectors and time lags in the adjustment of capacity and production to demand as the main source of the slow-down. This idea is captured by the concept of disproportionate production:

> The means of production may be wrongly distributed, so that overproduction in one place corresponds to insufficient production in another (*disproportionate production*). Recent research has shown *overinvestment* to be the most important form. This kind of overproduction is concentrated in indirect consumption goods and is caused by an excess of investment for the construction of industrial plant and long-term public utilities (investment goods) over both demand and disposable savings. (Spiethoff 2002a: 113–14, original emphasis)

Moreover, the shortage of complementary input factors like working capital and labour of certain skills induces an upward pressure on wages and interest rates. This squeezes profit margins, frustrates investors and further decelerates expansion. Then, "self-propagating downswing forces" (Spiethoff 2002a: 196) unfold and lead the system into a crisis in which prices, interest rates and wages move down, re-establishing favourable conditions for an new upswing.

DAVID HAAS

See also:

Business and cycles and growth (III); German and Austrian schools (II); Historical economics (II); Joseph Alois Schumpeter (I).

References and further reading

Clausing, G. (1958), 'Arthur Spiethoff's wissenschaftliches Lebenswerk', *Schmollers Jahrbuch für Gesetzgebung, Verwaltung und Volkswirtschaft*, **78**, 257–90.
Gioia, V. (1997), 'Historical changes and economics in Arthur Spiethoff's theory of Wirtschaftsstil (style of an economic system)', in P. Koslowski (ed.), *Methodology of the Social Sciences, Ethics, and Economics in the Newer Historical School. From Max Weber and Rickert to Sombart and Rothacker*, Berlin and Heidelberg: Springer, pp. 168–90.
Kamp, M.E. (1969), 'Arthur Spiethoff', in M.E. Kamp and F.H. Stamm (eds), *Bonner Gelehrte. Beiträge zur Geschichte der Wissenschaften in Bonn. Staatswissenschaften*, Bonn: H. Bouvier und Co. Verlag – Ludwig Röhrscheid Verlag, pp. 26–44.
Kurz, H.D. (2013), 'The beat of the economic heart. Joseph Schumpeter and Arthur Spiethoff on business cycles', *Journal of Evolutionary Economics*, **25** (1), 147–62.
Schumpeter, J.A. (1954), *History of Economic Analysis*, London: Allen & Unwin.
Spiethoff, A. (1902), 'Vorbemerkungen zu einer Theorie der Überproduktion', *Schmollers Jahrbuch für Gesetztgebung, Verwaltung und Volkswirtschaft im Deutschen Reiche*, **26**, 721–59.
Spiethoff, A. (1925), 'Krisen', *Handwörterbuch der Staatswissenschaft*, **6**, 8–91.
Spiethoff, A. (1952), 'The "historical" character of economic theories', *Journal of Economic History*, **12** (2), 131–9.
Spiethoff, A. (1953), 'Pure theory and economic Gestalt theory: ideal types and real types', in F.C. Lane and J.C. Riemersma (eds), *Enterprise and Secular Change: Readings in Economic History*, London: George Allen & Unwin, pp. 444–63.
Spiethoff, A. (1955), *Die wirtschaftlichen Wechsellagen. Aufschwung, Krise, Stockung, with a preface by Edgar Salion*, 2 vols, Tübingen and Zürich: Polygraph.
Spiethoff, A. (2002a), 'Business cycles', in H. Hagemann (ed.), *Business Cycle Theory. Selected Texts 1860–1939, II, Structural Theories of the Business Cycle*, London: Pickering & Chatto, pp. 109–205, paper first published 1953.
Spiethoff, A. (2002b), 'Preliminary remarks to a theory of overproduction', in H. Hagemann (ed.), *Business Cycle Theory. Selected Texts 1860–1939, II, Structural Theories of the Business Cycle*, London: Pickering & Chatto, pp. 45–76, paper first published 1902.

Albert Aftalion (1874–1956)

Albert Aftalion was born in Bulgaria (Roustchouk) in 1874 into a Jewish Sephardi family. He came to France in 1876 when his parents decided to settle in Nancy. He completed a doctorate in law at the University of Paris, where he was appointed as "Chargé de conference" (lecturer) and embarked on a doctorate in political economy (defended in 1899) on the economics of Sismondi. Somewhat surprisingly, at this time, his preoccupation with Sismondi was driven only by his interest in poverty in relation to the industrializing countries, and in interrogating the objectives of political economy more widely (Demals 2002b). In 1900, he moved to the University of Lille and in 1901, after success at the French national academic competition, the "Concours national d'agrégation", he was appointed "Professeur adjoint". He went on to take up a chair in Political Economy and the History of Economic Doctrines in 1906 in the same university. In 1923 he accepted a chair in Statistics at the University of Paris, and in 1934 he succeeded Charles Rist as Professor of Political Economy. Throughout his successful academic career he was deeply respected by his peers. However, during the dark episode in French academia in 1940 (the Jew status laws were enacted on 3 October, 1940), he was dismissed by the Paris University Council (Delmas 2002a). He was not allowed back into the university until 1944, and in 1946 he retired.

Aftalion was one of the most influential French economists in the first half of the twentieth century (Guitton 1957; Lhomme et al. 1957): he had a major influence on the way economics developed in France, and despite the fact that his contributions were not systematically translated into English, he rapidly became well known internationally (Schumpeter 1954, LLP 1914, Persons 1914). His reputation was attributable mainly to his 1909 and 1913 contributions to business cycle theory although he also made contributions in other economic areas.

Aftalion first published in 1896. At that time, he was writing on various topics (married women's rights, the development and regulation of sea ports in Germany and Sismondi). From 1903 (after moving to Lille), he started to focus on industry – mainly the textile industry where his empirical investigations included the conflicting relationships between workers and owners of the firms (1907, 1912). His first publication on this topic appeared in 1908 and was to continue to figure in his work although progressively he included monetary as well as international dimensions in his economic analysis. His interest in monetary issues really began in 1924 with a paper on exchange rates variations, and in 1927 he published a book on monetary theory (Dangel and Rainelli 2000; Dangel in Dormard 2002). This book was very successful and in 1937 was translated into Japanese. Also in 1927 he seemingly published his first paper in English. It is also notable that Aftalion published a paper in 1923 on the foundations of Socialism (Frobert 1999). For the rest of his academic career, Aftalion continued to be interested in monetary and business cycle theories, and he produced an interesting analysis of the crises during the chaotic period between 1930 and 1932 (see, for example, the detailed bibliography in the *Cahiers Lillois d'Economie et de Sociologie* special issue; Dormard 2002).

Nevertheless, Aftalion is known essentially for his contribution to business cycle theory. Although he did not invent the concept, he is acknowledged as the economist who devised the accelerator principle, a very sophisticated pre-Keynesian version of business cycle analysis developed under the influence of marginalism (Dangel and Raybaut 1997; Raybaut in Dormard 2002). Like Clément Juglar, Aftalion relied on empirical analysis, and systematically tested his theory. He studied intensively and also taught statistics. His first empirical work on the industries of Northern France had a profound influence on his theory (Dormard 2002). Following Juglar (to whom he refers explicitly in his first essay in 1908–09), Aftalion considered that crises were general and periodic. He then logically rejected exogenous business cycle theories. He argued that while causes have consequences, they nevertheless provide only superficial explanations of business cycles: fundamental elements need to be identified from among the inherent characteristics of industrialized countries. Referring explicitly to the contributions of E. von Böhn-Bawerk, A. Marshall and J.B. Clark, Aftalion insisted that the core element of business cycles lay in the structure of the production process. Moreover, he supposed that: "To the consumer the value of goods purchased depends on the satisfaction which he expects to receive from them. To the producer the value of materials depends on the price which he expects to obtain for them upon resale after transformation . . . on his forecast of future prices" (Aftalion 1927: 165). Those expectations are alternately (overly) optimistic or (overly) pessimistic, and it is the length of the production process of capital goods that prevents entrepreneurs from making the "right" decisions. Indeed, modern production processes are characterized by two distinct stages: the production of capital goods, and the production of consumption goods. As long as the effective level of capital is lower than the expected level, the demand for additional capital will increase in all sectors (because of inter-sectorial interactions) as activity develops: this is the prosperity phase. The economy is naturally and progressively led to overcapitalization, and finally overproduction:

> In the modern capitalistic technique the actual state of demand and prices is a bad index of future demand and prices, because of the long interval which separates the moment when new constructions are undertaken from that when they satisfy the demand. So long as the fixed capital under construction is not finished, demand may continue to be unsatisfied and prices may remain high. (Aftalion 1927: 166)

It was exactly in order to represent this mechanism that Aftalion used *stove* metaphor. It should be noted that entrepreneurs repeat their mistakes (which means fluctuations recur) not because they are irrational but because they face uncertainty (Dangel and Raybaut 1997). A crisis starts when the prices are decreasing which is interpreted as a general decrease in the intensity of the need for the goods produced. During the recession phase, the forecasting error is reversed: the amount of capital dedicated to the construction of production capacity is smaller than is required by the secular trend. The progressive diminution of stocks is interpreted as a positive signal: "New orders are given . . . A new cycle begins" (Aftalion 1927: 166).

Aftalion argued that fluctuations in the economy were inevitable, and were magnified by the structure of modern economies, that is, the social and technical organization of production. His objective was to refute Classical theory which denies the possibility of general overproduction. Although not wholly successful in this aim, he was an undoubted contributor to this debate.

MURIEL DAL PONT LEGRAND

See also:
Eugen von Böhm-Bawerk (I); John Bates Clark (I); Alfred Marshall (I); Paul Anthony Samuelson (I); Jean-Charles Léonard Simonde de Sismondi (I).

References and further reading

Aftalion, A. (1903), 'La décadence de l'industrie linière et la concurrence victorieuse de l'industrie cotonnière', *Revue d'Economie Politique*, May, July, October–November, 420–557, 616–36, 827–53.
Aftalion, A. (1907), *La conciliation dans les conflits entre patrons et ouvriers*, Paris: Publication de l'Association pour la protection légale des travailleurs.
Aftalion, A. (1908–09), 'Essai d'une théorie des crises périodiques; La réalité des surproductions générales', *Revue d'Economie Politique*, October 1908, 696–706 and February, March and April 1909, 81–117, 201–29, 241–59.
Aftalion, A. (1912), 'Le salaire réel et sa nouvelle orientation', *Revue d'Economie Politique*, September–October, 124–46.
Aftalion, A. (1913), *Les crises périodiques de surproduction*, vol. 1, *Les variations périodiques des prix et des revenus, les théories dominantes*, vol. 2, *Les mouvements périodiques de la production, essai d'une théorie*, Paris: M. Rivière.
Aftalion, A. (1927), 'The theory of economic cycles based on the capitalistic technique of production', *Review of Economic Statistics*, 9 (4), 165–70.
Aftalion, A. (1927), *Monnaie, prix et change. Expériences récentes et théorie*, 2nd edn 1933; 3rd edn 1935, 4th edn 1937, Paris: Sirey.
Dangel, C. and M. Rainelli (2000), 'Albert Aftalion, théoricien de la monnaie et des changes', in P. Dockès, L. Frobert, G. Klotz, J.P. Potier and A. Tiran (eds), *Les traditions économiques françaises 1848–1939*, Paris: CNRS Editions.
Dangel, C. and A. Raybaut (1997), 'Albert Aftalion's macrodynamic theory of endogenous business cycles', *Journal of the History of Economic Thought*, 19 (1), 71–92.
Delmas, B. (2002a), 'Albert Aftalion 1874–1956. Jalons et enjeux d'une biographie', in S, Dormard (coord.), *Albert Aftalion. Redécouverte d'un économiste français du XXe siècle. Cahiers Lillois d'Economie et de Sociologie*, no. 39, Paris: L'Harmattan, pp. 16–35.
Demals, T. (2002b), 'Les deux Sismondi d'Aftalion' in S. Dormard (coord.), *Albert Aftalion. Redécouverte d'un économiste français du XXe siècle. Cahiers Lillois d'Economie et de Sociologie*, no. 39, Paris: L'Harmattan, pp. 37–59.
Dormard, S. (ed.) (2002), *Albert Aftalion, redécouverte d'un économiste français du XXe siècle*, special issue of *Cahiers Lillois d'Economie et de Sociologie*, n. 39, Paris: L'Harmattan.
Frobert, L. (1999), 'Albert Aftalion on socialism', *Journal of the History of Economic Thought*, 21 (2), 145–61.
Guitton, H. (1957), 'Aftalion 1874–1946', *Revue d'Economie Politique*, 68, 161–3.
Lhomme, J., J. Lecaillon and G. Hosmalin (1957), 'L'influence intellectuelle d'Albert Aftalion', suivi d'une liste des travaux d'Albert Aftalion par J. Lecaillon et G. Hosmalin, *Revue Economique*, no. 3, 353–66.
LLP [Langford, Lovell Price] (1914), 'Les crises périodiques de surproduction by Albert Aftalion; Good and Bad Trade: An Inquiry into the Causes of Trade Fluctuations by R.G. Hawtrey; Business Cycles by Wesley Clair Mitchell', *Journal of the Royal Statistical Society*, 77 (2), 217–21.
Persons, W.M. (1914), Review, 'Books on Business Cycles: Mitchell, Aftalion, Bilgram', *Quarterly Journal of Economics*, 28 (4), 795–810.
Schumpeter, J.A. (1954), *History of Economic Analysis*, London: Allen & Unwin.

Wesley Clair Mitchell (1874–1948)

Mitchell's great contributions to economics lie in his pioneering work on business cycles, his broad promotion of empirical work in economics, his role in the development of research organizations, and in the students he inspired. He was one of the major figures within the institutionalist movement in American economics.

Mitchell was born in Rushville, Illinois, on 5 August 1874, and brought up in Decatur, Illinois. His university education was at the University of Chicago (AB 1896; PhD 1899), with one year spent at Halle and Vienna taking lectures from Johannes Conrad and Carl Menger. At Chicago, Mitchell came under the influence of Thorstein Veblen and John Dewey, but it was Laurence Laughlin who supervised Mitchell's PhD thesis on the Greenback issues of the Civil War (Mitchell 1903). Laughlin inspired Mitchell's empiricism, Veblen his institutionalism, and Dewey his pragmatic reformism.

Mitchell worked for a year in the Census Office and for two years at Chicago as an instructor before being recruited to Berkeley in 1903. He continued to work on the Greenbacks, but, influenced by Veblen, expanded his horizons to write on the issue of rationality in economics (Mitchell 1910), the economic problems of the household (Mitchell 1912), and embark on a project concerning the evolution and functioning of the "money economy". This last project grew too large, and in 1910 he decided to focus on just one part. In a remarkably short time Mitchell produced his most important book *Business Cycles* (Mitchell 1913). The book provided an empirically based "analytic description" of the course of the cycle, presented as four phases – prosperity, crisis, depression, and revival – with each phase creating the conditions for the transition into the next, and the cycle as a whole growing out of the institutions of the "money economy" in the form of the interaction of business decisions based on profit expectations, the behaviour of the banking system, and the leads and lags in the movement of wages and prices. The book also contained a critical discussion of the adequacy of existing theories of cycles in terms of their consistency with the empirical evidence.

In 1913 Mitchell and his new wife, Lucy Sprague Mitchell, moved to New York where he was appointed to a position at Columbia University. Initially his work focused on index numbers, and the history of economic thought. The First World War took him to the Prices Section of the War Industries Board, work on price and production indexes, and an appreciation of the potential of statistical work for government policy making as expressed in his Presidential Address to the American Statistical Association (Mitchell 1919). Mitchell became involved with the founding of the New School for Social Research in 1919, but returned to Columbia three years later. He was the major figure in the founding of the National Bureau of Economic Research (NBER) in 1920, and acted as its Director of Research from 1920 until 1945, when he was succeeded by his student, Arthur F. Burns. He was also closely involved with the establishment and operation of the Social Science Research Council (SSRC). In these endeavours Mitchell was attempting to provide an institutional foundation for an empirical economics, that would inform and be informed by other social sciences, and that could provide the basic information necessary for improved economic policy making.

Mitchell's 1924 Presidential Address to the American Economic Association (AEA) forcefully expressed his belief in the combination of institutional and quantitative analysis. For Mitchell quantitative analysis complements the institutional approach to economics, as it is institutions that standardize behaviour and create those patters of mass behaviour that quantitative work observes. Quantitative work will thus provide the basis for a constructive criticism of the institutions of the money economy, capable of guiding efforts to make the economic system better fitted to serve human needs (Mitchell 1925).

The NBER under Mitchell began by investigating the size and distribution of national income, work later assigned to Simon Kuznets who went on to develop the system of national income accounting for the US government. From 1922 onwards, however, the major focus of Mitchell's and the NBER's work was on business cycles, a project designed to update and expand on Mitchell's 1913 book. Mitchell produced *Business Cycles: The Problem and Its Setting*, in 1927. This book provided a review of theories of the business cycle; a historical section linking the phenomenon of business cycles to the rise of the institutions of the money economy; a discussion of business cycles in relation to business decision-making, the system of prices, and the monetary mechanism; and a survey of data sources, both from statistics and business annals. The book concluded with a working concept of business cycles and a plan of work. As Mitchell stated: "The ultimate aim of our business-cycle program is clearer understanding of the complicated processes that bring about financial crises and industrial depressions. Such knowledge we think prerequisite to intelligent efforts to prevent, or even to mitigate appreciably, these recurring disasters" (Mitchell 1939: 23–4).

The NBER business cycle project produced a vast collection of data series; many empirical studies of cyclical behaviour in specific economic variables, industries, or sectors; the development of business cycle indicators; and methods of dealing with an array of measurement issues relating to timing, amplitude, and rates of change across successive cycles, which resulted in what became known as the "NBER method" of specific and reference cycles (Morgan 1990: 44–56). The outcome of much of this work was published as *Measuring Business Cycles* in 1946 (Burns and Mitchell 1946). *Measuring Business Cycles* was attacked by Tjalling Koopmans of the Cowles Commission as "measurement without theory" (Koopmans 1947). Mitchell's approach was not based on a structural economic model, but it was informed by existing theories and had theoretical objectives. Rutledge Vining defended the NBER approach by arguing that their methods were designed to discover new and improved hypotheses (Vining 1949: 85). Nevertheless, the final, theoretical, volume that Mitchell had planned was never completed, although a part was published after Mitchell's death as *What Happens during Business Cycles* (Mitchell 1951).

The NBER under Burns carried on the business cycle project, ultimately producing such well known work as Milton Friedman and Anna Schwartz's *A Monetary History of the United States, 1867–1960* (Friedman and Schwartz 1963).

MALCOLM RUTHERFORD

See also:

Institutionalism (II); Thorstein Bunde Veblen (I).

References and further reading

Biddle, J. (1998), 'Social science and the making of social policy: Wesley Mitchell's vision', in M. Rutherford (ed.), *The Economic Mind in America: Essays in the History of American Economics*, London: Routledge, pp. 43–79.

Burns, A.F. (ed.) (1952), *Wesley Clair Mitchell: The Economic Scientist*, New York: NBER.
Burns, A.F. and W.C. Mitchell (1946), *Measuring Business Cycles*, New York: NBER.
Friedman, M. and A.J. Schwartz (1963), *A Monetary History of the United States, 1867–1960*, Princeton, NJ: Princeton University Press.
Koopmans, T.C. (1947), 'Measurement without theory', *Review of Economic Statistics*, **29** (August), 161–72.
Mitchell, L.S. (1953), *Two Lives: The Story of Wesley Clair Mitchell and Myself*, New York: Simon and Schuster.
Mitchell, W.C. (1903), *A History of the Greenbacks, with Special Reference to the Economic Consequences of Their Issue, 1862–65*. Chicago, IL: University of Chicago Press.
Mitchell, W.C. (1910), 'The rationality of economic activity', pts I and II, *Journal of Political Economy*, **18** (February), 97–113, **18** (March), 197–216.
Mitchell, W.C. (1912), 'The backward art of spending money', *American Economic Review*, **2** (June), 269–81.
Mitchell, W.C. (1913), *Business Cycles*, Berkeley, CA: University of California Press.
Mitchell, W.C. (1919), 'Statistics and government', *Quarterly Publications of the American Statistical Association*, **16** (March), 223–36.
Mitchell, W.C. (1925), 'Quantitative analysis in economic theory', *American Economic Review*, **15** (March), 1–12.
Mitchell, W.C. (1927), *Business Cycles: The Problem and Its Setting*, New York: NBER.
Mitchell, W.C. (1939), *The National Bureau's Social Function*, NBER Annual Report, New York: NBER.
Mitchell, W.C. (1951), *What Happens during Business Cycles: A Progress Report*, New York: NBER.
Morgan, M.S. (1990), *The History of Econometric Ideas*, Cambridge: Cambridge University Press.
Vining, R. (1949), 'Methodological issues in quantitative economics: Koopmans on the choice of variables to be studied and on methods of measurement', *Review of Economics and Statistics*, **31** (May), 77–86.

Edwin Walter Kemmerer (1875–1945)

Edwin Walter Kemmerer was an American economist born in Scranton, Pennsylvania. In 1899, he obtained his Master's degree in economics at Wesleyan University with Phi Beta Kappa honours. He also joined the Delta Kappa Epsilon fraternity and during a fraternity meeting he met Rachel Dickele, who would become his wife two years later.

While Kemmerer was working on his Master's degree in economics (1895–99) the debates about money between Republicans and Democrats were at the centre of public life. In 1896, the presidential campaign between William McKinley (Republican) and William Jennings Bryan (Democrat) centred on the monetary question. The Democrats defended bimetallism while the Republicans along with "gold-Democrats" – a minority of Democrats who defended the gold standard – proposed the definitive adoption of the gold standard (GS). Kemmerer became interested in the campaign debates and studied the principle works of the protagonists – Harvey (*Coin's Financial School*, 1894) and Laughlin (*Facts about Money*, 1895, and *Coin's Financial Fool*). Kemmerer found himself near the heart of the Republican Party and became an ardent defender of the GS, so, he decided to take it upon himself to convert the Democrats to monometallism. In 1899 Kemmerer started a PhD at Cornell University. He chose to work on the quantity theory of money (QTM), a choice that would be pivotal for his professional future: Kemmerer was a quantity theorist, but also a defender of gold-monometallism, putting him at odds with several other quantity theorists who favoured bimetallism.

An Economist in a Class of his Own

On the theoretical questions, Kemmerer appears to be in a class of his own. From his 1903 doctoral thesis published in its revised form in 1907, to his last work in 1944, Kemmerer consistently defended the GS system and the QTM. However, he also advocated certain principles of the real bills doctrine and believed that money issuing and credit allowance should meet the needs of trade. One of Kemmerer's first professors of economics, Willard Fisher, was one of the major American bimetallists, and like most bimetallists, defended QTM. Jeremiah Jenks, Kemmerer's PhD adviser, was a monometallist and quantity theorist. He strongly influenced Kemmerer who continued to work on the QTM as his PhD thesis topic, developing a statistical test to prove its long-term validity in the United States between 1879 and 1901.

In his thesis, Kemmerer introduced a concept that was to recur throughout his work, that of business confidence. High business confidence enables a bank's money supply to meet the needs of trade in the long term, and stabilizes the ratio of a bank's money supply to the primary money supply (coins and bank notes) in the short term. When there is business confidence, the QTM is verified: the fluctuation of the ratio between money supply and commodity supply matches the fluctuation of the general level of prices, except over the periods characterized by a business distress.

In an attempt to prove that money value is determined just like any other product, Kemmerer wrote the exchange equation yielding the value of money as an equilibrium condition between money supply and money demand. He drew on John S. Mill to define the concept of money demand, but moved away from him for the concept of money supply. He defined money supply as a stock of money, including bank money, multiplied by its rapidity of circulation. As underlined in Gómez Betancourt (2010a), the concept of money demand used by Kemmerer does not anticipate that developed by Cambridge School. Indeed, it refers to money to be spent rather than to be kept. Kemmerer does not by any means anticipate liquidity preference theory or any other reasons accounting for money retention. Rather, he remains at odds with what will become the Keynesian Revolution.

After being named Financial Adviser to the US Philippine Commission (from 1904 to 1906) when only 28 years old, he became a professor at Cornell University (1906–12) and then at Princeton University until he retired emeritus in 1943. In 1906 Kemmerer was already known as an international "money doctor" and was capable enough to advise on behalf of the US government. Kemmerer's contribution to the creation of the Federal Reserve System is significant but not sufficiently acknowledged (Gómez Betancourt 2010b). As early as 1909, he started a study on the variation of short-term interest rates on the money market of the main American cities. This study revealed the weaknesses of the National Banking System in place since 1863, and advocated in favour of a more elastic money and credit issuing system that would allow farmers greater access to liquidity. According to him, a central bank system for the US was needed in order to ensure the elasticity of money and credit, as well as the liquidity of the money market. In exchanging bank notes for real bills, the central bank puts an end to the considerable and often erratic fluctuation of the interest rate. Kemmerer was not a strong supporter of the currency board, but rather envisioned the central bank as a lender of last resort. Kemmerer, who was a member of the Progressive Party from 1912, played an important political part in supporting the reforms proposed, on the one hand, by bankers and Republican groups, and, on the other, by the Democratic administration of the period, followed by the signature of the Federal Reserve Act on 23 December 1913.

The Theoretician of the Gold Exchange Standard and the "Money Doctor"

Kemmerer devoted his last book to the GS. The question of the stability of the value of money was at the heart of the debate at the turn of the twentieth century in the United States. American economists were wondering how they could prevent such significant fluctuations in the value of the dollar. According to Kemmerer the GS was the system that could best minimize the instability of the value of money. The aim of the GS was to reinforce the confidence in money and in the exchange system in order to stimulate trade between countries and attract foreign investments. For the "money doctor", confidence in money is guaranteed by fixing the price of gold and ensuring the convertibility of bank money at this price whether in coins (Gold Coin Standard), in bullion (Gold Bullion Standard), or in a currency convertible to gold (Gold Exchange Standard).

Kemmerer believes that its instability is inherent in money itself: like any other commodity, it depends on the law of supply and demand. Rather than searching for a system capable of fixing the value of money, Kemmerer admits several criticisms of the GS such that the value of gold was unstable (that is, the purchasing power of the dollar went down) after the First World War. While being aware of its impact on debt, he does not provide any solution to the problem. Instead, he only argues that the other types of standards are even less stable than the GS.

The issue that Kemmerer does not address in his 1944 work, although he was aware of it, is that the international GS is not a symmetrical system. Indeed, the countries under the GS and those under the Gold Exchange Standard are not exposed in the same way to the exchange risk since the former are creditors while the latter are debtors. In addition, the major drawback of the gold standard was the high cost of maintaining the necessary gold reserves. Rich countries could establish a gold coin standard and poor countries could only wish for a gold exchange standard. As European countries, and then the United States, came to suspend the GS, the money doctor began to lose his patients.

Kemmerer was a Republican albeit a progressive one, an advocate of the Monroe Doctrine, a supporter of dollar diplomacy, and eventually an anti-New Deal economist. He approved of Theodore Roosevelt's policies but rejected Franklin D. Roosevelt's. During the first three decades of the twentieth century his ideas as a theoretician and economic adviser were in line with mainstream thinking, and he was much sought after by those in power. He helped to establish the Central Banks of Bolivia, Chile, Colombia, Equator and Peru and advised more than 20 countries on monetary policy. As the Great Depression took hold, his monetary reforms became unpopular and he soon sank into oblivion. He died in 1945, leaving a mark on economic history as practitioner as well as a theoretician, as a politician as well as an economist.

REBECA GÓMEZ BETANCOURT

See also:

Balance of payments and exchange rates (III); Irving Fisher (I); Money and banking (III).

References and further reading

Gómez Betancourt, R. (2010a), 'Edwin Walter Kemmerer's contribution to quantity theory of money', *European Journal of the History of Economic Thought*, **17** (1), 115–40.

Gómez Betancourt, R. (2010b), 'Edwin Walter Kemmerer and the origins of the Federal Reserve System', *Journal of the History of Economic Thought*, **32** (4), 445–70.

Harvey, W.H. (1894), *Coin's Financial School*, Chicago, IL: Coin Publishing Company.

Kemmerer, E.W. (1905), 'The establishment of the gold exchange standard in the Philippines', *Quarterly Journal of Economics*, **19** (4), 585–609.

Kemmerer, E.W. (1907), *Money and Credit Instruments in their Relation to General Prices*, New York: Henry Holt and Co., 2nd edn 1909.

Kemmerer, E.W. (1916), *Modern Currency Reform. A History and Discussion of Recent Currency Reform in India, Porto Rico, Philippine Islands, Strait Settlements and Mexico*, New York: Macmillan.

Kemmerer, E.W. (1923), 'Monetary standards in South American countries', *Proceedings of the Academy of Political Science in the City of New York*, **10** (2), 45–56.

Kemmerer, E.W. (1927), 'Economic advisory work for governments', *American Economic Review*, **17** (1), 1–12.

Kemmerer, E.W. (1934), *Kemmerer on Money: An Elementary Discussion of the Important Facts and Underlying Principles of the Money Problems Now Confronting the American People*, Chicago, IL: Winston.

Kemmerer, E.W. (1938), *Money. The Principles of Money and their Exemplification in Outstanding Chapters of Monetary History*, New York: Macmillan.

Kemmerer, E.W. (1944), *Gold and the Gold Standard*, New York: Macmillan.

Laughlin, J.L. (1895), *Facts about Money. Including the Debate with W.H. Harvey at the Illinois Club*, Chicago, IL: E.A. Weeks & Company.

Arthur Cecil Pigou (1877–1959)

Arthur Cecil Pigou, Marshall's successor in the chair of Political Economy and the executor of the Marshallian heritage, may with good reason be regarded as the paradigm of an "old", pre-Keynesian Cambridge economist. It is this Marshallian point of departure from which he progressed into new spheres of analysis, some of which still play an important role in present-day economics.

Pigou was born in 1877 on the Isle of Wight, he died in 1959 in Cambridge. Personally, he has been characterized as eccentric and shy, especially towards women. After winning a scholarship to King's his scientific career began as a lecturer at Cambridge University on general economic topics in 1904. In 1908 he was appointed as Marshall's successor at the age of just 30 and against such an established contender as Herbert Foxwell. His work on industrial and labour economics turned into *Wealth and Welfare* (1912), the first edition of a work the themes of which determined the direction of Pigou's research for the rest of his life. In this sense, not only *The Economics of Welfare* (1920) but also *Industrial Fluctuations* (1927a) and *The Theory of Unemployment* (1933) with their focus respectively on the business cycle and the labour market should be considered as elaborations and extensions of the concepts laid down in his welfare economics. Yet in the late 1920s his intellectual capacity and the energy to put it to full use slowly faded away, owing to ill health, disillusionment stemming from the horrible experiences of war – which he shared as a voluntary ambulance worker in World War I – and the comparative lack of success within the politics of the interwar period. Eventually he had to recognize that the kind of Pigovian economics that he had propagated as a consistent continuation of Marshall was abandoned for the neoclassical synthesis of Keynesian and Hicksian thought.

In the following, three fields from Pigou's work are selected for closer scrutiny. These are his all-encompassing treatment of welfare economics and as a kind of application his contributions to microeconomics, in particular to the controversy on the laws of returns, and to monetary theory, in particular as a foil against the Keynesian conquest of macroeconomics.

Welfare Economics

Pigou's venture into welfare economics represents an innovative extension of the economics of Marshall, possibly inspired by Henry Sidgwick's contribution to ethics. In his definition, Pigou identifies social welfare, the subject of his inquiry, with economic welfare, the "limited group of satisfactions and dissatisfactions" that "can be brought directly or indirectly into relation with the measuring-rod of money" (1920 [1932]: 14, 11) – to be distinguished from noneconomic welfare. The indicator used for economic welfare is the "national dividend", a measure rather similar to present-day's net national product: other things being equal, increases in the size of the national dividend as well as increases in the share of the poor are to be considered improvements in economic welfare, so that there is in effect a double criterion; furthermore a decrease in the variability over time of the national dividend is also considered an improvement thus providing a rationale for dealing with the business cycle (Pigou 1912: 66). Against this background Pigou's most innovative idea, still alive and well today, is the distinction between social and private costs, or in his own terminology between "marginal social" and "marginal private net product". The social net product indicates the contribution to the national dividend while the private net product the contribution to profit or loss from the individual's point of view. Thus when these two products diverge it becomes possible to reallocate the resources of the economy so as to increase the national dividend, that is, economic welfare. In his writings Pigou lists many examples of such distortions, ranging from land tenancy and the diminished incentive for tenants to invest with a fixed contract length, to air pollution, and finally to the alleged discrepancy between actual and ideal output in industries not subject to long-run constant costs (see below). From the latter emerged Pigou's famous tax-bounty solution, that is, to levy a tax on activities where actual output lies above ideal output and vice versa. It is this general argument of a Pigou tax on which many well-known proposals of modern environmental policy are based, for example, the recommendation of a carbon tax for addressing the danger of global warming.

In the ensuing theoretical debate Pigou's specific type of "old" welfare economics and its proposed solution to divergences between social and private cost encountered two main criticisms. The first criticism is based on the rejection of interpersonal comparisons of utility (and also of the cardinal measurability of individual utilities) as put forward by Robbins's methodological essay (1932) and implied by Hicks's revision of the foundations of demand theory (1934). Ultimately this attack resulted in a "new" welfare economics, with its criterion of Pareto efficiency, an approach almost purged from any considerations of distributional equity. The source of the second criticism is Coases's famous questioning of the problem of social costs (1960). Accordingly, discrepancies between social and private cost originate from the lack of well-defined property rights or, on the other side of the same coin, from excessive transaction costs. Rather than imposing taxes (or granting subsidies) that might in effect aggravate existing distortions, the direct remedy lies in the establishment of property rights to realign private incentives with social benefits. Although both types of criticism appear incontrovertible as far as abstract theory goes, their impetus derived possibly as much from their quest to remedy logical shortcomings as from the scepticism towards the belief in the prevalence of "market failures" and in the neglect of government failure. Yet for practical purposes of economic policy debate, the tool-kit of Pigovian welfare economics appears still to provide an important benchmark.

Microeconomics

Central and most typical of Pigou's contribution to microeconomics, or the economics of industry, is his participation in the so-called cost controversy. The starting point of the controversy lies in Marshall's enigmatic presentation of the "laws of returns", distinguishing diminishing, increasing and constant returns, and deriving therefrom industries characterized by rising, falling and constant (long-run) supply price. In the quest for practical relevance, for example, with regard to falling supply price, Marshall's analysis made use of internal as well as external economies, of technological as well as pecuniary effects, of technical improvements giving rise to an increase of output as well as of output growth giving rise to such improvements, and finally, of a "representative firm" situated in an industry composed of firms of different sizes and in different phases of their individual life cycles. Furthermore, Marshall introduced, and Pigou in the early editions of *Economics of Welfare* elaborated, the idea that with non-constant returns an industry's actual would as a rule deviate from its ideal output, and thus taxes on increasing-costs-industries might be justified as well as bounties for industries with decreasing costs. When in this situation the economic historian Clapham (1922) doubted that this classification might contain only "empty economic boxes", the ensuing debate soon transgressed the realm of history and turned into a fundamental critique of the whole Marshallian (and Pigovian) edifice.

The controversy, in which Piero Sraffa, Allyn Young and Joseph Schumpeter stood out as critics (against the British, Dennis Robertson, Gerald Shove and Pigou), dragged on well through the 1920s and exposed the inevitable tension between the phenomena to be analysed and – as Schumpeter (1928: 379) put it – "the cracking frame" of an approach of static and partial equilibrium. First, turning to the problem of pecuniary effects, these are owing to the feedback from an industry's output to the demand for its factors of production and to factor prices, and thereby back to its production costs. Yet these effects cannot justify a discrepancy between actual and ideal output, nor can they be legitimately analysed within a partial equilibrium framework as the change in factor prices may work back both on the distribution of income and on the prices of substitutes in demand. Second, it became clear that in a modern setting, with profit-maximizing firms choosing in the long-run the optimum firm size, economies internal to the firm generating a downward sloping marginal cost curve are incompatible with equilibrium of perfect competition – in this regard Sraffa's critique (1926) coincided with the development of the "imperfect competition revolution" of Chamberlin and Robinson. The only way to salvage the coexistence of decreasing-costs industries and perfect competition is by the artifice of economies external to the firm but internal to the industry; yet although this solution is logically consistent, its realism soon appeared doubtful. Third, the defenders of the Marshallian (and Pigovian) framework also realized the necessity to distinguish between historical and analytical cost curves, that is, those to be traced out in historical investigations and those derived in static conditions, with a given state of knowledge. The concentration on analytical cost curves, however, eliminated aspects from the analysis that some economists believed to be crucial for the dynamics of the capitalist system, for example, innovations as shifts of production functions (Schumpeter) or increasing returns deriving from the division of labour (Young).

Pigou's contributions to the cost controversy were manifold (1922, 1927b, 1928): he suggested replacing Marshall's "representative firm" with the "equilibrium firm"; he emphasized external (instead of internal) economies for making both increasing returns compatible with perfect competition and actually diverge from ideal output; to keep the analysis within the bounds of partial equilibrium he discarded pecuniary effects as a cause of rising (or falling) supply prices and was thus compelled to restrict this explanation to "unimportant" goods; he integrated profit maximizing firms and the optimal choice of firm size into the analysis of industry supply price; and finally, he was among those participants who clearly identified supply price with the aggregate of marginal (and not, as others did, average) costs. However, in Pigou's writings imperfect competition is notable by its absence. In sum, what Pigou did to the Marshallian edifice was to reshape or "purify" it, sacrificing Marshall's vent for descriptive realism for the logical consistency of a static model of perfect competition. He thus paved the way for the codification of this type of analysis, which in the geometrical presentation introduced by Viner (1931) is still enshrined in present-day elementary textbooks.

Money, Business Cycles and Macroeconomics

In monetary theory proper, concerned with the determination of "the value of money", Pigou's (1917) contribution consisted in a refinement of Marshall's approach towards a stock demand for money. His well-known formula of the cash-balance approach, $P = kR/M$, marks an important step towards, but does not fully anticipate, the modern idea of money demand as the solution to a portfolio allocation problem as in Keynes's liquidity preference theory. In particular, it lacks the explicit recognition of wealth as a balance-sheet constraint and it confuses the demand schedule with that of equilibrium loci (when M signifies an exogenous money supply).

In his explanation of the business cycle Pigou (1927a) combined "psychological" and monetary factors with expectations, the optimism and pessimism of the business community, playing the active role and money merely an accommodating, passive role. Thus the initiating cause of the cycle were fluctuations in investment demand, and not the banking system's arbitrary injections of money into the economy, that is, in modern terms, he considered the cycle to be due to real and not monetary shocks. *The Theory of Unemployment* (1933), a treatise on labour economics, in which Pigou focused on the macroeconomics of the labour market and wage formation, owed him the label of a "classical economist". It is, indeed, "classical" inasmuch as it explains unemployment by the interaction of a fluctuating demand for labour (which in his theory of the business cycle Pigou had derived from the changing expectations driving investment demand) and a fixed real or money wage, which combined with a given value of full employment produces an inversely L-shaped supply curve of labour. Accordingly it confirmed the accepted classical view on the causes of unemployment in attributing it to wage rigidity. Furthermore, taking his earlier monetary analysis of the cycle for granted, Pigou over-emphasized the capacity of a purely real analysis to capture the significant aspects of unemployment, for example, by confining the concern with money wage rigidity to a small part of the whole book. Yet Pigou's approach was not "classical" in the specific sense in which Keynes (1936) used the term in the *General Theory*, especially in his chapter 19 attack on Pigou, because nowhere did Pigou deny the possibility of involuntary unemployment. Moreover, with regard to business-cycle policy, Pigou was ready to refine and supplement his theoretical structure so as to accommodate for expansionist policy proposals, "proto-Keynesian" in nature, in extraordinary circumstances like the Great Depression of the 1930s, when he aligned with Keynes and other advocates of expansionist policy against the orthodox prescriptions put forward by London School of Economics (LSE) economists.

Within the field of macroeconomics most of Pigou's fame or notoriety derives from his controversy with Keynes. After having been singled out in the *General Theory* as the archetype of a "classical economist" and Pigou's striking back in a highly critical review, the conflict culminated in the debate between Pigou, Keynes and Kaldor in the *Economic Journal* (1937). Here Pigou's aim was to demonstrate the effectiveness of wage cuts in expanding employment in general, and specifically to show that "a money wage cut is not simply a piece of ritual that enables the real cause of employment expansion – a fall in the rate of money interest – to take effect" (Pigou 1937: 411). In defending the framework of the *General Theory*, Kaldor (1937) responded by proving, by means of a small "Keynesian" macro model, that indeed the reaction of the rate of interest, later termed the "Keynes effect", is crucial; and in fact Pigou (1938) conceded this point. Nevertheless Pigou (1943) soon reconfirmed his belief in the principal stability of the economic system by pointing out that a decline in wages and prices will in the end generate an increase in the real value of cash balances, which may directly affect consumption expenditures, later termed the "Pigou effect". Typically the verdict on the Pigou effect has been to accept its logical validity but to deny it empirical relevance. Thus, although in the contemporary debate Pigou obviously lost his case against Keynes, there is some irony in this judgement. First, Kaldor's refutation relied on just that type of model (IS–LM combined with a supply side modelled on the principle of profit maximization and marginal productivity) that later on came to be denounced as "Bastard Keynesianism". Second, Pigou's ideas appear as surprisingly resilient: the combination of short-run sticky wages giving rise to unemployment and long-run wage flexibility bringing the economy back to full employment is as much Pigovian as it is familiar from present-day introductory macroeconomics textbooks. Possibly Pigou himself would readily recognize in this framework analytically polished, yet familiar, elements from his own thought.

In conclusion, both failure and accomplishment can be found in Pigou's work. He failed in his attempts to preserve the skeleton of Marshallian analysis, even at the price of thinning out its vent for descriptive realism, in particular when facing the onslaught of the Keynesian revolution in macroeconomics and the neo-Walrasian approach propagated by Hicks's introduction of a general equilibrium framework. Yet Pigou, the classical economist, has resurfaced, veiled in modern clothes, in the new types of theorizing about the macro economy that have turned away from the Keynesian diagnosis and instead emphasize all kinds of frictions as the sources of (transitory) deviations from equilibrium. In this respect, part of present-day economics comes rather close to Pigou's, although it apparently does not share his presumption of the prevalence of market failures and his view of welfare economics as the basis for interventionist economic policy.

HANSJÖRG KLAUSINGER

See also:

Cambridge School of economics (II); Macroeconomics (III); Alfred Marshall (I); Piero Sraffa (I); Theory of the firm (III); Welfare economics (III).

References and further reading

As a highly selective sample from the secondary literature on which the foregoing has drawn, see Collard (1999) and de Graaff (1987) on biographical information, Aslanbeigui and Medema (1998) on Pigou's versus Coases's welfare economics, Aslanbeigui (1996) on the cost controversy, and Klausinger (2003) on Pigou's macroeconomics.

Aslanbeigui, N. (1996), 'The cost controversy: Pigouvian economics in disequilibrium', *European Journal of the History of Economic Thought*, **3** (2), 275–95.
Aslanbeigui, N. and S.G. Medema (1998), 'Beyond the dark clouds: Pigou and Coase on social cost', *History of Political Economy*, **30** (4), 601–25.
Clapham, J.H. (1922), 'Of empty economic boxes', *Economic Journal*, **32** (127), 305–14.
Coase, R.H. (1960), 'The problem of social cost', *Journal of Law and Economics*, **3** (October), 144.
Collard, D. (1999), 'Introduction', A.C. Pigou, *Collected Economic Writings*, 14 vols, Houndmills and London: Macmillan, pp. v–xlvii.

De Graaff, J. (1987), 'Pigou, Arthur Cecil', in J. Eatwell, M. Milgate and P. Newman (eds), *The New Palgrave Dictionary of Economics*, vol. 3, London: Macmillan, pp. 876–9.

Hicks, J.R. (1934), 'A reconstruction of the theory of value, part 1', *Economica*, new series, **1** (1), 52–76.

Kaldor, N. (1937), 'Prof. Pigou on money wages in relation to unemployment', *Economic Journal*, **47** (188), 745–53.

Keynes, J.M. (1936), *The General Theory of Employment, Interest and Money*, London: Macmillan, reprinted in A. Robinson and D. Moggridge (eds) (1971), *The Collected Writings of John Maynard Keynes*, vol. 7, London: Macmillan, and Cambridge: Cambridge University Press.

Klausinger, H. (2003), 'Pigou, Neisser, and Machlup on wage cuts: how great a gap between Keynes and the pre-Keynesians?', *History of Economic Ideas*, **11** (2), 53–73.

Marshall, A. (1890), *Principles of Economics*, London: Macmillan, reprinted in the 9th variorum edn with annotations by C.W. Guillebaud, 1961, 2 vols.

Pigou, A.C. (1912), *Wealth and Welfare*, London: Macmillan; reprinted as A.C. Pigou (1999), *Collected Economic Writings*, vol. 2, Houndmills and London: Macmillan.

Pigou, A.C. (1917), 'The value of money', *Quarterly Journal of Economics*, **32** (1), 38–65.

Pigou, A.C. (1920), *The Economics of Welfare*, London: Macmillan, 4th edn 1932, reprinted as A.C. Pigou (1999), *Collected Economic Writings*, vol. 3, Houndmills and London: Macmillan.

Pigou, A.C. (1922), 'Empty economic boxes: a reply', *Economic Journal*, **32** (128), 458–65.

Pigou, A.C. (1927a), *Industrial Fluctuations*, London: Macmillan, 2nd edn 1929, reprinted as A.C. Pigou (1999), *Collected Economic Writings*, vol. 6, Houndmills and London: Macmillan.

Pigou, A.C. (1927b), 'The laws of diminishing and increasing cost', *Economic Journal*, **37** (146), 188–97.

Pigou, A.C. (1928), 'An analysis of supply', *Economic Journal*, **38** (150), 238–57.

Pigou, A.C. (1933), *The Theory of Unemployment*, London: Macmillan; reprinted as A.C. Pigou (1999), *Collected Economic Writings*, vol. 8, Houndmills and London: Macmillan.

Pigou, A.C. (1937), 'Real and money wage rates in relation to unemployment', *Economic Journal*, **47** (187), 405–22.

Pigou, A.C. (1938), 'Money wage rates in relation to unemployment', *Economic Journal*, **48** (189), 134–8.

Pigou, A.C. (1943), 'The classical stationary state', *Economic Journal*, **53** (212), 343–51.

Pigou, A.C. (1999), *Collected Economic Writings*, 14 vols, Houndmills and London: Macmillan.

Robbins, L. (1932), *An Essay on the Nature and Significance of Economic Science*, London: Macmillan.

Schumpeter, J. (1928), 'The instability of capitalism', *Economic Journal*, **38** (151), 361–86.

Sraffa, P. (1926), 'The laws of returns under competitive conditions', *Economic Journal*, **36** (144), 535–50.

Viner, J. (1931), 'Cost curves and supply curves', *Zeitschrift für Nationalökonomie*, **3** (1), 23–46.

Young, A.A. (1928), 'Increasing returns and economic progress', *Economic Journal*, **38** (152), 527–42.

Ralph George Hawtrey (1879–1975)

Although he was neither banker nor politician, neither academic nor university professor, Ralph George Hawtrey (1879–1975) was an influential British monetary economist during the interwar period. According to Schumpeter (1954: 1121): "Throughout the twenties . . . [his theory] enjoyed a considerable vogue". Hawtrey joined the British administration when he was 24 years of age, in 1903, then moved to the Treasury in 1904, where he was appointed Director of Financial Enquiries from 1919 until his retirement in 1947. He played a leading role in the 1921 Genoa Conference and was invited to Harvard for the 1928–29 academic year, on Allyn Abbott Young's initiative. He was seen as a representative of the so-called Treasury View concerning a return to the gold standard with an exchange rate at the level of pre-war parity and the denial that public expenditure could resolve unemployment. Nevertheless, Keynes (1937: 202) regarded him as his "grandparent . . . in the paths of errancy". His approach was unorthodox.

Hawtrey studied mathematics at Trinity College, Cambridge, from which he graduated in 1901. He was a member of the Apostles and the Bloomsbury group, and was close to George Edward Moore (see Donnini Macciò 2015). He first studied economics when applying for a Civil Service position. He then devoted most of his time to economics. However, he continued to regularly attend the Apostles' meetings. He was working on two books on philosophy – *Right Policy: the Place of Value Judgments in Politics* and *Thoughts and Things* – when he died at the age of 96. He was a prolific writer in economics, publishing 12 books and 44 articles. His most important book is *Currency and Credit*; the first edition appeared in 1919 and the second in 1928. It is also important to mention *Good and Bad Trade* (1913), his first publication, in which some of his key original notions are already present; *Gold Standard in Theory and Practice* (1927), devoted to the restoration of the gold standard after WWI; *The Art of Central Banking* (1932), which focuses on the lender-of-last-resort function of central banks and presents his comments on Keynes's *Treatise on Money* (1930); *Capital and Employment* (1937), devoted to the economics of depression, with comments on Keynes's *General Theory* (1936), and *A Century of Bank Rate* (1938), in which he examined the history of British interest rate policy in the management of money. Most of Hawtrey's monetary ideas were already present in his 1919 book. Hawtrey was influential, but he was not open to the influence of others. He used his own terms – "unspent margin", "consumers' income and outlay", "capital outlay", and so on. He never integrated Marshall's vocabulary or analysis of the demand for money into his theory, nor did he accept Pigou's (1913, 1933) and Keynes's (1936) public expenditure proposals, or Keynes's ideas about the monetary determination of the long-term interest rate. Hawtrey developed a monetary theory of the credit cycle, but it differs markedly from those of Marshall, Wicksell or Fisher.

According to Hawtrey, money is not derived from barter, but from credit. It does not provide a means for the circulation of goods, but for the payment of debts. Consequently, it is the regulator of credit. To that end, it must be managed. More precisely, money has to be issued by the central bank acting as a lender of last resort. At the same time, the central bank must modify its discount rate and actively intervene on the open market. According to this view, the gold standard system is not self-equilibrating; it has to be managed. Without monetary policy, economic activity would be unstable, resulting in cycles, crises and unemployment. Accurate monetary policy, not government spending, is the solution, according to Hawtrey. This policy is not passive or neutral; it is an active and effective art, the art of central banking.

For Hawtrey, the key figures in the exchange economy are the trader and the banker, rather than the individual with initial endowments, the entrepreneur or the capitalist. The trader buys and sells goods and uses credit as a means of circulation. He trades according to two factors: his anticipations about the demand for goods, and the cost of financing his stock, that is, the short-term interest rate. When the interest rate falls, traders expand their debt and their stock. Therefore, their orders to industry increase, production increases, incomes increase, the demand for goods increases, the sales of dealers increase, and when full employment is reached, prices increase. The process is cumulative. The reverse process holds in the case of a rise in the interest rate. Both processes show that credit is inherently unstable. According to Hawtrey, because it is the legal tender, money puts an end to this instability of credit. Credit inflation requires more means of payment and consequently encounters the problem of the limited quantity of legal tender money.

Thanks to traders and commercial credit, the goods produced and supplied by industry are marketable. Thanks to banks, commercial credit is liquid. Banks are in fact the dealers of traders' debts; they compensate these debts, and substitute their own debt for the traders' debt. Furthermore, bank debt is payable at sight, whereas traders' debt is payable at term. Households do not spend all their income (on purchases of consumer goods and financial assets) – therefore, they retain an "unspent margin" in legal tender (coins and Bank of England notes) and bank deposits. So, through the intermediation of the banking system, households finance the traders' stocks. Because inflation leads households to increase their demand for coins and Bank of England notes, bank credit also faces the problem of the limited supply of legal tender money.

As long as the quantity of legal tender is strictly limited, the limit it applies to commercial and bank credit will give rise to sudden commercial and banking crises, which degenerate into recessions. This was the case with the gold specie standard without central bank lending in last resort. On the contrary, if there is a central bank that grants credit in order to issue bank notes that are legal tender, trade and bank crises can be limited or avoided. However, the central bank should not wait until the limit is reached, but intervene actively beforehand, by raising its interest rate in order to remedy the inherent instability of credit. Therefore, the gold standard establishes a limit to credit, but it can be destabilizing if it is not managed by a central bank that permanently issues debt and lends in last resort. So Hawtrey stood outside British monetary orthodoxy. He improved Thornton's and Bagehot's analyses: on the one hand, the central bank demands commercial assets on the credit market, thus regulating credit through its interest rate policy; on the other hand, the central bank supplies money on the market for cash balances, thus ending the liquidity crisis.

Furthermore, Hawtrey expressed the clear view that the international gold standard system before World War I was not symmetrical, but dominated by London. This permitted British banks to manage international commercial credit so that the Bank of England discount rate was the benchmark rate at the international level. According to Hawtrey, after World War I, the restoration of London's leading financial role was a political priority, even if the role was to be shared with New York. This meant restoring the dollar–pound exchange rate to the level of pre-war parity, which meant a return to the gold standard at the pre-war fixed legal price of gold. For Hawtrey, the necessary 8–10 per cent deflation of prices was tolerable. In addition, he argued that the monetary uses of gold should be limited in order to avoid global deflation. To achieve this goal, he promoted the idea of an international gold exchange standard. Finally, attention should be drawn to Hawtrey's 1932 plea for the establishment of an international lender of last resort in order to remedy twin (exchange and banking) crises.

JÉRÔME DE BOYER DES ROCHES

See also:

Walter Bagehot (I); Balance of payments and exchange rates (III); Bullionist and anti-bullionist schools (II); John Maynard Keynes (I); Money and banking (III); Arthur Cecil Pigou (I); Joseph Alois Schumpeter (I); Henry Thornton (I).

References and further reading

de Boyer des Roches, J. (2003), *La pensée monétaire, histoire et analyse*, Paris: Les Solos.
de Boyer des Roches, J. and R. Solis Rosales (2011), 'R.G. Hawtrey on the national and international lender of last resort', *European Journal of the History of Economic Thought*, **18** (2), 175–202.
Deutscher, P. (1990), *R.G. Hawtrey and the Development of Macroeconomics*, London: Macmillan
Donnini Macciò, D. (2015), 'G.E. Moore's philosophy and Cambridge economics: Ralph Hawtrey on ethics and methodology', *European Journal of the History of Economic Thought*, **22** (2), 163–97.
Hawtrey, R.G. (1913), *Good and Bad Trade: An Inquiry into the Causes of Trade Fluctuations*, London: Constable.
Hawtrey, R.G. (1919), *Currency and Credit*, 2nd edn 1928, London: Longmans, Green and Co.
Hawtrey, R.G. (1927), *The Gold Standard in Theory and Practice*, London: Longmans, Green and Co.
Hawtrey, R.G. (1932), *The Art of Central Banking*, London: Longmans, Green and Co.
Hawtrey, R.G. (1937), *Capital and Employment*, London: Longmans, Green and Co.
Hawtrey, R.G. (1938), *A Century of Bank Rate*, London: Longmans, Green and Co.
Keynes, J.M. (1930), *A Treatise on Money, in Two Volumes: 1 The Pure Theory of Money; 2 The Applied Theory of Money*, London: Macmillan.
Keynes, J.M. (1936), *The General Theory of Employment, Interest and Money*, London: Macmillan.
Keynes, J.M. (1937), 'Alternative theories of the rate of interest', *Economic Journal*, reprinted 1973 in *The Collected Writings of John Maynard Keynes*, vol. XIV, London: Macmillan and St. Martin's Press, pp. 201–15.
Pigou, A.C. (1913), *Unemployment*, London: William and Norgate.
Pigou, A.C. (1933), *The Theory of Unemployment*, London: Macmillan.
Schumpeter, J.A. (1954), *History of Economic Analysis*, London: George Allen and Unwin.

Evgeny Evgenievich Slutsky (1880–1948)

Evgeny Evgenievich (Eugen) Slutsky was born on 7 April 1880, in Novoye Selo in Yaroslavskaya province into a teacher's family. From early childhood he was very impulsive and inconsistent. He graduated from high school in 1899 in Zhitomir and then studied in the Mathematics Department of the Physics and Mathematics Faculty of the University at Kiev. Being expelled several times from the University owing to political motives, he finally graduated from its Law Faculty in 1911, at the age of 31, receiving a golden medal for his diploma thesis on "The theory of marginal utility". This theme was probably the result of his stay for three years (1902–05) at the Munich Polytechnic Institute, where he had a chance to learn about the latest trends in economic thought. At that time he was interested in mathematical economics and specific economic researches. This interest was developed in close friendship with N.A. Svavitsky (1879–1936), an expert in local (*zemskaya*) statistics. An important event was Slutsky's marriage to Ylia N. Volodkevich, the daughter of the principal in one of Kiev's private schools. This was a happy alliance, solidly maintained through many of life's troubles.

Slutsky had numerous abilities: he was talented in mathematics, but also in the arts, especially painting and writing poems. After graduation from the university an academic career was not an option (owing to his reputation as a "red student"). Slutsky therefore started to work as a freelance teacher at his father-in-law's school.

At the same time his mathematical talent gained new momentum: in 1911–12 he came across mathematical statistics introduced by A.V. Leontovich's book, *Elementary Guidelines to Gauss and Pearson Methods in the Assessment of Errors in Statistics and Biology* (Leontovich 1909–11). Slutsky was fascinated by the ideas of K. Pearson and already in 1912 published his own book entitled *Theory of Correlation and Elements of Distribution Curves Theory*, first in a publication series of Kiev Commercial Institute and later as a separate publication (Slutsky 1912). At the time this work represented the best introduction to the English school of mathematics and statistics.

The same year he had to go to St Petersburg to the Ministry of Commerce and Industry in order to get permission to continue teaching. On this occasion he met Professor A.A. Tchuprov at the Polytechnical Institute of Peter the Great. Tchuprov came up with the idea of translating into Russian the widely known book by G.U. Yule, *An Introduction to the Theory of Statistics*, whose second edition was published in London in 1911. Slutsky and N.S. Tchetverikov, a student of Tchuprov, were supposed to translate the book. Although the project could not be realized owing to the outbreak of World War I, the intellectual friendship of the three statisticians lasted.

Because of good reviews of the *Theory of Correlation*, Slutsky was invited to join the Kiev Commercial Institute from January 1913, where he stayed until 1926. In order to be able to continue his teaching career, he had to take the exam for a Master's degree in political economy and statistics at Moscow University in 1917. On 14 November 1913, at the meeting of the Economists' Society, he presented an article devoted to the contributions of William Petty. This article was first published in a student journal of the Commercial Institute in 1914 and later as a separate book (Slutsky 1914).

A result of his intensive work on economic theory was his article "On the theory of the balanced consumer budget" which was published in the Italian journal *Giornale degli economisti e rivista di statistica* (Slutsky, 1915). The article brought him world recognition. The Slutsky equation relates changes in Marshallian demand to changes in Hicksian demand. It demonstrates that demand changes owing to price changes are the result of two effects: the substitution effect as the result of a change in the exchange rate between two goods; and the income effect, which relates to the change of the consumer's purchasing power consequent upon a change in price. Each element of the Slutsky matrix is given by:

$$\frac{\partial x_i(p,w)}{\partial p_j} = \frac{\partial h_i(p,u)}{\partial p_j} - \frac{\partial x_i(p,w)}{\partial w} x_j(p,w), \tag{1}$$

where $h(p, u)$ is the Hicksian demand and $x(p, w)$ is the Marshallian demand, at price level p, wealth level w, and utility level u. The first term on the right-hand side of the equality sign represents the substitution effect, and the second term represents the income effect. In this article, Slutsky developed some ideas by Francis Ysidro Edgeworth and Vilfredo Pareto about the relation between the utility function, prices, income and consumption. Slutsky's article was published in Russian for the first time only in 1963 (Slutsky 1963).

Before World War I, Slutsky became interested in psychology and sociology, but still stayed close to mathematics. He taught a variety of subjects – from mathematical statistics to economic history and social studies. However, teaching did not bring him satisfaction. After his Master's degree at Moscow University he left Volodkevich's school in 1918. The first half of the 1920s was very productive for Slutsky as an economist. In 1923 his work "On the issue of calculation of state income from emission" was published as a mathematical supplement to an article by L.N. Yasnopolsky. In it Slutsky presented a graph of money emission as a curve on a logarithmic scale (Slutsky 1923).

In 1926 Slutsky moved to Moscow to work in the Central Statistical Office. In February 1926 he started to work as a consultant at the Business Cycle Institute of the National Committee of Finance of the USSR, where he studied economic cycles in capitalistic countries. At the same time he was the head of the Agricultural Section of the Institute of Experimental Statistics and Statistical Methodology of the Central Statistical Office of the USSR. In 1930 Slutsky worked in institutions related to geophysics and meteorology. The subject of his research was the impact of solar activity on crop yields. In the early 1930s he also worked on the problem of times series. In the mid-1920s his article about stochastic asymptote and limit was published in the journal *Metron*. It became the basis of the theory of random functions – one of the most important directions of the modern theory of probability (Slutsky 1925). His contribution on the summation of random causes was the source of cyclical processes research (Slutsky 1927 in Russian; Slutsky 1937 in English). He showed that the observed quasi-periodicity may be the result of statistical stationarity, rather than real periodicity. In 1939 he started working at the Research Institute of Mathematics and Mechanics of Moscow State University. There he was awarded the degree of Doctor in Physics and Mathematical Sciences. In 1939 Slutsky began the development of the theory of random processes at the V.A. Steklov Institute of Mathematics of the USSR Academy of Sciences.

During World War II he was evacuated to Tashkent. After coming back to Moscow he was diagnosed with lung cancer. Nevertheless, he continued to build the tables of incomplete Γ-functions until his last days. He died in Moscow on 10 March 1948.

IRINA ELISEEVA

See also:

John Richard Hicks (I); Vilfredo Pareto (I); Russian School of mathematical economics (II).

References and further reading

Barnett, V. (2006), 'Changing an interpretation: Slutsky's random cycles revisited', *European Journal of the History of Economic Thought*, **13** (3), 411–32.

Barnett, V. (2011), *E.E. Slutsky as Economist and Mathematician: Crossing the Limits of Knowledge*, London: Routledge.

Chipman, J.S. and J.-S. Lenfant (2002), 'Slutsky's 1915 article: how it came to be found and interpreted', *History of Political Economy*, **34** (3), 553–97.

Leontovich, A.V. (1909–11), *Elementarnoye posobie k primeneniyu metodov Gauss'a i Pearson'a pri otsenke oshibok v statistike i biologii* (*Elementary Guidelines to Gauss and Pearson Methods in the Assessment of Errors in Statistics and Biology*), 3 vols, Kiev: tip. S.V.Kuldzhenko.

Seneta, E. (2001), 'Evgenii Evgenievich Slutsky (Slutskii)', in C.C.Heyde, E. Seneta, P. Crepel, S.E. Fienberg and J. Gani (eds), *Statisticians of the Centuries*, New York: Springer, pp. 343–5.

Slutsky, E.E. (1912), 'Teoriya korrelyatsii i elementy ucheniya o krivykh raspredeleniya (posobiye k izucheniyu nekotorykh vazhneyshykh metodov sovremennoi statistiki)' ('Theory of correlation and elements of distribution curves theory'), *Journal of Kiev Commercial Institute*, book XVI.

Slutsky, E.E. (1914), 'Sir William Petty: kratkaya stat'ya o ego economicheskikh vzglyadakh s prilozheniem naibolee vazhnykh otryvkov iz ego rabot' ('Sir William Petty: short article about his economics views with supplement of most important passages from his works'), *Student Journal of Kiev Commercial Institute*, no.16–18, 5–48.

Slutsky, E.E. (1915), 'Sulla teoria del bilancio del consumatore', *Giornale degli economisti e rivista statistica*, **51** (1), 1–26.

Slutsky, E.E. (1923), 'K voprosu o vychislenii dohoda gosudarstva ot emissii' ('On the issue of calculation of state income from emission'), *Mestnoe Khozyastvo*, Kiev, no. 2, November (Supplement I to the article by N.P. Yasnopolsky, "Nashe denezhnoe obraschenie v epokhu revolyutsii" ('Our monetary circulation in the era of revolution').

Slutsky, E.E. (1925), 'Ueberstochastische Asymptoten und Grenzwerte', *Metron*, Padova, **V** (3), 3–89.

Slutsky, E.E. (1927), 'Slozhenie sluchainykh prichin kak istochnic tsyklicheskikh protsessov', *Voprosy Kon'yunktury*, Moscow, **3** (1), 34–64.

Slutsky, E.E. (1937), 'The summation of random causes as the source of cyclic processes', *Econometrica*, **5** (2), 105–46.

Slutsky, E.E. (1960), *Izbrannye trudy. Matematicheskaya statistika. Teoriya veroyatnostei*, eds B.V. Gnedenko and N.V.Smirnov, Moscow: Academy of Sciences of USSR.

Slutsky, E.E. (1963), 'K teorii sbalansirovannogo byudjeta potrebitelya', *Narodno-hozyastvennye Modeli. Teoreticheskie voprosy potrebleniya*, trans. from the Italian by N.S. Chetverikov, Moscow: Academy of Sciences of USSR: 241–71.

Slutsky, E.E. (2009), *Theory of Correlation and Elements of the Doctrine of the Curves of Distribution. Manual for Studying Some Most Important Methods of Contemporary Statistics* (1912), trans. O.B. Sheynin, Berlin: NG Verlag.

Slutsky, E.E. (2010), Economicheskie i Statisticheskie proizvedeniya. Isbrannoe (*Selected Works in Economics and Statistics*), ed. P. Klyukin, Moscow: ECSMO.

Tchuprov, A.A. (1914), 'Leontovich A. "Elementarnoye posobie k primeneniyu metodov Gauss'a i Pearson'a pri otsenke oshibok v statistike i biologii, Chasti 1-3 Kiev, 1909–1911", Slutsky E.: "Teoriya korrelyatsii i elementy ucheniya o krivykh raspredeleniya (posobiye k izucheniyu nekotorykh vazhneyshykh metodov sovremennoi statistiki) Kiev, 1912"' (review article), *Russkie Vedomosti*, 14 November, 4.

Yule, G.U. (1911), *An Introduction to the Theory of Statistics*, London: Griffin.

Ludwig Heinrich von Mises (1881–1973)

Ludwig Heinrich von Mises was born in Lemberg (capital of Galicia, then a province of the Habsburg empire, today Lviv, Ukraine) on 29 September 1881 and died in New York 18 October 1973. His father was a Jewish-Austrian railroad engineer. The family moved to Vienna soon after Ludwig's birth, where he attended an elite grammar school and the University of Vienna (1900–1906). Like most other Austrian economists, he enrolled in the Faculty of Law, earning his doctoral degree in 1906 and becoming a member of Eugen von Böhm-Bawerk's famous seminar. Mises's professional achievements in academia remained modest in comparison to his scholarly accomplishments. After his habilitation in 1913, he taught as *Privatdozent* and later as "extraordinary" professor without a salary. Until he left Austria in 1934, he spent most of his professional life as an economist for the Viennese chamber of commerce. In the 1920s and early 1930s, he became influential as an adviser to the centre-right coalition governments of the First Austrian Republic. In the 1920s, he inaugurated a private seminar, attracting brilliant young economists and social theorists such as Gottfried Haberler, Friedrich August von Hayek, Felix Kaufmann, Fritz Machlup, Oskar Morgenstern, Paul Rosenstein-Rodan and Alfred Schütz. As a consequence of the surge of the Nazi movement in Germany and the concomitant menace regarding the political situation in Austria, Mises moved to the Institut Universitaire des Hautes Études Internationales in Geneva in 1934, where he was offered a paid professorship.

After the defeat of the French army in 1940, Switzerland was no longer a comfortable safe haven for a Jewish emigrant. The border of the German Occupied Zone was alarmingly close to Geneva. Mises, aged 59, emigrated to the US. Mises's reception by the academic establishment in the US was not entirely reassuring. His eccentric position vis-à-vis the mainstream of economics and the fact that he was approaching retirement age made it difficult to find an academic position, which would match his credits as a theorist. From 1945 to 1969, he taught at New York University as an externally funded professor. Even though he never achieved a regular professorship, Mises again attracted disciples and again held a private seminar. Compared with the Mises Seminar in Vienna with its remarkably heterogeneous membership composed of original and independent thinkers, many of which were to become eminent scholars, the seminar groups in New York can be considered as the nucleus of a more narrowly defined Mises School characterized by a libertarian-conservative agenda. Mises's US disciples, such as Murray Rothbard, were staunch adherents of a free-market stance. Yet while Mises himself believed that a minimal state is defensible on the grounds of its role in enforcing private property rights and contractual obligations, some of his US followers endorsed "anti-statist" anarcho-capitalistic views. In terms of academic reputation, his most important American student is Israel Kirzner, who developed an arguably Misesian theory of entrepreneurship.

While other Austrian economists teaching in the US, such as Schumpeter, Machlup, Morgenstern and Haberler did not put great emphasis on promoting a distinct Austrian School, Mises and his thought becomes the focal point of the emergence of contemporary currents now known as the Austrian School (see Vaughn 1994: 62–99). The development of those currents gained momentum in the 1960s and 1970s.

Mises's early reputation as an economist was built on his work on money and credit

(*Theorie des Geldes und der Umlaufsmittel*, 1912). He attempts to explain monetary phenomena on the basis of Austrian marginal utility theory. Topics include:

1. *The spontaneous, market-based origin of commodity money*. Regarding the origin of money, Mises elaborates on Carl Menger's pertinent line argument: the so called regression theorem implies a rejection of theories explaining money as a collective institution built on contract or convention.
2. *The foundational role of precious metals as reserves in the monetary and financial system*. Mises advocates the gold standard, or, more precisely, the privatization of money, which, he is convinced, would lead to the gold standard.
3. *Problems of non-neutral money, expansionary credit and inflationary banking*. In the 1920s he pursues this line of investigation in his monetary theory of the business cycle (cf. 1949 [1963]: ch. 20).

While some of the tenets developed in Mises (1912) had considerable impact on later discussions (for example, on Hayek's business cycle theory), Mises's most influential contributions are related to the so-called German language "calculation debate", including economics of socialism and state interventionism. Mises (1920, 1922) famously stated the impossibility of rational economic calculation in a socialist commonwealth without private property. As he puts it, socialist planners would be "groping in the dark". He predicts a sharp decline in productivity after a transition period following the socialist revolution. During this transition period, economic planning would still benefit from the allocation mechanism prevalent in the market economy. However, the information once made available by the system of market prices would fade away or become obsolete. The era of darkness, low productivity and mass starvation would begin. This is stated with apodictic certainty. In Mises's *Human Action* (1949 [1963]: 680) we read: "The choice is between capitalism and chaos. . . . To stress this point is the task of economics as it is the task of biology and chemistry to teach that potassium cyanide is not a nutriment but a deadly poison."

Mises's arguments in the German language debate on economic calculation were to a large extent directed against Otto von Neurath's concept of planning in-kind (that is, planning without prices and money), which had been inspired by experiences of the war economy. Hence money is an issue for Mises also in his contributions on economic planning. In the 1920s, it became clear that not many socialists did advocate this type of comprehensive planning in-kind. They, rather, endorsed a price-guided planning process or some kind of a mixed economy. Both of those hybrid types of economic system would entail important interventions by the state at one or the other level. Consequently, Mises (1929) concentrates his efforts on the rejection of interventionism. He argues that it would not be possible to limit interventions to some particular kind of problems or to some specific level of decisions, as it may appear desirable in the view of some moderate reformists who wish to cure the ills of capitalism without abolishing markets. This idea is fundamentally flawed, Mises argues. One single well-meant intervention rather would trigger a whole epidemic of interventions, eventually leading to the total destruction of the price system and to a centrally planned economy. Hence one better steer clear of the slippery slope unavoidably following any intervention.

In the 1930s, Mises wrote his foundational magnum opus *Nationalökonomie:*

Theorie des Handelns und des Wirtschaftens (Mises 1940 [1980]). In a modified version, this is published in English as *Human Action: A Treatise on Economics* (Mises 1949 [1963]). In *Human Action*, the traditional Austrian tenets of methodological individualism, subjectivism and causal-genetic explanation are supplemented by an aprioristic epistemology. Mises's so-called praxeology is represented as the encompassing science of human action, comprising catallactics (the theory of market exchange) and economics (price theory). Mises emphasizes the non-psychological character of the basic ingredients of economics. While positing instrumental rationality as the aprioristic pivot of the human condition, Mises at the same time rejects the axiomatic choice-theoretic foundations of microeconomics, which can be considered as the basis for economics as a mathematical, quantitative science. On the basis of his praxeology, Mises attempts to establish a kind of free market-doctrine in which the stability of private property rights is of pivotal importance. If private property rights are guaranteed, lack of competition is not a major problem. In the context of an adequate market process theory of the economy (instead of mistaken Walrasian equilibrium analysis), monopolies are temporary phenomena. Notice, though, that Mises employs equilibrium constructs (the state of rest and the evenly rotating economy) to establish static reference scenarios, against which process-related aspects such as entrepreneurship can be better understood. This invites a comparison with Schumpeter.

   Coordination failures brought about by malfunctioning of markets are not really a theme for Mises. In his view, major disturbances occurring in contemporary economies are always either owing to misplaced government intervention or the failure of government to close gaps in the existing system of private property rights. The main thrust of this view is to be found already in Mises's writings of the interwar period. In Mises's later writings, the political element becomes ever more prominent. While some of his books (for example, on bureaucracy or on economic evolution; Mises 1944b, 1957) broaden the topical scope of Mises's economics, writings such as *The Anti-Capitalistic Mentality* (Mises 1956) are worth noting because of their fervent polemic against left-leaning intellectuals rather than for their contribution to economic analysis or to social theory. The fact that some intellectuals endorse socialism, even though they should know better, and even though they have every reason to be grateful to capitalism (no other system created sufficient wealth to feed so many of them), apparently becomes a major problem for Mises. In similar mood, he develops a kind of contempt for the masses who are ignorant of the enormous advantages that the capitalist system confers upon them, as they benefit from the wealth created by the highly productive capitalist elite. An extreme version of this view is promoted in the novel *Atlas Shrugged* by Ayn Rand, which is avowedly endorsed by Mises (see Mises 1958). Rand recommends Mises's economics to her libertarian followers, even though she endorses an objectivist philosophy while Mises's economics is renowned for its uncompromising subjectivism.

RICHARD STURN

See also:

Eugen von Böhm-Bawerk (I); German and Austrian schools (II); Friedrich August von Hayek (I); Non-Marxist socialist ideas in Germany and Austria (II); Friedrich von Wieser (I).

References and further reading

Boettke, P.J. (ed.) (1994), *The Elgar Companion to Austrian Economics*, Cheltenham, UK and Northampton, MA, USA: Edward Elgar.

Mises, L. von (1912), *Theorie des Geldes und der Umlaufsmittel*, Munich and Leipzig: Duncker & Humblot.

Mises, L. von (1919), *Nation, Staat und Wirtschaft: Beiträge zur Politik und Geschichte der Zeit*, Vienna: Manzsche Verlags- und Universitätsbuchhandlung.

Mises, L. von (1920), 'Die Wirtschaftsrechnung im sozialistischen Gemeinwesen', *Archiv für Sozialwissenschaft und Sozialpolitik*, **47**, 86–121.

Mises, L. von (1922), *Die Gemeinwirtschaft. Untersuchungen über den Sozialismus*, Jena: Gustav Fischer.

Mises, L. von (1922), *Socialism. An Economic and Sociological Analysis*, reprinted 1981, Indianapolis, IN: Liberty Fund.

Mises, L. von (1927), *Liberalismus*, Jena: Gustav Fischer.

Mises, L. von (1929), *Kritik des Interventionismus. Untersuchungen zur Wirtschaftspolitik und Wirtschaftsideologie der Gegenwart*, Jena: Gustav Fischer.

Mises, L. von (1933), *Grundprobleme der Nationalökonomie. Untersuchungen über Verfahren, Aufgabe und Inhalte der Wirtschafts- und Gesellschaftslehre*, Jena: Gustav Fischer.

Mises, L. von (1940), *Nationalökonomie*, Theorie des Handelns und Wirtschaftens, München, reprinted 1980, Geneva: Editions Union.

Mises, L. von (1944a), *Omnipotent Government. The Rise of the Total State and Total War*, New Haven, CT: Yale University Press.

Mises, L. von (1944b), *Bureaucracy*, New Haven, CT: Yale University Press.

Mises, L. von (1949), *Human Action. A Treatise on Economics*, New Haven, CT: Yale University Press, revised and expanded 2nd edn 1963.

Mises, L. von (1952), *Planning for Freedom. Let the Market System Work*, Indianapolis, IN: Liberty Fund.

Mises, L. von (1956), *The Anti-Capitalist Mentality*, Princeton, NJ: D. van Nostrand.

Mises, L. von (1957), *Theory and History. An Interpretation of Social and Economic Evolution*, New Haven, CT: Yale University Press.

Mises, L. von (1958), 'Letter to Mrs. Ayn Rand', accessed 27 November 2015 at http/www.mises.org/etexts/misesatlas.pdf.

Mises, L. von (1978), *Erinnerungen*, Stuttgart and New York: Gustav Fischer.

Prychitko, D. (1994), 'Praxeology', in P.J. Boettke (ed.), *The Elgar Companion to Austrian Economics*, Cheltenham, UK and Northampton, MA, USA: Edward Elgar, pp. 77–83.

Vaughn, K. (1994), *Austrian Economics in America*, Cambridge: Cambridge University Press.

Wieser, F. von (1884), *Über den Ursprung und die Hauptgesetze des Wirtschaftlichen Werthes*, Vienna: Alfred Hölder.

John Maynard Keynes (1883–1946)

Life

John Maynard Keynes was born in Cambridge, England, the eldest of three children. His father, John Neville Keynes, was a Cambridge don (and later Registrary of the University) who lectured in logic and political economy. His *Scope and Method of Political Economy* (1891) remains an important text in economic methodology. Maynard's mother, Florence Ada Keynes, was the daughter of a Congregationalist minister. She was educated at Newnham College in the pioneering days of women's education at Cambridge. She was active in progressive social projects and became a magistrate and the first woman mayor of Cambridge.

Maynard's father supervised his early studies; they worked together in the father's study. Maynard was perceived as exceptionally intelligent from an early age and was pushed rather hard, but where a lesser child might have found this onerous or have rebelled, he revelled in the work and excelled. He won a scholarship to Eton, where he developed his knowledge of philosophy and began to collect rare books. (He later made a substantial contribution to the history of science by collecting Newton's alchemical papers.) He went from there to King's College, Cambridge, where philosophy and ethics claimed his attention more than the subject he was reading: mathematics. He and those in his circle were much influenced by the philosophy of G.E. Moore, for whom the contemplation of beauty and the enjoyment of friendship were the true purposes of life, a view deeply subversive of Victorian values of duty and convention.

Keynes took a first class degree in 1905 and then, with Alfred Marshall's encouragement and supervision, stayed on in Cambridge with a view to studying for the (then new) economics examinations. In the end he elected to sit the Civil Service examinations instead. He came second and joined the India Office, where he spent just two years. He found the work less than a challenge and began to write his dissertation for a fellowship at King's. From 1908 he was back in Cambridge, lecturing in economics and revising his dissertation, which was accepted the following year and published much later (*A Treatise on Probability*, 1921). In 1911 (aged 28) he was appointed editor of the *Economic Journal* and in 1913 published his first book, *Indian Currency and Finance*. Cambridge was his centre of gravity until the outbreak of the First World War, though he kept up his friendships with what became known as the Bloomsbury Group, including the painters Duncan Grant and Vanessa Bell, and the writers Virginia Woolf and Lytton Strachey, sharing a series of houses with several of them.

Whether by association with these people, exposure to Moore's ideas, or natural inclination, Keynes embraced the arts with enthusiasm. His artistic interests spanned theatre, ballet, painting and rare books. His greatest contributions to the arts were to establish the Arts Council and to give the Arts Theatre to Cambridge. He also secured some very important pictures for the National Gallery; his own collection is now on long loan from King's College to the Fitzwilliam Museum. In Keynes's personality these goals were balanced by the acceptance of a duty to contribute to public life, which he did in abundance.

Keynes went to the Treasury in January 1915 to work on wartime internal and external finance, and at the end of the war he was the Treasury's chief representative at the Paris peace conference. He strongly opposed the punitive settlement France wanted to impose on Germany, arguing that the attempt to pay what France was asking would first bankrupt Germany and then embitter her, and a bitter Germany was dangerous (as it proved).

When his view made no headway, Keynes resigned in protest and spent the summer at Charleston, the farmhouse in Sussex that Vanessa Bell and Duncan Grant had leased, writing *The Economic Consequences of the Peace* (1919). The book was a sensation, both for the depth of its analysis of the economic background to the war and the consequences of the proposed peace settlement, but also for its vivid depiction of the strong political forces at work in the conference and its devastating characterization of the chief participants. Keynes was now famous, not as an academic but in world affairs (he became a subject of David Low's cartoons). In official circles, however, the book was (understandably) deeply offensive. He left the Treasury to return only when the next war, which he had predicted, broke out.

In the 1920s, Keynes returned to lecturing at Cambridge (unpaid, in order to leave time for writing – he now made his money mainly by playing various financial and commodity markets). But he was not only a don: journalism, financial dealings, chairmanship of a life assurance company and the pursuit of the good life enriched his days – and sometimes his pocket. He served King's as Bursar. As Skidelsky (1992) put it, the academic was balanced by the man of affairs, the manager by the aesthete.

Recovery from the First World War, price instability and the debate over the related questions of whether Britain should return to the gold standard (to which he was strongly opposed) and, if so, at what parity were key issues for Keynes in the early 1920s, while he revised and published his fellowship dissertation (*A Treatise on Probability*, 1921). He returned to the reparations issue (*A Revision of the Treaty*, 1922), collected up his writings on price stability and the gold standard into *A Tract on Monetary Reform* (1923) and in 1924 began work on *A Treatise on Money* (1930).

He spent part of each week at King's and part in London at 46 Gordon Square in Bloomsbury. During the 1920s, Diaghilev's Ballets Russes had captivated London – and Keynes, after a lifetime of homosexual affairs, fell deeply in love with its prima ballerina, Lydia Lopokova. They married in 1925, took sole possession of 46 Gordon Square and also took a lease on Tilton, a farmhouse in Sussex very near Charleston.

He kept up a close relationship with the Liberal Party. He took a particularly active role in the 1929 election campaign, in which he advised and wrote pamphlets on unemployment policy and its finance (for example, the pamphlet written with Hubert Henderson, *Can Lloyd George Do It?*, Keynes 1929 [1972]), and spoke on the hustings in support of Liberal candidates. He was urged to stand for the Cambridge University constituency but refused.

Britain left the gold standard in 1931, which left interest rates free to fall. Keynes organized the conversion of the huge War Loan, issued in 1917 at 5 per cent, to a much lower rate. But neither of these events did much to alleviate the high unemployment that Britain had suffered since 1921, now intensified by the Wall Street crash and the collapse of American prosperity and world trade. Arguing from *A Treatise on Money* in the Macmillan Committee on Finance and Industry, Keynes realized that neither he nor his contemporaries could explain the persistence of unemployment. Keynes began to work toward *The General Theory of Employment, Interest and Money* (1936), aided by the criticisms of his younger Cambridge colleagues.

In 1937, Keynes suffered his first heart attack, by which his activities were much reduced. By the time war was declared, his health had improved. He returned to the Treasury and devoted himself first to *How to Pay for the War* (1940) with low interest costs and limited inflation. He made several trips to the United States to negotiate the Lend Lease agreement. He was elevated to the peerage in 1942. When he turned to preparing for post-war arrangements for trade and international payments, his Clearing Union became the official British proposal at the Bretton Woods conference in 1944. Its core proposal was defeated by the Americans. Later that year he had another serious heart attack.

In late 1945, he returned to America to negotiate a loan. The terms were harsh, but he defended them in the House of Lords as the best that could be got. He returned to the US for the inauguration of the International Monetary Fund (IMF) and the World Bank and suffered another heart attack on the way back. The next heart attack, at Tilton on 21 April 1946, was fatal.

From Early Philosophy to *A Treatise on Probability*

Keynes came to economics after he took his degree and, informally, learning from Marshall while preparing for the Civil Service examination. As an undergraduate, while formally reading mathematics, it was philosophy that grabbed his attention. He was a member of a "secret" society called The Apostles, where students read papers on a wide range of subjects. In Keynes's time they were much influenced by the philosophy of G.E. Moore, for whom the contemplation of beauty and the enjoyment of friendship were the true purposes of life. Keynes responded to Moore with an essay on beauty and three papers on ethics. He also wrote a long essay on political philosophy, taking much (but not his conservatism) from Edmund Burke. Under the influence of Moore, he developed an Ideal, which included not only Moore's concept of the good life but also his acknowledgement that nothing in personal life or society can be considered as certain; history does not repeat itself, and therefore the future is unknown and unknowable. This poses a challenge both to ethical conduct when we do not know the consequences of our actions and to the meaning we attach to knowledge and rationality.

Moore's answer to the ethical problem was to fall back on convention as the repository of accumulated wisdom. Keynes's critique of this position led him to develop a theory of rationality under uncertainty, which he first submitted to King's College as a fellowship dissertation in 1908. It was published in 1921 as *A Treatise on Probability* (hereafter *TP*).

In an uncertain world, all knowledge is only probable. Economics had inherited the idea, which comes down from Greek philosophy, that rationality can only coexist with certainty. A later modification allowed for "certainty equivalents" derived from classical probability – the sort of probability that pertains to repeated throws of fair dice. For Keynes, the fact that the future is uncertain takes us beyond the limited sphere to which classical probability applies. Radical uncertainty, as it has come to be known, was simply a fact, but a fact that need not paralyse action or defeat rationality: rather, rationality and rational action had to be redefined. A rational approach to decision-making under uncertainty was to establish a "rational belief" in the link between a proposition and its probable outcome, by scrutinizing the available evidence, weighted according to its (probable) reliability and relevance.

The logic of this process is not watertight, not demonstrable, as in classical logic. It belongs to "human logic", and its rationality conforms to the meaning of rationality in ordinary language. In the ever-changing world in which we live, it is irrational to apply the "rationality" of certainty and perfect knowledge.

Rational belief, however, is an insufficient guide to ethical conduct. Since the consequences of our actions are at best only probable, Keynes proposed that rational ethics should be based on motive rather than consequences. For example, Keynes accepted the profit motive but decried the love of money for its own sake. For him, "being good" is the key ethical principle: an action is good if it is directed to something intrinsically worthwhile rather than toward some ulterior goal. Even Keynes's pragmatism had its roots in ethical principles. To him, both economics and politics dealt only with means. They were facilitators of the good life, never ends in themselves.

Keynes developed early the philosophical foundations on which his economic thinking stands but went on exploring its ramifications. It took a long time for the philosophical thinking of *TP* to become fully incorporated into his economic theory; not until *The General Theory* in fact. The journey through economic analysis to the point where his earliest work and his last book are united is a long and tortuous one. We now trace the main signposts of that journey.

Indian Currency and Finance (1913): The Role of Institutions

Keynes was in the India Office for less than two years. He not only wrote the first version of his fellowship dissertation in that time but also closely studied the peculiarities of India's financial system. His analysis in the resulting book, *Indian Currency and Finance* (hereafter *ICF*, Keynes 1913 [1971]), established his method of theorizing from the known facts – not the usual procedure in economics, then as (even more) now. Although the book reads as a coherent whole, once Keynes was invited to participate in the Royal Commission on Indian Finance and Currency, it was sent to print without some of its intended chapters, in order to establish the book's independence from the Commission's deliberations.

India's gold standard was effectively based on sterling, and the system functioned differently from the gold standard in Britain also because of their different financial institutions and real economies. The emphasis on institutional factors that characterizes *ICF* is only equalled in Keynes's later work on commodity markets, but we would argue that institutional knowledge is at the back of his mind at all times and can be detected in his later theoretical propositions, for example, the theory of liquidity preference and the causal priority of investment over saving.

The most striking difference in the system's operation arose from the strong seasonal fluctuations in interest rates in India, driven by the variable liquidity needs of her agricultural economic base. India at that time had no central bank but was entirely dependent on London for its liquidity. Before the advent of rapid communication, the time lost in the transfer of funds from London cost interest, which India could ill afford. Keynes recommended that India have its own central bank, which would issue paper money to accommodate seasonal liquidity needs while maintaining its currency's gold parity. This possibility of using credit to alleviate the gold standard's rigidity and to economize on the expense of minting and shipping precious metal recommended the gold-exchange standard to Keynes as a future system more generally. The existing one-to-one relationship between gold reserves and the supply of currency in a "proper" gold standard led to instability; a managed currency would be better.

Keynes's objection to the gold standard went beyond its unnecessary rigidity. The conventional wisdom was that the second half of the nineteenth century was a wonderful age of stability and prosperity and that the gold standard was largely responsible for its success. A return to gold was seen as the best hope of recapturing prosperity. Keynes argued for the opposite causality: that the apparent success of the gold standard as an international payments system depended on the particular historical circumstances of the period, which were unlikely to be repeated in the post-war world economy.

The Economic Consequences of the Peace (1919)

The book that made Keynes famous was best known for its unflattering characterizations of the main participants in the peace negotiations at Versailles and its description of their narrow aims, motivated by (mis-)perceived national advantage. In Keynes's view those aims were self-defeating; the proposed reparations were designed to cripple Germany, but he argued that they would also undermine the prosperity of the victors. His analysis, based on data whose collection he had directed while in the Treasury, of the relationship between Germany's rapid industrialization and the structure of European trade before the war showed that the pre-war structure of activity and trade between the combatants was fragile but benefited all participants. The Versailles treaty put this interdependent system in jeopardy.

Keynes's analysis in *Economic Consequences of the Peace* (hereafter *ECP*, Keynes 1919 [1971]), was truly macroeconomic and forward-looking; it was concerned with the future health of the European economy as a whole. He argued that from that point of view the political aim should have been to establish an international framework for a stable European economy rather than pursuing national interests dominated by a desire for revenge.

A Tract on Monetary Reform (1923) and the Gold Standard

British prices just after the war were more volatile than ever before or since. The monthly cost of living index (1913 average = 100) rose from 242 in August 1919 to 319 the following March and then fell to 158 by February 1922 (*A Tract on Monetary Reform*, hereafter *TMF*, Keynes 1923 [1971]: 84). Wholesale prices followed a similar pattern. These huge fluctuations in the price level, deflation as well as inflation, had a destabilizing effect on production and employment: unemployment rose to 14 per cent in 1922 and, as other problems arose, never fell below 10 per cent for the entire interwar period – more on that persistent imbalance below. In *TMR*, based on previously published newspaper articles, Keynes attempted to explain these dramatic short-term price fluctuations.

The quantity theory of money

The only theory of prices available to Keynes at the time was the quantity theory of money. Detailed formulations of the theory varied. Unsurprisingly, Keynes preferred the oral Cambridge tradition inherited from Marshall (see Keynes 1911 [1983]). However, all proposed an equiproportional link between changes in prices and changes in the money supply in long-run equilibrium. Keynes at this time thought this proposition incontrovertible, although there was clearly no tight relationship between the money supply, which had changed little, and price changes observed in the post-war years.

Part of Keynes's explanation involved a shift of focus from state-supplied money (notes and coin), still thought to be the only proper money, to their close substitute, bank deposits. Although the note issue was broadly speaking unchanged, private bank lending could break the link between central bank money and deposits, so the velocity of circulation of central bank money had become unstable and unpredictable. Once again, Keynes's empirical observation and institutional insight gave rise to a new approach.

Keynes argued that the enhanced importance of the banking system called for a more active monetary policy, directed towards stability of the domestic price level rather than the exchange rate. This was feasible as long as Britain was de facto off gold. (This recommendation echoes the thinking in *ICF*.)

The quantity theory failed to explain the course of prices not only because it ignored bank lending: more importantly, it was a long-run, equilibrium theory. The quantity theory was at one with the rest of economics at the time, which saw the short run as transitory and therefore not worth the theorist's attention. Keynes ventured into short-run territory to attempt to explain post-war price fluctuations. He expressed his dissatisfaction with the quantity theory's equilibrium method forcefully: "But the long run is a misleading guide to current affairs. In the long run we are all dead. Economists set themselves too easy, too useless a task if in tempestuous seasons they can only tell us that when the storm is long past the ocean is flat again" (*TMR*, Keynes 1923 [1971]: 65). However, he left its long-run theoretical proposition unchallenged: he had not yet given up the quantity theory altogether.

The gold standard

Keynes had always been opposed to the rigid gold standard: beginning with *ICF*, he favoured managed money. Now, having argued that deflation had even worse consequences than inflation, he could argue against gold even more strongly: a return at pre-war parity would entail the continuation of the deflationary policies already in place, as British wages and prices were still about 10 per cent above American levels at the old exchange rate.

Keynes was in a minority of one among prominent economists, and his view was not considered respectable by most politicians at home or abroad. The gold standard was widely perceived as the key to stability and the return to pre-war parity as honouring one's debts. Once again, Keynes lost the political argument: Britain returned to gold convertibility at pre-war parity in 1925. He expressed his discontent in a pamphlet, *The Economic Consequences of Mr Churchill* (Keynes 1925 [1972]), in which he continued his earlier argument that, if sterling was tied to gold, the overvaluation of sterling could only be rectified by further deflation and unemployment.

These analytical conclusions came true. The policy of deflation continued, provoking the General Strike of 1926. But it took a world recession and a collapse of world trade to make the gold standard finally untenable. Britain went off gold in 1931.

The Liberal Party

Throughout the 1920s Keynes was an active member of the Liberal Party, reaching a peak in the run-up to the 1929 election. He wrote *We Can Conquer Unemployment* (not reproduced in the *Collected Writings*) and *Can Lloyd George Do It?* (Keynes [1929] 1972), the latter with Hubert Henderson. These spelled out a programme of public works to alleviate unemployment, with due attention to the financing of the programme. Emphasis was laid on the second and further rounds of expenditure, which would result in what there was called "indirect employment" – what we now know as multiplier effects. In unpublished notes for a speech on the hustings in support of a candidate, even a rudimentary formal multiplier had been found (Kent 2008). The multiplier would be developed, but the idea came too late to be included in his next book, which after six years' work was about to be published.

A Treatise on Money (1930): Interest and Prices

As soon as *TMR* was published, Keynes was dissatisfied with the theory there presented. Work on what would become *A Treatise on Money* (hereafter *TM*, Keynes 1930 [1971]) began the following year. The result was a scholarly work in two volumes following the traditional separation of the "pure theory" of money from "applied theory". His original intention was to present his accumulated knowledge of the working of money and finance in the economy as a whole. The analysis was more far-reaching than that.

Keynes still took the quantity theory as his starting point, but he states his intention to address the cardinal flaw acknowledged in *TMR*: "My object has been to find a method which is useful in describing, not merely the characteristics of static equilibrium, but also those of disequilibrium" (*TM*, Keynes 1930 [1971], I: xvii). The tempestuous seasons as well as the flat ocean should be the subject of analysis.

He was traditional also in taking Marshallian long-period normal profit and the consequent price level as his definition of equilibrium. Deviations from the equilibrium position were characterized as "windfall" profits or losses. The associated fluctuations in prices were analysed by an expanded version of the quantity theory which he called the "Fundamental Equations". The link between money and prices was no longer simple and direct but involved three main elements: the level of money income relative to "efficiency" (that is, productivity), which determined factor costs, the expectations of holders of financial assets and, most importantly, disparities between voluntary savings and real investment, the latter measured in terms of cost of production.

The treatment of the saving–investment nexus marked a radical departure from the conventional wisdom, in which the two were brought into equilibrium by the rate of interest and analytically considered as Siamese twins. In *TM*, saving and investment are undertaken by different people with different motives, and there is no specific "financial market" or single variable (such as a rate of interest) that coordinates these two separate activities. (This separation is also central to *The General Theory*.) At its simplest, an excess of investment over saving produces windfall profits and higher prices; an excess of saving produces losses and deflation. However, money is used not only in the "industrial circulation" but also in the "financial circulation", where an increase in bearishness (pessimistic expectations) can result in money being withheld from the industrial circulation, causing a rise in the rate of interest and deflationary pressures on real investment. Bullishness (optimism) could have the opposite effect. This is a precursor of the "liquidity preference theory" fully unfolded in *The General Theory*. The rate of interest is mainly determined by expectations of participants in the financial circulation, and monetary fluctuations now affect the real economy: they were no longer neutral. Only when the money value of voluntary saving and investment are equal will normal profits and equilibrium prices prevail. The quantity theory holds in this equilibrium; but there are no automatic market mechanisms to bring it about.

Besides this admixture of traditional and innovative theory, *TM* contains a wealth of institutional and historical detail and a thorough exploration of the theory of monetary policy. Keynes's analysis showed that interest rate policy was not helpful in combating cost inflation but could be used to counteract or, preferably, ward off inflation or deflation caused by a misalignment of saving and investment. Monetary policy could stabilize the economy as a whole by bringing the market rate into line with the (Wicksellian) natural rate of interest.

A Treatise on Money was developed alongside Keynes's work on the Macmillan Committee on Finance and Industry (1929–31), and his contribution there was based on its framework. However, the Committee found it less than convincing, because it could not explain persistent unemployment, a crucial problem visible to all in interwar Britain and now intensified since the Wall Street crash of 1929. In *TM*, persistent unemployment could be seen as an imbalance between saving and investment in the context of an inappropriate exchange rate. The over-saving could not be eliminated by reducing the rate of interest, due to the fixed exchange rate and the predominance of bear speculators. Ingenious though *TM* was, the equilibrium level of output had been taken as given at full employment; all variation was perceived as a deviation from this level.

Once again, as soon as *TM* was published, Keynes began to think his way to the next book: *The General Theory*. He brooded over it for six years, and it was his crowning theoretical achievement. Two of *TM*'s conclusions will be overturned there, that a slump is due to lack of entrepreneurial optimism and that an increase in employment requires a fall in wages. And Keynes will at long last have put the quantity theory behind him.

The General Theory of Employment, Interest and Money (1936): Unemployment Equilibrium

A Treatise on Money was written more or less in isolation, but it was exposed even before publication to the criticism of members of the Macmillan Committee. Keynes also received criticism from Hayek, but they were not on the same wavelength: Hayek expected a theory which would encompass capital theory in the manner of Böhm-Bawerk, but Keynes's frame of reference was different. Keynes did reply concerning the quantity theory, showing that Hayek retained loanable funds theory, which Keynes rejected on the grounds that it was incompatible with the facts of modern money and finance (Keynes 1931a [1973]).

Some of his younger Cambridge colleagues, among other Richard Kahn, Piero Sraffa, Austin Robinson, Joan Robinson and (on leave from Oxford) James Meade, formed a group known as "The Circus", to discuss *TM* in detail. They soon found themselves debating and contributing to the development of Keynes's new ideas, which he began to introduce into his Cambridge teaching as early as 1931. The following year he changed the title of his lectures (Skidelsky 1992: 460) from 'The pure theory of money' to 'The monetary theory of production', reflecting the contrast he made with the real theory of exchange (the subject of neoclassical theory) in a short forthcoming article (Keynes 1933a

[1973]). Kahn developed the idea of the multiplier, which Keynes had introduced in 1929, into a formal system (Kahn 1931); it becomes a central concept in *The General Theory*.

There is both continuity and great change between *TM* and *The General Theory of Employment, Interest and Money* (hereafter *GT*, Keynes 1936 [1973]). The main problem with *TM* was that it followed tradition in taking for granted a "long run", full-employment equilibrium as its reference point. This was dispensed with in *GT* and the concept of equilibrium had to change as a consequence. These changes were only the beginning of the radical shift in method that the *GT* presents.

Methodology
Long-run, full-employment equilibrium occupied a central role in the thinking of those economists Keynes called "classical" (by which he meant all those who believed that the economy would adjust automatically to full employment). The prevailing long-run analysis was static and therefore abstracted from historical time. Deviations from long-run equilibrium or the processes that might bring the system back to equilibrium were rarely entertained, let alone analysed (Wicksell, and Keynes in *TM*, are notable exceptions). It was simply assumed that the economy would return to equilibrium if disturbed. (Keynes's objection to this assumption is the subject of a very important article in 1934: "Poverty in plenty: is the economic system self-adjusting?", Keynes 1934 [1973]: 485–92.)

In the *GT*, Keynes changed all that. The long run in the *GT* emerges organically out of the processes that unfold in a succession of (Marshallian) "short periods". Trend and cycle are not seen as separate but as part of the same process. Features which his contemporaries had assumed to hold in the long run, most importantly, full employment and the validity of the quantity theory, were no longer to be treated as articles of faith but as proper subjects for analysis, and they turned out to hold only in circumstances so special as to be nearly irrelevant.

Instead of a preconceived long run and transitory disturbances, Keynes adopted Marshall's three "periods" (not "runs" – the short run refers to historical time and the long run is timeless): the market period (the "day"), when output is fixed (*GT*, Keynes 1936 [1973]: ch. 5); the short period, when output could vary but capital is given (ibid.: most of the book); and the long period, when even capital is variable (ibid.: mainly chs 16 and 17). These are analytical constructs, allowing the theorist to separate factors which adjust quickly from those that move more slowly. Although artificial, the relevance of the separate periods is assured by their strong correspondence with processes in actual time. Keynes made one modification to Marshall's short period: net new investment was a contribution to aggregate demand, but the resulting change in the capital stock was not allowed to affect the cost of producing output (aggregate supply).

Uncertainty   Immediately in *GT*'s chapter 3, (Keynes 1936 [1973]) we see how an uncertain future shapes the determination of output and employment, the central concerns of the book. Output is decided by producers whose capital equipment is given: the decision takes place in the short period. Output takes time to produce, so the market for it lies in the future, which by definition is uncertain. Producers must form expectations of what the market will be like and decide their output and employment accordingly. For the first time we have an explicit link to Keynes's earliest scholarly work, the *Treatise on Probability*; here is an exploration in economics of rational decision-making in the face of uncertainty. Also, for the first time in economics, we have a method which is consistent with the world economic actors actually live in.

The expectations of producers are central, but Keynes carefully reflects also on what expectations are important for other macroeconomic groups: households (*GT*, Keynes 1936 [1973]: chs 8 and 9), the investors in real capital (ibid.: ch. 11) and the financial speculators (ibid.: ch. 12). Economic activities with the shortest time horizons are in general the least uncertain; for instance, daily consumption is quite predictable, while investment decisions are made in the light of longer-term, and therefore more uncertain, expectations. This is the opposite of the theory of *TM* and of neoclassical theory today, where unexpected events (for example, windfalls) can occur in the short term, but long-run equilibrium is certain and known. (Financial speculation is an exception, in having a short time horizon but being very uncertain.)

The path-dependent system that Keynes created in the *GT* is an example of an open system, in this case open to future developments, which cannot be known.

Equilibrium   With this new method comes a redefinition of equilibrium. It is not an end-point or a configuration existing out of time, but a configuration contingent on the analytical constraints imposed (for example, the short period) or the policy stance assumed (monetary policy is mentioned explicitly); these are held constant for the purpose of the analysis. Equilibrium can pertain to a part of the system or to the whole: for example, "the equilibrium level of employment [is] the level at which there is no inducement to employers as a whole either to expand or to contract employment" (*GT*, Keynes [1936] 1973: 27), and chapter 18 outlines the equilibrium of the system as a whole (ibid.: 249). There is no suggestion of market clearing; this is important, for unemployment had continued at a high level for 15 years when the *GT* was published. Keynes characterized persistent unemployment as unemployment equilibrium and in the *GT* provided a theory which could explain how such an equilibrium (as he defined it) could occur.

For large parts of the analysis Keynes takes expectations as given. This allows him to get definite results. However, he relaxes this assumption, to show where greater realism will lead. First he varies short-term expectations, then also long-term expectations. The latter is "Keynes's model of shifting equilibrium [which describes] an actual path of an economy over time chasing an ever changing [analytical] equilibrium – it need never catch it" (Kregel 1976: 217).

The fallacy of composition   Finally we must mention the appropriate level of analysis when analysing the economy as a whole.

> Though an individual whose transactions are small in relation to the market can safely neglect the fact that demand is not a one-sided transaction, it makes nonsense to neglect it when we come to aggregate demand. This is the vital difference between the theory of the economic behaviour of the aggregate and the theory of the behaviour of the individual unit . . . (*GT*, Keynes 1936 [1973]: 85)

Keynes indicated in the above passage that if one were to argue from individual behaviour to developments in the economy as a whole, the wrong answer is likely to be obtained. This occurs because the economy as a whole is not the same as the sum of its parts, and to argue from the part to the whole in such a circumstance is to commit the fallacy of composition. The most famous example of the conflict between the individual and aggregate levels in the *GT* concerns saving behaviour. Collectively, aggregate saving must equal aggregate investment, and investment is the variable determined by factors outside the theoretical system, so saving must conform to investment. Neither individually nor collectively do savers know this, but if there is a rise in the desire to save while investment stays the same, the shift away from consumption will decrease sales and firms will cut back output. Aggregate income will fall and savers will not be able to realize their original saving plans. Simply to aggregate the plans is to ignore the feedback which is forthcoming from other actors in the economy. This little story is known as the paradox of thrift, but it is not really a paradox, rather an example of applying the wrong level of analysis.

Another example concerns the labour "market". Keynes's contemporaries reasoned that if the supply of labour exceeded demand (that is, there is unemployment), the price of labour – the wage – must be "too high", above its equilibrium level. Therefore to reduce unemployment, reduce wages. This is an example of the method practised by Marshall of looking at one market at a time: partial equilibrium analysis. Significantly, he did not apply this method to the labour market. Marshall understood that labour is only hired by producers if they expect to be able to sell the output the labour will produce. He referred to the derived demand for labour. Keynes generalized this principle to the macroeconomic level. When the demand for labour is correctly perceived as dependent on producers' expectations of the future market for output, the policy conclusion is to stimulate demand, not to cut wages.

Macroeconomic theory

The principle of effective demand   Keynes's contemporaries were used to thinking that at the aggregate level demand could not be distinguished from supply: whatever was produced would generate an equal demand to absorb that output ("You will not find [aggregate demand] mentioned even once in the whole works of Marshall, Edgeworth and Professor Pigou"; *GT*, Keynes 1936 [1973]: 32). Keynes saw empirically that aggregate supply did not create its own demand and provided the theoretical justification for treating supply and demand as independent of each other. He also saw that in real time producers must form expectations about the future level of demand to combine with their (known) cost structure to determine the profit-maximizing level of output and thus employment. If the result for the economy as a whole was less than full employment, there was nothing labour could do about it. This "Principle of Effective Demand", as Keynes called it, was perhaps the most important contribution of the *GT*: it asserted the independence of demand from supply at the aggregate level, showed the importance of producers' expectations and established the systemic dependence of employment on producers' output decisions: the labour market should not be analysed in isolation.

If expectations are not fulfilled, profits are larger or smaller than expected, and firms may alter their expectations, and their output decisions, but only in future (*GT*, Keynes 1936 [1973]: ch 5). Current employment is determined by those earlier expectations, whether or not they are correct (ibid.: ch 3). If expectations are fulfilled, the output and employment decisions are likely to be repeated unchanged. This result is called an equilibrium, whether full employment or not.

Aggregate demand If the level of activity is stable, it is assumed that firms' expectations of demand will converge to the actual level of aggregate demand expressed in expenditure. Keynes continued the convention of dividing aggregate demand into consumption and investment, but in the *GT* he made much more of that distinction than earlier theory had done. Consumption, he argued, was mainly responsive to changes in income and thus could not drive changes in income by itself. Consumption moved in the same direction as income but not to the full amount, because some income is saved: the marginal propensity to consume (mpc) is hypothesized to be less than one. This assumption gave Keynes powerful ammunition, for it put a stop to the automatic expansion of economic activity independently of (and most likely before) full employment, contrary to the classical idea of self-adjustment to full-employment equilibrium.

Investment, the purchase of real productive capital, was, by contrast, not determined by current income, for two reasons: the purpose of investment is to expand the capacity to meet expected future, not current, demand; and (in Keynes's time) much investment was initially financed by bank loans. The first point is the source of Keynes's stress on long-term expectations as the main driving force of investment: expectations of future profits must be made for the entire life of the equipment. The second point overturns the classical causality between saving and investment. Bank loans are independent of current or prior saving; therefore investment can take place without prior saving (Chick 1983: ch. 9). Investment raises income and desired saving, but realized saving includes new bank deposits created when investment expenditure is made. ("The investment market can be congested through shortage of cash. It can never be congested through shortage of saving"; Keynes 1937b [1973]: 222). (Any change in expenditure not dependent on current income will be amplified according to the multiplier.)

The rate of interest Along with long-term expectations, the other major factor influencing investment was the rate of interest. This represented the cost of obtaining funds to carry out the projects. Here, again, Keynes departed from conventional wisdom, which had treated interest and returns on real capital as synonymous. The rate of interest in *GT* is a purely monetary phenomenon, mainly determined by the degree of preference for liquid over illiquid financial assets. This preference will depend not only on the need for cash for routine transactions with a cushion for the unexpected but will also, sometimes largely, be determined by the expectations of future capital gains and losses on the part of speculators (*GT*, Keynes 1936 [1973]: ch. 12), the bulls and bears introduced in *TM*. The capital value of securities is inversely related to the rate of interest. Keynes framed liquidity preference in terms of expected interest rates and showed that an excessive preference for liquidity could keep rates too high to stimulate enough investment to provide full employment. The root cause of unemployment was not high wages but high rates of interest.

Liquidity preference and unemployment equilibrium gave Keynes the means finally to escape the quantity theory. He showed (*GT*, Keynes 1936 [1973]: ch. 21) that only at full employment and with zero preference for liquidity would the quantity theory hold.

Both the speculators and those investing in real capital were subject to sudden changes in their expectations of an uncertain future, periods of optimism and pessimism which they often shared. This made investment potentially volatile. However, investment was also the economy's engine of growth. A rise in investment would cause consumption to rise, in accordance with the mpc, as the new income circulated around the economy. If the process were to work its way out in full, the extent to which the change in income exceeded the rise in investment would be given by the "multiplier", which depended on the mpc. With Keynes's new methodological perspective, such a boom was no longer seen as a deviation from long-run equilibrium, and thus deplored, but something to be welcomed and, if possible, prolonged. Far from the classical economist's instinct to raise interest rates to choke off a boom, Keynes would lower interest rates to facilitate it as long as unemployment prevailed. Indeed, he favoured a general policy of low interest rates, as these would stimulate investment and, by making loans easier to pay off, prevent debt from accumulating. This is his characteristic policy conclusion (Tily 2009), far more than the policy usually associated with his name: fiscal stimulus. The latter policy might be the only thing to take an economy out of a slump, but it was not a policy for all seasons.

The long run   The bulk of *GT* is occupied with short-period analysis, but the long-run effects of capital accumulation do claim Keynes's attention, mainly in chapters 16 and 17. Although he looked forward to the time when capital was no longer scarce, he saw that the existence of money as an alternative store of value presented a problem: that as capital accumulates, its diminishing scarcity value reduces the marginal efficiency of capital (mec, or expected return) – even to zero if scarcity ceases altogether. But the liquidity premium commanded by money, which is cheap to store and does not require any effort to generate the return that liquidity affords, will prevent the rate of interest from falling to zero. If the mec falls to zero but the desire to save is still positive at full employment, the only way to reduce saving to zero, to match investment, is for income (and employment) to fall. A zero rate of new investment and saving at just full employment would be a fluke: the classical theorem that full employment characterizes the long run is refuted.

The General Theory: a revolution?

The *GT* constitutes a sea-change in macroeconomic analysis. Keynes demonstrated that unemployment equilibrium was a logical outcome of a macroeconomic system in which decisions are taken by many firms acting independently, all facing uncertain markets.

A revolution in economic method was needed to come to that conclusion, as the prevailing method ruled out any but temporary and self-correcting unemployment. In developing a path-dependent, open-system analysis, Keynes created a theory which reflected reality better than the theories of his predecessors (and most of his successors). There were many possible equilibria, depending on the constraints imposed and, more importantly, policies assumed, and there was no presumption that an actual economy would ever settle into any equilibrium, let alone one in which full employment prevailed.

Monetary factors were allowed their full economic impact, affecting all areas of "real" economic life instead of being confined to determining prices. The "classical dichotomy" between monetary and real factors was abolished and the quantity theory shown to characterize only a very special case.

The *GT* amounted to a revolution in both economic theory and method. It was an intellectually stunning achievement – so stunning that its path-breaking contributions have either not yet been understood by the majority of economists or have proved unpalatable and been transformed into something else. Whatever the cause, although mainstream textbooks in macroeconomics may claim that their short-run analysis is

"Keynesian" or "New Keynesian", it is easily demonstrated that the theory presented is confined within a neoclassical analytical and methodological framework quite similar to that which Keynes thought he had overturned.

Today, Keynes's macroeconomic thinking is mainly represented by the national income accounts, which are in use worldwide.

National Income Accounting

With war again looming, the need to assess available resources and the tax base became urgent. The *GT* provided the framework. In his pamphlet, *How to Pay for the War* (Keynes 1940 [1972]: 367–439), Keynes regretted the poor standard of the official statistics on national income and output. During the war, the Treasury set up a unit for the development of national accounts, headed by James Meade and Richard Stone. Keynes used their calculations to estimate how much purchasing power could be left for private consumption without causing excess demand (and inflation) and thus the required level of taxation and deferment of purchasing power by forced saving. These measures helped to secure public borrowing at low cost and reduce inflationary pressure, in sharp contrast to the situation during the 1914–18 war.

The Dutch economist Jan Tinbergen used national accounting data from the interwar period in a pioneering income–expenditure model of the Dutch economy (Tinbergen 1939) using econometric methods. Keynes was sceptical of using econometric methods to illuminate the present situation, let alone to predict the future, on the grounds that the stability of economic relationships which these methods presuppose is not present. To him a model should rather be part of a way of thinking, an aid to the organization of perceptions and ideas. However, economists found the attractions of econometric techniques more compelling than Keynes's argument.

There was a flurry of comments and objections to the *GT* shortly after its publication, but poor health and later preparations for war and the war itself meant that Keynes would never write another book of major importance to economic analysis. However, he responded to some of the main critiques of *GT* by writing a number of papers where he elaborated on, among other issues, methodology (see especially, Keynes 1938 [1973]), the rate of interest and theory of finance Keynes 1937a, 1937b [1973].

Bretton Woods

When war broke out, Keynes once again was asked to return to the Treasury to work on the annual national budget. He began to turn his mind to post-war arrangements. In 1941 Keynes prepared the first of many drafts of a plan for the post-war international financial system. The "Keynes plan" for an international clearing union became the official British position at the Bretton Woods Conference in 1944. All international payments were to be settled through a Clearing Union in an artificial book-entry currency, which Keynes called bancor. Exchange rates between national currencies and bancor would be fixed but from time to time adjusted to correct payments imbalances. According to the plan, surplus as well as deficit countries were required to take steps to eliminate their foreign imbalances at a feasible pace. The Clearing Union could create loans in bancor to ease adjustment, but penalties were payable on cumulative bancor positions, either debit or credit, above a certain amount. These adjustment mechanisms were an application of liquidity preference theory to international money: their purpose was to prevent the deflationary influence on economic activity of the desire to accumulate foreign reserves. From a world perspective this was sound, but the USA was in a strong creditor position at the end of the war and did not accept enforced adjustment. The Clearing Union was replaced with the USA's proposed International Monetary Fund, which had more limited credit-creating powers and did not impose adjustment requirements on creditor countries. A separate institution, the World Bank, was founded to deal first with reconstruction and then with lending for development.

Keynes was more successful when it came to restrictions on international financial transactions. His arguments were that credit and finance for domestic activities should be left to national institutions, regulated by each country's central bank. Therefore, member countries were left free to restrict purely financial cross-border transactions. In sum, Keynes was concerned that participating countries should benefit as much as possible from foreign trade, without putting the ability to pursue national full employment monetary and fiscal policies at risk.

The Social Philosophy towards which Keynes might Lead

The development of Keynes's macroeconomic analysis, from the very first contribution in *ICF*, via *TMR* and *TM* to the *GT*, eventually provided the insight needed to realize his vision: to "combine economic efficiency, social justice, and individual liberty" ("Liberalism and labour", Keynes 1926 [1972]: 311). After the war, part of his social philosophy became for a couple of decades accepted in mainstream thinking in Western economics and politics with regard to the operation of the international monetary system and national commitments to full employment.

At the end of his life his view was still that individuals should have the possibility, but also the responsibility, to pursue their aspiration of a good life (*My Early Beliefs*, Keynes 1949 [1972]). This presupposed organization by the state and semi-official institutions of a reasonably stable macroeconomic and political environment for the good of the system as a whole. One might call it a philosophy of holistic individualism.

VICTORIA CHICK AND JESPER JESPERSEN

See also:
Cambridge School of economics (II); Keynesianism (II); Post-Keynesianism (II).

References and further reading
Chick, V. (1983), *Macroeconomics after Keynes: A Reconsideration of the General Theory*, Cambridge, MA: MIT Press.
Fitzgibbons, A. (1988), *Keynes's Vision: A New Political Economy*, Oxford: Clarendon Press.
Jespersen, J. (2009), *Macroeconomic Methodology: A Post-Keynesian Perspective*, Cheltenham, UK and Northampton, MA, USA: Edward Elgar.
Kahn, R. (1931), 'The relation of home investment to unemployment', *Economic Journal*, **41** (June), 173–96.
Kent, R.J. (2008), 'A 1929 application of multiplier theory in Keynes', *History of Political Economy*, **39** (Fall), 551–60.
Keynes, J.M. (1911), 'Review of *The Purchasing Power of Money* by I. Fisher', in E. Johnson and D. Moggridge (eds) (1983), *The Collected Writings of John Maynard Keynes*, vol. XII, London: Macmillan and Cambridge University Press, pp. 375–84.

Keynes, J.M. (1913), *Indian Currency and Finance*, in E. Johnson and D. Moggridge (eds) (1971), *The Collected Writings of John Maynard Keynes*, vol. I, London: Macmillan and Cambridge University Press.
Keynes, J.M. (1919), *Economic Consequences of the Peace*, in E. Johnson and D. Moggridge (eds) (1971), *The Collected Writings of John Maynard Keynes*, vol. II, London: Macmillan and Cambridge University Press.
Keynes, J.M. (1921), *A Treatise on Probability*, in E. Johnson and D. Moggridge (eds) (1971), *The Collected Writings of John Maynard Keynes*, vol. VIII, London: Macmillan and Cambridge University Press.
Keynes, J.M. (1922), *A Revision of the Treaty*, in E. Johnson and D. Moggridge (eds) (1971), *The Collected Writings of John Maynard Keynes*, vol. III, London: Macmillan and Cambridge University Press.
Keynes, J.M. (1923), *A Tract on Monetary Reform*, in E. Johnson and D. Moggridge (eds) (1971), *The Collected Writings of John Maynard Keynes*, vol. IV, London: Macmillan and Cambridge University Press.
Keynes, J.M. (1925), *The Economic Consequences of Mr Churchill*, in E. Johnson and D. Moggridge (eds) (1972), *The Collected Writings of John Maynard Keynes*, vol. IX, London: Macmillan and Cambridge University Press, pp. 207–30.
Keynes, J.M. (1926), 'Liberalism and labour', in E. Johnson and D. Moggridge (eds) (1972), *The Collected Writings of John Maynard Keynes*, vol. IX, London: Macmillan and Cambridge University Press, pp. 307–11.
Keynes, J.M. (1929), *Can Lloyd George Do It?*, in E. Johnson and D. Moggridge (eds) (1972), *The Collected Writings of John Maynard Keynes*, vol. IX, London: Macmillan and Cambridge University Press, pp. 86–125.
Keynes, J.M. (1930), *A Treatise on Money*, in E. Johnson and D. Moggridge (eds) (1971), *The Collected Writings of John Maynard Keynes*, vols V and VI, London: Macmillan and Cambridge University Press.
Keynes, J.M. (1931a), 'The pure theory of money: a reply to Hayek', in E. Johnson and D. Moggridge (eds) (1972), *The Collected Writings of John Maynard Keynes*, vol. XIII, London: Macmillan and Cambridge University Press, pp. 243–56.
Keynes, J.M. (1931b), *Essays in Persuasion*, in E. Johnson and D. Moggridge (eds) (1972), *The Collected Writings of John Maynard Keynes*, vol. IX, London: Macmillan and Cambridge University Press.
Keynes, J.M. (1933a), 'The monetary theory of production', in E. Johnson and D. Moggridge (eds) (1973), *The Collected Writings of John Maynard Keynes*, vol. XIII, London: Macmillan and Cambridge University Press, pp. 408–11.
Keynes, J.M. (1933b), *Essays in Biography*, in E. Johnson and D. Moggridge (eds) (1972), *The Collected Writings of John Maynard Keynes*, vol. X, London: Macmillan and Cambridge University Press.
Keynes, J.M. (1934), 'Poverty in plenty: is the economic system self-adjusting?', in E. Johnson and D. Moggridge (eds) (1973), *The Collected Writings of John Maynard Keynes*, vol. XIII, London: Macmillan and Cambridge University Press, pp. 485–92.
Keynes, J.M. (1936), *The General Theory of Employment, Interest and Money*, in E. Johnson and D. Moggridge (eds) (1973), *The Collected Writings of John Maynard Keynes*, vol. VII, London: Macmillan and Cambridge University Press.
Keynes, J.M. (1937a), 'Alternative theories of the rate of interest', in E. Johnson and D. Moggridge (eds) (1973), *The Collected Writings of John Maynard Keynes*, vol. XIV, London: Macmillan and Cambridge University Press, pp. 201–15.
Keynes, J.M. (1937b), 'The "ex ante" theory of the rate of interest', in E. Johnson and D. Moggridge (eds) (1973), *The Collected Writings of John Maynard Keynes*, vol. XIV, London: Macmillan and Cambridge University Press, pp. 215–23.
Keynes, J.M. (1938), Correspondence with Roy Harrod, commenting on Harrod's presidential address to the Royal Economic Society, in E. Johnson and D. Moggridge (eds) (1973), *The Collected Writings of John Maynard Keynes*, vol. XIV, London: Macmillan and Cambridge University Press, pp. 296–301.
Keynes, J.M. (1940), *How to Pay for the War*, in E. Johnson and D. Moggridge (eds) (1972), *The Collected Writings of John Maynard Keynes*, vol. IX, London: Macmillan and Cambridge University Press, pp. 367–439.
Keynes, J.M. (1949), *My Early Beliefs*, in E. Johnson and D. Moggridge (eds) (1972), *The Collected Writings of John Maynard Keynes*, vol. X, London: Macmillan and Cambridge University Press, pp. 433–51.
Keynes, J.N. (1891), *The Scope and Method of Political Economy*, London: Macmillan.
Kregel, J. (1976), 'Economic methodology in the face of uncertainty: the modelling methods of Keynes and the post-Keynesians', *Economic Journal*, **86** (June), 209–25.
Moggridge, D.E. (1992), *Maynard Keynes: An Economist's Biography*, London: Routledge.
Skidelsky, R. (1983), *John Maynard Keynes*, vol. 1: *Hopes Betrayed, 1883–1920*, London: Macmillan.
Skidelsky, R. (1992), *John Maynard Keynes*, vol. 2: *The Economist as Saviour, 1920–37*, London: Macmillan.
Skidelsky, R. (1995), 'Keynes and the quantity theory of money', in M. Blaug (ed.), *The Quantity Theory of Money from Keynes to Locke and Friedman*, Cheltenham, UK and Northampton, MA, USA: Edward Elgar.
Skidelsky, R. (2001), *John Maynard Keynes*, vol. 3: *Fighting for Britain, 1937–46*, London: Macmillan.
Tily, G. (2009), *The General Theory, the Rate of Interest and 'Keynesian' Economics: Keynes Betrayed*, London: Macmillan.
Tinbergen, J. (1939), *Statistical Testing of Business Cycle Theories*, 2 vols, Geneva: League of Nations.

Joseph Alois Schumpeter (1883–1950)

Life

Joseph Alois Schumpeter (hereafter JAS) was born on 8 February 1883 in the little town of Triesch in Moravia (today Czech Republic) which at that time was part of the Austrian Habsburg Empire. The family of his father had an entrepreneurial background in textile manufacturing and trade. After the early death of her husband, JAS's mother Johanna moved to Graz, where she married the retired army general Sigmund von Kéler, whose social status was a major advantage for her gifted son: it opened the doors of the Theresianum, Austria's elite grammar school for the offspring of the nobility, including the imperial family. JAS made good use of the Theresianum's rich and demanding curriculum and the partly excellent teaching staff. He graduated not only with fluency in six languages, but with a remarkable degree of intellectual maturity.

This was certainly a precondition for his subsequent successful study of economics at the University of Vienna. For students with a certain breadth and depth of education, this university was an excellent place for the study of economics, even though an official curriculum in economics did not exist at that time; economics was a part of the law curriculum. The professorial staff of the law faculty included the founding fathers of Austrian economics – Carl Menger, Friedrich von Wieser and Eugen von Böhm-Bawerk. The members of this triad of Austrian economics shared some basic tenets, but disagreed on substantial issues, such as the theory of capital and interest. Beyond that, the senior teaching staff was diverse, including not only protagonists of the Austrian School with its emphasis on pure theory, but also scholars such as Eugen von Philippovich (advocating a synthesis of theory and history) and Karl Inama von Sternegg, a statistician with historical interests. JAS's first published essays were written under the supervision of Inama and Sternegg, but soon he turned to theory, benefiting in particular from Wieser and Böhm-Bawerk. In addition to the works of his Viennese teachers, he studied Walras's (1874 [1988]) *Pure Economics* and absorbed much of what is on offer outside economics in the vibrant intellectual climate of post-1900 Vienna with its stark contrasts between the preservation of the delicate equilibrium of an old order and multi-level revolutionary challenges and provocations. These challenges included the theories of Karl Marx, the target of an important critical treatise by Böhm-Bawerk and the intellectual hero of JAS's socialist classmates in Böhm-Bawerk's famous seminar, such as Otto Bauer, Rudolf Hilferding and Emil Lederer. From early on, Marx's analysis of capitalism's economic dynamism became a major source of inspiration for him.

So, JAS found himself in the middle of several fundamental controversies regarding the relations between theory, empirics, history, and politics. From early on, he felt that he had a mission with regard to those controversies. After graduation in 1906, he spent some months in Berlin (where he attended Schmoller's seminar) and in England, where he met Marshall and Edgeworth and married Gladys Ricarde Seaver. The young couple moved to Cairo, where JAS earned his living as a lawyer and a financial counsellor for an Egyptian princess. He wrote a programmatic and ambitious book (*Das Wesen und der Hauptinhalt der theoretischen Nationalökonomie – The Nature and Scope of Theoretical Economics*, 1908). There he explained how to make sense of the hits and misses of contemporary economics, and what had to be done for its future advances. This work of the 25-year old earned him the habilitation at Vienna University and a position as an extraordinary professor at the University of Czernowitz, the capital of the province of Bukowina in the South-East of the Habsburg Empire (today Western Ukraine). In Czernowitz he wrote *Theorie der wirtschaftlichen Entwicklung* (1912). A substantially revised second edition became available in an English translation (1934, *Theory of Economic Development*) and became the seminal work for Schumpeterian economics. In 1911, he was appointed to a chair at the University of Graz, which he held until 1921.

During the Graz period he published important works on the history and the method of economics (1914, 1915), and the fiscal sociology of the tax state (1918 [1952]). However, the focus of his attention was shifting to the drama unravelling in the theatre of politics. As a student at Theresianum he had imbibed the spirit of non-partisan civil service, a virtue which is desperately needed to preserve the delicate balances of the complex multilingual order of the Danube monarchy. As the deadly threats posed by growing nationalism are cumulating in World War I, he felt obliged to support that order. JAS was (and remained throughout his live) convinced that no attractive alternative to the values defining that order was available. He wrote several memoranda dealing with political agenda related to inter-ethnic equilibrium in the Habsburg monarchy and pragmatic steps towards peace, with conservative circles as addressees who might consider him for a position in the war cabinet. While those hopes were frustrated, he was appointed finance minister in the first government of the Republic of Austria in 1919, established by a coalition between Socialists and Christian-Democrats. His essentially sound proposal of a capital levy in order to deal with the financial consequences of the transition from the war economy was not put into practice. He left office after only seven months on the grounds of fundamental disagreements regarding Austria's future: against all contemporary currents, JAS favoured an economic federation of the states of the former Habsburg Empire.

Still on leave from Graz, he was engaged in converting the time-honoured Biedermann-Bank into a joint stock company and eventually became its president. His engagement in private business was accompanied by only transitory successes; it culminated in huge private debts amounting to the equivalent of 2 million 2014 euros in 1925 (Peneder and Resch 2015: 19). Apart from the difficult business environment in the aftermath of a major war, hyperinflation, and the downturn of the stock exchange in 1924, three almost simultaneous specific developments contributed to his financial disaster: first, failed private speculations (notably against the French franc) which had been leveraged by money borrowed from his Biedermann-Bank; second, the bankruptcy of a venture capitalist industrial group of industry start-ups, where JAS's former Theresianum colleague Rudolf-Maria Braun-Stammfest was his partner (JAS again was involved with his private money); third, the heterogeneous shareholder structure and concomitant inconsistent business strategies of the Biedermann-Bank, which went bankrupt in 1926, while JAS had already resigned as president in 1924. He was in desperate need of a job.

Dealing with his heavy debts, he gave paid lectures to non-academic audiences and wrote articles for the Austrian and German weekly *Der Volkswirt* (a kind of German-language *The Economist*) edited by his friend Gustav Stolper (see Schumpeter 1985, 1993). Most fortunately, on the initiative of Arthur Spiethoff he managed to get a chair at Bonn University. From autumn 1926 until 1932, JAS taught in Bonn, where his students included August Lösch, Erich Schneider, Hans Singer, Wolfgang Stolper, and

Cläre Tisch. Publications of that period included a paper on the instability of capitalism (1928). Moreover, he was concerned with the revision and English translation of *Theory of Economic Development* and a manuscript on monetary theory, which were not published in his lifetime (Schumpeter 1970). His time in Bonn was overshadowed by the loss of his beloved second wife Annie who died in childbirth.

Starting in 1927, Frank Taussig (whom JAS had met during his 1913–14 stay in the US as a visiting professor at Columbia) initiated recurrent visits for him to Harvard University, and in 1932 JAS accepted an offer for a permanent position at this institution. However, the 1930s are not an altogether happy decade for JAS: on the positive side was his success in promoting the foundation of the Econometric Society. As a by-product he published an essay on the role of econometrics (1933). He is also successful in shaping Harvard's recruitment policy by promoting appointments such as the one of Wassily Leontief. Not least due to those efforts, Harvard was on the way to become one of the leading research universities, attracting visiting economists and graduate students from all over the world. The group of JAS's excellent Harvard students is fascinating not least in its diversity, including Paul Samuelson and James Tobin, Hyman Minsky and Nicolas Georgescu-Roegen, Paul Sweezy, Richard Goodwin, but also the Jesuit Father Bernard Dempsey, with whom he may have had discussions on medieval scholasticism (which he found interesting from early on) and on catholic corporatism, which he began to see as a system suitable to balance over-centralizing forces inherent in modern capitalist development. Catholic corporatism also stresses the secular convergence of interest between industrial capitalists and workers, a theme which is also to be found in JAS's own writings. In 1937, he married his third wife Elizabeth Boody Firuski, an economist who specialized in Japanese studies. Her support would become essential for JAS's success in producing three major works in his Harvard period, including his unfinished *History of Economic Analysis*, which was posthumously published by her (1954a). In 1939, he published another magnum opus (*Business Cycles*), followed by his bestselling *Capitalism, Socialism, and Democracy* (1942).

Yet prospects were darkened by political developments at both national and international levels, in particular by tendencies that were gaining ground inside and outside the economic discipline in the wake of the economic crisis. Of course, JAS worried about the development in Germany, but he also disliked Roosevelt's New Deal. Above all, he regretted the success of John Maynard Keynes, whose *General Theory* dealt with phenomena of the business cycle while abstracting from the kind of pervasive change which is the most salient aspect of capitalist development, including its discontinuous nature. Despite this major deficiency, the *General Theory* carried the day in two respects: as a guide to the economic policy of demand management, and as a starting point for the development of macroeconomic modelling (cf. Keynes 1936; Schumpeter 1952b: 260–91), attracting also the attention of some of JAS's best Harvard students. By contrast, his own work on business cycles was received with little enthusiasm in the discipline. In particular, neither his own efforts to express his subtle and encompassing reasoning on the complexities of capitalist development by means of theoretical concepts of formalized economics, and to support it by systematized empirical material, nor his cautious encouragement of quantitative elaboration by younger economists were really successful (see, for example, Andersen 2011: chs 9–12).

Apart from his two major publication projects (1942, 1954a), Schumpeter's work in the 1940s was being reflected by a number of important essays, dealing *inter alia* with the future of capitalism in the post-war world (1950) and the role of economic history as an integral part of socio-economic research (1949b). The pieces collected in the posthumously published volume *Ten Great Economists* (1952a) were to a great part written in the 1940s. He was elected President of the Econometric Society in 1942 and of the American Economic Association in 1948. As president-elect of the newly founded International Economic Association he planned to attend its annual meeting in Paris in 1950, which would bring him to Europe for the first time since the war. With important unfinished works on his agenda, he died on 8 January 1950 in Taconic, Connecticut.

Works

Das Wesen und der Hauptinhalt der theoretischen Nationalökonomie (1908)

This work combines a grandiose programmatic architecture including foundational methodological considerations with a service part: it makes accessible what JAS calls the Magna Carta of economics (that is, the multi-equational Walrasian system of general market equilibrium) to a German-language audience in a non-technical way. The foundational considerations include perceptive passages implying an encompassing vision of the social sciences, emphasizing in particular the division of labour between empirical-historical and theoretical research. However, they also include passages written in a provocative tone, in which he attempts to express as crisply as possible some principles pertinent to the scientific logic of pure, exact economics: he resolutely anticipates the increasing role of mathematics in economics (cf. also Schumpeter 1906) as well as Friedman's instrumentalist methodology (cf. Schumpeter 1908: 93–4), emphatically denying the relevance of questions as to whether some model premises adequately capture "the nature" of the economic process. He proclaims "a kind of Monroe doctrine" (ibid.: 536), referring to the epistemological independence of pure economics from disciplines such as psychology, biology, philosophy or other kinds of social theory. Economics is a body of knowledge that increasingly adopts methods and procedures typical for modern natural science and on that basis increases its explanatory and predictive power. The programmatic outlook of the book emphasizes dynamic theory as the Promised Land for future research.

Basic tenets and core features of JAS's scientific style already find expression in this book, not least the air of "cool, scientific detachment" (Haberler 1951: 338) with which he is stressing the relative autonomy of economic science vis-à-vis economic policy, and with which he is judging the relative merits of the various kinds of scholarly endeavours while consistently resisting any adherence to a particular school. "I have come to the conviction that almost every orientation (*Richtung*) and each individual writer are right in their propositions: as they are meant, from the standpoint of the purposes for which they are intended" (Schumpeter 1908: v–vi). This quotation could be taken as a prelude to boring eclecticism which is somehow attempting to give everybody his due. However, throughout his career, JAS offered something quite different: Apart from the integrative architecture across the various levels and "purposes" which was already indicated in that statement, he developed bold new combinations, such as that between Walrasian equilibrium analysis and a dynamic perspective on capitalist development *à la* Marx. Sometimes such combinations come closer to a chemical synthesis of heterogeneous theoretical elements which are amalgamated without too much ado: an example in case is the introduction of Austrian elements (cf. Streissler 1983) in the Walrasian system. All this is complemented by provocation as a didactic device for stressing the logic of some specific argument related to a specific theoretical context.

Theorie der wirtschaftlichen Entwicklung (1912)

Here Schumpeter's grand overarching goal as a scientist is clearly brought to the fore: contributing to the explanation of the modern "social process" which "is really one indivisible whole" (Schumpeter 1934: 3) by developing an economic theory of economic change, which (in modified ways and complemented by other elements) may also be helpful for the understanding of social, cultural or political change. He attempts to approach that goal by means of a bold new combination, including (1) the representation of the circular flow according to Walrasian equilibrium analysis complemented by some Austrian elements, (2) Marxian emphasis on restless change and power asymmetries (including morally arbitrary re-distribution processes) as crucial features of capital(ism), and (3) a theorization of the entrepreneur as an agent of change who is upsetting the equilibrium of the circular flow, conceptualized in a way reminiscent of early twentieth-century literature emphasizing leadership, elite-mass distinctions, and notions of energetic action reminiscent of Henri Bergson's élan vital. Towards the end of the book, JAS discusses possible extensions of the sketched theory of change to spheres outside economics.

JAS is relating his analysis of dynamism to the core economic concepts of capital, interest, and to the financial system. He claims that his new theory is required (1) for an adequate "dynamic" rejection of Marxist exploitation theory and (2) for a proper understanding of capital and interest as essentially dynamic phenomena and as core elements of the capitalist process of change. His critical point of reference is Böhm-Bawerk's (1889) theory of capital and interest developed in a static setting, which also had been employed in criticizing Marx. In the subsequent debate, Böhm-Bawerk (1913a, 1913b) argued that JAS's new paradigm (including the provocative claim that the rate of interest must be zero under static conditions) was fatally flawed. In a rejoinder, JAS (Schumpeter 1913) attempted to minimize the differences: he emphasized his understanding of Böhm-Bawerk's tenets and their context, while arguing that Böhm-Bawerk's critique was almost entirely beside the point, as it missed the implications of the dynamic framework (Kurz and Sturn 2012: 161–9).

Epochen der Dogmen- und Methodengeschichte (1914; **English:** *Economic Doctrine and Method* 1954b) and *Vergangenheit und Zukunft* (1915)

Both books (which in a sense complement each other) clarify some of the reasons why JAS held the history of the subject important for the latter's current development. Unlike the posthumously published *History of Economic Analysis* (1954a), *Epochen* (1914) tends to highlight the character of classical economics as a distinct paradigm and generally pursues a broader approach to the history of *economic thought*. Notice, though, that the evolution of economic analysis as a narrower and specifically modern phenomenon within the history of knowledge systems is present from early on (Schumpeter 1908, 1915).

Economic Development: An Inquiry into Profits, Capital, Credit, Interest and the Business Cycle (1926, 1934)

The revised and shortened second edition of *Entwicklung* (1912) is the basis for the English translation. In addition to removing the final passages on change outside the sphere of economics, more emphasis is put on the *economic functions* of entrepreneurs and bankers, whereas the strongly personalized drama of creative destruction in *Entwicklung* (1912) is presented in a somewhat more neutral tone in *Economic Development*. Moreover, there are some terminological adjustments: "in deference to Professor (Ragnar) Frisch" (Schumpeter 1934: lxiii), the notions "static" and "dynamic" are substituted by the concepts "circular flow" and "development".

Business Cycles: A Theoretical, Historical, and Statistical Analysis of the Capitalist Process (1939)

This is the first of the three main works of the Harvard period. Seen together, they are a comprehensive effort to deal with processes of modernization and rationalization in the very long period, with the evolution of modern capitalism at its core. In *Business Cycles* he wishes to demonstrate that this multifaceted process can be studied by means of modern science: the more than 1000 pages of the book represent JAS's attempt to deal with the complex phenomenon of change by means of a combination of the tools of modern economics (theory plus historical and statistical empirics). This endeavour gets close to the attempt of squaring the circle, in particular when one keeps in mind the following aspects: (1) capitalist development is a unique historical process, even though we observe cyclical patterns; (2) change and innovation are endogenous phenomena; (3) JAS emphasizes heterogeneity of agents and goods, rendering the work with statistical aggregates problematic; and (4) JAS emphasizes discontinuity in keeping with Austrian views on the limited usefulness of continuous functions. Anyway, JAS reconstructs the wave-like secular development of modern capitalism since its beginnings on the basis of the entrepreneurial model of economic change. This account includes the famous model which superimposes long Kondratieff waves on medium Juglar and short Kitchin waves and the story of railroadization with its pervasive effects on the economy as "our standard example by which to illustrate the working of our model" (Schumpeter 1939: 304).

Capitalism, Socialism, and Democracy (1942)

As indicated by the title, this work provides an encompassing panorama of modern social development. It resumes ideas pursued from early on, notably the integration of explanatory approaches to political, cultural and economic development within a comprehensive theory of the modern social process (cf. Schumpeter 1934: 3), conceived of as a process of ubiquitous rationalization in the sense of Max Weber. Pertinent earlier work includes an essay on the sociology of imperialism written at the end of World War I (see Schumpeter 1955). Imperialism (and war as a mode of conflict solution) is insolubly linked to "atavistic structures and dispositions". In contrast to Lenin's or Rosa Luxemburg's theories, JAS's specific focus of analysis implies that imperialism is not a product of mature capitalism and rational modernity, whatever its economic consequences may be under particular historic circumstances. In *Capitalism* (1942), he argues that pre-modern values and dispositions are extremely important in the history of capitalist modernization. In this book, provocative and paradoxical claims according to which capitalism cannot survive as a consequence of its pervasive economic success, are employed to sharpen our understanding of characteristic features of modern capitalist development. (Remember that in earlier works provocations were primarily employed in order to sharpen our understanding of theoretical and meta-theoretical issues, including the character of economics which proceeds by using abstractive assumptions that strike the layman as odd.) Beyond the provocative thesis absorbing much of the attention of most commentators, the book includes in-depth considerations on: (1) the co-evolution of economic and non-economic rationalization – some aspects of rationalization turn out to be inimical to the core of the entrepreneurial mechanism of creative destruction as conceptualized in earlier works (Schumpeter 1912, 1934, 1939), which is called Schumpeter Mark I in the secondary literature; (2) concomitant tendencies of the routinization and managerialization of innovation processes in big firms (called Schumpeter Mark II), making innovation independent of the heroic entrepreneur and the birth and decay of firms; (3) the culmination of those developments in the form of socialist tendencies which according to JAS are promoted more by the "Carnegies and Rockefellers" than by socialist agitators; (4) the logic of democratic politics in its relation to capitalist and socialist regimes, and (5) a rich and inspired characterization of Marx, highlighting his intellectual debts to Marx as the theorist of capitalist change. After the mixed success of his business cycles, where he made a remarkable attempt to deal with the multifaceted and complex phenomenon of capitalistic development by means of theory-guided "statistical analysis", the discussion is not supported by the use of technical tools.

History of Economic Analysis (1954a)

This book is based on manuscripts assembled and systematized by the editorial effort of Elizabeth Boody. *History* is an intellectually much more ambitious work than it may appear at first sight. JAS reconstructs the history of economic analysis as an account of the modernization and rationalization process of economic knowledge. In that process, economic analysis (understood as a box of tools developed in close analogy to the natural sciences) assumes a prominent place, always keeping in mind that the subject matter of this specific field of analytical work is itself evolving in history, including the evolution of the cultural setting, of policy issues and of the agents of policy. In the context of JAS's other work, this project is to be seen in two perspectives: (1) History of modern knowledge represents a part of the overall rationalization within the modern "social process" which "is really one indivisible whole" (Schumpeter 1934: 3), and (2) the conditions that must be met in order to transform pre-analytic visions of economic thought into "economic analysis" come to the fore. This view of economic analysis as embedded in a broader context of knowledge and practices is especially relevant for innovation processes in economics: despite a well-understood emphasis on economics as a technical subject, progress in economics cannot be reduced to the perfection of tools and techniques. Nonetheless, some of the provocative and questionable judgements in *History* may to a certain extent be related to the emphasis of the toolbox-aspect. A case in point is Adam Smith, whose status is no doubt unjustly minimized. Yet it may be argued that Smith was not excelling in the provision of new tools, notwithstanding his overall importance in summarizing and combining pieces of knowledge and analysis.

There is no comprehensive edition of Schumpeter's works, either in English or in German. This may reflect the fact that there is no such thing as a Schumpeter school.

In fact, a number of economists with multifarious backgrounds have done editorial work, including Elizabeth Boody and Wolfgang Stolper. Schumpeter's students and Schumpeterian economists are a minority among them. Unpublished manuscripts and interesting biographical details have been made available in recent years by Ulrich Hedtke (see http://www.schumpeter.info).

Schumpeter's Uniqueness as an Economist and Historian of Economics

The history of economic thought was one of JAS's favourite subjects which is surprising for someone who claimed that economic research should be pursued as a quasi-natural science. So why was history important to JAS? First, he develops a specific approach to the historical dimension of the subject: the subject matter of the discipline is economic development, that is, the economic process evolving in historical time. Second, the history of the subject is posing intricate challenges, analogous to the dialectic of modernization at large: on the one hand, the modern development of economic analysis can be regarded as the relatively autonomous development of a scientific tool-box; on the other hand, various historically contingent phenomena are playing a role in the formation of economic theories, including ideologies (cf. Schumpeter 1949a). Their effects are ambivalent: they are sources of distortion and obstacles to progress, but they may frame certain issues and develop "pre-analytic visions" enhancing theoretical developments. In the following, pertinent ambivalences will be discussed, as JAS's way of dealing with them makes him unique in the history of economic thought.

Referring to Karl Marx, JAS (Schumpeter 1942: 3) wrote:

> Most of the creations of the intellect or fancy pass away for good after a time that varies between an after-dinner hour and a generation. Some, however, do not. They suffer eclipses, but they come back again, and they come back not as unrecognizable elements of cultural inheritance, but in their individual garb and with their personal scars which people may see and touch. These we may well call the great ones – it is no disadvantage of this definition that it links greatness to vitality. . . . But there is an additional advantage to defining greatness by revivals: it thereby becomes independent of our love or hate.

Given his own definition of greatness, JAS is certainly making the grade. Gaining momentum in the 1980s, a veritable wave of Schumpeter-revivals took place. Schumpeter's influence is now visible in a great variety of scholarly discourses, including Schumpeterian growth theories (Aghion et al. 2013), evolutionary economics (Andersen 2009, 2011; Witt 2002), entrepreneurship as a subject of management studies and economic history (McCraw 2007), or the broader perspectives of economic dynamism *à la* Edmund Phelps in his more recent works. Those almost simultaneous but distinct kinds of revivals indicate JAS's unique place in the history of economic thought. His role is specific in more than one respect, and it is a specific challenge for the history of modern economics: first, there is hardly another theorist who so resolutely motivates and pursues a research agenda in which dynamism and open-ended development assumes centre stage, while at the same time paying genuine and emphatic tribute to the achievements of static equilibrium theory (namely, the theory of the circular flow). Second, there is hardly another economist whose whole oeuvre is abounding with various kinds of explicit and implicit references pertinent to the double nature of economics as a system of knowledge: as a body of knowledge which is evolving (and ought to evolve) not different from modern natural science, on the one hand, and, on the other hand, is so intricately intertwined with a richer array of discourses and sources of knowledge regarding socio-economic live. Apart from his emphasis on economic history (1949b), JAS (1954a: 16) thinks that in economics "one source of information . . . denied to physics, namely, man's extensive knowledge of the *meanings* of economic actions" is available. Hence the vision of economics as a specialized toolbox of social physics is complemented by broader and richer domains of knowledge regarding socio-economic interdependences.

This is reflected in a number of observations and implications to be found throughout JAS's oeuvre:

1.   Historically, economics needed quite a long time to emancipate itself from other disciplines, notably from theology and philosophy (Schumpeter 1915).
2.   Schools and paradigms play a more important role than in the natural sciences. That role is in need of clarification (Schumpeter 1908; 1915). In the future, modern economics should leave behind the straightjackets imposed by schools.
3.   The evolution of economics is often influenced by political issues, which determine the problem setting (Schumpeter 1954a).
4.   Pre-analytic visions or ideologies play a role as a background for formulating questions or endowing them with a sense of importance, but also as a source of distortion or as an obstacle for further development (Schumpeter 1949a; 1954a).
5.   In order to identify economics as a discipline separated from others such as sociology, we cannot rely on the distinction between "rational" and "irrational" behaviour.

Agents of change

The last point is of particular importance in the light of Schumpeter's entrepreneurial theory of change. Pareto and others considered rationality as the core of the foundational distinction between economics and sociology. But this is at odds with the main thrust of Schumpeter's own entrepreneurial theory of economic change which is not modelled on the basis of neoclassical rational choice. For Schumpeter, drawing the line according to the distinction between preference-guided optimizing (*homo oeconomicus*) versus routine-/ norm-induced behaviour (*homo sociologicus*) would impede the formation of a theory of change. In his economic theory, both routine-induced behaviour as well as energetic action plays a role. Constrained optimization is not taken to capture all economically important aspects of human action. As already becomes clear in *Entwicklung* (1912), JAS's classes of agents exhibit a significant degree of heterogeneity, with the behavioural patterns corresponding to functional roles: the static agents sustaining the circular flow follow routines and adapt their behaviour to given circumstances; others (the entrepreneurs) mobilize superior energies to change those circumstances by disrupting the circular flow, engaging in creative destruction in terms of new products, production methods, markets, price systems, organizational patterns, and norms. An intermediate type of agent (the early follower) has capabilities allowing him or her to swiftly recognize successful innovations and imitate them. Somewhat similar capabilities of judgement (albeit in a different decision context) are ascribed to "the banker", who is responsible for channelling scarce resources (which are assumed to be fully employed in the circular flow) to some of the would-be innovators. While the powerful innovative agency of entrepreneurs certainly cannot be reduced to the kind of perfect hedonic rationality under conditions of full information, it would be a big mistake to equate it with irrationality. On the contrary, rationality may play a larger role in the context of the behaviour of innovators than of those who are mainly following routines or at best adapt to changing circumstances. Innovative entrepreneurs are not necessarily rational in a neoclassical sense, but rationalizing agents in a systemic sense. Their agency ("creative destruction") is pivotal for forward-looking disruption of routinized behaviours and structures. For innovation to become a pervasive and systemic phenomenon, agents such as "the early follower" or "the banker" play an important subsidiary role. In that process of experimentation and creative destruction, boundedly rational agents of change employ their creative energies. In historical perspective, semi-rational entrepreneurial capitalism unleashes most powerful forces of rationalization which eventually transform the economic process: in the whole process, enterprises and societies learn to organize and routinize change.

Tensions and ambivalences
From the beginning of JAS's career to his last writings, his work mirrors the tensions which he diagnoses with respect to the reality of modern capitalism: he has a genuine taste for distinctions to be used for purely analytical purposes, suggesting concepts such as "methodological individualism" or "analytical egalitarianism". He moreover puts forward strong statements emphasizing the development of modern economics as a modern quasi-natural science more and more emancipated from the vestigial traces of metaphysics and ideology as well as from the intellectual parochialism of "schools". According to his version of a "Monroe doctrine", the continent of modern economics should be kept free of foreign influences. He emphasizes the hegemony of a specific economic methodology and its independence from other disciplines: biology, psychology and philosophy have nothing to offer (Schumpeter 1908: 553), whereas mathematical methods and tools of quantitative analysis are (correctly) predicted to carry the day. Later, he readily adopts Joan Robinson's apt phrase of economics as a tool box.

Those declarations notwithstanding, Schumpeter does not pay much tribute to his "Monroe doctrine" in his main contributions to economics and social theory. The various types of agency relevant in the context of innovation processes make it impossible to steer clear of culture and psychology as determinants of behavioural tendencies. From the beginning of his career to his last writings, JAS takes recourse to economic sociology, psychology and history (cf. Schumpeter 1949b) whenever he thinks that the methods of pure economics and econometrics are insufficient. Examples include not only the characterization of entrepreneurial agency, but also the fiscal sociology introduced in his great essay on the fiscal crises of the tax state (1918), and the kind of behavioural public choice reasoning suggested in *Capitalism, Socialism and Democracy* (1942). This methodological pluralism is hardly compatible with his "Monroe doctrine".

As indicated above, Schumpeter's perception of the intricate nature of economics and of rationalization as a unique historical process with contradictions and unintended turns is the basis of subtle reflections. But in his work as an economist, it leads to tensions which remain unresolved. In his ambitious project of an explanatory approach to the historical process of capitalist development (cf. Schumpeter 1949b), the divergent theoretical perspectives are reflected by tension, such as the tension between entrepreneur-led creative destruction and the rationalized process of managed innovation (see Andersen 2009: 167). Those tensions are situated at the core of Schumpeter's uniqueness. They are deeply related to his character as a thinker. Moreover, they are related to profound questions regarding theoretical knowledge of socio-economic affairs: Schumpeter is a theorist of the seamless whole of the social process evolving in historical time, but he also emphatically endorses the principles (and the dos and don'ts) of economics as a special-ized science. Unfortunately, the socio-economic theory of the seamless whole can hardly be approached by research strategies guided exclusively by those dos and don'ts. When approaching the seamless whole, a theoretical horizon beyond the specialized discipli-nary research programmes (which are necessarily based on bold abstractions) seems not only useful, but indispensable.

Those tensions cannot be easily reconciled. What can be done is the following: (1) extend the scope of pure economics towards a wider set of phenomena, including dynamic and evolutionary processes; and (2) develop theoretical discourses in which the interdepend-ences of the seamless whole beyond the purely economic sphere can be approached and theorized. The latter requires a high degree of intellectual alertness in order to facilitate suitable changes of levels, frameworks and perspectives, and it requires a rough archi-tecture organizing the various levels of argument and perspectives within a provisional order. Under those preconditions, (2) may facilitate the finding of new combinations. It is obvious that strategy (1) is pursued in *Entwicklung* (1912, 1934) and in *Business Cycles* (1939). Elements of (2) can be found in all of his major works and are looming particu-larly large in his writings on the history of the subject. Indeed, Schumpeter's references to the specific nature of economics are not confined to tangential hints and implicit mes-sages scattered throughout his oeuvre. Important and explicit references can be found in his works on the history of economic thought and in shorter essays on the foundations of modern economics (Schumpeter 1915, 1949a).

The double nature of economics and its history
Most important for historians of economic thought, the double nature of economics as a pure analytical science and as a more encompassing body of knowledge is the deeper reason for the specific and important role of the history of the subject as well as the history of the modern socio-economic process. The main thrust of *History* (Schumpeter 1954a) can be summarized as follows: in a long process that exhibits various kinds of vicissitudes and detours, where all the above-sketched manifold influences and con-straints play their role, economic thought eventually evolved towards a scientific body of economic analysis, with its specific models, methods and techniques. The latter are necessary conditions for a systematic treatment of the quantitative aspects of socio-economic life. They moreover set the stage for the kind of cumulative progress and sys-tematic improvement of economics which is a characteristic of modern science at large. It is of the utmost importance that all this is kept in mind. However, as already indicated, that story of progress in economics is not the whole story, and it is certainly not the main reason why JAS is important as a historian of economics even today. Given his over-arching research agenda formulated and pursued from early on, the story of cumulative progress is hardly a plausible motive for investing so much energy towards the end of his career in what was to become his monumental, unfinished *History*. The perspective of a Whig story of cumulative progress could be a motive only for specialists and those

who love the old work for its own sake, or those who are concerned with the provision of some kind of history-based identity for their discipline. For JAS, history widens the horizon in specific respects: it enhances the powers of judgement in the realm of competing new ideas, theories and models. It offers a unique opportunity to gain insights into the ingredients and the logic of discovery processes, as in their work scientists report their mental processes. Moreover, the subject matter of economics is a "unique historical process", and the "filiation of ideas has met with more inhibitions in our field than it has in almost all others . . . results have been lost on the way or remained in abeyance for centuries. We shall meet with instances that are little short of appalling" (Schumpeter 1954a: 6).

This suggests that a motive for studying history is a better understanding of the current development and the future perspectives of economics. This is specifically important in economics as a field in which a powerful apparatus of analysis was developed along the lines of core principles of modern science, even though the specific form of this development was, is and remains conditioned by a set of complex extra-scientific and extra-disciplinary forces and influences; forces and influences which are poorly understood when they are perceived only as distortions (1949a), as they are preparing the stage for various combinations of questions, concepts, models, and empirical approaches. Incidentally, the double nature of economics is also reflected in the definition of greatness quoted above, in so far as it invokes multiple revivals which are not plausible within the framework of Whig history of linear progress in economics.

Put in that way, it can be easily seen that, for Schumpeter, history of economics is not a hobby or a welcome opportunity for the display of erudition, but an integrative part of a comprehensive research programme with the goal of understanding the whole of the social process. It specifically refers to the modern process of rationalization at large, which he perceives not as a process of linear progress in which rationality and efficiency more and more rule all over the place, but as a process of change and vicissitudes. This process is conditioned by non-rational elements and eventually produces unintended outcomes. As he explains in *Socialism* (1942), those outcomes may subvert the institutional and cultural basis of the agents of change who were responsible for past episodes of the rationalizing process.

JAS's habit of swiftly moving across a diverse landscape of different frameworks, levels and perspectives is challenging, and it poses problems in still another respect: there is hardly another economist or social theorist whose overall role in the development of twentieth-century economics is as puzzling to friends and foes. Specific discussions related to such "puzzles" include the question as to which extent this "enfant terrible" was an Austrian economist (Sturn 2014), or an unfinished precursor of evolutionary economics (Andersen 2009, 2011). "Although he was an Austrian by birth and training, he was not an 'Austrian economist'", writes Stolper (1968). This is true, but does not invalidate Erich Streissler's observation (1983: 358) that "he took up so many ideas then current only in the Austrian economic tradition that any hypothetical historian of economic thought, not knowing Schumpeter to be an Austrian, could immediately trace him to this school". Caldwell (2004) summarizes Schumpeter's seemingly surprising turns as "Schumpeter's multiple apostasies". Apostasies presuppose orthodoxies. Perhaps the deepest of JAS's conviction as a theorist is that innovative theorizing inevitably means transcending orthodoxies.

But how to prevent modern economics from becoming orthodox? In the light of this question, the coexistence of his late terminological shift emphasizing the character of scientific economics as a tool box and his re-affirmation of the importance of history (Schumpeter 1949b) can be taken as an acknowledgement of the problems of axiomatic "pure" economics which may tend to develop an aprioristic pretence of knowledge. An economist considering himself or herself "merely" a master of a tool box may be inclined to be interested in various other sources of knowledge relevant for the socio-economic domain. By contrast, if an economist believes him or herself to be in the possession of a deductive apparatus which allows him or her to derive results from axioms that are considered as aprioristically true, he or she may be less inclined to step out of the model-based orthodoxy.

JAS had a price to pay for the tensions which characterized his uniqueness. As aptly expressed by Andersen (2011: 239), his work is in an important sense unfinished, or – to use a phrase coined by Streissler (1972: 441), referring to Carl Menger – he ended in doubt and not in positive theorems.

RICHARD STURN

See also:

Eugen von Böhm-Bawerk (I); Evolutionary economics (III); German and Austrian schools (II); John Maynard Keynes (I); Public economics (III); Friedrich von Wieser (I).

References and further reading

Aghion, P., U. Akcigit and P. Howitt (2013), 'What do we learn from Schumpeterian growth theory?', NBER Working Paper No. 18824, February, National Bureau of Economic Research, Cambridge, MA.
Andersen, E.S. (2009), *Schumpeter's Evolutionary Economics. A Theoretical, Historical and Statistical Analysis of the Engine of Capitalism*, London and New York: Anthem Press.
Andersen, E.S. (2011), *Joseph A. Schumpeter. A Theory of Social and Economic Evolution*, Basingstoke and New York: Palgrave Macmillan.
Bergson, H. (1907), *L'évolution creatrice*, Paris: Holt.
Böhm, S. (2009), 'Joseph A. Schumpeter (1883–1950)', in H.D. Kurz (ed.), *Klassiker des ökonomischen Denkens*, vol. 2, Munich: Beck, pp. 137–60.
Böhm-Bawerk, E. von (1889), *Kapital und Kapitalzins*, Vol. 2: *Positive Theorie des Kapitals*, Innsbruck: Verlag der Wagner'schen Universitätsbuchhandlung.
Böhm-Bawerk, E. von (1913a), 'Eine "dynamische" Theorie des Kapitalzinses', *Zeitschrift für Volkswirtschaft, Sozialpolitik und Verwaltung*, **22**, 520–85.
Böhm-Bawerk, E. von (1913b), 'Eine "dynamische" Theorie des Kapitalzinses'. *Zeitschrift für Volkswirtschaft, Sozialpolitik und Verwaltung*, **23**, 640–57.
Caldwell, B. (2004), *Hayek's Challenge*, Chicago, IL: University of Chicago Press.
Haberler, G. (1951), 'Joseph Alois Schumpeter, 1883–1950', in S.E. Harris (ed.), *Schumpeter: Social Scientist*, Cambridge, MA: Harvard University Press, pp. 24–7.
Hayek, F.A. von (1952), *The Counter-Revolution of Science*, Glencoe, IL: Free Press.
Hayek, F.A. von (1968), 'Economic thought: the Austrian School', in D.L. Sills (ed.), *International Encyclopedia of the Social Sciences*, vol. 4, New York: Macmillan, pp. 458–62.
Keynes, J.M. (1936), *The General Theory of Employment, Interest and Money*, London: Macmillan.
Kurz, H.D. (ed.) (2009), *Klassiker des ökonomischen Denkens*, vol. 2. Munich: Beck.
Kurz, H.D. and R. Sturn (2012), *Schumpeter für jedermann*, Frankfurt am Main: Frankfurter Allgemeine Buch.
McCraw, T. (2007), *Prophet of Innovation: Joseph Schumpeter and Creative Destruction*, Cambridge, MA and London: Belknap Press.
Peneder, M. and A. Resch (2015), 'Schumpeter and venture finance; radical theorist, broke investor, and enigmatic teacher', *Industrial and Corporate Change*, online 15 March, 1–38, doi: 10.1093/icc/dtv004.
Rosenberg, N. (2000), *Schumpeter and the Endogeneity of Technology: Some American Perspectives*, The Graz Schumpeter Lectures, vol. 3, London: Routledge.
Samuelson, P. (1983), 'Marx, Keynes, and Schumpeter', *Eastern Economic Journal*, **9** (3), 166–79.

Schumpeter, J.A. (1906), 'Über die mathematische Methode der theoretischen Ökonomie', *Zeitschrift für Volkswirtschaft, Sozialpolitik und Verwaltung*, **15**, 30–49.
Schumpeter, J.A. (1908), *Das Wesen und der Hauptinhalt der theoretischen Nationalökonomie*, Leipzig: Duncker & Humblot.
Schumpeter, J.A. (1912), *Theorie der wirtschaftlichen Entwicklung*, Leipzig: Duncker & Humblot.
Schumpeter, J.A. (1913), 'Eine "dynamische" Theorie des Kapitalzinses. Eine Entgegnung', *Zeitschrift für Volkswirtschaft, Sozialpolitik und Verwaltung*, **22**, 411–51.
Schumpeter, J.A. (1914), *Epochen der Dogmen- und Methodengeschichte*, in M. Weber et al. (eds), *Grundriss der Sozialökonomik*, vol. I, Tübingen: J.C.B. Mohr, pp. 19–124.
Schumpeter, J.A. (1915), *Vergangenheit und Zukunft der Sozialwissenschaften*, Munich and Leipzig: Duncker & Humblot.
Schumpeter, J.A. (1918), *Die Krise des Steuerstaates*, Graz and Leipzig: Leuschner & Lubensky, reprinted in E. Schneider and A. Spiethof (eds) (1952), *Aufsätze zur ökonomischen Theorie*, Tübingen: J.C.B. Mohr pp. 1–71.
Schumpeter, J.A. (1926), *Theorie der wirtschaftlichen Entwicklung*, revised and shortened 2nd edn, Munich and Leipzig: Duncker & Humblot.
Schumpeter, J.A. (1928), 'The instability of capitalism', *Economic Journal*, **38** (September), 361–86.
Schumpeter, J.A. (1933), 'The common sense of econometrics', *Econometrica*, **1** (1), 5–12.
Schumpeter, J.A. (1934), *The Theory of Economic Development. An Inquiry into Profits, Capital, Credit, Interest, and the Business Cycle*, Cambridge, MA: Harvard University Press.
Schumpeter, J.A. (1936), 'J.M. Keynes: *General Theory of Employment, Interest and Money*', *Journal of the American Statistical Association*, **31** (December), 791–5.
Schumpeter, J.A. (1939), *Business Cycles. A Theoretical, Historical and Statistical Analysis of the Capitalist Process*, 2 vols, New York and London: McGraw-Hill.
Schumpeter, J.A. (1942), *Capitalism, Socialism and Democracy*, New York: Harper & Brothers.
Schumpeter, J.A. (1949a), 'Science and ideology', *American Economic Review*, **39** (2), 345–59.
Schumpeter, J.A. (1949b), 'The historical approach to the analysis of business cycles', in J.A. Schumpeter (1989), *Essays*, ed. R.V. Clemence, intro. R. Swedberg, New Brunswick, NJ: Transaction, pp. 322–9.
Schumpeter, J.A. (1950), 'The march into Socialism', *American Economic Review*, **40** (2), 446–56.
Schumpeter, J.A. (1952a), *Ten Great Economists*, London: George Allen & Unwin.
Schumpeter, J.A. (1952b), *Aufsätze zur ökonomischen Theorie*, eds E. Schneider and A. Spiethof, Tübingen: J.C.B. Mohr.
Schumpeter, J.A. (1953), *Aufsätze zur Soziologie*, eds E. Schneider and A. Spiethoff, Tübingen: J.C.B. Mohr.
Schumpeter, J.A. (1954a), *History of Economic Analysis*, London: George Allen & Unwin.
Schumpeter, J.A. (1954b), *Economic Doctrine and Method*, New York: Cambridge University Press.
Schumpeter, J.A. (1955), *Imperialism and Social Classes*, Cleveland, OH and New York: World.
Schumpeter, J.A. (1970), *Das Wesen des Geldes*, ed. F.K. Mann, Göttingen: Vandenhoeck & Ruprecht.
Schumpeter, J.A. (1985), *Aufsätze zur Wirtschaftspolitik*, eds C. Seidl and W. Stolper, Tübingen: J.C.B. Mohr.
Schumpeter, J.A. (1987), *Beiträge zur Sozialökonomik*, ed. S. Böhm, Vienna: Böhlau.
Schumpeter, J.A. (1989), *Essays*, ed. R.V. Clemence, intro. R. Swedberg, New Brunswick, NJ: Transaction.
Schumpeter, J.A. (1992), *Politische Reden*, eds C. Seidl and W.F. Stolper, Tübingen: J.C.B. Mohr.
Schumpeter, J.A. (1993), *Aufsätze zur Tagespolitik*, eds C. Seidl and W.F. Stolpe, Tübingen: J.C.B. Mohr.
Schumpeter, J.A. (2000), *Briefe/Letters*, eds U. Hedtke and R. Swedberg. Tübingen: J.C.B. Mohr.
Simpson, D. (1983), 'Joseph Schumpeter and the Austrian School of economics', *Journal of Economic Studies*, **10** (4), 18–28.
Stolper, W. (1968), 'Schumpeter, Joseph A.', *International Encyclopedia of the Social Sciences*, accessed 27 November 2015 at http://www.encyclopedia.com/doc/1G2-3045001111.html.
Streissler, E. (1972), 'To what extent was the Austrian School marginalist?', *History of Political Economy*, **4** (2), 426–41.
Streissler, E. (1983), 'Schumpeter and Hayek: on some similarities of their thought', in F. Machlup, G. Fels and H. Müller-Groeling (eds), *Reflections on a Troubled World Economy. Essays in Honour of Herbert Giersch*, London: Palgrave-Macmillan, pp. 357–64.
Sturn, R. (2013), 'Schumpeter und die österreichische Theorie der Nationalökonomie', in I. Pies and M. Leschke (eds), *Joseph Schumpeters Theorie gesellschaftlicher Entwicklung*, Tübingen: Mohr Siebeck, pp. 37–65.
Walras, L. (1874), *Eléments d'économie politique pure: Ou théorie de la richesse sociale*, Lausanne: L. Corbaz, facsimile reproduction 1988, Düsseldorf: Verlag Wirtschaft und Finanzen.
Weber, M. (ed.) (1914), *Grundriss der Sozialökonomik*, vol. I, Tübingen: J.C.B. Mohr.
Witt, U. (2002), 'How evolutionary is Schumpeter's theory of economic development?', *Industry and Innovation*, **9** (1–2), 7–22.

Frank H. Knight (1885–1972)

Born and raised on a farm in McLean County, Illinois, Frank Knight (1885–1972) lived most of his life in the American Mid-West. After the completion of his university studies in eastern Tennessee and upstate New York (Cornell PhD, 1916), he returned to the Mid-West for an academic career spent at either The University of Iowa (1919–28) or The University of Chicago (1917–19, and 1928 until his death). His most famous contribution – grounding the theory of profit in the existence of uncertainty – was contained in *Risk, Uncertainty, and Profit* (Knight 1921), his doctoral dissertation. His subsequent defence of neoclassical theory against American institutionalism (Knight 1999a: 1–39, 112–32), his evaluation of economic ethics and the morality of competition (Knight 1999a: 40–60, 61–93), and his classic articulation of the price system in a market economy (eventually published in Knight 1951) led to his appointment at the University of Chicago in the late 1920s.

From Hyde Park, he launched an attack on Austrian capital theory, resuscitated alternative/opportunity cost theory, and criticized the classical tri-partite division of productive factors, all in the context of the initiation of the Chicago price theory tradition. The group of like-minded scholars who gathered around Knight during the 1930s – Henry C. Simons and Lloyd Mints, plus students Allen Wallis, Milton Friedman, George Stigler, Homer Jones, and Aaron Director – formed the basis on which the post-war Chicago School of economics was built. Knight himself is often identified as the "dominant intellectual influence" (Stigler 1987: 56) of post-war Chicago economics, although by that time he was occupied almost exclusively with broader themes of economic and social philosophy than with the Chicago School's development of economics as an applied policy science. His last published contributions to economic theory were written prior to the conclusion of World War II. Knight was selected as the recipient of the American Economic Association's Francis A. Walker Medal in 1947, and named president of the association three years later. He was granted honorary degrees by several European and American universities, elected to membership in the American Academy of Arts and Sciences and the Accademia Nazionale Dei Lincei, and awarded the prize for distinguished service to humanistic scholarship by the American Council of Learned Societies.

Risk, Uncertainty and Profit

Knight is best known for Knightian uncertainty. Frequently described as a context for decision-making in which not even the probability distributions of the outcomes of future actions are known, uncertainty is also sometimes distinguished from risk by its uninsurability (Knight 1999b: 345). If the outcomes of future actions can be quantified in any way, market participants can find ways to insure themselves against future risks, converting them into known costs. If the outcomes cannot be measured in some way, insurance markets will not emerge, and entrepreneurs will have to bear negative outcomes themselves. Human action in the context of Knightian uncertainty, then, is based on subjective estimates of the future outcomes of potential actions. Knightian uncertainty is often called an epistemological problem because it identifies the limit of human knowledge. However, Knight's discussion of uncertainty as the grounds for entrepreneurial action, and hence the reason for the existence of economic profit, also makes it an interpersonal, even moral, problem. The "true uncertainty," he says, is our uncertainty about the capacity of others to "meet uncertainty" (Knight 1921: 309). The entrepreneur accepts that challenge, making judgements about the capabilities of those hired, even though they may cost the entrepreneur dearly.

Because Knight identified economic decision-making in the context of uncertainty as the fundamental departure of actual economic life from perfect competition theory, Knightian uncertainty is generally considered a foundational contribution to the theory of entrepreneurship and is indirectly linked to the development of non-neoclassical theories of the firm. Douglass North has made the concept integral to his historical work on the process of economic change (North 2005), and it has come to be used in financial economics as a counter to the use of Bayesian subjective probabilities in market forecasting.

Methodology: From Successive Approximation to Weberian "Verstehen"

Risk, Uncertainty, and Profit (Knight 1921) introduced another key theme of Knight's economic thinking: the tension between the analytical relevance of economic principles to understanding and participation in economic life and, at the same time, the mistake of viewing economics as a predictive science. In *Risk, Uncertainty, and Profit*, the distance between the realm of perfect competition and the realm of actual economic life was traversed for Knight by the relaxation of one assumption at a time. The assumption of perfect knowledge was the first to be relaxed, and the most important, but other assumptions would need to be relaxed, altered or replaced to enable economists to speak more directly about the relevance of economic principles to policy matters. T.W. Hutchison later described this approach as the method of "successive approximation" (1938: 73).

In the mid-1920s, however, Knight began reading intensively in the literature of the German Historical School, and translated Max Weber's *General Economic History*, the first of Weber's work to be translated into English (Weber 1927). Shortly thereafter, he re-evaluated his conception of equilibrium theorizing; instead of traversing from perfect competition to actual competition via successive approximation, Knight argued that there was an "impassable gulf" between the two, and hence, that economic theory could not predict the dynamics of actual economic activity (Knight 1999a: 149–71). However, non-predictability does not mean that economic theory is not scientific or relevant to understanding economic life (Knight 1999a: 372–99). Like Weber, Knight ends up arguing that fundamental concepts in a social science provide a way of understanding the economy even if they cannot be turned into predictive models (a good summary is Knight 1961). The transition in his economic methodology can be seen in his theory of comparative economic organization, and his re-evaluation of capital and cost theory, in which he developed an approach that generated further controversies and/or theoretical developments.

Comparative Economic Organization and the Re-Evaluation of Economic Theory

Convinced by Weber that competitive price theory provided only an archetype of actual competition, Knight began to synthesize neoclassical theory and Weberian comparative history over the 1930s and 1940s. The final form of his synthesis is summarized for a general audience in the third and fourth chapters of Knight (1960), but pieces of it appear earlier in Knight (Knight 1951; Knight and Merriam 1945). The purpose of the synthesis was to accomplish two tasks simultaneously: (1) distinguish between those aspects of economic analysis which treat conditions as given, and those which provide an analysis under conditions of progress; and (2) use an analysis of individual organization of activity as the context for identifying the fundamental principles of economic rationality and key aspects of competitive theory, while allowing a concurrent examination of the states of social economic organization. The analysis of individual action under given conditions produced a sole individual allocating resources among competing wants according to the equimarginal principle, and drawing upon a Crusonia plant for the replacement of all those aspects of the production process that deteriorated and needed replacement. Savings from current resource use and investment into future resource use not only determined the rate of interest, but also created the conditions for social economic organization to move from exchange of basic necessities among largely self-sufficient units to expand into the organized production of modern economic life. However, it was the "entrepreneur function" that Knight had first identified in *Risk, Uncertainty, and Profit* that provided the opposite of Crusoe's life alone on an island with given resources. By investing in new products and re-organizing existing production, entrepreneurs created new conditions for human activity, thereby facilitating the progress of economy and society.

The theory of capital and the interest rate embedded in Knight's theory of economic organization had emerged originally in the context of his debate with Austrian economists. During the 1930s, Knight wrote a sequence of almost a dozen articles on capital theory, specifically targeting Austrian theory. After the initial broadside (Knight 1933), the articles are written in the context of exchanges with Fritz Machlup (Machlup 1935; Knight 1935b), Kenneth Boulding (Knight 1935d), F.A. Hayek (Hayek 1934, 1935; Knight 1935c), and Nicholas Kaldor (Kaldor 1937; Knight 1938). At the end, he wrote a two part article summarizing his view (Knight 1999a: 290–344). At the heart of his argument is the effort to show how the "period of production" concept of Austrian theory is incompatible with pure equilibrium analysis because it changes, in real historical time, the conditions of production while maintaining that all given conditions remain the same – everything remains the same; yet capital has changed.

In cost theory, as in capital theory, Knight set out to reformulate neoclassical theory by stripping away elements of change that had slipped into static equilibrium contexts. Cost became measured in terms of alternative or displaced product (Knight 1928, 1935a), with no mention of the classical theory of abstinence or sacrifice (Knight 1999a: 237–89). Knight's formulation of cost has become the standard version of opportunity cost theory in economics today (see Buchanan 1969).

Mechanical and Ethical Limitations of Competitive Theory

Knight's discussion of the entrepreneur's function in modern economic organization also allowed him to recast a distinction he had made early in his career between the "mechanical" and the "ethical" limitations of competition (Knight 1999a: 61–93; and Knight 1951). At the time, he said in passing that the market had the means to overcome the mechanical limitations – things like monopoly power, externalities and public goods.

For example, in his article on social cost that criticizes A.C. Pigou's theory of externalities, Knight (1924) argued that competition would not only better serve the public, but would, over time, find ways to internalize whatever externalities that occurred. In Knight (1960) he argues that entrepreneurial action over relatively short time horizons will reduce any monopoly that is not sanctioned by government to the status of just another competitor.

Unlike the mechanical limitations – which competitive forces would overcome through internalization and innovation, the ethical limitations of competition were, for Knight, serious obstacles for a free enterprise economy. Next to *Risk, Uncertainty, and Profit*, Knight is perhaps best known for the essay "Ethics of Competition" (Knight 1999a: 61–93) in which he argued that a competitive economy did not – indeed, could not – be reconciled to the ethical requirements of either classical or Christian moral philosophy. "We appear" he concludes, "to search in vain for any really ethical basis of approval for competition as a basis for an ideal type of human relations, or as a motive to action." The only justification for competitive society "is that it is effective in getting things done; but any candid answer to the question, "what things," compels the admission that they leave much to be desired" (Knight 1999a: 89). Knight's conclusion, however, did not leave him any more satisfied with non-economic conceptions of value; in 1939 he published a scathing criticism of a wide range of moral theories as they applied to consideration of economic reform (Knight 1999b: 1–75). Perhaps the best summary of his ethics is provided by his adaption of Talleyrand's famous line that "the best principle is to have no principles". In his presidential address to the American Economic Association in 1950, Knight said that a better expression would be: "The right principle is to respect all the principles, take them fully into account, and then use *good judgment* as to how far to follow one or another in the case in hand" (Knight 1999b: 366, original emphasis).

From Economics to Social Philosophy

Although philosophical themes run all the way back in Knight's work to his days as a philosophy graduate student at Cornell in 1913, his remarks about the state of liberal society in the 1930s gained him a reputation for pugnacious realism (Knight 1947: 19–34, 370–402; 1991), and by the 1940s the majority of his work concerns three themes in social philosophy. The first was the historical origins of the Liberal Revolution, especially the history of the epistemological break of scientific thinking from organized religion and its implications for social science (Knight and Merriam 1945). The second was the political autonomy of democratic deliberation from the threat of social control in either the name of moralism or scientism. The third was the need for a social scientific approach to intelligent social action grounded in the principles of economics, but incorporating as well an understanding of democratic politics and an affirmation of the independence of ethical judgements. From the end of World War II until his death in 1972, he lectured, wrote and revised on the threefold nature of democratic social philosophy – economics, politics and ethics. That work, along with his earlier economic theorizing, is his legacy.

ROSS B. EMMETT

See also:

British classical political economy (II); Chicago School (II); German and Austrian schools (II); Institutionalism (II).

References and further reading

Buchanan, J.M. (1969), *Cost and Choice: An Inquiry into Economic Theory*, Chicago, IL: University of Chicago Press.
Hayek, F.A. (1934), 'On the relationship between investment and output', *Economic Journal*, **44** (174), 207–31.
Hayek, F.A. (1935), 'The mythology of capital', *Quarterly Journal of Economics*, **50** (2), 199–228.
Hutchison, T.W. (1938), *The Significance and Basic Postulates of Economic Theory*, London: Macmillan.
Kaldor, N. (1937), 'Annual survey of economic theory: the recent controversy on the theory of capital', *Econometrica*, **5** (3), 201–33.
Knight, F.H. (1921), *Risk, Uncertainty and Profit*, Boston, MA: Houghton Mifflin.
Knight, F.H. (1924), 'Some fallacies in the interpretation of social cost', *Quarterly Journal of Economics*, **38** (August), 582–606.
Knight, F.H. (1928), 'A suggestion for simplifying the statement for a general theory of price', *Journal of Political Economy*, **36** (3), 353–70.
Knight, F.H. (1933), 'Capitalistic production, time and the rate of return', in *Economic Essays in Honour of Gustav Cassel*, London: George Allen & Unwin, pp. 327–42.
Knight, F.H. (1935a), 'Bemerkungen über Nutzen und Kosten', *Zeitschrift für Nationalökonomie*, **6** (1), 28–52, and (3), 315–36.
Knight, F.H. (1935b), 'Comment', *Journal of Political Economy*, **43** (5), 625–27.
Knight, F.H. (1935c), 'Professor Hayek and the theory of investment', *Economic Journal*, **45** (March), 77–94.
Knight, F.H. (1935d), 'The theory of investment once more: Mr. Boulding and the Austrians', *Quarterly Journal of Economics*, **50** (1), 36–67.
Knight, F.H. (1938), 'On the theory of capital: in reply to Mr. Kaldor', *Econometrica*, **6** (1), 63–82.
Knight, F.H. (1947), *Freedom and Reform: Essays in Economics and Social Philosophy*, New York: Harper & Bros.
Knight, F.H. (1951), *The Economic Organization, with an Article 'Notes on cost and utility'*, New York: Augustus M. Kelley.
Knight, F.H. (1960), *Intelligence and Democratic Action*, Cambridge, MA: Harvard University Press.
Knight, F.H. (1961), 'Methodology in economics', *Southern Economic Journal*, **27**, pt 1 (3), 185–93, pt 2 (4), 273–82.
Knight, F.H. (1991), 'The case for communism: from the standpoint of an ex-liberal', *Research in the History of Economic Thought and Methodology* (archival supplement 2), 57–108.
Knight, F.H. (1999a), *Selected Essays by Frank H. Knight*, R.B. Emmett (ed.), Vol. 1, *"What is truth" in Economics?*, Chicago, IL: University of Chicago Press.
Knight, F.H. (1999b), *Selected Essays by Frank H. Knight*, R.B. Emmett (ed.), Vol. 2, *Laissez-Faire: Pro and Con*, Chicago, IL: University of Chicago Press.
Knight, F.H. and T.W. Merriam (1945), *The Economic Order and Religion*, New York: Harper & Bros.
Machlup, F. (1935), 'Professor Knight and the "period of production"', *Journal of Political Economy*, **43** (5), 577–624.
North, D.C. (2005), *Understanding the Process of Economic Change*, Princeton, NJ: Princeton University Press.
Stigler, G.J. (1987), 'Frank Hyneman Knight', in J. Eatwell, M. Milgate and P. Newman (eds), *The New Palgrave: A Dictionary of Economics*, New York: Stockton Press, pp. 55–9.
Weber, M. (1927), *General Economic History*, trans. F.H. Knight, London: George Allen & Unwin.

Karl Polanyi (1886–1964)

Karl Polanyi was born 1886 in Vienna into a Jewish family and grew up in Budapest. As one commentator (Block 2001: xix) noted, the family was "remarkable for its social engagement and intellectual achievements". He studied philosophy and law at the universities of Budapest and Kolozsvár in Hungary. As a student in Budapest he founded the radical Club Galilei, in which he became acquainted with Georg Lukács, Karl Mannheim and other intellectuals who should gain fame. In 1914 he was involved in the foundation of the Hungarian Radical Party.

After the war he supported the Republican government in Hungary, but when this was overthrown and transformed into a Soviet republic in 1919 (which lasted only four months) he fled to Vienna. There he worked from 1924 until 1933 as a journalist, mainly for *Der Österreichische Volkswirt* (*The Austrian Economist*), a renowned economic and financial weekly. In his publications during that period he dealt with a whole host of economic problems, *inter alia* he participated in the socialist accountancy debates with Ludwig von Mises. In 1925 he married Ilona Duczynska, a sympathizer of the Communist Party.

The rise of fascist trends in Austria long before its *Anschluss* to Germany in 1938 caused Polanyi to emigrate in 1933. He moved to London where he made a living from the little money he earned as journalist and lecturer for the Workers' Educational Association. During that time he began his research for *The Great Transformation* (*TGT*) and accepted invitations for lectures in the United States. However, the writing of his magnum opus had to wait until he moved in 1940 to Vermont, USA, where he got a position at Bennington College.

From 1947 to 1953 Polanyi held a teaching position at Columbia University in New York City. Polanyi had to commute; owing to his wife's former communist affiliation, a US visa for her was withheld and they had to settle in Canada, where Polanyi died in 1964.

Polanyi's intellectual development took place in the bracing climate of the final stage of the Austro-Hungarian Empire with its cornucopia of new approaches in science and the arts. As far as economics was concerned, marginalists (and representatives of the Austrian School), advocates of the Historical School and Marxists struggled in his formative years for supremacy in the German-speaking countries. Polanyi was well aware of the alternatives, but no clear-cut adherent of any of them – in fact, he criticized strongly some aspects of them – but each exerted some influence on him. He received additional stimuli, *inter alia*, from G.D.H. Cole's *Guild Socialism*, from the sociologist Ferdinand Tönnies with his distinction between community (*Gemeinschaft*) and society (*Gesellschaft*) and, in subsequent years, from his studies of history, social theory and anthropology. In *TGT* he made use of all these strands.

The Great Transformation, Polanyi's magnum opus, was published in 1944 – the same year as Hayek's *The Road to Serfdom* appeared, which in several respects heralds the opposite standpoint. Its subtitle is *The Political and Economic Origins of Our Time* and provides the clue to *TGT*'s intention: to demonstrate why after World War I a great transformation took place that destroyed the order which had ruled before and had lasted for a century (1815–1914). Decisive for the understanding of this transformation is, in his eyes, to realize the peculiarity of the order in the nineteenth century.

According to Polanyi it rested on four pillars: an international balance of power system which, by and large, took care of peace; the gold standard; the liberal state and the self-regulating market. Most important, and at the same time "a stark utopia", is the last mentioned: "Such an institution could not exist for any length of time without annihilating the human and natural substance of society" (Polanyi 2001: 3). In contrast to societal organizations, which are characterized by reciprocity and redistribution, a market system tends to subordinate society to the logic of the market and to turn human beings and the natural environment into commodities – fictitious commodities in Polanyi's words. Making use of anthropological studies, he tries to show that this is in contradiction to former societies where the economy was embedded in social relations. In addition, he tries to demonstrate that in primitive societies markets played only an accessory role.

The utopian character of a self-regulating market system results from the fact that society sooner or later will revolt against it: Because the devastating consequences of a subordination to the imperatives of a market system are not accepted, counter-movements emerge. The development of a market system is therefore characterized by a "double movement". This term was coined by Polanyi and explained as follows: "the market system expanded continuously but this movement was met by a countermovement checking the expansion in definite directions. Vital though such a countermovement was for the protection of society, it was incompatible with the self-regulation of the market, and thus with the market system itself" (2001: 130). The tension between the two will either destroy the system completely, as the Soviet Union or Nazi Germany demonstrated, where freedom was abolished and the market substituted by central planning or subjected to political purposes; or a considerable realignment in the relationship between economy and society will take place, as was the case with the New Deal, the establishment of welfare states and the adoption of Keynesian full-employment policies. Most likely, Polanyi would not have been surprised that adherents of a self-regulating market would do their best to turn back these changes. However, it is highly probable that he would have been very astonished about their success in re-establishing something like a self-regulating market system in the last decades of twentieth century.

The economic historian Gregory Clark has remarked: "*The Great Transformation* has attained the status of a classic in branches of sociology, political science, and anthropology. . . . Yet in economics the work is unknown – or, when discussed, derided" (Clark 2008). While this is an exaggeration, it is true that mainstream economics has, by and large, neglected Polanyi's contributions which comprises, in addition to *TGT*, numerous publications (see the extensive bibliography in Karl Polanyi Institute of Political Economy n.d.). Only a few economists, including Kindleberger (1974), Stiglitz (Foreword in Polanyi 2001) and Kuttner (2014) have discussed his ideas. Economic historians often objected that he romanticized archaic societies. The greatest impact he had was undoubtedly in economic sociology and economic anthropology. Especially his concept of (dis)embeddedness (Wikipedia: "embeddedness refers to the degree to which economic activity is constrained by non-economic institutions") – meanwhile subjected to a great transformation itself – has made a remarkable career. Outside academia Polanyi's arguments still have considerable influence among the adversaries of globalization and critics of the policies of international financial organizations.

PETER KALMBACH

See also:

Development economics (III); Institutional economics (III); Karl Heinrich Marx (I); Non-Marxian socialist ideas in Britain and the United States (II); Non-Marxist socialist ideas in Germany and Austria (II); Joseph Alois Schumpeter (I).

References and further reading

Block, F. (2001), 'Introduction', in K. Polanyi, *The Great Transformation. The Political and Economic Origins of Our Time*, Boston, MA: Beacon Press, pp. xix–xxxviii.

Block, F. and M.F. Somers (2014), *The Power of Market Fundamentalism. Karl Polanyi's Critique*, Harvard, MA: Harvard University Press.

Clark, G. (2008), 'Reconsiderations: "The Great Transformation" by Karl Polanyi', *The New York Sun*, accessed 5 September 2014 at http://www.nysun.com/arts/reconsiderations-the-great-transformation-by-karl/79250/.

Dale, G. (2010), *Karl Polanyi. The Limits of the Market*, Cambridge: Polity Press.

Karl Polanyi Institute of Political Economy (n.d.), accessed 23 September 2014 at http://www.concordia.ca/research/polanyi/archive.html.

Kindleberger, C.P. (1974), 'The Great Transformation by Karl Polanyi', *Daedalus, Journal of the American Academy of Arts and Sciences*, **103** (1), 45–52.

Kuttner, R. (2014), 'Karl Polanyi explains it all', *The American Prospect*, 15 April, accessed 23 September 2014 at http://www.prospect.org/article/karl-polanyi-explain-it-all.

Polanyi, K. (2001), *The Great Transformation. The Political and Economic Origins of Our Time*, Foreword by J.E. Stiglitz, Introduction by F. Block, Boston, MA: Beacon Press, first published 1944.

Stanfield, J.R. (1986), *The Economic Thought of Karl Polanyi*, Basingstoke: Macmillan.

Walter Eucken (1891–1950)

Walter Eucken, born in Jena on 17 January 1891, was the son of the philosopher and Nobel laureate Rudolf Eucken. He studied economics and obtained a doctoral degree in Bonn in 1913. After World War I, he followed his professor, Hermann Schumacher, to Berlin. He was appointed to a professorship in Tübingen in 1925, and from 1927 to 1950 he taught in Freiburg.

After the Nazi seizure of power, a group formed in Freiburg that discussed questions of ethics and resistance from a Christian perspective. Eventually the circle around Eucken developed plans for a restructuring of the economy and the legal system. Some of them were arrested after the attempted assassination of Adolf Hitler in 1944; Eucken was among those who were interrogated. Members of the circle were later among the close advisers to Ludwig Erhard, the first West German economics minister and the "father" of the social market economy. While giving lectures as a visiting professor in London, Eucken died of a heart attack on 20 March 1950.

Eucken's early studies were still written in the descriptive style of the historical school. However, when he wrote his *Kritische Betrachtungen zum deutschen Geldproblem*, published in 1923 at the time of the Great Inflation, he was already discussing the quantity theory of money and the purchasing power parity of money espoused by the Swedish economist Gustav Cassel. He opposed Georg F. Knapp, whose work *Staatliche Theorie des Geldes* (1905) had ignored the risks coming from governments printing money. By expressing these views, he became one of those who inculcated in the Germans a deep-seated fear of any government-induced expansion of the money supply.

At this time, the notion began gaining ground that the creation of credit was the key causal factor behind the fluctuations in economic activity. Eucken's study "Kredit und Konjunktur" (1929) focused attention on this question. Contrary to the non-monetary over-investment theory of the German doyen of business cycle research, Arthur Spiethoff, he did not believe that the depression made a sufficient amount of unused capital available and automatically supplied the forces for the recovery – "additional credit" was a necessary requirement for the change from a downturn to an upswing.

With the 1931 banking crisis, the demand for "productive credit creation" was suddenly high on the agenda. Eucken's friend Wilhelm Röpke, who had also lost confidence in the market's ability to self-adjust, proposed a credit-financed programme. In doing so, he coined the term "initial ignition", which was to jump-start the engine of the economy. But Eucken remained sceptical. Cartel pricing and wage rigidity had to be broken first. Pointing the way to a new liberal economic order instead of directing economical processes, the creed of the later so-called ordoliberalism began to take shape.

In this environment, the first manifestos of ordoliberalism emerged in 1932: a speech by Alexander Rüstow at the Verein für Sozialpolitik and Eucken's essay "Staatliche Strukturwandlungen und die Krise des Kapitalismus" about changes in the structure of the state and the crisis of capitalism. Both men complained that in the course of democratization, the state had degenerated into a tool of various interest groups and their calls for intervention. Eucken argued that the regulatory effect of the price system had been reversed by government intervention. This was the cause of the crisis, and now the government had to find the strength to "liberate itself from the influence of the masses" once again. Although Eucken proved to be a critic of the Weimar Republic, this did not make him sympathetic to the Nazis.

When Eucken's most important work, *Die Grundlagen der Nationalökonomie*, was first published in 1940, Germany was celebrating Hitler's successes, Stalin had established a planned economy and Roosevelt's New Deal had been put to work. The question of what was the right economic system was up for debate, and Eucken was going against the flow.

Methodologically, Eucken's *Grundlagen* is a late contribution to the *Methodenstreit* between the historical and the marginalist school, a debate especially over whether the inductive or the deductive method should be adopted. Eucken wanted to overcome this "great antinomy". According to him, Gustav Schmoller was justified in charging the theorists with being out of touch with reality, because they sought only the one natural order in historical diversity and limited themselves to the analysis of perfect competition. This, Eucken argued, had created a divide between theory and reality. However, Schmoller, he added, was making the opposite mistake when he told his students to describe a given economy in detail, not in the abstract. Instead, Eucken wrote, it was necessary to establish universally valid theories by means of "emphasizing abstraction", irrespective of the change in historical life. Thus Eucken examined the economic orders visible in the course of history and isolated pure forms, based on the polar opposition of the centrally planned economy and the exchange economy.

In the exchange economy, individual plans are coordinated via markets and prices. Exactly how this process works depends on the economic subjects' position of power, and on the respective dominant market forms. According to Eucken, perfect competition, partial oligopolies, oligopolies, partial monopolies and monopolies were conceivable on both the supply and the demand side, and this led him to distinguish between 25 market forms in terms of which all economic systems at all times and in all places can be understood. Which of these forms existed "when" and "where" was a question of empiricism, while the clarification of the laws applicable in them was the task of theory.

According to Eucken, the distribution resulting from the free market leads to social problems when the levels of prices and incomes are not based on scarcity relationships but on positions of power resulting from imperfect markets. For this reason, he favoured a strong state that guaranteed an economic order in which wages and prices develop according to the rules of functioning markets. He argued in favour of a properly functioning and humane economic order and criticized central planning as a system that did not correspond to "the essence of man and his concern".

According to Eucken, private property could and collective property must lead to abuses, because the free development of prices was impossible. The political consequences were serious: Eucken agreed with Hayek's view that the planned economy was subject to a tendency toward state slavery. However, with his critique of laissez-faire he was closer to the classic liberalism of a John Stuart Mill than to the neoliberalism of a Friedrich Hayek.

When considering the small number of great German economists of the twentieth century, the name Eucken stands out. His work had the greatest influence on the course of economics and the structuring of the economic order in Germany after World War II. Eucken's importance lies in the combination of theory and policy, of academic and moral integrity in search of answers to the pressing questions of a difficult time. He offered a starting point, particularly to those who refused to accept the enforced conformity of the universities after the Nazi takeover and aspired to a new, free economic order. Against this historical background, his ability to establish a school of thought in Germany becomes understandable. In addition to the "Freiburgers" Franz Böhm, Hans Großmann-Doerth, Friedrich Lutz and Leonard Miksch, Rüstow and Röpke are also part of this group. Some would also include Erhard and Alfred Müller-Armack.

Ordoliberalism survived both the heyday of Keynesianism and the monetarist revolution. Eucken's defining influence in Germany started to wane noticeably in the 1970s. With the advent of the financial crisis in 2008–09, his criticism of laissez-faire policies has gained a new relevance.

HAUKE JANSSEN

See also:

Gustav Cassel (I); German and Austrian achools (II); Friedrich August von Hayek (I); Historical economics (II); Gustav Friedrich von Schmoller (I); Arthur Spiethoff (I).

References and further reading

Eucken, W. (1923), *Kritische Betrachtungen zum deutschen Geldproblem*, Jena: Gustav Fischer.
Eucken, W. (1929), 'Kredit und Konjunktur', *Schriften des Vereins für Sozialpolitik 175*, Munich and Leipzig: Duncker & Humblot, pp. 287–305.
Eucken, W. (1932), 'Staatliche Strukturwandlungen und die Krise des Kapitalismus', *Weltwirtschaftliches Archiv*, **36** (2), 297–321.
Eucken, W. (1940), *Die Grundlagen der Nationalökonomie*, Berlin, Göttingen and Heidelberg: Springer, 6th edn 1950.
Janssen, H. (2009), 'Walter Eucken', in H.D. Kurz (ed.), *Klassiker des ökonomischen Denkens II*, Munich: Beck, pp. 187–204.
Knapp, G.F. (1905), *Staatliche Theorie des Geldes*, Leipzig: Duncker & Humblot.
Rieter, H. and M. Schmolz (1993), 'The ideas of German Ordoliberalism 1938–45: pointing the way to a new economic order', *European Journal of the History of Economic Thought*, **1** (1), 87–114.

Erik Lindahl (1891–1960)

Erik Lindahl was born on 21 November 1891 in Stockholm and died on 6 January 1960 in Uppsala, Sweden. He was a pioneer of the modern theory of public finance and a leading member of the "Stockholm school" of economics, which in the interwar period elaborated on Knut Wicksell's approach to macroeconomics and monetary theory. Further members of this loosely organized group of Swedish economists were Dag Hammarskjöld, Alf Johansson, Erik Lundberg, Gunnar Myrdal, Bertil Ohlin, and Ingvar Svennilsson (see Jonung 1991).

Lindahl grew up in Jönköping and then studied humanities and law, from 1910 to 1914, at the University of Lund. He was encouraged by his economics teacher, Emil Sommarin, to study carefully Knut Wicksell's writings, which became a major source of inspiration for most of his subsequent work. He had, however, no personal contact with Wicksell until the public defence of his doctoral dissertation in 1919, when the latter acted as one of the official "challengers" (Steiger 2008). Lindahl was a *docent* (reader) in public finance at Lund University from 1920 to 1924, and a reader in economics and fiscal law at the University of Uppsala from 1924 to 1926. In 1926, Lindahl became responsible for the planning of an extensive empirical study on 'Wages, Cost of Living and National Income in Sweden 1860–1930', financed by the Rockefeller Foundation and carried out in the following decade at the Institute for Social Sciences at Stockholm University. Thereafter, he held professorial positions at the Gothenburg School of Business Economics (1932–39) and at the Universities of Lund (1939–42) and Uppsala (1942–58). He was a consultant to the Swedish central bank (in 1931) and to the Swedish ministry of finance (1935–43), an economic adviser to the League of Nations (1936–39) and to the United Nations (from 1949–50 and 1952–54), and also served as President of the International Economic Association (1956–59).

Lindahl's writings, from his doctoral dissertation in 1919 to his last publication in 1959, cover four main areas: public finance, dynamic economic theory (that is, capital theory), macroeconomics, and monetary theory. In public finance, Lindahl's rigorous application of the benefit principle to taxation facilitated the integration of public economics and neoclassical economic theory; it also paved the way for integrating public goods into general equilibrium theory. In capital theory, he was the first to provide a mathematical analysis of an "intertemporal equilibrium" and to introduce the concept of a "temporary equilibrium". In the field of macroeconomic theory, he anticipated some of the insights of Keynes's *General Theory* and of the Kaldor–Pasinetti theory of income distribution. In monetary theory he contributed, together with Gunnar Myrdal, to the development of cumulative process analysis. While Lindahl's main contributions were in the area of pure economic theory, he was also interested in fostering empirical studies of prices and income, and in developing national accounting standards.

Public Finance

In his doctoral dissertation of 1919, *Die Gerechtigkeit der Besteuerung*, and in a subsequent paper (1928), Lindahl elaborated on Wicksell's approach to public finance (Wicksell 1896) and proposed an individualized tax, now known as a "Lindahl tax", for financing the provision of public goods and services in accordance with individual benefits. This tax is determined from so-called "Lindahl prices", which are calculated for each individual consumer (or group of consumers) and set according to the consumer's marginal benefit, evaluated at the equilibrium quantity. According to Lindahl, these prices can be viewed in the same way as implicit prices for joint products, which in equilibrium reflect differences in the relative demand for jointly produced commodities. Analogously, different individuals (or groups of homogenous individuals) who jointly consume a public good have different demand prices or willingness to pay for a marginal unit of government expenditure. In "Lindahl equilibrium" the total quantity of the public good satisfies the requirement that the *aggregate* marginal benefit equals the marginal cost of providing the good (Böhm 1987).

Lindahl's path-breaking contribution was properly appreciated only in the 1950s, when the main part of his dissertation appeared in an English translation (Lindahl 1958) and Paul A. Samuelson, Richard A. Musgrave and others harked back to it in their own contributions to the modern theory of public finance. In the 1970s Lindahl's approach, which originally had been formulated in a partial equilibrium setting, was reformulated in a general equilibrium framework (Foley 1970). Despite its great theoretical appeal, practical use of the benefit approach is considerably restricted by the information problems that arise from determining the individual marginal benefits, because taxpayers have no incentives to reveal their preferences for public goods.

Capital Theory and Dynamic Methods

Lindahl's contributions to the development of dynamic methods emanated from the elaboration of his macroeconomic theory in the late 1920s and early 1930s. In his essay "The place of capital in the theory of price" (1929 [1939]) Lindahl was led to the formulation of the concept of an "intertemporal equilibrium" from a critique of Wicksell's treatment of capital. He pointed out that Wicksell's approach, in both the Austrian version of *Value, Capital and Rent* (1893 [1954]) and in the formulation which he later adopted in his *Lectures* (1901 [1934]), involves that "the measure of capital is made dependent on the prices of the services invested and on the rate of interest – which belong to the unknown factors of the problem" (1929 [1939]: 317). Lindahl concluded:

> The difficulties here mentioned are associated with the stationary setting of the problem. On account of its artificial and very special assumptions the static problem has little or no connection with the phenomena determining prices in the real world. Therefore the attempt must be made to build up on this foundation an improved analysis which will have more general validity. (1929 [1939]: 317)

This he attempted to do by formulating an intertemporal equilibrium model which extends over a finite number of periods (1929 [1939]: 322–8). Lindahl's model has been praised by Gérard Debreu as a precursor of his own (1959: 35), but exhibits some important conceptual differences with regard to the Arrow–Debreu model. Lindahl conceived of an intertemporal equilibrium as a depiction of an efficient adjustment path to an unexpected change in the long-period data, which (in the absence of further changes in data) terminates in a stationary state. He noted explicitly that this way of approaching the problem of capital and interest opens up the possibility of treating "all existing capital equipment [in the initial period] as original", while capital goods which are "produced in the periods included in the analysis . . . cannot be included among the given factors. Their production is, on the contrary, one of the quantities that, together with prices, are determined by the given factors" (1929 [1939]: 321). Lindahl thus adopted the novel concept because it allowed him to start out, as in the Walras–Cassel model, from given initial endowments with capital goods (specified in physical terms) and then to determine endogenously the quantities of the capital goods which are produced in the following periods before the system finally approaches a stationary equilibrium. He thus avoided the need to specify a given aggregate amount of capital in value terms in the initial period, but nevertheless preserved the traditional idea of a "centre of gravitation" towards which the economic system tends in the absence of further changes in the long-period data.

However, in the last section of the essay (Lindahl 1929 [1939]: 348–50) he substituted imperfect for perfect foresight, and in his next essay, *Penningpolitikens Medel* (*The Aims of Monetary Policy*) (1930 [1939]), he abandoned the intertemporal equilibrium method, for the case of imperfect foresight, and replaced it with the notion of a sequence of temporary equilibria. This concept was soon afterwards adopted (and slightly reformulated) by John Hicks in *Value and Capital* (1946: ch. 9, first published in 1939), but Lindahl was not satisfied with it. Because the method of temporary equilibrium could not handle unforeseen events that occur during a period, and thus failed to generate causal sequences, he replaced it with the method of "sequence analysis" in the first part of his *Studies* (1939: 21–69). Lindahl sought to develop such a causal sequence analysis by incorporating Myrdal's distinction between *ex ante* and *ex post*: he first analysed a single period, in which *ex ante* plans determine *ex post* results, and then linked the periods together by means of a continuation analysis, in which the *ex post* events of the preceding period lead to revised *ex ante* plans in the subsequent period. Hansson (1982) provides a comprehensive account of the development of dynamic methods in the interwar period by members of the Stockholm school.

Monetary Theory and Macroeconomics

In his monetary theory, Lindahl also started out from a critical appraisal of Wicksell's approach, but here his critique was so severe as to lead effectively to its abandonment. Lindahl approved of Wicksell's general approach to monetary analysis, according to which the same sort of mechanisms should be used to explain monetary and "real" phenomena, and stressed that "changes of the price level as well as of relative prices should be explained by the relationship between demand and supply of goods" (1930 [1939]: 245). However, he dismissed Wicksell's concept of the "natural rate of interest", together with the associated idea that it acts as an attractor for the money rate of interest:

> Only under very special assumptions is it possible to conceive of the natural or real rate of interest determined purely by technical considerations, and thus independent of the price system. For this to be true it must be supposed that the productive process consists only in investing the units of goods or services of the same type as the final product, the latter increasing with the passage of time without the cooperation of other scarce factors. . . . Under more realistic assumptions it is not possible to measure the investment and the product in the same real unit. To compare services invested and the resulting products, they must be expressed in a common unit which presupposes that the price relation is given. *Then the real rate of interest does not depend only on technical conditions, but also on the price situation, and cannot be regarded as existing independently of the loan rate of interest.* (1930 [1939]: 247–8; emphasis added)

In *Penningpolitikens Medel* (1930 [1939]) Lindahl investigated the consequences of cumulative processes that are triggered by a lowering of the money rate of interest. Following Wicksell, he, for simplicity, assumed a pure credit economy, in which the monetary authority sets the money rate of interest autonomously (Lindahl 1930 [1939]: 139–41), and then explored in a variety of scenarios the effects on the price level, income, savings, and investment by varying the assumptions regarding investment periods (rigid, non-rigid), resource constraints (fully employed, unemployed resources), expectations formation (static, adaptive, forward-looking), and the state of information (perfect, imperfect foresight). In one of those scenarios Lindahl argued that the credit expansion consequent upon the lowering of the money rate would induce an income redistribution mechanism by means of which savings *ex post* are adapted to the increased level of investment. The rise in the price level that follows from the credit expansion reduces the purchasing power of fixed nominal incomes, but tends to raise the incomes of entrepreneurs, inducing them to plough back their inflationary windfall profits into further investment: "The shift in the price level will be sufficiently large to cause such a change in the distribution of incomes that total savings in the community will correspond to the value of real investment" (1930 [1939]: 175). Lindahl stressed that the amount of "unintentional saving" depends on the assumptions regarding expectations formation: with static expectations, the cumulative price rise "need not continue indefinitely, but comes to an end when the supply of capital has been increased until it corresponds to the new rate of interest" (1930 [1939]: 181). Obviously, savings and investment are here envisaged as being equilibrated not by changes in aggregate income but by variations in income distribution. Lindahl thus anticipated important elements of the Kaldor–Pasinetti theory of distributive shares (see Chiodi and Velupillai 1983; Velupillai 1988). In his later contributions to monetary theory, Lindahl (1957) adopted a monetarist perspective and anticipated the Phelps–Friedman "accelerationist hypothesis" in inflation theory (Boianovsky and Trautwein 2006).

CHRISTIAN GEHRKE

See also:

John Richard Hicks (I); Keynesianism (II); Gunnar Myrdal (I); Post-Keynesianism (II); Stockholm (Swedish) School (II); Knut Wicksell (I).

References and further reading

Böhm, P. (1987), 'Lindahl on public finance', in J. Eatwell, M. Milgate, and P. Newman (eds), *The New Palgrave. A Dictionary of Economics*, vol. 3, London: Macmillan.

Boianovsky, M. and H.-M. Trautwein (2006), 'Price expectations, capital accumulation and employment: Lindahl's macroeconomics from the 1920s to the 1950s', *Cambridge Journal of Economics*, **30** (November), 881–900.

Chiodi, G. and K. Velupillai (1983), 'A note on Lindahl's theory of distribution', *Kyklos*, **36** (1), 103–11.

Debreu, G. (1959), *Theory of Value. An Axiomatic Analysis of Economic Equilibrium*, New York: Wiley.

Foley, D.K. (1970), 'Lindahl's solution and the core of an economy with public goods', *Econometrica*, **38** (1), 66–72.

Hansson, B. (1982), *The Stockholm School and the Development of Dynamic Method*, London: Croom Helm.

Hicks, J. (1946), *Value and Capital. An Inquiry into Some Fundamental Principles of Economic Theory*, 2nd edn, Oxford: Clarendon Press, first published 1939.

Jonung, L. (ed.) (1991), *The Stockholm School of Economics Revisited*, Cambridge: Cambridge University Press.

Lindahl, E. (1919), *Die Gerechtigkeit der Besteuerung. Eine Analyse der Steuerprinzipien auf der Grundlage der Grenznutzentheorie*, Lund: Gleerupska Universitetsbokhandeln and Hakan Ohlsson, English trans. of ch. 4,

'Just taxation – a positive solution', in R.A. Musgrave and A.T. Peacock (eds) (1958), *Classics in the Theory of Public Finance*, London and New York: Macmillan, pp. 168–176.

Lindahl, E. (1928), 'Einige strittige Fragen der Steuertheorie', in: H. Mayer (ed.), *Die Wirtschaftstheorie der Gegenwart*, vol. IV, Vienna: J. Springer, pp. 282–304, English trans. in R.A. Musgrave and A.T. Peacock (eds) (1958), *Classics in the Theory of Public Finance*, London: Macmillan.

Lindahl, E. (1929), 'Prisbildningsproblemets uppläggning från kapitalteoretisk synpunkt', *Ekonomisk Tidskrift*, **31**, 31–81, English trans. 'The place of capital in the theory of price' in E. Lindahl (1939), *Studies in the Theory of Money and Capital*, London: Allen & Unwin, pp. 269–350.

Lindahl, E. (1930), *Penningpolitikens Medel*, Malmö: Förlagsaktiebolaget, English partly trans. as 'The rate of interest and the price level', in E. Lindahl (1939), *Studies in the Theory of Money and Capital*, London: Allen & Unwin, pp. 137–268.

Lindahl, E. (1939a), 'The dynamic approach to economic theory', in E. Lindahl, *Studies in the Theory of Money and Capital*, London: Allen & Unwin, pp. 20–136.

Lindahl, E. (1939b), *Studies in the Theory of Money and Capital*, London: Allen & Unwin.

Lindahl, E. (1957), *Spelet om penningvärdet*, Stockholm: Kooperativa Förbundet, German trans. 1961, 'Das Spiel mit dem Geldwert', *Weltwirtschaftliches Archiv*, **87** (1), 7–53.

Lindahl, E. (1958), 'Just taxation – a positive solution', in R.A. Musgrave and A.T. Peacock (eds), *Classics in the Theory of Public Finance*, London: Macmillan, pp. 98–123.

Steiger, O. (2008), 'Lindahl, Erik Robert (1891–1960)', in S.N. Durlauf and L.E. Blume (eds), *The New Palgrave Dictionary of Economics*, vol. 6, pp. 120–29.

Velupillai, K. (1988), 'Some Swedish stepping stones to modern macroeconomics', *Eastern Economic Journal*, **14**, 87–98.

Wicksell, K. (1893), *Über Wert, Kapital und Rente nach den neueren nationalökonomischen Theorien*, Jena: G. Fischer, English trans. 1954, *Value, Capital and Rent*, London: Allen & Unwin.

Wicksell, K. (1896), *Finanztheoretische Untersuchungen nebst Darstellung und Kritik des Steuerwesens Schwedens*, Jena: G. Fischer.

Wicksell, K. (1901), *Föreläsningar i nationalekonomi*, vol. 1, Stockholm: Fritzes, Lund: Berlingska, English trans. 1934, *Lectures on Political Economy, Volume 1: General Theory*, London: Routledge & Sons.

Adolph Lowe (1893–1995)

Adolph Lowe was born Adolf Löwe on 4 March 1893 to a liberal Jewish family in Stuttgart and died in Wolfenbüttel, Germany on 3 June 1995. Lowe was one of the outstanding political economists of the twentieth century. Unlike most modern economists, he did not separate economics from the other social sciences, so that Kenneth Boulding (1965: 139) characterized Lowe, who during his whole life was striving for a humanist middle way between liberalism and socialism, as an "economic philosopher".

The concern with a viable order, both stable and free, permeates Lowe's entire economic, sociological and philosophical work: from the early analysis in *Arbeitslosigkeit und Kriminalität* (*Unemployment and Criminality*) (1914) via his London School of Economics (LSE) lectures *Economics and Sociology* (1935) making a strong plea for cooperation in the social sciences, his analysis of "spontaneous conformity" in liberal Britain as central for balancing freedom and order successfully for a large-scale society in his essay *The Price of Liberty* (1937), and his elaborations of "Political Economics" as the science of controlled economic systems in *On Economic Knowledge* (1965), up to his last work *Has Freedom a Future?* (1988), in which Lowe has become more sceptical due to many destabilizing factors at work, such as technological unemployment, enormous inequalities of income and wealth, and ecological crises. Here Lowe stresses the danger that the failures of a free market system could be aggravated by failures of the political system, a danger which has become real in the current financial and economic crisis. This peril could only be avoided by revitalizing the Western tradition (going back to Aristotle's philosophy) properly understood: an individualism rooted in social responsibility which balances the private and the public domains, that is, freedom and order (Hagemann and Kurz 1990).

Lowe strongly argues for an ethics in which individualism is combined with social responsibility. Although he shares his birthplace with Hegel, Lowe thus stands much more in a Kantian tradition. His social liberalism is deeply rooted in his biography and has much in common with Keynes who also favoured governmental interventionism in periods of great economic and political crises to safeguard the democracy. The ends of these interventions are themselves subject to the checks and balances of the democratic process. Political economics and the social sciences are essentially recognized as moral sciences. The work of Lowe, who had been an active member of the group of religious socialists around his close friend Paul Tillich – the most distinguished Protestant theologian in Weimar Germany – to defend the young Republic, is deeply rooted in a common Jewish-Christian culture.

From 1911 to 1915 Lowe studied law, economics and philosophy at the universities of Munich, Berlin and Tübingen where he received his doctorate in law in November 1918. The main stimulus as an economist Lowe received from Lujo Brentano in Munich and Franz Oppenheimer in Berlin. At the end of World War I Lowe became a chief economic adviser to the young Weimar Republic. From 1919 to 1924 he served as Section Head in the Ministry of Economics, being involved with issues of reparation policy and drafting the memoranda which the German government presented at the conferences in Genoa 1922 and Paris 1924 (Dawes plan; see also Krohn 1996).

From 1924 to 1926 he was Head of the International Division of the German Bureau of Statistics and assisted the President Ernst Wagemann to found the first German

Institute for Business Cycle Research in Berlin in 1925. In early 1926 Lowe accepted an offer by Bernhard Harms, the President of the Kiel Institute of World Economics, to become Director of Research of a new department of statistical international economics and international trade cycles. Owing to outstanding scholars such as Gerhard Colm, Hans Neisser, Fritz (Frank) Burchardt (who in 1949 became Director of the Oxford Institute of Statistics), Wassily Leontief and Jacob Marschak, the department soon obtained international reputation and substantial research money from the Rockefeller Foundation. In October 1931 Lowe, who had been appointed Professor of Economic Theory and Sociology at the University of Kiel in February 1930, moved to the Goethe University in Frankfurt, where in April 1933 he was among the first professors to be dismissed by the Nazis for racial and political reasons.

The first hosting country in exile was the United Kingdom where Lowe became special Honorary Lecturer in economics and political philosophy at the University of Manchester in 1933 and, together with Marschak in Oxford, one of the main advisers of the Rockefeller Foundation on émigré economists. In England Lowe also became a naturalized citizen in September 1939: 'Löwe' mutated to 'Lowe'. In summer 1940 he accepted a renewed offer from the New School for Social Research in New York. There Lowe served as Professor of Economics until his retirement in 1963, and also as Director of Research at the Institute of World Affairs between 1943 and 1951. He continued teaching until the late 1970s and remained a very active researcher which is best reflected in the fact that his two main works *On Economic Knowledge* (1965) and *The Path of Economic Growth* (1976) were published rather late. After the death of his wife Beatrice Loewenstein, Lowe returned to Germany in March 1983, exactly half a century after his forced departure.

Lowe played a major role in the debates on business cycles in the 1920s. It was particularly his seminal Kiel habilitation thesis with the Kantian-inspired question "How is business cycle theory possible at all?" which had a significant impact on subsequent debates in the German language area and to some extent also internationally (see, for example, Kuznets 1930a, 1930b). In his "brilliant article" (Kuznets 1930b: 128) Lowe pointed out a fundamental methodological dilemma of business-cycle theory: how can the traditional equilibrium concept in economics – which Lowe, inspired by Schumpeter, also called static system – cope with an essentially disequilibrium phenomenon such as cyclical fluctuations? Lowe's conclusion is clear: "Those who wish to solve the business cycle problem must sacrifice the static system. Those who adhere to the static system must abandon the business cycle problem" (Lowe 1926 [1997]: 267). Lowe was fully endorsed by Kuznets who concluded that "equilibrium economics was . . . adding the dead weight of a barren doctrine to the burdens of a complex reality" (1930a: 390) and regarded "the equilibrium approach . . . to be a blind alley from the point of view of business-cycle theory" (ibid.: 399).

Hayek took up Lowe's fundamental methodological challenge concerning the (in) compatibility of business-cycle theory with the equilibrium approach in the first chapter of his *Monetary Theory and the Trade Cycle*. He agrees with Lowe "that the incorporation of cyclical phenomena into the system of economic equilibrium theory, with which they are in apparent contradiction, remains the crucial problem of Trade Cycle theory" (Hayek 1929 [1933]: 33). However, in the conclusions drawn, Hayek differed substantially from Lowe (see Hagemann 1994). Whereas Lowe wanted to abandon the equilibrium approach in business-cycle theory, Hayek adhered to the equilibrium concept as an indispensable tool. In contrast to Lowe (and Schumpeter) who emphasized technical progress as the decisive impulse, Hayek (and Mises) attributed the cycle to monetary factors. Both, Lowe and Hayek, emphasized the importance of the underlying structure of production. However, whereas Lowe had found the basis of his later works on the structural theory of economic growth very early in Marx's scheme of expanded reproduction, in which emphasis is on the "horizontal" or sectoral treatment of production, Hayek remained in the Austrian tradition, originated by Böhm-Bawerk, with a "vertical" treatment of production structures and emphasis on the time dimension.

In more than 60 years of research, Lowe focused on technological change as the mainspring of destabilizing tendencies in industrial economies. His attempt to develop a theory of accumulation, technical progress, and structural change culminated in his *The Path of Economic Growth* (1976). It shows Lowe as a pioneer of traverse analysis along with John Hicks who in his *Capital and Time* (1973) had also been fascinated by Ricardo's analysis of the machinery problem. However, whereas Hicks investigates the short- and medium-run consequences of innovations on the basis of a neo-Austrian representation of production structures, Lowe uses a horizontal model in which inter-sectoral interdependencies and the existing stock of capital goods as a decisive physical bottleneck are emphasized. Lowe had developed the structural model of production which he used for his traverse analysis already in two articles (Lowe 1952, 1955), written in the wake of the foundation of modern growth theory by Harrod and Domar. He modified Marx's schemes of reproduction by splitting up the investment goods sector into two parts, thus extending the two-sectoral into a three-sectoral model (see also Hagemann 1990). Lowe's instrumental analysis (Lowe 1965), the core of which consists in deriving suitable means from given ends – such as a successful compensation of technological unemployment – has two parts: structural analysis and force analysis, which reveals the crucial role of expectations and the significance of a functioning price mechanism in market economies.

HARALD HAGEMANN

See also:
Friedrich August von Hayek (I); John Richard Hicks (I); Wassily W. Leontief (I); Jacob Marschak (I).

References and further reading
Boulding, K.E. (1965), 'Is economics obsolescent?', *Scientific American*, **212** (May), 139–43.
Hagemann, H. (1990), 'The structural theory of economic growth', in M. Baranzini and R. Scazzieri (eds), *The Economic Theory of Structure and Change*, Cambridge: Cambridge University Press, pp. 144–71.
Hagemann, H. (1994), 'Hayek and the Kiel School: some reflections on the German debate on business cycles in the late 1920s and the early 1930s', in M. Colonna and H. Hagemann (eds), *Money and Business Cycles. The Economics of F.A. Hayek*, vol. 1, Aldershot, UK and Brookfield, VT, USA: Edward Elgar, pp. 101–20.
Hagemann, H. and H.D. Kurz (1990), 'Balancing freedom and order: on Adolph Lowe's political economics', *Social Research*, **57** (3), 734–53.
Hagemann, H. and H.D. Kurz (1998), *Political Economics in Retrospect. Essays in Memory of Adolph Lowe*, Cheltenham, UK and Northampton, MA, USA: Edward Elgar, contains a full bibliography of Lowe's published writings.
Hayek, F.A. (1929), *Geldtheorie und Konjunkturtheorie*, Vienna, English trans. 1933, *Monetary Theory and the Trade Cycle*, London: J.J. Cape.
Hicks, J. (1973), *Capital and Time. A Neo-Austrian Theory*, Oxford: Clarendon Press.
Krohn, C.-D. (1996), *Der Philosophische Ökonom. Zur intellektuellen Biographie Adolph Lowes*, Marburg: Metropolis.

Kuznets, S. (1930a), 'Equilibrium economics and business-cycle theory', *Quarterly Journal of Economics*, **44** (3), 381–415.

Kuznets, S. (1930b), 'Monetary business cycle theory in Germany', *Journal of Political Economy*, **38** (2), 125–63.

Löwe, A. (1914), *Arbeitslosigkeit und Kriminalität*, Berlin: J. Guttentag.

Löwe, A. (1926), 'Wie ist Konjunkturtheorie überhaupt möglich?', *Weltwirtschaftliches Archiv*, **24**, 165–97, English trans. 1997, 'How is business cycle theory possible at all?', *Structural Change and Economic Dynamics*, **8** (2), 245–70.

Löwe, A. (1935), *Economics and Sociology*, London: Allen & Unwin.

Löwe, A. (1937), *The Price of Liberty. An Essay on Contemporary Britain*, London: Hogarth Press.

Lowe, A. (1952), 'A structural model of production', *Social Research*, **19** (1), 135–76.

Lowe, A. (1955), 'Structural analysis of real capital formation', in M. Abramovitz (ed.), *Capital Formation and Economic Growth*, Princeton, NJ: Princeton University Press, pp. 581–634.

Lowe, A. (1965), *On Economic Knowledge. Towards a Science of Political Economics*, New York: Harper and Row.

Lowe, A. (1976), *The Path of Economic Growth*, Cambridge: Cambridge University Press.

Lowe, A. (1988), *Has Freedom a Future?*, New York: Praeger.

Ragnar Anton Kittil Frisch (1895–1973)

Ragnar Anton Kittil Frisch was born on 3 March 1895 in Kristiania (Oslo), Norway. His father, Anton Frisch, was a jeweller descending from a mining specialist from Saxony who had come to Norway in the seventeenth century. Ragnar was the only child and groomed to continue the family business. He credited his mother, Ragna Fredrikke Kittilsen, for having influenced his general outlook on life and for having insisted that he took up a university study along with his apprenticeship to become a silversmith. The short (two-year) study of economics was chosen (Nobel Foundation 1969b).

Ragnar Frisch is known in particular for his role in creating econometrics. He coined 'econometrics' as the name of a new discipline in economics outlining an ambitious research program (Frisch 1926). He gathered support for the idea by initiating and being the driving force behind the establishment of the Econometric Society in 1930, for a long time the only international organization in economics. Frisch launched during 1926–36 a number of ground-breaking ideas for the new econometric discipline, one of which was his propagation-impulse explanation of business cycles (Frisch 1933a), alluded to in the caption for the first *Sveriges Riksbank Prize in Economic Sciences in Memory of Alfred Nobel* awarded to Ragnar Frisch in 1969 (jointly with Jan Tinbergen) "for having developed and applied dynamic models for the analysis of economic processes" (Nobel Foundation 1969a).

At his graduation in economics in 1919, Frisch ended his examination paper in public finance as follows: "Man must not be deterred by the apparently impossible. History has shown that the human beings have had a wonderful ability for obeying the maxim of Aristotle: *Make the unmeasurable measurable!*". By these unusual words in an examination paper Frisch stated an overriding concern in his future work, not least in the measurement of utility.

Shortly after graduation Frisch completed his probation work as a silversmith. His father made him partner in the jeweller's shop which at the time was a flourishing business. This allowed the newlywed Ragnar and Marie Frisch to spend two to three years abroad for Ragnar's studies, mostly in Paris but also visiting England, Germany and Italy. In 1926 the doctoral degree was conferred on Ragnar Frisch at the University of Kristiania for a dissertation in mathematical statistics.

During 1927–28 Frisch visited the United States on a Rockefeller Fellowship. It allowed him to propagate the idea of an association and a journal to promote econometrics in the USA. He found partners for this venture in Irving Fisher, Charles Roos, and Joseph Schumpeter. Soon after his return to Europe his father died while the jeweller's shop was in dire economic straits. Frisch was facing having to give up a scientific career. A generous offer from Irving Fisher for Frisch to visit Yale University 1930–31 became decisive. During the visit Fisher and Frisch joined forces in founding the Econometric Society. Frisch was later elected as Editor of *Econometrica*, a position he held for 22 years. While Frisch was still in the USA he was appointed professor in Oslo in an effort to pre-empt Frisch from accepting an offer from Yale University. Frisch returned to Norway, negotiated a grant from the Rockefeller Foundation allowing him to establish the Institute of Economics in 1932. It became his econometric laboratory. His student Trygve Haavelmo became a co-worker and his later well-known contribution to econometrics was rooted in the fertile research environment of Frisch.

As author of path-breaking econometric works, a most forceful participant of the early European meetings of the Econometric Society, and at the same time Editor of *Econometrica*, Ragnar Frisch put a strong mark on the emerging econometric community. In Paul Samuelson's words "Frisch dominated analytical economics from the early 1930's founding of the Econometric Society to his wartime internment . . . combining fertility and versatility with depth" (Samuelson 1974: 7). Frisch's small laboratory institute, which served as a model for research facilities in other countries, was visited by a number of young scholars until World War II subdued the activity. In 1943 Frisch was arrested and put in a detention camp by the wartime Nazi regime. In the long postwar period until his death in 1973 Frisch continued to be very active in research but no longer at centre stage on the international scene. Some of his old ideas appeared in new and fruitful settings. He vented his dissatisfaction with aspects of the development within econometrics – labelling it playometrics – at the first World Congress of the Econometric Society in 1965.

Frisch's econometric research program may in general terms best be described as turning economics into a real science "by constructive and rigorous thinking similar to that which has come to dominate in the natural sciences" (as quoted from the Constitution of the Econometric Society). The tenor of this pursuit can best be assessed from lecture series at Yale 1930 and at the Sorbonne 1933, recently issued as Bjerkholt and Qin (2010) and Bjerkholt and Dupont-Kieffer (2009). The remarkable early work of Frisch (1926) was devoted to demonstrating that marginal utility could be "quantified" as a theoretical concept, as had been the "dream of Jevons". The approach, influenced by Irving Fisher, was to establish a set of choice axioms from which the existence of a utility indicator could be derived. Frisch's further work on measuring utility comprised *New Methods of Measuring Marginal Utility* (Frisch 1932) and a penetrating contribution to index theory (Frisch 1936). Frisch's utility measurement ebbed out in the mid-1930s at criticism that his results were based on too narrow assumptions and under the impact of the new demand theory of Hicks, Allen and others which rejected the implied cardinalism of Frisch's approach. A late spin-off was the much cited Frisch (1959).

Frisch (1933a) in "Propagation problems and impulse problems", embodying Knut Wicksell's deceptively simple simile of the rocking-horse, explained economic fluctuations as the interaction of a system of dynamic structural equations and a stream of random shocks hitting the economy. The penetrating analysis of the role of random shocks in the economy was inspired by Eugen Slutsky. Methodologically, Frisch was way ahead of all other attempts at the time of explaining business cycles. His article introduced the idea of a macroeconomic model with macroeconomic aggregates quantified from (not yet existing) national accounts.

Ragnar Frisch made profound contributions towards developing statistical methods for use in economics. He realized at an early stage the limitations inherent in economic observations being "passive observations" resulting from economic mechanisms representing simultaneous equations. He criticized sharply empirical analysis applying regression methods in studies not properly guided by theory and for neglecting that economic relationships typically are part of a system of simultaneous relations. Another early work, the "Pitfalls" treatise (Frisch 1933b) was the first analytic discussion of the identification problem in the two-variable, two-equation problem of supply/demand curves. Then followed *Statistical Confluence Analysis* (Frisch 1934a), designed as a general tool for the determination of structural economic relations. The non-probabilistic approach of the confluence analysis caused it to be left by the wayside when the Cowles Commission approach became popular in the late 1940s.

In the area of production theory Frisch pursued the general econometric programme of providing a conceptually rich mathematized structure of production suitable for applied theoretical work and applicable to empirical quantification. Frisch's innovative mathematization of production theory stemmed from around 1930 but was not published internationally until much later. Frisch applied the production theory in an analysis which is recognized as the first specimen of an "engineering production function" approach (Førsund 1999).

After World War II, Frisch's interest shifted towards issues relevant for national (and international) economic development and he took little part in the international theoretical development. Frisch developed at his institute a series of policy-oriented models, his own term was "decision models". The first of these, "Price-wage-tax-subsidy policies as instruments in maintaining optimal employment" (Frisch 1949), was developed while Frisch was chairing a UN Commission on Employment and Economic Stability and designed to address the unemployment problems in constrained post-war economies. Frisch's modelling approaches and modelling philosophy was set out in a number of papers; see Kloc (1972). Frisch spent a year in India in the mid-1950s working with Prasanta Mahalanobis on the Indian five-year plan. He exerted an influence on national planning in the United Arab Republic through several visits during the 1960s.

Important elements in Frisch's concept of national economic modelling were (1) objective functions reflecting the policy makers' preferences, and (2) computational methods for achieving optimal solutions. He put considerable effort into developing methods for eliciting explicit macroeconomic preference functions through a sophisticated interview technique (Bjerkholt and Strøm 2002). On optimization, Frisch pioneered in the mid-1950s new approaches to the solution of linear programming problems. Frisch's interest in this field can be traced back to his formulation of linear and linear-quadratic programming problems in the 1930s. His logarithmic potential method from 1956 for solving linear programming problems anticipated by 28 years Karmarkar's interior-point algorithm beating the simplex method for all large problems (Konker 2000). In both these accounts Frisch's ventures were much ahead of their time.

Frisch was more of a methodological problem solver than a theoretician. His general attitude towards problem solving is revealed in a quote from a 1934 paper on remedies counteracting market collapse during a depression: "We have here one of those cases – so frequent in economic practice – where it can be 'proved' by abstract reasoning that a solution is not possible, but where life itself compels us nevertheless to find a way out" (Frisch 1934b: 274). Examples of originality in Frisch's work can be found in Frisch (1933c), an early work outlining a game-theoretic approach to market solutions, and the intriguing "On welfare theory and Pareto regions" (Frisch 1954 [1959]). Frisch's rather unusual Nobel speech (Frisch 1970) touched upon a number of widely different topics, including his epistemological view suggesting that the regularities we observe in economics are really figments of the human mind, while the outer world is entirely chaotic.

Many of Frisch's theoretical contributions and ideas were accompanied with new terms and concepts, some of which entered the basic vocabulary of economics, such as econometrics, macroeconomics, and microeconomics. In production theory he introduced, for example, isoquant, isocline, substitumal, pari-passu, ultra-passum, and passus coefficient. Frisch (1959) gave us Slutsky elasticity and Slutsky equation. It also introduced want elasticity, in the literature later renamed as Frisch elasticity. Samuelson (1974: 8) made the remark that the term "model" as used in economics had been introduced by Frisch. It may seem to hint at an argument in Bjerkholt and Qin (2010: 31–2) comprising the following passage:

> The observational world itself, taken as a whole in its infinite complexity . . . is impossible to grasp. . . . we make an intellectual trick: In our mind we create a little model world of our own, a model world which is not too complicated to be overlooked . . . And then we analyze this little model world instead of the real world. This mental trick is the thing which constitutes the rational method, that is, theory.

Frisch was born into the liberal bourgeoisie. At the depth of depression in the 1930s he affiliated with the Labour Party of Norway, which he abandoned in the 1960s. Frisch joined forces with Joan Robinson (but was opposed by Jan Tinbergen) in scepticism toward the Treaty of Rome, denoting it as representing "unenlightened financialism". The wringing pains of the European monetary union in recent years would hardly have surprised him.

Outside economics Frisch had other passionate callings. He kept bees, specializing on queen bee rearing; it was more than a hobby and also a field for publication. Frisch seemed quite dependent upon spending weeks in often remote mountain areas, hiking by day and working on economic and econometric problems at night.

OLAV BJERKHOLT

See also:

Business cycles and growth (III); Econometrics (III); Economic dynamics (III); Macroeconomics (III).

References and further reading

Arrow, K. (1960), 'The work of Ragnar Frisch, econometrician', *Econometrica*, **28** (2), 175–92.

Bjerkholt, O. and A. Dupont-Kieffer (eds) (2009), *Problems and Methods of Econometrics. The Poincaré Lectures of Ragnar Frisch 1933*, London: Routledge.

Bjerkholt, O. and D. Qin (eds) (2010), *A Dynamic Approach to Economic Theory. The Yale Lectures of Ragnar Frisch, 1930*, London: Routledge.

Bjerkholt, O. and S. Strøm (2002), 'Decision models and preferences: the pioneering contribution of Ragnar Frisch', in A.S. Tangian and J. Gruber (eds), *Constructing and Applying Objective Functions*, Berlin: Springer, pp. 17–36.

Førsund, F.R. (1999), 'On the contribution of Ragnar Frisch to production theory', *Rivista Internazionale di Scienze Economiche e Commerciali*, **46** (1), 1–34.

Frisch, R. (1926), 'Sur un problème d'économie pure', *Norsk Matematisk Forenings Skrifter*, series I (16), 1–40.

Frisch, R. (1932), *New Methods of Measuring Marginal Utility*, Tübingen: Verlag von J.C.B. Mohr (Paul Siebeck).

Frisch, R. (1933a), 'Propagation problems and impulse problems in dynamic economics', in K. Koch (ed.), *Economic Essays in Honour of Gustav Cassel*, London: Allen & Unwin, pp. 171–205.

Frisch, R. (1933b), 'Pitfalls in the statistical construction of demand and supply curves', *Veröffentlichungen der Frankfurter Gesellschaft für Konjunkturforschung*, New Series, no. 5, Leipzig: Hans Buske Verlag.

Frisch, R. (1933c), 'Monopole – Polypole – La notion de force dans l'économie', *Nationaløkonomisk Tidsskrift*, **71**, supplement, 241–59.

Frisch, R. (1934a), *Statistical Confluence Analysis by Means of Complete Regression Systems*, Publication no. 5, Institute of Economics, Oslo.

Frisch, R. (1934b), 'Circulation planning: proposal for a national organisation of a commodity and service exchange', *Econometrica*, **2** (3), 258–336, (4 October), 422–35.
Frisch, R. (1936), 'Annual survey of general economic theory: the problem of index numbers', *Econometrica*, **4** (1), 1–38.
Frisch, R. (1949), 'Price-wage-tax-subsidy policies as instruments in maintaining optimal employment. A memorandum on analytical machinery to be used in discussions on causes of and remedies to unemployment', E/CN.1/Sub.2/13, 18 April, United Nations.
Frisch, R. (1954), 'La théorie de l'avantage collectif et les régions de Pareto', *Économie Appliquée*, **7**, 211–80, English trans, 1959 'On welfare theory and Pareto regions', *International Economic Papers*, no. 9, 39–92.
Frisch, R. (1959), 'A complete scheme for computing all direct and cross demand elasticities in a model with many sectors', *Econometrica*, **27** (2), 177–96.
Frisch, R. (1970), 'From utopian theory to practical applications: the case of econometrics', *Réimpression de Les Prix Nobel en 1969*, 213–43.
Kloc, E.M. (1972), 'The planning models of Ragnar Frisch', *Socio-Economic Planning Sciences*, **6** (5), 437–55.
Konker, R. (2000), 'Galton, Edgeworth, Frisch, and prospects for quantile regression in econometrics', *Journal of Econometrics*, **95** (2), 347–74.
Nobel Foundation (1969a), 'The Sveriges Riksbank Prize in Economic Sciences in Memory of Alfred Nobel 1969', Nobelprize.org, accessed 27 November 2015 at http://www.nobelprize.org/nobel_prizes/economic-sciences/laureates/1969/.
Nobel Foundation (1969b), 'Ragnar Frisch – Biographical', Nobelprize.org, accessed 27 November 2015 at http://www.nobelprize.org/nobel_prizes/economic-sciences/laureates/1969/frisch-bio.html.
Samuelson, P.A. (1974), 'Remembrances of Frisch', *European Economic Review*, **5** (1), 7–23.

Jacob Marschak (1898–1977)

Marschak was born in Kiev, Russia on 23 July 1898 and died in Los Angeles on 27 July 1977. He had one of the most adventurous biographies of an economist in the twentieth century (Arrow 1979; Hagemann 1997; Radner 1984). At the age of 19 Marschak became Secretary of Labour in a revolutionary government of the Terek Republic in the Northern Caucasus (Marschak 1971). When he died Marschak was President Elect of the American Economic Association. He was twice forced to emigrate: after the Bolshevist revolution in January 1919, and after the Nazis' rise to power in March 1933.

Marschak's professional career extended over 58 years and across three countries: Weimar Germany (1919–33), the United Kingdom (1933–38) and the United States. He got his PhD from the University of Heidelberg in 1922. His thesis on the quantity equation (Marschak 1924b) indicated already his lifelong interest in monetary macroeconomics. Marschak later was open to an independent reception of Keynes's theory, as reflected in his Chicago lectures *Income, Employment and the Price Level* (Marschak 1951), and his two outstanding PhD students, Franco Modigliani and Don Patinkin, who both made substantial contributions to modern macroeconomics.

In his first major publication Marschak (1924a) critically investigates Mises's thesis of the impossibility of economic calculation in the socialist commonwealth because there is no price formation in free markets. Marschak objects to Mises empirically that in capitalist economies with an increasing number of cartels and trusts the requirements of price formation on free markets are not fulfilled, and theoretically that this growing number of trusts shows that the advantages of monopolistic calculation exist mainly in the economic calculation for goods of higher order and in the sphere of dynamics, that is, those two areas which are particularly affected by Mises's scepticism. Marschak's analysis, which Arrow (1979: 502) classifies as one of his "papers with the greatest permanent interest", has much in common with Schumpeter's view on the subject and links up well with his later theory of teams (Marschak and Radner 1972), which provided a powerful tool for the analysis of the relative informational efficiencies of decentralized price expectations and emphasized the importance of communications and its limits in the transmission of information.

In the wake of a longer visit to Italy Marschak (1924c) gave one of the first well-informed analyses of Italian fascism, which also reveals the comprehensive socio-economic training he had received with his teachers Emil Lederer and Alfred Weber at Heidelberg. This is also brought to the fore in joint studies with Lederer on the role of the new middle classes which they regarded as critical for a greater stability of democracy.

From 1924 to 1926 Marschak worked as an economic journalist in the editorial staff of the leading liberal newspaper *Frankfurter Zeitung*, and from 1926 to 1928 on the staff of the Research Centre for Economic Policy, sponsored by the German trade unions and the Social-democratic parliamentary group of the Reichstag in Berlin. There, in 1927, he married Marianne Berta Kamnitzer with whom he had two children: Angela (Ann Jernberg), who became a psychotherapist, and Thomas, who became a long-time professor at the Haas School of Business at the University of California in Berkeley.

From 1928 to 1930 Marschak worked as a research supervisor for a parliamentary commission on exporting industries in the department on business cycles founded by Adolph Lowe at the Kiel Institute for World Economics. During that period he became increasingly interested in the new econometric movement. In Kiel he also wrote his habilitation thesis *Elasticity of Demand* (1931) which Marschak submitted to the University of Heidelberg. There he became Privatdozent on 22 February 1930, a position from which he was dismissed for his 'non-Aryan descent' by the Nazis on 20 April 1933.

Marschak also played a major role among the minority group of German economists arguing strongly against a deflationary wage policy as the central element of economic policy in the Great Depression (Hagemann 1999). In particular Marschak (1930) was a differentiated defender of the purchasing power argument emphasizing that a reallocation of purchasing power owing to wage reductions (increases) is associated with a change in the structural composition of production and that the goods consumed by workers are subjected to the law of mass production to a higher degree than those goods consumed by capitalists.

The Nazis' rise to power caused Marschak's second emigration in March 1933. In autumn 1933 he became Chichele Lecturer in Economics at All Souls College in Oxford. In 1935 Marschak was appointed Reader of Statistics, and became the founding Director of the Oxford Institute of Statistics (OIS) which was financially supported by the Rockefeller Foundation. In September 1936 the OIS hosted the famous conference of the Econometric Society where Hicks (1937) first presented his IS–LM model. Marschak had become a charter member of the Econometric Society in 1931, and was appreciated by Frisch and Tinbergen alike as a leading young scholar in this field. During his British period Marschak was involved in studies on the mobility of labour, and published his article "Money and the theory of assets" (1938), which was the first out of a series on the theory of portfolio choice influencing later work by Harry Markowitz and James Tobin. Marschak's later attempts to clarify the concept of liquidity show the importance of acquisition of new information for economic behaviour. The roots of his interest on these issues date back to the early experiences Marschak made with substitutes of money in the revolutionary and hyperinflationary period in the Northern Caucasus (Marschak 1971: 31–2, 48–9).

Marschak, who had gone to the United States with a one-year fellowship by the Rockefeller Foundation in December 1938, did not return to Britain after the outbreak of World War II. In September 1939 he was appointed Professor at the New School for Social Research as the successor of Gerhard Colm who had joined the Roosevelt administration. In New York Marschak organized a seminar on econometrics and mathematical economics on behalf of the National Bureau of Economic Research which was a kind of prelude to the Chicago period "that brought out his leadership qualities in full strength" (Koopmans 1978: XI). In January 1943 Marschak became professor at the University of Chicago and director of the Cowles Commission for Research in Economics.

Under the directorship of Marschak (1943–49) and Koopmans, the Cowles Commission soon became the world centre of the 'econometric revolution' in economics (Christ 1994). The statistical estimation of systems of simultaneous equations, as explored in the pioneering contributions by Haavelmo (1943), Mann and Wald (1943) and Marschak and Andrews (1944), as well as the probability approach in econometrics (Haavelmo 1944), soon became the trademark of the Cowles Commission. Marschak attracted a remarkable staff of researchers of whom many later received the Nobel Prize. During this period he was elected Vice President (1944–45) and President (1946–47) of the Econometric Society and Vice President of the American Statistical Association, and later (1967) became Distinguished Fellow of the American Economic Association. When in 1955 Tobin took over the directorship of the Cowles Commission, now renamed the Cowles Foundation and shifted to Yale, Marschak also left Chicago and became professor at Yale. From there he moved in 1960 to his final destination, the University of California at Los Angeles, where he was from 1965 until his retirement in 1971, also Director of the Western Management Science Institute.

Marschak's work since 1950 focused on economic decision-making in the face of uncertainty and the economic value and the costs of information (see volumes I and II of Marschak 1974, Radner 1984). Inspired by John von Neumann and Oskar Morgenstern's development of game theory, Marschak introduced the concept of a "team" into economics which he later elaborated with Roy Radner into an *Economic Theory of Teams* (Marschak and Radner 1972). The theory of teams provided a powerful tool for the analysis of the relative informational efficiencies of decentralized price mechanisms. It thus links up well with his first scientific contribution on the socialist calculation debate. Just as Koopmans has pointed out that Marschak "was a citizen of the World" who "remained very Russian and very Jewish throughout these changes" (1978: X), we thus can identify in Marschak's concern with the value and theory of money and of decision-making under uncertainty by individuals, institutions and policy-makers a remarkable element of path-dependency and continuity throughout his whole professional life.

HARALD HAGEMANN

See also:

Kenneth Joseph Arrow (I); Econometrics (III); Adolph Lowe (I); Ludwig Heinrich von Mises (I); Don Patinkin (I).

References and further reading

Arrow, K.J. (1979), 'Marschak, Jacob', in D.L. Sills (ed.), *International Encyclopedia of the Social Sciences, Vol. 18: Biographical Supplement*, New York and London: Macmillan, pp. 500–507.
Christ, C. (1994), 'The Cowles Commission's contributions to econometrics at Chicago, 1939–1955', *Journal of Economic Literature*, **32** (1), 30–59.
Haavelmo, T. (1943), 'The statistical implications of a system of simultaneous equations', *Econometrica*, **11** (1), 1–12.
Haavelmo, T. (1944), 'The probability approach in econometrics', *Econometrica*, **12** (1), 1–115.
Hagemann, H. (1997), 'Jacob Marschak (1998–1977)', in R. Blomert, H.U. Esslinger and N. Giovannini (eds), *Heidelberger Sozial- und Staatswissenschaften. Das Institut für Sozial- und Staatswissenschaften zwischen 1918 und 1958*, Marburg: Metropolis, pp. 219–54.
Hagemann, H. (1999), 'The analysis of wages and unemployment revisited: Keynes and economic "activists" in pre-Hitler Germany', in L.L. Pasinetti and B. Schefold (eds), *The Impact of Keynes on Economics in the 20th Century*, Cheltenham, UK and Northampton, MA, USA: Edward Elgar, pp. 117–30.
Hicks, J.R. (1937), 'Mr. Keynes and the "Classics": a suggested interpretation', *Econometrica*, **5** (2), 147–59.
Koopmans, T.C. (1978), 'Jacob Marschak, 1898–1977', *American Economic Review*, **68** (2), IX–XI.
Mann, H.B. and A. Wald (1943), 'On the statistical treatment of linear stochastic difference equations', *Econometrica*, **11** (2), 173–220.
Marschak, J. (1924a), 'Wirtschaftsrechnung und Gemeinwirtschaft. Zur Mises'schen These von der Unmöglichkeit sozialistischer Wirtschaftsrechnung', *Archiv für Sozialwissenschaft und Sozialpolitik*, **51**, 501–20.
Marschak, J. (1924b), 'Die Verkehrsgleichung', *Archiv für Sozialwissenschaft und Sozialpolitik*, **52**, 344–84.
Marschak, J. (1924c), 'Der korporative und der hierarchische Gedanke im Fascismus I + II', *Archiv für Sozialwissenschaft und Sozialpolitik*, **52**, 695–72, **53**, 81–140.
Marschak, J. (1930), 'Das Kaufkraft-Argument in der Lohnpolitik', *Magazin der Wirtschaft*, **6** (11), 1443–7.

Marschak, J. (1931), *Elastizität der Nachfrage*, Tübingen: J.C.B. Mohr.
Marschak, J. (1938), 'Money and the theory of assets', *Econometrica*, **6** (4), 311–25.
Marschak, J. (1951), *Income, Employment and the Price Level*, New York: Sentry Press.
Marschak, J. (1971), 'Recollections of Kiew and the Northern Caucasus, 1917–18', an interview conducted by Richard A. Pierce, University of California, Regional Oral History Office, Bancroft Library, Berkeley, CA.
Marschak, J. (1974), *Economic Information, Decision, and Prediction. Selected Essays*, 3 vols, Dordrecht and Boston, MA: Reidel.
Marschak, J. and W.H. Andrews (1944), 'Random simultaneous equations and the theory of production', *Econometrica*, **12** (3 and 4), 143–205.
Marschak, J. and R. Radner (1972), *Economic Theory of Teams*, New Haven, CT: Yale University Press.
Radner, R. (1984), 'On Marschak', in H.W. Spiegel and W.J. Samuels (eds), *Contemporary Economists in Perspective*, Greenwich, CT and London: JAI Press, pp. 443–60.

Gunnar Myrdal (1898–1987)

When Gunnar Myrdal (born 1898) had passed away in 1987, the *New York Times* wrote:

> Mr. Myrdal has been called the leading economist and social scientist of his epoch. Statesman, reformer, dissenter, pacifist and foe of inequality, an architect of the Swedish welfare state, he literally left his mark in a footnote to history – the famous footnote 11 to the United States Supreme Court's 1954 ruling that segregation in public schools was unconstitutional. (*New York Times*, 18 May 1987)

It might be disputed that Myrdal was the leading economist in his epoch, which lasted for almost half a century from the early 1930s onwards. Yet he was certainly one of the most prominent representatives and critics of his discipline. His success derived largely from applying the principle of circular and cumulative causation to different economic and social contexts.

Myrdal was a student of Gustav Cassel, whom he succeeded as professor of political economy and public finance at the University of Stockholm in 1933. In his doctoral dissertation on "price formation and changeability", Myrdal (1927) attempted to transform Cassel's static framework of general equilibrium analysis into a dynamic theory. Myrdal's innovation was to include expectations in the set of data that determine prices, in addition to tastes, technology and factor endowments. Various constellations of expectations and their interaction in the markets lead to different disequilibria and to multiple equilibria. This became a recurrent theme in Myrdal's later work, and it was the first step towards the conceptualization of circular and cumulative processes.

The second step was *Monetary Equilibrium* (1931 [1939]), a critical reconstruction of Knut Wicksell's theory of interest and prices (1898). Wicksell had argued that inflation and deflation are caused by divergences of the money rate of interest from the "natural rate", defining the latter as the yield on real capital that brings investment in line with planned saving, independently of changes in the monetary sphere. In Wicksell's theory, the changes in the price level continue in a cumulative fashion until the money rate converges on the natural rate. Myrdal (1931 [1939]: 45–53) demonstrated that, outside a stationary barter economy, the yield on real capital cannot be captured in terms of marginal physical productivity, but needs to be expressed as expected profitability in terms of exchange value productivity. This implies feedbacks from changes in the price level and the market rate of interest to the (no longer) "natural rate". In his redefinition of the equilibrium rate of interest as the rate at which the "cost of production of new investment" equals "free capital disposal", Myrdal (1931 [1939]: 84–97) anticipated the formulation of Tobin's q. While the idea of cumulative processes was Wicksell's, the term was Myrdal's creation; and while causation in Wicksell's cumulative process of inflation ran only in one direction (from interest-rate gaps to prices), circularity was Myrdal's innovation. In the German version of *Monetary Equilibrium*, Myrdal (1931 [1933]) also coined the famous twin term "*ex ante – ex post*", in order to distinguish between the formation of plans in accordance with expectations, and their coordination through unplanned adjustments. Both Myrdal's 1927 dissertation and his 1931 treatise greatly influenced the development of the Stockholm School.

Throughout his academic life, Myrdal combined the analysis of economic issues with methodological critique of neoclassical economics. His book on *The Political Element in the Development of Economic Theory*, first published in 1930, was soon translated into many languages (yet, in English only in 1953). Myrdal criticized "economic orthodoxy" for its tautological "explanations" of profits and its teleological theories of development. He argued that economic orthodoxy suffered from self-referential and "spurious objectivity", confusing "what is" with "what ought to be" (Streeten 1998: 542). Yet he conceded that all work in the social sciences is based on value premises, and recommended therefore to disclose these, so as to give readers a chance to control for distorting biases.

His critique of biases in economics made Myrdal take a sociological view on his discipline. He acquired an even wider interest in sociological issues in the 1930s, when he, together with his wife Alva, propagated welfare-state policies and became active in the Social Democratic Party, the parliament and the government. He contributed to debates on population policy and education, and to the design of countercyclical fiscal policies in 1933–36. From 1945 until 1947 he was Swedish minister of commerce (Barber 2008: chs 4, 5, 7).

Myrdal's breakthrough as an academic sociologist came in the years between with *An American Dilemma: The Negro Problem and Modern Democracy* (1944), a large study he undertook in the United States by invitation from the Carnegie Foundation. Working on the value premises of the "American Creed of liberty, equality, justice, and fair opportunity for everybody" (1944: xlviii), he confronted these ideals with the discrimination and poverty of black people. For the latter's explanation, Myrdal took recourse to his principle of circular and cumulative causation, "also commonly called the 'vicious circle.' This principle has a much wider application in social relations. It is, or should be developed into, a main theoretical tool in studying social change" (1994: 75).

At the next stage, in the 1950s, Myrdal came to find an even wider application for this tool. From the explanation of social inequality within one nation he took it to the explanation of economic inequalities between regions and between nations. Based on his experience as executive secretary of the United Nations Economic Commission for Europe (1947–57), Myrdal advanced a theory of polarizing development under the title *Economic Theory and Under-Developed Regions* (1957). In his description of the conditions under which the development of some regions leads to the underdevelopment of other regions, he stressed the role of institutions, both for polarization and for counteracting it. His explicit value premise was that egalitarian welfare state policies are the best strategy to foster development and to reverse underdevelopment. Myrdal developed his institutional approach further in his 2300-page *Asian Drama: An Inquiry into the Poverty of Nations* (1968). His contributions to development economics helped to create an anti-neoclassical mind frame that was highly influential in academia and politics in the 1960s and 1970s.

In 1974, Myrdal was awarded the Nobel Prize (officially: Sveriges Riksbank Prize in Economic Sciences in Memory of Alfred Nobel), together with Friedrich A. von Hayek. As the Prize Committee put it, they had been selected jointly "for their pioneering work in the theory of money and economic fluctuations and for their penetrating analysis of the interdependence of economic, social and institutional phenomena". This must have left the co-laureates with mixed feelings, as their economic and political views differed fundamentally in almost every respect. It is said that you always meet twice in a lifetime: the paths of Myrdal and Hayek had crossed before, in 1933, when Hayek published the German version of Myrdal's *Monetary Equilibrium* in his anthology of contributions to monetary theory. In combination with the translation of *The Political Element in the Development of Economic Theory*, this had made Myrdal known outside Sweden.

HANS-MICHAEL TRAUTWEIN

See also:

Gustav Cassel (I); Development economics (III); Erik Lindahl (I); Macroeconomics (III); Stockholm (Swedish) School (II); Knut Wicksell (I).

References and further reading

Barber, W.J. (2008), *Gunnar Myrdal: An Intellectual Biography*, Basingstoke: Macmillan.

Myrdal, G. (1927), *Prisbildningen och föränderligheten*, Uppsala: Almqvist & Wiksell.

Myrdal, G. (1930), *Vetenskap och politik i nationalekonomien*, Stockholm: P.A. Norstedt, English trans. 1953, *The Political Element in the Development of Economic Theory*, London: Routledge & Kegan Paul.

Myrdal, G. (1931), 'Om penningteoretisk jämvikt. En studie över den "normala räntan" i Wicksells penninglära', *Ekonomisk Tidskrift*, **33** (5 and 6), 191–302, German trans. 1933, 'Der Gleichgewichtsbegriff als Instrument der geldtheoretischen Analyse', in F.A. von Hayek (ed.), *Beiträge zur Geldtheorie*, Vienna: Julius Springer, English trans. 1939, *Monetary Equilibrium*, London: William Hodge.

Myrdal, G. (1944), *An American Dilemma: The Negro Problem and Modern Democracy*, New York: Harper.

Myrdal, G. (1957), *Economic Theory and Under-Developed Regions*, London: Gerald Duckworth.

Myrdal, G. (1968), *Asian Drama: An Inquiry into the Poverty of Nations*, New York: Twentieth Century Fund.

Streeten, P. (1998), 'The cheerful pessimist: Gunnar Myrdal the dissenter (1898–1987)', *World Development*, **26** (3), 539–50.

Lionel Charles Robbins (1898–1984)

Lionel Charles Robbins was born in London in 1898. His education at the University College London was interrupted by World War I. He served in the Royal Artillery from 1916 to 1918. From 1920 to 1923 he studied at the London School of Economics (LSE). There he ran the Economics Department from 1929 to 1962 (with interceptions) after alternately lecturing at New College, Oxford and at the LSE from 1924 to 1929. Even after his retirement he remained associated with the LSE until 1980. He worked as an adviser to the British government in the aftermath of the Great Depression and his scientific career was interrupted only during World War II when he was director of the Economic Section of the British government. His tasks included the development and implementation of activities aiming at post-war recovery, and he also attended the Bretton Woods Conference in 1944 as a member of the British delegation. In the post-war period Robbins influenced the British educational system as chairman of the Committee on Higher Education. He authored the Robbins Report (Committee on Higher Education 1963), where he stated the "Robbins Principle": "courses of higher education should be available for all those who are qualified by ability and attainment" (ibid.: 8).

As an economist Lionel Robbins was interested in questions of economic theory, economic methodology and the history of economic thought. Within today's economic community he is best known for his definition of economics in his *Essay on the Nature and Significance of Economic Science*: "Economics is a science which studies human behaviour as a relationship between ends and scarce means which have alternative uses" (Robbins 1932: 15). This definition involves a renunciation of the definition of the classical economists, according to which economics studies the production, distribution and disposition of the wealth of a nation, and indicates the rise to dominance of the marginalist school. Its alleged generality and force of expression helped its entry into many contemporary textbooks (Backhouse and Medema 2009). In Robbins's view (1932: viii) this definition grasped the contemporary practice of economic research. Whether this depicted accurately an actual practice is a matter for discussion. On the one hand, Robbins puts the focus on rational choice, which obviously narrows the subject matter of economics compared with what economists did at that time and had done in the past. This can be seen as an attempt to oppose Marshallian economics and especially the view that economic theory is concerned with material welfare. On the other hand, the scope of economics is extended by Robbins's definition to all social phenomena which involve some kind of scarcity (Backhouse and Medema 2009: 805).

Given the scope of economics, Robbins asked which kind of propositions economic theory can provide. Whether tendencies (of imprecise concepts such as aggregate output, for example) or economic laws can be deduced depends on the topics to be discussed:

> The Ricardian System which . . . provides the archetype of all subsequent systems, is essentially a discussion of the tendencies to equilibrium of clear-cut quantities and relationships. It is no accident that wherever its discussions have related to separate types of economic goods and ratios of exchange between economic goods, there the generalisations of Economics have assumed the form of scientific laws. (Robbins 1932: 67)

Robbins was also concerned with the aggregation problem, which was pivotal in his controversy with John Maynard Keynes in the aftermath of the Great Depression. He advocated a disaggregated analysis of the economy in terms of industries. He was looking for explanations of economic depressions, which went beyond an aggregate view. In his book about *The Great Depression* (1934 [1971]) he argued that an economic crisis develops if in many industries profits vanish, the pivotal questions being: "Why do . . . simultaneous changes take place? Why is there over-production in many lines of industry?" (Robbins 1934 [1971]: 16). Robbins also kept up this critical view of aggregate economic concepts when stating that economic laws can only be derived for well-defined concepts. As an example he discussed the problems of economic indices as a means for economic reasoning: "[T]he idea of changes in the total volume of production has no precise content. We may, if we please, attach certain conventional values to certain indices and say that we define a change in production as a change in this index; for certain purposes this may be advisable. But there is no analytical justification for this procedure" (Robbins 1932: 66).

This led to consequences concerning economic policy advice. Robbins deviated from the Keynesian approach based on the concept of effective demand, which he saw as belonging to the tradition of under-consumption theory. Keynes, in his 1936 *The General Theory of Employment, Interest and Money*, looked at the economic system as a whole, employing concepts such as the propensity to consume and asking for sufficient investment to get full employment. His economic policy advice was governmental deficit spending to increase effective demand. Robbins (1934 [1971]: 160), on the other hand, focused on the restoration of confidence: "The first essential of any recovery from the position in which the world now finds itself is a return of business confidence", which would increase investment without Keynesian deficit spending. To him it was clear that a fall of prices "is not the cause – it is the effect – of the fundamental fluctuation. In the search for ultimate causes it constitutes the problem, not the solution" (ibid.: 13). As a consequence, any explanation of the Great Depression "must look either to commodity supply or to demand expressed in terms of money" (ibid.). Robbins stressed that over-production cannot last "[s]o long as there remain anywhere wants which are unsatisfied" (ibid.). However, over-production exists in times of economic depression in the sense that "in wide groups of important markets, at the price prevailing, the supply cannot be sold at a profit" (ibid.: 13–14).

Besides his explanation of the Great Depression, Robbins also studied class relations and international relations and rejected the under-consumption theory of recessions as the prime mover of social and international struggle (Robbins 1939 [1968]). He outlined his laissez-faire policy and advocated free markets. What he wanted to debunk was the "thought that the institutions of private property and the market, in their present stage of development, tend inevitably to breed international conflict – that war is a necessary by-product of the capitalist system" (Robbins 1939 [1968]: 17). Robbins's basic premise in terms of policy incentives is the observation that the driving force of international relations is "to conserve (or increase) our power. Such and such an action will affect our power in such and such a way. This action is therefore to be commended (or rejected)" (Robbins 1939 [1968]: 61). This implies that economic factors are at work, since the attainment of any kind of power "involves the control of scarce resources" (Robbins 1939 [1968]: 61). That he dealt with questions of war might be owed to his service in the Royal Field Artillery from 1916 to 1918 in World War I, and it was nurtured by the political situation of the 1930s in Europe. By expounding his laissez-faire attitude Robbins also opposed Keynesian recovery policy advice. At that time Robbins was affiliated with the LSE, whereas Keynes was affiliated with the University of Cambridge. Their differences had consequences on the perception of certain decisions Robbins made, especially on his advocacy of Friedrich August von Hayek to join the LSE in 1931: "It is all too often claimed that Robbins invited Hayek to LSE to 'fight Keynes' and to establish a 'school' of economists in opposition to the Cambridge economists" (Howson 2011: 1028). According to Howson this cannot be sustained. However, she provides no compelling evidence to the contrary. Despite their differences of opinion Robbins (1947 [1957]: 68) and Hayek (1994: 80) were on good personal terms with Keynes. In his post-war book Robbins (1947 [1957]: 68) even changed his mind concerning the concept of aggregate demand:

> I grew up in a tradition in which, while recognition was indeed given to the problems created by the ups and downs of the trade cycle and the fluctuations of aggregate demand, there was a tendency to ignore certain deep-seated possibilities of disharmony, in a way which, I now think, led sometimes to superficiality and sometimes to positive error. I owe much to Cambridge economists, particularly to Lord Keynes and Professor Robertson, for having awakened me from dogmatic slumbers in this very important respect.

Robbins's change of attitude towards government interventions was not at odds with his laissez-faire policy and advocacy of free markets. He was against central planning but this did not prevent him from opting for sound institutional design in the tradition of the *Ordnungsökonomik*. Pivotal for his evaluation of government action was the actual economic and political environment. A broad discussion of his ideas can be found in his *Politics and Economics* (1963), and his ideas on proper economic policy action can also be found in *The Theory of Economic Policy* (1965), where he critically reviews English classical political economy. This book is a part of Robbins's writings about the history of economic ideas, which comprises *The Theory of Economic Development in the History of Economic Thought* (1968), *The Evolution of Modern Economic Theory* (1970) and his LSE lectures posthumously published in *A History of Economic Thought* (2000).

ANDREAS RAINER

See also:

British marginalism (II); Friedrich August von Hayek (I); John Maynard Keynes (I).

References and further reading

Backhouse, R.E. and S.G Medema (2009), 'Defining economics: the long road to acceptance of the Robbins definition', *Economica*, **76** (S1), 805–20.

Committee on Higher Education (1963), 'Higher education: report of the Committee appointed by the Prime Minister under the Chairmanship of Lord Robbins 1961–63', Cmnd. 2154, London: HMSO.

Hayek, F.A. (1994), *Hayek on Hayek: An Autobiographical Dialogue*, Chicago, IL: University of Chicago Press.

Howson, S. (2011), *Lionel Robbins*, Cambridge: Cambridge University Press.

Keynes, J.M. (1936), *The General Theory of Employment, Interest and Money*, London: Macmillan.

Robbins, L. (1932), *An Essay on the Nature and Significance of Economic Science*, London: Macmillan.

Robbins, L. (1934), *The Great Depression*, New York: Books for Libraries Press, reprinted 1971.

Robbins, L. (1939), *The Economic Causes of War*, New York: Howard Fertig, reprinted 1968.

Robbins, L. (1947), *The Economic Problem of Peace and War*, London: Macmillan, reprinted 1957.

Robbins, L. (1963), *Politics and Economics*, New York: St Martin's Press.

Robbins, L. (1965), *The Theory of Economic Policy*, London: Macmillan.

Robbins, L. (1968), *The Theory of Economic Development in the History of Economic Thought*, London: Macmillan.

Robbins, L. (1970), *The Evolution of Modern Economic Theory*, Chicago, IL: Aldine Publications.

Robbins, L. (2000), *A History of Economic Thought: The LSE Lectures*, S.G. Medema and W.J. Samuels (eds), Princeton, NJ: Princeton University Press.

Piero Sraffa (1898–1983)

Life

Piero Sraffa was born on 5 August 1898 in Turin, Italy. His father, Angelo Sraffa, was an eminent professor of commercial law and later rector of Bocconi University in Milan. Throughout his life Piero had a very close relationship with his mother, who after his father's death moved to Cambridge to stay near to her son who remained a bachelor. He studied law in Turin and discussed his thesis in 1920 with Luigi Einaudi, who became the President of the Italian Republic in 1948. In the thesis he dealt with the inflation in Italy during and after World War I (Sraffa 1920 [1993]). A year earlier he met Antonio Gramsci, who later was one of the founders of the Italian Communist Party (PCd'I). The two connected a deep friendship that lasted until Gramsci's death. Sraffa remained close to the party but never became its member.

After graduating in Turin he spent a year at the London School of Economics (LSE), where he attended lectures by Edwin Cannan and Herbert Foxwell. He met John Maynard Keynes, who was deeply impressed by the young Italian and invited him to write an essay about the Italian banking system. Keynes published the paper "The bank crisis in Italy" in the *Economic Journal*, whose editor he was, and asked Sraffa to compose a shorter article for the supplement to the *Manchester Guardian Commercial*. In it Sraffa, who was possessed of detailed information, uncovered the critical position of the three main Italian banks. Benito Mussolini, who had just taken office as Prime Minister, telegraphed Sraffa's father and requested in vain the withdrawal of the piece.

At the time the power of the fascists had not yet fully extended to the universities. In November 1923, Sraffa was appointed to a temporary lectureship in political economy and public finance at the University of Perugia. In preparing his lectures he studied intensively the partial equilibrium analysis of Alfred Marshall. In 1925 he published "Sulle relazioni fra costo e quantità prodotta" ("On the relationships between cost and quantity produced") in the recently founded journal *Annali di Economia* (Sraffa 1925 [1998]). The essay contains a detailed criticism of Marshall's version of the marginalist theory and established Sraffa's reputation as a brilliant economist. In 1926 he won the competition for a chair at the University of Cagliari, Sardinia. At the suggestion of Francis Y. Edgeworth he published "The laws of returns under competitive conditions" in the *Economic Journal* (Sraffa 1926). Four years later he concluded his contribution to the 1930 *Economic Journal* symposium on "Increasing returns and the representative firm" with the remark that Marshall's theory "should be discarded" (Sraffa 1930: 93).

In November 1926 Gramsci was arrested and in 1928 condemned to 20 years in gaol. He died in 1937. During these years Sraffa played a crucial role in assisting Gramsci, sending books, maintaining a relationship with the family and especially with the sister-in-law Tatiana, organizing legal and medical support, and maintaining links with the party (see Sraffa 1991; Napolitano 2005).

In 1927 Sraffa was offered a lectureship at the University of Cambridge, UK. He became a member of King's College, of which Keynes was a fellow. Over the summer he prepared his "Lectures on advanced theory of value", which were scheduled for the autumn term. But he asked for a postponement for a year. It was not only his meticulousness that prompted him to do so. As we know from his hitherto unpublished manuscripts, it became clear to him that Marshall's analysis could not be salvaged by putting the "forces" of supply and demand on solid, objective grounds. Rather an entirely fresh start was needed in the theory of value and distribution. The situation at the time was rendered a great deal more complicated by the fact that the sought new beginning soon turned out to require a return to the approach advocated by the classical economists from Adam Smith to David Ricardo. Criticizing Marshall's theory, elaborating an alternative to it and uncovering its historical roots were tasks too big for scrupulous Sraffa to lecture on. "Whereof one cannot speak, thereof one must be silent", as Wittgenstein put it famously. However, as we know from his papers, from mid-1927 until the second half of 1930, Sraffa worked hard on what was to become his magnum opus, *Production of Commodities by Means of Commodities* (Sraffa 1960). After three years of lecturing on value theory (in the same period he also gave lectures on the continental banking system and compared it with the English banking system) he asked to be released from the task and assumed the position of librarian in the Marshall Library. Later, the Faculty entrusted him also with the graduate studies programme and made him Assistant Director of Research in Economics.

In 1929 Sraffa met the Austrian philosopher Ludwig Wittgenstein upon the latter's return to Cambridge, with whom he got on friendly terms and on whose thinking he had a great influence (see Kurz 2009). As Wittgenstein acknowledged, his transition from the *Tractatus logico-philosophicus* to the *Philosophical Investigations* was first and foremost due to Sraffa's criticism. Wittgenstein admired Sraffa's breadth of knowledge and astuteness, but he also suffered from him. Sraffa, on the other hand, found it difficult to cope with his friend's narcissism and political naivety. In 1943 Sraffa, to Wittgenstein's dismay, terminated their regular meetings and discussions. Sraffa was also on friendly terms with several other scholars in Cambridge, especially Keynes, the philosopher and mathematician Frank P. Ramsey, the mathematician Abram S. Besicovitch and the economist Maurice Dobb.

In early 1930 the Royal Economic Society entrusted Sraffa with the edition of *The Works and Correspondence of David Ricardo* because of which he had to interrupt his constructive work on his book. Sraffa rushed with passion at the job. Reflecting his expertise, in 1930 he published in the *Quarterly Journal of Economics* a note in which he showed that an "oversight" on the principle of comparative cost that John Stuart Mill had attributed to Ricardo was indeed an error committed by James Mill and repeated by the latter's son John Stuart himself (Sraffa and Einaudi 1930).

At the suggestion of Sraffa, in 1930 the so-called "Cambridge Circus" formed in order to work through Keynes's *Treatise on Money* (1930). He, Richard Kahn, James Meade, Joan and Austin Robinson met regularly and formulated questions and criticisms, which were then communicated to Keynes, who in the meantime had started to work on *The General Theory of Employment, Interest and Money* (Keynes 1971–88, *Collected Writings*, hereafter *CW* VII). Sraffa's impeccable logic was both extolled and feared. For example, in 1932 Joan Robinson wrote to Keynes:

> I believe that like the rest of us you have had your faith in supply curves shaken by Piero. But what he attacks are just the one-by-one supply curves that you regard as legitimate. His objections do not apply to the supply curve of output [as a whole] – but Heaven help us when he starts thinking out objections that do apply to it! (Keynes *CW* XIII: 378)

As we know from Sraffa's papers and library, he did indeed formulate objections to Keynes's new theory, especially to its core piece, the theory of liquidity preference (see below).

Keynes appreciated Sraffa not only because of his quick mind and erudition, but also because of his intimate knowledge of the banking system and the stock exchange. Variously Sraffa demonstrated his skills and sound judgement during discussions Keynes had with him and Kahn in the preparation of transactions at the stock exchange. On at least one occasion Keynes would have been well advised to follow Sraffa's reasoning (see Keynes *CW* XII: 22–4). Otherwise, Sraffa's collaboration with Keynes was largely restricted to only two areas: the Ricardo edition (see Gehrke and Kurz 2002) and in tracing the author of an *Abstract of a Treatise on Human Nature*. It was Sraffa, "from whom nothing is hid" (Keynes *CW* X: 97), who established the fact that the author was Hume, and not Adam Smith (see the introduction by Keynes and Sraffa in Hume 1938).

In 1931 Friedrich August von Hayek published, upon Lionel Robbins's invitation, in *Economica* a frontal assault on Keynes's *Treatise* (Hayek 1931a). In the same year Hayek published *Prices and Production* (Hayek 1931b), the written version of four lectures the Austrian had given at the LSE. Keynes, unfamiliar with the building blocks of Hayek's attack – Eugen von Böhm-Bawerk's theory of capital and interest and Vilfredo Pareto's theory of general economic equilibrium – asked Sraffa to bail him out. In 1932 Sraffa published "Dr. Hayek on money and capital", in which he criticized Hayek's monetary overinvestment theory of the business cycle (Sraffa 1932a). Hayek replied in the same year (1932), followed by a rejoinder by Sraffa (1932b). The acerbic controversy did not prevent the two scholars from getting on good terms again with one another via their common bibliophile interests.

In 1939 Sraffa became a fellow of Trinity College, Cambridge, where he stayed until the end of his life. In 1940 he was for several months interned together with other aliens living in Great Britain on the Isle of Man. It was thanks to Keynes's intervention that a few months later he was released. Back in Cambridge he worked feverishly on the Ricardo edition and resumed his work on the reconstruction of the classical approach to the theory of value and distribution. He felt he could accomplish both tasks before long. He was offered positions at the University of Chicago and the New School for Social Research, but he turned both offers down. During 1942–43 he gave lectures in Cambridge on "Industry", in which he discussed *inter alia* the problem of the separation of ownership and control in modern joint stock companies. Upon the surprising discovery of Ricardo's letters to James Mill in 1943 he was forced to rearrange the Ricardo volumes, which were already available in lead typesetting. Between 1951 and 1955 he at long last managed to publish, with the assistance of Maurice Dobb, volumes I–X of *The Works and Correspondence of David Ricardo* (volume XI, containing the index, had to wait until 1973). For his achievement the Royal Swedish Academy of Sciences awarded him in 1961 the Söderström medal, a prize given only on the occasion of exceptional scholarly achievements.

After another interruption for a decade or so, Sraffa finally, from 1956 until 1958, put together, on the basis of his old notes and manuscripts, his 1960 book. The work of barely 100 pages was published in English and almost at the same time in an Italian edition elaborated with the help of an Italian friend, the banker Raffaele Mattioli. The book was swiftly translated into several languages and formed the linchpin of the controversies in the theory of capital in the 1960s and 1970s. Sraffa did not himself intervene directly in the controversy. He replied however to Roy F. Harrod, who had suggested a particular interpretation of Sraffa's equations of production (Sraffa 1962).

Sraffa was offered honorary PhD degrees by several universities from all over the world, but typically he did not accept them when his personal presence at the ceremony was requested. He still tinkered with the idea of complementing the "Prelude to a critique of economic theory", the subtitle of his book, with the critique itself in a further book. However, his vigour and stamina had weakened and he suffered from illnesses.

Sraffa died on 3 September 1983 in Cambridge. He left Trinity College a considerable amount of money, a most precious library of several thousand books (see De Vivo 2014) and huge literary remains of several thousand pages, slips of paper and notes. A judicious edition of Sraffa's papers and correspondence is currently in preparation.

Theoretical Contributions

Criticism of Marshall's partial equilibrium analysis

In 1925 and 1926 Sraffa published a thorough and devastating criticism of Marshall's method of partial equilibrium of competitive prices. The second paper starts with the following observation:

> A striking feature of the present position of economic science is the almost unanimous agreement at which economists have arrived regarding the theory of competitive value, which is inspired by the fundamental symmetry existing between the forces of demand and those of supply, . . . represented by a pair of intersecting curves of collective demand and supply. This state of things is in such marked contrast with the controversies on the theory of value by which political economy was characterized during the past century that it might almost be thought that from these clashes of thought the spark of an ultimate truth had at length been struck. (Sraffa 1926: 535)

Sraffa did not share this view. He objected that in "the tranquil view which the modern theory of value presents us there is one dark spot which disturbs the harmony of the whole" – the supply curve, based upon the combination of the laws of increasing and diminishing returns. Its foundations, he maintained, "are actually so weak as to be unable to support the weight imposed upon them" (1926: 536).

Consider the usual textbook partial equilibrium argument. A change in one market (for example, a shift in the demand curve for wine) is taken to have first an effect on the equilibrium in that market (for example, a change in the price and in the quantity of wine produced), and then perhaps an effect on other markets as a consequence of this change in price and quantity (for example, a shift in the demand for grapes and in the demand for beer, for some a wine substitute). If it can be assumed that the effects on the other markets are of a second order of magnitude with respect to the effect obtained on the equilibrium of the market in which the original change took place, and if these former effects are assumed to be so small that they can be neglected, at least at a first stage, then the supply and demand curves of a given market can be considered, in regard to small variations, as independent both of each other and of the supply and demand curves of all other commodities.

Both logical and empirical aspects are tightly intertwined in Sraffa's critique of

Marshall: by reconstructing, in a logically consistent way, the Marshallian partial equilibrium model of competitive markets, Sraffa was able to identify the boundaries of its explanatory domain. Which potentially observable facts may be analysed by means of Marshall's model? The result of Sraffa's investigation was that the explanatory power of Marshall's model is extremely limited, which may explain why the Marshallian boxes on returns to scale remained obstinately empty, as Clapham (1922) observed. Sraffa distinguished between variable returns that are (1) internal to the firm; (2) external to the firm but internal to the industry; and (3) external to both the firm and the industry. Variable returns of type (1) are incompatible with perfect competition, whereas variable returns of type (3) are incompatible with the method of partial equilibrium. Only variable returns of type (2), whose empirical importance is dubious, turn out to be compatible with Marshall's analysis of the supply curve of an industry in competitive conditions (see Signorino 2000, 2001; Freni and Salvadori 2013).

In his two papers Sraffa (1925, 1926) did not base his criticism on the fact that commodities are produced by means of commodities, that is, there is a tight interdependence between industries, each industry selling its product(s) as necessary input(s) to many other industries and buying the products of many other industries as necessary inputs (see Steedman 1988; Freni 2001). The type of sectoral interdependence considered in his two papers is, rather, a consequence of the fact that commodities are produced either by means of technologies employing the same primary inputs (in the decreasing returns case) or characterized by the same external economies (in the increasing returns case).

Sraffa (1925) concluded from this that with regard to small variations in the quantity produced the assumption of constant returns is the most convenient for the analysis of the supply curve of an industry in competitive conditions. This view is repeated in his 1926 paper and interpreted as rendering support to the classical doctrine: "the old and now obsolete theory which makes it [the competitive value] dependent on the cost of production alone appears to hold its ground as the best available" (1926: 541). Yet, if in competitive conditions cost of production determines values in the long period, it follows that the symmetric theory of value loses its appeal: demand has no role to play in determining value.

For several reasons this conclusion did not satisfy Sraffa. Could Marshall's approach perhaps be remedied, and, if yes, how? Was it necessary to abandon the assumption of perfect competition or that of partial equilibrium analysis, or both? How do costs of production determine values in the classical authors? Was the substance or only the form of the classical theory unsound?

Here we cannot enter into a detailed discussion of how Sraffa responded to these questions. A few observations must suffice. In assessing Marshall's analysis Sraffa had at the back of his mind some form of general analysis of economic interdependence. It was a stripped-down version of such an analysis, because it did not take into account the fact that commodities are produced by means of commodities. Sraffa motivated this neglect of a most important fact in terms of the observation that "the conditions of simultaneous equilibrium in numerous industries" are far too complex and that "the present state of our knowledge . . . does not permit of even much simpler schema being applied to the study of real conditions" (Sraffa 1926: 541). Interestingly, he concluded the paper by pointing out that "the process of diffusion of profits throughout the various stages of production and of the process of forming a normal level of profits throughout all the industries of a country . . . is . . . beyond the scope of this article" (ibid.: 550). It is precisely this problem that Sraffa began to tackle in the late 1920s. However, before we turn to this we must first, following a chronological order, recall some other works he published or edited.

Criticism of Hayek's overinvestment theory of the business cycle
Sraffa succeeded in warding off Hayek's (1931a, 1931b) attack on Keynes. (For the following, see Kurz 2000.) He rejected Hayek's basic proposition that a divergence between the actual or money rate of interest and the "natural" or "equilibrium rate" is a characteristic feature of a monetary economy (Sraffa 1932a: 49). With reference to Wicksell's definition that interest is the surplus in real units of the exchange of physically homogeneous goods across time, he emphasized:

> If money did not exist, and loans were made in terms of all sorts of commodities, there would be a single rate which satisfies the conditions of equilibrium, but there might be at any moment as many "natural" rates of interest as there are commodities, though they would not be 'equilibrium' rates. (Sraffa 1932a: 49)

He added:

> The "arbitrary" action of the banks is by no means a necessary condition for the divergence; if loans were made in wheat and farmers (or for that matter the weather) "arbitrarily changed" the quantity of wheat produced, the actual rate of interest on loans in terms of wheat would diverge from the rate on other commodities and there would be no single equilibrium rate. (Ibid.)

Sraffa illustrated his argument in terms of two economies, one with and the other without money, and exemplified the main idea with regard to a cotton trader:

> The rate of interest which he pays, per hundred bales of cotton, is the number of bales that can be purchased with the following sum of money: the interest on the money required to buy spot 100 bales, plus the excess (or minus the deficiency) of the spot over the forward prices of the 100 bales. (Sraffa 1932a: 50)

Let $i_{t,\theta}$ be the money rate of interest for θ periods, M the sum of money under consideration, p^t and $p^{t+\theta}$ the spot and forward price, and $\rho_{t,\theta}$ the commodity rate of interest of cotton between t and $t + \theta$, we have:

$$\rho_{t,\theta} = \frac{M}{p^{t+\theta}} = \frac{(1 + i_{t,\theta})p^t - p^{t+\theta}}{p^{t+\theta}} = \frac{(1 + i_{t,\theta})p^t}{p^{t+\theta}} - 1 \tag{1}$$

In equilibrium the spot and forward price coincide for all commodities, and all commodity rates are equal to one another and equal to the money rate.

> But if, for any reason, the supply and the demand for a commodity are not in equilibrium (*i.e.* its market price exceeds or falls short of its cost of production), its spot and forward prices diverge, and the "natural" rate of interest on that commodity diverges from the "natural" rates on other commodities. (Sraffa 1932a: 50)

He added that "under free competition, this divergence of rates is as essential to the effecting of the transition [to a new equilibrium] as is the divergence of prices from the costs of production; *it is, in fact, another aspect of the same thing*" (ibid.: 50; emphasis added).

In terms of classical economics we are confronted with the problem of the gravitation of "market prices" towards their "natural" levels. These are equal to costs of production (including the general rate of profits on the capitals employed), which Sraffa had analysed in the late 1920s in his "second" (with surplus) equations (see below). The idea of gravitation is clearly spelled out:

> [I]mmediately some [commodities] will rise in price, and others will fall; the market will expect that, after a certain time, the supply of the former will increase, and the supply of the latter fall, and accordingly the forward price, for the date on which equilibrium is expected to be restored, will be below the spot price in the case of the former and above it in the case of the latter; in other words the rate of interest on the former will be higher than on the latter (Sraffa 1932a: 50).

In addition, Sraffa criticized Hayek's view that, as a consequence of the banking system's eventual abandonment of its mistaken interest rate policy, the economy will return to its old equilibrium. This will not be the case, because in the meantime the policy will have changed wealth and income distribution and thus one of the data defining an equilibrium (the other two being preferences of agents and technical alternatives of production). Hayek's idea that "voluntary savings" can be strictly separated from "forced savings", caused by the reduction in the output of consumer goods consequent upon a lowering of the money rate of interest and the shifting of productive resources away from the consumption goods and to the investment goods industries, is naive. Hayek had not argued correctly and was unable to explain the facts he purported to explain.

Keynes was very pleased with Sraffa's performance: it had effectively countered the assault on his intellectual project launched by Lionel Robbins and his circle at the LSE, and had allowed him to develop the *General Theory* undisturbed by any further interventions by the Austrian economist. In chapter 17 of the *General Theory*, "The essential properties of interest and money", Keynes thanked Sraffa (see *CW* VII: 223 fn.), adopted what he considered the concept of commodity rates of interest to be and based his argument upon it. He contended that the "money own rate of interest", determined by liquidity preference, is sticky downwards and prevents the volume of investment to attain a level equal to full employment savings (see Keynes *CW* VII: 222–44).

Criticism of Keynes's theory of liquidity preference

Sraffa was not at all pleased with Keynes's respective argument. He felt that Keynes had seriously misunderstood the concept of commodity rate of interest and had grossly misapprehended its explanatory potential. Sraffa's objections are contained in his annotations in chapter 17 of his working copy of the *General Theory* and in two short manuscript fragments that were found in the latter after Sraffa had passed away in 1983. These objections have far-reaching implications because in Sraffa's assessment the theory of liquidity preference "involves *all* the functions considered in the system: it is, in fact, Keynes's system!" (Sraffa Papers: I100) (see Ranchetti 2002; Kurz 2010).

In his annotations Sraffa made the following objections. First, Keynes used two contradictory definitions of the concept of commodity rate, Sraffa's and a new one according to which the latter is made up of three characteristics of any durable asset that supposedly can all be translated into interest rate equivalents and then added up: (1) the "yield" of the asset q, (2) its "carrying cost" c, and (3) the "liquidity premium" l, that is, $q + c + l$ (see Keynes *CW* VII: 226). As against this, Sraffa insisted that the concept is only defined in terms of an expected change of the price of the asset. Secondly, as regards Keynes's choice of money as standard of value, Sraffa drew attention to an important implication Keynes had overlooked: "The point is, that in the case of the rate of the article chosen as standard, *the effect upon it of the expected depreciation is concealed*" (ibid.: 227, emphasis added). Thus, an expected fall in the value of money implies a high "money-rate of wheat interest", which, alas, Keynes did not take into account. Third, Keynes did not reason correctly and variously arrived at conclusions that are exactly the opposite of what results from a cogent argument. His contention that the money rate of interest cannot fall to a level compatible with full employment savings, because the elasticity of production of money is zero and its elasticity of substitution close to zero, cannot be sustained.

The two manuscript fragments confirm the assessment that the chapter is a mess. Sraffa argues in particular: (1) Keynes' concept of liquidity is vague and ambiguous; (2) there is no reason to presume that a higher liquidity is *always* a good thing for each and every agent; and (3) Keynes erroneously admits Fisher's effect for all commodities except money. (In the following, all quotations are from folder I100 of the Sraffa Papers.)

With regard to (2), Sraffa observes that the liquidity preference curve – the inverse relationship between holding cash and the rate of interest – is reminiscent of the usual marginal utility curve: "liquidity is always an advantage, though diminishing". Sraffa objects that while for some agents it may be the case in a particular situation, for others it may be otherwise. Banks, for example, must remain solvent and liquid, but they must also make profits. When their income consists almost exclusively of interest, they must, with a lower rate of interest, get less liquid in order to keep up their income. Therefore it is impossible to say in general that there is a definite relationship between the quantity of money and the rate of interest or liquidity preference curve.

Advantages associated with carrying an asset, Sraffa insists, have nothing to do with its commodity rate. People who borrow money or any other asset typically do this not in order to carry what is being borrowed until the expiration of the contract. They, rather, borrow money to buy with it other things. What is being borrowed is not what is being kept, but the standard in which the debt is fixed. Therefore, it is irrelevant whether a person pays in money or wheat and whether what is borrowed is durable or perishable. Sraffa is convinced "that K. has in the back of his mind two wrong notions, which have entirely misled him", namely, that only durables can be borrowed and are so for the sake of keeping them.

There remains the fact that a large quantity of money (cash) and a low rate of interest often go together, which gives the curve some plausibility. Yet according to Sraffa the "causation is the other way round": it is a low rate of interest that is responsible for a large quantity of money, not a large quantity of money that causes a low rate of interest. Attention ought to focus on those who demand loans (investors) and not on those who provide them with liquid funds (banks and savers). Keynes's theory of liquidity preference, Sraffa concludes, is similar to the old long-period theory of the supply of savings that is elastic with respect to the rate of interest carried over to a short-period framework.

The commodity rate of interest, Sraffa observes, is defined with respect to the forward price of a commodity and nothing else. There are two ways in which the commodity rates can become uniform again: via changes in prices and/or quantities. Surprisingly,

Keynes allows for both possibilities with regard to all commodities except money. To see this, contemplate the case in which people suddenly develop a large propensity to hoard money. This will depress the economy and commodity prices will start to fall, that is, the value of money will rise. Now, an expected further increase in the value of money implies a lower "own rate of money interest", using Keynes' peculiar concept. Sraffa concludes from this that "therefore the money rate will be *lower* than other rates and not higher". He observes that this is "Fisher's effect, which K. admits for all commodities except money". The reference is to Irving Fisher (see especially 1907), who first put forward the concept of own rates. Sraffa summarizes his criticism of Keynes: "Thus in the K. case, the result on rates of int[erest] is opposite to K.'s conclusion."

The Ricardo edition
The first volumes of *The Works and Correspondence of David Ricardo* (Ricardo 1951–73, hereafter *Works*) were published in 1951, 31 years after Sraffa had been appointed to the editorship by the Royal Economic Society. (For the causes of this delay, see Pollit 1990; Gehrke and Kurz 2002.) The edition substantiated Sraffa's interpretation of the classical economists as advocating a surplus approach to the theory of value and distribution. Sraffa had begun in the late 1920s to reformulate this approach in a coherent way, an endeavour that culminated in his 1960 book. Here we focus attention especially on the "corn-ratio theory" of profits of Sraffa's new interpretation of Ricardo.

In his Introduction to the *Principles* in *Works* volume I, Sraffa interprets Ricardo's 1815 *Essay on Profits* as being based on the idea that there is a sector in the economy that is "in the special condition of not employing the products of other trades while all the others must employ *its* product as capital" (*Works* I: xxxi, emphasis in the original). The sector is corn (wheat) production. Sraffa therefore speaks of the "corn-ratio theory". It allows determination of the rate of profit in the corn sector in purely material terms as the surplus (exclusive of rent) obtained, a quantity of corn, divided by the capital advanced in the sector, another quantity of corn – without any reference to values. However, the rate of profit so determined is also the general rate of profits since, in the case of free competition, all other sectors that need corn as an input yield the proprietors of capital the same rate of profit via an adjustment of the prices of their products relative to that of corn.

In his 1960 book Sraffa writes: "It should perhaps be stated that it was only when the Standard system and the distinction between basics and non-basics had emerged in the course of the present investigation that the [corn-ratio] theory suggested itself as a natural consequence" (Sraffa 1960: 93). Corn in this interpretation is what Sraffa in his book was to call a "basic" commodity (and actually the only basic commodity in the system), since it is needed directly or indirectly in the production of all commodities (Sraffa 1960: 7), whereas all the other commodities are non-basics. This distinction plays a crucial role in the concepts of the standard system and standard commodity, which Sraffa had succeeded in elaborating (with the help of Abram S. Besicovitch) by May 1944, and in which non-basics have been eliminated.

With these findings at the back of his mind, Sraffa (with the help of Dobb) then composed his Introduction to volume I of the *Works*, in which he interpreted Ricardo's *Essay* of 1815, which revolves around a numerical example contained in a table, as reflecting the corn-ratio theory. Sraffa also draws attention to Malthus's criticism of "the fault of Mr. Ricardo's table", since circulating capital (which includes real wages) typically does not only consist of corn, but includes "tea sugar cloaths &c for the labourers" (*Works* I: xxxii, n. 4). With the price of corn as the standard of value, the prices of manufactured products are bound to decrease in terms of corn as less and less fertile lands have to be cultivated. Ricardo had, of course, not to be convinced by Malthus that capital and wages in agriculture consist of several commodities and not only of corn (a term, which, by the way, stood for a composite commodity like "bread" in the Bible). But then, in the *Essay*, after having stated the obvious in the text himself, Ricardo in the table, simply ignored it. This may be seen to reflect his basic vision that the rate of profits could be conceived of in purely physical terms. A deeper analysis than Malthus's shallow proposition, which Ricardo paraphrased as saying that "the profits of the farmer no more regulate the profits of other trades, than the profits of other trades regulate the profits of the farmer" (*Works* VI: 104), was needed. This proposition was of no use at all in understanding how that regulation was actually meant to work.

A particularly clear expression of his basic vision Ricardo formulated some six years later in his letter to McCulloch of 13 June 1820 – to Sraffa (*Works* I: xxxiii) "an echo of the old corn-ratio theory". In it Ricardo insisted: "After all the great questions of Rent, Wages, and Profits must be explained by the proportions in which the whole produce is divided between landlords, capitalists, and labourers, *and which are not essentially connected with the doctrine of value*" (*Works* VIII: 194; emphasis added).

In the *Principles* Ricardo sought to deal with the heterogeneity of commodities in terms of the amounts of labour bestowed upon them in their production. The labour theory of value was the device by means of which he intended to overcome as best as he could the impasse in which he found himself. However, this did not make him entirely abandon his basic vision. Interestingly, in all three editions of the *Principles* we encounter a numerical example, which satisfies the homogeneity condition of output and capital, but now no longer with regard to a single industry only, but with regard to the aggregate of several industries taken together (see *Works* I: 50, 64–6).

Taking into account a multiplicity of wage goods, as Malthus had requested, does not spell trouble for Ricardo's grand vision of the factors affecting the general rate of profits and the possibility of conceiving of it in physical terms. The rate depends on the conditions of production in all industries that directly or indirectly contribute to the production of wage goods, but does not depend on the conditions of production of "luxuries" (see *Works* I: 132, 143). Ricardo's above example elevates the corn-ratio theory from its previous single commodity conceptualization to an explicitly multi-commodity conceptualization.

Clearly, both the corn-ratio theory and the labour theory of value are makeshift solutions Ricardo adopted lacking a fully satisfactory theory. In a letter to Malthus dated 17 April 1815 he spoke of his "simple doctrine", designed to "account for all the phenomena in an easy, natural manner" and thus stay away from "a labyrinth of difficulties" (*Works* VI: 214).

We now turn to Sraffa's work on the reconstruction and rectification of the classical theory of value and distribution, which began in late 1927 and extended over three periods of time, roughly the years 1927–31, 1942–45 and 1956–58.

Revisiting the classical theory of value and distribution

At the latest in 1927, Sraffa saw that the Marshallian interpretation of the classical economists as early and crude precursors of the marginalists could not be sustained. However, what precisely was the classical point of view and why had it been abandoned? Covered by thick layers of (mis)interpretation, Sraffa had first to lay bare the analytical structure of the surplus explanation of profits. In a second step he then had to remove the deficiencies because of which it had been abandoned prematurely. In a third step it had to be shown that the reformulated classical theory provided "the basis for a critique of that [the marginalist] theory" (Sraffa 1960: vi).

A main reason why the classical theory had been abandoned, Sraffa was convinced, was because the analytical tools at the disposal of its advocates were not up to the complexity of their sophisticated view of the capitalist economy. They conceived of production as a circular flow in a system characterized by a social division of labour, with inputs advanced at the beginning of the production period and consisting of heterogeneous commodities. This process generated a surplus above and beyond the necessary means of sustenance in the support of workers and the means of production that were of necessity used up, or "destroyed", in the course of production. The surplus represented the material basis of all non-labour or non-wage incomes, rents, profits and interest. In competitive conditions profits were distributed at a uniform rate on all capitals employed in the economy. How to deal with such a system?

The mismatch between tools and concepts landed these authors in an impasse, with which they tried to cope as best as they could. The result of this was the labour theory of value. Whereas Smith and Ricardo insisted that it held exactly true in explaining relative prices in exceptional circumstances only and Ricardo thought it was a reasonably good approximation to a correct theory of value otherwise, Marx contended that both the general rate of profits, the key variable of the system, and prices of production of commodities corresponding to this rate could be ascertained on the basis of the "law of value".

When Sraffa scrutinized the writings of the classical authors he concluded that the labour theory of value involved a "corruption" of their approach. In a note entitled "Degeneration of cost and value", probably written in November 1927, he insisted: "A. Smith and Ricardo and Marx indeed began to corrupt the old idea of cost, – from food to labour. But their notion was still near enough to be in many cases equivalent." (Sraffa Papers D3/12/4: 2(1)). In what sense did the labour theory of value involve a "corruption" of classical theory? (For the following see, in particular, Kurz and Salvadori 2005a, 2005b, Gehrke and Kurz 2006 and Kurz 2012.)

Sraffa rejected Marshall's concept of "real costs", which involved subjectivist elements (disutility, abstinence, waiting, and so on). While he had sensed at an early time that the classical economists' analyses differed in important respects from those of the later marginalists, he was far from clear wherein precisely the difference consisted. He now grasped that a characteristic feature of their theory of value was that it was based on what he called "physical real cost", or "physical cost" for short, to distinguish it from Marshall's "real cost": the value of a commodity reflected the amounts of commodities (raw materials, means of production and means of subsistence of workers) that had of necessity to be used up in its production. Such costs reflected the "difficulty" of producing a particular commodity, and value had to do with the amounts of commodities that had be "destroyed" in order to overcome the difficulty.

Sraffa encountered numerous expressions in the writings of the classical authors of the physical cost approach. For example, William Petty had advocated a "physician's outlook" on economic matters and had decided "to express my self in terms of *Number, Weight*, or *Measure* . . . and to consider only such Cases, as have visible Foundations in Nature, leaving those that depend upon the mutable Minds, Opinions, Appetites, and Passions of particular Men, to the Consideration of others" (Sraffa Papers D3/12/4: 3). Petty's statement is particularly interesting, because it confronts the physical cost point of view neatly with an early expression of the subjectivist one. Even more physicalist in character is James Mill's (1826: 165) remarkable proposition: "The agents of production are the commodities themselves . . . They are the food of the labourer, the tools and the machines with which he works, and the raw materials which he works upon."

Echoing these statements, Sraffa in December 1927 called classical economics explicitly a "science of things" (D3/12/61: 2) as opposed to Marshall's economics, which was a science of motives. But how could one ascertain the values of commodities in terms of physical costs? In order to determine the value of commodity A one had to know the values of commodities X, Y, Z . . . used up in its production. In short, it appeared as if one was trapped in circular reasoning, explaining values by values. How did the classical economists (and Marx) try to avoid the pitfall? They sought to render all commodities commensurable by reducing each to an "ultimate measure of value".

Sraffa in his early manuscripts followed the classical economists and attempted to reduce commodities to some such measure. He did so by starting from systems of simultaneous equations and quickly discovered that several commodities could serve as such a measure: in the case of a system without a surplus product, all commodities produced are "necessaries", that is, they are indispensable in each and every line of production. Hence each and every commodity enters into the production of each and every commodity. Relative prices, Sraffa had convinced himself in late 1927, could be ascertained without being trapped by circular reasoning that had Smith and Ricardo prompted to endorse the labour theory of value. This could be done by formulating and solving a system of simultaneous equations, in which only quantities of commodities appear as known magnitudes. This was the tool the classical economists had badly missed.

Beginning in November 1927, Sraffa developed at first square systems of equations (dealing with single production) in which no more is produced of the different commodities than is consumed productively, that is, systems without a surplus product. This is what he called his "first equations". He swiftly moved on, in the late 1920s, to investigate systems with a surplus product, without and with durable instruments of production (fixed capital) and with given and constant real wages in his "second equations", followed by an investigation of the impact of a variation in real wages on the "rate of interest" and relative prices in his "third equations". He analysed the mathematical properties of the following systems (taking gross output quantities as defining one unit of the respective output).

Without a surplus product

$$\mathbf{p} = \mathbf{A}^*\mathbf{p} \tag{2}$$

Here **p** is the price vector and **A*** is the input matrix (per unit of output) of the means of production-cum-means of subsistence consumed productively during the annual cycle of production.

With a surplus product

$$\mathbf{p} = (1 + R)\, \mathbf{A}^{**}\mathbf{p} \qquad (3)$$

Here R is the general rate of profits and **A**** is the input matrix in the new situation. With real wages given (and included in **A****), R gives the rate of return supported by the socio-technical conditions under consideration.

Studying the impact of a rise in real wages on the rate of profits and prices, Sraffa at first followed Ricardo, who had contemplated a redistribution that is proportional to the surplus product in the initial situation. If the entire surplus becomes wages, we are back to a system like equation (2) with **A**** in the place of **A***.

While Sraffa at first does not appear to have been aware of the fact that with wages absorbing the entire surplus product, relative prices of commodities can be shown to be proportional to the relative quantities of labour embodied in the various commodities, or labour values (properly defined; see Kurz and Salvadori 2009). Hence labour values reflect but a very special constellation of the sharing out of the surplus product among workers and capitalists. To emphasize this fact, Sraffa in the early 1940s coined the term "value theory of labour" (see Sraffa Papers D3/12/44: 3). Labour values, far from being simple things, require the solution of a system of simultaneous equations.

As Sraffa's interpretation of the classical authors shows, if their physical cost approach is developed coherently, there is no problem of the "transformation" of values into prices of production, with which Marx had struggled in vain. This does not mean that one cannot get, in certain cases, in a logically consistent way from labour values to prices. It only means that the latter can be determined totally independently of the former, which are therefore redundant in the analysis (Steedman 1977). Interestingly, in non-trivial cases in which one can go from labour values to prices of production the use of Sraffa's standard commodity is required (see Kurz and Salvadori 2009). In this perspective the labour theory of value is not an indispensable building block of classical economics.

Production of Commodities by Means of Commodities

Sraffa vacillated whether to publish the manuscript, which for some time he had given the title "Production of Commodities by Commodities", echoing James Mill's dictum above. Originally he had planned to write a much more comprehensive work, which was supposed to provide not only a prelude to a critique of marginalist theory, but of the critique itself, and a history of economic thought, explaining the reasons for the abandonment of the classical doctrine. The latter Sraffa considered to be an even more important task than the critique itself (see Sraffa Papers D3/12/4: 14). Besicovitch eventually convinced him to publish the results of his work, because it contained "new results".

The book was finally published in 1960. Sraffa followed the classical authors not only in terms of the method adopted and the general approach chosen, but broadly also in terms of the two-part structure of the argument. In one part he is concerned with investigating *given* "systems of production". The relationship between relative prices, the general rate of profits and the wage rate implicit in the given system of production, or "technique", is analysed partly in formal terms. Subsequently Sraffa turns to the choice of technique problem. Hence, what was initially taken as given is now an unknown. This is dealt with in chapter XII, "Switch in methods of production", on the assumption that the choice between alternative techniques "will be exclusively grounded on cheapness" (1960: 83); that is, he is concerned with determining cost-minimizing system(s) of production.

The basic premise from which Sraffa starts is that commodities are produced by means of commodities. This then leads to the concept of surplus, to the distinction between basic and non-basic products, and to the assumption that there exists at least one basic commodity (chapters I and II, §§. 1–12). The main aim of chapter III (§§. 13–22) is to provide a "preliminary survey" (§. 20) of price movements consequent upon changes in distribution on the assumption that the methods of production remain unchanged. Sraffa concludes this preliminary survey of the subject by asserting that

> the relative price-movements of two products come to depend, not only on the 'proportions' of labour to means of production by which they are respectively produced, but also on the 'proportions' by which those means have themselves been produced, and also on the 'proportions' by which the means of production of those means of production have been produced, and so on. (1960: 15)

He adds that the relative price of two products may behave in a non-expected way, and that "further complications arise" (Sraffa 1960: 15).

The complete analysis of price movements in the case of single production is provided in chapter VI (§§. 45–9), showing that the difference between the prices of two commodities can be positive or negative depending on income distribution. The analysis is significantly simplified by the use of the "Standard commodity" as numéraire. Chapters IV and V of Sraffa's book are in fact devoted to the introduction of this tool of analysis and to the study of its properties.

While Part I of Sraffa's book is devoted to single-product industries and circulating capital, Part II deals with joint production (chapters VII–IX), fixed capital (chapter X) and land (chapter XI). These chapters will be discussed later, jointly with the literature to which they gave rise. Part III of Sraffa's book is devoted to the choice of technique problem.

In the Preface to his book Sraffa stressed that he had not made any assumption about returns since it was *not* concerned with changes either in the scale of production or in the proportions in which the "factors of production" are employed (1960: v). In Parts I and II of the book it is clear that the quantities produced of the various commodities and the methods of production operated are taken as given. This is particularly clear in chapter XI, devoted to "Land" and diminishing returns. The exposition of extensive rent (§. 86), of intensive rent (§. 87), and of the problem of a multiplicity of agricultural products (§. 89) starts from given quantities and methods. Only in section 88 it is explicitly stated that the results presented in sections 86–87 (and 89) are the outcome of a process of diminishing returns, and the connection that exists "between the employment of two methods of producing corn on land of a single quality and a process of 'intensive' diminishing returns" is fully explained. This connection is considered "less obvious" than the connection between the employment of n methods of producing corn on n

different qualities of land and a process of "'extensive' diminishing returns", which is considered to be "readily recognized". It is only in this context that Sraffa actually does not consider gross output quantities as given. Interestingly, the process of diminishing returns described in section 88 is exactly the same as in Sraffa's (1925) paper; diminishing returns

> must of necessity occur because it will be the producer himself who, for his own benefit, will arrange the doses of the factors and the methods of use in a decreasing order, going from the most favourable ones to the most ineffective, and he will start production with the best combinations, resorting little by little, as these are exhausted, to the worst ones. (Sraffa 1925: 288, [1998]: 332)

Reception and Impact

Each of Sraffa's publications had a considerable immediate impact on the profession, but the long-term legacy of his work cannot be assessed as yet. His criticism of Marshall's theory was at first received enthusiastically. Leading authorities in economics such as Edgeworth or Morgenstern (1931) praised Sraffa's papers as masterpieces. The papers paved the way to the theory of monopolistic competition, but soon the profession returned to old modes of thought. His criticism of Hayek dealt a serious blow to Austrian economics. The Ricardo edition has fundamentally changed our view of the doctrine of the classical economists and of the history of economic thought more generally. It has also made the profession aware of the fact that certain doctrines may be prematurely abandoned not because of irremediable defects, but because of a form that cannot be sustained. Sraffa put into sharp relief that the "market for economic ideas" is not an efficient selection mechanism that abandons whatever is untenable and preserves whatever is correct.

While the controversy in the theory of capital took off from a paper by Joan Robinson (1953), she stressed that she had picked up ideas coming from Sraffa. The latter was the mentor of two major combatants in the controversy, Pierangelo Garegnani and Luigi Pasinetti. For summary accounts of the controversy, which revolved around the phenomena of "reswitching" and "reverse capital deepening" and their implication for the marginalist or neoclassical theory, see Garegnani (1970, 2012), Harcourt (1972) and Kurz and Salvadori (1995: ch. 14). For assessments of the impact of Sraffa's book, see Roncaglia (1978) and more recently Aspromourgos (2004).

While the problem of single production has been investigated swiftly after the publication of Sraffa's book (1960), the problems of joint production, fixed capital and land were studied only after 1978 (see Salvadori and Steedman 1990). A common aspect of Sraffa's treatment of these issues is that he takes the number of processes involved to be equal to the number of commodities. However, is that necessarily so? Schefold (1978) and Bidard (1986), among others, proved that while in some cases the answer is yes, in others it is no. This led to the adoption of the treatment of the problem in terms of inequalities (von Neumann 1945).

In appendix D of his book, Sraffa (1960) explains how the method of treating what is left of fixed capital at the end of the year as a kind of joint product is foreshadowed in some classical economists (see on this Kurz and Salvadori 2005a). In chapter X Sraffa presents his analysis of fixed capital, but limits it to the case in which only one machine is used, the efficiency of this machine is constant, and the machine is not transferable between sectors. The subsequent literature generalized the theory to cover the cases of variable efficiency, the joint utilization of machines and their transferability and varying degrees of capital utilization; for a summary account, see Kurz and Salvadori (1995: chs 7 and 9) and Salvadori (1999).

In chapter XI Sraffa (1960) presents his analysis of land. Actually Sraffa (1960: 74) refers to "Natural resources which are used in production, such as land and mineral deposits." However, we know from the correction of the proofs of his book that in the last minute he dropped parts of a section devoted to what in his preparatory notes he had called "wasting assets" (see Kurz and Salvadori 2001: 290–93). The case of scarce natural resources such as land(s) makes it abundantly clear that relative prices and income distribution cannot be ascertained independently of the gross output levels of the different commodities. In the case of intensive diminishing returns a rent will emerge if the land under consideration is scarce, which is typically reflected in the coexistence of two methods of production by means of which either land itself or an agricultural product is utilized. It has also been confirmed that "fertility" (in the sense of the order according to which different lands are cultivated) is not an intrinsic property of lands, but depends on the rate of profits.

In a case in which output quantities change over time, the scarcities of lands are bound to change and with them prices, the rates of rent, and the rate of profits (or, alternatively, the real wage rate). A similar problem arises when exhaustible resources, such as oil or minerals, are taken into consideration. These have been investigated starting from a classical-Sraffian framework of the analysis (see Kurz and Salvadori 2015: ch. 16 for a review of the whole debate).

In appendix A Sraffa (1960: 90) explains how from the economic system one can extract a "smaller self-replacing system the net product of which consists of only one kind of commodity". Sraffa calls such a miniature system a "sub-system". It is also known as a "vertically integrated system"; for a formalization and elaboration of the concept, see Pasinetti (1988).

Sraffa's book also provided the basis for a reformulation of the pure theory of international trade, paying special attention to the fact that capital consists of heterogeneous produced means of production and showing that several theorems derived within the Heckscher–Ohlin–Samuelson trade model cannot be sustained anymore; see in particular the collection of essays in Steedman (1979).

Production of Commodities by Means of Commodities was an important tool in investigating issues in the history of economic analysis and has led to a reassessment and frequently the rejection of received views. A few examples must suffice. Steedman (1977) scrutinized Marx's labour value-based reasoning and showed that it cannot generally be sustained. Kurz and Salvadori (2002) refuted Walras's criticism of Ricardo and showed that the classical and the marginalist theory are fundamentally different. In a number of contributions Kurz and Salvadori (see, for example, 1998: ch. 4) related some of the so-called "new growth models" to the classical approach. They pointed out that there is an analogy between the classical assumption of labour being generated from within the system and the replacement of labour in new growth models by "human capital" or "knowledge", a producible commodity.

HEINZ D. KURZ AND NERI SALVADORI

See also:

Ladislaus von Bortkiewicz (I); Cambridge School of economics (II); Capital theory (III); Vladimir Karpovich Dmitriev (I); Income distribution (III); John Maynard Keynes (I); Alfred Marshall (I); Karl Heinrich Marx (I); Neo-Ricardian economics (II); John von Neumann (I); William Petty (I); François Quesnay and Physiocracy (I); David Ricardo (I); Joan Violet Robinson (I); Paul Anthony Samuelson (I); Adam Smith (I); Robert Torrens (I); Value and price (III).

References and further reading

Aspromourgos, T. (2004), 'Sraffian research programmes and unorthodox economics', *Review of Political Economy*, **16** (2), 179–206.

Bidard, C. (1986), 'Is von Neumann square?', *Zeitschrift für Nationalökonomie*, **46** (4), 401–19.

Clapham, J.H. (1922), 'Of empty economic boxes', *Economic Journal*, **32** (127), 305–14.

De Vivo, G. (2014), *Catalogue of the Library of Piero Sraffa*, Milan: Fondazione Raffaele Mattioli.

Freni, G. (2001), 'Sraffa's early contribution to competitive price theory', *European Journal of the History of Economic Thought*, **8** (3), 363–90.

Freni, G. and N. Salvadori (2013), 'The construction of the long-run market supply curves: some notes on Sraffa's critique of partial equilibrium analysis', in E.S. Levrero, A. Palumbo and A. Stirati (eds), *Sraffa and the Reconstruction of Economic Theory*, vol. 3, *Sraffa's Legacy: Interpretations and Historical Perspectives*, Basingstoke and New York: Palgrave Macmillan, pp. 189–216.

Garegnani, P. (1970), 'Heterogeneous capital, the production function and the theory of distribution', *Review of Economic Studies*, **37** (3), 407–36.

Garegnani, P. (2012), 'On the present state of the capital controversies', *Cambridge Journal of Economics*, **36** (6), 1417–32.

Gehrke, C. and H.D. Kurz (2002), 'Keynes and Sraffa's "difficulties with J.H. Hollander": a note on the history of the RES edition of *The Works and Correspondence of David Ricardo*', *European Journal of the History of Economic Thought*, **9** (4), 644–71.

Gehrke, C. and H.D. Kurz (2006), 'Sraffa on von Bortkiewicz: reconstructing the classical theory of value and distribution', *History of Political Economy*, **38** (1), 91–149.

Harcourt, G.C. (1972), *Some Cambridge Controversies in the Theory of Capital*, Cambridge: Cambridge University Press.

Hayek, F.A. von (1931a), 'Reflections on the pure theory of money of Mr. J. M. Keynes', *Economica*, **11** (33), 270–95.

Hayek, F.A. von (1931b), *Prices and Production*, London: Routledge and Kegan Paul.

Hayek, F.A. von (1932), 'Money and capital: a reply', *Economic Journal*, **42** (2), 237–49.

Hume, D. (1938), *An Abstract of a Treatise on Human Nature*, ed. and introduced by J.M. Keynes and P. Sraffa, Hamden, CT: Archon Books.

Keynes, J.M. (1971–88), *The Collected Writings of John Maynard Keynes*, 30 vols, A. Robinson and D. Moggridge (eds), London: Macmillan. (In the text abbreviated as *CW*.)

Kurz, H.D. (ed.) (2000), *Critical Essays on Piero Sraffa's Legacy in Economics*, Cambridge and New York: Cambridge University Press.

Kurz, H.D. (2009), '"If some people looked like elephants and others like cats, or fish ..." On the difficulties of understanding each other: the case of Wittgenstein and Sraffa', *European Journal of the History of Economic Thought*, **16** (2), 361–74.

Kurz, H.D. (2010), 'Keynes, Sraffa, and the latter's "secret scepticism"', in B. Bateman, T. Hirai and C. Marcuzzo (eds), *The Return to Keynes*, Cambridge, MA: Belknap Press of Harvard University Press, pp. 184–204.

Kurz, H.D. (2012), 'Don't treat too ill my Piero! Interpreting Sraffa's papers', *Cambridge Journal of Economics*, **36** (6), 1535–69.

Kurz, H.D. and N. Salvadori (1995), *Theory of Production: A Long-Period Analysis*, Cambridge: Cambridge University Press.

Kurz, H.D. and N. Salvadori (1998), *Understanding 'Classical' Economics: Studies in Long-Period Theory*, London: Routledge.

Kurz, H.D. and N. Salvadori (2001), 'Sraffa and the mathematicians: Frank Ramsey and Alister Watson', in T. Cozzi and R. Marchionatti (eds), *Piero Sraffa's Political Economy: A Centenary Estimate*, London, Routledge, pp. 187–216.

Kurz, H.D. and N. Salvadori (2002), 'One theory or two? Walras's critique of Ricardo', *History of Political Economy*, **34** (2), 365–98.

Kurz, H.D. and N. Salvadori (2005a), 'Removing an "insuperable obstacle" in the way of an objectivist analysis: Sraffa's attempts at fixed capital', *European Journal of the History of Economic Thought*, **12** (3), 493–523.

Kurz, H.D. and N. Salvadori (2005b), 'Representing the production and circulation of commodities in material terms: on Sraffa's objectivism', *Review of Political Economy*, **17** (3), 413–41.

Kurz, H.D. and N. Salvadori (2009), 'Sraffa and the labour theory of value: a few observations', in J. Vint, J.S. Metcalfe, H.D. Kurz, N. Salvadori and P.A. Samuelson (eds), *Economic Theory and Economic Thought: Festschrift in Honour of Ian Steedman*, London, Routledge, pp. 187–213.

Kurz, H.D. and N. Salvadori (2015), *Revisiting Classical Economics: Studies in Long-Period Analysis*, London: Routledge.

Mill, J. (1826), *Elements of Political Economy*, 3rd edn, London: Henry G. Bohn.

Morgenstern, O. (1931), 'Offene Probleme der Kosten- und Ertragstheorie', *Zeitschrift für Nationalökonomie*, **2** (4), 481–522.

Napolitano, G. (2005), 'Sraffa and Gramsci: a recollection', *Review of Political Economy*, **17** (3), 407–412.

Neumann, J. von (1945), 'A model of general economic equilibrium', *Review of Economic Studies*, **13** (1), 1–9.

Pasinetti, L.L. (1988), 'Growing subsystems, vertically hyper-integrated sectors and the labour theory of value', *Cambridge Journal of Economics*, **12** (1), 125–34.

Pollit, B.H. (1990), 'Clearing the path for "Production of Commodities by Means of Commodities": notes on the collaboration of Maurice Dobb in Piero Sraffa's edition of the "Works and Correspondence of David Ricardo"', in K. Bharadwaj and B. Schefold (eds), *Essays on Piero Sraffa: Critical Perspectives on the Revival of Classical Theory*, London: Unwin Hyman, pp. 516–28.

Ranchetti, F. (2002), 'On the relationship between Sraffa and Keynes', in T. Cozzi and R. Marchionatti (eds), *Piero Sraffa's Political Economy. A Centenary Estimate*, London and New York: Routledge, pp. 311–31.

Ricardo, D. (1951–73), *The Works and Correspondence of David Ricardo*, 11 vols, ed. P. Sraffa with the collaboration of M.H. Dobb, Cambridge: Cambridge University Press.

Robinson, J.V. (1953), 'The production function and the theory of capital', *Review of Economic Studies*, **21**, 81–106.

Roncaglia, A. (1978), *Sraffa and the Theory of Prices*, New York: Wiley, first published in Italian in 1975.

Salvadori, N. (1999), 'Transferable machines with uniform efficiency paths', in G. Mongiovi and F. Petri (eds), *Value, Distribution and Capital*, London and New York: Routledge, pp. 297–313.

Salvadori, N. and I. Steedman (eds) (1990), *Joint Production of Commodities*, Aldershot: Edward Elgar.

Schefold, B. (1978), 'On counting equations', *Zeitschrift für Nationalökonomie*, **38**, 253–85.

Signorino, R. (2000), 'Method and analysis in Piero Sraffa's 1925 critique of Marshallian economics', *European Journal of the History of Economic Thought*, **7**, 569–94.

Signorino, R. (2001), 'An appraisal of Piero Sraffa's "The laws of returns under competitive conditions"', *European Journal of the History of Economic Thought*, **8**, 230–50.

Sraffa Papers, Trinity College Library, Cambridge, catalogued by Jonathan Smith, archivist; the references follow the Trinity College catalogue.

Sraffa, P. (1920), 'Monetary inflation in Italy during the war', thesis obtained in November 1920, Premiata Scuola Tip. Salesiana, Turin, trans. from the Italian by W.J. Harcourt and C. Sardoni (1993), *Cambridge Journal of Economics*, **17** (1), 7–26.

Sraffa, P. (1925), 'Sulle relazioni fra costo e quantità prodotta', *Annali di Economia*, **2**, 277–328, English trans. L.L. Pasinetti (ed.) (1998), *Italian Economic Papers*, Bologna: Il Mulino, pp. 323–63, reprinted in H.D. Kurz and N. Salvadori (eds) *The Legacy of Sraffa*, vol. 1, Cheltenham, UK and Northampton, MA, USA: Edward Elgar, pp. 3–43.

Sraffa, P. (1926), 'The laws of returns under competitive conditions', *Economic Journal*, **36** (144), 535–50.

Sraffa, P. (1930), 'A criticism. A rejoinder', *Economic Journal*, **40** (March), 89–93.

Sraffa, P. (1932a), 'Dr. Hayek on money and capital', *Economic Journal*, **42** (1), 42–53.

Sraffa, P. (1932b), 'A rejoinder', *Economic Journal*, **42** (2), 249–51.

Sraffa, P. (1960), *Production of Commodities by Means of Commodities*, Cambridge: Cambridge University Press.

Sraffa, P. (1962), 'Production of Commodities: a comment', *Economic Journal*, **72** (286), 477–9.

Sraffa, P. (1991), *Lettere a Tania per Gramsci*, ed. V. Gerratana, Rome: Editori Riuniti.

Sraffa, P. and L. Einaudi (1930), 'An alleged correction of Ricardo', *Quarterly Journal of Economics*, **44** (3), 539–45.

Steedman, I. (1977), *Marx after Sraffa*, London: New Left Books.

Steedman, I. (ed.) (1979), *Fundamental Issues in Trade Theory*, London: Macmillan.

Steedman, I. (1988), 'Sraffian interdependence and partial equilibrium analysis', *Cambridge Journal of Economics*, **12** (1), 85–95.

Edward Hastings Chamberlin (1899–1967)

Edward Hastings Chamberlin was an American economist. He was born in La Conner, Washington, on 18 May 1899, and died in Cambridge, Massachusetts, on 16 July 1967. His book, *The Theory of Monopolistic Competition*, and Joan Robinson's *The Theory of Imperfect Competition*, both published in 1933, are unanimously acknowledged as the two path-breaking contributions that paved the way to the (so-called) imperfect/ monopolistic competition revolution, whose basic aim was freeing economic analysis from the straitjacket of perfect competition theory. Insomuch as it was presented as a revolution in microeconomic theory – on a par with the almost contemporaneous Keynesian revolution in macroeconomic theory – the monopolistic competition literature of the 1930s–1950s was a revolution that failed to dethrone perfect competition from its privileged status within economics (Tsoulfidis 2009). Yet, taking the clue from Dixit and Stiglitz (1977), a second wave of monopolistic competition literature has blossomed with much more profound impact on various quarters of economic analysis such as international trade, macroeconomics, growth theory and economic geography (Brakman and Hijdra 2004).

While Joan Robinson soon lost any interest in the subject, Chamberlin devoted his entire intellectual life to (1) report and rectify (what he considered to be) "misconceptions" of his own theory and (2) differentiate his own contribution from that of his Cambridge (UK) counterpart. At least on this latter point, his efforts were largely ineffective: Kaldor's scathing remark – "Professor Chamberlin has fallen a victim to the general tendency among producers in an imperfectly competitive market – a tendency he so convincingly describes – and is trying to differentiate his product too far" (Kaldor 1938: 525) – epitomizes the mainstream view that Chamberlin's and Robinson's analyses are but an instance of a multiple discovery of the same set of ideas, a phenomenon not uncommon in economics. (On Chamberlin's multivariate tactics to gain precedence over Joan Robinson, see Aslanbeigui and Oakes 2011.)

As we know from Chamberlin's personal recollections, his interest in value theory, in general, and on the relationship between perfect competition and monopoly, in particular, dates back to 1921 when, as a graduate student at the University of Michigan, he "took a course in Railway Transportation under Professor I.L. Sharfman, and wrote a course paper on the Taussig–Pigou controversy over railway rates" (Chamberlin 1961: 517). He then moved to Harvard where he devoted the years 1924–26 to writing his PhD dissertation, successfully defended in 1927 under the guidance of Allyn Young. Reading Chamberlin's acknowledgement of his intellectual debt to Young in the Preface to the first edition of his 1933 book, the latter seemed deeply involved in the project, more than a simple supervisor. (On Young's influence on Chamberlin, see Reinwald 1977, 1985; Blitch 1985.)

Until retirement in 1966, Chamberlin spent almost all his academic career at Harvard (where he became full professor in 1937) also serving as editor of the *Quarterly Journal of Economics* from 1948 to 1958 (Kuenne 2008). Together with Wassily Leontief, Gottfried Haberler, Alvin Hansen and, of course, Joseph Alois Schumpeter, he was one of the leading figures who contributed to establishing the Harvard Department of Economics in the 1930s. A balanced assessment of Chamberlin's scholarship is provided by two of his Harvard colleagues:

As a scholar Chamberlin was a "lone wolf" whose work owed remarkably little to the extensive literature of the 1920s on increasing returns. He was not much interested in developments in areas of economics other than his own. Macroeconomic analysis in particular left him cold, and the fact the Keynes and other macroeconomists, in general, assumed that markets were competitive was enough to turn him off. But his influence on the study of the structure and functioning of markets and on the theory of the firm was profound. (Mason and Lamont 1982: 423)

In the Introduction to her 1933 book Joan Robinson pointed to Sraffa's intimation to "abandon the path of free competition and turn in the opposite direction, namely, towards monopoly" (Sraffa 1926: 542) as her primary source of inspiration. By contrast, as the opportunity arose, Chamberlin minimized or even denied his intellectual debt to the literature concerning the increasing returns-perfect competition debate of the late 1920s. Conversely, he was much less explicit on the "ultimate origins and influences contributing to the development of *The Theory of Monopolistic Competition*", as he plainly admitted in his 1961 *Quarterly Journal of Economics* paper, where he tried to fill such a lacuna. There, besides "classic" references to perfect competition and duopoly literature (from Cournot to Marshall and J.M. Clark), he focused on the "Competing Monopolists and the Literature of Business" (1961: 524 ff) and stressed the abysmal chasm between the view of market competition proposed by pure economic theorists, on the one hand, and by the applied scholars working on goodwill, patents, trademarks, advertisement, selling costs and so on, on the other. For Chamberlin, received economic theory, based on the perfect competition/pure monopoly dichotomy, presented a basically false representation of actual competition in real-world markets: its two polar models rigidly separated the forces which tend towards monopoly (the tireless effort by individual undertakers to create their own "special markets" – as Marshall would say – by means of product differentiation) and those, which tend towards competition (the invasion of someone else's "special market" through product imitation). For Chamberlin, these two forces are deeply interwoven, though in varying degrees in different markets, to the effect that a rigid taxonomy of market structures turns out to be definitely misleading:

> "Monopolistic competition" is a challenge to the traditional viewpoint of economics that competition and monopoly are alternatives and that individual prices are to be explained in terms of either the one or the other. By contrast, it is held that most economic situations are composites of both competition and monopoly, and that, wherever this is the case, a false view is given by neglecting either one of the two forces and regarding the situation as made up entirely of the other ... To say that each producer in an industry has a monopoly of his own variety of product is not to say that the industry is monopolized. On the contrary, there may be a very intense competition within the industry, not of the sort described by the theories of pure competition to be sure, but different by virtue of the fact that each producer has a monopoly of his own variety of product. (Chamberlin 1937: 570–71; see also Chamberlin 1951: 352–3)

According to Chamberlin's (implicit) methodology, the predictive content of a theory depends on the realism of its assumptions. That is the reason why he thought that perfect competition, based on an utterly unrealistic description of the firm, ought to be banished from the realm of economics:

> if we are to have any respect as scientists for the economic system which it is our duty to explain, the correct procedure would seem to be not to assume pure competition and then to bring the firm into line by Procrustean methods, but rather to build up the system from the firms which

compose it, *discovering from the facts what assumptions are appropriate as to competition and monopoly*, and therefore as to structure. (Chamberlin 1951: 349, emphasis added)

(It hardly needs to be stressed that such a methodological standpoint dramatically flies in the face of a positive economist *à la* Friedman and played a non-negligible role in provoking Chicago economists to react vehemently against the monopolistic competition literature. Keppler (1998) provides a methodological assessment of the "Chamberlin *vs* Chicago" controversy. A different view is entertained by Latsis (1972: 207), who considers such controversy but "a family quarrel between two slightly differing branches of the same dominant research programme, namely, situational determinism".)

Once consumers perceive goods as differentiated and brand loyalty is created, competing firms may control and optimally choose price(s), product quality, design and packaging, store location, retail contracts, advertisement expenditure, after-sales services and so on. In short, competition becomes a multi-dimensional activity, far removed from the passive quantity-adjustment envisaged by the perfect competition model. While any realistic description of how competition actually works cannot dispense with the notion of "product as a variable" (Chamberlin 1953), it is fair to say that Chamberlin was not able to achieve definite analytical results beyond the narrow field of price-competition.

In what follows, attention focuses on Chamberlin's analysis of firm's equilibrium in the large-group case, that is, when producers "whose goods are fairly close substitutes" (Chamberlin 1933 [1962]: 81) are so numerous that "any adjustment of price . . . by a single producer spreads its influence over so many of his competitors that the impact felt by any one is negligible and does not lead him to any readjustment of his own situation" (ibid.: 83). Moreover, Chamberlin's analysis of the large-group case is carried out "under the heroic assumption that both demand and cost curves for all the 'products' are uniform throughout the group" (ibid.: 82) and that "conditions of constant cost obtained for the group as a whole" (ibid.: 85). (The debate following the publication of *The Theory of Monopolistic Competition* focused on the large-group case as Chamberlin's main analytical innovation. Chamberlin did not ignore the small-group case, both with homogeneous and differentiated products, but his analysis of oligopolistic competition was not up to the task; see Kuenne 2008.)

Figure 6 reproduces with only slight modifications to Figure 14 on page 91 of *The Theory of Monopolistic Competition* (1933 [1962])). AC is the long-run U-shaped average cost curve of firm 1, dd' is its (perceived) demand curve. Since products are differentiated, the dd' curve is downward-sloping and not horizontal, as in the perfect competition model. For Chamberlin, "the divergence of the demand curve for his product from the horizontal imposes upon the seller a price problem, absent under pure competition, which is the same as that ordinarily associated with the monopolist" (Chamberlin 1933 [1962]: 71). Yet, unlike the pure monopoly case where the monopolist faces no close substitutes, in Chamberlin's large-group case the position of firm 1's demand curve depends, *inter alia*, on the prices of its substitutes. How to tackle analytically such an interdependence problem? Chamberlin's solution is a very Marshallian one: "[within] any group of closely related products . . . the demand and cost conditions (and hence the price) of any one are defined only if the demand and cost conditions with respect to the others are taken as given" (ibid.: 69). Accordingly, the dd' curve is drawn on the assumption that firm 1 believes that all its competitors will keep their prices constant, irrespective of its

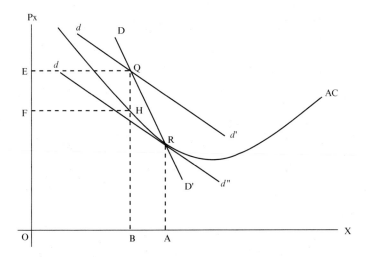

Figure 6   Short- and long-run equilibriums of a firm in Chamberlin's large-group case

price policy. In particular, firm *i* believes that if it reduces its price, its competitors will not retaliate by cutting their prices. (By contrast, *DD'* is firm 1's demand curve when all its competitors follow its same price-cutting policy so to keep their market shares unaltered.) BQ is firm 1's initial price and EQHF its initial profit.

(Note that, unlike Joan Robinson and her emphasis on the marginal revenue curve, Chamberlin wittingly did not make use of marginal analysis to determine firm's equilibrium price BQ and quantity 0B. He disparagingly defined the marginal revenue curve as "a piece of pure technique unrelated to the central problem". For Chamberlin the major drawback of the marginal revenue curve is that "it does not by itself reveal the price" while price is "the category with reference to which business decisions are most usually taken" (Chamberlin 1952: 321–2). The (alleged) irrelevance of marginalism in *The Theory of Monopolistic Competition* is the basic foundation of Chamberlin's claim that his analysis, unlike Joan Robinson's, is wholly compatible with full-cost pricing theories *à la* Hall and Hitch.)

BQ is not an equilibrium price for firm 1: the latter may increase its profit by cutting its price, that is, moving to the right of BQ along *dd'*. For Chamberlin "any individual seller [has no fear] of ultimately reducing his gain [by a price cut] through forcing others to follow him because his competitors are so numerous that the market of each of them is inappreciably affected by his move" (Chamberlin 1933 [1962]: 91). Thus, since all firms within the group are assumed to have the same demand and cost conditions and the same belief on their rivals' reaction, all firms have an incentive to, and actually will, cut their prices. As a consequence, firm 1's demand curve will shift downwards (from *dd'* to *dd''*) until it becomes tangent to AC. At this tangency point the price cutting policy ceases to be profitable and the equilibrium price AR is finally determined. Although its profit is annihilated, firm 1 is producing in the downward-sloping region of its average cost curve. Hence, firm 1's equilibrium is characterized by unexploited scale economies (that is, excess capacity).

RODOLFO SIGNORINO

See also:

British marginalism (II); Cambridge School of economics (II); Chicago School (II); Competition (III); Antoine-Augustin Cournot (I); Industrial organization (III); Alfred Marshall (I); Joan Violet Robinson (I); Piero Sraffa (I); Theory of the firm (III).

References and further reading

Aslanbeigui, N. and G. Oakes (2011), 'Hostage to fortune: Edward Chamberlin and the reception of the theory of monopolistic competition', *History of Political Economy*, **43** (3), 471–512.

Blitch, C.P. (1985), 'The genesis of Chamberlinian monopolistic competition theory: addendum', *History of Political Economy*, **17** (3), 395–400.

Brakman, S. and B.J. Hijdra (eds) (2004), *The Monopolistic Competition Revolution in Retrospect*, Cambridge: Cambridge University Press.

Chamberlin, E.H. (1933), *The Theory of Monopolistic Competition. A Re-orientation of the Theory of Value*, Cambridge, MA: Harvard University Press, 8th edn 1962.

Chamberlin, E.H. (1937), 'Monopolistic or imperfect competition?', *Quarterly Journal of Economics*, **51** (4), 557–80.

Chamberlin, E.H. (1951), 'Monopolistic competition revisited', *Economica*, **18** (72), 343–62.

Chamberlin, E.H. (1952), '"Full cost" and monopolistic competition', *Economic Journal*, **62** (246), 318–25.

Chamberlin, E.H. (1953), 'The product as an economic variable', *Quarterly Journal of Economics*, **67** (1), 1–29.

Chamberlin, E.H. (ed.) (1954), *Monopoly, Competition, and Their Regulation. Papers and Proceedings of a Conference held by the International Economic Association*, London: Macmillan.

Chamberlin, E.H. (1957), *Towards a More General Theory of Value*, New York: Oxford University Press.

Chamberlin, E.H. (1961), 'The origin and early development of monopolistic competition theory', *Quarterly Journal of Economics*, **75** (4), 515–43.

Dixit, A.K. and J.E. Stiglitz (1977), 'Monopolistic competition and optimum product diversity', *American Economic Review*, **67** (3), 297–308.

Kaldor, N. (1938), 'Professor Chamberlin on monopolistic and imperfect competition', *Quarterly Journal of Economics*, **52** (3), 513–29.

Keppler, J.H. (1998), 'The genesis of "positive economics" and the rejection of monopolistic competition theory: a methodological debate', *Cambridge Journal of Economics*, **22** (3), 261–76.

Kuenne, R.E. (2008), 'Chamberlin, Edward Hastings (1899 – 1967)', in S.N. Durlauf and L.E. Blume (eds), *The New Palgrave Dictionary of Economics*, 2nd edn, London: Macmillan.

Latsis, S.J. (1972), 'Situational determinism in economics', *British Journal for the Philosophy of Science*, **23** (3), 207–45.

Mason, E.S. and T.S. Lamont (1982), 'The Harvard Department of Economics from the beginning to World War II', *Quarterly Journal of Economics*, **97** (3), 383–433.

Reinwald, T.P. (1977), 'The genesis of Chamberlinian monopolistic competition theory', *History of Political Economy*, **9** (4), 522–34.

Reinwald, T.P. (1985), 'The genesis of Chamberlinian monopolistic competition theory: addendum – a comment', *History of Political Economy*, **17** (3), 400–402.

Robinson, Joan V. (1933), *The Economics of Imperfect Competition*, London: Macmillan.

Sraffa, P. (1926), 'The laws of returns under competitive conditions', *Economic Journal*, **36** (144), 535–50.

Tsoulfidis, L. (2009), 'The rise and fall of monopolistic competition revolution', *International Review of Economics*, **56** (1), 29–45.

Friedrich August von Hayek (1899–1992)

> Nobody can be a great economist who is only an economist – and I am even tempted to add that the economist who is only an economist is likely to become a nuisance if not a positive danger. (F.A. Hayek, "The dilemmas of specialization", 1956, echoing J.S. Mill)

Friedrich A. Hayek passed away on 23 March 1992, at the age of 92. His first academic publication was in the 1920s and his last was in the late 1980s. As Bruce Caldwell has put it:

> The volume of Hayek's work provides another daunting challenge for interpreters. Hayek lived from 1899 to 1992, and his writings span seven decades. Worse, he was incredibly prolific. Even worse, he did not restrict himself to economics, making contributions in fields as diverse as psychology, political philosophy, the history of ideas, and social-science methodology. (Caldwell 2004: 4)

Hayek's depth and breadth was probably unmatched among twentieth-century economists, and was more in keeping with the grand tradition of moral philosophy and political economy as it was practised from Adam Smith to J.S. Mill. There certainly can be little doubt that Hayek was among the most prodigious classical liberal scholars of the twentieth century. Though he was awarded the 1974 Sveriges Riksbank Prize in Economic Sciences in Memory of Alfred Nobel, his scholarly endeavours extended well beyond economics. At the time of his death, he had published 130 articles and 25 books on topics ranging from technical economics to theoretical psychology, from political philosophy to legal anthropology, and from the philosophy of science to the history of ideas. Hayek was no mere dabbler; he was an accomplished scholar in each of these fields of inquiry. On Google Scholar, his article "The use of knowledge in society" has been cited over 11 000 times, while his classic works in political economy *The Road to Serfdom*, *The Constitution of Liberty*, and *Law, Legislation and Liberty* all have over 5000 citations each. Finally, his work in theoretical psychology, *The Sensory Order* (Hayek 1952b), has also received close to 1000 citations. Moreover, in a study by David Skarbek (2009) on the Nobel Prize lectures, Hayek was the second most cited author by the other Sveriges Riksbank Prize winners in their own official Nobel lectures, behind only Kenneth Arrow. Hayek's impact, as I have argued elsewhere (Boettke 1999: xiv–xv), has been felt more in the broad social scientific community than in scientific economics. Further, as Boettke and O'Donnell (2013) argue, Hayek's main insights have been fundamentally misunderstood when discussed within formalist renderings of economic theory.

Hayek was born into a family of intellectuals in Vienna on 8 May 1899. He earned doctorates from the University of Vienna (1921 and 1923). During the early years of the twentieth century the theories of the Austrian School of Economics, sparked by Menger's *Principles of Economics* (1871), were gradually being formulated and refined by Eugen von Böhm-Bawerk, his brother-in-law, Friedrich von Wieser, Joseph Schumpeter and Ludwig von Mises. Hayek's grandfather was an academic colleague and friends with Böhm-Bawerk and Wieser. His father was a physician and botanist. Hayek grew up in an atmosphere of science and scholarship.

Economics at the University of Vienna was integrated with the study of law. Hayek began his studies at the University of Vienna in November 1918 and earned his first doctorate in law in 1921, and his second doctorate in political economy in 1923. As a student, Hayek studied law, psychology and economics, before specializing in economic theory. As a student during his first doctorate, he recalled attending one of Mises's classes, but found Mises's anti-socialist position too strong for his liking. Wieser, who was more interventionist with respect to economic policy and a very distinguished professor, offered an approach that was more attractive to Hayek at the time, and Hayek became his pupil. Hayek would eventually do his first original work in economic theory dealing with the problem of imputation under the guidance of Wieser. Yet, ironically it was Mises, through his devastating critique of socialism published in 1922, who would become his mentor throughout the 1920s and set Hayek on the research path that he would pursue in philosophy, politics and economics throughout his long career. At the time, while Menger, Böhm-Bawerk and Mises were well known for their liberalism, this was not seen as essential to the scientific project of the school in furthering marginal utility analysis; the science of economics, not commitment to any political philosophy, was the defining characteristic of the Austrian school (see Myrdal 1929).

After graduating in 1921, Hayek via an introduction from Wieser was hired by Mises to work in a government office set up for the primary purpose of the settlement of pre-war private debts between nations as part of the peace treaty of 1919. Hayek worked under Mises's direct supervision in this office, interrupted only by his visit to the US, until 1927. In 1927, Mises helped Hayek establish the Austrian Institute for Business Cycle Research, which Hayek directed after Mises was able to secure the necessary funds. Hayek would in turn bring in Oskar Morgenstern as his collaborator. When Hayek left for the London School of Economics (LSE) in 1931, Morgenstern would assume the directorship until he himself emigrated to the US.

The best way to understand Hayek's vast contributions to economics and classical liberalism is to view them in light of the programme for the study of social cooperation laid out by Mises. Mises, the great system builder, provided Hayek with the research programme. Hayek became the great dissector and analyser. His life's work can best be appreciated as an attempt to make explicit what Mises had left implicit, to refine what Mises had outlined, and to answer questions Mises had left unanswered. Of Mises, Hayek stated: "There is no single man to whom I owe more intellectually" (1978 [1983]: 17). The Misesian connection is most evident in Hayek's work on the problems with socialism. However, the insights derived from the analysis of socialism permeate the entire corpus of his work, from business cycles to the origin of social cooperation. In Hayek's own depiction of his intellectual relationship with Mises he stressed how working in close collaboration with someone for an extended period of time with whom you agree so strongly with their conclusions but do not find the analysis by which they ended up with those conclusions completely satisfying was for him a great stimulus for original thought.

In 1923, after Mises had secured Hayek the necessary leave of absence on financial terms favourable enough to make the plan possible, Hayek travelled to the US to observe and study the latest statistical techniques that were being developed to study industrial fluctuations. Hayek spent time both at New York University (NYU, where he worked as a research assistant to Jeremiah Jenks, and actually submitted work towards earning a PhD) and Columbia during that year in NYC. He was interested in the work at Columbia, where Wesley Claire Mitchell was pioneering the empirical approach to business cycles that would define the early National Bureau of Economic Research (NBER) approach. Upon his return to Vienna, Hayek continued his work with Mises, and, as already mentioned, they established the Austrian Institute for Business Cycle Research, which Hayek would direct. During his trip to the US, Hayek had already begun to draft "The monetary policy of the United States after the recovery from the 1920s crisis" (1925), which sought to apply the Mises–Wicksell theory of the business cycle to contemporary events.

Building on Mises's *The Theory of Money and Credit* (1912), Hayek refined both the technical understanding of capital coordination and the institutional details of credit policy. Seminal studies in monetary theory and the trade cycle followed. Hayek's first book, *Monetary Theory and the Trade Cycle* (1929), analysed the effects of credit expansion on the capital structure of an economy.

Publication of that book prompted an invitation from Lionel Robbins for Hayek to lecture at the LSE. His lectures there were published in a second book on the "Austrian theory of the trade cycle", *Prices and Production* (1931), which was cited by the Nobel Prize Committee in 1974.

Hayek's 1930–31 lectures at the LSE were received with such great acclaim that he was called back and appointed Tooke Professor of Economic Science and Statistics. At age 32, Hayek had secured one of the more prestigious appointments in the economics profession. As he has said in an interview with Axel Leijonhufvud, when you get an appointment as a professor in London at 32, you take it (Hayek 1979b).

The Mises–Hayek theory of the trade cycle explained the "cluster of errors" that characterizes the cycle. Credit expansion, made possible by the artificial lowering of interest rates, misleads businessmen; they are led to engage in ventures that would not otherwise have appeared profitable. The false signal generated by credit expansion leads to mal-coordination of the production and consumption plans of economic actors. This mal-coordination first manifests itself in a "boom," and then, later, in the "bust" as the time pattern of production adjusts to the real pattern of savings and consumption in the economy.

Hayek versus Keynes

Soon after Hayek's arrival in London he crossed swords with John Maynard Keynes. Keynes, a prominent member of the British civil service then serving on the governmental Committee on Finance and Industry, was credited by the academic community as the author of serious books on economics. The Hayek–Keynes debate was perhaps the most fundamental debate in monetary economics in the early twentieth century. Beginning with his essay, *The End of Laissez Faire* (1926), Keynes presented his position in the language of pragmatic liberalism. As a result, Keynes was heralded as the "saviour of capitalism," rather than being viewed as a critic of the existing order. So the Hayek–Keynes debate was of a different nature than Hayek's debate with the market socialists, but ultimately turned on similar issues related to the nature of the price system and the institutional infrastructure within which economic activity takes place.

Hayek believed he had pinpointed the fundamental problems with Keynes's economics – his failure to understand the role that interest rates and capital structure play in a market economy. Because of Keynes's habit of using aggregate (collective) concepts, he failed to address these issues adequately in *A Treatise on Money* (1930). Hayek pointed out that Keynes's aggregation tended to redirect the analytical focus of the economist away from examining how the industrial structure of the economy emerged from the economic choices of individuals.

Keynes did not take kindly to Hayek's criticism. Hayek had accused Keynes of dropping the capital theory and microeconomic analysis of intertemporal coordination from the Wicksellian system; but of course, those elements in the Wicksellian system were being developed by Mises and Hayek. So in essence, Hayek was criticizing Keynes for not incorporating the Mises–Hayek work into his analysis, despite the fact that Keynes's work was written before Mises's *Theory of Money and Credit* had been translated into English (1953), and before Hayek had published *Prices and Production* (1931). Keynes chose to respond at first by attacking Hayek's *Prices and Production*. As Keynes wrote:

> The book, as it stands, seems to me to be one of the most frightful muddles I have ever read, with scarcely a sound proposition in it beginning with page 45, and yet it remains a book of some interest, which is likely to leave its mark on the mind of the reader. It is an extraordinary example of how, starting with a mistake, a remorseless logician can end up in bedlam . . . (1931: 394)

So rather than judging the Mises–Hayek theory of industrial fluctuations as one of the first systemic attempts to integrate micro and macro and provide a choice-theoretic foundation for industrial fluctuations and economic coordination more generally, Keynes judged the effort as a muddle.

Keynes's second intellectual move was to ally himself with fellow Cambridge economist Piero Sraffa against Hayek's suggested adoption of Böhm-Bawerkian capital theory. As Kurz explains, "When Sraffa was confronted with Hayek's argument, he knew already that its theoretical core – Böhm-Bawerk's theory of capital and interest – was shaky" (Kurz 2015: 111). It is thus unsurprising that Sraffa argued that he found internally contradictory Hayek's attempt at construction of a monetary theory upon a foundation that was in his estimation unsound. Hayek's emphasis on the coordination in a monetary economy provided by the "natural rate of interest" was one such faulty step in the construction, as there simply was no such singular rate but rather a collection of natural rates. Considered within the economics profession at the time to be obscure if not incomprehensible, the exchange between Hayek and Sraffa (Hayek 1932; Sraffa 1932a, 1932b) regarding the perceived flaws in Hayek's theoretical arguments blunted the force of Hayek's call for Keynes to adopt Hayek's own capital theory in the medium-term. Only later, in light of the evolution of the theoretical systems developed by Hayek and Sraffa following the debate, were these articles seen as providing insights into the nature of each thinker's understanding of the roles played by capital theory, interest rates, and equilibrium in the economic system (Lachmann 1986).

Finally, Keynes's third intellectual move was equally interesting and proved very effective as well. Keynes claimed that he no longer believed what he had written in *A Treatise on Money*, and turned his attention to writing another book, *The General Theory of Employment, Interest, and Money* (1936), which in time became the most influential book on economic policy in the twentieth century. As Mark Blaug (1997: 642) remarks, never before had we seen such a quick and complete conversion of the profession to the new paradigm as we saw in the decade after the publication of the *General Theory*.

Throughout the US and Europe, Keynesian thought dominated economic discourse from the basic teaching of the discipline to the highest level deliberations of public policy. The entire discipline of economics was transformed as a result, and the discipline that Hayek was trained in, and practised, seemed to vanish as he was still working out the implications of his own thinking.

Rather than attempting to criticize directly what Keynes presented in his *General Theory*, Hayek turned his analytical attention to refining capital theory. Hayek was convinced that the essential point to convey to Keynes and the rest of the economics profession concerning monetary policy lay in working out the implications of a consistent and coherent capital theory. Thus Hayek proceeded to set forth his thesis in *The Pure Theory of Capital* (1941). However correct his assessment may have been, this book, Hayek's most technical, was his least influential. In the eyes of the public Keynes had defeated Hayek. Hayek lost standing in the profession and with students. If in the early 1930s almost every one of his students at the LSE was a Hayekian, then by the end of the decade barely a Hayekian could be found.

During this time, Hayek was also involved in another grand debate in economic policy, the socialist calculation debate, triggered by a 1920 article by Mises that stated that socialism was technically impossible because in abolishing private property in the means of production it would lack market prices for capital goods. Without prices guiding production decisions, economic planning would be lost amid the sea of economic possibilities. Socialist planning, Mises demonstrated, would not be able to engage in rational economic calculation of the alternative investment plans. The socialist planner would not know, for example, whether to build railroad tracks out of platinum or steel owing to the inability to engage in rational economic calculation. Mises had refined this argument in 1922 in *Socialism: An Economic and Sociological Analysis*, the book which had profoundly impressed the young Hayek (and the young Lionel Robbins) when it appeared. Hayek developed Mises's argument further in several articles during the 1930s. In 1935, he collected and edited a series of essays on the problems of socialist economic organization, *Collectivist Economic Planning*, in which Mises's original 1920 article was published in English for the first time. Hayek and Robbins also worked to get Mises's *Socialism* translated and published in English, which it was in 1936. Robbins would publish *Economic Planning and the International Order* in 1937, and additional Hayek essays on the problems of socialism, and specifically the model of "market socialism" developed by Oskar Lange and Abba Lerner in their attempt to answer Mises and Hayek, were later collected in *Individualism and Economic Order* (Hayek 1948).

Again, the economics profession and the intellectual community in general did not view Hayek's criticism as decisive in the dispute. The socialist calculation debate of the 1930s took place on two levels – as a technical question of economic theory and as an outgrowth of the progressive social, cultural, and philosophical approach to modernity. As a proposition of economic theory, since Mises's original challenge in 1920, economists had developed in more detail the perfectly competitive model and refined the general equilibrium concept central to neoclassical economics. While the early Austrian economists had viewed themselves as squarely in the scientific mainstream of the then emerging neoclassical economics in the late nineteenth and early twentieth centuries, by the 1930s it was becoming increasingly clear to Mises, and especially Hayek, that in the context of the socialist calculation debate the neoclassical tradition of price determination modelled as a simultaneous system of equations within a perfectly competitive economy had diverged significantly from the Austrian school's understanding of the theory of price formation through the "higgling and bargaining" in the entrepreneurial and competitive market economy (Lavoie 1985). Competition in the model of perfect competition was no longer seen as a rivalrous activity, but instead as an equilibrium state of affairs with a set of corresponding optimality conditions. To the Austrian economists, in contrast, the competitive market process emerges out of the ongoing exchange relations and productive activities that are engaged in by economic participants and the institutions within which these activities take place.

The strategic move made by Oskar Lange and Abba Lerner in developing the model of market socialism was to substitute for the Walrasian auctioneer and the *tâtonnement* process the Central Planning Board and the establishment of the optimality rule of price equals marginal cost and the directive to produce at that level that minimizes average costs as the guide to socialist enterprises. If the essence of either the capitalist or socialist system was captured in the simultaneous equation system of general competitive equilibrium, then the institutional background of private property or collective ownership should not matter for the achievement of optimality in allocation and production decisions. They argued that such a response to Mises (and to Hayek) effectively answered the challenge of economic calculation and production could in fact be rationalized under socialism. Lange argued that his model had demonstrated that socialist economies in theory could achieve the same optimality results as those achieved in the market, but also that since under socialism the problems of monopolistic exploitation and the instability of business cycles would be eliminated socialist planning would outperform capitalist economies in practice. In addition, since distribution would be determined through socialist and democratic deliberation, the injustice of the capitalist system would be overcome.

Alongside of the technical economic theory arguments for market socialism, there was also a general cultural sense that modern science and technology had delivered mankind into such an advanced state of affairs that more rational control over the economy was not only possible, but a moral imperative. Had not modern science given man the ability to control and design society according to moral rules of his own choosing? The planned society envisioned under socialism was supposed to be not only as efficient as capitalism (especially in view of the chaos capitalism was said to generate with its business cycles and monopoly power), but socialism, with its promise of social justice, was expected to be morally superior. Moreover, it was considered the wave of the future. Only a reactionary, it was argued, could resist the inevitable tide of history. Not only had Hayek appeared to lose the technical economic debate with Keynes and the Keynesians concerning the causes of business cycles, but, in view of the rising tide of socialism throughout the world, his general philosophical perspective was increasingly seen as decidedly out of step with the march of progress.

The experience of the 1930s and 1940s dramatically shaped Hayek's subsequent research programme. Why was it that economists trained in the early neoclassical tradition that Hayek's teachers were responsible for developing, and to which he thought his own original contributions were directed at advancing, got so off-track from his perspective on the fundamental questions of the monetary economy, the capital structure, the price system, and the competitive market process? The discerning reader of Hayek will see in his "Trend of economic thinking" (1933) the claim that neoclassical economics provides the proper analytics for studying the problems of economic coordination in a systematic way; yet by the time that same reader is confronting "Economics and knowledge" (1937), let alone "The use of knowledge in society" (1945), he or she will see that Hayek is arguing that the preoccupation among neoclassical theorists with the equilibrium conditions is causing confusion rather than illumination.

In order to understand the events of the previous decade, Hayek undertook two important foundational scientific and scholarly moves in the 1940s, both beginning his "Abuse of reason" project critical of the underlying philosophical and methodological underpinnings of modern social science, and an "institutional turn" in his research to draw attention to the institutional framework within which economic activity takes place. Both new directions are interrelated, and deeply connected to his analytical perspective as a technical economist. As I have argued elsewhere, "the most productive reading of Hayek is one which sees the common thread in his work from psychology to economics to the philosophy of science to political science to law and finally to philosophical anthropology and social theory. The common thread is decisive *epistemic* turn to *comparative institutional analysis*" (Boettke 1999: xv, original emphasis).

The Road to Serfdom

In response to the debate first with Keynes and then with the market socialists, Hayek kept refining the argument for economic liberalism. The problems of socialism that he had observed in Nazi Germany and that he saw beginning in Britain led him to write *The Road to Serfdom* (1944). If socialism required the replacement of the market with a central plan, then, Hayek pointed out, an institution must be established that would be responsible for formulating this plan, which Hayek referred to as the Central Planning Bureau. To implement the plan and to control the flow of resources, the bureau would have to exercise broad discretionary power in economic affairs. Yet the Central Planning Bureau in a socialist society would have no market prices to serve as guides. It would have no means of knowing which production possibilities were economically feasible. The absence of a pricing system, Hayek said, would prove to be socialism's fatal flaw. Mises's essential criticisms were correct and had to be the starting point of any discussion of the economic problems of socialism.

In *The Road to Serfdom*, Hayek argued that since the Central Planning Bureau could not base decisions on economic criterion, those in positions of power would base decisions on some other basis. The economic logic of the situation would give rise to the organizational logic of socialist planning. Thus, there was good reason to suspect that those who would rise to the top in a socialistic regime would be those who had a comparative advantage in exercising discretionary power and were willing to make unpleasant decisions. Also it was inevitable that these powerful men would run the system to their own personal advantage. The economic problem with socialism led directly to the political problem of socialism. The *Road to Serfdom* thus presented to advocates of socialism an additional problem beyond that of the technical economic problem, the political realities inherent in granting a single institution these kinds of powers over economic affairs.

Totalitarianism is not a historical accident that emerges solely because of a poor choice of leaders under a socialist regime. Totalitarianism, Hayek shows, is the logical outcome of the institutional order of socialist planning.

Why was it so hard to penetrate not only the popular imagination with this message, but more importantly for him the intellectual imagination of professional economists who he thought would be his ally in the battle of ideas against historicism and collectivism? To answer this question Hayek turned his attention away from technical economics and concentrated on restating the principles of classical liberalism. Hayek had pointed out the need for market prices as conveyors of dispersed economic information. He showed that attempts to replace or control the market lead to a knowledge problem. Hayek also described the totalitarian problem associated with placing discretionary power in the hands of a few. This led him to examine the intellectual prejudices that blind men from seeing the problems of government economic planning.

During the 1940s, Hayek published a series of essays in professional journals examining the dominant philosophical trends that prejudiced intellectuals in a way that did not allow them to recognize the systemic problems that economic planners would confront. These essays were later collected and published as *The Counter-Revolution of Science* (1952a). It provides a detailed intellectual history of "rational constructivism" and the problems of "scientism" in the social sciences. It is in this work that Hayek articulates his version of the Scottish Enlightenment project of David Hume and Adam Smith of "using reason to whittle down the claims of Reason". Modern civilization was not only threatened by irrational zealots hell-bent on destroying the world, but was also threatened by the abuse of reason by rational constructivists trying to consciously design the modern world that had placed mankind in chains of its own making.

In 1950, Hayek moved to the University of Chicago, where he taught until 1962 in the Committee on Social Thought. While there, he wrote *The Constitution of Liberty* (1960). This work represented Hayek's first systemic treatise on classical liberal political economy. Beginning with the work that had resulted in *The Road to Serfdom*, Hayek had wanted to call attention to the framework assumed in economic analysis and highlight its importance. Basic economics begins with the assumption of clearly defined and strictly enforced private property rights which forms the basis of mutually beneficial exchange between parties. Private property and freedom of contract embodied in the rule of law is the assumed background. However, it was so far in the background of analysis by the 1930s and 1940s that it was easy for thinkers to forget. They proceeded as if economic relationships were merely technical optimality conditions and could be determined under a variety of institutional settings. In fact, institutional differences did not matter as the explicit goal of mid-twentieth century theorists was to derive a pure institutionally antiseptic theory of economic optimality.

What Hayek had accomplished in *The Road to Serfdom* was to demonstrate the incompatibility of socialist planning with democracy and the rule of law. What he sought to derive in *The Constitution of Liberty* was a historical explanation for co-evolution of Western civilization and the rule of law, and then to develop an approach to contemporary public policy grounded in the generality norm upon which the rule of law is based. It is important to stress that for Hayek, the rule of law was not merely rule by laws, but had specific content associated with the generality norm that bound not only the actors within the system but the governors that were called to provide oversight of the system. Hayek's conception of the "good society" was one that exhibited neither dominion nor discrimination.

In 1962, Hayek moved to Germany, where he had obtained a position at the University of Freiburg. He then increasingly centred his efforts on examining and elaborating the "spontaneous" ordering of economic and social activity. Hayek set about reconstructing liberal social theory and providing a vision of peaceful social cooperation and productive specialization among free individuals.

With his three-volume study, *Law, Legislation and Liberty* (1979a) and his final book *The Fatal Conceit* (1988), Hayek extended his analysis of society to an examination of the "spontaneous" emergence of legal and moral rules. His political and legal theory emphasized that the rule of law was the necessary foundation for peaceful coexistence. He contrasted the tradition of the common law with that of statute law, that is, legislative decrees. He showed how the common law emerges, case by case, as judges apply to particular cases general rules that are themselves products of cultural evolution. Thus, he explained that embedded within the common law is knowledge gained through a long history of trial and error. This insight led Hayek to the conclusion that law, like the market, is a "spontaneous" order – the result of human action, but not of human design. (Hayek 1967)

Conclusion

Hayek had a long and productive career. He had to endure the curse of achieving fame at a young age and then having that fame turn to ridicule as the intellectual and political world moved away from his ideas. However, he lived long enough to see his original ideas recognized again. In many ways all his intellectual opponents at a methodological, analytical and, dare we say, ideological level were eventually challenged by the tide of events and the penetrating logic of Hayek's analysis. At the time of his death, classical liberalism was once again a vibrant body of thought. The Austrian school of economics had re-emerged as a major school of economic thought, and younger scholars in law, history, economics, politics, and philosophy are pursuing Hayekian themes. Since his death, these trends have grown in momentum. Consider the renewed interest in Hayek's work in monetary theory and the trade cycle in the wake of the global financial crisis of 2008, or the critique of development planning found in works such as William Easterly (2014), or the focus on the institutional infrastructure in the development of the West found in such works at North et al. (2009).

Finally, any discussion of Hayek for contemporary readers would be incomplete if the work by Bruce Caldwell, both in terms of his own scholarship on Hayek (for example, *Hayek's Challenge*, 2004) but also in editing the *Collected Works of F.A. Hayek*, was not mentioned. This ongoing project is estimated to be 19 volumes with some supplemental material, and there is also the extensive oral history interviews that Hayek did at the University of California, Los Angeles (UCLA) that are available now online at the Universidad Francisco Marroquin digital resources. Scholars are judged not only by the answers they provided to the problems they tackled during their careers, but the questions they motivate others to ask and the avenues of new lines of inquiry their work opens up. Hayek's work continues to serve as the basis for a progressive research programme in the social sciences from technical economics to social philosophy.

Peter Boettke

See also:

Eugen von Böhm-Bawerk (I); Business cycles and growth (III); Capital theory (III); Economics and philosophy (III); German and Austrian schools (II); John Maynard Keynes (I); Abba Ptachya Lerner (I); Carl Menger (I); Ludwig Heinrich von Mises (I); Money and banking (III); Political philosophy and economics: freedom and labour (III); Lionel Charles Robbins (I); Joseph Alois Schumpeter (I); Piero Sraffa (I).

References and further reading

Blaug, M. (1997), *Economic Theory in Retrospect*, 5th edn, Cambridge: Cambridge University Press.
Boettke, P. (1999), 'Which enlightenment, whose liberalism: F.A. Hayek's research program for understanding the liberal society', in P.J. Boettke (ed.), *The Legacy of F.A. Hayek: Politics, Philosophy, Economics*, vol. 1, Cheltenham, UK and Northampton, MA, USA: Edward Elgar, pp. xi–lv.
Boettke, P.J. and K.W. O'Donnell (2013), 'The failed appropriation of F.A. Hayek by formalist economics', *Critical Review*, **25** (3–4), 305–41.
Caldwell, B. (2004), *Hayek's Challenge: An Intellectual Biography of F.A. Hayek*, Chicago, IL: University of Chicago Press.
Easterly, W. (2014), *The Tyranny of Experts: Economists, Dictators, and the Forgotten Rights of the Poor*, New York: Basic Books.
Hayek, F.A. (1925), 'The monetary policy of the United States after the recovery from the 1920 crisis', reprinted in R. McCloughry (ed.) (1984), *F.A. Hayek: Money, Capital and Fluctuations: Early Essays*, Chicago, IL: University of Chicago Press.
Hayek, F.A. (1929), *Monetary Theory and the Trade Cycle*, reprinted 1975, New York: Augustus M. Kelley.
Hayek, F.A. (1931), *Prices and Production*, reprinted 1967, New York: Augustus M. Kelley.
Hayek, F.A. (1932), 'Money and capital: a reply', *Economic Journal*, **42** (166), 237–49.
Hayek, F.A. (1933), 'The trend of economic thinking', *Economica* (May), 121–37.
Hayek, F.A. (1935), *Collectivist Economic Planning*, London: Routledge.
Hayek, F.A. (1937), 'Economics and knowledge', reprinted in F.A. Hayek (1948), *Individualism and Economic Order*, reprinted 1996, Chicago, IL: University of Chicago Press, pp. 33–56.
Hayek, F.A. (1941), *The Pure Theory of Capital*, Chicago, IL: University of Chicago Press.
Hayek, F.A. (1944), *The Road to Serfdom*, Chicago, IL: University of Chicago Press.
Hayek, F.A. (1945), 'The use of knowledge in society', reprinted in F.A. Hayek (1996), *Individualism and Economic Order*, Chicago, IL: University of Chicago Press, pp 77–91.
Hayek, F.A. (1948), *Individualism and Economic Order*, reprinted 1996, Chicago, IL: University of Chicago Press.
Hayek, F.A. (1952a), *The Counter-Revolution of Science*, Indianapolis, IN: Liberty Fund, reprinted 1979.
Hayek, F.A. (1952b), *The Sensory Order*, Chicago, IL: University of Chicago Press.
Hayek, F.A. (1956), 'The dilemma of specialization', reprinted in F.A. Hayek (ed.) (1967), *Studies in Philosophy, Politics, and Economics*, Chicago, IL: University of Chicago Press, pp. 122–32.
Hayek, F.A. (1960), *The Constitution of Liberty*, Chicago, IL: University of Chicago Press.
Hayek, F.A. (1967), 'The results of human action but not of human design', in F.A. Hayek (ed.), *Studies in Philosophy, Politics, and Economics*, Chicago, IL: University of Chicago Press, pp. 95–105.
Hayek, F.A. (1978), 'Coping with ignorance', in F.A. Hayek (ed.) (1983), *Knowledge, Evolution, and Society*, London: Adam Smith Institute, pp. 1–6.
Hayek, F.A. (1979a), *Law, Legislation, and Liberty*, 3 vols, Chicago, IL: University of Chicago Press.
Hayek, F.A. (1979b), Interview with Axel Leijonhuvfud, accessed 19 May 2015 at http://hayek.ufm.edu/index.php/Axel_Leijonhufvud.
Hayek, F.A. (1988), *The Fatal Conceit: The Errors of Socialism*, in F.A. Hayek, *Collected Works*, vol. 1, Chicago, IL: University of Chicago Press.
Keynes, J.M. (1926), *The End of Laissez-Faire*, London: Hogarth Press.
Keynes, J.M. (1930), *A Treatise on Money*, New York: Harcourt, Brace and Company.
Keynes, J.M. (1931), 'The pure theory of money: a reply to Dr. Hayek', *Econometrica*, **11** (November), 387–97.
Keynes, J.M. (1936), *The General Theory of Employment, Interest, and Money*, London: Palgrave Macmillan.
Kurz, H.D. (2000), 'The Hayek–Keynes–Sraffa controversy reconsidered', in H.D. Kurz (ed.), *Critical Essays on Piero Sraffa's Legacy in Economics*, Cambridge: Cambridge University Press.
Kurz, H.D. (2015), 'Keynes, Sraffa, and the latter's "secret scepticism"' in H.D. Kurz and Neri Salvadori (eds), *Revisiting Classical Economics: Studies in Long-Period Analysis*, New York: Routledge, pp. 102–22.
Lachmann, L. (1986), 'Austrian economics under fire: the Hayek–Sraffa duel in retrospect', in D. Lavoie (ed.) (1994), *Expectations and the Meaning of Institutions: Essays in Economics by Ludwig Lachmann*, London: Routledge.

Lavoie, D. (1985), *Rivalry and Central Planning: The Socialist Calculation Debate Reconsidered*, Cambridge: Cambridge University Press.

Menger, C. (1871), *Principles of Economics*, reprinted 1950, New York: Free Press.

Mises, L. von (1912), *The Theory of Money and Credit*, reprinted 1953, New Haven, CT: Yale University Press.

Mises, L. von (1922), *Socialism: An Economic and Sociological Analysis* reprinted 1951, New Haven, CT: Yale University Press.

Myrdal, G. (1929), *The Political Element in the Development of Economic Theory*, translated 1953, London: Routledge.

North, D.C., J.J. Wallis and B. Weingast (2009), *Violence and Social Orders: A Conceptual Framework for Interpreting Recorded Human History*, Cambridge: Cambridge University Press.

Robbins, L. (1937), *Economic Planning and International Order*, London: Macmillan.

Skarbek, D. (2009), 'F.A. Hayek's influence on Nobel prize winners', *Review of Austrian Economics*, **22** (1), 109–12.

Sraffa, P. (1932a), 'Dr. Hayek on money and capital', *Economic Journal*, **42** (165), 42–53.

Sraffa, P. (1932b), 'A rejoinder', *Economic Journal*, **42** (166), 249–51.

Michał Kalecki (1899–1970)

Michał Kalecki is certainly one of the most enigmatic economists of the twentieth century. Besides anticipating Keynes's *General Theory* (1936) he is credited with paving the way for connecting imperfect competition to business-cycle analysis, designing the first macro-dynamic model unifying mathematics, statistics, and economic theory, as well as developing a theory of the political business cycle (Lopez and Assous 2010; Toporowski 2013).

Michał Kalecki was born on 22 June 1899 in Lodz into a Polish-Jewish family, and died in Warsaw on the 17 April 1970. He began mathematical studies in 1917 – going on to publish several papers in that field – at the Warsaw University and later studied civil engineering at the Gdansk University Engineering College. In 1923, because of the failure of his father's cotton business, Kalecki interrupted his studies and decided to work for a credit rating agency. It was then that he started working on economic problems. At the same time, his socialist political inclinations led him to study Marx's *Capital* (1976) as well as the works of Rosa Luxemburg and Mikhail Tugan-Baranovsky. In the late 1920s, he started contributing regularly to two Polish economics journals, denying in several articles the existence of self-correcting market mechanisms likely to eliminate mass unemployment, and arguing that the way to escape from crises was by stimulating aggregate demand.

Thanks to his mathematical and economics background, Kalecki obtained his first academic job at the Institute for the Study of Business Cycles and Prices in late 1929. His task was twofold. With Erik Landau he produced the first estimates of prices, investment, consumption and social income in Poland; meanwhile, Kalecki also focused on crafting a formal mathematical treatment of the business cycle. In July 1933, he published a booklet entitled *An Essay in the Theory of the Business Cycle* in which he attempted to explain observed cycles with a system whose solutions are deterministic cycles. This contribution constitutes an important step in the history of macroeconomics. For the first time, the functioning of a constrained demand economy had been described mathematically and estimated statistically.

In 1936, thanks to a Rockfeller scholarship, he went to Sweden, Norway and then England. From there, Kalecki established scholarly contacts with Bertil Ohlin, Erik Lindahl, Tjalling Koopmans, Ragnar Frisch, Piero Sraffa, Richard F. Kahn, John Maynard Keynes and Joan Robinson. In the same year, he embarked on the supervision of the Cambridge Research Scheme of the National Institute of Economic and Social Research into Prime Costs, Proceeds and Output. During the Second World War, he moved to the Oxford University Institute of Statistics. In March 1945, he left for Montreal to take a post at the International Labour Office before in 1946 taking a position as Assistant Director in the Department of Economic Affairs of the United Nations Secretariat, in New York City. His work, set out in the *World Economic Report* series, was mainly dedicated to the study of problems of full employment and inflation in both developed and underdeveloped countries, including the socialist ones.

In 1954, Kalecki resigned in protest against the McCarthyism which swept the United Nations secretariat. At the end of February 1955, he returned to Poland where, after the death of Stalin, the political situation had become more positive. During the period up until the beginning of 1960, he served as an adviser on matters concerning economic planning, and during 1958 and 1959 was especially deeply involved in the Outline Perspective Plan for the years 1961–75. However, this plan was severely criticized for departing from the communist orthodoxy as regards, in particular, the relative size of consumption and investment. At the same time, Kalecki was very active in teaching and research at the Polish Academy of Sciences. In 1961 he began lecturing at the Central School of Planning and Statistics, where he eventually took a full-time job.

Kalecki and Underemployment Equilibrium

Kalecki's argument regarding the functioning of a constrained demand economy had two strands. The first was an explanation of why, for a given capital stock and given money wages, the economy can become stuck in a stable short-period equilibrium with unemployment. The second was an explanation of why, when the capital stock and money wages are variable, the economy is bound to fluctuate.

Kalecki's first point serves to deny the existence of self-correcting market mechanisms which would eliminate excess supplies of productive resources. Moreover, he denied that these would exist even in a competitive economy. Joan Robinson claimed that it was precisely because Kalecki had remained outside the mainstream of traditional economics that he succeeded in developing a new macroeconomic analysis (see, for example, Robinson 1966). She maintained that Kalecki, unlike Keynes, did not have to free himself from the mainstream theoretical framework, simply because he did not know it. However, a close look at his 1934 paper "Three systems" reveals that he was indeed familiar with important authors of both the Marshallian and Wicksellian traditions, as well as business-cycle theorists such as Albert Aftalion and Joseph Schumpeter.

According to Kalecki, there are theoretically conceivable circumstances in which, with fixed money wages and a constant capital stock, the economy will become stuck in a "quasi-equilibrium" with mass unemployment. The essence of Kalecki's theory of employment consists in a distinction between endogenous components of aggregate demand (for example, worker's consumption) and exogenous components (for example, investment outlays, exports surpluses, budget deficits). Along these lines, in a model that integrates the real and monetary sectors of the economy, Kalecki (1934) demonstrates that any disequilibrium between aggregate demand and aggregate supply causes a change in output (and hence income), which leads the economy to an equilibrium position. A crucial assumption of both Keynes's and Kalecki's analysis is that the marginal propensity to spend is less than one. Therefore Patinkin's claim that Kalecki had not anticipated Keynes's central message has to be rejected (Chapple 1995; Assous 2007).

However, even if a demand-constrained economy behaves differently from an economy in which Say's law applies, the proof of the possibility of a continuum of equilibriums parameterized by a given money wage does not suffice in itself to demonstrate the possibility of persistent unemployment. His point was that to show that unemployment is persistent, it is necessary to resort to dynamic analysis. He thought the phenomena of underemployment had to be considered as a case of disequilibrium dynamics.

Kalecki described a mechanism showing that the real equilibrium of the economy is not independent from the level of money wages and prices. This adjustment mechanism was the so-called Keynes effect (Leijonhufvud 1968), by which a lower price level increases the real money supply and so lowers the interest rate, and then stimulates investment until, through a multiplier effect, income and production reach a level that ensures an equilibrium in all markets.

Realizing that equilibrium analysis and comparative statics are not the best tools for demonstrating the possibility of mass unemployment, Kalecki developed a double argument. He first emphasized that the adverse effect of lower prices on debtors via an increased real debt burden can provoke bankruptcies and lead ultimately to lower aggregate demand because debtors have a higher propensity to spend than do creditors. Second, deflation generates expectations of falling prices and lower future prices which materialize in a higher real rate of interest and thus lower spending. Unlike Keynes, Kalecki was ready to accept that this last argument matters only during the adjustment process: "your point on the rising real rate of interest is valid only in the period of adjustment. Once a new equilibrium is achieved the wages and prices stop falling" (Kalecki 1944 [1990]: 568). From that point of view, Kalecki's employment theory is more in line with the dynamic Keynesian approach later developed by Tobin (1975) than with the static Keynesian analysis of Hicks (1937) and Modigliani (1944).

Imperfect Competition, Income Distribution and the Multiplier Analysis

From 1936, Kalecki (1936) resorted exclusively to imperfect competition. Initially, in reference to Edward Chamberlin's framework (1933), his purpose was to clarify the problem of the micro foundations of the *General Theory*, in which Keynes considered the degree of competition as one of the "givens" for the determination of the levels of employment and output.

The macro equilibrium is shown in a figure presenting micro curves, which are summed to bring about the macro aggregates. Each imperfectly competitive firm produces so as to equate the marginal "value added" and marginal cost. The marginal "value added" curve is the marginal revenue curve of any firm, given the conjecture the other firms' prices are given. The intersection of the curves of marginal revenue and marginal cost is thus a representation of profit maximization. Once the costs of material inputs are deduced from both curves, we obtain Kalecki's figure (Figure 7).

In the labour market, workers are price takers at a given nominal wage $\overline{W}$. Looking at the first unit of output along the horizontal axis in Figure 7, the marginal revenue curve shows the revenue produced by that unit of output. The wage component is the marginal cost $\overline{W}/MPL$ where MPL represents the marginal product of labour. The remainder, the difference between marginal revenue and marginal cost, is the amount of profit associated with the first unit of output. Similarly, each subsequent unit of output is associated with an amount of profit. Total profit at the equilibrium is equal to the sum of the profits associated with each unit of output up to equilibrium, and is hence equal to the area under the marginal revenue curve and above the marginal cost.

On scaling from micro to macro, Figure 7 reconciles micro analysis and macro aggregates. The area OABC is national income, the area above the marginal cost, global profits, and the residual area, aggregate wages. The distributive shares can be deduced directly as the ratio of both areas.

When aggregate demand from capitalists changes, the area of profits changes correspondingly. At the new equilibrium point, the shift of the marginal revenue curve

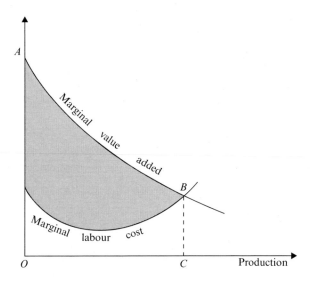

Figure 7   Kalecki's 1936 diagram

is precisely such that the sum of shaded areas is just equal to aggregate profits, which corresponds, via the multiplier of capitalist autonomous expenditure, to investment and capitalists' consumption, and what is left is made up of wages which bring about a demand for consumption goods equal to their amount. We hence see that while workers spend what they earn, capitalists earn what they spend.

It is clear from Figure 7 that any attempt to explain the observed cyclical behaviour of distributive shares requires us to question the determinants of the shape of the cost functions, as well as the evolution of the degree of competition. Under monopolistic competition – Kalecki (1939) coined the term "pure imperfect competition" – the micro demand curves are a family of equations $y_i = \left(\frac{p_i}{P}\right)^{-\varepsilon}\frac{Y}{m}$ where y_i is the micro quantity, p_i the individual demand price, P the general price level, ε the elasticity of demand, Y the aggregate demand, and m the number of firms present in the economy. Any change in aggregate demand entailing iso-elastic shifts in the marginal revenue curve along with increasing marginal real costs provokes a change in income distribution in favour of profits. Thus, taking into account a given degree of competition and accepting the assumption of increasing marginal cost allows him to establish the procyclicality of the profit share.

Looking at the problem from the point of view of costs, monopolistic competition allows us to do without the classical assumption of increasing marginal real cost in the short term. In the presence of excess capacity, it is indeed possible to refer to the idea that marginal cost can be taken as approximately constant, an idea first presented by Harrod (1936) and developed by Kalecki in 1938 in a paper quoted by Keynes (1939). This is the assumption that the marginal cost and average cost coincide up to a point where the normal utilization of capacity is reached, and begins to rise afterwards.

Under the assumption of a constant degree of competition, one can move directly to a relation between pricing processes via the mark-up and demonstrate the constancy of distributive shares. With constant distributive shares, the social propensity to spend is now constant and one can obtain a model isomorphic to the Keynesian model, with a linear aggregate demand curve, which can be reproduced by the familiar 45-degree figure which served to express the core of the *General Theory*. At the micro level, this mechanism implies a relationship between the location of the micro demand curves and the aggregate demand curve. This was accomplished by Kalecki by assuming that a shift in aggregate demand was materialized as an income effect, entailing either rightward or leftward shifts in the micro demand curve and producing successively higher or lower micro equilibriums.

It is worth emphasizing here that a change in the degree of monopoly – and thus in income distributive shares – has no effect on the level of profits. Assume the degree of monopoly has increased. By redistributing income in disfavour of workers, global consumption falls, which entails a decrease in output. Yet as long as the capitalists' expenditures remain unchanged, the level of profit does not change: capitalists just earn a greater part of a lower gross domestic product. Graphically, this means that individual demand curve shifts leftwards until the equilibrium is restored.

Cycles and Growth

Kalecki's analysis was explicitly dynamic. Since net investment varies, so does total capital, which influences output, investment, and savings. Kalecki did not ignore these effects, and treated the stocks of production factors and technology as variable. Taking into account the existence of a gestation period of investment, he described cycles as a succession of temporary equilibriums parameterized by a given money wage and a given capital stock, both variables resulting from investment decisions taken in the past. The model was based on the capital stock adjustment (or "flexible accelerator") principle: current investment equals some fraction of the gap between the desired and the actual capital. The desired stock varies directly with output (taken as a proxy for the expected demand for output that the capital is to help produce). Net investment therefore depends positively on output and inversely on the initially available stock of capital.

In his 1933 version, the dynamics of Kalecki's models came mainly from lags. Two important distinctions were introduced: one between investment decisions and actual expenditures of investment, and another between investment orders and the deliveries of equipment. With a linear mixed difference and differential system, Kalecki first thought he could explain self-sustained cycles. Owing to remarks he received from Ragnar Frisch and Nicholas Kaldor, Kalecki later made important use of non-linearities. In 1943, he assumed investment to be of the S-shape form with much lower positive slopes at both extremes than the broad middle range of the output scale: investment being assumed to be deterred both by surplus capacity and by pessimistic expectations when activity is respectively low or high. The saving curve, on the contrary, is assumed (as long as the degree of monopoly is constant) to have a constant slope. Given the output, investment depends inversely on the capital stock. Thus there are three possible equilibria, two of which are stable while the stationary one is unstable. The result is a self-sustained cycle in the real aggregates, describing how the economy moves from a stable to an unstable to another stable equilibrium. Without any reference to random shocks and Frisch's swinging system, Kalecki hence developed a new endogenous model in which fluctuation results from waves of optimism and pessimism and the market power of firms.

Later, admitting the dampened nature of fluctuations, Kalecki explained the constant amplitude of the cycle by referring to exogenous shocks. In 1954, and finally in 1968, he returned to a linear system and introduced important modifications which have to do with the influence of development factors such as innovations and "rentiers" savings, the long-run development of a capitalist economy being positive only if technical progress exerts a stronger influence than "rentiers" savings.

Socialism

While from the 1930s to the 1960s Kalecki was associated with the socialist movement, he always stood apart from political parties, serving mainly as a consultant on economic problems.

Kalecki thought that savings were likely to increase faster than the investment necessary to expand productive capacity proportionately to full employment. As a result, if private investment was stimulated to the level of saving at full employment, there would be a continuous fall in the degree of utilization of equipment and thus a continuous fall in the rate of profit. In order to prevent the fall in the rate of profit, the government should thus intervene by increasing its spending either on public investment or on subsidies to consumption, according to social priorities. A redistribution of income from the rich to the poor would adversely affect the propensity to save. The growing interest on the National Debt he proposed to meet from an annual capital tax or from a "modified income tax", designed so as to offset any adverse effect of additional taxation on the propensity to invest.

Convinced that full employment policies could be secured by appropriate fiscal and budgetary policies, he did not ignore the political aspects which these policies were likely to raise. Because of financial imperfections – which are implicit in Marx's schemes of reproduction, and to which Kalecki constantly referred – capitalists as a class have great power in the determination of the growth rate. Being alone in determining the level of investment and thus the level of activity, capitalists as a class have control over the level of employment. However, the preservation of their social position comes before the quest for profit. This is why, because government interventions are likely to weaken their political influence by achieving full employment and thus increasing the workers' bargaining power, the capitalist may accept a higher rate of unemployment in order to restore "the discipline in the factories", even if this comes with a lower rate of profit. It is thus only by profound institutional changes that the class conflicts can be overcome, but, in that case, the economy will be more socialist than capitalist.

MICHAËL ASSOUS

See also:

Business cycles and growth (III); Roy Forbes Harrod (I); Keynesianism (II); Marxism(s) (II); Post-Keynesianism (II).

References and further reading

Assous, M. (2007), 'Kalecki's 1934 model vs. the IS–LM model of Hicks (1937) and of Modigliani (1944)', *European Journal of the History of Economic Thought*, **14** (1), 97–118.
Chamberlin, E. (1933), *Theory of Monopolistic Competition*, Cambridge, MA: Harvard University Press.
Chapple, S. (1995), 'The Kaleckian origins of the Keynesian model', *Oxford Economic Papers*, **47** (2), 525–37.

Feiwel, G.R. (1975), *Michał Kalecki. A Study in Economic Theory and Policy*, Knoxville, TN: University of Tennessee Press.

Harrod, R.-F. (1936), *The Trade Cycle. An Essay*, Oxford: Clarendon Press.

Hicks, J. (1937), 'Mr. Keynes and the "Classics": a suggested interpretation', *Econometrica*, **5** (2), 147–59.

Kalecki, M. (1934), 'Trzy układy', *Ekonomista*, **34**, 54–70, English trans. 'Three systems', in J. Osiatynski (ed.) (1990), *Collected Works of Michał Kalecki*, vol. 1, *Capitalism, Business Cycles and Full Employment*, Oxford: Clarendon Press, pp. 201–19.

Kalecki, M. (1936), 'Pare uwag o teorii Keynesa', *Ekhonomista*, **36**, 18–26, English trans. 'Some remarks on Keynes's theory', in J. Osiatynski (ed.) (1990), *Collected Works of Michał Kalecki*, vol. 1, *Capitalism, Business Cycles and Full Employment*, Oxford: Clarendon Press, pp. 223–32.

Kalecki, M. (1938), 'The determinants of the distribution of national income', *Econometrica*, **6** (2), 97–112.

Kalecki, M. (1939), 'The supply curve of an industry under imperfect competition', *Review of Economic Studies*, **7** (2), 91–112.

Kalecki, M. (1944), 'Prof. Pigou on "the classical stationary state". A comment', *Economic Journal*, **54** (2), 131–2.

Kalecki, M. (1990), *Collected Works of Michał Kalecki*, vol. 1, *Capitalism, Business Cycles and Full Employment*, J. Osiatynski (ed.), Oxford: Clarendon Press.

Keynes, J.M. (1936), *The General Theory of Employment, Interest and Money*, London: Macmillan.

Keynes, J.M. (1939), 'Relative movements of real wages and output', *Economic Journal*, **49** (March), 34–51.

Leijonhufvud, A. (1968), *On Keynesian Economics and the Economics of Keynes*, New York: Oxford University Press.

Lopez, J. and M. Assous (2010), *Michał Kalecki: An Intellectual Biography*, Basingstoke: Palgrave Macmillan.

Marx, K. (1976), *Capital, Volume I*, trans. B. Fowkes, Harmondsworth: Penguin.

Modigliani, F. (1944), 'Liquidity preference and the theory of interest and money', *Econometrica*, **12** (1), 44–88.

Robinson, J. (1966), 'Kalecki and Keynes', in P.A. Baran (ed.), *Problems of Economic Dynamics and Planning: Essays in Honour of Michał Kalecki*, London: Pergamon Press.

Tobin, J. (1975), 'Keynesian models of recession and depression', *American Economic Review*, **65** (2), 195–202.

Toporowski, J. (2013), *Michał Kalecki: An Intellectual Biography*, vol. 1, *Rendez-vous in Cambridge 1899–1939*, New York: St Martin's Press, Palgrave Macmillan.

Roy Forbes Harrod (1900–1978)

Harrod was born in Norfolk on the 13 February 1900 to Henry Dawes Harrod, businessman, and his wife Frances (née Forbes-Robertson), novelist. Following the ruin of his father's business, Harrod won a scholarship to go up to St Paul's, leaving two years later to enter Westminster as a King's Scholar. In 1919, he began studies in philosophy and modern history at Oxford, which led him in 1922 to take up a Tutorial Fellowship at Christ Church. In order to learn more about economics, Harrod was allowed to spend his first term at Cambridge where he took weekly essays on money and international trade to John Maynard Keynes. Once back at Oxford, he attended Francis Y. Edgeworth's lectures on microeconomics. In the early 1930s Harrod came to grips with the theories of imperfect competition developed by Edward Chamberlin and Joan Robinson (Harrod 1934). Meanwhile, drawn into the Circus – a group of young economists involved in the elaboration of Keynes's *General Theory* – he got deep insight into Keynesian economics (Eltis 2008). In 1936, drawing on both his microeconomic and macroeconomic backgrounds, he published his first book, *The Trade Cycle* (1936), in which he laid out for the first time the analytical foundations for the multiplier-accelerator model. This book, as well as "An essay in dynamic theory" (1939), marks an important step in the history of macroeconomics. Here, Harrod set the research agenda of the post-war work on economic dynamics.

His work on the theory of the firm occupied a good deal of his attention in the post-war decades. As part of the Oxford Economists' Research Group, Harrod took a great interest in how firms set their prices by adding a margin they consider satisfactory to their average or "full" cost of production. In addition, throughout his academic career he published extensively on international monetary theory and economic policies. Meanwhile, he had also published major works on philosophy. In his *Foundations of Inductive Logic* (1956) – which he regarded as his greatest achievement – he claimed that inductive arguments could be given a rational basis.

Imperfect Competition, Income Distribution and the Trade Cycle

Harrod's argument for resorting to imperfect competition had two strands. The first was an explanation why, under increasing returns, the equilibrium approach was well suited for explaining fluctuations. Under decreasing marginal costs, there exists a multiplicity of long period equilibriums. Because any equilibrium is determined by correct producer's expectations, any sudden revision of expectations will lead the economy to a new equilibrium position. Waves of optimism and pessimism may thus explain how the economy moves from low to high equilibrium outputs and vice versa. The second was an explanation of the behaviour of costs relative to prices during business cycles. Harrod's point of departure was Keynes's advocacy for public spending. Keynes made two important assumptions. First, he assumed imperfect competition in the product markets, admitting that the degree of competition in the economy can be taken as given. Second, he supposed that there was a decreasing short-run marginal product of labour. Along these lines, Keynes concluded that there existed an inverse relation between real wages and output. For that reason, Harrod thought that Keynes's policies could cause inflationary conditions by generating demands for money-wage rises to offset falling real wages, which were likely to justify reversing the policy before much headway had been made in reducing unemployment. If, however, increasing return prevails, as long as the degree of competition remains unchanged, Keynesian policies could be implemented without bearing the risk of rising inflation and being interrupted prematurely.

Despite the effect of decreasing costs, Harrod was convinced that there existed an inverse relation between the real wage and output. His argument relies on what he called the "law of diminishing elasticity of demand", implying that the degree of monopoly increases in the upswing and falls in the downswing. He thought that in the upswing, the rise in the mark-up will dominate the fall in real cost, entailing what he called a "shift to profit", that is to say a change in income distribution in favour of profit earners. Since profit earners save a greater proportion of their income than workers, this results in an increased propensity to save by the whole community. Jointly with other factors, such an evolution was likely to play a critical role in dynamics.

Instability, Cycles and Growth

Harrod's works on dynamics are based on the concepts of natural growth, warranted growth and actual growth. The natural growth is the rate required to maintain full employment. The warranted rate of growth is

> the rate of growth which, if it occurs, will leave all parties satisfied that they have produced neither more nor less than the right amount. Or, to state the matter otherwise, it will put them into a frame of mind which will cause them to give such additional orders as will maintain the same rate of growth. (Harrod 1939: 16)

This results from the interaction of the multiplier and the accelerator. The multiplier determines by how much income increases as a consequence of an increase in investment, depending on the proportion of income saved s; the accelerator, or "the relation" as he called it, determines how many units of capital, C, are needed to produce an extra unit of output, given the state of technology and the rate of interest. Each of these relations feeds on the other: if actual demand exceeds anticipated demand, firms would have underinvested and would respond by increasing investment. This would itself cause actual growth rate to rise, requiring even further investment.

Harrod explored the consequences of a divergence both between the warranted and natural rates and the actual and warranted rates. The problem, in accordance with the "principle of instability", was that anything that would make the warranted rate move towards the natural rate would also drag along with it a fall in the actual rate. Suppose the warranted rate rises towards the natural rate. If entrepreneurs continue to expect the same rate of growth (equal to the previous and smaller value of the warranted rate), the actual rate of growth will actually be smaller, so that the actual and warranted rates of growth will move in opposite directions. It is only because the parameters determining the warranted rate will change that this cumulative movement will be reversed. Harrod's point was that a falling actual growth rate resulting from variations in income distribution, the saving rate or in the capital coefficient, will ultimately reduce the warranted rate to the point of making it lower than the actual rate of growth. A process of cumulative expansion will then start and a phase of expansion will take place. However, as soon as the actual rate reaches its natural limit the warranted rate will eventually grow larger.

Once this happens, a reverse cumulative movement is set in motion. In this respect, Harrod's dynamics strongly differ from Solow's (1956) or Kaldor's (1957) growth models. While the former focused exclusively on the adjustments of the warranted (assumed equal to the actual rate) and natural rate, Harrod was equally concerned with the adjustment between the actual and warranted rates. This explains partly why, in Harrod's theory, the non-linear character of the investment and saving functions resulting from changes in the saving rate and the capital coefficients are supposed to produce both cycles and growth (Besomi 2001: 82). Unfortunately, although noticed by most of his contemporaries (Sember 2010), this important aspect of Harrod's theory remained largely ignored in subsequent interpretations.

MICHAËL ASSOUS

See also:

Business cycles and growth (III); Michał Kalecki (I); Keynesianism (II); Jacob Marschak (I).

References and further reading

Besomi, D. (2001), 'Harrod's dynamics and the theory of growth: the story of a mistaken attribution', *Cambridge Journal of Economics*, **25** (1), 79–96.
Eltis, W. (2008), 'Harrod, Roy Forbes (1900–1978)', in St N. Durlauf and L.E. Blume (eds), *The New Palgrave Dictionary of Economics*, 2nd edn, vol. 3, Basingstoke: Palgrave Macmillan, pp. 836–45.
Harrod, R.-F. (1934), 'Doctrines of imperfect competition', *Quarterly Journal of Economics*, **48** (3), 442–70.
Harrod, R.-F. (1936), *The Trade Cycle. An Essay*, Oxford: Clarendon Press.
Harrod, R.-F. (1939), 'An essay in dynamic theory', *Economic Journal*, **49** (193), 14–33.
Harrod, R.-F. (1956), *Foundations of Inductive Logic*, London and New York: Macmillan.
Kaldor, N. (1957), 'A model of economic growth', *Economic Journal*, **67** (December), 591–624.
Kregel, J. (1985), 'Harrod and Keynes: increasing returns, the theory of employment and dynamic economics', in G.C. Harcourt (ed.), *Keynes and his Contemporaries*, London: Macmillan, pp. 67–88.
Sember, F. (2010), 'Closing the model? The Harrod–Marschak correspondence on the draft of the *Essay in Dynamic Theory*', *Journal of the History of Economic Thought*, **32** (4), 583–608.
Solow, R. (1956), 'A contribution to the theory of economic growth', *Quarterly Journal of Economics*, **70** (1), 65–94.

Abba Ptachya Lerner (1903–1982)

Abba P. Lerner was born into a Jewish family in Romania on 28 October 1903. In 1912 the family emigrated to London. Growing up in London's East End, he became familiar with the conditions of the working class when he himself worked as a machinist and a cap maker at the age of 16. An early association with the different socialist movements prevalent in the 1920s in Great Britain brought him into contact with economics. In 1929 he enrolled to study economics at the London School of Economics (LSE). He quickly earned several scholarships for his outstanding essays, many of which were published while he was still an undergraduate. With one of these scholarships, he financed a six-month stay at Cambridge University (1934–35), where he made contact with "the Circus", a group of young economists associated with John Maynard Keynes. Together with other graduate students from the LSE – among them P. Sweezy and U. Webb (later Hicks) – in 1933 he founded the *Review of Economic Studies* (*RES*), one of today's leading economics journals. His appointment as assistant lecturer at the LSE in 1936 was the first of many teaching positions he held, all the others in the United States, where he emigrated in 1937 endowed with a Rockefeller grant. He taught *inter alia* at Columbia University, the New School for Social Research, Johns Hopkins University, and the University of California at Berkeley. He died on 27 October 1982 in Tallahassee, Florida, one day before his seventy-ninth birthday.

Lerner made numerous contributions to economics. One even bears his name: the so-called Marshall–Lerner condition explains the influence of the currency exchange rate on the balance of payments. As one of the founders of the *RES* he also contributed to the inaugural volume with the article "The concept of monopoly and the measurement of monopoly power" (1934a). The paper's main contribution is its clear account of requirements for efficiency in the allocation of scarce resources, well known to economists as the Pareto condition. Deviations from allocative efficiency can be measured by the "Lerner Index" (or Lerner's degree of monopoly), that is, $\frac{p - mc}{p}$, where p is the price and mc the marginal cost of a commodity.

Lerner's second contribution to the *RES*, "Economic theory and socialist economy" (1934b), was the first of several influential papers he published on the theoretical foundations of "market socialism" between 1934 and 1938. Together with Oskar Lange, who was his classmate at the LSE, he shared the view that markets will help to improve the allocation in socialist economies (socialist market economies). According to the first welfare theorem, if perfect competition prevails, prices are equal to marginal costs, which implies a Pareto optimal allocation. Whereas in capitalism deviations from perfect competition are regular, in socialism the planning can conform to the "price equals marginal cost" rule. The allocative efficiency of socialism compared to capitalism seems to be vindicated. The second aspect of Lerner's contribution to "market socialism" concerns the distribution of incomes. While in capitalism the means of production and other resources are privately owned, in socialism they are owned by the public. Consequently, in socialism the income of the citizens consists of wages plus the "social dividend". According to which rule should the "social dividend" be distributed so that it does not interfere with the optimal allocation of labour? Lerner persuaded Oscar Lange that a lump sum would not disturb the allocation on the labour market.

In Lerner's early years, his research focus was in the field of welfare economics. His thoughts on welfare economics, international trade and the functioning of markets are contained in his magnum opus *The Economics of Control* (1944), which was his PhD thesis submitted to the LSE in 1934. In addition to the aforementioned topics, Lerner elucidates in his book Keynes's *General Theory*, especially the liquidity preference theory. He also helped to clarify the loanable funds versus liquidity preference debate between Keynes and Bertil Ohlin and he developed his own ideas about the principles of "functional finance", which start from the premise that government expenditure should be designed to obtain full employment output and price stability regardless of whether it increases public debt. He argued against the idea of the "burden of the debt" and against crowding out effects commonly used against deficit spending.

His contributions to Keynesian themes, particularly remedies against unemployment and inflation, were published in 1951 in *Economics of Employment*. In this book Lerner advocated a policy to achieve full employment referring to his concept of functional finance. He argues that monetary economies are inherently demand constrained. The general shortage of aggregate demand should be compensated by government spending. The government should increase spending up to a level where aggregate demand equals potential output. Government spending should be financed by non-interest bearing government bonds, which are sold to private banks or to the central bank. This is almost equivalent to pump priming by printing money. Similarities to the policy of the Federal Reserve System (FED) in 2010 after the financial crisis are perhaps more than mere chance. Why did Lerner not consider that the expectations of future inflation would be self-fulfilling? Because he thought wages did not rise until full employment was reached. Interestingly, Lerner recommends what he called a "low level of full employment", where labour unions' bargaining power is not too strong, so that wages will not increase faster than labour productivity. Such a "low level of full employment" equilibrium has similar properties as the "natural rate of unemployment" in recent macroeconomics, where the remaining unemployment is essentially only the result of frictions. However, if the economy moves into a situation of "high full employment" a wage-price spiral may build up and lead to inflation.

Lerner was a staunch supporter of Keynesianism and yet capable of explaining the stagflation phenomenon, which occurred much later. It seems that his ideas were not acknowledged by the then leading neoclassical synthesis Keynesians. One may speculate why Lerner remained an outsider in the US economics academia with little influence on the development of mainstream economics. Tibor Scitovsky mentioned Lerner's pedagogical device to use paradoxes in his papers and lectures. This was irritating for

the not-so-young, in whom the profession's conventional wisdom was often too deeply ingrained to be examined afresh. They were merely alienated by Lerner's paradoxes and deceptively simple ideas and quite frequently looked upon him as a crank. That was all the easier, because he dressed the part, with his open neck, bare toes and (later in life) his prophet's beard. In short, Lerner was a great teacher but a bad salesman. (Scitovsky 1984: 1548)

VOLKER CASPARI

See also:

Competition (III); John Maynard Keynes (I); Oskar Ryszard Lange (I); Welfare economics (III).

References and further reading

Keynes, J.M. (1936), *The General Theory of Employment, Interest and Money*, London: Macmillan.
Landes, D.S. (1994), 'Abba Ptachya Lerner (1903–1982)', *Biographical Memoirs*, **64**, Washington: National Academy of Sciences, pp. 208–31.
Lerner, A.P. (1934a), 'The concept of monopoly and the measurement of monopoly power,' *Review of Economic Studies*, **1** (3), 157–75.
Lerner, A.P. (1934b), 'Economic theory and socialist economy', *Review of Economic Studies*, **2** (1), 51–61.
Lerner, A.P. (1936), 'A note on socialist economics', *Review of Economic Studies*, **4** (1), 72–6.
Lerner, A.P. (1937), 'Statics and dynamics in socialist economics,' *Economic Journal*, **47** (186), 253–70.
Lerner, A.P. (1938), 'Theory and practice in socialist economics', *Review of Economic Studies*, **6** (1), 71–5.
Lerner, A.P. (1943), 'Functional finance and the federal debt', *Social Research*, **10** (1), 38–51.
Lerner, A.P. (1944), *The Economics of Control*, New York: Macmillan,
Lerner, A.P. (1951), *Economics of Employment*, New York: McGraw-Hill.
Scitovsky, T. (1984), 'Lerner's contribution to economics', *Journal of Economic Literature*, **22** (4), 1547–71.

John von Neumann (1903–1957)

Two Contributions?

The impact of John von Neumann's "model of general economic equilibrium" could be evaluated by the number and names of laureates of the Sveriges Riksbank Prize in Economic Sciences in Memory of Alfred Nobel who refer to this work: Kenneth Arrow, Gérard Debreu, Paul Samuelson, Tjalling Koopmans, Leonid Kantarovich, and Robert Solow. Weintraub (1983: 13) claims that von Neumann's "A model of general economic equilibrium" (GE) is "the single most important article in mathematical economics" while Baumol (1972) labels GE "the most remarkable virtuoso performance" in this field. Indeed, GE is a virtuoso performance, but one can easily get advanced degrees in economics without having heard of this paper. This is not to say that advanced students of economics do not study both general equilibrium theory and growth theory, but they might never learn that the mathematical treatment of both has one of its roots in von Neumann's GE. Von Neumann presented this paper at the Mathematical Seminar of Princeton University in 1932 and in Karl Menger's Mathematical Colloquium at the University of Vienna in 1936. It was published in German in 1937 and in English in 1945, see von Neumann (1937 [1945]).

This is quite different to the second area of economics that von Neumann inspired with his work, that is, game theory. Of course, we cannot answer the question of how game theory would look today, or whether there would be any game theory at all, if von Neumann had never presented the minimax theorem in Hilbert's seminar at the University of Göttingen in 1926, and published it in his article "Zur Theorie der Gesellschaftsspiele" in 1928 (published as "On the theory of games of strategy" in 1959). In the 1920s, Emile Borel also analysed games "in which the winnings depend simultaneously on chance and the skill of the player" (Borel quoted by Rives 1975: 559), but he did present a convincing solution concept like the minimax theorem. (See Leonard 2010: 57ff.) The collaboration between von Neumann and Oskar Morgenstern that resulted in the volume *Theory of Games and Economic Behavior* (*TGEB*) in 1944 was a consequence of von Neumann's 1928 paper.

The proof of the minimax theorem in the 1928 paper inspired the proof of the existence of an "expanding general equilibrium" of the GE model. In this context, von Neumann used game theory as a mathematical technique, "as a calculus" (Morgenstern 1976: 810). Do we have to conclude that von Neumann's "work reflects a belief in the relevant role mathematics could play in science and society rather than a genuine interest in economic issues" (De Pina Cabral 2003: 127)? The focus on Brouwer's fixed point theorem in the GE paper, emphasized in its German title, supports this hypothesis. A fixed point argument is also central to the proof of the minimax theorem in the 1928 paper. It was Morgenstern who raised the question of rationality and expectations that directed the *TGEB* towards economics (see Morgenstern 1949). If von Neumann's contribution to economics was meant to enhance the status of mathematics, the use of Brouwer's fixed point theorem and its extensions indeed enriched the tool box of economists and even entered advanced textbooks in microeconomics and game theory. Moreover, the *TGEB* had a strong impact on the development of axiomatic analysis in economics, especially demonstrated by the formalization and proof of the expected utility function. The first five axioms of Nash's (1950b) solution to the bargaining problem correspond to the axioms that von Neumann and Morgenstern proposed for expected utility. However, the proof of existence of a corresponding utility function was not published in the first edition of *TGEB*, although the authors already had the proof "of course" (Morgenstern 1976: 809). It is fair to say that the empirical testing of theoretical results of expected utility theory and game theory became one of the roots of experimental economics – an extremely popular branch of today's economics.

The game theoretical work of von Neumann never left the zero-sum world "of perfect conflict" in which the advantage of one player implies an equally large disadvantage of the other player, even when there are more than two players. In an earlier paper on *TGEB* and its authors (Holler 2009) I argued that the focus on conflict and zero sum that even entered the analysis of N-person games in *TGEB* via the concept of fictitious players reflects an important feature of von Neumann's personality. Von Neumann was very sceptical towards the Nash equilibrium that generalized the minimax theorem for variable sum games that may represent situations of both conflict and coordination and applies to more than two players. For Nash, however, the zero sum limitation of *TGEB* was the motivation to develop his equilibrium concept (Nash 1950a) and propose a solution to the bargaining problem (Nash 1950b). In *TGEB*,

> a theory of n-person games is developed which includes as a special case the two-person bargaining problem. But the theory there developed makes no attempt to find a value for a given n-person game, that is, to determine what it is worth to each player to have the opportunity to engage in the game. This determination is accomplished only in the case of the two-person zero sum game. (Nash 1950a: 157)

Note that Nash (1951) used Brouwer's theorem to prove the existence of an equilibrium for all games with a finite number of pure strategies.

A Short Vitae

Obviously, von Neumann's scientific interest strongly focused on mathematics and its applications. He has delivered substantial contributions to quantum physics, functional analysis, set theory, topology, numerical analysis, cellular automata, and computer science, and his work in economics looks just like another field of application of mathematics.

He was born Neumann János Lajos in 1903 in Budapest and died in 1957 in Washington, DC. At the age of 6, he could exchange jokes in Classical Greek, memorize telephone directories, and was able to divide two eight-digit numbers in his head. His first mathematics paper, written jointly with Michael Fekete, then assistant at the University of Budapest who had been tutoring him, was published in 1922. At the age of 25, he had published ten major papers in mathematics.

In 1926, aged 23, he received his PhD in mathematics from the University of Budapest and a diploma in chemical engineering from the ETH Zurich (the Swiss Federal Institute of Technology in Zurich). He taught as a Privatdozent at the University of Berlin, today's Humboldt-Universität, from 1926 to 1929 and at the University of Hamburg from 1929 to1930. In 1930 he became a visiting lecturer at Princeton University, being appointed professor there in 1931. In 1933, he became professor of mathematics at the newly founded Institute for Advanced Study in Princeton – a position he kept for the remainder of his life.

Morgenstern (1976) reports that on 1 February 1939, when he gave an after-lunch talk on business cycles at the Nassau Club, he had a first chance to talk to von Neumann about games. Over the year their discussion and friendship progressed. In 1944, their *Theory of Games and Economic Behavior* was published, a volume of more than 600 pages.

During the years of collaboration with Morgenstern and after World War II, von Neumann served as a consultant to the armed forces. In 1940 he became a member of the Scientific Advisory Committee at the Ballistic Research Laboratories and in 1941 a member of the Navy Bureau of Ordnance. He was a consultant to the Los Alamos Scientific Laboratory from 1943 to 1955. In this function he was a leading contributor to the development of the nuclear and, along with Edward Teller and Stanisław Ulam, of the hydrogen bomb. In 1956 he received the presidential Medal for Freedom – being America's highest civilian award, recognizing exceptional meritorious service. Von Neumann died on 8 February 1957, "after much suffering" (Morgenstern 1976: 814).

Von Neumann's Expanding General Equilibrium Model

In the first line of his GE article, von Neumann states that the subject matter of this paper is "the solution of a typical economic equation system". (The von Neumann citations in this section are taken from the English version, von Neumann 1945.) This equation system assumes that there are n goods which can be produced by m different processes being characterized by constant returns to scale. Moreover, a good "can be produced only jointly with certain others". There are natural factors of production but the emphasis is on produced goods that enter production as inputs. Thus production is circular and the distinction of primary factors and outputs, substantial to the dominant Walrasian general equilibrium model, is not valid. Natural factors of production, including labour and land, are abundant and "can be expanded in unlimited quantities". Labour is remunerated with the "necessities of life". There are no savings: "consumption of goods takes place only through the processes of production" and "all incomes in excess of necessities of life will be reinvested".

After having defined the intensities of production x_i ($i = 1, \ldots, m$), expressing to what degree a process i is applied, and the prices y_j ($j = 1, \ldots, n$), x_i and y_j being non-negative, von Neumann proposes the following equations:

$$\alpha \sum_{i=1}^{m} a_{ij} x_i \le \sum_{i=1}^{m} b_{ij} x_i \tag{1}$$

If < applies in (1) then $y_j = 0$, and j is a free good.

$$\beta \sum_{j=1}^{n} a_{ij} y_j \ge \sum_{j=1}^{n} b_{ij} y_j \tag{2}$$

If > applies in (2) then $x_i = 0$, that is, process i is unprofitable and will not be used.

In (1) and (2), a_{ij} and b_{ij} quantify inputs and outputs in the production of good j, given at any point in time. α and β represent "the coefficient of the expansion of the whole economy" and the interest factor, respectively. Condition (1) says that it is impossible to consume more of a good j in the total production than is being produced. Condition (2) assumes perfect competition: in equilibrium there are no profits with any process i.

Quantities a_{ij} and b_{ij} are given, variables α, β, x_i and y_j are unknown. Von Neumann's proof demonstrates that for the given system α, β, x_i and y_j can always be determined. Even with constant ratios of intensities, there could be several solutions for x_i and y_j while α and β are uniquely determined. It turns out that $\alpha = \beta$.

Von Neumann's GE tries to answer the question "which processes will be actually used and which not". As such it is the first paper of what has been subsequently called activity analysis, and "the first use in economics of . . . explicit duality arguments, explicit fixed-point techniques for an existence proof, and convexity arguments" (Weintraub 1983: 13). Economists may regret that no preferences were needed to explain demand, and money did not matter as there was no saving and still, for positive prices, inputs and outputs balanced. The interest factor is not determined by time preference or demand and supply of money but by the expansion coefficient, that is, the supply of goods. This suggests that the model is in the classical and not in the neoclassical tradition (see Kurz and Salvadori 1993, 1995: 403ff).

Game Theory

In GE, von Neumann has an extensive footnote referring to the minimax theorem and his 1928 paper "Zur Theorie der Gesellschaftsspiele" (TG) that contains its proof. Despite the time difference between the publication of TG and GE it has been argued that the two papers were not developed independently from each other.

"Zur Theorie der Gesellschaftsspiele" introduces all instruments that are essential for non-cooperative game theory, but it also gives a definition of the characteristic function that is applied to analyse coalition formation. More fundamental, however, is the introduction of the concept of strategy as a complete plan of moves that a player can choose, including mixed strategies. The strategy sets reflect the rules of the game and the possible information that a player has at the beginning of a game and that he collects in its course. This introduces the extensive form of a game.

For the case of two-person zero-sum games with finitely many pure strategies for each player, that is, if the advantage of one player implies an "equally" large disadvantage of the other, TG contains a proof of the minimax theorem which says: there is always a pair of strategies, pure or mixed, such that none of the players can deviate and achieve a higher "payoff" (see below). Thus, the theorem guarantees a value for each player which is independent of the behaviour of the other.

In the case of more than two players, the problem of coalition formation exists. "Zur Theorie der Gesellschaftsspiele" proposes a solution concept that prescribes outcomes such that no pair of players can guarantee itself a higher value then the utilities that the solution allocates to them. This condition is satisfied by the core, but not by the "solution" introduced in *TGEB*.

Apart from a large variety of applications, the *TGEB* adds two essentials to TG: an axiomatization of the expected utility (EU) hypothesis and a solution concept for games with more than two players, called "solution" by the authors. Often, the second concept is considered as a poor substitute for the core and has hardly any relevance in economics. However, there are arguments in favour of this concept (see Aumann 1987; Binmore 1998: 40f.). Expected utility became an indispensable tool to modern microeconomics, and not only in its game theoretical applications. It says that given a lottery $L = (A, p; B, 1 - p)$ where A and B are sure alternatives and p and $1 - p$ are the probability by which they occur, then we can write $u(L) = pu(A) + (1 - p)u(B)$. Utility functions u(.) that satisfy this property are called von Neumann Morgenstern utilities or payoffs. (The use of the term payoff is, however, not unambiguous: some authors use it, for example, for money instead of utilities.) Obviously, EU applies to the evaluation of risky outcomes, for instance, as a result of playing mixed strategies. It might be helpful to know that this concept has an axiomatic basis, but more often the axioms are used to identify some properties of EU and submit them to empirical tests and theoretical speculation. Allais's (1953) early critique on the EU concept was mainly based on introspection – Allais's label "l'école américaine" has a certain charm: its authors conversed in German when writing the *TGEB* (see Morgenstern 1976).

One of the achievements of *TGEB* was to make von Neumann's TG article and its results known. Even Morgenstern had not read the article before he met von Neumann at Princeton. However, he had heard of von Neumann: "The principal reason for my wanting to go to Princeton was the possibility that I might become acquainted with von Neumann and the hope that this would be a great stimulus for my future work" (Morgenstern 1976: 807).

MANFRED J. HOLLER

See also:

Economics and philosophy (III); Formalization and mathematical modelling (III); Game theory (III); Growth (III); Input–output analysis (III); Social choice (III).

References

Allais, M. (1953), 'Le comportement de l'homme rational devant le risque: critique des postulats et axiomes de l'école américaine', *Econometrica*, **21** (4), 503–46.
Aumann, R.J. (1987), 'Game theory', in J. Eatwell, M. Milgate and P. Newman (eds), *The New Palgrave, A Dictionary of Economics*, vol. 2, London and Basingstoke: Macmillan, pp. 460–82.
Baumol, W.J. (1972), *Economic Theory and Operations Analysis*, 3rd edn, Englewood Cliffs, NJ: Prentice Hall, first published 1961.
Binmore, K. (1998), *Just Playing: Game Theory and the Social Contract II*, Cambridge, MA and London: MIT Press.
De Pina Cabral, M.J.C. (2003), 'John von Neumann's contribution to economic science,' *International Social Science Review*, **78** (3–4), 126–37.
Holler, M.J. (2009), 'John von Neumann und Oskar Morgenstern', in H.D. Kurz (ed.), *Klassiker des ökonomischen Denkens*, Munich: Verlag C.H. Beck, pp 250–67.
Kurz, H.D. and N. Salvadori (1993), 'Von Neumann's growth model and the "classical tradition"', *European Journal of the History of Thought*, **1** (1), 129–60.
Kurz, H.D. and N. Salvadori (1995), *Theory of Production: A Long-Period Analysis*, Cambridge, Melbourne and New York: Cambridge University Press.
Leonard, R. (2010), *Von Neumann, Morgenstern, and the Creation of Game Theory*, New York: Cambridge University Press.
Morgenstern, O. (1949), 'Economics and the theory of games', *Kyklos*, **3** (4), 294–308.
Morgenstern, O. (1976), 'The collaboration between Oskar Morgenstern and John von Neumann on the theory of games', *Journal of Economic Literature*, **14** (3), 805–16.

Nash, J.F. (1950a), 'Equilibrium points in N-person games', *Proceedings of the National Academy of Sciences*, **36** (1), 48–9.
Nash, J.F. (1950b), 'The bargaining problem', *Econometrica*, **18** (2), 155–62.
Nash, J.F. (1951), 'Non-cooperative games', *Annals of Mathematics*, **54**, 286–95.
Neumann, J. von (1928), 'Zur Theorie der Gesellschaftsspiele', *Mathematische Annalen*, **100** (1), 295–320, English trans. (1959), 'On the theory of games of strategy', in A.W. Tucker and R.D. Luce (eds), *Contributions to the Theory of Games*, vol. 4, Princeton, NJ: Princeton University Press.
Neumann, J. von (1937), 'Über ein ökonomisches Gleichungssystem und eine Verallgemeinerung des Brouwerschen Fixpunktsatzes', in K. Menger (ed.), *Ergebnisse eines Mathematischen Seminars*, vol. 8, Vienna, English trans. (1945), 'A model of general economic equilibrium', *Review of Economic Studies*, **13** (1), 1–9.
Neumann, J. von and O. Morgenstern (1944), *Theory of Games and Economic Behavior*, Princeton, NJ: Princeton University Press.
Rives, N.W. Jr (1975), 'On the history of the mathematical theory of games', *History of Political Economy*, **7** (4), 549–65.
Weintraub, E.R. (1983), 'On the existence of a competitive equilibrium: 1930–1954', *Journal of Economic Literature*, **21** (1), 1–39.

Frank Plumpton Ramsey (1903–1930)

> If I was to write a *Weltanschaung* I should call it not "What I believe" but "What I feel." This is connected with Wittgenstein's view that philosophy does not give us beliefs, but merely relieves feelings of intellectual discomfort. . . . I don't feel the least humble before the vastness of the heavens. The stars may be large, but they cannot think or love; and these are qualities which impress me far more than size does. (Ramsey 1931: 290–91)

In one of those extraordinary serendipities with which greatness is tinged, and Frank Ramsey – despite the cruelty of a life cut short at its prime – was blessed with an abundance of it, he was born in Cambridge on 22 February 1903, the year the defining works of the twentieth century in ethics and the foundations of mathematics were published: *Principia Ethica* by G.E. Moore and the *Principles of Mathematics* by Bertrand Russell, the latter presaging the monumental *Principia Mathematica* (written jointly with Whitehead). With equal irony, Ramsey died in London, on 19 January 1930, the year Kurt Gödel announced his famous incompleteness theorem(s) in Königsberg. With the celebrated Paris–Harrington results (Paris and Harrington 1977), the connection between Ramsey's posthumously published classic, *On a Problem of Formal Logic* (Ramsey 1928a, 1928b), and Gödel's pioneering results have been shown to be woven from the same foundational fabric of the *Entscheidungsproblem* that Hilbert had formulated, to settle, decisively, the *grundlagenkrise* of the 1920s, precipitated by Brouwer's intuitionistic and constructive challenges. It may be that Ramsey himself veered towards intuitionism, in mathematical philosophy at the end of his short life (Braithwaite's 'Introduction' to Ramsey 1991; Ramsey 1991: chs 53, 54).

The bare bones of Frank Ramsey's family background are simple enough to document, although behind this simplistic account there is a richness that deserves to be expanded. He was the eldest of Agnes Mary – née Wilson – and Arthur Stanley Ramsey's four children. His brother, Michael, later to become the Archbishop of Canterbury, was born one year later and his sisters, Bridget and Margaret were, respectively, four and 14 years younger. Frank's father, Arthur Stanley, was also a mathematician, Fellow, Tutor, Bursar and President of Magdalene College, Cambridge. Frank himself, at the time of his death, was a Fellow of King's College, Cambridge. He had been a scholar at Winchester, from 1915 and went up to Trinity College, Cambridge, in 1920, graduating as a Wrangler in 1923. He was elected to a Fellowship at King's College in 1924, to a University Lectureship in Mathematics in 1926 and took over as the Director of Studies in Mathematics at King's. He married Lettice Barker (d. 12 July 1985), five years his senior in age, in September 1925 and they had two daughters, Jane and Sarah; only the latter survived the deaths of her parents, separated by 55 years, to produce three grandchildren, Stephen, Belinda and Matthew Burch.

Moore's *Principia Ethica*, Russell's (and Whitehead's 1913) *Principia Mathematica*, Hardy's *Pure Mathematics* (1908), Keynes' *Treatise on Probability* (1921) and Wittgenstein's *Tractatus Logico Philosophicus* (1921–22; the manuscript version of which was placed at Frank Ramsey's disposal by C.K. Ogden, with whom he eventually translated it while still a teenager) redefined the intellectual landscape of their respective fields, as Ramsey himself reached his precociously youthful maturity in the approaching postwar period. To these themes, in which he excelled and made what can only be described as outstanding contributions, he added, under the influence of Maynard Keynes (and A.C. Pigou, also a Fellow at King's), a mastery of economics that few, then or since, matched for analytical brilliance and originality.

The "Eponymous F.P. Ramsey" (Mellor 1983) has given birth to Ramsey economics, Ramsey pricing and the Ramsey taxation formula, the Ramsey sentence, the Ramsey theorem (Wang 1981), Ramsey problem, Ramsey theory and Ramsey number. Beyond these, there are the contributions to a simplified theory of types (Ramsey 1925, 1926; Chwistek 1949: ch. 6, whose work Ramsey was acquainted with, claims priority on this point) to resolve the perplexities of the logical and semantic paradoxes that plagued *Principia Mathematica* and the discussions and debates with Wittgenstein on finitism and the role of tautologies and the definition of identity in mathematics. Finally, there is the acknowledged influence of Ramsey on *Production of Commodities by Means of Commodities* (Sraffa 1960).

Since it is impossible to discuss all of the above in any kind of justifiable detail within the restricted space we have at our disposal, we confine ourselves to five core contributions, with economic relevance, past, present and, we are sure, future.

"Officially", in the past and the present, Ramsey's contributions to economics have been confined to his three articles on "Truth and probability" (1926), "A contribution to the theory of taxation" (1927a) and "A mathematical theory of saving" (1928c). With hindsight at our disposal, we can see that "Ramsey's theorem" (1928b) has become relevant for various frontiers in economic theory. Then, there is the explicit acknowledgement by Sraffa, in the preface to his magnum opus, of Ramsey's "mathematical help".

"Truth and probability", written as a critical review of *A Treatise on Probability* (Keynes 1921; incidentally, many insist that Keynes accepted Ramsey's criticisms and gave up on "partial orders", which simply cannot be true, given the many ways in which Keynes insisted on the unbridgeable formal gap between "risk" and "uncertainty", particularly in the *General Theory*), is justly celebrated as the original contribution to the axiomatization of subjective probability – predating the equally important work of Bruno De Finetti by many years and anticipating the more orthodox von Neumann–Morgenstern work by almost two decades – and providing foundations for expected utility maximization underpinning for rational behaviour. However, it is rarely – if ever – remembered that Ramsey added an important caveat (De Finetti, was also explicit in his rejection of σ-algebras and the embracing of finite-additivity when axiomatizing subjective probability) to this classic contribution (Ramsey 1926: 85): "[N]othing has been said [in my paper] about degrees of belief when the number of alternatives is *infinite*. About this I have nothing useful to say, except that I doubt if the mind is capable of contemplating more than a *finite* number of alternatives."

Similarly, Ramsey's injunctions (perhaps "Pigou-inspired"?) against discounting the future, as "a practice which is ethically indefensible and arises merely from the weakness of the imagination" (Ramsey 1928: 261), are no longer even added as a footnote qualification when deriving the Keynes–Ramsey Rule within the framework of the "Ramsey–Cass–Koopmans" model of optimal aggregate economic growth in neoclassical economics. Moreover, the published version of this modern classic omitted two additional sections (document # 006-07-01 in the "Ramsey Collection" held in the Hillman Library of the University of Pittsburgh), where it can be seen that Ramsey thought hard and deeply about the problem of discounting the future. It is our firm belief that Keynes's *Economic Possibilities for our Grandchildren*, given not only in 1928, the year Ramsey's "Saving" paper was published in the *Economic Journal*, but also at Winchester College, Ramsey's old school, was consistent with the problem of discounting the infinite future, solved with the notion of "bliss" by Ramsey.

Ramsey (1927a) has spawned two strands of optimal pricing research in economics: the classic optimal taxation literature, linking up with the work that originates with Mirrlees and Diamond; the other, more along the lines of public utility and public goods, pricing has resulted in the Ramsey–Boiteux inverse elasticity formula (which, though famously also derived in Robinson 1933, has no reference to Ramsey!). However, it remains a puzzle to us that the link with Lindahl pricing has never been developed.

The Ramsey–Sraffa interaction is clearly and, so far as we can tell, exhaustively, presented in Kurz and Salvadori (2001). The only comment we would like to add here is the following. The first of the three comments by Ramsey, summarized by Sraffa on 26 June, 1928 (Kurz and Salvadori 2001: 262), refers essentially to the Ruffini–Abel result on the unsolvability of the *quintic*, which Ramsey would, as a student of mathematics (particularly of Hardy), have known very well. The point here is the affinity of Abel's approach to his unsolvability proof with Gödel's later unsolvability proof strategies and the present understanding of the relevance of such things to variations of 'Ramsey's theorem' (cf. Paris and Harrington 1977).

We come now to what we think will be Ramsey's lasting contribution to economic theory, in the future: the growing influence of Ramsey (1928a, 1928b) on graph theory, combinatorics, recursion theory and computational complexity theory. We are convinced that Ramsey theory – that is, "Ramsey's Theorem" – will come to play an increasingly important computational role in these fields. To substantiate this conjecture we have to refer to what are called the two principles of Ramsey theory. However, to state them we have, first, to state, in some minimally formal way, the Ramsey theorem:

> Ramsey's theorem (Ramsey, 1928b [1978]: 233, theorem A):
> For $A \subseteq N$, where N: the set of natural numbers, $[A]^n$ the class of all n-element subsets of A; Partition $[N]^n$ into *finitely* many sub-classes, C_i, $i = 1, 2, \ldots, p$ and call the partition P.
> $H(P)$: the class of those *infinite* sets $A \subseteq N$, s.t., $[A]^n \subseteq C_i$ for some i.
> Then, $H(P)$ is nonempty for every such partition.
> Ramsey theory's first principle:
> Structure (of P, for example) is preserved under finite partitions.
> Ramsey theory's second principle:
> There is always an appropriate notion of *size*, s.t., any sufficiently large structure always contains the desired well-organized sub-structure.

Now, suppose we endow P with a recursive structure, then we ask what we can say about $H(P)$, from many points of view: computational complexity theory, for example. Recent research shows that this kind of question can be answered using proof strategies developed in Kolomogorov complexity theory.

Ramsey's remarkable theorem, in being a source for the derivation of the celebrated

Paris–Harrington theorem, also links up with Goodstein's algorithm and the more recent development in rational-valued nonlinear dynamics (Paris and Tavakol 1993). This latter class of dynamical systems goes beyond the sensitive dependence on initial conditions nonlinear dynamics and a new class, labelled "super sensitive dynamical systems", has been defined. The attractors of such dynamical systems are invariably trivial.

In conclusion, the Ramseyan precept for intellectual adventures that we have culled out of our research on the remarkable work of this prodigal genius can be summarized by his own paraphrasing of Wittgenstein's well known aphorism: "What we can't say, we can't say and we can't whistle it either."

K. Vela Velupillai and Ragupathy Venkatachalam

See also:

Cambridge School of economics (II); Public economics (III).

References and further reading

Chwistek, L. (1949), *The Limits of Science*, London: Routledge & Kegan Paul.
Hardy, G.H. (1908), *Pure Mathematics*, Cambridge: Cambridge University Press.
Keynes, J.M. (1921), *A Treatise on Probability*, London: Macmillan.
Kurz, H. and N. Salvadori (2001), 'Sraffa and the mathematicians: Frank Ramsey and Alister Watson', pt IV, ch 17, in T. Cozzi and R. Marchionatti (eds), *Piero Sraffa's Political Economy – A Centenary Estimate*, London: Routledge, pt IV, ch 17.
Mellor, D.H (1983), 'The eponymous F.P. Ramsey', *Journal of Graph Theory*, 7 (1), 9–13.
Moore, G.E. (1903), *Principia Ethica*, Cambridge: Cambridge University Press.
Paris, J. and L. Harrington (1977), 'A mathematical incompleteness in Peano arithmetic', in J. Barwise (ed.), *Handbook of Mathematical Logic*, Amsterdam and New York: North-Holland, pp. 1133–42.
Paris, J. and R. Tavakol (1993), 'Goodstein algorithm as a super-transient dynamical system', *Physics Letters A*, **180** (1–2), 83–6.
Ramsey, F.P. (1925), 'The foundations of mathematics', in F.P. Ramsey (1978), *Foundations – Essays in Philosophy, Logic, Mathematics and Economics*, D.H. Mellor (ed.), London: Routledge & Kegan Paul, pp. 154–212.
Ramsey, F.P. (1926), 'Truth and probability', in F.P. Ramsey (1978), *Foundations – Essays in Philosophy, Logic, Mathematics and Economics*, ed. D.H. Mellor, London: Routledge & Kegan Paul, pp. 58–100.
Ramsey, F.P. (1927a), 'A contribution to the theory of taxation', in F.P. Ramsey (1978), *Foundations – Essays in Philosophy, Logic, Mathematics and Economics*, ed. D.H. Mellor, London: Routledge & Kegan Paul, pp. 242–60.
Ramsey, F.P. (1927b), 'Facts and propositions', in F.P. Ramsey (1978), *Foundations – Essays in Philosophy, Logic, Mathematics and Economics*, ed. D.H. Mellor, London: Routledge & Kegan Paul, pp. 40–57.
Ramsey, F.P. (1928a), 'On a problem of formal logic', in F.P. Ramsey, *The Foundations of Mathematics, and other Logical Essays*, ed. and Introduction by R.B. Braithwaite, Preface by G.E. Moore, London: Kegan Paul, Trench, Trubner and Company, pp. 82–111.
Ramsey, F.P. (1928b), 'Ramsey's theorem', in F.P. Ramsey (1978), *Foundations – Essays in Philosophy, Logic, Mathematics and Economics*, ed. D.H. Mellor, London: Routledge & Kegan Paul, pp. 233–41.
Ramsey, F.P. (1928c), 'A mathematical theory of saving', in F.P. Ramsey (1978), *Foundations – Essays in Philosophy, Logic, Mathematics and Economics*, ed. D.H. Mellor, London: Routledge & Kegan Paul, pp. 261–81.
Ramsey, F.P. (1931), *The Foundations of Mathematics, and other Logical Essays*, ed. and Introduction by R.B. Braithwaite, Preface by G.E. Moore, London: Kegan Paul, Trench, Trubner and Company.
Ramsey, F.P. (1978), *Foundations – Essays in Philosophy, Logic, Mathematics and Economics*, ed. D.H. Mellor, London: Routledge & Kegan Paul.
Ramsey, F.P. (1991), *Notes on Philosophy, Probability and Mathematics*, ed. M.C. Galavotti, Naples: Bibliopolis.
Robinson, J. (1933), *The Economics of Imperfect Competition*, London: Macmillan.
Russell, B. (1903), *The Principles of Mathematics*, vol 1, Cambridge: Cambridge University Press.

Russell, B.A.W. and A.N. Whitehead (1913), *Principia Mathematica*, vol. 3, Cambridge: Cambridge University Press, vol. 1 (1910), vol. 2 (1912).

Sraffa, P. (1960), *Production of Commodities by Means of Commodities: Prelude to a Critique of Economic Theory*, Cambridge: Cambridge University Press.

Wang, H. (1981), *Popular Lectures on Mathematical Logic*, New York: Van Nostrand Reinhold.

Wittgenstein, L. (1921–22), *Tractatus Logico-Philosophicus*, trans C.K. Ogden and F.P. Ramsey, Introduction by B. Russell, London: Routledge & Kegan Paul.

Joan Violet Robinson (1903–1983)

For Joan Robinson, there was "no such thing as a 'purely economic' problem [to be] settled by purely economic logic; political interest and political prejudices are involved in every discussion of actual questions" (Robinson 1951–79, *Collected Economic Papers*, hereafter *CEP*, V: 1). Indeed, "the answers to economic problems are only political questions" (Robinson 1975: iv), rooted in morality and ethics. Besides the political, you find, throughout Robinson's work, that the answers to economic questions are mired in epistemic ambiguities, the basis for her insistence on a distinction between history and equilibrium.

An instinct for the ethical dimensions of economic problems is evident from the beginning. "Beauty and the beast" (*CEP*, I: 225–33), an undergraduate essay, reflecting a deep understanding of what she had learned from Marshall's *Principles* (1920), ends in a "happy union of producer's and consumer's surplus", but what sparks our interest is an ethical problem with a decidedly modern ring.

> [The] speculator who by intelligent foresight anticipates the future, and who makes his gains by shrewd purchases and sales, renders thereby a public service of no small importance, but when to a normal degree of foresight is added [the Beast's] supernatural [inside] information, the speculator is in a position to enhance his own gains at the expense of less enlightened members of the community. Such malignant forms of speculation are a grievous hindrance to progress. (*CEP*, I: 230)

Then there is the enduring moral question of what ought to be for sale. The father of the Beauty "had never been accustomed to regard his daughters either as capital or as stock-in-trade". Not slow to realize the exorbitant price he was about to pay in fulfilment of the contract entered into, he was only

> for a moment in some doubt as to the advisability of repudiating his obligations . . . [reflecting on his long held belief] that the structure of modern industry could only be maintained by that rigid observance of contracts which is the essential basis for all commercial progress . . . [and by] the scrupulous integrity with which every member of the business community must refrain from yielding to the vast temptations to fraud which lie in his way. (*CEP*, I: 231)

Unearthing a discomfiting subtext in the moralizing aspects of Marshall's *Principles* (1920) would come naturally to a dissenting member of a dissenting family. At the age of 15, Joan witnessed the consequences of the public accusation by her father, Major-General Sir Frederick Maurice, to the effect that the War Cabinet had intentionally misrepresented to Parliament the strength of British troop levels on the Western Front. Standing on principle in her own fight for answers to the problems of unemployment and poverty would be a mark of Joan Robinson's entire academic life.

She had read history at St Paul's Girls' School, followed by economics at Girton College, from 1922 to her graduation in 1925. Her marriage in 1926 to fellow economist Austin Robinson was followed by a two-year stint in India, to which she often returned in later life. Austin had been appointed to a university lectureship in 1928 and it was in that year that Joan began in earnest to establish her own international reputation as an academic economist. All agree that *The Economics of Imperfect Competition* (Robinson 1933) would have figured prominently in the award to Joan Robinson of the

Sveriges Riksbank Prize in Economic Sciences in Memory of Alfred Nobel, had it ever come to pass. Still, her appointment in 1934 to an assistant lectureship was not accompanied then or later by a college teaching fellowship, and even that first step caused some grousing (Harcourt and Kerr 2009: 8). The quality of her articles and books, numbering well over 400 items (Marcuzzo 2002), overcame the obstacles standing in the way of academic women. She became university lecturer in 1937; reader in 1949, a year after being granted, upon a change in the rules, her 1925 degree; and professor in 1965, six years prior to her retirement from teaching duties. Her standing in Cambridge and throughout the world prompted Kings College unanimously to grant to her its first female Honorary Fellowship in 1970. Her standing in the economics profession was evident in the reception she received upon giving the Richard Ely Lecture to the American Economic Association in 1971.

The engaging style of writing which infused "Beauty and the Beast" became a hallmark. No potted versions of her essays or books (in many cases a series of essays) measure up to the originals, rich tapestries of impressions and arguments reflecting the contradictory facts of economic life. Even in self-criticism of her first book (*CEP*, II: 222–45), Robinson offered complex insight into the distinction between firm and industry and the nature and sphere of competition, concluding that there are many ways other than sub-optimum scales of production in which imperfect competition generates waste, while noting that the main benefit of price competition imposed by perfect markets is to be found, not in some notion of Pareto optimality, but in the spur it gives to the introduction of new commodities and new methods of production. In an early paper (*CEP*, I: 20–34), she grapples with a problem not adequately handled even now. In the presence of abnormal profits in a competitive industry, how many and how large are the new firms? Marshallian economics, freed from the notion of an optimum size firm, underlies Robinson's insistence on the role of history, bequeathing inconsistencies between stocks and flows, and setting the stage for the myriad ways in which present action causes the future to unfold.

Robinson played a major role in the discussions in Cambridge leading up to Keynes's *General Theory* (1936). These began with the formation of the "Circus" in 1930 (Harcourt and Kerr 2009: 23). Her own influential *Essays in the Theory of Employment* appeared in 1937, followed by a pamphlet, "The problem of full employment", published in various versions during the 1940s. An intuition "that there was a certain sympathy between Keynes's theory of employment and effective demand and Marx's theory of crises" (Harcourt and Kerr 2009: 33) resulted in *An Essay on Marxian Economics* (Robinson 1942). Lectures given in 1955 on "Marx, Marshall and Keynes" (*CEP*, II: 1–17) signal Robinson's enduring belief that all economic theory contains an ideological point of view which must be ferreted out before the theory can be made useful. This is as true of Marx, the revolutionary, who gives the best defence of capitalism, as it is of Marshall, the complacent defender who exposes its greatest defect, and of Keynes, seeking to "devise means to save it from destroying itself" (*CEP*, II.: 1) while setting the stage for policy initiatives of the most pernicious sort.

Towards a Dynamic Economics (Harrod 1948), though critically reviewed by Robinson (*CEP*, I: 155–74), became the inspiration for her first attempt at a "Generalisation of the General Theory" (Robinson 1952 [1979]). In an effort to move on, she had drawn the distinction between capital as a fund of finance and as a stock of equipment in a paper universally regarded (Robinson 1953) as the first volley in a long and surprisingly bitter controversy, a paper "met, not only with incomprehension, but with ridicule and indignation" (Robinson 1975: vi). Paul Samuelson's attribution to J.B. Clark of the concept of a capital to labour ratio, "continuously squeezed up or spread out, as [capital] accrues, so as always to preserve equilibrium", ruled out "every objective of Keynesian and post-Keynesian analysis . . . straddling like the impenetrable Boyg [Ibsen, *Peer Gynt*, act II, sc. 7] across the path to reasoned argument" (Robinson 1975: vii; cf. Robinson 1962: 1). In giving her own answer to the question of how capital is substituted for labour as accumulation takes place in the absence of technological change, Robinson acknowledged Ruth Cohen for pointing out the possibility of what would later be called the reswitching of techniques (Robinson 1953: 106). She did not make much of it, calling it a "curiosum" in *The Accumulation of Capital* (Robinson 1956: 109), while acknowledging, in a postscript to the third edition of her magnum opus, that it was not to be "unduly deprecated" (Robinson 1969: 427). However, by then, following an unsuccessful effort to prove its impossibility, reswitching had become a cause célèbre. True to form, within a few years, she warned that her analysis was "not recommended to anybody . . . [for it had not] repudiated the concept of accumulation in a given state of knowledge nearly thoroughly enough" (Robinson 1975: ix).

Thus there came a double parting of the ways. Reswitching implies no general presumption that a reduction in the real wage, however brought about, can be guaranteed to make an economy more labour intensive, however measured. This result, if not given prominence, risks leaving in place the argument that it is only the rigidity of wages that explains the prevalence of unemployment as substitution of labour for capital is held up by market "imperfections". Partly for this reason, those who continue the work of reviving the standpoint of "the old Classical economists from Adam Smith to Ricardo" (Sraffa 1960: v) and who might be expected to find in Robinson's work much upon which to build, rarely cite her. As for mainstream theorists, they have long ceased to concern themselves with Robinson's questions, putting past controversies down to the inability of a literary economist to appreciate the subtleties of dynamic programming. However, her questions were never answered. Samuelson left hanging in the air, in his reply to Robinson's paper on "The unimportance of reswitching" (*CEP*, V: 76–89), a telling reference to the "Hahn problem", failing to grant to her precisely the points he had himself made (Samuelson 1967: 228–30) and which so well expressed her own theoretical concerns.

It has been said that Robinson became "more and more pessimistic, even nihilistic" (Harcourt and Kerr 2009: 223) about the prospect of grafting onto the Keynesian approach a Marxian/Kaleckian analysis of historical economic development, taking into account the ethical and moral dimensions of economic problems. Yet, what emerges from her penchant for drawing a sharp distinction between history and equilibrium may be something quite hopeful. Throughout her work there are constant reminders, often thrown out only as hints, that what matters most for the future development of economic theory is the role of firms in creating technological change, for good or ill. Citing Kaldor (1972), she writes: "The growth of output itself creates opportunities for specialization and 'increasing returns' in Allyn Young's sense and new inventions and discoveries are continually being adapted to industrial processes" (Robinson 1975: x). Brian Loasby, whom Robinson cited in connection with the problem of knowledge (*CEP* V: 7–8), has long argued for all manner of connections between the epistemic questions underlying her distinction between history and equilibrium and the work of Smith, Young, Shackle, Schumpeter, and Penrose, all of whom Robinson recognized at various points in her work.

HARVEY GRAM

See also:

Cambridge School of economics (II); Capital theory (III); Economics and philosophy (III); Roy Forbes Harrod (I); Richard Ferdinand Kahn (I); John Maynard Keynes (I); Alfred Marshall (I); Karl Heinrich Marx (I); Piero Sraffa (I).

References and further reading

Harcourt, G.C. and P. Kerr (2009), *Joan Robinson*, London: Palgrave Macmillan.
Harrod, R. (1948), *Towards a Dynamic Economics*, London: Macmillan.
Kaldor, N. (1972), 'The irrelevance of equilibrium economics', *Economic Journal*, **82** (328), 1237–55.
Keynes, J.M. (1936), *The General Theory of Employment, Interest and Money*, London: Macmillan.
Marshall, A. (1920), *Principles of Economics, an Introductory Volume*, 8th edn, London: Macmillan.
Robinson, J.V. (1933), *The Economics of Imperfect Competition*, London: Macmillan.
Robinson, J.V. (1937), *Essays in the Theory of Employment*, Oxford: Basil Blackwell.
Robinson, J.V. (1942), *An Essay on Marxian Economics*, London: Macmillan.
Robinson, J.V. (1949), *The Problem of Full Employment*, London: The Workers' Educational Association.
Robinson, J.V. (1951–79), *Collected Economic Papers*, 5 vols, Oxford: Basil Blackwell.
Robinson, J.V. (1952), *The Rate of Interest and Other Essays*, London: Macmillan, republished 1979 as *The Generalisation of the General Theory and Other Essays*.
Robinson, J.V. (1953), 'The production function and the theory of capital', *Review of Economic Studies*, **21** (2), No. 55; partially reprinted in J.V. Robinson (1951–79), *Collected Economic Papers*, vol. II, Oxford: Basil Blackwell.
Robinson, J.V. (1956), *The Accumulation of Capital*, London: Macmillan, 2nd edn 1969.
Robinson, J.V. (1962), *Economic Philosophy*, London: C.A. Watts.
Robinson, J.V. (1975), 'Introduction 1974', *Collected Economic Papers*, vol. II, Oxford: Basil Blackwell.
Samuelson, P.A. (1967), 'Indeterminacy of development in a heterogeneous-capital model with constant saving propensity', in K. Shell (ed.), *Essays on the Theory of Optimal Economic Growth*, Cambridge, MA: MIT Press.
Sraffa, P. (1960), *Production of Commodities by Means of Commodities*, Cambridge: Cambridge University Press.

George Lennox Sharman Shackle (1903–1992)

George Shackle was born in Cambridge on 14 July 1903. Following his father to Perse School, he gained entrance to his father's college, St Catherine's, but could not take it up because he failed to win a scholarship. Instead he became a bank clerk. This prompted a crucial change of focus: at St Catherine's he would probably have read modern languages, but for banking the study of economics seemed more appropriate. Though subsequently moving to a tobacco company and then becoming a schoolteacher, he persisted, eventually gaining a London external degree in 1931. By then he was contemplating a lifetime commitment. Thus a distressing failure became a precondition of unimagined success, and Shackle's own career an exemplar of his own system of thought.

Private study of Keynes's *Treatise on Money* (1930) and Hayek's *Prices and Production* (1933) prompted an article which was published in the first issue of the *Review of Economic Studies* (Shackle 1933). This led to a research studentship at the London School of Economics (LSE), a PhD and his first book, published in 1938. By then he had moved to Oxford, working with Henry Phelps Brown and writing papers for which he was awarded a DPhil in 1940. Soon after the outbreak of war he was called from a lectureship at St Andrews to join Lindemann's team working for Churchill, transferring after the war to the Economics Section of the Cabinet Secretariat. In 1950, at the age of 47, he was appointed Reader at Leeds, moving after four terms to the Brunner Chair at Liverpool, from which he retired in 1969 to Aldeburgh and a daily routine of writing. He died on 3 March 1992, and so a conference in Aldeburgh designed in his honour became a memorial. Revised versions of some papers from that conference appear in Earl and Frowen (2000).

Shackle's life between 1920 and 1935 had demonstrated how unpredictable are the consequences of both events and decisions; and this double unpredictability provided the theme for all his work. Shackle arrived at the LSE just in time to hear Brinley Thomas's inspirational account of the new Swedish approach to the functioning of economic systems through a sequence analysis which incorporated the essential fallibility of expectations, and Hicks's lectures on economic dynamics, in which the entrepreneur contemplates possible actions, soon followed by expositions of Keynes's then forthcoming *General Theory* (1936). All three experiences were striking illustrations of the process of generating new ways of thinking in economics.

The shared context was uncertainty, which as Knight had observed was a precondition, not only of enterprise and the firm, but even of human intelligence. Shackle's work is a celebration of intelligence, which combines reason and creativity. Knight (1921: 348) had concluded that "a life with uncertainty eliminated ... would not appeal to us"; Shackle (1966a: 133) described it as "the reverse of hope, the opposite of freedom" (see also Shackle 1953: 1). Humans are "originative, ambitious, reckless and insecure, ... they do not know what they are next going to attempt" (Shackle 1974: 67); therefore "the future is not there to be discovered, but must be created" (Shackle 1969: 16). Shackle focused on the creative role of entrepreneurs – "what ... is economics about, if it is not about business psychology" (Shackle 1966b: 287) – and of economists. However, the necessary complement to enterprise is the dissolution of order, both in economic systems and schools of thought.

The combination of economic depression and the emergence of exciting new theories to explain it naturally first focused his attention on the threats of unpredictability to economic order, and Shackle is likely to be primarily associated with macroeconomic theorizing in the spirit of Keynes, with particular emphasis on the necessarily fragile basis of our views about the future and the consequent possibility of their sudden transformation (most forcefully expressed in Keynes 1937), although he persisted in regretting Keynes's refusal to incorporate *ex ante/ex post* reasoning – see especially *Keynesian Kaleidics* (Shackle 1974), lectures delivered with Brinley Thomas in the audience. However he was no less impressed by the opportunities inherent in unpredictability for business enterprise and theoretical innovation, which provided him with more intellectual excitement than one might expect from his demeanour and his reluctance to engage in debates on policy.

His first book, *Expectations, Investment and Income* (Shackle 1938) develops the ideas of Hicks and the Swedes and anticipates the aspiration/achievement model of Cyert and March (1963) in constructing a theory in which the divergence between expectations and outcomes for each producer (in part because of the consequences of other producers' decisions) leads to a new set of decisions which are also not pre-reconciled; combined with a ratchet effect of experience on consumption (anticipating Duesenberry) this generates an asymmetric business cycle. His second book, *Expectation in Economics* (Shackle 1949) focuses on the problems of making unique decisions when there is no adequate basis for probabilistic reasoning, which assumes repeated trials within a closed system. He suggests an alternative built on the decision-maker's judgement of the possibilities of various future events, assessed by the degree of potential surprise, which is a non-additive measure.

The underlying issue is the nature and potential of human knowledge, too often neglected in both microeconomics and macroeconomics by recourse to facile notions of "rationality" which assume the sufficiency of knowledge. In *The Years of High Theory* (1967) Shackle unconsciously reinvented Adam Smith's account of the development of science (as Andrew Skinner (1979) pointed out – to Shackle's delight) in order to explain the "landslide of invention" in economics between 1926 and 1939. We have a powerful motivation to incorporate phenomena and experience within existing schemes of order, and to create new schemes when these fail, both to set our minds at rest and to make practical life possible (Shackle 1967: 288, 286). Order is not a product of rationality, but a precondition. The patterns on which we rely are generated by our imagination (as, Smith noted, was Newton's great theory); they are unrefuted conjectures, which set bounds to our perceived uncertainty and allow decisions to be made (Shackle 1969: 224.) However each "will exist by sufferance of the things which it has excluded" (Shackle 1972: 354) and is consequently subject to disruption by forces outside our probability sets, but which may be the product of someone else's imagination.

Shackle shared Marshall's (1920: 1) view that economics is both a study of wealth and "on the . . . more important side, a part of the study of man". It is a theory of change which, in the tradition of Adam Smith, is driven by the differential imagination of new connections, facilitated by variation both between and within forms of organization. Shackle (1965: 36) recognized that Marshall used his concept of equilibrium to describe a process of adjustment which revealed new possibilities and created new resources, thus facilitating further change. This conception provided the basis for Shackle's own exposition of the theory of the firm, *Expectation, Enterprise and Profit* (1970), which, while respecting the constraints of the short run, makes – like Marshall – no attempt to present a long-run equilibrium of an individual firm but explores, in detail which Keynes never attempted, the problem for every agent of deciding, according to their conceptions of particular circumstances, what durable commitments to make for use in future situations which (as Keynes insisted) cannot be foreseen.

There are striking affinities, still unexplored, with Penrose's (1959) account of how firms grow, including the crucial role of imagination. For Shackle, as for Marshall – and for the outstanding analyst of management Peter Drucker, who commended Shackle's approach (Drucker 1969: 210) – the role of the firm is to make "committed conjectures" (Shackle 1974: 5), and to take the losses if, for whatever reason, their conjectures are falsified (Drucker 1969: 293). Equilibrium as a set of pre-reconciled choices does not describe either a possible or an ideal economy. In *Epistemics and Economics* (1972) Shackle's extensive "critique of economic doctrines" makes a powerful case for a proper recognition of uncertainty, which would allow us to explore how locally sufficient organizations and institutions frame the evolution of knowledge by imaginative conjectures.

BRIAN J. LOASBY

See also:

Friedrich August von Hayek (I); John Maynard Keynes (I); Frank H. Knight (I); Alfred Marshall (I); Adam Smith (I).

References and further reading

Cyert, R.M. and J.G. March (1963), *A Behavioral Theory of the Firm*, Englewood Cliffs, NJ: Prentice-Hall.
Drucker, P.F. (1969), *The Age of Discontinuity*, London: Heinemann.
Earl, P.E. and S.F. Frowen (eds) (2000), *Economics as an Art of Thought*, London and New York: Routledge.
Hayek, F.A. (1933), *Prices and Production*, London: Routledge and Kegan Paul.
Keynes, J.M. (1930), *A Treatise on Money*, London: Macmillan.
Keynes, J.M. (1936), *The General Theory of Employment, Interest and Money*, London: Macmillan.
Keynes, J.M. (1937), 'The general theory of employment', *Quarterly Journal of Economics*, **51** (February), 209–23.
Knight, F.H. (1921), *Risk, Uncertainty and Profit*, Boston, MA: Houghton Mifflin.
Marshall, Alfred (1920), *Principles of Economics*, 8th edn, London: Macmillan.
Penrose, E.T. (1959), *The Theory of the Growth of the Firm*, Oxford: Basil Blackwell.
Shackle, G.L.S. (1933), 'Some notes on monetary theories of the trade cycle', *Review of Economic Studies*, **1** (1), 27–38.
Shackle, G.L.S. (1938), *Expectations, Investment and Income*, Oxford: Oxford University Press.
Shackle, G.L.S. (1949), *Expectation in Economics*, Cambridge: Cambridge University Press.
Shackle, G.L.S. (1953), 'Economics and sincerity', *Oxford Economic Papers*, **1** (1), 1–19.
Shackle, G.L.S. (1965), *A Scheme of Economic Theory*, Cambridge: Cambridge University Press.
Shackle, G.L.S. (1966a), 'Theory and the business man', in G.L.S, Shackle, *The Nature of Economic Thought: Selected Papers 1955–1964*, Cambridge: Cambridge University Press, pp. 131–43.
Shackle, G.L.S. (1966b), 'Battles long ago', in G.L.S, Shackle, *The Nature of Economic Thought: Selected Papers 1955–64*, Cambridge: Cambridge University Press, pp. 285–90.
Shackle, G.L.S. (1967), *The Years of High Theory*, Cambridge: Cambridge University Press.
Shackle, G.L.S. (1969), *Decision, Order and Time in Human Affairs*, Cambridge: Cambridge University Press.
Shackle, G.L.S. (1970), *Expectation, Enterprise and Profit*, London: Allen and Unwin.
Shackle, G.L.S. (1972), *Epistemics and Economics*, Cambridge: Cambridge University Press.
Shackle, G.L.S. (1974), *Keynesian Kaleidics*, Edinburgh: Edinburgh University Press.
Skinner, A.S. (1979), *Scottish Journal of Political Economy*, **26** (2), 109–24.

Jan Tinbergen (1903–1994)

Jan Tinbergen was an early pioneer in developing the field of econometrics and building macro-econometric models that could describe business cyclical behaviour as well as stabilization policy and long-term economic planning. Born on 12 April 1903 in The Hague, Jan Tinbergen studied mathematics and theoretical physics at Leiden University, where he completed a doctorate under the supervision of Paul Ehrenfest in 1929. The core of his thesis was on minimization problems in mathematics, but he provided an appendix where he also considered economic problems, which was added because of his desire to combine mathematics with his political views on social democracy. Tinbergen was Statistician for Business Cycle Research at the Central Bureau of Statistics (CBS) from 1929 to 1945, and from 1933 he was Professor of Economics at The Netherlands School of Economics, Rotterdam, until his retirement in 1973; but he also served as an expert to the League of Nations from 1936 to 1938 and Director of the Central Planning Bureau (CPB) from 1945 to 1951. In 1969, he shared the first Bank of Sweden Prize in Economic Sciences in Memory of Alfred Nobel with Ragnar Frisch for "having developed and applied dynamic models for the analysis of economic processes". Tinbergen died on 9 June 1994 in The Hague, Netherlands.

Tinbergen made several seminal contributions to the mathematical theory of the business cycle and macro-econometric model building while doing business cycle research at the CBS. The CBS was a good place to be as he had access to large amounts of data and was able to test and develop different theoretical models. In his early research, Tinbergen focused on developing an endogenous theory of the business cycle, which included an application of Arthur Hanau's cobweb-dynamics to agricultural product cycles, and an extension of this analysis to the shipbuilding industry, in which gestation lags in the investment process imply that the dynamics be represented by a mixed difference-differential equation. The method had an important influence on Frisch and Michał Kalecki, who both used it in their later models of the national business cycle.

An invitation by the Royal Economic Association in 1936 to discuss the deteriorating economic conditions and policy problems in the Netherlands prompted Tinbergen (1959) to build and estimate the first large-scale macro-econometric business cycle model. The model was highly novel, containing 24 linear equations, six of which contained lagged endogenous variables that generated dynamics, and a number of non-estimated coefficients. Tinbergen explored several policy scenarios, one of which supported the initiative to abandon the gold parity of the guilder, effectively allowing the guilder to devalue by 20 per cent. Several policy implications were also incorporated into the alternative policy agenda of the Social Democratic Labour Party.

In the same year, Tinbergen was commissioned by the League of Nations to carry out statistical tests of existing business cycle theories. This research, published in two volumes in 1939, was novel in its extensive use of testing procedures (Morgan 1990). The first volume contained an exposition of his econometric method, essentially classical multiple regression analysis combined with Frisch's confluence analysis, and then applied this method to fluctuations in investment, in general, and in residential building and in railway rolling-stock, in particular. In the second volume, Tinbergen set up a large-scale macro-econometric model of business cycles in the United States that contained 71 variables and 48 equations and covered the period from 1919 to 1932.

A precursor of the giant computer models, the dynamic model was novel in that it could be used to better understand past business cycles as unified, single phenomenon, forecast future trends, and identify policy instruments that can change the direction of the cycle. It was proposed in the preface to carry out a parallel study of the United Kingdom, which Tinbergen carried out in the 1940s and published in 1951.

While these models represent a fundamental contribution to macro-econometric model building, it also sparked a lively debate with several economists, including John Maynard Keynes. Keynes was very sceptical of the methodology underlying the League of Nations study and published a long review of it in the September 1939 issue of the *Economic Journal*. Keynes's main concern was the application of multiple regression analysis to non-homogeneous series in real time, and the consequent problem of independence and misspecification of the economic model. He believed that the complexity and variability observed over the cycle meant that some influences on the cycle could not be reduced to statistical form, such as long-term profit expectations. Keynes elicited a response from Tinbergen who maintained that his model was comprehensive and contained the most important variables, other influences that changed over the course of the cycle were included in the residual variable, and that it is possible to base expectations on the past and thus be extrapolated. He also maintained that explanatory factors only needed to be uncorrelated in statistical relations rather than independent in an economic sense. Overall, Tinbergen (1940: 154) rejected Keynes's sceptical view of econometrics, not because he considered his criticism irrelevant, but because he believed that the method "promises – and actually yields – much more than Mr. Keynes thinks". Tinbergen received a life subscription to the journal for his contribution, for which he later commented, "I've never been paid that generously" (Magnus and Morgan 1987: 129).

The Keynes–Tinbergen debate marked an important milestone in the development of macro-econometric model building, but the urgent need to reconstruct much of Europe after World War II made it essential to the development of a theory of economic policy. As the first director of the CPB and a key policy adviser to the Social Democrats, Tinbergen was highly influential in shaping economic policy of the Netherlands, but he was also essential to the development of the methodology underlying policy-making. Tinbergen's (1952, 1956) novel approach to the problem was to combine large-scale macro-econometric models with instrumental analysis. What he had done was to invert the economic problem so that the desired goal or policy objective becomes the datum of the theory, and the objective analysis is to identify the economic means suitable for the attainment of the desired macro-goal (Löwe 1965). Variables in these types of models can either be controlled (instruments), whose values are chosen directly by the policy-maker given certain constraints, or be uncontrolled, whose values are only influenced indirectly by the policy-maker given their choice of instrumental variables. Some of the variables are defined as the targets, which is what the policy-maker wants influence through the use of policy instruments. Any number of policy instruments can be used within a stated economic policy, but consistent policy requires that the number of independent instruments must equal the number of policy targets.

Policy advice based on the large-scale structural macro-econometric models received much criticism from the new classical economic perspective. The "Lucas critique", named after Robert Lucas (1976), focuses on the Tinbergen model, particularly on the way it represents expectations, because it does not consider the dependence of individual behaviour on perceived government policy rules, potentially misleading policy-makers as to the effectiveness and desirability of their policy choices. Lucas maintained that these models were not adequately grounded in dynamic economic theory and suggested that a theory of economic policy should always start from the basic neoclassical parameters that govern individual behaviour, namely, preferences, technology and resource endowments. The issue of policy neutrality is at the centre of the Lucas critique, with instrumental analysis its main target, but the solution it offers is to require overly restrictive assumptions about individual behaviour, which may not be empirically relevant, as Tinbergen would point out.

Tinbergen continued to do policy-relevant research for the rest of his life. After the mid-1950s, most of his research centred on the problem of economic development, developing and applying his modelling methodology to low-income countries. Tinbergen (1968) developed a novel multistage approach to development planning, based on the Harrod–Domar growth model, which involved private and public decision-makers at the national, sectoral and project levels. These models focused not only on the need for physical capital and a transport infrastructure but also on the need for education and skill development. Tinbergen (1959) also made original contributions to the theory of income distribution, focusing on the issue of the distribution of personal income well after retirement. Throughout his life, Tinbergen was concerned with economic and social problems, placing particular importance on empirically based and policy relevant research. For this reason it is difficult to place him in a particular school of economic thought, but instead to consider the important role he played in making economics more empirically relevant.

MARK KNELL

See also:

Econometrics (III); Ragnar Anton Kittil Frisch (I); John Maynard Keynes (I); Macroeconomics (III).

References and further reading

Alberts, G. (1994), 'On connecting socialism and mathematics: Dirk Struik, Jan Burgers, and Jan Tinbergen', *Historia Mathematica*, **21** (3), 280–305.
Keynes, J.M. (1939), 'Professor Tinbergen's method', *Economic Journal*, **49** (September), 558–68.
Lucas, R. (1976), 'Econometric policy evaluation: a critique', *Carnegie-Rochester Conference Series on Public Policy*, **1** (1), 19–46.
Löwe, A. (1965), *On Economic Knowledge: Toward a Science of Political Economics*, New York: Harper and Row.
Magnus, J.R. and M. Morgan (1987), 'The ET interview: Professor J. Tinbergen', *Econometric Theory*, **3** (1), 117–42.
Morgan, M. (1990), *The History of Econometric Ideas*, New York: Cambridge University Press.
Tinbergen, J. (1939), *Statistical Testing of Business-Cycle Theories*, vol. 1, *A Method and Its Application in Investment Activity*, vol. 2, *Business Cycles in the USA, 1919–1932*, Geneva: League of Nations.
Tinbergen, J. (1940), 'On a method of statistical business research. A reply', *Economic Journal*, **50** (197), 141–54.
Tinbergen, J. (1951), *Business Cycles in the United Kingdom, 1870–1914*, Amsterdam: North-Holland.
Tinbergen, J. (1952), *On the Theory of Economic Policy*, Amsterdam: North-Holland.
Tinbergen, J. (1956), *Economic Policy: Principles and Design*, Amsterdam: North-Holland.
Tinbergen, J. (1959), *Selected Papers*, Amsterdam, North-Holland.
Tinbergen, J. (1968), *Development Planning*, London: Wiedenfeld and Nicolson.

John Richard Hicks (1904–1989)

Life

Hicks was the first British economist who was awarded the Sveriges Riksbank Prize in Economic Sciences in Memory of Alfred Nobel in 1972. He jointly won the prize with Kenneth Arrow "for their pioneering contributions to general equilibrium theory and welfare theory". Hicks was one of the last great decathletes in economics with good medal chances in many specific areas.

He was born on 8 April 1904 at Warwick, England, where his father was a journalist at a local newspaper. From 1917 to 1922 he was educated at Clifton College, and thereafter he studied at Balliol College, Oxford. Having first specialized in mathematics, Hicks moved to the new programme in "philosophy, politics and economics" (PPE) in 1923. After working as a junior reporter for the *Manchester Guardian* for six months, Hicks received a temporary lectureship at the London School of Economics (LSE) in 1926, where he finally taught until 1935. It was the LSE, where Robbins in fall 1929 started a research seminar that made him an economist.

In 1935 Hicks married Ursula Webb, a distinguished scholar in public finance, who remained his closest intellectual companion until her death in 1985. Through his friendship with Dennis Robertson, he accepted Pigou's offer of a university lectureship in Cambridge in summer 1935 where he stayed for three years, also as a Fellow of Gonville and Caius College. While at Cambridge he finished his work on *Value and Capital* (1939) but also wrote his two well-known articles reviewing Keynes's *General Theory* (1936, 1937). However, Hicks was alienated by the intellectual climate and personally disharmonious atmosphere in Cambridge, and in 1938 he moved to the University of Manchester where he stayed as William Stanley Jevons Professor of Political Economy until 1946. In Manchester he did his main work on welfare economics (1981, pt I), with some application to national income accounting.

In 1946 Hicks returned to Oxford, first as a research fellow of Nuffield College, from 1952 to 1965 as Drummond Professor of Political Economy and finally, after retiring from teaching and administrative duties, as research fellow of All Souls College (1965–71).

Hicks became a Fellow of the British Academy in 1942, a foreign member of the Royal Swedish Academy in 1948, of the Italian Accademia dei Lincei in 1952, and of the American Academy in 1958. He was President of the Royal Economic Society from 1960 to 1962, and was knighted in 1964 when "JR" became "Sir John". He received an honorary doctoral degree from more than a dozen universities and was made an honorary Senator of the University of Vienna in 1971. He died in his home in Blockley, Gloucestershire, on 20 May 1989.

Work

Hicks has made important contributions to various subfields of economics. His early work as a labour economist culminated in *The Theory of Wages* (Hicks 1932), which despite some shortcomings, later openly conceded in the commentary by the author in the revised second edition of his "juvenile opus", introduced some innovative concepts into theoretical economics. Building on the marginal productivity theory, Hicks introduced the new concepts of the "elasticity of substitution" and "Hicks-neutral", "labour-saving" and "capital saving" inventions in the famous chapter 6 on "Distribution and economic progress". It was Hicks (1934) who in his joint work with Allen – which was "*Werttheorie* in the sense of Menger" (1934 [1981]: 4) and thereby had an Austrian as well as a Paretian origin – building on Edgeworth's first drawing of indifference curve diagrams, integrated indifference curves and budget constraints into standard microeconomic analysis. He demonstrated how indifference curves could be used to construct a downward-sloping demand curve for any good and to separate the income effect from the substitution effect of a price change. In part I of *Value and Capital* (Hicks 1939) he expanded his pioneering analysis to investigate the role of income effects and substitution effects of price changes for the economy as a whole.

In his early phase Hicks benefited enormously from the international atmosphere at the LSE and from his own language skills in French, Italian, and German which allowed him to read authors such as Walras, Pareto, Cassel, Myrdal and Wicksell in the original. During his whole life Hicks kept a strong interest in history, literature (with Dante as the poet most loved), music and philosophy. As an eminent economist he was very modest and self-reflective, constantly re-examining his own earlier work. Hicks was never a member of any school of thought nor did he intend to create his own.

The Nobel Prize citation puts *Value and Capital* as Hicks's magnum opus into the centre, the foundation of modern general equilibrium theory on which subsequent work by Samuelson, Arrow, Hahn and Debreu was built. In particular the question of stability of a general equilibrium in the presence of external shocks is at issue.

> General equilibrium theory had, earlier, essentially the character of formal analysis. . . . Hicks abandoned this tradition and gave the theory an increased economic relevance. He presented a complete economic equilibrium model with aggregated markets for commodities, factors of production, credit and money. The construction of this model included a number of innovations, i.e., a further development of older theories of consumption and of production, the formulation of conditions for multimarket stability, an extension of the applicability of the static method of analysis to include multiperiod analysis, and the introduction of a capital theory based on profit maximization assumptions. By being deeply anchored in theories of the behaviour of consumers and of entrepreneurs, Hicks's model offered far better possibilities to study the consequences of changes in externally given variables than earlier models in this field, and Hicks succeeded in formulating a number of economically interesting theorems. His model became of great importance also as a connecting link between general equilibrium theory and current theories of business cycles. (Nobelprize.org 1972)

Hicks identified a certain "sterility" (1939: 60) in the Walrasian system of general equilibrium. Unlike Arrow he did not take the existence problem beyond the counting of equations and variables but entered into a pioneering analysis of the stability of a system of multiple exchange.

In parts III and IV of *Value and Capital* stronger elements from the Marshallian–Keynesian tradition of the short-run enter into Hicks's formerly static analysis to create "The foundations of dynamic economics" and to analyse "The working of the dynamic system". Most important for later economic analysis are Hicks's method of equilibrium and the related concept of the elasticity of expectations.

Hicks re-examined "Methods of dynamic analysis" time and again until the end of his life (1956a, 1965, pt I, 1985). He came to consider perfect foresight models as essentially static and disliked steady state models as they became prominent in post-war growth economics. He confessed that he did not give a genuine definition of dynamics in *Value and Capital*, identified many assumptions (for example, assuming capital to be homogeneous or all capital to be circulating) how economists fall into static method, and pointed out that dynamics comprises more than that every variable must be dated. For a critical assessment of Hicks's capital theory in *Value and Capital* see Garegnani (2012), for the analysis of his early advocacy and the appropriateness of his use of the method of temporary equilibrium, Hicks's later recantation of this method owing to its elimination of dynamics and lags from analysis, that is, the impermanence problem, and the limited impact Hicks's moving away from the temporary equilibrium method had on mainstream economics see also Petri (1991).

In his *A Contribution to the Theory of the Trade Cycle* Hicks (1950) combines Harrod's growth theory with a Hansen–Samuelson model of the business cycle based on the interaction between multiplier and accelerator. Hicks's approach gave some inspiration to Richard Goodwin to modify and extend the analysis to deal with the difficult problems of economic dynamics in a more proper way of non-linear growth-cycles interaction.

Hicks's seminal articles to welfare theory, mainly published in 1939–46, contain four main contributions, founding the "New welfare economics" or "Kaldor–Hicks welfare economics" (see also, Bliss 1987; and the modern reassessment by Chipman in Hagemann and Hamouda 1994). First, at a time when cardinal utility was not generally accepted by economists anymore, Hicks critically examined the compensation principle, that is, the possibility of Pareto improvements when the welfare beneficiaries fully compensate the losers and still would be better off. He later (Hicks 1981: xiii) confessed that at the time of formulating the "Kaldor–Hicks criterion" he was not aware of the Scitovsky paradox, that is, that the hypothetical compensation is not necessarily reversible. He also emphasized that his most fundamental shortcoming of his contemporary work on welfare economics was that it fell short of the "revealed preference" theory developed by Samuelson (1948). Samuelson's approach stimulated Hicks to write his *A Revision of Demand Theory* (1956b). Second, the issue of welfare improvements is closely related to the problem of measurement of real national income as an index of economic welfare. Hicks concluded that the two types of measurement of income, in terms of utility and in terms of cost, are quite different, and he rejected the utility approach to measure welfare. On the important question how to treat government expenditures and indirect taxation in the valuation of social income Hicks was engaged in a major controversy with Kuznets, which he comments *ex post* (1981: 96–9, 142–88). Unlike Arrow, Hicks never developed an interest in the formulation of a social welfare function, probably also due to a lack of faith in the optimality of the market process and its results. Third, Hicks aimed at rehabilitating the Marshallian concept of consumers' surplus, most commonly referred to as the area under an individual's demand curve between two prices. In its revised Hicksian formulation with the famous compensating and equivalent variations it had a great impact in subsequent cost–benefit analysis and other areas of applied economics to approximately measure changes in welfare. Fourth, a particular controversial question is the measurement of capital, a problem to which Hicks made his most important contribution to the 1958 Corfu conference of the International Economic Association on capital theory (1981: ch. 8), a topic he took up again in his two subsequent books on *Capital* (1965: ch. 24; 1973b: ch. 13).

The four letters that students of several generations have associated with Hicks after their first basic course in macroeconomics are IS–LM (after Hansen's modification of Hicks's original SI–LL terminology). The IS (LM) curve is the schedule specifying the combinations of interest rates and levels of national income which ensure equilibrium in the goods (money) market. The point of intersection between the two curves determines simultaneous equilibrium on both markets but leaves the labour market outside. So is Keynesian unemployment compatible with a Walrasian interpretation, when in Walras all markets are cleared?

Despite the great influence of his interpretation of Keynes's *General Theory* (1936) through the IS–LM diagram and the ensuing development of modern macroeconomic theory, and students being trained on the effects of monetary and fiscal policies on the basis of this standard model of macroeconomic textbooks, Hicks never had been convinced that the whole Keynesian theory could be confined to the model he was responsible for establishing in his "suggested interpretation", "Mr. Keynes and the 'classics'" (Hicks 1937).

This 1937 article, which Hicks first presented to the meeting of the Econometric Society at Oxford in September 1936, was not the first but the second interpretation of the *General Theory* by Hicks, after he had written his review article "Mr. Keynes's theory of employment" for the *Economic Journal* of which Keynes was the editor. "I was asked because it was hoped that I should be a sympathetic but independent critic; and such, at that date, were not easy to find" (Hicks 1974: 6). Nevertheless it was his second article, which captured those parts of Keynes's theory most accessible to formalization, which exerted the enormous influence. "Keynes's own version of Keynesian economics, is by no means easy to determine" (ibid.: 5).

From the mid-1960s onwards Hicks came back time and again to a reinterpretation of Keynesian economics (1974, 1977: ch. VI, 1980), and he increasingly drifted away from the "neoclassical synthesis" (Samuelson) mainstream he himself had helped to established in younger years, and which was strongly disliked by Keynes's disciples such as Kahn and Joan Robinson, who, for example, could rightly criticize that the IS–LM model with its focus on equilibrium does not capture the uncertainty that characterizes a monetary economy.

Hicks himself later pointed out that the IS–LM diagram "is now much less popular with me than I think it still is with many other people. It reduces the *General Theory* to equilibrium economics; it is not really *in* time" (1982: 289–90). Among the three parts he considered as the essential building blocks of Keynes's theory, the marginal efficiency of capital and liquidity preference unquestionably are in time, whereas the multiplier theory is out of time. In his widely perceived article "IS–LM: an explanation" (Hicks 1980) he accordingly emphasized the hybrid character of his own construction that the IS curve is a flow relation whereas the LM curve is a stock relation referring to a point of time. The IS–LM analysis therefore could only survive "in application to a particular kind of causal analysis, where the use of equilibrium methods . . . is not inappropriate" (ibid.: 152). Leijonhufvud (1983) came to the conclusion that the hybrid character of the IS–LM apparatus, which ignores the sequence of events within the period, is due to the fact that it combines a Walrasian element of a simultaneous equilibrium on interdependent markets with Marshallian microfoundations. The problem was that Marshallian economics was in time, whereas theory in the Walrasian tradition was not, as Hicks only later came to recognize.

Hicks grappled with an adequate treatment of time in economic theory for almost six decades. According to him the movement of an economy through time is the central subject of macroeconomics. The relevance of the time dimension is particularly important in the taking-up process of a new technology. By the late 1960s he became fascinated by the Ricardo machinery effect, that is, the employment consequences of a different more mechanized method of production. He defended what he considered the core of Ricardo's analysis, namely, that there exist important cases – "strongly forward-biased" innovations according to his newly developed "index of improvement in efficiency" (1973b) – that reduce real output in the short run and make the existence of temporary technological unemployment unavoidable, but the detrimental effects are overcome due to real capital formation as the consequence of higher profits resulting from the greater efficiency of the new methods of production.

Throughout his professional life Hicks maintained a deep interest in capital theory, as is reflected in his famous trilogy *Value and Capital*, *Capital and Growth* and *Capital and Time*. In his view, "[C]apital . . . is a very large subject, with many aspects; wherever one starts, it is hard to bring more than a few of them into view" (1973b: v). In *Capital and Time* Hicks switched to a neo-Austrian model to analyse the problem of a traverse caused by a change in technology, after he soon had become dissatisfied with the embryonic theory of traverse which he studied in chapter 16 of his *Capital and Growth* (1965) on the basis of a two-sectoral fixed coefficient model, and the critique raised by Kennedy (1968). Implicit in *Capital and Time* is the concept of the "impulse", which is developed in his Nobel lecture "The mainspring of economic growth" (1973a) and particularly in his essay on "industrialism" (1977: ch. 2).

The decisive Austrian elements in Hicks's "*neo*-Austrian" theory are the focusing on the time structure of the production process and the special treatment of capital goods as intermediate products in a vertical model (see also Burmeister 1974). Capital is a medium for sequential production. By dealing explicitly with fixed capital goods Hicks's neo-Austrian approach, in contrast to Böhm-Bawerk and Hayek, considers production processes to be of the flow input–flow output type. As has already been emphasized in his "The Hayek story" (Hicks 1967: ch. 12) not only the economics of Keynes but also the economics of Hayek were a lifelong challenge for Hicks in developing his own theory. Hicks always had been sceptical about Hayek's claim that the economy would be in equilibrium if there were no monetary disturbances. Altough he took over from Hayek the idea that the impact of an impulse on the real structure of production is most important, he argued against Hayek that technological change is "more fundamental" (Hicks 1973b: 133–4).

As Hagemann and Kurz (1976) have shown, Hicks's view of the choice of technique problem vis-à-vis fixed capital cannot generally be sustained. The neo-Austrian model does not contain basic products and thus does not possess a finite maximum rate of profits. The return of the same length of the production process (utilization time of the fixed capital good) at varying rates of profits is proved to be a "curiosum" only in the neo-Austrian model but not in a more general von Neumann–Sraffa model, while reswitching of processes (techniques) is perfectly normal in both models.

History had already been Hicks's favourite subject at school and in his library

(Hamouda 1993: ch. 10). With increasing age Hicks emphasized more and more the relationship between economic history and economic theory as of fundamental methodological significance. This holds in particular for fields such as monetary economics (Hicks 1967, ch. 9), but he also considered Keynes and his ideas mainly as a product of his own era. He not only had a deep sense of the historical origins and time related character of economic models, thereby also identifying their intrinsic limits, but also made ample use of the materials of economic history and the history of economic thought (see also Hicks 1983) as necessary tools in the process of economic theorizing. A good example is the chapter on the Industrial Revolution in his *A Theory of Economic History* (1969), which he wrote when he was on his own personal traverse to *Capital and Time*. The constancy of the level of wages as an important stylized fact in Ricardo's time is referred to as a rationale for providing the fixwage path as a proper replication of Ricardo's analysis of the machinery problem. The careful distinction between fixprice and flexprice models, as his repeated reflections on risk and uncertainty, are just two out of many topics which indicate Hicks lifelong awareness of methodological issues in economics.

Hicks has left his mark almost everywhere in the many subfields of the economic discipline, not least so in monetary economics. His achievements date from his early contribution to the evolution of a theory of liquidity preference and portfolio selection in "A suggestion for simplifying the theory of money" (1935) via *Critical Essays in Monetary Theory* (1967) to his final *A Market Theory of Money* (1989) in which he treated money as an integral part of the institutional framework and elaborated a neo-Wicksellian approach for a modern overdraft economy.

Hicks himself made his conversion from J.R. to Sir John public:

> Clearly I need to change my name. Let it be understood that *Value and Capital* was the work of J.R. Hicks, a "neoclassical" economist now deceased; while *Capital and Time* – and *A Theory of Economic History* – are the work of John Hicks, a non-neoclassic who is quite disrespectful towards his "uncle". (1975: 365)

He did not become a "revolutionary" as Keynes in his *General Theory* but he remained an independent mind considering his 1956 contribution to the Lindahl Festschrift (Hicks 1956a) as the "turning-point" (1982: 217) for the development of his own thinking. Thereafter he increasingly kept at a distance from his earlier works, but more for the use American and other neoclassicals (who never liked the work of Sir John) made of them than for the ideas he had developed himself and continuously re-examined and modified. Nevertheless it is characteristic that Hicks dedicated his Nobel lecture to "The mainspring of economic growth" and not to the two topics, general economic equilibrium and welfare theory, for which the prize was awarded.

HARALD HAGEMANN

See also:

Kenneth Joseph Arrow (I); Eugen von Böhm-Bawerk (I); Economic dynamics (III); General equilibrium theory (III); Nicholas Kaldor (I); John Maynard Keynes (I); Vilfredo Pareto (I); David Ricardo (I); Paul Anthony Samuelson (I); Marie-Esprit-Léon Walras (I); Welfare economics (III); Knut Wicksell (I).

References and further reading

Bliss, C. (1987), 'Hicks, John Richard', in J. Eatwell, M. Milgate and P. Newman (eds), *The New Palgrave. A Dictionary of Economics*, vol. 2, London: Macmillan, pp. 641–6.
Burmeister, E. (1974), 'Synthesizing the neo-Austrian and alternative approaches to capital theory', *Journal of Economic Literature*, **12** (2), 413–56.
Collard, D.A., D.R. Helm, M.F.G. Scott and A.K. Sen (eds) (1984), *Economic Theory and Hicksian Themes*, Oxford: Clarendon Press.
Garegnani, P. (2012), 'On the present state of the capital controversy', *Cambridge Journal of Economics*, **36** (6), 1417–32.
Hagemann, H. and O.F. Hamouda (eds) (1994), *The Legacy of Hicks. His Contributions to Economic Analysis*, London and New York: Routledge (with full bibliography).
Hagemann, H. and H.D. Kurz (1976), 'The return of the same truncation period and reswitching of techniques in neo-Austrian and more general models', *Kyklos*, **29** (4), 678–708.
Hagemann, H. and R. Scazzieri (eds) (2009), *Capital, Time and Transitional Dynamics*, London and New York: Routledge.
Hamouda, O.F. (1993), *John R. Hicks: The Economist's Economist*, Oxford: Blackwell.
Hicks, J.R. (1932), *The Theory of Wages*, 2nd edn 1963, London: Macmillan.
Hicks, J.R. (1933), 'Gleichgewicht und Konjunktur', *Zeitschrift für Nationalökonomie*, **4**, 441–55, trans. 1980, 'Equilibrium and the trade cycle', *Economic Inquiry*, **18**, 523–34, reprinted in J.R. Hicks (1982), *Money, Interest and Wages, Collected Essays on Economic Theory*, vol. 2, Oxford: Basil Blackwell, pp. 28–41.
Hicks, J.R. (1934), 'A reconsideration of the Theory of Value', part I, *Economica*, New Series, **1** (February), 52–76, part II by R.G.D. Allen, *Economica*, New Series, **1** (May), 196–219, reprinted in J.R. Hicks (1981), *Wealth and Welfare. Collected Essays on Economic Theory*, vol. 1, Oxford: Basil Blackwell, pp. 5–29, 30–55.
Hicks, J.R. (1935), 'A suggestion for simplifying the theory of money', *Economica*, New Series, **2** (February), 1–19.
Hicks, J.R. (1936), 'Mr Keynes's theory of employment', *Economic Journal*, **46**, 238–53, reprinted in J.R. Hicks (1982), *Money, Interest and Wages, Collected Essays on Economic Theory*, vol. 2, Oxford: Basil Blackwell, pp. 84–99.
Hicks, J.R. (1937), 'Mr. Keynes and the "classics"', *Econometrica*, **5** (2), 147–59.
Hicks, J.R. (1939), *Value and Capital*, Oxford: Clarendon Press.
Hicks, J.R. (1942), *The Social Framework: An Introduction to Economics*, Oxford: Clarendon Press.
Hicks, J.R. (1950), *A Contribution to the Theory of the Trade Cycle*, Oxford: Clarendon Press.
Hicks, J.R. (1956a), 'Methods of dynamic analysis', in *Twenty-Five Economic Essays in Honour of Erik Lindahl*, Stockholm: Ekonomisk Tidskrift, reprinted with addendum in J.R. Hicks (1982), *Money, Interest and Wages, Collected Essays on Economic Theory*, vol. 2, Oxford: Basil Blackwell, pp. 219–35.
Hicks, J.R. (1956b), *A Revision of Demand Theory*, Oxford: Clarendon Press.
Hicks, J.R. (1965), *Capital and Growth*, Oxford: Clarendon Press.
Hicks, J.R. (1967), *Critical Essays in Monetary Theory*, Oxford: Clarendon Press.
Hicks, J.R. (1969), *A Theory of Economic History*, Oxford: Oxford University Press.
Hicks, J.R. (1973a), 'The mainspring of economic growth', *Swedish Journal of Economics*, **75** (December), 336–48.
Hicks, J.R. (1973b), *Capital and Time. A Neo-Austrian Theory*, Oxford: Clarendon Press.
Hicks, J.R. (1974), *The Crisis in Keynesian Economics*, Oxford: Basil Blackwell.
Hicks, J.R. (1975), 'Revival of political economy: the old and the new', *Economic Record*, **51** (September), 365–7.
Hicks, J.R. (1977), *Economic Perspectives: Further Essays on Money and Growth*, Oxford: Clarendon Press.
Hicks, J.R. (1979), *Causality in Economics*, Oxford: Basil Blackwell and New York: Basic Books.
Hicks, J.R. (1980), 'IS–LM: an explanation', *Journal of Post Keynesian Economics*, **3** (2), 139–54.
Hicks, J.R. (1981), *Wealth and Welfare. Collected Essays on Economic Theory*, vol. 1, Oxford: Basil Blackwell.
Hicks, J.R. (1982), *Money, Interest and Wages, Collected Essays on Economic Theory*, vol. 2, Oxford: Basil Blackwell.
Hicks, J. (1983), *Classics and Moderns, Collected Essays on Economic Theory*, vol. 3, Oxford: Basil Blackwell.
Hicks, J.R. (1985), *Methods of Dynamic Economics*, Oxford: Clarendon Press.
Hicks, J.R. (1989), *A Market Theory of Money*, Oxford: Clarendon Press.
Helm, D.R. (ed.) (1984), *The Economics of John Hicks*, Oxford: Basil Blackwell.
Kennedy, C. (1968), 'Time, interest and the production function', in J.N. Wolfe (ed.), *Value, Capital and Growth. Papers in Honour of Sir John Hicks*, Edinburgh: Edinburgh University Press, pp. 275–90.
Keynes, J.M. (1936), *The General Theory of Employment, Interest and Money*, London: Macmillan.
Leijonhufvud, A. (1983), 'What was the matter with IS–LM?', in J.-P. Fitoussi (ed.), *Modern Macroeconomic Theory*, Oxford: Blackwell, pp. 64–90.

Nobelprize.org (1972), 'The Prize in Economics 1972 – press release', *Nobelprize.org*, 25 October, Nobel Media AB 2014, accessed 8 December 2015 at http://www.nobelprize.org/nobel_prizes/economic-sciences/laureates/1972/press.html.

Petri, F. (1991), 'Hicks's recantation of the temporary equilibrium method', *Review of Political Economy*, **3** (3), 268–88.

Samuelson, P.A. (1948), 'Consumption theory in terms of revealed preference', *Economica*, New Series, **15** (November), 243–53.

Scazzieri, R., A. Sen and S. Zamagni (eds) (2008), *Markets, Money and Capital. Hicksian Economics for the Twenty-First Century*, Cambridge: Cambridge University Press.

Wood, J.C. and R.N. Woods (eds) (1989), *Sir John Hicks: Critical Assessments*, 4 vols, London: Routledge.

Oskar Ryszard Lange (1904–1965)

Lange was born in Poland in July 1904 into the family of a German-born, assimilated textile manufacturer, and died in London in 1965. After studying law and economics in Poznan and Cracow, he did a PhD on business cycles in the Polish economy based on new statistical tools. In 1934, he moved to Harvard to work with Joseph Schumpeter, returning to Europe two years later to spend seven months at Cambridge.

During his academic career, he lectured in statistics in Cracow (1927–37), Chicago (1938–45) and Warsaw (1948–65). Politically involved since his youth, he was active at the Independent Socialist Youth Union in the interwar period. During the Second World War he pushed the cause of Soviet–American rapprochement and socialist–communist cooperation. He served as the first ambassador of the Polish People's Republic in Washington (1945–46) and as the Polish delegate to the United Nations (UN) Security Council (1946–47). Later, he was a member of parliament and a member of the State Council in Poland (Kowalik 2008).

His economic works mainly addressed two topics: the evolution of capitalism and the functioning of the market mechanism in a socialist system. In two major studies, "The rate of interest and the optimum propensity to consume" (Lange 1938) and "Say's law: a criticism and restatement" (Lange 1942), Lange prepared the ground for an ambitious analysis of capitalist dynamics that he finally achieved in his 1944 *Price Flexibility and Full Employment*. In the post-war period, still focusing on capitalist dynamics, he tried to establish a connection between the Marxian schemes of reproduction and Harrod's and Kalecki's growth-cycle theory. The second direction of research found its major expression in Lange's (in collaboration with Taylor) 1938 essay *On the Economic Theory of Socialism*. The main argument of this work was that welfare economics was better suited to studying the functioning of socialist rather than capitalist economies. In addition to the papers he published on the subject, in the late 1950s Lange played a leading part in the work of the Polish Economic Council, which aimed at increasing the role of incentives for socialist firms within the framework of central planning. Here, Lange outlined some of the main ingredients of the post-war research programme on socialist economies.

Finally, apart from economic theory, Lange received serious critical success for his work on sociology and mathematics.

Dynamics of Capitalist Economies

Lange manifested his interest in dynamics very early in his career. In his seminal article "Marxian economics and modern economic theory" (Lange 1935), he set out the methodological foundations of reasoning using dynamics. He asserted that the methodologically correct dynamic approach is to explain in detail the evolution of the economy as resulting from "within" the economic process in a capitalist society (Assous and Lampa 2014).

The marginalist approach, and the traditional theory of economic equilibrium developed mainly by Walras, Lange believed to give a good enough description of the system as it is. As it prescinds from any institutional data, it has the merit of being abstract and therefore universal, its basic notions holding true in any kind of economic system including a socialist system. Consequently, it provides "a scientific basis" for the current administration of many aspects of the economy, such as prices, market-structure or allocation of resources. Its fault, however, is that it investigates the economic process "under a system of constant data", thus completely ignoring both the characteristics of the data themselves (which become the object of economic statistics) and the change in the data (which is the object of economic history); therefore, static analysis relegates any laws or tendencies discoverable in the evolution of the economic facts to outside the boundaries of economics.

In opposition to the traditional static theory, Lange thought that Marxian economics, but also Schumpeter's *Theory of Economic Development* (1911) as well as Kalecki's (1939) and Kaldor's (1940) cycle theories, offered an adequate framework in so far as it allows us to deduce the existence and the direction of certain changes in economic variables from the intrinsic instability of the economic process. The merit of these approaches would pertain especially to their institutional dimension, particularly in the light of the existence of different classes of people: "The institutional datum, which is the corner-stone of the Marxian analysis of Capitalism, is the division of the population into two parts, one of which owns the means of production, while the other owns only labour power" (Lange 1935: 197).

Lange was well aware that the distinction between two social classes was inseparable from the existence of imperfection in the financial markets. If workers who supply labour and capitalists who own the capital stock could indeed borrow through a complete and fully competitive set of financial markets, both could invest effectively and nothing would hence differentiate them. Incidentally, it is the message of Lange's 1944 book that under uncertainty and incomplete financial markets, price flexibility – and in particular flexible prices of production factors, mainly of labour – do not result necessarily in the automatic restoration of equilibrium.

Socialism

In collaboration with Marek Breit, in 1934 Lange wrote the first outline of a corporate market economy under socialism (Breit and Lange, English trans. 2003). The chief purpose of that study was to design a system for Poland which would be different from the command-planning system existing at this time in the Soviet Union. It rested on the rule that political authority should be separated from economic organization. Property rights should be transferred to a public bank and industrial branches should be organized in trusts. Trusts, organized into "an appropriate system of workers councils", would hence be the basic units of the economy whose autonomy would be limited by the public bank's supervision and coordination functions. Basic planning instruments would then include accumulation fund management and trust financing. Perceiving the danger of inflation resulting from the market power of trusts, Lange and Breit proposed to resort to a mechanism that might insure labour mobility and, finally, low wages and inflation rates.

Lange presented a second model in a book from 1938 (Lange and Taylor 1938), the chief purpose of which was now to define the outlines of a socialist organization to show theoretically and practically the feasibility of economic calculus in the absence of a genuine capital market. The model shared several features with the 1934 model, especially as regards the separation of political power from economic units. The 1934 model was, however, more "market oriented," in so far as all prices of goods and services were to be determined by trusts under the assumption that the public bank would react to changes in employment. On the contrary, in the 1938 model, the role of the Central Planning Board (CPB) was basically to imitate the market. Acting as an auctioneer, the CPB was hence assumed to perform the role of the market by reacting to changes in inventories.

Aware of the danger of the bureaucratization of economic life, in later works Lange suggested several ideas for devising institutional guarantees for democratic control.

MICHAËL ASSOUS

See also:

Business cycles and growth (III); Michał Kalecki (I); Keynesianism (II).

References and further reading

Assous, M. and R. Lampa (2014), 'Lange's 1938 model: dynamics and the "optimum propensity to consume"', *European Journal of the History of Economic Thought*, **21** (5), 871–98.
Breit, M. and O. Lange (2003), 'The way to the socialist planned economy', trans. J. Toporowski, *History of Economics Review*, **37** (Winter), 51–70.
Kaldor, N. (1940), 'A model of the trade cycle', *Economic Journal*, **50** (197), 78–92.
Kalecki, M. (1939), *Essays in the Theory of Economic Fluctuations*, London: Allen and Unwin.
Kowalik, T. (2008), 'Lange, Oskar Ryszard (1904–1965)', *The New Palgrave Dictionary of Economics*, 2nd edn, S.N. Durlauf and L.E. Blume (eds), Basingstoke and New York: Palgrave Macmillan; *The New Palgrave Dictionary of Economics Online*, accessed 14 December 2015 at http://www.dictionaryofeconomics.com/article?id=pde2008_L000024.
Lange, O. (1935), 'Marxian economics and modern economic theory', *Review of Economic Studies*, **2** (3), 189–201.
Lange, O. (1938), 'The rate of interest and the optimum propensity to consume', *Economica*, **5** (17), 12–32.
Lange, O. (1942), 'Say's law: a criticism and restatement', in O. Lange, F. McIntyre and T.O. Yntema (eds), *Studies in Mathematical Economics and Econometrics*, Chicago, IL: University of Chicago Press, pp. 49–68.
Lange, O (1944), *Price Flexibility and Employment*, Bloomington, IN: Principia Press.
Lange, O. and F.M. Taylor (1938), *On the Economic Theory of Socialism*, Minneapolis, MN: University of Minnesota Press.
Schumpeter, J.A. (1911), *The Theory of Economic Development: An Inquiry into Profits, Capital, Credit, Interest and the Business Cycle*, trans. from the German by R. Opie (2008), New Brunswick, NJ, and London: Transaction.

Richard Ferdinand Kahn (1905–1989)

Richard Kahn was Maynard Keynes's favourite pupil. At the end of his life Kahn said he was happy to be regarded as a disciple of Keynes. However, it may be argued that Kahn was much more than either of these (which is not meant to downgrade either of them).

Kahn was born in London in 1905 into a Jewish family of German origin. His family combined strict religious observance with a passion for education. Kahn went to St Paul's School for Boys. (Joan Robinson, his greatest intellectual friend, went to St Paul's School for Girls.) He came up to Cambridge in 1926, to King's College. For the first three years he read mathematics, obtaining a First, and then physics, in which he obtained a Second and a notorious reputation for clumsiness and breakages at laboratory practicals. He stayed on for a fourth year, reading for Part II of the Economics Tripos. Kahn was supervised by Gerald Shove and Keynes. He obtained a First, a remarkable performance. This was followed by an even more remarkable achievement. He wrote, in just over one and a half years, a Fellowship dissertation for King's, "The economics of the short period", which was highly praised by Pigou and Keynes.

In his dissertation Kahn (1929) made the short period a topic worthy of study in its own right, especially in periods of recession or depression when the *ceteris paribus* assumption of a given stock of capital goods held for long stretches of calendar time. In the dissertation, sadly only published in English in 1989, just after Kahn died, are to be found the principal propositions of the imperfect/monopolistic competition "revolutions", including the kinked demand curves of competing oligopolists. Moreover, the theoretical propositions are supported by empirical data on the UK staple industries, especially textiles, which Keynes made available to Kahn. When Joan Robinson was writing her *Economics of Imperfect Competition* (1933), Kahn was her most invaluable guide and critic, selflessly putting many of his own findings and methods into her book. In her preface she refers to his "constant assistance" and writes that the "whole technical apparatus was built up with his aid [, that] major problems . . . were solved . . . by him" (Robinson 1933: v).

Keynes had Kahn read the proofs and prepare the index of *A Treatise of Money* (Keynes 1930), and then subsequently to provide the formal arguments to back up the conjectures of Hubert Henderson and Keynes in their 1929 pamphlet "Can Lloyd George do it?". This led Kahn, together with James Meade, who was in Cambridge at this time and who was a member of the "Circus" which met to discuss Keynes's 1930 volumes, to formulate the multiplier. The latter is a precise expression, under explicit conditions, of how much secondary employment would be created by a given rise in primary employment associated with, say, public works expenditure (Kahn 1931). The article became an integral part of the structure of *The General Theory* (Keynes 1936), especially in Keynes's formulation of the consumption function.

Kahn was always sceptical of the quantity theory of money as constituting a causal mechanism in the determination of the general price level. He thought that the "fundamental equations" of *A Treatise of Money* could explain both the general price level and its sectorial counterparts without any need to refer to the quantity of money – even though Keynes himself argued that he was working within the quantity theory framework. Kahn's emphasis on the short period and his scepticism about the quantity theory were the greatest direct influences on Keynes as he moved from the system of

A Treatise on Money to the revolutionary system of *The General Theory*. Kahn was also the most important influence by far of the small group of people Keynes consulted while writing *The General Theory*. For example, Keynes wrote to Joan Robinson on 29 March 1934 that he was "going through a stiff week's supervision from RFK ... there never was anyone in the history of the world to whom it was so helpful to submit one's stuff" (*C.W.*, vol XIII, 1973, 422).

Kahn published important papers in a number of areas in the 1930s – on the elasticity of substitution, on ideal output, and on duopoly, for example. When war came he took to the Civil Service like a duck to water. He had an excellent war, being much in demand for his wise help in policy making combined with his meticulous attention to detail. During the war years he wrote a full-length manuscript on buffer stock schemes to stabilize the prices of primary products which alas was never published.

After the war he was mostly in Cambridge in a splendid set of rooms in Webb's Court, King's. He was appointed to a Chair in 1951 when he gave up the senior bursarship of King's, a post he was appointed to following Keynes's death in 1946. He was made a life peer in 1965, Baron Kahn of Hampstead. Kahn worked closely with Joan Robinson and later Luigi Pasinetti in developing post-Keynesian theories of distribution and growth, what Joan Robinson called generalizing *The General Theory* to the long period. His 1959 paper in *Oxford Economic Papers* is the clearest account of the nature, achievements and limitations of Golden Age – steady state – growth theory. He was also closely associated with the parallel critique of the conceptual foundations of the mainstream theory of value and distribution. Kahn wrote an important paper on the concept of the valuation ratio (a close cousin of Tobin's q) in the 1960s (though it was not published until 1972; Kahn 1972a).

In the 1950s Kahn extended Keynes's liquidity preference theory of the rate of interest to the stock market. He was one of the most important contributors to the Radcliffe Committee on the monetary system in 1958, in effect feeding into its pages a qualitative version of endogenous money theory. He also gave lectures on the need to establish a permanent incomes policy if full employment was to be sustained. In the 1970s and 1980s, in his British Academy Keynes Lecture (1975), an article in the *Journal of Economic Literature* (1978), and his Mattioli lectures (1984), he set out his accounts of the making of *The General Theory*, accounts which are insightful and definitive. A selection of his most important articles were brought together in 1972 by Cambridge University Press (Kahn 1972b). Had his dissertation been published in the 1930s (he later wished that it had been), it and his 1931 multiplier article would surely have meant the award of a (akin to) Nobel Prize in economics.

Especially in later years when he was very deaf and suffering ill health, Kahn seemed outwardly a forbidding and remote figure. However, to his friends he was as loved as ever for his thoughtfulness, consideration and loyalty, albeit all were still wary of his notoriously fierce temper when he was displeased. He had been a byword for orthodoxy as a young man. He returned to the beliefs of his youth in his old age and was buried with his prayer shawl and phylacteries in the Jewish section of the Cambridge cemetery. Kahn never married but he never lacked agreeable female company either.

G.C. HARCOURT

See also:

Cambridge School of economics (II); Nicholas Kaldor (I); Michał Kalecki (I); John Maynard Keynes (I); Keynesianism (II); Macroeconomics (III); Joan Violet Robinson (I).

References and further reading

Kahn, R.F. (1929), *The Economics of The Short Period*, English trans. 1989, Basingstoke: Macmillan.
Kahn, R.F. (1931), 'The relation of home investment to unemployment', *Economic Journal*, **41** (164), 173–98.
Kahn, R.F. (1954), 'Some notes on liquidity preference', *Manchester School of Economic and Social Studies*, **22** (3), 229–57.
Kahn, R.F. (1958), 'Memorandum of evidence', submitted to the Radcliffe Committee on the Working of the Monetary System, *Principal Memoranda of Evidence*, vol. 3, London: HMSO, pp. 138–46.
Kahn, R.F. (1959), 'Exercises in the analysis of growth', *Oxford Economic Papers*, New Series, **11**, 146–63.
Kahn, R.F. (1972a), 'Notes on the rate of interest and the growth of firms', in R.F. Kahn, *Selected Essays on Employment and Growth*, Cambridge: Cambridge University Press, pp. 208–32.
Kahn, R.F. (1972b), *Selected Essays on Employment and Growth*, Cambridge: Cambridge University Press.
Kahn, R.F. (1975), *On Re-Reading Keynes. Fourth Keynes Lecture in Economics, 6 November 1974*, London: The British Academy and Oxford University Press.
Kahn, R.F. (1978), 'Some aspects of the development of Keynes's thought', *Journal of Economic Literature*, **16** (2), 545–59.
Kahn, R.F. (1984), *The Making of Keynes' General Theory*, Cambridge: Cambridge University Press.
Keynes, J.M. (1930), *A Treatise on Money*, 2 vols, London: Macmillan, reprinted in D.E. Moggridge (ed.) (1973), *Collected Writings of John Maynard Keynes*, vols V and VI, London: Macmillan.
Keynes, J.M. (1936), *The General Theory of Employment, Interest and Money*, London: Macmillan, reprinted in D.E. Moggridge (ed.) (1973), *Collected Writings of John Maynard Keynes*, vol. VII, London: Macmillan.
Keynes, J.M. (1973), *The General Theory and After. Part I Preparation*, London: Macmillan; reprinted in D.E. Moggridge (ed.) (1973), *Collected Writings of John Maynard Keynes*, vol. XIII, London: Macmillan.
Keynes, J.M. and H. Henderson (1929), 'Can Lloyd George do it?', reprinted 1972 in *Collected Writings of John Maynard Keynes*, vol. IX, *Essays in Persuasion*, London: Macmillan, pp. 86–125.
Robinson, J. (1933), *The Economics of Imperfect Competition*, London: Macmillan, 2nd edn 1969.

Wassily W. Leontief (1905–1999)

Wassily W. Leontief was born on 5 August 1905 in Munich, where his father, also named Wassily W. Leontief, at the time was completing a doctorate in political economy. Leontief was born into a merchant family established in St Petersburg since before 1750 (Kaliadina and Pavlova 2006). Leontief's mother, born Zlata Bekker, was from Odessa and of Jewish extraction, renamed Evgeniia after conversion to the Orthodox faith in 1906.

Wassily Leontief is best known as the originator of input–output analysis, which, although rooted in his interwar work, he introduced around 1950 as "a method of analysis that takes advantage of the relative stable pattern of the flow of goods and services . . . to bring a much more detailed statistical picture of the system into the range of manipulation by economic theory" (Leontief 1986: 4). In 1986 he defined it more briefly and generally as "a method of systematically quantifying the mutual interrelationships among the various sectors of a complex economic system" (Leontief 1986: 19). The Sveriges Riksbank Prize in Economic Sciences in Memory of Alfred Nobel 1973 was awarded to Wassily Leontief "for the development of the input–output method and for its application to important economic problems". The applications of Leontief's invention have been very many and increasingly diversified. Leontief was a very gifted theoretical and mathematical economist whose interests and contributions covered a wide range of topics. Before proceeding with his scholarly contributions we sketch his path through life.

Wassily Leontief grew up in St Petersburg (from 1914 Petrograd). He entered Petrograd State University in 1921 and studied, according to his own account, philosophy, sociology and finally economics, receiving the degree Learned Economist in 1924. He also acquired considerable mathematical expertise. Leontief excelled in his studies and his talent for research was recognized. He was singled out for retention at the university with the following recommendation from one of his teachers: "In his work, Leontief revealed excellent research capacities in the field of political economy, good capacities in the field of economics work, good knowledge in the literature in theoretical economics, a subtle understanding of the basics of economic Marxism, and great assiduity in and love of science". (For further details of his studies, see Kaliadina 2006; Kaliadina and Pavlova 2006.) At the university Leontief completed an essay entitled "Laws in the social sciences – the experience of abstract-logical analysis", accepted for journal publication but censored before it could be published.

Leontief's study period in Petrograd was interrupted twice by often recounted incidents. After putting up posters protesting against the suspension of teachers from the university in 1922, Leontief and fellow students were arrested and interrogated by the Cheka. The other incident was a cancer diagnosis in 1923, a sarcoma in the jaw, resulting in surgery. Leontief in retrospect surmised that the bleak prospects for a recovery from the cancer might have been the major reason for the issuance to him of passport and permission to leave the country at the beginning of 1925. At that time he was listed for work at the university (which had become Leningrad State University) and simultaneously at a research institute in Moscow. However, Leontief left the Soviet Union in March 1925 and applied for permanent residency in Germany. He settled down in Berlin to study.

At the University of Berlin he was a doctoral student with Walter Sombart and later, and more importantly, with Ladislaus von Bortkiewicz. The doctoral degree was conferred in 1928 for a dissertation submitted in 1927 (Leontief 1991). After Berlin, Leontief was a staff member of the Institute for World Economy in Kiel 1927–30 in a research group comprising Adolph Lowe, Hans Neisser and others. Leontief was engaged in research on a new method for the determination of supply and demand curves (Leontief 1929). At this point a curious interlude took place in Leontief's life, an accidental meeting with a Chinese delegation led to an invitation to advise on railway trajectories in China. Leontief spent most of a year in China in 1929–30.

Leontief moved to the United States in 1931 as he won a one year fellowship as research associate at National Bureau of Economic Research (NBER) in New York City. Simon Kuznets, who was on the research staff of NBER, and Mordecai Ezekiel were helpful in advising Leontief on how to get the fellowship. After having given a lecture in Harvard's Economic Seminar Leontief was offered a position as instructor in 1932/33 and then in succession became Assistant Professor (1933), Associate Professor (1939) and Professor in Economics (1946). Joseph Schumpeter had played a role in easing Leontief's entry into Harvard. Leontief established the Harvard Economic Research Project in 1948 with the Rockefeller Foundation and US Air Force as sponsors. He left Harvard in 1975 and became head of the Institute for Economic Analysis at New York University from which he retired at a very great age.

In his 1928 dissertation Leontief set out "a general scheme of the circular flow of an economy", that is a representation of the economy as a reproductive process of causal relationships leading to a system of economic interrelationships represented as "a long path describing a wide circle and ending up again at its starting point" (Leontief 1991: 181). The stationary system of production of commodities by means of commodities included, naturally, prices accompanying the commodity flows. The largely verbal presentation, also discussing how shocks would reverberate through the system, was enhanced by formulae for increased precision and illuminated by ingenious graphs. Key concepts were coefficients characterizing the input structure as well as the output distribution. The dissertation also dealt with the treatment of capital within the system, dealing critically with the capital concept of contemporary authors. The dissertation had no empirical part but a stated intention of extending the scheme to empirical analysis: "The object of our analysis has not been the economic process itself, but rather a model of a system of economic flows. Our next task is to undertake the transition from this general scheme to empirical facts" (Leontief 1991: 198).

From a history perspective, Leontief's 1928 scheme has classical roots as argued convincingly by Kurz and Salvadori (1995, 2000), going back to François Quesnay and the *Tableau économique* or even further back to Petty and Cantillon. Kurz and Salvatori (2000) point out similarities between Leontief's work and that of Achille-Nicolas Isnard and survey other authors within the same classical vein, such as Karl Marx, V.K. Dmitriev and G. von Charasoff. Leontief's work had similarities with contemporary work by Piero Sraffa (see Kurz and Salvadori 2006).

Leontief's invention and development of input–output analysis took place after his arrival in America. It has often been interpreted as more or less directly related to the 1928 dissertation but can also be viewed as his current research concerns. In retrospect Leontief gave somewhat different clues about the historical roots of his input–output analysis. In 1965 he wrote that input–output analysis was "an adaptation of the neo-classical theory of general equilibrium to the empirical study of the quantitative interdependence between interrelated economic activities" (Leontief 1966: 134). Similar statements emphasizing the Walrasian roots made this the commonly accepted view. However, he also asserted in places that input–output analysis was "a practical extension of the classical theory of general interdependence which view the whole economy . . . as a single system and sets out to describe and to interpret its operation in terms of directly observable basic structural relationships" (Leontief 2008). Both views can be given a rationale.

Already at the NBER in 1931/32 Leontief conducted theoretical and empirical studies of the US industrial economy. This continued at Harvard where he got research assistance grants for using the Census of Manufactures and other data for 1919 and 1929 for constructing input–output tables, an idea apparently regarded with great scepticism. The outcome was a pair of articles (Leontief 1936, 1937), commonly regarded as the cornerstones of input–output analysis. Compared with Walras's vision of a determinate general equilibrium system, the input–output system launched by Leontief was a simplification but with a shift in emphasis by putting the inter-industrial transactions at the centre, and above all a vitalization of a theoretical conception idea by filling in numbers based on direct observations.

The outcome was the input–output analysis. Leontief's development of input–output analysis, from the very first steps until it had matured into a new sub-discipline of economics, falls naturally into two phases. The first phase, which was completed with Leontief (1941), displayed what in the input–output terminology became known as a "closed input–output model" where the demand side was taken as given and the use of the operationalized equilibrium system was fairly limited. This phase showed however the viability of Leontief's visionary idea as long as it could be supported by computational capacity. Leontief's early work comprised by far the most comprehensive computations in the history of economic analysis. However, there were recognized shortcomings, such as large amounts of unspecified inputs, unsatisfactory treatment of saving and investment, and others in addition to the non-existence so far of adequate computers.

At the beginning of World War II the US Bureau of Labor Statistics (BLS) had been assigned the task of preparing for the post-war situation. Attention was paid to Leontief's work and the input–output approach was found highly suitable for the task. A close cooperation followed between Leontief and the BLS which prepared the 1939 input–output table and later a huge table for 1947 (see Kohli 2001). It also led to the slight, but very important, reformulation of the theoretical structure as an "open input–output model", turning out to be an immensely versatile tool for a wide range of policy analyses, when supported by computer tools increasingly available after World War II.

The second phase was marked by a new edition of the 1941 monograph enhanced by four papers introducing the possibilities and potential of the open input–output model (Leontief 1951). From here it was straightforward to worldwide distribution of input–output analysis.

Leontief continued as a leader of input–output developments and new applications, in particular in the analysis of military expenditure, environmental analysis, world development issues, implications of demographic development, and automation.

In his early years Leontief had written and published penetrating studies on a number of issues, see Dorfman (1973). A repeated theme was methodology. Leontief was sharply opposed to the increasing separation between theoretical and empirical economics and expressed this view most prominently in his presidential address to the American Economic Association in 1970 (Leontief 1971), much of which may be read as equally valid today. Leontief's methodological views were expressed throughout his career. He criticized the "implicit theorizing" of the circuit around Keynes, favoured detailed "direct observation" as exemplified by the input–output tables, and the use of engineering information, rather than econometric analysis of aggregates he tended to be doubtful about. In the famous methodological controversy between the Cowles Commission and the NBER in the immediate post-war period, Leontief was a bystander whose methodological position clearly differed substantially from both sides. Leontief had triumphed on his use of the highly simplistic assumption of constant input coefficients, basically because it worked in practice, although many felt called upon to denigrate his achievement. The relationship between Leontief and the Cowles Commission under Koopmans soured. Leontief defended his position in characteristic and polemic style: "The very process of aggregation obscures the sharp outlines of the underlying structural relationships to such an extent that one is naturally forced to give up the simpler methods of direct induction and take recourse to 'blind flying' by the complicated but hardly foolproof instruments of indirect statistical inference" (Leontief 1951: 210).

We finally deal with an oddity in Leontief's curriculum vitae. Leontief's passport stated that he was born in 1906. After visiting Russia in the early 1990s Leontief let his associates know that a Russian scholar interested in the Leontief family history had unearthed documents showing that the correct birth year was 1905 (Duchin 1995: 267). A similar confusion arose about his birthplace. At the time of Leontief's death, in 1999, obituaries and encyclopedia entries displayed all four possible combinations of birth year 1905/1906 and birthplace St Petersburg/Munich. The core of the confusion about his birth year was later found to be that when the Leontief family returned to St Petersburg from Munich in August 1906 their one-year-old child was baptized and registered – with or without the connivance of the authorities – as born only three weeks earlier. By this deception it would appear as if the conversion of Zlata Bakker to the Orthodox faith had taken place prior to the childbirth. The story that Leontief passed on is hardly convincing; most likely he knew throughout his life his correct birth year and birthplace and just wanted to put things right towards the end of his life. Leontief died in 1999. A remnant of this curious confusion remains, as his gravestone in Connecticut, next to that of Schumpeter, gives correct birth year but states incorrectly his birthplace as St Petersburg.

Olav Bjerkholt

See also:

Vladimir Karpovich Dmitriev (I); Input–output analysis (III); François Quesnay and Physiocracy (I); Piero Sraffa (I).

References

Dorfman, R. (1973), 'Wassily Leontief's contribution to economics', *Swedish Journal of Economics*, **75** (4), 430–49.
Duchin, F. (1995), 'In honor of Wassily Leontief's 90th birthday', *Structural Change and Economic Dynamics*, **6** (3), 267–9.

Kaliadina, S.A. (2006), 'Leontief and the repressions of the 1920s: an interview', ed. and annotated by C. Wittich, *Economic Systems Research*, **18** (4), 347–56.

Kaliadina, S.A. and N.I. Pavlova (2006), 'The family of W.W. Leontief in Russia', trans. and annotated by C. Wittich, *Economic Systems Research*, **18** (4), 335–46.

Kohli, M.C. (2001), 'Leontief and the Bureau of Labor Statistics, 1941–54: developing a framework for measurement', *History of Political Economy*, **33** (Supplement 1), 190–212.

Kurz, H.D. and N. Salvadori (1995), *Theory of Production. A Long-Period Analysis*, Cambridge: Cambridge University Press.

Kurz, H.D. and N. Salvadori (2000), '"Classical" roots of input–output analysis: a short account of its long prehistory', *Economic Systems Research*, **12** (2), 153–79.

Kurz, H.D. and N. Salvadori (2006), 'Input–output analysis from a wider perspective: a comparison of the early works of Leontief and Sraffa', *Economic Systems Research*, **18** (4), 373–90.

Leontief, W. (1929), 'Ein Versuch zur statistischen Analyse von Angebot und Nachfrage', *Weltwirtschaftliches Archiv – Chronik und Archivalien*, **30**, 1–53.

Leontief, W. (1936), 'Quantitative input–output relations in the economic system of the United States', *Review of Economic Statistics*, **18** (3), 105–25.

Leontief, W. (1937), 'Interrelations of prices, output, savings and investment: a study in empirical application of economic theory of general interdependence', *Review of Economic Statistics*, **19** (3), 109–32.

Leontief, W. (1941), *The Structure of American Economy, 1919–1929*, Cambridge MA: Harvard University Press.

Leontief, W. (1951), *The Structure of American Economy, 1919–1939. An Empirical Application of Equilibrium Analysis*, 2nd enlarged edn, New York: Oxford University Press.

Leontief, W. (1966), *Input–Output Economics*, New York: Oxford University Press.

Leontief, W. (1971), 'Theoretical assumptions and nonobserved facts', *American Economic Review*, **61** (1), 1–7.

Leontief, W. (1986), *Input–Output Economics*, 2nd edn, Oxford: Oxford University Press.

Leontief, W. (1991), 'The economy as a circular flow', *Structural Change and Economic Dynamics*, **2** (1), 181–212, abbreviated version, trans. R. Aylett from W. Leontief (1928), 'Die Wirtschaft als Kreislauf', *Archiv für Sozialwissenschaft und Sozialpolitik*, **60**, 577–623.

Leontief, W. (2008), 'Input–output analysis', in S.N. Durlauf and L.E.Blume (eds), *The New Palgrave. A Dictionary of Economics*, 2nd edn, London: Palgrave Macmillan, doi:10.1057/9780230226203.0805.

Heinrich von Stackelberg (1905–1946)

Life

Heinrich von Stackelberg was born 31 October 1905 in Kudinow near Moscow, into a noble Baltic-German family from Estonia. After the October Revolution the family fled to Germany, first to Ratibor in Silesia and later to Cologne, where they settled down. Heinrich von Stackelberg studied economics and mathematics at the University of Cologne as an undergraduate and graduated in 1927 with a thesis on the quasi-rent in Alfred Marshall's work ("Die Quasirente bei Alfred Marshall"). He continued his studies as a PhD student in economics under Erwin von Beckerath. Only three years after his diploma he graduated in 1930 with a dissertation on cost theory ("Die Grundlagen einer reinen Kostentheorie"), which was published in 1932 in Vienna and which received international recognition. In 1932 he went on several research trips to Vienna, where he worked together for a couple of months with the founders of the New Vienna School such as Gottfried von Haberler, Friedrich August von Hayek, Fritz Machlup, Oskar Morgenstern, Hans Mayer, and Richard von Strigl. Afterwards he went to Italy where he wrote works on imperfect competition under the influence of Luigi Amoroso (see Konow 1994: 148). In 1934, von Stackelberg completed his habilitation with the title "Marktform und Gleichgewicht" ("Market structure and equilibrium") published in 1934. After his habilitation he worked as a lecturer at the University of Cologne for one term before he became associate professor at the University of Berlin, where he taught until 1941. He was one of the co-founders of the *Archiv für mathematische Wirtschafts- und Sozialforschung* that was issued between 1935 and 1942. In 1941, von Stackelberg became full professor of economics at the University of Bonn. During the war, he was twice recruited as a soldier for a few months. For the rest of the time, he was exempted from military service in order to be able to proceed with his teachings. In 1943, because of the difficult teaching and research conditions in Germany, he accepted an invitation as a visiting professor at the Complutense University of Madrid in Spain, where he worked for the following three years (see Fuertes 1996). Heinrich von Stackelberg died on 12 October 1946, just before his forty-sixth birthday, from the incurable Hodgkin's disease.

In his minority group of German-Baltic descent, German-nationalist and right-wing conservative attitudes were widespread (see Möller 1992). Owing to these influences, von Stackelberg turned to nationalist and conservative groups. In 1931, he joined the Nationalsozialistische Deutsche Arbeiterpartei (NSDAP). In June 1933, he became a member of the SS. At about the same time, he became leader of the lecturers at the University of Cologne. However, as early as 1935, von Stackelberg tried to quit the SS. He also insisted on a wedding in church, which contradicted the NS ideology and further alienated him from the NS regime (see Senn 1996). He was in contact with Jens Jessen and Ulrich von Hassell, who were murdered after the assassination attempt against Hitler. While the war was still going on, he stayed in contact with the Freiburg Circle (Erwin von Beckerath, Walter Eucken and Constantin von Dietze) – an oppositional and illegal group (see Eucken 1948). Another sign of his alienation from the NS ideology was his taking part in the probably last doctoral proceedings of a Jewish doctoral student (see Senn 1996).

Works

Von Stackelberg was one of the most talented German economists in the 1930s. He had a deep mathematical understanding that enabled him to use mathematical methods to analyse complex problems. The topics he dealt with are mostly microeconomic in nature. His first scientific work is his doctoral thesis that combines traditional cost accounting with marginal analysis. His most important extension of traditional analysis is its application to joint production. He decomposes the optimization problem of the firm into two steps: first, the derivation of the optimal level of production for any possible composition of output and, second, the choice of the profit-maximizing level of production. Another contribution is his analysis of transfer prices within a firm. The last chapter of his thesis contains some reflections on dynamic development, for example, owing to technological progress. When technological progress causes a decrease in average cost, market concentration can be expected to increase, that is, an oligopolistic or monopolistic market structure is likely to occur.

These reflections point towards future focuses of his research, that is, the analysis of market structures with imperfect competition and the examination of dynamic developments in an economy. A first analysis of imperfect competition was presented in an essay in 1933 that had been written during his cooperation with Luigi Amoroso in Italy. The essay turned out to be preliminary work to his habilitation thesis *Marktform und Gleichgewicht*. It also contains his most famous contribution, an analysis of markets with imperfect competition, a prevalent area at the time (see Scherer 1996). The main interest is the analysis of the stability of markets with imperfect competition, especially the case of a supply duopoly. Each firm may be either dependent or independent. In the former case, the duopolist assumes that its rival will not react to its behaviour, that is, the rival's quantity supplied is taken as given. In the latter case, a duopolist assumes that its rival's behaviour depends on its own decision. There are three cases to consider: (1) both firms believe the rival's behaviour to be independent of its own; (2) both firms believe that the rival reacts to its own choice of strategy; and (3) an asymmetric situation where one firm is dependent while the other is independent. In the first case, each firm will maximize its profits, given the other firm's reaction function. Since both firms act in the same way, the competitive quantity will be supplied, and profits are very small. According to von Stackelberg, however, this situation is unstable since one of the firms could increase its profit by reducing its quantity supplied. But it remains unclear which of the firms should act accordingly. Further, it may be the case that the firm increases its quantity again at a later stage. In the second case, each firm assumes that the other reacts to its behaviour. This is the Cournot case. The expectations on the rival's quantity are confirmed, since one firm's quantity corresponds to the other's supply according to its reaction function. However, this situation is not an equilibrium either, since, given the dependent position of one firm, the other would prefer to be independent. The third case, which von Stackelberg refers to as an asymmetric oligopoly, may constitute an equilibrium since it is in one firm's interest to act according to the other firm's will. However, this will be an equilibrium only if there are substantial asymmetries between the firms with respect to costs or technology. However, this equilibrium has to be considered an exception – in general, oligopoly is a market form without equilibrium.

The analysis is then extended to the relationship between two or several markets, and the profitability of the duopolistic market positions of the firms is examined. Von Stackelberg uses the concept of a reaction function, and introduces isoprofit lines as a new analytical tool. He considers price and quantity competition in different market forms. The analysis confirms the general instability of oligopolistic market structures. These results gave rise to his far-reaching call for an interventionist state that acts as an equilibrating force, for example, by creating and regulating cartels, trade unions, or trade associations.

Besides oligopoly theory, von Stackelberg also analysed questions of spatial economics and provided contributions to the theory of price discrimination. He was particularly interested in intertemporal and dynamic aspects of an economy. In his essay "Beitrag zur Theorie des individuellen Sparens" ("Contribution to the theory of individual saving") (1938), he deals with the question of why a household should save, and analyses the effects of the expected interest rate on household savings. Referring to John Hicks and Roy Allen, he analyses the allocation of expenses over time in a framework of intertemporal utility maximization (see Krelle 2008). He derives the law of Böhm-Bawerk on the underestimation of future goods from the law of the decreasing marginal rate of substitution, and shows in what way it affects the optimal allocation of expenses over time. In the framework of the Austrian theory of capital, the time structure of production is of central importance. Defining the per se problematic concept of an average production period in a manageable way may be considered his main contribution. Thus, in his contribution "Kapital und Zins in der stationären Verkehrswirtschaft" ("Capital and interest in a stationary economy") (1941), he suggests the approach of defining the average production period in an economy by the solution of the equation $w = \frac{y}{(1+r)^t}$ where w denotes the factor income, r is the interest rate, and y denotes output. That is, the average period is defined by that period over which the output has to be discounted in order to be equal to the factor income.

His last major work is *Die Grundzüge der theoretischen Volkswirtschaftslehre* (*Principles of Economic Theory*) (1943), which was republished in 1948, after his death, in a significantly extended version with the title *Grundlagen der theoretischen Volkswirtschaftslehre* (*Fundamentals of Economic Theory*). The work consists of six chapters that deal with large parts of contemporary economic research and makes it accessible to the German public (see Maks and Haan 1996). He shows that, given the initial endowments, utility and profit maximization induces an efficient allocation. The distribution of income may, however, be devised by the government according to the political ideas of fairness and equality.

Impact

Jürg Niehans dubbed von Stackelberg a "creative eclectic" who made contributions to each topic he concerned himself with (Niehans 1992: 204). Today, especially his works on oligopoly theory form an important part of industrial organization. They belong to the classical models of imperfect competition, where the approach is of major importance in the framework of sequential decision making when an individual or a firm has the option to commit itself to some action. Numerous models are built on the approach developed by von Stackelberg, and it is applied to various economic problems. Because of the formal methods and concepts, he was of major importance for German economic theory as, besides Wilhelm Krelle and Erich Schneider, he was one of the few German economists that kept up the connection to mainstream economic research.

ULRICH SCHWALBE

See also:

Eugen von Böhm-Bawerk (I); Capital theory (III); Competition (III); Antoine-Augustin Cournot (I); Game theory (III); Industrial organization (III).

References and further reading

Eucken, W. (1948), 'Heinrich von Stackelberg (1905–1946)', *Economic Journal*, **58** (229), 132–5.
Fuertes, J.V. (1996), 'Stackelberg and his role in the change in the Spanish economic policy', *Journal of Economic Studies*, **23** (5–6), 128–40.
Kloten, N. and H. Möller (eds) (1992), *Heinrich Freiherr von Stackelberg: Gesammelte wissenschaftliche Abhandlungen*, 2 vols, Regensburg: Transfer Verlag.
Konow, J. (1994), 'The political economy of Heinrich von Stackelberg', *Economic Inquiry*, **32** (1), 146–65.
Krelle, W. (2008), 'Stackelberg, Heinrich von (1905–1946)', in S.N. Durlauf and L.E. Blume (eds), *The New Palgrave Dictionary of Economics*, 2nd edn, London: Palgrave Macmillan.
Maks, J.A.H. and M. Haan (1996), 'Heinrich von Stackelberg's textbook *Grundlagen der theoretischen Volkswirtschaftslehre* revisited', *Journal of Economic Studies*, **23** (5–6), 40–47.
Möller, H. (1992), 'Heinrich von Stackelberg – Leben und Werk', in N. Kloten and H. Möller (eds), *Heinrich Freiherr von Stackelberg: Gesammelte wissenschaftliche Abhandlungen*, Regensburg: Transfer Verlag, pp. 1–65.
Niehans, J. (1992), 'Heinrich von Stackelberg: relinking German economics to the mainstream', *Journal of the History of Economic Thought*, **14** (2), 189–208.
Scherer, F.M. (1996), 'Heinrich von Stackelberg's *Marktform und Gleichgewicht*', *Journal of Economic Studies*, **23** (5–6), 58–70.
Senn, P.R. (1996), 'A short sketch of Stackelberg's career', *Journal of Economic Studies*, **23** (5–6), 9–14.
Stackelberg, H. von (1932), *Grundlagen einer reinen Kostentheorie*, Vienna: Julius Springer.
Stackelberg, H. von (1934), *Marktform und Gleichgewicht*, Vienna and Berlin: Springer.
Stackelberg, H. von (1938), 'Beitrag zur Theorie des individuellen Sparens', *Zeitschrift für Nationalökonomie*, **9**, 167–200.
Stackelberg, H. von (1941), 'Kapital und Zins in der stationären Verkehrswirtschaft', *Zeitschrift für Nationalökonomie*, **10**, 25–61.
Stackelberg, H. von (1943), *Grundzüge der theoretischen Volkswirtschaftslehre*, Stuttgart and Berlin: Kohlhammer.
Stackelberg, H. von (1948), *Grundlagen der theoretischen Volkswirtschaftslehre*, 2nd edn of *Grundzüge der theoretischen Volkswirtschaftslehre*, Berne: Francke, English trans. 1952, *The Theory of the Market Economy*, London: Hodge.

James Edward Meade (1907–1995)

James E. Meade was born on 23 June 1907 in Swanage, Dorset, brought up in Bath, Somerset, and died on 22 December 1995 in Cambridge (UK). He studied philosophy, politics and economics at Oriel College in Oxford. After his graduation he was immediately appointed to a fellowship in Economics at Hertford College. The college allowed him to go away to learn more about economics. In 1930 he went to Cambridge on the invitation of by Dennis Robertson, whom he had met in Bath some years before. Robertson introduced Meade to Richard Kahn who was working on his paper on the multiplier – "The relation of home investment to unemployment" – which was published in the *Economic Journal* in 1931. Working with Kahn, Meade became a member of the "Circus", a group of young economists who discussed Keynes's (1930) *A Treatise on Money*. The other members of the group were Piero Sraffa and Austin and Joan Robinson. In 1931 Meade went back to Oxford and taught economics at Hertford College. From 1938 till 1940 he worked at the Economic Intelligence Service of the League of Nations in Geneva. During the war he was employed in the Economic Section of the War Cabinet Offices, where he prepared, together with Richard Stone, the first estimates of national income accounts. In 1946 Meade followed L. Robbins as director of the Economic Section and a year later he happily accepted Robbins's offer of the Cassel Professorship of Commerce with special reference to International Trade at the London School of Economics. Ten years later he succeeded his close friend Dennis Robertson as Professor of Political Economy at Cambridge University, the chair once held by Pigou, who himself had succeeded Marshall.

The move to Cambridge confronted him with the embittered conflicts within the Economics Faculty, which he very much disliked. Looking back, it is clear that the debates reflected not only the combative personality of some of the key participants – particularly Joan Robinson, Kahn and Kaldor, on the one hand, and Frank Hahn and his followers, on the other – but also fundamental intellectual differences on how Keynes's original insights should be interpreted and developed. Tired of the Cambridge Faculty politics, Meade decided in 1968 to resign from his chair and devote more time to research and writing. Christ's College offered him a position as Senior Research Fellow, which he held until 1974. In 1977, together with Bertil Ohlin, James Meade was awarded the Sveriges Riksbank Prize in Economic Sciences in Memory of Alfred Nobel "for their path breaking contribution to the theory of international trade and international capital movements".

One of Meade's important contributions to economics was in international trade theory and in the field of the theory of the balance of payments, where he clarified under which conditions a country can simultaneously achieve an equilibrium both internally as well as a balance in its international payments. He pointed out the conflict between the goals of ensuring full employment and bringing the balance of payments into equilibrium. To resolve this conflict he proposed a combination of various economic policy instruments leading to the simultaneous attainment of both goals. His analysis of the impacts of the rate of interest and monetary policy on the balance of payments was path breaking, as was his analysis of the importance of exchange-rate systems for the effective operation of stabilization policy. He coined the notions of "internal balance" and "external balance". To attain "internal balance" price stability and full employment should be obtained. He mentions demand management and wage-fixing as instruments. In his Nobel Lecture (Meade 1977b) he emphasized that many "industrialised countries have failed to find appropriate national institutional ways of combining full employment with price stability". Also, referring to "external balance" he continued: "with full employment and price stability at home the balance of payments could with much more confidence be left to the mechanism of flexible foreign exchange rates" (ibid.).

Meade's most important works, *The Balance of Payments* (1951b) and *Trade and Welfare* (1955, also 1952), had two most influential sources: Keynes's *General Theory* and modern welfare economics, mirroring the two persons – Keynes and Robbins – who both had a strong intellectual influence on him.

A second field of his research was the theory of economic policy, particularly economic policy for an open economy. The Tinbergen–Meade approach is quite simple: suppose government spending is a policy instrument under the control of government. Then one can achieve a particular level of gross national product (GNP) by inputting the target value of the GNP and then inverting the equation for the policy variable. As a result one gets the optimal setting for the instrument. Then, the question arises as to how to achieve this in practice. Starting from the rule that to each macro-goal (external equilibrium, full employment and price stability) there should be a corresponding policy instrument, then you have to look for the institution which will make use of the instrument. Regarding external equilibrium, Meade takes it for granted that there exists a certain separation of power between national governments and international institutions. National governments should be responsible for national monetary, fiscal and wage policy ensuring full employment and a stable price level, while external equilibrium should be maintained by foreign exchange policy under the supervision of international institutions.

In the 1960s Meade wrote extensively on growth economics assuming a neoclassical position, which was one reason why he came into conflict with Keynesians such as Kaldor, Robinson and Champernowne. However, Meade belonged to a group of economists, like Harrod or Hicks, who were not hostile to Keynesian economics. Instead of regarding Keynes's theory as a dissenting approach, they reconciled it with the mainstream and contributed to the neoclassical synthesis.

With the appearance of the stagflation phenomenon in the 1970s, Meade became interested in this issue and in 1978 started a major research project on "stagflation" with younger economists in the Department of Applied Economics at Cambridge University. According to him the main cause for stagflation was a reduction of the rate of profit brought about by the growth of wage costs and "imported costs". He identified the three driving forces behind this as the over-extended use of traditional Keynesian policies to stimulate aggregate demand, the policy of the trade unions to increase the money wages, and monopolistic markets with inflexible prices.

Given these conditions Meade concludes that traditional Keynesian policies became severely limited particularly to fight inflation. According to Meade's "new Keynesianism" countries have to create "appropriate institutions" for a social regulation of wage rates, that is, independent salary commissions and arbitration proceedings.

James Meade contributed to many areas of macroeconomics, to international trade, and to the theory of economic policy. Meade was a broad-minded social scientist and not a narrow specialist. Besides economics, his interests spanned social policy, history and politics. He was convinced that specialization would not lead to an understanding of the working of the economic system as a whole. In his autobiography he wrote:

> The frontiers of knowledge in the various fields of our subject are expanding at such a rate that, work as hard as one can, one finds oneself further and further away from an understanding of the whole. I believe this experience to illustrate the basic problem of our subject. Sane economic policy must take into account simultaneously all aspects of the economy; but a soundly based understanding of the whole and of the relationship between its parts becomes more and more difficult, if not impossible, to attain. (Meade 1977a)

VOLKER CASPARI

See also:

Balance of payments and exchange rates (III); Cambridge School of economics (II); Richard Ferdinand Kahn (I); John Maynard Keynes (I); Keynesianism (II); Macroeconomics (III).

References and further reading

Howson, S. (2000), 'James Meade', *Economic Journal*, **110** (461), Features, F122–F145.
Johnson, H.G. (1978), 'James Meade's contribution to economics', *Scandinavian Journal of Economics*, **80** (1), 64–85.
Kahn, R.F. (1931), 'The relation of home investment to unemployment', *Economic Journal*, **41** (162), 173–98.
Keynes, J.M. (1930), *A Treatise on Money*, London: Macmillan.
Meade, J.E. (1944), *National Income and Expenditure*, London: Oxford University Press.
Meade, J.E. (1951a), *The Theory of International Economic Policy*, London: Oxford University Press.
Meade, J.E. (1951b), *The Balance of Payments*, London: Oxford University Press.
Meade, J.E. (1952), *Geometry of International Trade*, London: George Allen & Unwin.
Meade, J.E. (1955), *Trade and Welfare*, London: Oxford University Press.
Meade, J.E. (1958), *The Control of Inflation*, Cambridge: Cambridge University Press.
Meade, J.E. (1964), *Efficiency, Equality and the Ownership of Property*, London: George Allen & Unwin.
Meade, J.E. (1977a), 'Autobiography', accessed 7 December 2015 at http://www.nobelprize.org/nobel_prizes/economic-sciences/laureates/1977/meade-bio.html.
Meade, J.E. (1977b), 'The meaning of "internal balance"', accessed 7 December 2015 at http://www.nobelprize.org/nobel_prizes/economic-sciences/laureates/1977/meade-lecture.html.
Meade, J.E. (1982), *Wage-fixing*, London: Unwin Hyman.
Meade, J.E. (1984), 'Structural changes in the rate of interest and the rate of foreign exchange to preserve equilibrium in the balance of payments and the budget balance', *Oxford Economic Papers*, **36** (1), 52–66.
Meade, J.E. (1986), *Alternative Systems of Business Organization and of Workers' Remuneration*, London: Unwin Hyman.

Nicholas Kaldor (1908–1986)

Nicholas Kaldor was one of the most prominent of the "Cambridge Keynesians" who defended and developed the revolutionary macroeconomics of John Maynard Keynes in the half-century after Keynes's death (Pasinetti 2007). He became an influential post-Keynesian critic of neoclassical theory, and was a lifelong advocate of democratic socialist economic policies.

Born in Budapest on 12 May 1908, Kaldor came to the London School of Economics in 1927 and remained there for 20 years, first as an undergraduate and then as a research student and lecturer. After a brief post-war spell at the United Nations in Geneva he moved to Cambridge in 1949 as a Fellow of King's College, and spent the rest of his life there; he was belatedly promoted to Professor in 1966. Active as a writer and controversialist until the very end of his life, he died in Cambridge on 30 September 1986. The core of Kaldor's voluminous writings can be found in the nine volumes of his selected economic essays (Kaldor 1960–89), supplemented by the posthumously published 1984 Mattioli lectures (Kaldor 1996); an excellent sample of his work is provided by Targetti and Thirlwall (1989). There are three intellectual biographies (Thirlwall 1987; Targetti 1992; King 2009).

Kaldor made many important contributions to economic theory. In the 1930s he wrote on capital theory and on the theory of the firm under imperfect competition; developed a penetrating critique of equilibrium theorizing, the full significance of which only became apparent decades later; produced the first published statement of the compensation principle in welfare economics; made a detailed analysis of the way in which speculative markets operate; and formulated an ambitious early Keynesian model of the business cycle. During the 1940s he wrote extensively on policy issues, including popular pieces suggesting social democratic solutions to post-war economic problems. He also arranged for his friend John von Neumann's important paper on the theory of economic growth to be translated and published in the *Review of Economic Studies* (von Neumann 1945–46). Kaldor was an enthusiastic advocate of William Beveridge's proposals for the creation of a comprehensive welfare state. With his young Hungarian colleague Tibor Barna, he wrote a brilliant technical appendix to Beveridge's 1944 report on *Full Employment in a Free Society*, exploring alternative fiscal policy measures for maintaining full employment without demand inflation after the war. He considered a range of taxation and expenditure options, with and without budget deficits, and also discussed issues related to fiscal sustainability. The entire analysis has an amazingly modern ring (see Buiter 2010: 60–61). In Geneva he also advised the United Nations on the international dimensions of policies to promote full employment.

On his return to academic life Kaldor re-established himself as a leading macroeconomic theorist. In the 1950s and early 1960s he published a series of formal models of economic growth, which combined severe criticism of neoclassical theory with a distinctively Keynesian approach to the distribution of income. Kaldor rejected as incoherent the neoclassical analysis of capital and the aggregate production function, and therefore also dismissed the marginal productivity theory of distribution. His extremely influential 1956 *Review of Economic Studies* paper on "alternative theories of distribution" set out a distinctive macroeconomic theory of relative shares in which everything depended on the ratio of investment to income and on the (very different) class propensities of workers and capitalists to save out of wages and profits. Beginning in 1966 Kaldor produced some much less formal but equally provocative and original ideas on economic growth, emphasizing dynamic increasing returns to scale and the critical role of manufacturing in the process of economic growth. Here he anticipated subsequent mainstream thinking on "endogenous growth".

Applying these ideas to the problems of economic growth in backward regions, Kaldor derived a "North–South" model of global development in which poor countries that relied heavily on exports of primary products were systematically disadvantaged in their trade with the rich industrialized countries. He became a strong critic both of neoclassical trade theory and more generally of equilibrium theorizing in economics, which he believed to neglect dynamic increasing returns, the principle of cumulative causation, and the resulting path-dependence of many important macroeconomic variables. He came to regard exports as the only genuinely exogenous component of aggregate demand, since domestic consumption, investment and government expenditure were all, in the final analysis, determined by income. Thus Kaldor explained Britain's relatively poor growth performance after 1945 in terms of its poor export performance, and inspired a substantial international literature on the theory of balance-of-payments-constrained growth (McCombie and Thirlwall 1994).

He was also heavily involved in policy debates. In 1950 he set out the fundamental principles of a prices and incomes policy to permit full employment to be maintained without the risk of serious cost inflation. After a flirtation with free market liberalism in the early 1930s, Kaldor was a lifelong supporter of moderate democratic socialism. He believed in a mixed economy, with progressive redistributive taxation (preferably levied on expenditure, not on income) rather than extensive nationalization as the most useful egalitarian measure open to a social democratic government. As an adviser to British Labour governments between 1964 and 1976 he grappled with the seemingly insoluble problems of slow economic growth, balance of payments deficits and accelerating inflation. He was never afraid to suggest unorthodox and controversial policies, including the short-lived Selective Employment Tax on jobs in the service sector; this was intended to promote growth in manufacturing, where he believed the prospects for productivity growth to be much greater. Kaldor consistently opposed membership of the then Common Market (now the European Union), on the grounds that through cumulative causation it would increase Britain's economic disadvantages, rather than reducing them.

After 1979 he became the most influential intellectual opponent of monetarist ideas, rejecting Milton Friedman's version of the quantity theory in favour of the post-Keynesian theory of endogenous money and fiercely criticizing the deflationary consequences of Margaret Thatcher's monetarist experiment from the Labour benches in the House of Lords (he was made a life peer in 1974). The disastrous economic consequences of Mrs Thatcher, Kaldor maintained, could only be reversed by a return to the first principles of Keynesian macroeconomic management. To restore full employment he therefore urged a policy of low interest rates ("cheap money") and an expansionary fiscal policy. Appropriate monetary and fiscal policies could be relied upon to restrain demand inflation, Kaldor believed. To control cost inflation he proposed a return to the centralized incomes policy that he had consistently advocated since 1950, and also argued for international agreement on commodity price stabilization schemes to prevent a repetition of the explosion in the prices of oil and grains that had generated high and increasing rates of inflation throughout the world in the 1970s (Kaldor 1996).

In endorsing these "Old Labour" policies Kaldor was swimming against a very strong neo-liberal tide, which was highly influential even in what professed to be parties of the Left. His fundamental critique of neoclassical economic theory was no more successful, and in the last decade of his life Kaldor was largely ignored by a mainstream economics profession that was increasingly intolerant of any dissent. However, he remains an inspiration to post-Keynesians, and to institutionalists, social economists and other dissident groupings in twenty-first century heterodox economics.

JOHN E. KING

See also:

Business cycles and growth (III); Cambridge School of economics (II); Growth (III); Roy Forbes Harrod (I); Income distribution (III); Richard Ferdinand Kahn (I); Keynesianism (II); Macroeconomics (III); Post-Keynesianism (II); Joan Violet Robinson (I).

References and further reading

Beveridge, W.H. (1944), *Full Employment in a Free Society: A Report*, London: Allen & Unwin.
Buiter, W.H. (2010), 'The limits to fiscal stimulus', *Oxford Review of Economic Policy*, **26** (1), 48–70.
Kaldor, N. (1960–89), *Collected Economic Essays*, London: Duckworth.
Kaldor, N. (1996), *Causes of Growth and Stagnation in the World Economy*, Cambridge: Cambridge University Press.
King, J.E. (2009), *Nicholas Kaldor*: Basingstoke: Palgrave Macmillan.
McCombie, J.S.L. and A.P. Thirlwall (1994), *Economic Growth and the Balance-of-Payments Constraint*, Basingstoke: Macmillan.
Neumann, J. von (1945–46), 'A model of general economic equilibrium', *Review of Economic Studies*, **13** (1), 1–9.
Pasinetti, L.L. (2007), *Keynes and the Cambridge Keynesians: A 'Revolution in Economics' to be Accomplished*, Cambridge: Cambridge University Press.
Targetti, F. (1992), *Nicholas Kaldor: the Economics and Politics of Capitalism as a Dynamic System*, Oxford: Clarendon Press.
Targetti, F. and A.P. Thirlwall (eds) (1989), *The Essential Kaldor*, London: Duckworth.
Thirlwall, A.P. (1987), *Nicholas Kaldor*, Brighton: Harvester.

Ronald Harry Coase (1910–2013)

In 1991, Ronald Harry Coase was awarded the Sveriges Riksbank Prize in Economic Sciences in Memory of Alfred Nobel, for his introduction of transaction costs and property rights to explain the functioning of the economic system. Two articles were cited: "The nature of the firm" (Coase 1937) – seminal for recent theories of the firm – and "The problem of social cost" (1960) – seminal for the Law and Economics movement. These articles are sometimes contrasted, illustrating Coase's political evolution from Socialism to membership of the Mont Pèlerin Society: the 1937 article, focusing on the costs of the market, can be read as defending economic planning, while the latter, from which originated the "Coase theorem", is typically interpreted as defending a market solution to externalities. Despite their divergences, both articles illustrate the main features of Coase's approach to economics. First, they develop a comparative institutional method, that is, they compare the production value yielded by alternative arrangements net of the costs of their operation. Second, they are based on empirical material and call for realism in the analysis, leading to the introduction of transaction costs as an explanation of the firm, and the economic role of the law, respectively.

These articles were the source of a renewed interest in institutions among economists, and paved the way for the different trends of institutional economics. Coase, however, contributed to other fields of economic theory (Medema 1994; Ménard and Bertrand 2016): he is cited as being the originator of the concept of rational expectations; his reflection on accounting (Coase 1938) is considered a crucial step in the development of the notion of subjective opportunity cost; he was one of the first to propose a multi-part tariff for firms with decreasing average costs in "The marginal cost controversy" (1946); and he claimed as early as 1972 that a monopoly selling durable goods would set a perfectly competitive price and output, what is known today as the "Coase conjecture".

The Firm and the Producer's Decision

Coase was born on 29 December 1910 in a London suburb and was the only child of a rather humble family (Coase 1995; Wang 2014). His career as an economist results, in his own words, from "a series of accidents" (Coase 1988b: 5) that led him to graduate in 1932 with a commerce degree from the London School of Economics (LSE), where he came back to teach two years later. There he was influenced by Arnold Plant, who introduced him to economic reasoning and the benefits of a competitive system. Also influential were Lionel Robbins and Friedrich Hayek, and his fellow student Ronald Fowler.

It was during his studies at the LSE that Coase began wondering why an alternative coordination mode – hierarchy – existed, if the pricing system was functioning as perfectly as claimed by economists. Thanks to a scholarship he spent the last year of his LSE degree travelling around the United States and looking for answers to his questions about lateral and vertical integration. As early as 1932 he ended up with the famous answer: the pricing system is costly to operate. "The nature of the firm" was not published until 1937 because during the same period he and Fowler were using some statistics on the cycle of the pork price, usually explained by the cobweb theorem, to show that producers' expectations were not static (Coase and Fowler 1935). Moreover his work within Plant's research group resulted in a series of articles calling for the inclusion of economic concepts in accounting, specifically the notion of subjective opportunity cost (Coase 1938). The subjectivity of the producers' decisions under uncertainty explains some of his criticisms of imperfect competition theory from this period too (see Bertrand 2015a).

At first "The nature of the firm" went unnoticed, but thanks to the instant success of "The problem of social cost" (1960) and, then, of Oliver Williamson's use of Coase's insights, it has become the obligatory standard reference for any theory of the firm.

Law, Government and the Market

As early as 1935, while in charge of a course on public utilities, Coase began a series of empirical studies on the management of water, gas, electricity, postal office and broadcasting services in Great Britain. Leaving the LSE for the USA in 1951, he extended his empirical studies to US radio and television institutions. In an article on the Federal Communications Commission (1959), he criticized the then dominant Pigovian theory of externalities, an argument that was developed in "The problem of social cost". This article is often reduced to the "Coase theorem" (a name actually given by Stigler 1966: 113), which claims that if transaction costs are zero and property rights are defined, exchanges of rights will lead to an optimal allocation of resources that is independent of the initial distribution of these rights. Coase's argument, however, went further: when transaction costs are introduced, the initial distribution of rights may influence the result and other solutions than the market, such as the firm or public regulation, are to be considered. This is why Coase vehemently criticized the economists' focus on his eponymous theorem, which was only a first step in his reasoning (Bertrand 2010).

Coase eventually arrived at the Law School of the University of Chicago in 1964, where he stayed until his retirement in 1981. His colleagues there were Harold Demsetz, Frank Knight, George Stigler and Milton Friedman. He became the editor of the *Journal of Law and Economics* (first with Aaron Director), in which he favoured the publication of articles dealing with the influence of law on the economic system and consisting of empirical studies on the actual effects of public regulation – studies that made him doubtful about the actual benefits of regulation (Campbell and Klaes 2005). Among his own empirical studies criticizing public intervention in case of so-called market failures, one became well known: "The lighthouse in economics" (1974) suggested that English lighthouses were privately and efficiently provided between the seventeenth and the nineteenth centuries.

During the 1970s and 1980s, he wrote some articles in methodology and the history of economic thought, particularly on Adam Smith and Alfred Marshall (they are collected in Coase 1994). Just before his death on 2 September 2013, with the aid of Ning Wang, he published a book on China's transition to capitalism (Coase and Wang 2012) and launched a new journal, *Man and the Economy*.

A Plea for Realism in Economics

The diversity of the themes studied by Coase does not hide the unity of his method. His early call for realism permeates all of his works and in "How should economists choose?" (1982), he explicitly opposed it to Friedman's instrumentalist manifesto (see Mäki 1998). This realism explains his criticism of standard microeconomics, of its abstract assumption of rational utility maximizers and its design of policies by comparison to an ideal world devoid of institutions: a "blackboard economics" in which "we have consumers without humanity, firms without organization, and even exchange without markets" (Coase 1988a: 3). Opposing Robbins's formalist definition of economics, and more influenced by Smith, Marshall and Plant, Coase gives his preference to theories that explain the working of the actual economic system and to policies designed by comparing alternative institutional arrangements (see Coase 1992). This accounts for the importance in his work of empirical studies, even if they are guided by political and theoretical presuppositions (Pratten 2001; Bertrand 2015b).

ÉLODIE BERTRAND

See also:

Chicago School (II); Institutional economics (III); Public economics (III); Theory of the firm (III).

References and further reading

Bertrand, E. (2010), 'The three roles of the "Coase theorem" in Coase's works', *European Journal of the History of Economic Thought*, **17** (4), 975–1000.

Bertrand, E. (2015a), 'From the firm to economic policy: the problem of Coase's cost', *History of Political Economy*, **47** (3), 481–510.

Bertrand, E. (2015b), 'Coase's choice of methodology', *Cambridge Journal of Economics*, doi: 10.1093/cje/bev072.

Campbell, D. and M. Klaes (2005), 'The principle of institutional direction: Coase's regulatory critique of intervention', *Cambridge Journal of Economics*, **29** (2), 263–88.

Coase, R.H. (1937), 'The nature of the firm', *Economica*, New Series, **4** (16), 386–405.

Coase, R.H. (1938), 'Business organization and the accountant' (a series of 12 articles), *The Accountant*, October–December, 470–72, 505–7, 537–8, 559–60, 607–8, 631–2, 665–66, 705–6, 737–9, 775–7, 814–15, 834–5.

Coase, R.H. (1946), 'The marginal cost controversy', *Economica*, New Series, **13** (51), 169–82.

Coase, R.H. (1959), 'The Federal Communications Commission', *Journal of Law and Economics*, **2** (October), 1–40.

Coase, R.H. (1960), 'The problem of social cost', *Journal of Law and Economics*, **3** (October), 1–44.

Coase, R.H. (1972), 'Durability and monopoly', *Journal of Law and Economics*, **15** (1), 143–9.

Coase, R.H. (1974), 'The lighthouse in economics', *Journal of Law and Economics*, **17** (2), 357–76.

Coase, R.H. (1982), 'How should economists choose?', G. Warren Nutter Lecture in Political Economy, Washington, DC: American Enterprise Institute for Public Policy Research.

Coase, R.H. (1988a), *The Firm, the Market and the Law*, Chicago, IL: University of Chicago Press.

Coase, R.H. (1988b), 'The nature of the firm: origin, meaning, influence', *Journal of Law, Economics, and Organization*, **4** (1), 3–47.

Coase, R.H. (1992), 'The institutional structure of production', *American Economic Review*, **82** (4), 713–19.

Coase, R.H. (1994), *Essays on Economics and Economists*, Chicago, IL: University of Chicago Press.

Coase, R.H. (1995), 'Lives of the laureates: thirteen Nobel economists: Ronald H. Coase', in W. Breit and R.W. Spencer (eds), *Lives of the Laureates. Thirteen Nobel Economists*, 3rd edn, Cambridge, MA: MIT Press, pp. 227–49.

Coase, R.H. and R.F. Fowler (1935), 'Bacon production and the pig-cycle in Great Britain', *Economica*, **2** (6), 142–67.

Coase, R.H. and N. Wang (2012), *How China Became Capitalist*, London: Palgrave Macmillan.

Mäki, U. (1998), 'Is Coase a realist?', *Philosophy of the Social Sciences*, **28** (1), 5–31.

Medema, S.G. (1994), *Ronald H. Coase*, London: Macmillan.

Ménard, C. and E. Bertrand (2016), *The Elgar Companion to Ronald H. Coase*, Cheltenham, UK and Northampton, MA, USA: Edward Elgar.

Pratten, S. (2001), 'Coase on broadcasting, advertising and policy', *Cambridge Journal of Economics*, **25** (5), 617–38.

Stigler, G.J. (1966), *The Theory of Price*, 3rd edn, New York: Macmillan.

Wang, N. (2014), 'In memoriam: Ronald H. Coase, December 29, 1910–September 2, 2013', *Man and the Economy*, **1** (1), 125–40.

Richard Abel Musgrave (1910–2007)

Musgrave (14 December 1910–15 January 2007) was born into a family with partially Jewish background in Königstein im Taunus, a small town north of Frankfurt am Main. In his family, endorsement of liberal and cosmopolitan ideals was accompanied by Anglophile sentiments. His father, Curt Abel-Musgrave, held a degree in chemistry, but published widely on socio-political themes and was a translator for his friends Sir Arthur Conan Doyle and Rudyard Kipling, while the writings of his grandfather, Carl Abel, include German translations of Shakespeare. Richard Abel Musgrave's scholarly achievements in combining heterogeneous traditions and "translating" economic concepts from German-language public economics to Anglo-Saxon market failure theory have a background in the cosmopolitan stance as well as in the sense of the value of plurality and wider horizons characteristic of his family. Autobiographical notes inform us about Richard's youthful hopes for the Weimar Republic, "that ill-fated yet noble experiment in German democracy" (Musgrave 1986, 1: vii). In 1930, he went to the University of Munich to begin his study of economics. Here he heard Adolf Weber lecturing on economics along the lines of Cassel's (1923) *Theory of Social Economy*, and was impressed by Otto von Zwiedeneck-Südenhorst, an Austrian economist renowned for publications on social policy and wages whose teaching programme included capital theory à la Böhm-Bawerk. Lasting influences date back to his Heidelberg years (1931–33) where he earned his diploma degree in 1933. Three names stand out: Jacob Marschak (whose work with Emil Lederer and the Kiel Institute contributed to a timely emphasis on macroeconomic problems, making Musgrave aware of stabilization as a core function of government); Alfred Weber (who gave seminars discussing the contributions of his brother Max, whose reasoning on fact and value in social science remained a fixed point of Musgrave's thought); and Otto Pfleiderer, the author of a book on public sector-related accounting containing a crisp summary of the German-language literature on the conceptual basis of social wants and public goods. The intellectual and political environment of the Heidelberg economics department (which under Weber's leadership was clearly anti-Nazi) was congenial to his father's foresight in leading to Musgrave's successful application for a fellowship of the International Institute of Education, which brought him to the University of Rochester in the USA in fall 1933. Having been trained there in Marshallian economics, he moved to Harvard where he became a member of a group of brilliant graduate students, among them Paul Samuelson. Musgrave received his MA in 1936 and his PhD in 1937. He became a US citizen and served on the Board of Governors of the Federal Reserve System, eventually as assistant to Chairman Marriner Eccles. He returned to academia in 1947, teaching first at Swarthmore College. Musgrave moved to the University of Michigan at Ann Arbor in 1949, where he worked on what was to become his magnum opus (Musgrave 1959) in a stimulating intellectual environment, including theorists such as Kenneth Boulding, Wolfgang Stolper and Lawrence Klein. Positions at Johns Hopkins University (1958–61) and Princeton preceded Musgrave's return to Harvard in 1965, where he retired in 1981.

Musgrave (1986, 1: viii) summarizes his early work on public good provision as a PhD student in Harvard (culminating in Musgrave's 1939 seminal paper on public goods) in the following way: "In contrast to the Lindahl model, the Pigovian framework offered an alternative approach, and the puzzle was how to merge the two strands". Indeed, an outstanding characteristic of Musgrave's achievements is his ability to integrate distant paradigms and approaches: the organization of synthesis. He is aware of his specific background: "I could claim the comparative advantage (and what an advantage it was) of acquaintance with the continental literature – Austrian, Italian, and Swedish" (Musgrave 1986: viii). It was an absolute advantage and the starting point for public good theory as the core micro base of the public sector: the concepts of public (that is, non-excludable and non-rival) goods and of merit wants were foreign to the Anglo-Saxon tradition, whose pertinent reasoning since Hume was based solely on non-excludability. Pigou introduced externalities as the core concept of market failure, but public good theory was not further developed.

Musgrave (1996: 149) writes that he "likes to think that his own initial paper on the Wicksell–Lindahl model . . . helped to bring the problem to Paul Samuelson's attention, then a fellow graduate student at Harvard" who derived the summation rule for non-rival goods in the 1950s. In Musgrave (1959) public goods and merit wants are integrated in the market failure framework. Musgrave was aware of the tension embodied in the concept of merit wants in the context of neoclassical economics. While sticking to the project of an individualistic explanation of the public sector, he takes seriously the arguments of German writers who emphasized the limits of purely individualist accounts of the state: certain valuations, particularly regarding basic patterns of core public institutions in areas such as law enforcement, defence or education, cannot be fully understood in terms of purely individualist consumer preferences. Individual valuations regarding those issues make sense if, and only if, individuals are considered as members of communities. In addition, consumer sovereignty may be a problematic assumption in cases of endogenous preferences (addictive goods, learning-by-using intensive goods), or of systematic cognitive difficulties of the kind recently stressed by advocates of "libertarian paternalism". To capture all those concerns, Musgrave suggested the concept of merit wants.

Concerning the overall development of modern public economics, a further dimension of Musgrave's contribution must be stressed; he suggested the well-known architecture of the branches of the public sector as three naves of the cathedral: allocation, distribution, and stabilization, which partly complemented and partly superseded the traditional distinction of revenue and expenditure side of the public budget related to a narrower conception of public finance. As put by Musgrave (1983), one or the other "chapel" (such as fiscal federalism, to be further pursued by his student Charles Tiebout) was added to this cathedral in the course of time.

Musgrave's approach to synthesis is clearly combinatorial rather than amalgamating. He prefers a transparently organized cathedral (with three naves and several chapels, to use his own metaphors) to a monolithic building whose complex structuring elements are hidden behind a more or less richly ornamented façade. A quick look to the table of contents of Musgrave (1986), a two-volume collection of his articles, shows that he provided contributions to almost all of the concepts, issues and questions which turned out to be important within the encompassing edifice of modern public economics. Musgrave stresses issues of distribution in the 1980s and 1990s when allocation theory carried the day, whereas he emphasized the role of the state regarding allocation in the late 1950s, when "the theory of Public Finance has been dominated by the study of the effects of fiscal policy upon the levels of income, employment and prices." (Musgrave and Peacock 1958: ix).

Musgrave's overall theoretical architecture has profound implications for the view of the relation between state and market. "To ask by how much the state should be restrained . . . leaves the state as the defendant who must prove his innocence", says Musgrave (for example, Buchanan and Musgrave 1999: 129) and argues that this perspective is flawed. Instead, he sticks to the German tradition of conceptualizing the state as a set of institutions complementary to the market system (ibid.: 37). While admitting the dangers of distortions in the public sector, Musgrave insists that integrating policy failure into the modelling premises is theoretically unsound, and that the propagation and popularization of suchlike views in the last quarter of the twentieth century "has been destructive of good government" (ibid.: 1999: 35). A priori pessimistic visions of public choice mechanisms are not appropriate, while at the same time using idealized models of market exchange. He thinks that we should aim at a neutral framework in which distortions/imperfections related to both types of institutions may be dealt with symmetrically. Following Wicksell (1896), for Musgrave the logic and problems of political provision belong to the core of the theory.

Last but not least, Musgrave was not only an architect of and a prolific contributor to modern public economics, but also one of its most eminent historians. Regarding "that most exciting aspect of history which is the history of ideas" (Musgrave 1983: 1), he is not only "historian by osmosis" (a term self-referentially invoked with characteristic understatement as "the prime benefit of growing older"): his seminal paper on "The voluntary exchange theory of the public economy" (1939) employs the history of ideas in the development of theory, dealing with pertinent contributions of Sax, Wicksell (1896) and Lindahl (1919). In *The Theory of Public Finance*, Musgrave (1959) succinctly summarizes the historical background of key concepts in carefully crafted footnotes. The introduction to the collection *Classics in the Theory of Public Finance* (Musgrave and Peacock 1959) consists of the most useful ten pages for anybody who seeks a first orientation with respect to the various paths along which modern public economics developed from the diverse traditions of the nineteenth century. In more recent contributions, Musgrave (1983, 1996) systematically deals with the emergence of modern public economics as well as with its pre-history, particularly the role of German, Austrian, Italian and Swedish influences. "With the '20s, what has here been called the tradition of Finanzwissenschaft had largely come to an end. When German economists resumed fiscal analysis after the close of the war it was in the spirit of the English language model", writes Musgrave (1996: 164). This is rather downplaying Musgrave's own role in bringing about the foundational synthesis of modern public economics.

RICHARD STURN

See also:

German and Austrian schools (II); Public economics (III); Public choice (II); Adolph Heinrich Gotthilf Wagner (I); Knut Wicksell (I).

References

Buchanan, J.M. and R.A. Musgrave (1999), *Public Finance and Public Choice: Two Contrasting Visions of the State*, Cambridge MA: MIT Press.
Cassel, G. (1923), *The Theory of Social Economy*, rev. trans. of the 5th German edn, New York: Harcourt, Brace & Co.
Lindahl, E. (1919), *Die Gerechtigkeit der Besteuerung*, Lund: Gleerupska Universitets-Bokhandeln.

Musgrave, R.A. (1939), 'The voluntary exchange theory of public economy', *Quarterly Journal of Economics*, **53** (February), 213–17.

Musgrave, R.A. (1959), *The Theory of Public Finance*, New York: McGraw-Hill.

Musgrave, R.A. (1983), 'Public finance, now and then', *Finanzarchiv*, NF, **41** (1), 1–10.

Musgrave, R.A. (1986), *Collected Papers: Public Finance in a Democratic Society*, vol. 1, *Social Goods, Taxation and Fiscal Policy*, vol. 2, *Fiscal Doctrine, Growth, and Institutions*, Brighton: Wheatsheaf Books.

Musgrave, R.A. (1996), 'Public finance and Finanzwissenschaft: traditions compared', *Finanzarchiv*, NF, **53** (2), 145–93.

Musgrave, R.A. and A.T. Peacock (eds) (1958), *Classics in the Theory of Public Finance*. London and New York: Macmillan.

Sinn, H.-W. (2007), *Please Bring Me the New York Times: On the European Roots of Richard Abel Musgrave*, CESifo Working Paper No. 2050, Munich.

Wicksell, K. (1896), *Finanztheoretische Untersuchungen*, Jena: Gustav Fischer.

Tibor Scitovsky (1910–2002)

Tibor Scitovsky (3 November 1910–1 June 2002) lived a varied life, both in the private sphere and in his public activity as an economist. Born into a rich Hungarian family of aristocratic origins, he was raised in a pre-capitalist society, in which money flowed freely and was there to be spent, not saved. His father, Tibor de Scitovszky Senior was a senior civil servant and banker, becoming Minister of Foreign Affairs for the ultra-conservative government of Count István Bethlen (1924–25), and then president of one of Hungary's largest banks. His mother, Hanna, was related to the noble La Rochefoucauld family, and her Thursday-afternoon "at homes" were a meeting place for Budapest's political and artistic elite, occasionally being attended by such notable guests as Paul Valéry and Thomas Mann, Cardinal Pacelli (later Pope Pius XII) and the provocative Colette.

Having enrolled in the Faculty of Law at the University of Budapest, in 1928 Scitovsky was seized by the desire for emancipation from a family he found suffocating, and obtained permission to continue his studies abroad. Arriving at Cambridge in October 1929, and looking for a field of study more interesting than international law, he switched to economics. Thus he met Maurice Dobb and Joan Robinson. He would later thank the latter for encouraging independent thought and a critical spirit:

> I had just started on economics a month earlier and did not even know there was a theory about money. . . . Joan read [my paper] while I watched her and waited with bated breath for her to deliver the verdict. There was no harm, she said, in listing what other people had to say about money but she looked in vain for my theory about it. So she suggested that I write the paper again, this time presenting my own ideas on the subject. (Scitovsky n.d.: 40; hereafter *Memoirs*)

Under Lionel Robbins and Friedrich von Hayek at the London School of Economics (1935–38), Scitovsky advanced further in his studies. He would later remember being impressed by "the elegant logic of the perfectly competitive model's self-equilibrating mechanism, but equally disturbed by its unreality and apparent uselessness" in explaining crises and unemployment (*Memoirs*: 54).

He first arrived in the USA in the fall of 1939 on a Leon Travelling Fellowship, and stayed there until 1943. These were the most trying years, with cultural integration proving difficult. Thus he wrote to Nicholas Kaldor: "It seems to be primarily the long tradition of culture which makes life so very pleasant in England and in France and it seems to have less to do with the particular form of government than I thought. I feel very home-sick for England" (letter from Scitovsky to Kaldor. 11 December 1939, King's College Archives, Cambridge University). His position in the USA during this time was precarious. He did not have a job and, for a time, had to depend for support on his new wife. Having been arrested on the suspicion of being a "premature anti-fascist", that is, a communist (*Memoirs*: 68), he escaped deportation by being drafted into the US Army (1943–46) and, as a result, being granted citizenship. Thanks to his good knowledge of German and French, he was first sent to Europe as a truck driver in a team along with J.K. Galbraith, E.F. Schumacher and his friend Kaldor. There he was involved in the capture of a dozen leading Nazis, including Hermann Göring and Albert Speer. Later he worked on the US Strategic Bombing Survey.

At the end of the war, he decided to stay in the USA, first receiving an appointment at Stanford, where he began teaching the new macroeconomics of Keynes, and was awarded tenure in 1949. He spent most of his career at Stanford (1946–58, 1970–76 and 1978–81), with an interim decade at Berkeley (1958–68), and appointments at several places, including the London School of Economics (1976–78). While at Berkeley, he was visiting professor at Harvard (1965–66) and research fellow at the Organisation for Economic Co-operation and Development in Paris (1966–68). Scitovsky went on teaching after his retirement at the University of California, Santa Cruz until the mid-1980s. He remained intellectually active to the end of his life, publishing articles on economics throughout the 1990s. He died in 2002, in Palo Alto, California.

Theoretical Contributions

For much of his life, Scitovsky worked on subjects related to welfare economics. His most famous and universally praised work was "A note on welfare propositions in economics" (1941), which contained what later came to be known as the "Scitovsky reversal paradox": that is, an economic policy innovation designed to redistribute wealth can, even if giving rise to a Pareto optimum, lead the individuals to be worse off to give money to those benefiting from the redistribution in order to persuade them to return to the original allocation. Among the other articles worthy of mention are "The political economy of consumers' rationing" (1942a) and "A reconsideration of the theory of tariffs" (1942b). The first explained the reasons for wartime rationing, which led James Tobin of Yale to write a dissertation on the subject; the second, which was reprinted and translated in foreign languages, pointed out the difference and relations between tariffs and producers' profit margins. With the publication of *Welfare and Competition* in 1951, Scitovsky's international reputation as standard welfare economist was established. Beginning in the early 1950s, however, and especially with the security of a permanent post, his publications progressively began to reflect a growing personal interest in ethical and cultural questions.

In "Ignorance as a source of oligopoly power" (1950), he claimed that the increasing complexity of consumer goods, caused by technological progress, leaves the majority of their buyers unable to judge the quality of the products, something that favours the formation of oligopolies. "What price economic progress?" (1959) deals with Erich Fromm's concept of alienation in a mass-consumption society in order to show the political implications and effect on human well-being of the growing specialization of knowledge, and "A critique of the present and proposed standards" (1960) elaborates on Galbraith's mistrust of the judgement of the consumer as guide and arbiter of resource allocation, in order to develop a critique of the conventional theory of consumer choice. In "On the principle of consumer sovereignty" (1962), it is asserted that the increasing neglect by the mass production system of an informed minority's preferences might have undesirable effects upon the development of majority preferences as well.

It was only shortly before retirement that Scitovsky wrote *The Joyless Economy* (1976), his successful, though controversial, monograph, which summarizes his inquiry into the sources of human satisfaction. The first part of the book presents a simple account of the theories of arousal by the motivational psychologists Donald O. Hebb (1955) and Daniel E. Berlyne (1960). These theories relate feelings of pain and pleasure to the physiology of the brain, showing paradoxically that the absence of pain, that is, comfort, leads to pain in terms of boredom, and that pleasantly stimulating activities, undertaken for no particular reason other than recreational ones, were major sources of satisfaction. The second part moves from individual psychology to social analysis, documenting the excessive demand for comfort in the American lifestyle and showing how mass production and the Puritan work ethic combine to deprive people of the skills and tastes necessary for the enjoyment of creative leisure.

If Scitovsky's earlier theoretical contributions were well received, the same cannot be said of *The Joyless Economy* (see Aufhauser 1976; Friedman 1976; Peacock 1976; Zikmund 1977). First, it contained too much psychology for the average economist of the time. Although Hebb's and Berlyne's theories on the origins of behaviour were well received in their own discipline, economics in the 1970s was simply not ready for such innovative change. Secondly, by emphasizing the distinction between pleasure and comfort, in keeping with the psychological theory of arousal, Scitovsky was distancing himself from the hedonistic-utilitarian perspective and thus criticizing the neoclassical theory of consumer behaviour. Thirdly, Scitovsky's analysis of modern consumer choices represented an open attack on a value system based on conspicuous consumption, on a vestigial Puritan ethic and on an educational philosophy that favoured technical specialization over the cultivation of the liberal and performing arts. The book's popular style, too, saw him lose status among academics.

It took an almost 20-year lapse, and the publication of the second edition in 1992, for *The Joyless Economy* to be praised. By then, thanks to the experimental work on rational choice theory by behavioural psychologists Daniel Kahneman and Amos Tversky (1979), economics was slowly opening itself to interdisciplinary research, and, thanks to the investigations of Richard Easterlin (1974), the economics of happiness was now beginning to be viewed as a new, promising approach to the study of welfare. Scitovsky is now cited as a forerunner of happiness studies in economics (Frey and Stutzer 2002; Easterlin 2003) and listed among the precursors of behavioural economics (Angner and Loewenstein 2012). However it must be noted that the appropriation of Scitovsky as precursor by the behavioural economists overlooks significant differences between them. Whereas Kahneman sought to modify the rationality axioms in the light of empirically observed systematic deviation, Scitovsky implicitly rejected the theoretical edifice of axiomatic rationality. His proposed revision of economics called for an entirely different conception of economic behaviour, one informed by psychology of a different kind. Furthermore, and different from the behavioural economists, Scitovsky's recourse to experimentation stopped with his appropriation of the psychological findings. Once he had drawn on Berlyne and Hebb in elaborating his theory, he offered no obvious further role for experimental investigation. With regard to the economics of happiness, Scitovsky was critical of Easterlin's emphasis on the effect of ranking in the income scale, or relative consumption, on reported well-being, implying that it overlooked the main basis of true happiness, namely, what Hannah Arendt (1958) described as the "productive life", or *vita activa*. If Scitovsky's influence on the economics profession has been diffuse, it has been more substantial in the literature of consumer sociology, informing the work of contemporary critics such as Juliet Schor, author of *The Overworked American* (1991).

VIVIANA DI GIOVINAZZO

See also:

Behavioural and cognitive economics (III); Nicholas Kaldor (I); Welfare economics (III).

References and further reading

Angner, E. and G. Loewenstein (2012), 'Behavioral economics', in U. Mäki (ed.), *Handbook of the Philosophy of Science: Philosophy of Economics*, Amsterdam: Elsevier, pp. 641–90.

Arendt, H. (1958), *The Human Condition*, Chicago, IL: University of Chicago Press.

Aufhauser, K. (1976), 'Review of *The Joyless Economy*', *Economic Journal*, **86** (344), 911–13.

Berlyne, D. (1960), *Conflict, Arousal, and Curiosity*, New York: McGraw-Hill.

Easterlin, R.A. (1974), 'Does economic growth improve the human lot? Some empirical evidence', in P.A. David and M.W. Reder (eds), *Nations and Households in Economic Growth: Essays in Honor of Moses Abramovitz*, New York: Academic Press, pp. 89–125.

Easterlin R.A. (2003), 'Explaining happiness', *Proceedings of the National Academy of Science*, **100** (19), 11176–83.

Frey, B.S. and A. Stutzer (2002), *Happiness & Economics*, Princeton, NJ: Princeton University Press.

Friedman, J.W. (1976), 'Review of *The Joyless Economy*', *Journal of Political Economy*, **84** (6), 1372–4.

Hebb, D.O. (1955), 'Drives and the C.N.S. (Conceptual Nervous System)', *Psychological Review*, **62** (4), 243–54.

Kahneman, D. and A. Tversky (1979), 'Prospect theory: an analysis of decision under risk', *Econometrica*, **47** (2), 263–92.

Peacock, A. (1976), 'Review of *The Joyless Economy*', *Journal of Economic Literature*, **14** (4), 1278–80.

Schor, J.B. (1991), *The Overworked American: The Unexpected Decline Of Leisure*, New York: Basic Books.

Scitovsky, T. (1941), 'A note on welfare propositions in economics', *Review of Economic Studies*, **9** (1), 77–88.

Scitovsky, T. (1942a), 'The political economy of consumers' rationing', *Review of Economic Studies*, **24** (3), 114–24.

Scitovsky, T. (1942b), 'A reconsideration of the theory of tariffs', *Review of Economic Studies*, **9** (2), 89–110.

Scitovsky, T. (1950), 'Ignorance as a source of oligopoly power', *American Economic Review*, **40** (2), 48–53.

Scitovsky, T. (1951), *Welfare and Competition: The Economics of a Fully Employed Economy*, Chicago, IL: Richard D. Irwin.

Scitovsky, T. (1960), 'A critique of the present and proposed standards', *American Economic Review*, **50** (2), 13–20.

Scitovsky, T. (1962), 'On the principle of consumer sovereignty', *American Economic Review*, **52** (2), 262–8.

Scitovsky, T. (1972), 'What's wrong with the arts is what's wrong with society', *American Economic Review*, **62** (1/2), 62–9.

Scitovsky, T. (1976), *The Joyless Economy: An Inquiry into Human Satisfaction and Consumer Dissatisfaction*, Oxford: Oxford University Press.

Scitovsky, T. (1992), *The Joyless Economy: The Psychology of Human Satisfaction*, 2nd edn, Oxford: Oxford University Press. First published 1976 (see above).

Scitovsky, T. (n.d.), 'Memoirs of a joyful economist', undated typescript, Tibor Scitovsky Papers, Rare Book, Manuscript, and Special Collections Library, Duke University, Durham, NC.

Scitovsky, T. and A. Scitovsky (1959), 'What price economic progress?', *The Yale Review*, **49** (Autumn), 95–110.

Sen, A.K. (1996), 'Rationality, joy and freedom', *Critical Review*, **10** (4), 481–93.

Zikmund, W.J. (1977), 'Review of *The Joyless Economy*', *Journal of Marketing*, **41** (2), 137–8.

Maurice Allais (1911–2010)

Maurice Allais was born in Paris on 31 May 1911 and died in Saint-Cloud on 9 October 2010. He was admitted to the École Polytechnique in 1931, studied also at the École des Mines from 1934 to 1936 and then started to work in Nantes as an engineer. But since his time as a student, his interests had changed. His first interests were in theoretical physics – he was to come back to this subject at the end of his life – but he turned to economics. In 30 months, from January 1941 to July 1943, he wrote his *Traité d'économie pure*. This work was intended to be the first of eight volumes, a series entitled *À la recherche d'une discipline économique*, supposedly to deal successively with pure economics, real economy and the economy of the future. He gave up his ambitious project but it is possible to find in *Économie et intérêt*, published in 1947, part of the material he had prepared for his magnum opus, that is, the areas which dealt with interest, money and disequilibria affecting the real economy.

In 1946 Allais became a senior research fellow at the Centre National de la Recherche Scientifique. He also lectured at the Paris École des Mines (1944–88), at the Institut de Statistiques of the University of Paris (1947–68) and at the University of Paris X Nanterre (1970–85). He was awarded the 1988 Sveriges Riksbank's Prize in Economic Sciences in Memory of Alfred Nobel for his contribution to the theory of markets and efficient use of resources, with the nominating committee explicitly referring to *Traité d'économie pure* and *Économie et intérêt*. It stressed that "Allais' distinguished contribution may to some extent be regarded as a parallel to two important works published around the same time . . . : *Value and Capital* (1939) by Sir John Hicks and *Foundations of Economic Analysis* by Paul A. Samuelson (1947)" (in Allais 1989: 2).

Allais (1989: 5) affirmed that his subsequent works are only developments and complements to the *Traité*. However his discourse evolved. In 1943, he maintained that the complexity of the problems was such that they could only be analysed with mathematics. In the 1950s, he was more cautious. The problem lies in the fact that "in a science like economics, the rigour of the mathematical deductions can be deceptive. What matters is only the discussion of the premises and the results" (Allais 1954: 68).

The *Traité* is an important step in the renewal of general equilibrium models. But, at the end of the 1960s, Allais also developed a radical critique of such models and proposed a dynamic approach based on the search of obtainable surpluses. And while his first publications deal with pure economics, at the end of his life he devoted more time to empirical works and to questions of economic policy.

The Theory of Equilibrium

Allais dedicated his *Traité* to Léon Walras, Vilfredo Pareto, Irving Fisher and François Divisia. He wanted to make a synthesis and go farther. He thought that their theories were essentially static and his ambition was to introduce time in order to obtain a dynamics of equilibrium. In such a model, the choices of the agents depend on actual and future prices. However, at this stage Allais wanted to eliminate risk; he thus supposed that "any decision taken now and implying the future is verified" (1943 [1994, 3rd edition]: 60). This hypothesis led him to think that there exist as many elementary markets as future goods and services.

When, in the first parts of *Éléments d'économie politique pure* (Walras 1874–77 [1988]), Walras studies an economy deprived of circulating money, he does not explain how exchanges and payments are made. Allais (1943 [1994, 3rd edition]: 536) is more explicit. He deals with an "économie de compte", different from a barter economy. Prices are expressed in a money detached from all material connotation. Exchanges are centralized; a clearing house counts the revenues and expenses of the agents and settles the accounts through transfers.

Allais thus defines the framework of the majority of general equilibrium models. He did not pose the questions of the existence and uniqueness of equilibrium. The problem that interests him is stability. In an exchange economy, he supposes that the utility functions of the agents are separable. The process of adjustment depends on four restrictive hypotheses, typical of the Walrasian model: (1) the price system is unique, whether the system in equilibrium or not; (2) if in a market supply exceeds (falls short of) demand, the price diminishes (increases); (3) prices do not simultaneously adjust in all markets, but successively; and (4) exchanges are only made at equilibrium prices. To study convergence, Allais introduces a characteristic function defined as the sum of the absolute values of the differences between the values of supplies and demands:

$$Z = \sum_{i=1}^{n} p_i |z_i| \tag{1}$$

If, for all individuals, the value of demand of a good varies inversely to its price, the value of the characteristic function diminishes when its price adjusts, and equilibrium is stable. If this is not the case, but if, in the neighbourhood of equilibrium, the value of the global demand of a good increases less rapidly than the value of the global supply when the price rises, equilibrium is stable (Allais 1943 [1994, 3rd edition]: 477). Negishi (1962: 656) showed that Allais's hypotheses boils down to the assumption that goods are gross substitutes; if the price of a commodity rises while all other prices are unchanged, the demand for the other commodities increases.

Surplus, Social Return and Dynamics of the System

Pareto had rejected the Marshallian notion of surplus. But, in his *Manuele* (1906: 655–6), he proposed a new, somewhat sibylline, definition of it. Allais – who became aware of the work of Dupuit in 1973 only and thought very high of it – picked it up. Let h be an individual who, in the initial situation, has a quantity x_i^h of good i. Suppose that, in a new situation, it has a quantity $x_i^h + \delta_i^h$ thereof. Allais measures the surplus from which this individual benefits in the new situation with the quantity $\delta\sigma_1^h$ of good 1 which, if it were withdrawn from it, would bring back the individual's satisfaction to the level it was in the initial situation:

$$u^h(x_1^h + \delta x_1^h - \delta\sigma_1^h, \ldots, x_i^h + \delta x_i^h, \ldots, x_n^h + \delta x_n^h) = u^h(x_1^h, \ldots, x_i^h, \ldots, x_n^h) \tag{2}$$

The available surplus due to the change in the economy is the sum of the surpluses $\delta\sigma_1 = \sum_h \delta\sigma_1^h$. The maximum available surplus σ_1^* is defined as the greatest among the available surpluses when the whole set of the possible changes of the economy are considered, which leave unchanged the indices of the satisfaction of the agents. When the maximal available surplus is nil, it is impossible to improve the situation of a person without worsening that of another person, and the efficiency of the economy is at a maximum.

Allais then states, in 1943, the two propositions of what he calls the "Théorème du rendement social" – later known as the two theorems of welfare economics – (1) any situation of maximum efficiency is a market equilibrium, and (2) any market equilibrium is a situation of maximum efficiency. In *Économie et intérêt*, he generalizes the notion of social return to take future generations into account. The social return is said to be at maximum when any change of the state considered, which increases the satisfaction of some individuals in certain periods, diminishes the satisfaction of the same or other individuals but in some other periods.

What are the consequences of these propositions? Allais discards at the same time planning and laissez-faire. The maximization of the social return, he stresses, cannot be realized in laissez-faire conditions. In industries with increasing returns, monopolies will prevail and, fixing a price greater than the marginal cost, prevents the realization of the optimum. In the other activities, the imperfection of competition – and particularly the absence of markets for future goods – leads to a suboptimal allocation of resources. Against planning, Allais stresses that the determination of prices is a central question, which can only be solved by markets. To deprive oneself of this mechanism means to forbid any rigorous economic calculation. However, the necessity to resort to markets leaves the question of the property of the means of production completely open.

> The economic organization must rely on autonomous economic agents, having, each according to its share, the free disposal of the economic goods . . . But one can imagine a society . . . in which the various company managerial staffs could have . . . this free disposal . . . without the ownership of the means of production ceasing to be collective. (Allais 1943 [1994]: 663)

At that time many French companies were nationalized and Allais thought that the system could work smoothly provided that the managing staffs of the public firms had an effective power of decision.

Neo-Walrasian models of general equilibrium deal with an economy, in which agents' supply and demand goods in a centralized market in function of a general and centralized system of prices, which is announced to them. Allais (1971: 369; 1981 [1989]: 359) proposes instead a model of a decentralized search for surplus. He imagines an economy, where each agent is looking for one or more partners, who would accept an exchange susceptible to generate a surplus to be shared. Equilibrium is thus defined as the situation where there is no possibility to generate a surplus. It is an optimum. While, in a Walrasian economy, exchanges are made at the same time, at equilibrium prices determined by the *tâtonnememt*, Allais describes the path to equilibrium, which results from successive exchanges made at different prices.

Choices under Uncertainty

In *Traité*, Allais abstracted from uncertainty, but he studied the question in 1953 when he discussed the analyses made at that time of the behaviour of a rational man facing risk. Bernoulli's idea that the agents maximize the mathematical expectation of their utility had been picked up and transformed (Friedman and Savage, 1948). An ordinal index of preferences had been substituted for the measure of cardinal utility and it was admitted that the probabilities taken into account in choices were subjective and not objective. To formalize the behaviour of a rational agent, Paul Samuelson (1952) had introduced an independence axiom. Suppose that an individual prefers lottery p to lottery q. Let r be some other lottery, and α a probability. The independence axiom states that:

$$\alpha p + (1 - \alpha)r > \alpha q + (1 - \alpha)r \tag{3}$$

This implies that if two lotteries have a common part $(1 - \alpha)r$, the preference order is not modified by a change in this part. To show that this axiom is not self-evident, Allais proposed the following experiment. One first asks a person whether he or she prefers to receive 100 million euro (situation A) – the size of the sum is crucial in the experiment – or to participate in a lottery where there is a 10 per cent probability of winning 500 million, 89 per cent of winning 100 million and 1 per cent of not winning anything (situation B). Then this person is asked whether he or she prefers to receive 100 million with a probability of 11 per cent and nothing with a probability of 89 per cent (situation C) or to receive 500 million with a 10 per cent probability and nothing with a probability of 90 per cent (situation D). The independence axiom implies that the individual who prefers C to D will prefer A to B, and conversely: when shifting from C to A or from D to B, only the common part is modified, which, with a probability α equal to 89 per cent, allows a gain of 100 million in lotteries A and B, and nothing in lotteries C and D. However, many persons among those who took part in the test, preferred D to C while preferring A to B. This result is often presented as a paradox – Allais's paradox. But Allais stresses that this is no paradox and that the problem with the theory of the expected utility is that it neglects the dispersion of the gains. When important sums of money are at stake, many choose security in the neighbourhood of certainty, and this explains that they prefer A to B, that is, the certainty to have 100 million rather than to participate in a lottery where they could win 500 million but also lose everything. The expected utility theory does not only lack an empirical foundation, it is also based on an arbitrary definition of rationality.

Money and Cycles

In *Économie and intérêt*, Allais tries to explain why the economic agents prefer to keep money rather than buy assets likely to bring them an interest. He thinks that "the reason why economic agents have cash balances is the existence of costs for . . . the negotiation of assets or the realization of investments or bonds according to their needs" (Allais 1947 [1998]: 256). He then establishes the "Rule of the square root": the average cash balance M of an agent is $M = \sqrt{(Y\Gamma)}/2r$, where Y is the income, r the interest rate and Γ the costs inherent to the investment.

In an appendix to this book Allais develops a scheme to analyse the factors, which determine the interest rate. The economy is supposed to entail a single category of agents, whose life consists of two periods of equal duration. During each period, two generations of agents coexist: the younger and the elder. Each individual works only during his youth, and there is no inheritance. Money is introduced as a means of payment and store of value. Owing to the non-synchronization of incomes and expenses, the young agents need a cash balance, which will allow them to buy consumption goods during their old age. In this context, Allais establishes a series of results:

1. The use of a medium of circulation increases the interest rate above the level it would have in an account economy because holding money satisfies in part the propensity to save and thus slows the accumulation of real capital.
2. The equilibrium interest rate is an increasing function of the preference for the liquidity, but does not depend on the quantity of money.
3. The depreciation of money diminishes the values of the interest rate, which correspond to stable equilibria.

In 1953, Allais developed a monetary theory of the business cycle. For him, "there are only two 'sine qua non' factors for the cycle: the fact that the circulating medium can be hoarded, and the possible issuing of overdraft money" (Allais 1953b [2001]: 228). The model has four central equations. (1) During a period, the global expense is equal to the revenue of the previous period plus the excess of the actual over the desired cash balances. (2) The ratio of the total desired cash balance on the total expense is a decreasing function of the rate of growth of the total expense: agents diminish their balances during expansion and increase them during recessions. It is the classical phenomenon of hoarding. (3) The global quantity of circulating medium (notes plus deposits) is an increasing function of the rate of growth of the total expense: during expansions, commercial banks lower their rate of reserves and they increase it during recessions. (4) Finally, in each period, expense equals income. Under very general hypotheses, there is no stable equilibrium and, from any state of the system, the economy tends to a limit cycle.

In this context, Allais (1965 [2001]) proposed a new version of the quantity theory of money, based on a restatement of the function of demand for money – hereditary, relative and logistic. The demand for money is hereditary in the sense that the relative demand for money – defined as the ratio of the desired cash balance on the expense – is a function of the past evolution of the global expense; it is relative because the rate of oversight is not a constant but depends on the business cycle: the past is forgotten even more rapidly as the historical context was troubled; it is logistic because the relative demand for money is a logistic function of a coefficient of psychological expansion. Allais thus shifted from an essentially theoretical approach in the 1940s to another approach, which puts emphasis on the statistical analysis of empirical data.

ALAIN BÉRAUD

See also:

John Richard Hicks (I); Vilfredo Pareto (I); Paul Anthony Samuelson (I); Marie-Esprit-Léon Walras (I).

References and further reading

Allais, M. (1943), *À la recherche d'une discipline économique*, première partie, *L'économie pure*, vol. 1, Paris: Chez l'auteur, 2nd edn 1952 as *Traité d'économie pure*, Paris: Imprimerie nationale, 3rd edn 1994, Paris: Clément Juglar.
Allais, M. (1947), *Économie et intérêt*, Paris: Imprimerie nationale, 2nd edn 1998, Paris: Clément Juglar.

Allais, M. (1953a), 'Le comportement de l'homme rationnel devant le risque: critique des postulats et axiomes de l'école américaine', *Econometrica*, **21** (4), 503–46.

Allais, M. (1953b), 'Illustration de la théorie des cycles économique dans un modèle monétaire non linéaire', Communication au Congrès Européen de la Société d'Économétrie, reproduced in M. Allais (2001), *Fondements de la dynamique monétaire*, Paris: Clément Juglar.

Allais, M. (1954), 'Puissance et dangers de l'utilisation de l'outil mathématique en Économique', *Econometrica*, **22** (1), 58–71.

Allais, M. (1965), *Reformulation de la théorie quantitative de la monnaie*, Paris: SEDEIS, reproduced in M. Allais (2001), *Fondements de la dynamique monétaire*, Paris: Clément Juglar.

Allais, M. (1971), 'Les théories de l'équilibre économique général et de l'efficacité maximale. Impasses récentes et nouvelles perspectives', *Revue d'économie politique*, **81** (3), 331–409.

Allais, M. (1981), 'La théorie générale des surplus', *Économies et Sociétés*, série Économie Mathématique et Économétrie, **8** and **9**, new edn 1989, Grenoble: Presses Universitaires de Grenoble.

Allais, M. (1989), 'Les lignes directrices de mon œuvre', Nobel Conference, *Annales d'économie et de statistique*, **14**, 1–23.

Allais, M. (2001), *Fondements de la dynamique monétaire*, Paris: Clément Juglar.

Béraud, A. (2014), 'Le développement de la théorie de l'équilibre général. Les apports d'Allais et de Hicks', *Revue économique*, **65** (1), 125–58.

Drèze, J. (1989), 'Maurice Allais and the French Marginalist School', *Scandinavian Journal of Economics*, **91** (1), 5–16.

Friedman, M. and L.J. Savage (1948), 'The utility analysis of choices involving risk', *Journal of Political Economy*, **56** (4), 279–304.

Grandmont, M. (1989), 'Rapport sur les travaux scientifiques de Maurice Allais', *Annales d'économie et de statistique*, **14**, 25–36.

Lenfant, J.-S. (2005), 'Psychologie individuelle et stabilité d'un équilibre général concurrentiel dans le Traité d'économie pure de Maurice Allais', *Revue économique*, **56** (4), 855–88.

Munier, B. (1991), 'Nobel laureate: the many other Allais paradoxes', *Journal of Economic Perspectives*, **5** (2), 179–99.

Munier, B., T. de Montbrial and M. Boiteux (1986), *Marchés, capital et incertitude. Essais en l'honneur de Maurice Allais*, Paris: Economica.

Negishi, T. (1962), 'The stability of competitive economy: a survey article', *Econometrica*, **30** (4), 635–69.

Pareto, V. (1906), *Manuale d'economia politica*, Milan: Società editrice libraria, French trans. 1966 in *Œuvres complètes de Vilfredo Pareto*, Geneva: Droz.

Raybaut, A. (2014), 'Toward a non-linear theory of economic fluctuations: Allais's contribution to endogenous business cycle theory in the 1950s', *European Journal of the History of Economic Thought*, **21** (5), 899–919.

Royal Swedish Academy of Sciences (1989), 'The Nobel memorial prize in economics 1988', *Scandinavian Journal of Economics*, **91** (1), 1–4.

Samuelson, P.A. (1952), 'Probability, utility, and the independence axiom', *Econometrica*, **20** (4), 670–78.

Walras, L. (1874–77 [1988]), *Éléments d'économie politique pure ou Théorie de la richesse sociale*, Lausanne: Corbaz, Paris: Guillaumin, Bale: Georg, reprint in A. Walras and L. Walras (1988), *Œuvres économiques complètes*, Paris: Economica.

Milton Friedman (1912–2006)

Life

Milton Friedman was born in Brooklyn, New York, on 31 July 1912, the fourth child of Jewish immigrants from today's Ukraine. At 13 months old, his family moved to New Jersey, where Friedman spent his youth in school and helping out at the family's store. While his parents never attracted great wealth – his father was a jobber commuting to New York and, at some point, a merchant, his mother led a few attempts at small businesses run from their home – they managed to keep the family solvent, placed a high value on education and probably gave Milton his perspective of a producer in a competitive environment when talking about the economy or politics. After high school, he went to Rutgers University and completed his undergraduate studies of mathematics and economics in 1932. Under the influence of the Great Depression, Friedman decided to further pursue economics. He was granted a scholarship at the University of Chicago, where he met his future wife Rose. Having already spent a year at Columbia University in his second year of graduate studies, he returned there in 1945 to receive his PhD.

In spite of his difficult economic background, Friedman always regarded and admired a market economy as the only social order capable of combining personal freedom with individual as well as collective prosperity. Nevertheless, his view on US capitalism was still differentiated: after holding a research position at the National Bureau of Economic Research (NBER), he worked at the Treasury and helped introduce an income-tax withholding system whose main purpose was to finance the United States' war expenses. Later, he would come to criticize this tax collection at the source – as well as his involvement in developing it – as intrusive and a severe political mistake.

Over time, defending the free play of market forces against interventions and regulations became a personal research project (Ebenstein 2007), which made him a maverick in the political-economic debate. *Capitalism and Freedom*, published in 1962, was an effort to counter US American tendencies towards a welfare state, but remained unsuccessful upon publication. However, when Ronald Reagan at the beginning of the 1980s introduced his supply-side economics, Friedman's views on the relationship of state and markets were to some extent embodied in economic policy. While he acted as economic adviser in many instances, he always refused to take a position as member of the government.

All this puts him in stark contrast to the other overarching economic figure of the time, John Maynard Keynes, who, as part of the United Kingdom's elite and (temporarily) executive of HM's Treasury, was concerned with monetary theory as well as policy early on, and was appointed by his country to negotiate the foundations of the postwar monetary order. At the same time, Keynes's economic policy agenda was oriented towards the interests of the working man, namely, achieving full employment. Friedman, in turn, always propagated free and undisturbed entrepreneurship. However, he never displayed a direct animosity towards Keynes, even though the latter gave him possible grounds by refusing publication of his first paper in the *Economic Journal*.

After a short episode at the University of Wisconsin from 1940 to 1941, where not every faculty member approved of Friedman's appointment, and working for the government during World War II, Friedman took over Jacob Viner's chair at the University of Chicago which he held until his retirement in 1976. He and von Hayek were the founders of the informal Chicago School of economics which promoted free-market liberalism and bred a number of laureates of the Sveriges Riksbank Prize in Economic Sciences in Memory of Alfred Nobel. Also, Friedman developed his interest for monetary topics there, founding the Workshop in Money and Banking and returning to the NBER under Arthur Burns. During this time, he came to meet Anna Jacobson Schwartz, with whom he ultimately co-authored the seminal *Monetary History of the United States, 1867–1960* (Friedman and Schwartz 1963).

One of the recurring themes in Friedman's scientific, journalistic and political work was freedom in the form of a market society without governmental interference. He promoted capitalism as a necessary (yet not sufficient) condition for political freedom not only in the United States but also abroad, including non-democratic countries. One of his journeys took him to Chile in 1975 where he advised Augusto Pinochet to act against inflation and take back the recent nationalizations of important businesses. Critics blamed him for aiding a dictatorship, but Friedman always characterized himself as a mere expert and added that dictatorial regimes were more likely to convert to democracies than totalitarian communist societies (among which he counted the regime of Pinochet's predecessor Salvador Allende).

The presentation of the Sveriges Riksbank Prize in Economic Sciences to Friedman in 1976 was overshadowed by protests against him. He then retreated from the University of Chicago and took a position at the Hoover Institution on War, Revolution and Peace at Stanford University in California and stayed there until his death in November 2006.

Work

Friedman was awarded the Sveriges Riksbank Prize "for his achievements in the fields of consumption analysis, monetary history and theory, and for his demonstration of the complexity of stabilization policy". Not mentioned was what might be called his decade-long crusade for a "pure" market economy, which he saw endangered by a well-meaning welfare and tax state. See his essays on the abolishment of the military draft as well as the mail monopoly, on the privatization of social security, the legalization of drugs, or the promotion of private schools (Friedman 1962).

Consumption theory

Chronologically, consumption analysis was Friedman's first important field of interest. In the beginning, he approached the area empirically, working on *The Study of Consumer Purchases* for the National Resources Committee in Washington, DC (United States Resource Committee 2009) and, after Simon Kuznets invited him to work at the NBER in 1937, on the income of freelancers. Part of the resulting *Income from Independent Professional Practitioners* (Friedman and Kuznets 1954) also formed his dissertation at Columbia; however, publication was delayed from 1941 until 1945 by intense discussions of certain implications it held, namely that the regulation of entry into medicine increased its price and impaired its supply.

His first major work, *A Theory of the Consumption Function*, was published in 1957. From a theoretical point of view, it marked a counterpoint to the then common mathematic representation of consumption used in Keynesian macroeconomics, which saw households' expenditures proportional to current income and seemed somewhat mechanistic and unfounded. Friedman instead described the consumption level as a function of "permanent income": rational households discount their real wealth with the interest rate in order to yield an estimate of future, or lifetime, income. Even though empirical economics by and large kept using the Keynesian concept, Friedman managed to introduce the fundamentally different perspective of an intertemporally optimizing individual agent (as opposed to the conventional household routine of consuming a certain proportion of every increase in income).

Thus he provided "microeconomic foundations" to consumption as a macroeconomic aggregate. In this respect, Friedman built on Irving Fisher whose time preference theory had already linked optimal distribution of consumption over several periods to interest rates – from which Keynes had deviated deliberately.

A disagreement about assumptions concerned the inherent stability of the economy, leading to full employment through market forces, which Friedman always claimed, but never established. This is directly connected to consumption because if economic agents are hindered in employing their abilities (their wealth) in the markets – for example, by involuntary unemployment – they are forced to adjust expenditures in the short term, that is, regardless of their longer-term permanent income. Nonetheless, the abolishment of a constant propensity to consume puts in doubt the existence of a (government expenditures) multiplier effect since households are not thought to react proportionally to current-income increases anymore, thus potentially making demand management less effective.

Further discussion revolved around an implicit assumption stemming from the divergence of current and permanent income: in order to maintain an even consumption level over time, agents need to be able to obtain credit and invest money without restrictions on perfect financial markets. However, concepts like risk aversion, information asymmetry and reputational deficits render this assumption invalid. Expected income and human capital are not (or only to a very small extent) eligible as collateral in credit contracts so that households in fact have to rely on their current instead of their permanent income. Furthermore, modern micro theory found more arguments in favour of the Keynesian consumption function by integrating norms into the utility function (Akerlof 2007).

Money demand

Friedman entered into a constructive dispute with Keynesianism by reviving the quantity theory of money. At its heart is the quantity equation $MV \equiv PY$ which describes the tautological relationship of the nominal transaction value, that is, (real national product Y times price level P), and its "technical" funding by an amount of money M that circulates through the economy with a certain velocity V (Fisher had used the sum of nominal transactions instead of nominal income). The quantity theory states that if velocity is stable and real aggregate output cannot be influenced by monetary policy, prices move along with the amount of money.

The velocity of money is the inverse of agents' propensity to hold real balances, that is, money demand; the approach thus builds on the traditional Cambridge k. In 1956, Friedman published a "Restatement" of money demand theory and explained the difference from the old quantity theory as follows: "For the transactions version [of the quantity theory], the most important thing about money is that it is transferred. For the income version, the most important thing is that it is held" (Friedman 1974: 8). Money demand is seen as an element of portfolio selection concerning a wide range of assets, and depends on income and on the vector of market returns.

Friedman's restatement made two important contributions. First, it made clear that transmission of interest rate changes not only runs from net investment to consumption: since securities and long-lived consumption goods are substitutes, a change in asset prices induced by interest rate policy can affect goods demand directly. Thus, the often unpredictable investment reaction as a potential weak spot in monetary macroeconomic stabilization can be circumvented. Second, and in contrast to classical economics, the velocity of money V is no longer constant but a stable function of other macroeconomic variables.

According to Keynes (1936: 164), a monetary expansion (rising M) can seep away in the "liquidity trap" (which implies a decreasing V). In this case, economic activity cannot be influenced by monetary policy anymore. During the world economic crisis of the 1930s, both production and prices fell. However, Friedman ascribed this to a significant decrease in the amount of money instead of an unstable velocity: because the Federal Reserve, in a blend of ignorance and misconceived competition policy, had let several struggling banks fail, broad money was diminished and chains of payment disrupted, leading to income and wealth decreases, bank runs, and hoarding of money. In his eyes, the crisis was just proof not of the market system's instability (as many Keynesians saw it) but of the incompetence of economic policy. His conclusion was that "money is much too serious a matter to be left to the Central Bankers" (Friedman 1962: 51). Ever since, he demanded a limit to central bank autonomy and money to be subject to a fixed percentage growth, which he deemed sufficient for growth, full employment, and price stability.

Monetary policy

As president of the American Economic Association, Friedman worked on the stabilizing "Role of monetary policy" (1968) more intensively, building on the negative relationship between inflation and unemployment as described by the Phillips curve which was discovered empirically only a few years earlier. Against this background, there was a discussion about the idea that economic policymakers could possibly choose any point on the curve, that is, for example, lower unemployment at the cost of accepting a higher rate of inflation. Friedman now analysed such a monetary expansion, assuming a "natural rate" of unemployment which is not cyclical but structural, that is, caused by inefficient markets and social structures such as insufficient workforce mobility. In this situation in which employment is at its short-term maximum, excess demand on labour markets leads to wage and price increases, with inflation expectations becoming increasingly important for wage demands. Hence, an additional motive (apart from and independent of the level of employment) enters the determination of wage and price growth rates – the Phillips curve is therefore only valid for given inflation expectations and moves up if they increase, resulting in higher inflation for any given rate of unemployment.

A monetary expansion can increase employment temporarily at most, namely, if nominal-wage growth stays below the actual rate of inflation. In the long run, there is no choice between inflation and unemployment, but only between low and high inflation at a given "natural rate" of unemployment that can be moved by supply-side measures (for example, aimed at flexibility, education, and productivity). This core message – demand-side policies cannot push the economy beyond full-employment for long – is considered trivial today and had already been advanced earlier by Keynes (1936: 289). Still, it received a lot of attention at the time and was fought heavily in the 1960s, especially by Keynesians.

Several explanations are conceivable. First, the "natural rate" is not a clear-cut point estimate, making it desirable for policymakers to "try" the supply restrictions imposed by the labour market. However, Friedman abstracts from such a lack of information in his model. Second, as Tobin (1972: 17) had already mentioned, cyclical underemployment can become structural. Under certain conditions, this process can also be reversed, that is temporary over-employment could lower the "natural rate" by re-qualifying formerly structurally unemployed in the production process and thus increasing the marketable labour force potential. However, this argument was developed only in the "hysteresis" debate in the 1980s (Jenkinson 1987). Third, Keynesians in the 1960s were so used to the assumption of unemployment that they overlooked Friedman's starting point – full employment – and subsequently engaged in a pointless argument. "Keynesians were concerned with the problem of pushing the economy to its natural rate, not beyond it. If the economy is already there, we can all go home" (Hahn 1982: 74–5) – Friedman merely added that unemployment rates below the "natural level" cannot be sustained.

Based on his work, the monetarist economic school of thought developed – the term "monetarism" goes back to Brunner (1968) – which considers the amount of money as the driving force of economic activity. In contrast to his monetarist peers, however, Friedman preferred simple models and clear messages, for example, his famous "helicopter money" parabola (Friedman 1969). This is in accordance with his position on methodology (Friedman 1953a): from his point of view, economic science is not about the realism of assumptions but instead about empirical validity of hypotheses, in this specific case a predictable relationship between money and prices. However, Friedman's use of theories was rather eclectic, using ad hoc either Walras's or Marshall's equilibrium theory, or even the Keynesian IS–LM model. This produced an open debate about his "Theoretical framework for monetary analysis" (1974) and led Hahn (1971: 62) to criticize his "lack of seriousness".

Impact

How are Friedman's scientific works and his economic policy advice to be assessed? The academic profession displays an ambiguity in this respect that is surprising for a world-renowned Sveriges Riksbank Prize laureate. Krugman (2007) attributed to Friedman three different personalities: while he is said to have attracted universal admiration as an economist, his other two personae – as a "policy entrepreneur" advocating monetarism and an ideologue demanding liberalization and deregulation in many respects – were met with stronger opposition. Krugman even calls Friedman "intellectually dishonest" in defending his views on policy. A closer look at Friedman as a person as well as his works reveals a consistency in his beliefs, publications and activities. Clear speech, the inclination to taper and simplify whenever possible, but also often describing problems only monocausally, explain his success in transferring his arguments from theory into practice.

The invisible hand of competition and the macroeconomic power of the amount of money are recurring motives while governing the economy is always criticized fiercely: "benevolent dictatorship is likely sooner or later to lead to a totalitarian society" (Friedman 1997: 22). At the centre of his economic concept stands ultimately a *homo oeconomicus* who is *Free to Choose* (which is the title of a television series aired in the 1980s, and also of a book jointly written with his wife Rose – Friedman and Friedman 1980). Friedman thus counts among the pioneers of the microfoundation of macroeconomics. However, he did not follow what was made of this by fellow economists afterwards: in combination with rational expectations, and pushing his Phillips curve analysis ever further, they arrived at new classical macroeconomics or, as Tobin (1980) called it, "Monetarism Mark II", in which rational agents know about the long-term effects of a monetary expansion and therefore only adjust prices but no real variables even in the short run. By contrast, Friedman always opposed such model-driven implications and emphasized the short- and medium-term non-neutrality of monetary policy on growth and employment. However, he did so not to steer central banks' attention towards day-to-day business but, rather, to indicate the economic costs of monetary policy when targeting the short term.

The transition towards money supply control was without doubt Friedman's greatest achievement with respect to (monetary) policy. In the mid-1970s, central banks in Germany and Switzerland, later also in England and the United States, implemented a monetary strategy that, at least at first sight, conformed to his demand for a slow, rule-based expansion of money supply. The "monetarist counter-revolution" put price stability before employment again, which also required central banks to be independent of foreign exchange markets, that is, required a system of flexible exchange rates (Friedman 1953b); however, Friedman like many economists did not anticipate the at times very strong exchange rate movements after the collapse of the Bretton Woods system. In 1975, the German Bundesbank was the first central bank to introduce money supply control, and its success in keeping inflation in check added greatly to the reputation of Friedman's ideas.

On a closer look, however, neither the Bundesbank nor other central banks actually followed Friedman's guideline of an optimal money growth. Instead, they practised interest rate policy and used the monetary target (which was missed about half of the time) merely as a means of "public relations". Since the European Central Bank has become Europe's first monetary authority, the role of money supply as an intermediate policy goal was diminished even further.

Having had very little success in predicting inflation rates using the quantity theory in the 1980s, Friedman became more flexible towards the end of his life. In his latest scientific work (2005) he shifted focus from goods to asset price inflation. He also predicted in a German newspaper severe political and economic tensions that might well lead to the breakdown of a future European Monetary Union.

CHRISTIAN PHILIPP SCHRÖDER AND PETER SPAHN

See also:

Chicago School (II); Monetarism (II); Money and banking (III).

References and further reading

Akerlof, G.A. (2007), 'The missing motivation in macroeconomics', *American Economic Review*, **97** (1), 5–36.
Brunner, K. (1968), 'The role of money and monetary policy', *Review*, Federal Reserve Bank of St Louis, 9–24.
Ebenstein, L. (2007), *Milton Friedman. A Biography*, London: Palgrave Macmillan.
Friedman, M. (1953a), 'The methodology of positive economics', in M. Friedman, *Essays in Positive Economics*, Chicago, IL: Chicago University Press, pp. 3–43.
Friedman, M. (1953b), 'The case for flexible exchange rates', in M. Friedman, *Essays in Positive Economics*, Chicago, IL: Chicago University Press, pp. 157–203.
Friedman, M. (1956), 'The quantity theory of money: a restatement', in M. Friedman (ed.), *Studies in the Quantity Theory of Money*, Chicago, IL: Chicago University Press, pp. 3–21.
Friedman, M. (1957), *A Theory of the Consumption Function*, Princeton, NJ: Princeton University Press.
Friedman, M. (1962), *Capitalism and Freedom*, Chicago, IL: Chicago University Press.
Friedman, M. (1968), 'The role of monetary policy', *American Economic Review*, **58** (1), 1–17.
Friedman, M. (1969), 'The optimum quantity of money', in M. Friedman, *The Optimum Quantity of Money and Other Essays*, Chicago, IL: Aldine, pp. 1–50.
Friedman, M. (1974), 'A theoretical framework for monetary analysis', in R.J. Gordon (ed.), *Milton Friedman's Monetary Framework – A Debate with His Critics*, Chicago, IL: Chicago University Press, pp. 1–62.
Friedman, M. (1997), 'John Maynard Keynes', *Economic Quarterly*, **83** (2), Federal Reserve Bank of Richmond, 1–23.
Friedman, M. (2005), 'A natural experiment in monetary policy covering three episodes of growth and decline in the economy and the stock market', *Journal of Economic Perspectives*, **19** (4), 145–50.
Friedman, M. and R. Friedman (1980), *Free to Choose: A Personal Statement*, New York: Harcourt.
Friedman, M. and S. Kuznets (1954), *Income from Independent Professional Practice*, Cambridge, MA: National Bureau of Economic Research.
Friedman, M. and A.J. Schwartz (1963), *A Monetary History of the United States, 1867–1960*, Princeton, NJ: Princeton University Press.
Hahn, F.H. (1971), 'Professor Friedman's views on money', *Economica*, **38** (149), 61–80.
Hahn, F.H. (1982), *Money and Inflation*, Oxford: Blackwell.
Jenkinson, T. (1987), 'The natural rate of unemployment: does it exist?', *Oxford Review of Economic Policy*, **3** (3), 20–26.
Keynes, J.M. (1936), *The General Theory of Employment, Interest and Money*, London: Macmillan.
Krugman, P. (2007), 'Who was Milton Friedman?', *New York Review of Books*, **54** (2), 27–30.
Tobin, J. (1972), 'Inflation and unemployment', *American Economic Review*, **62** (1/2), 1–18.
Tobin, J. (1980), *Asset Accumulation and Economic Activity*, Oxford: Basil Blackwell.
United States National Resources Committee (2009), *Study of Consumer Purchases in the United States, 1935–1936*, Ann Arbor, MI: Inter-university Consortium for Political and Social Research.

Abram Bergson [Abram Burk] (1914–2003)

Abram Bergson (21 April 1914–23 April 2003) has been famous both for welfare economics and for Soviet economics. It is worth noticing that two of his most well-known papers, published in 1936 and 1938, are authored by Burk while referred to as Bergson's. At a time when being a Jew was not easy in Europe and being Russian was not popular in the US, his older brother Gus Burk and himself, Abram Burk, were both students in Harvard. They voluntarily decided to change their surname into Bergson in order to assert themselves as sons of Russian immigrant Jews. This is just one story about the change from Burk to Bergson as it is described by his great friend Paul A. Samuelson. The latter recalls that Abram Bergson was known as "Honest Abe" in Harvard; he describes him as very modest yet not shy, straight arrow, upright, and as "a man of the center with a personal preference toward less economic inequality" (2004: 27, 29).

Abram Bergson spent his youth in Baltimore. He was married to Rita Macht Bergson, herself trained in Baltimore, with whom he had three daughters Judy, Mimi and Lucy. After an undergraduate training at Johns Hopkins University, he studied economics at the Harvard Graduate School. He started to learn the Russian language and he made a lengthy visit to Moscow in 1937. He published his Harvard PhD thesis in 1940, by which time he had already gained a wide recognition as a mathematical economist. During World War II, he worked between 1940 and 1942 at the University of Texas, Austin. He then became head of the Russian desk at the Office of Strategic Services (OSS). He played a major role in establishing and maintaining close links between US academic studies of the Soviet economy and the intelligence community of the Federal government. After the end of the war, he had an economics chair at Columbia, and worked in the RAND Corporation in Santa Monica. He became a Harvard Professor in 1956, where he was the director of the Harvard Russian Research centre from 1964 to 1968 and during 1969–70. He was also chairman of the Social Science Advisory Board of the US Arms Control and Disarmament Agency, consultant to various federal agencies, the President of the Association for Comparative Studies, and he several times gave testimony before the US Congress.

His contributions to economics are numerous, important and diverse. In economic theory, his famous 1936 article discusses techniques to measure marginal utility and its importance for the general index number theory. He found an earliest formulation of the constant elasticity of substitution function, which outside consumer utility analysis, became widely used in production theory and in modern finance theory, for instance, in case optimal portfolio ratios are independent to wealth.

In welfare economics, Bergson's uncontroversial celebrity derives from his 1938 *Quarterly Journal of Economics* article in which he defines and discusses individualistic social welfare function, as a method of ranking different Pareto-optimal allocations. Social welfare is expressed as a function of the amounts of commodities allocated to individuals as well as the allocation of factor services, the latter defined with reference to the particular uses of labour services and of particular industries in which labour was employed. With such an individualistic social welfare function, Pareto optimality conditions are derived as necessary but not sufficient conditions for defining interpersonal normative equity. Besides providing a representation of social welfare and a framework for welfare economics, this social welfare function notably provides a sound answer to

Robbins's critics according to which value judgements should be thrown out of economics, for interpersonal comparisons of utility are not testable empirical relations. Such function should indeed provide coherent interpretations of ethical value judgements. Samuelson considerably simplified Bergson's presentation by adding further postulates in his 1947 book. Even though the now so called Bergson–Samuelson social welfare function in its actual shape is due to Samuelson, the latter has always been very cautious to attribute its actual origin to Bergson.

For the history of welfare economic thought, we should recall Bergson's strong statements as whether we should use the word "Pareto optimality" since it appeared before, however vaguely, in Mill, Smith and Edgeworth. In a critical approach, he has also contributed to the analysis of compensation variations and consumer surplus. He introduced the concept of marginal rate of income substitution (MRIS), which amounts to a distributional weight; he showed that any results based on that framework depend on the price structure that hence require a general equilibrium context. He also points out its redundancy by establishing a connection between the analysis of variations and index number theory.

In comparative economics, he is often considered to be the father of the US economic Sovietology. His works on the Soviet economy include description and analysis of the Soviet economic institutions, measurement of economic growth, and a deep knowledge of the Soviet statistics. One of his main contributions concerns the measurement of economic growth in Soviet systems. Such advances made it possible to compare growth rates between USSR and other economic systems. It was indeed a difficult task: no market prices are obviously available, and the methods of evaluation used in Soviet economies at this time made Soviet growth appear unrealistically high. Bergson fostered dependable comparisons by applying the adjusted factor cost method for the USSR for 1928–55, which consisted in adjusting actual Soviet transactions prices to what they would be according to the neoclassical theory. These prices are used as weights to aggregate the physical outputs in each branch and economic sector. Such data are then comparable to aggregates from systems of national accounts (SNAs), and, as argued by Bergson, provide possible welfare interpretations. Here again, Bergson's results have been undoubtedly influential, yet controversial.

In both domains of research, whether Sovietology or welfare economics, Bergson has always put forward that any evaluation of social states or any assessment of the superiority of one system should mainly rest on value judgements rather than on objective quantitative economic data. Comparisons indeed induce weighting different activities into an index, and eventually rely on ethical values.

ANTOINETTE BAUJARD

See also:

Paul Anthony Samuelson (I); Welfare economics (III).

References and further reading

Bergson, A. (1948), 'Socialist economics', in H.S. Ellis (ed.), *A Survey of Contemporary Economics*, Philadelphia, PA: Blakiston, pp. 412–48.
Bergson, A. (1961), *Real National Income of Soviet Russia, Since 1928*, Cambridge, MA: Harvard University Press.
Bergson, A. (1966), *Essays in Normative Economics*, London: Oxford University Press.
Bergson, A. (1967), 'Market socialism revisited', *Journal of Political Economy*, **75** (5), 655–73.

Bergson, A. (1973), 'On monopoly welfare losses', *American Economic Review*, **63** (5), 853–70.

Bergson, A. (1976), 'Social choice and welfare economics under representative government', *Journal of Public Economics*, **6** (3), 171–90.

Bergson, A. (1978), *Productivity and the Social System: The USSR and the West*, Cambridge, MA: Harvard University Press.

Bergson, A. (1980), 'Consumer's surplus and income redistribution', *Journal of Public Economics*, **14** (1), 31–47.

Bergson, A. (1982), *Welfare, Planning, and Employment: Selected Essays in Economic Theory*, Cambridge, MA and London: MIT Press.

Burk [Bergson], A. (1936), 'Real income, expenditure proportionality, and Frisch's "new methods of measuring marginal utility"', *Review of Economic Studies*, **4** (1), 33–52.

Burk [Bergson], A. (1938), 'A reformulation of certain aspects of welfare economics', *Quarterly Journal of Economics* **52** (2), 310–34.

Samuelson, P.A. (1947), *Foundations of Economic Analysis*, Cambridge, MA: Harvard University Press.

Samuelson, P.A. (2004), 'Abram Bergson, 1914–2003', in National Academy of Sciences (ed.), *Bibliographical Memoirs*, vol. 84, Washington, DC: National Academies Press, pp. 21–34.

Paul Anthony Samuelson (1915–2009)

Life

Paul Anthony Samuelson was born in Gary, a steel town near Chicago, on 15 May 1915. His father ran a small pharmacy. During his childhood, Samuelson saw the plight of the workers labouring in the steel works without any welfare provision whatsoever. As a young man in the early 1930s, he was able to observe the effects of the Great Depression, and this had a profound impact on him and on his lifelong view of the world. In 1932, aged 16, Samuelson began his studies as an undergraduate at the University of Chicago. Aaron Director, Jacob Viner, Frank Knight and Henry Schultz were among his teachers. After his BA, he went on to study at Harvard University with a scholarship. At the age of 21, in 1936, he published his first article in a scientific journal. Shortly afterwards, he was elected Junior Fellow at Harvard University, which allowed him to conduct research freely for three years. During this time, he published a number of further essays, completing his dissertation in 1941, which he rewrote and published as *Foundations of Economic Analysis* after the war. In 1938 he married his fellow student Marion Crawford, whom he had met while at university. They had six children together.

Among Samuelson's teachers at Harvard University were the economists Alvin Hansen, Wassily Leontief and Joseph Schumpeter, as well as the mathematician and physicist Edwin Bidwell Wilson. Abram Bergson, Lloyd Metzler and James Tobin were among his fellow students. Despite his brilliance, which was obvious to all, he found it difficult to pursue a career at Harvard University, an institution that, like all Ivy League universities at the time, was tainted by strong anti-Jewish prejudice (on this, see Samuelson 2002). He therefore decided to accept a position at the nearby Massachusetts Institute of Technology (MIT), a university to which he remained faithful until his death in 2009. During the war, Samuelson interrupted his research to work on the National Resources Planning Board and, following that, at the MIT Radiation Laboratory and the War Production Board.

The publication of his *Foundations* soon established Samuelson as one of the leading mathematical economists of his generation (Samuelson 1947). Ralph Freeman, the chairman of his department at MIT, dispensed with some of Samuelson's teaching duties after the war, requesting him to write a modern introductory textbook. This textbook, given the title *Economics*, was published in 1948 and very quickly became a bestseller and a model for the entire textbook literature in economics. On the one hand, the book is imbued with the new Keynesian spirit; on the other, there is a neoclassical approach in modernized form, developed by Samuelson himself. Since the book dispenses with mathematical derivations and is written in an extremely skilful didactic manner, it very soon made known all over the world the idea of "neoclassical synthesis", that is, the concept of integrating the Keynesian macroeconomic revolution into neoclassicism.

In the social sciences, as far as I can tell, this textbook is a unique experience: Samuelson, belonging to a younger generation, knew exactly how to change profoundly, and in a very short period of time, the broad effect of an entire field. Perhaps there was a renewed sense, following the Depression, of orthodox teaching absorbing Keynesian thought. However, the fact that this neoclassical synthesis was able to spread so smoothly is due in no small part to Samuelson's textbook. Despite its accessibility, it avoided misleading simplifications, introducing students to economic thinking in such a convincing way as to show them just how all this could be useful to economic policy.

As mentioned before, Samuelson remained faithful to MIT, arguably making its Economics Department the leading department in the world, alongside his colleagues. One crucial reason for this was that he produced a string of scientific publications that developed, improved and even revolutionized the standard of knowledge in several branches of economics. In 1970, aged 55, he was awarded the Sveriges Riksbank Prize in Economic Sciences in Memory of Alfred Nobel. His huge output continued incessantly, and even at the age of over 90, Samuelson remained very much a public figure whose commentaries on current events continued to meet with huge attention and interest.

Two characteristics are central to Samuelson's research. First, the rigorousness of his argumentation; and secondly, the embedding of specific results in a greater context. The combination of these two characteristics makes Samuelson distinguishable from most of his peers. There are certainly some economists, including important ones, who retain a sense of the greater picture, although most of them lack the rigorous argumentation based on the mathematical model. On the other hand, there are scores of economists who will develop and publish innumerable mathematical models, albeit without displaying any sense of the greater picture. Samuelson's way of working also means he cannot be pigeonholed as either a "market disciple" or a "state disciple". In his work, Samuelson is able to demonstrate in crystal-clear fashion what market processes and competition can do in different contexts; at the same time, however, he uses the same methods to point out the limits of the market principle – limits that call for the state to make adjustments. Perhaps, therefore, Samuelson may be regarded, more than any other economist, as a theorist of the "mixed economy". The neoclassical synthesis between Keynes and a modernized neoclassicism is only one example for this. Analogous examples can be found in his ground-breaking work on welfare economics, on international trade theory, on risk and financial economics or on the theory of public goods.

In this sense, he is quite different from his long-time rival Milton Friedman, the intellectual leader of the Chicago School and a fervent critic of state activity and of Keynesianism. Samuelson frequently accused Friedman of oversimplification. However, it is certainly not wrong to say that in public debates between the two economists, such as those broadcast on television, Milton Friedman had greater success in making his arguments sound convincing.

Despite his huge public impact and his influence on economic policy, in particular that of the Democratic Party and its presidential candidates, Samuelson's political influence rests mainly on his teaching and research. Part of this is due to the broad effect of his textbook that was emulated in one form or another by those who came after him. A much larger part is due to his teaching, and that of his colleagues at the MIT Economics Department. There, graduate and doctoral students learned how to combine rigorous theory with empirical relevance in economics. They were introduced to an incentive structure that proved particularly conducive to research. Samuelson spread a spirit in the department, so that all graduate students could expect their own original research results to be appreciated and to have a positive effect on furthering their careers. The MIT would become able to choose the cream of the crop for its own graduate school, but even for young people who are above average it is certainly a stroke of good fortune to become involved, on the one hand, in the strict discipline of rigorous theoretical derivations and, on the other, to experience a stimulating discussion environment in which new ideas are appreciated and not stifled.

The spirit that reigned at the MIT Economics Department may be illustrated by a Samuelson anecdote, of which there are many. This anecdote was told by Cary Brown and Robert Solow in their preface to a Festschrift for Samuelson dating back to 1983 (Brown and Solow 1983b). In the mid-1950s, Seymour Harris, who was then chairman of the Harvard Economics Department, had organized a nationwide survey among the economics departments in order to establish what people thought about the quality of their departments. Harvard ended up in first place, while MIT scored a place in the upper third of the list. When Samuelson heard about this, he is supposed to have said: "We may not be the best department, but we certainly are the happiest." Perhaps this could be an interesting result for modern-day happiness research, considering that only ten years later the MIT moved on to become the best department, too, well ahead of Harvard.

In the 1950s and 1960s, the Economics Lunch Table at the MIT Faculty Club (located in the same building as the Economics Department) was renowned. Every day, the subject and its current condition would be debated at a big round table, without a formally elected chair, albeit under Samuelson's informal guidance. Subjects for debates would include current controversies within economics or in the economic policy of the day, questions of methodology or content, the scene in the United States and the rest of the world, with a particularly critical glance towards England (especially Cambridge) and the famous neighbour, Harvard, and the intellectual opposition in Chicago. Samuelson's encyclopaedic knowledge, his capacity to follow other people's thought processes, his unsurpassed memory for anecdotes and stories, his quick-wittedness and sense of humour that bristled with self-mockery all made these intellectual forays at lunchtime extremely gratifying. At the same time, they were also intensive courses in which one could learn – by speed-listening, as it were – outside of the dry old system. This laughing lunch table, lasting about an hour or an hour and a half, was very close to Humboldt's ideal for university life, at least with regard to the field of economics (on this see Brown and Solow 1983: xif.).

Thus, the MIT School produced a large number of important economists and advisers to governments and international organizations. Today's apparent obsession to evaluate everything means that we also look at the number of Nobel laureates connected with a particular institution. Well, there is no doubt that among the more recent Sveriges Riksbank Prizes in Economic Sciences in Memory of Alfred Nobel, the share of MIT PhDs, and professors is larger than at any other school.

Work

The *Foundations*
Shortly after World War II, in 1947, Samuelson published his *Foundations*. The work would become the most important reference, in the years following publication, for any research in theoretical economics. It was certainly not the first book on mathematical economics, but it is no exaggeration to say that it revolutionized the way in which economic theory was conducted. It was this book that laid the foundation for the axiomatic method that became the dominant method of economic theory during the following

decades and to this day. This book is a classic. It became a model for how an economic theorist should conduct research. Nowadays, it is generally referred to as *Foundations*, abbreviated in the same way that the titles of Adam Smith's *Wealth of Nations* and Keynes' *General Theory* are shortened.

The epigraph Samuelson used for *Foundations* is a quote from the American physicist Willard Gibbs, "Mathematics is a language", and there is no doubt that Samuelson saw the increasing reliance of theoretical physics on mathematics and wished to apply this model to economics. The first part of the book takes up 70 per cent of its entire volume. It is dedicated to themes that the field of economics has since then been referring to as comparative statics. The second, shorter part deals with themes related to dynamics. However, it is primarily the first part that forms the basis for the way in which economic theory, particularly microeconomics, develops models.

Two relatively abstract terms are central to the first part of *Foundations*: maximization and equilibrium. Of course, neither term was new to economic theorists. Yet, they were primarily applied in concrete contexts; the field had not yet recognized what the various cases in which they were used had in common. Samuelson brought the theories of utility maximization and profit maximization or cost minimization together to show the formal characteristics they have in common, namely, those resulting from the principle of maximization itself. He views the term equilibrium in a similar vein, namely, as a solution to a system of equations, only to discover then what statements can be derived at the abstract level about the relation between the exogenously given parameters (describing, for instance, the available production technology) and the values of the variables, determined endogenously in equilibrium (for example, the quantities produced).

Samuelson understands his theory as empirically refutable: by deriving certain conclusions from the theoretical approach, for example, the hypothesis of utility maximization, on the relation between variables and parameters, or on different variables among each other, these results may be compared to empirical findings. If these contradict the theoretical information, then the basic hypotheses have not passed the empirical test. From this point of view, it was also wrong to refer to this axiomatic approach as "modelling Platonism", as was done later.

One of the central results of Samuelson's approach is a proposition he himself refers to as the "Le Chatelier principle", thereby indicating the close proximity to findings in theoretical physics. In the mathematical model, this Le Chatelier principle proves an insight that had already been intuitively grasped by economic theorists since the time of Alfred Marshall. At the same time, this insight is substantially generalized, so that this already known insight turns out to be a special case of a general principle. Since Alfred Marshall's studies, the following empirically rather robust statement has been known: reaction elasticities are higher in the long term than in the short term. An example for this lies in the price elasticity of demand: in case of a change in price, the demanded amount declines less dramatically in the short term than in the long term. The Samuelson–Le Chatelier principle now says the following: we assume a maximization task in several variables with additional constraints. We examine how the optimal values react to parameter changes. We look at one point that maximizes the target with and without a particular additional constraint. Then, in the case when the constraint ceases to apply, reaction elasticity to a parameter change is higher than when the constraint applies. This mathematical statement, which can also be generalized, has multiple applications in economics. One of these is the relation of the long-term to the short-term marginal cost curve. Similar results are reached in consumer theory. The fact that it makes sense, in time of war, to ration food consumption – without deducing from this that the same makes sense in normal times – can also be ascribed to the insight that adaptive reactions require time. Samuelson's Le Chatelier principle provides these intuitions with a general structural theory that can be used as a basis for all economic contexts. On the Samuelson–Le Chatelier principle, see Milgrom (2006). On the principle of maximization or minimization in economics and physics, see Samuelson's Nobel lecture (Samuelson 1971a).

There is not enough room here to analyse the individual chapters of Samuelson's *Foundations* in depth. I shall highlight merely one further chapter, on "welfare economics". On the one hand, it is a masterpiece of "*Dogmengeschichte*" (history of thought) from the beginnings of this field with Bentham and Adam Smith up to the current state of knowledge before Samuelson himself contributed his work. At the same time, Samuelson's work successfully brings a much-needed clarity to an area that had hitherto fallen victim to a host of misunderstandings. The "social welfare function" he develops here is the point of departure of a continued development and application of welfare economics in the post-war world. Even today, it remains the theoretical foundation for the efficiency criterion, which is almost universally used in applied economics, be it in a cost–benefit analysis or in modern industrial economics. We should, however, not fail to mention that this theoretical foundation is not very solid. The limits to a "new welfare economics" that wants to do without an interpersonal benefit comparison were quite clearly outlined by Samuelson. In practice, they are mostly forgotten nowadays, or even consciously ignored. One of Samuelson's important later contributions to welfare economics is Samuelson (1956).

In the following, I discuss selectively a few of Samuelson's contributions, published mainly in scholarly journals over the course of several decades.

Revealed preference
Even before World War II, Samuelson developed the seminal idea of "revealed preference". In economic theory, we take the axiom as given that people act rationally in the sense that the actions they select orient themselves along the principle of achieving as far as possible most of the goals they have set for themselves. Then, however, it should be possible in principle to draw conclusions from individuals' observed actions to their goals or preferences. Samuelson and later Houthakker were able to show that complete knowledge of an individual's demand curve allows us to unlock that individual's complete preference order if a particular rationality axiom, the strong axiom of revealed preference, can be assumed.

In a similar vein to the Samuelson–Le Chatelier principle, the Samuelson–Houthakker theory of revealed preference confirms a long-existing intuition: liberal social philosophy always knew that a society of free human beings can only remain stable if the consequences of a citizen's actions, resulting from his or her own free will, are ascribed to a substantial degree to that individual. Let us call this the principle of responsibility. Now, what exactly does this principle mean? What is the exact content of the term "private autonomy"? Even today, we have no clear answer to this yet. However, in its axiomatization undertaken by Samuelson and continued by others, the revealed preference principle is the beginning of the answer: the consequences of his or her actions may be attributed to the acting individual, as an expression of the individual's preferences, which are assumed to remain consistent; preferences thus deduced can serve as a benchmark for benefit and cost of a public investment project or changes to legislation or a particular external trade policy (see Samuelson 1938, 1948a; Houthakker 1950).

The concept of revealed preference has not been without criticism from within the field. Consider Hayek's fundamental critique of the "constructivism" of all welfare-economic approaches, as criticism "from the right", as it were (Hayek 1974); or, on the "left", Amartya Sen's relativization of the idea in the context of his reference to the orientation of behaviour along norms that limit purely preference-oriented decisions (Sen 1977). Revealed preference nonetheless remains an innovation of theoretical thought on the possibilities of the coexistence of free citizens. At its core, it remains indispensable to a modern society.

On Marx
Only a handful of great researchers in economics have studied intensively the work of their predecessors. Among these we must certainly count George Stigler. However, it is perhaps Samuelson who can lay claim to have tried, more than anyone else, to understand and honour his predecessors. This is expressed by the string of names that can be found in his work, referring to certain earlier findings and their advancement in the field. Almost every work of Samuelson's is imbued with references to the achievements of earlier scholars; and perhaps some readers of Samuelson's works have only truly appreciated the importance of certain earlier scholars after reading Samuelson. Without Samuelson's influence, I for one would never have grasped the significance of Knut Wicksell or Alfred Marshall.

Apart from the references to heroes of the past, Samuelson also dealt extensively with theories of the past. Such articles were very often written with the express purpose of engaging in "*Dogmengeschichte*" and concern, for instance, such figures as David Ricardo and Karl Marx. The following paragraphs focus only on Karl Marx.

Among sensible people, the significance of Karl Marx as a social theorist, an economist, a philosopher and a person who influenced the course of mankind like barely anyone else is undisputed. However, his works on economic theory (in the sense of an understanding of economic theory as developed by "bourgeois" economics) have always been controversial. One important early critic of Karl Marx's theoretical approach was Eugen von Böhm-Bawerk. Over the course of time, there have been numerous debates between Marxist theorists and those stemming from the "bourgeois" camp.

In an article he published in 1957, Samuelson developed a new analytical set of tools, particularly the wage-interest curve, in order to conclude logically that three different statements made by Marx in his work are contradictory. The statements in question are (1) in capitalism, there is constant technical progress (the Marxist production of relative surplus value); (2) in capitalism, the real wage does not rise, but instead always remains near the margin of subsistence; and (3) in the long term, the profit rate falls in capitalism (Samuelson 1957). Technical progress means that, as Marx himself stressed, the "degree of exploitation" and the profit rate rise. Thus, it is impossible for the real wage to remain stagnant, or even fall, and for the profit rate to fall at the same time.

Since each of these three statements are indispensable for a complete analysis of capitalism in Marxist theory, Samuelson's proof of their inconsistency constitutes a blow to the Marxist worldview. It was this essay by Samuelson that so concisely managed to condense the contradictory nature of the Marxist theoretical approach. I consider this essay one of the high points of the debate between traditional bourgeois economics and Marxism.

When the essay appeared in 1957, Marxism had not yet experienced its renaissance in the intellectual debate. In the western world, this only happened in the 1960s in particular. That probably prompted Samuelson to engage with Marxism once again at a later stage, in particular in the context of the famous transformation problem and, in the same context, the study of the labour theory of value. These further essays also demonstrate Samuelson's willingness to deal in depth with Marx's extensive "sociological" analyses (see Samuelson 1971b).

International trade theory
Samuelson contributed to international trade theory for seven decades. Not long ago, he published an essay that was subject to much public debate; however, his first analytical approaches to international trade theory date back to the 1930s. In the following, I wish merely to refer to two of these contributions, one very early and another very recent. It can be stated quite generally that the theory of foreign trade was one of Samuelson's favourite fields. For him, it was particularly fertile ground, enabling him to approach the more abstract theory of welfare economics and thereby influencing his own welfare-economic way of thinking.

The best-known work is probably his joint work with Wolfgang Stolper, which was published in 1941 under the heading "Protection and real wages" (Samuelson and Stolper 1941). Using analytical methods that were fairly new at the time, the authors show in this article that certain perceptions on the effect of foreign trade on wage distribution were not correct. They use a two-country model in which there are two goods and two production factors (for example, labour and capital). The production functions exhibit constant returns to scale and – apart from one proportionality factor – are the same for both countries. Factor inputs are different for the two goods. The two countries differ in terms of their domestic supply of the two production factors. With these hypotheses, it is possible to show that, after a transition from a state without external trade to a regime of free trade, real wages of that production factor fall which is scarcer at home than abroad. Thus, despite the overall economy profiting from the introduction of free trade, the production factor that is scarcer at home than abroad suffers.

The Samuelson–Stolper theorem became a milestone in the advancement of foreign trade theory. It showed that more care had to be taken when deriving the advantages of a system of free trade, as most economists do, than had traditionally been the case. Incidentally, Samuelson never used this theorem to defect to the protectionist camp. The specific assumptions of the model are not meant to mirror reality, merely serving instead to demonstrate that distribution effects of foreign trade play a significant role. At the same time, they can also serve to understand which groups in a country support protectionism.

It is worth keeping in mind that Samuelson attracted much attention with another article he wrote on international trade, aged 89 (Samuelson 2004). This article appeared at the height of the controversial discussion on globalization, in 2004. Samuelson was then seen by many media as a critic of free international trade. However, this is not correct. What Samuelson was absolutely right to note was that the advantages of international trade, for example, between two countries such as the United States and China, can diminish over time if the production technologies at the disposal of both countries gradually reach the same level. This is obviously the case, as China's productivity in industrial production is making huge progress and, in this sense, is approaching the level of the United States. However, it is quite natural for the advantage of international trade – which rests on the effect of comparative advantage – to decline over time, if this effect can be traced back to the difference in the technologies at the disposal of both countries. Put simply, the advantage of cheap textiles from China diminishes for the American consumer if wages rise in China. Samuelson's entire contribution to international trade theory is well appreciated by Jones (1983).

Public-goods theory
As in so many other cases, Samuelson was just as adept in public-goods theory at formulating a problem as clearly as possible. The renowned public-finance scholar Richard Musgrave wrote in a Festschrift for Samuelson in 1983: "The modern theory of public goods may be dated from June 1954, when Samuelson's 'Pure theory of public expenditures' appeared. Never have three pages had so great an impact on the theory of public finance" (Musgrave 1983: 139–56).

In these three pages, Samuelson develops the mathematical structure of the optimal provision of a public good; this structure made its way into all public-finance and economics textbooks that followed. Even today, it remains the reference point for innumerable articles on public-goods theory. Samuelson also demonstrates here why the invisible hand of the market fails in providing public goods (Samuelson 1954).

The overlapping generations (OLG) model
In 1958, Samuelson published the essay entitled "An exact consumption-loan model of interest with or without the social contrivance of money" (Samuelson 1958). In this article he develops a model in which it is possible, without physically creating capital, to optimize inter-temporal consumer decisions. The "trick" here is the introduction of a model in which a new generation emerges in each period. Each generation lives for three periods, each individual working in the first two of these periods, albeit wishing to consume in all three periods. Samuelson now shows how a quasi-credit system makes saving for the third period individually possible without the economy requiring physical capital. Different institutional arrangements are examined, and it is demonstrated that they influence the result. The fundamental insight, however, is that the process of saving, conducted by one generation, can be synchronized with the process of dissaving, conducted by the other generation. This allows every generation to substitute and optimize inter-temporally, even though an inter-temporal substitution is not possible in the economy as a whole. On Samuelson's model from today's perspective, see Solow (2006) and Kotlikoff (2006).

Perhaps the true significance of this work of Samuelson's lies not so much in his answering the specific question that had initially been his reason for developing the OLG model. Rather, I believe that the idea of the model as such is the truly seminal part. It took some time before economic theory realized the true potential of this OLG concept.

Only in the late 1970s, and then increasingly in the 1980s and 1990s and up until today, have innumerable works using that idea been written.

Risk and capital-market theory
In his later years, Samuelson dealt intensively with the stochastics of markets that redistribute risks, that is, with the financial markets. We cannot go into the details here. However, just as in welfare economics, where he warned of over-simplistic recipes – such as the term consumer surplus – he also warned of simplifications here, such as the idea of maximizing the expected value of a logarithm of a portfolio in a multi-period model being an investment strategy that should be recommended at all times. He is also a pioneer of the option pricing theory, which led to the famous Black–Scholes–Merton formula in the early 1970s. The tempestuous growth of the markets for financial derivatives goes back to the existence of this formula. Samuelson devoted intensive and mathematically highly complex work to the "efficient market hypothesis" in its various guises. Samuelson is one of the fathers, if not *the* father, of modern finance as an academic field (see Samuelson 1965a, 1965b, 1971c). An excellent appraisal of Samuelson's contributions to this prospering field was written by one of his students, Sveriges Riksbank Prize laureate Robert Merton (2006).

Further contributions
It is impossible to sketch Samuelson's extensive scientific research work here in its entirety. Contributions to the following further fields are therefore merely mentioned: stability theory of market processes, induced technical progress, neoclassical capital theory, in particular his part in the famous Cambridge–Cambridge controversy, the non-substitution theorem, the turnpike theorem, consumer and utility theory, theory of index numbers, the relation of linear programming and economic theory, multiplier and acceleration theory, Say's law, fiscal policy, the theory of money, methodology, in particular on the role of mathematics in economics, population theory and mathematical models of biology.

Impact

Every analysis of impact or effect is a search for causes. With innovations in economic or scientific areas, there is always the difficulty of not knowing whether the concrete creator made something that might have been created by others at a later stage, had the creator not got there first. In a sense, thus, the attribution of discoveries to a single discoverer – as has been the routine in the history of science – overestimates somewhat that single person's significance for the progress of science. On the other hand, the indirect effect of the eminent researcher is often underestimated when his or her successes are depicted. This indirect effect lies in the fact that later research results, obtained by later researchers, could not have been achieved had it not been for the earlier researcher achieving the earlier results.

   Like barely anyone else, Samuelson always explicitly acknowledged the previous work of others who either made his own research results possible or else merely kindled in him an interest in a problem. If his successors in the field – in other words, virtually every economist working since World War II – all documented their debt to earlier scientists, as Samuelson did, then it would become instantaneously obvious to all just how immense the indirect effect of Samuelson's output is. We may surmise that it is much larger than any potential downgrading of his significance or stature, which may occur if we consider that others could have made the same discoveries later. Perhaps that is a characteristic of the truly great in a field; that their overall effect is underestimated if their direct research results, first and foremost, are attributed to them. In that sense, Samuelson is a truly great scientist. On the other hand, the significance of performances by lesser men and women is overrated if we attribute their direct research results to them and forget that most of what they have been researching would most likely have been researched by others, albeit later, even if they had not done their work. Thus, there is a kind of "re-distribution" from the top to the bottom, if we measure the importance of a researcher by the number of works published, as is commonly done nowadays in the ubiquitous evaluation campaigns.

CARL CHRISTIAN VON WEIZSÄCKER

See also:

Kenneth Joseph Arrow (I); Abram Bergson [Abram Burk] (I); Growth (III); John Richard Hicks (I); Income distribution (III); International trade (III); John Maynard Keynes (I); Keynesianism (II); Macroeconomics (III); Public economics (III); Frank Plumpton Ramsey (I); David Ricardo (I); Adam Smith (I); Robert Merton Solow (I); Piero Sraffa (I); Welfare economics (III).

References and further reading

Brown, E.C. and R.M. Solow (eds) (1983a), *Paul Samuelson and Modern Economic Theory*, New York: McGraw Hill.

Brown, E.C. and R.M. Solow (1983b), 'Preface', in E.C. Brown and R.M. Solow (eds), *Paul Samuelson and Modern Economic Theory*, New York: McGraw Hill, pp. ix–xiii.

Hayek, F.A. von (1974), 'The pretence of knowledge', Nobel Lecture, 11 December, Stockholm.

Houthakker, H.S. (1950), 'Revealed preference and the utility function', *Economica*, **17** (66), 159–74.

Jones, R.W. (1983), 'International trade theory', in E.C. Brown and R.M. Solow (eds), *Paul Samuelson and Modern Economic Theory*, New York: McGraw Hill, pp. 69–103.

Kotlikoff, L.J. (2006), 'Paul Samuelson's amazing intergenerational transfer', in M. Szenberg, L. Ramrattan and A. Gottesman (eds), *Samuelsonian Economics and the Twenty-First Century*, Oxford, Oxford University Press, pp. 42–53.

Merton, R.C. (2006), 'Paul Samuelson and financial economics', in M. Szenberg, L. Ramrattan and A. Gottesman (eds), *Samuelsonian Economics and the Twenty-First Century*, Oxford, Oxford University Press, pp. 262–300.

Milgrom, P. (2006), 'Multipliers and the Le Chatelier principle', in M. Szenberg, L. Ramrattan and A. Gottesman (eds), *Samuelsonian Economics and the Twenty-First Century*, Oxford, Oxford University Press, pp. 303–10.

Musgrave, R.A. (1983), 'Public goods', in E.C. Brown and R.M. Solow (eds), *Paul Samuelson and Modern Economic Theory*, New York: McGraw Hill, pp. 139–56.

Samuelson, P.A. (1938), 'A note on the pure theory of consumer behaviour', *Economica*, **5** (17), 61–71, addendum 353–4; also in P.A. Samuelson (1966), *Collected Scientific Papers*, vol. 1, ed. J.E. Stiglitz, Cambridge, MA: MIT Press, paper no. 1.

Samuelson, P.A. (1947), *Foundations of Economic Analysis*, Cambridge, MA: Harvard University Press, enlarged edn 1983.

Samuelson, P.A. (1948a), 'Consumption theory in terms of revealed preference', *Economica*, **15** (36), 243–53, also in P.A. Samuelson (1966), *Collected Scientific Papers*, vol. 1, ed. J.E. Stiglitz, Cambridge, MA: MIT Press, paper no. 9.

Samuelson, P.A. (1948b), *Economics*, New York: McGraw-Hill, and P.A. Samuelson and W. Nordhaus (2004), *Economics*, 18th edn, New York: McGraw Hill.

Samuelson, P.A. (1954), 'The pure theory of public expenditure', *Review of Economics and Statistics*, **36** (4), 387–9, also in P.A. Samuelson (1966), *Collected Scientific Papers*, vol. 2, ed. J.E. Stiglitz, Cambridge, MA: MIT Press, paper no. 92.

Samuelson, P.A. (1956), 'Social indifference curves', *Quarterly Journal of Economics*, **70** (1), 1–22, also in P.A. Samuelson (1966), *Collected Scientific Papers*, vol. 2, ed. J.E. Stiglitz, Cambridge, MA: MIT Press, paper no. 78.

Samuelson, P.A. (1957), 'Wages and interest: a modern dissection of Marxian economic models', *American Economic Review*, **47** (December), 884–912, also in P.A. Samuelson (1966), *Collected Scientific Papers*, vol. 1, ed. J.E. Stiglitz, Cambridge, MA: MIT Press, paper no. 29.

Samuelson, P.A. (1958), 'An exact consumption loan model of interest with or without the social contrivance of money', *Journal of Political Economy*, **66** (6), 467–82, also in P.A. Samuelson (1966), *Collected Scientific Papers*, vol. 1, ed. J.E. Stiglitz, Cambridge, MA: MIT Press, paper no. 21.

Samuelson, P.A. (1965a), 'Proof that properly anticipated prices fluctuate randomly', *Industrial Management Review*, **6** (2), 41–9, also in P.A. Samuelson (1966), *Collected Scientific Papers*, vol. 3, ed. R.C. Merton, Cambridge, MA: MIT Press, paper no. 198.

Samuelson, P.A. (1965b), 'Rational theory of warrant pricing', *Industrial Management Review*, **6** (2), 13–39, also in P.A. Samuelson (1966), *Collected Scientific Papers*, vol. 3, ed. R.C. Merton, Cambridge, MA: MIT Press, paper no. 199.

Samuelson, P.A. (1966–86), *The Collected Scientific Papers of Paul A. Samuelson*, 5 vols, vols 1–2 (1966) ed. J.E. Stiglitz, vol. 3 (1972) ed. R.C. Merton, vol. 4 (1977) eds H. Nagatani and K. Crowley, vol. 5 (1986) ed. K. Crowley, Cambridge, MA: MIT Press.

Samuelson, P.A. (1971a), 'Maximum principles in analytical economics', in *Les Prix Nobel en 1970*, Stockholm: Nobel Foundation, also in P.A. Samuelson (1966), *Collected Scientific Papers*, vol. 3, ed. R.C. Merton, Cambridge, MA: MIT Press, paper no. 130.

Samuelson, P.A. (1971b), 'Understanding the Marxian notion of exploitation: a summary of the so-called transformation problem between Marxian values and competitive prices', *Journal of Economic Literature*, **9** (2), 399–431 also in P.A. Samuelson (1966), *Collected Scientific Papers*, vol. 3, ed. R.C. Merton, Cambridge, MA: MIT Press, paper no. 153.

Samuelson, P.A. (1971c), 'The "fallacy" of maximizing the geometric mean in long sequences of investing or gambling', *Proceedings of the National Academy of Sciences*, **68** (10), 2493–6, also in P.A. Samuelson (1966), *Collected Scientific Papers*, vol. 3, ed. R.C. Merton, Cambridge, MA: MIT Press, paper no. 207.

Samuelson, P.A. (2002), 'Pastiches from an earlier politically incorrect academic age', in H. Lim, U.K. Park and G.C. Harcourt, *Editing Economics*, New York, Routledge, pp. 47–55.

Samuelson, P.A. (2004), 'Where Ricardo and Mill rebut and confirm arguments of mainstream economists supporting globalization', *Journal of Economic Perspectives*, **18** (Summer), 135–46.

Samuelson, P.A. and W. Stolper (1941), 'Protection and real wages', *Review of Economic Studies*, **9**, 58–73; also in P.A. Samuelson (1966), *Collected Scientific Papers*, vol. 2, ed. J.E. Stiglitz, Cambridge, MA: MIT Press, paper no. 66.

Sen, A. (1977), 'Rational fools: a critique of the behavioural foundations of economic theory', *Philosophy and Public Affairs*, **6** (4), 317–44.

Solow, R.M. (1997), 'How did economics get that way and what way did it get?', *Daedalus, Journal of the American Academy of Arts and Sciences*, **126** (1), 39–58.

Solow, R.M. (2006), 'Overlapping generations', in M. Szenberg, L. Ramrattan and A. Gottesman (eds), *Samuelsonian Economics and the Twenty-First Century*, Oxford, Oxford University Press, pp. 35–41.

Szenberg, M., L. Ramrattan and A. Gottesman (eds) (2006), *Samuelsonian Economics and the Twenty-First Century*, Oxford, Oxford University Press.

Herbert Alexander Simon (1916–2001)

No other single person has won the Nobel Memorial Prize for Economics (1978), the Turing Award of the Association for Computing Machinery (Newell and Simon 1972), the Orsa/Tims John von Neumann Theory Prize (1988), the Distinguished Scientific Contribution Award of the American Psychological Association (1969) and the National Medal of Science (1986). Perhaps this renaissance man's outlook on the scientific spirit he nurtured can be summarized in his characterization of 'the central task of natural science' to be (Simon 1996: 1–2):

> [T]o make the wonderful commonplace: to show that complexity, correctly viewed, is only a mask for simplicity; to find pattern hidden in apparent chaos. . . . This is the task of natural science: to show that the wonderful is not incomprehensible, to show how it can be comprehended – but not to destroy wonder. For when we have explained the wonderful, unmasked the hidden pattern, a new wonder arises at how complexity was woven out of simplicity. The aesthetics of natural science and mathematics is at one with the aesthetics of music and painting – both inhere in the discovery of a partially concealed pattern.

In an academic life spanning more than six decades, Simon managed, almost single-handedly, to create the wholly new disciplines of behavioural economics and the cognitive sciences and nurture through to growth and prosperity one of the great academic institutions, the Graduate School of Industrial Administration (GSIA) at the Carnegie Institute of Technology (now the Carnegie Mellon University – CMU) in Pittsburgh, where these disciplines were fostered with immense dedication. The eminent proof theorist, metamathematician and philosopher, Wilfried Sieg, recalled during a memorial event that Simon was also instrumental in the creation of a department of philosophy at CMU and went on to observe:

> How intimately theoretical issues and practical affairs were intertwined for Herb! Having discussed some difficult administrative problems with him, he remarked without further explanation: *Proceed, as if you were proving a theorem*! I followed his advice and, lo and behold, it worked: proving a theorem requires, after all, to look at the problem from a variety of perspectives and to expend lots of patience. (Sieg 2001, emphasis added)

Of course, Simon would not have suggested this metaphor to a Bourbakist or an Hilbertian Formalist, but only to a proof-theorist like Sieg, who would have thought of a proof as a procedure, in the same sense in which Simon extolled the virtues of procedural decision-making in all aspects of administrative and economic life. Incidentally, Sieg's colleague in the philosophy department at CMU, Teddy Seidenfeld, is the current holder of the Herbert Simon Professorship of Philosophy and Statistics.

Herbert Simon (born 15 June 1916, Milwaukee, Wisconsin, died 9 February 2001, Pittsburgh, Pennsylvania) was the second son of Arthur Carl Simon, a German émigré electrical engineer, inventor and patent lawyer, and Edna Marguerite Merkel, pianist and a second-generation descendant of immigrants from Prague and Cologne. He was wholly Jewish on his father's side; partly Lutheran on his mother's. His brother Clarence was five years older. He was introduced to Dorothea Isabel Pye by William W. Cooper (of "Charnes–Cooper" fame and coincidentally also the man who helped establish the School of Urban and Public Affairs at CMU, serving also as its Dean from 1969 to 1975) and they married on Christmas day in 1937. Their daughter Kathie was born in 1942, followed by son Peter in 1944 and another daughter Barbara in 1946.

From the public elementary and high schools in Milwaukee, he won a full scholarship ($300 per year) to the University of Chicago, taking the examination in physics, mathematics and English. His maternal uncle, Harold Merkel, "an ardent formal debater [whom] I followed in that activity too", who had died young, at the age of 30, in 1922, was an early intellectual influence. Uncle Harold had graduated with distinction in law from the University of Wisconsin, having also studied economics under the legendary John R. Commons and leaving behind copies of *The Federalist Papers* and William James's *Psychology* in the family library, both of which were devoured by the young Herbert, leaving indelible impressions on the future civil libertarian, behavioural economist, computer scientist and cognitive psychologist. His first publication was a letter to the Editor of the *Milwaukee Journal*, defending atheism.

To buttress his debating skills he began to read widely in the social sciences. Two books in particular were decisively influential: Richard T. Ely's *Outlines of Economics* (1893) and Henry George's *Progress and Poverty* (1879). By the time he was ready to embark upon a university career, he had developed a clear sense of the general direction he intended to take in his studies. He would devote himself to becoming a "mathematical social scientist". We cannot imagine anyone else encapsulating and wearing this mantle with more grace and justification.

He obtained his BA in political science from Chicago in 1936 and a PhD in 1943 and decided to major in political science because his first choice of major, economics, required him to take an obligatory course in accounting, which he detested.

The undergraduate-term paper, written for graduation, led to a research assistantship at the Milwaukee City Government in the field of Municipal Administration, which in turn led to a Directorship at the Bureau of Public Measurement in the University of California at Berkeley, from 1939 to 1942. For Milwaukee he undertook a study of how the municipal employees made budget decisions, for example, when deciding between planting trees and hiring a recreation director. From this work grew his PhD thesis that, subsequently, became one of the fountainheads for the whole field of organization theory: *Administrative Behavior*, published first in 1947 and still in print.

Simon's main intellectual impulses during the Chicago years came from Henry Schultz in mathematical economics and econometrics, who was also a mentor, from Rudolf Carnap, in the philosophy of science, from Nicholas Rashevsky, in mathematical biophysics and from Harold Lasswell and Charles Merriam, in political science.

Simon observed, when writing an appreciation of Allen Newell, that the four great questions of human intellectual endeavour are those on the nature of matter, the origins of the universe, the nature of life and the working of the mind. There is little doubt that he himself devoted the whole of his professional life to various aspects of the problem of the working of the mind. How does the mind perceive the external world? How does perception link up with memory? How does memory act as a reservoir of information and knowledge in interacting with the processes that are activated in human decision-making, in individual and social settings? In short, human problem solving (the title of his 1972 book with Newell): in the face of internal constraints emanating from the working of the mind; and constraints, imposed on its workings, by the external, perceived, world.

Much is made these days of "ecological rationality" and "ecological cognitive computing", by which is meant that any internal constraints on the working of the mind should be taken in conjunction with the "external constraints of the environment" in which the mind is situated for its interaction with the external world. Simon's definition of bounded rationality – the term, although not the concept, was introduced in the Introduction to part IV of Simon (1957: 198), while the analytical content, together with its conceptual underpinnings, were fully developed in Simon (1955, 1956) – from the outset, was to encapsulate both of these aspects of the workings of the mind, in its rational, decision-making, incarnation.

Nothing, and no one, in the burgeoning field of modern behavioural economics (see Velupillai and Kao 2014 for the definitions of modern and classical behavioural economics) seem to have ever underpinned any of their theories on a model of computation. Thus they are unable to comprehend the nature of the decision problem framework, intrinsically framed with an underlying algorithmic basis, within which Simon first advanced, and then developed, boundedly rational and satisficing decisions.

George Polya's influential little book *How to Solve It?* (Polya 1945) introduced generations of students to heuristics – the art of guided search. Simon and Newell (1983) felt that the Polya framework provided a starting point for investigating, experimentally, the creative aspects of the workings of the mind in two formally and rigorously definable areas – human problem solving and in the art of discovery. From lessons that could be learnt in understanding the formal aspects of human problem solving they felt they could move on to more ambitious tasks: to an understanding of human thinking, in general. From there it would be a natural step to a formal understanding of the underpinnings of human decision-making in general.

The art of discovery, based on heuristics as guided search, led Simon to develop *Models of Discovery* (1977), resurrecting the Peirce–Hanson (Hanson 1958) emphasis on retroduction (or abduction; thus, circumventing the tiresome dichotomy between induction and deduction) and, simultaneously, taking a well-aimed attack on the nihilism in Karl Popper's stance that there was no scientific basis for a "logic of scientific discovery" (see, in particular, Simon, 1977: ch. 5.4).

Simon used "experimentally" in the sense of exploring by computer simulation, guided by programmed heuristics. These were, for Simon, algorithms that were not necessarily constrained by the Church–Turing thesis of computability theory. In this sense his lifelong adherence to heuristic methods in human problem-solving, models of discovery, design of organizations and evolutionary dynamics, had more in common with the notion of algorithms as proofs in constructive mathematics. A lack of appreciation of this subtle difference may have been the reason for even the great Hao Wang to be critical of the way Newell, Shaw and Simon automated proofs in *Principia Mathematica*, in contrast to the way he had done the same (Wang 1970: 227; emphasis added): "There is no need to kill a chicken with a butcher's knife. Yet the net impression is that Newell–Shaw–Simon failed even to kill the chicken with their butcher's knife. . . . To argue the superiority of '*heuristic*' over *algorithmic methods* by choosing a particularly *inefficient algorithm* seems hardly just." What is a heuristic, if not an algorithm?

Simon was a member of the Cowles Foundation for Economic Research in its early Chicago days, before its move to Yale in New Haven; he was also a member of the Rand Corporation in its glory days, the early 1950s. The former nurtured, in Simon's own words, the econometric "mafia"; the latter fostered the mathematical economics "mafia". He remained a gadfly inside these citadels of orthodoxy while enjoying the respect, perhaps even the envy, of his distinguished and eminent peers.

His contributions to formal and traditional economic theory – both to micro and macro variants – and to econometric theory were fundamental and path-breaking. At a very early stage in the mathematization of economics he deduced, in joint work with the mathematician David Hawkins (Hawkins and Simon 1949), conditions for stability, which came to be known as the Hawkins–Simon conditions in the folklore of the subject, for linear multi-sectoral models of the economy. This led to an amusing episode with the House Un-American Committee hearings, during the "McCarthy era", because Hawkins – whom Simon had never met and with whom he had written the famous paper entirely by correspondence – was a paid-up member of the Communist Party.

During the Great Depression, Simon had seen a chart on the walls of his father's study, tracking the dismal progress of a faltering American economy. This chart was constructed on the basis of a model of the macroeconomy and its flows built on the principles of servomechanism theory, using hydrodynamic analogies devised by an imaginative engineer, with a doctorate in sociology, A.O. Dahlberg. Inspired by the memories of the Dahlberg chart in his father's study, he began to look at the economy from the point of view of the theory of servomechanisms and feedback control. This line of research led him to his celebrated results on certainty equivalence in the devising of optimal policy in decisions on production scheduling in firms. He did not pursue the servomechanism metaphors for too long, because he felt, by then, that analogue simulations were a distinct second best to the digital possibilities he was pioneering.

The origins of the inspiration that led to the influential work with his eminent Japanese student Yuji Ijiri on the size distributions of the growth and decay of business firms and organizations are narrated with humour and candour in his charming autobiography, *Models of My Life* (Simon 1991). It is also a tale of academic bloody-mindedness, recounted without rancour, and revisited with nostalgia and regrets on the fallibility of memory.

In 1946 Richard Goodwin (1947) had begun interpreting economic agents, markets and the economic system as (nonlinear) oscillators, analysing markets as coupled oscillators with hierarchies of coupling strengths. All of them were linked by economy-wide, common, expenditure impulses (and averaged expectations). In a series of papers, extending over half a century, Simon exploited this simple idea in many fertile ways: to study causality in economic models; to formalize causality and link it with identifiability in econometric models; to theorize about aggregation in economic models; and to formalize the idea of the hierarchy of complexity utilizing near decomposability in hierarchical organizations (Simon 1996: 173–216); to study counterfactuals in scientific theorizing, and on using the idea of near-decomposability to study evolutionary aspects of mind, thought, organizations and nature.

The idea of "near decomposability", extracted from Goodwin's notion of unilateral coupling in markets with production lags, was made mathematically rigorous by the idea of approximately decomposable (or indecomposable) matrices. It was in Goodwin's own pioneering work on multi-sectoral dynamic models (in the late 1940s and early 1950s) that both the link between indecomposability and the Perron–Frobenius theorem(s) and, indeed, the use and introduction of the Perron–Frobenius theorem(s) first appeared. The Goodwin–Simon analytical nexus straddled both inter-industrial and macroeconomic dynamics, in that Simon's work on applying servomechanism theory to the modelling of macroeconomic systems was also inspired by the former's classics on aggregate nonlinear macrodynamics (see Goodwin 1951: Simon 1952).

In *Models of My Life*, he takes this particular example of the inspiration he got from Goodwin's attempt to represent markets interacting with delayed responses as hierarchically coupled oscillators to wonder about the kinds of representations scientists use in thinking about research problems: where do the metaphors for scientific representations come from? How are they represented and retained in the human mind? How are they recalled – when, and why at that particular juncture? What are the triggering mechanisms and the catalysts? He had answers, tentative, testable and, as always, interesting and provocative.

In his *Raffaele Mattioli Lectures* of 1993 (Simon 1997), he argued for a study of economies in terms of organizations as the basic unit rather than the traditional device of markets. His case was based on solid empirical and theoretical results. He felt – justified by empirical and experimental data and results – the reliance on markets led to the unnecessary and false claims for their optimality properties (true only in one of many possible mathematical worlds and false in all others) as well as the propagation of the false dichotomy between the virtues of decentralization and the vices of centralization, without forgetting the merits of the former and the disadvantages of the latter.

Finally, it is rarely recognized that Simon, in his imaginative experimental approach to human problem-solving was one of the undisputed pioneers of so-called agent-based modelling. He always made clear, for example, in studying and automating chess, that understanding the difference between the rules determining the exact dynamics of an individual chessman, say the rook, and its particular position in the configuration of a game, was formally – that is, algorithmically – indeterminate (without going as far towards claiming algorithmic undecidability for this "aggregation" problem).

He was optimistic about the future of economics and even more so of computer science and the interaction between the two and psychology. In a letter written after reading Velupillai (2000), he wrote that "the battle has been won, at least the first part, although it will take a couple of academic generations to clear the field and get some sensible textbooks written and the next generations trained".

The precept that may have guided his astonishingly fertile scientific life may well have been, in his own words (Simon, 1996: 28; original emphasis): "What a person *cannot* do he or she *will not* do, no matter how strong the urge to do it."

At the time of his death he was the Richard King Mellon Professor of Computer Science and Psychology at Carnegie-Mellon University, a post he had held since 1966.

K. VELA VELUPILLAI AND YING-FANG KAO

See also:

Behavioural and cognitive economics (III); Economic dynamics (III); Evolutionary economics (III).

References and further reading

Ely, R.T (1893), *Outlines of Economics*, New York: Hunt and Eaton.
George, H. (1879), *Progress and Poverty: An Enquiry into the Cause of Industrial Depressions, and of Increase of Want with Increase of Wealth. The Remedy*, New York: K. Paul, Trench & Company.
Goodwin, R.M. (1947), 'Dynamical coupling with especial reference to markets having production lags', *Econometrica*, **15** (3), 181–204.

Goodwin, R.M (1951), 'The nonlinear accelerator and the business cycle', *Econometrica*, **19** (1), 1–17.

Hanson, N.R. (1958), *Patterns of Discovery*, Cambridge: Cambridge University Press.

Hawkins, D. and H.A. Simon (1949), 'Note: some conditions of macroeconomic stability', *Econometrica*, **17** (3/4), 245–8.

Newell, A. (1983), 'The heuristic of George Polya and its relation to artificial intelligence', in R. Groner, M. Croner and W.F. Bischof (eds), *Methods of heuristics*. Hillsdale, NJ: Lawrence Erlbaum Associates, pp. 195–243.

Newell, A. and H.A. Simon (1972), *Human Problem Solving*, Englewood Cliffs, NJ: Prentice-Hall.

Polya, G. (1945), *How to Solve It: A New Aspect of Mathematical Method*, Princeton, NJ: Princeton University Press.

Sieg, W. (2001), 'Remembrances of Herbert Simon', accessed 27 December 2015 at http://www.cs.cmu.edu/simon/all.html.

Simon, H.A. (1947), *Administrative Behavior: A Study of Decision-Making Processes in Administrative Organization*, New York: Macmillan.

Simon, H.A. (1952), 'On the application of servomechanism theory in the study of production control', *Econometrica*, **20** (2), 247–68.

Simon, H.A. (1955), 'A behavioral model of rational choice', *Quarterly Journal of Economics*, **69** (1), 99–118.

Simon, H.A. (1956), 'Rational choice and the structure of the environment', *Psychological Review*, **63** (122), 129–38.

Simon, H.A. (1957), *Models of Man: Social and Rational*, New York: John Wiley & Sons.

Simon, H.A. (1977), *Models of Discovery*, Dordrecht: D. Reidel.

Simon, H.A. (1991), *Models of My Life*, Cambridge, MA: MIT Press.

Simon, H.A. (1996), *The Sciences of the Artificial*, 3rd edn, Cambridge, MA: MIT Press.

Simon, H.A. (1997), *An Empirically Based Microeconomics, The Raffaele Mattioli Lectures*, delivered on 18 and 19 March 1993, Cambridge: Cambridge University Press.

Velupillai, K. (2000), *Computable Economics*, Oxford: Oxford University Press.

Velupillai, K.V. and Y.-F. Kao (2014), 'Computable and computational complexity theoretic bases for Herbert Simon's cognitive behavioural economics', *Cognitive Systems Research*, **29–30** (September), 40–52.

Wang, H. (1970), *Logic, Computers and Sets*, New York: Chelsea.

James Tobin (1918–2002)

The American economist James Tobin was awarded the 1981 Royal Bank of Sweden Prize in Economic Science in Memory of Alfred Nobel for his contributions to monetary economics and macroeconomics (Purvis 1982; Myhrman 1982). Among the generation of American Keynesians who came to economics in the 1930s and 1940s, which included his fellow Nobel laureates Paul Samuelson, Robert Solow, Lawrence Klein and Franco Modigliani, Tobin stood out for his exploration of the working of the monetary system and especially of the transmission mechanism through which monetary policy affects the real economy (Tobin 1980, 1971–96; Purvis 1991; Buiter 2003; Dimand 2014). Tobin's contributions ranged from models of the transactions demand for money (Tobin 1956) and demand for money as a store of value (Tobin 1958b) to the extension of the investment saving–liquidity preference money supply (IS–LM) macroeconomic framework to multi-asset portfolio balance models (Brainard and Tobin 1968; Tobin 1969, 1982a), introducing money in long-run growth theory (Tobin 1965), and scepticism about the macro efficiency of the financial system (Tobin 1984). Within the economics profession, he was best known for Tobin's q theory of investment (Tobin's q is the ratio of the market value of equity to the replacement cost of capital; Brainard and Tobin 1968), Tobit estimators for limited dependent variables (Tobin 1955b, 1958a), and the Tobin separation theorem (Tobin 1958b: if a riskless asset exists, differing degrees of risk aversion just affect the fraction of the portfolio to be placed in risky assets, but do not change the optimal combination of risky assets). Beyond the economics profession, he was famed for the Tobin tax, a proposed small tax on international currency transactions to inhibit speculative "hot money" flows (Tobin 2003; Haq et al. 1996). His contributions to economics beyond monetary economics included pioneering work in "green accounting" to move beyond gross domestic product (GDP) to a Measure of Economic Welfare (Nordhaus and Tobin 1972) and in the creation of neoclassical growth theory (Tobin 1955a; Solow 1956; Swan 1956). Describing himself as an "Old Keynesian" (Tobin 1993) rather than a new, neo- or post-Keynesian, Tobin served on President Kennedy's Council of Economic Advisors and argued for activist macroeconomic stabilization policies and for income redistribution to fight poverty (see essays collected in Tobin 1989, 1996). "Tobin's way of combining rigor and relevance, intelligence and passion, theory and common sense, has stayed green in my memory for more than 40 years," wrote Robert Solow (2004: 658).

James Tobin was born on 5 March 1918, in Champaign–Urbana, Illinois, to a journalist, who later handled publicity for the University of Illinois Athletic Association, and a social worker. After attending the university's experimental high school, Tobin went to Harvard on a scholarship in 1935, receiving his BA in 1939, his MA in 1940, and his PhD, after a year working in Washington and then wartime service in the US Navy, in 1947. When Tobin took Ec A (Principles of Economics),

> [t]he same crazy graduate student [Spencer Pollard] who was my Ec A instructor was also my tutor ... My tutor wanted us to read "this new book that people are saying is important" [Keynes 1936] ... I found it pretty exciting because this whole idea of setting up a macro model as a system of simultaneous equations appealed to my intellect ... So my introduction to economics, taking the elementary course and reading Keynes, were simultaneous in my sophomore year. (Interview in Shiller 1999: 870)

Coming to economics by reading Keynes's *General Theory*, and hearing his mother's experiences as a social worker in the Depression, shaped Tobin's approach to macro-economics as a discipline relevant to public policy and the real world, not just intellectual puzzle-solving.

Tobin's PhD dissertation (1947a) investigated why the simple Keynesian consumption function, which showed an almost perfect fit between aggregate consumption and aggregate disposable income in the interwar United States, failed to predict the post-war surge in consumption. His main contribution in his thesis, adding wealth as an argument in the saving function, was published as Tobin (1951) and added an inter-temporal dimension to modelling of consumption and saving – the implications of Irving Fisher's 1907 two-period optimal consumption diagram were not then generally recognized. As Willem Buiter (2003: F609) observes, section 3.3 of Tobin (1952), "The public debt as private wealth," considered the possibility of what is now called debt neutrality or Ricardian equivalence, but Tobin (like David Ricardo) considered this unlikely to hold in practice. As late as the 1960s, Tobin was invited to contribute to the *International Encyclopaedia of the Social Sciences* as an authority on the consumption function, rather than as a monetary economist. But even as a graduate student, Tobin worked in monetary economics, making Keynes's liquidity preference function operational and estimating its parameters (Tobin 1947b). Hansen (1949), source of what became known as the Hicks–Hansen IS–LM diagrams, "relied heavily upon [Tobin's] analysis" (and on Hicks 1937) in the more technical parts of the book, and Tobin was the only person Hansen thanked for prepublication comments (Hansen 1949: vi, 126 n., 168n).

After his PhD, Tobin was elected to a three-year term in Harvard's Society of Fellows, with no responsibilities except his own research. He spent the last of those academic years, 1949–50, visiting Richard Stone's Department of Applied Economics in the other Cambridge. Tobin (1950) pioneered pooling aggregate time-series data with cross-section budget studies to estimate the demand for food in the United States, a landmark study that held up well when revisited by later econometricians using current methods (Magnus and Morgan 1999). Noting that in any data for purchases of consumer durables (such as automobiles), most observations would be zero (most households do not buy a car in any given year), Tobin (1955b, 1958a) extended probit analysis to examine simultaneously the decision whether to spend and how much to spend, a procedure econometrician Arthur Goldberger named Tobit analysis.

Tobin joined Yale University as associate professor in 1950 (full professor from 1955, Sterling Professor of Economics from 1957), retiring in 1988 but teaching undergraduate courses for another decade and remaining active in research until his death on 11 March 2002. He won the American Economics Association's John Bates Clark Medal, for an outstanding American economist below the age of 40, in 1955, and was president of the Econometric Society in 1958. After Tobin declined to move to the University of Chicago to succeed Tjalling Koopmans as director of the Cowles Commission, Koopmans and Cowles moved to Yale with Tobin as the first director of the renamed Cowles Foundation for Research in Economics.

Tobin (1956, 1958b) asked why rational agents hold fiat money yielding zero interest when bonds paid strictly positive nominal returns. Like Baumol (1952), Tobin (1956) modelled transactions demand for money as an optimizing trade-off between transactions cost of selling bonds for money to make payments and interest foregone by holding cash instead of bonds. The resulting square root rule, familiar in the literature on inventories, had been derived by Maurice Allais (1947: 238–41, translated in Baumol and Tobin 1989), but this was ignored by English-speaking economists. Drawing on Harry Markowitz's concept of an optimally diversified portfolio that minimized risk for any given level of expected return (Markowitz 1952), Tobin (1958b) modelled demand for money as an asset as a trade-off between expected return and risk (measured as the mean and variance, respectively, of the distribution of returns on an efficient portfolio of risky assets), solving for the fraction of the portfolio to be held as riskless, zero-return money. Whereas Keynes (1936) assumed that each investor held a different point-expectation of returns, so each investor held either all cash or all securities, Tobin (1958b) posited that investors share a probability distribution over expected returns, so that a change in the interest rate would cause each investor to hold a slightly larger or smaller proportion of his or her wealth as money, rather than some investor switching entirely between money and securities while others did not adjust their portfolios at all. Markowitz (1952) examined how a rational investor should act, Tobin (1958b) the money demand function and asset market equilibrium that would result from investors following Markowitz's prescription.

On sabbatical in 1958, Tobin began a comprehensive statement of his approach to monetary theory that four decades later became *Money, Credit and Capital* (Tobin with Golub 1998). Tobin's account of endogenous creation of money through optimizing portfolio choices of commercial banks facing risk (Tobin 1982b; Tobin with Golub 1998:ch. 7) was a part of that manuscript that was completed by 1960. The project was interrupted when President-elect John F. Kennedy chose Tobin for the President's Council of Economic Advisers. "I remember your protesting, in our telephone conversation prior to your appointment, that you were an 'ivory tower' economist," recalled Kennedy when Tobin left the Council (Yale University Library, Manuscripts and Archives 1999 [2010]: Kennedy to Tobin, 12 July 1962, Tobin Papers 2004-M-088, Box 7):

> If so, you have convincingly demonstrated that the ivory tower can produce public servants of remarkable effectiveness. Your ideas – on domestic policies for stability and growth and on many other economic issues – have been lucid and reasoned, and your advocacy of them has been forceful and persuasive. I have both enjoyed and benefited from our exchange . . . Your advice, whether from within or without the Government, will always be received with interest and respect in this Administration.

Tobin (1955a) was a founding contributor to neoclassical growth theory. Like Pilvin (1953), Solow (1956) and Swan (1956), Tobin (1955a) eliminated the knife-edge instability property attributed to Harrod–Domar growth models by allowing smooth substitution between capital and labour instead of fixed proportions in production. However, Tobin (1955a) was overshadowed by Solow (1956) and Swan (1956), partly because Tobin's paper did too many things at once, for example, introducing portfolio substitution between money and capital in long-run growth, and considering long-run growth in a model with unemployment due to a rigid money wage. Trying again, but making one contribution at a time, Tobin (1965) argued that monetary policy has long-run non-neutral effects through capital intensity even if full employment is assumed. While Tobin (1965) treated money and capital as substitutes in portfolios, so that faster increase of the nominal money supply and price level (raising the opportunity cost of holding real money balances) would increase capital intensity, Stanley Fischer and others later modelled money and capital as complementary factors inputs for firms (see Dimand 2014). While money is thus not necessarily neutral even in the long run without price or wage rigidities, the direction of the non-neutrality is sensitive to how the model is specified. Nordhaus and Tobin (1972), a founding work of "green accounting", stressed the growth of a Measure of Economic Welfare rather than growth of GDP.

Tobin (1974, 1978, 2003) proposed a small tax on international currency transactions to curb speculative capital flows that inhibit use of national demand management to stabilize employment and output (Keynes 1936: 160, proposed a small tax on stock market trades to limit speculation). Such a small tax would have inconsequential effects on trade in goods and services and on long-term direct and portfolio investments, but would cumulate on high-frequency short-term "hot money" flows: "A tax of 0.05 per cent is negligible, for a one-time transfer but, if paid once a week, it cuts 2.5 percentage points off the annual rate of return and much more off the yield of day trading" (Tobin 2003: 62 – automated trading algorithms now trade at much higher frequencies). To Tobin's dismay, he was acclaimed by opponents of globalization: two of the pieces reprinted in Tobin (2003) are entitled "They are misusing my name" and "An idea that gained currency but lost clarity". Similarly, Jagdish Bhagwati has been lionized by advocates of globalization, yet Tobin and Bhagwati agreed in supporting free trade in goods and services while wishing to control short-term capital flows (Dimand 2014).

Encountering economics through Keynes and the Depression, Tobin rejected the natural rate hypothesis of Milton Friedman (1968) that the economy would be at the natural rate of unemployment in the absence of unexpected inflation and that reducing unemployment below the natural rate involves fooling people into giving up valuable leisure for lower real wages than they think they are getting (see Friedman and Tobin in Gordon 1974; also Tobin 1980; Lucas 1981). Inspired by Irving Fisher (1933) as well as Keynes (1936: ch. 19), Tobin (1975, 1980, 1993, 1997) argued that, because aggregate effective demand depends on (expected) inflation as well as on the price level, the economy is only self-adjusting within a corridor of stability (Palley 2008; Bruno and Dimand 2009). In Tobin's model, the economy returns automatically to potential output after small shocks, but large negative demand shocks push the economy outside the corridor, moving further away from full employment unless government policy introduces an offsetting demand shock – that is, Great Depressions are possible. In such a model faster adjustment of prices and money wages can be destabilizing.

Tobin's q theory of investment made net investment depend on q, the ratio of the market value of equity to the replacement cost of capital (Brainard and Tobin 1968), providing a channel for monetary policy (and stock market bubbles and crashes) to affect investment by changing asset prices (see also Tobin 1961). If q exceeds one, net investment is positive and the capital stock grows. If q is less than one, it is more profitable for firms to buy existing assets than to invest in creating new ones, so gross investment is less than depreciation, and net investment is negative. At $q = 1$, the capital stock is at its desired level. Since asset prices were the channel through which monetary policy could affect real investment, Tobin (1969, 1982a) turned to the determination of asset prices through his "general equilibrium approach to monetary theory," with money as one of several assets that are imperfect substitutes for each other. Money differs from other assets by having an institutionally fixed nominal return. Hicks (1935) crucially influenced Tobin's approach. The later new classical usage of "general equilibrium" refers to markets linked through the budget constraint of a representative agent (or in overlapping-generations models, two agents, one old and one young). For Tobin "general equilibrium" implied market linked by the adding-up constraint that asset demands had to sum to total wealth and that stocks and flows had to be consistent. Tobin developed choice-theoretic foundations of each component of aggregate demand: consumption (Tobin 1947a, 1951), investment (Tobin's *q*), money supply (Tobin 1982b), and money demand and portfolio balance (Tobin 1956, 1958b).

Keynesian macroeconomics lost ground to monetarism, new classical economics, and real business cycle theory in the 1970s and even more in the 1980s for several reasons: greater concern with inflation rather than unemployment, emphasis on long-run growth of potential output rather than short-run stabilization, instability of parameters in large macro-econometric models used for forecasting and policy evaluation, conservative shifts in the political environment. In addition, correlation among the many, imperfectly substitutable assets in the multi-asset modelling approach of Tobin (1969, 1982a) led to high standard deviations and low t-statistics in attempts at empirical implementation such as Backus et al. (1980), while, as Tobin noted (in Shiller 1999: 889), "The whole idea of modern finance does not include imperfect substitution. I suppose in defense of ignoring it is the fact that we weren't actually able to solve the nonlinear equations with these adjustment mechanisms." Recent events, showing that depressions and financial crises can still happen in advanced industrial countries, suggest renewed relevance for the corridor of stability of Tobin (1975, 1980, 1993, 1997) as a middle ground between models that automatically re-adjust to a unique full employment equilibrium, not matter how large the shock, and models that are always unstable – particularly since Tobin's result does not depend on wage rigidity but only on noting that aggregate demand depends on the rate of change of prices as well as on the level (see also Fisher 1933; Keynes 1936: ch. 19). Beyond his role as an "Old Keynesian" in macroeconomic debates (for example, the corridor of stability) and public policy (for example, the Tobin tax), Tobin's contributions to economics range from Tobin's *q* and his modelling of money demand and endogenous money creation to the Tobit estimator, pooling of time series and cross-section data, the Tobin separation theorem in portfolio choice, and his role in the creation of the capital asset pricing model (CAPM) and the neoclassical growth model.

ROBERT W. DIMAND

See also:

Econometrics (III); Growth (III); John Maynard Keynes (I); Keynesianism (II); Macroeconomics (III); Money and banking (III).

References and further reading

Allais, M. (1947), *Economie et Intérêt*, Paris: Imprimerie Nationale.
Backus, D., W.C. Brainard, G. Smith and J. Tobin (1980), 'A model of US financial and nonfinancial economic behavior', *Journal of Money, Credit and Banking*, **12** (2), 259–93.
Baumol, W.J. (1952), 'The transactions demand for cash: an inventory-theoretic approach', *Quarterly Journal of Economics*, **66** (November), 545–56.
Baumol, W.J. and J. Tobin (1989), 'The optimal cash balance proposition: Maurice Allais's priority', *Journal of Economic Literature*, **27** (3), 1160–62.
Brainard, W.C., and J. Tobin (1968), 'Pitfalls in financial model building', *American Economic Review*, **58** (2), 99–122.

Bruno, R. and R.W. Dimand (2009), 'The corridor of stability in Tobin's Keynesian model of recession and depression', *International Journal of Applied Economics and Econometrics*, **17** (1), 17–25.
Buiter, W.H. (2003), 'James Tobin: an appreciation of his contribution to economics', *Economic Journal*, **113** (November), F585–F631.
Colander, D. (1999), 'Conversations with James Tobin and Robert Shiller on the 'Yale Tradition' in macro-economics', *Macroeconomic Dynamics*, **3** (1), 116–43.
Dimand, R.W. (2014), *James Tobin*, London and Basingstoke: Palgrave Macmillan.
Fisher, I. (1933), 'The debt-deflation theory of great depressions', *Econometrica*, **1** (3), 337–57.
Friedman, M. (1968), 'The role of monetary policy', *American Economic Review*, **58** (1), 1–17.
Gordon, R.J. (ed.) (1974), *Milton Friedman's Monetary Framework: A Debate with his Critics*, Chicago, IL: University of Chicago Press.
Hansen, A.H. (1949), *Monetary Theory and Fiscal Policy*, New York: McGraw-Hill.
Haq, M. ul, I. Kaul and I. Grunberg (eds) (1996), *The Tobin Tax: Coping with Financial Volatility*, with pro-logue by J. Tobin, New York: Oxford University Press.
Hicks, J.R. (1935), 'A suggestion for simplifying the theory of money', *Economica*, n.s. **2** (1), 1–19.
Hicks, J.R. (1937), 'Mr. Keynes and the classics: a suggested interpretation', *Econometrica*, **5** (2), 147–59.
Keynes, J.M. (1936), *The General Theory of Employment, Interest and Money*, London: Macmillan.
Lucas, R.E. Jr (1981), 'Tobin and monetarism: a review article', *Journal of Economic Literature*, **19** (2), 558–67.
Magnus, J.R. and M.S. Morgan (eds) (1999), *Methodology and Tacit Knowledge: Two Experiments in Econometrics*, New York: John Wiley & Sons.
Markowitz, H. (1952), 'Portfolio selection', *Journal of Finance*, **7** (1), 77–91.
Myhrman, J. (1982), 'James Tobin's contributions to economics', *Scandinavian Journal of Economics*, **84** (1), 89–100.
Nordhaus, W. and J. Tobin (1972), 'Is growth obsolete?', in *Economic Growth: Fiftieth Anniversary Colloquium V*, New York: Columbia University Press for the National Bureau of Economic Research, pp. 1–80.
Palley, T.I. (2008), 'Keynesian models of recession and depression revisited', *Journal of Economic Behavior and Organization*, **68** (2), 167–77.
Pilvin, H. (1953), 'Full capacity versus full employment growth', *Quarterly Journal of Economics*, **67** (4), 545–52.
Purvis, D.D. (1982), 'James Tobin's contributions to economics', *Scandinavian Journal of Economics*, **84** (1), 61–88.
Purvis, D.D. (1991), 'James Tobin's contributions to economics', in W.C. Brainard, W. Nordhaus and H.W. Watts (eds), *Money, Macroeconomics, and Economic Policy: Essays in Honor of James Tobin*, Cambridge, MA: MIT Press, pp. 1–42.
Shiller, R.J. (1999), 'The ET interview: Professor James Tobin', *Econometric Theory*, **15** (6), 867–900.
Solow, R.M. (1956), 'A contribution to the theory of economic growth', *Quarterly Journal of Economics*, **70** (1), 65–94.
Solow, R.M. (2004), 'The Tobin approach to monetary economics', *Journal of Money, Credit and Banking*, **36** (4), 657–63.
Swan, T.W. (1956), 'Economic growth and capital accumulation', *Economic Record*, **32** (63), 334–61.
Tobin, J. (1947a), 'A theoretical and statistical analysis of consumer saving', PhD dissertation, Harvard University.
Tobin, J. (1947b), 'Liquidity preference and monetary policy', *Review of Economics and Statistics*, **29** (2), 124–31, and 'Rejoinder' (1948), *Review of Economics and Statistics*, **30** (4), 314–17.
Tobin, J. (1950), 'A statistical demand function food in the USA', *Journal of the Royal Statistical Society*, Series A, **113** (2), 113–41.
Tobin, J. (1951), 'Relative income, absolute income, and saving', in *Money, Trade and Economic Growth: Essays in Honor of John Henry Williams*, New York: Macmillan, pp. 135–56.
Tobin, J. (1952), 'Asset holding and spending decisions', *American Economic Review: AEA Papers and Proceedings*, **42** (2), 109–23.
Tobin, J. (1955a), 'A dynamic aggregative model', *Journal of Political Economy*, **63** (April), 103–15.
Tobin, J. (1955b), 'The application of multivariate probit analysis to economic data', Cowles Foundation Discussion Paper No. 1, published as 'Multiple Probit Regression of Dichotomous Economic Variables' in J. Tobin (1971–96), *Essays in Economics*, vol. 2, Cambridge, MA: MIT Press, ch. 43, first published 1975 Amsterdam: North-Holland.
Tobin, J. (1956), 'The interest elasticity of transactions demand for cash', *Review of Economics and Statistics*, **38** (1), 41–7.
Tobin, J. (1958a), 'Estimation of relationships for limited dependent variables', *Econometrica*, **26** (1), 24–36.
Tobin, J. (1958b), 'Liquidity preference as behaviour towards risk', *Review of Economic Studies*, **25** (67), 65–86.
Tobin, J. (1961), 'Money, capital, and other stores of value', *American Economic Review: AEA Papers and Proceedings*, **51** (2), 26–37.

Tobin, J. (1965), 'Money and economic growth', *Econometrica*, **33** (4), 671–84.

Tobin, J. (1969), 'A general equilibrium approach to monetary theory', *Journal of Money, Credit and Banking*, **1** (1), 15–29.

Tobin, J. (1971–96), *Essays in Economics*, 4 vols, Cambridge, MA: MIT Press, vol. 1 first published 1972 Chicago: Markham, vol. 2 first published 1975 Amsterdam: North-Holland.

Tobin, J. (1974), *The New Economics One Decade Older*, Princeton, NJ: Princeton University Press.

Tobin, J. (1975), 'Keynesian models of recession and depression', *American Economic Review: Papers and Proceedings*, **65** (2), 175–82.

Tobin, J. (1978), 'A proposal for international monetary reform', *Eastern Economic Journal*, **4** (3–4), 153–9.

Tobin, J. (1980), *Asset Accumulation and Economic Activity*, Oxford: Blackwell and Chicago: University of Chicago Press.

Tobin, J. (1982a), 'Nobel lecture: money and finance in the macroeconomic process', *Journal of Money, Credit and Banking*, **14** (2), 171–204.

Tobin, J. (1982b), 'The commercial banking firm: a simple model', *Scandinavian Journal of Economics*, **84** (4), 495–530.

Tobin, J. (1984), 'On the efficiency of the financial system', *Lloyds Bank Review*, **153** (June), 1–15.

Tobin, J. (1989), *Policies for Prosperity: Essays in a Keynesian Mode*, Cambridge, MA: MIT Press.

Tobin, J. (1993), 'Price flexibility and output stability: an Old Keynesian view', *Journal of Economic Perspectives*, **7** (1), 45–65.

Tobin, J. (1996), *Full Employment and Growth: Further Keynesian Essays on Policy*, Cheltenham, UK, and Northampton, MA, USA: Edward Elgar Publishing.

Tobin, J. (1997), 'An overview of *The General Theory*: behaviour of an economic system without government intervention', in G.C. Harcourt and P.A. Riach (eds), *A 'Second Edition' of the General Theory*, vol. 2, London and New York: Routledge, pp. 3–27.

Tobin, J. (2003), *World Finance and Economic Stability: Selected Essays of James Tobin*, with foreword by J. Yellen, Cheltenham, UK and Northampton, MA, USA: Edward Elgar.

Tobin, J. with S.S. Golub (1998), *Money, Credit and Capital*, Boston, MA: Irwin McGraw-Hill.

Yale University Library, Manuscripts and Archives (1999), *Preliminary Guide to the James Tobin Papers MS 1746*, revised 2010, New Haven, CT: Yale University Library.

James M. Buchanan (1919–2013)

James M. Buchanan is one of the main founders of public choice theory, the leading head of the so-called Virginia School of Political Economy and principal originator of the research programme of constitutional economics.

Buchanan was born on 3 October 1919 in Murfreesboro, Tennessee. He earned a BA from Middle Tennessee Teachers College in 1940, and an MSc from the University of Tennessee in 1941. After serving in the United States Navy from 1941 to 1945 he entered the economics doctoral programme at the University of Chicago and received his PhD in 1948. From 1948 to 1951 he taught at the University of Tennessee and from 1951 to 1956 at Florida State University. From 1956 on – except for a brief interlude at the University of California in Los Angeles (1968–69) – he held appointments at state universities in Virginia, at the University of Virginia from 1956 to1968, at Virginia Polytechnic Institute and State University from 1969 to 1983, and at George Mason University from 1983 until his retirement in 1999. In 1986 he was awarded the Sveriges Riksbank Prize in Economic Sciences in Memory of Alfred Nobel for his eminent role as paradigm builder in the fields of public choice and constitutional economics.

What is most remarkable about Buchanan's work is the coherence and continuity of the research programme that he has pursued throughout his life, the basic contours of which are already visible in his first major paper "The pure theory of government finance" (1949). Starting as a public finance economist, Buchanan felt "intellectual frustration" with orthodox theorizing in his own field as well as in its close neighbour, welfare economics. The intellectual independence that allowed him, as a young scholar, to keep a critical distance from mainstream thinking Buchanan himself attributes in particular to two sources: to Frank Knight, "his professor" at Chicago, and to Knut Wicksell's *Finanztheoretische Untersuchungen* (1896), a book he came across in the summer of 1948, during the interim period between his graduation and his first appointment.

Buchanan's "intellectual frustration" was caused by what he diagnosed as "methodological confusion", namely, an inconsistency between the fundamental theoretical and methodological principles that economists applied in their principal field, the study of market processes, and the perspective they tacitly adopted when, in such fields as public finance and welfare economics, they extended their analysis into the realm of politics. In their study of markets, economists adhere to methodological individualism, explaining collective phenomena as the aggregate outcome of individual actions and their interaction-effects, and assume individuals to be self-interested, advantage-seeking agents. Yet, so Buchanan charged, when they do public finance and welfare economics, they tacitly shift into a paradigmatically different framework. They tend to adopt an organicist view of society, looking at the state as if it were a supra-individual entity with its own value-scale, and to phrase their policy recommendations as if they were advising "benevolent despots" whose only aim is to maximize social welfare. For Buchanan, to diagnose what he regarded as fundamental flaws in mainstream theorizing in such manner also meant identifying the strategy that had to be adopted in order to rectify the "methodological confusion". What needed to be done was to consistently extend the methodological individualism and the behavioural model that had formed the core of the Smithean tradition in economics from the study of market processes into the realm of politics and collective decision-making more generally. Carrying out this project was to become Buchanan's lifelong research agenda. The scholarly work that emerged from this research agenda – assembled in *The Collected Works of James M. Buchanan* (Buchanan 1999–2001) – can be broadly subsumed under two interrelated but separable rubrics: public choice and constitutional economics.

In early 1957, shortly after arriving at the University of Virginia, Buchanan founded with his colleague Warren Nutter the Thomas Jefferson Center for Studies in Political Economy. It can be viewed as the precursor of the Center for Study of Public Choice that Buchanan established in 1969 with Gordon Tullock at Virginia Polytechnic Institute in Blacksburg and that he and his colleagues relocated in 1983 to George Mason University, its current home. It is because of this affiliation with three Virginian state universities that the research tradition associated with Buchanan's work is often labelled as the Virginia School of Political Economy. Public choice theory began largely as a response to the market failure theory of welfare economics, a theory that diagnosed real world markets as "deficient" and in need of political correction whenever they fall short of the theoretical ideal of perfect competition. Buchanan and his fellow public choice theorists accused this approach of a fundamental analytical asymmetry. Its advocates, after diagnosing that real world markets fail when measured against an unattainable theoretical ideal, jump to the conclusion that government intervention is advisable, without ever asking if real world governments are likely to act in the ideal manner that they implicitly presume. Yet, so Buchanan argued, before government intervention can responsibly be recommended, this question needs to be answered, requiring a realistic theory of real world politics. The public choice project that he promoted was to develop, and apply in various ways, such a theory, an economic theory of politics that is on an equal footing with the economics of markets.

While public choice was the primary focus of Buchanan's research in the early part of his Virginia career, later on his interest increasingly shifted towards constitutional economics, even if his pioneering contribution to the field, *The Calculus of Consent* (co-authored with Gordon Tullock), dates back to 1962. The two fields are closely related, but their emphasis is different. Both are about extending economic analysis beyond its traditional domain, the study of markets, but they do so in different "dimensions". Public choice theory extends economics "horizontally" from the market arena to the arena of politics, but it maintains its standard approach, namely, explaining how self-interested individuals seek their advantage within given constraints, be it the constraints they face in markets or the constraints they face in the realm of politics. By contrast, constitutional economics extends economics "vertically" by drawing attention to the fact that human beings are not confined to choosing within given constraints, but can to some extent choose their constraints, in other words, that they can choose at differ-ent levels of choice. In particular, collectively, as politically organized groups, they can choose the "rules of the game" under which they act and interact.

The distinction between the constitutional and the sub-constitutional level of choice, between the choice among rules and the choice within rules is foundational for constitu-tional economics as the economics of rules. It is the trademark of a research programme that enquires into how self-interested agents, just as they can realize mutual gains from trade in markets, may realize mutual benefits by adopting better "rules of the game". Its generalization of the gains from trade paradigm from the market arena to the level of political choice, and constitutional choice in particular, is in fact the very paradigmatic core of Buchanan's constitutional economics. It is this outlook that distinguishes it categorically from a welfare economics that seeks to bridge the theoretical gap between the study of markets and the study of politics by supposing that policy choice is about maximizing a social welfare function, just as behaviour in markets is about maximizing individual utility functions. The inappropriate generalization of the maximization paradigm from the level of individual choice to the level of collective-political choice is, as Buchanan charges, the root cause of the "methodological confusion" that he diagnosed as a young public finance economist in his own field and in welfare economics. With the research programme of constitutional economics he has suggested an alternative theoretical outlook the central message of which is that economists should recognize the gains from trade paradigm as the principal insight of their discipline that ought to be applied consistently to politics no less than to markets. Just as in markets, the voluntary consent of the trading parties is the only conclusive evidence of mutual gains, and hence of "efficiency". In the realm of collective-political choice, voluntary consent, so Buchanan argues, must be considered the ultimate criterion of mutual gains, and hence of "efficiency" as well. The mission of constitutional economics is about dealing with the manifold analytical and empirical issues that a consistent and rigorous application of this alternative theoretical outlook raises.

VIKTOR J. VANBERG

See also:

Public choice (II); Welfare economics (III).

References and further reading

Brennan, G., H. Kliemt and R.D. Tollison (eds) (2002), *Methods and Morals in Constitutional Economics. Essays in Honor of James M. Buchanan*, Berlin, Heidelberg and New York: Springer.
Buchanan, J.M. (1949), 'The pure theory of government finance', *Journal of Political Economy*, **57** (December), 496–505.
Buchanan, J.M. (1960), *Fiscal Theory and Political Economy*, Chapel Hill, NC: University of North Carolina Press.
Buchanan, J.M. (1979), *What Should Economists Do?*, Indianapolis, IN: Liberty Press.
Buchanan, J.M. (1987), *Economics – Between Predictive Science and Moral Philosophy*, College Station, TX: Texas A&M University Press.
Buchanan, J.M. (1992), *Better than Plowing and Other Personal Essays*, Chicago, IL: University of Chicago Press.
Buchanan, J.M. (1999–2001), *The Collected Works of James M. Buchanan*, 20 vols, Indianapolis, IN: Liberty Fund.
Buchanan, J.M. and G. Tullock (1962), *The Calculus of Consent: Logical Foundations of Constitutional Democracy*, Ann Arbor, MI: University of Michigan.
Reisman, D. (1990), *The Political Economy of James M. Buchanan*, College Station, TX: Texas A&M University Press.
Wicksell, K. (1896), *Finanztheoretische Untersuchungen nebst Darstellung und Kritik des Steuerwesens Schwedens*, Jena: Gustav Fischer.

Hyman Philip Minsky (1919–1996)

Hyman P. Minsky (1919–1996) studied at the University of Chicago and, after a stint in World War II, earned his PhD at Harvard University. His biggest influences were the Chicago School's intuitionalist tradition (especially Henry Simons, but he also worked with Oscar Lange, Paul Douglas and Frank Knight) and Harvard's Joseph Schumpeter. He taught at Brown University, the University of California at Berkeley, and Washington University. When he retired from teaching in 1990, he moved to the Levy Economics Institute as Distinguished Scholar, where he remained until his death.

While he served as Alvin Hansen's teaching assistant at Harvard, he later remarked that the "mechanistic" approach of what Joan Robinson called the "Bastard Keynesians" did not appeal to him. Although J.M. Keynes clearly influenced him, he did not have much affinity with the post-war American "Keynesians". From his earliest work, he was more interested in dynamic, evolutionary change with institutional constraints. Indeed, in one of his first papers he took Paul Samuelson's linear-accelerator model and added institutional "ceilings and floors". Minsky's approach to banking drew heavily on Jack Gurley and E.S. Shaw while adapting Schumpeter's theory of innovation to analysis of the financial sector. During the 1960s he was involved in major studies of monetary policy formation and banking regulation, doing research for the Federal Reserve's (the Fed) Board of Governors and for the California state banking commission. Later, after moving to Washington University, he served on the board of a Missouri bank holding company, and he developed close relations with financial markets participants, among whom he counted Henry Kaufman as a friend. All of this provided a deep understanding of real world financial institutions and practices that influenced his writing and thinking. After he moved to the Levy Institute, he used Wall Street connections to establish a long-running research project titled "The reconstitution of the financial system" that led to the creation of the annual "Minsky Conference" held every year in April.

Minsky is best known for his development of the "financial instability hypothesis" (FIH), but it was by no means his only contribution. This entry will also examine his work in three other areas: his analysis of money and banking; his employer of last resort proposal; and his views on the longer-term evolution of the economy.

Money and Banking

Minsky (1957) analysed the development of the "fed funds" market in the US – the interbank market for lending reserves – arguing that banks economize on reserves, making it difficult for the Fed to influence lending activity, or "money creation", which is actually determined by the willingness of banks to lend, and of their customers to borrow. If the central bank wants to influence bank lending, it must affect that decision. For example, it can raise required underwriting standards – forcing banks to require more collateral and better credit histories. Stemming from his research conducted for the Fed, Minsky came to the conclusion that reserves should be provided mostly at the discount window – forcing banks to borrow them directly from the central bank, rather than obtaining them from other banks or through open market purchases by the central bank. This would allow the central bank to more closely supervise banks, and to favour safer bank activities by choosing what could serve as collateral against loans of reserves.

Minsky took a broad approach to money creation, arguing that "everyone can create money; the problem is to get it accepted" (1986 [2008]: 255). Money is really just an IOU denominated in the money of account, but there is a hierarchy of monies – some are more widely accepted than others – with the monetary IOUs issued by the treasury and the central bank sitting at the top of the money pyramid. He saw banking as essentially the business of "accepting" IOUs, making payments on behalf of customers and holding their liabilities. Banks make payments in their own IOUs, which are then cleared using the central bank's reserves. Further, "(b)ecause bankers live in the same expectational climate as businessmen, profit-seeking bankers will find ways of accommodating their customers; this behaviour by bankers reinforces disequilibrating pressures. Symmetrically, the processes that decrease the prices of capital assets will also decrease the willingness of bankers to finance business" (Minsky 1986 [2008]: 255). In other words, the "money supply" expands and contracts as bankers accommodate the demands of their customers in a pro-cyclical manner.

Financial Instability Hypothesis

This pro-cyclical behaviour amplifies the business cycle, increasing the thrust toward instability. Minsky's theory can be summarized as an investment theory of the cycle and a financial theory of investment; the first is the usual Keynesian view, and the second stresses that modern investment is expensive and must be financed – and it is the financing that generates structural fragility. During an upswing, profit-seeking firms and banks become more optimistic, taking on riskier financial structures. Firms commit larger portions of expected revenues to debt service. Lenders accept smaller down-payments and lower-quality collateral. Financial institutions innovate new products and finesse rules and regulations imposed by supervisory authorities. Borrowers use more external finance (rather than retained earnings), and increasingly issue short-term debt that is potentially volatile (it must be "rolled-over" so there is risk that lenders might refuse to do so). As the boom heats up, the central bank hikes its interest rate – and with greater use of short-term finance, borrowers face higher debt service costs.

Minsky developed a famous classification for fragility of financing positions. The safest is called "hedge" finance (note this is not related to so-called hedge funds). In a hedge position, expected income is sufficient to make all payments as they come due, including both interest and principle. A "speculative" position is one in which expected income is sufficient to make interest payments, but principle must be rolled-over. It is "speculative" in the sense that income must increase, or an asset must be sold to cover the principle payment. Finally, a "Ponzi" position (named after a famous fraudster, Charles Ponzi, who ran a pyramid scheme – much like Bernie Madoff's more recent fraud) is one in which even interest payments cannot be met, so the debtor must borrow to pay interest (the outstanding loan balance grows by the interest due). Speculative positions turn into Ponzi positions if income falls, or if interest rates rise. Ponzi positions are inherently problematic as default is avoided only so long as the lender allows the loan balance to grow. Beyond some point, the lender will cut losses by forcing default.

Over the business cycle, fragility rises, exposing the system to the possibility of a crisis – coming from a variety of directions: income flows turn out to be lower than expected, interest rates rise, lenders curtail lending, or a prominent firm or bank defaults on payment commitments. Just as finance accelerates the boom, it fuels the collapse as debtors need to cut back spending and sell assets to make contractual payments. As spending falls, income and employment fall; as assets are sold, their prices fall. In the extreme, debt-deflation dynamics that Irving Fisher saw in the Great Depression can be generated – asset values plummet and widespread bankruptcies occur.

However, following his early training in Chicago, Minsky recognized that institutional "ceilings and floors" can help to attenuate the cycle. The most obvious of these come from government, although there are also private institutional constraints, such as stock market rules that suspend trading when prices fall too far. The two most important constraining institutions are the "Big Government" (national treasury) and the "Big Bank" (central bank). The first helps to stabilize the economy through a countercyclical budget: spending falls and taxes rise in a boom, while spending rises and taxes fall in a bust – so surpluses in expansion and deficits in recession constrain the cycle. The central bank can try to constrain lending in a boom (although Minsky was sceptical since profit-seeking banks innovate around constraints), but more importantly it can act as lender of last resort when a financial crisis hits. This prevents a run on financial institutions, which reduces pressure on banks to engage in firesales of assets to meet withdrawals.

Employer of Last Resort

While Minsky's work on poverty and unemployment is not well known, from the 1960s through to the mid-1970s he actually wrote as much on this topic as he did on financial instability. At Berkeley he worked with labour economists to formulate an anti-poverty strategy focusing on employment rather than welfare. Minsky criticized the Kennedy–Johnson war on poverty, warning that without a significant job creation component it would fail to reduce poverty even as it created a welfare-dependent and marginalized class. He showed that offering one full-time job per low-income household instead – even at the minimum wage – would raise two-thirds of all poor families above the poverty line. Further, he estimated that the output created by putting people to work would more than provide for the extra consumption by increasing gross domestic product (GDP) by a multiple of the extra wages.

Minsky argued a legislated minimum wage is effective only with an employer of last resort, for otherwise the true minimum wage is zero for all those who cannot find a job. Hence, he proposed that the national government stand ready to fund a job for anyone ready and willing to work at the minimum wage. Only the national government can afford to offer an "infinitely elastic" supply of jobs at the minimum wage. The government as employer of last resort serves as a bookend to the central bank as lender of last resort – just as the lender of last resort sets a floor to asset prices (by lending so that banks do not have to engage in firesales), the employer of last resort sets a floor to wages (anyone willing to work can get the minimum wage) and thus also to aggregate demand and consumption. In this manner countercyclical fiscal policy is enhanced (government spending rises in recession and falls in expansion when workers are hired away by the private sector) and supplements countercyclical monetary policy interventions.

Long-Term Evolution of the Economy

While Minsky's FIH is usually interpreted as a theory of the business cycle, he also developed a theory of the long-term transformation of the economy. Briefly, capitalism evolves through several stages, each marked by a different financial structure. The nineteenth century saw "commercial capitalism" where commercial banking dominated – banks made short-term commercial loans and issued deposits. This was replaced by the beginning of the twentieth century, with "finance capitalism", after Rudolf Hilferding, where investment banks ruled. The distinguishing characteristic was the use of long-term external finance to purchase expensive capital assets. The financial structure was riskier, and collapsed into the Great Depression – which he saw as the failure of finance capitalism. We emerged from World War II with a new form of capitalism, "managerial welfare-state capitalism", in which financial institutions were constrained by New Deal reforms, and with large oligopolistic corporations that financed investment out of retained earnings. Private sector debt was small, but government debt left over from war finance was large – providing safe assets for households, firms, and banks. This system was financially robust, unlikely to experience deep recession because of the Big Government and Big Bank constraints discussed above.

However, the relative stability of the first few decades after World War II encouraged ever-greater risk-taking as the financial system was transformed into "money manager capitalism", where the dominant financial players are "managed money" – lightly regulated "shadow banks" like pension funds, hedge funds, sovereign wealth funds, and university endowments – with huge pools of funds in search of the highest returns. Innovations by financial engineers encouraged growth of private debt relative to income, and increased reliance on volatile short-term finance.

The first US post-war financial crisis occurred in 1966 but it was quickly resolved by swift government intervention. This set a pattern: crises came more frequently but government saved the day each time. As a result, ever more risky financial arrangements were "validated", leading to more experimentation. The crises became more severe, requiring greater rescue efforts by governments.

Finally, the entire global financial system crashed in fall 2008 – with many calling it the "Minsky Moment" or "Minsky Crisis". Unfortunately, most analyses relied on his FIH rather than on his "stages" approach. If, as Minsky believed, the financial system had experienced a long-term transformation toward fragility, then recovery would only presage an even bigger collapse – on a scale such as the 1929 crash that ended the finance capitalism stage. In that case, what will be necessary is fundamental – New Deal style – reforms.

Following his institutionalist roots, Minsky argued there are "57 varieties" of capitalism, so the death of money manager capitalism might be replaced with a new, more stable form. However, as he insisted, there is no final once-and-for-all solution for the inherent tendency to instability of capitalism.

L. Randall Wray

See also:

Business cycles and growth (III); Institutional economics (III); John Maynard Keynes (I); Oskar Ryszard Lange (I); Abba Ptachya Lerner (I); Post-Keynesianism (II); Joseph Alois Schumpeter (I).

References and further reading

Cassidy, J. (2008), 'The Minsky moment', *The New Yorker*, 4 February, accessed 29 January 2008 at http://www.newyorker.com/.

Chancellor, E. (2007), 'Ponzi nation', *Institutional Investor*, 7 February.

McCulley, P. (2007), 'The plankton theory meets Minsky', *Global Central Bank Focus*, March, PIMCO Bonds, accessed 6 February 2015 at http://media.pimco.com/Documents/GCB%20Focus%20MAR%2007%20WEB.pdf.

Minsky, H.P. (1957), 'Central banking and money market changes', *Quarterly Journal of Economics*, **71** (2), 171.

Minsky, H.P. (1965), 'The role of employment policy', in M.S. Gordon (ed.), *Poverty in America*, San Francisco, CA: Chandler.

Minsky, H.P. (1975), *John Maynard Keynes*, reprinted 2008, New York: Columbia University Press.

Minsky, H.P. (1982), *Can it Happen Again?*, Armonk, NY: M.E. Sharpe.

Minsky, H.P. (1986), *Stabilizing an Unstable Economy*, reprinted 2008, New Haven, CT and London: Yale University Press.

Minsky, H.P. (1987), 'Securitization', Levy Economics Institute of Bard College, Policy Note No. 2, 12 May, reprinted 2008, Annandale-on-Hudson, NY.

Minsky, H.P. (1996), 'Uncertainty and the institutional structure of capitalist economies', The Levy Economics Institute of Bard College, Working Paper No. 155, Annandale-on-Hudson, NY.

Nersisyan, Y. and L.R. Wray (2010), 'Transformation of the financial system: financialization, concentration, and the shift to shadow banking', in D. Tavasci and J. Toporowski (eds), *Minsky, Crisis and Development*, Basingstoke: Palgrave Macmillan, pp. 32–49.

Papadimitriou, D.B. and L.R. Wray (1998), 'The economic contributions of Hyman Minsky: varieties of capitalism and institutional reform', *Review of Political Economy*, **10** (2), 199–225.

Whalen, C. (2007), 'The U.S. credit crunch of 2007: a Minsky moment', Levy Economics Institute Public Policy Brief, No. 92, Annandale-on-Hudson, NY, accessed 27 December 2015 at http://www.levyinstitute.org/pubs/ppb_92.pdf.

Wray, L.R. (2009), 'The rise and fall of money manager capitalism: a Minskian approach', *Cambridge Journal of Economics*, **33** (4), 807–28.

Kenneth Joseph Arrow (b. 1921)

Kenneth J. Arrow's name is associated with two famous components of microeconomic theory: Arrow's (im)possibility theorem of social choice and the so-called Arrow–Debreu model. The publication of Arrow's impossibility theorem in 1950 marks the birth of a whole scientific field (social choice theory) that goes well beyond economics and overlaps with several other subjects, including political science, political philosophy and social ethics.

Arrow's scientific life is well documented. There are, among others, two papers authored by Arrow himself (1992, 2009), a number of interviews – for example, Kelly (1987 [2010]) and Feiwel (1987a, 1987b) – and the prefaces to the six volumes of his collected papers as well as the short historical introductions to many individual papers in this collection (Arrow 1984a, 1984b, 1984c, 1984d, 1985a, 1985b).

In the book edited by Szenberg (1992), eminent economists were asked to write a 20-page essay on their life philosophy. Arrow responded with a beautifully written piece. We learn there about his interest in literature (Proust, Joyce, Kafka, Shelley and Keats) and in music (Wagner). His interest or even passion for abstraction had implications for his taste regarding the fine arts, which is also reflected in his admiration of Mondrian.

Life

Arrow was born in New York on 23 August 1921, into a wealthy family. He told Feiwel (1987b): "my first ten years were spent in considerable affluence, my next ten years in very considerable poverty". After high school, he attended the City College of New York because it was then an institution that did not charge tuition fees. He graduated in 1940 with a degree of Bachelor of Science in Social Science, but with a major in mathematics. During his high school and college years he was particularly interested in mathematics and more specifically in mathematical logic. According to Arrow (2009), fear of unemployment led him to supplement his abstract interests in mathematics and logic with several alternative practical pursuits including high school teaching, actuarial work and statistics. While at City College he could attend a course on logic (on the calculus of relations) given by Alfred Tarski. For practical reasons, he did his graduate studies at Columbia University where mathematical statistics was developing with Harold Hotelling and Abraham Wald. When he asked Hotelling to write a recommendation letter for a fellowship in mathematics, Hotelling told him that such a letter would have probably no effect, but if he rather switched to economics he could become a fellow. As a consequence, Arrow switched to economics. From 1942 to 1946 he served as a weather officer in the US Army Air Corps. His first published paper, "On the use of winds in flight planning", appeared in 1949 in the *Journal of Meteorology*.

Back in Columbia, he had difficulties finding a dissertation topic. He contemplated the idea of redoing Hicks's *Value and Capital* from a more rigorous standpoint, using second-order properties and so on. Although he heard about the problem of the existence of a general competitive equilibrium, it was not from Wald who had made major advances in this area while he was still in Vienna before the Second World War (see Weintraub 1985; Düppe and Weintraub 2014). However, Wald discouraged him from working on this question because of its difficulty. In the spring of 1947, Arrow got a position at the Cowles Commission then located in Chicago. There he met Jacob Marschak, Tjalling Koopmans, Leonid Hurwicz (with whom he collaborated later on several major projects), Lawrence Klein and others. He spent the summer 1948 at the RAND Corporation. Summers at RAND are now famous among laymen since the publication of Nash's biography (Nasar 1998). It is at RAND that Arrow had the definite idea leading to his impossibility theorem. It is also at RAND that he met a number of game theorists (Shapley, Nash and von Neumann), applied mathematicians (Bellman), and statisticians (Blackwell). It is also at Cowles and at RAND that he understood the importance of mathematical notions in combinatorial and general topology, convex analysis and so on that later have proven crucial in general equilibrium theory. His PhD dissertation – in fact Arrow (1951a) – was completed while he was already Assistant Professor at Stanford. He stayed at Stanford until 1968 and again from 1979 onwards. In between he was at Harvard, an institution for which he expressed mixed feelings. He held a number of visiting positions, for instance, at MIT and Churchill College (Cambridge), and received many prizes, including, in 1972, the Sveriges Riksbank Prize in Economic Sciences in Memory of Alfred Nobel.

In Breit and Hirsch (2009), Arrow identifies his three major contributions: social choice, general equilibrium, and asymmetric information. A fourth is added, even if it is based on a short paper: the abstract approach to revealed preference theory.

Social Choice

Surprisingly, Arrow's interest in collective decision-making was prompted by his desire to write a PhD dissertation whose objective ("grandiose" as he wrote in Arrow 1984a) was to redo Hick's *Value and Capital*. One of the points he wished to improve upon concerned the theory of the firm. In Hicks, there is a single owner, which does not apply to most actual firms, in particular large ones. In a firm with several owners, even if we can accept that they have a common objective, maximization of profits, they may have different expectations of the future, and, consequently, different preferences regarding, say, investments. Decisions should then be taken using majority rule, possibly weighted according to shares. Arrow quickly discovered the Condorcet paradox and, even though he was fairly sure that this was known, he did not know that it was attributed to Condorcet. He considered at that time that this type of intransitivity/cycle was a nuisance and he did not pursue his research until, in the winter of 1947–48, he had the idea that, if we assume some homogeneity in individual preferences – for instance, on the basis of a political spectrum left-right – we could obtain a transitive collective ranking. This was the condition now known as single-peakedness. He discovered a little later that Duncan Black had had the same idea (Black 1948) a few months before him. While at RAND during the summer of 1948, he was asked by Olaf Elmer, one of the logicians there, to write an exposition showing how Abram Bergson's social welfare function could be used as a payoff function for an international game. It is on this occasion that, wishing to adopt an ordinalist viewpoint, he started to develop what would become his famous impossibility theorem. This eventually became his doctoral dissertation and a book (Arrow 1951a). Arrow (1950) contains a brief presentation of his results.

To simplify the presentation, assume that everything is finite, both the set of options (social states, candidates, allocations, and so on, depending on the context) and the set of agents – this is a crucial assumption that is needed not only to make the proofs simpler: with an infinite set of agents, the theorem is no longer true. Each agent is rational in the sense that he or she can rank the options with possible ties (indifferences). Given that each agent has a ranking of the options, the Arrovian social choice problem is to determine a (unique) social ranking. Rules or procedures that associate a social ranking with a list of individual rankings (one ranking per individual) are called Arrovian social welfare functions, or social welfare functions for short. The list of individual rankings will be called a "profile". Of course, you can imagine that the social ranking is systematically the ranking of a specific individual. This would be a dictatorial social welfare function. Arrow (1963) imposes four conditions on the social welfare function.

The first condition states that individuals can have any ranking, so that there is no super-rationality condition as in the case of Black's single-peakedness. Admitting ties, this means that, for three options, one has 13 rankings (six rankings without ties, three with two top options, three with two bottom options and one where the three options are tied).

The second condition concerns the level of information that should be used in the aggregation process. This information is purely ordinal, or, more precisely, binary within individuals and non-comparable across individuals. Given two profiles and two options, if we have the same binary information regarding these two options in the individual rankings, then the binary collective relation regarding the two options must be identical. For instance, consider options *a* and *b*, if individual 1 prefers *a* to *b* in the first and the second profile, individual 2 is indifferent between *a* and *b* in the first and the second profile, individual 3 prefers *b* to *a* in the first and the second profile, and so on, then the social/collective preference between *a* and *b* must be identical, say, *a* is collectively preferred to *b* for both profiles. This is obtained in case, say, individual 1 ranks *a* first and *b* last (supposing we have 20 options) in the first profile and *a* third and *b* fourth in the second profile. What is taken into consideration is only the fact that individual 1 prefers *a* to *b* in both profiles. This is independent of the fact that there are 18 options ranked between *a* and *b* in the first profile and none in the second profile. This is the reason why Arrow called this condition "independence of irrelevant alternatives".

The third condition is very simple. It says that the collective preference must respect unanimity. If in a profile every individual agrees that some option is better than some other option, the social preference must be identical to the unanimous preference. In spite of appearing innocuous, this condition has an important consequence. Given a very small amount of diversity among the individual rankings, this condition excludes constant social welfare functions. Such constant functions would give the same collective ranking for every profile, that is, the social ranking would be independent of the agents' preferences. In the 1951 version of the theorem, this unanimity (sometimes called Pareto) condition was the consequence of a condition of non-imposition associated with independence of irrelevant alternatives and some monotonicity assumption.

Loosely speaking, the fourth condition excludes that the social preference be systematically the preference of a specific individual; it excludes dictatorship. More precisely it says that there is no individual (a dictator) whose "strict" preference becomes the social "strict" preference. There is an indeterminacy in case the dictator is indifferent.

The theorem states that if there are at least two agents and three options, there is no social welfare function satisfying the four conditions. With three options and three individuals there are 13^{2197} possible social welfare functions, a really huge number. The four conditions are sufficient to annihilate all these functions: no function among this huge number satisfies the four conditions.

In Arrow (1951a), there is also a discrete version of single-peakedness and a possibility theorem for majority rule (majority rule is then a social welfare function satisfying the last three conditions).

General Equilibrium

The Walrasian description of an economy as a system of simultaneous equations representing the consumers' demands and producers' supplies with the equilibrium condition that for each market demand is equal to supply largely left aside the fundamental problem of existence. A prevalent idea was that it was sufficient to have a number of equations equal to the number of unknowns. At the end of note XXI in the mathematical appendix to Marshall's *Principles of Economics* (1920: 856) we read: "Thus, however complex the problem may become, we can see that it is theoretically determinate, because the number of unknowns is always exactly equal to the number of the equations which we obtain." According to Schumpeter (1954: 1006), Walras did not believe this. Schumpeter writes: "Of all the unjust or even meaningless objections that have been leveled at Walras, perhaps the most unjust is that he believed that this existence question is answered as soon as we have counted 'equations' and 'unknowns' and have found that they are equal in number" (ibid.). The best we had at the beginning of the 1940s were Wald's papers in German, in particular Wald (1936 [1951]). Wald was one of Arrow's teachers at Columbia, but his interests had switched to mathematical statistics. From Wald, Arrow learnt that the existence problem was very difficult and, given Wald's mathematical expertise, this was rather discouraging. Arrow's visit to RAND in 1948 was crucial because it is there that he learnt a great deal about convex analysis, in particular results about hyperplanes separating convex sets that would reveal fundamental tools for the second theorem of welfare economics. What was also crucial was Nash's very short paper (Nash 1951), which uses Kakutani's fixed point theorem to prove the existence of an equilibrium point in n-person games. While he was working on this existence problem, Arrow learnt that Debreu had obtained essentially similar results. Arrow and Debreu then decided to write a joint paper (Arrow and Debreu 1954). At about the same time, McKenzie also had very similar intuitions (see McKenzie 2002; Düppe and Weintraub 2014).

Although recent advances in mathematics were important for this result, Arrow and Debreu (1954) cannot be evaluated only on the basis of the use of the relevant technical tools. In fact Arrow and Debreu – in this paper but also in two previous papers about the so-called welfare economics theorems (Arrow 1951b; Debreu 1951) – created the basic framework that would pervade modern microeconomic theory.

To simplify consider an exchange economy. The supply side is given by the initial endowments of agents. Agents have a budget set, defined in terms of a given vector of prices and their initial endowments, and maximize their preference relation over this budget set. Formal conditions of convexity and continuity guarantee that there is a vector of quantity of goods (not necessarily unique) that maximizes this preference relation. This defines the individual demand (a correspondence or with more restrictive conditions a function). A simple operation of vector addition (one can also define the addition of sets of vectors) gives the (global) demand. Subtracting the global supply (the sum of the individual initial endowments), one gets the excess demand correspondence. The equilibrium existence question is then to find a vector of prices such that the nul-vector belongs to the excess demand correspondence.

The relations between equilibrium allocations and Pareto optimality are known as the classical theorems of welfare economics. An allocation is a vector composed of vectors of quantities of goods, one vector for each agent, such that their sum is equal to the sum of the agents' initial endowments. If the allocation corresponds to a zero of the excess demand function, given an equilibrium vector of prices, it is said that it is an equilibrium allocation. An allocation is Pareto optimal if there is no other vector such that each individual finds his vector component at least as good and one individual finds his vector component better. The first welfare economics theorem states that an equilibrium allocation is Pareto optimal. The second welfare economics theorem states that, given a Pareto optimal allocation, one can find a vector of prices and a distribution of total resources as initial endowments that will guarantee that the given allocation is an equilibrium allocation. Although the proof of the first theorem is elementary, to prove the second one, one has to use the mathematical results about hyperplanes separating convex sets.

Arrow and Hahn (1971) offers a detailed view of Arrow's work in general equilibrium theory with further developments on stability.

The Economics of Information

The Arrow–Debreu model of a competitive economy of 1954 does not consider uncertainty. Of course, both Arrow and Debreu knew that this was a limitation of their analysis. As mentioned previously, Arrow's interest in social choice was indirectly prompted by problems related to uncertainty in the decision-making process in the theory of the firm. In a paper published in French (Arrow 1953 [1963–64]), Arrow proposed to deal with uncertainty via contingent contracts. Arrow (1953 [1963–64]) is often considered as the foundational paper for the theory of incomplete markets and the theory of finance. The following description is in Debreu (1959: 98): "A contract for the transfer of a commodity now specifies, in addition to its physical properties, its location and its date, an event on the occurrence of which the transfer is conditional." The purpose was to have a treatment of uncertainty that was not reducible to probabilities and would allow a straightforward generalization of the results of Arrow–Debreu (1954).

A number of economists were not satisfied by this treatment of uncertainty, in spite of its elegance. Arrow was one of them. At the beginning of the 1960s, he was asked by the Ford Foundation to survey medical economics from a theoretical point of view. In his historical introduction to Arrow (1963) he explains that he "started the survey in a conscientious catalogue fashion, but felt that the whole study lacked focus" (Arrow 1985b: 15). He knew that a "key component" was asymmetric information, between the physician and the patient, as well as between both of them and the insurer. Arrow noted that health insurance creates an incentive to spend more freely than necessary, a phenomenon known as "moral hazard". In 1963 the question of asymmetric information was hardly mentioned in microeconomic theory. Nowadays, it is one of the major topics of the microeconomic textbooks as exemplified by Mas-Colell et al. (1995) and Jehle and Reny (2001). Arrow played an instrumental role in this development.

Revealed Preference Theory

Feiwel (1987a) rightly mentions that Arrow's work on choice theory is underappreciated. Arrow himself is rather modest saying, "It has certainly been surpassed by Sen and Richter" (Feiwel 1987a: 223). However, one may wonder whether without his short paper (1959) the set-theoretic treatment of revealed preference theory would have seen this major development that culminates (at this time) in Bossert and Suzumura (2010).

In standard microeconomic theory of the consumer, the basic concept is the agent's (ordinal) utility function (or her preference in the Arrow–Debreu model). Given her initial endowment and the price system, the agent maximizes this utility function over her budget set. Given appropriate assumptions, we know that there is a point (a vector of quantities of each good) in the budget set that does maximize the function. Making further assumptions (for instance, strict quasi-concavity) this point can be unique. We have then a demand function that associates this maximizer to a price-vector and income (the income is the value of the initial endowment given this price-vector). In a fundamental paper, Samuelson (1938: 71) proposed to inverse the analysis "to develop the theory of consumer's behavior freed from any vestigial traces of the utility concept." In his 1950 paper, Samuelson stated the weak axiom of revealed preference in the following way: "If at a price and income of situation A you could have bought the goods actually bought at a different point B and if you actually chose not to, then A is defined to be 'revealed better than' B. The basic postulate is that B is never to reveal itself to be also 'better than' A" (Samuelson 1950: 370). The idea was then to go from a demand function (that would satisfy this axiom and other conditions) to a utility function having all the properties necessary for its maximization. This is the integrability problem. This problem is quite demanding from a mathematical point of view (see Chipman et al. 1971).

Arrow's purpose was to develop revealed preference theory in a more general framework than the framework of consumer theory. He defines a binary relation of revealed preference in terms of choice (a choice function is defined over subsets of a general set and selects, for each subset in its domain, some options belonging to the subset). Then an option a is revealed preferred to an option b if there is a subset in which a is selected and b is not. The weak axiom of revealed preference asserts that if a is revealed preferred to b, then there is no subset to which a belongs in which b is chosen. Arrow introduced other consistency conditions on choice functions and on the binary relation of revealed preference. In particular, one of these consistency conditions on choice functions was shown to be equivalent to the weak axiom of revealed preference. It states that if A and B are two subsets in the domain of the choice function and if A is included in B the options selected in the larger subset that also belongs to the smaller one are the options that are selected in the smaller subset. To give a clarifying illustration, consider a department store that includes a food department. You are doing your weekly shopping. What you are buying includes food and, say, household products, clothes and toilet products. Let us suppose that you have to leave all these products and are asked to do your shopping again but only within the food department. Then you will buy exactly the same food products as when it was possible to visit all the departments. Arrow suggested that on the basis of a choice function you can derive a binary relation of (normal) preference by saying that *a* is chosen in a subset that is limited to *a* and *b* if and only if *a* is at least as good as *b*. Arrow then demonstrated that if the choice function satisfies the weak axiom of revealed preference, the binary relation derived from this choice function is a complete pre-order (a complete ranking with possible ties). The complete pre-order is said to rationalize the choice function, and one can, loosely speaking, consider that this rationalizability corresponds in the set-theoretic framework to the integrability *à la* Samuelson.

Other Works

There are many other important contributions by Arrow. These include his works on growth theory, capital and production theory, technical progress theory (learning by doing), stability of equilibrium, risk analysis (Arrow 1970), multicriterion decision-making (Arrow and Raynaud 1986), public investments (Arrow and Kurz 1970), applied mathematics (quasi-concave programming), health economics, and so on.

MAURICE SALLES

See also:

Jeremy Bentham (I); Abram Bergson [Abram Burk] (I); James M. Buchanan (I); Marie-Jean-Antoine-Nicolas Caritat de Condorcet (I); Gérard Debreu (I); Formalization and mathematical modelling (III); General equilibrium theory (III); John Richard Hicks (I); Lausanne School (II); John Stuart Mill (I); John Forbes Nash Jr (I); Arthur Cecil Pigou (I); Public choice (II); Paul Anthony Samuelson (I); Amartya Kumar Sen (I); Social choice (III); Uncertainty and information (III); Utilitarianism and anti-utilitarianism (III); Welfare economics (III).

References and further reading

Arrow, K.J. (1950), 'A difficulty in the concept of social welfare', *Journal of Political Economy*, **58** (4), 328–46.
Arrow, K.J. (1951a), *Social Choice and Individual Values*, 2nd edn 1963, New York: Wiley.
Arrow, K.J. (1951b), 'An extension of the basic theorems of classical welfare economics', in J. Neyman (ed.), *Proceedings of the Second Berkeley Symposium on Mathematical Statistics and Probability*, Berkeley, CA: University of California Press, pp. 507–32.
Arrow, K.J. (1953), 'Le rôle des valeurs boursières pour la répartition la meilleure des risques', in *Économétrie*, Colloques Internationaux du Centre National de la Recherche Scientifique, vol. 11, pp. 41–7, Paris: Editions du CNRS, English trans. (1963–64), 'The role of securities in the optimal allocation of risk-bearing', *Review of Economic Studies*, **31** (2), 91–6.
Arrow, K.J. (1959), 'Rational choice functions and orderings', *Economica*, **26** (102), 121–7.
Arrow, K.J. (1963), 'Uncertainty and the welfare economics of medical care', *American Economic Review*, **53** (5), 941–73.
Arrow, K.J. (1970), *Essays in the Theory of Risk-Bearing*, Amsterdam: North-Holland.
Arrow, K.J. (1984a), *Collected Papers 1: Social Choice and Justice*, Oxford: Blackwell.
Arrow, K.J. (1984b), *Collected Papers 2: General Equilibrium*, Oxford: Blackwell.
Arrow, K.J. (1984c), *Collected Papers 3: Individual Choice under Certainty and Uncertainty*, Oxford: Blackwell.
Arrow, K.J. (1984d), *Collected Papers 4: The Economics of Information*, Oxford: Blackwell.
Arrow, K.J. (1985a), *Collected Papers 5: Production and Capital*, Oxford: Blackwell.
Arrow, K.J. (1985b), *Collected Papers 6: Applied Economics*, Oxford: Blackwell.
Arrow, K.J. (1992), '"I know a hawk from a handsaw"', in M. Szenberg (ed.), *Eminent Economists: Their Life Philosophies*, Cambridge: Cambridge University Press, pp. 42–50.
Arrow, K.J. (2009), 'Kenneth J. Arrow', in W. Breit and B.T. Hirsch (eds), *Lives of the Laureates: Twenty Six Nobel Economists*, Cambridge, MA: MIT Press, pp. 35–47.
Arrow, K.J. and G. Debreu (1954), 'Existence of an equilibrium for a competitive economy', *Econometrica*, **22** (3), 265–90.
Arrow, K.J. and F.H. Hahn (1971), *General Competitive Analysis*, San Francisco, CA: Holden-Day.

Arrow, K.J. and M. Kurz (1970), *Public Investment, the Rate of Return, and Optimal Fiscal Policy*, Baltimore, MD: Johns Hopkins Press.
Arrow, K.J. and H. Raynaud (1986), *Social Choice and Multicriterion Decision-Making*, Cambridge, MA: MIT Press.
Black, D. (1948), 'On the rationale of group decision making', *Journal of Political Economy*, **56** (1), 23–34.
Breit, W. and B.T. Hirsch (2009), *Lives of the Laureates: Twenty Six Nobel Economists*, Cambridge, MA: MIT Press.
Bossert, W. and K. Suzumura (2010), *Consistency, Choice and Rationality*, Cambridge, MA: Harvard University Press.
Chipman, J.S., L. Hurwicz, M.K. Richter and H.F. Sonnenschein (eds) (1971), *Preference, Utility, and Demand*, New York: Harcourt, Brace, Jovanovich.
Debreu, G. (1951), 'The coefficient of resource utilization', *Econometrica*, **19** (3), 273–92.
Debreu, G. (1959), *Theory of Value. An Axiomatic Analysis of Economic Equilibrium*, New York: Wiley.
Düppe, T. and E.R. Weintraub (2014), *Finding Equilibrium. Arrow, Debreu, McKenzie and the Problem of Scientific Credit*, Princeton, NJ: Princeton University Press.
Feiwel, G.R. (1987a), 'Oral history I: an interview with Kenneth J. Arrow', in G.R. Feiwel (ed.), *Arrow and the Ascent of Modern Economic Theory*, Basingstoke: Macmillan, pp. 191–242.
Feiwel, G.R. (1987b), 'Arrow on Arrow: an interview with Kenneth J. Arrow', in G.R. Feiwel (ed.), *Arrow and the Foundations of the Theory of Economic Policy*, Basingstoke: Macmillan, pp. 637–57.
Hicks, J.R. (1939), *Value and Capital*, 2nd edn 1946, Oxford: Oxford University Press.
Jehle, G.A. and P.J. Reny (2001), *Advanced Microeconomic Theory*, 2nd edn, Boston, MA: Addison-Wesley.
Kelly, J.S. (1987), 'An interview with Kenneth J. Arrow', *Social Choice and Welfare*, **4**, 43–62, reprinted in K.J.Arrow, A.K. Sen and K. Suzumura (eds) (2010), *Handbook of Social Choice and Welfare*, vol. 2, Amsterdam: Elsevier, pp. 4–24.
Marshall, A. (1920), *Principles of Economics*, 8th edn, London: Macmillan.
Mas-Colell, A., M.D. Whinston and J. Green (1995), *Microeconomic Theory*, New York: Oxford University Press.
McKenzie, L.W. (2002), *Classical General Equilibrium Theory*, Cambridge MA: MIT Press.
Nasar, S. (1998), *A Beautiful Mind*, New York: Simon & Schuster.
Nash, J.F. (1951), 'Equilibrium points in *n*-person games', *Proceedings of the National Academy of Sciences*, **36** (1), 48–9.
Samuelson, P.A. (1938), 'A note on the pure theory of consumer's behaviour', *Economica*, **5** (17), 61–71.
Samuelson, P.A. (1950), 'The problem of integrability in utility theory', *Economica*, **17** (68), 355–85.
Schumpeter, J.A. (1954), *History of Economic Analysis*, London: Allen and Unwin.
Szenberg, M. (ed.) (1992), *Eminent Economists: Their Life Philosophies*, Cambridge: Cambridge University Press.
Wald, A. (1936), 'Über einige Gleichungssysteme der mathematischen Ökonomie', *Zeitschrift für NationalÖkonomie*, **7**, 637–70, English trans. 1951, 'On some systems of equations of mathematical economics', *Econometrica*, **19** (4), 368–403.
Weintraub, E.R. (1985), *General Equilibrium Analysis: Studies in Appraisal*, Cambridge: Cambridge University Press.

Gérard Debreu (1921–2004)

Gérard Debreu was an austere man who brought that austerity to economics. He, almost single-handedly, introduced the axiomatic approach to economic theory. He never speculated about what might be true and confined himself to saying what he knew to be true. His approach was essentially that of a mathematician and he used that to protect himself from getting involved in debates about economic matters. His reserved attitude to the profession and to the world can, at least in part, be attributed to the sad events that marked his early years (see Düppe 2012).

Life

Born in Calais in 1921, he was orphaned at a very young age and spent most of his youth in boarding schools, until, with the outbreak of the war, he was evacuated to the unoccupied part of France where he prepared for the competition to enter a "Grande École". He succeeded and was admitted to the École Normale Supérieure in Paris, then occupied by the Germans, to study mathematics. When he had finished he was going to take the aggrégation to become a mathematics teacher but went into the army until the end of the war when he finally took the examination and was also admitted as a researcher in the Centre national de la recherche scientifique (CNRS). He had been heavily influenced by the Bourbaki School of mathematics and his research reflects that school's approach.

His interest, nevertheless, turned to economics and followed the courses given in Paris by Maurice Allais, who was later also to obtain the Sveriges Riksbank Prize in Economic Sciences in Memory of Alfred Nobel. He was offered, through the good offices of Maurice Allais, a Rockefeller fellowship to go to the United States. Allais could propose two candidates, but one would have to wait a year. Marcel Boiteux was the other potential candidate and the two decided on the toss of a coin. Boiteux went on to become the Chief Executive Officer of Électricité de France, and never took up the scholarship. Debreu spent six months at Harvard, then a summer at Berkeley before going to the Cowles Commission in Chicago. He visited Ragnar Frisch before accepting a permanent position at the Cowles Commission. When the Commission moved to Yale, Debreu was appointed as an associate professor. In 1954 he was elected as a Fellow of the Econometric Society and defended his PhD thesis at the Sorbonne in 1956. This thesis was the first version of his seminal work, *Theory of Value* published in 1959. He spent a sabbatical year at Stanford in 1960–61 before becoming full professor of economics at Berkeley and later, in 1975, also professor of mathematics. He was elected president of the Econometric Society in 1972 and was named Chevalier de la Légion d'Honneur in 1976. He received the Sveriges Riksbank Prize in Economic Sciences in 1983. Gérard Debreu returned to France at the end of his career and died in Paris on the last day of 2004.

Debreu's Contributions to Economics

In addition to Debreu's own interest in economics from an abstract and mathematical point of view, we should not forget the strong influence that the Second World War and its aftermath had on all those involved in economics at the time. There was a general sentiment that the wartime experience had, to an important extent, vindicated economic planning. Thus there was a certain confidence in the government as a resource manager. Furthermore, rightly or wrongly, the Marshall Plan was held up as a shining example of successful government intervention. It is not surprising then that Debreu's first published contribution was entitled "The coefficient of resource utilization" (1951) and involved a discussion of the nature of Pareto optimality and measuring the extent to which an economy approached that situation. At the same time, the major thrust in pure economic theory to which Debreu devoted his whole career was general equilibrium theory and the notion of social optimality derived from the earlier work of Walras and Pareto. This tradition had been extended and developed by Maurice Allais in his book published in 1943 and entitled *A la recherche d'une discipline économique* which was revised and then republished in 1953 with the title *Traité d'économie pure*. Debreu's interest in the efficient allocation of scarce resources had then two origins, one being the impact of the wartime experience in France and the other being that of the intellectual tradition of refining and perfecting the basic mathematical structure of economic theory.

From his earliest encounters with economics, Debreu already saw the major task in economic theory as being that of showing that the general equilibrium model, which originated with Walras and Pareto, was internally consistent. He was later to say, in his Nobel lecture that "the highest prominence will be given in this lecture to Léon Walras (1834–1910), the founder of the mathematical theory of general economic equilibrium, to Francis Y. Edgeworth (1845–1926), and to Vilfredo Pareto (1848–1923)" (Debreu 1983 [1992]: 87).

For Debreu, the basic problem boiled down to showing that there exists a vector of prices which will clear all markets simultaneously. This amounts to finding a solution to a set of equations and had already, in large part, been solved by Wald (1935). Framing the problem in these terms was very much in the spirit of the Bourbaki tradition and it is not surprising that it should have been Debreu who pushed Walrasian theory in this direction. He was following on from Maurice Allais, his mentor, who was clearly oriented in the direction of mathematical purity rather than realism. "The fundamental Anglo-Saxon quality is satisfaction with the accumulation of facts. The need for clarity, for logical coherence and for synthesis is, for an Anglo-Saxon, only a minor need, if it is a need at all. For a Latin, and particularly a Frenchman, it is exactly the opposite" (Allais (1953: 58).

However, in thinking in this way Allais was encouraging the distancing of economics from reality. This was exactly in the Bourbaki tradition for as Bourbaki (1949: 2) wrote:

> Why do applications [of mathematics] ever succeed? Why is a certain amount of logical reasoning occasionally helpful in practical life? Why have some of the most intricate theories in mathematics become an indispensable tool to the modern physicist, to the engineer, and to the manufacturer of atom-bombs? Fortunately for us, the mathematician does not feel called upon to answer such questions.

Already, when Debreu received the Sveriges Riksbank Prize the message was clear, the way forward was to use the mathematical approach that he introduced. As the Sveriges Riksbank Prize committee said at the time,

Gérard Debreu symbolizes the use of a new mathematical apparatus, an apparatus compre-
hended by most economists only abstractly. Nevertheless, his work has given us an improved
intuitive understanding of the underlying economic relevance. His clarity and analytical rigor,
as well as the distinction drawn by him between an economic theory and its interpretation, have
given his work important bearing on the choice of methods and analytical techniques within
economic theory on a par with any other living economist. (Sveriges Riksbank 1983)

Undoubtedly Debreu's contribution that will mark the history of economic thought
the most is that with Arrow (Arrow and Debreu 1954), where they gave a proof of the
existence of an equilibrium for an economy under rather general conditions. But, more
importantly, what were the specific contributions made by Gérard Debreu which convinced an important part of the economics profession to accept his methodology in the
1960s and 1970s?

The *Theory of Value*
The most symbolic of these was his *Theory of Value* (Debreu 1959). This slim book was,
during that period, a sort of bible for all mathematically inclined economists. This for
two reasons: the axiomatic approach seemed to provide the rigorous foundations that
put economics on a par with the "hard sciences", and secondly, it gave the impression
of limiting the assumptions to a minimum. The first of these was, in large measure, an
illusion. Physics, for example, which had provided the theoretical structure for Walras
and Pareto, had moved in quite a different direction, and what Debreu wanted to achieve
was to place economics firmly in the field of abstract mathematics. Nowhere, in Debreu's
work, is there any reference to an empirical phenomenon and all the emphasis is on
building an internally consistent model without any concern for its use in explaining
economic data.

The second reason for the admiration for Debreu's approach, that it minimized the
assumptions used to arrive at his basic results, is also, in retrospect erroneous. Debreu
made great play, in the *Theory of Value*, with the absence of any assumption of differentiability, "the differential calculus and its compromises with logic". This seemed like a
major and even revolutionary step. The whole marginal revolution had been formalized
in terms of marginal products, or marginal utility, which were formally interpreted as
derivatives of the relevant production, cost, or utility functions. Thus, to dispense with
this assumption gave the impression of a significant advance. Yet as Mas-Colell (1990),
in many ways a disciple of Debreu, showed later, given the other assumptions that
Debreu made, it is always possible to approximate any of the functions in question by a
differentiable function. Thus, the period that a generation of young theoretical economists spent wrestling with the mathematical structure that Debreu had imposed was, in
large part, wasted.

However, what was the structure of the economy that Debreu worked with and what
were its basic properties? The first pillar was the definition of goods, of which there were
a finite number, and were characterized by their physical characteristics, and the time
and place at which they were available. Of course, if time is continuous the assumption that there is only a finite number of good is contradictory; or, again, even if time is
discrete, if no limit is put on the lifespan of the individuals in the economy, the fact that
goods are dated will make them infinite in number.

The second pillar of the economy is provided by the characteristics of the consumers who were assumed to have preferences over the goods which satisfied certain axioms. These axioms were not based on observing people's choices but on the introspection of economists who had preceded Debreu. Although each of them, such as continuity, convexity and monotonicity can be given an intuitive explanation, they are essentially imposed for mathematical convenience. Given these assumptions, one can derive the individual and aggregate demand of the consumers, that is, what they would like to consume at any given prices. Although Debreu did not use utility functions in the *Theory of Value*, one question of some importance to theoretical economists in this connection is, under what conditions can one represent the ordinal preferences that he used, by a continuous utility function? The idea, that it was enough to know how individuals order bundles of goods, rather than attribute quantities of utility to those bundles, was developed by Pareto. To analyse choices one has only to know whether bundle x is preferred or indifferent to bundle y, written $x \gtrsim y$. Then the question becomes, under what conditions can one find a function $u(x)$ such that $u(x) \geq u(y) \Leftrightarrow x \gtrsim y$? Debreu had already given the conditions for this earlier, in Debreu (1954), but chose not to work with this notion even if it is more familiar to economists, because it entails some restrictions that can be dispensed with if one works with preferences alone.

The third pillar is given by the producers, who are present in a fixed number and who are characterized by their production possibilities. The latter specify all the possible production plans, that is, all the possible combinations of inputs and outputs. Given the prices of the inputs and outputs the producer simply chooses the production plan that generates the maximum profit. These choices define the individual and aggregate supplies of the economy. Debreu made a number of assumptions about the set of production possibilities, or technologies. Perhaps the most important of these is that this set is convex. This rules out the inconvenient possibility of increasing returns to scale. However, it does not rule out the possibility that firms will make positive profits and then, to complete the model, what happens to those profits has to be specified. Debreu's answer was to assume that every consumer, at the outset, is somehow endowed with a share in each firm's profits and that they include this in their income. There is an obvious simultaneity problem here and, if Debreu's general equilibrium model is thought of as a model of how individuals make their choices, it is not clear how consumers are supposed to know what the profits of the firms will be at equilibrium. In fact, Debreu ignored this problem by simply viewing an equilibrium as a set of prices and choices such that aggregate demand is equal to aggregate supply, or, put another way, the excess demands for all goods are zero. No question is asked as to how such an equilibrium is established; the statement is simply, if these were the prices and these were all the choices made by the individual consumers and producers in the economy at those prices then the economy would be in equilibrium. The examination of the properties of an equilibrium state was Debreu's fundamental contribution in the *Theory of Value*. He showed that a competitive equilibrium allocation of resources is efficient by the Pareto criterion and, what is more, that for any such efficient allocation, one can always redistribute initial resources in the economy so that, for the new resources, the efficient allocation in question is the competitive allocation. These are the basic fundamental theorems of welfare economics, which were to lead the Figaro newspaper (Le Figaro 1984), to claim, when Debreu received the Sveriges Riksbank Prize, that he had shown that free markets were socially optimal.

However, all of this raises an important question, for much of the justification for the market economy which the general equilibrium model is supposed to epitomize rests on the idea that the economy will somehow organize itself into an equilibrium state. Given this, one is then interested in what the properties of such states are. Yet, Debreu, unlike many of his contemporaries, such as Arrow and Fisher, did not concern himself with the "stability" problem, that of how an economy would reach equilibrium, but instead just assumed that it would do so. Indeed, he asserted in private conversations that the problem was fundamentally intractable. He also considered that global uniqueness of equilibrium was out of reach with the standard assumptions. The idea that the equilibrium of an economy is unique is not just an abstract consideration. Macroeconomists, in seeking to determine the effects of a policy measure, rely on the comparative statics approach. This means considering "the equilibrium" of an economy and then changing some parameter, and analysing the new equilibrium that results from the change. However, this makes little sense if there are several equilibria since it is not known from where one starts and where one would end up. Yet, the use or misuse of economic theory was never something which interested Debreu; he simply ignored work which he thought made unjustified claims.

The core of an economy
One of the major figures cited by Debreu was Edgeworth. The latter argued that one should not be interested, as was Walras, in showing how a vector of prices, one for each good, converged to an equilibrium but one should consider haggling between individuals as reflecting the process involved. He then went on to develop a solution to this negotiation process which later was known as the core of an economy. When formalized, this amounts to considering allocations of goods to which no group, or "coalition" of agents could object. Such a group could object if they could take their own resources and distribute them among themselves, and, in so doing, make all the members of their group better off. What Edgeworth showed, in a very limited case, was that allocations with this property were competitive equilibria if the number of agents was large enough. This has led some to suggest, erroneously, that a bargaining process consisting of proposed allocations and objections to them would lead to an equilibrium. All that it, in fact, says is that an allocation to which no coalition has an objection is a competitive equilibrium when the number of agents in the economy becomes arbitrarily large. Nothing is said about how the economy gets there. Nevertheless, the result is a curiosity since, whether or not there is an objection to an allocation, it in no way involves prices, yet this criterion gives the same result as the more familiar price mechanism. Debreu, and Herbert Scarf (1963), showed that Edgeworth's result holds for a reasonably general class of economies. Later, Debreu (1975) discussed how fast this would happen, in the sense of asking how close this result was to holding as the number of agents increased. Although Lloyd Shapley (1975) had shown that the convergence could be arbitrarily slow, Debreu showed that for a certain class of economies the "core converges to the competitive equilibrium" at the rate of $1/N$ where N is the number of agents in the economy. This has sometimes been misinterpreted as saying how fast a bargaining process would lead to competitive equilibrium and this is, of course, not true.

This work shows again clearly how fascinated Debreu was with the beauty of proving results for very abstract economies rather than being concerned with analysing real economic phenomena. Yet it has also to be said that the refined puzzles on which he worked, usually had their origins in the work of leading figures in the history of economic theory.

Uniqueness of equilibrium

Debreu (1970) showed in a paper, again reverting to differentiability, that economies, in general, only have a finite set of equilibria. This means that even if there are many of them they will each be isolated and, in that sense, locally unique. This result is not particularly comforting for macroeconomists but does introduce an interesting notion, the idea that something may be true in general for economies but does not always hold. Somewhat inaccurately it can be said that the probability of finding an economy with an infinite number of equilibria is zero. Such a property is referred to as being "generic". This idea is not as innocent as it might seem and such results should be treated with caution (see Grandmont et al. 1974). Nevertheless, this was an innovation in a discipline in which researchers had been concerned with proving results that held without exception, albeit for a very limited class of economies.

Undermining the foundations

The general equilibrium framework which Debreu was, in large measure, responsible for perfecting, turned out to be extremely fragile. A reflection of this is seen in his 1974 paper, where he contributed to the results obtained by Sonnenschein (1972) and Mantel (1974) by showing that, even with the restrictive standard assumptions on the individual participants in the economy, neither stability nor uniqueness could be guaranteed. Ironically, this paper was heavily dependent on a differentiability assumption, something which he had disdained earlier. Here Debreu's major contribution was to refine in an elegant way the insight provided by Sonnenschein's contribution. He essentially showed that the only properties that could be deduced from the standard assumptions on individuals in an economy were the continuity of the aggregate excess demand function, Walras's Law, and the homogeneity of degree 0 of the economies aggregate excess demand function (increasing all prices by a multiple has no effect on excess demand). If not confined to prices that are bounded away from zero, it has to be added that if the price of any good goes to zero then the average excess demand for all commodities goes to infinity. Since it is easy to give examples of functions which satisfy these conditions but which have neither unique nor stable equilibria, then the usefulness of general equilibrium models for macroeconomists, for example, is obviously limited. It took some time before the devastating implications of this result for general equilibrium theory were realized, and there are still many economists who refer to their models as general equilibrium models but who, in reality, simplify away the difficulties by making some special assumption, such as assuming the existence of a "representative agent". Debreu never approved of this.

Conclusion

Debreu provides a very special and very important example of the relationship between economics and mathematics in what might be thought of as the golden age of high theory in economics. He felt that he had provided a method which, even if destructive in some ways, enforced clear and rigorous thinking in economics and even had an influence on mathematics. As he said in his Nobel lecture:

> [T]he axiomatization of economic theory has helped its practitioners by making available to them the superbly efficient language of mathematics. It has permitted them to communicate with each other, and to think, with a great economy of means. At the same time, the dialogue between economists and mathematicians has become more intense. The example of a mathematician of the first magnitude like John von Neumann devoting a significant fraction of his research to economic problems has not been unique. Simultaneously, economic theory has begun to influence mathematics . . . (Debreu 1983 [1992]: 99)

Yet, looking at the recent evolution of the world's economy, it is perhaps legitimate to enquire whether the edifice that Debreu contributed so much to building has produced much insight into the working of that economy. Hildenbrand (1981) speaking of Debreu's contribution to general equilibrium theory said that while Walras was the architect, Debreu was the master builder. Yet more recently it has been said (Kirman 1998), that this magnificent building, once full of fervent believers is now only visited by curious tourists. This was said in a volume in honour of Debreu's seventy-fifth birthday, and his response was characteristic; he was happy that the weaknesses of the structure, to which he had contributed so much, were revealed by those who had built it.

ALAN KIRMAN

See also:

Maurice Allais (I); Kenneth Joseph Arrow (I); Competition (III); Francis Ysidro Edgeworth (I); Formalization and mathematical modelling (III); Game theory (III); General equilibrium theory (III); Lausanne School (II); Vilfredo Pareto (I); Adam Smith (I); Value and price (III); Marie-Esprit-Léon Walras (I).

References and further reading

Allais, M. (1953), *Traité d'économie pure*, Paris: Imprimerie Nationale.
Arrow, K.J. and G. Debreu (1954), 'Existence of an equilibrium for a competitive economy', *Econometrica*, **22** (3), 265–90.
Bourbaki, N. (1949), 'The foundations of mathematics for the working mathematician', *Journal of Symbolic Logic*, **14** (1), 1–8.
Debreu, G. (1951), 'The coefficient of resource utilization', *Econometrica*, **19** (3), 273–92.
Debreu, G. (1954), 'Representation of a preference ordering by a numerical function', in R.M. Thrall, C.H. Coombs and R.L. Davis (eds), *Decision Processes*, New York: Wiley, pp. 159–65.
Debreu, G. (1959), *Theory of Value: An Axiomatic Analysis of Economic Equilibrium*, New York: Wiley.
Debreu, G. (1970), 'Economies with a finite set of equilibria', *Econometrica*, **38** (3), 387–92.
Debreu, G. (1974), 'Excess demand functions', *Journal of Mathematical Economics*, **1** (1), 15–21.
Debreu, G. (1975), 'The rate of convergence of the core of an economy', *Journal of Mathematical Economics*, **2** (1), 1–7.
Debreu, G. (1983), 'Economics in the mathematical mode', Nobel Memorial lecture, in K.-G. Mäler (ed.) (1992), *Nobel Lectures, Economics 1981–1990*, Singapore: World Scientific.
Debreu, G. and H. Scarf (1963), 'A limit theorem on the core of an economy', *International Economic Review*, **4** (3), 235–46.
Düppe, T. (2012), 'Gerard Debreu's secrecy: his life in order and silence', *History of Political Economy*, **44** (3), 413–49.
Grandmont, J.-M., A. Kirman and W. Neuefeind (1974), 'A new approach to the uniqueness of equilibrium', *Review of Economic Studies*, **41** (2), 289–91.
Hildenbrand, W. (1981), 'Introduction', in W. Hildenbrand (ed.), *Mathematical Economics: Twenty Papers of Gerard Debreu*, Cambridge: Cambridge University Press.
Kirman, A. (ed.) (1998), *Elements of General Equilibrium Analysis*, Oxford, Basil Blackwell.

Le Figaro (1984), 'Entretien avec Gerard Nobel', *Le Figaro*, 10 March.

Mas Colell, A. (1990), *The Theory of General Economic Equilibrium: A Differentiable Approach*, Cambridge, Cambridge University Press.

Mantel, R. (1974), 'On the characterization of aggregate excess demand', *Journal of Economic Theory*, **7** (3), 348–53.

Shapley, L.S. (1975), 'An example of a slow-converging core', *International Economic Review*, **16** (2), 345–51.

Sonnenschein, H. (1972), 'Market excess demand functions', *Econometrica*, **40** (3), 549–63.

Sveriges Riksbank (1983), presentation of the Sveriges Riksbank Prize in Economic Sciences in Memory of Alfred Nobel to Gérard Debreu, 17 October, Stockholm.

Wald, A. (1935), 'Über die eindeutige positive Lösbarkeit der neuen Produktionsgleichungen', *Ergebnisse eines mathematischen Kolloquiums*, **6**, 12–20.

Don Patinkin (1922–1995)

Don Patinkin (born 1922 in Chicago, died 1995 in Jerusalem) was the author of *Money, Interest and Prices* (1956), a book widely considered as the epitome if not the apex of the "neoclassical synthesis". He entered Chicago University in 1941 and was trained in the Marshallian tradition by the figures of the old Chicago School, Knight, Simons, Mint and Viner. However, he was also the student of Hurwicz, Lange and Marschak – mathematical economists and prominent members of the Cowles Commission. As a fellow of this institution, in 1947, Patinkin completed a PhD thesis titled "On the consistency of economic models: a theory of involuntary unemployment".

Patinkin emigrated to Israel in 1949 where he became a professor at the Hebrew University of Jerusalem. According to Barkai (1993: 3), he "single-handedly established economics as an academic discipline and, at the same time, showed how this discipline could be applied to the analysis of Israel's pressing economic problems". In 1956, with Simon Kuznets, he created what became the Maurice Falk Institute for Economic Research in Israel in order to provide Israeli economists with macroeconomic data. Patinkin was its research director from 1956 to 1972. He was deeply involved in the making of Israel's economic policy until the 1970s, either directly or through his students, the "Patinkin boys", serving in the administrations.

The Integration of Money into General Equilibrium Theory

Patinkin's contribution to monetary theory came as a reaction to the works of Lange (1942, 1944) and Modigliani (1944), works actively discussed at the Cowles Commission.

Lange (1942) claimed that, in order to account for an overproduction crisis, general equilibrium theory had to incorporate money. Combining Walras's and Say's laws, Lange showed that the level of money prices was indeterminate in the classical theory of prices. The "traditional approach", determining relative prices in the real sector and money prices by use of the cash balance equation, was no escape since the equation was inconsistent with Say's law. Both had to be abandoned in favour of a truly general equilibrium treatment of the issue, a move supposed to imply the rejection of money neutrality. In 1944, Modigliani challenged Lange's conclusions and claimed that the hallmark of the classics was their view that "all the supply and demand functions [except the ones for money] must be homogeneous of zero degree, if people behave rationally" (1944: 46). Once Say's law had been put aside, the traditional approach and money neutrality remained intact. The same year, Lange (1944) published an attempt to develop the depression theory hinted at in 1942 and, like Modigliani, he adopted the zero degree homogeneity postulate.

From Patinkin (1949: 1, 9), one can infer that Hurwicz discovered an inconsistency in Lange's system of equations and that Haavelmo convinced Patinkin to work on the issue. Using the work of Hurwicz, Patinkin showed that the indeterminacy disclosed by Lange was a direct consequence of the assumption of zero degree homogeneity. Besides, this assumption was inconsistent with the Cantabrigian cash balance equation. The thrust of the argument was that if commodity excess demands were independent of the level of money prices, by virtue of Walras's law, it should also be true of the real excess demand for money. The 1944 models of Lange and Modigliani were both inconsistent.

In his thesis and the two articles extracted from it, Patinkin (1948a, 1949) widened his critique to the monetary theories of the "classics" – mainly Cassel, Pareto and Walras. Inspired by Hicks (1935), Patinkin criticized Pareto and Walras for their supposed refusal to introduce money in agents' utility functions. He showed that this approach was consistent only if the stock of money was nil and concluded that "any realistic attempt to describe this world must provide for the inclusion of money in the utility function" (Patinkin 1948a: 154).

Patinkin's demonstration of the inconsistencies affecting the classics' monetary theories left an open question: how could one solve the indeterminacy of money prices without violating the neutrality of money? The solution, introduced in the end of Patinkin's 1949 article, was developed in *Money, Interest and Prices*. To realize the "integration of monetary and value theory", one had to take account of the real balance effect, "the sine qua none of monetary theory" (Patinkin, 1956: 22).

Patinkin started from the simplest framework to focus on the essential features of his theory. He analysed a pure exchange economy with goods and fiat money. The temporality of the economy was defined by the Hicksian week. Each Monday morning, agents were endowed with given quantities of goods "falling from heaven" and with cash balances carried over from the preceding week. Then they had to determine the quantities of goods they would sell and purchase and the money balances with which they would start the following week. A *tâtonnement* process would take place and by the end of the day general equilibrium prices were determined and contracts were signed. At this stage, Patinkin assumed that contracts were placed in a common pool and randomly drawn from it in order to fix the day and the hour of their completion. As a result, agents had to face the risk of discrepancies between payments and receipts. In order to insure against the "embarrassment of default" they would keep some reserves of the medium of exchange. This narrative was not formalized but it vindicated the introduction of real balances in the utility function.

The assumption that each agent determines his optimum level of real balances led Patinkin to supplement the Hicksian demand theory with the real balance effect. A modification of the price of a particular commodity triggered the traditional substitution and income effects but it also affected the real value of cash balances. In order to restore their optimum level, agents modify their expenditures on goods. Patinkin noted that money demand was also subject to this effect. A price level increase leads agents to demand more money. However, since the real value of their money holdings decreases, the budget constraint implies a reduction of this optimum level. The Cantabrigian assumption of a unit elasticity of money demand with respect to prices is false.

On this basis, Patinkin analysed the "determination of the price level" or the stability of general equilibrium in a money economy. Assuming that there was an equilibrium, Patinkin considered a situation in which real balances are higher than their equilibrium levels. In this case, there would be an excess demand on the goods market pressing prices upward. Real balances and demands for goods would decline until equilibrium is restored on the goods markets and, due to Walras's law, also on the money market. Patinkin also showed that in the absence of distribution effects and money illusion, a doubling of the quantity of money would cause a proportionate increase of money prices without affecting real magnitudes. His approach was supposed to offer the "ultimate, rigorous validation of the classical quantity theory of money itself" (1956: 99). In chapter 8 of *Money,*

Interest and Prices, Patinkin examined systematically how his new approach overcomes the limits and the errors involved in the older versions of monetary theory. In contrast with his earlier works he carefully distinguished the "classicals" from the various sorts of "neoclassicals" and documented all his claims with "notes and studies in the literature".

Patinkin's works on the integration of money had a deep influence on the debates of the 1950s and 1960s. Several economists opposed his rejection of the classical dichotomy. The contribution of Archibald and Lipsey (1958) marked the higher point of the resulting "Patinkin controversy" leading to a special issue of the *Review of Economic Studies* (1960). Patinkin's indictment of the dichotomy was finally accepted, except in the case of an inside money economy (Modigliani, 1963). But deeper critiques were gradually formulated. Hahn (1965) showed that nothing in Patinkin's models guarantees that the accounting price of money is strictly positive. The foundations for a monetary theory were still to be found. Different alternatives were offered over the years but none settled the issue.

Macroeconomics

"Macroeconomics" was the title of the second part of *Money, Interest and Prices*. There, Patinkin submitted the investment saving–liquidity preference money supply (IS–LM) framework to the discipline of the Walrasian method and used it to extend the neutrality results of the first part of the book to an economy with production.

Until the mid-1950s, the numerous versions of IS–LM had been plagued by confusions in the formulation of their equations and in the analysis of their properties. Despite its success, Modigliani's 1944 model illustrates the issue (Rubin 2004). For instance, he made behaviour functions dependent on money instead of real income and the signification of the IS equation remained unclear. When he analysed the dynamics of his model, Modigliani actually presented IS as the long-run equilibrium condition for the money market. Some basic principles borrowed from the Walrasian methodology allowed Patinkin to formulate a superior version of IS–LM. The model was presented as a four-market system with three unknowns. Then Walras's law and a set of simplifying assumptions related to the labour market was introduced to show how this four equation model could be reduced to the interaction between two different markets (preferably goods and bonds). Thanks to his *tâtonnement* method Patinkin clarified the adjustment process leading to the equilibrium in his various versions of IS–LM. He also resolved a number of issues that would seem obvious afterwards. For instance, he showed that Keynes's introduction of the rate of interest in the demand for money was not enough to discard the neutrality of money in a full employment model unless the speculative demand for money featured money illusion as it did in the *General Theory* (Keynes 1936). Incorporating the distinction of internal and external money developed by Gurley and Shaw (1960), Patinkin offered a detailed discussion of the introduction of a banking system in his model. Following Hicks (1939), he closed the long debate over the determination of the rate of interest stating that if the rate of interest is primarily related to the bonds market, it is generally determined, like all prices, by all the equations of the model. He showed that the usual definition of the liquidity trap as the consequence of an "infinite demand for money" is mistaken for it implies the violation of the agents' intertemporal budget constraints. All this explains why, in the 1960s, "at the London School of Economics and at MIT, the two essential books in macroeconomics were the *General Theory* and *Money, Interest and Prices*" (Fisher 1993: 25).

In his introduction of *Money, Interest and Prices*, Patinkin presented "the theory of a monetary economy with involuntary unemployment" as the "second major theme" of his book (1956: 2–3). This issue was actually the starting point of his PhD dissertation in 1946. Lange presented Keynes's concept of involuntary unemployment as the consequence of a horizontal supply curve for labour. For Patinkin, since this assumption implied labour market clearing, the position of workers could hardly be called involuntary. Involuntary unemployment could only arise when workers were "off their supply curve". Patinkin developed this line of thought in the second part of his thesis, giving rise later to the disequilibrium theories of the 1970s (Rubin 2012). Within a framework supposed to derive from a Walrasian model, he tried to account for the possibility of an unemployment equilibrium with price and wage flexibility. He argued that, in a disequilibrium context, agents were faced with "additional restraints" so that the choice theoretic basis of the general equilibrium models had to be modified. He identified correctly the additional constraint of unemployed workers as the level of employment and came very close to Clower's dual decision concept. Yet, Patinkin did not see how to give an operational content to his intuition. His reasoning suffered from a partial equilibrium perspective and, ironically, his model left the interest rate and the price level indeterminate. These problems forced him to revise his position.

From 1948 on, Patinkin claimed that Keynesian economics were about unemployment disequilibrium. This position was supported by chapter 13 of *Money, Interest and Prices*, the beginning of the history of disequilibrium economics and the result of a long process of elaboration (see Boianovsky 2006). In this chapter, Patinkin applied the concept of "spillover effect" in a Keynesian context and finally captured the operational intuition missed in his thesis. He submitted his four-market system to an aggregate demand decline and assumed that the adjustment process was slow. Faced with a sales constraint on the market for goods, firms would have to revise their demand for labour whatever the real wage level. This in turn would create an excess supply of labour and involuntary unemployment. Analysing different scenarios on the basis of the relative adjustment speeds of wages and prices, Patinkin's claimed that unemployment could appear even if the real wage is still at its market clearing level. Chapter 13 was a decisive source of inspiration for Clower (1965) (Rubin 2005). The concept of spillover was taken up by Barro and Grossman (1971) and played a crucial role in the literature on disequilibrium that developed in the 1970s. Patinkin's involuntary unemployment theory was far from being conclusive. In a famous footnote, he admitted the inconsistency of an analysis combining the assumption of a sales constraint with perfect competition and hoped that someone would find a consistent way of modelling the behaviour of firms in disequilibrium.

Patinkin's approach supported a new definition of the frontier between the classics and Keynes. A chapter 19 Keynesian, Patinkin always claimed that involuntary unemployment was not a consequence of wage rigidity. According to him, both the classics and Keynes admitted that even though prices and wages were flexible their adjustments were not instantaneous. Assuming the same speeds of adjustment for wages, prices and the rate of interest, they differ in their evaluation of the elasticity of aggregate demand with respect to the rate of interest and the price level. For the classics, this elasticity is high. As a result, a small price decline would restore equilibrium on goods' markets in a short time. For the Keynesians, the elasticity is low and, even if the real balance effect pushes the system back towards full employment, this process is a "long, drawn out one" (Patinkin 1956: 216). A market economy left on its own is prone to chronic disequilibrium and unemployment. The length of time of the adjustment process is enough to vindicate the use of public expenditure to maintain full employment. The debate between the two camps was a matter of "empirical considerations" (ibid.: 237) and the Keynesian stance was freed from its dependence on extreme theoretical scenarios like the liquidity trap.

Patinkin as a Historian of Economic Thought

As already noted above, Patinkin's commitment to history of economic thought was a distinctive characteristic of *Money, Interest and Prices*. His "Notes on the literature" with the studies on Fisher, Walras or Wicksell were a remarkable contribution to the history of the quantity theory. In the 1970s, Patinkin devoted his research to the history of the Keynesian revolution in the 1930s. Since his days as a student, he had tried to find out the nature of Keynesian economics. Patinkin pursued this quest on the basis of the newly published volumes of Keynes's collected writings (Backhouse 2002). In 1976 he published *Keynes' Monetary Thought*, a book that examines the development of Keynes's ideas from the *Tract* to the *General Theory*. Patinkin argued that Keynes's central message in 1936 is the theory of effective demand. For him, Keynes's book is the "first practical application of the Walrasian theory of general equilibrium" and the *General Theory* is a "dynamic theory of unemployment disequilibrium". In his *Anticipations of the* General Theory? (1982) Patinkin argued that the Keynesian revolution was not a case of multiple discoveries. All these works were condensed in Patinkin's entry on Keynes's for the *New Palgrave Dictionary of Economics* (Patinkin 1991). Another important contribution to the field was Patinkin's study on the Chicago tradition (1981). The fierce polemic it triggered with Friedman stimulated a whole stream of research.

GOULVEN RUBIN

See also:

Chicago School (II); General equilibrium theory (III); Keynesianism (II); Oskar Ryszard Lange (I); Macroeconomics (III); Jacob Marschak (I); Money and banking (III).

References and further reading

Archibald, G.C. and R.G. Lipsey (1958),'Monetary and value theory: a critique of Lange and Patinkin', *Review of Economic Studies*, **26** (1), 1–22.
Backhouse, R. (2002), 'Don Patinkin: interpreter of the Keynesian revolution', *European Journal of History of Economic Thought*, **9** (2), 186–204.
Barkai, H. (1993), 'Don Patinkin's contribution to economics in Israel', in H. Barkai, S. Fisher and N. Liviatan (eds), *Monetary Theory and Thought: Essays in Honour of Don Patinkin*, London: Macmillan, pp. 3–15.
Barro, R.J. and H.I. Grossman (1971), 'A general disequilibrium model of income and employment', *American Economic Review*, **61** (1), 82–93.
Boianovsky, M.(2006), 'The making of chapter 13 and 14 of Patinkin's *Money, Interest and Prices*', *History of Political Economy*, **38** (2), 193–249.
Clower, R. (1965), 'The Keynesian counter-revolution: a theoretical appraisal', in F.H. Hahn and F.P.R. Bretchling (eds), *The Theory of Interest Rates*, London: Macmillan, pp. 103–25.
Fisher, S. (1993), 'Money, interest, and prices', in H. Barkai, S. Fisher and N. Liviatan (eds), *Monetary Theory and Thought: Essays in Honour of Don Patinkin*, London: Macmillan, pp.15–31.
Gurley, J.G. and E.S. Shaw (1960), *Money in a Theory of Finance*, Washington, DC: Brooking Institution.

Hahn, F.H. (1965), 'On some problems of proving the existence of an equilibrium in a monetary economy', in F.H. Hahn and F.P.R. Bretchling (eds), *The Theory of Interest Rates*, London: Macmillan, pp. 103–25.

Hicks, J.R. (1935), 'A suggestion for simplifying the theory of money', *Economica*, New Series, **2** (5), 1–19.

Hicks, J.R.(1939), *Value and Capital. An Inquiry into Some Fundamental Principles of Economic Theory*, 2nd edn 1946, Oxford: Clarendon Press.

Keynes, J.M. (1936), *The General Theory of Employment, Interest and Money*, London: Macmillan.

Lange, O. (1942), 'Say's law: a restatement and criticism', in O. Lange, F. McIntyre and T.O. Yntema (eds), *Studies in Mathematical Economics and Econometrics*, Chicago, IL: University of Chicago Press, pp. 4–68.

Lange, O. (1944), *Price Flexibility and Employment*, Cowles Commission for Research in Economics Monograph no. 8, San Antonio: Principia Press of Trinity University.

Modigliani, F. (1944), 'Liquidity preference and the theory of interest and money', *Econometrica*, **12** (1), 45–88.

Modigliani, F. (1963), 'The monetary mechanism and its interaction with real phenomena', *Review of Economics and Statistics*, **45** (1), 79–107.

Patinkin, D. (1948a), 'Relative prices, Say's law, and the demand for money', *Econometrica*, **16** (2), 135–54.

Patinkin, D. (1948b), 'Price flexibility and full employment', *American Economic Review*, **38** (4), 543–64.

Patinkin, D. (1949), 'The indeterminacy of absolute prices in classical economic theory', *Econometrica*, **17** (1), 1–27.

Patinkin, D. (1956), *Money, Interest and Prices: An Integration of Monetary and Value Theory*, Evanston, IL: Row, Peterson.

Patinkin, D. (1976), *Keynes' Monetary Thought: A Study of its Development*, Durham, NC: Duke University Press.

Patinkin, D. (1981), *Essays On and In the Chicago Tradition*, Durham, NC: Duke University Press.

Patinkin, D. (1982), *Anticipations of the* General Theory? *And Other Essays on Keynes*, Chicago, IL: University of Chicago Press.

Patinkin, D. (1991), 'Keynes, John Maynard', in J. Eatwell, M. Milgate and P. Newman (eds), *The New Palgrave a Dictionary of Economics*, vol. 3, London: Macmillan, pp. 19–41.

Review of Economic Studies (1960), 'A symposium on monetary theory', *Review of Economic Studies*, **28** (1), contributions by W.J. Baumol et al.; F. H. Hahn; R.J. Ball and R. Bodkin; and G.C. Archibald and R.G. Lipsey.

Rubin, G. (2004), 'Patinkin on IS–LM: an alternative to Modigliani', *History of Political Economy*, **36** (Annual Supplement), 190–216.

Rubin, G. (2005), 'La controverse entre Clower et Patinkin au sujet de la loi de Walras', *Revue économique*, **56** (1), 5–24.

Rubin, G. (2012), 'Don Patinkin's PhD dissertation as the prehistory of disequilibrium theories', *History of Political Economy*, **44** (1), 235–76.

Michio Morishima (1923–2004)

Michio Morishima (1923–2004) is an internationally renowned Japanese mathematical economist, although his base was the London School of Economics (LSE) in England rather than Japan for a long time. He was born in 1923 in Japan, and entered Kyoto Imperial University (currently Kyoto University) as a student in the midst of World War II (1942). In Kyoto, he studied sociology under the guidance of the distinguished sociologist Yasuma Takata and studied Western mainstream economic theory (in particular, Hicks's 1939 *Value and Capital*) under the guidance of Hideo Aoyama. After World War II, he taught economic theory at Kyoto University and Osaka University in Japan. In 1969, he shifted his base from Japan to England, and taught economic theory at the University of Essex. He was a professor of economic theory at the LSE from 1970 to 1988. He contributed to the establishment of the Suntry and Toyota International Centre for Economic and Related Disciplines (STICERD) at the LSE and became the first chairman of STICERD. After retiring from the LSE, he taught economics at the University of Siena, Italy. He became the first Japanese economist to undertake the role of the president of the Econometric Society in 1965 when he was a professor at Osaka University. (Later two Japanese economists, Hirofumi Uzawa and Takashi Negishi, followed him to become the president of the Econometric Society.)

He has published numerous creative papers on mathematical economic theory both in Japanese and in English since the 1950s. In particular, he contributed in the field of nonlinear macrodynamic theories of economic fluctuations in the 1950s, and multisectoral dynamic theories of economic growth in the 1960s. His first book entitled *Dogakuteki Keizai Riron* (*Dynamic Economic Theory*) was published in Japanese by Kobundo, Tokyo in 1950, and a revised version of this book was published in English 46 years later (Morishima 1996). In this book he studied stability, instability, and cyclical fluctuations of dynamic general equilibrium system by means of linear and nonlinear differential equations, and his theoretical achievements surpassed those of J.R. Hicks, P.A. Samuelson and O. Lange at that time. On the basis of these theoretical achievements, he contributed to the development of multisectoral theories of economic growth which were originated in the seminal work by von Neumann (Morishima 1964, 1969). In the 1970s and the 1980s, he published a series of works which tackled the economic theories of the past great economists such as Marx, Walras and Ricardo from the point of view of modern mathematical economics (Morishima 1973, 1977, 1989; see also Kurz 2011). From the 1980s to the 2000s, he published a series of socio-economic essays on the Japanese society (Morishima 1982, 2000).

Although his socio-economic essays on Japan during the 1980s to 2000s contributed to his success in getting popularity among the non-academic world, his main contribution in economics is the development of the mathematically rigorous dynamic economic theory. As already noted, Morishima (1950) is the starting point of his research of dynamic economic theory, and it was already a highly creative contribution to economic theory. After the publication of this book, he wrote a series of original papers on the nonlinear macrodynamic theory of the business cycles at almost the same period as Goodwin's contribution appeared (Morishima 1953, 1958). His contribution together with contributions by Yasui and Ichimura in this period was referred to as "Japanese contributions to nonlinear cycle theory" by Velupillai (2008).

His main contribution in the 1960s is the mathematical studies of the multisectoral models of economic growth that was inspired by von Neumann's model of general economic equilibrium in a growing economy (Morishima 1964, 1969). His contribution in this period was much influenced by Hicks's (1965) study. Morishima's study of the capital theory in the 1990s is also based on the multisectoral dynamic models *à la* von Neumann (Morishima 1992). Even his highly original studies of the past great economists by means of rigorous mathematical method in the 1970s and the 1980s are based on von Neumann type multisectoral models (Morishima 1973, 1977, 1989).

It was already noted that Morishima contributed to the mathematical formulation of Marxian economic theory in the 1970s (see Morishima 1973). It is also worth noting, however, that his contribution of mathematical Marxian economics was influenced by the contributions by another pioneering Japanese mathematical Marxian economist, Nobuo Okishio (see Okishio 1963, 1993).

In the 1990s, Morishima challenged the new approach to synthesize the growth theory and the monetary theory based on the analytical framework of von Neumann's multisectoral model (see Morishima 1992), which became his last major contribution to economic theory.

TOICHIRO ASADA

See also:

Economic dynamics (III); Formalization and mathematical modelling (III); Growth (III); John Richard Hicks (I); Oskar Ryszard Lange (I); Karl Heinrich Marx (I); John von Neumann (I); David Ricardo (I); Paul Anthony Samuelson (I); Value and price (III); Marie-Esprit-Léon Walras (I).

References and further reading

Hicks, J.R. (1939), *Value and Capital*, Oxford: Clarendon Press.
Hicks, J.R. (1965), *Capital and Growth*, Oxford: Clarendon Press.
Kurz, H.D. (2011), 'The contributions of two eminent Japanese scholars to the development of economic theory: Michio Morishima and Takashi Negishi', in H.D. Kurz, T. Nishizawa and K. Tribe (eds), *The Dissemination of Economic Ideas*, Cheltenham, UK and Northampton, MA, USA: Edward Elgar, pp. 337–64.
Morishima, M. (1950), *Dougakuteki Keizai Riron* (*Dynamic Economic Theory*), Tokyo: Kobundo (in Japanese).
Morishima, M. (1953), 'Mittsu no hisenkei moderu' ('Three nonlinear models'), *Kikan Riron Keizaigaku* (*Economic Studies Quarterly*), **4** (3–4), 213–19, in Japanese.
Morishima, M. (1958), 'A contribution to the nonlinear theory of the trade cycle', *Zeitschrift für Nationalökonomie*, **18** (March), 165–73.
Morishima, M. (1964), *Equilibrium, Stability and Growth: A Multi-Sectoral Analysis*, Oxford: Oxford University Press.
Morishima, M. (1969), *Theory of Economic Growth*, Oxford: Oxford University Press.
Morishima, M. (1973), *Marx's Economics: A Dual Theory of Value and Growth*, Cambridge: Cambridge University Press.
Morishima, M. (1977), *Walras' Economics: A Pure Theory of Capital and Money*, Cambridge: Cambridge University Press.
Morishima, M. (1982), *Why Has Japan Succeeded?*, Cambridge: Cambridge University Press.
Morishima, M. (1989), *Ricardo's Economics: A General Equilibrium Theory of Distribution and Growth*, Cambridge: Cambridge University Press.
Morishima, M. (1992), *Capital and Credit: A New Formulation of General Equilibrium Theory*, Cambridge: Cambridge University Press.
Morishima, M. (1996), *Dynamic Economic Theory*, Cambridge: Cambridge University Press.
Morishima, M. (2000), *Japan as a Deadlock*, London: Macmillan.
Okishio, N. (1963), 'A mathematical note on Marxian theorems', *Weltwirtschaftliches Archiv*, **91** (2), 287–99.
Okishio, N. (1993), *Essays on Political Economy*, M. Krueger and P. Flaschel (eds), Frankfurt am Main: Peter Lang.
Velupillai, K.V. (2008), 'Japanese contributions to nonlinear cycle theory in the 1950s', *Japanese Economic Review*, **59** (March), 54–74.

Robert Merton Solow (b. 1924)

Robert M. Solow was born on 23 August 1924 in Brooklyn, New York. He was the oldest of three children of parents who were children of immigrants. A scholarship allowed him to enrol in Harvard College from 1940 and he became, as he formulated it many years later, "curious about what made society tick". After two years and at only 18 years of age he left the college and became a soldier for a three-year period, which he spent mainly in Italy.

After the end of the war he studied at Harvard University and came in contact with Wassily Leontief who had a lasting influence on him and who hired him as a research assistant. Solow's thesis was about changes in the size distribution of labour income and won him a prize. At Columbia University he enhanced his statistical and econometrical abilities, and in the early 1950s he became an assistant professor (later full professor) at the Massachusetts Institute of Technology (MIT), where he stayed for his whole academic career. There he developed a close friendship and productive collaboration with Paul A. Samuelson, who had the office next to him. In 1995 he retired but continued to do research, lecture and participate in public discussions – often with handy formulations on complicated issues.

Solow received a number of important awards and prizes. In 1961 he was awarded the John Bates Clark Medal, which goes annually to the best economist under 40 years of age. In 1987 he was awarded the Nobel Memorial Prize in Economics and in 1999 he received the National Medal of Science of the United States. The most important award, the Nobel Memorial Prize of the Sveriges Riksbank was awarded to him "for his contributions to the theory of economic growth" (see especially Solow 1956, 1957, 1970).

In contrast to the founders of modern growth theory, Roy F. Harrod and Evsey Domar, Solow was not interested in the process of how equality between investment (I) and saving (S) is achieved. In his opinion this was a short-run problem not to be dealt with when long-run questions such as economic growth are on the agenda. He assumed therefore that $I = S$ is always fulfilled, which amounts to adopting Say's law. However, he went further. Postulating a linear homogeneous macroeconomic production function with substitutive factors of production and perfect factor markets with flexible prices, he excluded problems such as unemployment and under-utilization of capital. Since the price mechanism is assumed to take care that all factors of production are fully used, the growth of real income in this world is completely determined by the growth of the factors of production. The decisive task of growth theory therefore is to investigate the determinants of the growth of the factors of production.

In Solow's basic model, without technical progress there are only two factors of production, labour and capital. As far as the labour force is concerned, he assumed that it is a constant share of population and that it increases with a constant rate, which is given from the outside. Net saving (identical with net investment or increase of the capital stock) is assumed to be proportional to income. It is quite obvious that three different situations can be distinguished: (1) capital and labour grow with an identical rate – the situation of steady-state growth – (2) capital grows with a higher rate than labour, and (3) labour grows with a higher rate than capital.

The first situation implies that real income grows at the same rate as labour and capital. We are in the situation of a steady state, in which capital intensity and per capita income are constant.

When capital increases more swiftly than labour, the assumptions of substitutability and of constant returns to scale imply that the growth rate of real income is smaller than capital's growth rate but larger than labour's. We are in a situation in which capital intensity as well as the capital coefficient increase. However, the growth rate of capital is

$$\frac{I}{K} = \frac{sY}{K} = \frac{s}{\dfrac{K}{Y}} \tag{1}$$

where K is the capital stock, s is the propensity to save and Y is the social product. Since in the situation under consideration the denominator on the right-hand side increases, it is obvious that the rate of accumulation (I/K) will fall. In other words: as long as the rate of accumulation exceeds the (constant) growth rate of the labour force, it is declining. This decline takes place until the growth rate of capital is equal to the growth rate of the labour force.

When labour grows at a faster rate than capital, we have the reverse situation: capital intensity and the capital coefficient decrease until the growth rate of capital has become equal to that of labour.

A remarkable feature of the model is the following: an increase (decrease) in the saving or investment rate can only temporarily but not permanently influence society's rate of growth. This can again be clarified with the equation above. A higher s will increase the accumulation rate I/K and at the same time the growth rate of income. But the latter will be lower than the former as the elasticities of production of substitutive production functions have values between zero and one. As a consequence the capital coefficient increases and that will decrease I/K, which finally will again coincide with the exogenously give rate of population growth. Only during the process of transition does a higher investment rate have a positive effect on the rate of growth.

This result challenged the conventional wisdom that an increase in the rate of investment is decisive for economic growth, which had instructed development policy.

The model in its basic form has an irritating feature because growth of per capita income is only a transitional phenomenon. However, statistics tell us that highly industrialized countries have long been experiencing growing per capita incomes. Therefore, an important ingredient explaining per capita growth is missing. Some economists spoke of this missing ingredient of a "third factor", some of technical change or technical progress. In an empirical investigation (Solow 1957), which supplemented his theoretical contribution (Solow 1956), Solow showed that capital intensification had contributed only a small part to the growth of per capita income, whereas the predominant part had to be attributed to "technical progress", which was not taken into account in the basic model. He stressed that this is a catch-all for the totality of influences we are not able to identify exactly; Moses Abramovitz (1956: 11) spoke of a "measure of our ignorance".

Technical change, as introduced by Solow, raises several questions. The first concerns the special form of it. As can be shown, the only form of technical progress compatible with steady-state growth is so-called labour-augmenting or Harrod-neutral progress which in a macro-economic production function has the form (β stands for the rate of efficiency growth of labour):

$$Y = F(K, A(t)L) \tag{2}$$

$$\text{with} \quad A(t) = A(0)\, e^{\beta t}$$

Solow does not discuss the question of why this form of technical change should dominate and only a few later contributions were concerned with this question.

A further feature of Solow's technical change is that it is disembodied, that is, it occurs without the necessity of introducing new capital goods. In a later paper (Solow et al. 1966) he discussed the consequences of embodied technical change in which gross investment is necessary to introduce new capital goods (so-called vintage models).

Finally it has to be mentioned that technical change in Solow's model is completely exogenous, it is simply a function of time. During the revival of growth theory ("neo-neoclassical growth theory") in the second part of the 1980s, attempts were made to endogenize technical progress, often using Solow's model as the point of departure.

Solow also made important contributions to other fields of economics. To mention but a few: (1) in Dorfman et al. (1958) the authors offered not only a rigorous introduction to the then new field of linear programming but showed at the same time that important messages of marginal analysis were not restricted to "well-behaved" twice differentiable functions but can also be formulated in the framework of linear equations subject to constraints as they are characteristic of linear programming approaches; (2) together with Samuelson (Samuelson and Solow 1960) he transformed the Phillips curve into a relation between the rate of unemployment and the rate of inflation, which seemed to offer politicians a choice between different options; (3) in McDonald and Solow (1981), taking up an idea of Leontief, the solution of the so-called monopoly union model (the union first chooses the wage and then the firm chooses employment subject to this wage) is shown to be Pareto inefficient and can be improved when the firm and the union negotiate an efficient contract; (4) in Solow (1990) he showed that the conventional market model has to be modified with respect to the labour market and he demonstrated why unemployed workers in general do not even try to undercut wages, so applying a game theoretic approach shows that it may be rational for workers to behave in that way, and (5) Hahn and Solow (1998), dissatisfied with the ruling representative–agent models in macroeconomics, tried to put macroeconomics on another track, with little success, as Solow himself admitted.

In contrast to the latter publication, Solow's contributions had a tremendous effect on economics and economic policy. This holds true first and foremost for his contributions to the theory of economic growth. They triggered innumerable theoretical and empirical studies and had, beyond that, a significant influence on economic policy because they challenged the previous view that an increase in the rate of investment of physical capital is crucial for economic growth. (However, things have come full circle: in new growth theory much of the attention focuses on the share of investment.) Although in Solow's model technical change was exogenous, it suggested that it would be beneficial for society to allocate resources to research and development, on the one hand, and to an enlargement of human capital on the other. With the burgeoning neo-neoclassical growth models these messages became a run-of-the-mill wisdom.

PETER KALMBACH

See also:

Capital theory (III); Economic dynamics (III); Growth (III); Labour and employment (III); Paul Anthony Samuelson (I); Technical change and innovation (III).

References and further reading

Abramovitz, M. (1956), 'Resources and output trends in the United States since 1870', *American Economic Review*, **46** (2), 5–23.
Dorfman, R., P.A. Samuelson and R.M. Solow (1958), *Linear Programming and Economic Analysis*, New York: McGraw-Hill.
Hahn, F. and R.M. Solow (1998), *A Critical Essay on Modern Macroeconomic Theory*, Oxford: Blackwell.
McDonald, I.M. and R.M. Solow (1981), 'Wage bargain and employment', *American Economic Review*, **71** (5), 896–908.
Samuelson, P.A. and R.M. Solow (1960), 'Analytical aspects of anti-inflation policy', *American Economic Review*, Papers and Proceedings, **50** (May), 177–94.
Solow, R.M. (1956), 'A contribution to the theory of economic growth', *Quarterly Journal of Economics*, **70** (February), 65–94.
Solow, R.M. (1957), 'Technical change and the aggregate production function', *Review of Economics and Statistics*, **39** (August), 312–20.
Solow, R.M. (1970), *Growth Theory. An Exposition*, Oxford: Oxford University Press.
Solow, R.M. (1990), *The Labor Market as a Social Institution*, Cambridge, MA: Blackwell.
Solow, R.M., J. Tobin, C.C. von Weizsäcker and M.E. Yaari (1966), 'Neoclassical growth with fixed factor proportions', *Review of Economic Studies*, **33** (2), 79–115.

John Forbes Nash Jr (1928–2015)

The mathematician John Forbes Nash Jr, shared the Royal Bank of Sweden Prize in Economic Science in Memory of Alfred Nobel with John Harsanyi and Reinhard Selten in 1994 for his contributions in the early 1950s to the theory of strategic games: his proof of the existence of Nash equilibrium in non-cooperative games with compact strategy spaces, the Nash bargaining solution for cooperative games (games in which binding agreements are possible among players, with costless enforcement of contracts), and the Nash programme linking non-cooperative and cooperative games. Nash equilibrium as a solution concept for non-cooperative games has been fundamental to the expansion of game theory from a small sub-field within mathematical economics to increasingly pervasive influence throughout economics, the other social sciences, law, business strategy, and evolutionary biology. In the words of Nobel laureate Roger Myerson (1991: 105), "Nash's (1951) concept of equilibrium is probably the most important solution concept in game theory" (see also Myerson 1999).

John Forbes Nash Jr was born on 13 June 1928, in Bluefield, West Virginia, to an electrical engineer and his wife, a retired school teacher. Nash showed an early aptitude for mathematics and enrolled in advanced mathematics courses at Bluefield College while still in high school. He continued on to the Carnegie Institute of Technology in Pittsburgh (now Carnegie Mellon University) on a full scholarship, initially majoring in chemical engineering but switching to mathematics during his first year. He completed his studies in only three years, graduating in 1948 with both a BSc. and an MSc. in mathematics, making such an impression in the Mathematics Department that he continued on to Princeton University for a PhD in mathematics with a one-sentence reference letter from his adviser: "This man is a genius." Nash submitted his doctoral dissertation in 1950, and was academically active for ten years, teaching at the Massachusetts Institute of Technology (MIT) and doing research at the RAND Corporation. During that decade he published five seminal papers in game theory and ten papers, viewed by many mathematicians as being of perhaps even greater significance, in topology and differential equations (Kuhn and Nasar 2002 reprint Nash's most important mathematical articles on the imbedding problem for Riemannian manifolds and on continuity of solutions of parabolic and elliptic equations, as well as his papers in game theory). His decade of productivity was followed by an illness-induced absence from research of some 25 years, during which he was diagnosed as paranoid schizophrenic, and then had a remarkable recovery (see Nasar 1998). A movie about his life, *A Beautiful Mind* (Howard 2001), won the Academy Award for Best Picture.

In 1928, John von Neumann proved the minimax theorem that, as long as mixed strategies are allowed (a linear combination of each player's possible actions, attaching a probability to each possible pure strategy), at least one equilibrium point exists for any two-person, zero-sum game: a proof simplified by Jean Ville in 1938 (see von Neumann and Morgenstern 1944). This result, together with von Neumann and Morgenstern's *Theory of Games and Economic Behavior*, is widely credited with laying the foundations of game theory. However, von Neumann and Morgenstern (1944) did not have any existence proof for the stable set, their solution concept for *n*-person games (and in the 1960s William Lucas demonstrated that the stable set solution does not always exist). John Nash (1950b, 1950c, 1951) proved that any non-cooperative, normal form game has at least one equilibrium point, regardless of the number of players or whether the sum of the payoffs is constant, provided only that mixed strategies are allowed and that the space of strategies available to the players is compact (bounded and closed). Nash used the Brouwer fixed point theorem (any continuous function mapped from a compact and convex subset of Euclidean space to the same subset maps at least one point to itself) to prove existence of equilibrium in his thesis (1950b, 1951). At David Gale's suggestion, Nash (1950c) used the Kakutani fixed point theorem (extending Brouwer's result to multi-valued mappings) for a more elegant and more general proof in a published note. Nash (1950b: 1, 3) defined a non-cooperative game as one in which "each participant acts independently, without collaboration or communication with any of the others" and the equilibrium of a non-cooperative game as "an n-tuple *S* such that each player's mixed strategy maximizes his pay-off if the strategies of the others are held fixed". For the outcome of a game to not be a Nash equilibrium would violate the assumption of individual rationality, since at least one player could increase his or her payoff by acting differently. A second interpretation of Nash equilibrium in Nash's unpublished dissertation (but not in his articles), in terms of statistical populations ("mass action") rather than individual rationality, later proved useful in evolutionary biology, in the words of the Nobel Prize citation, "in order to understand how the principles of natural selection operate in strategic interaction within and among species".

After Nash published, Martin Shubik and other economists reinterpreted A.A. Cournot's 1838 analysis of equilibrium among oligopolists, each maximizing profit taking the output of the others as given, as a special case of Nash equilibrium. When Nash told von Neumann (a fellow at the Institute for Advanced Study in Princeton) about his stronger and more general proof of existence of equilibrium, von Neumann dismissed the young graduate student's result as "just another fixed point theorem" and as "trivial" which it isn't (quoted by Kuhn and Nasar 2002: xix and caption to photograph no. 4). The preface to the 1953 third edition of von Neumann and Morgenstern (1944) made a bare mention of Nash (1951) in connection with "further developments" of *n*-person game theory in the direction of non-cooperative games. Not distinguishing between cooperative and non-cooperative games, and hence not ruling out coalitions with binding agreements, was the stumbling block that kept von Neumann and Morgenstern from proving existence of equilibrium for *n*-person games.

Nash (1950a, 1953) proposed the Nash bargaining solution for cooperative games. His first published article, "The bargaining problem" (1950a), was written while taking Albert Tucker's game theory seminar at Princeton, but was based on an idea Nash had while taking an international trade course at Carnegie Institute of Technology, the only economics course he ever took. Nash suggested four conditions that two players might plausibly wish an arbitrator to follow in dividing the gains from cooperation between them: Pareto efficiency, symmetry (it does not matter if the identities of the two players are switched), independence of a positive linear transformation of a player's utility function, and independence of irrelevant alternatives (that is, if a point that is neither the threat point or the solution becomes infeasible, the solution is not altered). He then proved that the only solution that satisfies all four conditions is to maximize the product of each player's gain in utility relative to the threat point (the threat point being the fallback utilities that the players would receive if no agreement was reached). Of the four conditions, independence of irrelevant alternatives is the one usually omitted by proponents of other solution concepts for cooperative games. The Nash programme linked cooperative and non-cooperative games by identifying the threat point of a cooperative game as the Nash equilibrium of the non-cooperative game that would be played if no agreement was reached. One other Nash contribution has been relevant for economics: methods developed in a 1958 article by Nash (reprinted in Kuhn and Nasar 2002: ch. 12) are used to solve a class of parabolic partial differential equations that occur in certain finance problems. After his remarkable recovery from decades of illness, John Nash received a National Science Foundation grant in 2001 to work on a new evolutionary solution concept for cooperative games. He died on 23 May 2015, in an automobile accident.

Robert W. Dimand and Khalid Yahia

See also:

Formalization and mathematical modelling (III); Game theory (III); John von Neumann (I).

References and further reading

Howard, R. (director) (2001), *A Beautiful Mind* (movie), Hollywood, CA: Universal Studios.
Kuhn, H.W. and S. Nasar (eds) (2002), *The Essential John Nash*, Princeton, NJ: Princeton University Press.
Myerson, R.B. (1991), *Game Theory: Analysis of Conflict*, Cambridge, MA: Harvard University Press.
Myerson, R.B. (1999), 'Nash equilibrium in the history of economic theory', *Journal of Economic Literature*, **37** (3), 1067–82.
Nasar, S. (1998), *A Beautiful Mind*, New York: Simon and Schuster.
Nash, J.F. Jr (1950a), 'The bargaining problem', *Econometrica*, **18** (2), 155–62.
Nash, J.F. Jr (1950b), 'Non-cooperative games', PhD dissertation, Princeton University, facsimile reprint in H.W. Kuhn and S. Nasar (eds) (2002), *The Essential John Nash*, Princeton, NJ: Princeton University Press, pp. 53–84.
Nash, J.F. Jr (1950c), 'Equilibrium points in *n*-person games', *Proceedings of the National Academy of Sciences*, **36** (1), 48–9.
Nash, J.F. Jr (1951), 'Non-cooperative games', *Annals of Mathematics*, **54** (2), 286–95.
Nash, J.F. Jr (1953), 'Two-person cooperative games', *Econometrica*, **21** (1), 128–40.
Nash, J.F. Jr (2008), 'The agencies method for modeling coalitions and cooperation in games', *International Game Theory Review*, **10** (4), 539–64.
Nash, J.F. Jr (2014), 'Research studies approaching cooperative games with new methods,' in R.M. Solow and J. Murray (eds), *Economics for the Curious: Inside the Minds of 12 Nobel Laureates*, Basingstoke: Palgrave Macmillan, pp. 112–22.
Rubinstein, A. (1995), 'John Nash: the master of economic modeling', *Scandinavian Journal of Economics*, **97** (1), 9–13.
Von Neumann, J. and O. Morgenstern (1944), *Theory of Games and Economic Behavior*, Princeton, NJ: Princeton University Press, 3rd edn 1953, sixtieth anniversary edn with introduction by H.W. Kuhn and afterword by A. Rubinstein 2004.

Robert Alexander Mundell (b. 1932)

Robert Mundell is most widely known for his work on monetary dynamics in different exchange rate systems and the analysis of optimum currency areas. Developed in the early 1960s, his ideas laid the foundation to further theoretical as well as empirical research which still prevails today.

Robert Alexander Mundell was born in 1932, in Kingston, Canada. After his undergraduate studies at the University of British Colombia, Vancouver and the University of Washington, he completed his education at the London School of Economics and the Massachusetts Institute of Technology (MIT) where he received a doctorate in 1956 for his research on international capital movements. During this time, he was attracted to and influenced by the works of Paul Samuelson, Charles Kindleberger, Lionel Robbins and James Meade who would later became his doctoral father at the MIT. During the following years, he taught at several universities, such as the University of Chicago where he was made professor in 1966. Other stations included Stanford University, the Johns Hopkins Bologna Center of Advanced International Studies in Italy and the Graduate Institute of International Studies in Geneva, Switzerland. From 1974 he was affiliated with the University of Columbia, New York.

He was the author of numerous articles and functioned as an adviser to the staff of several international institutions and governments, such as the International Monetary Fund, the United Nations, the World Bank and the European Commission. During his time at the University of Chicago he also became the editor of the *Journal of Political Economy*.

In 1999, after receiving several other prizes, awards and titles of honorary doctor, he was awarded the Bank of Sweden Prize in Economic Sciences in memory of Alfred Nobel, "for his analysis of monetary and fiscal policy under different exchange rate regimes and his analysis of optimum currency areas". The prize was especially devoted to Mundell's work in the 1960s. At this time, most of the world was still operating in a fixed exchange rate system, while free capital mobility was just in its infancy. His anticipation of the evolution of an international capital market as well as his work on currency unions were praised for their "almost prophetic foresight". His extensions of the investment saving–liquidity preference money supply equilibrium (IS–LM) model to show the effect of monetary and fiscal policy in an open economy were described as both simple and decisive. His works on optimum currency areas were used intensively in the early efforts to create a common currency in Europe.

Owing to his versatility, Mundell is also the co-originator of supply-side economics, most prominent during the Reagan administration. His work covers economic theory in various areas such as international trade, transition economies and the history of the monetary system. According to the Mundell–Tobin effect, a rise in expected inflation will reduce the demand for real money balances. Owing to an incomplete adjustment of the nominal rate, real interest rates will fall, leading to a portfolio shift in favour of real capital investment. Therefore, Mundell's model shows that inflation expectations could have real economic effects. Nevertheless, he is clearly most renowned for his "Nobel works" concerning exchange rate policy and optimum currency areas, both of which have been developed further over the years.

Building on the closed economy IS–LM model of John Hicks, Mundell incorporates foreign trade and capital movements, hence opening up the model for a multi-country analysis. He complements the goods demand and money market equations with a balance-of-payment equation that captures trade and capital flows. For non-perfect capital markets, where domestic and foreign financial assets are no perfect substitutes, permanent interest rate differences thus create a flow of assets at a steady rate. This simple setting allows Mundell to extend the analysis of the IS–LM model in order to explain the (non-)autonomy and (non-)effectiveness of fiscal and monetary policy in an open economy under fixed or flexible exchange rates. With perfect international capital markets, the balance-of-payment equation reduces to the no-arbitrage condition of interest rate parity.

Rising domestic demand would traditionally raise the domestic interest rate, which in an open economy would trigger capital movements, resulting in an inflow of foreign capital, therefore forcing the local currency to appreciate. Mundell shows that, under fixed exchange rates, monetary policy is degraded to merely manage the composition of assets, whereas fiscal stimuli are amplified by the monetary policy measures induced by the goal of defending a given exchange rate level. The opposite holds for the case of flexible exchange rates; where in turn fiscal policy is dampened by exchange rate adjustments and the monetary policy becomes a powerful tool.

This leads to two conclusions: the first is known as the assignment problem and asks whether the central bank or the fiscal authority is responsible for internal or external balances, respectively. According to Mundell, this depends on the respective impact. Therefore, the speed of adjustment as well as the implied interest rate sensitivity is of special focus for his work. The second is known as the incompatible trinity and states that free capital mobility either allows for an external target, such as the exchange rate, or an internal target, such as the price level, but not for both simultaneously.

The open-economy IS–LM model (also named Mundell–Fleming model) played an indispensable role in teaching, research and economic policy advice for many years (Frenkel and Razin 1987). However, his theory has also been subject to debate. Obstfeld and Rogoff (1995) criticize the atemporal character of the model, leading to problems concerning budget constraints or external balances. Furthermore, from a contemporary point of view, the model is not micro-founded and thus – some would argue – of minor (normative) explanatory power owing to its ad-hocery tendencies.

Mundell's second major work is devoted to the question of whether or not a single country should aspire to enter a monetary union. A major stimulus for his theory was the signing of the Treaties of Rome in 1957, which led to his 1961 article "A theory of optimum currency areas".

If a country has the choice to join a monetary union, it has to compare the advantage of lower transaction costs with the disadvantage of forgoing its monetary sovereignty. Theoretically you could ask whether it is more favourable to go for several different currencies – in the extreme, one currency for each good which implies a barter economy – or to go for a single currency, leading to only one large integrated monetary area.

In his original version, Mundell singles out labour mobility as the most important criterion. He shows that not country borders, but economic regions matter for a successful optimum currency area. If these are not congruent, a system of flexible exchange rates is superior, at least if no labour mobility is given. Thus from a stability point of view, small regions would be more desirable, while from a transaction cost view, large areas would be favoured.

The model is quite restrictive in terms of expectations, does not elaborate on the trade-off between prices and employment and assumes a homogeneous stock of labour quality. Since then, Mundell's ideas have been developed in different directions. There have been several works focusing on issues such as capital mobility, inflation rate and business cycle synchronization and the political will for an integrated currency area. Mundell himself has developed his idea further in his two 1973 papers.

Mundell's theory played an important role during the preparing debates on the European Monetary Union (EMU). Incidentally his work was honoured the same year as EMU was brought into existence. However, the criteria used to select the participating countries were different from those suggested by Mundell. There have been attempts to promote a modern theory of optimal currency areas, suited to the apparent success of EMU in its first decade (Tavlas 1993; Mongelli 2008; Beetsma and Giuliodori 2010). Mundell's arguments were often used to criticize the EMU project and to propose a flexible-exchange-rate solution owing to the heterogeneous structure of the European economies. In spite of various drawbacks and the non-optimality of Europe as assessed against his own standards, Mundell has always emphasized the political component in this process and is to this day a promoter of EMU.

Mundell's ideas seem to be novel and unconventional, on the one hand, and standard, on the other. In his Nobel Prize lecture, he condemned economic policy norms of the gold standard. "Had the price of gold been raised in the late 1920s, or, alternatively, had the major central banks pursued policies of price stability instead of adhering to the gold standard, there would have been no Great Depression, no Nazi revolution, and no World War II" (Mundell 1999: 230). However, later he advocated a return of the USA to the gold standard and a resurrection of a (modified) Bretton Woods system of fixed exchange rates. To his followers this is neither untypical nor inconsistent, it underlines his unorthodox – out of the box – way of thinking.

OLIVER SAUTER AND PETER SPAHN

See also:

Balance of payments and exchange rates (III); Open economy macroeconomics (III); Post-Keynesianism (II).

References and further reading

Beetsma, R. and M. Giuliodori (2010), 'The macroeconomic costs and benefits of the EMU and other monetary unions – an overview of recent research'. *Journal of Economic Literature*, **48** (3), 603–41.
Frenkel, J.A. and A. Razin (1987), 'The Mundell–Fleming model a quarter century later', NBER Working Paper Series No. 2321, National Bureau of Economic Research, Cambridge, MA, pp. 1–87.
Mongelli, F.P. (2008), *European Economic and Monetary Integration, and the Optimum Currency Area Theory*, Economic Papers No. 302, Brussels: European Commission, Directorate-General for Economic and Financial Affairs.
Mundell, R. (1961), 'A theory of optimum currency areas', *American Economic Review*, **51** (4), 657–65.
Mundell, R. (1963), 'Capital mobility and stabilization policy under fixed and flexible exchange rates', *Canadian Journal of Economics*, **29** (4), 475–85.
Mundell, R. (1968), *International Economics*, New York: Macmillan.
Mundell, R. (1973a), 'Uncommon arguments for common currencies', in H.G. Johnson and A.K. Swoboda (eds), *The Economics of Common Currencies*, London: Allen and Unwin, pp. 114–32.
Mundell, R. (1973b), 'A plan for a European currency', in H.G. Johnson and A.K. Swoboda (eds), *The Economics of Common Currencies*, London: Allen and Unwin, pp. 143–72.

Mundell, R. (1999), 'A reconsideration of the twentieth century', The Sveriges Riksbank Prize in Economic Sciences in Memory of Alfred Nobel 1999, Prize Lecture, accessed 28 December 2015 at http://www.nobel-prize.org/nobel_prizes/economic-sciences/laureates/1999/mundell-lecture.html.
Obstfeld, M. and K. Rogoff (1995), 'The intertemporal approach to the current account', in G.M. Grossman and K. Rogoff (eds), *Handbook of International Economics*, vol. 3, Amsterdam: Elsevier, pp. 1731–99.
Tavlas, G.S. (1993), 'The "new" theory of optimum currency areas', *The World Economy*, **16** (6), 663–85.

Takashi Negishi (b. 1933)

Takashi Negishi (born 1933) is a distinguished Japanese economic theorist and a historian of economic theory. In 1963 he received a PhD in economics from the University of Tokyo in Japan, and he was professor of economics at the University of Tokyo from 1976 to 1994. After retiring from the University of Tokyo, he taught economics at Aoyama Gakuin University in Tokyo and some other universities. He became the president of the Econometric Society in 1993. He published numerous papers in English; his main contributions were republished in Negishi (1994a, 1994b).

He started his career in economic research as a general equilibrium theorist. In the late 1950s and the early 1960s he published a series of pioneering mathematical papers on stability analysis, welfare analysis and on the theory of imperfect competition in the context of general equilibrium theory. In particular, the following three papers are important: (1) "A note on the stability of an economy where all goods are gross substitutes" (1958), (2) "Welfare economics and existence of an equilibrium for a competitive economy" (1960) and (3) "Monopolistic competition and general equilibrium" (1961).

Paper 1 is a seminal paper that provided a mathematical proof of the dynamic stability of the Walrasian price adjustment by means of *tâtonnement* (trial and error). Walrasian price adjustment process implies that the prices of the goods with excess demand increase and the prices of the goods with excess supply decrease. However, the dynamic stability of the equilibrium point is not ensured, unless some restrictive assumptions on the excess demand functions are imposed. Hicks (1939) proposed some mathematical "stability condition", but Samuelson (1944) pointed out that Hicks's condition is not equivalent to the "true" condition for the dynamic stability of the equilibrium point of a system of differential equations. Metzler (1945) found that Hicks's condition becomes equivalent to Samuelson's "true" condition of dynamic stability if it is assumed that all goods are "gross substitutes". Negishi's paper 1 provided a mathematical proof that the "true" condition of dynamic stability is automatically satisfied if all goods are "gross substitutes". Negishi's contribution in paper 1 was written independently of the contributions of Hahn (1958) and Arrow and Hurwicz (1958), all of which were published in *Econometrica* in 1958.

Paper 2 is also a seminal paper that provided a new method of the proof of the existence of a general equilibrium of a competitive economy. Gale (1955) and Nikaido (1956) utilized the excess demand correspondence and the fixed-point theorem to prove the existence of the general equilibrium solution. On the other hand, Negishi's paper 2 utilized the Pareto optimality condition that is expressed by the maximization of the weighted average of the utilities of the consumers subject to the production possibility constraint to prove the existence of the general equilibrium solution. His method of proof, which is called "Negishi's method", turned out to be more efficient than the alternative method for the numerical computation of the general equilibrium solution.

Paper 3 is a seminal paper that constructed a model of general equilibrium with monopolistic competition. Before this paper was published, general equilibrium theory tended to concentrate on the analysis of a perfectly competitive economy, and the theory of imperfect competition was concentrating on partial equilibrium analysis. Negishi's paper filled this gap. In fact, Nikaido's (1975) book on the general equilibrium approach to monopolistic competition owes much to the idea that is expressed in Negishi's paper.

He also made some important theoretical contributions to international economics and public economics (see Negishi 1994a).

In the 1970s, Negishi utilized the mathematical method of general equilibrium analysis to consider the microeconomic foundation of Keynesian macroeconomics, which turned out to be an important predecessor of the "new Keynesian" theory that flourished in the 1980s and the 1990s (Negishi 1979). In Negishi (1979), he suggested the concept of the "kinky perceived demand curves" to prove the existence of "Keynesian" equilibria with involuntary unemployment, which are called "Keynes–Negishi equilibria" (see Drèze and Hering 2008).

In the 1980s, his attention shifted to the study of the history of economic theory against the background of modern economic analysis (Negishi 1985, 1989, 1994b). In this area of research, he applied modern mathematical methods to the theories of great economists of the past, such as Adam Smith, Ricardo, Malthus, Marx, Mill, Walras, Jevons, Menger, Marshall, Böhm-Bawerk, von Thünen and Keynes. His approach to the history of economic theory resembles that of Michio Morishima, another major Japanese economist, who examined the theories of Marx, Walras and Ricardo from the viewpoint of modern analytical economics (see Kurz 2011).

TOICHIRO ASADA

See also:

Competition (III); Formalization and mathematical modelling (III); General equilibrium theory (III); John Maynard Keynes (I); Keynesianism (II); Karl Heinrich Marx (I); Michio Morishima (I); New Keynesianism (II); David Ricardo (I); Marie-Esprit-Léon Walras (I).

References and further reading

Arrow, K.J. and L. Hurwicz (1958), 'On the stability of the competitive equilibrium', *Econometrica*, **26** (October), 522–52.
Drèze, J. and P.J.J. Hering (2008), 'Kinky perceived demand curves and Keynes–Negishi equilibria', *International Journal of Economic Theory*, **4** (June), 207–46.
Gale, D. (1955), 'The law of supply and demand', *Mathematica Scandinavica*, **3**, 155–69.
Hahn, F.H. (1958), 'Gross substitutes and the dynamic stability of general equilibrium', *Econometrica*, **26** (January), 169–70.
Hicks, J.R. (1939), *Value and Capital*, Oxford: Clarendon Press.
Kurz, H.D. (2011), 'The contributions of two eminent Japanese scholars to the development of economic theory: Michio Morishima and Takashi Negishi', in H.D. Kurz, T. Nishizawa and K. Tribe (eds), *The Dissemination of Economic Ideas*, Cheltenham, UK and Northampton, MA, USA: Edward Elgar, pp. 337–64.
Metzler, L. (1945), 'Stability of multiple market: the Hicksian condition', *Econometrica*, **13** (October), 277–92.
Negishi, T. (1958), 'A note on the stability of an economy where all goods are gross substitutes', *Econometrica*, **30** (July), 445–7.
Negishi, T. (1960), 'Welfare economics and existence of an equilibrium for a competitive economy', *Metroeconomica*, **12** (June), 92–7.
Negishi, T. (1961), 'Monopolistic competition and general equilibrium', *Review of Economic Studies*, **28** (June), 196–201.
Negishi, T. (1979), *Microeconomic Foundations of Keynesian Macroeconomics*, Amsterdam: North-Holland.
Negishi, T. (1985), *Economic Theories in a Non-Walrasian Tradition*, Cambridge: Cambridge University Press.
Negishi, T. (1989), *History of Economic Theory*, Amsterdam: North-Holland.
Negishi, T. (1994a), *The Collected Writings of Takashi Negishi*, vol. 1 *General Equilibrium Theory*, Aldershot, UK and Brookfield, VT, USA: Edward Elgar.

Negishi, T. (1994b), *The Collected Writings of Takashi Negishi*, vol. 2 The History of Economics, Aldershot, UK and Brookfield, VT, USA: Edward Elgar.

Nikaido, H. (1956), 'On the classical multilateral exchange problem', *Metroeconomica*, **8** (June), 135–45.

Nikaido, H. (1975), *Monopolistic Competition and Effective Demand*, Princeton, NJ: Princeton University Press.

Samuelson, P.A. (1944), 'The relation between Hicksian stability and true dynamic stability', *Econometrica*, **10** (July–October), 1–25.

Amartya Kumar Sen (b. 1933)

Amartya Sen was born on 3 November 1933 in Santiniketan where he went to school. From 1951 to 1953 he studied at Presidency College in Calcutta where he received a Bachelor Degree. In 1953 Sen moved to Cambridge, England, where he wrote his doctoral dissertation on "The choice of techniques". From 1963 to 1971 Sen taught at the Delhi School of Economics. In 1971, he accepted a chair at the London School of Economics. From 1977 to 1987 he held a professorship at Oxford and was Fellow at All Souls College. In 1987 Sen accepted a chair at Harvard University and became a member of both the economics department and the philosophy department. In 1998 he returned to Cambridge, England, and became "Master of Trinity College". In the same year, he received the Sveriges Riksbank Prize in Economic Sciences in Memory of Alfred Nobel. Sen returned to Harvard University in 2004. He published numerous books and articles both in economic theory and development economics, in philosophy, political theory and public policy, the latter with an emphasis on the history and culture of India.

The Informational Basis of Social Choice

Sen received the Sveriges Riksbank Prize in particular for his contributions to welfare economics and the theory of social choice. The latter area has its modern origin in Arrow's famous monograph *Social Choice and Individual Values* from 1951 (2nd edition 1963) where the author proved that under certain rather intuitive conditions, a so-called social welfare function does not exist. This negative result, often called "Arrow's impossibility result", had a huge impact on economics but also on philosophy and political science.

Sen's own reaction to Arrow's findings culminated in his monograph from 1970 *Collective Choice and Social Welfare*, though in the second half of the 1960s already, Sen had published a couple of fundamental articles on this topic in economics journals that emphasize the formal or mathematical approach, such as *Econometrica*, *Journal of Economic Theory* and the *Review of Economic Studies*. Sen's book, which turned out to be the gateway into the field of collective decisions for many who, in the course of time, became distinguished social choice theorists, highlighted at least three fundamental aspects within the area: the informational parsimony within the Arrovian approach and various escape roads therefrom, the role of individual rights and liberties within collective decisions, and the effectiveness of the majority method and related rules under various domain conditions of voters' preferences.

The informational basis in Arrow's set-up is a set of individual ordinal preferences to be mapped into a unique social ordering. Preference intensities not only make no sense in such a framework, they cannot even be expressed meaningfully in an ordinal framework. Arrow also excluded the interpersonal comparability of preference rankings. Once ordinal preferences are combined with the possibility to compare levels of utility across persons so that it is, for example, possible to say that under a certain policy x, let's say, person i is better off than person j, the maximin or leximin rule (that is, the lexicographic extension of maximin) à la Rawls (1971) focusing on the worst-off in society is a non-contradictory and, perhaps, attractive aggregation rule. If preferences are assumed to be cardinal so that utility differences are measurable, bargaining solutions à la Nash or Kalai–Smorodinsky may be considered as social choice rules. These are defined with respect to a status-quo point. If utilities are not only cardinal but also comparable across persons, classical utilitarianism and its modern version based on the Bayesian concept of rationality, as proposed by Harsanyi (1953, 1955, 1977), do not run into the Arrovian impossibility. In other words, the informational aspect, the degree of available utility information, is a powerful tool to distinguish among different approaches, and it was Sen in particular who made us aware of this "taxonomy" very convincingly. As is argued above, Arrow's approach is parsimonious and, in a certain sense, unsuccessful, ending in a cul de sac.

Sen (1970a, 1970b) was the first to combine the mechanism of aggregating preferences with the idea that individuals or citizens within a community should be able to exercise certain personal rights. While Arrow showed the existence of a global dictator, Sen asked whether it would be possible to permit individuals to be "local dictators" over purely private matters. The latter was called a libertarian right. To the surprise of many, Sen came up with another impossibility result, the "impossibility of a Paretian libertarian". Under an unrestricted domain of individual preferences, the weak Pareto principle and the right to be individually decisive over a minimal personal sphere are incompatible. The number of papers that tried to circumvent this negative finding runs into hundreds. Individuals' rights can be restricted, though Sen's requirement is already minimal, the application of the weak Pareto rule can be limited or the domain of individual preferences can be restricted. However, are these proposals satisfactory? Sen's negative result has an analogy in non-cooperative game theory where it is well known that Nash equilibria can be Pareto inefficient.

That the majority rule can lead to cyclicity if preferences are not restricted has been known for several centuries. The Marquis de Condorcet had already suggested ways out of this dilemma. It was only around 1950 that Arrow (1951) and Black (1948) independently came forward with a domain condition on individual preferences that is not only easily interpretable but can also be witnessed in certain real-life situations, the property of single-peaked preferences. Given a certain number of alternatives arranged along the real line, individuals have a most preferred object somewhere along the line, and to the left and to the right of this object, preferences decline. This can be taken literally. One of the examples that depict this structure comes from the left-to-right structure of political parties. The mirror-image of single-peakedness is single-cavedness. Sen (1966) proposed his condition of value restriction which encompasses both properties and a third of "not being in the middle" between the other two alternatives, given any triple of options, and showed that this condition is sufficient for the existence of a majority or Condorcet winner under the simple majority rule. If the number of voters who are not indifferent among all alternatives is odd, the simple majority rule yields a social ordering. In Arrow's terminology, under value restriction plus oddness, the method of simple majority decision is a social welfare function. Various other sufficient conditions, for example, limited agreement and dichotomous preferences, such that the simple majority rule becomes an Arrow social welfare function were formulated, but space does not allow us to go into greater detail.

Functionings and Capabilities

The aspect of informational parsimony may have led Sen, in collaboration with Mahbub ul Haq, to devise and construct the so-called human development index. This index, as a rival to gross domestic product (GDP), was meant to serve as a more humane measure of development than a purely income-based (or commodity-based) measure like GDP, to reflect the "life chances" people have. The idea was to divert attention from the single-focus GDP indicator to aspects that are fundamental ingredients of the freedom of living and well-being. For Sen, what defines the latter are the functionings of a person, his or her achievements and not just the accumulation of primary goods as in Rawls' (1971) *Theory of Justice*. What a person manages to do or to be (for example, being well-nourished, well-clothed, taking part in community life, and having access to medical care) are functionings that are important for a person's life. The total number of functionings that are available to a person or household define the advantages of that person, his or her real opportunities. According to Sen (1985), these make up the person's capability set.

Preferences over outcomes such as commodity allocations miss what is of primary importance, namely, that individuals are deeply concerned with what substantive opportunities are available to them. The opportunity set that is offered to an individual is as important to evaluating his freedom as is his autonomy in making decisions and his freedom from interferences imposed by others. Of course, measuring an individual's freedom and the capability set available to him is not an easy task – there is both a measurement problem and a shortage of reliable data – but it should be done (and has already been attempted by a number of researchers). That the GDP as a measure for well-being is largely unsatisfactory had already been demonstrated by Sen in his book *Commodities and Capabilities* from 1985 where he showed that, at that time, India and China were close together in terms of gross national product per head but quite far apart in terms of criteria such as the ability to live long, the ability to avoid mortality during infancy and childhood, and the ability to read and write. All of these are of utmost importance for developing countries in particular.

Poverty and Famines

An area that has not yet been mentioned in this review but which has propelled Sen's reputation and fame in third world countries is development economics. In his investigation on *Poverty and Famines* from 1981, Sen tried to shed some light on the causes of famines. The author focused in particular on large-scale famines in Africa and Asia in recent times. Frequently, famines and a drastically restricted availability of food products go hand in hand. In the large-scale famine in Bangladesh in 1974, however, there were other factors that increased the suffering of the population. Owing to an earlier flooding of the country, the price of rice, a basic food product, increased considerably. At the same time, large numbers of rural workers lost their work as no harvest was possible in the flooded areas. Real wages fell dramatically among the rural population so that starvation took its death toll. Sen argued that in order to prevent a deterioration of the situation of those who did not possess much anyway, public interventions would have been needed These could have taken the form of distributing cash money to the poor, starting publicly financed employment programmes and even intervening in the formation of food prices. During recent decades, this recommendation was followed by a larger number of developing countries. There is still another aspect to which Sen drew attention. He asserted that multi-party democracies never witnessed serious famines. Both a free press and a functioning opposition in parliament would force the ruling party to introduce effective measures against the threat of a beginning famine.

Before proposing his capability approach, Sen offered contributions to the measurement of economic inequality and suggested a new poverty measure. In 1974, he published an alternative characterization of the Gini Index which has been widely used as a measure of inequalities in income and wealth. His characterization is based on an equi-distanced weighting scheme à la Borda. The new poverty measure, suggested by Sen in 1976, combined the Gini Index with two hitherto used measures, the "headcount ratio", which determines the ratio between the number of people who have an income below or equal to the poverty line and the total number of people in a country, and the "income-gap ratio" which focuses on the ratio between the average poverty gap and the poverty line. While the headcount ratio does not measure the actual distance of the individual incomes below the poverty line to this line, the income-gap ratio does not consider the absolute number of the poor. Sen combined both indexes with the Gini coefficient of the income distribution of the poor. Doing this results in an index number that reflects the exact structure of the income distribution of the poor. Analogous to Sen's axiomatization of the Gini coefficient, an ordinal weighting scheme is needed such that the weight attached to the income gap of a particular person below the poverty line is the same as the rank number of this person in the interpersonal welfare ordering among the poor.

Consistency and Menu-Dependence

In much of modern economics, individual agents are assumed to be fully rational, maximizing their own personal gain. Sometimes, it is said that the person, in his or her maximizing behaviour, considers the immediate neighbourhood as well, in other words, family and close friends. This being conceded, it is the self-seeking behaviour which is being presumed. Sen (1977) couched the assumption of purely self-seeking behaviour into the following situation of two people who meet in the street. Here is their conversation. "Where is the railway station?" asks one of them. "There", says the other, pointing at the post office, "and would you please post this letter for me on the way?" "Yes", the first person answers, determined to open the envelope and check whether it contains something valuable.

Sen states that it is often argued that economic theory of utility has too much structure. His view is that there is too little structure. A person's behaviour is reduced to whether the concept of internal consistency is fulfilled. This is a property which is directly linked to choices from different sets of options. When you choose alternative x, for example, from a larger set, and this alternative is also contained in a smaller set, then this option should be picked from the smaller set as well. Sen's example from 1997 which violates internal consistency without any trace of pathology runs as follows. Let x be an apple from a fruit basket containing this apple, another apple and the option to choose nothing. The individual to whom this fruit basket is offered picks one of the apples. Now let us suppose that a smaller basket just contains one of the two apples and nothing else. This apple is offered to our individual and the person politely says "No, thanks". Clearly, this apple, having become the only or last apple, is definitely different from being one of the two apples in the first basket.

Choices frequently depend on what else is offered on a plate – Sen calls this phenomenon "menu-dependence". The choice of a median element (for example, with respect to the price of a bunch of flowers or a bottle of wine to be offered as a gift) depends on the number of available alternatives. Such a decision violates the postulate of internal consistency (Gaertner and Xu, 1999). The aspect of menu-dependence is particularly striking in one of Sen's (1997: 753) own examples. Imagine that at a cocktail party, some other guest who you have met asks you whether you would like to come over to his flat the following afternoon, for a cup of tea or a cup of coffee or a hot chocolate. Since the conversation during the party was interesting, you gladly accept this invitation. Imagine that besides tea, coffee and hot chocolate, cocaine is offered as well. Would you accept the invitation now? Sen speaks of the epistemic value of the menu – the alternatives offered contain valuable information per se that may influence an agent's decision. This example supports his assertion very convincingly that we need more and not less structure in our theories of decision making.

Sen (1997: 763) proposes that maximization be considered ("choose an element such that in comparison no better element exists") instead of optimization ("always pick the best element from the set of available options"). He argues that it is often the case that the assumption of complete comparability of all objects is not fulfilled. Then a best element does not exist whereas a maximal element is always given.

The Idea of Justice

The argument of incompleteness is a recurrent theme in Sen's writings, notably put forward in one of his most recent publications, *The Idea of Justice*, from 2009. In this book, Sen attempts to devise a counter-position to Rawls' theory of justice (1971). Rawls's basic claim was that a unique set of principles of justice would emerge in a so-called original position where the individual members of society are under a veil of ignorance, not knowing their place in society, that is, their position or social status. The Rawlsian principles are meant to shape just institutions constituting the basic structure of society. Sen is very sceptical about the assumption that a unanimous agreement on one set of principles of justice will be brought about in the original position. He argues that there may be a plurality of reasons for justice, and if this is the case, how could one then arrive at one unique set of principles of justice?

Sen denotes the derivation of an ideal theory of justice such as that by Rawls or, for example, the utilitarian philosophy as the transcendental approach. His own claim is "less elevated" or more humble. It is to,

> address questions about advancing justice and compare alternative proposals for having a more just society, short of the utopian proposal of taking an imagined jump to a perfectly just world. Indeed, the answers that a transcendental approach to justice gives . . . are quite distinct and distant from the type of concerns that engage people in discussions on justice and injustice in the world (for example, inequities of hunger, poverty, illiteracy, torture, racism, female subjugation, arbitrary incarceration or medical exclusion as social features that need remedying). (Sen 2009: 96).

On page 2 of this book, Sen (2009) already formulates one of his main messages: "What is important, as central to the idea of justice, is that we can have a strong sense of injustice on many different grounds, and yet not agree on one particular ground as being the dominant reason for the diagnosis of injustice".

This being so, you cannot expect to arrive at a complete social ordering. Since the members of society vary to some degree in their views of what a more just society should be like, we have to look for non-empty intersections among the individuals' preference orderings, the shared beliefs of the different members of society and, from there, derive some partial ordering for society. Sen writes that "such incompleteness would not prevent making comparative judgments about justice in a great many cases ... about how to enhance justice and reduce injustice" (2009: 105). Sen views his approach as comparative in contrast to the transcendental framework of Rawls and others. The economist, the social choice theorist in particular, may find the comparative approach more appealing than the transcendental perspective, while the philosopher may have the opposite view.

WULF GAERTNER

See also:

Kenneth Joseph Arrow (I); Abram Bergson [Abram Burk] (I); Economics and philosophy (III); Public choice (II); Paul Anthony Samuelson (I); Social choice (III); Utilitarianism and anti-utilitarianism (III); Welfare economics (III).

References and further reading

Arrow, K.J. (1951), *Social Choice and Individual Values*, 2nd edn 1963, New York: John Wiley.
Black, D. (1948), 'On the rationale of group decision making', *Journal of Political Economy*, **56** (1), 23–34.
Gaertner, W. and Y. Xu (1999), 'On rationalizability of choice functions: a characterization of the median', *Social Choice and Welfare*, **16** (4), 629–38.
Harsanyi, J.C. (1953), 'Cardinal utility in welfare economics and in the theory of risk-taking', *Journal of Political Economy*, **61** (5), 434–5.
Harsanyi, J.C. (1955), 'Cardinal welfare, individualistic ethics, and interpersonal comparisons of utility', *Journal of Political Economy*, **63** (4), 309–21.
Harsanyi, J.C. (1977), *Rational Behaviour and Bargaining Equilibrium in Games and Social Situations*, Cambridge: Cambridge University Press.
Rawls, J. (1971), *A Theory of Justice*, Cambridge, MA: Harvard University Press.
Sen, A.K. (1966), 'A possibility theorem on majority decisions', *Econometrica*, **34** (2), 491–9.
Sen, A.K. (1970a), *Collective Choice and Social Welfare*, San Francisco, CA: Holden-Day.
Sen, A.K. (1970b), 'The impossibility of a Paretian liberal', *Journal of Political Economy*, **78** (1), 152–7.
Sen, A.K. (1974), 'Informational bases of alternative welfare approaches. Aggregation and income distribution', *Journal of Public Economics*, **3** (4), 387–403.
Sen, A.K. (1976), 'Poverty: an ordinal approach to measurement', *Econometrica*, **44** (2), 219–31.
Sen, A.K. (1977), 'Rational fools: a critique of the behavioural foundations of economic theory', *Philosophy and Public Affairs*, **6** (4), 317–44.
Sen, A.K. (1981), *Poverty and Famines. An Essay on Entitlement and Deprivation*, Oxford: Clarendon Press.
Sen, A.K. (1985), *Commodities and Capabilities*, Amsterdam: North-Holland.
Sen, A.K. (1997), 'Maximization and the act of choice', *Econometrica*, **65** (4), 745–79.
Sen, A.K. (2009), *The Idea of Justice*, London: Allen Lane.

Robert E. Lucas (b. 1937)

Robert Emerson Lucas was born in 1937, the same year his father's small business was wiped out by the Great Depression. In his autobiographical notes for the committee of the Sveriges Riksbank Prize in Economic Sciences in Memory of Alfred Nobel, that honoured him in 1995, Lucas highlights the supportive role of his parents in his outstanding intellectual development (see also Lucas 2001). Young Robert showed an early interest and talent in science, mathematics, and engineering. After graduating in Seattle, he received a scholarship from the University of Chicago in 1955. There, he was attracted to liberal arts courses, especially to those on Western History. He soon realized, however, that economic education is a prerequisite for good historical judgement. He found his way to economics through Paul Samuelson's *Foundations of Economic Analysis* (1947). Lucas owes his enthusiasm for mathematical economics in general, and general equilibrium analysis in particular, to Samuelson. His first contact with macroeconomics in terms of simple investment saving–liquidity preference money supply equilibrium (IS–LM) dynamics left him unimpressed (see Lucas 2004).

It is hard to overestimate the impact of Robert Lucas on modern macroeconomics. To him more than to anyone else does the representative macroeconomist owe his methodological judgement, his toolset, and his theoretical point of view. Lucas enters macroeconomics through the back door, by way of his collaboration with Leonard Rapping on labour economics. In *Real Wages, Employment, and Inflation* (1969) they apply the notion of intertemporal optimization, a cornerstone of general equilibrium analysis since Irving Fisher, to the labour supply function. They thereby provide a rigorous (Walrasian) foundation for Milton Friedman's permanent income hypothesis.

Although still endowed with adaptive expectations, otherwise rational households choose between opportunities to allocate their labour supply over time. For instance, given sufficiently convex preferences, an expected productivity hike suggests a reduction in today's labour supply. Whereas macroeconomics before Lucas was focused on involuntary unemployment such that employed labour was unidirectionally determined by aggregate demand, macroeconomics since Lucas places great emphasis on voluntarily induced changes in labour supply. Today, the inconvenience to explain empirical variations in labour supply in terms of shifting preferences and expectations is overcome by the introduction of market frictions, accounted for by costly search and matching processes. It is this versatility of his micro-founded toolset that accounts for the productivity of Lucas's research programme.

Lucas's possibly most important contributions are "Expectations and the neutrality of money" (1972) and its extension to "An equilibrium model of the business cycle" (1975). He merges his earlier contribution with John F. Muth's notion of rational expectations in a stochastic general equilibrium setting. The information sets of intertemporally optimizing agents are augmented by a generally understood and accepted macroeconomic model and the "true" probability distributions of the variables specified by the model. Exploiting all such knowledge, agents optimally forecast future equilibrium values such that remaining errors are "white noise". Labour hours and aggregate output remain unaffected by observed nominal values and money is always and by necessity ineffective and neutral.

Such is the equilibrium benchmark. The music comes from the frictions that Lucas imposes on his agents. They are locally dispersed and in effect isolated so that they have no access to real-time price-level data. Assuming that transmission is immediate, he shows that if agents also lack knowledge of actual money supply, they have to rely on past data to forecast the ruling price level and thereby to isolate changes in relative prices. If policy exploits this little window to surprise the market, agents face a signal-extracting problem since the reliance on all but the present nominal data generates inefficient predictions of their actual values. To the extent that agents make mistakes that could be avoided by augmenting the information set, real macroeconomic variables deviate from their rational expectations equilibrium values. Thus, a real friction accounts for monetary short-run non-neutrality.

The significance of Lucas's island model is that it does not rely on the representative agent, a concept that cannot withstand theoretical scrutiny and that nevertheless has become a standard assumption in applied macroeconomics. On the contrary, Lucas makes use of the Walrasian apparatus and the decentralization properties of competitive equilibria. In fact, he makes a subtle distinction between private and public information. Only the latter is the subject-matter of optimal forecasts, imposing already high individual information-processing capabilities.

The alternative would be to extend the notion of rational expectations to the forecast of private information. We know from general equilibrium analysis that such a rational expectations equilibrium is the only permissible alternative to the complete-markets economy. If markets are missing and, therefore, price systems are incomplete, then general equilibrium exists only if each agent is globally informed. Whereas the goal of Walrasian analysis is to conceptualize the coordination of only locally informed agents, which thus places emphasis on the intelligence and information-processing capabilities of the system rather than on individuals, rational expectations with respect to private information suggest superhuman skills and downgrade the anonymous system. Because Lucas avoids this assumption, the decentralization properties of price systems remain intact in his framework.

However, even if rational expectations only extend to public information, it is still overly restrictive. It needs Friedman's instrumentalist viewpoint, also adhered to by Lucas, to remain unimpressed by the information-processing capabilities still imposed on each agent. Even worse, as Roman Frydman (1983) has shown, there is nothing that could ever decentralize the computation of macroeconomic variables. In particular, rational expectations equilibria cannot be learned in a Walrasian setting. The information additionally required to ensure convergence in such disequilibrium processes is that agents have access to other agents' aggregate forecast functions and average opinions. Certainly, asking for agents that do know each other strictly violates Walrasian standards.

From a purely theoretical perspective, the alliance of rational expectations and general equilibrium analysis is no success. So Lucas's toolset is certainly less restrictive than the "new Keynesian" workhorse, that is, the class of representative–agent–based real business cycle models equipped with nominal rigidities, which substitute for the real frictions in Lucas's semi-decentralized model.

More important for the evaluation of his contributions, however, are the conclusions he draws for empirical analysis and which culminate into the so-called "Lucas critique". In "Econometric policy evaluation – a critique" (1976), Lucas formulates his opposition to the then ruling econometric practices, especially with regard to their ability to record market adjustments to shifts in policy regimes. Without microfoundations, so his argument goes, it is impossible to isolate changes in data owing to policy shifts from changes owing to shifts of primitive or "deep" data. It follows that forecasts of the then dominant models systematically fail whenever they are specified for time series that have memorized some policy regime and are applied to periods with another regime. The Lucas critique led to radical adjustments of all those economists, who believed in structural models in empirical analysis. It may be owing to the dominance of applied work that Lucas's research programme still dominates macroeconomics. He has developed the tools and has shown how to apply them in his many empirical contributions. He thereby unequivocally improved the practice of doing macroeconomics.

From a pure theory perspective, however, his impressive contribution still fails. Either it is not permissible by his own Walrasian standards or it suffers from the same negative results that struck down the even more impressive contributions to general equilibrium theory associated in the Cowles Commission.

ARASH MOLAVI VASSÉI AND PETER SPAHN

See also:

Macroeconomics (III); New classical macroeconomics (II).

References

Frydman, R. (1983), 'Individual rationality, decentralization and the rational expectations hypothesis', in R. Frydman and E.S. Phelps (eds), *Individual Forecasting and Aggregate Outcomes – 'Rational Expectations' Examined*, Cambridge: Cambridge University Press, pp. 97–122.

Lucas, R.E. Jr (1972), 'Expectations and the neutrality of money', reprinted in R.E Lucas Jr (1981), *Studies in Business Cycle Theory*, Cambridge, MA: MIT Press, pp. 66–89.

Lucas, R.E. Jr (1975), 'An equilibrium model of the business cycle', reprinted in R.E Lucas Jr (1981), *Studies in Business Cycle Theory*, Cambridge, MA: MIT Press, pp. 179–214.

Lucas, R.E. Jr (1976), 'Econometric policy evaluation – a critique', reprinted in R.E Lucas Jr (1981), *Studies in Business Cycle Theory*, Cambridge, MA: MIT Press, pp. 104–30.

Lucas, R.E. Jr (2001), 'Professional memoir', mimeo, accessed 14 December 2015 at http://coin.wne.uw.edu.pl/rkruszewski/memoir.pdf.

Lucas, R.E. Jr (2004), 'My Keynesian education', in M. De Vroey and K. Hoover (eds), *The IS–LM Model: Its Rise, Fall, and Strange Persistence*, Durham, NC: Duke University Press, pp. 12–24.

Lucas, R.E. Jr and L.A. Rapping (1969), 'Real wages, employment, and inflation', reprinted in R.E Lucas Jr (1981), *Studies in Business Cycle Theory*, Cambridge, MA: MIT Press, pp. 19–58.

Samuelson, P. (1947), *Foundations of Economic Analysis*, Cambridge, MA: Harvard University Press.

George Akerlof (b. 1940)

George Akerlof was born in Newhaven (Connecticut, USA) on 17 June 1940. His father was a Swedish immigrant and his mother was from a family that had immigrated from Germany. He received his BA at Yale University in 1962, and his PhD at the Massachusetts Institute of Technology (MIT) in 1966. He spent the whole of his career at the University of California at Berkeley, with some breaks at the Indian Statistical Institute (1967–68), the Council of Economic Advisors (1973–74), the Federal Reserve Board (1977–78) and the London School of Economics (1978–80). He was a joint recipient of the Sveriges Riksbank Prize in Economic Sciences in Memory of Alfred Nobel in 2001, with Michael Spence and Joseph Stiglitz.

Akerlof is one of the most original economic theorists in recent times – beginning with "The market for lemons" (1970), the paper for which he received the above mentioned Nobel prize, to his last book *Animal Spirits: How Human Psychology Drives the Economy and Why It Matters for Global Capitalism* (co-authored with Robert Shiller 2009). What is remarkable is the gradual emergence of a new paradigm in economics, which is by now quite explicit but which could not be expected, when reading his 1970 paper. The importance of information asymmetries (of which he was one of the three modern "discoverers", as the 2001 Bank of Sweden Prize committee rightly acknowledges) could have driven him towards the waters of the nowadays standard mainstream economics, with its extreme hypotheses on calculative rationality and sophisticated equilibria. However, it was, as his readers gradually discovered when reading the subsequent steps in Akerlof's work, upon the methodological (rather than substantial) foundations of the "lemons" paper that he built his research programme towards the "pragmatic economics" and the "behavioural macroeconomics", which he now advocates.

Theoretical Contributions

The theoretical contributions of Akerlof could be retrospectively summarized in an intellectual pilgrimage with four main steps, consisting in four discoveries: the importance of asymmetric information, the possibility of code equilibria, the presence of an identity component within utility, and the macroeconomic negative consequences of norms.

The importance of asymmetric information
On the used car model (Akerlof 1970), it is obvious that the sellers know more about the quality of their cars than the buyers:

> If good and bad cars are sold at the same price, owners are more likely to offer a bad car for sale than a good one. Potential buyers of used cars suspect that the cars on the market are bad. Accordingly they reduce the price they are willing to pay, reducing further the incentive to put a good car up for sale. In a vicious circle, such interactions between the buyers and the sellers may even cause a total market collapse. (Akerlof 2005: 4)

The next point to understand is that this problem is a general one, potentially pervading all kinds of markets (credit, products, labour, and so on). However, perhaps the right conclusion is not so much a problem about information, as about the quality of information. Markets with quality as an unknown are a much more fragile machinery than markets without.

The existence of code equilibria

We should pay attention to the following warning, if we are tempted to think that Akerlof's subsequent discoveries are not as important as the first discovery: "The truth we see from caste regarding economic equilibrium are as fundamental as those in 'Lemons'" (Akerlof 2005: 6). Codes of caste behaviour – to be retrospectively read as a generic term for any norm-dependent economic equilibrium – modify demand and supply decisions, in a sense that prevents the equality of supply and demand as determined by economic considerations. Obedience to the codes of caste behaviour is contrary to economic motivation, but not to self-interest, if our conceptions of costs and benefits are enlarged to include those that are non-economic. People may fear to be outcast or boycotted for breaking the code (Akerlof 1976, 1985).

In another line of research, to follow the code of the group may be economically profitable for each member of the group, as when workers reward their employer who gives them more than the minimum wage (and/or who demands less than the maximum effort), by giving their employer a counter-gift of an effort above the minimum level. It still remains that this kind of "efficiency wage" may be too high to clear the labour market (Akerlof 1982), confirming that market equilibria with quality are a much more fragile machinery.

The presence of an identity component within utility

The next step was to go further into the re-definition of standard *homo œconomicus*. "Self-interest" had just been enlarged by extending the field of this "interest": now it will be changed through a revision of the "self": but formally as an extension, too, in order to preserve the mathematics of the utility function. Up to a certain extent, people can choose their identity by choosing the social category to which they belong. Also, "social categories have ideal-types that exemplify how people in those social categories *should* behave" (Akerlof 2005: 8, original emphasis). People are then supposed to maximize utility functions with new arguments (beside the traditional ones), positive (identity of their social category) as well as negative (the gap between the corresponding ideal behaviour). With this seemingly technical extension, Akerlof is able to give account of a host of hitherto unexplained facts, and as diverse as the efficiency of management by objectives compared to the use of monetary incentives (Akerlof and Kranton 2005b), or the prevalence of self-destructive behaviour among dominated groups (Akerlof and Kranton 2000). It gives credit to active and preventive social policies, at variance with the prevalent neo-liberal political philosophy. An economic agent caring about his or her own quality is likely to be a more fragile machinery than the same one only concerned by prices and quantities.

The macroeconomic negative consequences of norms

The immediate consequence of the third step is that now the way people should behave becomes an essential part of the explanation of how people do behave – Akerlof is probably the economist in the world who makes the greatest use of the normative conditional "should". When going from microeconomics to macroeconomics, he strongly rehabilitates, first, Keynes's economics, exactly for those reasons why new classical economists despise it – that is, the use of psychological factors, including "animal spirits" (Akerlof and Shiller 2009); and second, Keynesian economics, because the norms followed by economic agents – on consumption, savings, investment, wages, prices, and nominal values – can be shown to destroy the five neutralities upon which the new mainstream orthodoxy is built (life cycle, Modigliani–Miller theorem, Ricardian equivalence, rational expectations, and natural rate of unemployment) (Akerlof 2007). Sometimes this might look like new wine in old bottles: unemployment is due to downward rigidity of wages, which restore a possible macroeconomic role for monetary policy. However, those old bottles are now illuminated by their affiliation to the new paradigm of behavioural macroeconomics (Akerlof 2002). A market economy with quality is also much more complex a machinery than a market economy without it.

Methodological Prescriptions

It should be clear by now that Akerlof would not have reached these results – more precisely these kinds of results – had he not experienced a new style of economic research, characterized by a paradoxical set of features: a sharp discontinuity with Friedman's methodology of positive economics, and a strong continuity with the usual practice of mainstream economists.

The discontinuity with mainstream practices

Back to realism! The objective is no longer to make sense only of some quantitative facts with a parsimonious model, but rather of some (often) obvious facts, including qualitative ones, with a plausible microeconomic model. Therefore it is essential to study specific markets or behaviours instead of looking for the highest generality. It becomes relevant to use (careful) case studies, where individuals are asked for the reasons of their decisions: they should no longer be systematically banned by scientists suspecting deceptive answers because of asymmetric information.

Farewell to imperialism! The relationships between economics and the other social sciences is now more balanced, with the former trying to give its own account of facts collected by the latter due to their traditional expertise in case studies and their absence of scorn toward fine-grained descriptions, especially in fields implying normative behaviours. Sometimes the economist may even proceed to a direct theoretical import from anthropology (Mauss) or social psychology (social identity theory).

The continuity
There is at least one thing in the practice of mainstream economists that Akerlof does not even think of criticizing: doing economic theory amounts to building a formal model – with individuals maximizing their utility, and coordinated through market or game equilibria. Of course it is not standard utility, but that may point to the Achille's heel of Akerlof's influence. The heart of his message about economic agents is that their rationality is not only of a calculative type, but also of an interpretative one: "social category", for instance, is clearly not an argument of the same logical type as consumption

or leisure. It was shrewd to insert identity inside utility and to keep on maximizing. Nevertheless it has a cost as high as its benefit: the equilibrium techniques belong to the standard tool kit, whereas we would have expected, as well as the usual economic variables, the emergence of some semantic concepts such as meaning. That should be the task of Akerlof's followers, including a richer view of institutions, strangely lacking in his framework. A consistent economic theory with quality is too complex a task to be mastered in one life, be it as innovative as the intellectual life of Akerlof.

OLIVIER FAVEREAU

See also:

Kenneth Joseph Arrow (I); Economic sociology (III); Milton Friedman (I); John Maynard Keynes (I); Robert E. Lucas (I); Macroeconomics (III); New Keynesianism (II); Robert Merton Solow (I); Joseph Eugene Stiglitz (I); James Tobin (I); Uncertainty and information (III).

References and further reading

Akerlof, G. (1970), 'The market for lemons: quality uncertainty and the market mechanism', *Quarterly Journal of Economics*, **84** (3), 488–500.
Akerlof, G. (1976), 'The economics of caste and of the rat race, and other woeful tales', *Quarterly Journal of Economics*, **90** (4), 599–617.
Akerlof, G. (1982), 'Labor contracts as partial gift exchange', *Quarterly Journal of Economics*, **97** (4), 543–69.
Akerlof, G. (1985), 'Discriminatory status-based wages among tradition-oriented stochastically based coconut producers', *Journal of Political Economy*, **93** (2), 265–76.
Akerlof, G. (2002), 'Behavioral macroeconomics and macroeconomic behavior', *American Economic Review*, **90** (3), 411–33.
Akerlof, G. (2005), *Explorations in Pragmatic Economics: Selected Papers of George A. Akerlof and Co-Authors*, Oxford: Oxford University Press.
Akerlof, G. (2007), 'The missing motivation in macroeconomics', *American Economic Review*, **97** (1), 3–36.
Akerlof, G. and R. Kranton (2000), 'Identity and economics', *Quarterly Journal of Economics*, **115** (3), 715–53.
Akerlof, G. and R. Kranton (2005), 'Identity and the economics of organization', *Journal of Economic Perspectives*, **19** (1), 9–32.
Akerlof, G. and R.J. Shiller (2009), *Animal Spirits: How Human Psychology Drives the Economy, and Why It Matters for Global Capitalism*, Princeton, NJ: Princeton University Press.

Joseph Eugene Stiglitz (b. 1943)

Joseph Eugene Stiglitz was born in 1943 to Charlotte and Nathaniel Stiglitz and grew up in the small Manufacturing Belt town of Gary, Indiana. Legend has it that Paul Samuelson, who was also born there, once recommended Stiglitz in a letter as "the best economist from Gary". According to his own account, the problems of unemployment, poverty and racial discrimination that plagued his hometown provoked an interest for Joseph Stiglitz in social sciences. Born into a politically active family he also developed a liking for political debates at an early age.

After finishing a public school in Gary, where he trained as a printer and an electrician, he decided in 1960 to join his older brother at Amherst College. At Amherst, Stiglitz took courses in physics, mathematics, history, and philosophy, served as the president of the Student Council, and was an enthusiastic participant in college debates. His attraction to economics arose primarily from the fact that it allowed him to apply his outstanding skills in mathematics to important questions of economic and social policy. When he informed his teachers about his decision to major in economics, they arranged for him to skip the senior year so he could go on to graduate school immediately. Without a degree, he left Amherst for the Massachusetts Institute of Technology (MIT) in 1963.

At that time, MIT was at the pinnacle of prominence with its staff including Paul Samuelson, Robert Solow, Franco Modigliani and Kenneth Arrow. Among his fellow students were George Akerlof, and Avinash Dixit with whom Stiglitz frequently collaborated during his later career. Only one year into graduate school, Stiglitz, at the age of 21, was asked to edit Paul Samuelson's collected papers. The MIT school of economics, and Samuelson's writings in particular, had a profound influence on his own work both with regard to method and style. Above all, Stiglitz, like his MIT mentors, always insisted on deducing practical policy advice from small, abstract models centred on the maximizing behaviour of economic agents.

Between the Cambridges: Early Work on Growth Theory

In the summer of 1964, Joseph Stiglitz was invited by Hirofumi Uzawa to join a group of young researchers (including George Akerlof among others) at the University of Chicago to work on the theory of growth. The mid-1960s were, of course, the heydays of growth theory with the heated debate between the neoclassicals of Cambridge, Massachusetts, and their critics at Cambridge, United Kingdom, reaching its climax. Feeling he had heard enough of one side of this debate, Stiglitz went to Cambridge, UK, to learn more about the other side. There he met Piero Sraffa, James Meade, Nicholas Kaldor, and Joan Robinson, the latter of whom was originally assigned to be his tutor. However, Robinson's attempts at re-education were greatly complicated by Stiglitz's self-confident scepticism and forwardness. Stiglitz's academic supervision was eventually taken over by Frank Hahn. Under Hahn's guidance, the two years in Cambridge turned out to be a highly stimulating experience yielding a series of papers that helped to build his reputation as a theorist.

Stiglitz's main concern in the 1960s growth literature was to spell out the theoretical implications of various amendments to the neoclassical theory of growth. Most of this work centred on the question of transitional dynamics (that is, economic systems outside their long-run steady-state growth path) and the efficiency and stability of these. Even if these early contributions came to be overshadowed by his later work on information economics, they are still interesting for the history of economic thought as they marked a key stage in the Cambridge–Cambridge capital controversy. A typical contribution from that stage is Cass and Stiglitz (1969). It builds a model with heterogeneous capital-goods which in the long run behaves essentially like the basic Solow–Swan one-good model, but allows for a richer variety of transitional dynamics. What happens in the transition towards the steady state crucially depends on the assumptions placed on saving behaviour and expectation formation.

Some years later Stiglitz (1974a) also aired his take on the capital controversy. In his opinion the Cambridge, UK, side of the argument fundamentally misunderstood the role of economic theory: "A model which is appropriate for illuminating one class of problems may not be adequate for illuminating another: we know that Newtonian physics is only a first approximation . . . Yet for most of the questions we wish to discuss in elementary physics courses, it is perfectly adequate" (Stiglitz 1974a: 901). The neoclassical one-good growth model should hold a similar place in economics. Whether or not a theory is adequate is essentially an empirical matter: is the theory able to predict real-world phenomena with a reasonable degree of precision?

The early work on growth theory also highlights a general feature of Stiglitz's approach to economic theorizing: starting from one fairly simple model that relied on a range of restrictive assumptions, he explored the consequences of relaxing those assumptions one at a time. This technique allowed him to develop a deeper understanding of the internal logic of economic models and made him more sensitive to the role of implicit assumptions in existing neoclassical theory. Among the most consequential of those was the assumption of perfect information.

Out of Kenya: The Economics of Imperfect Information

In 1969 Stiglitz went on an extensive research visit to Kenya, which had just won independence from British colonial power. The manifold social and economic problems he encountered there caused a shift in interest away from the purely academic disputes in growth theory towards what he felt were more relevant issues.

One of those issues was the peculiar phenomenon of "sharecropping" which was widespread in many developing countries. Under a sharecropping arrangement, the farmer had to deliver a fixed share (typically half) of his produce to the landlord in return for the use of his land. This appeared to pose a significant disincentive for farmers to work, similar to a tax on the farmers' labour. However, Stiglitz (1974b) showed that sharecropping is one particular solution to the problem of imperfect information. While the input of the farmer cannot be directly observed, his output can, but his output is subject to chance. Renting the land would mean that the farmer shoulders all the risk of a bad crop; employing the farmer for a fixed wage would leave the landlord with all the risk. Sharecropping can thus be understood as a partial insurance contract: farmer and landlord share the risk of a bad crop among them.

Stiglitz realized that a very similar incentive problem is found in large corporations in which there is a separation between ownership and management. The board of directors cannot observe what the manager does, but they can observe the company's profit, which is (imperfectly) correlated with the manager's effort. Paying the manager a fixed salary would attenuate his incentives to run the company well; paying him a share of the company's profit would expose the manager to a lot of risk. Hence the equilibrium contract will, under certain assumptions, consist of a combination of both. Stiglitz's work (together with Richard Arnott) on these incentive problems opened up an extensive research project that revolutionized both the theory and practice of corporate governance.

A central issue for the Kenyan government, aiming to lift the country out of poverty, was how much it should invest in education. It had been recognized that the social return to education need not coincide with the private return, since the value of education to an individual partly comes from making him or her "stand out from the crowd". If the population as a whole becomes more educated, the private return may become larger (it becomes even more important to stand out through more education) than the social return.

Stiglitz (1975) focused attention on what came to be called the "screening" function of education and its role in wage determination. Employers typically cannot know the skills of a worker prior to employment. Hence the wage rate for any given group of workers is determined by the expected marginal productivity given the available information about the skill level of that group. How much information will be made available? A job applicant may have an incentive to disclose her true skills to prospective employers – but only if she thinks her skills are above average. Below-average workers would prefer to hide their true abilities. Stiglitz was able to show that one possible equilibrium outcome involved full revelation of the entire distribution of skills: the best workers have an incentive to disclose their abilities, setting themselves apart from the others. Then the second-best workers will try to separate themselves from the rest, and so on until all skill levels are revealed.

What happens if applicants cannot fully disclose their true skills? If an employer can choose from a pool of job applicants whose observable characteristics, and hence whose market wages, are the same, she may have an incentive to single out the most highly skilled worker. However, this incentive only exists if the employer can keep the knowledge of an applicant's true skill to herself. If the information on the true skills of an applicant becomes known to other employers, the wage of that applicant will be bid up. In technical language, the incentive to "screen" (that is, to gather information on the true characteristics of individuals) depends on whether the screener can appropriate the value of the information gathered through screening. The basic concept of screening turned out to apply, as Stiglitz soon realized, to a broad array of problems including insurance (insurers screening the risk attributes of the insured) and banking (bankers screening the creditworthiness of borrowers).

Another problem Stiglitz witnessed in Kenya was the prevalence of urban unemployment. Conventional theory held that if unemployment exists, wages fall so as to equalize the demand and supply of labour. How could one explain then that employers continued to pay fairly high wages even though there was a large pool of unemployed workers? Here, Stiglitz drew on an old idea, which can be traced back to Alfred Marshall and even to Adam Smith: paying higher wages can make workers more productive. If firms find it profitable to pay wages over and above the market-clearing rate, there could be unemployment in equilibrium. Stiglitz dubbed this the efficiency wage theory.

In his later work with Carl Shapiro (Shapiro and Stiglitz 1984), which became the classic treatment of efficiency wages, he emphasized the threat of unemployment as a substitute for monitoring the work effort of employees. If wages were set at the market-clearing level, workers could be sure to quickly find another job once they get fired, so they have no incentive to work hard. Consequently, workers will "shirk". In this situation, it is profitable for an individual firm to raise wages above the ruling market wage rate, since this increases the cost of getting caught shirking. As all firms follow the same logic, the general wage rate will rise, reducing the incentive not to shirk. However, the increase in wages creates unemployment, which in turn creates a penalty for shirking. In equilibrium, all firms pay above-market-clearing wages and all workers work hard for fear of becoming unemployed. Thus unemployment fulfils, in the words of Shapiro and Stiglitz (1984), the role of a "disciplining device".

The various research projects that grew out of Kenya all had one thing in common: they all undermined crucial tenets of the economic orthodoxy of the time. At the same time, Stiglitz's research agenda employed the same methodology on which that very orthodoxy was built: analysing the interaction of maximizing agents in equilibrium.

According to orthodox theory, prices move so that markets clear. Efficiency wage theory showed that this result is not generally valid. If the price of the good influences the quality of the good (like the productivity of labour), demand may not equal supply in equilibrium. If the wage affects the quality of labour, there will be equilibrium unemployment; if the interest rate affects the quality of the pool of borrowers, credit will be rationed in equilibrium (Stiglitz and Weiss 1981).

Another subversive result of Stiglitz's research was the inefficiency of market outcomes. Before the advent of information economics, market failures were discussed as exceptions to the rule. With imperfect information, market failure seemed to be the rule. The analysis of sharecropping pointed to one source of this inefficiency, the principal–agent problem; the theory of screening highlighted another, the problem of appropriation. Some years later Greenwald and Stiglitz (1986) demonstrate that economies with information imperfections would generally not be Pareto efficient, even when the costs of obtaining information were taken into account. Hence there almost always exist, in principle, government interventions that would leave everyone better off.

Beyond Information Economics

Apart from his pioneering work on the economics of imperfect information, Joseph Stiglitz also contributed to a vast variety of loosely related issues ranging from industrial organization to macroeconomic policy.

In the 1930s and 1940s, the development of an alternative to the theory of perfect competition was a major research project, led by Edward Chamberlin and Joan Robinson. The shortcoming of this early effort was that it remained confined to partial equilibrium analysis. In 1977, Avinash Dixit and Joseph Stiglitz developed the first general equilibrium model of monopolistic competition (Dixit and Stigliz 1977). They envisaged a large number of firms each producing one variety of a differentiated good, each facing a downward sloping demand curve for its output. This model proved to be extremely influential in two quite distinct branches of economic theory. In international economics, the Dixit–Stiglitz model provided the basis for much of the new trade theory as well as the new economic geography. In macroeconomics, it became a crucial ingredient in new Keynesian models of the business cycle.

In his work on public finance, Stiglitz helped develop the theory of optimal taxation pioneered by Frank Ramsey in the 1920s and revived by James Mirrlees and Peter Diamond. He took issue with some implications of this theory, for instance, the proposition that goods with a low price elasticity (such as food) should be taxed heavily, because they seemed to suggest that regressive taxes were optimal. Together with Tony Atkinson, he showed that once distributional concerns are explicitly taken into account in the design of tax policy, the counter-intuitive results tended to disappear (Atkinson and Stiglitz 1972). In later work, he aimed at merging information economics with the optimal taxation literature. The key insight was that imperfect information imposed restrictions on the set of taxes that could be imposed by the government, and taking these restrictions into account could drastically alter the conclusions (for example, corporate taxes could become optimal).

During the 1970s and 1980s, while the information revolution was reshaping microeconomics, macroeconomics underwent its own revolution following the advent of rational expectations models. These models not only suggested that government stabilization policies were ineffective, but that unemployment was not a real problem. Stiglitz, together with his former student Peter Neary, argued (Neary and Stiglitz 1984) that these results depended not so much on the rational expectations assumption, but on the assumption of perfectly flexible prices. They showed that, under the assumption of sticky prices, government policy was likely to be more effective with rational expectations than without it.

Policy Making and Public Writing

Up until the early 1990s, Joseph Stiglitz was an economist's economist. He was widely known among professional economists as a brilliant theorist, but engaged rarely in public policy debates. This would change when he was invited in 1992 by President Bill Clinton to chair the Council of Economic Advisers. For Stiglitz, this was an opportunity to put his theoretical insights to action in solving real-world problems. In this new role as policy adviser, Stiglitz was instrumental in defining the "third way" philosophy of the Clinton era, which constituted a marked departure from both free-market enthusiasm of the Reagan years and the interventionism of traditional socialists.

In 1996, Stiglitz left the Clinton administration to become the chief economist of the World Bank. The really important policy issues of the time, he felt, were on a global rather than on a national scale. Among those issues was the transition of the formerly Communist countries of Eastern Europe and the rapidly progressing process of globalization.

In *Whither Socialism?* (Stiglitz 1994) he had already submitted his interpretation of the fall of Communism and made suggestions of how the conversion from central planning to a market-based economy should be effected. The root of the failure of socialism, he argued, was an erroneous theory of the market system. The neglect of information imperfections not only resulted in a misleading image of the market, it also led to the belief that "market socialism" (that is, a system in which the state tries to simulate the price mechanism) could work. On the question of transition, Stiglitz came out in favour of a gradualist approach and in opposition to the "shock therapy" that was being applied by the International Monetary Fund (IMF). In particular, Stiglitz cautioned against an excessively rapid and careless privatization of state-owned industries.

His views on globalization led to an open conflict with the IMF whom Stiglitz accused of pushing a market-fundamentalist agenda, commonly referred to as the "Washington consensus". Against the backdrop of the East Asian financial crisis of the late 1990s, the dispute focused on the issue of capital market liberalization. Whereas the IMF adhered to the view that such liberalization would facilitate a more efficient international sharing of risks, Stiglitz, drawing on his work of asymmetric information in financial markets, argued to the contrary.

In *Globalization and Its Discontents* (Stiglitz 2002), he summarized his critique of the IMF, its handling of the crises of the 1990s, and more broadly the political management of globalization. The book was controversial not so much for its substantive criticisms with which many economists agreed, but for its personal attacks on some of the IMF staff. Outside academic circles the book was, strangely, received as an endorsement of the anti-globalization movement. However, Stiglitz never argued against the process of global economic integration. What he criticized was the macroeconomic policy prescriptions of the Washington consensus that, in his opinion, impeded developing countries to reap the full benefits of globalization.

In 2001, Joseph Sitglitz was awarded the Sveriges Riksbank Prize in Economic Sciences in Memory of Alfred Nobel together with George Akerlof and Michael Spence "for their analyses of markets with asymmetric information". The award added to his status as a celebrity economist, which he used successfully to make his voice heard in political debates.

Joseph Stiglitz was and continues to be one of the most innovative economic theorists of his time. His contributions to the economics of information changed the way economists think about the price mechanism and the proper role of government. In a time of great enthusiasm for the "magic of the marketplace", Joseph Stiglitz constantly reminded both economists and policy makers of the manifold shortcomings of market systems and showed how an intelligent government could overcome these shortcomings.

MAX GÖDL

See also:

George Akerlof (I); Growth (III); Income distribution (III); Paul Anthony Samuelson (I); Uncertainty and information (III).

References and further reading

Atkinson, A.B. and J.E. Stiglitz (1972), 'The structure of indirect taxation and economic efficiency', *Journal of Public Economics*, **1** (1), 97–119.
Cass, D. and J.E. Stiglitz (1969), 'The implications for alternative saving and expectation hypotheses for choices of technique and patterns of growth', *Journal of Political Economy*, **77** (4), 586–627.
Dixit, A.K. and J.E. Stiglitz (1977), 'Monopolistic competition and optimum product diversity', *American Economic Review*, **67** (3), 297–308.
Greenwald, B.C. and J.E. Stiglitz (1986), 'Externalities in economies with imperfect information and incomplete markets', *Quarterly Journal of Economics*, **101** (2), 229–64.
Neary, J.P. and J.E. Stiglitz (1983), 'Toward a reconstruction of Keynesian economics: expectations and constrained equilibria', *Quarterly Journal of Economics*, **98** (3), 199–228.

Shapiro, C. and J.E. Stiglitz (1984), 'Equilibrium unemployment as a worker discipline device', *American Economic Review*, **74** (3), 433–44.

Stiglitz, J.E. (1974a), 'The Cambridge–Cambridge controversy in the theory of capital: a view from New Haven', *Journal of Political Economy*, **82** (4), 893–903.

Stiglitz, J.E. (1974b), 'Incentives and risk sharing in sharecropping', *Review of Economic Studies*, **41** (2), 219–55.

Stiglitz, J.E. (1975), 'The theory of "screening" education, and the distribution of income', *American Economic Review*, **65** (3), 283–300.

Stiglitz, J.E. (1994), *Whither Socialism?*, Cambridge, MA: MIT Press.

Stiglitz, J.E. (2002), *Globalization and Its Discontents*, New York: W.W. Norton.

Stiglitz, J.E. and A. Weiss (1981), 'Credit rationing in markets with imperfect information', *American Economic Review*, **71** (3), 393–410.

Paul Robin Krugman (b. 1953)

Paul Robin Krugman was born in 1953 in Albany, New York, the only child of Anita and David Krugman, an insurance industry manager, and grew up in a middle-class neighbourhood in Long Island.

Krugman began studying economics at Yale where he soon attracted the attention of his professors. In 1973, he became a research assistant to William Nordhaus. After graduating from Yale in 1974, Krugman went on to the Massachusetts Institute of Technology (MIT) to study under Paul Samuelson, Robert Solow, and Rüdiger Dornbusch, the latter of whom became his PhD adviser. During this time Krugman was introduced to the distinctive MIT variant of neoclassical economics with its emphasis on small-scale theoretical models tailored around a set of stylized empirical observations. The MIT economics department was rather sceptical toward the rational expectations revolution that was sweeping through macroeconomics at that time and continued to teach "old" Keynesian theory. In particular, Dornbusch's brand of international macroeconomics, which had a strong influence on Krugman, was largely Keynesian in character.

The years at MIT were formative not only for Krugman's understanding of economic theory but also for his intellectual style. From Samuelson and Solow he learnt to combine a mathematically rigorous way of thinking with a light and playful style of exposition. From Dornbusch he inherited a strong affinity for policy-oriented issues. In 1977, Krugman finished his doctoral thesis on flexible exchange rates and took a position as assistant professor at Yale where he began to work on what would become the foundation of "new trade theory". His seminal papers on increasing returns and international trade propelled Krugman to the status of an economic wunderkind and secured him a place among the leading international economists of his generation.

The Increasing Returns Revolution in Trade Theory

Towards the end of the 1970s, international economics was in an unfortunate state. On the one hand, there was a growing sense of dissatisfaction with the dominating neoclassical (Heckscher–Ohlin–Samuelson, HOS) trade model. This dissatisfaction arose primarily from its inability to explain trade within industries or within firms as opposed to trade between industries. During the 1960s and 1970s, evidence was mounting that intra-industry trade was quantitatively much more important than inter-industry trade.

On the other hand, the only explanations for intra-industry trade available at that time, such as those of Staffan Burenstam Linder (1961), relied implicitly or explicitly on increasing returns to scale. As economists knew since the days of Alfred Marshall, increasing returns to scale cannot be reconciled with the assumption of price-taking behaviour and hence call for a theory of imperfect competition. However, the only available models of non-perfect competition at the time were partial equilibrium models and therefore ill-suited for the analysis of international trade.

This changed in the mid-1970s when Avinash Dixit and Joseph Stiglitz (1977) generalized Chamberlin's theory of monopolistic competition. It was Paul Krugman who used this innovation to build a new theory of trade. Like so often in the history of economic thought, Krugman was not alone in this discovery. Kelvin Lancaster (1980), among others, had independently developed similar ideas at around the same time. In fact, the distinguishing feature of Krugman's contribution is not so much its originality but its analytical elegance.

The core of Krugman's trade theory (Krugman 1979b) is a Chamberlin–Dixit–Stiglitz view of competition in which there is a large number of differentiated goods, which may be interpreted as varieties of a good. Each firm produces a distinct variety under econo-mies of scale internal to the firm and therefore faces a downward sloping demand curve for its product. The price of each variety is then a mark-up over marginal costs depend-ing on the elasticity of demand for the variety. As long as existing firms are making profits, new firms with new varieties will enter the market reducing demand for existing varieties. This ensures that firms earn zero pure profits in equilibrium and prices equal average costs. Because of increasing returns, the no-profits condition implies an inverse relationship between the price and the output of each variety. Full employment of labour implies another inverse relationship between the number of varieties produced and the amount produced of each variety.

The effects of trade are straightforward. Through foreign trade, consumers have access to more varieties compared with autarky, so they can distribute their expendi-tures over a greater range of differentiated goods. Hence trade occurs in this model even though there are no comparative advantages, and this trade involves shipping very similar goods between countries. The increased choice of differentiated goods for con-sumers is one source of gains from trade in Krugman's model. Surprisingly, as long as the elasticity of demand for each variety is not affected by this greater choice, it is also the only gain from trade. In particular, with constant demand elasticities, trade has no effect on the scale of production of individual firms. Only if one assumes, as Krugman (1979b) did, that the demand for each variety becomes more elastic as the number of available varieties increases, there is also a beneficial scale effect of trade. If, after opening to trade, the demand curve for each variety becomes flatter, the price for each variety will be lower than in autarky. A lower price can only be achieved if firms move down along their average cost curves by increasing output. However, since labour supply is fixed, not all the firms that exist in autarky can actually increase output, so some of them must go out of business as the economy adapts to the new equilibrium. This also means that the number of varieties produced in each country decreases through trade.

The new trade theory, as it was soon to be called, was different from the HOS approach in substance as well as in method. It provided a firm theoretical explanation of a range of phenomena that had hitherto seemed puzzling and it confirmed some of the hypotheses of earlier writers, such as Linder's home market effect (Krugman 1980). It was different in method as well in so far as it relied on very special ad hoc assumptions on consumer preferences and cost structures in a way traditional theory did not. Krugman defended such ad-hocery on the grounds that it allowed his theory to remain both rigorous and tractable. He also argued that, although the neoclassical model was indeed more general than his, this generality was bought at the price of making the "big untrue assumption" of constant returns to scale.

Krugman's contributions to the new trade theory reveal a certain pattern that also appears in his later academic work and distinguish him as a theorist. He typically starts by picking up a heterodox idea that seems outlandish and untenable to mainstream economists, reformulates it in a simple but fully specified general equilibrium model and pushes it to new and sometimes astonishing implications. In this process, he often pays little attention as to whether his is a fair or historically correct interpretation of the original idea.

His treatment of "uneven development" is a case in point. In the 1950s Gunnar Myrdal (1957), among others, had argued that international trade has a tendency to increase worldwide economic inequality, that rich countries become richer at the expense of poor ones. Krugman (1981) reconstructs their argument in a dynamic two-sector two-country model, in which the country with the larger initial capital stock has a higher rate of profits and a higher rate of growth. Owing to increasing returns to scale in the manufacturing sector, faster capital accumulation in the "developed" country reinforces its comparative advantage in manufacturing, leading ultimately to the extinction of the industrial sector in the "underdeveloped" country. The remarkable feature of this model is that it lends support to Lenin's theory of the two-stage evolution of capitalism. In the first stage, capital accumulation in the developed world is sustained by drawing labour from the agricultural sector into manufacturing. This stage relies on the export of industrial goods to the poor country. As soon as the richer country is completely specialized in manufacturing, wages start to rise driving down the rate of profits. This in turn induces capital to flow to the underdeveloped country, giving rise to the second "imperialist" stage of accumulation. The lesson Krugman wants to teach here is not that Lenin was right, but rather that the tools of orthodox economics can be employed both to support and to sharpen the ideas of capitalism's most radical critics.

While Krugman enjoyed exploring unorthodox ideas, he was also striving to reconcile new trade theory with the "old" comparative advantage paradigm. In *Market Structure and Foreign Trade* (Helpman and Krugman 1985) he, together with Elhanan Helpman, attempted an integrated treatment of the factor endowments and the economies of scale theories of trade. The central insight from their analysis is that the new theory poses no threat to the neoclassical factor endowments approach but can be viewed as complementary to it. Furthermore, and in contrast to some of his fellow "new traders", Krugman (1987) emphasized that his model did not invalidate but even strengthens the classical view that free international trade is beneficial for all and that protectionist policies are generally harmful.

New Economic Geography

Krugman's second major contribution to international economics came with his celebrated 1991 paper "Increasing returns and economic geography" which sparked new interest in the economics of spatial concentration of industries. The primary achievement of this research project is perhaps best described as providing microeconomic foundations to "agglomeration economies", that is, deriving from optimizing behaviour of economic agents general conditions under which industries will disperse or concentrate in space.

As with new trade theory, the idea of agglomeration economies was far from new. Alfred Marshall had written extensively about the tendency of certain industries to agglomerate. Even before that, Johann Heinrich von Thünen had developed his famous ring theory of land use, which was extended by German economists to a "theory of central places". These theories went a long way towards describing how various economic activities locate around urban centres. But they did not provide a satisfactory explanation as to why and how these core–periphery patterns emerge endogenously. That was precisely the goal of the new economic geography (NEG).

The ingredients for NEG models, as exemplified by Krugman (1991), are threefold. First, there are two regions with two sectors: perfectly competitive constant-returns agriculture and monopolistic increasing-returns manufacturing. Second, while industrial workers are fully mobile between regions, agricultural workers are not. Third, trade of manufacturing goods incurs transportation costs of the so-called "iceberg" form: some given fraction of goods disappears when being shipped from one place to another. Now imagine an initial equilibrium in which "footloose" industrial workers are spread evenly across regions and ask: what happens if this equilibrium is disturbed by one manufacturing firm entering region A? There are three effects to consider:

1. Increased competition in region A tends to lower the price index of manufacturing goods and thus lowers demand for each individual firm. This price index effect acts to reduce profits in region A relative to region B and therefore exerts a centrifugal force to restore the initial equilibrium.
2. Increased labour demand invites immigration of industrial workers into region A which in turn increases the demand for varieties produced in this region. This counteracts the price index effect and exerts a centripetal force towards a "concentrated" equilibrium.
3. Since the drop in the price index increases real manufacturing wages in region A, the influx of "footloose" labour into region A must lead to a drop in nominal manufacturing wages there such that real wages stay equalized across regions. This decreases costs for manufacturing firms in A and thus reinforces the tendency to agglomerate.

As Krugman (1991) shows, the relative strength of these effects depends on three parameters. The forces towards agglomeration are stronger the lower the transport costs, the higher the expenditure share of manufacturing goods and the higher the degree of increasing returns to scale. For one set of parameter values the model exhibits diversification, for another set it exhibits agglomeration.

Krugman also showed that if simple dynamics are added to the basic model, it exhibits "order from instability": starting from a small deviation from the uniform, "disordered" equilibrium, the economy self-organizes into a highly structured landscape. In *The Self-Organizing Economy* (Krugman 1996) he elaborated on the idea of spontaneous order that arises from a symmetric but unstable initial state and demonstrated how it can help explain things like size distribution of cities or the emergence of business cycles. In *The Spatial Economy* (Fujita et al. 1999), co-authored by Masahisa Fujita and Anthony Venables, Krugman synthesized the various models that NEG had produced during the first decade of its existence.

Currency Crises, the Liquidity Trap and Depression Economics

A third theme in Krugman's *œuvre* is the macroeconomics of financial crises. His contributions in this field do not constitute a cohesive theoretical structure as they were mainly motivated by contemporary economic events.

Krugman (1979a) argued that the attempt of a government to peg the exchange rate is similar to a government trying to control the price of an exhaustible resource: at some point, the government may run out of resources (or of foreign exchange reserves) and can then no longer maintain the price control (or the exchange rate peg). When that happens, the currency will suddenly depreciate leaving investors with a windfall capital loss, which they will naturally try to avoid. Hence forward-looking investors will "flee" from the pegged currency before the foreign exchange reserves are actually depleted and thus trigger a speculative attack on the currency. Such an attack necessarily occurs at a point where the government would have had sufficient reserves to uphold the peg for some time, but the anticipating behaviour of investors forces the government to liquidate its foreign exchange reserves.

Krugman's model served as a starting point for the first of three "generations" of currency crisis models. In first generation models, speculative attacks are the natural consequence of rational investors anticipating an inevitable future crisis in the balance of payments. However, the crisis of the 1990s in East Asia and Latin America led him to reconsider the possibility of purely self-fulfilling crises that occur regardless of fundamental economic conditions. Krugman (1999) conceded that those crises could not be adequately explained by his 1979 model, but are best understood in terms of multiple equilibria: the economy remains in the "good" equilibrium as long as everybody believes so and can suddenly, through a minor change in expectations, shift to a "bad" equilibrium and hence suffer a crisis.

Japan's financial crash in the early 1990s and its subsequent stagnation caused another change of opinion in Krugman. Prior to the Japanese experience, Krugman shared the consensus view of the time that recessions can, at least in principle, always be avoided by expansionary monetary policy and that John Maynard Keynes' idea of the "liquidity trap" – a situation where nominal interest rates have sunk so low that ordinary monetary policy ceases to be effective – was a mere theoretical anomaly. He was at first certain that a liquidity trap could never arise in a fully "micro-founded" model, and discovered to his own surprise that this was not so.

In his 1998 paper (Krugman 1998b) he demonstrated how such a trap could arise in a simple macroeconomic model with maximizing agents: consider an economy in which individuals must hold money to pay for consumption and can invest their savings in riskless bonds, and assume that output, price level and interest rate are fixed from the second period onwards. In the first period, consumption smoothing implies an inverse relationship between current output and the (real) interest rate. If the price level in period one is fixed, monetary policy can choose any point on this curve by controlling the nominal interest rate via open market operations. However, there is a natural limit to such operations when the interest rate has dropped to zero. In this event, individuals hold money, at the margin, not to purchase goods but as a store of value, so any expansion in the money supply has no effect on output. The economy will be caught in such a trap whenever present consumption demand is sufficiently depressed either by fears of future deflation or an expected decline in future output.

This analysis, not least because of its immediate importance for the Japanese crisis, led to a return of the liquidity trap to macroeconomic theory. The relevance of the subject became even more apparent after the global financial crisis of 2008 and the deep recession that followed it. The rediscovery of the liquidity trap entailed a turn in Krugman's thinking on macroeconomics in general. The existence of a "zero lower bound" on interest rates implies, in his view, that there are two kinds of economics: one for normal times when the central bank can prevent major deviations from full-employment and another for depression times when it cannot. Whereas in normal times government deficits are harmful, they stimulate the economy in depression times. Whereas in normal times monetary policy should keep inflation down, it should try to generate inflation expectations in depression times.

Popular and Political Writings

Beginning in the mid-1990s, Krugman shifted more and more towards writing for a broader audience. *The Age of Diminished Expectations* (Krugman 1990), intended as a primer on the state of the US economy, became the first in a series of treatises on current issues of economic policy. In these books Krugman, on the one hand, provided his own pessimistic account of America's economic history and, on the other, attacked popular writers who, in his judgement, were spreading fallacies and falsehoods about economic matters, comprising both supply-side economists and left-wing critics of globalization.

The controversial election of George W. Bush in 2000 marked a turning point in Krugman's career, leading him to focus almost exclusively on political writing. In his biweekly opposite the editorial page (op-ed) columns for the *New York Times*, Krugman vigorously attacked the economic and social policies of the Bush administration. In *The Conscience of a Liberal* (Krugman 2007) he elaborated on his critique of the ruling conservative political agenda which, he argued, rooted in free-market dogmatism and aimed at rolling back the welfare state. He was also a pioneer of the economic "blogosphere", a rapidly growing network of internet blogs covering economic issues that emerged during the 2000s.

Krugman's celebrity status received a further boost in 2008 when he was awarded the Sveriges Riksbank Prize in Economic Sciences in Memory of Alfred Nobel "for his analysis of trade patterns and location of economic activity". During the global financial crisis that broke out the same year, Krugman took a leading role in advocating expansionary fiscal and monetary policies to fight unemployment, harshly criticizing those economists who, in his opinion, had discarded the lessons of the Great Depression and clung to a "Panglossian" world-view of self-correcting markets (Krugman 2009).

In his popular writings, Krugman frequently commented on more "philosophical" issues, including questions of methodology in economics, about which he had remained rather mute in his academic work. His approach to economic theory is perhaps best described in this remark:

> You can't do serious economics unless you are willing to be playful. Economic theory is not a collection of dictums laid down by pompous authority figures. Mainly, it is a menagerie of thought experiments – parables, if you like – that are intended to capture the logic of economic processes in a simplified way. (Krugman, 1998a: 19)

MAX GÖDL

See also:

Balance of payments and exchange rates (III); Economic geography (III); International trade (III); New Keynesianism (II).

References and further reading

Burenstam Linder, S. (1961), *An Essay on Trade and Transformation*, New York: John Wiley and Sons.
Dixit, A.K. and J.E. Stiglitz (1977), 'Monopolistic competition and optimum product diversity', *American Economic Review*, **67** (3), 297–308.
Fujita, M., P.R. Krugman and A. Venables (1999), *The Spatial Economy. Cities, Regions, and International Trade*, Cambridge, MA: MIT Press.
Helpman, E. and P.R. Krugman (1985), *Market Structure and Foreign Trade. Increasing Returns, Imperfect Competition, and the International Economy*, Brighton, UK: Wheatsheaf Books.
Krugman, P.R. (1979a), 'A model of balance of payments crises', *Journal of Money, Credit, and Banking*, **11** (3), 311–24.
Krugman, P.R. (1979b), 'Increasing returns, monopolistic competition, and international trade', *Journal of International Economics*, **9** (4), 469–79.
Krugman, P.R. (1980), 'Scale economies, product differentiation, and the pattern of trade', *American Economic Review*, **70** (5), 950–59.
Krugman, P.R. (1981), 'Trade, accumulation, and uneven development', *Journal of Development Economics*, **8** (2), 149–61.
Krugman, P.R. (1987), 'Is free trade passé?', *Journal of Economic Perspectives*, **1** (2), 131–44.
Krugman, P.R. (1990), *The Age of Diminished Expectations. U.S. Economic Policy in the 1990s*, Cambridge, MA: MIT Press.
Krugman, P.R. (1991), 'Increasing returns and economic geography', *Journal of Political Economy*, **99** (31), 483–99.
Krugman, P.R. (1996), *The Self Organizing Economy*, Hoboken, NJ: Wiley-Blackwell.
Krugman, P.R. (1998a), *The Accidental Theorist and Other Dispatches from the Dismal Science*, New York: W.W. Norton.
Krugman, P.R. (1998b), 'It's baaack: Japan's slump and the return of the liquidity trap', *Brookings Papers on Economic Activity*, **29** (2), 137–87.
Krugman, P.R. (1999), 'Balance sheets, the transfer problem, and financial crises', *International Tax and Public Finance*, **6** (4), 459–72.
Krugman, P.R. (2007), *The Conscience of a Liberal*, New York: W.W. Norton.
Krugman, P.R. (2009), 'How did economists get it so wrong?', *New York Times*, 6 September.
Lancaster, K. (1980), 'Intra-industry trade under perfect monopolistic competition', *Journal of International Economics*, **10** (2), 151–75.
Myrdal, G. (1957), *Economic Theory and Underdeveloped Regions*, London: Duckworth.

Index

Abeille, Louis-Paul 34
Académie de Bordeaux 24
Académie de Chirurgie 28
Académie de Grenoble 174
Académie des Sciences 28, 42, 83
Académie des Sciences Morales et Politiques
    164, 234, 247
Académie Française 24, 83
Accademia dei Lincei 498, 602
Acta Borussica 275
Adam Smith Society 323
Adams, Henry Brooks 374
Addington, Henry 95
Aftalion, Albert 443–4
agriculture 13–14, 21, 29–30, 32–4, 55, 131,
    168, 177, 225, 256, 395, 427, 471, 543, 547,
    549, 750–51
    crises 14
    investment in 76
    production/productivity 14, 30, 75–7, 153–4,
        263
        product cycles 599
        spatial models of 159
        surplus 54
    rural 374
    urban 161
Akerlof, George 737–41, 746
    Animal Spirits: How Human Psychology
        Drives the Economy and Why It Matters
        for Global Capitalism (2009) 737
    theories of
        asymmetric information 737
        code equilibria 737–8
        identity component in utility 737–8
        macroeconomic negative consequences of
            norms 737–9
    used car model of 737–8
Alembert, Jean Le Rond d' 28, 83–5
    Encyclopédie ou dictionnaire raisonné des
        sciences, des arts et des métiers 28, 73, 83
Algeria
    Algiers 215
Allais, Maurice 337, 642–3, 645, 677, 698–9
    À la recherche d'une discipline économique
        642, 699
    Économie et intérêt (1947) 642, 645–6
    role in development of general equilibrium
        models 643

    role in development of welfare economics
        644
    theory of business cycle 646
    Traité d'économie pure (1943) 642–5, 699
Allen, Roy 623
Allende, Salvador 649
allocation theory 364, 635
    welfare-theoretic approach to 365
Althoff, Friedrich 272
American Academy 602
American Academy of Arts and Sciences
    498
American Council of Learned Societies
    498
American Economic Association (AEA) 321,
    367, 410, 446, 501, 523, 525, 619, 651
    Francis A. Walker Medal 498
    John Bates Clark Medal 676, 714
    Richard Ely Lecture 593
American Statistical Association 411, 419,
    446
Amherst College 320–21, 741
Amoroso, Luigi 337, 622
Ampère, André-Marie 174
Ancient Greece 50
Ancient Rome 24–5, 49, 51, 80
Anderson, James
    Observations on the Means of Exciting a
        Spirit of National Industry (1777) 98
Annuaire de l'économie politique et de la
    statistique 234
Anti-Corn Laws League 171
Aoyama Gakuin University 725
The Apostles 470
applied economics 250, 253, 256–7, 259, 325,
    393, 604, 662
    Pareto's law 329–30, 337
Arbetarföreningen (Workers' Association) 348
arbitrary functions 179
Archiv für mathematische Wirtschafts- und
    Sozialforschung 621
Archiv für soziale Gesetzgebung und Statistik
    394
Archiv für Sozialwissenschaft und Sozialpolitik
    394
Aristotle 284, 286, 291, 514, 518
    Nicomachean Ethics 79, 312
    Politics 90

Arrow, Kenneth Joseph 84, 91–2, 523, 557,
581, 602–3, 690, 694–6, 702, 728–30, 741
Arrow–Debreu model of general
equilibrium 408, 510, 690, 693–5,
700–701, 703
Collective Choice and Social Welfare 728
impossibility theorem of social choice theory
91, 690–93, 729
revealed preference theory 695
Social Choice and Individual Values (1951)
728
Aspromourgos, T. 6, 8, 548
Assemblée Législative 83
Athénée 114
Aubrey, John 7
Augustine of Hippo, St. 10
Auspitz, Rudolf 290, 412, 435
Investigations on the Theory of Price (1889)
410
Australia 153, 263
Sydney 262
Austria 273, 485
Christian-Democrat Party 485
Graz 484–5
Salzburg 363
Vienna 268, 277, 283, 341, 348, 351, 363,
395–6, 408, 419, 446, 503, 559
Austrian Institute for Business Cycle Research
558–9
Austrian School of Economics 275, 283, 363,
365, 484, 548
Austro-Hungarian Empire 503
Brünn (Brno) 341
Prague 283

Bachelier, Louis 436–8
Le jeu, la chance et le hazard 438
principle of independence 436–7
principle of uniformity 437
Bacon, Francis 5, 7
Bagehot, Walter 242
banking reform proposals 242–3
Economic Studies (1880) 242
The English Constitution (1867) 242
*Lombard Street: A Description of the Money
Market* (1873) 242
Bakunin, Michail 212
balance of payments 21–2, 127, 243, 263, 341,
625–6, 752
deficit in 105, 629
influence of currency exchange rate on
578
monetary approach to 50
Bangladesh
Famine (1974) 730

Bank of England 22, 104–5, 120, 122, 149, 243,
459
personnel of 104
Banking School 63, 104, 242, 257
Baran, Paul A. 229
Baring, Francis 243
Barna, Tibor 628
Barnard, T.C. 8
Barone, Enrico 327, 337, 367–8, 370, 388–90,
410, 412
*Essay on the Coordination of the Laws of
Distribution* (1894) 389
"Il Ministro della Produzione nello Stato
Collettivista" (1908) 337, 389
Bastiat, Frédéric 171, 194, 237, 287
Les harmonies économiques 171
theory of labour 172
Baudeau, Nicolas 34
Baudrillart, Henri 181
Bauer, Bruno 211
Bavarian Academy of Sciences 206
Bayle, Pierre 10
Beard, Charles Austin 377
Beckerath, Erwin von 621
behavioural economics 640, 669, 671
social preferences 270
Belgium 213, 238
Adinkerque 237
Antwerp 237
Brussels 16, 212–13
Liège 237
Benini, Rudolfo 337
Bennington College 503
Bentham, Jeremy 95–6, 114, 187, 196, 280,
317, 662
Defence of Usury (1787) 96, 99
essays of 96
Fragment on Government (1776) 98
greatest happiness principle (GHP) 95, 99
*An Introduction to the Principles of Morals
and Legislation* (1780) 95, 98–9
Manuel d'économie politique 96–8, 99
*Projet d'un corps de loix complet à l'usage
d'un pays quelconque* 98
A Protest against Law Taxes 96–7
Surs les prix 96–7
Théorie des peines et des récompenses (1811)
96, 98
Traités de législation civile et pénale (1802)
98
Writings on Political Economy 95
Berdyaev, N.A. 400
Bergson, Abram (Abram Burk) 655, 658, 691
concept of marginal rate of income
substitution (MRIS) 656

Bergson, Henri 488
Berlyne, Daniel E. 639–40
Bernoulli, Daniel 40–42, 44–6, 174, 326, 644
  Bernoulli's hypothesis 44–5
  Exercitationes Quaedam Mathematicae (*Mathematical Exercises*) 41–2
  Hydrodynamica (1738) 42, 46
  Saint Petersburg Paradox 42–3
  "Specimen Theoriae Novae de Mensura Sortis" ("Proposal of a new theory of the measure of chance") 42
Bernoulli, Jakob 41, 43, 88
  Ars Conjectandi 40–41, 86
Bernoulli, Johann 40–41
Bernoulli, Niklaus 40
Bernoulli, Nikolaus 40–43
  Dissertatio inauguralis mathematico-juridica de usu artis conjectandi in jure 41, 86
Bertrand, Joseph 178
Besant, Annie 348
Besicovitch, Abram S. 535, 542
Beveridge, William
  Beveridge Report (1944) 628
Bharadwaj, Krishna 140, 307
Bibliothèque de l'homme public 83
Bicquilley, Charles-François de
  Théorie élémentaire du commerce 86
Biedermann-Bank 485
Bismarck, Otto von 268
Black, Duncan 84, 691
Blackstone, William 144
  Commentaries on the Laws of England (1765–69) 98
Blanqui, Jérôme-Adolphe 146
Blaug, Mark 140
Boccardo, Gerolamo 248
Böhm, Franz 508
Böhm-Bawerk, Eugen von 76, 139, 216, 292, 341, 343–5, 347, 355, 363, 410, 415, 422, 444, 464, 484, 488, 516, 536, 557, 634, 663, 726
  Kapital und Kapitalizins (1880) 341
  Positive Theory of Capital (1889) 342, 348, 422
  temporal capital theory of 342–3, 354, 421, 428, 560
  theory of interest 404
  "Zum Abschluß des Marxchen Systems" (1886) 227
Boisguilbert, Pierre le Pesant de 9–15, 76
  Dissertation de la nature des richesses, de l'argent et des tributs 99
  Dixme Royale 9

  Le Détail de la France (1695) 9
  Traité de la nature, culture, commerce et intérêt des grains 9
Bolivia 451
Bonald, Louis de 164
Bonaparte, Louis-Napoléon 164, 192, 237
Bonaparte, Napoleon 120, 121, 145
  coup d'état (1799) 114
Bonn University 211, 485
Bonnot de Condillac, Étienne, *see* Condillac, Étienne Bonnot de
Bonnot de Mably, Gabriel, *see* Mably, Gabriel Bonnot de
Boody, Elizabeth 490–91
Bordeaux Faculty of Law 24
Bordin, Arrigo 337
Bortkiewicz, Ladislaus von 139, 223, 227, 248, 344, 617
  critiques made by 419–28
  Das Gesetz der kleinen Zahlen (*The Law of Small Numbers*) (1898) 420
  theory of interest/profits 421–2
Boukharin, Nikolaï
  Economic Theory of the Leisure Class (1927) 227
Boulding, Kenneth 500, 514
Bowley, Arthur 298
Braun-Stammfest, Rudolf-Maria 485
Breit, Marek 611
Brentano, Ludwig Joseph (Lujo) 272–3, 277, 395, 514
Bretton Woods Conference (1944) 470, 481–2, 530, 653
Brewer, A. 75
British Association 265
  Section F 263, 315
British Economic Association (BEA) 367
Brockhaus and Efron Encyclopedic Dictionary 400–401
Brown, Cary 660
Brown, Henry Phelps 596
Brown University 320, 685
Brownian motion 438
  development of 438
Bryan, William Jennings 449
Brydges, James 19
Buchanan, James M. 682–4
  The Calculus of Consent (1962) 683
  The Collected Works of James M. Buchanan 683
Buddhism 1
The Budget 153
Buffon, Georges-Louis Leclerc de 43–4
  "Essai d'arithmétique morale" 43

Bulgakov, S.N. 400
Bulgaria 443
Bullion Controversy 127
Bund der Kommunisten (the Communist
    League) 213
Burke, Edmund 470
    Thoughts and Details on Scarcity (1795) 98
Burns, Arthur F. 446
Bush, George W. 753
business cycle theory 234–5, 358, 406, 408–9,
    440, 443–4, 447, 452, 455, 536, 558, 569,
    583, 599, 686, 744
    analysis 400–401, 444
    endogenous 441
    equilibrium approach to 515–16
    macroeconomic model of 599
    Mises–Wicksell theory of 559
    monetary theory of 646
    phases of 446
    political 568
Byzantine Empire 396

Calvinism 40
Cambridge–Cambridge controversy 666, 742
Cambridge University 107, 295, 351, 359, 469,
    475, 532, 578, 602, 638, 741
    Christ's College 625
    Churchill College 691
    Department of Applied Economics 626
    Faculty of Economics and Politics 281
    King's College 468, 470, 534, 587, 593, 613,
        628
    Magdalene College 587
    Newnham College 295, 468
    St John's College 311
    Trinity College 280, 458, 536–7, 587, 728
cameralism 205, 291
    German 55
Canada 18
    Kingston 721
    Montreal 568
Canard, Nicolas-François
    Principes d'économie politique 86
Cannan, Edwin 60, 534
Cantillon, Richard 16–17, 19, 22–3, 73, 81
    analysis of monetary economy 21–2
        Cantillon Effect 22
    Essai sur la nature du commerce en général 20
    landed estate economic model of 20
        focus on entrepreneurs 20–21
capital/capital theory 33, 61–2, 64, 69, 75, 77,
    97, 116, 129–30, 135, 151, 213, 221, 253,
    329, 341–2, 350, 354, 356, 382, 416, 419,
    421, 484, 498, 500, 509, 548, 560, 572, 592,
    603–5, 617, 623, 664, 677, 714–15, 721–2

accumulation of 62, 67, 76, 126, 132, 137–8,
    159, 223–4, 229, 480, 750
circulating 33–4, 252
coefficient 577
constant 222
conversion of revenue to 112
demand 345
financial 401
fixed 33, 152, 423–5, 433
flows 678
formation of 160, 326
goods 160, 420, 441, 444, 516, 606
    heterogeneous 160, 742
human 44, 160, 168, 549, 650
inflows 21
invested 238
marginal efficiency of 416
marginal productivity of 357, 422
markets 238, 611, 746
money 33
national 115
neoclassical 359, 666
non-wage 152
original 227
physical 601
private ownership of 274
real 162, 479
replacement cost of 675, 678
returns on 30, 161, 479
services 354
Solow model of 343
supply of 345, 512
transfers 105
variable 222, 427
capital asset pricing model (CAPM) 679
capitalism 6, 9, 125, 130, 145, 193, 226, 228–9,
    320–21, 375, 391, 394, 396, 399, 402, 440,
    465–6, 485, 487–8, 490, 493, 544, 559, 570,
    573, 611, 632, 663
    agrarian 392, 396
    anarcho- 464
    development 489, 493–4
    entrepreneurial 493
    evolution of 687–8, 750
    liberal 65
    production relations 212, 221
Caritat de Condorcet, Marie-Jean-Antoine-
    Nicolas, *see* Condorcet, Marie-Jean-
    Antoine-Nicolas Caritat de
Carleton College 320
Carlyle, Thomas 144, 187
Carnegie Foundation 528
Carnegie Mellon University (CMU) 673, 718
    Graduate School of Industrial
        Administration (GSIA) 669

School of Urban and Public Affairs 669
Cassel, Gustav 342, 344, 349, 351, 357, 404–9, 506, 527, 603, 707
  business cycle theory of 406–7
  In the Service of Reason (1940–41) 405
  The Nature and Necessity of Interest (1903) 404
  purchasing power parity (PPP) theory 408
  Sozialökonomie (1918) 407, 408
  Theory of Social Economy (1918) 404, 407, 634
  The World's Monetary Problems (1921) 405
Catholicism 196–7
  Immaculate Conception 349
  Irish 19
  Spanish 40
Central Bureau of Statistics (CBS) 599
Central School of Planning and Statistics 569
Centre National de la Recherche Scientifique (CNRS) 642, 698
Chamberlin, Edward Hastings 552–4, 570, 575, 744
  The Theory of Monopolistic Competition (1933) 552–5, 748
Chamfort, Sébastien-Roch de 114
Chamillart, Michel 9
Champernowne, David Gawen 338, 626
Chandos, Duke of 19
Chapman, Sydney 280
Charasoff, Georg von 617
Charles II, King 5
Cherbuliez, Antoine-Elisée 200
Chicago School of Economics 498, 554, 649, 659
Child, Josiah 73
Chile 451, 649
China, People's Republic of 1, 396, 632, 665
China, Republic of 617
Chipman, John 337
choice theory
  development of 331
Christaller, Walter 162
Christian-Social Party 268
Christianity 40, 66, 78, 281, 506, 514
  Bible 347
    New Testament 7
  Lutheran 347
Churchill, Winston 596
Clark, E.A. 268
Clark, Gregory 504
Clark, John Bates 322, 342, 351, 422, 444, 594
  Christianity and Modern Economics (1887) 320
  The Control of Trusts (1901) 321

The Distribution of Wealth. A Theory of Wages, Interest and Profits (1899) 320–21
The Essentials of Economic Theory (1907) 321
The Philosophy of Wealth (1886) 320
Clavière, Étienne 114
Clearing Union 481–2
Clinton, Bill 745
closed economy 721–2
  models of 157–8
Club of German Communists 203
Coase, Ronald Harry 633
  Coase theorem 631–2
  "How should economists choose?" (1982) 632
  "The lighthouse in economics" (1974) 632
  "The nature of the firm" (1937) 631
  "The problem of social cost" (1960) 631
Cobb, Charles 352
Cobden, Richard 171
Cohn, Gustav 277
Cole, G.D.H.
  Guild Socialism 503
Collège de France 114
Collège de Navarre 83
College of Juilly 24
College of Surgery of Saint-Côme 28
Colm, Gerhard 515, 524
Colombia 451
Columbia University 321–2, 446, 558, 578, 690, 693, 714
commodities 7, 11–12, 20, 25–6, 36, 55, 62–3, 80–81, 102, 110–12, 121, 123, 125, 129–37, 148, 151, 175–6, 194, 215–24, 238, 247, 249–53, 256–7, 264, 281, 289, 302–3, 305, 312, 407, 412–13, 416, 423, 426–7, 431–2, 449–50, 465, 504, 510, 531, 538–9, 543–5, 593, 617, 655, 694, 706–7, 730
  composite 152, 543
  connected 372
  contradictions of 218–19
  exchange values of 215
  market 21, 469, 471
  prices of 52, 60–61, 69, 77, 116, 126, 128, 138, 171, 179, 190, 292, 423–5, 546–9, 578, 629, 643
    equilibrium 251
  rate of interest 540–42
  supply and demand
    curves 537
    functions for 68
  trading 392–3
Commons, John Roger 168

communism 197, 745
  Marxian 257
Communistisches Korrespondenz-Kommittee
    (Communist Correspondence Committee)
    213
competitive price theory 499–500
Comte, Charles 96, 164, 171, 192–3
Condillac, Étienne Bonnot de 28, 73
  *Le commerce et le gouvernement considérés
      relativement l'un à l'autre* (1776) 81, 98
  Traité des sensations (1754) 78
Condorcet, Marie-Jean-Antoine-Nicolas
    Caritat de 37, 74, 77, 83–92, 108, 729
  "Condorcet effect" 91–2
  Éléments du calcul des probabilités 86
  *Esquisse d'un tableau historique des progrès
      de l'esprit humain* (1795) 84
  *Essai sur l'application de l'analyse à la
      probabilité des décisions rendues à la
      pluralité des voix* (1785) 83, 86, 89, 91
  *Essai sur la constitution et les fonctions des
      assemblées provinciales* (1788) 83
  *Lettres d'un bourgeois de New Haven à
      un citoyen de Virginie, sur l'utilité
      de partager le pouvoir legislatif entre
      plusieurs corps* (1788) 83
  jury theorem 90–91
  Réflexions sur le commerce des blés (1776) 83
  Sur la forme des élections (1789) 83
  *Tableau historique des progrès de l'esprit
      humain* 84
  theory of taxation 87–9
  Vie de Voltaire (1789) 83
  Vie de M. Turgot (1786) 74, 83
Congrès international de l'impôt (International
    Congress on Taxes) (1860) 246, 254
Conrad, Johannes 274
Conseil des Cinq-Cents
  Legislative Committee 114
Conservatoire des Arts et Métiers 114
Constant, Benjamin 115
constitutional economics 682–4
consumer theory 326–7, 662, 695
  pure theory in 337
Convention Nationale 83
Cooper Union Forum 322
cooperative equilibrium 177
cooperatives 246–7
  credit 203
Coquelin, Charles 240–41
Cornell University 374, 377, 449
cost theory 499–501, 621
  agency 292
  alternative/opportunity 498
  production 161

Cournot, Antoine-Augustin 174–6, 178–9, 181,
    190, 290, 434, 553, 622
  Essai sur les fondements de nos connaissances
      (1851) 174–5
  *Exposition de la théorie des chances et des
      probabilités* (1843) 174
  Principes de la théorie des richesses (1863)
      174
  *Recherches sur les principes mathématiques
      de la théorie des richesses* (1838) 174–5,
      178, 200, 248
  theory of consumption 431, 434
  theory of "Loi du debit" 176–7
  *Traité de l'enchaînement des idées
      fondamentales dans les sciences et dans
      l'histoire* (1861) 174–5
  *Traité élémentaire de la théorie des fonctions
      et du calcul infinitesimal* (1841) 174
Cowles Commission for Research in
    Economics 447, 520, 524–5, 619, 676, 691,
    698, 706, 736
Cowles Foundation for Economic Research
    671
Cramer, Gabriel 43–4
credit 204, 257–8, 357, 376, 401, 458, 464–5
  bank 22
  bubble 411
  commercial 459
  creation of 506
  economy 204
  paper 104
  public 51
  rationing 105
  risks 104
  systems of 97
Credit School 104
crises 16–17, 117, 149, 154, 204, 242, 258–9,
    360, 379, 399–400, 440, 443–4, 447,
    458–60, 493, 514, 568, 638, 679, 688, 746,
    752
  agricultural 13–14
  commercial 235, 262, 459
  credit 243
  sales 208
  theories of 224
Crispi, Francesco 367
Cromwell, Oliver 5
Currency School 149, 154
Czech Republic 484

Dahlberg, A.O. 672
Daire, Eugène 74
D'Alessandro, S. 131
Darwin, Charles 263, 273, 347
Darwin, George 263

Dauphin, Jeanne-Catherine 28
Davidson, David 347, 350, 357
Debreu, Gérard 510, 581, 603, 691–3, 698–9, 702–4
  Arrow–Debreu model of general equilibrium 408, 510, 690, 693–5, 700–701, 703
  Theory of Value (1959) 698, 700–701
debt 411–12, 450, 459, 473, 480, 541, 570, 666, 686–8
  debt–deflation relationship 687
  government 18
  interest on 26
  national 122–3, 573
  private 485, 558, 668
  public 26, 51, 84, 242, 255, 258, 345, 380, 579, 676
deflation 350, 356, 360, 405, 411–12, 414, 460, 472–3, 475, 527, 570, 629
  cumulative 358
  debt–deflation relationship 687
  global 460
Delbrück, Rudolf 273
demand and supply 96, 116–17, 123, 190, 250
  Hicksian theory of 707
  King–Davenant law 266, 313
  partial equilibrium analysis of 312
  Say's Law 117, 133, 145, 234, 401, 405, 407, 569, 666, 706, 714
    opposition to 208, 610
  supply curve 304–5, 312
demand economy 568–9
demand function
  inverse 177–8
Dempsey, Bernard 486
Denmark
  Copenhagen 348
De Viti de Marco, Antonio 368, 379–80
  I primi principî dell'economia finanziaria (1928) 380
  Il carattere teorico dell'economia finanziaria (1888) 379
  Principî di economia finanziaria (1934) 380
  use of marginal analysis 380
De Vivo, Giancarlo 140
De Witt, Jan 86
Der Österreichische Volkswirt (*The Austrian Economist*) 503
Der Volkswirt 485
Desmarets, Nicolas 9
Deutsch-Französische Jahrbücher 212
The Dial 377
Diamond, Peter 745
Diderot, Denis 28, 83

Encyclopédie ou dictionnaire raisonné des sciences, des arts et des métiers 28, 73, 83
Dilthey, Wilhelm 275
Director, Aaron 658
Dissenting Academy 107
distribution theory 321
  unit costs 327
Divisia, François 642
Dixit, Avinash K. 552, 741, 744
  Dixit–Stiglitz partial equilibrium model of monopolistic competition 744–5, 748
Dmitriev, Vladimir Karpovich 139, 227, 423, 431–2, 617
  Economic Essays. First Series: Attempt at an Organic Synthesis of the Labour Theory of Value and the Theory of Marginal Utility 431–3
  theory of profit and production 432–4
Dobb, Maurice H. 139, 535–6, 638
Dodgson, Charles Lutwidge (Lewis Carroll) 84
Domar, Evsey 714
Domat, Jean 10–11
Dornbusch, Rüdiger 748
Douglas, Paul 352, 685
Drysdale, George
  Elements of Social Science (1878) 347
Du Tot, Nicolas 16
Duclos, Charles Pinot 28
Duke University 290
Dumont, Étienne 96–8
Dunoyer de Segonzac, Barthélemy-Charles 96, 115, 164–5, 171, 239
duopoly 175–9, 553, 614
  supply 622
Dupont, Pierre-Samuel 27, 34, 37, 74–5
  Physiocratie, ou constitution naturelle du gouvernement le plus avantageux au genre humain 35
Dupuit, Jules 181–2
  analysis of utility 181–3
Dussard, Hippolyte 74
Dutch Academy of Science 273

East India Company 104
Easterlin, Richard 640
Eatwell, John 140
Eccles, Marriner 634
Eckhardt, Julius 274
École de Droit 164
École de Lausanne 260
École des Mines 642
École des Ponts 181
École Normale 174, 245
École Polytechnique 642

École royale des Ponts et Chaussées 101
Econometrica 518
Econometrics Society 411, 486, 519, 524–5,
    605, 676, 698, 712, 725
  Constitution of 519
  establishment of (1930) 518
  First World Congress of (1965) 519
Economic Journal 315, 363–4, 455, 534, 600,
    605, 648
Edgeworth, Francis Ysidro 248, 263–4, 298,
    312–13, 315, 317–19, 330, 337, 367, 382,
    389, 410, 412, 421, 462, 484, 534, 548, 575,
    699, 702
  "Edgeworth box" 315
  *Mathematical Psychics: An Essay on the
    Application of Mathematics to the
    Moral Sciences* 265, 298, 315, 317
  *Metretike: or the Method of Measuring
    Probability and Utility* (1887) 315
  New and Old Methods of Ethics (1877)
    317
  trading theory of 315–18
Edgeworth, Maria 140, 178–9
Edinburgh Encyclopedia 144–5
Edinburgh Review 59, 109, 144
Egypt
  Cairo 484
Elmer, Olaf 691
Ely, Richard T.
  Outlines of Economics (1893) 670
Empson, William 107
*Encyclopédie des Sciences Mathématiques
    Pures et Appliqués* 330
Encyclopédie méthodique 86
Engel, Ernst 274
Engels, Friedrich 204, 214–15, 226, 426
  The Communist Manifesto 213
  Die deutsche Ideologie (*The German
    Ideology*) (1845–6) 212
  Die Lage der arbeitenden Klasse in England
    (1845) 204
  "Umrisse zu einer Kritik der
    Nationalökonomie" ("Outlines of a
    Critique of Political Economy") 212
Engländer, Oskar 162
Enlightenment 36
  French 10, 83
entrepreneurship 20–21, 29–30, 203, 292, 365,
    464, 466, 499, 648
Éphémérides du citoyen 35
États Généraux du Royaume 83
Eucken, Walter 506–8, 621
  Die Grundlagen der Nationalökonomie (1940)
    507
  "Kredit und Konjunktur" (1929) 506

*Kritische Betrachtungen zum deutschen
    Geldproblem* (1923) 506
  "Staatliche Strukturwandlungen und die
    Krise des Kapitalismus" 506
Euler, Leonhard 42
  Euler's theorem 311
European Central Bank 415, 653
European Monetary Union (EMU) 521, 653,
    723
European Union (EU) 629
exchange rates 104–5, 217, 451, 459–60, 462,
    471, 473, 481, 578, 625–6, 653
  determination 408
  fixing of 405, 475
  purchasing power theory of 127
  variations 443

Faccarello, Gilbert 9, 11, 14, 36–7, 46, 74–5,
    77, 84, 87–8, 136, 138, 216, 220, 227
Faculty of Pont-à-Mousson 28
Fascism 379, 503, 523, 534
Faulkner, William 3
Faurie, François 171
Fechner, Gustav 289
Feldman, G.A. 229
Ferraris, Galileo 388
Ferri, Enrico 374
Ferry, Jules 247
Fireman, P. 227
First World War (1914–18) 242, 272, 277, 350,
    368, 395, 404–5, 411, 446, 450, 452, 458–9,
    469, 481, 489, 503, 506, 514, 530, 534
  Paris Peace Conference (1919) 468
  Treaty of Versailles (1919) 278, 377, 405,
    469, 472
Fisher, Irving 161, 179, 251, 342, 344, 380,
    410–11, 413, 415–16, 458, 518, 542, 642,
    676, 687, 702, 710, 734
  Appreciation and Interest 412–13
  Boom and Depressions (1932) 411
  Constructive Income Taxation (1942) 412
  Elementary Principles of Economics (1911)
    411
  general equilibrium system of 412
  *How to Live. Rules for Healthful Living
    Based on Modern Science* (1915) 411
  Introduction to Economic Science (1910) 411
  The Making of Index Numbers (1922) 415
  *Mathematical Investigations in the Theory of
    Value and Prices* (1892) 410, 412
  The Nature of Capital and Income (1906) 411
  The Purchasing Power of Money (1911) 411,
    413–14
  The Rate of Interest (1907) 411
  separation theorem 415

theory of investment 416–17
time preference theory 342–3, 650
use of quantity theory 413–15
Fisk, Eugene Lyman
*How to Live. Rules for Healthful Living
Based on Modern Science* (1915) 411
Flux, Alfred 280, 311
Foerster, Norman
concept of "provincialism of time" 2
Fontenelle, Bernard Le Bovier de 9
Forbonnais, François Véron de 33, 35–6
Observations sur l'esprit des loix (1753) 27
Ford Foundation 694
Fossati, Eraldo 337
Foxwell, Herbert 534
France 12, 18, 25–7, 30, 54, 57, 59, 83, 107–8,
212, 247–8, 297, 443, 464, 468, 639, 698
Anjou 48
Assemblée Constituante 171
Assemblée Législative 171
Bordeaux 24
Calais 698
Dijon 436
February Revolution (1848) 171–2, 194, 213,
237
government of
debt 18
July Revolution (1830) 164
Lille 443
Lyon 114, 174
Méré 28
National Assembly 96
Normandy 9
Paris 9, 20, 28, 42, 48, 73, 101, 114, 164, 167,
171, 174, 181, 187, 192, 212–13, 234,
237, 247, 323, 348, 514, 518–19, 639,
642, 698
Paris Commune 237
Rennes 436
Revolution (1789–99) 83–4, 96, 101, 114,
117
Royal Bank 17–18
Sorbonne 81, 698
Strasbourg 348, 392
Versailles 28, 31, 37
Franco-Prussian War (1870–71) 242, 274
Frankfurter Zeitung 523
free market 363, 464
failure of 514
influence of 273
Friedman, Milton 17, 360, 413, 487, 632–3,
648, 652–3, 659, 678, 734
Capitalism and Freedom (1962) 648
focus on quantity theory 650–51
Free to Choose 653

*Income from Independent Professional
Practitioners* (1954) 649
*A Monetary History of the United States,
1867–1960* 447, 649
The Study of Consumer Purchases 649
A Theory of the Consumption Function
649–50
transfer of notions 360
variant of quantity theory 629
Frisch, Ragnar Anton Kittil 408, 518–19, 568,
572, 599–600, 698
influence in
econometrics 519
production theory 520–21
New Methods of Measuring Marginal Utility
(1932) 519
Statistical Confluence Analysis (1934) 519–20
Frisi, Paolo
Meditazioni sulla Economia Politica 86
Frobenius, Ferdinand Georg 410
Fromm, Erich
concept of alienation 639
Fujita, Masahisa
The Spatial Economy (1999) 751
full-employment equilibrium 477–9
long run 476, 480
Fundamental Law of Psychophysics 289

Gage, Joseph 20
Galbraith, J.K. 638–9
Gale, David 719
Gallani, Ferdinando
Dialogues sur le commerce des blés (1770)
74
game theory 525, 581–2, 584
development of 718–19
non-cooperative 729
Garegnani, Pierangelo 140
Garnier, Joseph 246
Gaussian distribution 437–8
Gdansk University Engineering College 568
general equilibrium (GE) 37, 79, 103, 162,
245, 247, 250, 252–3, 258, 266, 290, 296,
300–303, 308, 324–6, 328, 332, 337, 342,
345, 347, 355, 363, 372, 388, 408–9, 412,
510, 643, 656, 691, 707, 713, 725, 749–50
analysis 406, 735–6
Walrasian 406, 408
Arrow–Debreu model 408, 510, 690, 693–5,
700–701, 703
neoclassical 618
use of monopoly in 328
von Neumann model of 581, 583–4
Walras–Cassel model 511
Genocchi, Angelo 388

George, Henry
  Progress and Poverty (1879) 311, 670
Georgescu-Roegen, Nicolas 200, 486
German Bureau of Statistics
  International Division 514
German Democratic Party 395
German Historical Schools 167, 169, 200,
  203–5, 209, 275–7, 283, 289, 292, 320
German Institute for Business Cycle Research
  founding of (1925) 514–15
German Use Value School 209
German Workers' Association 213
Germany 54, 167, 226, 269, 272, 377, 400, 404,
  443, 469, 472, 514, 518, 564, 653
  Bad Harzburg 275
  Berlin 206, 211, 268, 272, 274–5, 277, 348,
    391–2, 410, 484, 515, 523, 616
  Bonn 211, 506
  Canarienhausen 157
  Cologne 196–7, 213, 621
  Düren 196
  Düsseldorf 440
  Erlangen 268
  Frankfurt 40, 158, 515, 634
  Freiburg 268
  Göttingen 206
  Hamburg 157, 268
  Hanover 206
  Heidelberg 320, 341, 393
  Jena 203, 341, 348, 506
  Köngstein im Taunus 634
  Leipzig 204, 341, 419
  Marburg 203
  Ministry of Education 272
  Munich 391, 616, 619
  National Assembly 158
  Naumburg 203
  Nuremberg 268
  Prussia 213, 272, 277, 329
    Upper House 275
  Reichstag 392, 523
  Reutlingen 167
  Silesia 621
  Stuttgart 514
  "Third Reich" (1933–45) 359, 464, 504,
    506–7, 515, 519, 524, 563, 634, 638, 723
    Schutzstaffel (SS) 621
  Tübingen 406, 440
  Wolfenbüttel 514
Gini Index 731
Giolitti, Giovanni 367
Giornale degli Economisti 323–4, 336, 367, 379,
  388–9
Giornale degli Economisti e rivista di statistica
  461

globalization 504, 664, 678
  opposition to 746
The Globe 150
Godolphin, Lord 16
Goethe University, Frankfurt 515
gold standard (GS) 16, 104, 127, 341, 405, 458,
  460, 465, 469, 471, 723
  adoption of 122, 449
  aims of 450
  departure of 405, 473
  opposition to 473
  suspension of 104, 350
Goldbach, Christian 42
Goldschmidt, Levin 392
Gómez Betancourt, Rebeca 449–50
Goodwin, Richard M. 229, 486, 672
  theory of unilateral coupling 672
Google, Inc.
  Google Scholar 557
Göring, Hermann 638
Gossen, Hermann Heinrich 196–7, 200, 209,
  255, 283, 290, 434
  *Entwickelung der Gesetze des menschlichen
    Verkehrs, und der daraus fließenden
    Regeln für menschliches Handeln* (1854)
    196–200
  Plan for the Nationalization of Land 200
Gothenburg School of Business Economics
  509
Gournay, Jacques-Claude-Marie Vincent
  de, *see* Vincent, Jacques-Claude-Marie
  (Marquis of Gournay)
Gramsci, Antonio 534
Granger, Gilles-Gaston 84, 89
Graslin, Jean-Joseph-Louis 35, 74
Graunt, John 86
Great Depression 404, 455, 524, 530–31, 658,
  672, 676, 678, 687, 723, 734, 753
  UK departure from gold standard 405,
    473
  Wall Street Crash (1929) 411
Great Recession (2007–9) 506, 508, 565, 579,
  688, 752–3
Grimm, Friedrich Melchior 27, 36
Griziotti, Benvenuto 380
Groenewegen, Peter 75
gross domestic product (GDP) 572, 675, 687,
  730
Grossmann, Henrik
  cycle and crises theories of 229
Großmann-Doerth, Hans 508
growth theory 552, 741
  Harrod–Domar 383, 408, 516, 601
  neoclassical 343, 677, 679, 716, 741–2
  Ramsey–Cass–Koopmans model 588

rate
  natural 576
  warranted 576
Solow–Swan one-good model 742
Grundriss der Sozialökonomik (Social Economics) 365, 394–5
Guérineau de Saint-Péravy, Jean-Nicolas 34, 37
Guilbaud, Georges-Théodule 84
Gurley, Jack 685

Haberler, Gottfried 464, 552, 621
Habsburg Empire 484
  Bukowina 485
  Galicia
    Lemberg 464
Hadley, Arthur Twining 410
Hahn, Frank 625, 694, 741
Halévy, Élie 98
Hamilton, William 59
Hammarskjöld, Dag 509
Hammond, Anthony 19
Hanau, Arthur
  cobweb-dynamics 599
Handelshochschulen (Merchants Superior Schools) 268
Handwörterbuch der Staatswissenschaften 365
Hansen, Alvin 235, 552, 658, 685
Haq, Mahbub ul 729–30
Hardy, G.H.
  Pure Mathematics (1908) 587
Harms, Bernhard 515
Harrod, Roy Forbes 537, 571, 575, 626, 714
  Foundations of Inductive Logic (1956) 575
  theory of
    dynamics 576–7
    imperfect competition 575–6
  Towards a Dynamic Economics (1948) 593
  The Trade Cycle (1936) 575
Hartlib, Samuel 7
Harvard University 359, 486, 489, 617–18, 634, 639, 658, 676, 685, 691, 728
  Department of Economics 552, 660
  Graduate School 655
Harvey, W.H.
  Coin's Financial School (1894) 449
Hawkins, David 672
Hawtrey, Ralph George 458–9
  The Art of Central Banking (1932) 243, 458, 460
  Capital and Employment (1937) 458
  A Century of Bank Rate (1938) 458
  Gold Standard in Theory and Practice (1927) 458

Right Policy: the Place of Value Judgments in Politics 458
Thoughts and Things 458
Hayek, Friedrich August von 104, 185, 190, 201, 284, 343, 363, 464, 475, 500, 507, 528, 532, 539, 557–62, 565, 606, 621, 631, 639
  Carl Menger Gesammelte Werke 284
  Collectivist Economic Planning (1935) 561
  The Constitution of Liberty (1960) 564
  The Counter-Revolution of Science (1952) 564
  criticisms of welfare economics 663
  "Economics and knowledge" (1937) 563
  The Fatal Conceit (1988) 565
  Law, Legislation and Liberty (1979) 565
  Monetary Theory and the Trade Cycle 515–16
  Prices and Production (1931) 536, 559–60, 596
  The Pure Theory of Capital (1941) 561
  The Road to Serfdom 503, 564
    Central Planning Bureau 563
  The Sensory Order (1952) 557
  "Trend of economic thinking" (1933) 562–3
  "The use of knowledge in society" (1945) 563
Hearn, W.E.
  Plutology (1864) 263
Hebb, Donald O. 639–40
Hebrew University of Jerusalem 706
Hecht, Jacqueline 9
Heckscher, Eli 350
Hegel, Georg Wilhelm Friedrich 212, 217–19, 298, 514
  Philosophy of Right 220
  Science of Logic 220
Helferich, J.A.R. 273
Helpman, Elhanan
  Market Structure and Foreign Trade (1985) 750
Helvétius, Claude-Adrien 28
Henderson, Hubert 613
  Can Lloyd George Do It? (1929) 469, 474
Herbert, Lady Mary 19–20
Herkner, Heinrich 277–8
Hermann, Friedrich Benedict Wilhelm 201, 209, 321
Herwegh, Georg 212
Hewins, W.A.S. 382
Hicks, John Richard 139, 263, 327, 337, 456, 519, 570, 602, 606–7, 623, 626, 678–9, 712
  Capital and Growth 605, 606
  Capital and Time. A Neo-Austrian Approach (1973) 343, 516, 605, 606

*A Contribution to the Theory of the Trade
    Cycle* (1950) 604
Critical Essays in Monetary Theory (1967)
    607
influence in macroeconomics 605
IS–LM, model of 524, 605, 721–2
A Market Theory of Money (1989) 607
theory of capital 602–4
The Theory of Wages (1932) 602–3
Value and Capital (1939) 344, 511, 603–4,
    606, 642, 690–91, 712
Hildebrand, Adolf von 203
Hildebrand, Bruno 203–4, 206, 363
*Die Nationalökonomie der Gegenwart und
    Zukunft* (*The Economics of the Present
    and the Future*) (1844) 203
"Umrisse zu einer Kritik der
    Nationalökonomie" 204–5
Hilferding, Rudolf 227, 229, 484, 688
Das Finanzkapital (1910) 227
Hirschman, Albert O. 25
Hitler, Adolf 507
Hitotsubashi University 284
Hobbes, Thomas 5
Hobson, John Atkinson 382
The Economics of Distribution (1900) 383–4
The Physiology of Industry (1889) 382–3
The Problem of the Unemployed (1896) 383
Hollander, Jacob H. 153
Hollander, Samuel 68, 118, 139–40
Hotelling, Harold
Hotelling model 133
Howard, Michael 226
Howlett, John
*Examination of Dr. Price's Essay on
    Population* (1781) 98
Hull, C.H. 7
humanism 66
civic 144
Humboldt University, Berlin 268
Hume, David 16, 48, 54, 58, 73, 77, 81, 105,
    564
Economic Writings (1955) 50
*An Enquiry Concerning Human
    Understanding* (1748) 48
*An Enquiry Concerning the Principles of
    Morals* (1751) 48
Essays Moral, Political and Literary 48–51
The History of England (1754–62) 48
Political Discourses (1752) 48
Political Essays (1751) 98
price-specie-flow theory of 148
A Treatise of Human Nature (1739–40) 48,
    52
Hungarian Radical Party 503

Hungary
    Budapest 503, 582, 628, 638
Hurwicz, Leonid 691
Huygens, Christiaan
    "De ratiociniis in ludo aleæ" 41
hydrodynamics 42

Ibsen, Henrik 347
Imperial Academy of Sciences 42
imperialism 206, 229, 331, 383, 489, 739, 750
income distribution 329, 350, 419
    functions 329–30
    Keynesian theory of 628
    neoclassical theory of 351–2
    relationship with capital accumulation 229
Independent Socialist Youth Union 610
index theory
    development of 519
India 242, 263, 396
    Calcutta 728
    Santiniketan 728
Indian Statistical Institute 737
Industrial Revolution 607
industrialism 146, 168, 605
inflation 17, 21–2, 26, 97, 120, 350, 356, 473, 679
    cost 629
    Phelps–Friedman accelerationist hypothesis
        512
    price 105
    theories of 105, 349
Innocent XI, Pope 81
input–output analysis 229, 433, 616–19
Institut Universitaire des Hautes Études
        Internationales 464
Institute for the Study of Business Cycle
        Research 568
Institute of Economics
    establishment of (1932) 518
Institute of World Affairs 515
institutionalism 168, 446, 630
    American 375, 498
insurance 46, 83, 114, 174, 196, 694, 742–3, 748
    marine 41, 45, 86–7
    markets 498
    social 268
interest 116, 341, 350, 354, 412–13, 421, 428,
    527
    rates of 26, 63, 358–9, 413, 416, 458–9, 479,
        500, 569–70
    determinants of 474–5
    equilibrium 344, 355
    gaps 350
    market 357
    monetary 161
    money 539

natural 511
nominal 414
real 343, 570
theories of 404
International Economic Association
Corfu Meeting (1958) 604
Paris Meeting (1950) 487
International Encyclopaedia of the Social Sciences 676
International Labour Office 568
International Monetary Conference for the Prolongation of the Latin Union (1884) 257
International Monetary Fund (IMF) 470, 482, 745–6
International Statistical Institute 419
International Workingmen's Association (First International) 194, 215
investment 30, 62, 64, 76, 123, 133, 136–7, 160, 183, 349, 354, 357–8, 360, 376, 382–3, 400–401, 408, 411, 413–17, 441, 455, 471, 475–80, 500, 506, 512, 516, 527, 531, 540, 561, 568–71, 576–7, 599, 618, 628–9, 648, 666, 675, 679, 686, 688, 691, 708, 714–16, 721, 734, 739
foreign 450
net 476, 572, 651, 678, 714
private 405, 573
public 181–2, 663, 696
rate of return 417
theories of 16
Ireland, Republic of 5–6, 8, 150
County Kerry
Ballyheigue 19
Portarlington 122
Islam 1
Isnard, Achilles-Nicolas 101, 617
Cathéchisme social (1784) 103
Traité des richesses (1781) 101–3
Israel 706
Italy 41, 268, 323, 329, 336–7, 363, 369, 379, 518, 523, 622, 712, 714, 721
Céligny 323
Florence 323, 410
Free State of Fiume 323
Genoa 323, 514
Italian Communist Party (PCd'I) 534
Naples 367, 388
Pisa 144
Rome 388, 410
Second War of Independence (1859) 363
Turin 388, 534
Tuscany 144–5
Venice 16
Izumo, Masashi 138

Jackson, Andrew 167
Jacobites 19, 84
Jaffé, Edgar 394
Jaffé, William 253
Jahrbücher für Nationalökonomie und Statistik 203
Jansenism 9–10
social theory 12
Japan 1, 138, 725, 752
Kyoto 712
Tokyo 284, 712
Jenkin, Fleeming 263
Jenks, Jeremiah 449
Jesuits 83
Jesus Christ 7
Jevons, William Stanley 138, 182, 198, 258, 262, 264, 266, 281, 283, 287, 312–13, 326, 348, 363, 423, 435, 519, 602, 726
The Coal Question (1865) 262
Elementary Lessons in Logic (1870) 262
exchange model 264–5
Investigations in Currency and Finance (1884) 262
law of indifference 264–5
Methods of Social Reform 262
Money and the Mechanism of Exchange (1875) 262
"Notice of a general mathematical theory of political economy" 263
A Primer on Political Economy (1878) 262
The Principles of Science (1874) 262
A Serious Fall in the Value of Gold (1863) 262
The State in Relation to Labour (1882) 262
theory of partial equilibrium 290, 454
Theory of Political Economy (1879) 182, 196, 263, 265, 311, 412
Johansson, Alf 509
Johns Hopkins Bologna Center of Advanced International Studies 721
Johns Hopkins University 321, 374, 578, 655
Johnson, Lyndon B. 687
Johnson, Samuel
Dictionary 59–60
Jones-Loyd, Samuel (Lord Overstone) 149
Journal d'agriculture, du commerce et des finances 35
Journal d'instruction sociale 83–4
Journal des économistes 171, 181, 237, 246, 256
Journal of Economic Literature 614
Journal of Economic Theory 728
Journal of Law and Economics 632
Journal of Political Economy 374, 721
Jovellanos, Gaspar Melchor de 96

Judaism 211, 385, 464, 503, 514, 525, 578, 613–14, 616, 634, 648, 655
  anti-Semitism 268, 368
  Sephardic 120
Juglar, Clément 234, 444
  Juglar cycle 234–5

Kahn, Richard Ferdinand 475–6, 535, 568, 605, 613–14, 625
  lectures of 614
  "The relation of home investment to unemployment" 625
Kahneman, Daniel 640
Kakutani fixed point theorem 719
Kaldor, Nicholas 343, 455–6, 500, 572, 594, 625–6, 628–30, 639, 741
  Full Employment in a Free Society 628
  global development model of 629
  growth models of 576–7, 611
Kalecki, Michał 568, 599
  cycles and growth models of 572–3, 610–11
  An Essay in the Theory of the Business Cycle 568
  theory of
    employment 569
    pure imperfect competition 570–71
Kant, Immanuel 121, 374, 402, 514–15
  theory of supreme value 402
Kantarovich, Leonid 581
Kardex Rand 411
Kaufmann, Felix 464
Kautsky, Karl 214
Kemmerer, Edwin Walter 449–50
  focus on QTM and GS 449–51
Kennedy, John F. 675, 677, 687
Kenya 742
  government of 743
Keynes, John Maynard 2, 26, 108, 112, 124, 138, 161, 189, 208–9, 245, 263, 281, 293, 384, 405, 413, 450, 452, 458, 468–73, 477–8, 514, 523, 531–2, 534–6, 540–41, 559, 562, 568–9, 571, 575, 578, 588, 597–8, 600, 613, 619, 625–6, 628, 638, 648, 651, 658–9, 677, 685, 726, 744, 748
  Can Lloyd George Do It? (1929) 469, 474
  concept of involuntary unemployment 407, 455, 650, 709–10, 726
  concept of liquidity 479, 541–2
  liquidity trap 752
  The Economic Consequences of Mr Churchill (1925) 473
  The Economic Consequences of the Peace (1920) 377, 469, 472
  Economic Possibilities for our Grandchildren 559

The End of Laissez Faire (1926) 559
  focus on QTM 472–4
  The General Theory of Money, Interest and Employment (1936) 360, 383, 416, 455–6, 458, 469, 471, 474, 476–82, 509, 531, 535, 540, 560, 568, 570, 572, 575, 579, 588, 593, 605, 607, 613–14, 626, 661, 676, 707, 710
  How to Pay for the War (1940) 470, 481
  Indian Currency and Finance (1913) 468, 471, 473, 482
  opposition to gold standard 473
  principle of effective demand 478–9
  A Revision of the Treaty (1922) 469
  A Tract on Monetary Reform (1923) 469, 472, 482
  A Treatise on Money (1930) 469, 474–6, 535–6, 560, 596, 613–14, 625
  A Treatise on Probability (1921) 420, 468–70, 476–7, 587–8
  We Can Conquer Unemployment 473–4
Keynes, John Neville 468
  Scope and Method of Political Economy (1891) 468
Khintchine, Alexandre 437
Kiel Institute of World Economics 515, 523–4, 617, 634
Kiev Commercial Institute 461
King, John 122, 124, 140, 226, 628
Kingdom of Saxony 167
Kirzner, Israel 292, 464
Klein, Lawrence 634, 675
Knapp, Georg Friedrich 274, 348
Knies, Karl 206, 285, 363, 393
  Das Geld (1885) 289
Knight, Frank H. 498, 500–501, 632, 658, 682, 685
  Knightian uncertainty 498–9
  Risk, *Uncertainty and Profit* (1921) 498–501
Koopmans, Tjalling 447, 524–5, 568, 581, 619, 676, 691
Kortum, Hermann 196
Krakow University 283
Krelle, Wilhelm 623
Krugman, Paul Robin 748
  The Age of Diminished Expectations (1990) 753
  The Conscience of a Liberal (2007) 753
  influence on trade theory 748–9
  Market Structure and Foreign Trade (1985) 750
  The Self-Organizing Economy (1996) 751
  The Spatial Economy (1999) 751
  theory of financial crises 751–3

Kurz, Heinz D. 103, 131–2, 136, 140, 160, 548–9, 560, 589, 606, 617
Kuznets, Simon 447, 515, 617, 649, 706
Kyoto University 712

La Décade philosophique, littéraire et politique, par une société de républicains 114
La Nation 237
La Presse 246
La Réforme 237
La Volpe, Giulio 337
labour 6–7, 20, 61, 64, 69, 107, 111, 115, 125–6, 128, 130–31, 133, 135–6, 151–2, 159–60, 171–2, 175, 181, 193–4, 215, 217, 220, 222, 306, 342, 345, 354, 402, 423, 431, 452, 583–4, 594, 655, 687, 714, 722, 734, 742–3, 750
    abstract 216–20
    common 61
    costs 136
    direct 128, 221
    division of 7, 13, 68, 75, 193, 197, 454
    market 14, 237–8, 478, 570, 652
    productive 62, 111, 165
    productivity 7, 225–6
    relationship with property 192–3
    remuneration of 116
    specialization 62
    units of 77–8
    universal social 217
    unproductive 62, 111, 165
    value 215–16, 425–6, 431–2, 546, 549
    wage 213–14
Labriola, Antonio 374
laissez faire 11–12, 97, 256, 508, 644
    opposition to 209, 273, 531–2
Lake Mohonk Conferences 322
Lange, Oskar Ryszard 562, 610–12, 685, 706, 712
    concept of "Walras's Law" 251, 703
    "Marxian economics and modern economic theory" (1935) 610
    model of central planning bureau 610, 612
    model of "market socialism" 561
    On the Economic Theory of Socialism 610
    Price Flexibility and Full Employment (1944) 610
Lansdowne, Marquis of 7
Laplace, Pierre-Simon 297, 319
    Mécanique Céleste 318
Lassalle, Ferdinand
    Allgemeiner Deutscher Arbeiterverein 215
Laughlin, James Laurence
    Coin's Financial Fool 449
    Facts about Money (1895) 449

Law, John 16–17, 19, 24
    "Essay on a land bank" 16
    Mississippi System 16–18
    Money and Trade Consider'd with a Proposal for Suppllying the Nation with Money (1705) 16–17
Le Bovier de Fontenelle, Bernard, *see* Fontenelle, Bernard Le Bovier de
Le Censeur 164
Le Censeur Européen 164
Le Courier français 237
Le Pesant de Boisguilbert, *see* Boisguilbert, Pierre le Pesant de
Le Travail, organe international des intérêts économiques de la classe laborieuse, revue du mouvement coopératif 246
Le Trosne, Guillaume-François 34
League of Nations 350, 405, 411, 509, 599–600
    Economic Intelligence Service 625
Leclerc de Buffon, Georges-Louis, *see* Buffon, Georges-Louis Leclerc de
Lederer, Emil 484, 634
Leibniz, Gottfried Wilhelm 40, 42, 197
Leirens, Constant 246
Lend Lease Agreement 470
Lenin, Vladimir I. 400, 489, 750
Leontief, Wassily W. 37, 229, 486, 515, 552, 616, 658, 714, 716
    "Die Wirtschaft als Kreislauf" (1928) 103
    role in development of input–output analysis 229, 616–19
Leontovich, A.V.
    Elementary Guidelines to Gauss and Pearson Methods in the Assessment of Errors in Statistics and Biology (1909–11) 461
Lerner, Abba Ptachya 562, 578–9
    "Economic theory and socialist economy" (1934) 578
    The Economics of Control (1944) 579
    Economics of Employment (1951) 579
    Lerner index 578
    Marshall–Lerner condition 578
    model of "market socialism" 561
Leroy, Charles-Georges 28, 31
Lessius, *see* Leys, Leonard de
Levy Economics Institute 685
Lévy, Paul 437
Lexis, Wilhelm 227, 419, 426
Leys, Leonard de (Lessius) 81
Liberal Revolution 501
liberalism 167, 185, 190, 205, 507, 514
    classical 564
    criticisms of 174
    ordoliberalism 508
    radical economic 292

liberty
    definitions of 164–5
Lieben, Richard 290, 435
    Investigations on the Theory of Price (1889)
        410
Liebknecht, Wilhelm
    Sozialdemokratische Arbeiterpartei 215
Life Extension Institute 411
Lindahl, Erik 359, 360, 405, 509, 568, 635–6
    Die Gerechtigkeit der Besteuerung 359, 509–10
        Lindahl equilibrium 510
        Lindahl prices 509–10
    monetary theory of 511–12
    Penningpolitikens Medel (*The Aims of
        Monetary Policy*) (1930) 511–12
    "The place of capital in the theory of price"
        (1929) 510
Linder, Staffan Burenstam 201
    home market effect theory of 748
Linguet, Simon-Nicolas-Henri
    Réponse aux docteurs modernes (1771) 36
liquidation 235
liquidity
    concepts of 541–2
    preference 479
    risks 104
List, Friedrich 167, 169, 174, 206
    concept of "mental capital/productive
        powers" 169
    *Das nationale System der politischen
        Ökonomie* (*The National System of
        Political Economy*) (1839–40) 167–9
Lloyd, William Forster 161
Locke, John 29, 73, 84, 269
London School of Economics (LSE) 455, 514,
    530, 532, 534, 558, 561, 578, 596, 602–3,
    625, 631–2, 638–9, 708–9, 712, 721, 728,
    737
    Toyota International Centre for Economic
        and Related Disciplines (STICERD)
        712
London Society for the Extension of
    University Teaching 382
Loria, Achille 227
Lösch, August 162, 485
Lothian, J.M. 59
Louis XIV 9
Louis XV 17, 28
Louis XVI 37
Louis XVIII
    "Charte octroyée" 164
Lowe, Adolph 514, 523, 617
    Arbeitslosigkeit und Kriminalität
        (*Unemployment and Criminality*) (1914)
        514

development of business cycle theory
    515–16
Economics and Sociology (1935) 514
Has Freedom a Future? (1988) 514
On Economic Knowledge (1965) 514–15
The Path of Economic Growth (1976) 515–16
The Price of Liberty (1937) 514
Lucas, Robert E. 48, 600, 734–5
    "Econometric policy evaluation – a
        critique" (1976) 735–6
    "An equilibrium model of the business
        cycle" (1975) 734
    "Expectations and the neutrality of money"
        (1972) 734
    island model of 735
    Lucas Critique 600–601, 735–6
    Real Wages, Employment, and Inflation
        (1969) 734
Lundberg, Erik 407, 509
    *Studies in the Theory of Economic
        Expansions* (1937) 408
Lutz, Friedrich 508
Luxemburg, Rosa 229, 489, 568
    Einführung in die Nationalökonomie (1925)
        227

Mably, Gabriel Bonnot de
    *Doutes sur l'ordre naturel et essentiel des
        sociétés politiques* 35
Maccabelli, Terenzio 338
Macgregor, D.H. 280
Machlup, Fritz 464, 500, 621
Macmillan Committee on Finance and
    Industry 469, 475
macroeconomics 16, 168–9, 229, 245, 343,
    349–50, 358, 376, 415, 452, 455, 478, 482,
    552, 560, 568, 599, 605, 626–7, 652–3, 675,
    703, 734, 736–7, 744–5, 752–3
    behavioural 739
    development of 359–60, 481
    financial crises 751–2
    investment saving–liquidity preference
        money supply framework (IS–LM) 605,
        652, 676, 708, 721–2, 734
    Keynesian 455, 629, 638, 649–50, 658, 679,
        726
    preference functions 520
    production 714
Madoff, Bernard 686
Mahalanobis, Prasanta 520
Maison de Sorbonne 73
Malthus, Daniel 107
Malthus, Thomas Robert 54, 96, 111–12, 118,
    121, 123–4, 129, 133, 145, 152, 157, 172,
    185, 188, 212, 269, 281, 348, 543, 726

The Crisis, a View of the Present Interesting State of Great Britain, by a Friend to the Constitution (1796) 107
Essay on the Principle of Population (1798) 84, 107–9
The Grounds of an Opinion on the Policy of Restricting the Importation of Foreign Corn (1815) 110
An Inquiry into the Nature and Progress of Rent (1815) 110, 151
An Investigation of the Cause of the Present High Price of Provisions (1800), 108
Observations on the Effects of the Corn Laws, and of a Rise or Fall in the Price of Corn on the Agriculture and General Wealth of the Country (1814) 110
"Pamphlets on the bullion question" (1811) 109–10
Principles of Political Economy (1820) 98, 109–11, 123
theory of population 208
Man and the Economy 632
Manchester Guardian 534, 602
Mandelbrot, Benoit 438–9
Mandeville, Bernard de 10, 198
Fable of the Bees 25
Maneschi, Andrea 329
Mangoldt, Karl-Hans von 287
Mantel, R. 703
manufacturing 17, 30, 111, 124, 131, 134–5, 168, 427, 629, 741, 750–51
competitive 308
development of 225
textile 484
Marchionatti, Roberto 336
marginal analysis 302, 352, 367, 369, 379
marginalism 68, 138, 367, 379, 388–9, 444, 610
Marivetz, Etienne-Claude de 31
market economies 20, 145, 164, 342, 465, 516, 559
price mechanism in 516
price system in 498
pure 649
social 506
market process theory 466
stability theory 666
Markowitz, Harry 677
Marschak, Jacob 515, 523, 691
Economic Theory of Teams (1972) 525
Elasticity of Demand (1931) 524
Income, Employment and the Price Level (1951) 523
Marshall, Alfred 2, 16–17, 68, 105, 139, 161–2, 280, 295–301, 305–9, 312, 315, 326, 351, 389, 404, 410, 414, 444, 458, 470, 472, 476,

478, 484, 530, 534–5, 548, 553, 569, 593, 597–8, 604, 621, 632–3, 643, 661, 706, 748, 750–51
analysis used by 300–304
concept of real costs 544–5
The Economics of Industry (1979) 295, 303
Industry and Trade (1919) 295, 304
marginal productivity theory 306
offer curve 317
Official Papers of Alfred Marshall 295
Principles of Economics 295, 297, 300, 304, 306–7, 592, 693
Money, Credit and Commerce (1923) 295
use of mathematics 297
use of partial equilibrium 301, 537–8
ceteris paribus clause 301–2
"Ye machine" 298–9
Marx, Karl Heinrich 5, 12, 16, 37, 54, 69, 77, 81, 107, 112, 132, 135, 138, 146, 152, 162, 167, 194, 204, 209, 211–29, 283, 293, 311, 320, 341, 343, 363, 374, 391, 400, 419, 421, 423–8, 433, 440, 484, 487–8, 490, 491, 516, 544, 545, 546, 549, 568, 573, 593, 617, 663–4, 712, 726
The Communist Manifesto 146, 204, 213
critiques of 227–9, 311
Das Kapital (*Capital*) 77, 81, 214, 216–24, 226–7, 341, 425–6, 568
Die deutsche Ideologie (*The German Ideology*) (1845–6) 212
Grundrisse der Kritik der Politischen Ökonomie (Rohentwurf) 1857–1858 214, 218
Misère de la Philosophie (*The Poverty of Philosophy*) (1847) 213
Ökonomisch-philosophische Manuskripte von 1844 (*Economic and Philosophic Manuscripts of 1844*) (1932) 212
Theorien über den Mehrwert (*Theories of Surplus Value*) 214
theory of capital
constant 222
variable 222
theory of labour 217, 219–20, 224
abstract 216–20
value 215–16, 222–3, 228, 534–5, 549
"Zur Judenfrage" ("On the Jewish question") 212
"Zur Kritik der Hegelschen Rechtsphilosophie" ("A contribution to the critique of Hegel's philosophy of right") 212

Zur Kritik der Politischen Ökonomie (Erstes Heft) (*A Contribution to the Critique of Political Economy*) (1859) 214, 216–17, 218–19
Marxism 205, 274, 399, 402, 503, 610, 616, 663–4, 713
   production of relative surplus value 663
Mas-Colell, Andreu 700
Massachusetts Institute of Technology (MIT) 438, 658–9, 691, 709, 714, 718, 721, 737, 741, 748
   Economics Department 659–60
   Faculty Club 660
   Radiation Laboratory 658
Matsukawa, S. 7
Mattioli, Raffaele 536
Maurice Falk Institute for Economic Research 706
Max Weber Gesamtausgabe (*MWG*) 391
Mayer, Hans 621
McCarthy, Joseph 568, 672
McCulloch, John Ramsey 103–4, 124, 145
McKinley, William 449
Meade, James Edward 475, 481, 535, 613, 625–7, 721, 741
   balance in international payments theory 625–6
   The Balance of Payments (1951) 626
   Trade and Welfare (1955) 626
Medlen, Craig
   The Evolution of Modern Capitalism (2012) 383
Melon, Jean-François
   Essai politique sur le commerce (1734) 26
Menger, Carl 168, 248, 262, 275, 283–6, 288–92, 341–2, 348, 363, 408, 410, 465, 484, 496, 603, 726
   Die Irrthümer des deutschen Historismus (*The Errors of German Historicism*) (1884) 276, 290
   Grundsätze der Volkswirthschaftslehre (1871) 209, 284–92, 557
   focus on utility 286–8
   Untersuchungen über die Methode der Socialwissenschaften und der Politischen Oekonomie insbesondere (1883) 290–91, 292
mercantilism 7, 61, 64
Mercier, Louis-Sébastien 36
Methodenstreit 168, 268, 275, 283, 289, 300, 507
microeconomics 168, 179, 183, 201, 376, 453–4, 466, 552, 581, 650, 661, 694
   applied 46
   consumer 695

Miksch, Leonard 508
Mill, James 114, 118, 121, 124, 136, 187, 374, 545
   Elements of Political Economy 187
   Essay on the Impolicy of a Bounty on the Exportation of Grain (1804) 98
Mill, John Stuart 136, 174, 186, 190, 245, 280, 312, 348, 380, 449, 507, 557, 726
   Autobiography 74, 186
   The Claims of Labour 188–9
   Essays on some Unsettled Questions of Political Economy (1844) 153, 186
   Principles of Political Economy 185, 188, 242
   A System of Logic, Ratiocinative and Inductive 186
   theory of value 189
Minsky, Hyman Philip 486, 685–6
   financial instability hypothesis (FIH) 685–8
Mir Bozhii (*God's World*) 399
Mirabeau, Gabriel-Honoré Riqueti, Count of 114
Mirabeau, Victor Riqueti, Marquis of 29, 31, 34, 36–7
   L'ami des hommes (1757) 31
   Philosophie rurale (1763) 29, 31, 34
   "Zig-Zag" model 31–2
   Tableau économique 31
   Théorie de l'impôt (1760) 31, 34
   Traité de la monarchie 31
Mirrlees, James 745
Mises, Ludwig Heinrich von 343, 357, 363, 464–5, 503, 523, 557, 561–2
   The Anti-Capitalistic (1956) 466
   Human Action: A Treatise on Economics (1949) 465–6
   Nationalökonomie: Theorie des Handelns und des Wirtschaftens (1940) 465–6
   Socialism: An Economic and Sociological Analysis (1922) 561
   Theorie des Geldes und der Umlaufsmittel (1912) 464–5, 559–60
Mississippi Company
   shares issued by 18–20
Mitchell, Wesley Clair 235, 377, 446–7, 559
   Business Cycles (1913) 446
   Business Cycles: The Problem and Its Setting (1927) 447
   Measuring Business Cycles (1946) 447
mixed economies 363, 365, 465, 629, 659
Modigliani, Franco 523, 570, 675, 706, 741
Molinari, Gustave de 237, 240, 434
   Les soirées de la rue Saint-Lazare (1849) 237, 239
   market reform theories of 238–9
   role of competitive firms 239–40

monetarism 17, 629, 652, 653, 679
monetary policy 17, 22, 105, 148, 149, 350,
  358, 360, 400, 404, 405, 451, 458, 473, 475,
  477, 559, 561, 625, 650, 651, 653, 675, 677,
  678, 685, 687, 722, 739, 752, 753
monetary theory 63, 126, 127, 148, 154, 160,
  161, 162, 248, 252, 253, 256, 289, 350, 354,
  358, 365, 379, 443, 452, 455, 458, 465, 475,
  486, 509, 515, 529, 559, 560, 565, 575, 646,
  648, 677, 678, 706, 707, 708, 713
  expansion 650–52
  international 575
  Lindahlian 511–12
  Ricardian 242–3
monopoly 177, 229, 257, 326, 337, 553, 578
  artificial 257
  natural 240–41
  pure 554
  use in general equilibrium 328
Monroe Doctrine 451, 493
Mont Pèlerin Society 631
Montesquieu, Charles-Louis de Secondat de
  24–6, 49, 164
  *Considerations on the Causes of the
    Greatness of the Romans and of their
    Decline* (*Considérations sur les causes
    de la grandeur des Romains et de leur
    décadence*) (1734) 24
  Lettres persanes (*Persian Letters*) (1721) 24
  The Spirit of the Laws (*De l'espirit des lois*)
    (1748) 24, 26–7, 98
Moore, George Edward 458, 468, 470
  Principia Ethica 587
Moral Sciences Tripos 280
Morellet, André
  Dictionnaire du commerce 74
  *Prospectus d'un nouveau dictionnaire de
    commerce* (1769) 81
Morgenstern, Oskar 464, 525, 548, 558, 588,
  621, 719
  Theory of Games and Economic Behavior
    (*TGEB*) (1944) 581–5, 718
Morishima, Michio 712–13, 726
  Dogakuteki Keizai Riron (*Dynamic
    Economic Theory*) (1950) 712
The Morning Chronicle 120
Morris, George S. 374
Moscow State University
  Research Institute of Mathematics and
    Mechanics 462
Moscow University 399, 461–2
Müller, Adam 204
  Elemente der Staatskunst (1809–10) 169
Müller-Armack, Alfred 508
Mummery, A.F. 382

Mun, Thomas 51
Mundell, Robert Alexander 721, 723
  Mundell–Tobin effect 721
  open-economy IS–LM model 722–3
Musgrave, Richard Abel 268, 359, 510, 634–6,
  665
  Classics in the Theory of Public Finance
    (1959) 636
  The Theory of Public Finance (1959) 636
Mussolini, Benito 534
Muth, John F. 734
Myrdal, Gunnar 360, 408, 509, 511, 527, 603,
  750
  *An American Dilemma: The Negro Problem
    and Modern Democracy* (1944) 528
  *Asian Drama: An Inquiry into the Poverty of
    Nations* (1968) 528
  *Economic Theory and Under-Developed
    Regions* (1957) 528
  Monetary Equilibrium (1931) 527–9
  *The Political Element in the Development of
    Economic Theory* (1930) 527–9

Nachalo (*The Beginning*) 399
Napoleonic Wars (1803–15) 105, 120, 122–3,
  145, 283
  Battle of Anholt (1811) 150
Nash Jr, John Forbes 179, 581–2, 691, 718, 720
  Nash equilibrium 718–20
  role in development of game theory 718–19
National Bureau of Economic Research
  (NBER) 446–7, 524, 559, 617–19, 648–9
National Institute of Economic and Social
  Research 568
National Socialism 169, 621
nationalism 167, 368, 485, 621
Nauchnoe obozrenie (*Scientific Review*) 399
Naumann, Friedrich 392
Neary, Peter 745
Negishi, Takashi 712, 725
  "Monopolistic competition and general
    equilibrium" (1961) 725–6
  Negishi's method 725
  "A note on the stability of an economy
    where all goods are gross substitutes"
    (1958) 725
  theory of kinky perceived demand curves
    726
  "Welfare economics and existence of an
    equilibrium for a competitive economy"
    (1960) 725
Neisser, Hans 408, 515, 617
Netherlands
  Amsterdam 120
  Central Planning Bureau (CPB) 599–600

The Hague 599
Holland 25
Rotterdam 599
Social Democratic Labour Party 599
Neue Annalen der Mecklenburgischen
    Landwirtschaftsgesellschaft 158, 161
Neue Rheinische Zeitung 213
Neumann, John von 525, 581–3, 588, 628, 691,
    712, 718–19
    model of general equilibrium 581, 583–4
    Theory of Games and Economic Behavior
        (*TGEB*) (1944) 581–5, 718
    "Zur Theorie der Gesellschaftsspiele" 584
Neurath, Otto von 465
The New Englander 320
New Palgrave Dictionary of Economics 710
New School for Social Research 536, 578
    founding of (1919) 446
New York Clearing House
    Coe Report (1873) 243
New York Daily Tribune 215
New York School for Social Research 377
New York Times 527
New York University (NYU) 558
Nicholson, Joseph Shield 280
Nicole, Pierre 10–12
North, Douglass 499
North, Lord Frederick 58
Norway 518, 568
    Labour Party 521
    Oslo 348, 518
Novoe slovo (*New World*) 399
Nutter, Warren 683

objectivism 466
Ogden, C.K. 587
Ohlin, Bertil 329, 360, 407, 509, 568, 579, 625
    theory of interregional trade 407
Okishio, Nobuo 713
    Okishio theorem 132
Older Historical School of Economics 206–7
oligopoly 376, 434, 622–3, 719
    formation of 639
Oppenheimer, Franz 514
option pricing theory
    Black–Scholes–Merton formula 666
Organisation for Economic Co-operation and
    Development (OECD) 639
Osaka University 712
Osborne, M.F. Maury 438
Ostrom, Elinor
    common property rights framework 161
Otter, Bishop William 107
Overstone, Lord, *see* Jones-Loyd, Samuel
Owens College, Manchester 185, 262

Oxford Economic Papers 614
Oxford Economists' Research Group 575
Oxford Institute of Statistics (OIS) 515, 524
Oxford University 5, 315, 475
    All Souls College 524
    Balliol College 57, 602
    Hertford College 625
    Institute of Statistics 568
    Lincoln College 382
    New College 530
    Nuffield College 367, 602
    Oriel College 625
    Queen's College 95

Palestine
    Jerusalem 706
Paley, Mary 281, 295
    The Economics of Industry (1979) 295
Palmer, J. Horsely 149
Palomba, Giuseppe 337
Panckoucke, Charles-Joseph
    Encyclopédie Méthodique 83
Pantaleoni, Maffeo 201, 287, 323, 325, 367–72,
    420
    Principii di economia puri (1889) 369
    theory of competition 370–72
Pareto, Vilfredo 216, 227, 248, 323, 325,
    367–71, 388, 412, 419, 462, 603, 642, 699,
    701, 707, 729
    application of general equilibrium 327–9
    Cours d'Économie Politique (1896–7) 323–5,
        327–30, 333
    "Economia sperimentale" (1918) 333
    "Économie mathématique" (1911) 330
    "Il Massimo di utilità dato della libera
        concorenza" (1894) 327
    "Il Massimo di utilità per una collettività in
        sociologia" 333–4
    "La Courbe de la repartition de la richesses"
        (1896) 329
    Les systèmes socialistes (1901–02) 323,
        331
    Manuale di Economia Politica (1906) 323,
        328, 330–33, 643
    methodology of 329–31
        dualistic 331
    Pareto efficiency 316–17, 453, 719
    role in development of welfare economics
        307, 317
    Sociologia (1916) 333–5
    theory of social equilibrium 334–6
    trade theory of 325–6
    Trattato di Sociologia Generale (1916) 323
Pascal, Blaise 10, 41
Pasinetti, Luigi 359, 548, 614

Patinkin, Don 523
  Anticipations of the General Theory? *And Other Essays on Keynes* (1982) 710
  Keynes' Monetary Thought 710
  Money, Interest and Prices (1956) 706–10
  "On the consistency of economic models: a theory of involuntary unemployment" (1947) 706, 709–10
  "Patinkin controversy" 708
Pattulo, Henry 31
Pearson, Karl 420
Permanent Mandates Commission 350
Perron–Frobenius theorem 672–3
Peru 329, 451
Petites Écoles de Port-Royal 9
Petrograd State University 616
Petty, William 5, 7–8, 17, 69, 86, 461
  concept of "political arithmetic" 5–6
  location theory of differential rent 6
  A Treatise of Taxes & Contributions (1662) 6–7
Phelps, Edmund 491
Philippe (duc d'Orléans) 17
Physiocracy 34–6, 60, 69, 74, 76–7, 246, 253
  criticisms of 114–15
  Éphémérides du citoyen 35
  Nouvelles éphémérides économiques 37
Pierce, Charles Sanders 374
Pigou, Arthur Cecil 1–2, 280, 307, 414, 452–3, 455–6, 458, 501, 588, 602, 613, 634
  The Economics of Welfare (1920) 452–4
  Industrial Fluctuations (1927) 452
  Memorials of Alfred Marshall 295
  The Theory of Unemployment (1933) 452, 455
  Wealth and Welfare (1912) 452
Pinochet, Augusto 649
Pitt the Younger, William 95, 107
Plant, Arnold 631, 633
Plutarch
  Lives 74
plutocracy 207
Pohle, Ludwig 277
Poisson distribution 420
Poisson, Siméon-Denis 41
Poland 153, 610
  Cracow 601
  Lodz 568
  Outline Perspective Plan 569
  Poznan 610
  Warsaw 610
Polanyi, Karl 503–4
  The Great Transformation 503–4
Polish Academy of Sciences 569
Polish Economic Council 610

political economy 5–6, 10, 12, 27–9, 35–6, 54, 66–7, 85, 96, 99, 192, 281–2, 347, 557
  classical 76, 138
  critique of 212–13
  practical 402
  prices 61
  proposed reform of 285
  theoretical 402
  theories of 276
Political Economy Club 123, 148, 150
  founding of 350
Polya, George
  How to Solve It? (1945) 671
Polytechnic Institute (St Petersburg) 399
Polytechnical Institute of Peter the Great 461
Ponzi, Charles 686
Pope, Alexander
  Essay on Man 319
Popper, Karl 671
Populism 146
Portugal 136–7
poverty 107, 145, 189, 245, 347, 443, 528, 592, 687, 690, 730–31, 741, 743
  measure of 687, 731
Predöhl, Andreas 162
Preußische Jahrbücher 273
Princeton University 582–3, 585, 718
principle of utility 117
probability theory
  development of 174
production/production theory 342, 352, 547–9
  capitalistic 215, 221
  definitions of 115
  development of 520
  modes of 214
  period of 343–5
  scales of 593
production function 96, 160, 327, 417
  Cobb–Douglas 157
productivity 55, 67, 76–7, 152, 189, 193, 198, 277, 342–4
  agricultural 35, 75, 111, 153
  exclusive 30, 33, 35, 75
  labour 7, 60, 62, 65–6, 68, 96, 225, 342, 344
  manufacturing 111
  marginal 69, 132, 157–60, 162, 208–9, 287, 295, 306, 311–12, 321, 326–7, 344, 347, 351–2, 357, 421
  theory of distribution 382
property 253–4
  landed 213
  relationship with labour 192–3
  rights 24
Prospective Review 242
Protestantism 10, 114, 206, 211, 396–7, 514

Proudhon, Pierre-Joseph 171, 192, 212, 246
  De la création de l'ordre dans l'humanité (1843) 192
  De la justice dans la revolution et dans l'Église (1858) 192
  De l'utilité de la célébration du Dimanche, considérée sous les rapports de l'hygiène publique, de la morale, des relations de famille et de cité (1839) 192
  Philosophie de la misère (*Philosophy of Poverty*) (1846) 213
  Système des contradictions économiques (1846) 192
  Théorie de la propriété (1866) 192–3
Prussian Academy of Sciences 275
public choice theory 682
public finance theory 352–3, 358–9, 380, 509, 636, 745
public goods theory
  development of 270, 665
pure equilibrium 337
pure public goods theory 359
pure theory 388, 484, 736
  development of 326–7

Quakerism 120
quantitative analysis 446–7, 493
quantity equation 523
quantity theory 105, 474, 629, 650–51
  of money (QTM) 449, 472–3, 613–14, 650, 707
Quarterly Journal of Economics 321, 383, 535, 552–3, 655
Quesnay, François 14, 21, 28–30, 33–7, 57, 69, 74–5, 76, 102, 285, 293
  Art de guérir par la saignée (1736) 28
  Encyclopédie 28–9
  Essai physique sur l'œconomie animale (1736) 28
  Essai sur l'oeconomie animale (1747) 29
  focus on agricultural productivity 29–31, 34–6
  Mémoires de l'Académie de chirurgie (1743) 28
  Philosophie rurale (1763) 29, 31, 34
  "Zig-Zag" model 31–2
  Problème économique (1766) 31
  Recherches philosophiques sur l'évidence des vérités géométriques (1773) 36–7
  Second problème économique (1767) 31
  Tableau économique 31, 102, 224, 617
  Théorie de l'impôt (1760) 31
  Traité de la gangrene (1749) 28

Traité de la monarchie 31
Traité de la suppuration (1749) 28
Traité des fièvres continues (1751) 28

Radner, Roy
  Economic Theory of Teams (1972) 525
Rae, John 415
Ramsey, Frank Plumpton 535, 587–9, 745
  influence of 588–9
    optimal pricing research 589, 745
  On a Problem of Formal Logic 587
  Ramsey's theorem 588–90
  "Truth and probability" 588
Rand, Ayn
  Atlas Shrugged 466
RAND Corporation 655, 671, 691, 718
Rapping, Leonard
  Real Wages, Employment, and Inflation (1969) 734
rates of return 76, 128, 329, 417, 546, 678
  internal 255
  marginal 415–16
  on capital 74, 161
  on investment 357, 417
  social 417
Rau, Karl-Heinrich 270, 287
Ravix, Joël-Thomas 75
Rawls, John 728
  Theory of Justice (1971) 730, 732–3
Reagan, Ronald 648, 721, 745
Rehn, Gösta 408
Remington Rand 411
Rémond de Montmort, Pierre 42
  Essay d'analyse des jeux de hazard (1708) 41–3
rent 255, 436, 542–3, 547, 549, 621
  absolute 427
  differential
    location theory of 6
  economic 329
  of land 116, 159, 255
  theories of 139, 269, 427, 433
Research Centre for Economic Policy 523
Review of Economic Studies (*RES*) 578, 596, 628, 708, 728
Revue socialiste 254
Rheinische Zeitung 211
Ricardo, David 62, 69, 96, 108–10, 111, 114–18, 120, 124–6, 128–35, 138, 140, 145, 155, 157, 162, 172, 185–6, 188, 212, 219–20, 222, 297, 306, 343, 347–8, 352, 356, 369, 380, 419, 423–4, 434, 516, 535, 546, 549, 606, 663, 676, 712, 726
  corn ratio theory of 129, 152, 542–3
  criticisms of 224–5

doctrine of value and distribution 124–7, 139, 154–5, 431

The Essay on the Influence of a Low Price of Corn on the Profits of Stock; Shewing the Inexpediency of Restrictions on Importation (1815) 121, 129, 134, 150–51, 542–3

The High Price of Bullion, a Proof of the Depreciation 109–10, 120

Ingot Plan 122

method of analysis 125–7

monetary theory of 127

Notes on Malthus 111–12

On the Principles of Political Economy, and Taxation (1817) 121–3, 126–7, 129–30, 132–5, 137–8, 151

rent theory 132, 139, 269, 383, 427, 433

Plan for the Establishment of a National Bank (1823) 122, 242

Proposals for an Economical and Secure Currency (1816) 122

Reply to Mr. Bosanquet's 'Practical Observations on the Report of the Bullion Committee' (1811) 109, 120–21

support for free trade 135–7

theorem of comparative advantage 137

theory of wages 190

use of mathematics 297

uses for Say's law 133

Rickert, Heinrich 275

Rist, Charles 443

Rivière, Pierre-Paul Lemercier de la 34, 37

L'ordre naturel et essential des sociétés politiques (1767) 36

Robbins, Lionel Charles 308, 311–12, 453, 530–31, 625–6, 631, 639, 656, 721

Economic Planning and the International Order (1937) 561

Essay on the Nature and Significance of Economic Science (1932) 530

The Evolution of Modern Economic Theory (1970) 532

The Great Depression (1934) 531

A History of Economic Thought (2000) 532

The Theory of Economic Development in the History of Economic Thought (1968) 532

The Theory of Economic Policy (1965) 532

Robertson, Dennis 2, 454, 625

Robinson, Austin 475, 535, 592, 625

Robinson, Joan Violet 359, 475, 493, 521, 535–6, 548, 553, 555, 568–9, 575, 592, 595, 605, 613–14, 625–6, 639, 741, 744

The Accumulation of Capital 594

Collected Economic Papers

"Beauty and the beast" 592–3

"The unimportance of reswitching" 594

The Economics of Imperfect Competition (1933) 592–3, 613

The Theory of Imperfect Competition (1933) 552

Rockefeller Foundation 509, 515, 518, 524, 617

Rodbertus, Karl 283, 427

Rœderer, Pierre-Louis 76–7

Romani, Paul-Marie 75

Romania 578

Roncaglia, Alessandro 8, 140

Roosevelt, Franklin D. 451

New Deal 504, 688

Röpke, Wilhelm 506

Roscher, Wilhelm Georg Friedrich 206–7, 274, 285, 363

Ansichten der Volkswirthschaft aus dem geschichtlichen Standpunkte (*Views of Economics from the Historical Point of View*) (1861) 207

Geschichte der National-Oekonomik in Deutschland (*History of Political Economy in Germany*) (1874) 206

Grundriß zu Vorlesungen über die Staatswirthschaft, nach geschichtlicher Methode (*Outline of Lectures on the Public Economy, Using the Historical Method*) (1842) 206

Politik: Geschichtliche Naturlehre der Monarchie, Aristokratie und Demokratie (*Politics: Historical Natural Doctrine of Monarchy, Aristocracy and Democracy*) (1892) 206–7

System der Volkswirthschaft. Hand- und Lesebuch für Geschäftsmänner und Studierende (*System of Economics. Hand- and Reading Book for Businessmen and Students*) 206

Die Grundlagen der Nationalökonomie (*The Foundations of Economics*), 208–9

"Zur Lehre von den Absatzkrisen" ("On the doctrine of sales crises") (1849) 208

Rossi, Pellegrino 96, 284, 434

Rothbard, Murray 292, 464

Rotwein, Eugene 50

Rousseau, Jean-Jacques 89–90, 91, 92, 164

concept of "general will" 89

Discours 59

Du contrat social (1762) 73, 89

Émile 107

Royal Agricultural Society of Brittany 34

Royal Economic Association 599

Royal Economic Society (RES) 535, 602
  *The Works and Correspondence of David
    Ricardo* 127, 535–6, 542
Royal Society 5, 28, 57
Royal Statistical Society 315, 419
Royal Swedish Academy of Sciences 139, 419,
  602
Rubin, Isaak Illich
  Essays on Marx's Theory of Value (1928)
    227
Ruchonnet, Louis 247
Ruge, Arnold 212
Russell, Bertrand
  Principles of Mathematics 587
Russian Empire 226, 523
  Cheka 616
  February Revolution (1917) 399
  Moscow 621
  October Revolution (1917) 395–6, 523
  Smolensk 431
  Solenoye 399
  St Petersburg 42, 148, 395, 419, 461, 616,
    619
Russian Federation 619
Rüstow, Alexander 506
Rutgers University 648

Saint-Péravy, Guérineau de 74, 76–8
Saint Petersburg Paradox 42–3
  solutions to 174
Saint Petersburg University 399
Saint-Simon, Claude-Henri de 165, 246
Salin, Edgar 209, 278
Salvadori, Neri 103, 131, 136, 140, 548–9, 589,
  617
Samuelson, Paul Anthony 139, 161, 227–8,
    337, 359, 438, 510, 519, 581, 594, 603–4,
    634, 645, 656, 658–9, 661, 664, 666–7, 675,
    695, 712, 714, 721, 725, 741, 748
  "An exact consumption-loan model of
    interest with or without the social
    contrivance of money" (1958) 665
  overlapping generations (OLG) model
    665
  Foundations of Economic Analysis (1947)
    642, 658, 660–62, 734
  influence on
    international trade theory 664
    public goods theory 665
    welfare economics 666
  "Pure theory of public expenditures" 665
  A Revision of Demand Theory (1956) 604
  Samuelson–Houthakker theory 662
  Samuelson–Le Chatelier principle 661–2
Sax, Emil 292, 379

Say, Jean-Baptiste 96, 114, 145, 157, 164–5,
    167, 171–2, 181, 187–8, 284, 569
  Traité d'économie politique (1803) 98, 101,
    114–15, 117
Say, Léon 246
Scarf, Herbert 702
Schabas, Margaret 50
Schäffle, Albert 268
Scheel, Hans von 292
Schefold, Bertram 134, 207, 276, 278, 343, 548
Schelle, Gustave 74
Schiller, Friedrich
  "An die Freude" 198
Schmidt, Conrad 227
Schmoller, Gustav Friedrich von 168, 272–3,
    275–7, 290–91, 404, 410
  "Die Volkswirtschaft, die
    Volkswirtschaftslehre und ihre
    Methode" (1893) 277
  founder of Verein für Socialpolitik 274
  *Grundriß der allgemeinen
    Volkswirtschaftslehre* 272, 275–6,
    277–8
Schmollers Jahrbuch 275
Schneider, Erich 485, 623
Schönberg, Gustav 292
  Handbuch der politischen Ökonomie 394
Schooten, Frans van
  Exercitationum mathematicarum (1657)
    41
Schor, Juliet
  The Overworked American (1991) 640
Schultz, Henry 327, 658
Schumacher, E.F. 638
Schumacher, Hermann 161
Schumpeter, Joseph Alois 2, 37, 95–6, 101,
    107, 125, 145, 185, 209, 234–5, 272, 283,
    289, 309, 388, 410, 413, 440, 458, 484,
    486–92, 496, 518, 552, 557, 595, 617, 619,
    658
  Business Cycles 486, 489, 494
  Capitalism, Socialism, and Democracy (1942)
    486, 489–90, 493, 495
  *Das Wesen und der Hauptinhalt der
    theoretischen Nationalökonomie* (*The
    Nature and Scope of Theoretical
    Economics*) (1908) 484, 487
  dynamic theory of capital 341
  entrepreneurial theory of change 492
  *Epochen der Dogmen- und
    Methodengeschichte* (*Economic Doctrine
    and Method*) (1914) 488
  History of Economic Analysis 48, 272, 440,
    486, 488, 490, 494–5
  Ten Great Economics (1952) 487

Theorie der wirtschaftlichen Entwicklung
(*Theory of Economic Development*)
(1912) 229, 485, 488–9
Theory of Economic Development (1934) 342,
485–6, 489, 611
Vergangenheit und Zukunft (1915) 488
Schütz, Alfred 464
Schütz, Carl von 273
Scitovsky, Tibor 638–9
"Ignorance is a source of oligopoly power"
(1950) 639
The Joyless Economy (1976) 639–40
"On the principle of consumer sovereignty"
(1962) 639
"The political economy of consumers'
rationing" (1942) 639
"A reconsideration of the theory of tariffs"
(1942) 639
Scitovsky Reversal Paradox 639
Welfare and Competition (1951) 639
"What price economic progress?" (1959) 639
Scorza, G. 333
Scuola Superiore di Commercio of Bari 367
Scuole Superiori di Commercio 368
Second World War (1939–45) 84, 388, 462,
482, 498, 501, 507, 519–20, 568, 583, 600,
610, 618, 648, 655, 660–62, 666, 685, 688,
698–9, 712, 714, 723
Seidenfeld, Teddy 669
Seligman, Edwin R. 153–4
Sen, Amartya Kumar 663, 728–31
Commodities and Capabilities (1985) 730
concept of "menu-dependence" 731–2
The Idea of Justice (2008) 732–3
influence on
social choice theory 728–30
welfare economics 728
Poverty and Famines (1981) 730
Senior, Nassau William 96, 434
Seton, Francis 227
Seven Years' War (1755–64) 48
Shackle, George Lennox Sharman 596–7
Epistemics and Economics (1972) 598
Expectations, Investment and Income (1938)
597–8
The Years of High Theory (1967) 597
Shanyavsky People's University (Moscow) 399
Shapiro, Carl 744
Shapley, Lloyd 691, 702
Shaw, Edward S. 685
Shaw, George Bernard 311
Shiller, Robert
*Animal Spirits: How Human Psychology
Drives the Economy and Why It Matters
for Global Capitalism* (2009) 737

Shove, Gerald 454, 613
Sidgwick, Henry 295, 452
The Economics of Industry (1879) 281, 295
The Elements of Politics 280
Methods of Ethics (1874) 280
Principles of Political Economy (1883)
280–81
Siebeck, Paul 394
Sieg, Wilfried 669
Signorino, Rodolfo 131, 137
Silva, Jean-Baptiste 28
Simmel, Georg 385–6
The Philosophy of Money 385–7
Simon, Herbert Alexander 669–70
Administrative Behavior (1947) 670
Models of Discovery (1977) 671
Models of My Life (1991) 672–3
Raffaele Mattioli Lectures (1993) 673
Singer, Hans 485
Sismondi, Jean-Charles Léonard Simonde de
77, 144, 204, 443
De la Richesse commercial (1803) 98, 145
Études sur l'économie politique (1837) 145
Études sur les sciences sociales 145
History of Italian Republics (1808–17) 144
Tableau de l'agriculture toscane (1801) 145
Skinner, Andrew S. 64, 67
Slutsky, Evgeny Evgenievich 327, 337, 412,
461, 519
Slutsky equation 461–2
*Theory of Correlation and Elements of
Distribution Curves Theory* (1912)
461–2
Smith, Adam 6, 10, 16, 57–8, 64–5, 68–70, 108,
114, 125, 127, 131, 133, 135, 144, 167, 185,
222, 273, 285, 293, 490, 535–6, 544, 557,
564, 594–5, 632–3, 662, 726, 743
"Considerations concerning the first
formation of languages, and the
different genius of original and
compounded languages" (1761) 60
Essays on Philosophical Subjects (1795)
59–60, 68
monetary theory of 62–3
theory of economic growth 61–2
theory of labour 165, 193
The Theory of Moral Sentiments (1759)
58–60, 67, 70
theory of natural and market price 20, 61,
115, 237
theory of value 99, 150–51
The Wealth of Nations (1776) 20, 48, 54, 57,
59–64, 66–70, 97–8, 104, 115, 118, 120,
349, 661
Smith College 320

social choice theory 728
  impossibility theorem 91, 690–93, 729
Social Democratic Party (SDP) 215
social equilibrium 334–6
social mathematic 87–8
  examples of 88–9
social product 125, 225
  annual 222
  distribution
    natural law of 321
  net 152
  share of 321
Social Science Research Council (SSRC) 446
socialism 9, 146, 171, 192, 197, 226, 237, 274,
    364, 389–90, 399, 465, 558, 561, 563, 568,
    573, 610–12, 631, 745
  democratic 629
  economic theory of 401–2
  evolutionary 190
  market 561, 578, 745
  opposition to 172
  revolutionary 215
Società Anonima delle Strade Ferrate
    (Railways Company Limited) 323
Société d'économie politique 234
Società delle Ferriere Italiane (Italian
    Ironworks Company) 323
Società dell'Industria del Ferro (Iron Industry
    Company) 323
Société de statistique de Paris 234
Society for Psychical Research 281
sociology 216–18, 227, 276, 292, 331, 333, 370,
    374, 385–7, 391, 395–6, 462, 489, 492, 504,
    528, 610, 616, 640, 672, 712
  development of 386–7
  fiscal 337, 485, 493
  political 330
Solow, Robert Merton 359, 417, 581, 660, 665,
    675, 677, 714, 741–2, 748
  growth models of 576–7, 714–17
Sombart, Werner 276–8, 374, 616–17
  Der modern Kapitalismus (1902) 396
Sonnenschein, H. 703
Sorel, Georges 194
South Africa 383
South Sea Bubble 22
Soviet Union (USSR) 504, 610, 656
  Central Statistical Office
    Institute of Experimental Statistics and
      Statistical Methodology 462
  economy of 655–6
  Moscow 462, 616, 655
  National Committee of Finance
    Business Cycle Institute 462
Sovietology 655–6

Spain 19, 25, 40
Speer, Albert 638
Spence, Michael 737, 746
Spencer, Herbert 363, 374
  Psychology 298
Spiethoff, Arthur 278, 400, 440–42
  Business Cycles (1953) 440
  Die wirtschaftlichen Wechsellagen.
    Aufschwung, Krise, Stockung (1955)
    440
Sraffa, Piero 48, 69, 123, 124, 127, 129, 131,
    139, 140, 152, 155, 159, 227, 228, 229, 308,
    343, 359, 368, 423, 427, 428, 454, 475, 532,
    534–49, 553, 560, 568, 589, 606, 617, 625,
    741
  "The bank crisis in Italy" 534
  critiques of 543
    Alfred Marshall 535–8, 544–5, 548
    David Ricardo 129, 152, 542–3
    Friedrich von Hayek 539–40
    John Maynard Keynes 540–42
  Production of Commodities by Means of
    Commodities (1960) 228, 535, 546–9,
    588
  "value theory of labour" 546
  The Works and Correspondence of David
    Ricardo (1951–73) 139, 154–5
Stackelberg, Heinrich von 408, 621–2
  Die Grundzüge der theoretischen
    Volkswirtschaftslehre (*Principles of*
    Economic Theory) (1943) 623
  "Kapital und Zins in der stationären
    Verkehrswirtschaft" ("Capital and
    interest in a stationary economy")
    (1941) 623
  market analysis by 622–3
  Marktform und Gleichgewicht 622
Staël, Germaine de 115
Stalin, Josef 568
Stanford University 649, 691, 698
  Hoover Institution on War, Revolution and
    Peace 649
Stark, Werner
  Jeremy Bentham's Economic Writings
    (1952–4) 95
state interventionism 405, 465
Steedman, Ian 201, 226, 228, 538, 546, 548–9
Stein, Lorenz von 268
Steindl, Josef 229
Steuart, James (James Denham-Steuart) 99
  An Inquiry into the Principles of Political
    Oeconomy (1767) 54–6, 98
Stewart, Dugald 70
Stigler, George J. 185, 188, 190, 632
Stiglitz, Joseph Eugene 552, 737, 741, 744

Dixit–Stiglitz partial equilibrium model of monopolistic competition 744–5, 748
Globalization and Its Discontents (2002) 746
influence on growth theory 741–2
Kenya research trip 742–4
Whither Socialism? (1994) 745
St Katherine's Dock Company 148
Stockholm School 360, 407–8, 509, 511
formation of 350
Stockholm University (University College of Stockholm) 348
stocks and shares 159, 266, 312–13, 316, 354, 444, 459, 572, 593, 679
capital 252
government 22
issuance of 376
precautionary 14–15
prices 436
speculative 13–14
Stoicism 67
Stolper, Wolfgang 485, 491, 634, 664
Stone, Richard 625, 676
Storch, Heinrich von 169
Cours d'économie politique 168
Strauß, David Friedrich 347
Streissler, Erich 209
Strigl, Richard von 621
subsistence wage theory 158, 160
Svavitsky, N.A. 461
Svennilsson, Ingvar 509
Sveriges Riksbank Prize in Economic Sciences in Memory of Alfred Nobel 518, 528, 557, 581, 592–3, 602, 616, 625, 631, 642, 649, 652, 659–60, 666, 682, 691, 698–701, 714, 728, 734, 737, 746, 753
Sweden 349, 358, 404, 529, 568
Social Democratic Party 528
Stockholm 347, 350
Uppsala 509
Sweezy, Paul M. 227, 229, 486
Swiss Federal Institute of Technology in Zurich (ETH Zurich) 582
Swiss Statistical Office 203
Switzerland 108, 323, 367, 653
Basel 40–41
Geneva 57, 145, 464, 625, 628
Jena 203
Lausanne 101, 245–8, 351, 410
systems of national accounts (SNAs) 656

Takata, Yasuma 712
Tarascio, Vincent 337
Tarde, Gabriel 374
Tarski, Alfred 690
Taussig, Frank 486

taxation 24, 26, 87–8, 126, 137, 268, 350, 352–4, 380, 509, 588, 678
development of 87–8
income 88
just 353
of property 123
optimal 745
Taylor, Fred M.
On the Economic Theory of Socialism 610
Tchetverikov, N.S. 461
Tchuprov, A.A. 461
Teller, Edward 583
Thomas (disciple of Jesus) 7
Thornton, Henry 104, 209, 243
An Enquiry into the Nature and Effects of the Paper Credit of Great Britain (1802) 104
gold points mechanism 105
theory of money 148
Thünen, Johann Heinrich von 157–62, 201, 283, 290, 321, 351, 726, 750
Der Isolierte Staat (1826) 157–8, 160–62
Description of the Agriculture in the Village of Gross-Flottbeck 157
Isolated State Model 157–9, 162, 208
components of 159
marginal productivity theory of 157–60
Tillich, Paul 514
Tinbergen, Jan 518, 599–601, 626
business cycle model of 600–601
Tisch, Cläre 486
Tobin, James 486, 570, 639, 658, 675–8
influence on neoclassical growth theory 677, 679
Money, Credit and Capital (1998) 677
q theory of investment 675, 678–9
theory of general equilibrium 679
Tobin tax 675
transactions demand for money models of 676–7
Tooke, Thomas 148, 243
Considerations on the State of the Currency (1826) 148
opposition to Bank Act 149
Torrens, Robert 124, 145, 150–55
The Economists Refuted (1808) 150, 152–3
Essay on Money and Paper Currency (1812) 154
Essay on the External Corn Trade (1815) 150–53
Essay on the Production of Wealth (1821) 151, 153
Letter to Lord Melbourne (1837) 154
Letters on Commercial Policy (1833) 153
Letters to Lauderdale (1816) 154

On the Operation of the Bank Charter Act of 1844, as it Affects Commercial Credit (1847) 154
Principles and Practical Operation of Sir Robert Peel's Bill of 1844 (1848) 154
theory of value and distribution 150–51
Tozer, John Edward 139
trade theory 11–12, 20, 24, 46, 96–7, 159, 329, 341, 449, 604, 749
  carrying 25
  foreign 14–15, 24, 55
  free 9–10, 13–14, 135–6, 171, 256, 292
  grain 29, 36
  imperfect competition 434, 454, 568, 575, 621–3, 628, 632, 725, 748–9
    pure 571
  international 25, 324, 626–7, 664, 750
    cycles 515
  intra-industry 748
  neoclassical theory of 407, 629
    Heckscher–Ohlin–Samuelson (HOS) model 748–9
  new economic geography (NEG) models of 751–2
  surplus 21
Treaty of Rome (1957) 521, 722
Tucker, Albert 791
Tucker, Josiah
  Elements of Commerce (1755) 98
  Reflections on the Expediency (1751) 73–4
Tugan-Baranovsky, Mikhail Ivanovich 399–401, 568
  cycle and crises theories of 228, 400–401
  Industrial Crises in Contemporary England (1894) 400
  Periodic Industrial Crises. A History of English Crises. A General Theory of Crises 400
  Russian Factory in Past and Present. Historical Development of the Russian Factory in the Nineteenth Century (1898) 399
Tullock, Gordon 683
  The Calculus of Consent (1962) 683
Turgot, Anne-Robert-Jacques 14, 34, 37, 57, 69, 73–4, 76–9, 81, 83–4, 89
  Mémoire sur les prêts d'argent (1770) 78–80
  Réflexions sur la formation et la distribution des richesses 74, 80
Turgot, Michel-Étienne 73
Tversky, Amos 640

Ukraine 399, 485, 648
  Kiev 399, 523

Lviv 283
Odessa 399, 616
Ulam, Stanisław 583
unemployment 17, 55, 107, 123, 134, 145, 273, 352–3, 356, 376, 382–3, 405, 441, 477–8, 569, 605, 687, 743–4
  involuntary 407, 455, 650, 706, 709–10, 726
  mass 568
  natural rate of 360, 652
  technological 135
United Arab Republic 520
United Kingdom (UK) 19, 25, 51, 59, 148–9, 263, 473, 515, 523, 536, 568, 613, 632
  Act of Union (1707) 16
  Bank Act 149
  Bank Charter Act (1844) 242
  Bank Restriction Act (1797) 117
  banking crises
    (1857) 242
    (1866) 242
  Bristol 48, 295
  Cambridge 534, 596, 728, 741–2
  Civil Service 458, 470, 559, 614
  Committee on Higher Education 530
  Corn Laws 110
  economic crisis (1857) 213–14
  Edinburgh 16, 48, 54, 58
  Glasgow 57
  government of
    Economic Section 530
  India Office 471
  Kirkcaldy 57
  Labour Party 629–30
  Liberal Party 383, 473–4
  London 16, 20, 22, 57, 95, 120, 148, 203, 213–15, 242, 311, 348, 382, 459, 471, 530, 559, 578, 587, 610, 613, 631
  London Stock Exchange 120–21
  Manchester 515
  Norfolk 575
  Oxford 295, 515
  Parliament 104, 121, 150, 592
    Committees of Secrecy 104
    House of Commons 120, 122
    House of Lords 470, 629
    Select Committee on the High Price of Gold Bullion 148
  Reform Bill (1832) 150
  Tory Party 104
    Whig Party 104, 110, 139, 494–5
  Treasury Department 458, 468, 648
  War Cabinet 485, 592, 625
  Warwick 602

United Nations (UN) 509
  Commission on Employment and Economic
    Stability 520
  Declaration of Human Rights 164
  Office of Secretariat 568–9
    Department of Economic Affairs 568
  Security Council 610
  World Economic Report 568
United States of America (USA) 167, 242, 268,
    295, 320, 375, 391, 470, 482, 503, 518, 523,
    528, 559–61, 617, 631–2, 665, 698
  Albany, NY 748
  Ann Arbor, MI 634
  Baltimore, MD 655
  Bluefield, WV 718
  Bureau of Labor Statistics (BLS) 618
  Cambridge, MA 359, 552, 741
  Cato, WI 374
  Champaign–Urbana, IL 675
  Chicago, IL 374, 376, 446, 610, 658
  Civil War (1861–5) 446
  Congress 655
    House of Representatives 405
  Council of Economic Advisors 675, 737, 745
  Declaration of Independence 57
  Democratic Party 449–50, 659
  economy of 320, 753
  Federal Communications Commission 632
  Federal Reserve 450, 579, 737
    Board of Governors 643, 685
  Gary, IN 741
  government of 447
  La Conner, WA 552
  Los Angeles, CA 523
  Murfreesboro, TN 682
  National Banking System 450
  National Resources Planning Board 658
  New Haven, CT 410, 737
  New York 617, 648, 714
  Northampton, MA 320
  Office of Strategic Services (OSS) 655
  Palo Alto, CA 377
  Progressive Party 450
  Providence, RI 320
  Republican Party 449, 451
  Rushville, IL 446
  Santa Monica, CA 655
  Scranton, PA 449
  Taconic, CT 487
  Tallahassee, FL 578
  US Arms Control and Disarmament Agency
    Social Science Advisory Board 655
  Washington DC 582, 610, 649, 675
University College London 262, 311–12
University of Berlin 275, 392, 582, 616–17, 621

University of British Colombia, Vancouver
    721
University of Budapest 582
  Faculty of Law 638
University of California, Berkeley 578, 639,
    685, 698, 737
  Haas School of Business 523
University of California, Los Angeles (UCLA)
    525, 565, 682
University of California, Santa Cruz 639
University of Camerino 379
University of Chicago 446, 498, 524, 536, 564,
    649, 658, 670, 682, 706, 721, 734, 741
  Committee on Social Thought 564
  Law School 632
University of Cologne 621
University of Edinburgh 48, 54, 186
University of Freiburg 391, 564–5
University of Glasgow 48, 57
University of Hamburg 582
University of Heidelberg 268, 385, 392, 523,
    634
University of Jena 211
University of Kiel 515
University of Kristiania 518
University of Lausanne 245, 249, 323, 327, 337
University of Lund 404, 509
University of Macerata 379
University of Marburg 203
University of Michigan 552, 634
University of Naples 367, 379
University of Paris 443, 642
University of Perugia 534
University of Prague 363, 440
University of Rochester 634
University of Rome 367–8, 379, 388
University of Stockholm 405
University of Strasbourg 274, 385, 419
University of Tennessee 682
University of Texas, Austin 655
University of Tokyo 725
University of Tübingen 273
  Faculty of State Sciences 167
University of Turin 323, 388
  Scuola di Applicazione per Ingegneri 323
University of Virginia 682
  Thomas Jefferson Center for Studies in
    Political Economy 683
University of Washington 721
University of Zurich 203
Uppsala University 348, 509
US Philippine Commission 450
USSR Academy of Sciences
  V.A. Steklov Institute of Mathematics 462
utilitarianism 98–9, 107, 316–19, 729

utility 337, 731–2
　analysis of 181–2
　expected (EU) 584–5
　functions 287, 581, 701, 707
　　Cobb–Douglas 327
　　social 334
　marginal 200, 287, 700
　　Austrian 465
　maximization 199
　measurement of 518
　public 183
Uzawa, Hirofumi 712, 741
Uzbekistan
　Tashkent 462

Vacherot, Étienne
　La métaphysique et la science ou principes de
　　métaphysique positive (1858) 258
value 78, 298, 351, 406–7
　esteem value 78–81
　labour theory of 664
　marginal valuation 364
　natural 364
　supreme 402
　theories of 175, 189, 350–51
　　neoclassical 351
Vaubourg, J.-B. Desmarets de 9
Veblen, Thorstein Bunde 168, 320, 374, 446
　The Engineers and Price System (1921) 377
　Imperial Germany and the Industrial
　　Revolution (1915) 377
　An Inquiry Into the Nature of Peace and the
　　Terms of its Perpetuation (1917) 377
　The Instinct of Workmanship and the State of
　　Industrial Arts (1914) 376
　social theory of 375–6
　The Theory of Business Enterprise 376
　The Theory of Leisure Class (1899) 374–5
　The Vested Interest and the State of
　　Industrial Arts (1919) 377
Venables, Anthony
　The Spatial Economy (1999) 751
Verein für Socialpolitik 272, 392, 394, 506
　founding of (1872) 274
　Vienna Conference (1909) 277
Véron de Forbonnais, François, *see*
　　Forbonnais, François Véron de
Verri, Piero 86
Vienna University 283–4, 464, 485, 557–8, 602
　Law Faculty 363
Vigne, Jean de la 28
Villeroy, Duke of 28
Vincent, Jacques-Claude-Marie (Marquis of
　　Gournay) 73–4
Viner, Jacob 64, 71, 648, 658

Vining, Rutledge 447
Virginia Polytechnic Institute 682–3
Virginia School of Political Economy 682–3
Vleugels, Wilhelm 268
Voltaire, François Marie Arouet de 29, 36, 57,
　　83, 89, 198

Wagner, Adolph Heinrich Gotthilf 268–70,
　　272, 274, 277, 348, 404, 410
　theories of 269–70
Wakefield, Edward Gibbon
　Colonization of South Australia (1835) 153–4
Wald, Abraham 408, 690, 693
Walras, Auguste 200, 246
　Œuvres économiques complètes 245, 253–5
Walras, Marie-Esprit-Léon 101, 139, 194, 196,
　　198, 245–7, 254–60, 266, 285, 287, 300,
　　312–13, 323, 325, 347, 352, 363, 388–9,
　　402, 406, 410, 419–21, 433, 435, 488, 549,
　　603, 610, 618, 699, 702, 704, 706–7, 710,
　　712, 725–6, 735
　Cours d'économie sociale 253, 256
　Cours d'économie politique appliquée 248,
　　253, 256
　Études d'économie sociales 252–4
　Éléments d'économie politique pure ou théorie
　　de la richesse sociale 247–50, 252–4,
　　256–9, 324, 389, 420–21, 642–3
　Francis Sauveur 246
　L'économie politique et la justice 246
　Notes d'humeur 253
　Œuvres économiques complètes 245, 253–5
　Pure Economics 484
　Théorie de la monnaie (1886) 252
　Théorie mathématique de la richesse sociale
　　(1877) 247–8
　theory of general equilibrium 103, 249–53,
　　259, 290, 296, 302–3, 368, 406, 421,
　　487
War of the Austrian Succession (1740–48) 28
Warsaw University 568
Washington University 685
Webb, Beatrice 404
Webb, Sidney 404
Weber, Alfred 162, 523, 634
Weber, Ernst 289
Weber, Max 276–8, 288, 385, 391–5, 397,
　　499–500
　Economy and Society 393–5
　General Economic History 499
　The Protestant Ethic and the Spirit of
　　Capitalism 393, 396–7
　Stunde Null 393
Wedderburn, Alexander 58
Weimar Republic 507, 514, 523, 634

welfare economics 201, 264, 280, 307, 324–5,
  328, 330, 332–3, 337, 452, 456, 578–9,
  655–6, 663, 666, 682, 694, 728
  compensation principle 190
  development of 307, 317, 347, 644
  Kaldor–Hicks 604
  new 389–90, 604
Wennerlind, Carl 52
Werturteilsstreit 277
Western Management Science Institute 525
Westphalen, Jenny von 212
Whewell, William 139
Wicksell, Knut 105, 132, 139, 161, 270, 342,
  347–50, 355, 404, 407, 413, 458, 509–10,
  512, 527, 569, 603, 636, 663, 710
  *Finanztheoretische Untersuchungen nebst
    Darstellung und Kritik des Steuerwesens
    Schwedens* (1896) 348–9, 353, 682
  influence in
    capital/monetary theory 354, 511
    income distribution theory 351–3
    public finance theory 353–4, 359–60
  Interest and Prices (1898) 356
  Lectures on Political Economy 349–52, 355,
    510
  On Value, Capital and Rent (1893) 354
  Selected Essays in Economics (1997) 359
  theory of
    capitalistic production 355–6
    cumulative deflation 358, 360
    inflation 359–60
    modernized quantity 356–7
    monetarism 358
    value 350
  Über Wert, Kapital und Rente 348, 510
  Wicksell effect 356
Wicksteed, Philip Henry 216, 227, 311–13, 327,
  351
  The Alphabet of Economic Science (1888)
    311
  Common Sense of Political Economy (1910)
    312
  demand and supply curve of 312–13
  *Essay on the Co-ordination of the Laws of the
    Distribution* (1894) 311
Wieser, Friedrich von 363–4, 410, 434, 484,
  557–8
  Das Gesetz der Macht (*The Law of Power*)
    (1926) 365

Der natürliche Werth (1889) 364
Law of Cost 364
Theorie der gesellschaftlichen Wirtschaft
  365
theory of
  marginal utility 364, 431, 435
*Über den Ursprung und die Hauptgesetze
  des wirtschaftlichen Werthes* (1884)
  364
Wilbrandt, Robert 277
Wilhelm, Kaiser 274
Willard Gibbs, Josiah 410, 661
Williamite–Jacobite War (1689–91) 19
  Treaty of Limerick (1691) 19
Wilson, Edward 16
Wilson, Edwin Bidwell 658
Wilson, James 242
Winch, Donald 109
Windelband, Wilhelm 275
Wittgenstein, Ludwig 535
  Philosophical Investigations 535
Wolf, Julius 227, 277
Wolowski, Louis 234, 247
Wooddeson, Richard 144
Woodford, Michael
  Interest and Prices (2003) 360
World Bank 470, 482, 745
Wundt, Wilhelm 290
Württembergische Jahrbücher 273

Xenophon 203

The Yale Review 320
Yale University 321, 374, 410, 412, 518–19,
  525, 639, 671, 676, 698, 737, 748
Yasnopolsky, L.N. 462
Young, Allyn 454, 458, 595
Young, Arthur
  Annals of Agriculture (1784–1815) 98
Young Hegelians 211
Younger Historical School 272
Yule, G.U.
  An Introduction to the Theory of Statistics
    461

Zeitschrift für das Gesammte Handelsrecht
  393
Zeuthen, Frederik 408
Zwiedeneck-Südenhorst, Otto von 634